5TH EDITION

LOOKING AT MOVIES

5TH EDITION

LOOKING AT MOVIES
AN INTRODUCTION TO FILM

RICHARD BARSAM & DAVE MONAHAN

W.W. NORTON & COMPANY
NEW YORK • LONDON

W. W. Norton & Company has been independent since its founding in 1923, when William Warder Norton and Mary D. Herter Norton first published lectures delivered at the People's Institute, the adult education division of New York City's Cooper Union. The firm soon expanded its program beyond the Institute, publishing books by celebrated academics from America and abroad. By midcentury, the two major pillars of Norton's publishing program—trade books and college texts—were firmly established. In the 1950s, the Norton family transferred control of the company to its employees, and today—with a staff of four hundred and a comparable number of trade, college, and professional titles published each year—W. W. Norton & Company stands as the largest and oldest publishing house owned wholly by its employees.

Editor: Spencer Richardson-Jones
Editorial assistant: Rachel Taylor
Project editor: Sujin Hong
Production manager: Andy Ensor
Design director: Rubina Yeh
Book and cover designer: Anna Reich
Marketing manager: Kimberly Bowers
Media editor: Carly Fraser Doria
Media designer: Colleen Caffrey
Associate media editor: Cara Folkman
Digital media project editor: Meg Wihoite
Photo editor: Evan Luberger
Permissions manager: Megan Jackson
Composition: Achorn International
Digital art file manipulation: Jay's Publishers Services
Manufacturing: Quad/Graphics Versailles
Development Editor for the First Edition: Kurt Wildermuth
Authors photograph taken by Joshua Curry

Library of Congress Cataloging-in-Publication Data

Barsam, Richard Meran.
    Looking at movies : an introduction to film / Richard Barsam & Dave Monahan.—5th Edition.
        pages cm
    Includes bibliographical references and index.

ISBN 978-0-393-26519-4 (pbk. : alk. paper)

1. Motion pictures. 2. Cinematography. I. Monahan, Dave. II. Title.
    PN1994.B313 2015
    791.43—dc23
                                                                                2015032210

W. W. Norton & Company, Inc., 500 Fifth Avenue, New York, N.Y. 10110
wwnorton.com

W. W. Norton & Company Ltd., Castle House, 75/76 Wells Street, London W1T 3QT

1 2 3 4 5 6 7 8 9 0

ABOUT THE AUTHORS

RICHARD BARSAM

(Ph.D., University of Southern California) is Professor Emeritus of Film Studies at Hunter College, City University of New York. He is the author of *Nonfiction Film: A Critical History* (rev. and exp. ed., 1992), *The Vision of Robert Flaherty: The Artist as Myth and Filmmaker* (1988), *In the Dark: A Primer for the Movies* (1977), and *Filmguide to Triumph of the Will* (1975); editor of *Nonfiction Film: Theory and Criticism* (1976); and contributing author to Paul Monaco's *The Sixties: 1960–1969* (Vol. 8 in the History of the American Cinema series, 2001) and *Filming Robert Flaherty's Louisiana Story: The Helen van Dongen Diary* (ed. Eva Orbanz, 1998). His articles and book reviews have appeared in *Cinema Journal, Quarterly Review of Film Studies, Film Comment, Studies in Visual Communication*, and *Harper's*. He has been a member of the Executive Council of the Society for Cinema and Media Studies and the Editorial Board of *Cinema Journal*, and he cofounded the journal *Persistence of Vision*.

DAVE MONAHAN

(M.F.A., Columbia University) is an Associate Professor and Department Chair of Film Studies at the University of North Carolina, Wilmington. His work as a writer, director, and editor includes *Things Grow* (2010), *Ringo* (2005), *Monkey Junction* (2004), *Prime Time* (1996), and *Angels Watching Over Me* (1993). His work has been screened internationally in over fifty film festivals and has earned numerous awards, including the New Line Cinema Award for Most Original Film (*Prime Time*) and the Seattle International Film Festival Grand Jury Prize for Best Animated Short Film (*Ringo*).

CONTENTS

TO STUDENTS

The movies, born in 1891, have flourished for 124 years, yet there have always been those who believed that they were a passing fancy, or a poor cousin of the more traditional arts like literature, painting, architecture, dance, and music. In 1996, shortly after cinema's one hundredth birthday, cultural pundit Susan Sontag mused on the state of the art:

> Cinema's 100 years seem to have the shape of a life cycle: an inevitable birth, the steady accumulation of glories and the onset in the last decade of an ignominious, irreversible decline. . . . the commercial cinema has settled for a policy of bloated, derivative film-making, a brazen combinatory or recombinatory art, in the hope of reproducing past successes. Cinema, once heralded as the art of the 20th century, seems now, as the century closes numerically, to be a decadent art.[1]

Yet, 60 years before that, the art historian Erwin Panofsky had a very different insight into the movies as a form of popular art:

> If all the serious lyrical poets, composers, painters and sculptors were forced by law to stop their activities, a rather small fraction of the general public would become aware of the fact and a still smaller fraction would seriously regret it. If the same thing were to happen with the movies the social consequences would be catastrophic.[2]

Both, of course, were right. The commercial cinema, driven by the box office, has not fulfilled the promise of cinema's potential, yet today, we would hardly know what to do without movies. They are a major presence in our lives, and an influential beneficiary of our technological age. Since their invention more than a hundred years ago, movies have become one of the world's largest industries and the most powerful art form of our time.

With each new technological development—sound, color, widescreen projection, television, 3-D, computer-generated imagery, DVDs, internet streaming, and digitization of the filmmaking process—the movies have changed. Indeed, looking at movies (and the audience that looks at them) has changed as well. Traditionally, we saw movies in a theater, separated from the outside world—although it was a communal experience, sitting in the dark on seats fixed to the floor and a huge image screen. Today, we see movies wherever we happen to be; with whomever we want to be with (but usually alone); standing with a handheld device, curled up on a sofa, or sitting at a desk; and usually with the lights on. The image can be as large as a home theater or as small as a smartphone screen.

A source of entertainment that makes us see beyond the borders of our experiences, movies have always possessed the power to amaze, frighten, and enlighten us. They challenge our senses, emotions, and sometimes, our intellect; pushing us to say, often passionately, that we love (or hate) them. It's easy to get excited by movies because they arouse our most public and private feelings and can overwhelm us with their sights and sounds. The challenge is to combine that enthusiasm with understanding, to be able to say why we feel so strongly about particular movies while others are easily forgotten. That's one reason why this book encourages you to go beyond the stories, and to understand how these stories are told. After all, movies are not reality but only illusions of reality, and as with most works of art, their form and content work as an interrelated system, one that asks us to accept it as a given rather than as the product of a process. As you read this book devoted to looking at movies—that is, not passively watching them but actively considering the relation of their form and their content—remember that there is no one way to look at film, no one critical perspective that is inherently better than another, and no one meaning that you can insist on after a single viewing. Indeed, movies are so diverse in their nature that no single approach could ever do them justice.

[1]. Susan Sontag, "The Decay of Cinema," *The New York Times*, Feb. 25, 1996.

[2]. Erwin Panofsky, "Style and Medium in the Motion Pictures," in *Film Theory and Criticism: Introductory Readings*, ed. Leo Braudy and Marshall Cohen, 5th ed. (New York: Oxford University Press, 1999), p. 280.

No other art form has had so many lives. The cinema is alive because it is constantly changing as it adapts to technological advances and audience expectations. Cinema evolves because everything we see on the movie screen—everything that engages our senses, emotions, and minds—results from hundreds of decisions affecting the interrelation of formal cinematic elements, such as narrative, composition, cinematography, editing, and sound, as well as the influence of film producers whose financial decisions determine which films are made and whose advertising decisions make audiences desire what's new. Audiences in turn encourage new trends with their ticket purchases and habits of consumption. This book encourages you to look at movies with an understanding and appreciation of how filmmakers make the decisions that help them tell a story and create the foundation for its meaning. After all, in the real life of the movies, it is not historians, theorists, or critics—important and invaluable as they are—but filmmakers who continually shape and revise our understanding and appreciation of the film art.

If Susan Sontag were alive today, she would probably still lament the decline of thoughtful content in movies. But in an industry driven by what the public wants, the movies are doing just fine, and their formal elements, history, business practices, and cultural impact remain fruitful fields for further study. So even as the technology for making movies continues to evolve, and the marketplace in which they are created grows and contracts and expands internationally, the principles of film art covered in this book remain essentially the same. The principles you learn and the analytic skills you hone as you read this book will help you look at motion pictures intelligently and perceptively throughout your life, no matter from which medium you view those pictures.

PREFACE

Students in an introductory film course who read *Looking at Movies* carefully and take full advantage of the materials surrounding the text will finish the course with a solid grounding in the major principles of film form as well as a more perceptive and analytic eye. A short description of the book's main features follows.

An Accessible and Comprehensive Overview of Film

Recognized from its first publication as an accessible introductory text, *Looking at Movies* covers key concepts in films studies as comprehensively as possible. In addition to its clear and inviting presentation of the fundamentals of film form, the text discusses film genres, film history, and the relationships between film and culture in an extensive but characteristically accessible way, thus providing students with a thorough introduction to the major subject areas in film studies.

Film Examples Chosen with Undergraduates in Mind

From its very first chapter, which features sustained analyses and examples from *The Hunger Games* and Jason Reitman's *Juno* (2009), *Looking at Movies* invites students into the serious study of cinema via films that are familiar to them and that they have a reasonable chance of having experienced outside the classroom prior to taking the course. Major film texts from the entire history of cinema are also generously represented, of course, but always with an eye to helping students see enjoyment and serious study as complementary experiences.

A Focus on Analytic Skills

A good introductory film book needs to help students make the transition from the natural enjoyment of mov-

ies to a critical understanding of the form, content, and meanings of movies. *Looking at Movies* accomplishes this task in several different ways:

Model Analyses

Hundreds of illustrative examples and analytic readings of films throughout the book provide students with concrete models for their own analytic work. The sustained analyses in Chapter 1 of *Juno* and *The Hunger Games*—films that most undergraduates will have seen and enjoyed but perhaps not viewed with a critical eye—discuss not only the formal structures and techniques of these films, but also their social and cultural meanings. These analyses offer students an accessible and jargon-free introduction to most of the major themes and goals of introductory film course, and show students that looking at movies analytically can start immediately, even before they learn the specialized vocabulary of film study.

Each chapter also concludes with an in-depth "Looking at Movies" analysis that offers a sustained look at an exemplar film through the lens of the chapter's focus. New analyses of *Donnie Darko*, *The Lego Movie*, and *Boyhood* join existing chapter summations on *Citizen Kane*, *Stagecoach*, and *City of God* to provide clear models for students' own analyses and interpretations of films.

Interactive Tutorials

New interactive tutorials created by the authors provide students with hands-on practice manipulating key concepts of filmmaking and formal analysis. Students can work at their own pace to see how elements such as lighting, sound, editing, composition, and color function within a film. Available in the ebook and on the *Looking at Movies* student website, both found at digital.wwnorton.com/movies5.

Video Tutorials

A series of video tutorials—written, directed, and hosted by the authors—complement and expand on the book's analyses. Ranging from 2 to 15 minutes in length, these tutorials show students via moving-image media what the book describes and illustrates in still images. Helpful as a quick review of core concepts in the text, these tutorials also provide useful models for film analysis, thus helping students further develop their analytical skills. Available in the ebook and on the *Looking at Movies* student website, both found at digital.wwnorton.com/movies5.

"Screening Checklists"

Each chapter ends with an "Analyzing" section that includes a "Screening Checklist" feature. This series of leading questions prompts students to apply what they've learned in the chapter to their own critical viewing, in class or at home.

The Most Visually Dynamic Text Available

Looking at Movies was written with one goal in mind: to prepare students for a lifetime of intelligent and perceptive viewing of motion pictures. In recognition of the central role visuals play in the film-studies classroom, *Looking at Movies* includes an illustration program that is both visually appealing and pedagogically focused, as well as an accompanying moving-image media that are second to none.

Hundreds of In-Text Illustrations

The text is accompanied by over 750 illustrations in color and in black and white. Nearly all the still pictures were captured from digital or analog film sources, thus ensuring that the images directly reflect the textual discussions and the films from which they're taken. Unlike publicity stills, which are attractive as photographs but less useful as teaching aids, the captured stills throughout this book provide visual information that will help students learn as they read and—because they are reproduced in the aspect ratio of the original source—will serve as accurate reference points for students' analyses.

Five Hours of Moving-Image Media

The ebook and student website that accompany *Looking at Movies* offer five hours of two different types of video content:

- The twenty-seven video tutorials described above were specifically created to complement Looking

at Movies and are exclusive to this text. The tutorials guide students' eyes to see what the text describes, and because they are viewable in fullscreen, they are suitable for presentation in class as "lecture launchers," as well as for students' self-study.

- A mini-anthology of thirteen complete short films, ranging from 5 to 30 minutes in length, provides a curated selection of accomplished and entertaining examples of short-form cinema, as well as useful material for short in-class activities or for students' analysis. Most of the films are also accompanied by optional audio commentary from the filmmakers. This commentary was recorded specifically for *Looking at Movies* and is exclusive to this text.

Accessible Presentation; Effective Pedagogy

Among the reasons that *Looking at Movies* is considered the most accessible introductory film text available is its clear and direct presentation of key concepts and unique pedagogical organization. The first three chapters of the book—Looking at Movies, Principles of Film Form, and Types of Movies—provide a comprehensive yet truly introductory overview of the major topics and themes of any film course, giving students a solid grounding in the basics before they move on to study those topics in greater depth in later chapters.

In addition, pedagogical features throughout provide a structure that clearly identifies the main ideas and primary goals of each chapter for students:

Learning Objectives

A checklist at the beginning of every chapter provides a brief summary of the core concepts to be covered in the chapter.

Extensive Captions

Each illustration is accompanied by a caption that elaborates on a key concept or that guides students to look at elements of the film more analytically. These captions expand on the in-text presentation and reinforce students' retention of key terms and ideas.

"Analyzing" Sections

At the end of each chapter is a section that ties the terms, concepts, and ideas of the chapter to the primary goal of the book: honing students' own analytical skills. This short overview makes explicit how the knowledge students have gained in the chapter can move their own analytical work forward. A short "Screening Checklist" provides leading questions that students can ponder as they screen a film or scene.

"Questions for Review"

"Questions for Review" section at the end of each chapter tests students' knowledge of the concepts first mentioned in the "Learning Objectives" at the beginning of the chapter.

Enhanced Ebook

Looking at Movies is also available as an enhanced ebook free with every new copy of the print book. This ebook works on all computers and mobile devices, and embeds all the rich media—video tutorials, interactive tutorials, and more—into one seamless experience. Instructors can focus student reading by sharing notes in the ebook, as well as embed images and other videos. Reports on student and class-wide access and time on task also enable instructors to monitor student reading and engagement.

Writing About Movies

Written by Karen Gocsik (University of California, San Diego) and the authors of *Looking at Movies*, this book is a clear and practical overview of the process of writing papers for film-studies courses. In addition to providing helpful information about the writing process, the new *Writing About Movies*, Fourth Edition, offers a substantial introduction-in-brief to the major topics in film studies, including an overview of the major film theories and their potential application to student writing, practical advice about note-taking during screenings and private viewings, information about the study of genre and film history, and an illustrated glossary of essential film terms. This inexpensive but invaluable text is available separately or in a significantly discounted package with *Looking at Movies*.

Resources for Instructors

Clip Guide

An invaluable class-prep tool, the Clip Guide suggests a wide range of clips for illustrating film concepts covered in the text. Each entry in the Clip Guide offers a quick overview of the scene, the idea, and crucially, time-stamp information on exactly where to find each clip. The *Looking at Movies* Clip Guide includes suggestions from not just the authors but a wide range of teachers, offering a broad perspective of insightful teaching tips that can inspire and save valuable prep time.

Instructor's Guide

The Instructor's Guide to *Looking at Movies* offers a concise overview of each chapter's main points and key concepts, as well as suggested learning exercises and recommended tutorials from the book's extensive media ancillaries.

PowerPoints

Ready-made lecture PowerPoint presentations for each chapter as well as art and image slides are available for download at Norton's instructor resource page: wwnorton.com/instructors.

Test Bank

Completely revised for this edition, each chapter of the Test Bank includes a "concept map," and 60–65 multiple-choice and 10–15 essay questions (with sample answer guides). Questions are labeled by concept, question type, and difficulty.

Coursepacks for Learning Management Systems

Ready-to-use coursepacks for Blackboard and other learning management systems are available free of charge to instructors who adopt *Looking at Movies*. These coursepacks offer unique activities that reinforce key concepts, chapter overviews and learning objectives, quiz questions, links to the video tutorials, questions about those tutorials and the short films, and the complete Test Bank.

A Note about Textual Conventions

Boldface type is used to highlight terms that are defined in the glossary at the point where they are introduced in the text. *Italics* are used occasionally for emphasis. References to movies in the text include the year the movie was released and the director's name. Members of the crew who are particularly important to the main topic of the chapter are also identified. For example, in the chapter on cinematography, a reference to *The Matrix* might look like this: Andy and Lana Wachowski's *The Matrix* (1999; cinematographer Bill Pope). Other relevant information about the films can be found in the chapter itself.

ACKNOWLEDGMENTS

Writing a book seems very much at times like the collaborative effort involved in making movies. In writing this Fifth Edition of *Looking at Movies*, we are grateful to our excellent partners at W. W. Norton & Company. Chief among them is our editor, Pete Simon, who has guided us and offered insightful ideas for every edition of this book. Other collaborators at Norton were Sujin Hong, project editor; Andy Ensor, production manager; Carly Fraser-Doria, media editor; Cara Folkman, associate media editor; Colleen Caffrey, media designer; Kimberly Bowers, marketing manager; and Emily Stuart and Gera Goff, editorial assistants. Thanks also to Spencer Richardson-Jones. It has been a pleasure to work with such a responsive, creative, and supportive team.

Richard Barsam thanks the friends and colleagues who have assisted and contributed suggestions over the course of five editions, including Kevin Harris Bahr, Luiz-Antonio Bocchi, Daniel Doron, Richard Koss, Emanuel Leonard, Vinny LoBrutto, Peter Maxwell, Gustavo Mercado, and Renato Tonelli. I am also grateful to Edgar Munhall for his continuing interest, patience, and companionship.

Dave Monahan would like to thank the faculty, staff, and students of the Film Studies Department at the University of North Carolina, Wilmington. My colleagues Mariana Johnson, Shannon Silva, Andre Silva, Tim Palmer, Todd Berliner, Carlos Kase, Nandana Bose, Chip Hackler, Lou Buttino, Glenn Pack, Terry Linehan, Ana Olenina, and Sue Richardson contributed expertise and advice. Film studies student Kevin Bahr excelled as my research assistant. My colleagues Nate Daniel, Glenn Pack, Aaron Cavazos, and Alex Markowski deserve special thanks for their production and postproduction help with the new video modules I directed for this edition. Nate was our camera operator, colorist, and postproduction supervisor; Glenn was our cinematographer, gaffer, and assistant director; Aaron did an amazing job on the animation and motion graphics for the new *The Hunger Games* tutorial; and Alex provided sound design and the sound module script. A number of talented UNCW students served on the crews that produced the new modules. Sarah Flores was our producer; Richard Martin, Adam Getz, Kim Szany, Savvas Yiannoulou, Ryne Seals, Patrick Johnson, and Adam Fackelman were the camera and lighting team; and Rebecca Rathier, Christina Lamia, and Tara Lymon-Dobson made up the art department. Cast members include Sarah Flores, Moriah Thomason, Christina Lamia, Chris Keefe, Cheyenne Puga, Kenneth Freyer, Tomasina Hill, Mariah Jarvis, Mikaela Fleming, John T. McDevitt, Gabby Adeoti, Daniel Adkins, and Adam O'Neill.

I would also like to thank my wife, Julie, for her patience, support, and encouragement; and my daughters, Iris and Elsa, for looking at a lot of movies with me.

Reviewers

We would like to join the publisher in thanking all the professors and students who provided valuable guidance as we planned this revision. *Looking at Movies* is as much their book as ours, and we are grateful to both students and faculty who have cared enough about this text to offer a hand in making it better.

The thoughtful comments from the following colleagues and fellow instructors helped shape both the book and media for this Fifth edition: Sandra Annett (Wilfred Laurier University), Richard Blake (Boston College), Laura Bouza (Moorpark College), Aaron Braun (Hofstra University), Derek Burrill (University of California, Riverside), Emily Carman (Chapman University), Megan Condis (University of Illinois), Angela Dancy (University of Chicago), Dawn Marie Fratini (Chapman University), Isabelle Freda (Oklahoma State University), Paul Gaustad (Georgia Perimeter College, Dunwoody), Michael Green (Arizona State University), David Kreutzer (Cape Fear Community College), Andrew Kunka (University of South Carolina, Sumter), G. S. Larke-Walsh (University of North Texas), Nee Lam (Chapman University), Elizabeth Lathrop (Georgia Perimeter College, Clarkston), Melissa Lenos (Donnelly College), Albert Lopez (University of Texas, San Antonio), Yuri Makino

(University of Arizona), Stephanie O'Brien (Ashville-Buncombe Technical Community College), Jun Okada (SUNY Geneseo), Mitchell Parry (University of Victoria), Frances Perkins (University of Wisconsin, Fox Valley), Christina Petersen (Eckerd College), George Rodman (Brooklyn College), Rosalind Sibielski (Bowling Green State University), Robert Sickels (Whitman College), Jason Spangler (Riverside City College), Suzie Young (York University), and Michael Zryd (York University).

The following colleagues provided extensive reviews of the Third Edition and many ideas for improving the book in its Fourth Edition: Katrina Boyd (University of Oklahoma), James B. Bush (Texas Tech University), Rodney Donahue (Texas Tech University), Cable Hardin (South Dakota State University), Christopher Jacobs (University of North Dakota), Tammy A. Kinsey (University of Toledo), Bradford Owen (California State University, San Bernadino), W. D. Phillips (College of Staten Island/New York University), Michael Rowin (Hunter College, CUNY), and Nicholas Sigman (Hunter College, CUNY).

The transition from our Second Edition to the Third was an especially momentous revision, and we wish to acknowledge once more the following people, all of whom provided invaluable input during this important stage in the evolution of *Looking at Movies*: Donna Casella (Minnesota State University), John G. Cooper (Eastern Michigan University), Mickey Hall (Volunteer State Community College), Stefan Hall (Defiance College), Jennifer Jenkins (University of Arizona), Robert S. Jones (University of Central Florida), Mildred Lewis (Chapman University), Matthew Sewell (Minnesota State University), Michael Stinson (Santa Barbara City College), and Michael Zryd (York University).

The following scholars and teachers responded to a lengthy questionnaire from the publisher several years ago, and their responses shaped the early editions of this book: Rebecca Alvin, Edwin Arnold, Antje Ascheid, Dyrk Ashton, Tony Avruch, Peter Bailey, Scott Baugh, Harry Benshoff, Mark Berrettini, Yifen Beus, Mike Birch, Robin Blaetz, Ellen Bland, Carroll Blue, James Bogan, Karen Budra, Don Bullens, Gerald Burgess, Jeremy Butler, Gary Byrd, Ed Cameron, Jose Cardenas, Jerry Carlson, Diane Carson, Robert Castaldo, Beth Clary, Darcy Cohn, Marie Connelly, Roger Cook, Robert Coscarelli, Bob Cousins, Donna Davidson, Rebecca Dean, Marshall Deutelbaum, Kent DeYoung, Michael DiRaimo, Carol Dole, Dan Dootson, John Ernst, James Fairchild, Adam Fischer, Craig Fischer, Tay Fizdale, Karen Fulton, Christopher Gittings, Barry Goldfarb, Neil Goldstein, Daryl Gonder, Patrick Gonder, Cynthia Gottshall, Curtis Green, William Green, Tracy Greene, Michael Griffin, Peter Hadorn, William Hagerty, John Harrigan, Catherine Hastings, Sherri Hill, Glenn Hopp, Tamra Horton, Alan Hutchison, Mike Hypio, Tom Isbell, Delmar Jacobs, Mitchell Jarosz, John Lee Jellicorse, Matthew Judd, Charles Keil, Joyce Kessel, Mark Kessler, Garland Kimmer, Lynn Kirby, David Kranz, James Kreul, Mikael Kreuzriegler, Cory Lash, Leon Lewis, Vincent LoBrutto, Jane Long, John Long, Jay Loughrin, Daniel Machon, Travis Malone, Todd McGowan, Casey McKittrick, Maria Mendoza-Enright, Andrea Mensch, Sharon Mitchler, Mary Alice Molgard, John Moses, Sheila Nayar, Sarah Nilsen, Ian Olney, Hank Ottinger, Dan Pal, Gary Peterson, Klaus Phillips, Alexander Pitofsky, Lisa Plinski, Leland Poague, Walter Renaud, Patricia Roby, Carole Rodgers, Stuart Rosenberg, Ben Russell, Kevin Sandler, Bennet Schaber, Mike Schoenecke, Hertha Schulze, David Seitz, Timothy Shary, Robert Sheppard, Charles Silet, Eric Smoodin, Ken Stofferahn, Bill Swanson, Molly Swiger, Joe Tarantowski, Susan Tavernetti, Edwin Thompson, Frank Tomasulo, Deborah Tudor, Bill Vincent, Richard Vincent, Ken White, Mark Williams, Deborah Wilson, and Elizabeth Wright.

Thank you all.

The Hunger Games: Mocking Jay, Part 1 (2014; director Francis Lawrence)

LOOKING AT MOVIES

Movies shape the way we see the world

No other movie featuring a homosexual relationship has earned the level of international critical acclaim and commercial success of *Brokeback Mountain* (2005). The Academy Award–winning independent film, made for a relatively paltry $14 million, grossed $178 million at the box office and eventually became the thirteenth highest-grossing romantic drama in Hollywood history. Academy Awards for Best Director (Ang Lee) and Best Adapted Screenplay (Diana Ossana and Larry McMurtry, from a short story by Annie Proulx) were among the many honors and accolades granted the independently produced movie. But even more important, by presenting a gay relationship in the context of the archetypal American West and casting popular leading men (Heath Ledger, Jake Gyllenhaal) in starring roles that embodied traditional notions of masculinity, *Brokeback Mountain* influenced the way many Americans perceived same-sex relationships and gay rights. Since the film's release, thirty-six states have lifted the ban on gay marriage, the U.S. Supreme Court made same-sex marriage a nationwide right, and LGBT characters and storylines have become increasingly commonplace in popular films and television. No movie can single-handedly change the world, but the accumulative influence of cinema is undeniable.

Looking at Movies

In just over a hundred years, movies have evolved into a complex form of artistic representation and communication: they are at once a hugely influential, wildly profitable global industry and a modern art—the most popular art form today. Popular may be an understatement. This art form has permeated our lives in ways that extend far beyond the multiplex. We watch movies on hundreds of cable and satellite channels. We buy movies online or from big-box retailers. We rent movies through the mail and from Redbox machines at the supermarket. We TiVo movies, stream movies, and download movies to watch on our televisions, our computers, our iPads, and our smart phones.

Unless you were raised by wolves—and possibly even if you were—you have likely devoted thousands of hours to absorbing the motion-picture medium. With so much experience, no one could blame you for wondering why you need a course or this book to tell you how to look at movies.

After all, you might say, "It's just a movie." For most of us most of the time, movies are a break from our daily obligations—a form of escape, entertainment, and pleasure. Motion pictures had been popular for fifty years before even most filmmakers, much less scholars, considered movies worthy of serious study. But motion pictures are much more than entertainment. The movies we see shape the way we view the world around us and our place in that world. Moreover, a close analysis of any particular movie can tell us a great deal about the artist, society, or industry that created it. Surely any art form with that kind of influence and insight is worth understanding on the deepest possible level.

Movies involve much more than meets the casual eye . . . or ear, for that matter. Cinema is a subtle—some might even say sneaky—medium. Because most movies seek to engage viewers' emotions and transport them inside the world presented onscreen, the visual vocabulary of film is designed to play upon those same instincts that we use to navigate and interpret the visual and aural information of our "real life." This often imperceptible **cinematic language**, composed not of words but of myriad integrated techniques and concepts, connects us to the story while deliberately concealing the means by which it does so.

Yet behind this mask, all movies, even the most blatantly commercial ones, contain layers of complexity and meaning that can be studied, analyzed, and appreciated. This book is devoted to that task—to actively *looking at* movies rather than just passively watching them. It will teach you to recognize the many tools and principles that filmmakers employ to tell stories, convey information and meaning, and influence our emotions and ideas.

Once you learn to speak this cinematic language, you'll be equipped to understand the movies that pervade our world on multiple levels: as narrative, as artistic expression, and as a reflection of the cultures that produce and consume them.

What Is a Movie?

Now that we've established what we mean by looking at movies, the next step is to attempt to answer the deceptively simple question, What is a movie? As this book will repeatedly illustrate, when it comes to movies, nothing is as straightforward as it appears.

Let's start, for example, with the word *movies*. If the course that you are taking while reading this book is "Introduction to Film" or "Cinema Studies 101," does that mean that your course and this book focus on two different things? What's the difference between a movie and a *film*? And where does the word *cinema* fit in?

For whatever reason, the designation *film* is often applied to a motion picture that critics and scholars consider to be more serious or challenging than the *movies* that entertain the masses at the multiplex. The still loftier designation of *cinema* seems reserved for groups of films that are considered works of art (e.g., "French cinema"). The truth is, the three terms are essentially interchangeable. *Cinema*, from the Greek *kinesis* ("movement"), originates from the name that filmmaking pioneers Auguste and Louis Lumière coined for the hall where they exhibited their invention; *film* derives from the celluloid strip on which the images that make up motion pictures were originally captured, cut, and projected; and *movies* is simply short for motion pictures. Since we consider all cinema worthy of study, acknowl-

edge that films are increasingly shot on formats other than film stock, and believe motion to be the essence of the movie medium, this book favors the term used in our title. That said, we'll mix all three terms into these pages (as evidenced in the preceding sentence) for the sake of variety, if nothing else.

To most people, a movie is a popular entertainment, a product produced and marketed by a large commercial studio. Regardless of the subject matter, this movie is pretty to look at—every image is well polished by an army of skilled artists and technicians. The finished product, which is about two hours long, screens initially in movie theaters; is eventually released to DVD and Blu-ray, streaming, download, or pay-per-view; and ultimately winds up on television. This common expectation is certainly understandable; most movies that reach most English-speaking audiences have followed a good part of this model for three-quarters of a century.

And almost all of these ubiquitous commercial, feature-length movies share another basic characteristic: narrative. When it comes to categorizing movies, the narrative designation simply means that these movies tell fictional (or at least fictionalized) stories. Of course, if you think of narrative in its broadest sense, *every* movie that selects and arranges subject matter in a cause-and-effect sequence of events is employing a narrative structure. For all their creative flexibility, movies by their very nature must travel a straight line. A conventional motion picture is essentially one very long strip of images. This linear quality makes movies perfectly suited to develop subject matter in a sequential progression. When a medium so compatible with narrative is introduced to a culture with an already well-established storytelling tradition, it's easy to understand how popular cinema came to be dominated by those movies devoted to telling fictional stories. Because these fiction films are so central to most readers' experience and so vital to the development of cinema as an art form and cultural force, we've made narrative movies the focus of this introductory textbook.

But keep in mind that commercial, feature-length narrative films represent only a fraction of the expressive potential of this versatile medium. Cinema and narrative are both very flexible concepts. Documentary films strive for objective, observed veracity, of course, but that doesn't mean they don't tell stories. These movies often arrange and present factual information and images in the form of a narrative, whether it be a predator's attempts to track and kill its prey, an activist's quest

Narrative in documentary

Just because a film is constructed from footage documenting actual events doesn't mean it can't tell a story. *The Imposter* (2012; director Bart Layton) tells the story of Frédéric Bourdin, a French con man who convinces an American family that he is their long-lost son. The film's interviews, reenactments, and archival footage are structured like a procedural crime thriller: once the impersonation seemingly succeeds, the imposter finds himself in over his head as increasingly skeptical investigators chip away at his masquerade and uncover troubling details about his adopted family.

to free a wrongfully convicted innocent, or a rookie athlete's struggle to make the big leagues. While virtually every movie, regardless of category, employs narrative in some form, cultural differences often affect exactly how these stories are presented. Narrative films made in Africa, Asia, and Latin America reflect storytelling traditions very different from the story structure we expect from films produced in North America and Western Europe. The unscripted, minimalist films by Iranian director Abbas Kiarostami, for example, often intentionally lack dramatic resolution, inviting viewers to imagine their own ending.[1] Sanskrit dramatic traditions have inspired "Bollywood" Indian cinema to feature staging that breaks the illusion of reality favored by Hollywood movies, such as actors that consistently face, and even directly address, the audience.[2]

Compared to North American and Western European films, Latin American films of the 1960s, like *Land in Anguish* (Glauber Rocha, 1967, Brazil) or *Memories of Underdevelopment* (Tomás Gutiérrez Alea, 1968, Cuba), are less concerned with individual character psychology and motivation. Instead, they present characters as social types or props in a political allegory.[3] The growing influ-

ence of these and other even less familiar approaches, combined with emerging technologies that make filmmaking more accessible and affordable, have made possible an ever-expanding range of independent movies created by crews as small as a single filmmaker and shot on any one of a variety of film and digital formats. The Irish director John Carney shot his musical love story *Once* (2006) on the streets of Dublin with a cast of mostly nonactors and a small crew using consumer-grade video cameras. American Oren Peli's homemade horror movie *Paranormal Activity* (2007) was produced on a miniscule $15,000 budget and was shot entirely from the point of view of its characters' camcorder. *Once* received critical acclaim and an Academy Award for best original song; *Paranormal Activity* eventually earned almost $200 million at the box office, making it one of the most profitable movies in the history of cinema. Even further out on the fringes of popular culture, an expanding universe of alternative cinematic creativity continues to flourish. These noncommercial movies innovate styles and aesthetics, can be of any length, and exploit an array of exhibition options—from independent theaters to cable television to film festivals to Netflix streaming to YouTube.

No matter what you call it, no matter the approach, no matter the format, every movie is a motion picture: a series of still images that, when viewed in rapid succession (usually 24 images per second), the human eye and brain see as fluid movement. In other words, movies *move*. That essential quality is what separates movies from all other two-dimensional pictorial art forms. Each image in every motion picture draws upon basic compositional principles developed by these older cousins (photography, painting, drawing, etc.), including the arrangement of visual elements and the interaction of light and shadow. But unlike photography or painting, films are constructed from individual **shots**—an unbroken span of action captured by an uninterrupted run of a motion-picture camera—that allow visual elements to rearrange themselves and the viewer's perspective itself to shift within any composition.

And this movie movement extends beyond any single shot because movies are constructed of multiple individual shots joined to one another in an extended sequence.

1. Laura Mulvey, "Kiarostami's Uncertainty Principle," *Sight and Sound* 8, no. 6 (June 1998): 24–27.

2. Philip Lutgendorf, "Is There an Indian Way of Filmmaking?" *International Journal of Hindu Studies* 10, no. 3 (December 2006): 227–256.

3. Many thanks to Dr. Mariana Johnson of the University of North Carolina Wilmington for some of the ideas in this analysis.

Cultural narrative traditions

The influence of Sanskrit dramatic traditions on Indian cinema can be seen in the prominence of staging that breaks the illusion of reality favored by Hollywood movies, such as actors that consistently face, and even directly address, the audience. In this image from the opening minutes of Rohit Shetty's *Chennai Express* (2013), the lonely bachelor Rahul (Shah Rukh Knan) interrupts his own voice-over narration to complain to viewers about attractive female customers who consider him only a "brother."

With each transition from one shot to another, a movie is able to move the viewer through time and space. This joining together of discrete shots, or **editing**, gives movies the power to choose what the viewer sees and how that viewer sees it at any given moment.

To understand better how movies control what audiences see, we can compare cinema to another, closely related medium: live theater. A stage play, which confines the viewer to a single wide-angle view of the action, might display a group of actors, one of whom holds a small object in her hand. The audience sees every cast member at once and continuously from the same angle and in the same relative size. The object in one performer's hand is too small to see clearly, even for those few viewers lucky enough to have front-row seats. The playwright, director, and actors have very few practical options to convey the object's physical properties, much less its narrative significance or its emotional meaning to the character. In contrast, a movie version of the same story can establish the dramatic situation and spatial relationships of its subjects from the same wide-angle viewpoint, then instantaneously jump to a composition isolating the actions of the character holding the object, then **cut** to a **close-up** view revealing the object to be a charm bracelet, move up to feature the character's face as she contemplates the bracelet, then leap thirty years into the past to a depiction of the character as a young girl receiving the jewelry as a gift. Editing's capacity to

isolate details and juxtapose images and sounds within and between shots gives movies an expressive agility impossible in any other dramatic art or visual medium.

The Movie Director

Throughout this book, we give primary credit to the movie's director; you'll see references, for example, to James Gunn's *Guardians of the Galaxy* (2014) or *Zero Dark Thirty* (2012; director Kathryn Bigelow). You may not know anything about the directorial style of Mr. Gunn or Ms. Bigelow, but if you enjoy these movies, you might seek out their work in the future.

Still, all moviegoers know—if only from seeing the seemingly endless credits at the end of most movies—that today's movies represent not the work of a single artist, but a collaboration between a group of creative contributors. In this collaboration, the director's role is basically that of a coordinating lead artist. He or she is the vital link between creative, production, and technical teams. The bigger the movie, the larger the crew, and the more complex and challenging the collaboration. Though different directors bring varying levels of foresight, pre-planning, and control to a project, every director must have a vision for the story and style to inform initial instructions to collaborators and to apply to the continuous decision-making process necessary in every stage of production. In short, the director must be a strong leader with a passion for filmmaking and a gift for collaboration.

The other primary collaborators on the creative team—screenwriter, actors, director of photography, production designer, editor, and sound designer—all work with the director to develop their contributions, and the director must approve their decisions as they progress. The director is at the top of the creative hierarchy, responsible for choosing (or at least approving) each of those primary collaborators. A possible exception is the screenwriter, though even then the director often contributes to revisions and assigns additional writers to provide revised or additional material.

The director's primary responsibilities are performance and camera—and the coordination of the two. The director selects actors for each role, works with those actors to develop their character, leads rehearsals, blocks performances in relationship with the camera on set, and modulates those performances from take to take and shot to shot as necessary throughout the shoot. He or she works with the director of photography to design an overall cinematic look for the movie and to visualize the framing and composition of each shot before and during shooting. Along the way, as inspiration or obstacles necessitate, changes are made to everything from the script to storyboards to blocking to edits. The director is the one making or approving each adjustment—sometimes after careful deliberation, sometimes on the fly.

On the set, the director does more than call "action" and "cut" and give direction to the actors and cinematographer. He or she must review the footage if necessary, decide when a shot or scene is satisfactory, and say that it's time to move on to the next task. In the editing room, the director sometimes works directly with the editor throughout the process but more often reviews successive "cuts" of scenes and provides the editor with feedback to use in revision.

In today's film industry, a director's qualifications may vary; she may have previous directorial credits on film or television, be a successful actor in her first position as a film director, or be a recent graduate of a film school. But the changing nature of film production (see Chapter 11, "How the Movies Are Made") and the increasing gender and ethnic diversity among directors makes defining the director's role a necessarily flexible thing.

Ways of Looking at Movies

Every movie is a complex synthesis—a combination of many separate, interrelated elements that form a coherent whole. A quick scan of this book's table of contents will give you an idea of just how many elements get mixed together to make a movie. Anyone attempting to comprehend a complex synthesis must rely on analysis—the act of taking apart something complicated to figure out what it is made of and how it all fits together.

A chemist breaks down a compound substance into its constituent parts to learn more than just a list of ingredients. The goal usually extends to determining how the identified individual components work together toward some sort of outcome: What is it about this particular mixture that makes it taste like strawberries, or grow hair, or kill cockroaches? Likewise, film analysis involves more than breaking down a sequence, a scene, or an entire movie to identify the tools and techniques that comprise it; the investigation is also concerned with

the function and potential effect of that combination: Why does it make you laugh, or prompt you to tell your friend to see it, or incite you to join the Peace Corps? The search for answers to these sorts of questions boils down to one essential inquiry: What does it mean? For the rest of the chapter, we'll explore film analysis by applying that question to some very different movies: first, and most extensively, the 2007 independent film *Juno*, and then the blockbuster Hunger Games film series.

Unfortunately, or perhaps intriguingly, not all movie meaning is easy to see. As we mentioned earlier, movies have a way of hiding their methods and meaning. So before we dive into specific approaches to analysis, let's wade a little deeper into this whole notion of hidden, or "invisible," meaning.

Invisibility and Cinematic Language

The moving aspect of moving pictures is one reason for this invisibility. Movies simply move too fast for even the most diligent viewers to consciously consider everything they've seen. When we read a book, we can pause to ponder the meaning or significance of any word, sentence, or passage. Our eyes often flit back to review something we've already read in order to further comprehend its meaning or to place a new passage in context. Similarly, we can stand and study a painting or sculpture or photograph for as long as we require to absorb whatever meaning we need or want from it. But until very recently, the moviegoer's relationship with every cinematic composition has been transitory. We experience a movie shot, which is capable of delivering multiple layers of visual and auditory information, for the briefest of moments before it is taken away and replaced with another moving image and another and another. If you're watching a movie the way it's designed to be experienced, there's little time to contemplate the various potential meanings of any single movie moment.

Recognizing a viewer's tendency (especially when sitting in a dark theater, staring at a large screen) to identify subconsciously with the camera's viewpoint, early filmmaking pioneers created a film grammar (or cinematic language) that draws upon the way we automatically interpret visual information in our real lives, thus allowing audiences to absorb movie meaning intuitively—and instantly.

The **fade-out/fade-in** is one of the most straightforward examples of this phenomenon. When such a

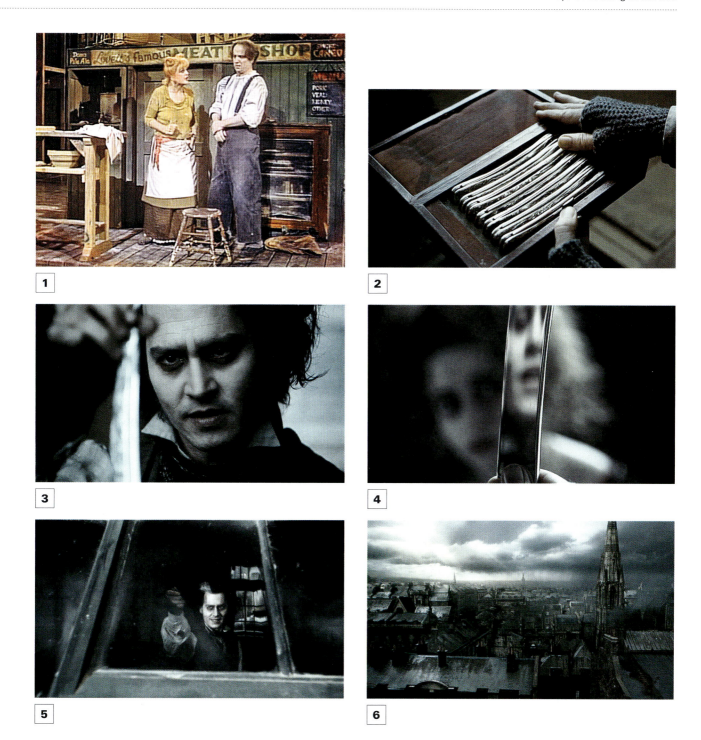

The expressive agility of movies

Even the best seats in the house offer a viewer of a theatrical production like Stephen Sondheim's *Sweeney Todd: The Demon Barber of Fleet Street* only one unchanging view of the action. The stage provides the audience a single wide-angle view of the scene in which the title character is reintroduced to the set of razors he will use in his bloody quest for revenge [1]. In contrast, cinema's spatial dexterity allows viewers of Tim Burton's 2007 film adaptation to experience the same scene as a sequence of fifty-nine viewpoints. Each one isolates and emphasizes distinct meanings and perspectives, including Sweeney Todd's (Johnny Depp) point of view as he gets his first glimpse of his long-lost tools of the trade [2]; his emotional reaction as he contemplates righteous murder [3]; the razor replacing Mrs. Lovett (Helena Bonham Carter) as the focus of his attention [4]; and a dizzying simulated camera move that starts with the vengeful antihero [5], then pulls back to reveal the morally corrupt city he (and his razors) will soon terrorize [6].

Cinematic invisibility: low angle
When it views a subject from a low camera angle, cinematic language taps our instinctive association of figures who we must literally "look up to" with figurative or literal power. In this case, the penultimate scene in *Juno* emphasizes the newfound freedom and resultant empowerment the title character feels by presenting her from a low angle for the first time in the film.

transition is meant to convey a passage of time between scenes, the last shot of a scene grows gradually darker (fades out) until the screen is rendered black for a moment. The first shot of the subsequent scene then fades in out of the darkness. Viewers don't have to think about what this means; our daily experience of time's passage marked by the setting and rising of the sun lets us understand intuitively that significant story time has elapsed over that very brief moment of screen darkness.

A **low-angle shot** communicates in a similarly hidden fashion. When, near the end of *Juno* (2007; director Jason Reitman), we see the title character happily transformed back into a "normal" teenager, our sense of her newfound empowerment is heightened by the low angle from which this (and the next) shot is captured. Viewers' shared experience of literally looking up at powerful figures—people on stages, at podiums, memorialized in statues, or simply bigger than them—sparks an automatic interpretation of movie subjects seen from this angle. Depending on context, we see these figures as strong, noble, or threatening.

This is all very well; the immediacy of cinematic language is what makes movies one of the most visceral experiences that art has to offer. The problem is that it also makes it all too easy to take movie meaning for granted.

The relatively seamless presentation of visual and narrative information found in most movies can also cloud our search for movie meaning. To exploit cinema's capacity for transporting audiences into the world of the story, the commercial filmmaking process stresses polished continuity of lighting, performance, costume, makeup, and movement to smooth transitions between shots and scenes, thus minimizing any distractions that might remind viewers that they're watching a highly manipulated, and manipulative, artificial reality.

Cutting on action is one of the most common editing techniques designed to hide the instantaneous and potentially jarring shift from one camera viewpoint to another. When connecting one shot to the next, a film editor often ends the first shot in the middle of a continuing action and starts the connecting shot at some point in the same action. As a result, the action flows so continuously over the cut between different moving images that most viewers fail to register the switch.

1

2

Invisible editing: cutting on action in *Juno*
Juno and Leah's playful wrestling continues over the cut between two shots, smoothing and hiding the instantaneous switch from one camera viewpoint to the next. Overlapping sound and the matching hairstyles, wardrobe, and lighting further obscure the audience's awareness that these two separate shots were filmed minutes or even hours apart and from different camera positions.

Invisible editing: continuity of screen direction

Juno's opening-credits sequence uses the title character's continuous walking movement to present the twenty-two different shots that comprise the scene as one continuous action. In every shot featuring lateral movement, Juno strolls consistently toward the left side of the screen, adding continuity of screen direction to the seamless presentation of the otherwise stylized animated sequence.

As with all things cinematic, invisibility has its exceptions. From the earliest days of moviemaking, innovative filmmakers have rebelled against the notion of hidden structures and meaning. The pioneering Soviet filmmaker and theorist Sergei Eisenstein believed that every edit, far from being invisible, should be very noticeable—a clash or collision of contiguous shots, rather than a seamless transition from one shot to the next. Filmmakers whose work is labeled "experimental"—inspired by Eisenstein and other predecessors—embrace self-reflexive styles that confront and confound conventional notions of continuity. Even some commercial films use techniques that undermine invisibility: in *The Limey* (1999), for example, Hollywood filmmaker Steven Soderbergh deliberately jumbles spatial and chronological continuity, forcing viewers to actively scrutinize the cinematic structures on-screen in order to assemble, and thus comprehend, the story. But most scenes in most films that most of us watch rely heavily on largely invisible techniques that convey meaning intuitively. It's not that cinematic language is impossible to spot; you simply have to know what you're looking for. And soon, you will. The rest of this book is dedicated to helping you identify and appreciate each of the many different secret ingredients that movies blend to convey meaning.

Luckily for you, motion pictures have been liberated from the imposed impermanence that helped create all this cinematic invisibility in the first place. Thanks to DVDs, Blu-rays, DVRs, and streaming video, you can now watch a movie in much the same way you read a book: pausing to scrutinize, ponder, or review as necessary. This relatively new relationship between movies and viewers will surely spark new approaches to cinematic language and attitudes toward invisibility. That's for future filmmakers, maybe including you, to decide. For now, these viewing technologies allow students of film like yourself to study movies with a lucidity and precision that was impossible for your predecessors.

But not even repeated DVD viewings can reveal those movie messages hidden by our own preconceptions and

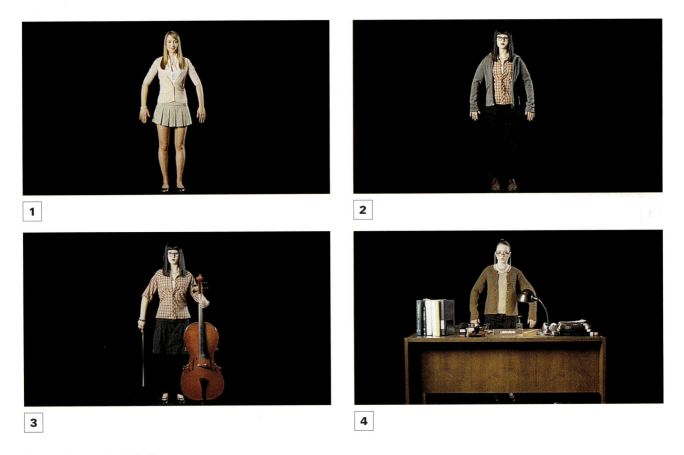

Exceptions to invisibility

Even *Juno* deviates from conventional invisibility in a stylized sequence illustrating a high-school jock's secret lust for "freaky girls." As Juno's voice-over aside detailing Steve Rendazo's (Daniel Clark) fetish begins, the movie suddenly abandons conventional continuity to launch into a series of abrupt juxtapositions that dress a generic girl posed like a paper doll in a rapid-fire succession of eccentric accessories. The moment Juno's diatribe ends, the film returns to a smooth visual flow of events and images. While this sequence is far from realistic, its ostentatious style effectively illustrates the trappings of teenage conformity and the ways that young women are objectified.

belief systems. Before we can detect and interpret these meanings, we must first be aware of the ways that expectations and cultural traditions obscure what movies have to say.

Cultural Invisibility

The same commercial instinct that inspires filmmakers to use seamless continuity also compels them to favor stories and themes that reinforce viewers' shared belief systems. After all, the film industry, for the most part, seeks to entertain, not to provoke, its customers. A key to entertaining the customers is to give them what they want—to tap into and reinforce their most fundamental desires and beliefs. Even movies deemed controversial or provocative can be popular if they trigger emotional responses from their viewers that reinforce yearnings or beliefs that lie deep within. And because so much of this occurs on an unconscious, emotional level, the casual viewer may be blind to the implied political, cultural, and ideological messages that help make the movie so appealing.

Of course, this cultural invisibility is not always a calculated decision by the filmmakers. Directors, screenwriters, and producers are, after all, products of the same society inhabited by their intended audience. Frequently, the people making the movies may be just as oblivious of the cultural attitudes shaping their cinematic stories as the people who watch them.

Juno's filmmakers are certainly aware that their film, which addresses issues of abortion and pregnancy, diverges from the ways that movies traditionally represent family structures and teenage girls. In this sense, the movie might be seen as resisting common cultural values. But these filmmakers may not be as conscious of the way their **protagonist** (main character) reinforces our culture's celebration of the individual. Her promiscuous, forceful, and charming persona is familiar

Cultural invisibility in _Juno_

An unrepentant former stripper (Diablo Cody) writes a script about an unrepentantly pregnant sixteen-year-old, her blithely accepting parents, and the dysfunctional couple to whom she relinquishes her newborn child. The resulting film goes on to become one of the biggest critical and box-office hits of 2007, attracting viewers from virtually every consumer demographic. How did a movie based on such seemingly provocative subject matter appeal to such a broad audience? One reason is that, beneath its veneer of controversy, _Juno_ repeatedly reinforces mainstream, even conservative, societal attitudes toward pregnancy, family, and marriage. Although Juno initially decides to abort the pregnancy, she quickly changes her mind. Her parents may seem relatively complacent when she confesses her condition, but they support, protect, and advise her throughout her pregnancy. When we first meet Mark (Jason Bateman) and Vanessa (Jennifer Garner), the prosperous young couple Juno has chosen to adopt her baby, it is with the youthful Mark [1] that we (and Juno) initially sympathize. He plays guitar and appreciates alternative music and vintage slasher movies. Vanessa, in comparison, comes off as a shallow and judgmental yuppie. But ultimately, both the movie and its protagonist side with the traditional values of motherhood and responsibility embodied by Vanessa [2], and reject Mark's rock-star ambitions as immature and self-centered.

because it displays traits we often associate with Hollywood's dominant view of the (usually male) rogue hero. Like Sam Spade, the Ringo Kid, Dirty Harry, and countless other classic American characters, Juno rejects convention yet ultimately upholds the very institutions she seemingly scorns. Yes, she's a smart-ass who cheats on homework, sleeps with her best friend, and pukes in her stepmother's decorative urn, yet in the end she does everything in her power to create the traditional nuclear family she never had. So even as the movie seems to call into question some of contemporary America's attitudes about family, its appeal to an arguably more fundamental American value (namely, robust individualism) explains in part why, despite its controversial subject matter, _Juno_ was (and still is) so popular with audiences.

Implicit and Explicit Meaning

As you attempt to become more skilled at looking at movies, try to be alert to the cultural values, shared ideals, and other ideas that lie just below the surface of the movie you're looking at. Being more alert to these things will make you sensitive to, and appreciative of, the many layers of meaning that any single movie contains. Of course, all this talk of layers and the notion that much of a movie's meaning lies below the surface may make the entire process of looking at movies seem unnecessarily complex and intimidating. But you'll find that the process of observing, identifying, and interpreting movie meaning will become considerably less mysterious and complicated once you grow accustomed to actively looking at movies rather than just watching them. It might help to keep in mind that, no matter how many different layers of meaning a movie may have, each layer is either implicit or explicit.

An **implicit meaning**, which lies below the surface of a movie's story and presentation, is closest to our everyday sense of the word _meaning_. It is an association, connection, or inference that a viewer makes on the basis of the **explicit meanings** available on the surface of the movie.

To get a sense of the difference between these two levels of meaning, let's look at two statements about _Juno_. First, let's imagine that a friend who hasn't seen the movie asks you what the film is _about_. Your friend doesn't want a detailed plot summary; she simply wants to know what she'll see if she decides to attend the movie.

In other words, she is asking for a statement about *Juno*'s explicit meaning. You might respond to her question by explaining:

> The movie's about a rebellious but smart sixteen-year-old girl who gets pregnant and resolves to tackle the problem head on. At first, she decides to get an abortion; but after she backs off that choice, she gets the idea to find a couple to adopt the kid after it's born. She spends the rest of the movie dealing with the implications of that choice.

It's not that this is the *only* explicit meaning in the film, but we can see that it is a fairly accurate statement about one meaning that the movie explicitly conveys to viewers, right there on its surface.

Now what if your friend hears this statement of explicit meaning and asks, "Okay, sure, but what do you think the movie is trying to say? What does it *mean?*" In a case like this, when someone is asking in general about an entire film, he or she is seeking something like an overall message or a point. In essence, your friend is asking you to *interpret* the movie—to say something arguable about it—not simply to make a statement of obvious surface meaning that everyone can agree on, as we did when we presented its explicit meaning. In other words, she is asking for your sense of the movie's implicit meaning. Here is one possible response: "A teenager faced with a difficult decision makes a bold leap toward adulthood but, in doing so, discovers that the world of adults is no less uncertain or overwhelming than adolescence." At first glance, this statement might seem to have a lot in common with your summary of the movie's explicit meaning, as, of course, it does—after all, even though a meaning is under the surface, it still has to relate to the surface, and your interpretation needs to be grounded in the explicitly presented details of that surface. But if you compare the two statements more closely, you can see that the second one is more interpretive than the first, more concerned with what the movie means.

Explicit and implicit meanings need not pertain to the movie as a whole, and not all implicit meaning is tied to broad messages or themes. Movies convey and imply smaller, more specific doses of both kinds of meaning in virtually every scene. *Juno*'s application of lipstick before she visits the adoptive father, Mark, is explicit information. The implications of this action—that her admiration for Mark is beginning to develop into some-

Explicit detail and implied meaning in *Juno*
Vanessa is the earnest yuppie mommy-wannabe to whom Juno has promised her baby. In contrast to the formal business attire she usually sports, Vanessa wears an Alice in Chains T-shirt to paint the nursery. This small explicit detail conveys important implicit meaning about her relationship with her husband, Mark, a middle-aged man reluctant to let go of his rock-band youth. The paint-spattered condition of the old shirt implies that she no longer values this symbol of the 1990s grunge-rock scene and, by extension, her past association with it.

thing approaching a crush—are implicit. Later, Mark's announcement that he is leaving his wife and does not want to be a father sends Juno into a panicked retreat. On her drive home, a crying jag forces the disillusioned Juno to pull off the highway. She skids to a stop beside a rotting boat abandoned in the ditch. The discarded boat's decayed condition and the incongruity of a watercraft adrift in an expanse of grass are explicit details that convey implicit meaning about Juno's isolation and alienation.

It's easy to accept that recognizing and interpreting implicit meaning requires some extra effort, but keep in mind that explicit meaning cannot be taken for granted simply because it is by definition obvious. Although explicit meaning is on the surface of a film for all to observe, viewers or writers likely will not remember and acknowledge every part of that meaning. Because movies are rich in plot detail, a good analysis must begin by taking into account the breadth and diversity of what has been explicitly presented. For example, we cannot fully appreciate the significance of Juno's defiant dumping of a blue slushy into her stepmother's beloved urn unless we have noticed and noted her dishonest denial when accused earlier of vomiting a similar substance into the same precious vessel. Our ability to discern a movie's explicit meanings directly depends on our ability to notice such associations and relationships.

Viewer Expectations

The discerning analyst must also be aware of the role expectations play in how movies are made, marketed, and received. Our experience of nearly every movie we see is shaped by what we have been told about that movie beforehand by previews, commercials, reviews, interviews, and word of mouth. After hearing your friends rave endlessly about *Juno*, you may have been underwhelmed by the actual movie. Or you might have been surprised and charmed by a film you entered with low expectations, based on the inevitable backlash that followed the movie's surprise success. Even the most general knowledge affects how we react to any given film. We go to see blockbusters because we crave an elaborate special effects extravaganza. We can still appreciate a summer movie's relatively simpleminded storytelling, as long as it delivers the promised spectacle. On the other hand, you might revile a high-quality tragedy if you bought your ticket expecting a lighthearted comedy.

Of course, the influence of expectation extends beyond the kind of anticipation generated by a movie's promotion. As we discussed earlier, we all harbor essential expectations concerning a film's form and organization. And most filmmakers give us what we expect: a relatively standardized cinematic language, seamless continuity, and a narrative organized like virtually every other fiction film we've ever seen. For example, years of watching movies has taught us to expect a clearly motivated protagonist to pursue a goal, confronting obstacles and antagonists along the way toward a clear (and usually satisfying) resolution. Sure enough, that's what we get in most commercial films.

We'll delve more deeply into narrative in the chapters that follow. For now, what's important is that you understand how your experience—and thus your interpretation—of any movie is affected by how the particular film manipulates these expected patterns. An analysis might note a film's failure to successfully exploit the standard structures or another movie's masterful subversion of expectations to surprise or mislead its audience. A more experimental approach might deliberately confound our

presumption of continuity or narrative. Viewers must be alert to these expected patterns in order to fully appreciate the significance of that deviation.

Expectations specific to a particular performer or filmmaker can also alter the way we perceive a movie.

1

2

Expectations and character in *Juno*

Audience reactions to Michael Cera's characterization of Juno's sort-of boyfriend, Paulie Bleeker, are colored by expectations based on the actor's perpetually embarrassed persona established in previous roles in the television series *Arrested Development* and films like *Superbad* [1]. We don't need the movie to tell us much of anything about Paulie—we form an almost instant affection for the character based on our familiarity with Cera's earlier performances. But while the character Paulie meets our expectations of Michael Cera, he defies our expectations of his character type. Repeated portrayals of high-school jocks as vain bullies, such as Thomas F. Wilson's iconic Biff in Robert Zemeckis's *Back to the Future* (1985) [2] have conditioned viewers to expect such characters to look and behave very differently than Paulie Bleeker.

For example, any fan of actor Michael Cera's previous performances as an endearingly awkward adolescent in the film *Superbad* (2007; director Greg Mottola) and television series *Arrested Development* (2003–2006) will watch *Juno* with a built-in affection for Paulie Bleeker, Juno's sort-of boyfriend. This predetermined fondness does more than help us like the movie; it dramatically changes the way we approach a character type (the high-school athlete who impregnates his teenage classmate) that our expectations might otherwise lead us to distrust. Ironically, audience expectations of Cera's sweetness may have contributed to the disappointing box-office performance of *Scott Pilgrim vs. the World* (2010; director Edgar Wright). Some critics proposed that viewers were uncomfortable seeing Cera play the somewhat vain and self-centered title character.

Viewers who know director Guillermo del Toro's commercial action/horror movies *Mimic* (1997), *Blade II* (2002), *Hellboy* (2004), and *Pacific Rim* (2013) might be surprised by the sophisticated political and philosophical metaphor of *Pan's Labyrinth* (2006) or *The Devil's Backbone* (2001). Yet all five films feature fantastic and macabre creatures as well as social commentary. An active awareness of an audience's various expectations of del Toro's films would inform an analysis of the elements common to the filmmaker's seemingly schizophrenic body of work. Such an analysis could focus on his visual style in terms of production design, lighting, or special effects, or it might instead examine recurring themes such as oppression, childhood trauma, or the role of the outcast.

As you can see, cinematic invisibility is not necessarily an impediment; once you know enough to acknowledge their existence, these potential blind spots also offer opportunities for insight and analysis. There are many ways to look at movies and many possible types of film analysis. We'll spend the rest of this chapter discussing the most common analytical approaches to movies.

Since this book considers an understanding of how film grammar conveys meaning, mood, and information as the essential foundation for any further study of cinema, we'll turn now to **formal analysis**—that analytical approach primarily concerned with film **form**, or the means by which a subject is expressed. Don't worry if you don't fully understand the function of the techniques discussed; that's what the rest of this book is for.

Formal Analysis

Formal analysis dissects the complex synthesis of cinematography, sound, composition, design, movement, performance, and editing orchestrated by creative artists like screenwriters, directors, cinematographers, actors, editors, sound designers, and art directors as well as the many craftspeople who implement their vision. The movie meaning expressed through form ranges from narrative information as straightforward as where and when a particular scene takes place to more subtle implied meaning, such as mood, tone, significance, or what a character is thinking or feeling.

While the overeager analyst certainly can read more meaning into a particular visual or audio component than the filmmaker intended, you should realize that cinematic storytellers exploit every tool at their disposal and that, therefore, every element in every frame is there for a reason. It's the analyst's job to carefully consider the narrative intent of the moment, scene, or sequence before attempting any interpretation of the formal elements used to communicate that intended meaning to the spectator.

For example, the simple awareness that *Juno*'s opening shot [1] is the first image of the movie informs us of the moment's most basic and explicit intent: to convey setting (contemporary middle-class suburbia) and time

LOOKING AT MOVIES
FILM ANALYSIS

VIDEO ▶

In this tutorial, Dave Monahan analyzes the "waiting room" scene from *Juno* and covers other key concepts of film analysis.

of day (dawn). But only after we have determined that the story opens with its title character overwhelmed by the prospect of her own teenage pregnancy are we prepared to deduce how this implicit meaning (her state of mind) is conveyed by the composition: Juno is at the far left of the frame and is tiny in relationship to the rest of the wide-angle composition. In fact, we may be well into the four-second shot before we even spot her. Her vulnerability is conveyed by the fact that she is dwarfed by her surroundings. Even when the scene cuts to a closer viewpoint [2], she, as the subject of a movie composition, is much smaller in frame than we are used to seeing, especially in the first shots used to introduce a protagonist. She is standing in a front yard contemplating an empty stuffed chair from a safe distance, as if the inanimate object might attack at any moment. Her pose adds to our implicit impression of Juno as alienated or off-balance.

Our command of the film's explicit details alerts us to another function of the scene: to introduce the recurring **theme** (or **motif**) of the empty chair that frames—and in some ways defines—the story. In this opening scene, accompanied by Juno's voice-over explanation, "It started with a chair," the empty, displaced object represents Juno's status and emotional state and foreshadows the unconventional setting for the sexual act that got her into this mess. By the story's conclusion, when Juno announces, "It ended with a chair," the motif—in the form of an adoptive mother's rocking chair—has been transformed, like Juno herself, to embody hope and potential.

All that meaning was packed into two shots spanning about 12 seconds of screen time. Let's see what we can learn from a formal analysis of a more extended sequence from the same film: Juno's visit to the Women Now clinic. To do so, we'll first want to consider what information the filmmaker needs this scene to communicate for viewers to understand and appreciate this pivotal piece of the movie's story in relation to the rest of the narrative. As we delve into material that deals with *Juno*'s sensitive subject matter, keep in mind that you don't have to agree with the meaning or values projected by the object of your analysis; you can learn even from a movie you dislike. Personal values and beliefs will undoubtedly influence your analysis of any movie. And personal views provide a legitimate perspective, as long as we recognize and acknowledge how they may color our interpretation.

1

2

Throughout *Juno*'s previous 18 minutes, all information concerning its protagonist's attitude toward her condition has explicitly enforced our expectation that she will end her unplanned pregnancy with an abortion. She pantomimes suicide once she's forced to admit her condition; she calmly discusses abortion facilities with her friend Leah; she displays no ambivalence when scheduling the procedure. As she approaches the clinic, Juno's nonchalant reaction to the comically morose pro-life demonstrator Su-Chin reinforces our expectations. Juno treats Su-Chin's assertion that the fetus has fingernails as more of an interesting bit of trivia than a concept worthy of serious consideration.

The subsequent waiting-room sequence is about Juno making an unexpected decision that propels the story in an entirely new direction. A formal analysis will tell us how the filmmakers orchestrated multiple formal elements, including sound, composition, moving camera,

and editing, to convey in 13 shots and 30 seconds of screen time how the seemingly insignificant fingernail factoid infiltrates Juno's thoughts and ultimately drives her from the clinic. By the time you have completed your course (and have read the book), you should be prepared to apply this same sort of formal analysis to any scene you choose.

The waiting-room sequence's opening shot [1] **dollies in** (the camera moves slowly toward the subject), which gradually enlarges Juno in frame, increasing her visual significance as she fills out the clinic admittance form on the clipboard in her hand [2]. The shot reestablishes her casual acceptance of the impending procedure, pro-

viding context for the events to come. Its relatively long 10-second **duration** sets up a relaxed rhythm that will shift later along with her state of mind. As the camera reaches its closest point, a loud sound invades the low hum of the previously hushed waiting room.

This obtrusive drumming sound motivates a somewhat startling cut to a new shot that plunges our viewpoint right up into Juno's face [3]. The sudden spatial shift gives the moment resonance and conveys Juno's thought process as she instantly shifts her concentration from the admittance form to this strange new sound. She turns her head in search of the sound's source, and the camera adjusts to adopt her **point of view** of a mother

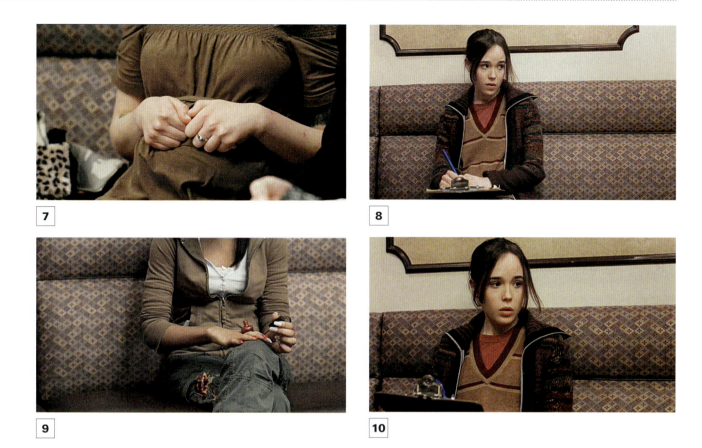

7

8

9

10

and daughter sitting beside her [4]. The mother's finger-nails drumming on her own clipboard is revealed as the source of the tapping sound. The sound's abnormally loud level signals the audience that we're not hearing at a natural volume level—we've begun to experience Juno's psychological perceptions. The little girl's stare into Juno's (and our) eyes helps to establish the association between the fingernail sound and Juno's latent guilt.

The sequence cuts back to the already troubled-looking Juno [5]. The juxtaposition connects her anxious expression to both the drumming mother and the little girl's gaze. The camera creeps in on her again. This time, the resulting enlargement initiates our intuitive association of this gradual intensification with a character's moment of realization. Within half a second, another noise joins the mix, and Juno's head turns in response [6].

The juxtaposition marks the next shot as Juno's point of view, but it is much too close to be her literal point of view. Like the unusually loud sound, the unrealistically close viewpoint of a woman picking her thumbnail reflects not an actual spatial relationship but the sight's significance to Juno [7]. When we cut back to Juno about a second later, the camera continues to close in on her,

and her gaze shifts again to follow yet another sound as it joins the rising clamor [8].

A new shot of another set of hands, again from a close-up, psychological point of view, shows a woman applying fingernail polish [9]. What would normally be a silent action emits a distinct, abrasive sound.

When we cut back to Juno half a second later, she is much larger in the frame than the last few times we saw her [10]. This break in pattern conveys a sudden intensification; this is really starting to get to her. Editing often establishes patterns and rhythms, only to break them for dramatic impact. Our appreciation of Juno's situation is enhanced by the way editing connects her reactions to the altered sights and sounds around her, as well as by her implied isolation—she appears to be the only one who notices the increasingly boisterous symphony of fingernails. Of course, Juno's not entirely alone—the audience is with her. At this point in the sequence, we have begun to associate the waiting-room fingernails with Su-Chin's attempt to humanize Juno's condition.

Juno's head jerks as yet another, even more invasive sound enters the fray [11]. We cut to another close-up point-of-view shot, this time of a young man scratching his arm [12]. At this point, another pattern is broken,

19

20

initiating the scene's formal and dramatic climax. Up until now, the sequence alternated between shots of Juno and shots of the fingernails as they caught her attention. Each juxtaposition caused us to identify with both Juno's reaction and her point of view. But now, the sequence shifts gears; instead of the expected switch back to Juno, we are subjected to an accelerating succession of fingernail shots, each one shorter and louder than the last. A woman bites her fingernails [13]; another files her nails [14]; a woman's hand drums her fingernails nervously [15]; a man scratches his neck [16]. With every new shot, another noise is added to the sound mix.

This pattern is itself broken in several ways by the scene's final shot. We've grown accustomed to seeing Juno look around every time we see her, but this time, she stares blankly ahead, immersed in thought [17]. A cacophony of fingernail sounds rings in her (and our) ears as the camera glides toward her for 3½ very long seconds—a duration six times longer than any of the previous nine shots. These pattern shifts signal the scene's climax, which is further emphasized by the moving camera's enlargement of Juno's figure [18], a visual action that cinematic language has trained viewers to associate with a subject's moment of realization or decision.

But the shot doesn't show us Juno acting on that decision. We don't see her cover her ears, throw down her clipboard, or jump up from the waiting-room banquette. Instead, we are ripped prematurely from this final waiting-room image and plunged into a shot that drops us into a different space and at least several moments ahead in time—back to Su-Chin chanting in the parking lot [19]. This jarring spatial, temporal, and visual shift helps us feel Juno's own instability at this crucial narrative moment. Before we can get our bearings, the camera has pivoted right to reveal Juno bursting out of the clinic door in the background [20]. She races past Su-Chin without a word. She does not have to say anything. Cinematic language—film form—has already told us what she decided and why.

Anyone watching this scene would sense the narrative and emotional meaning revealed by this analysis, but only a viewer actively analyzing the film form used to construct it can fully comprehend how the sophisticated machinery of cinematic language shapes and conveys that meaning. Formal analysis is fundamental to all approaches to understanding and engaging cinema—whether you're making, studying, or simply appreciating movies—which is why the elements and grammar of film form are the primary focus of *Looking at Movies*.

Alternative Approaches to Analysis

Although we'll be looking at movies primarily to learn the forms they take and the nuts and bolts they are constructed from, any serious student of film should be aware that there are many other legitimate frameworks for analysis. These alternative approaches analyze movies more as cultural artifacts than as traditional works of art. They search beneath a movie's form and content to expose implicit and hidden meanings that inform our understanding of cinema's function within popular culture as well as the influence of popular culture on the movies.

The preceding formal analysis demonstrated how *Juno* used cinematic language to convey meaning and tell a story. Given the right interpretive scrutiny, our case study film may also speak eloquently about social conditions and attitudes. For example, considering that the protagonist is the daughter of an air-conditioner repairman and a manicurist, and that the couple she selects to adopt her baby are white-collar professionals

Comparative cultural analysis

A comparison of *Juno*'s treatment of unwanted pregnancy with other films featuring the same subject matter is but one of many analytical approaches that could be used to explore cinema's function within culture, as well as the influence of culture on the movies. Such an analysis could compare *Juno* with American films produced in earlier eras, from D. W. Griffith's dramatic *Way Down East* (1920) [1] to Preston Sturges's 1944 screwball comedy *The Miracle of Morgan's Creek* [2] to Roman Polanski's paranoid horror film *Rosemary's Baby* (1968) [3]. An alternate analysis might compare *Juno* with the other American films released in 2007 that approached the subject with a similar blend of comedy and drama: Judd Apatow's *Knocked Up* [4] and Adrienne Shelly's *Waitress* [5]. A comparative analysis of the independent film *Obvious Child* (2014; director Gillian Robespierre) [6] might reveal evolving cultural attitudes toward abortion seven years after *Juno*, *Knocked Up*, and *Waitress* all concluded with a birth scene.

living in an oversized McMansion, a cultural analysis of *Juno* could explore the movie's treatment of class.

An analysis from a feminist perspective could concentrate on, among other elements, the movie's depiction of women and childbirth, not to mention Juno's father, the father of her baby, and the prospective adoptive father. Such an analysis might also consider the creative and ideological contributions of the movie's female screenwriter, Diablo Cody, an outspoken former stripper and sex blogger.

A linguistic analysis might explore the historical, cultural, or imaginary origins of the highly stylized slang spouted by Juno, her friends, even the mini-mart clerk who sells her a pregnancy test. A thesis could be (and probably has been) written about the implications of the T-shirt messages displayed by the film's characters or the implicit meaning of the movie's track-team motif.

Some analyses place movies within the stylistic or political context of a director's career. *Juno*'s young director, Jason Reitman, has made only three other feature films. But even that relatively short filmography provides opportunity for comparative analysis: all of Reitman's movies take provocative political stances, gradually generate empathy for initially unsympathetic characters, and favor fast-paced expositional montages featuring expressive juxtapositions, graphic compositions, and first-person voice-over narration.

Another comparative analysis could investigate society's evolving (or perhaps fixed) attitudes toward "illegitimate" pregnancy by placing *Juno* in context with the long history of films about the subject. These movies range from D. W. Griffith's 1920 silent drama *Way Down East*, which banished its unwed mother and drove her to attempted suicide, to Preston Sturges's irreverent 1944 comedy *The Miracle of Morgan's Creek* and its mysteriously pregnant protagonist, Trudy Kockenlocker (whose character name alone says a great deal about its era's attitudes toward women) to another mysterious, but ultimately far more terrifying pregnancy in Roman Polanski's 1968 horror masterpiece *Rosemary's Baby*.

Juno is only one in a small stampede of recent popular films dealing with this ever-timely issue. A cultural analysis might compare and contrast *Juno* with its American contemporaries *Knocked Up* (2007; director Judd Apatow) and *Waitress* (2007; director Adrienne Shelly). Both movies share *Juno*'s blend of comedy and drama as well as a pronounced ambivalence concerning abortion, but depict decidedly different characters, settings, and stories. What might such an analysis of these movies (and their critical and popular success) tell us about that particular era's attitudes toward women, pregnancy, and motherhood? Seven years later, in 2014, *Obvious Child* was initially marketed as an "abortion comedy." When the protagonist Donna (Jenny Slate) finds herself pregnant after a one-night stand, her decision to get an abortion is immediate and matter of fact. Unlike all of its 2007 predecessors, *Obvious Child* does not deliver a baby in the end. Was director Gillian Robespierre reacting to those earlier films, influenced by evolving attitudes, or simply offering her own perspective on the subject? *Knocked Up* is written and directed by a man, *Juno* is written by a woman and directed by a man, *Waitress* and *Obvious Child* are written and directed by a woman. Does the relative gender of each film's creator affect stance and story? If this comparative analysis incorporated Romanian filmmaker Cristian Mungiu's stark abortion drama *4 Months, 3 Weeks and 2 Days* (2007) or Mike Leigh's nuanced portrayal of the abortionist *Vera Drake* (2004), the result might inform a deeper understanding of the differences between European and American sensibilities.

An unwanted pregnancy is a potentially controversial subject for any film, especially when the central character is a teenager. Any extensive analysis focused on *Juno*'s cultural meaning would have to address what this particular film's content implies about the hot-button issue of abortion. To illustrate, let's return to the clinic waiting room. An analysis that asserts *Juno* espouses a "pro-life" (i.e., antiabortion) message could point to several explicit details in this sequence and to those preceding and following it. In contrast to the relatively welcoming suburban settings that dominate the rest of the story, the ironically named Women Now abortion clinic is an unattractive stone structure squatting at one end of an urban asphalt parking lot. Juno is confronted by clearly stated and compelling arguments against abortion via Su-Chin's dialogue: the "baby" has a beating heart, can feel pain, . . . and has fingernails. The clinic receptionist, the sole on-screen representative of the pro-choice alternative, is a sneering cynic with multiple piercings and a declared taste for fruit-flavored condoms. The idea of the fetus as a human being, stressed by Su-Chin's earnest admonishments, is driven home by the scene's formal presentation analyzed earlier.

On the other hand, a counterargument maintaining that Juno implies a pro-choice stance could state that the lone on-screen representation of the pro-life position is portrayed just as negatively (and extremely) as the clinic receptionist. Su-Chin is presented as an infantile simpleton who wields a homemade sign stating, rather clumsily, "No Babies Like Murdering," shouts "All babies want to get borned!" and is bundled in an oversized stocking cap and pink quilted coat as if dressed by an overprotective mother. Juno's choice can hardly be labeled a righteous conversion. Even after fleeing the clinic, the clearly ambivalent mother-to-be struggles to rationalize her decision, which she announces not as "I'm having this baby" but as "I'm staying pregnant." Some analysts may conclude that the filmmakers, mindful of audience demographics, were trying to have it both ways. Others could argue that the movie is understandably more concerned with narrative considerations than a precise political stance. The negative aspects of every alternative are consistent with a story world that offers its young protagonist little comfort and no easy choices.

Cultural and Formal Analysis in *The Hunger Games*

In the preceding discussion we demonstrated that a popular mainstream entertainment like *Juno* offers ample material for analysis. While many film scholars study unorthodox approaches to the movie medium, or explore old or even forgotten films in search of cinematic origins and innovations, many of these same scholars pay special attention to blockbusters and other popular entertainments. To begin with, they may seek the answer to an obvious question: Why do audiences like this movie? Or, to take it a step further, what form, themes, and messages does this film contain that contemporary audiences are so eager to receive? The more consumers see a movie—or even just see the advertising and witness public reaction to its success—the more likely that movie is to exert some kind of effect on those consumers' culture. Any movie capable of influencing society is surely worth a closer look.

For example, the Hunger Games films picked up where the Harry Potter series left off to become the biggest

VIDEO ▶

In this tutorial, Dave Monahan provides a detailed shot-by-shot analysis of a scene from *The Hunger Games*.

film franchise of this decade. The first two installments, *The Hunger Games* (2011; director Gary Ross) and *The Hunger Games: Catching Fire* (2013; director Francis Lawrence), each broke box office records for an opening weekend; together, the two films earned $1.5 billion at the box office, a staggering figure that doesn't even include the additional exposure and revenue generated by DVD and Blu-ray sales, digital downloads, video on demand, and television broadcasts. The $122 million opening weekend posted by *The Hunger Games: Mockingjay—Part 1* (2014; director Francis Lawrence) was the biggest of 2014 and one of the strongest in box office history.[4] Clearly, the Hunger Games series is an influential and important cultural phenomenon. But how can we even begin to explain its popularity?

To start with, unlike the virtually all-male Avengers and Hobbit movies, the Hunger Games features a strong female protagonist capable of attracting the same ticket sales among women and girls that boosted the box office of other recent hits like *Maleficent* (2014, director Robert Stromberg) and *The Fault in Our Stars* (2014, director Josh Boone).[5] Katniss Everdeen is an expert hunter and a deadly fighter who takes bold risks and suffers consequences with stoic resolve.

---

4. www.boxofficemojo.com.

5. With a production budget of just $12 million, *The Fault in Our Stars* earned over $124 million at the box office. Twentieth Century Fox reported that 82 percent of the audience was female. *The Hunger Games* generated $161 million in its North American opening weekend alone; an estimated 71 percent of those ticket buyers were female. Globally, opening weekend box office sales for *Maleficent* topped $171 million; females comprised 60 percent of that audience. (Sources: www.indiewire.com, www.nydailynews.com, www.nytimes.com, www.boxofficemojo.com.)

1

2

Is *The Hunger Games* feminist?

Feminism is a movement and ideology that advocates the social, political, and economic equality of the sexes. The Hunger Games films feature a strong female protagonist who rarely depends on men for anything. On the contrary, Katniss is much more likely to be either attacking or protecting her male counterparts. She relies on more than weapon skills and brute strength; her success in the arena hinges on forming bonds and nurturing relationships. She is made an object of beauty for the pleasure and consumption of others, but never willingly. On the other hand, Katniss does spend a great deal of time and energy trying to appease the two boys vying for her affections. An analysis might explore how this complex character manages to embody feminist principles and yet also reflect gender stereotypes.

A cultural analysis of *The Hunger Games* might ask if the saga's heroine and fan base qualify the movies as feminist. Unlike a surprising number of Hollywood movies, the Hunger Games films certainly pass the Bechdel test. This test is an evaluative tool, credited to feminist cartoonist and author Alison Bechdel, that qualifies films as woman-friendly only if they (a) have at least two women characters who (b) talk to each other (c) about something besides a man. Katniss Everdeen certainly has plenty of other pressing topics to discuss with her mother, her sister Prim, and the other female tributes she either enlists or attacks in her struggle to survive. And when it comes to romance, Katniss defies most gender roles assigned to female film characters. She plays the role of protector not just for her mother and sister, but for her primary love interest, the passive and lovestruck baker boy Peeta.

This combination of feminist tendencies and attributes traditionally associated with a male hero might help explain the wide appeal of the Hunger Games movies. They attract female audiences that don't typically attend action franchises like The Avengers, and they draw in action-oriented male audiences that normally avoid female-centered fare like the Twilight movies.

But a closer look at the Katniss character could reveal an even more powerful touchstone with a key demographic. Like the teenagers who make up the bulk of her viewers, Katniss embodies a complex set of often conflicting emotions and perspectives. She is both angry and afraid, self-centered and self-hating, antiauthoritarian and desperate for guidance. Like most high school seniors, she faces an uncertain future that she often feels powerless to control or predict. She is forced to live up to increasingly mounting outside expectations while struggling to discover her own identity. In the arena, she even has to cope with "careers," the Hunger Games version of jocks and mean girls. No wonder Katniss is so petulant, defiant, and violent. And no wonder teenage viewers flock to participate vicariously in the adventures imposed upon her.

A narrative analysis of the Hunger Games films and their resonance with audiences might explore Katniss's place in a classical storytelling tradition. She is the ordinary girl suddenly revealed as a sort of chosen one with extraordinary hidden talents and a special destiny. This secret savior is plucked from obscurity, undergoes training, and is tested by a series of dangerous challenges. In the end, our unlikely heroine defeats a seemingly invincible evil. This same description could be applied to characters at the heart of other recent popular serial adventures, including Neo in the Matrix movies, Luke Skywalker in the original Star Wars trilogy, and Harry Potter. Some scholars maintain that Jesus Christ belongs to the same narrative tradition; others may argue the character type is in fact inspired by Christ's actual experience. Regardless of religious beliefs, it's hard to deny that Katniss Everdeen's behavior and presentation reference the Christ archetype. She's anointed, questioned, betrayed, and redeemed. At the climax of *The Hunger Games: Catching Fire*, she even sacrifices herself. Ironically, she does so by shooting an arrow at the roiling (and artificial) heavens, which then fall to pieces. Nevertheless, the Christ comparison is explicitly reinforced when Katniss, arms splayed in a cruciform pose and swathed in a shaft of white light, is lifted skyward by a giant artificial hand.

Is Katniss a Christ figure?
Like the Star Wars, Matrix, and Harry Potter blockbuster franchises that preceded it, the Hunger Games movies reference one of Western culture's most admired and familiar figures. The climactic scene in *The Hunger Games: Catching Fire* visually associates Katniss with Jesus Christ. After sacrificing herself, she ascends into the heavens.

An analysis studying the appeal of the Hunger Games movies would likely examine the films' central themes and discuss how those ideas reflect the culture that produced and consumed the popular series. Celebrity is central to Panem: tributes like Katniss and Peeta are transformed by stylists into slick, attractive products, and then tirelessly marketed as stars of elaborate entertainments. This ubiquitously broadcast spectacle keeps the masses in check by distracting them from far more serious issues. Sound familiar? A critical analysis might examine the irony of this particular social critique being manufactured, marketed, and capitalized by one of its primary targets: Hollywood itself. It could be argued that the actor Jennifer Lawrence is as aggressively marketed and culturally omnipresent as the Katniss character she portrays. Perhaps the timeliness of this theme contributes to the films' popularity; paradoxically, the same audiences that idolize the stars and spectacle of the Hunger Games may also identify with a struggle against enforced celebrity. In fact, the striking parallels to contemporary society drawn by post-apocalyptic movies are almost certainly central to the popularity of the genre.

Further investigation into the reception of the Hunger Games series could look for political analogies in the movies' narrative. The districts of Panem are controlled by a powerful (and power hungry) centralized government located in a capital city (the Capitol) that is both physically and culturally isolated. This situation reflects the way many conservatives and libertarians view the U.S. federal government in Washington, D.C. Liberal political forces warn that U.S. economic policies have created a growing gap between wealthy and poor Americans, much like the rift between the Capitol's privileged, frivolous elites and the Districts' downtrodden working class. An analysis might attempt to parse the films' political stance. Is the Hunger Games series a liberal indictment of corporate oppression, a depiction of conservative distrust of big government, a sharp satire of commercial media, or a multifaceted reflection of a more collective cultural malaise?

Ultimately, audiences want to see Katniss and company bring down the government that stages the Hunger Games. Like melting the ring in *The Lord of the Rings* or defeating Voldemort in *Harry Potter*, the promise of witnessing the eventual destruction of President Snow's regime is what keeps us watching through multiple movies. But along the way, the Hunger Games movies make us complicit in the sins of the Capitol. We enjoy a good multiplayer fight to the death as much as the citizens of Panem. As much as any of these aforementioned factors, the popularity of the Hunger Games series may be driven by an intoxicating amalgam of the kind of primitive impulses that fuel the license-to-kill mayhem of zombie movies and first-person shooter games, and the same competitive instincts that propel sports fandom (and sports movies). We deplore the government that forces Katniss to kill other tributes, but we can't help enjoying the games while they last.

Like a great athlete in the heat of a big game, Katniss must rely on her instincts to make instant—and often consequential—decisions. She impulsively volunteers to take Prim's place at the first reaping. In the first games, she uses her last arrow to start an explosive chain reaction that destroys the enemy's hoarded supplies. At the end of those games, only Peeta and Katniss are still standing. Rather than kill her friend to give the Capitol a lone victor, she suddenly proposes double suicide, a bold choice that forces the Capitol to allow two victors for the first time in the history of the games—and makes Katniss a folk hero capable of sparking revolution. What makes these game-changing actions notable, and particular to this character and this series, is how these rash decisions and their outcomes combine unbridled emotion with global significance. One last critical analysis might attribute the success of the Hunger Games movies to this validating vision of teen empowerment.

As you can see, even mainstream crowd-pleasers like the Hunger Games films can offer a multitude of avenues for cultural and critical analysis. But this book is primarily dedicated to film form. Let's close this introduction

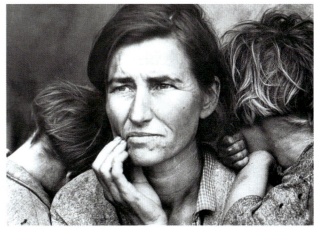

The Hunger Games references cultural touchstones

Like many speculative works of cinematic science fiction, the Hunger Games films project contemporary problems into a post-apocalyptic future. The movies also exploit powerful ideas and images from the past. The clothes, hairstyles, and settings in District 13 reference famous photographs of Depression-era America. The Capitol parade grounds and President Snow's podium feature the same spartan symmetry and graphic emblems favored by the Nazis and other World War II–era Fascists.

Are *The Hunger Games* and *The Hunger Games: Catching Fire* sports movies?

Sports genre movies from *Rocky* (1976; director John G. Avildsen) to *Hoosiers* (1986; director David Anspaugh) to *Cars* (2006; directors John Lasseter and Joe Ranft) all incorporate many of the same story elements that make sports themselves entertaining and compelling. An analysis of the first two Hunger Games films might discuss the ways that the post-apocalyptic sci-fi teen action films are also sports movies. Katniss and Peeta are inexperienced underdogs trained by a seemingly unreliable coach who later proves to be wise and caring. They face daunting competition and fall behind early, but cooperation, inner strength, and hidden talents ultimately lead them to victory.

with a formal analysis of one of the game-changers already mentioned—a pivotal scene from *The Hunger Games: Catching Fire*.

Infuriated by Katniss's defiance and District 12's unprecedented team win in the 74th Hunger Games, the sinister President Snow pays Katniss a surprise visit on the eve of her and Peeta's mandated victory tour. His message is alarmingly clear: if Katniss does not convince all of Panem that she is nothing more than a grateful and lovestruck citizen, everything and everyone she loves will be annihilated. But things go terribly wrong on the tour's very first stop. District 11, the home of slain tributes Roo and Thrush, who both sacrificed their own safety to aid Katniss, is even more oppressed than District 12. Shaken by the grim dignity in the faces of their forcibly assembled audience, both Katniss and Peeta go off script. Katniss's impromptu eulogy to the district's fallen tributes inspires a forbidden salute from a stoic old man. The crowd joins in the gesture of solidarity, which brings down the wrath of the "Peacekeeper" police. The revolution has begun.

The Hunger Games movies are full of speeches, interviews, and presentations. Usually, the action of an audience watching a speech is pretty straightforward.

Speakers speak, the audience watches and listens; the camera need only alternate between two shots to convey this simple exchange. But in this case, the participating characters' evolving thoughts and emotions are complex and narratively significant. Connections are made, perceptions evolve, choices are taken. To convey this complexity, the filmmakers have fragmented the 3½-minute scene into 56 shots, each one presenting its own particular cinematic take on the moment it conveys. While 56 shots is more than we need for the kind of comprehensive shot-by-shot breakdown we did for *Juno* earlier, we can still learn a lot from analyzing several representative shots and sequences.

As in nearly all films, color is used throughout the Hunger Games series to provide context and evoke mood. Scenes set in the Capitol are dominated by a spectrum of vibrant hues. Thanks to a combination of production design and digital visual effects known as color grading that were applied after the movie was shot, the districts are presented as virtually drained of color; what little there is consists of muted browns, grays, greens, and blues.

Katniss and Peeta's first view of the district [0] is typical of the virtually colorless look used to convey the hopeless hardship of the outer regions. This shot is also emblematic of the highly ordered, symmetrical composition the series employs to evoke the repressive power of the State. This same compositional depiction of au-

0

1

thority is employed in a number of shots interspersed throughout the speech scene, including the first shot [1].

The composition in that first shot is repeated twice more as the scene progresses. In all three examples, the representatives of the Capitol and the dais they stand on are composed in strict symmetry, as opposed to the relatively random arrangement of the District 11 workers in the foreground. The disparity between the presenters and their audience is further enforced with color and light. In the background, a dull blue shadow veils the symmetrical speakers and their armored entourage. In contrast, bright highlights rim each of the assembled workers, warming hues and giving the foreground crowd a dimension not present in the relatively flat background.

Like *Star Wars* Stormtroopers, the Peacekeepers on stage are dehumanized by armored uniforms and face-obscuring helmets. Later, in the moment the Peacekeepers move to attack the crowd in shot 44b, the camera dehumanizes them further by adjusting the frame to exclude their heads entirely. It's the same technique used by pioneering filmmaker Sergei Eisenstein to depict similarly brutal soldiers in his famous *Battleship Potemkin* "Odessa Steps" sequence eighty-eight years earlier [44a].

The impending threat of the Peacekeepers is emphasized at the beginning of the scene by placing an armed enforcer in the extreme foreground of shot 3. The figure obscures much of the frame and dominates the high-angle composition. The Peacekeeper dwarfs our heroes Katniss and Peeta, who are relatively tiny by compar-

3

6

ison, thanks to distance, camera angle, and a lens that exaggerates the effects of spatial perspective. The largest object in the frame is usually the subject of the shot, but here that is clearly not the case. The looming Peacekeeper casts a shadow that influences our interpretation of a shot that nonetheless clearly belongs to Katniss and Peeta. Context and movement make this evident, but what makes their narrative significance crystal clear is the fact that *they are crystal clear*. Unlike the Peacekeeper, our protagonists are in focus.

Filmmakers can manipulate how lenses and light interact to control what slice of the depth in front of the camera is in focus, and which portions of that space are out of focus. This cinematic property, known as **depth of field**, can be used expressively, or simply to emphasize the most significant action or subject in a particular composition. For example, Peeta opens the preapproved victory tour speech in shot 6. The most important part of this sequence is not his rote remarks but Katniss's growing emotional distress. So in this shot, and every other close-up featuring both victors, the speaker Peeta is a bit blurry; the silent Katniss is captured in sharp detail.

In the scene's 25th shot, Peeta withdraws, but Katniss hesitates. In doing so, she not only disobeys President Snow; she initiates a fascinating demonstration of the cinema's capacity to create vivid and meaningful connections between subjects seen separately on screen. We are so accustomed to interpreting and reacting to visual information in our daily lives that when we watch a

44a

44b

25

26

27a

27b

28

movie, we can't help identifying with the camera's viewpoint. This is especially true with shots that convey or imply another person's point of view by using an **eyeline match cut**. When a sequence repeatedly cuts back and forth between these point-of-view shots, our automatic identification with each of the alternating characters (via the camera) can dramatically intensify our narrative experience.

As Peeta drifts into the background of shot 25, Katniss lingers and looks offscreen. Her expression and eyeline generate expectation and mystery: she's looking at someone, but who? That question is answered in shot 26. The big-screen video projection of Roo looks back at Katniss, and by extension, the viewer. This juxtaposition, along with the magnified size of Roo's face and the direction and directness of her gaze, establishes a living connection with the dead girl. It's a remarkable moment, and an especially fitting one given the central role media plays in the films. The image of Roo is shot "over the shoulder" of Katniss; her soft-focus silhouette crops the frame to concentrate more directly on her martyred friend.

The connection is intensified as the back-and-forth pattern continues with a cut back to Katniss. Shot 27 is the first shot in the scene she has not shared with Peeta. Katniss is now larger in the frame, increasing the implied significance of her reaction [27a]. She grows larger still as she steps to the foreground microphone [27b].

The sequence again provokes apprehension: we sense that something important is about to happen.

As Katniss begins to speak, her gaze offscreen shifts, motivating a cut to a new point of view. In shot 28, we're looking over her shoulder again, but this time it's into the eyes of Thrush's video projection. As Katniss's offscreen voice expresses respect and gratitude, Thrush stares back at her (and us) with the same imposing strength he displayed in the games.

In shot 29, Katniss concludes her tribute to Thrush, looks again to her right, raises her chin, and says, "I did know Roo." This time, we are able to anticipate the next shot; and sure enough, shot 30 is of Roo again. But this time the frame is cropped a little tighter, and Roo is a little bigger. As we saw in the *Juno* analysis, filmmakers often use progressions in subject size to incrementally increase significance as sequences build toward a narrative crescendo.

That intensification temporarily plateaus in shot 31, as Katniss continues her heartfelt tribute in the same

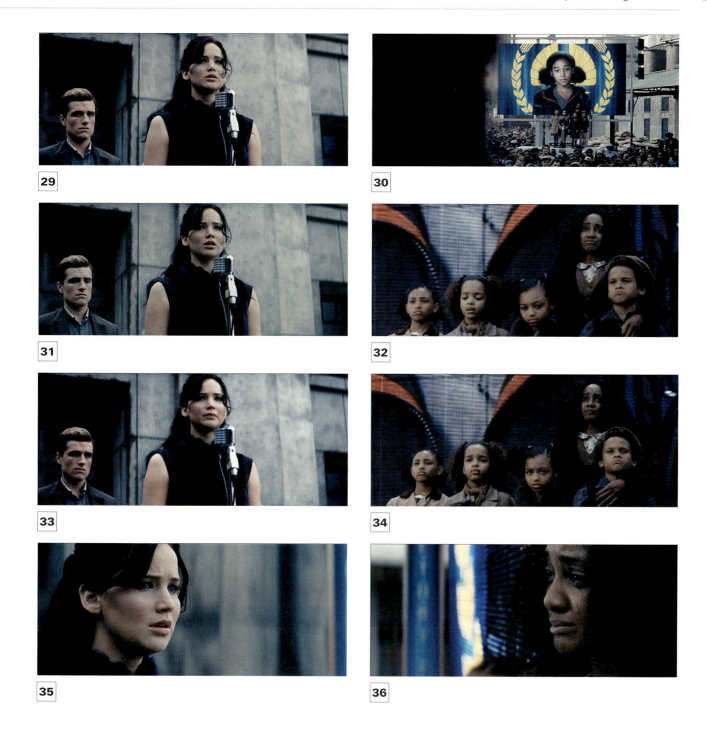

29

30

31

32

33

34

35

36

composition (probably the same **take**) that we saw in shot 29. But the sequence surprises us with the next cut. The pattern established in the previous seven shots taught us to expect another similar image of Roo, but shot 32 gives us her grieving family instead. For the first time in this interaction, Katniss's point of view does not convey her perspective from onstage. Katniss has not moved closer to the family; this enlargement reflects her state of mind as much as her point of view. Shots 33 and 34 repeat the juxtaposition—Katniss has not changed

the tone of her tribute, but cinematic language tells us that she is no longer addressing the crowd or the projection of Roo. She is now speaking directly to her friend's family.

The sequence shifts emphasis again with the next cut. In shot 35, Katniss's face—and the emotions it conveys—fills the frame in the scene's tightest close-up. The camera angle has moved up from the slightly lowered direction that previously helped evoke her elevated position on the speakers' platform. Whereas preceding shots

37

38b

38a

38c

had her looking offscreen in a more general direction, this virtual profile aims her eyeline specifically to the right.

The composition in shot 36 mirrors this composition; Roo's mother stares directly back at Katniss. The cut back to Katniss in shot 37 reinforces the effect—the two women are eye to eye. Nobody on the set has moved an inch, but these juxtapositions have transformed a ceremonial speech into an intimate confession. When Katniss apologizes for Roo's death, instead of bouncing back

as expected to Roo's mother's reaction, the sequence instead cuts to the older man. With this break in the pattern, shot 38a sends the scene in a new and unexpected direction, which is reflected in film form.

Before the salute, every image was smooth and stable; they were shot by a camera mounted on a fixed tripod or gliding dolly. Now, as the old man raises his hand [38b], the camera suddenly shifts to follow his three-fingered salute, then drops back down to his face [38c]. Thanks to personal and cinematic experience, viewers

39

41

40

42

45

46

47

48

49

50

51

52

53

54

55

56

instinctively associate this kind of spontaneous, slightly erratic movement with a handheld camera, a technique used to document unplanned and unpredictable events. After a brief four-shot sequence [39–42] in which the crowd follows the old man's courageous example, the Peacekeepers draw their weapons in shot 44b (on p. 27), and the extemporaneous instability of handheld camera returns to capture the ensuing chaos. The preceding forty-three shots covering the victor's speech were stable, composed, and patterned. The last twelve shots [45–56], capturing Katniss's anguished exit and the old man's immediate execution, are rough and rapid-fire.

The previous examples illustrate only a few of the virtually limitless approaches available to advanced students and scholars interested in how movies reflect and influence culture, and in how cinema functions as an art form. Formal analysis and cultural analysis are both useful and valid approaches to looking at movies.

LOOKING AT MOVIES

FILM ANALYSIS: *HARRY POTTER*

VIDEO ▶

In this tutorial, Dave Monahan discusses cultural analysis and looks closely at the Harry Potter series.

ANALYZING LOOKING AT MOVIES

As we said at the beginning of the chapter, the primary goal of *Looking at Movies* is to help you graduate from being a spectator of movies—from merely *watching* them—to actively and analytically *looking* at them. The chapters that follow provide specific information about each of the major formal components of film, information that you can use to write and talk intelligently about the films you view in class and elsewhere. Once you've read the chapter on cinematography, for example, you will have at hand the basic vocabulary to describe accurately the lighting and camera work you see on-screen.

As you read the subsequent chapters of this book, you will acquire a specialized vocabulary for describing, analyzing, discussing, and writing about the movies you see. But now, as a beginning student of film and armed only with the general knowledge that you've acquired in this first chapter, you can begin looking at movies more analytically and perceptively. You can easily say more than "I liked" or "I didn't like" the movie, because you can enumerate and understand the cinematic techniques and concepts the filmmakers employed to convey story, character state of mind, and other meanings. What's more, by cultivating an active awareness of the meanings and structures hidden under every movie's surface, you will become increasingly capable of recognizing the film's implicit meanings and interpreting what they reveal about the culture that produced and consumed it.

The following checklist provides a few ideas about how to start.

SCREENING CHECKLIST: LOOKING AT MOVIES

☐ Be aware that there are many ways to look at movies. Are you primarily interested in interpreting the ways in which the movie manipulates formal elements such as composition, editing, and sound to tell its story moment to moment, or are you concerned with what the movie has to say in broader cultural terms, such as a political message?

☐ Whenever you prepare a formal analysis of a scene's use of film grammar, start by considering the filmmakers' intent. Remember that filmmakers use every cinematic tool at their disposal; very little in any movie moment is left to chance. So before analyzing any scene, first ask yourself some basic questions: What is this scene about? After watching this scene, what do I understand about the character's thoughts and emotions? How did the scene make me feel? Once you determine what information and mood the scene conveyed, you'll be better prepared to figure out how cinematic tools and techniques were used to communicate the scene's intended meaning.

☐ Do your best to see beyond cinematic invisibility. Remember that a great deal of a movie's machinery is designed to make you forget you are experiencing a highly manipulated, and manipulative, artificial reality. One of the best ways to combat cinema's seamless presentation is to watch a movie more than once. You may allow yourself to be transported into the world of the story on your first viewing. Repeated viewings will give you the distance required for critical observation.

☐ On a related note, be aware that you may be initially blind to a movie's political, cultural, and ideological meaning, especially if that meaning reinforces ideas and values you already hold. The greater your awareness of your own belief systems (and those you share with your culture in general), the easier it will be to recognize and interpret a movie's implicit meaning.

☐ Ask yourself how expectations shaped your reaction to this movie. Does it conform to the ways you've come to expect a movie to function? How did what you'd heard about this movie beforehand—through the media, your friends, or your professor—affect your attitude toward the film? Did your previous experience of the director or star inform your prior understanding of what to expect from this particular film? In each case, did the movie fulfill, disappoint, or confound your expectations?

☐ Before and after you see a movie, think about the direct meanings, as well as the implications, of its title. The title of Roman Polanski's *Chinatown* (1974) is a specific geographic reference, but once you've seen the movie, you'll understand that it functions as a metaphor for a larger body of meaning. Richard Kelly's *Donnie Darko* (2001) makes us wonder if Darko is a real name (it is) or if it is a not-so-subtle clue that Donnie has a dark side (he does). Try to explain the title's meaning, if it isn't self-evident.

Questions for Review

1. What do you think of when you hear the word *movie*? Has your perception changed since reading this chapter? In what ways?

2. How is the experience of seeing a movie different from watching a play? Reading a book? Viewing a painting or photograph?

3. Why has the grammar of film evolved to allow audiences to absorb movie meaning intuitively?

4. In what ways do movies minimize viewers' awareness that they are experiencing a highly manipulated, artificial reality?

5. What do we mean by *cultural invisibility*? How is this different from *cinematic invisibility*?

6. What is the difference between *implicit* and *explicit* meaning?

7. How might your previous experiences of a particular actor influence your reaction to a new movie featuring the same performer?

8. What are some of the other expectations that can affect the way viewers react to a movie?

9. What are you looking for when you do a formal analysis of a movie scene? What are some other alternative approaches to analysis, and what sorts of meaning might they uncover?

10. At this point, would you say that learning what a movie is all about is more challenging than you first thought? If so, why?

STUDENT RESOURCES ONLINE

digital.wwnorton.com/movies5

▶ **VIDEO**

The tutorials for this chapter analyze scenes from *Juno* and *The Hunger Games* and they review important concepts covered in this chapter.

CHAPTER

PRINCIPLES OF FILM FORM

2

Film Form

Chapter 1's analyses of scenes from *Juno* and the Hunger Games series provided us with a small taste of how the various elements of movies work. We saw how the filmmakers coordinated performance, composition, sound, and editing to create meaning and tell a story. All of these elements were carefully chosen and controlled by the filmmakers to produce each movie's form.

If we've learned nothing else so far, we can at least now say with confidence that very little in any movie is left to chance. Each of the multiple systems that together become the "complex synthesis" that we know as a movie is highly organized and deliberately assembled and sculpted by filmmakers. For example, **mise-en-scène**, one elemental system of film, comprises design elements such as lighting, setting, props, costumes, and makeup within individual shots. **Sound**, another elemental system, is organized into a series of dialogue, music, ambience, and effects tracks. **Narrative** is structured into acts that establish, develop, and resolve character conflict. **Editing** juxtaposes individual **shots** (the product of one uninterrupted run of the camera) to create **sequences** (a series of shots unified by theme or purpose), arranges these sequences into **scenes** (complete units of plot action), and from these scenes builds a movie. The synthesis of all of these elemental systems (and others not mentioned above) constitutes the overall form that the movie takes. We'll spend some time

with each of these elemental formal systems in later chapters, but first let's take a closer look at the concept of form itself, beginning with the correlation between form and the content it shapes and communicates.

Form and Content

The terms *form* and *content* crop up in almost any scholarly discussion of the arts, but what do they mean, and why are they so often paired? To start with, we can define **content** as the subject of an artwork (what the work is about), and **form** as the means by which that subject is expressed and experienced. The two terms are often paired because works of art need them both. Content provides something to express; form supplies the methods and techniques necessary to present it to the audience.

And form doesn't just allow us to *see* the subject/content; it lets us see that content *in a particular way*. Form enables the artist to shape our particular experience *and interpretation* of that content. In the world of movies, form is **cinematic language:** the tools and techniques that filmmakers use to convey meaning and mood to the viewer, including lighting, mise-en-scène, cinematography, performance, editing, and sound—in other words, the content of most of this textbook.

If we consider the *Juno* scene analyzed in Chapter 1, the content is: *Juno in the waiting room*. We could be more specific and say that the content is *Juno thinking*

LOOKING AT MOVIES

FORM AND CONTENT

VIDEO ▶

This tutorial reviews the key concepts of form and content and illustrates their importance with additional examples.

Form and content

The *content* of the *Juno* "waiting room" scene analyzed in Chapter 1 is Juno thinking about fingernails and changing her mind. As we saw in that analysis, a great deal of *form* was employed to shape our experience and interpretation of that content, including sound, juxtaposition, pattern, point of view, and the relative size of the subject in each frame.

about fingernails and changing her mind. The form used to express that subject and meaning includes decor, patterns, implied proximity, point of view, moving camera, and sound.

The relationship between form and content is central not just to our study of movies; it is an underlying concern in all art. An understanding of the two intersecting concepts can help us to distinguish one work of art from another or to compare the styles and visions of different artists approaching the same subject.

If we look at three sculptures of a male figure, for example—by Praxiteles, Alberto Giacometti, and Keith Haring, artists spanning history from ancient Greece to the present—we can see crucial differences in vision, style, and meaning (see the illustrations on p. 38). Each sculpture can be said to express the same subject, the male body, but they clearly differ in form. Of the three, Praxiteles's sculpture, *Hermes Carrying the Infant Dionysus*, comes closest to resembling a flesh-and-blood body. Giacometti's *Walking Man* (1960) elongates and exaggerates anatomical features, but the figure remains recognizable as a male human. Haring's *Self*

Portrait (1989) smooths out and simplifies the contours of the human body to create an even more abstract rendering.

Once we recognize the formal differences and similarities among these three sculptures, we can ask questions about how the respective forms shape our emotional and intellectual responses to the subject matter. Look again at the ancient Greek sculpture. Although there might once have been a living man whose body looked like this, very few bodies do. The sculpture is an idealization—less a matter of recording the way a particular man actually looked than of visually describing an ideal male form. As such, it is as much an interpretation of the subject matter as—and thus no more "real" than—the other two sculptures. Giacometti's version, because of its exaggerated form, conveys a sense of isolation and nervousness, perhaps even anguish. Haring's sculpture, relying on stylized and almost cartoonlike form, seems more playful and mischievous than the other two. Suddenly, because of the different form each sculpture takes, we realize that the content of each has changed: they are no

1

2

3

Form and content

Compare these sculptures: [1] *Hermes Carrying the Infant Dionysus*, by Praxiteles, who lived in Greece during the fourth century BCE; [2] *Walking Man II*, by Alberto Giacometti (1901–1966), a Swiss artist; and [3] *Self Portrait*, by Keith Haring (1958–1990), an American. Although all three works depict the male figure, their forms are so different that their meanings, too, must be different. What, then, is the relationship between the form of an artwork and its content?

Focusing on content

Sometimes, of course, we might have good reasons, conceptually and critically, to isolate the content of a film from its form. The subject of Kathryn Bigelow's *Zero Dark Thirty* (2012, screenwriter Mark Boal) is the tracking and eventual killing of Osama Bin Laden by United States CIA agents and U.S. Navy Seals. That content is historical fact. But limited access to some specific details, and the demands of cinematic storytelling, compelled the filmmakers to take liberties with the original content when giving the movie its ultimate form. *Zero Dark Thirty* invents and combines characters, rearranges and condenses action, and speculates on events. Many critiques of *Zero Dark Thirty*, noting the significance and sensitivity of the content, questioned the film's completeness, accuracy, and reliability. Yet the movie could be considered a formal success; it received Academy Award nominations for Best Picture, Actress, Original Screenplay, Film Editing, and Sound Editing. By focusing solely on content, we may risk overlooking the aspects that make movies interesting as individual works of art.

longer *about* the same subject. Praxiteles's sculpture is somehow about defining an ideal; Giacometti's seems to reach for something that lies beneath the surface of human life and the human form; and Haring's appears to celebrate the body as a source of joy. As we become more attentive to their formal differences, these sculptures become more unlike each other in their content, too.

Thus form and content—rather than being separate things that come together to produce art—are instead two aspects of the entire formal system of a work of art. They are interrelated, interdependent, and interactive.

Form and Expectations

As we discussed in Chapter 1, our decision to see a particular movie is almost always based on certain expectations. Perhaps we have enjoyed previous work by the director, the screenwriter, or the actors; or publicity, advertisements, friends, or reviews have attracted us; or

the genre is appealing; or we're curious about the techniques used to make the movie.

Even if we have no such preconceptions before stepping into a movie theater, we will form impressions very quickly once the movie begins, sometimes even from the moment the opening credits roll. (In Hollywood, producers and screenwriters assume that audiences decide whether they like or dislike a movie within its first 10 minutes.) As the movie continues, we experience a more complex web of expectations. Many of them may be tied to the narrative—the formal arrangement of the events that make up the story—and specifically to our sense that certain events produce likely actions or outcomes.

We've learned to expect that most movies start with a "normal" world, which is altered by a particular incident, that in turn compels the characters to pursue a goal. And once the narrative begins, those expectations provoke us to ask predictive questions about the story's outcome, questions we will be asking ourselves repeatedly and waiting to have answered over the course of the film.

The nineteenth-century Russian playwright Anton Chekhov famously said that when a theater audience sees a character produce a gun in the first act, they expect that gun to be used before the play ends. Movie audiences have similar expectations. In the Coen brothers' 2010 version of *True Grit*, the villain Tom Chaney threatens young Mattie Ross: "That pit is one hundred feet deep and I will throw you in it." From that moment on, our interpretation of events is colored by the suggestion that Mattie is destined for the abyss. Later, when her would-be rescuer LeBoeuf says in passing, "Mind your footing, there is a pit here," our expectations are reinforced. We can't help but suppose that somebody is going down that hole. Screenwriters often organize a film's narrative structure around the viewer's desire to learn the answers to such central questions as, Will Dorothy get back to Kansas? or Will Frodo destroy the ring?

The first few scenes in *Short Term 12* (2013; director and screenwriter Destin Daniel Cretton) establish a series of interconnected expectations that will influence the way viewers engage and experience the story to come. Each event invests the audience with a certain predictive power. We anticipate—and desire—seeing these potentials develop into outcomes.

Short Term 12 takes place at a group home for troubled teenagers. Almost all of the characters are either

Formal expectations and *The Searchers*

Directors can subvert our most basic expectations of film form to dramatic effect. We have been conditioned to assume that the subject (or narrative focus) of any shot will be the largest or most noticeable element in the frame. At the point in John Ford's *The Searchers* (1956) illustrated here, the movie has devoted most of its screen time to Ethan Edwards's (John Wayne) thus-far fruitless five-year search for his kidnapped niece Debbie (Natalie Wood). Ford lends resonance to the climactic point when the searchers and their objective are finally (albeit briefly) reunited by reversing our formal expectations for such an important dramatic moment. As Ethan and his exasperated partner, Martin (Jeffrey Hunter), argue, the all-important Debbie appears not as the composition's featured visual element, but as a tiny figure in the background, distinguishable only by her movement across the stark sky and sand. Even though she is barely a speck on the screen, Debbie instantly becomes the focus of our attention. This unexpected formal approach allows the audience to spot the search's goal long before Ethan and Martin do, which creates suspense as we await her long-delayed arrival, anticipate her volatile uncle's reaction, and ask the story's central question one last time: Will the searchers ever find Debbie?

the kids confined for treatment or the workers who supervise them. In the movie's very first scene, the veteran staff person Mason (John Gallagher Jr.) is breaking in a new worker. Right in the middle of Mason's cautionary tale about escape attempts, a young detainee makes a break for it. We are only 3½ minutes into the story, but already we know this is a place that people try to get away from. And we can't help expecting that another attempted escape is in our future.

A few minutes later, Mason's tenacious supervisor Grace (Brie Larson) inducts a new resident, named Jayden (Kaitlyn Dever). She is hostile, miserable, smart, and seemingly immune to Grace's legendary powers of persuasion. The emphasis placed on Jayden's induction, combined with her apparently unshakable bad attitude, makes us anticipate a showdown—perhaps even one involving an attempted escape—between the troubled girl and her determined caseworker.

We learn that Grace is pregnant when she stops by a clinic after work to confirm her condition. Her feelings about the pregnancy are made clear when she immediately schedules an abortion. These actions raise expectations about her attitude toward the man responsible for her condition, but those expectations are complicated when she gets home and we discover she has an affectionate and supportive partner: her coworker, Mason. Grace doesn't tell Mason about the baby, but she does initiate a passionate encounter—only to abruptly and violently break off what she started. We can now recognize that Grace is struggling to overcome serious emotional problems of her own, problems that may either undermine or inform her attempts to help Jayden.

1

2

Expectations in *Bonnie and Clyde*

Much of the development and ultimate impact of Arthur Penn's *Bonnie and Clyde* (1967) depends on the sexual chemistry between the title characters [1], established through physical expression, dialogue, and overt symbolism. Early in the film, Clyde (Warren Beatty), ruthless and handsome, brandishes his gun threateningly and phallically [2]. Attracted by this display and others, the beautiful Bonnie (Faye Dunaway) is as surprised as we are when Clyde later rebuffs her obvious sexual attraction to him (at one point, he demurs, "I ain't much of a lover boy"). We may not like this contradiction, but it is established early in the film and quickly teaches us that our expectations will not always be satisfied.

And, as we learned in *Juno*, a pregnancy can be suggestive as Chekhov's hypothetical gun. We expect an end result, and we can't help wondering how that conclusion will affect the character concerned.

All of these developments lead us to adjust previous expectations about the movie's eventual outcome. In each of the cases described, the general expectation is ultimately fulfilled, but none of the situations play out exactly as we initially predict. Making, processing, and revising expectations is part of what makes watching movies a compelling participatory experience.

Director Alfred Hitchcock treated his audiences' expectations in ironic, even playful, ways—sometimes using the gun, so to speak, and sometimes not—and this became one of his major stylistic traits. Hitchcock used the otherwise meaningless term *MacGuffin* to refer to an object, document, or secret within a story that is vitally important to the characters, and thus motivates their actions and the conflict, but that turns out to be less significant to the overall narrative than we might at first expect.[1] In *Psycho* (1960; screenwriter Joseph Stefano), for example, Marion Crane (Janet Leigh) believes that the $40,000 she steals from her employer will help her start a new life. Instead, her flight with the money leads to the Bates Motel, the resident psychopath, and Marion's death. The money plays no role in motivating her murderer; in fact, the killer doesn't seem to know it exists. Once the murder has occurred, the money—a classic MacGuffin—is of no real importance to the rest of the movie. With the death of our assumed protagonist, Hitchcock sends our expectations in a new and unanticipated direction. The question that drew us into the narrative—Will Marion get away with embezzlement?—suddenly switches to Who will stop this murderously overprotective mother? As anyone who has seen *Psycho* knows, this narrative about-face isn't the end of the director's manipulation of audience expectations.

Even as the narrative form of a movie is shaping and sometimes confounding our expectations, other formal qualities may perform similar functions. Seemingly insignificant and abstract elements of film such as color schemes, sounds, shot length, and camera movement often cooperate with dramatic elements to either heighten or confuse our expectations. One way they do this is by establishing patterns.

Patterns

Instinctively, we search for patterns and progressions in all art forms. The more these meet our expectations (or contradict them in interesting ways), the more likely we are to enjoy, analyze, and interpret the work.

The penultimate scene in D. W. Griffith's *Way Down East* (1920; scenario Anthony Paul Kelly), one of the most famous chase scenes in movie history, illustrates

1. Hitchcock discusses the MacGuffin in François Truffaut, *Hitchcock*, rev. ed. (New York: Simon & Schuster, 1984), pp. 137–139.

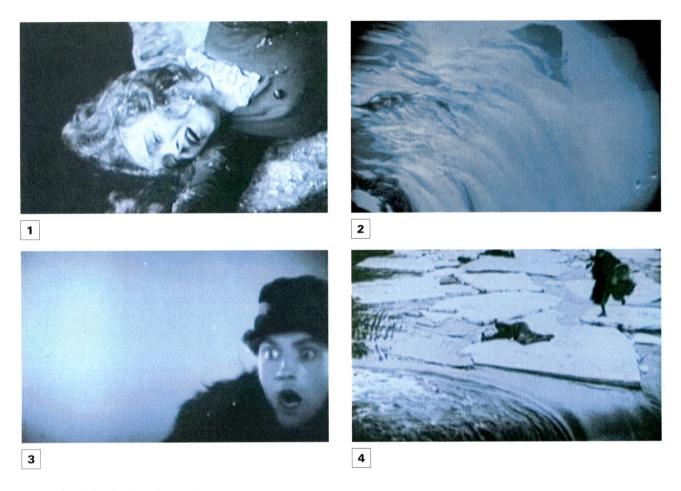

Parallel editing in *Way Down East*

Pioneering director D. W. Griffith risked the lives of actors Lillian Gish and Richard Barthelmess to film *Way Down East*'s now classic "ice break" scene—a scene that builds suspense by exposing us to a pattern of different shots called *parallel editing*. Griffith shot much of the blizzard and ice-floe footage along the Connecticut River, then edited it together with studio shots and scenes of Niagara Falls. Gish, thinly dressed, was freezing on the ice and was periodically revived with hot tea. Although the dangers during filming were real enough, the "reality" portrayed in the final scene—a rescue from the certain death that would result from a plunge over Niagara Falls—is wholly the result of Griffith's use of a pattern of editing that has by now become a standard technique in narrative filmmaking.

how the movies depend on our recognition of patterns. Banished from a "respectable" family's house because of her scandalous past, Anna Moore (Lillian Gish) tries to walk through a blizzard but quickly becomes disoriented and wanders onto a partially frozen river. She faints on an ice floe and, after much suspense, is rescued by David Bartlett (Richard Barthelmess) just as she is about to go over a huge waterfall to what clearly would have been her death.

To heighten the drama of his characters' predicament, Griffith employs parallel editing—a technique that makes different lines of action appear to be occurring simultaneously. Griffith shows us Anna on the ice, Niagara Falls, and David jumping from one floe to another as he tries to catch up with her. As we watch these three lines of action edited together (in a general

pattern of ABCACBCABCACBC), they appear simultaneous. We assume that the river flows over Niagara Falls and that the ice floe that Anna is on is heading down that river. It doesn't matter that the actors weren't literally in danger of going over a waterfall or that David's actions did not occur simultaneously with Anna's progress downriver on the floe. The form of the scene, established by the pattern of parallel editing, has created an illusion of connections among these various shots, leaving us with an impression of a continuous, anxiety-producing drama.

The editing in one scene of Jonathan Demme's *The Silence of the Lambs* (1991; screenwriter Ted Tally) takes advantage of our natural interpretation of parallel action to achieve a disorienting effect. Earlier in the movie, Demme has already shown us countless ver-

Patterns and suspense

Filmmakers can use patterns to catch us unawares. In *The Silence of the Lambs* (1991), Jonathan Demme exploits our sense that when shots are juxtaposed, they must share a logical connection. After FBI agents surround a house, an agent disguised as a deliveryman (Lamont Arnold) rings the doorbell [1]; a bell rings in the serial killer Buffalo Bill's (Ted Levine) basement [2]; Bill reacts to that ring [3], leaves behind the prisoner he was about to harm, goes upstairs, and answers his front door, revealing not the deliveryman we expect to see but Clarice Starling (Jodie Foster) [4]. As agents storm the house they've been staking out [5], Clarice and Bill continue to talk [6]. The agents have entered the wrong house, Clarice is now alone with a psychopath, and our anxiety rises as a result of the surprise.

sions of a formal pattern in which two elements seen in separation are alternated and related (ABABAB). So we expect that pattern to be repeated when shots of the serial killer Buffalo Bill (Ted Levine) arguing with his intended victim in his basement are intercut with shots of the FBI team preparing to storm a house. We naturally assume that the FBI has targeted the same house in which Buffalo Bill is going about his grisly business. When the sequence eventually reveals that the FBI is, in fact, attacking a different house, the pattern is broken, thwarting our expectations and setting in motion the suspenseful scene that follows.

Parallel editing is not the only means of creating and exploiting patterns in movies, of course. Some patterns

Breaking patterns for dramatic effect

The six consecutive underwater shots that open Terrence Malick's *The New World* (2005) establish a pattern of tranquility and affinity. Each shot conveys a harmonious fusion of indigenous people and their natural environment. The seventh shot rises from the blue waters to break the pattern and thus cinematically signal the Virginia Company's intrusion into the Algonquin paradise. Everything has suddenly changed: the light, the framing, the content, the world.

are made to be broken. The six consecutive underwater shots that open Terrence Malick's *The New World* (2005) establish a pattern of peace and affinity. Each shot conveys a harmonious fusion of indigenous people and their natural environment: fish glide past the camera, a smiling Pocahontas runs her hand across the shimmering surface, Algonquin natives swim hand in hand, and Pocahontas glides upward trailing a stream of air bubbles. The cumulative effect of this AAAAAA pattern is quietly powerful—it repeatedly reinforces a feeling of slow-motion tranquility. But the sequence's most expressive moment comes just when this pleasant pattern is broken. The seventh shot rises from the blue waters to cinematically signal the Virginia Company's intrusion into the Algonquin paradise. The underwater A shots were infused with blue; this open-air B shot is dominated by shades of brown. The opening A sequence featured close-framed human subjects; this pattern-breaking B shot is a wide angle of three large European ships. Everything has suddenly changed: the light, the framing, the content, the world.

The preceding examples offer a taste of how important patterns can be to our experience and interpretation of movies. Narrative patterns provide an element of structure, ground us in the familiar, or acquaint us with the unfamiliar; repeating them emphasizes their content. Shot patterns can convey character state of mind, create relationships, and communicate narrative meaning. As we will see in later chapters, nonnarrative patterns such as the repetition of a familiar image or a familiar sound effect (or motif from the movie's musical score) are also important components of film form.

Fundamentals of Film Form

The remaining chapters in this book describe the major formal aspects of film—narrative, mise-en-scène, cinematography, acting, editing, sound—to provide you with a beginning vocabulary for talking about film form more specifically. Before we study these individual formal elements, however, let's briefly discuss three fundamental principles of film form:

> Movies depend on light.

> Movies provide an illusion of movement.

> Movies manipulate space and time in unique ways.

Movies Depend on Light

Light is the essential ingredient in the creation and consumption of motion pictures. Movie images are made when a camera lens focuses light onto either film stock or a video sensor chip. Movie-theater projectors and video monitors all transmit motion pictures as light, which is gathered by the lenses and sensors in our own eyes. Movie production crews—including the cinematographer, the gaffer, the best boy, and many assorted grips and assistants—devote an impressive amount of time and equipment to illumination design and execution. Yet it would be a mistake to think of light as simply a requirement for a decent exposure. Light is more than a source of illumination; it is a key formal element that film artists and technicians carefully manipulate to create mood, reveal character, and convey meaning.

One of the most powerful black-and-white films ever made, John Ford's *The Grapes of Wrath* (1940), tells the story of an Oklahoma farming family forced off their land by the violent dust storms that plagued the region during the Great Depression of the 1930s (see p. 46). The eldest son, Tom Joad (Henry Fonda), returns home after serving a prison sentence, only to find that his family has left their farm for the supposedly greener pastures of California.

Tom and an itinerant preacher named Jim Casy (John Carradine), whom he has met along the way, enter the Joad house, using a candle to help them see inside the pitch-black interior. Lurking in the dark, but illuminated by the candlelight (masterfully simulated by cinematographer Gregg Toland), is Muley Graves (John Qualen), a farmer who has refused to leave Oklahoma with his family. As Muley tells Tom and Casy what has happened in the area, Tom holds the candle so that he and Casy can see him better [1], and the contrasts between the dark background and Muley's haunted face, illuminated by the flickering candle, reveal their collective state of mind: despair. The unconventional direction of the harsh light distorts the characters' features and casts elongated shadows looming behind and above them [2]. The story is told less through words than through the overtly symbolic light of a single candle.

Muley's flashback account of the loss of his farm reverses the pattern. The harsh light of the sun that, along with the relentless wind, has withered his fields beats down upon Muley, casting a deep, foreshortened shadow of the ruined man across his ruined land [3]. Such sharp contrasts of light and dark occur throughout the film, thus providing a pattern of meaning.

Expressive use of light in *The Grapes of Wrath*
Strong contrasts between light and dark (called chiaroscuro) make movies visually interesting and focus our attention on significant details. But that's not all that they accomplish. They can also evoke moods and meanings, and even symbolically complement the other formal elements of a movie, as in these frames from John Ford's *The Grapes of Wrath* (1940).

It is useful to distinguish between the luminous energy we call light and the crafted interplay between motion-picture light and shadow known as lighting. Light is responsible for the image we see on the screen, whether photographed (shot) on film or video, or created with a computer. Lighting is responsible for significant effects in each shot or scene. It enhances the texture, depth, emotions, and mood of a shot. It accents the rough texture of a cobblestoned street in Carol Reed's *The Third Man* (1949), helps to extend the illusion of depth in Orson Welles's *Citizen Kane* (1941), and emphasizes a character's subjective feelings of apprehension or suspense in such film noirs as Billy Wilder's *Double Indemnity* (1944). In fact, lighting often conveys these things by augmenting, complicating, or even contradicting other cinematic elements within the shot (e.g., dialogue, movement, or composition). Lighting also affects the ways that we see and think about a movie's characters. It can make a character's face appear attractive or unattractive, make the viewer like a character or be afraid of her, and reveal a character's state of mind.

These are just a few of the basic ways that movies depend on light to achieve their effects. We'll continue our discussion of cinema's use of light and manipulation of lighting later (Chapter 6 includes information and analysis of lighting's aesthetic role in cinematography; Chapter 11 covers how motion-picture technologies capture and use light). For now, it's enough to appreciate that light is essential to movie meaning and to the filmmaking process itself.

Movies Provide an Illusion of Movement

We need light to make, shape, and see movies, but it takes more than light to make *motion* pictures. As we learned in Chapter 1, movement is what separates cinema from all other two-dimensional pictorial art forms. We call them "movies" for a reason: the movies' expressive power largely derives from the medium's fundamental ability to move. Or, rather, they *seem* to move. As we sit in a movie theater, believing ourselves to be watching a continuously lit screen portraying fluid, uninterrupted movement, we are actually watching a quick succession of twenty-four individual still photographs per second. And as the projector moves one of these images out of the frame to bring the next one in, the screen goes dark. Although the movies are distin-

Lighting and character in *Atonement*

Filmmakers often craft the interplay between illumination and shadow to imply character state of mind. The tragic romance of *Atonement* (2007; director Joe Wright, cinematographer Seamus McGarvey) hinges on the actions of a precocious thirteen-year-old, Briony Tallis (Saoirse Ronan). Lives are irrevocably altered when Briony's adolescent jealousy prompts her to accuse the housekeeper's son Robbie of rape. As events unfold, a series of different lighting designs are employed to enhance our perception of Briony's evolving (and often suppressed) emotions as she stumbles upon Cecilia and Robbie making love in the library [1], catches a startled glimpse of her cousin's rape [2], accuses Robbie of the crime [3], guiltily retreats upon Robbie's arrival [4], contemplates the consequences of her actions [5], and observes Robbie's arrest [6].

guished from other arts by their dependence on light and movement, we spend a good amount of our time in movie theaters sitting in complete darkness, facing a screen with nothing projected on it at all!

The movement we see on the movie screen is an illusion, made possible by two interacting optical and per-

ceptual phenomena: persistence of vision and the phi phenomenon. **Persistence of vision** is the process by which the human brain retains an image for a fraction of a second longer than the eye records it. You can observe this phenomenon by quickly switching a light on and then off in a dark room. Doing this, you should see an afterimage of the objects in the room, or at least of whatever you were looking at directly when you switched the light off. Similarly, in the movie theater we see a smooth flow of images and not the darkness between frames. So the persistence of vision gives the *illusion of succession*, or one image following another without interruption. However, we must also experience the *illusion of movement*, or figures and objects within the image changing position simultaneously without actually moving.

The **phi phenomenon** is the illusion of movement created by events that succeed each other rapidly, as when two adjacent lights flash on and off alternately and we seem to see a single light shifting back and forth. The phi phenomenon is related to **critical flicker fusion**, which occurs when a single light flickers on and off with such speed that the individual pulses of light fuse together to give the illusion of continuous light. (Early movies were called *flicks* because the projectors that were used often ran at slower speeds than were necessary to sustain this illusion; the result was not continuous light, but a flickering image on-screen. The most acute human eye can discern no more than fifty pulses of light per second. Because the shutters of modern projectors "double-flash" each frame of film, we watch forty-eight pulses per second, close enough to the limit of perception to eliminate our awareness of the flicker effect.) The movie projector relies on such phenomena to trick us into perceiving separate images as one continuous image; and because each successive image differs only slightly from the one that precedes it, we perceive **apparent motion** rather than a series of jerky movements.

Movies Manipulate Space and Time in Unique Ways

Some of the arts, such as architecture, are concerned mostly with space; others, such as music, are related mainly to time. But movies manipulate space and time equally well, so they are both a spatial and a temporal art form. Movies can move seamlessly from one space to another (say, from a room to a landscape to outer space), or make space move (as when the camera turns around or away from its subject, changing the physical, psychological, or emotional relationship between the viewer and the subject), or fragment time in many different ways. Only movies can record real time in its chronological passing as well as subjective versions of time passing—slow motion, for example, or extreme compression of vast swaths of time.

On the movie screen, space and time are relative to each other, and we can't separate them or perceive one without the other. The movies give time to space and space to time, a phenomenon that art historian and film theorist Erwin Panofsky describes as the *dynamization of space* and the *spatialization of time*.[2] To understand this principle of "co-expressibility," compare your experiences of space when you watch a play and when you watch a movie. As a spectator at a play in the theater, your relationship to the stage, the settings, and the actors is *fixed*. Your perspective on these things is determined by the location of your seat, and everything on the stage remains the same size in relation to the entire stage. Sets may change between scenes, but within scenes the set remains, for the most part, in place. No matter how skillfully constructed and painted the set is, you know (because of the clear boundaries between the set and the rest of the theater) that it is not real and that when actors go through doors in the set's walls, they go backstage or into the wings at the side of the stage, not into a continuation of the world portrayed on the stage.

By contrast, when you watch a movie, your relationship to the space portrayed on-screen can be flexible. You still sit in a fixed seat, but the screen images move: the spatial relationships on the screen may constantly change, and the film directs your gaze. Suppose, for example, that during a scene in which two characters meet at a bar, the action suddenly flashes forward to their later rendezvous at an apartment, then flashes back to the conversation at the bar, and so on; or a close-up focuses your attention on one character's (or both characters') lips. A live theater performance can attempt versions of such spatial and temporal effects,[3] but a play can't do so as seamlessly, immediately, persuasively, or intensely as a movie can. If one of the two actors in that bar scene

---

2. Erwin Panofsky, "Style and Medium in the Motion Pictures," in *Film Theory and Criticism: Introductory Readings*, 5th ed., ed. Leo Braudy and Marshall Cohen (New York: Oxford University Press, 1999), pp. 281–283.

3. Film director Ingmar Bergman demonstrated spatial manipulation in his 1970 stage production of Henrik Ibsen's *Hedda Gabler* (1890), in which a spotlight left only the actor's face or lips visible, thus creating a kind of close-up; and Arthur Miller's *Death of a Salesman* (1949), in which past and present intermingle within scenes, demonstrating temporal manipulation.

were to back away from the other and thus disappear from the screen, you would perceive her as moving to another part of the bar—that is, into a continuation of the space already established in the scene. You can easily imagine this movement due to the fluidity of movie space, more of which is necessarily suggested than is shown.

The key to the unique power of movies to manipulate our sense of space is the motion-picture camera, particularly its lens. We identify with this lens, for it determines our perception of cinematic space. Indeed, if we didn't automatically make this identification—assuming, for example, that the camera's point of view is a sort of roving, omniscient one that we are supposed to identify with—movies would be almost incomprehensible. The key to understanding our connection to the camera lens lies in the differences between how the human eye and the camera eye see. The camera eye captures what's placed before it through a series of different pictures (shots), made with different lenses, from different camera positions and angles, using different movements, under different lighting, and so on. Although both the camera eye and the human eye can see the movements, colors, textures, sizes, and locations of people, places, and things, the camera eye is more selective in its view. The camera frames its image, for example, and can widen and foreshorten space. Through camera positioning, the lens can record a close-up, removing from our view the surrounding visual context that we see in real life, no matter how close we get to an object. In short, the camera mediates between the exterior (the world) and the interior (our eyes and brains).

We use the term **mediation**, a key concept in film theory, literally to mean the process by which an agent, structure, or other formal element, whether human or technological, transfers something from one place to another. No matter how straightforward the mediation of the camera eye may seem, it always involves selection and manipulation of what is seen. This is what mediation as a concept implies. Unlike a video surveillance camera or a webcam, the motion-picture camera eye is not an artless recorder of "reality." It is instead one of a number of expressive tools that filmmakers use to influence our interpretation of the movie's meaning.

Cinema's ability to manipulate space is illustrated in Charles Chaplin's *The Gold Rush* (1925). This brilliant comedy portrays the adventures of two prospectors: the "Little Fellow" (Chaplin) and his nemesis, Big Jim McKay (Mack Swain). After many twists and turns of the plot, the two find themselves sharing an isolated cabin. At night, the winds of a fierce storm blow the cabin to the brink of a deep abyss. Waking and walking about, the Little Fellow slides toward the door (and almost certain death). The danger is established by our first seeing the sharp precipice on which the cabin is located and then by seeing the Little Fellow sliding toward the door that opens out over the abyss. Subsequently, we see him and Big Jim engaged in a struggle for survival that requires them to maintain the balance of the cabin on the edge of the abyss.

The suspense exists because individual shots—one made outdoors, the other safely in a studio—have been edited together to create the illusion that they form part of a complete space. As we watch the cabin sway and teeter on the cliff's edge, we imagine the hapless adventurers inside; when the action cuts to the interior of the cabin and we see the floor pitching back and forth, we imagine the cabin perched precariously on the edge. The experience of these shots as a continuous record of action occurring in a complete (and realistic) space is an illusion that no other art form can convey as effectively as movies can.

The manipulation of time (as well as space), a function of editing, is handled with great irony, cinematic power, and emotional impact in the "baptism and murder" scene in Francis Ford Coppola's *The Godfather* (1972). This five-minute scene consists of thirty-six shots made at different locations. The primary location is a church where Michael Corleone (Al Pacino), the newly named godfather of the Corleone mob, and his wife, Kay (Diane Keaton), attend their nephew's baptism. Symbolically, Michael is also the child's godfather. Coppola cuts back and forth between the baptism; the preparations for five murders, which Michael has ordered, at five different locations; and the murders themselves.

Each time we return to the baptism, it continues where it left off for one of these cutaways to other actions. We know this from the continuity of the priest's actions, Latin incantations, and the Bach organ music. This continuity tells us not only that these actions are taking place simultaneously but also that Michael is involved in all of them, either directly or indirectly. The simultaneity is further strengthened by the organ music, which underscores every scene in the sequence, not just those that take place in the cathedral. The music goes up in pitch and loudness as the sequence progresses, rising to particular climaxes as the murders are committed. As the priest says to Michael, "Go in peace, and may the

Manipulating space in *The Gold Rush*

Film editing can convince us that we're seeing a complete space and a continuous action, even though individual shots have been filmed in different places and at different times. In Charles Chaplin's *The Gold Rush* (1925), an exterior shot of the cabin [1] establishes the danger that the main characters only slowly become aware of [2]. As the cabin hangs in the balance [3], alternating interior and exterior shots [4–6] accentuate our sense of suspense and amusement.

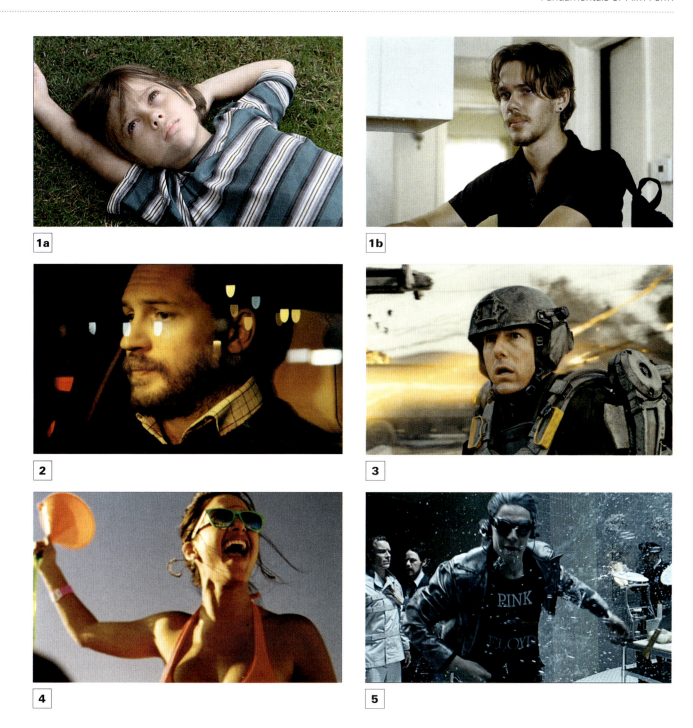

1a

1b

2

3

4

5

Movies manipulate time

A number of recently released films offer ample evidence that rearranging chronology isn't the only way movies manipulate time. Director Richard Linklater shot *Boyhood* (2014) using the same actors over a period of twelve years. The audience literally watches the boy in question (Ellar Coltrane) grow up on-screen [1]. In contrast, the 85-minute running time of *Locke* (2013; director Steven Knight) essentially matches the time it takes for the story to elapse. The entire film is confined to the restricted space and real time of a moving car as Locke (Tom Hardy) makes an 85-minute drive to London [2]. The alien-invasion action movie *Edge of Tomorrow* (2014; director Doug Liman) takes place all in one day, but that day is repeated (and repurposed) countless times as the protagonist Cage (Tom Cruise) exploits the involuntary time travel imposed on him [3]. *Spring Breakers* (2012; director Harmony Korine) employs slow motion to invest scenes of debauchery and brutality with a kind of dreamy transcendence that visually conveys the principal characters' deluded state of mind [4]. In *X-Men: Days of Future Past* (2014; director Bryan Singer), the film does more than jump back and forth between an apocalyptic future and a nostalgic past. One scene portrays the unique chronological perspective of the superfast character Quicksilver (Evan Peters) by a combination of ramped speed, a technique in which action speeds up and slows down within a single shot, and bullet time, a disorienting effect that combines real-time camera movement with slow-motion action [5].

Lord be with you," we are left to reconcile this meticulously timed, simultaneous occurrence of sacred and criminal acts.

The parallel action sequences in *The Silence of the Lambs, Way Down East*, and *The Godfather* are evidence of cinema's ability to use crosscutting to represent multiple events occurring at the same instant. Some movies, like *City of God* (2002; directors Fernando Meirelles and Kátia Lund), do parallel action one better, using a split screen to show the concurrent actions simultaneously.

Movies frequently rearrange time by organizing story events in nonchronological order. Orson Welles's *Citizen Kane* (1941) and Todd Haynes's *I'm Not There* (2007) both begin their exploration of a life with that character's death and, for the rest of the film, shuffle the events leading up to that opening conclusion. Movies like *Atonement* (2007; director Joe Wright) reorder time to present events from multiple perspectives and depict character memory. A number of films, most famously Christopher Nolan's *Memento* (2000) and Gaspar Noé's *Irréversible* (2002), transpose time by presenting their stories in scene-by-scene reverse chronological order. All of these approaches to rearranging time allow filmmakers to create new narrative meaning by juxtaposing events in ways linear chronology does not permit.

John Woo's 1989 action extravaganza *The Killer* maintains conventional chronology but uses many other expressive manipulations of time to tell its story of a kindhearted assassin (Yun-Fat Chow) and the relentless cop (Danny Lee) determined to capture him. Each of the film's many gun battle scenes features elegant slow-motion shots of either the antihero or one of his unfortunate rivals delivering or absorbing multiple bullets. The slow motion invites the audience to pause and savor an extended moment of stylized violence. The sequences also employ occasional bursts of fast motion that have the opposite effect. These sudden temporal shifts allow Woo and film editor Kung Ming Fan to choreograph cinematic patterns and rhythms that give their

Split screen and simultaneous action
Most movies use crosscutting techniques like parallel action to represent more than one event occurring at the same moment. The audience experiences only one event at a time, but the repeated crosscutting implies simultaneity. *City of God* (2002; directors Fernando Meirelles and Kátia Lund) sometimes breaks with convention and splits the screen into multiple frames to present a more immediate depiction of simultaneous action.

fight scenes a dizzying kinetic energy that borders on the outrageous.

Woo expands the audience's experience of time at key points in the story by fragmenting the moment preceding an important action. The film's climactic gunfight finds the hit man and the cop allied against overwhelming forces. The sequence begins with several shots of an army of trigger-happy gangsters bursting into the isolated church where the unlikely partners are holed up. The film extends the brief instant before the bullets fly with a series of twelve shots, including a panicked bystander covering her ears, a priest crossing himself, and the cop and killer exchanging tenacious glances. The accumulation of these time fragments holds us in the moment far longer than the momentum of the action could realistically allow. The sequence's relative stasis establishes a pattern that is broken by the inevitable explosion of violence. Later, a brief break in the combat is punctuated by a **freeze-frame** (in which a still image is shown on-screen for a period of time),

Manipulating time in *The Killer*
The world-weary title character in John Woo's *The Killer* (1989) is an expert assassin attempting to cash in and retire after one last hit. Woo conveys the hit man's reluctance to kill again by expanding the moment of his decision to pull the trigger. Film editor Kung Ming Fan fragments the dramatic pause preceding the action into a thirty-four-shot sequence that cuts between multiple images of the intended target [1], the dragon-boat ceremony he is officiating [2, 3], and the pensive killer [4, 5]. The accumulation of all these fragments extends what should be a brief moment into a tension-filled 52 seconds. When the killer finally does draw his weapon, the significance of the decision is made clear by the repetition of this action in three shots from different camera angles [6–8]. The rapid-fire repetition of a single action is one of cinema's most explicit manipulations of time.

Movement in *The Matrix*

For Andy and Lana Wachowski's *The Matrix* (1999), special effects supervisors Steve Courtley and Brian Cox employed a setup much like that used by early pioneers of serial photography (see Chapter 10). They placed 120 still cameras in an arc and coordinated their exposures using computers. The individual frames, shot from various angles but in much quicker succession than is possible with a motion-picture camera, could then be edited together to create the duality of movement (sometimes called bullet time) for which *The Matrix* is famous. The camera moves around a slow-motion subject at a relatively fast pace, apparently independent of the subject's stylized slowness. Despite its contemporary look, this special effects technique is grounded in principles and methods established during the earliest years of motion-picture history.

another of Woo's time-shifting trademarks. Bloodied but still breathing, the newfound friends emerge from the bullet-ridden sanctuary. The killer's fond glance at the cop suddenly freezes into a still image, suspending time and motion for a couple of seconds. The cop's smiling response is prolonged in a matching sustained freeze-frame. As you may have guessed, *The Killer* is an odd sort of love story. With that in mind, we can see that these freeze-frames do more than manipulate time;

they visually unite the two former foes, thus emphasizing their mutual admiration.

One of the most dazzling manipulations of both space and time the movies have to offer was perfected and popularized by Andy and Lana Wachowski with their 1999 science fiction film, *The Matrix*. This effect, known—for reasons that will become obvious—as bullet time, is critical to one of the film's pivotal scenes. In the scene, the hacker-turned-savior-of-humanity Neo

(Keanu Reeves) transcends real-world physics and bends the Matrix to his purposes for the first time. When one of the deadly digital henchmen known as agents shoots at Neo, the action suddenly reverts to stylized slow motion as Neo literally bends over backward to avoid the projectiles. The slow motion allows us to see "speeding" slugs, and lends a balletic grace to Neo's movements. But what makes the moment magical—and conveys our hero's newfound mastery—is the addition of an extra and unexpected time reference: a swooping camera that circumnavigates the slo-mo action at normal real-time speed. To achieve this disorienting and spellbinding combination of multiple speeds, the filmmakers worked with engineers to develop new technology in a process that resembled sequence photography experiments from the earliest days of motion-picture photography. Neo's dodging dance was shot not by one motion-picture camera, but by 120 still cameras mounted in a roller-coaster-style arc and snapping single images in a computer-driven, rapid-fire sequence. When all those individual shots are projected in quick succession, the subject appears to move slowly while the viewpoint of the camera capturing that subject maintains its own independent fluidity and speed.

Realism and Antirealism

All the unique features of film form we've just described combine to enable filmmakers to create vivid and believable worlds on the screen. Although not every film strives to be "realistic," nearly all films attempt to immerse us in a world that is depicted convincingly on its own terms. Moving-picture technology arose primarily from attempts to record natural images through photography, but it also was shaped by similar attempts in painting and literature. That is, the realist impulse of the visual arts—recording the visible facts of people, places, and social life for a working-class and growing middle-class audience—helped inspire the first motion pictures. However, it soon became clear that movies could be used to create antirealist as well as realist worlds.

Between 1895 and 1905, the French filmmakers Auguste and Louis Lumière and Georges Méliès established the two basic directions that the cinema would follow: the Lumières' **realism** (an interest in or concern for the actual or real, a tendency to view or represent things as they really are) and Méliès's **antirealism** (an interest in or concern for the abstract, speculative, or fantastic).

1

2

Lumière / Méliès
Whether presenting a scene from everyday life, as in Louis Lumière's *Employees Leaving the Lumière Factory* (1895) [1], or showing a fantastical scenario, as in Georges Méliès's *A Trip to the Moon* (1902) [2], motion pictures were recognized from the very beginning for their ability to create a feeling of *being there*, of seeing something that could actually happen. The Lumière brothers favored what they called *actualités*—mini-documentaries of scenes from everyday life; Méliès made movies directly inspired by his interest in magicians' illusions. Yet both the Lumières and Méliès wanted to portray their on-screen worlds convincingly.

Mixing the real and the fantastic

On its surface, *Beasts of the Southern Wild* (2012; director Benh Zeitlin) is very much a realist movie. The story of the volatile but ultimately loving relationship between a young girl named Hushpuppy (Quvenzhané Wallis) and her hotheaded father Wink (Dwight Henry) is populated with characters played mostly by residents of the rustic area of the Louisiana delta (dubbed "The Bathtub"), where the production used existing locations. The story is loosely structured, the camera is handheld, and everything is gritty: the setting, the characters, and the light-sensitive film stock. Most of the movie looks, sounds, and moves like the real world. And yet the filmmakers push this realism to an extreme that veers into the fantastic. The real-world locations are extraordinarily ramshackle; the working-class characters are ardent eccentrics. Events also reflect antirealism. Small children swim out into the ocean and are transported to a floating (and nurturing) brothel called "Elysian Fields." Hushpuppy has recurring visions of icebergs that crumble to reveal—and eventually free—gigantic horned beasts encased inside. Realism and antirealism come face to face when these awesome creatures make their way to the Bathtub and are confronted by the diminutive Hushpuppy.

Although in the following years a notion evolved that a movie was either realistic or fantastic, in fact movies in general and any movie in particular can be both. Today, many movies mix the real and the fantastic—especially those in the science-fiction, action, and thriller genres.

Let's start with realism. What makes a movie realistic? In the case of the Lumière brothers, it came down to subject matter and style. For the most part, these pioneering filmmakers documented unrehearsed scenes from everyday life. They did not stylize this "reality" with conspicuous camera angles, compositions, lighting, or edits. In doing so, they established some basic approaches that today's fiction film audiences still associate with cinematic realism. These components include naturalistic performances and dialogue; modest, unembellished sets and settings; and storylines that portray the everyday lives of "ordinary" people.

Technology and the appearance of realism

Movies as diverse as the stark drama *L'Enfant* (2005; directors Jean-Pierre Dardenne and Luc Dardenne, cinematographer Alain Marcoen) and the apocalyptic horror film *Cloverfield* (2008; director Matt Reeves, cinematographer Michael Bonvillain) create a sense of realism by employing camera formats and techniques that audiences associate with "reality." *L'Enfant* [1] is shot with a relatively smooth handheld technique on light-sensitive (and therefore "grainy") 16mm film stock for a look that resembles that of professional documentary films. *Cloverfield* [2] goes several steps further, shooting in a shaky handheld style and degrading the video image to resemble amateur home movies—the ultimate in unvarnished reality footage.

In most movie entertainments, every character and situation serves a preordained function in a highly organized plot structure. Because real life is often messy and complicated, movies striving for realism often take a more inclusive, less organized approach to story. These storylines are conveyed without obvious artistic flourishes like dramatic lighting or dazzling camera moves. But that does not mean that realism is devoid of style. On the contrary, fiction movies in this category often adapt techniques associated with documentary filmmaking.

Realism versus antirealism

These two paintings illustrate the difference between realism and antirealism. Thomas Gainsborough's eighteenth-century portrait *The Hon. Frances Duncombe* presents its subject in a form that conforms to our experiences and expectations of how a woman looks [1]. Compare this with *Nude Descending a Staircase, No. 2*, by the twentieth-century French artist Marcel Duchamp [2]. Duchamp has transformed a woman's natural appearance (which we know from life) into a radically altered form of sharp angles and fractured shapes. Both paintings represent women, and each took great technical skill and artistic talent to create; but they differ greatly in their relationship to realism.

The down-to-earth authenticity this approach projects makes realism a natural fit for films portraying social issues.

For example, *Fruitvale Station* (2013; director Ryan Coogler) is closely based on the true story of Oscar Grant III, an unemployed San Francisco grocery clerk who was shot and killed on a subway platform by Bay Area Transit Police on his way home from New Year's festivities in 2009. The script, which recounts the last day of Mr. Grant's life, includes multiple events and interactions that don't feed directly into the film's plot.

Instead they provide the everyday texture of the protagonist's life and personality. The director cast professional but not widely known actors. He shot the movie at actual locations with a handheld camera using the kind of light-sensitive (and thus grainy) 16mm film stock associated with documentary cinema.

Realism conforms to our real-world experiences and expectations. Antirealism uses our perceptions of reality as a starting point to expand upon or even purposely subvert them. Movies that can be considered antirealist may use highly stylized and distinctive camera work, editing, and lighting to convey sensational stories set in embellished or imaginary settings. Those settings are often filmed on highly designed sets that purposely reinvent or reject the look of everyday locations.

Wes Anderson's *The Grand Budapest Hotel* (2014) is located at the pinnacle of antirealism. The fanciful story of an impeccable concierge framed for murder is set in an ornate pink hotel located at the summit of a nearly perpendicular mountain peak above an imaginary town in a fictional country. The filmmakers make no effort to disguise the fact that the exterior set of the titular hotel is a miniature model. The plot is highly structured and includes absurd events like a high-speed sled chase. The larger-than-life characters wear whimsical costumes and makeup, and they are presented by (mostly) famous actors delivering deliberately mannered performances. The cinematography features dramatic lighting, saturated colors, and elaborately staged formal compositions.

Of course, it's important to keep in mind that the two movie examples given here exist at opposite ends of a realism spectrum. Most films fall somewhere between these two extremes. And the concept of realism should not be confused with a value judgment. Some of the most profound and heartfelt works in cinema could be called antirealist, just as creative innovation can be found in movies classified as realist. Often, our engagement with a movie has less to do with the appearance of realism and more to do with whether we believe it in the moment—which brings us to our next subject.

Verisimilitude

Whether a movie is realistic, antirealistic, or a combination of the two, it can achieve a convincing appearance of truth, a quality that we call **verisimilitude**. Movies are verisimilar when they convince you that the things on the screen—people, places, what have you, no matter how fantastic or antirealistic—are "really there." In other words, the movie's vision seems internally consistent, giving you a sense that in the world on-screen, things could be just like that. Of course, you can be convinced by the physical verisimilitude of the world being depicted and still be unconvinced by the "unreality" of the characters, their portrayal by the actors, the physical or logical implausibility of the action, and so on.

In addition, audiences' expectations of "reality" change over time and across cultures. A movie made in Germany in the 1930s may have been considered thoroughly verisimilar by those Germans who viewed it at the time, but it may seem utterly unfamiliar and perhaps even unbelievable to contemporary American viewers. Films that succeed in seeming verisimilar across cultures and times often enjoy the sort of critical and popular success that prompts people to call them timeless.

Some of the most popular and successful movies of all time convincingly depict imaginative or supernatural worlds and events that have little or nothing in common with our actual experiences. For example, Victor Fleming's *Gone with the Wind* (1939) treats the American South of the Civil War as a soap opera rather than important history; Steven Spielberg's *Jurassic*

1

2

Verisimilitude and the viewing experience

Verisimilitude plays a large role in the viewers' relationship with *Let the Right One In* (2008; director Tomas Alfredson) [1]. The authenticity of the bleak suburban apartment complex and its inhabitants brings an urgency to the horror and the camaraderie the adolescent vampire character inflicts on her new friends and neighbors. On the other hand, much of the fun of watching *Kick-Ass* (2010; director Matthew Vaughn) [2] must be credited to the action extravaganza's gleeful disregard for verisimilitude. The characters and performances are larger than life, the situations are absurd, and the violence is outlandish.

Park (1993) almost convinces us that the dinosaur amusement park of the title really exists, just as Matt Reeves's *Dawn of the Planet of the Apes* (2014) makes us believe in a postapocalyptic San Francisco dominated by a civilization of intelligent primates led by a talking chimpanzee.

In Ridley Scott's *Gladiator* (2000), people, places, and things look, sound, and move in ways that are believable and even convincing. This is not because they are true to our experiences but because they conform to what common knowledge tells us about how life might have been lived and how things might have looked in the ancient world. More to the point, *Gladiator* adheres to the cinematic conventions established by previous movies about the ancient world—dozens of them, ranging from Fred Niblo's *Ben-Hur: A Tale of the Christ* (1925) to William Wyler's remake of *Ben-Hur* (1959) to Stanley Kubrick's *Spartacus* (1960)—and thus satisfies our individual experiences with the subject matter of the film.

Cinematic Language

By cinematic language—a phrase that we have already used a few times in this book—we mean the accepted systems, methods, or conventions by which the movies communicate with the viewer. To fully understand cinema as a language, let's compare it with another, more familiar form of language—the written one you're engaged with this instant. Our written language is based, for the purpose of this explanation, on words. Each of those words has a generally accepted meaning; but when juxtaposed and combined with other words into a sentence and presented in a certain context, each can convey meaning that is potentially far more subtle, precise, or evocative than that implied by its standard "dictionary" definition.

Instead of arranging words into sentences, cinematic language combines and composes a variety of elements—for example, lighting, movement, sound, acting, and a number of camera effects—into single shots. As you work your way through this book, you will learn that most of these individual elements carry conventional, generalized meanings. But when combined with any number of other elements and presented in a particular context, that element's standardized meaning grows more individuated and complex. And the integrated arrangement of all of a shot's combined elements provides

even greater expressive potential. So, in cinema, as in the written word, the whole is greater than the sum of its parts. But the analogy doesn't end there. Just as authors arrange sentences into paragraphs and chapters, filmmakers derive still more accumulated meaning by organizing shots into a system of larger components: sequences and scenes. Furthermore, within sequences and scenes a filmmaker can juxtapose shots to create a more complex meaning than is usually achieved in standard prose. As viewers, we analyze cinematic language and its particular resources of expression and meaning. If your instructor refers to the *text* of a movie or asks you to *read* a particular shot, scene, or movie, she is asking you to apply your understanding of cinematic language.

The conventions that make up cinematic language are flexible, not rules; they imply a practice that has evolved through film history, not an indisputable or "correct" way of doing things. In fact, cinematic conventions represent a degree of agreement between the filmmaker and the audience about the mediating element between them: the film itself. Although filmmakers frequently build upon conventions with their own innovations, they nonetheless understand and appreciate that these conventions were themselves the result of innovations. For example, a dissolve between two shots usually indicates the passing of time but not the extent of that duration, so in the hands of one filmmaker it might mean two minutes, and in the hands of another, several years. Thus you will begin to understand and appreciate that the development of cinematic language, and therefore the cinema itself, is founded on this tension between convention and innovation.

In all of this, we identify with the camera lens. The filmmaker (here in this introduction, we use that generic term instead of the specific terms *screenwriter, director, cinematographer, editor,* and so on that we'll use as we proceed) uses the camera as a maker of meaning, just as the painter uses the brush or the writer uses the pen: the angles, heights, and movements of the camera function both as a set of techniques and as expressive material, the cinematic equivalent of brushstrokes or of nouns, verbs, and adjectives. From years of looking at movies, you are already aware of how cinematic language creates meaning: how close-ups have the power to change our proximity to a character or low camera angles usually suggest that the subject of the shot is superior or threatening.

[2] Design elements such as costumes, props, and set furnishings help communicate the story's early nineteenth-century time period, as well as the upper-class status of Jane's adoptive family.

[4] John Reed (Craig Roberts) is backlit, a lighting direction that renders a figure in silhouette. In this context, the technique differentiates John from our hiding heroine Jane, and visually reinforces his cruel and deceptive behavior.

[1] Young Jane (Amelia Clarkson) is the primary subject of this shot. She is the largest figure in the frame, and she is clearly in focus. She is lit with diffused light that softens her features. Her vulnerable situation—and state of mind—is conveyed via her downcast performance, her comparatively dour dress, and the framing that partially obscures her face.

[3] Jane's literal and figurative detachment is conveyed by the curtains, illumination, shadows, and depth that divides her half of the frame from that occupied by her abusive cousin and aunt.

[5] In contrast to the soft, diffused light that characterizes Jane, Mrs. Reed's portion of the frame is lit with direct, unfiltered light that casts deep shadows and bright highlights. Her distance from Jane, and perhaps even her insensitivity to her niece's situation, is emphasized by the different quality of light, relative size in frame, and indistinct focus.

Cinematic language

Looking at this single image, without even knowing what movie it is from or anything about the various characters pictured in the frame, we can immediately infer layers of meaning and significance. If we think of cinematic language as akin to written language, we can think of this single image from Cary Fukunaga's *Jane Eyre* (2011) as a richly layered "sentence" that communicates by combining and arranging multiple visual elements (or "words" in this analogy) that include lighting, composition, depth, design, cinematography, and performance.

All of the following chapters of this book will expand on this introduction to the language of cinema. And although they will focus mainly on the conventional meanings and methods of that language, you will also see exceptions. Soon you will understand how these and other elements of cinematic language help set movies apart from the other arts. Even as the technology used to make and display movies continues to evolve, the principles of film art covered in this book will remain essentially the same. So the knowledge and skill you acquire by reading this book will help you look at motion pictures intelligently and perceptively throughout your life, no matter which medium delivers those pictures to you.

Looking at Film Form: *Donnie Darko*

To better understand how some of these principles of film form function within a single movie, let's examine how they're used in Richard Kelly's *Donnie Darko*. The film was a box office dud in 2001, but it gained critical acclaim and what has proven to be an enduring cult following after its release on VHS and DVD the next year. This popularity—and intense audience interest in the

Who and what is Frank?
The grotesque bunny figure Frank plays a central role in the *Donnie Darko* viewing experience. His first appearance complicates expectations about Donnie's mental state, predicts the film's ending, and injects a horror movie mood to what might previously have been assumed to be a conventional troubled teenager story. Frank exists on the border between realism and antirealism. He is a cosmic hallucination dressed in a shaggy homemade costume; he's both a messenger from the future and Donnie's big sister's boyfriend dressed up for Halloween.

film's sometimes murky meaning—led to the issue of an extended director's cut in 2004. For consistency's sake, we will confine our evaluation to the original theatrical release.

Content

What is the content of *Donnie Darko*? That's an interesting question since the search for content is a large part of what makes the movie an absorbing cinematic experience. Throughout the film, events unfold and details emerge that force us as viewers to continually reevaluate our understanding of that content. We are repeatedly provoked to ask if Donnie's mind- and time-bending experiences are real, or simply a projection of his diagnosed mental illness. Audiences aren't used to working so hard for their content; the effort *Donnie Darko* demands probably played a part in both the tepid response it received in theaters and its increased popularity on DVD and VHS, formats that allow for repeated viewings. For the purpose of this analysis, let's keep it as simple as possible: the movie is about suburban hypocrisy, high school politics, adolescent alienation—and time travel between parallel universes. The story centers on a troubled and possibly schizophrenic teenager named Donnie Darko (Jake Gyllenhaal) who is haunted by a mysterious being that compels him to perform acts of retaliatory destruction.

Expectations

The first scenes of most films prompt basic expectations that shape an audience's engagement with the rest of the movie. These opening moments set the tone and let us know what style of story to expect. Viewers sense if this is reliable or an unpredictable world, determine whether they're watching serious drama or a playful comedy, and form instructive opinions about the characters.

Most movies establish expectations in order to involve and guide the audience. *Donnie Darko* exploits expectations to keep viewers off balance. The film opens with the title character waking from a sound sleep in the middle of a mountain road—a situation that is simultaneously dangerous and ridiculous. So we're still not exactly sure what we're in for as he rides his bike home and we head into the next scenes: a contentious family dinner erupting in political tension and teenage hostility, followed by a confrontation between Donnie and his mother in which we realize he is both in therapy and on medication.

At this stage, past movie experience leads us to presume we've entered a family drama that will chronicle Donnie's struggle with mental illness. That night, a strange disembodied voice summons Donnie to sleepwalk out to the front lawn, where he encounters Frank, a tall figure wearing a shaggy homemade costume topped with a grotesque rabbit mask. Based on the previous scenes, we assume that we are experiencing the hallucinations of a disturbed mind. And other, more conflicting expectations are in play as well: the absurdity of a man in a rabbit outfit may lead us to expect something comic, or at least innocuous. Yet there's something scary about the incongruity of the costume that triggers anxious expectations born of horror movie clowns and dolls. Then Frank tells Donnie the world will end in 28 days, 6 hours, 42 minutes, and 12 seconds.

Now, faced with a precise time frame and specific outcome, we instinctively begin to anticipate how this story will conclude, even as we doubt the reliability (and existence) of the source. The next morning, Donnie wakes up on a golf course and stumbles home, only to discover that during his absence a very real jet engine has fallen from the sky and crashed into his bedroom. This sudden intrusion of the undeniably tangible makes us reevaluate our expectations about what kind of movie we're watching, what's at stake, what is real, and what will happen.

Patterns

Like most other movies, *Donnie Darko* uses pattern to convey and compare simultaneous action, fragment dramatic situations for emphasis and juxtaposition, and establish—and then sometimes subvert—expectations. A sequence that occurs early in the film manages to fulfill all of these functions. Donnie's father Eddie (Holmes Osborne) is driving him home after school; father and son discuss the mysterious origin of the fallen jet engine. Until its startling conclusion, the scene is presented in a conventional AB shot/reverse shot pattern: we see Eddie [A] when he speaks, then cut to Donnie [B] for his reaction and response, and so on. On its surface, the pattern presents a practical approach to a two-person conversation filmed in the cramped confines of a moving automobile. But the choice provides opportunities for narrative expression as well. Each

A

B

C

Pattern in *Donnie Darko*

Donnie Darko uses a simple ABABAB pattern to lull viewers into a sort of cinematic complacency before jolting our senses. The fifteen-shot sequence shifts back and forth seven times between a shot of Eddie Darko [A] and his son Donnie [B] before a new shot of a woman in their path [C] interrupts their conversation. This jarring break in pattern dramatically visualizes the Darkos' sudden realization, allows the audience to experience a shock similar to that of the characters on-screen, and provides a striking introduction to a pivotal figure.

shot of Eddie represents the point of view of Donnie, or vice versa. Fragmenting the conversation empowers the filmmakers to select the best dramatic moments to concentrate on either character's dialogue or reaction.

This back-and-forth AB pattern continues for seven repetitions—long enough to lull the viewer into a certain complacency. We're so caught up in the conversation that we may not notice that we haven't been provided a view through the windshield. So when the established pattern is suddenly broken with a shot of the old lady standing in the middle of the street [C], we experience a shock comparable to that of the distracted characters about to run her over. This jarring transition also gives special emphasis to the character it introduces; the lady in the road is Rebecca Sparrow (Patience Cleveland), the one person alive who could have (before she lost her mind) solved the mystery of the fallen jet engine.

Manipulating Space

Pattern is also a component of *Donnie Darko*'s parallel action sequences. These sequences don't alternate shot by shot like the car scene, but they do exploit a more general back-and-forth pattern between two simultaneous

events occurring in distinctly separate spaces. By exploiting the cinema's ability to manipulate space, these sequences function in much the same way as *The Godfather*'s "baptism and murder" parallel action sequence described earlier in this chapter. Like that sequence, parallel action in *Donnie Darko* juxtaposes action that appears disturbingly incongruous, even incompatible, until the pattern of repeated juxtaposition compels viewers to perceive meaningful connections in the apparent contrasts. The viewer sees each event in light of the other alternated event and thus vividly experiences the duality of *Donnie Darko*'s universe.

One such sequence intersperses shots of Donnie's therapist telling his dismayed parents about their son's

1 **2** **3** **4** **5** **6**

Parallel action in *Donnie Darko*

The reality of the alternating events in another notable *Donnie Darko* parallel action sequence is not in question, but the juxtaposition—and the simultaneity—is just as significant. While the rest of the town is consumed with raptly watching an inane community talent show, Donnie is burning down the mansion of the charismatic motivational speaker who holds the townsfolk in his sway. The contrast here is less cosmic and more thematic: the sequence compares and contrasts teenage rebellion with slack-jawed conformity.

potentially violent hallucinations with shots of Donnie confronting a very real-seeming Frank using a very large knife. The content of each action undermines the credibility of the alternating other. In comparison to Donnie's experience, the parent/therapist discussion seems obtuse and oblivious; in light of the therapist's diagnosis, Frank's actual existence is in question. In the twisted world of Donnie Darko, these two perspectives don't cancel each other out; they represent an uneasy coexistence between dual realities.

Manipulating Time

It's only logical that a movie about the distortion of time would exploit cinema's ability to distort time. In the film's first high school scene, the filmmakers employ a relentlessly moving camera shifting between "normal," fast, and slow motion to introduce and connect all the characters associated with the setting. The scene starts in slow motion to show Donnie bursting out of the bus and entering the school, then spurts into fast motion to follow the hypervigilant gym teacher, Kitty Farmer (Beth Grant). Dreamy slo-mo returns when the camera pivots to Donnie's potential love interest, Gretchen Ross (Jena Malone). In this case, the technique serves as a visual representation of character qualities and state of mind, and it also emphasizes the fluid nature of time as posited in the movie's dual universe. Throughout the rest of the movie, shifts in motion speed will return in shots that transition between scenes to remind audiences that, in the *Donnie Darko* countdown to the end of the world, time is possibly malleable, seemingly unpredictable, and certainly unstoppable. Clouds fly across the sky in time-lapse fast motion. Donnie's little sister does slow-motion jumps on her trampoline. Sometimes students scurry out of high school in fast motion, and sometimes the daily ritual is portrayed in graceful slo-mo.

The manipulation of time can also be used to convey a character's thought process and state of mind. Things, temporally and otherwise, get more confused and conflicted for Donnie until it all goes tragically wrong on Halloween night. At his lowest point, Donnie suddenly realizes that he has the power to reset everything. The resulting rapid-fire, thirty-seven-shot sequence that conveys the jumble of memories and revelations flooding his consciousness features thirteen images that visualize time actually reversing itself, an expressive technique that is as straightforward as playing the shots backward.

Realism, Antirealism, and Verisimilitude

Donnie Darko's normal world is portrayed with relative realism. The locations, sets, costumes, and most of the performances are designed to look and sound like the real world viewers experience every day—or at least an affluent suburban version of it. Even Jake Gyllenhaal's behavior as the disturbed Donnie is what we would expect from a teenager in his situation. The filmmakers have good reason to ground their movie in realism: this is a story about a mundane existence infiltrated by the fantastic. If viewers did not recognize Donnie's world to begin with, it would be difficult to identify with his struggle to navigate the bizarre cosmic quest thrust upon him, or to fully appreciate the return to normalcy he ultimately accomplishes.

But as we explained earlier in this chapter, cinematic realism is not an absolute value, but falls into a broad spectrum. And Donnie Darko intersects this spectrum at multiple points. The film features stylized lighting and editing that falls outside the realm of pure realism, as do at least two broad characters, seemingly included to amplify the film's social commentary: the pompous self-help guru Jim Cunningham (Patrick Swayze) and his overzealous disciple Kitty Farmer. And Frank is only one of many examples of antirealism that intrude with increasing frequency as the movie progresses. Long, fluid tendrils emerge from peoples' chests, a black vortex sprouts from the clouds above Donnie's house, and Donnie's ultimate sacrifice resets time to the morning the story began.

But those antirealist elements do nothing to undermine Donnie Darko's ultimate believability. What makes this achievement in verisimilitude so remarkable is that so little of the film's internal logic is ever entirely explained. Even though few viewers can claim to fully comprehend exactly how the story's time loops function, Donnie Darko is a persuasive and engaging movie experience because we believe it when we see it. So much so that fans can now purchase the (fictional) *Philosophy of Time Travel* book that helps Donnie unlock the secrets of the parallel universe, or they can consult an abundance of websites and published articles devoted to the cult movie and its complex concept.

ANALYZING PRINCIPLES OF FILM FORM

At this early stage in your pursuit of actively looking at movies, you may still be wondering what exactly you are supposed to be looking for. For starters, you now recognize that filmmakers deliberately manipulate your experience and understanding of a movie's content with a constant barrage of techniques and systems known as film form and that this form is organized into an integrated cinematic language. Simply acknowledging the difference between form and content, and knowing that a deliberate system is at work, are the first steps toward identifying and interpreting how movies communicate with viewers. The general principles of film form discussed in this chapter can now provide a framework to help you focus your gaze and develop deeper analytical skills. The checklist below will give you some specific elements and applications of form to watch out for the next time you see a film. Using this and the screening checklists in upcoming chapters, you can turn every movie you watch into an exercise in observation and analysis.

SCREENING CHECKLIST: PRINCIPLES OF FILM FORM

☐ A useful initial step in analyzing any movie is to distinguish an individual scene's content from its form. First try to identify a scene's subject matter: What is this scene about? What happens? Once you have established that content, you should consider how that content was expressed. What was the mood of the scene? What do you understand about each character's state of mind? How did you perceive and interpret each moment? Did that understanding shift at any point? Once you know what happened and how you felt about it, search the scene for those formal elements that influenced your interpretation and experience. The combination and interplay of multiple formal elements that you seek is the cinematic language that movies employ to communicate with the viewer.

☐ Do any narrative or visual patterns recur a sufficient number of times to suggest a structural element in themselves? If so, what are these patterns? Do they help you determine the meaning of the film?

☐ Do you notice anything particular about the movie's presentation of cinematic space? What do you see on the screen? Lots of landscapes or close-ups? Moving or static camera?

☐ Does the director manipulate viewers' experience of time? Is this condensing, slowing, speeding, repeating, or reordering of time simply practical (as in removing insignificant events) or is it expressive? If it is expressive, just what does it express?

☐ Does the director's use of lighting help to create meaning? If so, how?

☐ Do you identify with the camera lens? What does the director compel you to see? What is left to your imagination? What does the director leave out altogether? In the end, besides showing you the action, how does the director's use of the camera help to create the movie's meaning?

Questions for Review

1. How and why do we differentiate between form and content in a movie, and why are they relevant to one another?

2. What expectations of film form can filmmakers exploit to shape an audience's experience?

3. What is parallel editing, and how does it use pattern?

4. In what other ways do movies use patterns to convey meaning? How do they create meaning by breaking an established pattern?

5. How do the movies create an illusion of movement?

6. How does a movie manipulate space?

7. How do movies manipulate time?

8. What is the difference between realism and antirealism in a movie, and why is verisimilitude important to them both?

9. What is meant by cinematic language? Why is it important to the ways that movies communicate with viewers?

10. Why do we identify with the camera lens?

STUDENT RESOURCES ONLINE

digital.wwnorton.com/movies5

▶ **VIDEO**

The tutorial for this chapter reviews the importance of form and content and features additional examples and illustrations.

LOOKING AT
MOVIES
CHAPTER 2:
PRINCIPLES OF FILM FORM

FORM AND CONTENT

▶ MAIN MENU

Mad Max: Fury Road (2015; director George Miller)

TYPES OF MOVIES

CHAPTER

3

LEARNING OBJECTIVES

After reading this chapter, you should be able to

✓ explain how and why movies are classified.

✓ define narrative, documentary, and experimental movies, and appreciate the ways these types of movies blend and overlap.

✓ understand the approaches to documenting actual events employed by documentary filmmakers.

✓ discuss the characteristics that most experimental films share.

✓ understand what genre is and why it is important.

✓ explain the most significant (or defining) elements of each of the six major American genres featured in this chapter.

✓ understand where animation fits into the movie types discussed in the chapter.

✓ explain the most commonly used animation techniques.

In this chapter, we will discuss the three major types of movies: narrative, documentary, and experimental. Within narrative movies, we will look at the subcategory of genre films, and we will explore six major American film genres in particular. Finally, we will look at a technique—animation—that is often discussed as if it were a type but that is actually used to make movies of all types.

The Idea of Narrative

The word *narrative* is much more than simply a general classification of a type of film. As you will soon see, depending on when and how we use the term, *narrative* might mean several slightly different things. Since we'll be using the term *narrative* in various ways throughout and beyond our exploration of the three essential types of movies, let's discuss some of the ways to approach the term.

When it comes to cinema, nothing is absolute. In the world of movies, a narrative might be a type of movie, the story that a particular film tells, the particular system by which a fictional story is structured, or a concept describing the sequential organization of events presented in almost any kind of movie. Once you become familiar with these different ways of looking at narrative, you will be able to recognize and understand almost any usage that you come across.

A narrative is a story. When people think of any medium or form—whether it's a movie, a joke, a commercial, or a news article—that tells a story, we consider that story a narrative. Journalists will often speak of finding the narrative in a news item, be it coverage of a city council meeting, a national election, or an Olympic swimming competition. By this, they mean that under the facts and details of any given news item is a story. It's the reporter's job to identify that story and organize his reporting in such a way as to elucidate that narrative.

Journalists do this because humans are a storytelling species. We use stories to arrange and understand our world and our lives. So, of course, news articles are not the only place you'll find narrative. Scientists, songwriters, advertisers, politicians, comedians, and teachers all incorporate narrative into the ways they frame and present information. This semester, you will likely hear your professor refer to the narrative of a particular movie. Depending on the context she uses, she might be talking about the story that the film tells, whether that movie is a science-fiction film or a documentary about science.

Narrative is a type of movie. Our most common perception of the word *narrative* is as a categorical term for those particular movies devoted to conveying a story, whether they are works of pure fiction like Alejandro González Iñárritu's *Birdman* (2014) or a fictionalized version of actual events such as *Selma* (2014; director Ava DuVernay). As we have made clear in previous chapters, these narrative films are the focus of this book. We'll discuss the narrative film as a type of movie (along with experimental and documentary films) later in this chapter.

Narrative is a way of structuring fictional or fictionalized stories presented in narrative films. Storytelling is a complicated business, especially when relating a multifaceted story involving multiple characters and conflicts over the course of two hours of screen time. Besides being a general term for a story or for a kind of movie, *narrative* is often used to describe the way that movie stories are constructed and presented to engage, involve, and orient an audience. This narrative structure—which includes exposition, rising action, climax, falling action, and denouement—helps filmmakers manipulate the viewer's cinematic experience by selectively conforming to or diverging from audience expectations of storytelling. Chapter 4 is devoted to this aspect of narrative.

Narrative is a broader concept that both includes and goes beyond any of these applications. Narrative can be defined in a broader conceptual context as

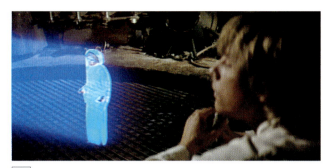

1

2

3

4

5

One thing leads to another

The most elemental way of looking at narrative is as a cinematic structure that arranges events in a cause-and-effect sequence. This causality is the basic organizing structure of most movie narratives. Consider the principal events in one of the best-known movies of all time, *Star Wars* (1977; director George Lucas): A starship is boarded by repressive Empire forces. The princess passenger records a plea for help on an android, which escapes to a desert planet. The roving android is captured by scavenging Jawas, who sell it to the farm family of Luke Skywalker, who discovers the message, which sends him in search of Obi-Wan Kenobi, who teaches him the way of the Force and accompanies him on a mission to rescue the princess. One event leads to another and another and another. Decisions are made, which lead to actions, which have consequences, which motivate reactions, which cause subsequent decisions, actions, and consequences. And so it goes. The viewer engages with this logical progression, anticipating probable developments, dreading some and hoping for others.

any cinematic structure in which content is selected and arranged in a cause-and-effect sequence of events occurring over time. Any time a filmmaker consciously chooses and organizes material so that one event leads to another in a recognizable progression, that filmmaker is employing narrative in its most basic sense. In this case, narrative is not simply the telling of a fictional story, it is a structural quality that nearly every movie possesses, whether it's an avant-garde art film, a documentary account of actual events, or a blockbuster Hollywood fantasy.

Movies do not have to arrange events in conventional order to employ narrative organization. In *21 Grams* (2003), director Alejandro González Iñárritu and screenwriter Guillermo Arriaga arrange the events comprising the intersecting stories of ex-convict Jack (Benicio Del Toro), dying heart patient Paul (Sean Penn), and recovering cocaine addict Cristina (Naomi Watts) in a

sequence motivated more by causality than chronology. A sequence in which Paul receives a heart transplant and Cristina loses her family propels the movie into a scene in which Paul approaches Cristina after he tracks her down as the person who saved his life by donating her recently deceased husband's heart. This personal connection is followed by the moments immediately preceding the death of Cristina's husband, the tragedy that ultimately brings these two lost souls together.

The next scene presents a devastated Jack resolving to turn himself in after leaving the scene of an accident that killed a man and his two daughters, knowing full well

Causal minimalism

A fiction movie need not have a traditional goal-driven plot to be considered narrative. Richard Linklater's *Slacker* (1991) has no central character, no sustained conflict, and tells no single story; yet its structure is very much built on cause-and-effect connections, however tenuous, between the young bohemians who drift in and out of the movie. Beginning with a man getting off a bus (played by Linklater himself), the camera follows one character to another, drifting through a succession of over a hundred individual participants as they cross paths in Austin, Texas. Each encounter leads to the next, and so forth, in an extended exercise in causal minimalism.

that his confession could send him back to prison. These events occur over time but are not connected by it. The scene-to-scene causality in this case is not motivated by chronology, but from the remorse, vulnerability, and sacrifice that bind the central characters. This approach to narrative demands a greater level of participation from viewers, who must actively engage with the movie to recognize the connections presented and reassemble events into a chronology that enables them to fully comprehend the story.

Although nonfiction filmmakers shooting documentary footage obviously can't always control the unstaged events happening before their cameras, contemporary documentary filmmakers often exploit their ability to select and arrange material in a cause-and-effect sequence of events. This very deliberate process may begin even before cameras roll.

Searching for Sugar Man (2012) director Malik Bendjelloul surely recognized the narrative potential of the disappearance and rumored death of Sixto Rodriguez. The American folk singer had never achieved anything approaching notoriety in his own country, but recordings he released in the 1960s made him a superstar in South Africa. Because his music, particularly a song titled "Sugarman," was associated with the country's antiapartheid movement, Rodriguez was still a major cultural figure there, even though he had not toured or recorded—or been heard from at all—in decades. Bendjelloul structured his film as a missing-person investigation filled with tantalizing clues and frustrating dead ends, as well as testimonials to Rodriguez's unique genius that feed the viewer's increasing hunger for a righteous resurrection. *Searching for Sugar Man* reaches its narrative climax with the discovery of Rodriguez, poor and obscure but very much alive, in Detroit, Michigan.

The nonfiction filmmaker's selective role is even more apparent in the Academy Award–winning documentary *Born into Brothels* (2004; directors Zana Briski and Ross Kauffman). The film's events are structured around co-director Briski's explicitly stated intent to use photography to reach and ultimately rescue the children of prostitutes in Calcutta's red-light district. The film's events are arranged in a cause-and-effect structure strikingly similar to that of a conventional fiction movie, where the filmmakers themselves not only select and arrange events, but actively participate in them. Briski engages the children first by photographing them, then by teaching them to take their own photographs. She works to convince the sex workers to allow her greater access to their children.

As the children's talents emerge, she leads them on photo-taking expeditions to the beach and the zoo, and eventually stages a series of public exhibitions of their work. As the children grow in confidence and ability, the sequence of events builds to a conclusion that engaged and gratified mainstream audiences, as well as the Academy of Motion Picture Arts and Sciences, which awarded the film an Oscar for Best Documentary Film. Those documentary filmmakers who strive to avoid influencing the events they record still exert a great deal of narrative influence during the editing process.

Most experimental, or avant-garde, movies try to break from the formulas and conventions of more mainstream narrative and documentary films. Even so, they employ narrative according to our most general definition of the concept, despite being more concerned with innovation and experimentation than accessibility and entertainment.

The complex process of making movies discourages purely random constructions. Filmmakers engaged with planning, capturing, selecting, and arranging footage tend to create sequences that grow logically in some way. The linear nature of motion pictures lends itself to structures that develop according to some form of progression, even if the resultant meaning is mostly impressionistic. Thus nearly every movie, regardless of how it is categorized, employs at least a loose interpretation of narrative.

Types of Movies

Films can be sorted into a variety of systems. The film industry catalogs films according to how they are distributed (theatrical, television, straight to DVD, streaming, etc.); how they are financed (by established studios or independent producers); or by their MPAA rating. Film festivals frequently separate entries according to running time. Film-studies curricula often group films by subject matter, the nation of origin, or the era or organized aesthetic movement that produced them.

The whole idea of breaking down an art form as multifaceted as motion pictures into strict classifications can be problematic. Although most movies fall squarely into a single category, many others defy exact classification by any standard. This is because cinematic expression exists along a continuum; no rule book enforcing set criteria exists. Throughout the history of the medium, innovative filmmakers have blurred boundaries and defied classification. Since this textbook is interested primarily in understanding motion-picture *form*, the categories of films that we'll discuss below—narrative, documentary, and experimental—are focused on the filmmaker's intent and the final product's relationship with the viewer.

Narrative Movies

As we learned earlier, the primary relationship of a narrative film to its audience is that of a storyteller. Narrative films are so pervasive, so ingrained in our culture, that before reading this book, you may never have stopped to consider the designation *narrative film*. After all, to most of us, a narrative movie is just a movie. We apply a label only to documentary or experimental films—movies that deviate from that "norm."

What distinguishes narrative films from these other kinds of movies, both of which also tell stories or use other formal aspects of narrative? The answer is that narrative films are directed toward fiction. Even those narrative movies that purport to tell a true story, such as David O. Russell's *American Hustle* (2013), adjust the stories they convey to better serve the principles of narrative structure that filmmakers use to engage and entertain audiences. Events are added or removed or rearranged, and characters are composited—actors (who are usually more attractive than the actual participants they play) add elements of their own persona to the role.

American Hustle acknowledges this necessary manipulation right up front; Russell's movie retelling of con artists caught up in a famous FBI sting operation opens with a title card that replaces the usual "based on a true story" claim with a more candid disclaimer: "Some of this actually happened." Audiences may be attracted to movies marketed as "based on a true story" due to the perception of immediacy or relevance that such a label imparts. But the truth is that very few "true stories" can deliver the narrative clarity and effect that audiences have come to expect from narrative films.

No matter what the source, typical narrative films are based on screenplays in which nearly every behavior and spoken line are predetermined. The characters are played by actors delivering dialogue and executing action in a manner that not only strives for verisimilitude but also facilitates the technical demands of the motion-picture production process. These demands include coordinating their activity with lighting design and camera movement, and performing scenes out of logical chronological sequence. This action typically takes place in artificial

1

2

3

Narrative commonality

Even those narrative films bearing an overt ideological message or a dark theme are designed to engage an audience with a story. A twisted formal exercise like David Lynch's *Mulholland Dr.* (2001) [1], an earnest political thriller like Stephen Gaghan's *Syriana* (2005) [2], and an animated crowd-pleaser like Gore Verbinski's *Rango* (2011) [3] all deliver different messages and are designed to appeal to different audiences. But they all employ the same narrative structures and techniques designed to transport viewers into a story, get them invested in the characters, and make them care about the end results, despite knowing up front that none of it is real.

worlds created on studio soundstages or in locations modified to suit the story and technical demands of production. The primary purpose of most narrative films is entertainment, a stance motivated by commercial intent.

Many narrative films can be broken down still further into categories known as genres. We'll explore that subject later in the chapter.

Documentary Movies

We might say that narrative film and documentary film differ primarily in terms of allegiance. Narrative film begins with a commitment to dramatic storytelling; documentary film is more concerned with recording reality, educating viewers, or presenting political or social analyses. In other words, if we think of a narrative movie as fiction, then the best way to understand documentary film is as nonfiction.

But it would be a mistake to think that simply because documentary filmmakers use actual people, places, and events as source material, their films always reflect objective truth. Whatever their allegiance, all documentary filmmakers employ storytelling and dramatization to some degree in shaping their material. If they didn't, their footage might end up as unwatchably dull as a surveillance video recording everyday comings and goings. As upcoming chapters will repeatedly illustrate, all elements of cinematic language—from the camera angle to the shot type to the lighting to the sound mix—color our perceptions of the material and so are subjective to some degree. And no documentary subject who knows she is being filmed can ever behave exactly as she would off camera.

So the unavoidable act of making the movie removes the possibility of a purely objective truth. And truth, of course, is in the eye of the beholder. Every documentary filmmaker has a personal perspective on the subject matter, whether she entered the production with a preexisting opinion or developed her point of view over the course of researching, shooting, and editing the movie. The informed documentary viewer should view these mediating factors thoughtfully, always trying to understand how the act of cinematic storytelling and the filmmaker's attitude toward the people and events depicted affect the interpretation of the truth up on the screen.

These complicating factors may have influenced film critic John Grierson, who originally coined the term *documentary* in 1926 to delineate cinema that observed life. Some time after he started making documentaries himself, Grierson described the approach as the "creative treatment of actuality."

Robert J. Flaherty's pioneering documentary *Nanook of the North* (1922) demonstrates the complex relationship between documentary filmmaking and objective truth. Flaherty's movie included authentic "documentary" footage but also incorporated a great deal of staged

reenactments. He reportedly encouraged the Inuit subjects to use older, more "traditional" hunting and fishing techniques for the film instead of their then current practices. However, no one who watches *Nanook* could argue that the film's portrayal of the Inuit and their nomadic northern lifestyle is a complete failure. The challenge for the viewer is to untangle *Nanook*'s nonfiction functions from its dramatic license, to view its anthropology apart from its artifice. Such a task requires a broad appreciation of both the movie and its subject from cinematic, historical, and scientific perspectives. We tend to assume that a wide separation exists between fact and fiction, historical reality and crafted story, truth and artifice. The difference, however, is never absolute in any film.

Historically, documentary films have been broken into four basic approaches: factual, instructional, persuasive, and propaganda. **Factual films**, including *Nanook of the North*, usually present people, places, or processes in straightforward ways meant to entertain and instruct without unduly influencing audiences. Early examples include some of the first movies made. In 1896, audiences marveled at the Lumière brothers' short, one-shot films documenting trains arriving, boats leaving, and soldiers marching off to the front. (At that time, the

Nanook of the North

Robert J. Flaherty's *Nanook of the North* (1922), a pioneering nonfiction film, gave general audiences their first visual encounter with Inuit culture. Its subject matter made it significant (and successful), and its use of narrative film techniques was pathbreaking. Flaherty edited together many different kinds of shots and angles, for example, and directed the Inuit through reenactments of life events, some of which—hunting with spears—were no longer part of their lives.

spectacle of moving images impressed viewers as much as, or more than, any particular subject matter.) More recent documentaries that could fall into the factual-documentary classification include Patrick Creadon's *Wordplay* (2006), an appreciation of the people who create and complete crossword puzzles, and *Finding Vivian Maier* (2014; directors John Maloof and Charlie Siskel), a portrait of an obscure nanny who was unveiled as a master photographer when her life's work was discovered after her death.

Instructional films seek to educate viewers about common interests, rather than persuading them to accept particular ideas. Today these movies are most likely to teach the viewer basic skills like cooking, yoga, or golf swings. They are not generally considered worthy of study or analysis.

Persuasive films were originally called *documentary films* until the term evolved to refer to all nonfiction films. The founding purpose of persuasive documentaries was to address social injustice, but today any documentary concerned with presenting a particular perspective on social issues or with corporate and governmental injustice of any kind could be considered persuasive. Director Gabriela Cowperthwaite's motivation in making *Blackfish* (2013) was not to simply entertain or inform audiences, but persuade them to oppose the practice of holding Orca whales in captivity at animal theme parks. Michael Moore's darkly humorous, self-aggrandizing documentaries take the persuasive documentary a step further. His confrontational and provocative movies address a series of left-of-center political causes, including health care (*Sicko*, 2007), gun control (*Bowling for Columbine*, 2002), and the Bush administration's role in the Iraq War (*Fahrenheit 9/11*, 2004).

When persuasive documentaries are produced by governments and carry governments' messages, they overlap with **propaganda films**, which systematically disseminate deceptive or distorted information. The most famous propaganda film ever made, Leni Riefenstahl's *Triumph of the Will* (1935), records many events at the 1934 Nuremberg rally of Germany's Nazi party. It thus might mistakenly be considered a "factual" film.

1

2

Triumph of the Will

The most accomplished (and notorious) propaganda film of all time, Leni Riefenstahl's *Triumph of the Will* (1935) is studied by historians and scholars of film. Much of the blocking of the 1934 Nuremberg Nazi rally was crafted specifically with the camera in mind. Riefenstahl, wearing a white dress and helping to push the camera [1], films a procession during the rally. Taken from a distant perspective, this shot conveys many concepts that the filmmaker and the Nazis wanted the world to see: order, discipline, and magnitude [2].

1

2

Documentary storytelling

Many documentary filmmakers select subjects that offer potential narrative development. The resulting movie may be considered factual, or even persuasive in some ways. But the content need not be "important." Rather, the movie's primary intent is to entertain and involve audiences with the struggles of goal-driven protagonists. The efforts of a hapless but relentless Wisconsin filmmaker to marshal the resources and support necessary to complete a low-budget horror film is the subject of Chris Smith's *American Movie* (1999) [1]. S. R. Bindler's *Hands on a Hard Body* (1997) [2] follows twenty-four desperate contestants through a grueling and often dehumanizing endurance contest to win a new pickup truck. Seth Gordon's *The King of Kong: A Fistful of Quarters* (2007) [3] explores the strange, obsessive world of classic arcade-game enthusiasts by chronicling the efforts of high school math teacher Steve Wiebe's attempts to achieve the official world record score in Donkey Kong, despite the efforts of the competitive gaming establishment to preserve that distinction for their hero, Billy Mitchell.

3

After all, no voice-over narration or on-screen commentator preaches a political message to the viewer. But through its carefully crafted cinematography and editing, this documentary presents a highly glorified image of Adolf Hitler and his Nazi followers for the consumption of non-German audiences before World War II.

Over a century of documentary innovation has blurred the distinctions between these four historical categories. Most documentary movies we consider worthy of study today are hybrids that combine qualities of two or more of these foundational approaches to non-fiction filmmaking. This versatility is one reason that documentary is enjoying a renaissance unprecedented in the history of cinema.

Barbara Kopple's *Harlan County USA* (1976) is an example of the nonfiction filmmaking style known as **direct cinema**. While many documentaries include on-screen or over-the-shoulder interviewers having conversations with subjects (in the segments on television's *60 Minutes*, for example), direct-cinema documentaries eschew interviewers and even limit the use of narrators. Instead of having voice-over narration to encourage the audience's indignation about the crime, scandal, or corruption being exposed, direct cinema involves placing small portable cameras and sound-recording equipment in an important location for days or weeks and recording events as they occur. The resulting documentary may never include a question from an interviewer; instead, it enables the audience to overhear conversations and interactions as they happen. *Harlan County USA* documents a yearlong Kentucky coal miners' strike in 1973–74. Risking her life and the lives of her crew, Kopple aligned herself with the United Mine Workers of America, who were intimidated and sometimes shot at by strikebreakers for the Eastover Mining Company.

During the film, Kopple's cameras begin to focus on the coal miners' wives, who encourage, cajole, and chastise their men to maintain the strike, walk the picket lines, and hold their families and communities together. While direct cinema can help reveal a subject in profound and unexpected ways, this technique may not remove the narrative voice and perspective as much as hide it or transfer its function to the more "invisible" power of other filmmaking systems. The editing process, for example, can include and exclude materials, ironically juxtapose people, events, and ideas, and arrange and order reality to suit the filmmaker's perspective.

Documentary filmmakers continue to employ conventional formal elements such as interviews, voice-over narration, and archival footage in innovative ways to create new and compelling nonfiction forms. Director Ken Burns seeks to bring history alive by presenting historical documents, archival photographs, painterly location shots, and posed artifacts to public-television audiences in a formalized style very different from the handheld "fly on the wall" perspective offered by direct-cinema documentaries. He has been known to film thousands of historical photographs in his signature manner, where the camera glides and the framing tightens; such "dramatic" camera movements emphasize details and link them to the narration and historical observations. Burns's use of the effect became so ubiquitous that Apple computers incorporated it into their home-movie-editing software iMovie and openly identified it as the "Ken Burns Effect."

Many documentaries investigate events that happened in the past, but some of these cinematic investigations are more personal than historical. The approach of films like Andrew Jarecki's *Capturing the Friedmans* (2003) rejects presenting a single "factual" interpretative stance in favor of offering a more ambiguous range of often-conflicting accounts. *Capturing the Friedmans* explores accusations of child molestation leveled at Arnold Friedman and his teenage son, Jesse, from multiple perspectives through a collage of home movies, archival media coverage, and interviews with both family members and alleged victims.

Director Errol Morris incorporates cinematic techniques normally associated with highly stylized narrative and experimental films into the typically spartan documentary form. *Fast, Cheap & Out of Control* (1997) implies profound associations between his seemingly diverse subjects—a topiary gardener, a lion tamer, a

1

2

Direct cinema

Documentaries made in the style known as direct cinema attempt to immerse the viewer in an experience as close as is cinematically possible to witnessing events as an invisible observer. Direct cinema films like Albert and David Maysles's *Grey Gardens* (1975; codirectors Ellen Hovde and Muffie Meyer) seek to avoid conventional documentary techniques such as interviews and voice-over narration, and instead rely on very small crews and lightweight, handheld camera and sound equipment to capture the action as unobtrusively as possible. As they filmed *Grey Gardens*, the Maysleses observed that their extroverted subject "Little Edie" Beale [1] was becoming more interested in performing for the filmmakers than in ignoring their presence. Some direct cinema purists may have discouraged or deleted her behavior, but the Maysleses saw Edie's need for recognition, and the delusions that fueled it, as a crucial part of her reality. The filmmakers acknowledged their own role in the situation by incorporating their own image (as captured in a mirror) into the movie [2].

robotics researcher, and a scientist studying naked mole rats—by intercutting interviews of all four men and lacing the movie with artfully crafted extreme close-ups, beautiful slow-motion effects, footage from old adventure films, abstracted reenactments, and original music by Caleb Sampson. Morris is famous for conducting his interviews using an Interrotron, a device of his own invention that projects the director's face onto a glass plate placed over the camera lens. The apparatus allows the subject to address responses directly into the lens, which establishes direct eye contact with the viewer.

Experimental Movies

Experimental is the most difficult of all types of movies to define precisely, in part because experimental filmmakers actively seek to defy categorization and convention. For starters, it's helpful to think of experimental cinema as pushing the boundaries of what most people think movies are—or should be. After all, *avant-garde*, the term originally applied to this approach to filmmaking,

comes from a French phrase used to describe scouts and pathfinders who explored ahead of an advancing army, implying that avant-garde artists, whether in film or another medium, are innovators who lead, rather than follow, the pack.

The term *experimental* falls along these same lines. It's an attempt to capture the innovative spirit of an approach to moviemaking that plays with the medium, is not bound by established traditions, and is dedicated to exploring possibility. Both *avant-garde* and *experimental* (and other terms) are still used to describe this kind of movie. But since *experimental* is the word most commonly used, is appropriately evocative, and is in English, let's stick with it.

In response to the often-asked question, "What is an experimental film?" film scholar Fred Camper offers six criteria that outline the characteristics that most experimental films share. While no criterion can hope to encapsulate an approach to filmmaking as vigorously diverse as experimental cinema, a summary of Camper's list of common qualities is a good place to start:

1

2

Boundary-pushing documentaries

Two recent documentaries test the boundaries between observation and exploitation, fiction and nonfiction. In *Exit Through the Gift Shop* (2010; director Banksy), what begins as a rambling archive of street art shot by a somewhat incompetent enthusiast named Theirry Guetta turns into a movie about Guetta himself when one of his subjects (the mysterious and wildly successful artist known as Banksy) appropriates the footage, takes over the camera, and turns Guetta into a pseudo-celebrity called Mr. Brainwash. Banksy uses his considerable clout to influence the art world and his subject, and he records the results as the fame-hungry Guetta (and a small army of paid assistants) mounts a huge exhibit of new artworks credited to Mr. Brainwash [1]. *The Act of Killing* (2012; directors Joshua Oppenheimer, Anonymous, and Christine Cynn) begins as a relatively conventional documentary look back at the politically motivated massacre of as many as 2.5 million Indonesian citizens in the 1960s and 1970s. What immediately stands out is that Anwar Congo, the former death squad leader being interviewed, makes no attempt to downplay his role in the genocide. On the contrary, he proudly demonstrates his favorite execution methods. The filmmakers harness their subject's brazen narcissism by facilitating (and filming) increasingly elaborate re-creations of torture and murder, all staged by and starring Anwar and his sidekick Herman Koto, a former paramilitary leader and self-described gangster [2]. The resulting spectacle is profoundly disturbing, yet inescapably amusing. Are Anwar, Herman, and Mr. Brainwash dupes or wily collaborators? Can a movie be a documentary when the filmmakers actively manipulate the people and events they document? Does the precise nature of truth matter, so long as the results are entertaining? Parsing these questions is a part of the experience of watching both *Exit Through the Gift Shop* and *The Act of Killing*.

1. *Experimental films are not commercial.* They are made by single filmmakers (or collaborative teams consisting of, at most, a few artists) for very low budgets and with no expectation of financial gain.

2. *Experimental films are personal.* They reflect the creative vision of a single artist who typically conceives, writes, directs, shoots, and edits the movie with minimal contributions by other filmmakers or technicians. Experimental film credits are short.

3. *Experimental films do not conform to conventional expectations of story and narrative cause and effect.*

4. *Experimental films exploit the possibilities of the cinema* and, by doing so, often reveal (and revel in) tactile and mechanical qualities of motion pictures that conventional movies seek to obscure. Most conventional narrative films are constructed to make audiences forget they are watching a movie, whereas many experimental films repeatedly remind the viewer of the fact. They embrace innovative techniques that call attention to, question, and even challenge their own artifice.

5. *Experimental films critique culture and media.* From their position outside the mainstream, they often comment on (and intentionally frustrate) viewer expectations of what a movie should be.

6. *Experimental films invite individual interpretation.* Like abstract expressionist paintings, they resist the kind of accessible and universal meaning found in conventional narrative and documentary films.[1]

Because most experimental films do not tell a story in the conventional sense, incorporate unorthodox imagery, and are motivated more by innovation and personal expression than by commerce and entertainment, they help us understand in yet another way why movies are a form of art capable of a sort of motion-picture equivalent of poetry. Disregarding the traditional expectations of audiences, experimental films remind us that film—like painting, sculpture, music, or architecture—can be made in as many ways as there are artists.

For example, Michael Snow's *Wavelength* (1967) is a 45-minute film that consists, in what we see, only of an exceedingly slow zoom lens shot through a loft. Although human figures wander in and out of the frame,

departing at will from that frame or being excluded from it as the camera moves slowly past them, the film is almost totally devoid of any human significance. Snow's central concern is space: how to conceive it, film it, and encourage viewers to make meaning of it. *Wavelength* is replete with differing qualities of space, light, exposures, focal lengths, and printing techniques, all offering rich possibilities for how we perceive these elements and interpret their meaning. For those who believe that a movie must represent the human condition, *Wavelength* seems empty. But for those who believe, with D. W. Griffith, that a movie is meant, above all, to make us see, the work demonstrates the importance of utterly unconventional filmmaking.

Su Friedrich's experimental films also "make us see," but in different ways. Friedrich's *Sink or Swim* (1990) opens abstractly with what seems to be scientific footage—a microscope's view of sperm cells, splitting cells, a developing fetus—inexplicably narrated by a young girl's voice recounting the mythological relationship between the goddess Athena and her father, Zeus. As the movie's remaining twenty-five segments unfold, the offscreen girl narrator shifts from mythological accounts of paternal relationships to third-person accounts of episodes between a contemporary girl and her father. The episodes are illustrated with candid documentary footage, often featuring men and girls at play, and with what appear to be home movies, edited in a way that obscures their origins. The footage sometimes enforces the narration's mood and content, but just as often conflicts with the girl's story or combines with it so that additional meaning is imparted to both image and spoken word. As the successive layers are revealed, what began as an apparent abstract exercise reveals itself as an autobiographical account of the filmmaker's troubled relationship with her distant and demanding father. Ironically, this experimental approach ultimately delivers a more emotionally complex and involving experience than most conventional narrative or documentary treatments of similar subject matter.

While *Wavelength* explores cinematic space and *Sink or Swim* focuses on personal expression, other experimental films are primarily concerned with the tactile and communicative qualities of the film medium itself. These movies scavenge found footage—originally

---

1. Fred Camper, "Naming, and Defining, Avant-Garde or Experimental Film" (n.d.), www.fredcamper.com/Film/AvantGardeDefinition.html (accessed March 19, 2015).

created by other filmmakers for other purposes—and then manipulate the gleaned images to create new meanings and aesthetics not intended by the artists or technicians who shot the original footage.

To create *Tribulation 99: Alien Anomalies under America* (1992), his feature-length satire of paranoid conspiracy theories, Craig Baldwin collected thousands of still and moving images from a wide variety of mostly vintage sources, including educational films, scientific studies, and low-budget horror movies. By combining, superimposing, and sequencing selected shots, and overlaying the result with ominous text and urgent voice-over narration, Baldwin changes the image context and meaning, thus transforming the way audiences interpret and experience the footage.

Experimental filmmaker Martin Arnold also manipulates preexisting footage to alter the viewer's interpretation and experience with a method that is in many ways the reverse of Baldwin's frenetic collage approach. Arnold's most famous film, *Passage à l'acte* (1993), uses only one sequence from a single source: a short, relatively mundane breakfast-table scene from Robert Mulligan's narrative feature *To Kill a Mockingbird* (1962). Using an optical printer, which allows the operator to duplicate one film frame at a time onto a new strip of film stock, Arnold stretched the 34-second sequence to over 11 minutes by rhythmically repeating every moment in the scene. The result forces us to see the familiar characters and situation in an entirely new way. What was originally an innocent and largely inconsequential exchange is infused with conflict and tension. Through multiple and rapid-fire repetitions, a simple gesture such as putting down a fork or glancing sideways becomes a hostile or provocative gesture, a mechanical loop, or an abstract dance. Like many experimental films, *Passage à l'acte* deliberately challenges the viewer's ingrained expectations of narrative, coherence, continuity, movement, and forward momentum. The resulting experience is hypnotic, musical, disturbing, fascinating, and infuriating.

It's easy to assume that films that test the audience's expectations of how a movie should behave are a relatively recent phenomenon. But the truth is that filmmakers have been experimenting with film form and reception since the early days of cinema. In the 1920s, the first truly experimental movement was born in France, with its national climate of avant-garde artistic expression. Among the most notable works were films by painters: René Clair's *Entr'acte* (1924), Fernand Léger

and Dudley Murphy's *Ballet mécanique* (1924), Marcel Duchamp's *Anémic cinéma* (1926), and Man Ray's *Emak-Bakia* (1926). These films are characterized uniformly by their surreal content, often dependent on dream impressions rather than objective observation; their abstract images, which tend to be shapes and patterns with no meaning other than the forms themselves; their absence of actors performing within a narrative context; and their desire to shock not only our sensibilities but also our morals. The most important of these films, the surrealist dreamscape *An Andalusian Dog* (1929), was made in France by the Spanish filmmaker Luis Buñuel and the Spanish painter Salvador Dalí. Re-creating the sexual nature of dreams, this film's images metamorphose continually, defy continuity, and even attack causality—as in one scene when a pair of breasts dissolves into buttocks.

Although an alternative cinema has existed in the United States since the 1920s—an achievement of substance and style that is all the more remarkable in a country where filmmaking is synonymous with Hollywood—the first experimental filmmakers here were either European-born or influenced by the French, Russians, and Germans. The first major American experimental filmmaker was Maya Deren. Her surreal films—*Meshes of the Afternoon* (1943), codirected with her husband, Alexander Hammid, is the best known—virtually established alternative filmmaking in this country. Deren's work combines her interests in various fields, including film, philosophy, ethnography, and dance, and it remains the touchstone for those studying avant-garde movies.

Concerned with the manipulation of space and time, which after all is the essence of filmmaking, Deren experimented with defying continuity, erasing the line between dream and reality. She used the cinematic equivalent of **stream of consciousness**, a literary style that gained prominence in the 1920s in the hands of such writers as Marcel Proust, Virginia Woolf, James Joyce, and Dorothy Richardson and that attempted to capture the unedited flow of experience through the mind. In *Meshes*, Deren is both the creative mind behind the film and the creative performer on the screen. She takes certain recognizable motifs—a key, a knife, a flower, a telephone receiver, and a shadowy figure walking down a garden path—and repeats them throughout the film, each time transfiguring them into something else. So, for example, the knife evolves into a key and the flower into

1

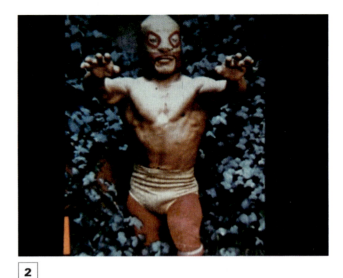

2

3

4

5

Rearranged footage

A sequence in Craig Baldwin's *Tribulation 99: Alien Anomalies under America* (1992) presents successive images of Mayan carvings [1], Lucha Libre masked wrestlers [2], natives in ceremonial woven suits [3], hooded prisoners [4], and nature footage of snakes [5] to illustrate the narration's breathless claim that displaced aliens hiding below the earth's surface have been forced to mate with reptiles. The power of editing to create meaning through juxtaposition allowed Baldwin to mutate his seemingly random collection of images of wildly disparate origins into a cohesive, if bizarre, story of the malevolent aliens emerging from their subterranean lair to attempt world domination.

a knife. These changing motifs are linked visually but also structurally. Deren's ideas and achievements bridge the gap between the surrealism of the French avant-garde films and such dream-related movies as Alain Resnais's *Last Year at Marienbad* (1961), Federico Fellini's *8½* (1963), Ingmar Bergman's *Persona* (1966), and Luis Buñuel's *The Milky Way* (1969).

Deren's work greatly influenced an American underground cinema that emerged in the 1950s. It has since favored four subgenres—the formal, the self-reflexive, the satirical, and the sexual—each of which tends to include aspects of the lyrical approach so typical of Deren. Works of pure form include John Whitney's early experiments with computer imagery in such films as *Matrix I* and *Matrix II* (both 1971); Shirley Clarke's *Skyscraper* (1960), one of several lighthearted, abstract tributes to city life; Peter Kubelka's *Arnulf Rainer* (1960), which created its images through abstract dots; Jordan Belson's *Allures* (1961), using abstract color animation; Robert Breer's *Fist Fight* (1964), which combines animation, images of handwriting, and other material; and Ernie Gehr's *The Astronomer's Dream* (2004), in which he speeds up the images so much that they become vertical purple lines.

Self-reflexive films, meaning those that represent their own conditions of production (movies, in other words, about movies, moviemaking, moviemakers, and so on), include Hans Richter's *Dreams That Money Can Buy* (1947), in the spirit of surrealism; Stan Brakhage's five-part *Dog Star Man* (1962–64), whose lyricism is greatly influenced by Deren's work; Bruce Baillie's *Mass for the Dakota Sioux* (1964), which combines a lyrical vision and social commentary; Hollis Frampton's *Zorn's Lemma* (1970), a complex meditation on cinematic structure, space, and movement; and Michael Snow's *Wavelength* (1967), which we already discussed.

Films that take a satirical view of life include James Broughton's *Mother's Day* (1948), on childhood; Stan van der Beek's *Death Breath* (1964), an apocalyptic vision using cartoons and other imagery; Bruce Conner's *Marilyn Times Five* (1973), which makes its comic points by compiling stock footage from other sources; and Mike Kuchar's *Sins of the Fleshapoids* (1965), an underground look at the horror genre.

Satirical and sexual films often overlap, particularly in their portrayal of sexual activities that challenge conventional ideas of "normality." Examples of these include Kenneth Anger's *Scorpio Rising* (1964), an explicit

Experimental film: style as subject

Among many other random repetitions and animations, Fernand Léger and Dudley Murphy's *Ballet Mécanique* (1924) repeatedly loops footage of a woman climbing stairs. This action lacks completion or narrative purpose and instead functions as a rhythmic counterpart to other sections of the film, in which more abstract objects are animated and choreographed in (as the title puts it) a "mechanical ballet."

1

2

3

4

Experimental film: image as shock

Luis Buñuel and Salvador Dalí collaborated to produce *An Andalusian Dog* (1929), one of the most famous experimental films. Through special effects, its notorious opening sequence can be summarized in four shots: [1] the title, "Once upon a time . . . ," which, under the circumstances, is an absurd use of the classic beginning of a nursery story; [2] an image of a man (who has just finished sharpening his straight razor); [3] an image of the hand of a differently dressed man holding a razor near a woman's eyeball with the implication that he will slit it; and [4] an image of a slit eyeball. There is no logic to this sequence, for the woman's eye is not slit; rather the slit eyeball appears to belong to an animal. The sequence is meant to shock the viewer, to surprise us, to make us "see" differently, but not to explain what we are seeing.

homosexual fantasy that is tame by today's standards; Jack Smith's *Flaming Creatures* (1963), a major test case for pornography laws; and many of Andy Warhol's films, including *Lonesome Cowboys* (1968). The directors who made these films tended to be obsessed, as was Deren, with expressing themselves and their subconscious through cinematic forms and images.

These days, movies that seem to be in direct opposition to Camper's experimental film criteria dominate our culture. Popular cinema is largely commercial, universal, and narrative. When most of us think of movies, we picture movies that conceal their artifice, reinforce viewer expectations, and seek a common, accessible interpretation.

While purely experimental cinema rarely penetrates into the mainstream, this highly personal and innovative approach to cinematic expression continues to thrive on the fringes of popular culture. A grassroots "micro-cinema" subculture has grown out of the affordability and accessibility of digital video formats, personal

Manipulated footage

Naomi Uman's *Removed* (1999) employs a reductive approach to found-footage filmmaking that made audiences reinterpret and reexamine previously existing footage. She used nail polish and bleach to remove the female character from the emulsion of all 10,000 frames of a 7-minute pornographic movie. The result forces the viewer to experience the objectification of women in a literal—or at least graphic—sense. The film's female character appears as an animated blank space that is physically manipulated by the male actors.

computer–based editing systems, and video-hosting Web sites like YouTube and Vimeo. Most film festivals, from the most influential international competitions to the smallest local showcases, feature experimental programs. Many prestigious film festivals specializing in experimental cinema, such as the Ann Arbor Film Festival, attract hundreds of submissions and thousands of patrons each year. International organizations like Flickr provide experimental filmmakers with an online venue to share and promote their work. Peripheral Produce and Invisible Cinema are among a growing number of companies and cooperatives that distribute experimental film and video compilations on DVD. Many art museums consider experimental applications of cinematic principles a fine-art form worthy of public display along with painting and sculpture.

Artists such as Bill Viola, Matthew Barney, Pierre Huyghe, and Douglas Gordon have attracted great attention to their avant-garde video installations, which change the traditional ways in which viewers experience and interact with moving images. Christian Marclay handled his experimental film *The Clock* (2010) like a limited edition fine-art print. The movie has never been distributed or broadcast; only seven copies have been sold to museums and collectors. *The Clock* is a precise assembly of thousands of images and lines of dialogue culled from existing movies and television shows, each one indicating a particular chronological moment in a 24-hour cycle.

And, finally, while truly experimental films rarely if ever reach mass audiences, experimental approaches to narrative construction, visual style, and editing techniques do often find their way into movies made by filmmakers sympathetic to the avant-garde's spirit of invention. Many of the Hollywood directors incorporating experimental techniques developed a taste for unconventional innovation in film school or art school, or while honing their craft on music videos, commercials, and independent art films. These filmmakers include David Lynch (*Inland Empire*, 2006), Spike Jonze (*Where the Wild Things Are*, 2009), Michel Gondry (*The Science of Sleep*, 2006), Richard Linklater (*A Scanner Darkly*, 2006), Charlie Kaufman (*Synecdoche, New York*, 2008), Gaspar Noé (*Enter the Void*, 2009), Nicholas Winding Refn (*Drive*, 2011), and Jonathan Glazer (*Under the Skin*, 2013). Experimental sensibilities have emerged in a growing number of mainstream productions, from Christian Wagner's wildly kinetic editing in Tony Scott movies like *Domino* (2005), to the abstracted images in the title sequences for David Fincher's *The Girl with the Dragon Tattoo* (2011), to the simulated found-footage sequence that opened each episode of the HBO dramatic series *True Blood* (2008–2014).

Hybrid Movies

The flexibility of film form has made cross-pollination among experimental, documentary, and narrative approaches an inevitable and desirable aspect of cinematic evolution. The resulting hybrids have blurred what were once distinct borders among the three primary film-type categories. For example, Roger Beebe's experimental movie *The Strip Mall Trilogy* (2001) documents a mile-long stretch of strip malls in Florida but so isolates and abstracts the images that he evokes meanings that transcend any architectural or anthropological investigation of commercial suburban development. Ray Tintori's narrative movie *Death to the Tinman* (2007) most certainly tells a story, but does so with narration, cinematography,

1

2

Documentary/narrative fusion

Larry Charles's *Borat: Cultural Learnings of America for Make Benefit Glorious Nation of Kazakhstan* (2006) [1] pushes the documentary/ narrative marriage to its extreme by placing the fictional character of Borat (Sacha Baron Cohen) in real-life situations with people who were led to believe that they (and Borat) were the subjects of a documentary about a foreign reporter's exploration of American culture. The result functions as both documentary and narrative: we experience a deliberately structured character pursuing a clearly defined goal, but that pursuit is punctuated with a series of spontaneous explosions of authentic human behavior provoked and manipulated by Borat/Cohen and captured by a documentary film crew. Director Jonathan Glazer took the hybrid a step further in *Under the Skin* (2013), his fiction film about an alien (Scarlett Johansson) who gradually begins to empathize with the humans she was sent to Earth to harvest. Glazer shot most of the movie using hidden cameras, so that many of the people appearing on-screen didn't know they were being filmed. The technique lends a sense of documentary realism to an otherwise fantastic situation. The men attracted to the beautiful extraterrestrial can't help convincingly portraying unsuspecting victims [2].

1

2

Film-type fusion

Perhaps the film that best exemplifies the fusion of narrative, documentary, and experimental film types is William Greaves's *Symbiopsychotaxiplasm: Take One* (1968). Greaves employed three camera crews and instructed the first crew to shoot only the series of actors performing the scripted scene, the second crew to film the first crew shooting the scene [1], and the third to shoot the entire multilevel production as well as anything else they judged footage-worthy going on around them. The edited film frequently uses split screen to present several of its multiple layers simultaneously [2]. Greaves intentionally provoked his various crews and casts with vague or contradictory directions, until what amounts to a civil war erupted as some of the film professionals involved began to question the director's intentions and methods. Greaves, who functioned as the director of the actors as well as a sort of actor himself in the dual layers of documentary footage, made sure that every aspect of the ensuing chaos—including private crew meetings criticizing the project—was captured on film and eventually combined into an experimental amalgam that breaks down audience expectations of narrative and documentary, artifice and reality.[2]

2. Amy Taubin, "*Symbiopsychotaxiplasm*: Still No Answers," The Criterion Collection (December 5, 2006), www.criterion.com/current/posts/460.

performance, and production-design stylings that subvert audience expectations as only an experimental film can.

We've already discussed the importance of narrative to many documentary films. A growing number of narrative feature films that incorporate documentary techniques demonstrate that the borrowing works in both directions. Contemporary directors such as Jean-Pierre and Luc Dardenne (*Two Days, One Night*, 2014), Lance Hammer (*Ballast*, 2008), Benh Zeitlen (*Beasts of the Southern Wild*, 2012), Ryan Coogler (*Fruitvale Station*, 2013), and Kelly Reichardt (*Night Moves*, 2014) use small crews, natural lighting, handheld cameras, and nonactors (alongside deglamorized professionals) to lend their gritty narrative films the sense of authentic realism associated with documentary aesthetics and techniques.[3]

Genre

Our brief survey of documentary and experimental cinema demonstrates that both of these primary types of movies can be further divided into defined subcategories. These distinctions are both useful and inevitable. Any art form practiced by ambitious innovators and consumed by a diverse and evolving culture can't help developing in multiple directions. When filmmakers and their audiences recognize and value particular approaches to both form and content, these documentary or experimental subcategories are further differentiated and defined. And the moment such a distinction is accepted, filmmakers and viewers will begin again to refine, revise, and recombine the elements that defined the new categorization in the first place.

Genre refers to the categorization of narrative films by the stories they tell and the ways they tell them. Commonly recognized movie genres include the Western, horror, science fiction, musical, and gangster film. But this is far from a complete list. The film industry continues to make action movies, biographies (biopics), melodramas, thrillers, romances, romantic comedies, fantasy films, and many others that fall within some genre or subgenre category.

Cinema of ideas

All cinema is about ideas—many about the idea of cinema itself—and there are many ways to make a film. Some filmmakers find nothing more challenging than making a movie about an idea for its own sake. With *The Tree of Life* (2011), writer/director Terrence Malick gently deals with such abstract ideas as life and death, love, family, joy and sorrow, the flow of time, and whether eternity exists. Its visual impact, produced by vivid images of our natural world, creates an overlaying structure. Under that he gently tucks a beautifully realized account of one family's life in the 1950s American Southwest, thus letting us experience the universe and the individual. But its principal purpose, like that of all cinema, is to make us see and help us understand its ideas.

A long list like that may lead you to believe that all films are genre movies. Not so. A quick scan of the movies in theaters during a single week in 2014 reveals many narrative films that tell stories and employ styles that don't fit neatly into any existing genre template. The nongenre titles filling out the top fifteen box office leaders during the last weekend in 2014, for example, included *Night at the Museum: Secret of the Tomb* (Shawn Levy), *The Gambler* (Rupert Wyatt), *Wild* (Jean-Marc Vallée), and *Top Five* (Chris Rock), as well as *The Hunger Games: Mockingjay—Part 1* (Francis Lawrence), which borrows from a number of genres but doesn't land directly in any.

Genre is certainly not the only way that narrative movies are classified. The film industry breaks down films according to studio of origin, budget, target audience, and distribution patterns. Moviegoers often make viewing decisions according to the directors and/or stars of the films available. Film scholars may categorize and analyze a movie based on a wide range of criteria, including its specific aesthetic style, the artists who created it,

3. Many thanks to Dr. James Kruel and University of North Carolina Wilmington professors Shannon Silva, Andre Silva, and Dr. J. Carlos Kase for some of the ideas in this analysis.

1

2

3

Genre study

Scholars find genre films to be especially rich artifacts that can reveal a great deal about the culture that produced and consumed them, as well as about the filmmakers who made them. How does Martin Scorsese, a director associated with gangster films such as *Mean Streets* (1973) [1] and *Goodfellas* (1990) [2], apply the conventions of that genre to the rise and fall of an unscrupulous stockbroker in *The Wolf of Wall Street* (2013) [3]? What do the forty-eight or so thrillers that Alfred Hitchcock produced in a prolific fifty-year span tell us about the evolution of our popular culture, film style, the movie business—and Hitchcock himself?

its country or region of origin, the apparent ideologies expressed by its style or subject matter, or the particular organized cinematic movement it emerged from.

Unlike these film movements (such as French New Wave or Dogme 95), in which a group of like-minded filmmakers consciously conspire to create a particular approach to film style and story, film genres tend to spring up organically, inspired by shifts in history, politics, or society. Genres are often brought about inadvertently—not through any conscious plan, but rather because of a cultural need to explore and express issues and ideas through images and stories. Many classic genres, including Westerns, horror, and science fiction, emerged in literature and evolved into cinematic form during the twentieth century. Others, such as the musical, originated on the Broadway and vaudeville stages before hitting the screen. Some, like the gangster film, were born and bred in the cinema. Cultural conditions inspire artists to tell certain kinds of stories (and audiences to respond to them), the nature of those narratives motivates certain technical and aesthetic approaches, and eventually the accumulation of like-minded movies is detected, labeled, studied, and explicated by cinema scholars.

And, of course, academic scholars are not the only movie lovers who find it useful to categorize films by genre. Genre significantly affects how audiences choose the movies they attend, rent, or purchase. Movie reviewers often critique a film based on how it stacks up against others in its genre. Most movie-rental retailers organize movies according to genre (along with more general catchall classifications like drama and comedy). Online and newspaper theater listings include a movie's genre alongside its rating, running time, and show time.

Of the aforementioned fifteen top-grossing movies for the weekend of December 26, 2014, at least ten could be considered genre films: *Interstellar* (Christopher Nolan) is science fiction; *The Hobbit: Battle of the Five Armies* (Peter Jackson) is fantasy; *Into the Woods* (Rob Marshall) and *Annie* (Will Gluck) are both musicals; and *Exodus: Gods and Kings* (Ridley Scott) updates the classic "sword and sandals" biblical epic. Two top-grossing animated kid's movies have adopted action film subgenres: *Big Hero Six* (Don Hall and Chris Williams) is a superhero movie, and *Penguins of Madagascar* (Eric Darnell and Simon J. Smith) is a James Bond–style spy thriller. *Unbroken* (Angelina Jolie), *The Imitation Game* (Morten Tyldum), and *Big Eyes* (Tim

Burton) are all biographical films, a genre that recounts a significant historical period of a notable person's life.

Since genre labels allow us to predict with reasonable certainty what sort of movie to expect, these classifications don't just help audiences make their viewing choices; the people that finance movies often must account for genre when deciding which projects to bankroll.

Genres offer familiar story formulas, conventions, themes, and conflicts, as well as immediately recognizable visual icons. Together, they provide a blueprint for creating and marketing a type of film that has proven successful in the past. Studios and distributors can develop genre-identified stars, select directors on the basis of proven ability in a particular genre; piggyback on the success of a previous genre hit; and even recycle props, sets, costumes, and digital backgrounds. Just as important, the industry counts on genre to predict ticket sales, presell markets, and cash in on recent trends by making films that allow consumers to predict they'll like a particular movie. In other words: give people what they want, and they will buy it. This simple economic principle helps us understand the phenomenal growth

of the movie industry from the 1930s on, as well as the mind-numbing mediocrity of so many of the movies the industry produces. The kind of strict adherence to genre convention driven solely by economics often yields derivative and formulaic results.

If genre films are prone to mediocrity, why are so many great filmmakers drawn to making them? Part of the answer can be found, of all places, in a statement by the Nobel Prize–winning poet T. S. Eliot, who wrote: "When forced to work within a strict framework, the imagination is taxed to its utmost—and will produce its richest ideas." Eliot was talking about poetry, but the same concept can be applied to cinema. Creatively ambitious writers and directors often challenge themselves to create art within the strict confines of genre convention.

A genre's so-called rules can provide a foundation upon which the filmmaker can both honor traditions and innovate change. The resulting stories and styles often expertly fulfill some expectations while surprising and subverting others as the filmmaker references, refutes, and revises well-established cultural associations. Genre has intrigued so many of our greatest American and

Genre masterpieces
Not all genre movies are disposable formula pictures churned out for the indiscriminate masses. Many of cinema's most revered films are also genre movies. Stanley Kubrick's *2001: A Space Odyssey* (1968) incorporates virtually every standard science-fiction genre element, including speculative setting, special effects, and a decided ambivalence toward the benefits of technology. Yet Kubrick's skills as a storyteller and stylist make *2001* a work of art that transcends conventional attitudes toward genre movies.

European filmmakers that numerous entries in the canon of important and transformative movies are genre films. *The Godfather* (1972; director Francis Ford Coppola), *Goodfellas* (1990; director Martin Scorsese), and *Bonnie and Clyde* (1967; director Arthur Penn) are all gangster films; Stanley Kubrick's *2001: A Space Odyssey* (1968) is science fiction; Carol Reed's *The Third Man* (1949) and even Jean-Luc Godard's *Breathless* (1960) could be considered film noir; Woody Allen's *Annie Hall* (1977) is a romantic comedy; John Ford's *The Searchers* (1956) is a Western, as is Sergio Leone's *The Good, the Bad and the Ugly* (1966); Stanley Donen and Gene Kelly's *Singin' in the Rain* (1952) is a musical; David Lean's *Lawrence of Arabia* (1962) is a biography and a war movie and an epic.

Still, audiences don't like just the classic films that transcend genre conventions. Genre films have been prevalent since the earliest days of cinema because, contrary to popular perceptions, most movie viewers value predictability over novelty. Elements of certain genres appeal to us, so we seek to repeat an entertaining or engaging cinema experience by viewing a film that promises the same surefire ingredients. We get a certain pleasure from seeing how different filmmakers and performers have rearranged and interpreted familiar elements, just as we are exhilarated by an unexpected deviation from the anticipated path. To put this relationship into gastronomic terms: the most common pizza features a flour-based crust topped with tomato sauce and mozzarella cheese, but it's the potential variety within that familiar foundation that has made pizza one of America's favorite foods.

A less obvious but perhaps more profound explanation for the prevalence of genre lies in the deep roots of genre in our society. Remember that any given genre naturally emerges and crystallizes not because Hollywood thinks it'll sell, but because it gives narrative voice to something essential to our culture. The film industry may ultimately exploit a genre's cultural resonance, but only after cultural conditions motivate enough individual artists and viewers to create the genre in the first place.

For example, no studio executive or directors' club decided to invent horror movies out of thin air. Horror movies exist due to our collective fear of death and the human psyche's need for catharsis. Westerns enact and endorse aspects of American history and the human condition that Americans have needed to believe about

themselves. We go to these movies not only to celebrate the familiar, but to enforce fundamental beliefs and passively perform cultural rituals. As our world evolves and audience perspectives change, genre movies adapt to reflect these cultural shifts. A Western made during the can-do patriotism of World War II is likely to express its themes differently than one produced at the height of the Vietnam War.

Genre Conventions

Movie genres are defined by sets of conventions—aspects of storytelling such as recurring themes and situations, setting, character types, and story formula, as well as aspects of presentation and visual style such as decor, lighting, and sound. Even the movie stars associated with a particular genre can be considered one of these defining conventions. Keep in mind that these conventions are not enforced; filmmakers don't follow mandated genre checklists. While every movie within any particular genre will incorporate some of these elements, few genre movies attempt to include every possible genre convention.

Story Formulas The way a movie's story is structured—its plot—also helps viewers determine what genre it belongs to. For example, gangster films—from Howard Hawks's *Scarface* (1932) to Ridley Scott's *American Gangster* (2007)—tend to share a plot structure in which an underprivileged and disrespected immigrant joins (or forms) an organized crime syndicate; works his way to the top with a combination of savvy, innovation, and ruthlessness; becomes corrupted by his newfound power and the fruits of his labors; and as a result is betrayed, killed, or captured.

Romantic comedy plots are structured around characters in love as they couple, break up, and reconnect. When they first meet, the two characters (usually a man and a woman) are at odds. They fall in love in spite of, or sometimes because of, this seeming incompatibility. Then they must overcome obstacles to their relationship in the form of misunderstandings, competing partners, social pressures, or friction caused by the aforementioned incompatibility. Eventually the romance will appear doomed, but one half of the couple will realize they are meant for each other and make a grand gesture that reunites the romantic duo.

Theme A movie's *theme* is a unifying idea that the film expresses through its narrative or imagery. Not every genre is united by a single, clear-cut thematic idea, but the Western comes close. Nearly all Westerns share a central conflict between civilization and wilderness: settlers, towns, schoolteachers, cavalry outposts, and lawmen stand for civilization; free-range cattlemen, Indians, prostitutes, outlaws, and the wide-open spaces themselves fill the wilderness role. Many classic Western characters exist on both sides of this thematic conflict. For example, the Wyatt Earp character played by Henry Fonda in John Ford's *My Darling Clementine* (1946) is a former gunfighter turned lawman turned cowboy turned lawman. He befriends an outlaw but falls in love with a schoolteacher from the east. Early Westerns tend to sympathize with the forces of civilization and order, but many of the Westerns from the 1960s and 1970s valorize the freedom-loving outlaw, cowboy, or Native American hero.

Gangster films from Howard Hawks's *Scarface* (1932) to Ridley Scott's *American Gangster* (2007) are shaped by three well-worn, but obviously resonant themes: rags to riches; crime does not pay; absolute power corrupts absolutely. The thematic complexity made possible by the tension between these aspirational and moralistic ideas can give viewers a more meaningful experience than we might expect from a genre dedicated to career criminals.

Character Types While most screenwriters strive to create individuated characters, genre films are often populated by specific character "types." Western protagonists personify the tension between order and chaos in the form of the free-spirited but civilized cowboy or the gunslinger turned lawman. Female characters also personify this tension, but only on one side or the other—as schoolmarm or prostitute, only rarely as a combination of both. Other Western character types include the cunning gambler, the greenhorn, the sidekick, and the settler. John Ford packed nearly every Western character type into a single wagon in his classic Western *Stagecoach* (1939).

The horror and science-fiction film antagonist is almost always some form of "other"—a being utterly different from the movie's protagonist (and audience) in form, attitude, and action. Many of these movie monsters are essentially large, malevolent bugs—the more foreign the villain's appearance and outlook, the better. When the other is actually a human, he often wears a mask designed to accentuate his otherness.

Setting Setting—where a movie's action is located and how that environment is portrayed—is also a common genre convention. Obviously, Westerns are typically set in the American West, but setting goes beyond geography. Most classic Westerns take place in the 1880s and 1890s, an era of western settlement when a booming population of Civil War veterans and other eastern refugees went west in pursuit of land, gold, and cattle trade. The physical location of Monument Valley became the landscape most associated with the genre, not because of any actual history that occurred there, but because the scenic area was the favorite location of the prolific Western director John Ford.

Since science-fiction films are speculative and, therefore, look forward rather than backward, they are usually set in the future; sometimes in space, sometimes in futuristic earth cities, sometimes in post-apocalyptic desolation, but almost always in an era and place greatly affected by technology. Unlike gangster films, which are almost always urban in setting, horror films seek the sort of isolated locations—farms, abandoned summer camps, small rural villages—that place the genre's besieged protagonists far from potential aid.

Presentation Many genres feature certain elements of cinematic language that communicate tone and atmosphere. For example, horror films take advantage of lighting schemes that accentuate and deepen shadows. The resulting gloom helps to create an eerie mood, but horror films are more than just dark; filmmakers use the hard-edged shadows as a dominant compositional element to convey a sense of oppression, distort our sense of space, and conceal narrative information. Film noir, a genre that also seeks to disorient the viewer and convey a sense of unease (although for very different thematic and narrative reasons), employs many of the same lighting techniques.

Ironically, science-fiction films use the latest high-tech special effects to tell stories that warn against the dehumanizing dangers of advanced technology. In fact, the genre is responsible for many important special effect innovations, from the miniatures and matte paintings that made possible the futuristic city of Fritz Lang's

Metropolis (1927) to the motion-control cameras and rotoscope animation that launched the spaceships of Stanley Kubrick's *2001: A Space Odyssey* (1968) to the special "virtual camera system" director James Cameron and his *Avatar* (2009) team used to capture actors' expressions and actions as the first step in a revolutionary technical process that transformed the film's cast into aliens inhabiting an all-digital world.

Westerns, a genre clearly associated with setting, feature a great many exterior shots that juxtapose the characters with the environment they inhabit. The human subject tends to dominate the frame in most movie compositions, but many of these Western exterior shots are framed so that the "civilized" characters are dwarfed by the overwhelming expanse of wilderness around them.

Movies in the action genre often shoot combat (and other high-energy action) from many different angles to allow for a fast-paced editing style that presents the action from a constantly shifting perspective. These highly fragmented sequences subject the viewer to a rapid-fire cinematic simulation of the amplified exercise presumably experienced by the characters fighting on-screen.

Stars Even the actors who star in genre movies factor into how the genre is classified, analyzed, and received by audiences. In the 1930s and 1940s, actors worked under restrictive long-term studio contracts. With the studios choosing their roles, actors were more likely to be "typecast" and identified with a particular genre that suited their studio-imposed persona. Thus John Wayne is forever identified with the Western, Edward G. Robinson with gangster films, and Boris Karloff with horror.

These days, most actors avoid limiting themselves to a single genre, but several contemporary actors have become stars by associating themselves almost exclusively with action films. Arnold Schwarzenegger, Jet Li, Jason Statham, and others have benefited from the genre's preference for physical presence and macho persona over acting ability. It's not that no genre stars can act. In fact, an actor who has become identified with one genre will often receive extra attention and accolades for performing outside of it. For example, Bill Murray became a star while acting in screwball comedies, but his subtle performances in the dramas *Lost in Translation* (2003; director Sofia Coppola) and *Broken Flowers* (2005; director Jim Jarmusch) made him an actor worthy of movie critics' praise.

Multigenre stardom

These days, few actors are associated with a single genre. Scarlett Johansson, since taking on the recurring superhero movie role of the Black Widow in *Iron Man 2* (2010; director Jon Favreau) [1]—a part she has reprised in three subsequent Avengers movies—starred in three very different science-fiction films as well: as a psychokinetic killer in the action-packed *Lucy* (2014; director Luc Besson), as a lonely alien in the artsy *Under the Skin* (2013; director Jonathan Glazer), and as the voice of a sentient computer operating system in the cerebral *Her* (2013; director Spike Jonze) [2]. During the same period, she also played the elegant movie star Janet Leigh in the biopic *Hitchcock* (2012; director Sacha Gervasi) [3], and a woman competing with her boyfriend's porn addiction in the raunchy romantic comedy *Don Jon* (2013; director Joseph Gordon-Levitt).

Compiling an authoritative list of narrative genres and their specific conventions is nearly impossible, especially in an introductory textbook. There are simply too many genres, too much cinematic variety and flexibility, and too little academic consensus to nail down every (or any) genre definitively. Nevertheless, the next section offers a closer look at six major American genres to help you begin developing a deeper understanding of how genre functions.

Six Major American Genres

Gangster

The gangster genre is deeply rooted in the concept of the American dream: anyone, regardless of how humble his origins, can succeed. For much of its history, America's wealth and political power have been wielded primarily by successive generations of a white, Anglo-Saxon, highly educated, and Protestant ruling class. American heroes like Daniel Boone, leaders like Andrew Jackson and Abraham Lincoln, and popular novelists like Horatio Alger Jr. challenged this tradition of power by birthright. Their example gave rise to the notion that anyone with intelligence and spunk can rise to great riches or power through hard work and bold action. The nation's expanding population of working-class American immigrants were eager to embrace this rags-to-riches mythology.

By the turn of the twentieth century, pulp-fiction accounts of the American West had already established the hero as an outsider who lives by his wits and is willing to break the rules to achieve his goals. Two historical events provided the remaining ingredients needed to turn these working-class notions into what we know now as the gangster genre.

First, the Eighteenth Amendment to the Constitution—passed in 1919—banned the manufacture, sale, and transport of alcohol. This ill-advised law empowered organized crime, which expanded to capitalize on the newfound market for the suddenly forbidden beverages. Many of the criminal entrepreneurs who exploited this opportunity were Irish, Italian, and Jewish immigrants.

What's more, Prohibition legitimized unlawful behavior by making outlaws out of common citizens thirsty for a beer after quitting time. As a result, common people—many of them immigrants themselves—began to identify with the bootleggers and racketeers. They were seen as active protagonists who took chances, risked the consequences, and got results—all surefire elements of successful cinema heroes. The stock market crash in 1929 and the resulting economic depression further cemented the public's distrust of authority (that is, banks and financiers) and the allure of the gangster.

In this specific cultural context, American audiences began to question the authority of discredited institutions such as banks, government, and law enforcement. This viewpoint fed their fascination with the outlaws who bucked those systems that had failed the rest of society. As the Depression deepened, the need for vivid, escapist entertainment increased. Hollywood was the ideal conduit for this emerging zeitgeist; the result was the gangster film.

Just as the gangster film emerged, however, the film industry adopted a production code that forbade movies from explicitly engaging audience sympathy with "crime, wrongdoing, evil or sin." As a result, while early gangster films were among the most violent and sexually explicit movies of their time, the central conflicts and themes they explored were often at odds with one another. For example, the stories were centered around outlaw entrepreneurs who empowered themselves, bucked the establishment, and grabbed their piece of the pie; yet, by the end of the story, this theme of success would give way to a "crime does not pay" message in which the enterprising hero is finally corrupted by his hunger for power and thus defeated by forces of law and order. In many of these films, violent crime was both celebrated and condemned. Movies that had audiences sympathizing with criminals (or at least their goals) at the start would ultimately turn an exhilarating rags-to-riches story of empowerment into a cautionary tale of the consequences of blind ambition. Central characters would achieve their goal, only to be killed either by the law or their own equally ruthless subordinates. Along the way, audiences enjoyed the vicarious thrills of a daring pursuit of power, as well as the righteous satisfaction of seeing order restored.

While modern gangster narratives have expanded to include a wide range of stories set within the milieu of organized crime, classic gangster plots typically follow this rags-to-riches-to-destruction formula. The protagonist

Gangster plot elements

Francis Ford Coppola's The Godfather trilogy (1972–90), perhaps the most famous gangster film series, includes many plot elements common to the genre, including the protagonist's humble origins and his rise to power through a combination of astute management and ruthless violence. But Coppola incorporated genre innovations that differentiated The Godfather movies from more typical gangster films. For example, the protagonist, Michael (Al Pacino), is an unwilling crime boss forced into syndicate leadership by circumstances and birthright. The plot elements of a humble origin and the rise to power are presented as flashbacks featuring not Michael, but his father, the man whose death propels Michael into a life of organized crime. Finally, Michael is unusual in that he attains power and prestige but is not destroyed (physically, at least) by corruption and greed.

is initially powerless and sometimes suffers some form of public humiliation that both emphasizes his vulnerability and motivates his struggle for recognition. (This humiliation can come at the hands of a governing institution or the ruling gang organization; often, the ensuing conflict pits the gangster hero against both the law and the criminals currently in control.) The hero gains status and eventually grabs power and riches through ingenuity, risk taking, and a capacity for violence.

Most gangster protagonists are killers, but their initial victims (such as the thugs responsible for the protagonist's initial humiliation) are usually portrayed as deserving of their fate. This pattern shifts as the hero reaches his goal to rule the criminal syndicate. His ambition clouds his vision; he becomes paranoid and power-hungry, and begins to resemble his deposed adversaries. Before he self-destructs, he often destroys—figuratively or literally—characters that represent his last remaining

ties to the earnest go-getter who began the story. Frequently, the protagonist expresses last-minute regret for what he has become, but by then it's almost always too late.

More sympathetic secondary characters often serve to humanize the gangster antihero. While the doomed protagonist is nearly always male, the secondary characters who provide a tenuous connection to the Old World values that he must sacrifice on his climb up the ladder usually take the form of a mother or sister. The only other female character typical to the genre is either a fellow criminal or a sort of gangster groupie known as a moll. Whereas the protagonist's mother loves him for his potential humanity, the gangster moll loves him for his potential power and wealth. She is a symbol of his aspirations—an alluring veneer concealing a rotten core.

The protagonist may also have a sidekick—a trusted companion from the old neighborhood—who makes

The antihero

The gangster movie gave the cinema some its first antiheroes. These unconventional central characters pursue goals, overcome obstacles, take risks, and suffer consequences—everything needed to propel a compelling narrative—but they lack the traditional "heroic" qualities that engage an audience's sympathy. While he may not be courteous, kind, and reverent, he is almost always smart (if uneducated), observant, and brave. More than anything, the gangster-hero is driven by an overwhelming need to prove himself. This need motivates his quest for power, fame, and wealth—and almost always proves to be the tragic flaw that brings about his inevitable downfall. In the final moments of Raoul Walsh's *White Heat* (1949), the psychopathic protagonist Cody Jarrett (James Cagney) declares "top of the world, Ma!" before blowing himself to bits rather than submitting to the policemen who have him surrounded.

the journey with him. This friend may be responsible for giving the protagonist his first break in the business, only to be eclipsed by the hero later. He is often instrumental in the protagonist's downfall, either as a betrayer or as a victim of the central character's greed and lust for power.

Antagonists come in two forms: law enforcement agents and fellow gangsters. In stark contrast to portrayals in traditional procedurals, the police in gangster movies are portrayed as oppressors who are corrupt, incompetent, or both. They are sometimes in league with the gangster antagonist, the current kingpin who lacks the imagination or courage of our hero. His overthrow is often one of the first major obstacles the protagonist must overcome. Of course, the ultimate antagonist in many gangster movies is the protagonist himself.

Legend has it that when the gangster Willie Sutton was asked why he robbed banks, he replied, "Because that's where the money is." The same sort of logic ex-

plains the setting of the vast majority of gangster films. Movies about organized crime are set in urban locations because organized crime flourishes primarily in large cities. The particulars of the setting evolve as the plot progresses. The story usually opens in a slum, develops on the mean streets downtown, and then works its way upward into luxury penthouses.

In contrast to most movie stars, the actors most closely associated with early gangster films were diminutive and relatively unattractive. The authority that actors like Edward G. Robinson and James Cagney conveyed on-screen was made all the more powerful by their atypical appearance. (In another twist of Hollywood logic, Cagney—whose gangster portrayals were among the most brutal in cinema history—was equally beloved as a star of happy-go-lucky musicals.)

Other notable gangster films include *Little Caesar* (1931; director Mervyn LeRoy); *The Public Enemy* (1931; director William A. Wellman); *Scarface* (1932; director Howard Hawks); *White Heat* (1949; director Raoul Walsh); *Touchez pas au grisbi* (1954; director Jacques Becker); *Rififi* (1955; director Jules Dassin); *Bonnie and Clyde* (1967; director Arthur Penn); *Le Samouraï* (1967; director Jean-Pierre Melville); *Battles without Honor or Humanity* (1973; director Kinji Fukasaku); *Scarface* (1983; director Brian De Palma); *Once upon a Time in America* (1984; director Sergio Leone); *The Krays* (1990; director Peter Medak); *Miller's Crossing* (1990; director Joel Coen); *Reservoir Dogs* (1992; director Quentin Tarantino); *Sonatine* (1993; director Takeshi Kitano); *Road to Perdition* (2002; director Sam Mendes); *City of God* (2002; directors Fernando Meirelles and Kátia Lund); and *Mesrine: Killer Instinct* and *Mesrine: Public Enemy #1* (2008; director Jean-François Richet).

Film Noir

In the early 1940s, the outlook, tone, and style of American genre films grew decidedly darker with the emergence of film noir (from the French for "black film"), a shift clearly denoted by its name. Not that movies hadn't already demonstrated a cynical streak. The gangster movies that surfaced in the previous decade featured antiheroes and less-than-flattering portrayals of our cities and institutions. World War I, Prohibition, and the Great Depression began the trend toward more realistic, and thus bleaker, artistic and narrative representations of the world, as evidenced in the written word of

1

2

Fatalism in film noir

Film noir movies sometimes present information and events in a way that heightens the audience's sense that the hard-luck protagonist is doomed from the moment the story opens. Director and screenwriter Billy Wilder pushed this technique to the extreme in two of his most famous noir movies, both of which reveal the demise of the protagonist. The first moments of *Double Indemnity* (1944) open with antihero Walter Neff (Fred MacMurray) stumbling wounded into his office to confess to the murder he will spend the rest of the story trying to get away with [1]. *Sunset Boulevard* (1950) goes one step further. The entire film is narrated in first-person voice-over by a protagonist (William Holden) presented in the opening scene as a floating corpse [2].

the time. Pulp-fiction writers like Dashiell Hammett had been publishing the hard-boiled stories that formed the foundation of film noir since the early 1930s.

In fact, if not for the efforts of Hollywood and the U.S. government during World War II, film noir might have come along sooner. Instead, gung-ho war movies were designed to build support for the war effort, and lighthearted musicals and comedies were produced to provide needed distractions from overwhelming world events. Yet the same war that helped delay the arrival of film noir also helped give birth to the new genre by exposing ordinary Americans to the horrors of war. Whether in person or through newsreels and newspapers, troops and citizens alike witnessed death camps, battlefield slaughters, the rise of fascism, and countless other atrocities.

Many of the genre's greatest directors, including Otto Preminger, Billy Wilder, and Fritz Lang, were themselves marked by the hardship and persecution they had experienced before leaving war-torn Europe for Hollywood. Others, like Samuel Fuller, fought as American soldiers. The atomic bomb that ended the war also demonstrated

that not even a nation as seemingly secure as the United States was safe from its devastating power. The financial boom that the war effort had generated ended abruptly as the soldiers returned home to a changed world of economic uncertainty. Film noir fed off the postwar disillusionment that followed prolonged exposure to this intimidating new perspective.

In part because many of the early noir movies were low-budget "B" movies (so called because they often screened in the second slot of double features), the genre was not initially recognized or respected by most American scholars. Its emphasis on corruption and despair was seen as an unflattering portrayal of the American character. It was left to French critics, some of whom went on to make genre films of their own, to recognize (and name) the genre.

In fact, the American critic Paul Schrader (himself a filmmaker who has written and directed noir films) feels that film noir is not a genre at all. He claims that "film noir . . . is not defined, as are the Western and gangster genres, by conventions of setting and conflict, but rather by the more subtle qualities of tone and mood."[4]

4. Paul Schrader, "Notes on *Film Noir*" (1972), in *Film Noir Reader,* ed. Alain Silver and James Ursini (New York: Limelight, 1996), pp. 53–64.

[1]

[2]

[3]

Modern film noir

While many modern noir films, such as Curtis Hanson's *L.A. Confidential* (1997), set their stories in places and times that directly reference the classic noir films of the 1940s, others offer a revised genre experience by relocating noir's thematic, aesthetic, and narrative elements to contemporary times and atypical locations. Rian Johnson's *Brick* (2005) [1] takes place within the convoluted social strata of a suburban high school. Joel Coen's *Fargo* (1996) [2] unfolds on the frozen prairies of rural North Dakota and the snow-packed Minneapolis suburbs. Erik Skjoldbjærg's *Insomnia* (1997) [3] trades ominous shadows for the unrelenting light of the midnight sun in a village above the Arctic Circle.

Regardless of how it is classified, film noir has continued to flourish long past the events that provoked its birth, thanks in part to a universal attraction to its visual and narrative style and a lasting affinity for its outlook. Like the eggs they are named for, the hard-boiled characters in film noir have a tough interior beneath brittle shells. The themes are fatalistic, the tone cynical. Film noir may not be defined by setting, but noir films are typically shot in large urban areas (such as Chicago, New York, or Los Angeles). They contain gritty, realistic night exteriors, many of them filmed on location, as opposed to the idealized and homogenized streets built on the studio back lot.

Like his counterpart in the gangster movie, the film-noir protagonist is an antihero. Unlike his gangster equivalent, he rarely pursues or achieves leadership status. On the contrary, the central noir character is an outsider. If he is a criminal, he's usually a lone operator caught up in a doomed attempt at a big score or a wrongdoer trying to elude justice. The private detectives at the center of many noir narratives operate midway between lawful society and the criminal underworld, with associates and enemies on both sides of the law. They may be former police officers who left the force in either disgrace or disgust; or they may be active but isolated police officers ostracized for their refusal to play by the rules. Whatever his profession, the noir protagonist is small-time, world-weary, aging, and not classically handsome. He's self-destructive and thus fallible, often suffering abuse on the way to a story conclusion that may very well deny him his goal and will almost certainly leave him unredeemed. All this is not to say that the noir protagonist is weak or unattractive. Ironically, the world-weary and wisecracking noir antihero is responsible for some of cinema's most popular and enduring characters. Humphrey Bogart was just a middle-aged character actor before his portrayal of the private detective Sam Spade in John Huston's *The Maltese Falcon* (1941) made him a cultural icon.

World War II expanded opportunities for women on the home front. They took over the factory jobs and other responsibilities from the men who left to fight in Europe and the Pacific. Perhaps as a reflection of men's fear or resentment of these newly empowered women, film noir elevated the female character to antagonist status. Instead of passive supporting players, the femme fatale (French for "deadly woman") role cast women as seductive, autonomous, and deceptive predators who use men for their own means. As a rule, the femme fatale is a far smarter—and thus formidable—opponent for the protagonist than other adversarial characters, most of whom are corrupt and violent though not necessarily a match for the hero's cynical intelligence.

More than virtually any other genre, film noir is distinguished by its visual style. The name *black film* references not just the genre's attitude, but its look as well. Noir movies employ lighting schemes that emphasize contrast and create deep shadows that can obscure as much information as the illumination reveals. Light sources are often placed low to the ground, resulting in illumination that distorts facial features and casts dramatic shadows. Exterior scenes usually take place at night; those interior scenes set during the day often play out behind drawn shades that cast patterns of light and shadow, splintering the frame. These patterns, in turn, combine with other diagonal visual elements to create a compositional tension that gives the frame—and the world it depicts—a restless, unstable quality.

Film noir plot structure reinforces this feeling of disorientation. The complex (sometimes incomprehensible) narratives are often presented in nonchronological or otherwise convoluted arrangements. Plot twists deprive the viewer of the comfort of a predictable plot. Goals shift, and expectations are reversed; allies are revealed to be enemies (and vice versa); narration, even that delivered by the protagonist, is sometimes unreliable. Moral reference points are skewed: victims are often as corrupt as their persecutors; criminals are working stiffs just doing their job. Paradoxically, this unsettling narrative complexity is often framed by a sort of enforced predictability. Fatalistic voice-over narration telegraphs future events and outcomes, creating a sense of predetermination and hopelessness for the protagonist's already lost cause.

Other notable film noir movies include *The Maltese Falcon* (1941; director John Huston); *Laura* (1944; director Otto Preminger); *Scarlet Street* (1945; director Fritz Lang); *Detour* (1945; director Edgar G. Ulmer); *The Big Sleep* (1946; director Howard Hawks); *The Postman Always Rings Twice* (1946; director Tay Garnett); *The Killers* (1946; director Robert Siodmak); *Out of the Past* (1947; director Jacques Tourneur); *The Naked City* (1948; director Jules Dassin); *Criss Cross* (1949; director Robert Siodmak); *Asphalt Jungle* (1950; director John Huston); *D.O.A.* (1950; director Rudolph Maté); *Panic in the Streets* (1950; director Elia Kazan); *Ace in the Hole* (1951; director Billy Wilder); *Pickup on South Street* (1953; director Samuel Fuller); *The Hitch-Hiker* (1953; director Ida Lupino); *Kiss Me Deadly* (1955; director Robert Aldrich); *Sweet Smell of Success* (1957; director Alexander Mackendrick); *Touch of Evil* (1958; director Orson Welles); *Chinatown* (1974; director Roman Polanski); *After Dark, My Sweet* (1990; director James Foley); *The Last Seduction* (1994; director John Dahl); *The Usual Suspects* (1995; director Bryan Singer); *Lost Highway* (1997; director David Lynch); *Memento* (2000; director Christoper Nolan); *The Man Who Wasn't There* (2001; director Joel Coen); *Sin City* (2005; director Frank Miller and Robert Rodriguez); *The Square* (2008; director Nash Edgerton); *Broken Embraces* (2009; director Pedro Almodovar); *Drive* (2011; director Nicolas Winding Refn); *Gone Girl* (2014; director David Fincher); and *Inherent Vice* (2014; director Paul Thomas Anderson).

Science Fiction

It seems logical to think of science fiction as being speculative fantasy about the potential wonders of technological advances. But most science-fiction films are not really about science. If we tried to prove the "science" that most sci-fi films present, much of it would be quickly exposed as ridiculous. Instead, the genre's focus is on humanity's relationship with science and the technology it generates.

Science fiction existed as a literary genre long before movies were invented. The genre began in the early nineteenth century as a reaction to the radical societal and economic changes spurred by the industrial revolution. At that time, the introduction of new technologies such as the steam engine dramatically changed the way Americans and Europeans worked and lived. What were once rural agrarian cultures were quickly transformed into mechanized urban societies. Stories are one way that our cultures process radical change, so it didn't take long for the anxiety unleashed by this explosion of technology to manifest itself in the form of Mary Shelley's 1818 novel *Frankenstein; or, The Modern Prometheus*. The subtitle makes evident the novel's theme: in Greek mythology, Prometheus is the Titan who stole fire from Zeu and bestowed this forbidden and dangerous knowl-

The other in science fiction
Science-fiction films often emphasize a malevolent alien's "otherness" by modeling its appearance on machines or insects. The benevolent visitors in Steven Spielberg's popular science-fiction film *Close Encounters of the Third Kind* (1977) [1] look much more reassuringly humanoid than the hostile invaders his collaborators created for *War of the Worlds* (2005) [2].

edge on mortals not yet ready to deal with its power. Shelley's "monster" represents the consequences of men using science and technology to play God.

Those of you familiar with twentieth-century movie versions may think of *Frankenstein* as a horror story. The genres are indeed closely related through their mutual exploitation of audience fears, but the source of the anxiety is different. Horror films speak to our fears of the supernatural and the unknown, whereas science-fiction movies explore our dread of technology and change. Both genres have their roots in folklore that articulates the ongoing battle between human beings and everything that is other than human. In ancient folklore, this "other" was anthropomorphized into monsters (trolls, ogres, etc.) that inhabited (and represented) the wilderness that humans could not control.

Ironically, the same advances in science and technology that allowed cultures to explain away—and thus destroy—all of these old monsters have given voice to the modern folklore of science fiction. For most of us, science is beyond our control. Its rapid advance is a phenomenon that we didn't create, that we don't entirely comprehend, and that moves too fast for us to keep up with. So when it comes to science fiction, the other represents—directly or indirectly—this technological juggernaut that can help us but also has the power to destroy us or at least make us obsolete.

We are not saying that science is an inherently negative force or even that anxiety dominates our relationship with technology. We all love our computers, appreciate modern medicine, and marvel at the wonders of space exploration. But conflict is an essential element of narrative. If everything is perfect, then there's no story. And unspoken, even unconscious, concerns are at the root of a great deal of artistic expression.

Science-inspired anxiety is behind the defining thematic conflict that unites most science-fiction movies. This conflict can be expressed in many ways, but for our purposes let's think of it as technology versus humanity or science versus soul.[5] This theme is expressed in stories that envision technology enslaving humanity, invading our minds and bodies, or bringing about the end of civilization as we know it. The antagonist in these conflicts takes the form of computers like the infamous HAL in Stanley Kubrick's *2001: A Space Odyssey* (1968); robots or machines in films like Ridley Scott's *Blade Runner* (1982), the Wachowski's The Matrix series (1999–2003), and James Cameron's Terminator movies (1984–2003); and mechanized, dehumanized societies in Fritz Lang's *Metropolis* (1927), Jean-Luc Godard's *Alphaville* (1965), and George Lucas's *THX 1138* (1971).

Alien invaders, another common science-fiction antagonistic other, are also an outgrowth of our innate fear of the machine. As soon as humankind was advanced

5. Per Schelde, *Androids, Humanoids, and Other Science Fiction Monsters: Science and Soul in Science Fiction Films* (New York: New York University Press, 1993).

Science fiction and special effects

James Cameron's *Avatar* (2009) put a new spin on the science-fiction genre by presenting humans as the cold-blooded alien invaders using superior technology to threaten an unspoiled world and its compassionate natives. The planet's symbiotic creatures and spectacular landscapes were created using the most sophisticated digital technology in the history of cinema. Ironically, the movie genre founded on audiences' dread of technology also happens to depend heavily on viewers' attraction to high-tech special effects. The speculative spectacle that audiences expect of science fiction means that most films in the genre feature elaborate sets, costumes, makeup, computer animation, and digital effects.

enough to contemplate travel outside the earth's orbit, we began to speculate about the possibility of life on other planets. Our fear of the unknown, combined with our tendency to see Earth as the center of the universe, empowered this imagined other as a threatening force, endowed with superior destructive technology, bent on displacing or enslaving us. The otherness of the most malevolent aliens is emphasized by designing their appearance to resemble machines or insects. In contrast, the science-fiction movies that reverse expectations and portray alien encounters in a positive light typically shape their extraterrestrials more like humans— or at least mammals. You need look no further than *Star Wars*' comfortably fuzzy Chewbacca (as opposed to Imperial storm troopers and Jabba the Hutt) for evidence of this tradition.

While most science-fiction movies stress the otherness of the antagonist, the opposite is true for the sci-fi protagonist. Science-fiction heroes are often literally and figuratively down-to-earth. They tend to be so compassionate and soulful that their essential humanity seems a liability—until their indomitable human spirit proves the key to defeating the malevolent other.

Because science-fiction narratives often deal with what-ifs, the setting is frequently speculative. If those sci-fi movies are set in the present day, they often heighten the dramatic impact of invasive aliens or time travelers. Most commonly, the genre places its stories in a future profoundly shaped by advances in technology. This setting allows filmmakers to hypothesize future effects of contemporary cultural, political, or scientific trends. These speculative settings may be high-tech megacities or postapocalyptic ruins. In movies like Ridley Scott's *Blade Runner* (1982), the setting suggests a combination of both. Of course, outer space is also a popular science-fiction setting for obvious reasons. In many of these examples, the technology-versus-humanity theme is presented in part by dramatizing the consequences of science taking us places we don't necessarily belong—or at least where we are not physically and spiritually equipped to survive. Science-fiction films made before the 1970s tended to feature sterile, well-ordered, almost utopian speculative settings. Movies like Scott's *Alien* (1979), with its grimy industrial space-barge interiors, reversed that trend by presenting a future in which living conditions had degraded rather than evolved.

The following are some notable science-fiction films: *A Trip to the Moon* (1902; director Georges Méliès); *Things to Come* (1936; director William Cameron Menzies); *The Day the Earth Stood Still* (1951; director Robert Wise); *It Came from Outer Space* (1953; director Jack Arnold); *Forbidden Planet* (1956; director Fred M. Wilcox); *Invasion of the Body Snatcher*s (1956; director Don Siegel); *On the Beach* (1959; director Stanley Kramer); *Village of the Damned* (1960; director Wolf Rilla); *Fahrenheit 451* (1966; director François Truffaut); *Solaris* (1972; director Andrei Tarkovsky); *The Man Who Fell to Earth* (1976; director Nicolas Roeg); *Stalker* (1979; director Andrei Tarkovsky); *Mad Max 2* (1981; director George Miller); *Nausicaä* (1984; director Hayao Miyazaki); *Brazil* (1985; director Terry Gilliam); *The Fly* (1986; director David Cronenberg); *Akira* (1988; director Katsuhiro Ôtomo); *Until the End of the World* (1991; director Wim Wenders); *Ghost in the Shell* (1995; director Mamoru Oshii); *Twelve Monkeys* (1995; director Terry Gilliam); *Gattaca* (1997; director Andrew Niccol); *Starship Troopers* (1997; director Paul Verhoeven); *The Iron Giant* (1999; director Brad Bird); *Donnie Darko* (2001; director Richard Kelly); *Children of Men* (2006; director Alfonso Cuarón); *The Host* (2006; director Joon-ho Bong); *Wall-E* (2008; director Andrew Stanton); *Avatar* (2009; director James Cameron); *Moon* (2009; director Duncan Jones); *District 9* (2009; director Neill Blomkamp); *Monsters* (2010; director Gareth Edwards); *Prometheus* (2012; director Ridley Scott); *Snowpiercer* (2013; Joon-ho Bong); *Interstellar* (2014; director Christopher Nolan); and *Edge of Tomorrow* (2014; director Doug Liman).

Horror

Like science fiction, the horror genre was born out of a cultural need to confront and vicariously conquer something frightening that we do not fully comprehend. In the case of horror films, those frightening somethings

are aspects of our existence even more intimidating than technology or science: death and insanity. Both represent the ultimate loss of control and a terrifying, inescapable metamorphosis.

To enact any sort of narrative conflict with either of these forces, they must be given a tangible form. And, like horror's sister genre, sci-fi, that form is the "other." Death takes the shape of ghosts, zombies, and vampires—all of which pose a transformative threat to the audience. The only thing scarier than being killed or consumed by the other is actually becoming the other. So it makes sense that the werewolves, demonic possessions, and homicidal maniacs that act as cinematic stand-ins for insanity also carry the threat of infection and conversion.

1

2

The infectious other

One reason we go to horror movies is to confront our fear of death and insanity, as well as the anxiety that arises out of our ultimate inability to control either condition. As a result, the other that fills the role of antagonist often carries the threat of infection and transformation. The raging zombies in Danny Boyle's *28 Days Later . . .* (2002) [1] are former humans changed into mindless killing machines by a runaway virus. In James Wan's *The Conjuring* (2013) [2], a loving mother is transformed into a demonic witch when she is possessed by a hateful ghost.

We could hypothesize that early, primitive religions—even the source of some modern religions—derive from the same essential human need to demystify and defeat these most basic fears. But the difference between movies and religious rituals is the intensity and immediacy that the cinema experience provides. While sitting in a darkened movie theater staring at oversized images of the other, movie viewers are immersed in a shared ritual that exposes them to dread, terror, and ultimately catharsis. We vicariously defeat death (even if the protagonist does not), because we survive the movie and walk back into our relatively safe lives after the credits roll and the lights come up. We experience the exhilaration of confronting the dreaded other without the devastating consequences.

Germany, with its strong tradition of folklore and more developed engagement with the darker aspects of existence (thanks in part to the devastation of World War I), created the first truly disturbing horror movies. Robert Wiene's *The Cabinet of Dr. Caligari* (1920) sees the world through the distorted perspective of a madman; F. W. Murnau's expressionist Dracula adaptation, *Nosferatu, a Symphony of Horror* (1922), associates its other with death and disease. The United States embraced the genre with the release of *Dracula* (1931; director Tod Browning), and thus began Hollywood's on-again, off-again relationship with the horror film. A golden age of Hollywood horror followed, with the monster others at its center taking top billing: *Frankenstein* (1931; director James Whale); *The Mummy* (1932; director Karl Freund); and *The Wolf Man* (1941; director George Waggner).

With the return of prosperity and the end of World War II, the classic "monster"-based horror film faded into mediocrity and relative obscurity until a new generation of audiences with their own fears resurrected the genre. Foreign and independent studios updated and moved beyond the original monster concept with low-budget productions created for the B-movie and drive-in markets. Horror did not return to the mainstream until veteran British directors Alfred Hitchcock and Michael Powell, both of whom were associated with very different motion-picture styles, each unleashed his own disturbing portrait of an outwardly attractive young serial killer. By subverting audiences' expectation of the other, Hitchcock's *Psycho* (1960) and Powell's *Peeping Tom* (1960) shocked audiences and revolutionized the horror genre. Ever since, as our culture's needs

Horror-movie settings
Most horror stories unfold in settings that isolate potential victims from potential help. Dario Argento's *Suspiria* (1977) goes one step further by placing the young protagonist, Suzy (Jessica Harper), in an unusually creepy ballet academy in rural Italy. As a newcomer and the only American student, Suzy is not only isolated from the relative security of a populated area, but must face considerable danger alone, without allies, in unfamiliar surroundings.

and attitudes change, and global awareness of real-life atrocities multiplies, horror has evolved to become one of cinema's most diverse and fluid genres.

A typical horror narrative begins by establishing a normal world that will be threatened by the arrival of the other. This monster must be vanquished or destroyed in order to reestablish normalcy. Often, the protagonist is the only person who initially recognizes the threat. Because the other is so far removed from normalcy, the protagonist may reject her own suspicions before she experiences the other more directly and announces the menace to those around her. When her warnings are ignored, the central character is directly targeted by the other. She must either enlist help or face the monster on her own. In the end, the protagonist may destroy the other—or at least appear to. Horror narratives tend to feature resurrections and other false resolutions. Originally, these open endings were meant to give the audience one last scare; now, they are just as likely intended to ensure the possibility of a profitable sequel.

This basic horror plot structure offers a number of typical variants: the protagonist may actually be directly or indirectly responsible for summoning the other, a violation that places even greater responsibility on her to restore the normal world. The protagonist may also have to enlist the help of a mentor or apprentice, or even sacrifice herself, to defeat the antagonistic other. Sometimes the protagonist actually becomes the other. She becomes infected and attempts to deny, and then hide, her encroaching transformation. She may pursue a solution, but ultimately faces the decision either to destroy herself or face a complete metamorphosis. Oftentimes, as in similar science-fiction stories, she is somehow saved by the power of her own humanity.

This protagonist is often a loner, someone socially reviled who must save the community that rejects her. We identify with her because she is (initially, at least) unusually fearful, a weakness that allows us the greatest possible identification with her struggle. This characteristic is certainly not limited to horror films. Many movie narratives center on flawed characters because they create high stakes and allow for the kind of character development that satisfies audiences.

While a significant number of horror-film antagonists are one-dimensional killing machines, many of these others are actually more compelling characters than the protagonists charged with destroying them.

Halloween lighting in *Bride of Frankenstein*
Like film noir, the horror genre utilizes a style of lighting (referred to as low-key, or chiaroscuro, lighting) that emphasizes stark contrasts between bright illumination and deep shadow. These shadows are used to create unsettling graphic compositions, obscure visual information, and suggest offscreen action. Lighting a subject from below, a technique often referred to as "Halloween lighting," distorts a subject's features by reversing the natural placement of shadows.

Vampires fascinate us because they can be as seductive as they are terrifying. Other monsters, such as Frankenstein's monster or his progeny, Edward Scissorhands, may actually display more humanity than the supposedly threatened populace. And, yes, the malevolent father in Stanley Kubrick's *The Shining* (1980) and Freddy Krueger of Wes Craven's *A Nightmare on Elm Street* (1984) may be evil, but they have undeniable personality. Even the masked, robotic killers at the center of the Halloween and Friday the 13th slasher franchises offer more complex histories and motives than their relatively anonymous victims.

Horror-movie settings tend to fall into two categories. The first is the aforementioned "normal world"—a hyperordinary place, usually a small town threatened by invasion of the other. This setting casts the protagonist as the protector of her beloved home turf and violates our own notions of personal safety. Other horror films set their action in remote rural areas that offer potential victims little hope for assistance. A related horror setting places the central character in a foreign, often exotic, environment that lacks the security of the familiar. The alien customs, language, and landscape disorient the protagonist (and the audience) and diminish any hope for potential support. And, as you may have guessed, regardless of where horror stories are located, they almost invariably stage their action at night.

Besides tapping into our instinctive fears, night scenes lend themselves to the chiaroscuro lighting—the use of deep gradations of light and shadow within an image—that most horror-movie cinematography depends upon. This lighting style emphasizes stark contrasts and shows large areas of deep shadow accented with bright highlights. The light is often direct or undiffused, which creates well-defined shadows and silhouettes, and low-key, meaning the dense shadows are not abated by additional "fill" lights. Horror-genre lighting is sometimes cast from below, an angle of illumination not typical of our everyday experience. The result is the distorted facial features and looming cast shadows known on film sets as "Halloween lighting." Canted camera angles that tilt the on-screen world off balance are used to disorient viewers. Horror-film staging also exploits the use of offscreen action and sound that suggests the presence of peril but denies the audience the relative reassurance of actually keeping an eye on the antagonist.

Some notable horror films include *Freaks* (1932; director Tod Browning); *Bride of Frankenstein* (1935; director James Whale); *Cat People* (1942; director Jacques Tourneur); *Black Sunday* (1960; director Mario Bava); *The Innocents* (1961; director Jack Clayton); *Carnival of Souls* (1962; director Herk Harvey); *The Birds* (1963; director Alfred Hitchcock); *Kaidan* (1964; director Masaki Kobayashi); *Rosemary's Baby* (1968; director Roman Polanski); *Night of the Living Dead* (1968; director George Romero); *The Exorcist* (1973; director William Friedkin); *The Texas Chain Saw Massacre* (1974; director Tobe Hooper); *Carrie* (1976; director Brian De Palma); *The Omen* (1976; director Richard Donner); *Dawn of the Dead* (1978; director George A. Romero); *Phantasm* (1979; director Don Coscarelli); *The Evil Dead* (1981; director Sam Raimi); *Poltergeist* (1982; director Tobe Hooper); *Evil Dead II* (1987; director Sam Raimi); *Hellraiser* (1987; director Clive Barker); *The Silence of the Lambs* (1991; director Jonathan Demme); *Braindead* (1992; director Peter Jackson); the TV miniseries *The Kingdom* (1994; directors Lars von Trier and Morton Arnfred); *Scream* (1996; director Wes Craven); *Ringu* (1998; director Hideo Nakata); *The Blair Witch Project* (1999; directors Daniel Myrick and Eduardo Sánchez); *The Sixth Sense* (1999; director M. Night Shyamalan); *The*

Others (2001; director Alejandro Amenábar); *28 Days Later . . .* (2002; director Danny Boyle); *Shaun of the Dead* (2004; director Edgar Wright); *Nightwatch* (2004; director Timur Bekmambetov); *Rec* (2007; directors Jaume Balagueró and Paco Plaza); *Paranormal Activity* (2007; director Oren Peli); *Let the Right One In* (2008; director Tomas Alfredson); *Drag Me to Hell* (2009; director Sam Raimi); *The Cabin in the Woods* (2012; director Drew Goddard); *The Woman in Black* (2012; director James Watkins); *The Conjuring* (2013; director James Wan); and *The Babadook* (2014; director Jennifer Kent).

The Western

Like most of the major genres, the Western predates the invention of motion pictures. The exploration and settlement of the western United States has fascinated

1

2

Wilderness and civilization

Although many Western narratives favor the forces of order, the outlaw is not always the bad guy. Revisionist Westerns like George Roy Hill's *Butch Cassidy and the Sundance Kid* (1969) mourn the inevitable loss of freedom that accompanies the civilization of the frontier. In that movie, and in many others that reconsidered Western mythology, the protagonists are good-natured outlaws [1]; the righteous avenging posse (presented as a faceless "other" in a technique borrowed from the horror and science-fiction genres) is the dreaded antagonist [2].

European Americans since the frontier was just a few hundred miles inland from the eastern coast. Set in 1757 and published in 1826, James Fenimore Cooper's *The Last of the Mohicans* is widely considered the first popular novel to explore the tension between the wilderness and encroaching civilization. But the considerably less reputable literature most responsible for spawning the Western movie didn't come along until about twenty-five years later. Dime novels (so called because of their low cost), short novellas written for young men and semi-literates, delivered sensational adventures of fictional cowboys, outlaws, and adventurers, as well as wildly fictionalized stories starring actual Western figures.

By the 1870s, stage productions and traveling circus-like shows featuring staged reenactments of famous battles and other events were capitalizing on the growing international fascination with the American West. Movies wasted no time getting into the act. Some of the earliest motion pictures were Westerns, including Thomas Edison's 46-second, one-shot vignette *Cripple Creek Bar-Room Scene* (1899) and Edwin S. Porter's groundbreaking *The Great Train Robbery* (1903).

American history inspired the Western, but the genre's enduring popularity has more to do with how Americans see and explain themselves than with any actual event. Westerns are a form of modern mythology that offers narrative representations of Americans as rugged, self-sufficient individuals taming a savage wilderness with common sense and direct action. The concept of the frontier as a sort of societal blank slate is at the heart of this mythology. The Wild West is a land of opportunity—both a dangerous, lawless country in need of taming and an expansive territory where anyone with the right stuff can reinvent himself and start a new life. The mythology label does not mean that these notions cannot be true. It simply acknowledges that certain aspects of the history of the American West have been amplified and modified to serve a collective cultural need.

Earlier in the chapter, we discussed the civilization-versus-wilderness conflict that provides the Western's thematic framework. The tension produced by this conflict is an essential ingredient in virtually every Western narrative. The wilderness can take the form of antagonistic forces in direct conflict with the civilizing settlers, such as the Apache Indians in John Ford's *The Searchers* (1956) and *Stagecoach* (1939), or the free-range cattleman of George Stevens's *Shane* (1953). Or it can manifest itself in more metaphorical terms. The wilderness of Ford's *3 Godfathers* (1948), for example, takes the form of the outlaw protagonists' self-interest, which is put in direct opposition with the civilizing effects of social responsibility when the bandits discover an infant orphaned in the desert.

But this sort of duality was nothing new. Many Western characters reverse or combine the thematic elements of order and chaos. Lawmen in movies like Clint Eastwood's *Unforgiven* (1992) are antagonists, and often even a lawman protagonist is a former outlaw or

1

2

Character duality in the Western

Western protagonists often embody both sides of the genre's thematic conflict between wilderness and civilization. Clint Eastwood's *Unforgiven* (1992) stars Eastwood himself as Bill Munny, a farmer and father enlisted as a hired gun on the basis of his faded (and dubious) reputation as a former gunslinger. Munny resists violent action until the murder of his friend and partner, Ned (Morgan Freeman), reawakens the ruthless desperado within him [1]. Johnny Depp's character in Jim Jarmusch's allegorical Western *Dead Man* (1995) begins his journey west as a hopelessly meek and inept accountant, but is gradually transformed into a deadly outlaw by both the figurative and literal wilderness [2].

Civilization and wilderness

This archetypal scene from John Ford's *My Darling Clementine* (1946) demonstrates the tension (and inevitable attraction) between encroaching civilization and the wide-open Wild West that lies at the heart of most Western-genre narrative conflicts. Deadly gunfighter turned reluctant lawman Wyatt Earp (Henry Fonda) escorts Clementine (Cathy Downs), a refined and educated woman from the East, to a community dance held in the bare bones of a not-yet-constructed church surrounded by desert and mountains.

gunfighter. Cowboys—quintessential Western characters—also embody the blurred borders between the Western's thematic forces. Cowboys may fight the Indians, but they are also symbols of rootless resisters of encroaching development. Whatever his particular stance and occupation, the Western hero is typically a man of action, not words. He is resistant—or at least uncomfortable—with the trappings of civilization, even in those common cases where he serves as a civilizing agent. *Shane*'s gunfighter protagonist sacrifices himself to defend the homesteader, but he rides off into oblivion rather than settling down and taking up a plow himself.

The actors associated with the genre reflect the quiet power of the laconic characters they repeatedly play.

Whereas gangster icons such as James Cagney are compact and manic, Western stars, from the silent era's William S. Hart through Henry Fonda and John Wayne and on up to Clint Eastwood, are outsized but relatively subdued performers.

All of the tertiary character types found in Westerns have a role to play in this overarching conflict between the wild and settled West. Native Americans are both ruthless savages and noble personifications of dignity and honor. Prostitutes are products of lawlessness but often long for marriage and family. Schoolmarms are educated and cultured, yet are irresistibly drawn to the frontier and the men who roam it. The greenhorn character may be sophisticated back East, but he is an inexperienced bumbler (and, as such, a perfect surrogate

LOOKING AT MOVIES

GENRE: THE WESTERN

VIDEO ▶ ━━━━━━━━━━●━━━━━━━━━

This tutorial explores the form and conventions of the Western.

for the viewer) when it comes to the ways of the West. His transformation into a skilled cowboy/gunfighter/lawman embodies the Western ideal of renewal.

More than any genre, the American Western is linked to place. But the West is not necessarily a particular place. The genre may be set on the prairie, in the mountains, or in the desert. But whatever the setting, the landscape is a dominant visual and thematic element that represents another Western duality: it's a deadly wilderness of stunning natural beauty. Because setting is of such primary importance, Westerns are dominated by daylight exterior shots and scenes. As a result, Westerns were among the first films to be shot almost exclusively on location. (When the Hollywood noir classic *Sunset Boulevard* needs to get a film-industry character out of town, it gets him a job on a Western.) The Western landscape is not limited to background information. The big skies and wide-open spaces are used to symbolize both limitless possibility and an untamable environment. For this reason, Westerns favor extreme long shots in which the landscape dwarfs human subjects and the primitive outposts of civilization.

The following list contains important Westerns: *The Iron Horse* (1924; director John Ford); *Tumbleweeds* (1925; director King Baggot); *The Big Trail* (1930; director Raoul Walsh); *Destry Rides Again* (1939; director George Marshall); *The Ox-Bow Incident* (1943; director William A. Wellman); *Duel in the Sun* (1946; director

King Vidor); *Fort Apache* (1948; director John Ford); *Red River* (1948; directors Howard Hawks and Arthur Rosson); *She Wore a Yellow Ribbon* (1949; director John Ford); *The Gunfighter* (1950; director Henry King); *Winchester '73* (1950; director Anthony Mann); *The Naked Spur* (1953; director Anthony Mann); *Johnny Guitar* (1954; director Nicholas Ray); *3:10 to Yuma* (1957; director Delmer Daves); *Forty Guns* (1957; director Samuel Fuller); *Man of the West* (1958; director Anthony Mann); *Lonely Are the Brave* (1962; director David Miller); *The Man Who Shot Liberty Valance* (1962; director John Ford); *Major Dundee* (1965; director Sam Peckinpah); *Hombre* (1967; director Martin Ritt); *Once upon a Time in the West* (1968; director Sergio Leone); *Will Penny* (1968; director Tom Gries); *The Wild Bunch* (1969; director Sam Peckinpah); *Little Big Man* (1970; director Arthur Penn); *McCabe & Mrs. Miller* (1971; director Robert Altman); *Silverado* (1985; director Lawrence Kasdan); *Dances with Wolves* (1990; director Kevin Costner); *The Ballad of Little Jo* (1993; director Maggie Greenwald); *Dead Man* (1995; director Jim Jarmusch); *The Missing* (2003; director Ron Howard); *Appaloosa* (2008; director Ed Harris); *True Grit* (2010; directors Ethan Coen and Joel Coen); *Rango* (2011; director Gore Verbinski); *Django Unchained* (2012; director Quentin Tarantino); and *The Hateful Eight* (2015; director Quentin Tarantino).

The Musical

The musical tells its story using characters that express themselves with song and/or dance. The actors sing every line of dialogue in a few musicals, such as Jacques Demy's *The Umbrellas of Cherbourg* (1964), and those musicals from the 1930s featuring Fred Astaire and Ginger Rogers focus more on dancing than singing. But for the most part, musicals feature a combination of music, singing, dancing, and spoken dialogue.

Unlike many genres, the musical film genre was not born out of any specific political or cultural moment or preexisting literary genre. But musical performance was already a well-established entertainment long before the invention of the movie camera. The long-standing traditions of religious pageants, opera, operetta, and ballet all present narrative within a musical context. Musical comedies similar in structure to movie musicals were popular on British and American stages throughout much of the nineteenth century.

Backstage and integrated musicals

Early Hollywood musicals like Harry Beaumont's *The Broadway Melody* (1929) [1] constructed their narratives around the rehearsal and performance of a musical stage show, a setting that provided an intriguing backdrop, narrative conflict, and a context that allowed the characters to sing and dance without testing verisimilitude. Within a few years, integrated musicals like Rouben Mamoulian's *Love Me Tonight* (1932) [2] proved that audiences were already willing to accept characters who burst into song in everyday situations, such as a tailor (Maurice Chevalier) who sings an ode to romantic love as he measures a customer for a suit.

So it was inevitable that the dazzling movement, formal spectacle, and emotional eloquence inherent in musical performance would eventually join forces with the expressive power of cinema. But two hurdles stood in the way of the union. First, the early film industry had to create a workable system for recording and pro-

jecting sound—a process over twenty-five years in the making. The next obstacle had less to do with mechanical engineering and more with audience perceptions. Because the new medium of motion-picture photography was closely associated with documentation and thus naturalism, the idea of otherwise realistic scenarios suddenly interrupted by characters bursting into song didn't seem to fit with the movies. Therefore, cinema had to establish a context that would allow for musical performance but still lend itself to relatively authentic performances and dramatic situations, as well as spoken dialogue.

The first major movie to incorporate extended synchronized sound sequences provided the solution. Alan Crosland's *The Jazz Singer* (1927) was a backstage musical. This kind of film placed the story in a performance setting (almost always Broadway), so that the characters were singers and dancers whose job it was to rehearse and stage songs anyway. By placing its narrative in this very specific setting, this early musical incarnation established some of the genre's most fixed plot and character elements. Backstage-musical stories typically revolved around a promising young performer searching for her big show-business break, or a talented singer/dancer protagonist pressured by a love interest or family member to leave show business, or a struggling company of singers and dancers determined to mount a big show. Many backstage narratives managed to combine two or more of these standard storylines. These musicals had their own set of character types, including the hard-bitten producer, the gifted ingenue, the insecure (i.e., less talented) star, and the faltering veteran with a heart of gold.

It might be assumed that since the backstage musical's songs were all performed as either rehearsals or productions within the framework of an externalized Broadway show, these songs would be missing the emotional power provided by a direct connection to the character's lives. But in practice, the lyrics and context were usually presented in such a way as to underscore the performing character's state of mind or personal situation.

Backstage musicals had been around for only a few years when so-called integrated musicals like Rouben Mamoulian's *Love Me Tonight* (1932) freed the genre from the Broadway setting. (Mamoulian also directed *Applause*, 1929, a pioneering backstage musical.) As the term implies, the integrated musical assimilated singing and dancing with conventional spoken dramatic action;

characters now could burst into song (or dance) as part of any situation. Of course, most of these musicals reserve musical performance for key dramatic moments, such as when a character declares her love, her goal, or her emotional state. Sometimes these songs are delivered to another character, but they may also be directed inward—a sort of sung soliloquy—or even aimed directly at the viewer.

Part of the pleasure of watching integrated musicals comes from the potentially dramatic shifts in tone and style required to move between dramatic and musical performance. Audiences have learned to appreciate the stylistic prowess required to balance these two seemingly incompatible entertainments, along with the whimsy or poignancy such combinations are capable of generating. Only in a musical can downtrodden factory workers erupt into a celebratory tune, as in Lars von Trier's *Dancer in the Dark* (2000), or a gang of rebellious college students sing and dance their way into a drunken, stoned stupor, as in Julie Taymor's *Across the Universe* (2007). The integrated musical, as these examples illustrate, freed the genre from the Broadway backdrop and allowed the musical to apply its unique stylings to a virtually limitless range of stories, characters, and settings.

While traditional musicals still tend to use the romantic comedy for their narrative template, contemporary movies have mixed the musical with a variety of other genres and cinema styles. Director Trey Parker has created credible musicals in the context of an extended *South Park* episode (*South Park: Bigger, Longer & Uncut*, 1999), a Michael Bay–style action movie performed by marionettes (*Team America: World Police*, 2004), and the only prosecuted case of cannibalism in United States history (*Cannibal! The Musical*, 1996). The genre dominated animated features from Walt Disney studios for almost sixty years. Even television programs have gotten into the act: *The Simpsons*, *Grey's Anatomy*, *Community*, and *How I Met Your Mother* have all created special musical episodes.

Notable musicals include *Le Million* (1931; director René Clair); *The Three Penny Opera* (1931; director G. W. Pabst); *42nd Street* (1933; director Lloyd Bacon); *Footlight Parade* (1933; director Lloyd Bacon); *Swing Time* (1936; director George Stevens); *The Wizard of Oz* (1939; director Victor Fleming); *Yankee Doodle Dandy* (1942; director Michael Curtiz); *Meet Me in St. Louis* (1944; director Vincente Minnelli); *On the Town* (1949; directors Stanley Donen and Gene Kelly); *An American*

Contemporary musicals

Bill Condon's *Dreamgirls* (2006) is set within a backstage musical situation that allows for staged performance of some musical numbers [1]. But a significant amount of the movie's most meaningful music is delivered in the style of the integrated musical: offstage and in character [2]. Julie Taymor's *Across the Universe* (2007) and Phyllida Lloyd's *Mamma Mia!* (2008) [3] represent a relatively new approach to the genre, one in which all of the music expresses character emotions and contributes to the narrative even though none of it was originally written for the movie. Both musicals select familiar songs from the catalogs of popular supergroups (the Beatles and ABBA, respectively) and create narratives to suit the appropriated music.

in Paris (1951; director Vincente Minnelli); *Singin' in the Rain* (1952; directors Stanley Donen and Gene Kelly); *The Band Wagon* (1953; director Vincente Minnelli); *French Cancan* (1954; director Jean Renoir); *A Star Is Born* (1954; director George Cukor); *Oklahoma!* (1955; director Fred Zinnemann); *The King and I* (1956; director Walter Lang); *West Side Story* (1961; directors Jerome Robbins and Robert Wise); *The Music Man* (1962; director Morton DaCosta); *The Sound of Music* (1965; director Robert Wise); *The Jungle Book* (1967; director Wolfgang Reitherman); *Cabaret* (1972; director Bob Fosse); *Jesus Christ Superstar* (1973; director Norman Jewison); *Grease* (1978; director Randal Kleiser); *Hair* (1979; director Milos Forman); *Blood Wedding* (1981; director Carlos Saura); *Pennies from Heaven* (1981; director Herbert Ross); *Moulin Rouge!* (2001; director Baz Luhrmann); *Chicago* (2002; director Rob Marshall); *Teacher's Pet* (2004; director Timothy Björklund); *Rent* (2005; director Chris Columbus); *The Muppets* (2011; director James Bobin); *Les Miserables* (2012; director Tom Hooper); *Pitch Perfect* (2012; director Jason Moore); *Black Nativity* (2013; director Kasi Lemmons); *Frozen* (2013; directors Chris Buck and Jennifer Lee); and *Into the Woods* (2014; director Rob Marshall).

Evolution and Transformation of Genre

Filmmakers are rarely satisfied to leave things as they are. Thus, as with all things cinematic, genre is in constant transition. Writers and directors, recognizing genre's narrative, thematic, and aesthetic potential, cannot resist blending ingredients gleaned from multiple styles in an attempt to invent exciting new hybrids. The seemingly impossible marriage of the horror and musical genres has resulted in a number of successful horror-musical fusions, including Jim Sharman's *The Rocky Horror Picture Show* (1975), Frank Oz's *Little Shop of Horrors* (1986), and Takashi Miike's *The Happiness of the Katakuris* (2001). Antonia Bird melded horror with another unlikely genre partner, the Western, for her 1999 film *Ravenous*. Sometimes the hybridization takes the form of a pastiche, as in Quentin Tarantino's *Kill Bill* cycle (*Vol. 1*, 2003; *Vol. 2*, 2004), films that borrow not only from the Japanese *chambara* (sword-fighting) genre but from many Hollywood genres, including the Western, musical, thriller, action, horror, and gangster.

1

2

The romantic vampire
Ever since Bela Lugosi first portrayed *Dracula* in Todd Browning's 1931 film, forbidden desire has been an essential ingredient of the vampire movie [1]. In recent years, much of the horror has been drained from the subgenre as audiences have fully embraced the vampire as a romantic figure. Films like *The Twilight Saga: Eclipse* (2010; director David Slade) [2] and television series like HBO's *True Blood* and CW's *The Vampire Diaries* feature attractive vampires who are ambivalent about their sinister appetites and dark powers—a contradiction that makes them irresistible to their mortal companions.

Genres develop inwardly as well. Subgenres occur when areas of narrative or stylistic specialization arise within a single genre. Thus Westerns can be divided into revenge Westerns, spaghetti Westerns, bounty-hunter Westerns, cattle-drive Westerns, gunfighter Westerns, cavalry Westerns, and so on. Zombie movies, slasher flicks, vampire films, the splatter movie, and torture porn are a few of the many manifestations of the horror genre.

To understand how complex a single genre can become, let's consider comedy. Movies are categorized as

Mixed genre

James Gunn's *Guardians of the Galaxy* (2014) is rife with Western genre archetypes, including righteous renegades, pitiless bounty hunters, a lawless frontier outpost, and a settlement threatened by ruthless savages. The outlaw protagonists risk their freedom (and their lives) to protect a civilization that wants no part of them or their wilderness ways. But this Western takes place in outer space, a speculative setting associated with the science-fiction genre. Showdowns are fought with laser blasters, and everyone rides rocket ships. The mysterious Infinity Stone the characters fight over epitomizes the menace of technology run amok behind the typical science-fiction antagonist.

comedies because they make us laugh, but we quickly realize that each one is unique because it is funny in its own way. Comedies, in fact, prove why movie genres exist. They give us what we expect, they make us laugh and ask for more, and they make money, often in spite of themselves. As a result, the comic genre in the movies has evolved into such a complex system that we rely on defined subgenres to keep track of comedy's development.

The silent-movie comedies of the 1920s featured such legends as Max Linder, Charlie Chaplin, Buster Keaton, Roscoe "Fatty" Arbuckle, Harry Langdon, and Harold Lloyd, many of whom worked for producer Mack Sennett. These films were known as slapstick comedies because aggression or violent behavior, not verbal humor, was the source of the laughs. (The term *slapstick* refers to the two pieces of wood, hinged together, that clowns used to produce a sharp noise that simulated the sound of one person striking another.)

After the arrival of sound, movie comedy continued the sight gags of the slapstick tradition (Laurel and Hardy, the Marx Brothers, W. C. Fields), and it also increasingly relied on verbal wit. Through the 1930s, a wide variety of subgenres developed: comedy of wit (Ernst Lubitsch's *Trouble in Paradise*, 1932); romantic

comedy (Rouben Mamoulian's *Love Me Tonight*, 1932), screwball comedy (Frank Capra's *It Happened One Night*, 1934), farce (any Marx Brothers movie), and sentimental comedy, often with a political twist (Frank Capra's *Meet John Doe*, 1941).

By the 1940s, comedy was perhaps the most popular genre in American movies, and it remains that way today, although another group of subgenres has developed, most in response to our changing cultural expectations of what is funny and what is now permissible to laugh at. These include light sex comedies (Billy Wilder's *Some Like It Hot*, 1959), gross-out sex comedies (Bobby and Peter Farrelly's *There's Something about Mary*, 1998), and neurotic sex comedies (almost any Woody Allen movie), as well as satire laced with black comedy (Stanley Kubrick's *Dr. Strangelove or: How I Learned to Stop Worrying and Love the Bomb*, 1964), outrageous farce (Mel Brooks's *The Producers*, 1968, and Susan Stroman's musical remake, 2005), and a whole subgenre of comedy that is associated with the name of the comedian featured—from Charlie Chaplin in the silent era to Jacques Tati and Jerry Lewis in the 1950s to Whoopie Goldberg and Jim Carrey in the 1990s to more recent headliners like Will Farrell and Seth Rogen.

The recent wave of what film critic Stephen Holden calls the "boys-will-be-babies-until-they-are-forced-to-grow-up school of arrested-development comedies"[6] seems to have spawned the beginnings of a new comic subgenre. These genre contenders include *The 40-Year-Old Virgin* (2005; director Judd Apatow); *Pineapple Express* (2008; director David Gordon Green); *The Hangover* (2009; director Todd Phillips); *Ted* (2012; director Seth MacFarlane); and *Neighbors* (2014; director Nicholas Stoller). Women characters broke into this formerly all-male subgenre in 2011 with the hit *Bridesmaids* (director Paul Feig).

On one hand, as a form of cinematic language, genres involve filmic realities—however stereotyped—that audiences can easily recognize and understand, and that film distributors can market (e.g., "the scariest thriller ever made"). On the other hand, genres evolve, changing with the times and adapting to audience expectations, which are in turn influenced by a large range of factors—technological, cultural, social, political, economic, and so on. **Generic transformation** is the process by which a particular genre is adapted to meet the expectations of a changing society. Arguably, genres that don't evolve lose the audience's interest quickly and fade away.

Horror movies' monsters have evolved from somewhat sympathetic literary figures like *Frankenstein* into increasingly prolific serial killers, then into seductive vampires, and on into apocalyptic zombies. Contemporary backstage musicals have moved off Broadway to the college a cappella singing competitions in *Pitch Perfect* (2012; director Jason Moore) and *Pitch Perfect 2* (2015; director Elizabeth Banks), and the offbeat live-album recording sessions in John Carney's *Begin Again* (2013).

Westerns began as reverent projections of how the United States saw itself: individualistic, entrepreneurial, and unambiguously righteous. But as perceptions of America grew more complex, so did the genre's depiction of the American West. For example, the protagonist of Robert Altman's *McCabe and Mrs. Miller* (1971), a Western released at the height of the Vietnam war, is an unscrupulous blowhard named McCabe (Warren Beatty). The civilization he brings to the wilderness is a house of prostitution. The resulting surrounding settlement is ultimately taken over by corrupt real estate speculators who hire hit men to eliminate McCabe. The movie ends with the newly erected church burning down and our bumbling hero forgotten and bleeding to death in a snowbank.

In 2005, the Western was transformed in a powerful new way in Ang Lee's *Brokeback Mountain* (2005). Set in the 1960s and 1970s, the film features many of the traditional genre elements, including wide open spaces, a taciturn loner incapable of living inside conventional settled society, and ranch hands herding livestock together under difficult conditions. But *Brokeback Mountain* took those elements a significant step further: the cowboys at the center of this story fall in love with one another. At first glance, it might seem that a same-sex romance has no place in a genre rooted in macho action and conservative values. But in fact the more essential components of character duality and the tension between conformity and individuality made the Western a meaningful vehicle for experiencing this passionate but doomed relationship.

And new genres continue to emerge. Superhero movies were first adapted from comic books in the 1930s and 1940s, finally hit the mainstream in 1978 with the big-budget hit *Superman* (director Richard Donner), and their cultural presence has grown ever since. The resulting genre dominates our twenty-first century multiplexes. Superhero movies feature protagonists with special powers that are either acquired via special suits and gadgets or imposed via some combination of freak accident, genetic mutation, immigration to Earth, and/or mad scientist. These protagonists wear costumes, have identity issues, and serve an often skeptical society by fighting super-villains who often have special powers of their own. Story formulas usually involve the origin of the protagonist's powers and/or a high-stakes struggle to defeat a villainous attempt to destroy a city, country, or universe. This mission is compromised by a combination of uncooperative authorities and the hero's love for a vulnerable mortal. The aforementioned identity issues are central to the themes explored by this genre; the same enviable abilities that make the hero super also isolate and burden the secretly flawed man (the superhero is almost always male) behind the mask. Out of necessity and by design, superhero movies offer dazzling special effects, elaborate costumes and makeup, extended action sequences, and stylized performances.

6. Stephen Holden, "Those Darn Kidults! The Menace of Eternal Youth," *New York Times* (November 7, 2008).

This antirealistic visual spectacle feeds a cultural craving for cinematic escapism, yet there is surely more to the genre's popularity. Secret heroes with hidden powers appeal to viewers' inner aspirations. Forward-looking protagonists capable of affecting meaningful change give vicarious satisfaction to audiences that feel powerless to influence a dauntingly complex universe. Any movie that resonates with audiences and inspires imitators that turn a profit could be the beginning of another new movie genre.

What about Animation?

Animation is regularly classified as a distinct type of motion picture. Even the Academy Awards separates the top honor for narrative feature films into "Best Picture" and "Best Animated Feature" categories. Undeniably, **animated films** look different from other movies. But it's important to recognize that, while animation employs different mechanisms to create the multitude of still images that motion pictures require, animation is just a different form of moviemaking, not necessarily a singular type of movie.

In a recent interview, director Brad Bird (*Ratatouille, The Incredibles, The Iron Giant*) stresses that process is the only difference between animation and filmmaking that relies on conventional photography. Bird explains: "Storytelling is storytelling no matter what your medium is. And the language of film is also the same. You're still using close ups and medium shots and long shots. You're still trying to introduce the audience to a character and get them to care."[7] In fact, animation techniques have been employed to make every type of movie described in this chapter. We are all familiar with animated narrative feature films; the animation process has been applied to hundreds of stories for adults and children, including examples from every major genre described earlier. In addition, a long tradition of experimental filmmaking consists entirely of abstract and representational animated images. Even documentaries occasionally use animation to represent events, ideas, and information that cannot be fully realized with conventional photography. Brett Morgen re-created undocumented courtroom scenes for portions of his documentary *Chicago 10* (2007); Ari Folman's war memoir *Waltz with Bashir* (2008) claims to be the first fully animated feature-length documentary. Michel Gondry's *Is the Man Who Is Tall Happy?* (2013) is a feature-length "animated conversation" with the linguist and philosopher Noam Chomsky.

Among the countless possible types and combinations of animation, three basic types are used widely today: hand-drawn (also known as traditional or cel animation), stop-motion animation, and computer animation (also known as 3-D animation). To create hand-drawn animation, animators draw or paint images that are then incorporated into a motion picture one drawing at a time. Since 24 frames equal 1 second of film time, the animator must draw 24 separate pictures to achieve 1 second of animation.

In 1914, Winsor McCay's classic animation *Gertie the Dinosaur* required over 5,000 drawings on separate sheets of paper.[8] The difficulty of achieving fluid movement by perfectly matching and aligning so many characters and backgrounds led, the next year, to the development of cel animation. Animator Earl Hurd used clear celluloid sheets to create single backgrounds that could serve for multiple exposures of his main character. Thus he needed to draw only the part of the image that was in motion, typically the character or a small part of the character. Contemporary "hand-drawn" animation is now produced almost exclusively on computers. The images are still two-dimensional drawings created by animation artists, and they still employ multiple layers (the digital equivalent of cels). But the process of drawing, combining, and capturing those images is now accomplished with a series of sophisticated software programs. This traditional method, once the animation standard, has largely been replaced by 3-D computer animation. But beautiful examples still reach theater screens, including Tomm Moore's *Song of the Sea* (2014) and *The Secret of Kells* (2009; codirected by Nora Twomey) and the movies produced by Japan's Studio Ghibli, such as *The Wind Rises* (2013; director Hayao Miyazaki) and *The Tale of Princess Kaguya* (2010; director Isao Takahata).

Stop-motion records the movement of objects (toys, puppets, clay figures, or cutouts) with a motion-picture camera; the animator moves the objects slightly for each

---

7. Brad Bird, interview with Elvis Mitchell, *The Business*, KCRW Public Radio (May 5, 2008).
8. Charles Solomon and Ron Stark, *The Complete Kodak Animation Book* (Rochester, NY: Eastman Kodak Co., 1983), p. 14.

1

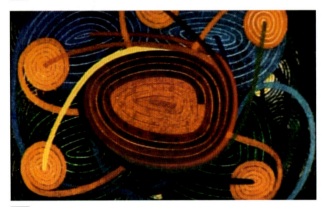

2

3

Alternative animation

Animation isn't just for narrative. *Waltz with Bashir*, Ari Folman's 2008 documentary portraying soldiers' recollections of the Lebanon war of 1982, uses animation to visualize his interview subjects' memories, dreams, and hallucinations [1]. The artist Oskar Fischinger began experimenting with abstract animation in 1926 [2]. The fifty avant-garde movies he animated, including *Motion Painting No. 1* (1947), influenced generations of animators and experimental filmmakers. Influential filmmakers like Jan Svankmejer and his stylistic progeny Stephen and Timothy Quay (better known as the Brothers Quay) employ stop-motion animation to create dark, surreal experimental movies like the Quays' *The Comb* (1990) [3].

recorded frame. The objects moved and photographed for stop-motion animation can be full-scale or miniature models, puppets made of cloth or clay, or cutouts of other drawings or pictures. Underneath some figures are armatures, or skeletons, with fine joints and pivots, which hold the figures in place between the animators' careful manipulations.

Among the first American stop-motion films was *The Dinosaur and the Missing Link: A Prehistoric Tragedy* (1915), by Willis O'Brien. He went on to animate stop-motion dinosaurs for Harry O. Hoyt's live-action adventure *The Lost World* (1925), then added giant apes to his repertoire with Merian C. Cooper and Ernest B. Schoedsack's *King Kong* (1933) and Schoedsack's *Mighty Joe Young* (1949). Inspired by O'Brien's work on *King Kong*, Ray Harryhausen set out at thirteen to become a stop-motion animator and is now most famous for his work on Don Chaffey's *Jason and the Argonauts* (1963), a Hollywood retelling of the ancient Greek legend. Feature-length animated narrative films that use this technique include Nick Park's *Wallace & Gromit in The Curse of the Were-Rabbit* (2005), Wes Anderson's *Fantastic Mr. Fox* (2009), and Tim Burton's *Frankenweenie* (2012). For the stop-motion films *ParaNorman* (2012; directors Chris Butler and Sam Fell) and *The Boxtrolls* (2014; directors Graham Annable and Anthony Stacchi), the filmmakers at the Laika animation studio adapted digital systems to the stop-motion process. The many interchangeable physical components they used to create different character expressions and poses are designed on computers and fabricated using 3-D printers.

Computer animation uses the virtual world of 3-D computer-modeling software to generate the animation. This technique is also known as 3-D animation, not because it produces an actual physical three-dimensional object or is necessarily screened using a 3-D projection system, but because the approach digitally constructs virtual characters, objects, and backgrounds in all three dimensions, so that these components can be composed and captured from any perspective or position. John Lasseter's *Toy Story* (1995), produced by Pixar, was the first feature-length computer-animated film. A commercial and critical success, it humanized computer animation and obliterated the fear that computer animation was limited to shiny, abstract objects floating in strange worlds. *Toy Story*'s focus on plastic toys, however, helped disguise the limitations of early digital animation techniques. Six more years of development

Persepolis

While digital animation now dominates the animated movie market, hand-drawn films like *Persepolis* (2007) still garner popular and critical attention. Marjane Satrapi's memoir of her childhood and adolescence in Iran and Paris (codirected with Vincent Paronnaud) broke with commercial animation practices by combining its adult subject matter with graphic, mostly black-and-white drawings that emphasized a two-dimensional universe.

enabled digitally animated movies such as Andrew Adamson and Vicky Jenson's *Shrek* (2001) to present compelling characters with visually interesting skin, hair, and fur.

The production of digitally animated features begins with less costly traditional techniques that allow filmmakers to test ideas and characters before starting the difficult and expensive computer-animation process. In the early phases, filmmakers use sketches, storyboards, scripts, pantomime, puppets, models, and voice performances to begin developing stories and characters. By creating a digital wire-frame character with virtual joints and anchor points, computer animators use technology to do some of the same work that stop-motion animators do by hand. Typically, a clay model is created and then scanned into the computer with the use of a digital pen or laser scanner. Animal and human actors can be dressed in black suits with small white circles attached to joints and extremities, allowing for "motion capture" of the distinctive actors' movements. The advanced motion-capture technologies developed to an-

imate the Na'vi natives in *Avatar* blur the line between animation and live action.

In digital animation, animators manipulate virtual skeletons or objects frame by frame on computers. To clothe the wire-frame figures with muscle, skin, fur, or hair, the animators use a digital process called texture mapping. Computer animators also "light" characters and scenes with virtual lights, employing traditional concepts used in theater and film. Specialists work on effects such as fire, explosions, and lightning. Compositing is the process of bringing all these elements together into one frame, and rendering is the process by which hundreds of computers combine all the elements at high resolution and in rich detail. Because the backgrounds, surface textures, lighting, and special effects require a tremendous amount of computer-processing power, animators typically work with wire-frame characters and unrendered backgrounds until all elements are finalized. At that point, a few seconds of screen time may take hundreds of computers many hours to render. Although the process is extremely expensive and labor intensive, computer animation's versatility and aesthetic potential have made it the method of choice for studio-produced feature animation. Aardman Animations, the Claymation production company behind the popular Wallace & Gromit movies, designed their project *Flushed Away* (2006; directors David Bowers and Sam Fell) with the stop-motion plasticine look of their popular Wallace & Gromit characters but created every frame of the film on a computer.

With the release of Hironobu Sakaguchi and Moto Sakakibara's *Final Fantasy: The Spirits Within* (2001), audiences were introduced to the most lifelike computer-animated human characters to date. To create these sophisticated representations, the filmmakers used an elaborate process (since dubbed "performance capture"): actors perform scenes in motion-capture ("mocap") suits that record millions of pieces of data that computers use to render the motion of **computer-generated imagery (CGI)** characters on-screen.

This process was so time-consuming and expensive that it contributed to the failure of the film's production company. Nonetheless, *Final Fantasy* gave birth to the first digitally animated human characters. But for many animators and audiences, "realistic" figures are not necessarily the ideal. In 2004, the stylized characters in Pixar's blockbuster *The Incredibles* (director Brad Bird) trumped the motion-capture-guided "lifelike" figures in Robert Zemeckis's *The Polar Express* in both box office and critical response.

Although there are many other potential reasons that audiences and analysts preferred *The Incredibles*, the key issue for many critics was an unsettling feeling that they couldn't shake while watching the characters in *The Polar Express*—a feeling that the whole thing wasn't heartwarming or endearing, but was instead simply creepy. Among fans of computer-generated imagery, there was considerable debate about why, exactly, *The Polar Express* left so many viewers feeling weird and uncomfortable rather than filled with the holiday spirit. Eventually, on blogs and listservs all over the Internet, a consensus was reached: *The Polar Express* had fallen into the "uncanny valley."

The uncanny valley is a theoretical concept first described in 1970 by a Japanese robotics engineer, Masahiro Mori. It states that the closer an object (a robot, an animated character) comes to resembling a human being in its motion and appearance, the more

The uncanny valley
If a filmmaker strives for a high level of verisimilitude in computer-generated characters, as Robert Zemeckis did in *The Polar Express* (2004), he may risk taking the humanlike resemblance too far, causing viewers to notice every detail of the characters' appearance or movement that doesn't conform to the way real human beings actually look or move. Our emotional response to these "almost human" characters will, therefore, be unease and discomfort, not pleasure or empathy—a negative reaction known as "the uncanny valley."

positive our emotional response to that object becomes until suddenly, at some point of very close (but not perfect) resemblance, our emotional response turns from empathy to revulsion. This revulsion or uneasiness, Mori says, is the result of a basic human tendency to look for anomalies in the appearance of other human beings. When an object such as a robot or an animated character is so anthropomorphic that it is nearly indistinguishable from a human being, we monitor the appearance of that object very closely and become extremely sensitive to any small anomalies that might identify the object as not fully human. For whatever reason, these anomalies create in many people a shudder of discomfort similar to the feeling we have when we watch a zombie movie or see an actual corpse. In both cases, what we see is both human and not fully human, and the contradiction produces a very negative reaction. As a result, viewers found it easy to identify and sympathize with the highly stylized characters in *The Incredibles* but responded to the much more realistic figures in *The Polar Express* with unease and discomfort.

Nevertheless, animation and photographed "reality" can and do get along. Animation has been incorporated into live-action movies since the 1920s. Today, many traditionally photographed movies integrate computer-generated animation into characters, backgrounds, and special effects. Computer-animated characters have been convincingly interacting on-screen with flesh-and-blood performers since Gollum in Peter Jackson's Lord of the Rings trilogy (2001–3). Gollum's digital descendants include Caesar in the Planet of the Apes series and the castaway tiger in Ang Lee's *Life of Pi* (2012).

This now commonplace intrusion into conventional motion pictures is only one example of the animation explosion made possible by the recent emergence of new technologies and growing audience demand. As a result, ten animated narrative features were given a major theatrical release in the United States in 2014. Countless more forgo the movie-house release and go straight to DVD. Network and cable television stations, including at least one dedicated entirely to cartoons, broadcast hundreds of animated series, specials, and advertisements. The video-game market exploits animation to create animated characters and situations that allow the viewer an unprecedented level of interaction. Viewers have always been drawn to cinema's ability to immerse them in environments, events, and images impossible in daily life. Animation simply expands that capacity.

Looking at the Types of Movies in *The Lego Movie*

Let's end this chapter by examining one film that borrows from many different types of movies. *The Lego Movie* (2014, directors Phil Lord and Christopher Miller) is the cinematic equivalent of a pastiche, a term applied to a work of art that imitates or appropriates recognizable stylistic elements from a previous work or works.[9] To help understand the concept, think of a pastiche as a collage in which pieces of preexisting drawings and paintings are snipped out and arranged on a new canvas into a cohesive assembly. Even though viewers may be able to identify the source of many of the different pieces,

we can still appreciate the new form and draw meaning specific to the resulting self-contained creation. In fact, we may get as much pleasure from recognizing the various appropriations as from experiencing the cohesive combination.[10]

The pastiche in *The Lego Movie* begins with the very specific (and unusual) way the film looks and moves. *The Lego Movie* is a big-budget computer-animated extravaganza made by a team of over 630 professionals, but it owes its distinct style to primitive homemade stop-motion videos. Amateur filmmakers began making short stop-motion animations using Lego bricks in the early 1970s. The interlocking bricks are ideal for building a wide variety of small-scale sets and props, and the Lego figures are easy to pose and position. The technique's unavoidable chunky look and jerky movement gave the movies an endearing common aesthetic. The method gained popularity in the 1990s as affordable consumer-grade digital cameras gave more people access to the technology necessary to make the movies and the Internet made it possible to share them. The new millennium brought a growing array of Lego products along with increased video streaming bandwidth; soon there were Web sites, film festivals, and YouTube channels dedicated to what had come to be known as *brickfilms*.

It wasn't long before market forces and creative minds saw the mutual benefit of bringing brickfilms to the big screen. But the producer Dan Lin and the codirectors Phil Lord and Christopher Miller realized that the labor-intensive stop-motion process would be unfeasible for the large scale they envisioned for what would become *The Lego Movie*. So 3-D computer animation was put to work creating an expansive action-packed universe built entirely of plastic bricks. Determined to keep the look and feel of a brickfilm, the animators retained the hand-made method's herky-jerky character movement and even digitally applied fingerprints, scratches, and dirt onto the animated bricks and figures.[11]

But the look wasn't the only element *The Lego Movie* borrowed. The pastiche approach that dominates the film's narrative also is rooted in the brickfilm. Because

9. Roland Green, ed., *Princeton Encyclopedia of Poetry and Poetics*, 4th ed. (Princeton, NJ: Princeton University Press, 2012), p. 1005.

10. Richard Dyer, *Introduction to Pastiche* (New York: Routledge, 2007).

11. http://io9.com/the-makers-of-the-lego-movie-take-apart-their-creation-1516662564 (accessed March 19, 2015).

The Lego Movie as genre pastiche

The Lego Movie combines a multitude of genre elements and cultural references to tell a classic quest story. A choreographed musical sequence introduces the primary setting of Bricksburg and establishes the unlikely hero Emmitt as a complacent conformist [1]. Later, when he attempts to live up to his "special one" status, Emmitt's awkward greenhorn posturing hushes a raucous saloon in a classic Western sequence [2]. Batman is his rival in a romantic comedy love story [3]. Finally, the villain President Business's climactic Kragle attack on Bricksburg unfolds like an epic science-fiction alien invasion [4].

Lego sets are often packaged with specific themes, many brickfilms incorporated Lego-version items and figures associated with pirates, police, and space travel, or film series like Star Wars, Lord of the Rings, Harry Potter, and Batman. Brickfilm narratives often referenced or re-created characters, situations, dialogue, and behavior associated with the incorporated components. As the brickfilm evolved, filmmakers increasingly combined elements from multiple, often disparate, sources. A pirate might team up with a spaceman; Harry Potter could duel Darth Vader.

The Lego Movie takes that approach to the extreme. The opening introduces Lord Business (voiced by Will Ferrell) and immediately establishes the film as a pastiche that samples a smorgasbord of cultural and genre sources. With his elaborate costume, diabolical bombast, and homogeneous henchmen, Lord Business is a combination of fantasy film evil wizard and superhero movie super-villain. Lord Business storms a castle for a showdown with Vitruvius (voiced by Morgan Freeman),

a character with his own fantasy origins: he is a wise, long-haired, magic-staff-wielding wizard in the mold of The Hobbit's Gandalf and Harry Potter's Professor Dumbledore. Vitruvius declares himself a "master builder," a *Lego Movie* character type with the power to build almost anything from the materials at hand—a disclosure that reveals still more cultural references. Vitruvius was the name of a notable first-century BCE Roman engineer; *The Master Builder* is the title of a famous nineteenth-century play by Henrik Ibsen about a successful but doomed architect. Lord Business defeats Vitruvius, then takes gleeful possession of the mysterious superweapon known as "the Kragle." Vitruvius interrupts the villain's triumphant gloating with a prophecy about a "piece of resistance" that can disarm the Kragle: one day, a "special one"—another master builder—will find a hidden piece of resistance and save the world.

Within two minutes, a familiar story formula has been established. Like Harry Potter, the original Star Wars saga, The Matrix, The Lord of the Rings, and even

The Hunger Games series, *The Lego Movie* is structured around an almost impossible quest led by a chosen one to save the world from a seemingly unstoppable evil. This story formula goes deeper than genre; the quest is rooted in what the eminent mythologist Joseph Campbell termed the "monomyth," or "hero's journey." According to Campbell, this basic pattern can be found in the folktales and myths—and movies—of multiple cultures:

> A hero ventures forth from the world of common day into a region of supernatural wonder: fabulous forces are there encountered and a decisive victory is won: the hero comes back from this mysterious adventure with the power to bestow boons on his fellow man.[12]

The cultural prevalence of the hero's journey archetype makes it likely that most viewers of *The Lego Movie* will recall the familiar story pattern the moment it's introduced. So when we meet the construction worker Emmitt Brickowoski (voiced by Chris Pratt) in the next scene, we instantly recognize him as our hero and anticipate his imminent departure on the aforementioned narrative excursion. He is an oblivious nincompoop, but that does nothing to undermine our assumption. On the contrary, Emmitt's incompetence reinforces our expectation. Cinematic history is full of protagonists who initially appear unfit for the challenges to come. So we immediately assume that Emmitt will discover the piece of resistance, amass allies, and ultimately prove his unlikely worth to save Bricksburg from President (aka Lord) Business. The predictability does not diminish either our pleasure or investment. When it comes to narrative and genre, much of a viewer's gratification comes not from unexpected revelations, but from experiencing how familiar elements and formulas operate and intersect within a particular scenario—in this case, a multilevel, magical universe constructed entirely out of interlocking plastic bricks and ruled by a meticulous tyrant determined to eliminate innovation by freezing everything in place with the Kragle (i.e., Krazy Glue).

The next few scenes assimilate genre elements and situations to launch Emmitt on his quest. First, the kind of elaborately choreographed song-and-dance sequence usually found in an integrated musical establishes Em-

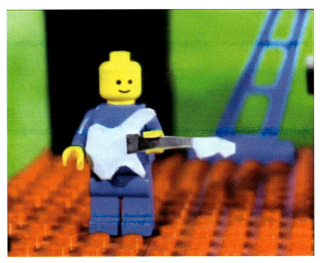

1

2

The Lego Movie origins

The computer-animated blockbuster borrowed the distinct style of low-budget stop-motion animations made using Lego bricks, like David Betteridge's 1989 music video for a British group called Ethereal [1]. Although *The Lego Movie* was computer animated, the filmmakers adapted the brickfilms' boxy look and restricted character movements. They even applied realistic-looking chips, scratches, and grime to their digital creations [2].

mitt and the rest of Bricktown's eager ignorance and instruction-following conformity. After stumbling upon the piece of resistance (which is the cap to the Kragle glue), Emmitt awakens in the glare of a spotlight to find himself in a spartan interrogation room being questioned by

---

12. Joseph Campbell, *The Hero with a Thousand Faces*, 2nd ed. (Princeton, NJ: Princeton University Press, 1949), p. 30.

a hostile policeman—a situation found in film noir crime movies and television police procedurals. Emmitt himself acknowledges the reference when he asks the Bad Cop: "I watch a lot of cop shows on TV . . . isn't there supposed to be a good cop?" Bad Cop (voiced by Will Arnett) straps Emmitt into the "melting chamber," an elaborate laser-shooting execution apparatus straight out of an early James Bond movie. A master builder named Wyldstyle (voiced by Elizabeth Banks) drops in just in time to rescue Emmitt in a scene dominated by action movie presentation elements like fast-paced editing, swooping moving camera, bullet time, and gravity-defying martial arts acrobatics. Emmitt and his savior flee a barrage of Bad Cop gunfire and land in an alley, where Wyldstyle immediately constructs a giant motorcycle from the objects at hand.

Wyldstyle's extravagant escape vehicle offers a visual metaphor for how *The Lego Movie* incorporates multiple types of movies into a somewhat cluttered, but ultimately cohesive, whole. None of the many and various components necessarily match, but each fulfills a function in service of a shared purpose. The movie conveys an entertaining cinematic story; the motorcycle propels our protagonists through a chase scene and out of a secret portal that leads to a stratified series of discrete worlds and genres. Emmitt's journey begins in a Western, adopts a romantic comedy love story, enlists superheroes and cyborg pirates, and culminates with a science-fiction apocalypse.

In the end, the narrative expands into a traditional live-action family drama. *The Lego Movie*'s segregated universe is revealed to be the creation of an adult Lego hobbyist with a strict sense of tradition and a striking resemblance to President Business. It turns out that the narrative's exuberant narrative hodgepodge is the product of his son, a boy too imaginative to be controlled by convention. Emmitt's quest is complete when both the father and his Lego counterpart accept the inevitability of innovation. It's only fitting that the humble brickfilm has the last word. *The Lego Movie*'s final credit sequence is a genuine stop-motion animation constructed entirely of actual plastic blocks.[13]

---

13. www.artofthetitle.com/title/the-lego-movie/ (accessed March 19, 2015).

ANALYZING TYPES OF MOVIES

This chapter's broad survey of the different types of movies should make clear that movies are divided into narrative, documentary, and experimental (and animation) categories, and that each of these has evolved a great variety of ways to express ideas, information, and meaning. What's more, the longer cinema is around, the more ways filmmakers find to borrow, reference, and blend elements from other types to best serve their own vision. Now that you have studied the various ways that movies are differentiated and classified, you should be able to identify what basic type or genre a movie belongs to, recognize how the movie uses the elements of form and content particular to its film type, and appreciate and understand instances when the filmmakers incorporate styles and approaches rooted in other film types.

SCREENING CHECKLIST: TYPES OF MOVIES

☐ If the film is a documentary, is it factual, instructional, persuasive, or propaganda—or a blend of two or more of these documentary approaches? Consider the movie's relationship with the spectator and with relative truth. Does it appear to be attempting to present events and ideas in as objective a manner as is cinematically possible, or does it make a specific persuasive argument? What elements of form or content lead you to this conclusion?

☐ Look for ways in which the documentary employs narrative. Are the events portrayed selected and organized so they tell a story?

☐ Ask yourself how this movie compares to other documentary films you've seen. Think about your formal expectations of nonfiction movies: talking-head interviews, voice-over narration, archival footage, and so on. Does this movie conform to those expectations? If not, how does it convey information and meaning in ways that are different from a typical documentary?

☐ To analyze an experimental movie, try to apply Fred Camper's criteria for experimental cinema. Which of the listed characteristics does the movie seem to fit, and which of them does it diverge from?

☐ Remember that experimental filmmakers often seek to defy expectations and easy characterization. So consider effect and intent. How does the movie make you feel, think, or react? Do you think the filmmaker intended these effects? If so, what elements of form and content contribute to this effect?

☐ When watching an experimental film, be especially aware of your expectations of what a movie should look like and what the movie experience should be. If the movie disappoints or confounds your expectations, do your best to let go of what you've been conditioned to assume, and try to encounter the movie on its own terms. Remember that many experimental movies, unlike documentaries and narrative films, are open to individual interpretation.

☐ Since most of the movies that you study in your introductory film class will be narrative films, you should ask whether a particular film can be linked with a specific genre and, if so, to what extent it does or does not fulfill your expectations of that genre.

☐ Be aware that many movies borrow or blend elements of multiple genres. Look for familiar formal, narrative, and thematic genre elements, and ask yourself how and why this film uses them.

Questions for Review

1. What are the four related ways we can define the term *narrative*?

2. What are the main differences among the three basic types of movies?

3. What are the four basic approaches to documentary cinema? How are these approaches blended and reinterpreted by contemporary documentary filmmakers?

4. What is direct cinema, and how does it differ in approach and technique from a conventional interview-based documentary?

5. What are Fred Camper's six characteristics that most experimental films share?

6. What is a hybrid movie? What are some of the ways that documentary, narrative, and experimental movies intersect?

7. What is genre? How does genre affect the way movies are made and received?

8. What are the six sets of conventions used to define and classify film genres?

9. What are the formal and narrative elements common to each of the six movie genres described in the chapter?

10. How does animation differ from the other three basic types of movies?

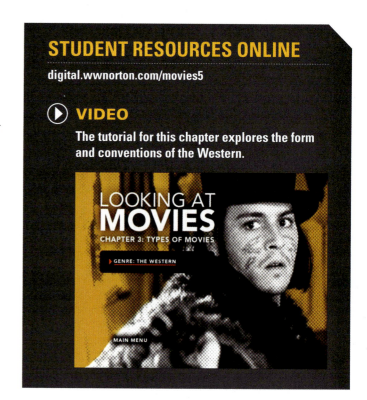

Snowpiercer (2014; director Bong Joon-ho)

ELEMENTS OF NARRATIVE

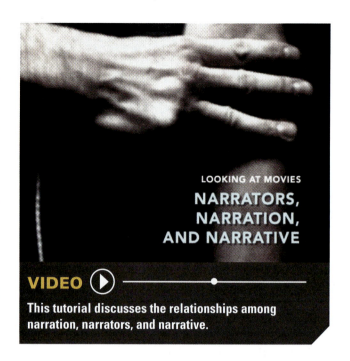

LOOKING AT MOVIES

NARRATORS, NARRATION, AND NARRATIVE

VIDEO ▶ ━━━━━━●━━━━━━

This tutorial discusses the relationships among narration, narrators, and narrative.

What Is Narrative?

We've already gotten a good start on exploring the question "What is narrative?" in Chapters 1 and 3. As we begin this chapter dedicated to the subject, we have already learned the following things about narrative:

> A narrative is a story.

> Narrative movies are fiction films, as opposed to other movie modes, such as documentary or experimental.

> At the broadest conceptual level, narrative is a cinematic structure in which the filmmakers have selected and arranged events in a cause-and-effect sequence occurring over time.

> When we think of it that way, almost all movies, even documentaries and experimental films, employ some level of narrative.

> In fact, narrative permeates more than just the world of movies—it infuses our culture and our lives. Whether we're describing a sporting event, relating a dream, recalling a memory, or telling a joke, we humans tend to order events so they will convey meaning and engage the recipient.

> Because story and storytelling are so ingrained in our everyday lives, including the movies we watch, it's all too easy to take narrative for granted.

To better recognize and understand how it works, we'll first need to break down narrative into the various components that contribute to telling a cinematic story. Let's start with two closely related (and potentially confusing) terms: *narration* and *narrator*.

Narration is the *act of telling* the story. The **narrator** is *who or what tells* the story. In other words, the *narrator* delivers the *narration* that conveys the *narrative*. Filmmakers employ different approaches to the concept of narrator (who or what tells the story) and narration (how that story is told) to shape the viewer's experience of the narrative (the story itself).

In every movie, the camera is the primary narrator. Its narration consists of the many visual elements it captures and arranges in every composition in every shot. A narrative moment in Alfred Hitchcock's *Notorious* (1946; screenwriter Ben Hecht) offers an easy example. In the previous scene, we watched the Nazi conspirator Alexander Sebastian (Claude Rains) discover that his wife, Alicia (Ingrid Bergman), is a U.S. government spy. Naturally, he tells his mother, and she begins brainstorming ways to discreetly eliminate his unfaithful spouse. A shot in the next scene begins focused on the

The camera as narrator

The camera (and everything that implies) is the primary narrator in every film. In this moving camera shot from Alfred Hitchcock's *Notorious*, the camera shows us the Nazi conspirator Alexander urging his wife Alicia to drink her coffee [1], moves to fill the screen with a close-up of her cup [2], follows it to her lips [3], and then turns to connect the action to her vengeful mother-in-law [4]. The next shot features Alicia holding her throbbing head [5]. The camera has told us a story: *Alexander and his mother are poisoning Alicia.*

betrayed husband as he urges his wife to drink her coffee. The camera drifts down from his smirking face and across the breakfast table until Alicia's coffee cup fills the screen. When she picks it up, the camera follows it to her lips. As Alicia begins to drink, the camera moves over to feature her scheming mother-in-law contentedly stitching her needlepoint. The next shot shows Alicia rubbing her forehead and looking decidedly under the weather. Throughout the sequence, the *camera narrator* tells us that Alicia's coffee is poisoned by selecting what we see and shaping when and how we see it. In other words, the camera tells the story.

And, of course, other cinematic elements contribute to the narration. The lighting, set design, makeup, and

Multiple narrators in *Stranger than Fiction*

In Marc Forster's *Stranger than Fiction* (2006; screenwriter Zack Helm), the third-person narrator doesn't just help *tell* the story—it becomes a player in the narrative itself. Harold Crick (Will Farrell) hears the voice-over narrating his own story and learns that his character is slated for an imminent demise. His goal of finding the source of the narration and changing his own tragic ending forms the basis of the rest of the story. As the story progresses, we meet the depressed novelist crafting Harold's destiny. Does knowing the character who wrote it make the narration first person, or is the novel's text a third-person narrator that exists apart from the novelist character? Or is it narration at all if a character can hear it? Participating in these inconsistencies is part of the fun—and playful strangeness—of *Stranger than Fiction*.

performances in each shot, as well as the associations achieved through the juxtaposition of images, all contribute to our engagement with the narrative. Maybe it would be more accurate to state that in every movie, the filmmakers and their creative techniques constitute the primary narrator. Nonetheless, it is a little more streamlined to think of all that as "the camera."

And the camera isn't always a movie's only narrator. Some movies use more than one narrator to deliver the narration. This narration can be in the form of a *character's* particular perspective on the narrative's events.

A **first-person narrator** is a character in the narrative who typically imparts information in the form of **voice-over narration**, which is when we hear a character's voice *over* the picture without actually seeing the character speak the words. This technique of a character speaking to the audience allows us to *hear* one narration—from the first-person character narrator—while simultaneously *watching* the narration provided by our narrator camera.

The combination of these narrator partners may be relatively straightforward, such as in Danny Boyle's *Trainspotting* (1996; screenwriter John Hodge), when the first-person voice-over primer to heroin addiction delivered by Renton (Ewan McGregor) plays over the opening sequences depicting the lives of the addicts that populate the story.

A richer, more complex experience of the narrative is possible when the first-person narration contrasts somehow with what we see on-screen. The first-person narrators of writer/director Terrence Malick's first two films (*Badlands*, 1973, and *Days of Heaven*, 1978) are naive and sometimes deluded young women who attempt to rationalize and even romanticize events and actions we can see for ourselves. The conflict between what the camera is telling us and the perspective provided by the first-person narrator can expand our relationship with the narrative beyond anything a camera alone can deliver.

And some movies push this relationship even further. These films don't limit the first-person narrative to voice-over narration. Instead, the first-person narrator character interrupts the narrative to deliver **direct address narration** directly to the audience, thus breaking the "fourth wall" that traditionally separates the viewer from the two-dimensional fiction on-screen.

Ferris Bueller's Day Off (1986; director/screenwriter John Hughes) features a charismatic slacker who seduces his fellow characters as well as his audience. Ferris (Matthew Broderick) frequently pauses the on-screen action to gaze into our eyes and charm us with his own personal take on the story he inhabits. Ferris Bueller follows in the footsteps of other smooth-talking scoundrels who break the fourth wall, most notably Tony Richardson's *Tom Jones* (1963; screenwriter John Osborne) and Lewis Gilbert's *Alfie* (1966; screenwriter Bill Naughton). Other direct address narration is more confrontational. Michel Haneke's *Funny Games* (2007; screenwriter Haneke) challenges the viewer to endure a brutal game of cat and mouse played by a pair of psychotic young men. After they take a young family hostage, the attackers goad their victims to wager on their own survival. When their prey try to refuse the bet, one of the attackers turns to confront the audience with a string of questions: "I mean, what do you think? Do you think they stand a chance? You're on their side, aren't you? Who are you betting on, huh?" By breaking the fourth wall in this way, Haneke forces the audience to acknowledge our participation in the violence. The filmmaker implies that, in watching this senseless cruelty, we're complicit in it.

Sometimes the voice-over narrator isn't even someone in the movie. Voice-over narration can also be expressed by a voice imposed from outside of the narrative. Standing at a remove from the action allows this **third-person narrator** to provide information not accessible to a narrator who is also a participant in the story. Like the author of the story, the third-person narrator knows all and can thus provide objective context to any situation.

Wes Anderson's *The Royal Tenenbaums* (2001) opens with a third-person voice-over relating the history of a family of eccentric geniuses delivered in the dispassionate tone of a documentary reporter. But even this seemingly remote narrator (voiced by Alec Baldwin) provides more than just information. The deadpan delivery layers a sort of literary seriousness over an extended series of comic scenes detailing the family's brilliant successes and staggering failures. Later, the third-person narrator interjects to let us into a character's head at a crucial narrative moment. Royal Tenenbaum, a manipulative con man, has wormed his way back into his estranged family by pretending to be dying of cancer. When he is caught in the lie, his non-apology is predictably slick: "Look, I know I'm going to be the bad guy on this one, but I just want to say that the last six days have been the best six days of probably my whole life." As the words leave his lips, he pauses as if momentarily confused. The third-person narrator speaks up to illuminate the situation: "Immediately after making this statement, Royal realized that it was true." All this goes to show that movies can use a number of possible narrators—even combinations of narrators. Likewise, movies employ more than one approach to *narration*.

Narration can be **omniscient**, meaning it knows all and can tell us whatever it wants us to know. Omniscient narration has *unrestricted* access to all aspects of the narrative. It can provide *any* character's experiences and perceptions, as well as information that *no* character knows. An omniscient camera shows the audience whatever it needs to in order to best tell the story.

An espionage thriller like *Notorious* involves deception, double crosses, and mixed motives. To fully exploit the intrigue, the camera narrator must show us what is going on with multiple characters and situations. We watch Alicia uncover evidence in the wine cellar proving her husband's Nazi plotting while he hosts a party in oblivious bliss upstairs. We see him plot her death after he learns she's an American spy. We writhe with

1

2

3

Narrators

In *The Royal Tenenbaums* (2001), the camera narrator tells us the story by displaying evidence of the children Royal abandoned, as well as the slick con man himself as he delivers what we assume to be the latest in a string of manipulative lies [1]. But the narrative deepens when the third-person voice-over interjects to tell the audience that he's telling the truth this time. In the opening and closing scenes of *The Spectacular Now* (2013, director James Ponsoldt, screenwriters Scott Neustadter and Michael H. Weber), Sutter Keely (Miles Teller) helps tell the story in a couple of ways. The camera shows us the character's image and actions on-screen, and his first-person narration (in the form of a surprisingly candid college admissions essay) is delivered in voice-over [2]. The sadistic home invader Paul (Michael Pitt) in *Funny Games* takes a more direct approach when he breaks the fourth wall to confront his audience with direct-address narration [3].

Restricted narration in *Black Swan*
Restricted narration makes watching *Black Swan* both excruciating and ultimately cathartic. The audience must endure every moment of the story locked inside the increasingly unreliable perspective of Nina (Natalie Portman), a prima ballerina, as the pressures of her role drive her insane. For many viewers, the ultimate experience of sharing Nina's transcendent final performance makes enduring her breakdown worthwhile.

frustration watching her fellow agent (and love interest) blame her disheveled appearance on a hangover, when we know that all she's been drinking is poisoned coffee. A large part of the pleasure in experiencing such a story comes from knowing more than the characters and anticipating what will happen if and when they learn the whole truth.

Another Hitchcock movie, *Rear Window* (1954; screenwriter John Michael Hayes), tells the story of Jeff Jeffries (James Stewart), a man of action stuck in his apartment in a wheelchair while recovering from a badly broken leg. To amuse himself, Jeff begins spying on his neighbors. The recreational snooping suddenly takes a dark turn when he witnesses what may—or may not be—a murder.

For the viewer, the pleasure of watching Jeff slowly unravel the mystery depends on being restricted to his incomplete understanding of the events unfolding outside his rear window. As a result, Hitchcock chose **restricted narration**, which limits the information it provides the audience to things known only to a single character. This approach encourages the audience to identify with the character's singular perspective on perplexing and frightening events—and invites us to participate in the gradual unlocking of the narrative's secrets.

Steven Soderbergh's *The Limey* (1999; screenwriter Lem Dobbs) uses a similar approach. For most of the film, the camera narrator restricts the narration. We see and hear only the thoughts, memories, perspectives, and experiences available to the character of Wilson (Ter-

rence Stamp) as he doggedly pursues the mystery behind the death of his daughter. In fact, as the narrative progresses, the viewer gradually realizes that the movie's highly stylized editing is not conveying the story events as they happened, but as they are recalled by Wilson on his way back to England after solving the mystery. It's a sort of visual first-person narration without voice-over.

Of course, nothing in cinema is absolute. Many films shift between restricted and omniscient narration depending on the needs of the story. Movies like *The Limey* enforce restricted narration for most of the story, only to switch to omniscient narration when it serves the narrative to expand our view on the action. For those few times when the narrative demands that the audience witness events outside Wilson's experience, the narration temporarily shifts into omniscient mode.

The deeper you look, the more complex and expressive cinema gets. But the general concepts at the foundation of cinematic storytelling are pretty straightforward. Just remember: the **narrative** is the story; narration is the act of telling the story; the narrator is who or what tells the story. In other words, the *narrator* delivers the *narration* that conveys the *narrative*.

Characters

Whether it's a pregnant teenager trying to find suitable parents to adopt her baby or a hobbit seeking to destroy an all-powerful ring, virtually every film narrative depends upon two essential elements: a **character** pursuing a **goal**.

The nature of that pursuit depends on the character's background, position, personality, attitudes, and beliefs. These traits govern how the character reacts to opportunities and problems, makes decisions, acts upon those decisions, and deals with the consequences of those actions. The allies and adversaries (all of whom have traits of their own) that the character attracts are influenced by these traits, as are all interactions between these other various characters. And that pursuit, and all the decisions, actions, consequences, relationships, and interactions that intersect and influence it, is the story.

Imagine how different the story of The Hunger Games series would have been if Katniss Everdeen had been cautious, confident, and privileged instead of the insecure, irreverent, and angry young woman who impulsively volunteers to take her little sister's place at the reaping. Or in the case of the Harry Potter series, what if Ron Weasley, the insecure and unrefined product of

1

2

Round and flat characters in *Precious*

Different types of stories, and even different roles within the same story, call for different approaches to character traits, behavior, and development. *Precious: Based on the Novel "Push" by Sapphire* (2009; director Lee Daniels, screenwriter Geoffrey Fletcher) features two remarkable characters: the illiterate teenager Precious (Gabourey Sidibe) and her abusive mother Mary (Mo'Nique). Each character is captivating in her own way, and the actresses who played them were both rightfully praised for their powerful performances. But the narrative requires that Mary be a flat character clearly defined by malicious anger and an inability to change [1]. In contrast, Precious must be a round character to drive a narrative built around revelation and transformation. At first glance, Precious appears to be slow-witted and apathetic, but as the story peels away at the layers of her complex personality, we (and Precious herself) learn that she's capable of imagination, ambition, bravery, intelligence, and insight [2].

a large rambunctious wizard family, had been the boy who lived, instead of the instinctive and strong-willed neglected orphan Harry Potter? Better still, what if the earnest, intelligent, overachieving child-of-muggles Hermione was the *girl* who lived? Even if the goal remained the same in each of these hypothetical narratives, the character's traits would inspire choices and behavior that would lead them to a different path, and thus tell a different story.

The profound effect characters have on narrative comes in handy. After all, there are only so many stories in the world—consider how many movies sound interchangeable when reduced to a short description—but character traits may be assembled in infinite combinations. Each new character makes possible a different take on the same old story. Think of all the love stories or murder mysteries you've watched. The individual personalities falling in love and/or solving (and committing) crimes play a large part in keeping those archetypal narrative approaches fresh. The directors, actors, cinematographers, and designers responsible for putting the characters and their story on-screen build upon the characterizations in the screenplay to develop how exactly each character looks, speaks, and behaves in the movie.

Of course, some characters are more complicated than others. In literature, complex characters are known as **round characters**. They may possess numerous subtle, repressed, or even contradictory traits that can change significantly over the course of the story—sometimes surprisingly so. Because they display the complexity we associate with our own personalities, we tend to see round characters as more lifelike. In contrast, relatively uncomplicated **flat characters** exhibit few distinct traits and do not change significantly as the story progresses.[1] This doesn't mean that one character classification is any more legitimate than the other. Different types of stories call for different approaches to character traits, behavior, and development.

For example, the flamboyant Jack Sparrow (Johnny Depp) is entertaining enough to drive the spectacular success of the Pirates of the Caribbean franchise; no one could call his character boring. But with Jack, what we see is what we get. His character is clearly and simply defined, and at the end of every installment he remains the same lovable scoundrel he was in the opening scene. The Pirates of the Caribbean movies benefit from Jack's flat character.

The coming-of-age drama *An Education* (2009; director Lone Scherfig, screenwriter Nick Hornby) calls

---

1. E. M. Forster, *Aspects of the Novel* (New York: Harcourt, Brace, 1927), pp. 103–118.

Character development in *District 9*

Progression is an essential narrative element, and the changes a character undergoes, especially when those changes involve some level of personal growth, are one of the most satisfying progressions movies have to offer. Neill Blomkamp's dystopian science-fiction thriller *District 9* (2009; screenwriters Blomcamp and Terri Tachell) explores the themes of racism and xenophobia with a story about the forced relocation of unwanted alien squatters. The posturing protagonist Wikus (Sharlto Copley) gets what's coming to him when his meddling results in his own inexorable transformation into one of the very aliens he persecuted. But it is the interior changes Wikus experiences that give his story meaning. The more he looks like a monster, the more human he becomes.

for a round character. Jenny Mellor (Carey Mulligan) is a complicated adolescent—she's smart but naive; she's both ambitious and insecure; she rebels against the same authorities whose approval she craves. Jenny falls in love with a charming older man who introduces her to a glamorous new lifestyle of concerts, art auctions, martinis, and sex. She quickly blossoms into a cosmopolitan sophisticate with no use for anything as inane as school. But she does receive an education when David turns out to be a thief and a con man—a married con man at that. Jenny enters the story as a bright girl and leaves it as a wise woman.

Of course, as with most things in the movies, round and flat characters exist not in absolutes, but along a continuum that adjusts according to narrative and cinematic needs. Some characters are rounder than others, and vice versa. And flat characters are no more limited to crowd-pleasing blockbusters than are round characters confined to sophisticated dramas.

No one could call the hyperkinetic and provocative *Black Swan* (2010; director Darren Aronofsky, screenwriter Mark Heyman) a simplistic movie. Natalie Portman's powerful performance as Nina, a ballerina driven to madness by her quest to inhabit a demanding role, de-

served the critical and popular acclaim it received. Yet in many ways, Nina could be considered a flat character. Her traits are straightforward; she's a fearful, driven perfectionist. Throughout her excruciating journey to the final performance, even as she (apparently) physically transforms, Nina stubbornly clings to the same insecurities and flaws that she carried into the story. Her final direct address declaration is evidence of her inability to change.

On the other hand, Peter Quill, the reckless smart aleck at the center of the comic adventure *Guardians of the Galaxy* (2014; director James Gunn, screenwriters Gunn and Nicole Perlman) would have to be considered at least somewhat rounded. After all, his seemingly selfish behavior is rooted in a tragic past that complicates any assessment of his actions and intentions. As the story unfolds, narrative events change Peter from an amoral (if amusing) thief to a hero willing to sacrifice himself to save the same civilization that condemned him to prison. Granted, he still steals—but with a strong sense of civic duty.

Whatever the shape of the character, narrative cannot exist if that character does not have a goal. The goal does not just give the character something to do (although that activity is important). It also gives the audience a chance to participate in the story by creating expectations that viewers want to see either fulfilled or surprised. More on that later—for now let's stick to how that goal affects our character.

The primary character who pursues the goal is known as the **protagonist**. The protagonist is sometimes referred to as the hero (or heroine), but this term can be misleading, since engaging narratives do not necessarily depend on worthy goals or brave and sympathetic characters. As Harry Potter or Katniss Everdeen can attest, it's certainly not a liability if the audience happens to like or admire the protagonist. But as long as the protagonist actively pursues the goal in an interesting way, the viewer cannot help becoming invested in that pursuit, and by extension, the story.

Seemingly unsympathetic protagonists chasing less than noble goals are sometimes called **anti-heroes**: Walter Neff is a cocky insurance agent whose quest is to murder his lover's husband so he can have her body—and her inheritance—all to himself. Walter's no Boy Scout, but when watching *Double Indemnity* (1944; director Billy Wilder, screenwriters Wilder and Raymond Chandler), it's tough not to root for him to get away with murder. Jordan Belfort doesn't kill anyone, but he does manipulate markets, cheat investors, and break innumerable laws to make outrageous profits (which he uses to fuel an aggressively excessive lifestyle). However, while watching *The Wolf of Wall Street* (2013, director Martin Scorsese, screenwriter Terrance Winter), we take some pleasure in Belfort's triumphs and can't help pitying him when his empire collapses.

In fact, impeccable characters are rare in modern movies. Narrative craves imperfect characters because those imperfections provide **obstacles**, another essential building block of storytelling. We'll discuss obstacles in the section on narrative structure. For now, simply consider that a romance about a shy, awkward boy in love with the head cheerleader is likely to be much more interesting than a love story between the two most beautiful and popular kids in school. Character imperfections and flaws also give characters room to grow. As the previous discussion of round and flat characters indicated, character development is central to many movie narratives.

In *Precious,* based on the novel *Push* by Sapphire, the title character's struggle to escape her violent mother and learn to read transforms her from a numbed victim into an assertive and expressive young woman. Precious's character development makes watching this often-harrowing movie a satisfying and rewarding narrative experience. On the other end of the entertainment spectrum, part of the pleasure of seeing *Big Hero Six* (2014; directors Don Hall and Chris Williams; screenwriters Jordan Roberts, Daniel Gerson, and Robert L. Baird) is the young inventor Hiro's progress from an embittered loner to the dynamic leader of a team of oddball crime-fighters. Even his sidekick Baymax (who is figuratively and literally a round character) experiences character growth. What begins as a benign, inflated health-care robot winds up a sentient superhero.

It's easy to understand what motivates these protagonists to pursue their goals. Precious is abused by her mother and inspired by her new teacher. Hiro discovers that a masked man has stolen his greatest invention. Baymax is programmed to heal. Most narrative relies on this character motivation. If the viewer doesn't believe or understand a character's actions, the story's verisimilitude, and thus the audience's identification with the protagonist's efforts, will be compromised. We believe and connect with the quest Mattie Ross (Hailee Steinfeld) undertakes to track down Tom Chaney in the Coen brothers' *True Grit* (2010; written and directed by Joel

Goals and needs

The intersection of narrative and character provides for a wide range of narrative structures and outcomes. Not every movie must have a happy ending, and the stories that do provide a happy ending are not always dependent on the protagonist achieving his or her goal. In *Rocky*, the ending is satisfying even though the underdog boxer loses the heavyweight match, because his gutsy performance gives him back the self-respect he was missing at the beginning of the story. Ultimately, the audience identifies with Rocky's psychological need even more than his goal of defeating the mighty Apollo Creed.

and Ethan Coen) because we know that he killed her father. Sonny Wortzik (Al Pacino), the protagonist of Sidney Lumet's *Dog Day Afternoon* (1975; screenwriter Frank Pierson), robs a bank (or tries to) because he needs money to pay for his lover's sex-change operation. We might not agree with Sonny's goal or his methods, but understanding the impulse behind his actions allows us to engage in his story.

Some storytellers use expectations of clear character motivation against their audience to create a specific experience of the narrative. In David Lynch's *Blue Velvet* (1986; screenwriter Lynch), Frank Booth's heinous behavior includes huffing a strange gas, stroking a swatch of velvet, and blurting "mommy" before assaulting his sex slave. Frank's bizarre behavior isn't motivated in a way that we can easily identify, but his outlandish actions only deepen our fascination with this disturbing movie's vivid mystery.

Characters are frequently motivated by basic psychological needs that can profoundly influence the narrative, even when the character is oblivious of the interior motivation directing his or her behavior. This character need often supports the pursuit of the goal. In John G. Avildson's classic boxing picture *Rocky* (1976, screenwriter Sylvester Stallone), the title character *wants* to win the big fight, but his *need* for self respect compels him to train hard and endure extraordinary physical punishment on his difficult road to the final bell of the championship bout. The narrative goes to great lengths to establish Rocky's need to regain his self-respect. The movie spends 54 minutes detailing Rocky's pathetic existence and degraded social status before he is offered a goal in the form of a serendipitous shot at a title fight. In the end, Rocky loses the big fight, but the audience still feels rewarded because his gutsy performance proves that he has fulfilled his need.

Sometimes, a story may gain a level of complexity by endowing a character with a need that is, in fact, in direct conflict with his goal. C. C. Baxter (Jack Lemmon), the protagonist of Billy Wilder's *The Apartment* (1960; screenwriters Wilder, I. A. L. Diamond), is a lonely man whose job is crunching numbers at a huge insurance company. C. C. *needs* love, but he *wants* to be a big shot. Sick of being a lowly cog in the company machine, C. C. does everything possible to achieve his goal of being promoted to an executive position, including letting his supervisors use his apartment as a base for their illicit affairs. C. C. is disheartened when he discovers that Fran (Shirley MacLaine), the office elevator operator he very much likes, is the mistress his boss Mr. Sheldrake (Fred MacMurray) has been entertaining in C. C.'s apartment. But C. C. continues to pursue his goal, even after he discovers the jilted Fran dying of a drug overdose in a suicide attempt. As he nurses Fran back to health, C. C.'s need for love progressively complicates his pursuit of corporate power. Ultimately, Sheldrake rewards C. C.'s discretion with the long-coveted job promotion, and our hero must choose between his goal and his need.

For the purposes of clarity, we've focused our discussion of character on the protagonist. But, of course, most stories require a number of players. And many of these secondary characters, including those who support or share the protagonist's objective as well as those who oppose it, may have their own goals and needs. Typically, the traits and storylines of these characters are not as developed as that of our protagonist. These characters' primary function is to serve the narrative by helping to move the story forward or flesh out the motivations of the protagonist.

Narrative Structure

Movies use a narrative structure that is very similar to the way that events are organized by novelists,

short-story writers, playwrights, comedians, and other storytellers. In all these cases, the basic formula that has evolved is calculated to engage and satisfy the receiver of the story.

The use of the word *formula* can be misleading. Most stories may follow the same general progression, but narrative is not a single simple recipe. Like pizza, among the many beauties of narrative structure is its malleability. We all know a pizza when we see it, but very few pies look or taste exactly the same. Once the chef knows the basic formula and the purpose of each individual ingredient, she has a certain amount of creative freedom when creating her own personal concoction—as long as it still tastes good when it comes out of the oven. Just as good cooks know when and how to bend the rules, so do the most effective cinematic storytellers recognize how to adjust narrative structure to serve their own particular style and story.

In order to organize story events into a recognizable progression, some screenwriters break the narrative into three acts, or sections; others prefer to divide the action into five acts; others—particularly television writers—employ a seven-act structure. Not that it really matters to the audience. Our experience of the story as a continuous sequence of events is not affected by any particular screenwriter's organizational approach to partitioning the narrative development.[2]

For our purposes, we might as well keep it simple. Most narratives can be broken into three basic pieces that essentially function as the beginning, middle, and end of the story. Each section performs a fundamental narrative task. The first act sets up the story; the second (and longest) act develops it; the third act resolves it. Of course, nothing as expressive and engaging as cinematic storytelling can be quite *that* simple. Each of these narrative components involves a few moving parts.

To begin with, the setup in the first act has to tell us what kind of a story we're about to experience by establishing the **normal world**. A movie's first few minutes lay out the rules of the universe that we will inhabit (or at least witness) for the next couple of hours. Once we as viewers know whether we've entered a world of talking dogs or wartime chaos—or whatever the case may be—we'll know how to appraise and approach the events to come. Our expectations of the story also depend on learning the movie's tone. Are we about to watch a grim drama, a whimsical fantasy, or something else alto-

2. David Howard and Edward Mabley, *The Tools of Screenwriting* (New York: St. Martin's Griffin, 1981), p. 24.

gether? It's up to the events and situations presented in the first act to let us know.

Character, which we already know to be the linchpin of the story, must also be established. The narrative often begins by revealing something about the protagonist's current situation, often by showing him engaged in an action that also reveals some of those essential character traits we discussed earlier in the chapter.

For example, in the Coen brothers' *The Big Lebowski* (1988; screenwriters Joel and Ethan Coen), we first meet Jeff Lebowski (Jeff Bridges)—known to his friends as The Dude—as he shuffles into a supermarket dairy section dressed in sunglasses, pajama shorts, flip-flops, and a well-worn bathrobe. The Dude scrutinizes the assortment like a connoisseur in a wine cellar, then cracks open a carton of half and half to sniff the contents. In the next shot, he pays for his selection with a check for 69 cents.

Before we even learn his name, we know that The Dude is a free spirit who plays by his own rules. He's a slob, is not necessarily smart, and is certainly not ambitious—but he does have standards. Thus we already have some of the essential information we'll need to anticipate and appreciate his particular response to the events and situations the narrative is about to present. We have been initiated into the story's comic, absurdist tone and are also becoming acquainted with the movie's normal world: Jeff Lebowski inhabits a decidedly unglamorous Los Angeles sprawl of dilapidated bungalows, strip malls, and bowling alleys.

Now that the character and his world have been established, it's time to get the story started. For this to happen, something must occur to change that normal world. The inciting incident (also known as the **catalyst**) presents the character with the goal that will drive the rest of the narrative.

In The Dude's case, the inciting incident happens the moment he gets home from the supermarket. Two thugs ambush him, shove his head in the toilet, and demand a large amount of missing money. It turns out that it's a case of mistaken identity—they're looking for a much richer Jeffrey Lebowski. To demonstrate his displeasure with this revelation, one of the attackers urinates on The Dude's beloved rug. The next day, our scruffy little Lebowski goes to see the big Lebowski about getting his rug replaced—and the story has begun.

Most inciting incidents and the resulting character goals are easy to spot. In *Black Swan*, Nina the ballerina is offered a chance at the lead role in *Swan Lake*, so she resolves to dance the part to perfection. When Tom

Establishing the normal world

The first scene of the Coen brothers' cult movie *The Big Lebowski* tells us what we need to know to understand and evaluate the narrative and its inhabitants. This offbeat comedy features a protagonist (Jeff Bridges) who wears a bathrobe in public, samples half and half in the supermarket, and writes checks for 69 cents. We are now armed with an understanding of the character that will help us appreciate The Dude's particular response to the situations the story presents to him.

Chaney guns down Mattie Ross's father in Fort Smith, Arkansas, in *True Grit*, the young girl swears vengeance. Dorothy, the protagonist of *The Wizard of Oz* (1939; director Victor Fleming, screenwriter Noel Langley), realizes that there's no place like home after a tornado deposits her among the munchkins.

Not all goals are this straightforward. Some goals shift—Luke Skywalker sets off to rescue a princess but winds up taking on the Death Star. The Dude sets off to replace a rug and winds up a pawn in someone else's mystery. The goal changes every day for William James, the danger-addicted protagonist of Kathryn Bigelow's Iraq war drama *The Hurt Locker* (2008; screenwriter Mark Boal)—but it's always the same goal: defuse the bomb before it explodes. Ultimately, James's toughest battle is with his own inner demons.

Whatever the goal, the nature of the pursuit depends on the individual character. Nina trains, panics, and sprouts black feathers. Mattie gets on the first train to Fort Smith and scours the frontier town for a lawman with true grit. Dorothy follows the Yellow Brick Road. This active pursuit of the goal signals the beginning of the second act.

The moment Dorothy is off to see the Wizard, the audience begins to ask themselves what screenwriters call the central question: Will she ever get back to Kansas? Whether the question whispers within our subconscious mind or we shout it at the screen, it is this expectation, this impulse to learn what happens and how it happens,

Plot points in *The Grand Budapest Hotel*

Screenwriting specialist Syd Field describes "plot points" as significant events that turn the narrative in a new direction.[3] For example, the development of *The Grand Budapest Hotel* (2014, director/screenwriter Wes Anderson) is profoundly influenced by the death of Madame D. (Tilda Swinton). The plot point leads to her convoluted last will and testament being contested by her greedy heirs, her lover Gustave stealing the priceless painting he believes is rightfully his, and a high-stakes search for the butler accused of her murder [1]. Likewise, the moment when Agatha (Saoirse Ronan) discovers Madame D.'s rightful will hidden in the stolen painting certainly qualifies as a plot point [2]. Gustave inherits her vast fortune, buys the Grand Budapest Hotel, and promotes his faithful protégé Zero (Tony Revolori) to head concierge.

that keeps us engaged with the narrative. We need to know if Nina will learn to let go and embrace the Black Swan inside her—and hold on to her sanity. We must find out if the spunky teenager Mattie can actually manage to wrangle Rooster Cogburn and track down the elusive Tom Chaney. We want to see if Rocky can beat the odds and defeat Apollo Creed to become heavyweight champ.

Naturally, in most cases, we want the answer to the central question to be yes. The irony, however, is that if the goal is quickly and easily attained, our story is over. This is where conflict comes in. Narrative depends on obstacles to block, or at least impede, our protagonist's quest for the goal. The person, people, creature, or force responsible for obstructing our protagonist is known as the **antagonist**. Sometimes, the identity and nature of the antagonist are clear-cut. The Wicked Witch is obviously the antagonist of *The Wizard of Oz* because she sets the scarecrow on fire, conjures a field of sleep-inducing poppies, and imprisons Dorothy. But we have to be careful with this term because, while most movies have a single—or at least primary—protagonist, the nature of the antagonist is much more variable. In *The Big*

Lebowski, The Dude is beaten and bamboozled by a host of oddballs who each use him for their own obscure purposes. Presumably, the fugitive Tom Chaney is the antagonist of *True Grit*. After all, he gunned down Mattie's beloved father. But he doesn't even appear on-screen until the last third of the movie. Before she discovers (and is taken hostage by) Chaney, Mattie's obstacles are imposed by mostly well-meaning characters concerned for the safety of the plucky young heroine. So, just as not every protagonist is a hero, not every antagonist is necessarily a villain. The imposing ballet director in *Black Swan* intimidates and manipulates Nina, but he also sincerely wants her to succeed. The restricted narration makes it difficult to determine any actual malice on the part of Nina's gifted understudy. Even the dark forces represented by Nina's apparent hallucinations play a role in pushing her toward greatness. Nina's greatest adversary is herself.

The antagonist need not even be human. Opposition and obstacles are supplied by a persistent shark in Steven Spielberg's *Jaws* (1975; screenwriters Peter Benchley and Carl Gottlieb); the harsh elements and

3. This description and elements of Figure 4.1 are based on Syd Field, *Screenplay: The Foundations of Screenwriting*, rev. ed. (New York: Delta, 2005), pp. 19–30.

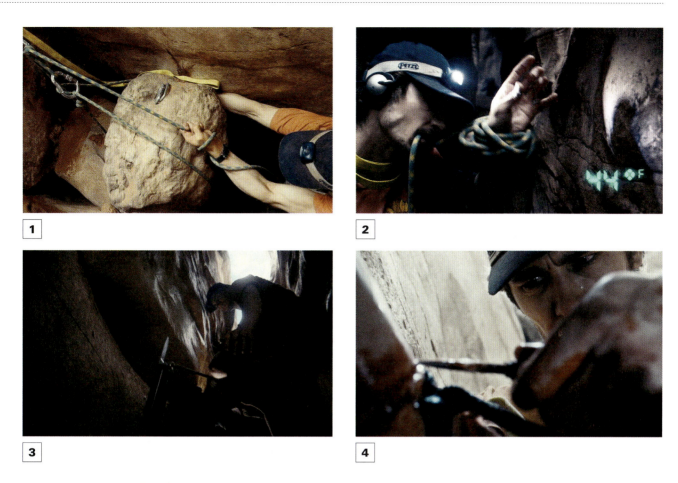

Narrative obstacles in *127 Hours*

Before the Aron Ralston character can finally achieve his narrative goal, he must first engage a series of obstacles. He tries (almost) every possible method of freeing his arm from the stubborn rock pinning it to a remote canyon wall [1], insulates himself from freezing temperatures with his otherwise useless climbing rope [2], and retrieves his dropped multi-tool with his toes [3]. The crisis comes when Aron must take dramatic action or die [4].

isolation of the Andes mountains in Frank Marshall's *Alive* (1993; screenwriter John Patrick Shanley); and a very stubborn rock in Danny Boyle's *127 Hours* (2010; screenwriters Boyle and Simon Beaufoy).

Whatever the source, obstacles are the second act's key ingredient. Let's take a closer look at *127 Hours* to see how obstacles help construct and drive the narrative. We'll start with a quick look at the setup in the first act: In the opening scene, the way the protagonist Aron Ralston (James Franco) packs establishes that he is a loner and an experienced, if overconfident, outdoorsman. As he scrambles around his spartan apartment throwing climbing gear and provisions into a day bag, he doesn't bother to locate his missing Swiss Army knife and ignores a call from his sister. Now that the narration has conveyed some of Aron's flaws, he has some room to grow, and we're prepared to chart and appreciate his development as the adventure unfolds.

Aron ventures into the desert wilds of the remote Canyonlands National Park. Along the way, he reaffirms his character traits by luring two novice hikers to an exhilarating but dangerous plunge into an underground pool before leaving them behind to trek still deeper into the wilderness. In the process of descending a deep slot canyon, Aron dislodges a small boulder. The man and the rock both tumble down the narrow ravine. When they meet again at the bottom, the rock pins Aron's arm to the canyon wall. This sudden event gives our protagonist a goal, supplies the story with conflict and an antagonist, and begins the second act.

The next hour of the movie is devoted to Aron's struggle to free himself. That struggle can be broken down into the series of obstacles he encounters. Aron will overcome some of them, circumvent others, and surrender to still more. Obviously, his tightly wedged arm is Aron's greatest obstacle. He attempts to yank it loose,

Figure 4.1 | NARRATIVE STRUCTURE SCHEMATIC

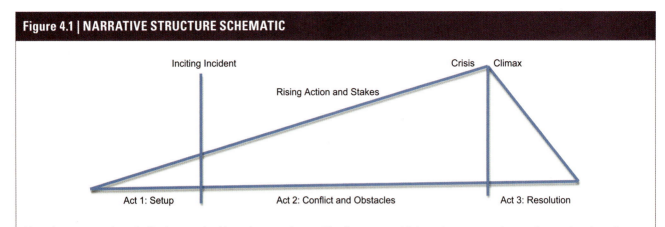

Narrative structure is typically characterized by a three-act format. The first act establishes character, setting, and tone, then introduces a goal with an inciting incident. The second act is structured around the protagonist's pursuit of the goal and the conflict and obstacles that must be confronted before the goal is either gained or lost at the peak of the rising action and stakes. The narrative then falls as the third act resolves the conflict, wraps up ongoing storylines, and gives the viewer a chance to either celebrate or mourn the dramatic result. Diagrams like this are helpful in visualizing a standard structure, but we should keep in mind that the shape any story takes is as flexible as the filmmakers want it to be.

he uses his cheap multi-tool to try to chip away at the rock, and he builds a pulley system with his climbing ropes. Nothing works.

Aron must confront other obstacles as well. When he drops his multi-tool, he retrieves it with a long stick gripped between his toes. He defeats the freezing night temperatures by wrapping his climbing ropes around his legs. He rations his water. As time goes on, Aron must also deal with memories, hallucinations, hopelessness, and regret.

And each time an attempt to dislodge the rock fails or a new obstacle presents itself, the audience asks itself the central question: Will Aron free himself and survive? When his water runs out and he begins to lose his grip on reality, a positive outcome seems increasingly unlikely and the question takes on greater urgency.

This is because the **stakes** are rising. In other words, the deeper we get into the story, the greater the risk to our protagonist. What begins as a possibility of getting lost progresses to the dangers of being trapped, which develops into what appears to be certain death. Of course, the ultimate magnitude of the stakes depends on the movie. By the end of *The Spectacular Now*, a troubled teenager may lose a meaningful friendship. Every life on Earth depends on the mission in *Interstellar* (2014, director Christopher Nolan, screenwriters Jonathan Nolan and Christopher Nolan).

The stakes are rising because the obstacles are becoming increasingly difficult for our protagonist to navigate. Over the course of the second act, narrative typically builds toward a peak, a breaking point of sorts, as the conflict intensifies and the goal remains out of reach. This **rising action** is illustrated in Figure 4.1. The tension it provokes enhances our engagement with the ongoing narrative. As the stakes and action rise in *127 Hours*, Aron undergoes character development. He reevaluates his selfish and solitary lifestyle, appreciates his family, and mourns a squandered relationship. In fact, Aron's encounters with memory provide some of the movie's most meaningful moments.

Eventually, our protagonist must face a seemingly insurmountable obstacle, and our story must reach a turning point and work its way toward resolution and the third and final act. This narrative peak is called the **crisis**. The goal is in its greatest jeopardy, and an affirmative answer to the central question seems all but impossible. In Aron Ralston's case, he's on the verge of death and out of options—almost.

The **climax** comes when the protagonist faces this major obstacle. In the process, usually the protagonist must take a great risk, make a significant sacrifice, or overcome a personal flaw. As the term implies, the climax tends to be the most impressive event in the movie. In *127 Hours*, Aron breaks the bone in his trapped arm, and then saws through what's left with a very dull blade. At the crisis point of *Star Wars: Episode IV—A New Hope* (1977; director/screenwriter George Lucas), Luke Skywalker's fellow fighter pilots have been decimated and the Death Star is within range of the rebel stronghold, so Luke uses the Force to drop two proton torpedoes into the evil Empire's exposed orifice. At the climax of *Black Swan*, Nina realizes she's been stabbed (by herself—it's complicated), but she dances onto the stage and gives the performance of her career.

Once the goal is either gained or lost, it's time for the **resolution**—the third act of falling action, in which the narrative wraps up loose ends and moves toward a conclusion. For some protagonists, the struggle continues well into this final act. After being trapped for 127 hours and amputating his own arm, Aron must still strike out in search of help. In *True Grit*, the recoil from the rifle that dispatches Chaney propels Mattie into a snake pit. She has to endure being bitten on the arm by rattlesnakes and carted across the prairie to a distant doctor. But sooner or later, virtually every story resolves the conflict and allows the audience a chance to celebrate and/or contemplate the final score before the credits roll. We see footage showing the real-life Aron Ralston (yes, it's a true story) as an active hiker with a wife and child. Luke, in blissful ignorance of his family history, enjoys a kiss from the princess. Surrounded by her adoring director and fellow dancers, the black swan declares her perfection. An elderly (and one-armed) Mattie pays homage to the crusty U.S. marshal whose true grit saved her life. Rocky hugs his girlfriend. The Dude abides—and bowls.

The Screenwriter

The screenwriter is responsible for coming up with this story, either from scratch or by adapting another source, such as a novel, play, memoir, or news story. Screenwriters build the narrative structure and devise every character, action, line of dialogue, and setting. And all this must be managed with the fewest words possible. Screenplay format is precisely prescribed—right down to page margins and font style and size—so that each script page represents one minute of screen time. The best screenwriters learn to craft concise but vivid descriptions of essential information so as to provide the director, cinematographer, designers, and actors a practical foundation that informs the collaborative creative process necessary to adapt the script to the screen. Many scripts are even described and arranged to take a step beyond written storytelling and suggest specific im-

ages, juxtapositions, and sequences. No rules determine how an idea should be developed or an existing literary property should be adapted into a film script, but the process usually consists of several stages and involves many rewrites. Likewise, no rule dictates the number of people who are eventually involved in the process. One person may write all the stages of the screenplay or may collaborate from the beginning with other screenwriters; sometimes the director is the sole screenwriter or co-screenwriter.

Before the breakdown of the Hollywood studio system and the emergence of the independent film, each of the major studios maintained its own staff of writers, each of whom were assigned ideas depending on their particular specialty and experience. Every writer was responsible by contract to write a specified number of films each year. Today, most scripts are written entirely by independent screenwriters (either as write-for-hires or on spec) and submitted as polished revisions. Many other screenplays, especially for movies created for mass appeal, are written by committee, meaning a collaboration of director, producer, editor, and others, including *script doctors* (professional screenwriters who are hired to review a screenplay and improve it). Whether working alone or in collaboration with others, a screenwriter significantly influences the screenplay and the completed movie and, thus, its artistic, critical, and box office success.

When the director is also the screenwriter, the screenplay is more likely to reflect and convey a consistent vision. This is true of films by directors such as François Truffaut, Werner Herzog, Chantal Akerman, Joel and Ethan Coen, Woody Allen, Akira Kurosawa, John Ford, and Satyajit Ray, to name a very few.

Seminars, books, and software programs may promise to teach the essentials of screenwriting overnight, but becoming a professional screenwriter requires innate talents and skills that can be enhanced by experience. Such skills include understanding the interaction of story, plot, and narrative; being able to write visually (meaning not only putting a world on the page but also foreseeing it on the screen); and being able to create characters and dialogue. Screenwriters must understand the conventions and expectations of the various genres, work within deadlines that are often unreasonable, and be able to collaborate, particularly with the producer and director, and to anticipate that their original ideas may be extensively and even radically altered before the shooting starts. In addition to creating a compelling story, engaging plot, and fascinating characters, screenwriters must have a solid understanding of what is marketable. Finally, if they are presenting a finished screenplay, it must conform to industry expectations regarding format and style.

Elements of Narrative

Narrative theory (sometimes called *narratology*) has a long history, starting with Aristotle and continuing with great vigor today. Aristotle said that a good story should have three sequential parts: a beginning, a middle, and an end—a concept that has influenced the history of playwriting and screenwriting. French New Wave director Jean-Luc Godard, who helped revolutionize cinematic style in the 1950s, agreed that a story should have a beginning, a middle, and an end—but, he added, "not necessarily in that order." Given the cinema's extraordinary freedom and flexibility in handling time (especially compared to the limited ways the theater can handle time), the directors of some of the most challenging movies ever made—including many contemporary examples—would seem to agree with Godard.

The complexities of narratology are beyond the scope of this book,[4] but we can begin our study by distinguishing between two fundamental elements: story and plot.

Story and Plot

Although in everyday conversation we might use the words *story* and *plot* interchangeably, they mean different things when we write and speak about movies. A movie's **story** consists of (1) all the narrative events that are explicitly presented on-screen plus (2) all the events that are implicit or that we infer to have happened but are not explicitly presented. The total world of the story—the events, characters, objects, settings, and sounds that form the world in which the story occurs—is called its **diegesis**, and the elements that make up the diegesis are called **diegetic elements**.

In the first scene of *The Social Network* (2010; director David Fincher, screenwriter Aaron Sorkin), we see

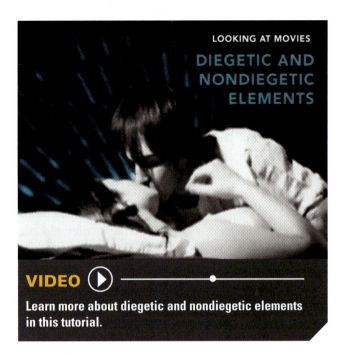

LOOKING AT MOVIES

DIEGETIC AND NONDIEGETIC ELEMENTS

VIDEO ▶

Learn more about diegetic and nondiegetic elements in this tutorial.

Mark Zuckerberg (Jesse Eisenberg) and Erica Albright (Rooney Mara) sitting together in a crowded bar. They are having a heated conversation—at least it's heated on one side. Mark is chattering a rapid-fire monologue involving SAT scores in China and rowing crew; Erica is struggling to clarify what exactly he's talking about. Everything we experience in this scene is part of the movie's diegesis, including the other bar patrons and the muffled dissonance of the crowd's chatter mixed with the White Stripes' "Ball and Biscuit" playing on an unseen jukebox. Of course, we pay special attention to what the featured characters say and how they look saying it. From this explicitly presented information, we are able to infer still more story information that we have not witnessed on-screen. They've been here a while—their beers are half empty, and they're in the middle of an ongoing conversation—and they're a couple. Watching their interaction, we can even guess the nature and duration of Mark and Erica's relationship. As the conversation intensifies, we can pick up on still more implicit information. Mark is obsessed with getting into a prestigious student club—his intensity implies that he is not exactly popular with the elite crowd. We learn Mark is going to Harvard and that he looks down on Erica for merely attending lowly (in his eyes) Boston University.

4. This discussion of narrative theory adapts material from, and is indebted to, Seymour Chatman, *Story and Discourse: Narrative Structure in Fiction and Film* (Ithaca, NY: Cornell University Press, 1978) and *Coming to Terms: The Rhetoric of Narrative in Fiction and Film* (Ithaca, NY: Cornell University Press, 1990). Other works of contemporary narrative theory are recommended in the bibliography at the end of this book.

The tone of her angry retort about Mark's Long Island roots lets us imagine a relatively humble upbringing that might be fueling his need for prestige. The story includes everything in the diegesis, every event and action we've seen on-screen, as well as everything we can infer from watching those events.

The **plot** consists of the specific actions and events that the filmmakers select and the order in which they arrange those events to effectively convey the narrative to the viewer. In this scene, what the characters do on-screen is part of the *plot*, including when Erica breaks up with Mark and stalks off, but the other information we infer from their exchange belongs exclusively to the *story*.

The distinction between plot and story is complicated because in every movie, the two concepts overlap and interact with one another. Let's continue exploring the subject by following the jilted Mark as he slinks out of the bar and makes his way back to his dorm. In this sequence, we hear the diegetic sounds of evening traffic, the tread of Mark's sneakers, and the muted chatter of his fellow pedestrians. We watch Mark trudge past the pub, trot across a busy street and down a crowded sidewalk, and jog across campus. As we can see in Figure 4.2, these *explicitly presented events*, and every image and sound they produce, are included in the intersection of story and plot.

But remember that story also incorporates those events *implied* by what we see (and hear) on-screen. In this particular sequence, implied events might involve the portions of Mark's journey that were not captured in any of the shots used to portray his journey. In addition, everything we infer from these images and sounds,

from the supremacy of the great university to the sophistication of the young scholars strolling its campus, is strictly story. The plot concerns only those portions of his journey necessary to effectively convey the Ivy League setting and the narrative idea of Mark's hurrying faster and faster the closer he gets to the sanctuary of his dorm room.

But the plot supplies more than simply this particular arrangement of these specific events. Plot also includes **nondiegetic elements**: those things we see and hear on the screen that come from outside the world of the story, such as score music (music not originating from the world of the story), titles and credits (words superimposed on the images on-screen), and voice-over comments from a third-person voice-over narrator.

For example, back in the bar, moments after Erica storms out, music begins to play over the shot of Mark alone at the table. This music is not the White Stripes song we heard in the background earlier in the scene. Whereas that *diegetic* music came from a jukebox from within the world of the story, this new music is *nondiegetic* score music that the filmmakers have imposed onto the movie to add narrative meaning to the sequence. The music begins as lilting piano notes that help convey the sadness Mark feels after getting unexpectedly dumped. Deeper, darker notes join the score as the music continues over Mark's journey home, allowing us to sense the thoughts of vengeance intruding on Mark's hurt feelings. As he trots up the steps to his dorm, a title announces the time and place of our story: Harvard University *Fall 2003*. These nondiegetic elements—score music and titles—are not part of the story. But they are an important piece of the plot: the deliberate selection

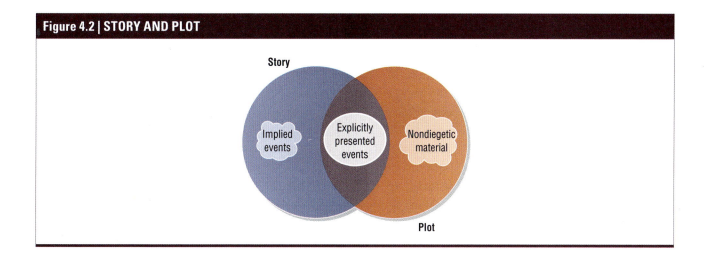

Figure 4.2 | STORY AND PLOT

1

2

3

4

5

Plot and story in *The Social Network*

The deliberate structure of selected events, as well as nondiegetic elements such as a rhythmic musical score and titles marking the passage of time, comprise the *plot* that delivers the *story* of Mark Zuckerberg's social networking epiphany. Causality guides the filmmakers' plot choices: Mark gets a diabolical idea [1], downloads dormitory resident photos [2], uses computer code and an algorithm to create an online game comparing relative female hotness [3], which rapidly escalates into an Internet sensation [4] that crashes the Harvard network—which delights Mark [5]. The specific events and their particular arrangement are plot; the events, along with other actions and meaning they imply but don't show, are the story.

and arrangement of specific events and elements the filmmakers employ to deliver the narrative.

A new sequence begins when Mark arrives home, cracks open a beer, and sits at his laptop. The next 8 minutes of *The Social Network* depict his discovery of the Internet's latent power to enthrall and connect its users.

The *story* conveyed in those 8 minutes includes the following: still stinging from Erica's rejection, Mark blogs a blistering critique of his now ex-girlfriend. Then, an offhand comment from one of his roommates gives Mark an idea. What if he could create a way for other students to compare pairs of female Harvard students and vote on which woman is hotter? Mark hacks into each of the university's dormitory "Face Book" photo rosters and downloads every possible female resident photo. His friend Eduardo (Andrew Garfield), having read Mark's blog, drops by to console him and winds up getting pressured into creating an algorithm to auto-

matically select and pair photos, then collate and come up with new pairings based on the results. Mark and Eduardo write the necessary code, and "Facemash" goes up on the campus network. Students all across Harvard discover and play and recommend Facemash. The explosion of online participation crashes the university's computer network.

Every event implied by the previous description, including every line of code Mark must write, every gathering happening across campus, every student who plays Facemash, every relative hotness vote they cast, and every roommate cheering them on or reacting with disgust are part of that *story*.

The filmmakers use *plot* to tell us that story. We can't possibly see every line of code, every game of Facemash, every campus activity interrupted and enlivened by the new Internet sensation. So specific events and elements are selected and ordered to present the cause-

1

2

Narrative form and the biopic

A biographical movie, or biopic, provides particularly rich opportunities to ask why the filmmakers chose to tell the story the way they did. After all, the facts of the main character's life are objectively verifiable and follow a particular order. But as two recent biopics about the beat poet Allen Ginsberg demonstrate, cinematic storytellers can select and shape that material in many different ways to convey a variety of narrative experiences and interpretations. *Howl* (2010; director Rob Epstein, screenwriters Epstein and Jeffrey Friedman) presents key ideas, sounds, and images from Ginsberg's life and work in a way that rejects the chronological order and cause-and-effect progression we expect from most narrative films. Stylized flashbacks from the poet's earlier life, Ginsberg (James Franco) performing his epic poem "Howl" [1], animation evoking the poem's imagery, and testimony in the obscenity trial incited by the ground-breaking poem are all juxtaposed in a fragmented montage that is just as interested in capturing the spirit of Ginsberg's poetry as it is with presenting a slice of his life. *Kill Your Darlings* (2013; director John Krokidas, screenwriters Krokidas and Austin Bunn) is a more conventional coming-of-age narrative that chronicles the young Ginsburg's first year at Columbia University in New York. Young Ginsburg (Daniel Radcliffe) [2] breaks free of his dysfunctional family, is drawn into the orbit of proudly decadent literary rebels, has a sexual awakening, gets his heart broken, and witnesses a crime of passion. Like many biopics, this narrative provides not just a compelling story; it offers viewers a revealing (and often fictionalized) peek at the events and associations that helped form a famous persona.

and-effect chain of events that enables the audience to experience and understand the narrative. Our engagement with the story on-screen is enhanced by the nondiegetic elements the plot layers onto this particular sequence of selected events, including a pulsating musical score and occasional titles announcing the time as the phenomenon spreads.

And, of course, the story and the plot overlap. Every event explicitly presented on-screen, and every diegetic sound generated by those events, qualifies as both story *and* plot.

The relationship between plot and story is important to filmmakers and to the audience. From the filmmaker's perspective, the story exists as a precondition for the plot, and the filmmaker must understand what story is being told before going through the difficult job of selecting events to show on-screen and determining in what order to present them. For us as viewers, the story is an abstraction—a construct—that we piece together as the elements of the plot unfold before us on-screen. Our impressions about the story often shift and adjust throughout the movie as more of the plot is revealed. The plots of some movies—classic murder mysteries, for example—lead us to an unambiguous sense of the story

by the time they are done. Other movies' plots reveal very little about the causal relationships among narrative events, thus leaving us to puzzle over those connections, to construct the story ourselves.

As you view movies more critically and analytically, pay attention not only to the story as you have inferred it but also to how it was conveyed through its plot. Understanding this basic distinction will help you to better appreciate and analyze the overall form of the movie.

To picture the relationship between plot and story slightly differently, and to become more aware of the deliberate ways in which filmmakers construct plots from stories, you might watch several different movies that tell a story you are familiar with—for example, Walt Disney's *Cinderella* (1950; screenwriters Ken Anderson et al.), Frank Tashlin's *Cinderfella* (1960, starring Jerry Lewis; screenwriter Tashlin), Garry Marshall's *Pretty Woman* (1990, starring Julia Roberts; screenwriter J. F. Lawton), Andy Tennant's *Ever After* (1998, starring Drew Barrymore; screenwriters Susannah Grant, Tennant, and Rick Parks), John Pasquin's *Miss Congeniality 2: Armed and Fabulous* (2005, starring Sandra Bullock; screenwriters Marc Lawrence, Katie Ford, and Caryn Lucas), and Kenneth Branagh's *Cinderella* (2015, starring

Lily James; screenwriter Chris Weitz). All of these movies rely on the basic story structure of the well-known fairy tale. This sort of critical comparison will enable you to see more clearly how the plots differ, how the formal decisions made by the filmmakers have shaped those differences, and how the overall form of each movie alters your perception of the underlying story.

When James Cameron planned to make a movie about the sinking of the HMS *Titanic*, he had to contend with the fact that there were already three feature films on the subject, as well as numerous television movies and documentaries. Moreover, everyone knew the story.

Adaptation of literary sources

David Lean's *Great Expectations* (1946; screenwriters Anthony Havelock-Allan, Lean, Cecil McGivern, Ronald Neame, and Kay Walsh) [1] takes place, as Dickens's novel does, in nineteenth-century England. The young protagonist (John Mills, *left*), a student in London named Pip (as in the novel), confronts his previously anonymous benefactor, Magwitch (Finlay Currie). Fifty-two years later, Alfonso Cuarón's version of the same story (*Great Expectations*, 1998; screenwriter Mitch Glazer) [2] is set in contemporary America. Finn (Ethan Hawke, *right*), a painter in New York City, confronts his previously anonymous benefactor, Arthur Lustig (Robert De Niro). An analysis of the differences between these two adaptations of the same novel can lead you to a deeper appreciation of the power of filmmakers' decisions regarding plot specifically and film form more generally.

So he created a narrative structure that was based on a **backstory**, a fictional history behind the situation existing at the start of the main story: the story of Rose Calvert's diamond. That device, as well as a powerful romantic story and astonishing special effects, made his *Titanic* (1997) one of the greatest box office hits in history.

Through plot, screenwriters and directors can give structure to stories and guide (if not control) viewers' emotional responses. In fact, a plot may be little more than a sequence of devices for arousing predictable responses of concern and excitement in audiences. We accept such a plot because we know it will lead to the resolution of conflicts, mysteries, and frustrations in the story.

Movies have always looked to literature as a proven source of narrative, style, and cultural resonance—as well as a built-in audience of readers eager to experience a favorite book on the big screen. For example, over 250 movies—many of them masterpieces in their own right—have been made from Shakespeare's plays, and producers continue to find imaginative ways of bringing other literary classics to the screen. In the last few years alone, cinematic adaptations have been made of the works of distinguished writers like Charlotte Brontë (*Jane Eyre*, 2011; director Cary Fukunaga), F. Scott Fitzgerald (*The Great Gatsby*, 2014; director Baz Luhrmann), and Thomas Pynchon (*Inherent Vice*, 2014; director Paul Thomas Anderson). *12 Years a Slave* (director Steve McQueen), the 2014 Best Picture Oscar winner, was adapted from a previously obscure but historically significant memoir by the abolitionist Solomon Northup. Popular films like *The Hunger Games*, *Gone Girl* (2014; director David Fincher) and *Fifty Shades of Grey* (2015; director Sam Taylor-Johnson) have been adapted from popular fiction. Some of the most popular films in recent history are adapted from comic books. Marvel Studios, a subsidiary of The Walt Disney Company, was formed to exploit Marvel Comic's huge accumulated (and copyrighted) library of characters and storylines. The company has released ten comic book adaptations since 2008's *Iron Man*, and has dozens more adaptations planned for the next fifteen years.

Movies are, by their nature, different from the books on which they are based. Peter Jackson's Lord of the Rings trilogy (2001–3) is relatively faithful to the spirit of J. R. R. Tolkien's novels, but Jackson had to eliminate or combine certain characters, details, and events in order to squeeze over 1,000 pages of source material into three movies. Jackson's subsequent decision to expand Tolkien's whimsical short novel *The Hobbit* into three epic movies had an opposite adaptation effect. Jackson and his fellow screenwriters (Fran Walsh, Philippa Boyens, and Guillermo del Toro) invented characters, inflated action sequences, and inserted new plot lines—including a tragic love story between and elf and a dwarf, and a revenge-fueled feud between the leader of the dwarves and an Orc chieftain. *The Hobbit: The Battle of the Five Armies* (2014) stretches a relatively modest five-page battle into a bombastic hour-long melee involving ten times the combatants described in the novel.[5]

Order

Bringing order to the plot events is one of the most fundamental decisions that filmmakers make about relaying story information through the plot. Most narrative film plots are structured in chronological order. But, unlike story order, which necessarily flows chronologically (as does life), plot order can be manipulated so that events are presented in nonchronological sequences that emphasize importance or meaning or that establish desired expectations in audiences. *Citizen Kane* (1941; director Orson Welles) presents the biography of Charles Foster Kane, a fictional character inspired by media mogul William Randolph Hearst. Welles and his co-screenwriter Herman J. Mankiewicz adopted an approach to plot order so radical for its time that it actually bewildered many viewers. The movie's plot consists of nine sequences, five of which are flashbacks. The film opens with Kane's death, followed by a newsreel that summarizes the major events of Kane's life in more or less chronological order. A third sequence introduces us to Mr. Thompson, a reporter assigned to get additional information about Kane's life—primarily about the meaning of his last word: "Rosebud." Thompson's subsequent investigation is a kind of detective story; each of the five sources he interviews or examines reveals a different perspective on different periods in Kane's life. The order of these sequences is determined not by chronology, but by the order of Thompson's investigation and the memory of his interview subjects. Just as Thompson tries to assemble clues about Kane's life, the audience

Plot order in *Citizen Kane*

To provide a straightforward account of Charles Foster Kane's life and help viewers get their bearings within a highly unconventional plot order, Orson Welles's *Citizen Kane* (1941) begins with a fictionalized mini-documentary. "News on the March" is a satire on the famous weekly newsreel series *The March of Time* (1935–51). The series, shown in movie theaters, mixed location footage with dramatic reenactments. Using this culturally familiar narrative device as an anchor for the rest of the movie, Welles tried to ensure that viewers wouldn't lose their way in the overall plot.

must assemble the jumbled chronology in which it is presented. The viewer participation required makes watching Citizen Kane an engaging, if sometimes disorienting, participatory experience. What's more, once freed from strict chronological order, Welles and Mankiewicz were able to juxtapose events in a way that provided additional context and meaning. For example, having just watched Kane die alone, we comprehend the significance of his leaving home at age eight on a level that would not have been possible if that earlier incident had been presented first. Likewise, our enjoyment of seeing Kane's exuberant idealism when he buys his first newspaper in 1892 is tempered by having previously watched him lose control of his media empire after the 1929 stock market crash.

However challenging it was for its time, the plot structure of *Citizen Kane* has been so influential that it is now considered conventional. One of the many movies that it influenced is Quentin Tarantino's *Pulp Fiction* (1994; screenwriters Tarantino and Roger Avary). The plot of *Pulp Fiction*, which is full of surprises, is constructed in

5. Rachel Nuwer, "The Tolkien Nerd's Guide to 'The Hobbit: The Battle of the Five Armies,'" December 19, 2014, www.Smithsonianmag.com (accessed February 9, 2015).

Plot order in *Memento*

In Christopher Nolan's *Memento* (2000), Leonard Shelby (Guy Pearce) suffers from a disorder that prevents him from forming short-term memories. To remember details of his life, he takes Polaroid snapshots, jots notes on scraps of paper, and even tattoos "The Facts" on his body. The movie's two-stranded plot order, both chronological and reverse chronological, likewise challenges us to recall what we've seen and how the parts fit together.

a nonlinear way and fragments the passing of time. We might have to see the movie several times before being able to say, for instance, at what point—in the plot and in the story—Vincent Vega (John Travolta) dies.

Christopher Nolan's *Memento* (2000) and Gaspar Noe's *Irreversible* (2002) take manipulation of plot order to the extreme by presenting the events in their respective narratives in reverse chronological order. Each film opens with the story's concluding event, then works its way backward to the occurrence that initiated the cause-and-effect chain. By inverting the sequence in which the audience is accustomed to experiencing events—in life as well as in movies—*Memento* and *Irreversible* essentially challenge viewers to relearn how to align expectation and decipher narrative context. We experience each presented event not in light of the string of actions and reactions that led up to it; our understanding comes only from what happened *after* the action we're currently watching. We start with resolution and work our way toward the inciting incident. In the case of *Memento*, our ignorance of previous events helps us identify with the limited perspective of the movie's protagonist, Leonard (Guy Pearce)—a man incapable of forming new memories.

In Akira Kurosawa's *Rashomon* (1950; screenwriters Kurosawa and Shinobu Hashimoto), we see an innovative variation on the idea of plot order. The same story—the rape of a woman—is told from four different points of view: a bandit, the woman, her husband, and a woodcutter (the only witness of the rape). Kurosawa's

purpose is to show us that we all remember and perceive differently, thus challenging our notions of perception and truth.

Events

In any plot, events have a logical order, as we've discussed, as well as a logical hierarchy. Some events are more important than others, and we infer their relative significance through the director's selection and arrangement of details of action, character, or setting. This hierarchy consists of (1) the events that seem crucial to the plot (and thus to the underlying story) and (2) the events that play a less crucial or even subordinate role.

The first category includes those major events or branching points in the plot structure that force characters to choose between or among alternate paths. Damien Chazelle's *Whiplash* (2014) tells the story of Andrew (Miles Teller), a talented young drummer who struggles to earn the approval of his demanding and abusive teacher Terrance Fletcher (J. K. Simmons). Andrew's performance in first-year band practice impresses Fletcher, who offers him a coveted spot in his studio band. Later, Fletcher humiliates Andrew for his inability to keep time on a challenging piece, so Andrew practices until his fingers bleed. Each following stage in the plot turns on such events, which force Andrew to take action and make consequential choices.

The second category includes those minor plot events that add texture and complexity to characters and actions but are not essential elements within the narrative. Andrew's relationships with people outside the competitive world of jazz performance create subordinate events. His submissive father, the antithesis of the domineering Fletcher, takes Andrew to old movies. Brimming with newfound confidence after a successful rehearsal, Andrew asks Nicole, the young woman working the concession stand, on a date. Later, Andrew's arrogance embarrasses his father; his ambition compels him to break up with Nicole. These minor or subordinate events enrich and complicate the diegesis (the world of the story) in a narrative film, but no single such event is indispensable to the story.

When filmmakers make decisions about which scenes to cut from a film during the editing phase, they generally look for minor events that, for one reason or another, don't contribute enough to the overall movie. As a critical viewer of movies, you can use this hierarchy

Hierarchy of events in *Whiplash*
In Damien Chazelle's *Whiplash* (2014), the student drummer Andrew impresses the school's most demanding teacher, who invites him to join the competitive studio band and thus sets the plot in motion [1]. Andrew's awkward romance with a woman outside the cutthroat culture of his music academy informs the plot through a series of minor events. Her conventional values lend perspective to Andrew's obsessive pursuit of percussion virtuosity [2].

of events in diagramming a plot (as a practical way of understanding it) or charting a course of the major and minor events confronting the characters.

Duration

Events, in life and in the movies, take time to occur. **Duration** is this length of time. When talking about narrative movies specifically, we can identify three specific kinds of duration: **story duration** is the amount of time that the implied story takes to occur; **plot duration** is the elapsed time of those events within the story that the film explicitly presents (in other words, the elapsed time of the plot); and **screen duration** is the movie's running time on-screen. In *Citizen Kane*, the plot duration is approximately one week (the duration of Thompson's search), the story duration is more than seventy years (the span of Kane's life), and the screen duration is

1 hour 59 minutes, the time it takes us to watch the film from beginning to end without interruption.

These distinctions are relatively simple in *Citizen Kane*, but the three-part relation of story, plot, and screen duration can become quite complex in some movies. Balancing the three elements is especially complex for a filmmaker because the screen duration is necessarily constrained by financial and other considerations. Movies may have become longer on average over the years, but filmmakers still must present their stories within a relatively short span of time. Because moviegoers generally regard films that run more than three hours as too long, such movies risk failure at the box office. Figure 4.3 illustrates the relationship between story duration and plot duration in a hypothetical movie. The story duration in this illustration—one week—is depicted in a plot that covers four discrete but crucial days in that week.

The relationships among the three types of duration can be isolated and analyzed, not only in the context of the entire narrative of the film but also within its constituent parts—in scenes and sequences. In these smaller parts, however, the relationship between plot duration and story duration generally remains stable; in most mainstream Hollywood movies, the duration of a plot event is assumed to be equivalent to the duration of the story event that it implies. At the level of scenes (a complete unit of plot action), the more interesting relationship is usually between screen duration and plot duration. We can generally characterize that relationship in one of three ways: (1) in a **summary relationship**, screen duration is shorter than plot duration; (2) in **real time**, screen duration corresponds directly to plot duration; and (3) in a **stretch relationship**, screen duration is longer than plot duration.

Both stretch and summary relationships are established primarily through editing techniques (discussed in detail in Chapter 8). The summary relationship is very familiar and occurs much more frequently in mainstream movies than do the other two. The summary relationship is depicted in Figure 4.4, which illustrates one scene in our hypothetical movie; the screen duration of this scene is 10 minutes, but the implied duration of the plot event is 4 hours.

In *Citizen Kane*, Welles depicts the steady disintegration of Kane's first marriage to Emily Norton (Ruth Warrick) through a rapid montage of six shots at the breakfast table that take two minutes on the screen

Figure 4.3 | DURATION: STORY VERSUS PLOT

Imagine a hypothetical movie that follows the lives of two people over the course of one week, starting with the moment that they first move into an apartment together as a couple and ending with their parting of ways seven days later.

Story duration = 1 week

Day 1   Day 3   Day 5   Day 7

Plot duration = 4 days out of that week

Although the movie's implied story duration is one week, the events that are explicitly part of the movie's plot take place during four discrete days within that week (the plot duration). Day 1 in the plot shows the couple moving and settling in. Day 3 shows them already squabbling. Day 5 shows the misguided couple getting ready for and throwing a housewarming party that concludes with a disastrous (but hilarious) argument. Day 7 shows them moving out and then having an amicable dinner over which they agree that the only way they can live with each other is by living apart.

Figure 4.4 | DURATION: PLOT VERSUS SCREEN

One portion of the plot in this hypothetical movie involves the housewarming party thrown by our ill-fated couple. The implied duration of this event (the plot duration) is 4 hours—from 8:00 in the evening to midnight of Day 5.

8:00 PM   Midnight

Day 5

Plot duration = 4 hours

Although the implied duration of the plot event is 4 hours, the actual duration on-screen of the shots that cover this 4-hour event is only 10 minutes (the screen duration). As you can see below, those 10 minutes are divided among 15 discrete shots, each of which features a specific event or discussion at the party.

Screen duration = 15 individual shots = 10 minutes

but depict seven years of their life together. Through changes in dress, hairstyle, seating, and their preferences in newspapers, we see the couple's relationship go from amorous passion to sarcastic hostility. Summary relationships are essential to telling movie stories, especially long and complicated ones.

Because it is less common than summary, the stretch relationship is often used to highlight a plot event, stressing its importance to the overall narrative. A stretch relationship can be achieved by special effects such as slow motion, particularly when a graceful effect is needed, as in showing a reunited couple running slowly toward one another. It can also be constructed

by editing techniques. The "Odessa Steps" sequence in Sergei Eisenstein's *Battleship Potemkin* (1925; screenwriters Nina Agadzhanova, Nikolai Aseyev, Eisenstein, and Sergei Tretyakov) uses editing to stretch the plot duration of the massacre: selected single moments are broken up into multiple shots that are overlapped and repeated so that our experience of each event on-screen lasts longer than it would have in reality. Eisenstein does this because he wants us to see the massacre as an important and meaningful event, as well as to increase our anxiety and empathy for the victims.

The real-time relationship is the least common of the three relationships between screen duration and plot

Real-time relationship in *Timecode*

Mike Figgis's *Timecode* (2000; screenwriter Figgis) offers a dramatic and daring version of real time. Split into quarters, the screen displays four distinct but overlapping stories, each shot in one continuous 93-minute take (the length of an ordinary digital videocassette), uninterrupted by editing.

Real-time relationship in *Birdman*

An innovative melding of summary and real-time relationships of plot to screen time compels viewers of *Birdman* (2014; director Alejandro González Iñárritu) to experience the same sort of over-stimulated exhaustion endured by Riggan (Michael Keaton), the film's protagonist. In a desperate attempt to restore his reputation, the former superhero franchise movie star is directing and starring in a Broadway play—and it's not going well. Riggan's last-ditch efforts to pull the play (and his life) together are presented in what appears (thanks to hidden edits) to be one very long continuous shot. Watching the movie, our visual senses—and our ingrained cinematic experience—tell us that this unbroken flow of action must represent a real-time relationship between plot and screen duration, but we soon realize that this single shot sneakily slides between and through multiple scenes that take place at different times: an actor injured in rehearsal, the arrival of his hot-shot replacement, a humiliating publicity interview, a disastrous preview performance, and on and on. What looks and feels like a real-time relationship is actually a summary relationship. The constant struggle to process a summary relationship disguised as a real-time relationship lets the viewer experience something comparable to Riggan's manic multitasking.

duration, but its use has always interested and delighted film buffs. Many directors use real time within films to create uninterrupted "reality" on the screen, but directors rarely use it for entire films. Alfred Hitchcock's *Rope* (1948; screenwriter Arthur Laurents) is famous for presenting a real-time relationship between screen and plot duration. In *Rope*, Hitchcock used the long take (discussed further in Chapter 6)—an unedited, continuous shot—to preserve real time. One roll of motion-picture film can record approximately 11 minutes of action, and thus Hitchcock made an 80-minute film with ten shots that range in length from 4 minutes 40 seconds to 10 minutes.[6] Six of the cuts between these shots are virtually unnoticeable because Hitchcock has the camera pass behind the backs of people or furniture and then makes the cut on a dark screen; four others are ordinary hard cuts from one person to another. Even these hard cuts do not break time or space, so the result is fluid storytelling in which the plot duration equals the screen duration of 80 minutes.

In most traditional narrative movies, cuts and other editing devices punctuate the flow of the narrative and

graphically indicate that the images occur in human-made **cinematic time**, not seamless real time. As viewers, we think that movies pass before us in the present tense, but we also understand that cinematic time can be manipulated through editing, among other means. As we accept these manipulative conventions, we also recognize that classic Hollywood editing generally goes out of its way to avoid calling attention to itself. What's more, it attempts to reflect the natural mental processes by which human consciousness moves back and forth between reality and illusion, shifting between past, present, and future.

6. Various critics have said that each shot in *Rope* lasts 10 minutes, but the DVD release of the film shows the timings (rounded off) to be as follows: opening credits, 2:09; shot 1, 9:50; shot 2, 8:00; shot 3, 7:50; shot 4, 7:09; shot 5, 10:00; shot 6, 7:40; shot 7, 8:00; shot 8, 10:00; shot 9, 4:40; shot 10, 5:40; closing credits, 00:28.

Summary relationship

A sequence in Martin Scorsese's *Raging Bull* (1980; screenwriters Paul Schrader and Mardik Martin) covers three years (story duration) in a few minutes (screen duration). Black-and-white shots of Jake La Motta's (Robert De Niro) most significant boxing matches from 1944 to 1947 are intercut with color shots from home movies that show La Motta and his second wife, Vickie (Cathy Moriarty), during the early years of their marriage.

Suspense versus Surprise

It's important to distinguish between suspense, which has been mentioned in the preceding discussions, and surprise. Although they are often confused, suspense and surprise are two fundamentally different elements in the development of many movie plots. Alfred Hitchcock mastered the unique properties of each, taking great care to ensure that they were integral to the internal logic of his plots. In a conversation with French director François Truffaut, Hitchcock explained the terms:

> We are now having a very innocent little chat. Let us suppose that there is a bomb underneath this table between us. Nothing happens, and then all of a sudden, "Boom!"
>
> There is an explosion. The public is *surprised,* but prior to this surprise, it has seen an absolutely ordinary scene of no special consequence. Now, let us take a *suspense* situation. The bomb is underneath the table and the public *knows* it, probably because they have seen the anarchist place it there. The public is *aware* that the bomb is going to explode at one o'clock and there is a clock in the decor. The public can see that it is a quarter to one. In these conditions this same innocuous conversation becomes fascinating because the public is participating in the scene. The audience is longing to warn the characters on the screen: "You shouldn't be talking about such trivial matters. There's a bomb beneath you and it's about to explode!"
>
> In the first scene we have given the public fifteen seconds of *surprise* at the moment of the explosion. In the second we have provided them with fifteen minutes of *suspense.* The conclusion is that whenever possible the public must be informed. Except when the surprise is a twist, that is, when the unexpected ending is, in itself, the highlight of the story.[7]

Because there are no repeat surprises, we can be surprised in the same way only once. As a result, a **surprise**, being taken unawares, can be shocking, and our emotional response to it is generally short-lived. By contrast, **suspense** is a more drawn-out (and, some would say, more enjoyable) experience, one that we may seek out even when we know what happens in a movie. Suspense is the anxiety brought on by a partial uncertainty:

Surprise versus suspense

Billy Wilder's *Some Like It Hot* (1959; screenwriters Wilder and I. A. L. Diamond) concerns two musicians who witness a mob murder, disguise themselves as women, and leave town to work in an all-woman band. Although their attempts to maintain this disguise are frustrated by their desires for the women who surround them, they persist through a series of hilarious turns that heighten the suspense. When will they be discovered? What will happen as a result? Eventually, a rich millionaire, Osgood Fielding III (Joe E. Brown, *left*) falls in love with Jerry/Daphne (Jack Lemmon, *right*), who frantically explains to Osgood that they can't marry because they are both men. As a surprise to cap the suspense, Osgood simply shrugs his shoulders and makes one of the greatest comebacks in movie history: "Well, nobody's perfect."

SUSPENSE AND SURPRISE

LOOKING AT MOVIES

VIDEO ▶ ──────●──────

In this tutorial, Dave Monahan discusses the differences between suspense and surprise.

7. Alfred Hitchcock, qtd. in François Truffaut, *Hitchcock*, rev. ed. (New York: Simon & Schuster, 1984), p. 73.

the end is certain, but the means is uncertain. Or, even more interestingly, we may know both the result and the means by which it's brought about, but we still feel suspense: we know what's going to happen and we want to warn and protect the characters, for we have grown to empathize with them (though we can intellectually acknowledge the fact that they aren't "real" people).

Repetition

The **repetition**, or number of times, that a story element recurs in a plot is an important aspect of narrative form. If an event occurs once in a plot, we accept it as a functioning part of the narrative's progression. Its appearance more than once, however, suggests a pattern and thus a higher level of importance. Like order and duration, then, repetition serves not only as a means of relaying story information but also as a signal that a particular event has a meaning or significance that should be acknowledged in our interpretation and analysis.

Story events can be repeated in various ways. A character may remember a key event at several times during the movie, indicating the psychological, intellectual, or physical importance of that event. The use of flashbacks or slow-motion sequences tends to give a mythical quality to memory, making the past seem more significant than it might actually have been. For example, in Atom Egoyan's *The Sweet Hereafter* (1997; screenwriter Egoyan), Mitchell Stephens (Ian Holm) is so troubled by his teenage daughter's drug addiction that he tries to put it out of his mind by frequently visualizing more pleasant memories of her as a child. In another form of repetition, the director relies on editing to contrast past and present.

The **familiar image** is defined by film theorist Stefan Sharff as any image (audio or visual) that a director periodically repeats in a movie (with or without variations) to help stabilize its narrative. By its repetition, the image calls attention to itself as a narrative (as well as visual) element. This familiar image repetition can be used as a sort of stabilizer within a single highly fragmented scene to help connect a complexity of narrative elements and imagery, as well as remind the viewer of the key ideas at play within the particular scenario. An example of a rhythmic use of identical images occurs in Eisenstein's repetition of a set of images (steps, soldiers, mother holding baby, mother with baby in carriage, woman shot in stomach, woman with broken glasses, etc.) in the "Odessa Steps" sequence of *Battleship Potemkin*.

Some familiar images are distributed throughout a film as thematic symbols, particularly those where a material object represents something abstract. In *Volver* (2006), director Pedro Almodóvar uses frequent shots of wind turbines in the Spanish landscape as a symbol to help us understand the meaning of the title, a Spanish word that means "turn," "return," or "revolution," as in a circle turning. On the literal level, the story itself turns on the cycle of genetic or behavioral influences that pass from one generation to the next.

The repetition of familiar images can also be used to influence how the audience interprets or experiences the narrative in multiple scenes. The first four shots in the scene depicting Kane's death in the opening minutes of *Citizen Kane* all feature the superimposed image of snow falling across the screen. This visual element is sourced in the snow globe Kane drops after he utters, "Rosebud." The snow image returns 16 minutes later during an event in Kane's childhood that changes his life forever. That familiar image evokes the audience's initial association with Kane's lonely death and last word, and thus colors the way we experience and interpret young Kane's separation from his mother. The falling snow returns once more in one of the film's final scenes. In a tantrum after his second wife leaves him, Kane tears her bedroom apart—until he stumbles upon the same snow globe we saw him clutching on his deathbed at the beginning of the movie. The snow globe, and the snow inside that swirls when Kane picks it up, reminds us of the two previous scenes featuring the familiar image: one portrayed the influential events that brought Kane to this moment, and the other revealed the eventual consequences of the actions we just witnessed.

Setting

The **setting** of a movie is the time and place in which the story occurs. It establishes the date, city, or country and provides the characters' social, educational, and cultural backgrounds and other identifying factors vital for understanding them—such as what they wear, eat, and drink. Setting sometimes provides an implicit explanation for actions or traits that we might otherwise consider eccentric, because cultural norms vary from place to place and throughout time. Certain genres are associated with specific settings—for example, Westerns with wide open country, film noirs with dark city streets, and horror movies with creepy houses.

Setting in science fiction

Based on Philip K. Dick's science-fiction novel *Do Androids Dream of Electric Sheep?* (1968), Ridley Scott's *Blade Runner* (1982) takes place in 2019 in an imaginary world where cities such as Los Angeles are ruled by technology and saturated with visual information. In most science-fiction films, setting plays an important part in our understanding of the narrative, so sci-fi filmmakers spend considerable time, money, and effort to make the setting come to life.

Besides giving us essential contextual information that helps us understand story events and character motivation, setting adds texture to the movie's diegesis, enriching our sense of the overall world of the movie. Terrence Malick's *Days of Heaven* (1978; screenwriter Malick) features magnificent landscapes in the American West of the 1920s. At first, the extraordinary visual imagery seems to take precedence over the narrative. However, the settings—the vast wheat fields and the great solitary house against the sky—directly complement the depth and power of the narrative, which is concerned with the cycle of the seasons, the work connected with each season, and how fate, greed, sexual passion, and jealousy can lead to tragedy. Here, setting also helps reveal the characters' states of mind. They are from the Chicago slums, and once they arrive in the pristine wheat fields of the West, they are lonely and alienated from themselves and their values. They cannot adapt and thus end tragically. Here, setting is destiny.

Other films tell stories closely related to their international, national, or regional settings, such as the specific neighborhoods of New York City that form the backdrop of many Woody Allen films. But think of the many different ways in which Manhattan has been photographed, including the many film noirs with their harsh black-and-white contrasts; the sour colors of Martin Scorsese's *Taxi Driver* (1976; screenwriter Paul Schrader); or the bright colors of Alfred Hitchcock's *North by Northwest* (1959; screenwriter Ernest Lehman).

Settings are not always drawn from real-life locales. An opening title card tells us that F. W. Murnau's *Sun-*

rise: A Song of Two Humans (1927; screenwriter Carl Mayer) takes place in "no place and every place"; Stanley Kubrick's *2001: A Space Odyssey* (1968; screenwriters Kubrick and Arthur C. Clarke) creates an entirely new space–time continuum; and Tim Burton's *Charlie and the Chocolate Factory* (2005; screenwriter John August) creates the most fantastic chocolate factory in the world. The attraction of science-fiction films such as George Lucas's *Star Wars* (1977; screenwriter Lucas) and Ridley Scott's *Blade Runner* (1982; director's cut released 1992; screenwriters Hampton Fancher and David Webb Peoples) is often attributed to their almost totally unfamiliar settings. These stories about outer space and future cities have a mythical or symbolic significance beyond that of stories set on Earth. Their settings may be verisimilar and appropriate for the purpose of the story, whether or not we can verify them as "real."

Scope

Related to duration and setting is **scope**—the overall range, in time and place, of the movie's story. Stories can range from the distant past to the narrative present, or they can be narrowly focused on a short period, even a matter of moments. They can take us from one galaxy to another, or they can remain inside a single room. They can present a rather limited perspective on their world, or they can show us several alternative perspectives. Determining the general scope of a movie's story—understanding its relative expansiveness—can

Scope

Bernardo Bertolucci's *The Last Emperor* (1987; screenwriters Mark Peploe and Bertolucci) recounts the comparatively small story of the title character, China's Pu Yi (John Lone), against the political changes enveloping China as it moved from monarchy to communism from 1908 to 1967. Even though the two stories occur simultaneously and are related causally, the expansive scope of the historical epic takes precedence over the story of the emperor's life.

help you piece together and understand other aspects of the movie as a whole.

For example, the *biopic*, a film about a person's life—whether historical or fictional—might tell the story in one of two ways: through one significant episode or period in the life of a person, or through a series of events in a single life, sometimes beginning with birth and ending in old age. Biopics remain one of the great staples of movie production. Think of the variety of subjects in these recent movies: the notorious Australian criminal Mark Brandon Read in *Chopper* (2000; director and screenwriter Andrew Dominik), the British antislavery advocate William Wilberforce in *Amazing Grace* (2006; director Michael Apted, screenwriter Stephen Knight), gay activist Harvey Milk in *Milk* (2008; director Gus Van Sant, screenwriter Dustin Lance Black), English poet John Keats in *Bright Star* (2009; directors and screenwriters Robert Epstein and Jeffrey Friedman), King George VI in *The King's Speech* (2010; director Tom Hooper, screenwriter David Seidler), or Marilyn Monroe in *My Week with Marilyn* (2011; director Simon Curtis, screenwriter Adrian Hodge).

Many war films have been limited in scope to the story of a single battle; others have treated an entire war. Steven Spielberg's *Saving Private Ryan* (1998; screenwriter Robert Rodat) covers two stories happening simultaneously: the larger story is that of the June 1944 D-Day invasion of Normandy, involving the vast Allied army; the more intimate story, and the one that gives the film its title, presents what happens from the time the U.S. government orders Private Ryan (Matt Damon) to be removed from combat to the time it actually happens. Both stories are seen from the American point of view, perceptually and politically.

By contrast, Ken Annakin, Andrew Marton, and Bernhard Wicki's *The Longest Day* (1962; screenwriters Romain Gary, James Jones, David Pursall, Jack Seddon, and Cornelius Ryan) relates the D-Day invasion to what was happening in four countries—the United States, France, England, and Germany—though also from the perspective of American politics. Thus its scope is broader, enhanced by the viewpoints of its large cast of characters. Although Terrence Malick's *The Thin Red Line* (1998; screenwriter Malick) focuses on the American invasion of the Japanese-held Pacific island of Guadalcanal, it ultimately uses the historical setting as a very personal backdrop for a meditation on war and its horrors.

Looking at Narrative: John Ford's *Stagecoach*

To better understand how these foundations and elements of narrative work together in a single movie, let's consider how they're used in John Ford's *Stagecoach* (1939; screenwriter Dudley Nichols). This movie is regarded by many as *the* classic Western, not only for its great entertainment value but also for its mastery of the subjects discussed in this chapter.

Story, Screenwriter, and Screenplay

The story of *Stagecoach* is based on a familiar convention sometimes called the "ship of fools." Such stories involve a diverse group of people—perhaps passengers traveling to a common destination or residents of a hotel—who must confront a common danger and, through that experience, confront themselves as individuals and as members of a group.

In *Stagecoach*, these people (male and female; weak and strong; from different places, backgrounds, and professions; with dissimilar temperaments) either have been living in or are passing through the frontier town of Tonto. Despite a warning from the U.S. Cavalry that Apache warriors, under the command of the dreaded Geronimo, have cut the telegraph wires and threatened the settlers' safety, this group boards a stagecoach to Lordsburg. In charge of the coach is Buck Rickabaugh (Andy Devine), the driver, and Marshal Curly Wilcox (George Bancroft), who is on the lookout for an escaped prisoner called the Ringo Kid (John Wayne). The seven passengers include (1) Lucy Mallory (Louise Platt), the aloof, Southern-born, and (as we later learn) pregnant wife of a cavalry officer whom she has come west to join; (2) Samuel Peacock (Donald Meek), a liquor salesman; (3) Dr. Josiah Boone (Thomas Mitchell), a doctor who still carries his bag of equipment, even though he has been kicked out of the profession for malpractice and now is being driven out of Tonto for drunkenness; (4) Mr. Hatfield (John Carradine), a Southern gambler, who is proud of having served in Lucy's father's regiment in the Civil War and leaves Tonto to serve as her protector on the trip; (5) Henry Gatewood (Berton Churchill), the Tonto bank president, who is leaving town with a mysterious satchel that we later learn contains money he stole from his bank; and (6) Dallas (Claire Trevor), a good-hearted prostitute, who has been driven out of

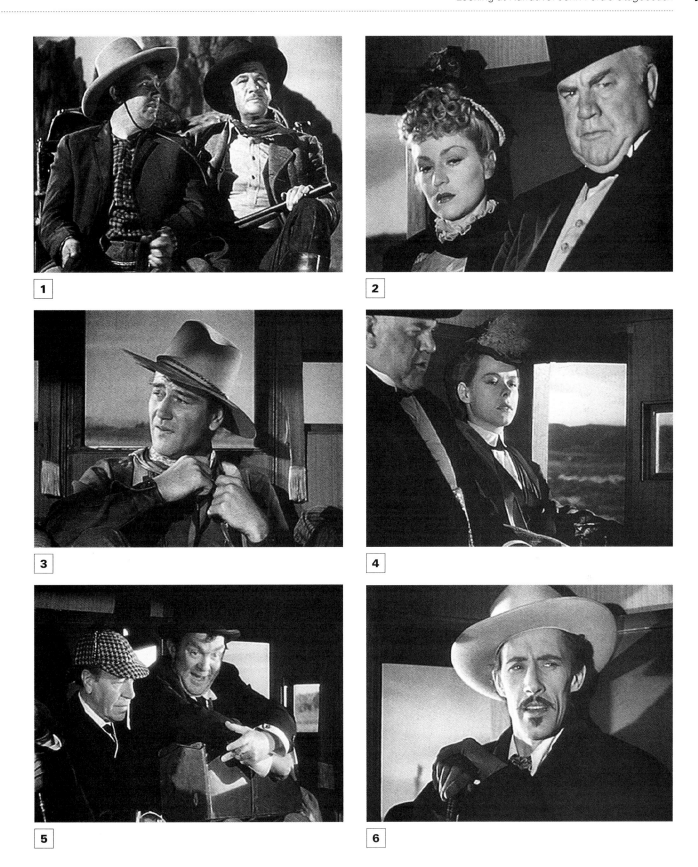

The cast of characters in *Stagecoach*

[1] Buck Rickabaugh (Andy Devine, *left*) and Marshal Curly Wilcox (George Bancroft); [2] Dallas (Claire Trevor) and Henry Gatewood (Berton Churchill); [3] the Ringo Kid (John Wayne); [4] Gatewood and Lucy Mallory (Louise Platt); [5] Samuel Peacock (Donald Meek, *left*) and Dr. Josiah Boone (Thomas Mitchell); and [6] Mr. Hatfield (John Carradine).

town by a group of Tonto's righteous women. The seventh passenger, Ringo, has been heading for Lordsburg to avenge his father's murder. But when his horse becomes lame outside Tonto, he stops the stagecoach and is arrested by the marshal before he boards. Each passenger has personal reasons for leaving Tonto (or, in Ringo's case, prison) and making the perilous journey. Lucy, Hatfield, Gatewood, and Peacock all have specific purposes for traveling to Lordsburg; Dallas and Dr. Boone are being forced to leave town; and the Ringo Kid has a grudge to settle.

The screenwriter Dudley Nichols, a veteran of working with Ford, based the screenplay on the story "Stage to Lordsburg," written by Ernest Haycox, who specialized in fiction based on Western themes.[8] Although this story is fiction, Ford usually sought to anchor his Western movies in historical reality by giving them a date; he does not do that in *Stagecoach*. Since Geronimo and his Apaches were most active between 1881 and 1886 in their encounters with the U. S. Army, we can locate the action sometime in this period. Haycox's story provides a basic plot and characters, but Ford and Nichols recognized in it the basis for a new kind of Hollywood Western, and made many alterations. They retained most characters, but added two new ones (Doc Boone and Gatewood) and changed all their names. Significantly, while Haycox had the Ringo character board the stagecoach with everyone else in Tonto, Nichols made him an escaped prisoner, thus strengthening the group of outcasts and contributing to the class consciousness at the heart of the story. Catering to the audience's expectations, Ford provides a spectacular Indian fight, but the movie's true strength lies in its magnificent imagery, as well as in the screenplay's sharp psychological portraits of vivid characters and pointed social commentary. At the end of the movie, we expect that Ringo, having gotten his revenge, will return to jail to complete his sentence. And we know that after his release, Ringo and Dallas plan to be married and live on his ranch across the border. Nichols made a significant addition to the story by giving it a happy ending—the couple escape into the night—and having Dr. Boone utter the movie's cynical last words: "Well, they're saved from the blessings of civilization."

Narration and Narrator

As was typical of John Ford's style throughout his career, he relies on visual images and dialogue, not a narrator, to tell the *Stagecoach* story. His narration is provided by an omniscient camera that sees and knows everything and can tell us whatever it wants us to know. You see this, for example, in the exterior shots of Geronimo on the hill, Gatewood robbing his own safe, the stagecoach racing across the territory, and the Luke Plummer scene. This camera has unrestricted access to all aspects of the narrative and, as a result, can provide the experiences and perceptions of any character, as well as information that no character knows. You see this in the medium and close-up shots of characters under stress. Ford's camera shows the audience whatever it needs to in order to best tell the story.

Although the movie uses neither narrator nor interior monologue, it features one especially interesting use of an auditory point of view when Lucy, a cavalry wife, is the first to recognize the bugle announcing the cavalry's impending arrival during the Apache attack. The situation is dire. She is praying, and Hatfield, who intends to

Auditory point of view as narration in *Stagecoach*
Upon hearing the cavalry bugle and knowing that help is near, Lucy reacts with great emotion. This is a key turning point in the journey from Tonto to Lordsburg, and the arrival of the cavalry means—or at least the members of the stagecoach party hope it means—that the travelers will end their journey safely.

8. Both the story and the screenplay are in Dudley Nichols, *Stagecoach: A Film by John Ford and Dudley Nichols* (New York: Simon & Schuster, 1971). See also Edward Buscombe's excellent analysis of the film in *Stagecoach* (London: British Film Institute, 1992), to which I am indebted.

shoot her so that she won't be captured by the Apaches, has pointed his revolver at her head. Just before he can pull the trigger, he is struck by an Apache bullet. Hearing the bugle at that moment, Lucy reacts with great emotion as she says, "Do you hear it? It's a bugle. They're blowing the charge." With a cut to the cavalry riding to save the stagecoach, the movie reaches its turning point. This powerful moment manipulates our expectations (we believe that Hatfield will perform the mercy killing), conventions of the Western genre (we would expect the cavalry to announce itself directly, not through a fragile woman's perception), and diegesis (particularly the characterization and explicitly presented events). Lucy unwittingly becomes one of the heroes of the movie.

When he needs to show that the characters do not form a community—for example, at the noontime lunch stop at Dry Fork, where underlying tensions flare up because Ringo has seated Dallas at the same table as Lucy—Ford establishes and reinforces ideological and emotional differences by alternating between shots from an omniscient point of view and shots from the characters' subjective points of view. As a result, the space at the dinner table, even though it is physically larger, is as socially and morally restricted as the space inside the stagecoach. The pattern of editing here establishes the camera's presence as narrator, the social stratification within the group, Lucy's inflexibility, Hatfield's protectiveness, and Gatewood's pretentiousness. But it also reveals Ringo's kindness, Dallas's vulnerability, and Ford's sympathy for them, which engages our sympathy.

Characters

All the characters inside the stagecoach—Dallas, Ringo, Hatfield, Peacock, Gatewood, Dr. Boone, and Lucy—are major, because they make the most things happen and have the most things happen to them. Dallas, Ringo, Dr. Boone, and Lucy are round characters: three-dimensional, possessing several traits, and unpredictable. The flat characters—one-dimensional, possessing one or very few discernible traits, and generally predictable—include Hatfield, Peacock, and Gatewood.

But Gatewood is somewhat more complicated. We know that when the Apaches cut the telegraph wires in the opening scene, they severed all communication between Tonto and Lordsburg. (Although the telephone was invented in 1876, it hadn't yet reached Tonto.) This incident helps to get the story under way. It's also the reason the marshal later realizes that Gatewood is guilty, since, as he enters the stagecoach, he claims to have "just" gotten a telegram.

Buck Rickabaugh and Marshal Wilcox, riding on the bench at the exterior front of the coach, are essentially minor (and flat) characters; they play less important roles and usually function as a means of moving the plot forward or of fleshing out the motivations of the major characters.

Ringo is the primary protagonist, with a goal to revenge his family and a (conflicting) need to find love and settle down. But you could argue that all of the passengers are protagonists, for they all have a common goal: Lordsburg.

The primary antagonist, for everyone on this journey, is Geronimo, even though he and his warriors appear on the screen briefly. One of the many things that makes *Stagecoach*'s narrative so interesting is that, while Geronimo is responsible for many of the narrative obstacles, much of the story's conflict originates in disputes between the characters who share a common goal. For Ringo, the Plummers are the antagonists. They loom large in the story, but do not appear on-screen until just before the movie ends.

Narrative Structure

The narrative structure employed by the screenwriter follows the familiar three-act model established earlier in this chapter. The first act, or setup, establishes the world of Tonto, presented as a typical frontier town: rough, prosperous, and ruled by a formidable force of social prejudice, the Ladies Law and Order League. The daily stagecoach, a lifeline to the outer world, stops for passengers, mail, news, and other necessities. Despite the U.S. Cavalry's warning about Geronimo and his troops, all its passengers have a reason for going to Lordsburg. Thus there are several inciting incidents: some want to leave (Mr. Hatfield, Mr. Gatewood), some are forced to leave (Doc Boone and Dallas), some are just passing through (Mrs. Mallory, Mr. Samuel Peacock), and some are just doing their jobs (Buck Rickabaugh, the stagecoach driver, and Curly Wilcox, the marshal). Ringo has his own reason for going to Lordsburg: revenge.

In the second act, we see what's at stake: delay and danger. While the characters share a common goal,

Lordsburg, they each have traits that color and shape their pursuits of it. However, they encounter major obstacles to their pursuit of this goal: Geronimo cuts the telegraph wires, the cavalry scout leaves them, the interior of the stagecoach is cramped and uncomfortable, and there are no fresh horses at the way station. What's more, there are social divisions among the passengers (so-called polite society versus the outcasts), Lucy Mallory's delivery of a baby, and, of course, the Apaches' attack. In addition to these impediments, Ringo has his own personal obstacles. Curly arrests him and takes his gun. Dallas tries to stop him from confronting the murderous Plummers, whom he must face even though he has only three bullets left. Ringo must convince Curly to give him ten minutes to say good-bye to Dallas. Ringo not only overcomes these obstacles but also sets an example of courage during the Apache attack with his willingness to sacrifice himself for the good of the group in successfully bringing the rampaging stagecoach horses under control. Hero that he is, he also gets lucky when the cavalry arrives to bolster the gutsy gunplay and determination he (and some others) use to fend off the Apaches. The group's crisis is averted, and the stagecoach proceeds toward Lordsburg. But Ringo's crisis is his showdown with the Plummers. He overcomes this seemingly insurmountable obstacle with guts and eagle-eye shooting. Dr. Boone tries to help by relieving Luke Plummer of his shotgun, but his girlfriend supplies him with one just before the gunfight.

In the third act, with Ringo's crisis solved, there are several resolutions: Gatewood is arrested, Mrs. Mallory implicitly asks Dallas's forgiveness, Mr. Mallory is all right, and Mr. Peacock has survived the Apache attack. But Doc, Curly, and Ringo and Dallas, especially, have another resolution. Doc stands up to the Plummers, but doesn't stop drinking; Ringo tells Dallas that he doesn't care about her past; Curly quietly lets Ringo elude his obligation to return to jail; and Ringo and Dallas ride off into the night.

Plot

The plot of *Stagecoach* covers the two-day trip from Tonto to Lordsburg and is developed in a strictly chronological way without flashbacks or flash-forwards. The

events follow one another coherently and logically, and their relations of cause and effect are easy to discern. Balance, harmony, and unity are the principal keys to understanding the relationship between the story and the plot. Indeed, the eminent French film theorist and critic André Bazin notes that

> *Stagecoach* (1939) is the ideal example of the maturity of a style brought to classic perfection. John Ford struck the ideal balance between social myth, historical reconstruction, psychological truth, and the traditional theme of the Western mise en scène. None of these elements dominated any other. *Stagecoach* is like a wheel, so perfectly made that it remains in equilibrium on its axis in any position.[9]

Order As already noted, Ford maintains strict chronological order in using the journey to structure the story events. The journey provides both chronological and geographical markers for dividing the sequences. Furthermore, it reveals a clear pattern of cause and effect created primarily by each character's desire to go to Lordsburg on this particular day. That pattern proceeds to conflict (created both by internal character interaction and by the external Apache attack, which frustrates the characters' desires), reaches a turning point (the victory over the Apaches), and concludes with a resolution (Ringo's revenge on the Plummers, whose testimony had put him in prison, and his riding off a free man with the woman he loves). Otherwise, the plot order is not manipulated in any way.

Diegetic and Nondiegetic Elements The diegetic elements are everything in the story except the opening and closing titles and credits and the background music, all of which are, of course, nondiegetic. One very important formal element in *Stagecoach* is American folk music, including the song "Bury Me Not on the Lone Prairie," most often heard in connection with Buck and representing his justifiable fears of dying on the range; a honky-tonk piano in the bar; and a symphonic score mixing many familiar folk tunes. The film's main theme is Stephen Foster's classic ballad "Jeanie with the Light Brown Hair." A song about remembering the past, perhaps with regret or loss, it is closely associated with the

9. André Bazin, "Evolution of the Western," in *What Is Cinema?* trans. Hugh Gray, 2 vols. (Berkeley: University of California Press, 1967–71), II, p. 149.

Old South and evokes the memories of Lucy Mallory and Hatfield: the devastating Civil War, the uncertain westward movement, the fragmented western territories, and, in all of this, a yearning for a simpler time and a woman with light brown hair.

Events The major events in *Stagecoach*—those branching points in the plot structure that force characters to choose between or among alternate paths—include (in the order of the plot; see images on pp. 156–157):

the passengers' decision to leave Tonto in spite of the cavalry's warning about Geronimo and his troops [1].

Marshal Wilcox's decision to let Ringo join the party [2].

the passengers' vote to leave the Dry Fork station for Lordsburg, even though a relief unit of cavalry has not yet arrived [3].

Dr. Boone's willingness to sober up and deliver the baby [4].

Dallas's decision at the Apache Wells station to accept Ringo's proposal [5].

the group's decision to delay departure from Apache Wells until Lucy has rested from childbirth and is ready to travel [6].

Ringo's attempt to escape at Apache Wells [7].

the passengers' decision at the burned-out ferry landing to try to reach Lordsburg, even though they realize that an Apache attack may be imminent [8].

Ringo's willingness to risk his life to bring the coach under control as the Apaches attack [9].

the arrival of the cavalry soon after the Apache attack has begun [10].

Marshal Wilcox's decision to reward Ringo's bravery by allowing him ten minutes of freedom in which to confront the Plummers [11].

the marshal's decision to set Ringo free [12].

The minor plot events that add texture and complexity to characters and events but are not essential elements within the narrative include (in plot order) the Apaches' cutting of the telegraph wires; Gatewood's anxiety about getting to Lordsburg no matter what happens along the route; Peacock's anxiety over Dr. Boone's helping himself to his stock of liquor; Buck's wavering enthusiasm for driving the stagecoach against the odds; Lucy's, Hatfield's, and Gatewood's demonstrations of their self-perceived social superiority, especially at the lunch table at Dry Fork; Hatfield's attempt to defend Lucy from Apache attack, which results in his being shot; Marshal Wilcox's distribution of weapons to the travelers for their self-defense during the Apache attack; Wilcox's arrest of Gatewood for embezzlement; and Ringo's successful killing of the three Plummer brothers.

Duration The story duration includes what we know and what we infer from the total lives of all the characters (e.g., Lucy's privileged upbringing in Virginia, marriage to a military officer, current pregnancy, and the route of her trip out West up until the moment the movie begins). The plot duration includes the time of those events within the story that the film chooses to tell—here the two days of the trip from Tonto to Lordsburg. The screen duration, or running time, is 96 minutes.

Repetition Although no story events recur in *Stagecoach*, character traits both recur (e.g., Gatewood's insensitive desire to keep moving, no matter what, puts in danger both individuals and the group as a whole) and are transformed as a result of the journey (e.g., Lucy tenderly acknowledges Dallas's invaluable assistance during childbirth: "Dallas, if there's ever anything I can do for . . ."). Ford also repeats a three-part editing pattern some dozen times in the movie: (shot 1) a *long shot* of the stagecoach rolling along the plain; (shot 2) a *two-shot* of Curly and Buck on the driver's seat; (shot 3) a *middle shot* or *close-up* of the passengers inside. We could broadly consider the recurrences of this series of shots as repetitions of familiar images.

Suspense

In the period depicted, it took two days for a fast stagecoach to make the trip from Tonto to Lordsburg, and the plot follows this two-day trip chronologically. However, the pace also serves other functions. The fear first

3

6

9

12

Major events in *Stagecoach*

These twelve images illustrate the major events in John Ford's *Stagecoach* (characters are listed from left to right): [1] Peacock, Curly, Hatfield, Lucy; [2] Buck, Curly, Ringo, cavalry captain; [3] Dallas, Ringo, Lucy, Buck, Curly, Peacock, Gatewood, Hatfield; [4] Curly, Peacock, Ringo; [5] Ringo and Dallas; [6] Gatewood, Buck, Curly, Hatfield, Peacock; [7] Ringo; [8] Buck, Curly, Dallas, Ringo; [9] Ringo; [10] cavalry flag bearer and bugler; [11] Ringo and Curly; [12] Curly, Ringo, and Dallas.

expressed in the opening moments at mention of the name Geronimo intensifies the suspense of the imminent Indian attack, thus providing a decisive crisis during which the characters respond to the challenges and rigors of the trip and reveal their true selves. Will Lucy stop acting like a spoiled rich woman? Will Dr. Boone sober up in time to deliver her child? Will Dallas accept Ringo's proposal? Because we know little of their origins, we must trust in what we see of their current surroundings, as well as their interactions with each other and with the community (both the community of Tonto and the "community" that develops on the journey).

Setting

The physical setting of *Stagecoach*—the desert and mountains, towns and stagecoach—also represents a moral world, established in its first minutes by the contrast between Geronimo and his Apaches (whom Ford portrays as evil) and the U.S. Army (portrayed as good). It was filmed on settings constructed in Hollywood—the interiors and exteriors of two towns and the stagecoach—and on actual locations in the spectacular Monument Valley of northern Arizona. Beautiful and important as Monument Valley and other exterior shots are to the film, the shots made inside the stagecoach as it speeds through the valley are essential to developing other themes in the movie. As the war with the Apaches signifies the territorial changes taking place outside, another drama is taking place among the passengers. In journeying through changing scenery, they also change through their responses to the dangers they face and their relations with, and reactions to, one another.

Understanding the setting helps us to understand many of the other aspects of the movie, especially its meanings. This may be a wilderness, but some settlers have brought from the East and the South their notions of social respectability and status, while others are

Settings in *Stagecoach*

[1] The main street of Tonto, where the horses are being attached to the stagecoach before the journey begins. [2] The stagecoach, with its cavalry escort, entering the first phase of the journey. [3] The Apache attack on the stagecoach. [4] The main street of Lordsburg, where residents watch the stagecoach arrive.

fleeing such constrictions. For the members of the Ladies Law and Order League, the setting offers them the opportunity to restore the town's moral balance, and Dallas and Dr. Boone are being sacrificed to underscore their efforts.

The physical setting is clearly depicted by sharp black-and-white cinematography, but Ford treats its darker side ironically, particularly in his choice of music, one of his favorite Christian hymns. "Shall We Gather at the River" (1864) offers a key to the movie's mood and meaning. (Those who know Ford's work will recognize it in at least four of his movies.) As you learn more about

ways to determine meaning, don't neglect the power of music. And identifying a movie's music is easy, for the information is usually in the closing credits and almost always cited in the IMDB.

As Dr. Boone starts to lead Dallas, the marshal, and the ladies toward the stagecoach, he says sarcastically that they are heading to death; his remark "to the guillotine" refers to the beheadings of those who provoked the French Revolution of 1789. Here, Ford's bouncy arrangement of the hymn's melody matches the pace of their walk. But the Ladies Law and Order League is composed of hypocrites who conveniently ignore the hymn's meaning. Its words suggest that believers and sinners who gather at the symbolic river to wash away their sins will be rewarded with grace.

Let's observe the effects of the trip on each of the seven passengers. Dallas, a prostitute, is being run out of town. Although the league sees her eviction as a triumph for its cause, Dallas actually becomes the heroine of the movie by showing dignity in the face of humiliation and compassion in helping to deliver Lucy's baby. Next comes Mr. Peacock, a traveling whiskey salesman, who by his brief appearance in Tonto does not much figure in the social scheme of things nor change during the journey. Following him closely, so that he can keep his hands on Peacock's sample case, is Dr. Boone, who is also being run out of town by the league (he tells Dallas, "We are the victims of a foul disease called social prejudice, my child"), but is redeemed during the journey when he sobers up and delivers Lucy's baby. Boone and Dallas are at one end of Tonto's social scale, but Lucy Mallory, stopping only for a change of horses in Tonto, is at the other, recognized by fellow army wives and treated as a respected southern aristocrat. She is cool and aloof throughout the journey, excluding her momentary acknowledgment of Dallas's kindness in helping Boone deliver her baby. But if Lucy is at the top of the social scale, Mr. Hatfield, a transient gambler, uses the opportunity to get out of town by playing the southern gentlemen who will protect Lucy during the journey; ironically, he dies in his efforts. Next comes Mr. Gatewood, the town's banker, a respected social pillar whose wife is a member of the Ladies Law and Order League. Initially, the viewer alone knows that he's leaving town with a $50,000 payroll, but later in Lordsburg, everyone gathers around to watch him being arrested for the robbery. Finally, Ringo, who has no social status when he joins the stagecoach party, becomes the hero of the story through his heroic defense of the stagecoach. At the movie's end, Dr. Boone, Dallas, and Ringo are redeemed by their kindness and charity. Ringo's valor encourages the law officers to turn a blind eye as he avenges his father's murder by killing the three Plummer brothers—this is, after all, the Wild West.

Scope

The story's overall range in time and place is broad, extending from early events—Dallas orphaned by an Indian massacre and the comparatively more pleasant childhood that Lucy enjoyed in Virginia—to those we see on-screen. And although we look essentially at the events on the two days that it takes the stagecoach to go from Tonto to Lordsburg, we are also aware of the larger scope of American history, particularly the westward movement, Ford's favorite subject. Made right before the start of World War II in Europe, *Stagecoach* presents a historical, social, and mythical vision of American civilization in the 1880s. Ford looked back at the movement west because he saw that period as characterized by clear, simple virtues and values. He viewed the pioneers as establishing the traditions for which Americans would soon be fighting: freedom, democracy, justice, and individualism.

Among the social themes of the movie is *manifest destiny*, a term used by conservative nationalists to explain that the territorial expansion of the United States was not only inevitable, but ordained by God. In that effort, embodied in the westward movement, the struggle to expand would be waged against the Native Americans. In his handling of the story, Ford strives to realistically depict settlers' lives in a frontier town and the dangers awaiting them in the wilderness. Although scholars differ in interpreting the politics of Ford's vision, particularly as it relates to his depictions of whites and Native Americans (depictions that vary throughout his many movies), here his Apaches, just like the white men, are noble (in their struggle) as well as savage (in war). Whether this particular story actually happened is not the point. As we understand American history, it could have happened. Ford accurately depicts the Apaches as well as the settlers—the stakes are high for each group—and though the cavalry rather theatrically arrives to save the stagecoach party, both sides suffer casualties and neither side "wins." In fact, Ringo's heroism during the Indian attack permits the stagecoach party to reach Lordsburg safely and earns him the freedom to avenge the deaths of his father and brother. That, of course, is one of the movie's personal themes: Ringo's revenge.

However, Ford sees many sad elements in the westward expansion: the displacement of the Native Americans, the migration of discriminatory social patterns from the East and South to the West, the establishment of uncivilized towns, and the dissolution of moral character among the settlers. These issues are related to the setting in which the story takes place. Here and in his other Westerns, Ford created his own vision of how the West was won. Most critics recognize that this vision is part real and part mythical, combining as it does the re-telling of actual incidents with a strong overlay of Ford's ideas on how people behaved (or should have behaved).

One of Ford's persistent beliefs is that civilization occurs as a result of a genuine community built—in the wilderness—through heroism and shared values. In Ford's overall vision, American heroes are always fighting for their rights, whether the fight is against the British, the Native Americans, or the fascists. Precisely because the beauty of Monument Valley means so many different things to different people, it becomes a symbol of the many outcomes that can result from exploration, settlement, and the inevitable territorial disputes that follow. But there seems little doubt that Ford himself is speaking (through Dr. Boone) at the end of the film. As Ringo and Dallas ride off to freedom across the border, Dr. Boone utters the ironic observation, "Well, they're saved from the blessings of civilization."

Dr. Boone's "civilization" includes the hypocritical ladies of Tonto, who force him and Dallas to flee the town; the banker, Gatewood, who pontificates about the importance of banks—"What's good for the banks is good for the country"—while embezzling $50,000 from a payroll meant for miners; and the culture of violence in towns such as Lordsburg. In the 1930s, when *Stagecoach* was made, President Franklin D. Roosevelt singled out the banks as a major cause of the Great Depression and increased the government's regulatory power of them, so we can see that Gatewood (who is not in the original story) gives the movie contemporary political relevance. In the year after John Ford made *Stagecoach*, in his adaptation of John Steinbeck's *The Grapes of Wrath* (1940)—the story of a dispossessed family journeying through dangerous country to reach a place of safety—the director again put himself fundamentally against the rich and powerful and on the side of the poor and weak.

ANALYZING ELEMENTS OF NARRATIVE

Most of us can hardly avoid analyzing the narrative of a movie after we have seen it. We ask, "Why did the director choose that story?" "Why did he choose to tell it in that way?" "What does it mean?" At the simplest level, our analysis happens unconsciously while we're watching a movie, as we fill in gaps in events, infer character traits from the clues or cues we receive, and interpret the significance of objects. But when we're actively looking at a movie, we should analyze their narratives in more precise, conscious detail. The following checklist provides a few ideas about how you might do this.

SCREENING CHECKLIST: ELEMENTS OF NARRATIVE

☐ Who is the movie's protagonist? What factors and needs motivate or complicate their actions? Can you characterize each of them according to their depth (round characters versus flat) and motivation?

☐ What is the narration of the movie? Does it use a narrator of any kind?

☐ What are the differences among omniscient, restricted, and unrestricted narration?

☐ Carefully reconstruct the narrative structure of the movie. What is the inciting incident? What goal does the protagonist pursue? How does the protagonist's need influence that pursuit? What obstacles (including the crisis) does the protagonist encounter, and how does she or he engage them?

☐ Keep track of nondiegetic elements that seem essential to the movie's plot (voice-overs, for example). Do they seem natural and appropriate to the film, or do they appear to be "tacked on" to make up for a shortcoming in the overall presentation of the movie's narrative?

☐ Are the plot events presented in chronological order? What is the significance of the order of plot events in the movie?

☐ Keep track of the major and minor events in the movie's plot. Are any of the minor events unnecessary to the movie overall? If these events were not included, would the movie be better? Why?

☐ Are there scenes that create a noticeable summary relationship between story duration and screen duration? Do these scenes complement or detract from the overall narrative? Do these scenes give you all the information about the underlying story that you need to understand what has happened in the elapsed story time?

☐ Do any scenes use real time or a stretch relationship between story duration and screen duration? If so, what is the significance of these scenes to the overall narrative?

☐ Is any major plot event presented on-screen more than once? If so, why do you think the filmmaker has chosen to repeat the event?

☐ How do the setting and the scope of the narrative complement the other elements?

Questions for Review

1. What is the difference between narration and narrator?

2. What are the differences between omniscient and restricted narration?

3. What are the differences between (a) the camera narrator and a first-person narrator and (b) a first-person narrator and a third-person narrator?

4. Can a major character be flat? Can a minor character be round? Explain your answer.

5. What is the climax, and how does it relate to the protagonist's pursuit of the goal?

6. How (and why) do we distinguish between the story and the plot of a movie?

7. What is meant by the diegesis of a story? What is the difference between diegetic and nondiegetic elements in the plot?

8. What are major and minor events each supposed to do for the movie's plot?

9. Which of the following is the most common relationship of screen duration to story duration: summary relationship, real time, or stretch relationship? Define each one.

10. What is the difference between suspense and surprise? Which one is more difficult for a filmmaker to create?

STUDENT RESOURCES ONLINE

digital.wwnorton.com/movies5

▶ **VIDEO**

The tutorials for this chapter cover narration, narrators, and narrative; diegetic and nondiegetic elements; and suspense and surprise.

LOOKING AT **MOVIES**
CHAPTER 4: ELEMENTS OF NARRATIVE

NARRATORS, NARRATION, AND NARRATIVE
DIEGETIC AND NONDIEGETIC ELEMENTS
SUSPENSE AND SURPRISE

▶ MAIN MENU

12 Years a Slave (2013; director Steve McQueen)

MISE-EN-SCÈNE

LEARNING OBJECTIVES

After reading this chapter, you should be able to

✓ define mise-en-scène overall and in terms of its constituent parts.

✓ describe the role of the production designer and the other personnel involved in designing a movie.

✓ understand the importance of design elements to our sense of a movie's characters, narrative, and themes.

✓ describe how framing in movies is different from framing of static images such as paintings or photographs.

✓ describe the relationship between on-screen and offscreen space, and explain why most shots in a film rely on both.

✓ accurately distinguish between the two basic types of movement—that of figures within the frame and that of the frame itself—in any film you watch.

✓ describe not only the details of any movie's mise-en-scène but also the effects that the mise-en-scène has on the movie's characters, narrative, and themes.

The best way to appreciate mise-en-scène—what it is, what it can do—is to experience it in a movie such as director Alfonso Cuarón's *Gravity* (2013), a science-fiction movie that overwhelms us with its look. Not only overwhelms us, but gives us the feeling of being there. The film opens with Dr. Ryan Stone (Sandra Bullock), a medical engineer, and astronaut Matt Kowalski (George Clooney) outside the American space shuttle *Explorer*, making repairs to the Hubble Telescope. This challenging task is sharply interrupted when a storm of space debris engulfs them, detaching Stone from the shuttle and sending her pinwheeling freely into the void before she is recovered and returned to the shuttle. This dizzying scene doesn't merely tell us what it's like to be lost in space, it *shows* us.

About this groundbreaking aspect of Cuarón's mise-en-scène, *New York Times* critic A. O. Scott wrote:

> Nothing in the movie—not hand tools or chess pieces, human bodies or cruise-ship-size space stations—rests within a stable vertical or horizontal plane. Neither does the movie itself, which in a little more than 90 minutes rewrites the rules of cinema as we have known them.[1]

Gravity is a stunning display of what cinema can do with its most fundamental properties: time and space.

It won't spoil your enjoyment of this movie to realize that the "outer space" we see on the screen is, as you know by now, an illusion. It is imaginatively conceived by the director and meticulously crafted by those responsible for the mise-en-scène: Andy Nicholson, production designer; Emmanuel Lubezki, director of photography; Mark Scruton, art director; and various costume, makeup, and hair designers. They use design, composition, elaborate camera setups, lighting, computer-generated imagery, and such practical effects as the rigging and wires that permit the director to move actors around the screen as easily as if they were puppets. *Gravity* is comparable to Stanley Kubrick's monumental *2001: A Space Odyssey* (1968) in making us feel the infinite vastness of space, the sense of gravity's pull as well as its absence. Since 1968, progress in cinematic technology has created advances in cinematic style. Alfonso Cuarón and his team are able to show us space from every conceivable angle and point of view, and seeing the film in 3-D and the IMAX format, as it was first released, further enhances the experience.

As a sci-fi epic, the movie is both scary and awesome (in the true sense of that overused word). But there are ideas here, too, about evolution and mortality as well as a woman who breaks through more than the glass ceiling. Dr. Ryan passes through the fiery reentry, lands in a lake that may not be on this earth, and crawls onto unfamiliar terrain as the movie ends. It's one small step for womankind, but we don't know where she is or where she's going. With its amazing special effects and powerful musical score, especially in the thrilling ending, *Gravity* goes beyond its basic value as entertainment and inspires our speculation with its ambivalence.

The movies are full of great scenes that allow us to observe a particular world, but *Gravity* virtually puts us *inside* its world. For those of us who will never experience outer space firsthand, *Gravity* is the next best thing.

What Is Mise-en-Scène?

The French phrase **mise-en-scène** (pronounced "meez-ahn-SEN") means literally "staging or putting on an

---

1. "Between Earth and Heaven," *New York Times* (October 3, 2013), www.nytimes.com/2013/10/04/movies/gravity-stars-sandra-bullock-and-george-clooney.html (accessed July 14, 2014).

Mise-en-scène creates a sense of being lost in space in *Gravity*
This image from *Gravity* records the moment before a devastating gale of debris changes the film's story. Kowalski (George Clooney, *right*), is trying to assist Dr. Stone (Sandra Bullock, *center*), get back safely into the "Explorer" before the storm hits. However, an omen (*left background*) shows us what they face: Shariff Dasari, the flight engineer, floats lifelessly, almost decapitated by a chunk of debris. The richly deployed elements of mise-en-scène create—along with the camera circling the action and the increasing complexity of sound—a terrifying reminder of the dangers of space exploration.

action or scene" and thus is sometimes called *staging.* Everything you see on the screen was *put* there for a reason: to help tell the story. In the critical analysis of movies, the term refers to the overall look and feel of a movie—the sum of everything the audience sees, hears,[2] and experiences while viewing it. A movie's mise-en-scène subtly influences our mood as we watch, much as the decor, lighting, smells, and sounds can influence our emotional response to a real-life place.

The two major visual components of mise-en-scène are design and composition. **Design** is the process by which the look of the settings, props, lighting, and actors is determined. Set design, décor, prop selection, lighting setup, costuming, makeup, and hairstyle design all play a role in shaping the overall design. **Composition** is the organization, distribution, balance, and general relationship of actors and objects within the space of each shot.

The visual elements of mise-en-scène are all crucial to shaping our sympathy for, and understanding of, the characters shaped by them. As you consider how a movie's mise-en-scène influences your thoughts about it, ask yourself if what you see in a scene is simply appealing decor, a well-dressed actor, and a striking bit of lighting, or if these elements improve your understanding of the narrative, characters, and action of the movie. Keep in mind that the director has a reason—related to the overall vision for the movie—for each thing put into a shot or scene (figures, objects, decor, landscaping, etc.), but each of these things does not necessarily have a meaning in and by itself. The combination of elements within the frame gives the shot or scene its overall meaning.

Every movie has a mise-en-scène. But in some movies the various elements of the mise-en-scène are so powerful that they enable the viewer to experience the aura of a place and time. A list of such films, chosen at random, might include historical spectacles such as Sergei Eisenstein and Dmitri Vasilyev's *Alexander Nevsky* (1938) or Stanley Kubrick's *Barry Lyndon* (1975);

2. As a scholarly matter, some critics and instructors, including us, consider sound to be an element of mise-en-scène. Other scholars consider mise-en-scène to be only the sum of *visual* elements in a film. Because of its complexity, we will discuss sound separately in Chapter 9. In this chapter, we will focus on the wholly visual aspects of mise-en-scène: on those filmmaking techniques and decisions that determine the placement, movement, and appearance of objects and people on-screen.

dramas such as *Jane Eyre* (2011; director Cary Fukunaga), *Amour* (2014; director Michael Haneke), and Richard Linklater's trilogy (*Before Sunrise*, 1995, *Before Sunset*, 2004, and *Before Midnight*, 2015). Mise-en-scène can also evoke unfamiliar places or cultures, such as hurricane-destroyed New Orleans in Benh Zeitlin's realistic and fantastic *Beasts of the Southern Wild* (2012), 1960s Greenwich Village in *Inside Llewin Davis* (2013; directors Ethan and Joel Coen), Europe between World Wars I and II in Wes Anderson's *The Grand Budapest Hotel* (2014), a racially divided town in the American South in *The Help* (2011; director Tate Taylor), or 1920s Paris in Woody Allen's *Midnight in Paris* (2011).

Allen and his longtime production designer Santo Loquasto are masters at conveying much of a story's dramatic thrust through the décor and settings in which their characters live, work, and play. His portrayals of New York City define many of his movies, such as *Annie Hall* (1978) and *Manhattan* (1980), and the characters look and feel so right for New York that one can imagine them as actual citizens, not actors.

All the movies we just listed challenge us to *read* their mise-en-scène and to relate it directly to the ideas and themes that the director is developing. Let's take a similar look at two more movies: Robert Mulligan's *To Kill a Mockingbird* (1962), an American classic, and Malgorzata Szumowska's *In the Name Of* (2013), a contemporary Polish movie. Each film helps us understand how its mise-en-scène works to develop its characters, plot, themes, and meanings. Both are concerned with major conflicts: the first with racial conflict in a small Southern town in the 1930s; the second, set in today's world, with a Catholic priest's conflict over his sexuality. Mulligan's film presents a social conflict, Szumowska's a personal one, and the settings of both films exemplify these struggles and are inseparable from them.

To Kill a Mockingbird is set in the small town of Maycomb, Alabama, a fictional place where racial discrimination, segregation, and lynching are part of everyday life. Maycomb is stuck in the Great Depression: poverty is rampant, its houses are dilapidated, and farmers can't find a market for their crops. The hero, Atticus Finch (Gregory Peck), is a trial lawyer and descendant of an old local family. He is one of the few people in town who believe that this situation is wrong and that it's time for a change. Most townspeople fear both African Americans and social change. Although Maycomb is surrounded by fields and forests, its heart is rotten to the core. The narrator, Atticus's daughter Scout (Mary Badham), is not burdened with racial prejudice; but even she fears night noises, cranky townsfolk, and the supposedly crazy neighbor Boo Radley (Robert Duvall).

Harper Lee's novel, and this movie based on it, are in the style of Southern Gothic, which emphasizes the backward, eccentric, disturbing, and grotesque elements of life in the American South. Despite its stereotypes and somewhat dated cinematic conventions (such as the overpowering musical score), the film is believable and moving. These elements suffuse the film's mise-en-scène, created in part by Henry Bumstead's design and Russell Harlan's dramatic black-and-white cinematography, which together recall Walker Evans's unforgettable photographs of the South in this period.[3] *To Kill a Mockingbird* owes much to Charles Laughton's *The Night of the Hunter* (1955), also shot in striking black and white. Indeed, both movies are among America's most enduring.

The conflict in *To Kill a Mockingbird* is rooted in the town's traditions and manners. Blacks and whites each have their place, separate and unequal, and tension hangs heavy. The situation erupts when Tom Robinson (Brock Peters), a black farmworker, is accused of raping a white woman. Atticus agrees to defend him; but throughout the trial, the town's soul is exposed in the attitudes of the prosecution, jury members, witnesses, and judge. Despite his eloquence, Atticus loses the case. Still not satisfied with the outcome, the community turns to vengeance. The conflict ends ambiguously: on a negative note, Robinson is shot by a deputy sheriff as he tries to escape. On a positive note, the supposedly crazy Boo Radley courageously saves Scout and her brother from Bob Ewell (James Anderson), the drunken madman responsible for fostering the posttrial chaos. Unfortunately, the movie ends where it started—in a Southern town fiercely split by racial tension. The movie is over, but the conflict continues. It leaves us to take sides.

The setting of *To Kill a Mockingbird* keeps us in one town, and we do not see other towns whose culture might provide an alternative to Maycomb's. By contrast, *In the Name Of* does recognize alternate worlds and

---

3. See James Agee and Walker Evans, *Let Us Now Praise Famous Men* (Boston: Houghton Mifflin, 1941).

1

2

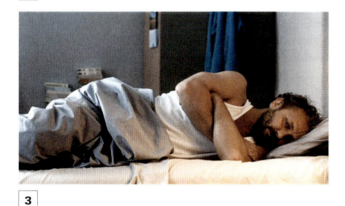

3

4

Mise-en-scène reinforces characters and themes

Both *To Kill a Mockingbird* and *In the Name Of* consider characters in conflict with their enclosed worlds: the first, a lawyer's social conflict with the racial discrimination of a small southern town in America; the second, a Catholic priest's personal conflict with his sexuality in a small Polish town. The confines of the town square of Maycomb in *To Kill a Mockingbird* [1] reflects its repressive ethos, which is echoed in an interior shot where we see Atticus Finch hemmed in on all sides [2] as he argues unsuccessfully for what he believes is right in a world he cannot escape. *In the Name Of* uses contrasting mise-en-scène to underscore its themes of entrapment and freedom, as shown in the interior of the priest's gloomy house [3, 4] contrasted with the freedom he feels playing with the boys whose school he supervises [5].

5

behaviors. It presents a similar conflict—conformity versus freedom—and is photographed in color, the way we naturally see the world.

The story is set in a small Polish village, particularly within the confines of a Catholic school for troubled teenagers. Adam (Andrezej Chyra), a young priest who has been assigned here, is dedicated to his daily work but has doubts about his calling as a priest. He hopes that being reassigned to a city parish will help him solve his conflict. Specifically, he cannot reconcile his vocation with his latent sexual attraction to men. Sexual temp-

tations surround him as he works with teenage boys who flaunt their muscular bodies as they work at farm duties and play rowdy games in the fields. He reveals no outward attraction to any of them, but jogs alone through the nearby woods in an attempt to clear his mind. However, he is also tempted by Eva (Maja Ostaszewska), who has married a former priest but is unsatisfied and tries to get Adam to have sex with her. She's as confused as he is, and Adam sends her away, saying ambiguously that he is "spoken for." (Their biblical names are ironic.) Adam's crisis occurs when Humpty (Mateusz Kosciukiewicz), one of the boys he supervises, slowly but aggressively seduces him into a sexual affair. This does not release Adam from his torment, and his superiors soon learn of his dilemma.

The subject of a priest confronting his sexuality is difficult to handle, but the mise-en-scène (Marek Za-wierucha's production design and Michal Englert's cinematography) establishes and reinforces the conflict through choice of film stock, composition, lighting, and imagery. As might be expected with a story like this, the setting involves contrasts: The countryside, with its abundant golden sunshine, represents freedom. The interiors of Adam's gloomy residence, the dim church, and shadowy forests where he runs represent the trap he is caught in. The cinematography contrasts soft interior imagery with documentary-style footage of the boys playing outside. While this film is not directly about the global problem of child abuse in the Catholic church, its turning point comes when a lay colleague reports Adam's illicit affair to the archbishop, who then rebukes Adam while apparently hiding from the realities of child abuse in his own jurisdiction. This scene helps us understand the film's title, which recalls the baptismal rites taken in the name of Jesus Christ. In *To Kill a Mockingbird*, there was plenty of talk in the courtroom about freedom, but to no reward; here, there is no discussion at all. Given the film's sparse dialogue, *In the Name Of* seems very much like a silent film, one where the visual images carry the weight of the story.

Atticus Finch seeks racial equality for his town, and he wins the argument but loses the battle. Adam and Eva seek free sexual expression and satisfaction but are also confined by their circumstances, and they also lose. The mise-en-scène defines each of these situations, the confined and tricky environments in which they unfold, and the inevitability of failure. These movies immerse us in mise-en-scène, creating a feeling completely in tune with their narrative and themes. At first, because this seems natural, we may not consciously notice it. Indeed, it simply feels natural.

French director René Clair said that the highest level of artistic achievement in movie design is reached when "the style relates so closely to that of the work itself that the audience pays no special attention to it."[4]

That description also fits the memorable Greenwich Village setting of Alfred Hitchcock's *Rear Window* (1954; art directors Joseph MacMillan Johnson and Hal Pereira). As the title credits roll, three bamboo shades rise, as if they were a curtain to reveal the stage beyond—an almost completely enclosed backyard space. The mise-en-scène is tightly controlled, and everything is photographed from the stationary point of view of L. B. Jefferies (James Stewart), a photographer with a broken leg who is sidelined in a wheelchair. As the camera next pans across the backyard in the early morning, we see the backs of the various structures that surround the open space: a glass-walled studio, a couple of brick apartment houses, and a small two-story house. An alley next to the house leads to the street beyond. It's located in the middle of New York City and, except for the alley, is isolated from the hubbub of street traffic. Within the first minutes, we have learned that this enclosed space embodies a world of differences: different structures, different tenants, and different lives. The tenants perceive that they live in a world of privacy, acting as if no one were watching; but (through Jefferies's eyes) we see them engaged in such private activities as shaving, getting out of bed, and dressing. Jefferies sees that in this enclosed space there are hidden, subtle clues that help him to solve the murder mystery at the heart of Hitchcock's narrative.[5]

Italian director Luchino Visconti's *The Leopard* (1963; production designer Mario Garbuglia) is an example of a film whose mise-en-scène perfectly complements its narrative and themes. The movie explores the gradual submergence and transformation of the aristocracy in Sicily after the unification of Italy, in 1861. More than anyone else in his family, Prince Don Fabrizio Salina (Burt Lancaster) makes sincere efforts to adjust to the emerging middle class, but at the same time he continues to enjoy the rituals he has always loved—masses in the family chapel, lavish banquets, travel to his other houses, and fancy balls. The 45-minute ball sequence (out of 185 minutes total), in fact, is the movie's set piece.

4. Qtd. in Léon Barsacq, *Caligari's Cabinet and Other Grand Illusions: A History of Film Design*, rev. and ed. Elliott Stein, trans. Michael Bullock (Boston: New York Graphic Society, 1976), p. vii.

5. For a superb analysis of the mise-en-scène and a fascinating account of the set's design and construction, see James Sanders, *Celluloid Skyline: New York and the Movies* (New York: Knopf, 2001), pp. 228–241.

1

2

3

4

Impressive mise-en-scène for Hitchcock's *Rear Window*

In *Rear Window*, director Alfred Hitchcock literally sets the stage by raising three bamboo window blinds one by one as the credits roll [1]. The principal mise-en-scène of the movie looks very much like a stage set; in fact, the single set was built to actual size—rising five stories—and filled one of the biggest soundstages on the studio lot. When completed, it included thirty-one individual apartments, twelve of them fully furnished, around a central courtyard [2], creating a memorable likeness of Greenwich Village in the early 1950s. The scope of this wonderful set permits the main character—Jeff Jefferies (James Stewart), who is temporarily immobilized in a wheelchair—to observe the activities of most of his neighbors. Indeed, he can do little else with his time. What we see is what he sees. Jeff becomes particularly interested in a married couple, seen here in their large apartment [3]. Lars Thorwald is in the kitchen (*left*) preparing a meal for his wife, a nagging invalid, who is in the bedroom (*right*). Over the next few days, Jeff will become preoccupied with Thorwald's behavior. His suspicions eventually lead to the police arresting Thorwald for the murder of his wife. Some less suspenseful things also occupy Jeff's voyeurism. Part of this courtyard complex is a small house with a terrace [4], where Jeff sees a young woman—Miss Torso, a dancer—entertaining several male friends. At the same time, the expansive set enables him to look through a passageway (*far left*) at people walking on a street. The street lamp and the human activity add the illusion of spatial depth and confirm that a world exists outside the courtyard.

Its length makes it more or less extraneous to the overall sequence of events in the movie, but its gorgeous surface beautifully reveals the social change beneath.

Visconti immerses us in the atmosphere of the ball: the grand rooms in the candlelit palazzo; the formalities of arrival and welcome; the ladies in elegant gowns and gentlemen in white-tie or military attire; the champagne and the food; the music; the room with a dozen chamber pots; the excitement of the young and the boredom of some of their elders; the endless gossiping and flirting; and the dancing of quadrilles, mazurkas, and waltzes. Visconti's care with the minute details of the decor, costumes, and characters' relationship to this environment is true to the time, space, and rhythm of life in the period.

The prince wanders from room to room, greeting old friends, reflecting on change. His only moment of real engagement in this sweepingly romantic ball is the powerful moment when he dances a waltz with Angelica (Claudia Cardinale), the fiancée of Tancredi (Alain Delon), the prince's nephew. The daughter of a crude but wealthy bourgeois, Angelica is unquestionably the most beautiful woman in the room, and the prince's dance with her is a sign to everyone at the ball of just how far the society has been transformed. He blesses the marital union as he accedes to the larger societal change. You can see and hear this transformation occurring, just as you can almost feel the silken texture of the gowns and the wall coverings and almost taste the wine and the food. Visconti's moving camera and changing angles bring us into the action and make us a participant, yet his control of the compositional elements keeps us focused on the main character. Throughout *The Leopard*, Visconti helps us to understand not only how his mise-en-scène has been constructed but also how it guides our reading of the scene's meaning. That room of colors, rituals, and music is a perfect lens through which to understand the change both inside and outside.

However, not all movies offer a mise-en-scène that successfully complements the movie's narrative and themes. Others overwhelm us with design, including Andy and Larry Wachowski's *The Matrix* (1999; production designer Owen Paterson), Martin Scorsese's *Gangs of New York* (2002; production designer Dante Ferretti), Michael Polish's *Northfork* (2003; production designers Brandee Dellaringa, Del Polish, and Ichelle Spitzig), and Christopher Nolan's *The Dark Knight* (2008; production designer Nathan Crowley). With *The Great Gatsby* (2013; production designer Catherine Martin), director Baz Luhrmann aspired to adapt a masterpiece of American literature into a musical. (This is the fifth film adaptation, and the first with a full musical score.)

Overpowering mise-en-scène in *The Great Gatsby*
The movies often make freewheeling adaptations of great novels. But the mise-en-scène of director Baz Luhrmann's adaptation of F. Scott Fitzgerald's novel is so overblown that it neither complements the narrative nor helps us understand it. While its razzle-dazzle style wowed some audiences as a fun night at the movies, it alienated others, such as critic Joe Morgenstern, who called it a "spectacle in search of a soul."[6]

The "novel into film" issue is not relevant here, for Luhrmann's treatment leaves the story far behind and replaces it with a garish mise-en-scène that continuously assaults our sensibilities. The design and overripe colors of the costumes have little to do with the 1920s, the period in which both the novel and film are set, although the makeup and hairstyles seem correct. Visually, the swirling movements of both camera and characters often disorient the viewer, calling more attention to graphic effects than plot or story. (It was even released in a 3-D version to heighten these effects.) Audibly, the film is very noisy. And musically, it is even more of an assault, blending musical references from many periods, movies,

Mise-en-scène as perfect complement to narrative in *The Leopard*
Luchino Visconti, one of the world's great masters of mise-en-scène, was at the height of his creative powers when he made *The Leopard*. Practically every setting, particularly the interiors of Prince Salina's palaces, is characterized by opulence and color. The rebellious activities in the streets outside are equally colorful. When Giuseppe Garibaldi, intent on unifying Italy and Sicily, swept through Sicily with his red-shirted forces [1], the aristocracy was overwhelmed. Princess Salina faints in her parlor as she hears the news; the orange flowers ironically echo the rebellion outside [2]. But life goes on: the prince reads aloud to his family in a sumptuous parlor, notable for the muted browns and purple tones [3]; supper is served in a magnificent dining room with walls covered in alternating orange and green fabrics [4]; the prince relaxes in his study with its red leather sofa, books bound in red, and red velvet draperies [5]; the family travels by coach through the comparatively barren landscape to their mountaintop palace [6], where Angelica, in a shocking pink dress, wanders through some of its abandoned rooms [7]. But it is in the 45-minute ballroom sequence that Visconti creates a virtual microcosm of how aristocratic Sicilian life has been altered in this time of great social transformation. This still image [8] from a sequence full of movement—swirling dancers, officers in splendid military uniforms with gold braid, active guests, and an almost constantly moving camera—features three of the principals: Tancredi (Alain Delon), in the far-left background in white-tie formal dress; Angelica (Claudia Cardinale), in a beautiful white gown; and Prince Don Fabrizio Salina (Burt Lancaster), dancing a waltz in the left middle ground. All of this is in a ballroom that has never changed, its walls covered by gold brocade fabric and lit entirely by candles. The prince stoically accepts the social changes, including the marriage of Angelica, who comes from a family of new wealth, and Prince Tancredi, his nephew, for his motto is "Things will have to change in order that they remain the same."

6. "The Grating 'Gatsby,'" *Wall Street Journal* (May 9, 2013).

1

2

3

4

5

6

7

8

1

2

Stanley Kubrick tightly controls mise-en-scène in *Eyes Wide Shut*

Two types of finely controlled mise-en-scène in Stanley Kubrick's *Eyes Wide Shut* (1999): [1] In this shot, which uses an indirect point of view, we see through the eyes of Dr. William Harford (Tom Cruise, not pictured) as he is brought before a ritualistic tribunal. Painterly framing concentrates our attention and thus accentuates the scene's harrowing, hallucinatory effects. Every particular in this image—the elaborate architecture, the beautiful masks and cloaks, the color scheme, the staging—makes clear that Harford is headed into the center of power within this cinematic underworld. [2] In contrast, a scene in which Harford searches for a costume in New York City's Greenwich Village seems natural, chaotic, even haphazard—but this illusion has been constructed as carefully as every other one in the movie. Here, the darkly clad Harford is the focal point amid more visual information than we can absorb. We note the urgency of his quest, not the details of the surroundings. (In fact, Kubrick filmed the Greenwich Village scenes not in his native New York but on sets in his adopted home, London. That the street names and shop names do not correspond to real ones in New York alerts sharp-eyed viewers to the sets' artificiality.)

and styles, including contemporary rap. Fortunately, the dignity of the novel remains unsullied for anyone who wants to read it. But the result has provoked some viewers to ask how much is too much before the mise-en-scène overwhelms the narrative. The movies can create the most imaginative spectacles, but when those spectacular effects do not help to tell the story, viewers are left with cinematic fireworks and little else.

The creation of a movie's mise-en-scène is nearly always the product of detailed planning of each shot in the movie. Planning a shot involves making advance decisions about the placement of people, objects, and elements of decor on the set; determining their movements (if any); setting up the lighting; figuring out the camera angles from which they will be photographed; determining the initial framing of the shot; choreographing the movement of the camera during the shot (if any); and creating the sounds that emanate from the shot. Mise-en-scène is the result of all that planning.

To be sure, impressive aspects of a movie's mise-en-scène can occur by chance, without planning, whether through an act of nature (a sudden rainstorm, for exam-

ple), an actor's deviating from the script, or some other accident. Although some directors display strict control of mise-en-scène and some don't, they generally collaborate with their teams to control every aspect of it. Consciously and deliberately put there by someone, staged for the camera, mise-en-scène happens because directors and their creative colleagues have envisioned it.

You should find the term *mise-en-scène* useful for explaining how all the formal elements of cinema contribute to your interpretation of a film's meanings. Indeed, the more familiar you become with film history, the more you will see that mise-en-scène can be used to distinguish the work of many great directors noted for their consummate manipulation of cinematic form. Among such directors are Wes Anderson, Tim Burton, John Ford, Alfred Hitchcock, Fritz Lang, Steve McQueen, Kenji Mizoguchi, F. W. Murnau, Yasujiro Ozu, Alexander Payne, Jean Renoir, Todd Solondz, Josef von Sternberg, and Orson Welles, to name but a few. Some directors (e.g., David Cronenberg, Lynne Ramsay, and Bela Karr) see the world differently—we often say that their vision of the world is different from what we ordinary mortals perceive—and when directors such as Paul Thomas Anderson (*The Master*, 2012), Terence Malick (*The Tree of Life*, 2011), and Alfonso Cuarón (*Pan's Labyrinth*, 2006) base their movies on dreamlike or mystical visions, we sometimes call their movies visionary. *Vision* and *visionary* are not terms to be used lightly.

Mise-en-scène can be highly personal and can help us distinguish one director's work from another's. But it can also be created through a predetermined formula, as it was, for instance, by the studios during the classical Hollywood studio era, when each studio typically had its own look. In addition, genre formulas can have a powerful influence on the mise-en-scène of individual films within that genre. Every director of a new film within a genre understands the pressure to make the mise-en-scène of that film correspond to the viewers' expectations of that genre. Nonetheless, each new film within a genre offers some new twist on the preceding formula, and those new twists may be the product of just a single collaborator's efforts.

Design

Sometimes the way the actors, setting, and decor in a movie look is the most powerful impression we take away from a first viewing. But design involves more than first impressions. Whatever its style and ultimate effect may be, design should help express a movie's vision; create a convincing sense of times, spaces, and moods; suggest a character's state of mind; and relate to developing themes.

Ideally, a movie's design should be appropriate to the narrative. So if the narrative strives to be realistic, then its look should have that quality too (as, for example, in Elia Kazan's *On the Waterfront* (1954; art director Richard Day). If its story is fantastic, then its design should mirror and complement the fantasy (Stuart Craig's production designs for all of the *Harry Potter* films to date are good examples). If a movie is of a particular genre, then its design should be suited to that genre. Every good designer knows that the Western needs open skies, the film noir relies on shadowy streets, and horror movies must have creepy, expressionistic effects. That does not mean using design clichés, as you can easily prove to yourself by watching a few great Westerns.

A movie's design should also be transparent, capable of transmitting light so that the audience can clearly see the actors, settings, objects, and so on within each setting. The director counts on a team of professionals to design the look of the movie with these important criteria in mind. Chief among these professionals is the production designer.

The challenge for the designers of James Cameron's *Avatar* (2009)—Rick Carter, Robert Stromberg, and Kim Sinclair—was to create a detailed vision of Pandora. Carter, the team's leader, has designed a number of science-fiction movies, including Steven Spielberg's *Jurassic Park* (1993) and *War of the Worlds* (2005). The extraterrestrial world of Pandora is populated by the blue-faced, thin-bodied Na'vi, a race that is physically superior to the technologically superior military and business interests that are mining valuable minerals in the area. Amid floating mountains, lush jungles, and cascading waterfalls, fly and gallop some of the most imaginative and gorgeous airborne and earthbound creatures ever seen on the screen. Using the most advanced cinematic technology to date—including Cameron's Reality Camera System (combining two cameras in a single camera body to create a heightened depth perception for the viewer)—the motion capture system, and other innovative visual effects, the designers created a world so awe-inspiring that their colleagues awarded them the Oscar for Best Art Direction.

The Production Designer

Generally one of the first collaborators that a director hires, the **production designer** works closely with the director as well as the director of photography in visualizing the movie that will appear on the screen. The production designer is both an artist and an executive, responsible for the overall design concept, for the look of the movie—its individual sets, locations, furnishings, props, and costumes—and for supervising the heads of the many departments involved in creating that look. These departments include

> art (developing the movie's look includes sketch artists, painters, and computer-graphics specialists)

> costume design and construction

> hairstyling

The twenty-second-century world of *Avatar*
Here we see Na'vi people as well as the human hybrids known as avatars in a jungle setting that was designed and lit to suggest an underwater realm. This is just one of the many ethereal jungle locations in the movie.

> makeup

> wardrobe (maintaining the costumes and having them ready for each day's shooting)

> location (finding appropriate locations, contracting for their use, and coordinating the transportation of cast and crew between the studio and the locations)

> properties (finding the right piece of furniture or object for a movie, either from a studio's own resources or from specialized outside firms that supply properties)

> carpentry

> set construction and decoration

> greenery (real or artificial greenery, including grass, trees, shrubs, and flowers)

> transportation (supplying the vehicles used in the film)

> visual effects (digital postproduction effects)

> special effects (mechanical effects and in-camera optical effects created during production)

During shooting, the production designer also works closely with the camera and lighting crews.

The title *production designer* is a relatively new one. In the classical Hollywood studio system of the 1930s, each studio had an art department headed by an executive (called the **art director**) who, in addition to creating and maintaining the studio's distinctive visual style, took full screen credit and any awards the film received for art direction. The art department collaborated with the other departments that bore any responsibility for a film's visual look. The supervising art director, though nominally in charge of designing all the studio's films, in fact assigned an individual art director to each movie. Most art directors were trained in drafting or architecture, and they brought to their work a fundamental understanding of how to draw and how to construct a building. Besides having a thorough knowledge of architecture and design, art directors were familiar with decorative and costume styles of major historical periods and were acquainted with all aspects of film production. As a result, the most accomplished art directors worked closely with film directors in a mutually influential and productive atmosphere.[7]

7. Despite their importance to the production process, most art directors worked in relative obscurity. Cedric Gibbons, supervising art director at MGM for thirty-two years, was the one art director for much of the twentieth century whom the general public knew by name, not only because the quality of MGM's style was so high but also because he was nominated forty times for the Academy Award for Art Direction, an honor he won eleven times.

By the 1960s, the title *production designer*, which we shall use, began to replace the title *art director*.[8] This shift in title wasn't merely a matter of ego or whim; it signaled an expansion of this important executive's responsibilities. In reality, yesterday's art director might not recognize the scope of responsibilities of today's production designer. The technological advances in all phases of production, as well as the increasing domination of computer-generated special effects, have completely changed the way movies are made. But even though today's production designers face more complicated challenges than their predecessors, their fundamental responsibility remains the same: to assist in realizing the overall look of a film.[9]

Design begins with the intensive previsualization done by the director and production designer—imagining, thinking, discussing, sketching, planning—that is at the core of all movies. If the collaboration succeeds, the production designer inspires the director to understand how the characters, places, objects, and so on will look as well as the relationships among these things. Responsible for everything on the screen except the actors' performances, the production designer helps create visual continuity, balance, and dramatic emphasis; indeed, the production designer "organizes the narrative through design."[10] Of course, the production designer's control over the final appearance of the movie is limited to a certain extent by the cinematographer's decisions about how to shoot the film.

The director and the production designer control, to paraphrase film theorist V. F. Perkins, everything we see *within* the image[11]; yet when they have different ideas about what a movie should look like, the design details can take precedence over the narrative and alter the relationship of the movie's formal elements. In all likelihood, this happened in Wes Anderson's *The Darjeeling Limited* (2007; production designer Mark Friedberg), a goofy, oddly touching movie about three brothers who are traveling together in India in an attempt to bond with one another against the odds.

The designer has paid meticulous attention to trains, clothes, luggage, personal belongings, and customs, but this is not sufficient to bolster the narrative or give meaning to it.

What about production design in animated films, which consist primarily, if not completely, of computer-generated imagery? While the relationship between the director and the production designer remains the same, the production designer and his staff have even greater control over the mise-en-scène and the entire look of the film than they could possibly have in nonanimated films. So, for example, in Brad Bird and Jan Pinkava's *Ratatouille* (2007; production designer: Harley Jessup), which has the visual perfectionism associated with Pixar Studios, the visual re-creation of Paris is magnificent, an integration of story and spectacle that recalls Vincente Minnelli's classic musical *An American in Paris* (1951; art directors E. Preston Ames and Cedric Gibbons).

Many art directors have become directors. Mitchell Leisen, for example, began his career designing films for Cecil B. DeMille and Ernst Lubitsch, who was the director of a long string of stylish studio films between 1934 and 1967. The Leisen style was pure glamour in interiors, clothes, and cars, as seen in the over-the-top Art Deco look of *Easy Living* (1937; art directors Hans Dreier and Ernst Fegté). Edgar G. Ulmer, who began his career designing several of the classic German Expressionist films—including F. W. Murnau's *The Last Laugh* (1924) as well as Murnau's Hollywood debut film, *Sunrise: A Song of Two Humans* (1927)—directed some fifty movies, most of which have cult status, including *The Black Cat* (1934). From his early career as an art director, Alfred Hitchcock learned much about creating visual and special effects, such as the powerful expressionist settings and lighting in *Number Seventeen* (1932; art director Wilfred Arnold). William Cameron Menzies was both a movie director (the futuristic *Things to Come* (1936; art director Vincent Korda) and a designer, whose most significant achievement was designing the entire production of Victor Fleming's *Gone with the Wind*

8. Actually, the title *production designer* was first used to acknowledge William Cameron Menzies's contributions to *Gone with the Wind* (1939), but it came into common use only in the 1960s. Menzies had drawn every shot of *Gone with the Wind*, and those meticulous drawings held the production together through four directors, many writers, and constant interventions by the producer, David O. Selznick. Before that—and through the 1950s—the credit title *art director* was generally used; in fact, Menzies won the first two Academy Awards for Art Direction, for movies made in 1927 and 1928.

9. See Cathy Whitlock and the Art Directors Guild, *Designs on Film: A Century of Hollywood Art Direction* (New York: Harper-Collins, 2010).

10. Charles Affron and Mirella Jona Affron, *Sets in Motion: Art Direction and Film Narrative* (New Brunswick, NJ: Rutgers University Press, 1995), p. 12.

11. V. F. Perkins, *Film as Film: Understanding and Judging Movies* (New York: Penguin, 1972), p. 74.

From director's drawing to screen
For *Hellboy II: The Golden Army*, director Guillermo del Toro made a clear drawing of how he thought Abe Sapien should appear [1]; you see how he actually looks on the screen in [2]. Obviously, this drawing was valuable to production designer Stephen Scott's on-screen conception.

(1939). Vincente Minnelli, who began his career as a theater designer, directed a host of lavish MGM musicals and dramas, all of which had outstanding production values (supervised by Cedric Gibbons, with whom Minnelli had legendary quarrels), including *Meet Me in St. Louis* (1944; art directors Gibbons, Lemuel Ayers, and Jack Martin Smith) and *Lust for Life* (1956; art directors Gibbons, Preston Ames, and Hans Peters). Ridley Scott began his career as a set designer for England's BBC television and has directed a series of visually stylish films, including *Prometheus* (2012). David Fincher, who began his career doing special effects and went on to do music videos for Madonna and other artists, has since directed *Se7en* (1995), *Fight Club* (1999), and *The Girl with the Dragon Tattoo* (2011).

Some directors make detailed drawings and storyboards to assist the production designer in fulfilling their vision. For example, the movies of Mexican director Guillermo del Toro are known, among other things, for the gruesome-looking beasts that populate them. His films include *Pan's Labyrinth* (2006; production designer Eugenio Caballero), *Hellboy* (2004; production designer Stephen Scott), and *Hellboy II: The Golden Army* (2008; production designer Scott). The "Hellboy" creatures resemble images from science fiction, Japanese anime, and horror movies. They originated in Mike Mignola's Dark Horse comic books, but del Toro sketched his own preproduction take on them. These meticulous drawings are accompanied by annotations that he enters in his diaries.

Elements of Design

During the process of envisioning and designing a film, the director and production designer (in collaboration with the cinematographer) are concerned with several

Movie sets are designed for the benefit of the camera

When a movie scene is shot in a studio (rather than at an actual location), the crew making a movie can give us the illusion of a whole room or building when, in fact, they construct only those aspects of a set needed for the benefit of the camera. David Fincher's *The Social Network* (2010; production designer Donald Graham Burt) was shot on actual locations in Massachusetts, Maryland, California, and England as well as in the Hollywood studio of Columbia Pictures. This set was designed and constructed to be a life-size representation of the Winklevoss brothers' dormitory rooms at Harvard; but as you can see, the principal room is missing its fourth wall, and lighting equipment is suspended from the ceiling (out of camera range). The wall with the window on the left clearly indicates that no shots will be made of the outside of the building in which this room is supposed to be. The camera is in the middle foreground, and through careful framing of each shot, the cinematographer will capture images that make us think this is an actual room. But fake as it is, the designers and decorators were meticulous about details, which one actor said helped him to better understand the characters and situation. The DVD release of *The Social Network* includes a supplementary disc that is unusually thorough in its detailed account of the film's making.

major elements. The most important of these are (1) setting, decor, and properties; (2) lighting; and (3) costume, makeup, and hairstyle.

Setting, Decor, and Properties The spatial and temporal **setting** of a film is the environment (realistic or imagined) in which the narrative takes place. In addition to its physical significance, the setting creates a mood that has social, psychological, emotional, economic, and cultural significance. The **set decorator**, who is in charge of all the countless details that go into furnishing and decorating a set, supervises a variety of specialists. The late Stephenie McMillan, a set decorator who worked with Stuart Craig, the production designer, on eight of the *Harry Potter* films, said that her job was to bring the production designer's vision to life. She believed that the look of a movie should never upstage the actors nor distract from the action.

Perhaps the most important decision that a filmmaker must make about setting is to determine when to shoot **on location** and when to shoot on a set. In the first two decades of moviemaking, the first preference was to shoot in exterior locations for both authenticity and natural depth. But location shooting proved expensive, and the evolution of larger studios made possible interiors (or sets) that were large, three-dimensional spaces that permitted the staging of action on all three planes and that could also accommodate multiple rooms. Interior shooting involves the added consideration of **decor**—the color and textures of the interior decoration, furniture,

1

2

Design of literary adaptations

Sir Arthur Conan Doyle's Sherlock Holmes detective stories have been adapted for nearly fifty movies. Some, like Guy Ritchie's 2009 version (*Sherlock Holmes*; production designer Sarah Greenwood and set decorator Katie Spencer), are set in designs of Holmes's Victorian London; others, like the BBC-TV series (*Sherlock Holmes*, 2010–2016; various directors, production designer Arwel Jones, and set decorators Joelle Rymbelow and Hannah Nicholson), are set in contemporary London. Both of these versions use existing locations as well as computer-generated imagery to reproduce the essentials of Holmes's elaborately messy apartment with its profusion of books, scientific equipment, and works of art—the true haunt of a man of many interests. In [1], Dr. Watson (Jude Law), accompanied by his fiancée Mary Morstan (Kelly Reilly), discovers Holmes (Robert Downey Jr.) hanging from the ceiling. Holmes has not taken his life but instead is testing a theory of how his antagonist could have escaped a hanging. The contemporary Holmes (Benedict Cumberbatch) [2] is every bit the match of his predecessor in deductive skills, using digital technology—including GPS, Twitter and other social media, and interactive maps—to locate his antagonists.

draperies, and curtains—and **properties** (or *props*), objects such as paintings, vases, flowers, silver tea sets, guns, and fishing rods that help us understand the characters by showing us their preferences in such things.

A movie set is not reality, but a fragment of reality created as the setting for a particular shot. It must be constructed both to look authentic and to photograph well. The first movie sets were no different from theater sets: flat backdrops erected, painted, and photographed in a studio, observed by the camera as if it were a spectator in the theater. Skylights and artificial lights provided indoor lighting. (Outdoors, filmmakers often left natural settings unadorned and photographed them realistically.) The first spectacular sets to be specifically constructed for a film were made in Italy; and with Giovanni Pastrone's epic *Cabiria* (1914; no credits for art director or costume designer), "the constructed set emerged completely developed and demanding to be imitated."[12] Indeed, its massive set was imitated in D. W.

Griffith's *Intolerance* (1916), which featured the first colossal outdoor sets constructed in Hollywood. Other directors soon began to commission elaborate sets constructed as architectural units out of wood, plaster, and other building materials or created from drawings that were manipulated by optical printers to look real. (Today, computers and computer-generated imagery—CGI—have replaced optical printers.)

The old Hollywood studios kept back lots full of classic examples of various types of architecture that were used again and again, often with new paint or landscaping to help them meet the requirements of a new narrative.[13] Today, the Universal Studios theme park in Hollywood preserves some of the sets from those lots. Sometimes, however, filmmakers construct and demolish a set as quickly as possible to keep the production on schedule. Only those aspects of a set that are necessary for the benefit of the camera are actually built, whether to scale (life-size) or in miniature, human-made or

12. Affron and Affron, *Sets in Motion*, p. 12.

13. See Stephen Binger et al., *M-G-M: Hollywood's Greatest Backlot* (Solana Beach, CA: Santa Monica Press, 2011).

1

2

3

First spectacular movie sets created for *Cabiria*

Giovanni Pastrone's extravagant and expensive *Cabiria* (1914) is regarded by many as the greatest achievement of the era of Italian blockbusters (roughly from 1909 through 1914). Its settings were the most complex and elaborate, yet they were created for a motion picture and, along with location shooting in Tunisia, Sicily, and the Alps, helped convince audiences that they were witnessing history in action (in this case, the Second Punic War between Rome and Carthage, which raged from 218 to 201 BCE). Italian pioneers of set design were later recruited by Hollywood producers and directors—including D. W. Griffith—to produce even more convincing (and expensive) backdrops for epic historical dramas. Three images give an idea of Pastrone's attempt at historical accuracy: [1] the Temple of Moloch; [2] Hannibal (Emilio Vardannes) and his troops crossing the Alps; and [3] Princess Sophonisba (Italia Almirante-Manzini) with her pet leopard, which is drinking milk.

computer-modeled. For example, the exterior front of a house may look complete with bushes and flowers, curtains in the windows, and so on, but there may be no rooms behind that facade. Constructed on a **soundstage**—a windowless, soundproofed, professional shooting environment that is usually several stories high and can cover an acre or more of floor space—will be only the minimum parts of the rooms needed to accommodate the actors and the movement of the camera: a corner, perhaps, or three sides.

On the screen, these parts will appear, in proper proportions to one another, as whole units. Lighting helps sustain this illusion. In *Citizen Kane* (1941; art directors Van Nest Polglase and Perry Ferguson), Orson Welles, like many others before him, was determined to make his sets look more authentic and thus photographed them from high angles (to show four walls) and low angles (to include both ceilings and four walls). In *The Shining* (1980; production designer Roy Walker), Stanley Kubrick mounted a special camera (called a Steadicam) on a wheelchair that could follow Danny (Danny Lloyd) on his Big Wheel to provide the boy's close-to-the-floor view of the Overlook Hotel sets, which included ceilings, rooms with four walls, and a seemingly endless series of corridors.

Lighting During the planning of a movie, most production designers include an idea of the lighting in their sketches. When the movie is ready for shooting, these sketches help guide the cinematographer in coordinating

1

2

Stark black-and-white lighting emphasizes a struggle between good and evil

In these images from *The Night of the Hunter*, which film critic Pauline Kael correctly calls "one of the most frightening movies ever made," the lighting underscores universal childhood fears. Before going to bed, John (Billy Chapin, *left*) is telling a story to his sister, Pearl (Sally Jane Bruce). Raised with the Bible in a fundamentalist home, he recounts a prophetic biblical tale that parallels the children's current situation. Just as he says, "The bad man came back," we see the ominous shadow of Harry Powell (Robert Mitchum) fall on the bedroom window [1]. These innocent children are deeply affected by his dark, menacing presence in their warm, cozy bedroom. Later, when confronting—almost trapping—John in a narrow hallway [2], Powell informs the boy that he will soon marry their mother and become their stepfather. Throughout the movie, elaborately staged, lit, and photographed shots contrast light and dark to reinforce the impending evil that is to change these children's lives.

the camera and the lighting. Light is not only fundamental to the recording of images on film but also has many important functions in shaping the way the final product looks, guiding our eyes through the moving image and helping to tell the movie's story. Light is an essential element in drawing the composition of a frame and realizing that arrangement on film. Through highlights, light calls attention to shapes and textures; through shadows, it may mask or conceal things. Often, much of what we remember about a film is its expressive style of lighting faces, figures, surfaces, settings, or landscapes. Both on a set and on location, light is controlled and manipulated to achieve expressive effects; except in rare instances, there is no such thing as wholly "natural" lighting in a movie.

The cinematographer Stanley Cortez said that in his experience only two directors understood the uses and meaning of light: Orson Welles and Charles Laughton.[14] Both directors began their careers on the stage in the 1930s, when theatrical lighting had evolved to a high degree of expressiveness. One of the great stage and screen actors of the twentieth century, Laughton directed only one film, *The Night of the Hunter* (1955; art director Hilyard Brown), an unforgettable masterpiece of suspense. For his cinematographer, he chose Cortez, a master of **chiaroscuro**—the use of deep gradations and subtle variations of lights and darks within an image.

Cortez once remarked that he "was always chosen to shoot weird things,"[15] and *The Night of the Hunter* is a weird film in both form and content. Its story focuses on Harry Powell (Robert Mitchum), an itinerant, phony preacher who murders widows for their money. His victims include the widow of a man who stole $10,000 to protect his family during the Depression, hid the money

14. See Charles Higham, "Stanley Cortez," in *Hollywood Cameramen: Sources of Light* (London: Thames & Hudson in association with the British Film Institute, 1970), p. 99.

15. Stanley Cortez, qtd. ibid., p. 102.

1

2

3

Expressive lighting in *City of God*

Lighting plays a powerful role in establishing the setting (as well as character and mood) in Fernando Meirelles and Kátia Lund's *City of God* (2002), a violent story of constantly changing moods that is told with equally rapid changes in style. [1] For a playful day on the beach, the lighting is bright sunlight, probably intensified by reflectors. [2] For a drug deal in a decaying slum building, the strong sunlight is filtered through a brick screen into the creepy hallway. [3] Strobe lights and reflections underscore the rapidly developing chaos at a disco party.

inside his daughter's doll, and swore both of his children to secrecy. After Harry marries and murders their widowed mother, the children flee. They end up at a farm downriver kept by Rachel Cooper (Lillian Gish), a kind of fairy godmother devoted to taking in homeless children. When Harry tracks down the kids and begins to threaten the safety of Rachel and her "family," Rachel sits on her porch, holding a shotgun to guard the house, while Harry, lurking outside, joins her in singing a religious hymn, "Lean on Jesus." Laughton uses backlighting that has a hard quality associated with the evil, tough Harry, but he also uses it on Rachel—not to equate her with his evil, but to intimate that she is a worthy adversary for him. Later in the same scene, she is suddenly lit differently—softer light, from a different direction, creates a halo effect through light behind her—because at this moment in the movie the director wants to emphasize not her resolve or her ability to stand up to Harry, but her purity of spirit.

The story and emotional tones of Fernando Meirelles and Kátia Lund's *City of God* (2002; cinematographer César Charlone), to cite another example, are closely linked with the movie's use of light. The codirectors and production designer, Tulé Peak, work with the contrasts between bright sunlight on the beach, the various kinds of lighting in the houses and apartments in the Brazilian slums, and in a climactic moment in the movie, in a crowded disco. The lighting in the disco is true to the source: the flickering spangles that come from the revolving mirrored ball high above the dancers; spotlights that are moved restlessly; banks of bright lights to which the camera returns again and again rhythmically, increasing our awareness that the situation is getting out of control. During this scene, Benny (Phellipe Haagensen), a drug dealer who has decided to go straight, is murdered by Neguinho/Blackie (Rubens Sabino) after a heated quarrel. The pulsating strobe lighting ramps up the chaos of the scene, and although it is perfectly natural to the world of the disco, it underscores the violent struggle between Benny's desire to get out of the terrible world he has been involved in so he can lead a good life and the evil forces that want to stop him from accomplishing his goal.

Costume, Makeup, and Hairstyle During the years of the classical Hollywood studio system, the actors' box-office appeal depended on their ability to project a screen image that audiences would love. Makeup and

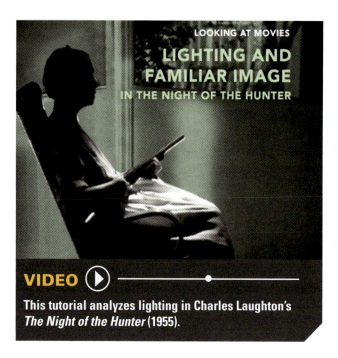

VIDEO

This tutorial analyzes lighting in Charles Laughton's *The Night of the Hunter* (1955).

many different parts, often changing her appearance (through costume, makeup, and hairstyle) to suit the roles. Theron has played Aileen Wuornos, a mentally ill prostitute who brutally kills seven of her clients in Patty Jenkins's *Monster* (2003); Gilda Bessé, a French Resistance fighter against the Nazis in John Duigan's *Head in the Clouds* (2004); the rebellious title character in Karyn Kusama's science-fiction thriller *Æon Flux* (2005); a police detective in Paul Haggis's *In the Valley of Elah* (2007), a provocative film about the aftereffects of the Iraq war on some U.S. soldiers; and in a **cameo** role, the character known as Woman in John Hillcoat's *The Road* (2009), about survival in a postapocalyptic world. Without the changes brought by costume, makeup, and hairstyle, she easily appears as her beautiful self in such films as Niki Caro's *North Country* (2005), Peter Berg's *Hancock* (2008), Guillermo Arriaga's *The Burning Plain* (2008), and Ivan Reitman's *Young Adult* (2011).

hair were the two most personal aspects of that image. The studios frequently took actors with star potential and "improved" their looks by having their hair dyed and restyled, their teeth fixed or replaced, or their noses reshaped or sagging chins tightened through cosmetic surgery. Such changes were based on each studio's belief that its overall look included a certain "ideal" kind of beauty, both feminine and masculine. To that end, each studio had the right to ask actors under contract to undergo plastic or dental surgery to improve their images on and off the screen. (Today's audiences have learned to love actors for their individual looks and styles, not for their conformity to ideals determined by the studios.) This classical approach led to the typecasting of actors in certain kinds of roles with which they became identified. An actor's ability to break out of stereotyped casting, when possible, was often due to the studio's design staff, whose work gave the actor a new look.

Today's actors, unfettered by rigid studio contracts, tend to play a wider variety of roles than they would have in the 1930s and 1940s. Although the actors' range and skill are important in making these different roles believable, perhaps even more important is the work of the art departments' professional staff to render the actors' appearance appropriate to the role. For example, Charlize Theron, a versatile actor who has won multiple awards for her talent, has taken on

Costume The setting of a film generally governs the design of the **costumes** (the clothing, sometimes known as *wardrobe*, worn by an actor in a movie). Costumes can contribute to that setting and suggest specific character traits, such as social station, self-image, the public image that the character is trying to project, state of mind, overall situation, and so on. Thus costumes are another element that helps tell a movie's story.

When the setting is a past era, costume designers may need to undertake extensive research to ensure authenticity. Even with such research, however, the costumes in historical films often do not accurately depict such details as women's necklines, breast shapes, and waistlines. Hats tend to look more contemporary and undergarments more lavish than they would have historically. Designing costumes for a movie set in the contemporary world is equally rigorous, perhaps even more so. Because the characters will wear clothes similar to our own, the designer understands that we will read these costumes more closely and interpret them on the basis of our experiences. The same can be said of makeup and hair design.

Although verisimilitude is a factor in costume design, other factors—style, fit, condition, patterns, and color of the clothing—can also define and differentiate characters. In Tim Burton's *Edward Scissorhands* (1990; costume designer Colleen Atwood; makeup designer

Costume, makeup, and hairstyle

Charlize Theron has created a memorable list of characters, ranging from comic and delightful to disturbing and tragic. No matter what role she plays, she is able to personify the character largely because of her acting talent, but also thanks to the artists who helped create her screen image. [1] In *Monster*, she plays Aileen Wuornos, a serial murderer, who is here driving frantically away from the scene of a near-accident. For this role, she put on weight, her makeup artists covered her face with freckles, and she wore a shabby wig. [2] In *Æon Flux*, a science-fiction thriller, she has an entirely different look: an asymmetrical black wig, perfectly applied eyeliner, and sculpted, black eyebrows all add to the mysteriousness of her character. [3] She plays a young French aristocrat who becomes the lover of a Nazi officer in *Head in the Clouds*, a political thriller set in the turmoil of late-1930s Europe. In such a role, we would expect her to be chic and sophisticated, and she does not disappoint, appearing here with a carefully coiffed wig, sculpted eyebrows, bright red lipstick and fingernails, and a neatly tailored suit. [4] In *North Country*, there are times when Theron, in the role of Josey Aimes, looks much as she does in real life. As one of few women working at a Minnesota mine, Josey rebels against the pervasive sexual harassment and eventually wins a landmark class action suit that changed the workplace forever. Here, at the trial and under pressure from the prosecuting attorney, she creates a distinctive impression with a casual wig and light, unobtrusive makeup. She is hated by most of the townspeople, who owe their livelihood to the mine, and she is the victim of witnesses who lie, yet she projects the image of an honest woman with a mission.

Ve Neill), Edward's (Johnny Depp) outsider status and otherness are emphasized by his costume and makeup. Other characters' traits, such as conformity, sexual neediness, and brutality are also portrayed through makeup and costume.

Two movies with brilliant costumes created for memorable actors impersonating other celebrities are Gus Van Sant's *To Die For* (1995; costume designer Beatrix

Aruna Pasztor), in which Nicole Kidman plays a delusional, driven "dumb blond" (almost a Marilyn Monroe imitation) who wants more than anything to be a TV star. Her costumes—pastel outfits that make her seem cute and cuddly—represent her vision of herself, but in fact she is a scheming backstabber who will do anything to get ahead. In Brian W. Cook's *Color Me Kubrick* (2005; costume designer Vicki Russell), a somewhat true

The importance of costume design in *Alice in Wonderland*

Tim Burton's adaptation of the classic story *Alice in Wonderland* (2010) is rendered with live action and computer-animated characters, all wearing whimsical costumes. John Tenniel's original drawings for Lewis Carroll's *Alice's Adventures in Wonderland* and *Through the Looking Glass* were in black and white, but Burton's conception is in full, rich color, very much in the tradition of his other highly imaginative movies, including *Edward Scissorhands* (1990) and *Charlie and the Chocolate Factory* (2005). Colleen Atwood won an Oscar for her design of the costumes, including those of the principal characters: [1] the Red Queen (Helena Bonham Carter), [2] the White Rabbit (voiced by Michael Sheen), [3] the Mad Hatter (Johnny Depp) and Alice (Mia Wasikowska), and [4] the White Queen (Anne Hathaway). Each of these costumes reinforces the uniqueness of the characters for whom they were created. But even costumes as good as these cannot exist by themselves. They are part of the film's larger world, particularly its overall production design (by Robert Stromberg) and set decoration (by Karen O'Hara). Both Stromberg and O'Hara also won Oscars for their achievements.

story, John Malkovich plays Alan Conway. Until he was caught and jailed, Conway masqueraded as movie director Stanley Kubrick in order to pick up young men in gay bars. In the first example, we are so familiar with Monroe's persona that it's a delight to see how she might have looked on the other side of stardom; in the second example, because Kubrick was a well-known recluse (and not known to be gay), the costume designer had free rein to create outrageous costumes for his impersonator.

Historical films tend to reflect both the years they hope to represent and the years in which they were

created. Nonetheless, they shape our ideas of historical dress. For example, although Walter Plunkett's clothing designs for Victor Fleming's *Gone with the Wind* (1939; production designer William Cameron Menzies) are often quite anachronistic, audiences usually see them as truly reflecting what people wore during the Civil War. Even though we have plenty of evidence to show what people wore in the mid-1800s, Vivien Leigh's appearance as Scarlett O'Hara only approximates how a woman of her social class might have dressed. Still, the costume design in *Gone with the Wind* often supports the narrative very well. Scarlett's green dress made from a curtain plays a major role in one scene and tells us a great deal about her character: the green reminds us of her Irish background, and the use of curtains reminds us of her newfound practicality and frugality. Ann Roth's costumes for Anthony Minghella's *Cold Mountain* (2003), another movie about the Civil War, were based on diligent research as well as on her belief that costumes help an actor to create character by either restricting or facilitating movement. For Joseph L. Mankiewicz's *Cleopatra* (1963), Irene Sharaff created spectacular costumes for Elizabeth Taylor that were basically contemporary gowns designed to accentuate the actress's beauty; experts agree that they bear little resemblance to the elaborate styles of the late Greco-Roman period.

When a film involves the future, as in science fiction, the costumes must reflect the social structure and values of an imaginary society. They also must look the way we expect "the future" to look. Ironically, these costumes almost always reflect historical influences. The characters may live on other planets, but the actors' costumes recall, for example, the dress of ancient Greeks and Romans (as in Richard Marquand's *Star Wars VI: Return of the Jedi*, 1983; costume designers Aggie Guerard Rodgers and Nilo Rodis-Jamero), Asian samurai and geisha (as in Daniel Haller's *Buck Rogers in the 25th Century*, 1979; costume designer Jean-Pierre Dorléac), or medieval knights and maidens (as in Leonard Nimoy's *Star Trek III: The Search for Spock*, 1984; costume designer Robert Fletcher).

The movies have always been associated with the greatest style and glamour. Beautiful clothes worn by beautiful people attract audiences, and since the earliest years filmmakers have invested considerable effort and expense in costume design. Giovanni Pastrone's Italian epic *Cabiria* (1914) was the first major film in which costumes were specifically designed to create the illusion of an earlier period (in this case, the Second Punic War, 218–201 BCE). That film influenced D. W. Griffith when he made *The Birth of a Nation* (1915; costume designer Robert Goldstein) and *Intolerance* (1916; costume designer Clare West, uncredited), both notable for their authentic costumes. *Birth of a Nation*, concerned with the Civil War, featured Ku Klux Klan robes that helped provoke the public outrage against the film. *Intolerance* told stories set in four different periods in history, each requiring its own costumes—some of which, as in the

Babylon sequence, were researched carefully and realized extravagantly. Before those films were made, actors wore their own clothes, whether or not those garments were appropriate for the setting of a film. During the 1920s, costume design became a serious part of the glamour of such stars as Gloria Swanson (in Erich von Stroheim's *Queen Kelly*, 1929), Theda Bara (in J. Gordon Edwards's *Cleopatra*, 1917), and Clara Bow (in Clarence G. Badger's *It*, 1927).

In the 1930s, with the studio and star systems in full swing, Hollywood began to devote as much attention to costume as to setting. One measure of the impact of such fashionable design work was that the public bought huge quantities of copies of the clothing originally created for movie stars. Yet Hollywood has tended to regard costume design less seriously than some of the other design areas in film. From its establishment in 1928, the Academy of Motion Picture Arts and Sciences gave awards for art direction, but it did not establish awards for costume design until 1948.

Makeup and Hairstyling The makeup used to enhance or alter (positively or negatively) an actor's appearance falls into two general categories: traditional materials and digital methods. Traditional materials cover the full range of facial and body cosmetics familiar to consumers, often specially blended to comply with camera and lighting requirements. Materials include prosthetics for creating aging effects or the frightening effects so common to horror movies; hair design, including wigs and other hairpieces; and all sorts of foam or plastic materials to increase the illusion of a character's weight, height, build, or walk.

The person responsible for all these effects is the **makeup artist**. This person must be experienced in using the traditional materials just outlined as well as able to work closely with the specialists involved in creating digital makeup, the production designer and art director, and the cinematographer. They must also work with actors themselves, usually accompanying them to the set and performing whatever touch-ups are necessary. To make a character convincing on the screen, they may also fit actors with false teeth, cover their bodies with tattoos and bruises, and restyle their hair.

For *Dallas Buyers Club* (2013; director Jean-Marc Vallée; makeup and hairstyling Adruitha Lee and Robin Mathews), the two lead actors, Matthew McConaughey

Transformative power of makeup, weight loss, hairstyle, and costume

In *Dallas Buyers Club*, the vivid makeup, hairstyles, and costumes created for Matthew McConaughey and Jared Leto help the actors realize their characters on-screen. In addition, each actor lost considerable weight to better reflect their HIV-positive condition. Here, these elements transform Leto into Rayon, a flamboyant transgender woman who is the perfect foil for McConaughey's cowboy character.

(Ron Woodroof) and Jared Leto (Rayon), play men stricken by AIDS. They were almost unrecognizable due to their weight loss (50 and 30 pounds, respectively) as well as the costumes, makeup, and hairstyling that transformed them into their characters. Ron Woodroof, a former rodeo rider, is in and out of the hospital during the movie; and though he looks emaciated and sick, he retains his macho behavior. He denies his homosexuality and is hostile to gay and lesbian people. The movie is set in 1985, when HIV drugs were still being tested and thus unapproved for use, and Woodroof runs a service that smuggles and sells these drugs to other HIV-positive patients. In this effort, he reluctantly recruits Rayon to help him. Rayon is a glamorous transgender woman whose appearance is partially created by distinctive wigs, makeup (skin blemishes and shaved eyebrows, in particular), and flamboyant costumes. Leto shows great commitment, focus, and consistency as an actor who stays solidly in character throughout the movie until Rayon's death. The movie won the Oscar for Best Makeup and Hairstyling.

The digital revolution has affected almost all areas of moviemaking, including makeup and hairstyling. Since the early 1990s, digital makeup has enabled makeup artists to achieve effects previously impossible to create. Virtually every fantasy, action, or science-fiction movie since then has employed digital effects for altering an actor's appearance. Digital artists scan photographic images of actors (faces or whole body) into a computer and alter them digitally. It seems simple, but in fact it is quite complicated. If you've ever used software such as Photoshop to alter a photograph, you have some idea of how

1

2

The expressive power of makeup

For Christopher Nolan's *The Dark Knight* (2008), a large team of makeup artists and hairstylists created the look of two remarkable characters. [1] The Joker (Heath Ledger) is a psychopathic criminal with a sick sense of humor, green hair, and a purple suit. But it's his face makeup that is most remarkable—that great, gashed red mouth, created through facial painting and prosthetics—a darkly comic deformation and a visual parallel to the character's dual traits of sadistic humor and true evil. In contrast, [2] Harvey Dent (Aaron Eckhart) appears normal in the first part of the movie as the handsome district attorney who attempts to eliminate organized crime from Gotham City. But toward the end, in a climactic struggle, Dent's face is badly burned by an explosion rigged by the Joker, and he is then known as "Two-Face." This horrifying face was created by a digital makeup process that essentially allowed the designers to remove half of Eckhart's face from a digital image and replace it with their creation.

it works. When done with great artistry, as in creating the character of Caesar (Andy Serkis), leader of the apes, in Matt Reeves's *Dawn of the Planet of the Apes* (2014; makeup artists Stacey Herbert and crew), the effects are astonishing. No less astonishing is the large team of digital artists needed to make these effects believable.

Although many directors favor makeup that is as natural as possible, audiences tend to notice makeup design when it helps create an unusual or fantastic character: Boris Karloff as the Monster in James Whale's *Frankenstein* (1931; makeup designer Jack P. Pierce); the self-transformation through science of Fredric March from the mild Dr. Jekyll into the evil side of his own character, the lustful and hideous Mr. Hyde, in Rouben Mamoulian's *Dr. Jekyll and Mr. Hyde* (1931; makeup designer Wally Westmore); James Cagney as the great silent-screen actor Lon Chaney in Joseph Pevney's *Man of a Thousand Faces* (1957; makeup designers Bud Westmore and Jack Kevan); the ape-men in Stanley Kubrick's *2001: A Space Odyssey* (1968; makeup designer Stuart Freeborn); or the varied creatures in the Lord of the Rings trilogy (makeup designer Peter King).

During the studio years, hairstyles were based on modified modern looks rather than on the period authenticity favored in costumes. Exceptions to this rule—such as Bette Davis's appearing as Queen Elizabeth I with shaved eyebrows and hairline in Michael Curtiz's *The Private Lives of Elizabeth and Essex* (1939) and with a bald head in the same role in Henry Koster's *The Virgin Queen* (1955)—are rare, because few studios were willing to jeopardize their stars' images. The idea of achieving historical accuracy in hairstyle was completely undercut in the late 1930s, when the studios developed a "Hollywood Beauty Queen" wig serviceable for every historical period. This all-purpose wig was worn by, among many others, Norma Shearer in W. S. Van Dyke's *Marie Antoinette* (1938) and Glynis Johns in Norman Panama and Melvin Frank's medieval comedy *The Court Jester* (1955). Generic as this wig was, hairstylists could obviously cut and style it to conform to the requirements of the individual production. Thus one hairstyle served to depict two different characters at two different times in history.

In fact, until the 1960s, actors in almost every film, whether period or modern, were required to wear wigs designed for the film for reasons both aesthetic and

Makeup as deception
In W. S. Van Dyke's *Marie Antoinette* (1938; costume designer Adrian), one of the most lavish costume epics ever made, the French queen (Norma Shearer) looks as glamourous as a movie star; Adrian, the designer, did everything in his power to embellish Shearer's screen image rather than make her resemble the queen, whose comparatively plain face is familiar from many paintings and other representations.

practical. In shooting out of sequence, which allows continuous scenes to be shot weeks apart, it is particularly difficult to re-create colors, cuts, and styles of hair. Once designed, a wig never changes, so at least an actor's hair won't be the source of a continuity "blooper." Such aspects of continuity are the responsibility of the **script supervisor**, who once kept a meticulous log of each day's shooting. Today, script supervisors use a tiny **video assist camera**, which is mounted in the viewing system of the film camera and provides instant visual feedback so they can view a scene (and thus compare its details with those of surrounding scenes) before sending the film to the laboratory for processing. Although wigs are still used frequently in the movies, hairstyling today reflects the more natural look of contemporary characters. Where historical expectations demand accuracy in hairstyling, wigs are used. Examples include Keira Knightley as Anna, the doomed Russian countess, in *Anna Karenina* (2012; director Joe Wright); Lupita Nyong'o as Patsey, a slave girl, in *12 Years a Slave* (2013; director Steve McQueen); and Ralph Fiennes as M. Gustave, a 1920s European hotel concierge in *The Grand Budapest Hotel* (2014; director Wes Anderson).

1

2

Hairstyles

Putting stars before the camera in hairstyles from, say, the Greek or Roman period, the Middle Ages, or even eighteenth-century France could threaten an actor's image with the public. Thus American studios in the 1930s devised the Hollywood Beauty Queen (HBQ) wig, which could be cut and styled to make it most flattering to the wearer. [1] The stylized HBQ wigs Vivien Leigh wore as Scarlett O'Hara in *Gone with the Wind* (1939) were, according to experts, more suggestive of the 1930s than the 1860s, the period in which the story is set. [2] The HBQ wig worn by Maid Jean (Glynis Johns) in *The Court Jester* (1955), however, has been styled more in keeping with the 1950s than the Middle Ages. Hubert Hawkins (Danny Kaye) is presumably wearing his own hair, but he also looks very contemporary.

International Styles of Design

Although there are as many styles of design as there are production designers, film design arguably uses only two fundamental styles: the realistic and the fantastic. These two styles were established in France in the very first motion pictures. The Lumière brothers pioneered the nonfiction film, shooting short, realistic depictions of everyday activities. Georges Méliès created the fictional film, using illusions he had learned in the theater. As Méliès employed all kinds of stage tricks, mechanisms, and illusions, he invented a variety of cinematic effects. In so doing, he also invented the film set, and thus we can consider him the first art director in film history.

In Russia, after the 1917 revolution, the avant-garde constructivists and futurists reshaped the entire concept of cinema: what it is, how it is shot, how it is edited, and how it looks. The great Russian filmmakers of the 1920s and 1930s—Dziga Vertov, Lev Kuleshov, Sergei Eisenstein, Vsevolod I. Pudovkin, and Aleksandr Dovzhenko—were influenced by two seemingly contradictory forces: (1) the nonfiction film, with its "docu-

mentary" look, and (2) a highly dynamic style of editing. The Russian films were masterpieces both of cinematic design and of political propaganda involving so-called socialist realism. They combined highly realistic exterior shots with an editing rhythm that, ever since, has affected the handling of cinematic time and space.

In 1922, Russian artists working in Paris introduced scenic conventions from the Russian realistic theater to French cinema. They also experimented with an array of visual effects influenced by contemporary art movements—cubism, dadaism, surrealism, and abstractionism. In the following decades, the look of the Russian film changed in many ways, including greater use of art directors, studio and location shooting, and constructed sets and artificial lighting. Notable are Isaak Shpinel's designs for two great Eisenstein films: *Alexander Nevsky* (1938), whose medieval helmets, armor, and trappings for horses rival any historical re-creation ever seen on the screen, and *Ivan the Terrible: Parts I* and *II* (1944, 1958). Much later, Yevgeni Yenej and Georgi Kropachyov designed two Shakespearean films: Grigori Kozintsev's adaptations of *Hamlet* (1964) and *King Lear* (1971). This version of *Hamlet*, in particular, is noteworthy for being filmed at Kronborg Castle in Elsinore, Denmark. The director uses the castle's mighty staircases for highly choreographed movement and the sounds and sights of the surrounding sea for emotional effect.

However, most important early developments in art direction took place in Germany. Expressionism, which emerged in the first decades of the twentieth century, influenced almost every form of German art, including the cinema. Its goal was to give objective expression to subjective human feelings and emotions by using objective design elements such as structure, color, or texture. It also aimed at heightening reality by relying on such nonobjective elements as symbols, stereotyped characters, and stylization. In German cinema, in the years immediately following World War I, expressionism gave rise to a new approach to composition, set design, and directing. The object was to create a totally unified mise-en-scène that would increase the emotional impact of the production on the audience.

Expressionist films were characterized by extreme stylization in their sets, decor, acting, lighting, and camera angles. The grossly distorted, largely abstract sets were as expressive as the actors, if not more so. To ensure complete control and free manipulation of the decor, lighting, and camera work, expressionist films were generally shot in the studio even when the script called for exterior scenes—a practice that was to have an important effect on how movies were later shot in Hollywood. Lighting was deliberately artificial, emphasizing deep shadows and sharp contrasts; camera angles were chosen to emphasize the fantastic and the grotesque; and the actors externalized their emotions to the extreme.

The first great German Expressionist film was Robert Wiene's *The Cabinet of Dr. Caligari* (1920). Designed by three prominent artists (Hermann Warm, Walter Reimann, and Walter Röhrig) who used painted sets to reflect the anxiety, terror, and madness of the film's characters, this movie reflected psychological states in exterior settings. *Dr. Caligari* gave space—interior and exterior—a voice. Its highly experimental and stylized setting, decor, costumes, and figure movement influenced the design of later German silent classics such as F. W. Murnau's *Nosferatu* (1922) and Fritz Lang's *Destiny* (1921), *Siegfried* (1924), *Kriemhild's Revenge* (1924), and *Metropolis* (1927). The influence of expressionist design is evident in such genres as horror movies, thrillers, and film noirs, and many films have paid hom-

LOOKING AT MOVIES

SETTING AND EXPRESSIONISM

VIDEO ▶ ━━━━━━━━━●━━━━

In this tutorial, Dave Monahan looks at setting in classic and contemporary films that have been influenced by German Expressionism.

age to the expressionist style, including James Whale's *Frankenstein* (1931; art director Charles D. Hall) and Woody Allen's *Shadows and Fog* (1992; production designer Santo Loquasto).

While the expressionist film was evolving, the Germans developed a realist cinema (known as *Kammerspielfilm*), the masterpiece of which is F. W. Murnau's *The Last Laugh* (1924; production designer Edgar G. Ulmer). This film radically changed the way shots were framed, actors were blocked, and sets were designed and built. It succeeded thanks mainly to Murnau's innovative use of the moving camera and the subjective camera. His "unchained camera" freed filmmakers from the limitations of a camera fixed to a tripod; his subjective camera used the camera eye as the eyes of a character in the film, so the audience saw only what the character saw. These new developments intensified the audience's involvement in events on-screen, extended the vocabulary by which filmmakers could tell and photograph stories, and thus influenced the conception and construction of sets.

From the 1920s on, Hollywood's idea of design became aesthetically more complex and beautiful as the studios hired foreign-born directors and art directors (e.g., Alfred Hitchcock, Erich von Stroheim, F. W. Murnau). In the early 1930s, some talented filmmakers fled the Nazis and went to work in California (Karl Freund, Fritz

1

2

3

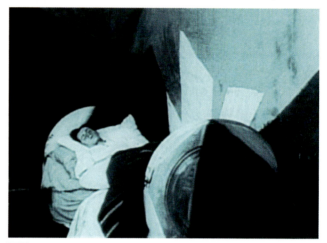

4

Expressionism

Highly stylized sets and **intertitles (insert titles)** added to the radical look of *The Cabinet of Dr. Caligari,* as in the following examples taken from the 1996 release of the restored movie. Image [1] is an abstract graphic intertitle—"The Annual Fair in Holstenwall"—tinted in beige, white, and brown; it immediately precedes image [2], an icy blue-tinted drawing that exaggerates the shape and height of the mountain town. Image [3] is also an abstract graphic—"Night"—tinted white, gray, and green, which precedes [4], another icy blue-tinted shot of a man asleep in his bed. In a convention used throughout the movie, the walls behind his bed are not actual walls but a painted image of them in a distorted perspective tinted in black, white, and gray. Rose-colored tints are used in other images. Such conventions ushered in an era of expressionist cinematography, design, and mise-en-scène in the United States and elsewhere. That influence is clear in, for example, Charles D. Hall's designs for James Whale's *Frankenstein* (1931) and *Bride of Frankenstein* (1935), Jack Otterson's designs for Rowland V. Lee's *Son of Frankenstein* (1939), Van Nest Polglase and Perry Ferguson's designs for Orson Welles's *Citizen Kane* (1941), and the designs of countless film noirs.

1

2

The powerful influence of German Expressionist design

The color design of *The Cabinet of Dr. Caligari* influenced many movies, including Dario Argento's *Suspiria* (1977; production designer Giuseppe Bassan). The plot of this popular slasher movie concerns Suzy Bannion (Jessica Harper), a young American ballet student who is studying at a supposedly prestigious German dance academy. She soon realizes that life there is not what she expected, for it includes murders, bizarre behavior, weird apparitions and noises, and an erratic director and ballet mistress. When Suzy investigates, she learns that a witches' coven rules the house and that they have tagged her for murder. Much like *Caligari*, in which Wiene used hand-tinted colors to externalize emotions, in *Suspiria* Argento saturated his shots (fifty-seven years after *Caligari*) with deep Technicolor reds and blues. In [1], these colors transform Suzy's paranoid fears into a surrealist stage setting. In [2], we see her escape this claustrophobic mise-en-scène as it collapses around her.

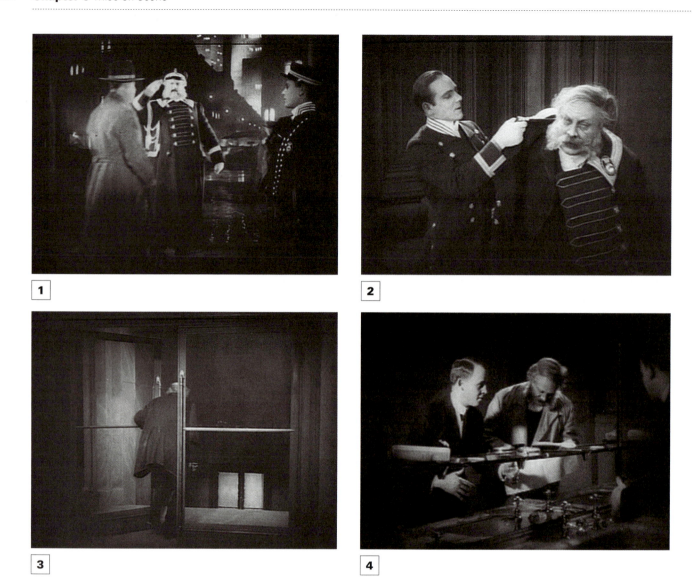

1

2

3

4

Camera use in *The Last Laugh*

F. W. Murnau's *The Last Laugh* (1924) is one of the most poignant, yet ultimately happy movies ever made. Emil Jannings plays an aging, weary hotel doorman who is demoted to the job of men's washroom porter; in the process, he is stripped of his magnificent uniform coat and given a simple white jacket to wear. Because the character has no name, we can assume that he is "everyman." With great sensitivity to this man's predicament, Murnau pays careful attention to camera point of view as he photographs the character's descent from a job of great dignity to one of humiliation. The drama begins when the hotel manager notices that the doorman is so weary that he has to sit down and rest. [1] From the manager's point of view, the camera looks through the glass revolving doors and sees the resplendent doorman formally greeting a guest; however, the manager has previously decided that the doorman is too old and tired to continue bearing these responsibilities. [2] Later, in the manager's office, from the manager's point of view, we see an assistant remove the doorman's symbolic coat—a shameful moment in which the old man's pride is stripped away from him, like the skin being flayed from an animal. [3] Still later, because the doorman does not want to be seen by anyone now, Murnau uses an objective camera to show us his descent to the basement to begin his new position; notice that, in contrast to image [1], the former doorman cowers in fear of being seen. [4] Once he is in the new job, because he is tired and weary here (just as he was when the manager decided to demote him), the former doorman dozes while holding a towel for a hotel guest, from whose point of view (through a mirror) this shot is photographed. Thus, with the exception of image [3], we see only what the characters see. The movie's title refers to the fact that, at the last moment, the doorman (through a plot twist you'll have to see to appreciate) becomes a rich man, returns to the hotel to dine, and has the last laugh.

Lang, Billy Wilder). Viennese-born von Stroheim—like D. W. Griffith and Orson Welles, a director, screenwriter, designer, and actor—was a master of realistic design in such movies as *Queen Kelly* (1929; art director Harold Miles). His demands for full-scale sets and lavish interiors cost millions to realize. That factor, in addition to his egotistical and tyrannical behavior on the set, led to his early retirement.

We need look no further than the extraordinary settings and costumes for *Queen Kelly* to understand von Stroheim's reputation as a perfectionist. In one scene, a banquet is given to announce a royal wedding. Most directors would have used a medium shot to show the splendidly dressed royal couple-to-be and enough guests sitting near them to suggest a much larger party. Not von Stroheim. After the announcement, he cuts to a reaction shot of the dinner guests, a very long shot that includes perhaps 100 people (guests and servants, all extras, appropriately costumed) in a lavish hall and a magnificent banquet table set with huge candelabra, china, silver, serving pieces, and flowers. The movie's producer and star, the legendary Gloria Swanson, said of this scene's extravagant cost, "Real caviar, real champagne to be sure."[16] Von Stroheim had a major influence on movie realism in general and, as can be seen in movies as diverse as Elia Kazan's *On the Waterfront* (1954; production designer Richard Day), Sergei Bondarchuk's *War and Peace* (1967; production designers Mikhail Bogdanov, Aleksandr Dikhtyar, Said Menyalshchikov, and Gennadi Myasnikov), and Martin Scorsese's *The Age of Innocence* (1993; production designer Dante Ferretti).

Other pioneering art directors who emigrated from Europe to Hollywood include German-born Hans Dreier, whose design career includes such memorable achievements as Rouben Mamoulian's *Dr. Jekyll and Mr. Hyde* (1931) and Billy Wilder's *Sunset Boulevard* (1950; co–art director John Meehan). Irish-born Cedric Gibbons supervised MGM's impressive art department for thirty-two years and, as supervisor, received screen credit as art director for hundreds of movies, even though his staff (who received other screen credit) did the actual work. He won eleven Oscars for Best Art Direction and was responsible for the studio's rich, glossy look in such movies as Edmund Goulding's *Grand Hotel* (1932), Ernst Lubitsch's *The Merry Widow* (1934), and W. S. Van

Narrative drives design in *Queen Kelly*
Ideally, the director and production designer (or art director) collaborate on creating a design scheme that is appropriate to the narrative. The art director for Erich von Stroheim's *Queen Kelly* (1929)—essentially a storybook romance—was nominally Harold Miles, but it's clear that von Stroheim, the consummate perfectionist, had his usual say about the overall look of the mise-en-scène. His extravagance forced producer-star Gloria Swanson to fire him. It was further obvious to the studio that, in the midst of the transition to sound, he was no longer in touch with what audiences wanted. Here, the art director's work serves the narrative with designs that are both appropriate and visually inseparable from it.

Dyke's *Marie Antoinette* (1938).[17] German-born Robert Siodmak had a distinctive talent for making great movies with MGM's superlative look, including *The Spiral Staircase* (1945; art directors Albert S. D'Agostino and Jack Okey), a suspenseful murder mystery set in a stylish, elaborate Victorian mansion.

The list of great Hollywood art directors and production designers is a long one, and it's impossible to include all of them. However, the names of certain production designers stand out. Mark-Lee Kirk (Orson Welles's *The Magnificent Ambersons*, 1942), Richard Sylbert (Roman Polanski's *Chinatown*, 1974), Ken Adam (Stanley Kubrick's *Barry Lyndon*, 1975), Tim Yip (Ang Lee's *Crouching Tiger, Hidden Dragon*, 2000), Grant Major (Peter Jackson's *Lord of the Rings* trilogy, 2001–3), Gemma Jackson (Marc Forster's *Finding Neverland*, 2004), Sarah Greenwood (Joe Wright's *Atonement*, 2007), Dante Ferretti (Anthony Minghella's *Cold Mountain*, 2003), and Jack Fisk (Paul Thomas Anderson's

16. See the interview with Gloria Swanson on the Kino Video DVD release of the movie (2003).

17. For a list of movies notable for their design, see "A Canon for Art Direction" in Affron and Affron, *Sets in Motion,* pp. 210–211.

There Will Be Blood, 2007) are all recognized as exceptional practitioners of the designer's craft.

British films of the 1930s and 1940s were in most instances indistinguishable in look from Hollywood films, but the two major exceptions were the films directed by Alfred Hitchcock and those designed by Vincent Korda. Because of his background as a designer, Hitchcock created films that were always unusually stylish, including such early works as the first version of *The Man Who Knew Too Much* (1934), *Sabotage* (1936), and *The Lady Vanishes* (1938). Korda's distinctive, lavish style can be seen in Ludwig Berger, Michael Powell, and Tim Whelan's *The Thief of Bagdad* (1940), a colorful adaptation of an Arabian Nights tale, and in most of the films produced by London Films, which was headed by Korda's brother Alexander, including the historical epics *The Private Life of Henry VIII* (1933) and *Rembrandt* (1936). In addition, Vincent Korda helped design the sets for designer-director William Cameron Menzies's stylish science-fiction film *Things to Come* (1936) and was one of several designers on Carol Reed's *The Third Man* (1949), set in a decadent Vienna after World War II and perhaps the most stylish of all black-and-white movies in the film noir style. Michael Powell and Emeric Pressburger, as creative partners, coproduced and codirected a body of major films that reflect serious attention to design elements, including *The Life and Death of Colonel Blimp* (1943; production designer Alfred Junge), *Black Narcissus* (1947; production designer Junge), and *The Red Shoes* (1948; production designer Hein Heckroth).

Italian neorealism, developed during World War II, influenced how cinema worldwide handled both narrative and design (or, in this case, absence of design). Its use of nonprofessional actors, handheld cameras, and location sets all diverged strongly from the practices of studio-bound productions, even those shot on location, and opened the door for new styles in Europe, India, and Hollywood. Its humanism and concerns with social conditions during and after the war broke away from conventional movie narrative and established a "new realism" in both story and style in the early films of Roberto Rossellini (*Rome, Open City,* 1945), Vittorio De Sica (*Shoeshine,* 1946, and *The Bicycle Thieves,* 1948), Michelangelo Antonioni (*L'Avventura,* 1960), and Federico Fellini (*I Vitelloni,* 1953).

Shooting in "real" locations—a seeming lack of design—actually reflects the work of an art director or a production designer who makes a well-orchestrated selection of streets and buildings. It produces a very

The Third Man

As already noted, many great movies, including Orson Welles's *Citizen Kane* (1941), owe visual and even thematic debts to Robert Wiene's *The Cabinet of Dr. Caligari* (1920). Among them is Carol Reed's hugely influential thriller *The Third Man* (1949; art directors Vincent Korda, Joseph Bato, and John Hawkesworth). In this masterpiece of design and mise-en-scène, a pulp writer, Holly Martins (Joseph Cotten), finds himself in a shadowy, angular, mazelike Vienna. Because Martins's investigation into the mysterious death of a long-lost friend yields as much deceit as truth, the city becomes not just a backdrop but a kind of major character, the troubled Martins's alter ego. The film's climactic chase scene—set in the labyrinthine sewer system, with bright lights revealing the sweating tunnel walls and police officers splashing through the dark waters—is one of the most memorable nightmare visions in movie history. That Harry Lime, the subject of the police chase, is played by Orson Welles has led some viewers to regard *The Third Man* as an homage to both *Dr. Caligari* and Welles's *Citizen Kane* (1941). Indeed, because of its characteristically Wellesian "look," some other viewers mistakenly think Welles directed it.

definite look and feel, a mise-en-scène as recognizable as the most elaborately designed picture. This approach has been influential in the design of countless films in Hollywood, where after 1950 the increasing production of stories set in real locations owed much to postwar Italian cinema. It was also notably influential in India, where Satyajit Ray, that country's most distinctive stylist, was deeply influenced by *The Bicycle Thieves* in making his classic "Apu" trilogy: *Pather Panchali* (1955), *The Unvanquished* (1956), and *The World of Apu* (1959).

Art direction and design are important elements in the films of the three Japanese directors best known in the West: Akira Kurosawa, Kenji Mizoguchi, and Yasujiro Ozu. Yoshirô Muraki and Shinobu Muraki's design brings visual simplicity and dramatic power to

Italian neorealism

Vittorio De Sica's *The Bicycle Thieves* (1948) is perhaps the best-loved movie from Italy's neorealist period, in part because its simple story speaks to many people by focusing on the details and chance events of ordinary lives. As Antonio Ricci (Lamberto Maggiorani) and his son Bruno (Enzo Staiola) pursue an old man who can identify the thief of Antonio's bicycle, for example, a rainstorm delays them and enables the old man to get away. The rainstorm was real, and the scene was filmed on location.

One type of Japanese mise-en-scène

A distinctive feature of many of Yasujiro Ozu's movies, including *Late Spring* (1949; art director Tatsuo Hamada), from which this image is taken, is the low but level camera angle that seems to imply the presence of a houseguest sitting on a traditional Japanese floor mat. The resulting mise-en-scène is intimate, relaxed, and generally very still.

Kurosawa's *Ran* (1985), for example. In Mizoguchi's *Sansho the Bailiff* (1954), Kisaku Ito and Shozaburo Nakajima's beautiful design is both poetic and realistic. Design credits seldom appear on Ozu's films, but we can discern a consistent visual style, austere and beautifully balanced in composition, in many of his films, including *An Autumn Afternoon* (1962) and *Late Spring* (1949). This style is based in part on Japanese culture itself—on the way Ozu's contemporaries lived, designed their houses and furniture, and ate their meals—and is therefore not exportable.

In India, the films of Satyajit Ray, who was successful as a graphic designer before he turned to film directing, are noted for their adherence to the principles of Italian neorealism, particularly the emphasis on shooting in real locations. But Ray was also influenced by the movies of Jean Renoir and John Ford. It is one reason his movies stand out from the traditional Indian cinema, which, like that of Japan or China, mostly reflects the uniqueness of its culture and so is not particularly influential on the filmmaking of other countries. Ray is highly esteemed by audiences and fellow film directors for his mastery of design details that reveal setting, a character's state of mind, and mood in such films as *The Music Room* (1958), *The Goddess* (1960), *Charulata* (1964), and *The Home and the World* (1984).

Chinese films display diverse visual styles. In the People's Republic of China, distinctive directors include Kaige Chen (*Yellow Earth*, 1984) and Yimou Zhang, whose films *Red Sorghum* (1987) and *Raise the Red Lantern* (1991) exploit color in impressive ways. In Hong Kong, a new cinema emerged in the 1960s characterized by its focus on the local Cantonese culture and on technological sophistication rather than style. Its distinctive achievements include Ann Hui's political *Ordinary Heroes* (1999); Hark Tsui's epic *Peking Opera Blues* (1986); and John Woo's superviolent *The Killer* (1989), which had a strong influence on director Quentin Tarantino and others.

Several important directors have emerged from Taiwan, including Edward Yang, whose *That Day, on the Beach* (1983) reflects Antonioni's austere style; and Hsiao-hsien Hou, whose *A City of Sadness* (1989) adheres to a more traditional Chinese cinematic style. Most famous internationally is Ang Lee, whose early films include *The Wedding Banquet* (1993) and *Eat Drink Man Woman* (1994). Since crossing over into mainstream Western film production, Lee has made movies set in utterly disparate worlds: *Sense and Sensibility* (1995), based on the 1811 novel by English writer Jane Austen; *The Ice Storm* (1997), based on the 1994 novel by American writer Rick Moody; and *Crouching Tiger, Hidden*

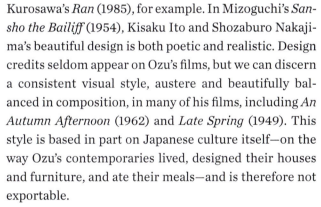

Dragon (2000), a Chinese love story told in the highly kinetic style reminiscent of Hong Kong martial arts films. Each of these movies displays a mastery of the principles of production design.

Apart from such postmodern filmmaking efforts as the Danish Dogme 95 movement (with its location shooting, handheld cameras, and natural light), most contemporary movie design tends to strive for the seamless integration of studio and natural settings. And except for the highly popular and hugely successful science-fiction and fantasy movies, most of today's stories involve recognizable people wearing recognizable clothes and moving through recognizable settings. The design work, however, is as challenging and involved as it was during the classical studio era. And the results, created with sophisticated technologies, are no less impressive.

Composition

Composition is part of the process of visualizing and planning the design of a movie. More precisely, composition is the organization, distribution, balance, and general relationship of stationary objects and **figures** (any significant things that move on the screen—people, animals, objects) as well as of light, shade, line, and color within the frame. Ensuring that such organization helps develop a movie's narrative and meanings requires much thought and discussion, so filmmakers use drawings and models—general sketches of the look of overall scenes, specific set designs, costume designs, storyboards for particular shot sequences, and so on—to aid them in visualizing each shot and achieving a unified whole.

As filmmakers visualize and plan each shot, they must make decisions about two aspects of composition: **framing** (what we see on the screen) and **kinesis** (what moves on the screen). This is true whether the movie strives for verisimilitude or fantasy. Certain visionary directors are known for making shots that resemble the canvas of an enormous painting and in doing so, they pay scrupulous attention to all aspects of composition. Such directors, to name only a few, include David Lynch (*The Elephant Man*, 1980; *Blue Velvet*, 1986; and *Mulholland Dr.*, 2001), Terry Gilliam (*Brazil*, 1985; *Fear and Loathing in Las Vegas*, 1998; and *The Brothers Grimm*, 2005), Roy Andersson (*World of Glory*, 1991; and *Songs from*

Composition and mise-en-scène

Two shots from William Wyler's *The Best Years of Our Lives* (1946; art directors Perry Ferguson and George Jenkins) illustrate the relationship between composition and mise-en-scène. In the movie, the lives of three veterans are intertwined, and triangular compositions reinforce that theme visually. [1] Early in the film, Fred Derry (Dana Andrews, *top*), Al Stephenson (Fredric March, *lower right*), and Homer Parrish (Harold Russell, *lower left*) return home after serving in World War II. Their tight physical grouping in the nose of a bomber reflects the tight emotional bond they have only recently established. [2] Much later, a similar tripoint pattern establishes a different relationship among the men. Here, a shot in Butch's bar has Derry using the phone in the background and inserts a noticeable gap between Stephenson and Parrish, reflecting the new and estranged relationship. Time has changed their lives, and the same old patterns have different meanings within the larger context.

the Second Floor, 2000), and Francis Ford Coppola (One from the Heart, 1982; and Apocalypse Now Redux, 2001 [director's cut of Apocalypse Now, 1979]).

Composition is important because it helps ensure the aesthetic unity and harmony of the movie as well as guide our looking—how we read the image and its component parts and, particularly, how we interpret the characters' physical, emotional, and psychological relationships to one another. Composition can produce a flat image, in which figures and objects are arranged and photographed in the foreground of the screen, or an image that has the illusion of depth.

Framing: What We See on the Screen

The frame is the border between what the filmmaker wants us to see and everything else—the dimensions of height and width that provide the shape of the movie's images. However, unlike the static frame around a painting, the frame around a motion-picture image can move and thus change its point of view (this process of **reframing** results from what is called a **moving frame**). The movie frame is therefore not merely a container for a movie's visual elements, it is itself an important and dynamic visual element.

Framing also implies **point of view (POV)**. At times, the framing seems to present us with the point of view of a single character (subjective POV). At other times, the framing implies a view that seems to be coming from no one in particular (omniscient POV). However, sometimes the framing can be so varied that it creates a desirable ambiguity that requires viewers to reach their own conclusions about the moral issues at hand. For example, Krzysztof Kieslowski's The Decalogue (1989; cinematographer Slawomir Idziak; art director Ewa Smal) is composed of 10 one-hour films, each devoted to a contemporary interpretation of one of the biblical commandments. The film pays particular attention to the point of view of the camera that visually narrates each of the stories. Kieslowski, a Catholic who experienced the Communist-controlled Poland of the 1960s and 1970s, was not overtly religious. Thus he espouses no particular doctrinal interpretation of the commandments, leaving interpretation to the viewer.

Thou Shalt Not Kill (1990), the fifth film, is perhaps the most demanding of the series, both because it deals with a murder so random and horrifying that it provokes our strongest moral outrage and because Kieslowski's

approach to the framing, which employs both traditional and innovative techniques, creates the sense of a coldly "objective" perspective on the crime even as it reveals subjective points of view. Kieslowski achieves this effect by shooting the actors and settings from a variety of angles, using a very close framing so that we become intimate with all of the characters. He shifts the camera's point of view so that, for example, as the murder is about to take place, we see shots of the murderer coiling a rope around his fist while drinking a cup of coffee and flirting with two young girls, hailing a taxi, staring at the driver's face in the rearview mirror, calmly looking out the window, and then murdering the driver. In other words, we see (1) the murderer's objective actions as observed by the camera, as if it were a documentary movie, including his garroting the driver, bludgeoning him, and dragging him to the riverside, where he smashes his face with a rock; (2) facial expressions that reveal some of the murderer's subjective thoughts; and (3) reaction shots of the driver as he picks up the passenger and discusses a change of route that leads him onto a deserted road, where he is killed. At other times, the scene begins with the murderer in one corner of the frame, so that we see what he's seeing, and then the camera reframes so that he is central to the action. Because he has no apparent motive, we are appalled at the extraordinary brutality that we see. Even he seems shocked by what he has done. Obviously, the director's choices in such techniques as camera angle, framing, and camera movement contribute to our reactions, but they do not lead those reactions in one way or another. In fact, the continual use of reflections in windows and mirrors makes us wonder which images to trust.

On-screen and Offscreen Space How filmmakers envision the look of a film and how the camera interprets that vision depend on the fundamental fact that cinematic seeing is framing. The frame of the camera's **viewfinder** (the little window you look through when taking a picture) indicates the boundaries of the camera's point of view. To demonstrate for yourself the difference between the camera's point of view and your everyday vision, put your hands together to form a rectangular frame, then look through it using one eye. If you move it to the left or the right, move it closer or farther away from your face, or tilt it up or down, you will see instantly how framing (and moving the frame) changes what you see.

Because the frame is dynamic, it often makes us aware of the **offscreen space** outside the frame as well as the **on-screen space** inside it. As the frame moves, it presents on the screen details that were previously offscreen, thus prompting us to be aware of the dynamic between offscreen and on-screen spaces. As the film theorist Noël Burch first suggested, the entire visual composition of a shot depends on the existence of both on-screen and offscreen spaces; both spaces are equally important to the composition and to the viewer's experience of it.[18] Burch divides offscreen space into six segments: the four infinite spaces that lie beyond the four borders of the frame; the spaces beyond the movie settings, which call our attention to entrances into and exits from the world of the frame; and the space behind the camera, which helps the viewer define the camera's point of view and identify a physical point beyond which characters may pass. Offscreen space has power, as Burch emphasizes: "The longer the screen remains empty, the greater the resulting tension between screen space and off-screen space and the greater the attention concentrated on off-screen space as against screen space."[19] In any movie—a verisimilar one, in particular—most shots depend on both on-screen and offscreen space, and our awareness of their interdependence reinforces the illusion of a larger spatial world than what is contained in any single frame.

In *Chinatown* (1974; production designer Richard Sylbert), Roman Polanski uses offscreen space to accentuate the suspense of the second meeting between the prying detective J. J. Gittes (Jack Nicholson) and the menacing tycoon Noah Cross (John Huston) at the house of Evelyn Mulwray (Faye Dunaway), who is both Cross's daughter and Gittes's client. Cross is a ruthless man who will do anything to keep his loathsome personal life and corrupt public activities from further notice, and Gittes knows he's now in danger when Cross arrives at the house. As the scene begins no one is in the frame, but a puff of cigarette smoke enters the left side of the frame and lets us know that Gittes is waiting there. This may be one of the rare instances when a puff of smoke can produce a powerful reaction from the viewers. Although it's been put there for a reason, its meaning is more metaphorical than literal: a transitional moment

1

2

3

On-screen and offscreen space in *Chinatown*
[1] Because of the smoke from his cigarette (*screen left*), we know that J. J. Gittes (Jack Nicholson) is in the space depicted here, and not being able to see him accentuates the suspense in this climactic scene from Roman Polanski's *Chinatown* (1974). [2] Noah Cross (John Huston) enters, looking for Gittes, and sees him (*offscreen left*). [3] Gittes enters the frame and begins their conversation.

of vagueness before a powerful confrontation between two antagonists. Cross steps onto the front porch, enters the house, crosses the foyer, appears on the terrace, looks offscreen at Gittes, and says, "Oh, there you are," as if he weren't prepared for the meeting. Gittes then enters the frame, and their conversation begins.

18. Noël Burch, *Theory of Film Practice*, trans. Helen R. Lane (1973; repr., Princeton, NJ: Princeton University Press, 1981), p. 25.
19. Ibid.

Open and Closed Framing The first and most obvious function of the motion-picture frame is to control our perception of the world by enclosing what we see within a rectangular border, generally wider than it is high. Because it shapes the image in a configuration that does not allow for peripheral vision and thus does not conform to our visual perception, we understand framing as one of the many conventions through which cinema gives form to what we see on the screen. Film theorist Leo Braudy, one of many writers to study the relationship between cinematic arrangement and viewer perception, distinguishes between open and closed films (or forms) as two ways of designing and representing the visible world through framing it, as well as two ways of perceiving and interpreting it.

Each of these cinematic worlds—open and closed—is created through a system of framing that should remain fairly consistent throughout the film so as not to confuse the viewer. The **open frame** is designed to depict a world where characters move freely within an open, recognizable environment, and the **closed frame** is designed to imply that other forces (such as fate; social, educational, or economic background; or a repressive government) have robbed characters of their ability to move and act freely. The open frame is generally employed in realistic (verisimilar) films, the closed frame in antirealistic films. In the realistic, or verisimilar, film, the frame is a "window" on the world—one that pro-

vides many views. Because the "reality" being depicted changes continuously, the movie's framing changes with it. In the antirealistic film, the frame is similar to the frame of a painting or photograph, enclosing or limiting the world by closing it down and providing only one view. Because only that one view exists, everything within the frame has its particular place. As with all such distinctions in film analysis, these differences between open and closed frames aren't absolute; they are a matter of degree and emphasis (as shown in Table 5.1).

Who or what decides whether the framing in a movie is open or closed? Sometimes it's the director; at other times, it's the narrative; in most movies, it's both. Directors choose the open frame to enable their characters to act freely, to come and go within the film's world. John Ford's *My Darling Clementine* (1946) is not only shot with an open frame, but concludes in open-ended ambiguity. In one sense, its characters (Wyatt Earp and company) face an existentialist dilemma: whether to live as uncivilized, lawless barbarians or to become lawful members of a civilized community. The town of Tombstone, set among the vast expanses of Monument Valley, can go one way or the other, depending upon the actions of individuals who live there. Ford seems to favor community, family, and organized religion; his hero, Earp, arrives in the lawless town, becomes the sheriff, establishes civic order, and then departs for his own reasons. This seems to be an ambiguous ending. It's noteworthy

Table 5.1 | OPEN AND CLOSED FRAMES

	Open	Closed
Visual characteristics	Normal depth, perspective, light, and scale. An overall look that is realistic, or verisimilar.	Exaggerated and stylized depth; out of perspective; distorted or exaggerated light and shadow; distorted scale. An overall look that is not realistic, or verisimilar.
Framing the characters	The characters act. They may move freely in and out of the frame. They are free to go to another place in the movie's world and return.	The characters are acted upon. They are controlled by outside forces and do not have the freedom to come and go as they wish. They have no control over the logic that drives the movie's actions.
Relationship of characters to design elements	The characters are more important than the sets, costumes, and other design elements. The design elements support the development of character and story.	Design elements call attention to themselves and may be more important than the characters. Design elements drive the story's development.
The world of the story	The world of the story is based on reality. It changes and evolves, and the framing changes with it. The frame is a window on this world.	The world of the story is self-contained; it doesn't refer to anything outside of itself. It is rigid and hierarchical: everything has its place. The frame is similar to a painting.

Source: Adapted from Leo Braudy, *The World in a Frame: What We See in Films* (1976; repr., Chicago: University of Chicago Press, 1984).

On-screen and offscreen space in *Stagecoach*

In John Ford's *Stagecoach* (1939; art director Alexander Toluboff), a scene set in the noontime lunch stop at Dry Fork illustrates social division among the characters through the use of on-screen and offscreen spaces. [1] The scene opens by establishing the location, showing two of the room's four walls. Following this establishing shot, a series of cuts fills in parts of the room not seen here. [2] Revealing a third wall but keeping us oriented by showing the chairs and part of the table, this shot takes us to what had been offscreen space and remains marginal territory, where Ringo (John Wayne) and Dallas (Claire Trevor) interact before he seats her at the table. [3] Opposed to Ringo and Dallas, on the other side of the room, are Gatewood (Berton Churchill, *seated left*), Hatfield (John Carradine, *standing right*), and Lucy (Louise Platt, *seated right*)—three characters who consider themselves socially superior to the others. [4] From yet another perspective we see the room's fourth wall and Lucy, who stares coldly and haughtily at [5] Dallas, who yields no ground. [6] When Ringo defies the anger rising across the table (a reinforcement of his position in [2]), [7] Hatfield escorts Lucy away from Dallas (a reinforcement of their position in [3]) to [8] the opposite end of the table, which we see from an entirely new perspective. Thus an area that had been largely offscreen, hardly registering, takes prominence, especially in contrast to the brightly lit, vacant, and exposed end of the table.

that both Kurosawa and Ford first studied to be painters, an art in which everything has its place and is enclosed within a frame. Although they both became film directors, their painting experience probably influenced their masterful sense of composition and attention to detail within the frame.

Directors choose the closed frame when their stories concern characters who are controlled by outside forces and do not have the freedom to come and go as they wish. Design elements frequently drive the story's development. Good examples include almost any Alfred Hitchcock movie (e.g., *Dial M for Murder*, 1954), Carol Reed's *The Third Man* (1949), Kelly Reichardt's *Wendy and Lucy* (2008) and *Meek's Cutoff* (2011), or King Vidor's silent classic *The Crowd* (1928).

Darren Aronofsky's *Black Swan* (2010) is a closed movie in which the design and framing are more important than the characters. The highly melodramatic story concerns a young ballet dancer, Nina Sayers (Natalie Portman), an artist with great technique who cannot become a prima ballerina until she realizes her soul as a dancer. In this case, that means fighting her demons, primarily her psychotic view of her world and colleagues. Her struggle occurs within a production design that is very claustrophobic; virtually all of its major scenes are shot in interiors: backstage, stage, dressing room, corridors, and Nina's bedroom at home. Despite her ambitions and her talent, Nina (as well as the other young dancers) seems caught in this labyrinth of spaces that define their world. Indeed, they are trapped in a world where their success is often determined more by destiny than talent. While some of the dancers are comfortable with this reality, those who aren't try to destroy it at their peril. Thomas Leroy (Vincent Cassel), the hard-driving director of the ballet company, controls

the repetitive rehearsals with an iron hand, calling our attention to the movie director's manipulation of the students' confining world.

An interesting paradox occurred when two different directors from different countries—Jean Renoir (France) and Akira Kurosawa (Japan)—each made their own cinematic adaptation of Russian writer Maxim Gorky's play *The Lower Depths* (1902). Gorky's work gives a pessimistic, dark view of lower-class Russians who share a boarding house, the principal setting of the play. In his 1936 version, Renoir, who generally favors the open frame, sets the story in a Parisian flophouse and allows his characters to move freely in and out of the frame as well as out of the house and into the city beyond. Kurosawa, in his 1957 version, sets the story in seventeenth-century

LOOKING AT MOVIES
COMPOSING THE FRAME

VIDEO ▶ ●────

In this tutorial, Dave Monahan discusses the core principles of composition within the frame.

Japan and, like Gorky, keeps the action inside the house. Renoir emphasizes that man's life is left to free will and chance, while Kurosawa allows his characters little freedom. Renoir's open frame is more relevant to the modern audience, while Kurosawa's relatively closed frame seems claustrophobic by contrast, perhaps reflecting the hierarchical society of the time.

The formulaic nature of these distinctions does not mean that you should automatically categorize movies that you see and analyze as open or closed, for there will be no profit in that. Instead, you can recognize the characteristics of each type of film (as described in Table 5.1), and you can be aware that certain directors consistently depict open worlds (Jean Renoir, John Ford, Robert Altman) while others are equally consistent in making closed ones (Alfred Hitchcock, Stanley Kubrick, Lars von Trier).

Kinesis: What Moves on the Screen

Because the movies move in so many ways, our perception of kinesis (movement) in a movie is influenced by several different factors at once—including the use of music in an otherwise static scene. But we perceive movement mainly when we see (1) the movement of objects and characters within the frame and (2) the apparent movement of the frame itself (the moving frame). Although their particular applications will differ depending on the specific work, both types of movement are part of any movie's composition and mise-en-scène.

Of course, all movies move, but some move more than others and differently. The kinetic quality of many movies is determined by their genre: action pictures, cartoons, and comedies tend to include more and faster movement than do love stories or biographical films. Many great films—Carl Theodor Dreyer's *The Passion of Joan of Arc* (1928), Robert Bresson's *Diary of a Country Priest* (1951), Yasujiro Ozu's *Tokyo Story* (1953), and Michelangelo Antonioni's *The Outcry* (1957), for example—use little movement and action. That lack of action represents not only a way of looking at the world (framing it) but also an approach to the movie's narrative and themes.

Which movie, then, is the more cinematic—one that moves all the time or one that moves hardly at all? Because kinetic power is only one of the inherent creative

Kinesis in action films
Throughout the history of film—from the swashbuckling of Hollywood legend Douglas Fairbanks, to the cinematic portrayals of Shakespeare's *Hamlet* by Laurence Olivier, Mel Gibson, Kenneth Branagh, and many others, to the movie careers of martial artists such as Bruce Lee and Jackie Chan—old-fashioned swordplay has always been one of the most exciting forms of movement on-screen. Ang Lee's *Crouching Tiger, Hidden Dragon* (2000), a contemporary update of Hong Kong sword-and-sorcery movies, combines martial arts with elaborate choreography. In playing the nobleman's-daughter-turned-warrior, Jen Yu, shown here in one of many fight sequences, actress Ziyi Zhang used her training in dance as well as her martial arts skills.

possibilities of movies, not an essential quality of every movie, we can answer this question only by examining the relationships among the movement, narrative, and overall mise-en-scène. In this way, we can determine what movement is appropriate and furthermore what movement works to control perceptions. To condemn *Tokyo Story*'s lack of movement when compared to the frenetic movement in, say, Yimou Zhang's *Hero* (2002; production designers Tingxiao Huo and Zhenzhou Yi) is like condemning Shakespeare for not writing in the style of contemporary playwright Harold Pinter. In other words, the comparison is unfair to both sides.

Movement of Figures within the Frame The word *figure* applies to anything concrete within the frame: an object, an animal, a person. The most important figure is usually the actor, who is cast, dressed, made up, and directed for the film and thus is a vital element in the composition and resulting mise-en-scène. Figures can move in many ways: across the frame (in a horizontal, diagonal, vertical, or circular pattern), from foreground to background (and vice versa), or from on and off the screen. A character can float weightlessly in outer space, as Frank Poole (Gary Lockwood) does in Stanley Kubrick's *2001: A Space Odyssey* (1968); dance without danger to himself up a wall and across the ceiling, as Tom Bowen (Fred Astaire) does in Stanley Donen's *Royal Wedding* (1951); or break free from leg braces and run like the wind, defying a childhood spinal problem and gravity itself, as the title character, played by Tom Hanks, does in Robert Zemeckis's *Forrest Gump* (1994). These and other kinds of figure movement, which can be as prosaic or as poetic as the story requires, show not only where a character is moving but also how (on foot, in a vehicle, through the air in a fight) and even sometimes (explicitly or implicitly) why.

The director and his team must plan the positions and movements of the actors and the cameras for each scene and, in rehearsals, familiarize the cast and camera operators with their plan. This process is known as **blocking**. In the early stages of blocking, the director often places pieces of tape on the floor to indicate the position of the camera and the actors; once crew and cast are familiar with their positions, the tape is removed. In designing a film, another essential element to be considered is how all the figures move within the space created to tell the story as well as how they are placed in relation to each other. The physical placement of characters can

Movement of figures within the frame
Movies can make anything and anyone move in any way the story calls for. All three movements in the images here are in the realm of the unbelievable. [1] Astronaut Frank Poole (Gary Lockwood), betrayed by an onboard computer that severs his lifeline, floats weightlessly to his death in *2001: A Space Odyssey* (1968). [2] Expressing his love for a woman, Tom Bowen (Fred Astaire) in *Royal Wedding* (1951) dances his way up a wall and eventually across the ceiling. [3] Forrest Gump (Tom Hanks), in the movie of that name (1994), acts from complete willpower to shed his leg braces and run free.

suggest the nature and complexity of whatever relationship may exist between them, and thus their placement and proximity are relevant to our understanding of how the composition of a shot helps to create meaning. (Analyzing placement and proximity is the study of *proxemics*.)

Ordinarily, close physical proximity implies emotional or other kinds of closeness. Federico Fellini's *I Vitelloni* (1953; cinematographers Carlo Carlini, Otello Martelli, and Luciano Trasatti; production designer Mario Chiari) goes against this convention by employing a rigorous compositional plan that involves placing the characters in symmetrical proximity. In one memorable shot, Fellini suggests group indolence by seating each character at a separate café table with half of them facing in one direction and the other half facing in the other. In *Love and Death* (1975; cinematographer Ghislain Cloquet; production designer Willy Holt), a low comedy about life's big issues, director Woody Allen shows that physical proximity between two characters can also mean the absence of romantic closeness. On the night before he is to fight a duel, Boris (Woody Allen) asks Sonja (Diane Keaton) to marry him. They are very tightly framed in the shot, and he starts intoning a nonsensical monologue: "To die before the harvest, the crops, the grains, the fields of rippling wheat—all there is in life is wheat." The shot continues as she, looking offscreen left, confesses her innermost feelings about him; and although he does not seem to hear what she is saying, his reaction is to mug all sorts of exaggerated facial reactions as he mumbles more nonsense about wheat. As he does with so many other aspects of film, Allen manipulates proxemics for brilliant comic effect.

Looking at Mise-en-Scène

The better the fit between mise-en-scène and the rest of a movie's elements, the more likely we are to take that mise-en-scène for granted. A movie's mise-en-scène may be so well conceived that it seems merely something there for the cinematographer to film rather than the deliberately produced result of labor by a team of artists and craftspeople. A fully realized mise-en-scène plays a crucial role in creating the illusion of naturalness that encourages our enjoyment of movies as spectators. But we must consciously resist that illusion if we hope to graduate from being spectators to being students of film, people who look at movies rather than just watch them. Looking at mise-en-scène critically does not mean taking the fun away from movies. You may still have as much fun as you like with (or is the better word *in*?) *The Matrix* (1999) while realizing that everything you see, hear, and feel in it was put there for a purpose.

Let's look closely at Tim Burton's *Sleepy Hollow* (1999), an enduring model of mise-en-scène that produces a rich viewing experience.

Tim Burton's *Sleepy Hollow*

Tim Burton is a director who has created imaginative fantasies that reveal great visual ingenuity and a wicked sense of humor. His movies are always a treat to look at, and they offer abundant opportunities for analyzing their design and mise-en-scène, even when these aspects do not always serve the narrative well. Among his most successful movies are *Batman* (1989), *Edward Scissorhands* (1990), *Ed Wood* (1994), *Sleepy Hollow* (1999), *Planet of the Apes* (2001), *Charlie and the Chocolate Factory* (2005), *Sweeney Todd: The Demon Barber of Fleet Street* (2007), *Alice in Wonderland* (2010), and *Big Eyes* (2014).

The highly stylized reimagining of Washington Irving's tale "The Legend of Sleepy Hollow" (1819–20) so totally transforms its source that, in effect, it leaves the text behind; it emphasizes instead the director's stunning vision and his production team's meticulous realization of that vision. The story concerns the efforts of Ichabod Crane (Johnny Depp), a forensic scientist, to solve three murders in the village of Sleepy Hollow where the victims were beheaded. The ending is so muddled that we don't really know if he succeeds, but at least he escapes with his head. The movie's unified design plan and mise-en-scène create the correct times, places, and moods—according to Burton's vision—and go beyond the superficial to reveal characters, provide the appropriate settings for the extraordinary action of the film, and develop its themes. Burton's overall goal in production design seems to have been to make this film as weird and scary as possible. Verisimilitude has nothing to do with it. Although Washington Irving's story describes the valley of Sleepy Hollow as a place filled with rippling brooks, cheerful birdcalls, and unchanging tranquility, Burton's version of Sleepy Hollow is dark

Mise-en-scène creates *Sleepy Hollow*'s unified look

[1] *Sleepy Hollow*'s primary palette, tending toward slate-gray and bluish-gray, and the overcast, forbidding look used in most of the outdoor shots enhance our sense of the mystery and danger lurking within the village. [2] Punctuating this overall grayness are magnificent homages to classic horror films, including a windmill straight out of James Whale's *Frankenstein* (1931).

and foreboding from the start. The visual presentation of the village is clearly inspired by the design vocabularies of horror and gothic movies.

Such movies include James Whale's *Frankenstein* (1931), which ends with an angry mob trapping the Monster in a windmill that they set afire. Burton similarly places the spectacular climax of his film in an ominous windmill, where Ichabod Crane lures the Headless Horseman (Christopher Walken), whose mysterious powers save him from death in the fiery explosion. In addition, Burton draws on Mario Bava's visually sumptuous vampire movie *Black Sunday* (1960), Roman Polanski's *The Fearless Vampire Killers* (1967), and films from Britain's Hammer Studios (the foremost producer of gothic horror films in movie history), whose style was characterized by careful attention to detail—including, of course, lots of blood—in such films as Terence Fisher's *The Curse of Frankenstein* (1957) and *Horror of Dracula* (1958). Burton also pays homage to the horror genre by casting Christopher Lee, who plays the Creature in *The Curse of Frankenstein*, as the Burgomaster in *Sleepy Hollow*.

Sleepy Hollow features many prominent characteristics of the horror and gothic genres, including

> a spooky setting—the almost colorless village of Sleepy Hollow and the creepy woods that surround it.

> a forensic scientist, Ichabod Crane (played by Johnny Depp, an actor whose fey style has added

much to several of Burton's movies), forced to struggle with a demonic antagonist (or perhaps the illusion of one), the Headless Horseman (Christopher Walken).

> a seemingly virginal heroine who dabbles in witchcraft—Katrina Anne Van Tassel (Christina Ricci)—and her wicked stepmother, Lady Mary Van Tassel (Miranda Richardson), the wife of the lord of the manor who moonlights as a witch.

> various other eccentric and deranged locals.

In addition, there are glimpses of the spirit world and other frightening, mysterious, and supernatural events.

Burton and his collaborators were also inspired by the visual style of the eighteenth-century British artists William Hogarth and Thomas Rowlandson. In such works as *A Rake's Progress* (1732–35), Hogarth created a series of anecdotal pictures (similar to movie storyboards) that had both a moral and a satirical message. Rowlandson created an instantly recognizable gallery of social types, many of whom seem to have served as models for the characters we meet at Van Tassel's mansion. When Crane steps into the house, a "harvest party" is taking place, and the guests are dancing, drinking, and quietly talking. The color palette changes from the exterior gloom to soft browns, grays, greens, and blacks. The interior colors are very subdued but warmed by a patterned tile floor, orange jack-o'-lanterns, candles, and firelight. (Here, as throughout the movie's interior scenes, candles seem to be the principal source of

Different characters in *Sleepy Hollow* require different looks

[1] Baltus Van Tassel (Michael Gambon, *standing left*) is among the many characters in *Sleepy Hollow* who might have stepped out of period paintings. Indeed, most of the village's residents seem stuck in an antiquated, vaguely European style of dress. [2] By contrast, the darkly and sleekly dressed Ichabod Crane (Johnny Depp) is a "modern" American man of science, here wearing the ambitious but wonderful instrument he has designed to perform forensic inspections. [3] In a flashback, the "Hessian" (Christopher Walken), who in death will become the Headless Horseman, is all spikes and sharp angles, looking very much like the vampire in F. W. Murnau's classic *Nosferatu* (1922).

illumination.) Baltus Van Tassel (Michael Gambon) wears a suit of beautiful dark-green velvet decorated with gold brocade, under which his cream-colored silk shirt is fastened with a bow; unlike many of the other men, he does not wear a wig. His beautiful younger wife, Lady Mary Van Tassel, wears an elaborate gown of yellow silk velvet decorated with an overlaid pattern in cut brown velvet. Her hair is swept back from her high forehead. The Van Tassels' dress and manner leave no question as to who heads society in Sleepy Hollow.

In a scene that could have come straight from Hogarth, Crane is introduced to the other ranking members of the community. We are in Van Tassel's study with its muted green wallpaper, leather chairs, books, portraits, Oriental carpet, blazing fire on the hearth, and candles mounted in wall sconces. Each man in the scene is striking in dress and manner. The Reverend Steenwyck (Jeffrey Jones) wears the most distinctive wig in the movie, and Magistrate Samuel Philipse (Richard Griffiths), seen pouring the contents of his flask into his teacup, has the stock red face of a drinking man that one sees so often in portraits of British aristocrats painted by George Romney, another of Hogarth's contemporaries.

Rick Heinrichs, the production designer, said of the design scheme for the village, "One of the things we were trying to do was inspire a sense of scary portentousness in the village. I think it's different from Irving's Sleepy Hollow which is described as a dozing Dutch farming community. If our Sleepy Hollow is asleep, it's a fitful sort of sleep, with nightmares."[20] *Sleepy Hollow* is clearly a closed film that depicts a singular, self-enclosed world in which almost everyone and everything are held in the grip of powerful personal, societal, and supernatural forces. Director Tim Burton is of course the strongest, most controlling force in this world.

To create this gloomy atmosphere, Burton and his collaborators use a muted, even drab, color palette, punctuated here and there by carefully placed bright details. (The only consistent deviation is in the sequences depicting Crane's dreams of his mother.) As the movie begins with prologue and title credits, however, the dominant color is not muted, but the red of dripping wax being used to seal a last will and testament—a red so evocative that we momentarily mistake it for blood.

20. Rick Heinrichs, qtd. in Denise Abbott, "Nightmare by Design," *Hollywood Reporter*, international ed., 361, no. 49 (February 29–March 6, 2000): S-6.

After sealing his will, Peter Van Garrett (Martin Landau, in an uncredited performance), a pale figure wearing a pale yellow silk jacket, flees by carriage with the Headless Horseman in pursuit. The Horseman lops off the head of the coachman and then of Van Garrett, whose blood spatters all over an eerie orange pumpkin head mounted on a stake. Decapitation, a central theme of *Sleepy Hollow*, produces lots of blood, and blood continually spurts throughout the movie in the murders committed by the Horseman as well as in self-inflicted wounds and the gory examinations of dead bodies.

As Ichabod Crane travels by a closed, black carriage between New York City and Sleepy Hollow in the opening scene of the film, we are introduced to the principal color palette of late fall and early winter: gray river, gray wintry skies, trees almost barren of leaves, and rime on the ground. As day turns to twilight, Crane arrives at the village entrance, marked by two pillars topped by stone stags' heads, and walks down the road through the village and across the fields to the Van Tassel mansion. The entire scene appears to have been shot in black and white rather than color, for Crane's extremely pale face provides the only color here, signifying, as we have already learned in theory but will now learn in fact, that the townspeople are drained of all life by their fear of the Horseman. Completely skeptical of what he considers the "myth" of the Horseman, Crane wears black and looks pallid, perturbed, and wary throughout the early part of the movie.

The village, the movie's most elaborate outdoor set, was constructed in England in a style that Heinrichs calls "Colonial Expressionism"; it includes a covered wooden bridge, church, general store, midwife's office, tavern, notary public, blacksmith, bank, mill house, warehouses, and several residences. Even the houses are scary with their gray facades, doors, and shutters. Recalling English and Dutch architecture of the seventeenth and eighteenth centuries, many of these exteriors were also duplicated inside London studios, where heavy layers of artificial fog and smoke and controlled lighting helped create the illusion of a dark, misty valley under a leaden sky.

This meticulously created mise-en-scène encourages us not only to escape into the past but also to suspend our disbelief. On this ground, two worlds collide: one is represented by Crane, a "modern" criminal investigator using the latest technology (most of it of his own invention); the other is represented by the

1

2

3

Contrasting colors emphasize narrative contrasts in *Sleepy Hollow*

Blood-red sealing wax [1] and blood spattered on a menacing jack-o'-lantern [2] are the sorts of bold design details that stand out against *Sleepy Hollow*'s generally muted palette, as evident in the "harvest party" scene [3] when Katrina Anne Van Tassel (Christina Ricci, *blindfolded*) first encounters Ichabod Crane (Johnny Depp). Note, in contrast to the smiling children on the right, the jack-o'-lantern in the upper left corner, echoing the sour expression on the face of Crane's eventual romantic rival, Brom Van Brunt (Casper Van Dien, *center*).

1

2

Expressive details define characters in *Sleepy Hollow*

In a movie as brilliantly stylized as Tim Burton's *Sleepy Hollow*, one in which the story hangs on the struggle between superstition and reason, many of the characters are defined in part by their costumes, makeup, or the props with which they are associated. For example, [1] Katrina Van Tassel's (Christina Ricci) book, *A Compendium of Spells, Charms and Devices of the Spirit World*, associates her clearly with the witchcraft that bedevils Sleepy Hollow, while [2] Ichabod Crane's (Johnny Depp) wonderful eyeglasses and bag of medical instruments, including some of his own devising, tell the town's inhabitants as well as the movie's viewers that he is a man of science.

community of Sleepy Hollow, which itself ranges from the rich to the poor, all afraid of the Headless Horseman. Burton tells the story in part through fantastic objects and details, including Crane's notebook containing his drawings and notes, various forensic instruments, and peculiar eyeglasses; Katrina's book of witchcraft and evil-eye diagrams, over which an ominous spider creeps; the fairy-tale witch's cave deep in the forest and her potions made of bats' heads and birds' wings; the mechanical horse used to propel the Horseman through the village and surrounding woods; the "Tree of Death," where the Horseman lives between murders; the windmill, where he almost meets his end; and the fountain of blood at the climactic moment, when the Horseman's head is restored to him and he returns to life. Impressionist, even expressionist, much of this creepy place, with its frightening inhabitants and their eccentric costumes and hairstyles, was created through special effects.

Although precision is necessary in analyzing all the design elements in a single scene or clip from a movie, we can only generalize in discussing them in a movie

as stylistically rich as *Sleepy Hollow*. Throughout, however, Burton's mise-en-scène reflects fairly consistent use of framing and camera movement. Reinforcing the closed nature of the movie, the frame is tightly restricted to the characters being photographed. Even many shots of the landscape are equally tight, providing little sense of the sky above or even the earth below; and when they do, the sky is invariably overcast.

The lighting creates a moody atmosphere. The exterior lighting—where mist, chimney smoke, and flashes of lightning are constant motifs—is slightly less dim than the interior lighting, which is provided seemingly by candles and firelight. The design elements in *Sleepy Hollow* produce distinct emotional responses in the viewers that perfectly complement our emotional responses to the narrative's twists and turns. We are repelled by the superstitious fears of the entire community and made uncomfortable by the conspiracy among the townspeople to hide the secret of the Horseman, and the mise-en-scène reinforces our discomfort even as it mesmerizes us.

ANALYZING MISE-EN-SCÈNE

This chapter has introduced the major elements that together form any film's mise-en-scène. You should now understand that the term *mise-en-scène* denotes all of those elements taken together—the overall look and feel of the film—and that mise-en-scène plays a crucial role in shaping the mood of the film. Using what you have learned in this chapter, you should be able to characterize the mise-en-scène of any movie (or any shot) in precise terms, referring to the framing, the composition in depth, the lighting, the setting, the design and use of objects, and the placement and appearance of characters.

SCREENING CHECKLIST: MISE-EN-SCÈNE

☐ As you watch the film or clip, be alert to the overall design plan and mise-en-scène and to your emotional response to them. Are you comforted or made anxious by them? Are your senses overwhelmed or calmed by what you see on-screen?

☐ Identify the elements of the mise-en-scène that seem to be contributing the most to your emotional response.

☐ Be alert to the framing of individual shots, and make note of the composition within the frame. Where are figures placed? What is the relationship among the figures in the foreground, middle ground, and background?

☐ Does the use of light in the movie or clip call attention to itself? If so, describe the effect that it has on the composition in any shot you analyze.

☐ Does the film or clip employ lots of movement? Very little movement? Describe how the use of movement in the film or clip complements or detracts from the development of the narrative.

☐ Note the type of movement (movement of figures within the frame or movement of the frame itself) in important shots. Describe as accurately as possible the effect of that movement on the relationships among the figures in the frame.

☐ Does the movie's design have a unified feel? Do the various elements of the design (the sets, props, costumes, makeup, hairstyles, etc.) work together, or do some elements work against others? What is the effect either way?

☐ Was achieving verisimilitude important to the design of this film or clip? If so, have the filmmakers succeeded in making the overall mise-en-scène feel real, or verisimilar? If verisimilitude doesn't seem to be important in this film or clip, what do you suspect the filmmakers were attempting to accomplish with their design?

☐ How does the design and mise-en-scène in this movie or clip relate to the narrative? Is it appropriate for the story being told? Does it quietly reinforce the narrative and development of characters? Does it partly determine the development of narrative and characters? Does it render the narrative secondary or even overwhelm it?

Questions for Review

1. What is the literal meaning of the phrase *mise-en-scène*? What do we mean by this phrase more generally when we discuss movies?
2. What are the two major visual components of mise-en-scène?
3. Does a movie's mise-en-scène happen by accident? If not, what or who determines it?
4. What are the principal responsibilities of the production designer?
5. Name and briefly discuss the major elements of cinematic design.
6. What is composition? What are the two major elements of composition?
7. What is the difference between the static frame and the moving frame?
8. Why do most shots in a film rely on both on-screen and offscreen spaces?
9. What are the essential differences between the open frame and the closed frame?
10. What are the two basic types of movement that we see on-screen?

STUDENT RESOURCES ONLINE

digital.wwnorton.com/movies5

▶ VIDEO

The tutorials for this chapter cover setting, lighting, and composition within the frame. An additional feature called *Drawing the Coke* looks at the Lumière brothers' short "actualité" to demonstrate the importance of mise-en-scène even at the very beginning of film history.

LOOKING AT
MOVIES
CHAPTER 5: MISE-EN-SCÈNE

SETTING AND EXPRESSIONISM
LIGHTING AND FAMILIAR IMAGE IN
THE NIGHT OF THE HUNTER
COMPOSING THE FRAME
THE LUMIÈRE BROTHERS' "ACTUALITÉS"

▶ MAIN MENU

INTERACTIVE

In this interactive tutorial on composition, see how many ways you can compose and capture a multitude of interactions and situations presented in a single scenario as you position and scale the camera frame.

Birdman (2014; director Alejandro González Iñárritu)

CINEMATOGRAPHY

LEARNING OBJECTIVES

After reading this chapter, you should be able to

✓ describe the differences among a shot, a setup, and a take.

✓ understand the role that a director of photography plays in film production.

✓ describe the basic characteristics of the cinematographic properties of a shot: film stock, lighting, and lenses.

✓ understand the basic elements of composition within the frame, including implied proximity to the camera, depth, camera angle and height, scale, and camera movement.

✓ define the *rule of thirds*.

✓ describe any shot in a movie by identifying

- its proximity to its subject.
- the angle of the camera.
- the nature of camera movement, if any, within the shot.
- the speed and length of the shot.

✓ understand the ways in which special effects are created and the various roles that special effects play in movies.

What Is Cinematography?

Cinematography is the process of capturing moving images on film or a digital storage device. The word comes to us from three Greek roots—*kinesis*, meaning "movement"; *photo*, meaning "light"; and *graphia*, meaning "writing"—but the word was coined only after motion pictures themselves were invented. Cinematography is closely related to still photography, but its methods and technologies clearly distinguish it from its static predecessor. This chapter introduces the major features of this unique art.

Although cinematography might seem to exist solely to please our eyes with beautiful images, it is in fact an intricate language that can (and in the most complex and meaningful films, does) contribute to a movie's overall meaning as much as the story, mise-en-scène, and acting do. The cinematographer (also known as the director of photography, or DP) uses the camera as a maker of meaning, just as the painter uses the brush or the writer uses the pen: the angles, heights, and movements of the camera function both as a set of techniques and as expressive material, the cinematic equivalent of brushstrokes or of nouns, verbs, and adjectives. So, to make an informed analysis and evaluation of a movie, we need to consider whether the cinematographer, in collaboration with the other filmmakers on the project, has successfully harnessed the powers of this visual language to help tell the story and convey the meaning(s) of the movie. As director Satyajit Ray puts it, "There is no such thing as good photography *per se*. It is either right for a certain kind of film, and therefore good; or wrong—however lush, well-composed, meticulous—and therefore bad."[1]

The Director of Photography

Every aspect of a movie's preproduction—writing the script, casting the talent, imagining the look of the finished work, designing and creating the sets and costumes, and determining what will be placed in front of the camera and in what arrangement and manner—leads to the most vital step: representing the mise-en-scène on film or video. Although what we see on the screen reflects the vision and design of the filmmakers as a team, the director of photography is the primary person responsible for transforming the other aspects of moviemaking into moving images.

DP Emmanuel Lubezki has collaborated with Terence Malick on three of his highly visual, almost abstract movies: *The New World* (2005), *The Tree of Life* (2011), and *To the Wonder* (2012). Malick makes movies like no one else today, and Lubezki finds that a strong, understanding relationship between him and the director helps make this possible. He says:

> It's been different every time. . . . The approach to shooting the movie is connected to the kind of movie he wants to make—the form and content are fundamentally connected. . . . We were trying to find a more cinematographic approach to filmmaking and a way of using film language that was less connected to theater

---

1. Satyajit Ray, *Our Films, Their Films* (1976; repr., New York: Hyperion, 1994), p. 68.

Setting up a shot

On an interior setting for *The Social Network* (2010), director David Fincher (*left*) and cinematographer Jeff Cronenweth (*center*)—aided by an unidentified camera operator or technician (*right*)—work with a video-assist camera to set up a shot. Fincher and Cronenweth also worked together on *Fight Club* (1999) and *The Girl with the Dragon Tattoo* (2011). Cronenweth was nominated for an Oscar for Best Cinematography on *The Social Network*.

and literature and other art forms. Terry wants this art form to have its own way of expressing ideas and emotions, and that's what was very exciting about the movie [*To the Wonder*]."[2]

Caleb Deschanel (DP for *Winter's Tale*, 2014) comments that the cinematography of *The Tree of Life* "records a small story, a celebration of the courage of everyday life. But it does it so up close and so effortlessly that it has the effect of elevating the intimacy of the story to a grand scale."[3]

In the ideal version of this working relationship, the director's vision shapes the process of rendering the mise-en-scène on film, but the cinematographer makes very specific decisions about how the movie will be photographed.

When the collaboration between the director and the cinematographer has been a good one, the images that we see on-screen correspond closely to what the director expected the DP to capture on film. As cinematographer John Alton explains,

The screen offers the advantage of an ability (although we do not always utilize it) to photograph the story from the position from which the director thinks the audience would like to see it. The success of any particular film depends a great deal upon the ability of the director to anticipate the desires of the audience in this respect. . . .

. . . [T]he director of photography visualizes the picture purely from a photographic point of view, as determined by lights and the moods of individual sequences

2. Qtd. in Jim Hemphill, "Lyrical Images," American Cinematographer, April 2013. See www.theasc.com/ac_magazine/April2013/TotheWonder/page1 .php (accessed July 22, 2014).

3. See www.brainyquote.com/quotes/quotes/c/calebdesch618537.html (accessed July 22, 2014).

and scenes. In other words, how to use angles, set-ups, lights, and camera as means to tell the story.[4]

As cinematographers translate visions into realities, however, they follow not inflexible rules but rather conventions, which are open to interpretation by the artists entrusted with them. But as Gordon Willis—who shot *The Godfather* movies and numerous Woody Allen films—puts it, there is no formula in preparing to shoot a film except a complete awareness of the art and craft of cinematography. He was known as the "prince of darkness" for his use of minimal light and maximum shadows. But he said that the DP's challenge is to "fit the punishment to the crime" in determining the cinematographic look that is artistically appropriate for the job at hand.

Many cinematographers succeed at meeting this challenge of fitting the photography to the story. For example, in *The Lives of Others* (2006; director Florian Henckel von Donnersmarck), the cinematographer Hagen Bogdanski employs a flat lighting scheme and color palette to portray an ugly world of surveillance in which citizens are fearful, paranoid, and humiliated into submission by the Stasi, the secret police in Communist East Germany in the 1980s. Todd Louiso's *Love Liza* (2002) concerns the anguish of a man (played by Philip Seymour Hoffman) whose wife has killed herself. Lisa Rinzler, the cinematographer—influenced by German Expressionist movies—observes the man from a 360-degree tracking shot and from striking angles shot with bold lighting to depict the emotional torment and physical clumsiness with which he confronts his despair.

See for yourself how this approach—fitting the photography to the story—works in Josef von Sternberg's *The Last Command* (1928; cinematographer Bert Glennon), where the soft studio style tempers the bite of this ironic movie about making movies; in Peter Ustinov's *Billy Budd* (1962; cinematographer Robert Krasker), where sharp black-and-white images underscore the moral dilemma of Herman Melville's story; in Martin Ritt's *The Spy Who Came in from the Cold* (1965; DP Oswald Morris), where the contrasts underscore the mysteries of this spy thriller; and in Ang Lee's *Life of Pi* (2012; cinematographer Claudio Miranda), whose digital tiger and startling 3-D color imagery bring us into the story's almost inconceivable situation—drifting in an open boat on the ocean with a tiger for a companion—as well as deepen its overall emotional power.

The three key terms used in shooting a movie are *shot, take*, and *setup*. A **shot** is (1) one uninterrupted run of the camera and (2) the recording on film, video, or other medium resulting from that run. A shot can be as short or as long as necessary, through it obviously cannot exceed the time limitations of the recording medium. The term **take** refers to the number of times a particular shot is taken. A **setup** is one camera position and everything associated with it. Whereas the shot is the basic building block of the film, the setup is the basic component of the film's production process, and the director and cinematographer spend the most time collaborating on the setup.

The cinematographer's responsibilities for each shot and setup, as well as for each take, fall into four broad categories:

1. cinematographic properties of the shot (film stock, lighting, lenses)

2. framing of the shot (proximity to the camera, depth, camera angle and height, scale, camera movement)

3. speed and length of the shot

4. special effects

Although these categories necessarily overlap, we will look at each one separately. In the process, we also examine the tools and equipment involved and discuss what they enable the cinematographer to do.

In carrying out these responsibilities, the DP relies on the assistance of the **camera crew**, which is divided into one group of technicians concerned with the camera and another concerned with electricity and lighting. The camera group consists of the **camera operator**, who does the actual shooting, and the **assistant camerapersons** (**ACs**). The **first AC** oversees everything having to do with the camera, lenses, supporting equipment, and the material on which the movie is being shot. The **second AC** prepares the **slate** that is used to identify each scene as it is shot, files camera reports, and when film stock is being used, feeds that stock into magazines that are then loaded onto the camera. The group concerned with electricity and lighting consists of the **gaffer** (chief electrician), **best boy** (first assistant electrician), other electricians, and **grips** (all-around handypersons who work with both the camera crew and the electrical crew to get the camera and lighting ready for shooting).

---

4. John Alton, *Painting with Light* (1949; repr., Berkeley: University of California Press, 1995), p. 33.

Cinematographic Properties of the Shot

The director of photography controls the cinematographic properties of the shot, those basics of motion-picture photography that make the movie image appear the way it does. These properties include the film stock, lighting, and lenses. By employing variations of each property, the cinematographer modifies the camera's basic neutrality as well as the look of the finished image that the audience sees.

Film Stock

The cinematographer is responsible for choosing a recording medium for the movie that has the best chance of producing images corresponding to the director's vision. Among the alternatives available are film stocks of various sizes and speeds, videotape, and direct-to-digital media. A skilled cinematographer must know the technical properties and cinematic possibilities of each option and must be able to choose the medium that is best suited to the project as a whole.

Even though more movies are being shot on digital media with each passing year, most feature films are still shot on traditional **film stock**. The two basic types of film stock—one to record images in black and white, the other to record them in color—are completely different and have their own technical properties and cinematic possibilities. Film stock is available in several standard **formats** (also called *gauges*; widths measured in millimeters): 8mm, Super 8mm, 16mm, 35mm, 65mm, and 70mm as well as special-use formats such as IMAX, which is ten times bigger than a 35mm frame (65mm film is used in the camera and then printed on 70mm film, which is used for projection; the additional space holds the sound track). Before the advent of camcorders, 8mm and Super 8mm were popular gauges for amateurs (for home movies). Many television or student movies, as well as low-budget productions, are shot on 16mm. Most

In Cold Blood: serendipity creates an unforgettable shot

Although the director of photography must strictly control the cinematographic properties of a movie's shots, every great cinematographer must also be alert to moments when an unplanned situation happens on the set that could make a shot even better than planned. In a climactic scene of *In Cold Blood* (1967; director Richard Brooks), based on Truman Capote's masterpiece, cinematographer Conrad Hall took advantage of a chance observation—the juxtaposition of rain running down a window with a condemned murderer's last-minute remembrance of his father—to create a memorable moment of cinema. Just before his execution for the brutal murders of a Kansas family, Perry Smith (Robert Blake) remembers his father. As he moves toward the window and looks out at the prison yard, heavy rain courses down the window, making it appear that he is crying. With the strong exterior lights directed at Smith's face, cinematographer Conrad Hall explains that he found the setup for this shot when he realized that this situation "created these avenues for the bright light outside to come in. . . . It was an accident I saw, and used, and capitalized on the moment." This scene is proof that a great shot can be the result of careful planning or, as in this case, serendipity.

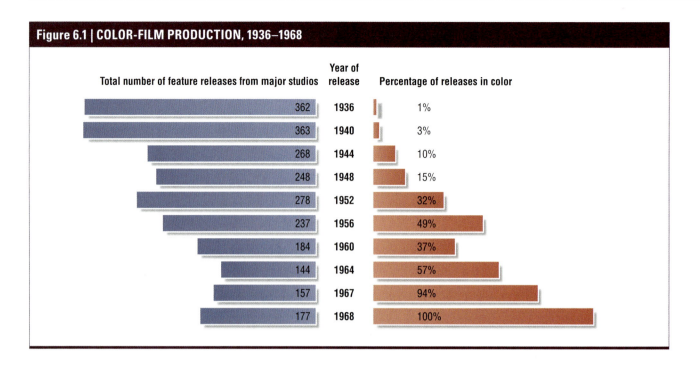

Figure 6.1 | COLOR-FILM PRODUCTION, 1936–1968

Total number of feature releases from major studios	Year of release	Percentage of releases in color
362	1936	1%
363	1940	3%
268	1944	10%
248	1948	15%
278	1952	32%
237	1956	49%
184	1960	37%
144	1964	57%
157	1967	94%
177	1968	100%

professional film productions use either 16mm or 35mm. Generally, the wider the gauge, the more expensive the film and, all other factors being equal, the better the quality of the image.

Another variable aspect of film stock is its **speed** (or exposure index)—how sensitive it is to light. Film stocks that are extremely sensitive to light and thus useful in low-light situations are called fast; those that require a lot of light are called slow. There are uses for both slow and fast film stock, depending on the shooting environment and the desired visual outcome. Fast films are grainy (larger grains of light-sensitive material need less light to record an image with a fast shutter speed), whereas slow films are fine-grained and require either a slow shutter speed, more light, or both. When a film's look must uniquely match the demands of the story, cinematographers will mix film stocks (e.g., Oliver Stone's *Natural Born Killers*, 1994; cinematographer Robert Richardson; or Tom Tykwer's *Run Lola Run*, 1998; cinematographer Frank Griebe) or intentionally use the wrong chemicals to process film stocks to achieve the desired look, as in David O. Russell's *Three Kings* (1999; cinematographer Newton Thomas Sigel).

Which stock is right for a particular film depends on the story being told. With only a few outstanding exceptions, however, virtually all movies are now shot in color, for that is what the public is accustomed to and there-

fore expects. As Figure 6.1 shows, when Hollywood began to use color film stock, only 1 percent of the feature releases from major studios in 1936 were in color. The growth of color production slowed during World War II because all film stock, especially color, was in short supply, but by 1968 virtually all feature releases were in color.

Although today the default choice for feature film production is color, in the period from 1940 to 1970 the choice between color and black and white needed to be carefully considered, and many films shot in color during that period might have been even stronger if they were shot instead in black and white. John Ford's *The Searchers* (1956; cinematographer Winton C. Hoch), a psychological Western that is concerned less with the traditional Western's struggle between good and evil than with the lead character's struggle against personal demons, might have been even more powerful shot in black and white instead of color. Doing so might have produced a visual mood, as in film noir, that complemented the darkness at the heart of the movie's narrative. Instead, the choice of color film stock for *The Searchers* seems to have been inspired by industry trends at the time—designed to improve flagging box-office receipts—rather than by strictly artistic criteria.

Ironically, audiences who had grown to love Ford's black-and-white movies set in Monument Valley reacted badly to his first color feature set there: *She Wore a Yellow Ribbon* (1949; cinematographer Winton C. Hoch). The vibrant colors they were seeing in this movie and in *The Searchers*—the reds and browns of the earth, the constantly changing blues of the sky—accurately captured the appearance of Monument Valley in real life, but for viewers whose expectations were shaped by Ford's earlier movies, such as *Stagecoach* (1939), Monument Valley existed only in black and white. In color, *The Searchers* is magnificent; we can only guess at what it might have been in black and white.

Black and White Black-and-white movies are not pictures that lack color, for black and white (and the range in between) *are* colors.[5]

Today's directors have rediscovered that black-and-white film stock offers compositional possibilities and cinematographic effects that are impossible with color film stock. Their movies include Pawel Pawlikowski's *Ida* (2013; DPs Pyszard Lenczewski and Lukasz Zal), Alexander Payne's *Nebraska* (2013; DP Phedon Papamichael), Josh Whedon's *Much Ado About Nothing* (2012; DP Jay Hunter), Marcel Gomes's *Tabu* (2012; DP Rul Poças),[6] and Bela Tarr and Agnes Hranitzky's *The Man from London* (2007; DP Fred Kelemen).

Because of its use in documentary films (before the 1960s) and in newspaper and magazine photographs (before the advent of color newspaper and magazine printing), audiences have ironically come to associate black-and-white photography and cinematography with a stronger sense of gritty realism than that provided by color film stock. But the distinct contrasts and hard edges of black-and-white cinematography can express an abstract world (a world from which color has been abstracted or removed) perfectly suited for the kind of morality tales told in Westerns, film noirs, and gangster films. In fact, although many excellent color films have been made in these same genres—such as Roman Polanski's neo-noir *Chinatown* (1974; cinematographer John A. Alonzo) or Quentin Tarantino's gangster film *Pulp Fiction* (1994; cinematographer Andrzej Sekula)—we generally view their distinctive black-and-white predecessors as the templates for the genres.

1

2

Black and white versus color

Stagecoach [1], made in 1939, was the first film that John Ford shot in Arizona's Monument Valley. Bert Glennon's black-and-white cinematography in *Stagecoach* portrayed an Old West that was different from Winton C. Hoch's depiction using color cinematography in *The Searchers* (1956) [2], one of the last films that Ford shot in Monument Valley. Although the expressive photography was state of the art in both films, the use of black and white and of color was not a matter of aesthetics but was dictated by industry standards.

Movies shot in black and white can also have moral or ethical implications. In theater throughout the ages, black-and-white costumes have been used to distinguish, respectively, between the "bad" and "good" characters. In the Western and film noir genres, this

---

5. For this book, we hold that position but acknowledge that for centuries people have debated whether black and white are colors. For those interested, a good introduction is "Are Black & White Colors?" www.colormatters.com/color-and-design/are-black-and-white-colors (accessed July 10, 2014).

6. Inspired by F. W. Murnau's movie *Tabu: A Story of the South Seas* (1931).

1

2

Black and white in *The Seventh Seal*

In the climactic battle between the allegorical figure of Death (Bengt Ekerot, *left*) and Antonius Block, the Knight (Max von Sydow, *right*) in *The Seventh Seal* (1957; cinematographer Gunnar Fischer), director Ingmar Bergman dresses both men in dark costumes but uses light and chess figures to distinguish between them [1]. Light from the upper left streams across the image, illuminating the Knight's blond-white hair, the Christian cross on his sword, and his chess pieces. There is just enough ambient light to outline the pale white face of the figure Death, shrouded in his hood. While this lighting and color strategy raises our expectations, we soon see that, in the chess game against Death, the Knight loses. The concluding shot [2] is one of the most iconic images in film history: Death leading the Knight and his squire, wife, and friends in a solemn dance of death. Again, notice Bergman's use of black and white: the dark-clad figures move upward on the mountain between the black earth and the white clouds. Death unites all.

has been a familiar pattern. In *The Seventh Seal* (1957; cinematographer Gunnar Fischer), set in the Middle Ages, Swedish director Ingmar Bergman uses high-contrast black-and-white cinematography to articulate a conflict between those who are devout Christians (dressed most often in white or gray costumes) and those nonbelievers who have only doubt and despair (dressed in black). But his color scheme goes beyond costuming to encompass distinct contrasts in lighting (both artificial and natural), settings (interior and exterior), and the chess pieces in a climactic game in which the figure of Death (in a black cowl) plays with black pieces while the Knight, who has returned from the Crusades to find his country ravaged by the Black Plague, plays with white pieces.

Tonality, the system of tones, is the distinguishing quality of black-and-white film stock. This system includes the complete range of tones from black to white. Anything on the set—furniture, furnishings, costumes, and makeup—registers in these tones. Even when a film is shot in black and white, its settings and costumes customarily are designed in color. Black-and-white cinematography achieves its distinctive look through such manipulation of the colors being photographed and through the lighting of them. At the height of the classical Hollywood studio system, set and costume designers closely collaborated with directors of photography to ensure that the colors used in their designs produced the optimal varieties of tones in black and white. Their goal was to ensure a balance of "warm" and "cold" tones to avoid a muddy blending of similar tones. Sometimes the colors chosen for optimal tonality on film were unattractive, even garish, on the set. Audiences were none the wiser, however, because they saw only the pleasing tonal contrasts in the final black-and-white movie.

Manipulation of tonal range makes black-and-white movies visually interesting, but that isn't all it does. For good or ill, tonality in black-and-white films often carries with it certain preconceived interpretations (e.g., black = evil, white = good). As simplistic, misleading, and potentially offensive as these interpretations may be, they reflect widespread cultural traditions that have been in effect for thousands of years. The earliest narrative films, which greatly appealed to immigrant audiences (most of whom could neither read nor speak English), often relied on such rough distinctions to establish the moral frameworks of their stories. Later, even though both audiences and cinematography became more sophisticated, these distinctions held together the narratives of countless films in diverse genres.

After tonality, the next thing we notice about black-and-white films is their use of, and emphasis on, texture and spatial depth within their images. The cinematographer can change the texture of an image by manipulating shadows and can control the depth of the image by manipulating lighting and lenses. The best-loved black-and-white movies employ such visual effects to underscore and enhance their stories. Looking at the work of cinematographer James Wong Howe on Alexander Mackendrick's *Sweet Smell of Success* (1957), for example, we are immediately struck by how his deft manipulation of tone, texture, and spatial depth have captured the sleazy allure of New York City's once notorious Times Square, and how the look of this movie is absolutely essential to its story of urban menace, corruption, and decay.

Color Although almost all movies today are shot in color, for nearly sixty years of cinema history color was an option that required much more labor, money, and artistic concession than black and white did. Color movies made before 1960 were typically elaborate productions, and in deciding to use color the producers expected the movies to justify the expense with impressive box-office returns. To gain a better understanding of the period before 1968, when color was not necessarily the default choice, let's take a moment to review briefly the history of color-film technology.

Although full-scale color production began only in the late 1930s, it was possible to create color images soon after the movies were invented, in 1895. The first methods were known as **additive color systems** because they added color to black-and-white film stock. These processes included hand-coloring, stenciling, tinting, and toning; but because they were so tedious, at first only selected frames were colored. Nonetheless, impressive achievements were made by such pioneers as Thomas A. Edison, Georges Méliès, Edwin S. Porter, and the filmmakers at Pathé Frères.

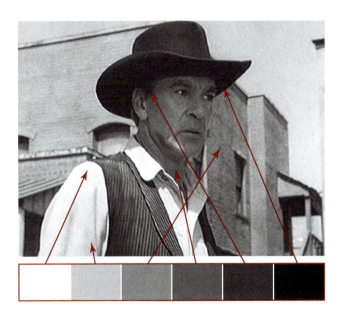

Tonal range

This shot from Fred Zinnemann's *High Noon* (1952; cinematographer Floyd Crosby) illustrates the tonal range possible in black-and-white cinematography: from absolute white (in the shirt) through a series of grays to absolute black (under the hat's brim). For the purposes of explanation, this illustration includes only six tones out of the complete range. Note that although he is the movie's protagonist, Marshal Will Kane (Gary Cooper) wears a black hat—typically, in less sophisticated morality tales, the symbolic mark of the bad guy.

Black-and-white tonality

The opening scene of Alexander Mackendrick's *Sweet Smell of Success* (1957; cinematographer James Wong Howe) takes place near midnight in Times Square, which is alive with activity. The thousands of incandescent and neon lights create a brash black-and-white environment in which the space lacks both depth and shadows. The people packed on the streets are members of a crowd, not individuals. In other movies, such bold blacks and whites might suggest the contrast of good and evil, but the lighting here gives no clue as to which is which.

D. W. Griffith used this technique very effectively in such films as *Broken Blossoms* (1919; cinematographer G. W. Bitzer), as did Robert Wiene in *The Cabinet of Dr. Caligari* (1920; cinematographer Willy Hameister). Toning, a chemical process distinct from tinting, offered greater aesthetic and emotional control over the image by coloring the opaque parts of an image to a general color. Tinting and toning were often used together to extend the color of a single image.

As imaginative as these processes are, they do not begin to accurately reproduce the range of colors that exist in nature. Further experimentation with additive color processing resulted in a crude two-color additive process that used two complementary colors, usually red-orange and blue-green. In 1915, the Technicolor Corporation introduced a two-color additive process, used effectively in aesthetic terms to photograph Albert Parker's impressive epic *The Black Pirate* (1926; cinematographer Henry Sharp).

By the early 1930s, the additive process was replaced by a three-color **subtractive color system** that laid the foundation for the development of modern color cinematography. How does it work in theory? Basically, color results from the physical action of different light waves on our eyes and optical nervous system, meaning that we perceive these different wavelengths of energy as different colors. Of these colors, three are primary—red, green, and blue; mixing them can produce all the other colors in the spectrum, and when added together they produce white. The subtractive process takes away unwanted colors from the white light. So when one of the additive primary colors (red, green, blue) has been removed from the spectrum on a single strip of film, what remains are the complementary colors (cyan, magenta, yellow). The first feature-length film made in the three-color subtractive process was Rouben Mamoulian's *Becky Sharp* (1935; cinematographer Ray Rennahan).

In practice, making a Technicolor movie was complicated, cumbersome, and cost almost 30 percent more than comparable black-and-white productions. The Technicolor camera, specially adapted to shoot three strips of film at one time, required a great deal of light. Its size and weight restricted its movements and potential use in exterior locations. Furthermore, the studios were obliged by contract to employ Technicolor's own makeup, which resisted melting under lights hotter than those used for shooting black-and-white films,

and to process the film in Technicolor's labs, initially the only place that knew how to do this work. In addition, production executives and personnel were required to tolerate the presence and meddling of Technicolor advisers on the set.

For all these reasons, in addition to a decline in film attendance caused by the Great Depression, producers were at first reluctant to shoot in color. By 1937, however, color had entered mainstream Hollywood production; by 1939 it had proved itself much more than a gimmick in movies such as Victor Fleming's *Gone with the Wind* (cinematographer Ernest Haller), *The Wizard of Oz* (cinematographer Harold Rosson), and John Ford's *Drums along the Mohawk* (cinematographers Bert Glennon and Ray Rennahan), all released that year.

In the early 1940s, Technicolor and Eastman introduced multilayered color film stocks that essentially replaced the earlier Technicolor system. These stocks, which were less expensive to process, could also be used in conventional cameras with less lighting and to shoot exterior shots. Eventually, Kodak's single-strip color film stock improved on these characteristics and became the standard. But just as Hollywood took several years to convert from silent film to sound, so too

Gone with the Wind and color filmmaking
Victor Fleming's *Gone with the Wind* (1939; cinematographer Ernest Haller) marked a turning point in Hollywood film production, ushering in an era of serious filmmaking in color. Its vibrant and nostalgic images of the antebellum South delighted audiences and earned it a special commendation at the 1939 Academy Awards for "outstanding achievement in the use of color for the enhancement of dramatic mood."

the movie industry did not immediately replace black-and-white film with color. During the 1950s, Hollywood used color film strategically, along with the **widescreen aspect ratio**, to lure people away from their television sets and back into theaters. (See "Framing of the Shot" on pp. 233–258.)

Now that color film dominates, a new naturalism has become the cinematographic norm, and what we see on the screen looks very much like what we would see in real life. By itself, however, color film stock doesn't necessarily produce a naturalistic image. Film artists and technicians can manipulate the colors in a film as completely as they can any other formal element. Ultimately, just like its black-and-white counterpart, color film can capture realistic, surrealistic, imaginary, or expressionistic images.

Much of Stanley Kubrick's *Barry Lyndon* (1975; cinematographer John Alcott), for example, has a color palette that reflects its temporal setting very well. It's the world of soft pastels and gentle shadows depicted in the paintings of such eighteenth- and nineteenth-century artists as Thomas Gainsborough, William Hogarth, and Adolph von Menzel. However, this palette wasn't achieved merely by pointing the camera in a certain direction and accurately recording the colors found there. Instead, the filmmakers specifically manipulated

Colors reflect and change lives in the movies

In Gary Ross's *Pleasantville* (1998; cinematographer John Lindley), a comic fable about the role of color in our lives, two contemporary teenagers (played by Reese Witherspoon and Tobey Maguire, *left to right*) are magically transported back into the world of a black-and-white television series called *Pleasantville*, set in 1958. Finding the town as realistically conformist, small-minded, and opposed to change as many small towns were in the late 1950s, they set about liberating their classmates and families. As they introduce love, sex, knowledge, modern art, self-expression, and freedom to the repressed black-and-white town, color begins to appear—slowly at first and then spreading as if it were a contagious disease. The town rebels, stages a witch hunt, and passes a law against all kinds of freedom, but the genie is out of the bottle and color is there to stay.

the images through careful planning, art direction, and technical know-how to render the naturally occurring colors in more subtle and "painterly" shades. In a different vein, the interplay of fantasy and reality is brilliantly and vibrantly conveyed in Christopher Nolan's sci-fi thriller *Inception* (2010; DP Wally Pfister) and Martin Scorsese's extravagant fantasy about the earliest years of filmmaking, *Hugo* (2011; DP Robert Richardson).

Today, when most all motion-picture postproduction (and much of the production, too) is done digitally, a great deal of any film's look, including its color, is completed on computers. This work is known as **color grading** (also called color correction), the process of altering and enhancing the color of a motion picture (or video or still image) with electronic, photochemical, or digital techniques. These days, filmmakers calibrate the way they capture footage to facilitate the technical and creative manipulation that happens largely in postproduction. Those manipulations include exposure, depth of shadows, brightness of highlights, saturation of colors, and color temperature. Filmmakers have been doing this for years, but it's now such a standard practice that

Evocative use of color

Because we experience the world in color, color films may strike us as more realistic than black-and-white films. Many color films, however, use their palettes not just expressively but also evocatively. For Stanley Kubrick's *Barry Lyndon* (1975), cinematographer John Alcott has helped convey both a historical period and a painterly world of soft pastels, gentle shading, and misty textures.

even prosumer (i.e., professional consumer) software—what is used to train students—is capable of creating the stylized visual looks that we see in big-budget features: desaturated, cold blue tints, sharp and high contrast, and soft warm and glowing tints, among others. For example, the warm saturated colors in the *Dogville* shots (see p. 228) or the cool blues of the shots from *The Devil's Backbone* (p. 232) are made or at least greatly enhanced in postproduction. Regarding the lights and camera on the set, cinematographers now have to be as knowledgeable about what happens on the computer after shooting as they are about what happens before. This need has created a new position on the professional camera crew: the **digital imaging technician (DIT)**, who is responsible for managing media capture with postproduction image manipulation in mind.

Lighting

During preproduction, most designers include an idea of the lighting in their sketches, but in actual production, the cinematographer determines the lighting once the camera setups are chosen. Ideally, the lighting shapes the way the movie looks and helps tell the story. As a key component of composition, lighting creates our sense of cinematic space by illuminating people and things,

LOOKING AT MOVIES
LIGHTING

VIDEO ▶ ━━━━━━━━●━━━━━━━━
This tutorial discusses the key properties of lighting.

creating highlights and shadows, and defining shapes and textures. Among its properties are its source, quality, direction, and style.

Source There are two sources of light: natural and artificial. Daylight is the most convenient and economical source, and in fact the movie industry made Hollywood the center of American movie production in part because of its almost constant sunshine. Even when movies are shot outdoors on clear, sunny days, however, filmmakers use reflectors and artificial lights because they cannot count on nature's cooperation. And even if nature does provide the right amount of natural light at the right time, that light may need to be controlled in various ways, as the accompanying photograph of reflector boards being used in the filming of John Ford's *My Darling Clementine* (1946) shows.

Artificial lights are called *instruments* to distinguish them from the light they produce. Among the many kinds of these instruments, the two most basic are **focusable spotlights** and **floodlights**, which produce, respectively, hard (mirrorlike) and soft (diffuse) light. A focusable spotlight can produce either a hard, direct spotlight beam or a more indirect beam. When equipped with black metal doors (known as *barn doors*), a spotlight can be used to cut and shape the light in a variety of ways. In either case, it produces distinct shadows. Floodlights produce diffuse, indirect light with very few to no shadows. The most effective floodlight for filmmaking is the

Suggestive use of lighting

In Billy Wilder's comedy *Some Like It Hot* (1959; cinematographer Charles Lang Jr.), the beam from a spotlight suggestively doubles as a virtual neckline for Marilyn Monroe during her famous performance of "I Wanna Be Loved by You." As he often did during his long career as a screenwriter and director, Wilder was playfully testing the boundaries of Hollywood moviemaking—seeing what he could get away with.

Reflector boards

Many scenes of John Ford's *My Darling Clementine* (1946; cinematographer Joe MacDonald) were shot in the sunny desert terrain of Monument Valley in Arizona and Utah. But as this photo shows, a large bank of reflector boards was used when the sunshine was insufficient or when the director wanted to control the lighting.

Softening shadows

Outdoor shots in direct sunlight pose a risk of casting harsh shadows on actors' faces. This shot from James Cameron's *Titanic* (1997; cinematographer: Russell Carpenter) shows the effect of using a reflector board to soften shadows and to cast diffuse light on the bottom of the chin and the nose and under the brow, thus giving Leonardo DiCaprio's face a softer, warmer look on-screen.

softlight, which creates a soft, diffuse, almost shadowless light.

Another piece of lighting equipment, the **reflector board**, is not really a lighting instrument because it does not rely on bulbs to produce illumination. Essentially, it is a double-sided board that pivots in a U-shaped holder. One side is a hard, smooth surface that reflects hard light; the other is a soft, textured surface that provides a softer fill light. Reflector boards come in many sizes and are used frequently, in interior and especially in exterior shooting; most often they are used to reflect sunlight into shadows during outdoor shooting.

Quality The quality of light on a character or situation is an important element in helping a movie tell its story. Quality refers to whether the light is hard (shining directly on the subject, creating crisp details and a defined border and high contrast between illumination and shadow) or soft (diffused so that light hits the subject from many slightly varying directions, softening details, blurring the line between illumination and shadow, and thus decreasing contrast). We can generally (but not always) associate hard, high-contrast lighting featuring deep shadows (known as *low-key lighting*) with serious or tragic stories and soft, even lighting (*high-key lighting*) with romantic or comic stories.

The way the cinematographer lights and shoots an actor invariably suggests an impression of the character to the audience. A good example of how the quality of lighting can affect how we look at and interpret characters in a scene can be found in Orson Welles's *Citizen Kane* (1941; cinematographer Gregg Toland). When Kane (Welles) first meets and woos Susan Alexander (Dorothy Comingore), the light thrown on their respective faces during close-up shots reveals an important distinction between them. Susan's face, lit with a soft light that blurs the border between illumination and shadow, appears youthful and naive. In contrast, Kane's face is lit with a hard and crisp light, making him appear older and more worldly.

Direction Light can be thrown onto a movie actor or setting (exterior or interior) from virtually any direction: front, side, back, below, or above. By direction, we also mean the angle of that throw, for the angle helps produce the contrasts and shadows that suggest the location of the scene, its mood, and the time of day. As with the other properties of lighting, the direction of the lighting must be planned ahead of time by the cinematographer in cooperation with the art director so that the lighting setup achieves effects that complement the director's overall vision.

1

2

Lighting and setting

A good way to understand the importance of how lighting influences our impressions of the setting is to compare the quality of two movies that were filmed in the same setting. Both Alexander Mackendrick's *Sweet Smell of Success* (1957; cinematographer James Wong Howe) and Woody Allen's *Manhattan* (1979; cinematographer Gordon Willis) use the Queensboro Bridge (or 59th Street Bridge, made famous in Simon and Garfunkel's song of the same name) for a key scene. Both scenes are shot at night in the environs of the bridge.

[1] This scene from *Sweet Smell of Success* takes place outside a nightclub located on a street that runs alongside and below the bridge. In this image, Sidney Falco, the unscrupulous assistant to J. J. Hunsecker, the city's most powerful gossip columnist, has just planted drugs in the coat of Steve Dallas, an innocent jazz guitarist who wants to marry Hunsecker's sister, Susan. We see Falco (Tony Curtis, *left*) confirming the setup with NYPD Lieutenant Harry Kello (Emile Meyer, *right*) and one of his assistants (unidentified actor, *center*). Hunsecker has ordered Falco—as well as Kello, whom he controls—to make Dallas the victim of this scheme to keep the musician from marrying his sister. Shadows are deep, and the streetlights cast sharp pools of light on streets wet with rain. This atmosphere is made even more menacing by the noisy sounds of the bridge traffic overhead.

[2] In *Manhattan*, two of the typically self-deprecating New Yorkers that populate Allen's movies—Isaac Davis (Woody Allen) and Mary Wilkie (Diane Keaton)—meet for the second time at a cocktail party, desert their dates and leave together, and take a joyous walk through the streets. They end up on a bench in Sutton Square, a quiet, elegant neighborhood a few blocks closer to the river than the site of the scene in image [1], but close enough that this scene is also set alongside and below the bridge. The world of *Sweet Smell of Success* could be a million miles away. The bridge stretches above the two characters and across the frame, its supporting cables twinkling with lights, the early morning sky soft and misty behind. The only sounds are the lovers' voices and George and Ira Gershwin's romantic ballad "Someone to Watch over Me." Woody Allen is no starry-eyed fool, but the Manhattan in this movie is all romance, soft lights, and human relationships that (mostly) end happily.

1

2

Soft versus hard lighting

Gregg Toland's use of lighting in *Citizen Kane* (1941) creates a clear contrast between Charles Foster Kane (Orson Welles) [1] and Susan Alexander (Dorothy Comingore) [2] that signals important differences between them in age (Kane is 45; Alexander is 22) and experience.

1

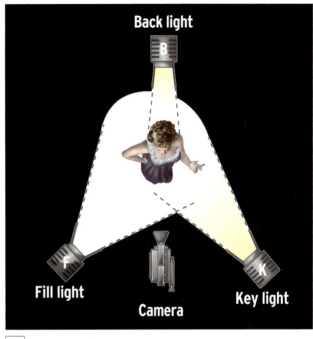

2

Three-point lighting

In the history of over-the-top mise-en-scène, few directors surpass Josef von Sternberg. *The Scarlet Empress* (1934; cinematographer Bert Glennon), a ravishing, high-camp historical drama, is also the director's visual tribute to the allure of Marlene Dietrich, who plays Russian empress Catherine the Great. Von Sternberg consistently photographs her with three-point lighting that accentuates her exquisite beauty. In this example, notice how the key light, positioned to the side and slightly below the actor, casts deep shadows around her eyes and on her right cheek. The fill light, which is positioned at the opposite side of the camera from the key light, softens the depth of the shadows created by the brighter key light. The backlight (a von Sternberg trademark in lighting Dietrich), which is positioned behind and above, lighting both sides of the actor, not only creates highlights along the edges of her hair but also separates her from the background and thus increases the appearance of three-dimensionality in the image.

The effects possible with any one lighting setup are extensive, but not limitless. If anything, the pioneering work of one cinematographer may make such an impression on moviegoers and filmmakers alike that it limits the freedom of subsequent filmmakers to use the same lighting setup in different ways. In other words, as with most other aspects of filmmaking, lighting is subject to conventions. Perhaps the best-known lighting convention in feature filmmaking is the **three-point system**. Employed extensively during the Hollywood studio era (1927–47), the three-point system was used to cast a glamourous light on the studios' most valuable assets during these years—their stars—and it remains the standard lighting for movies today.

The three-point system employs three sources of light, each aimed from a different direction and position in relation to the subject: key light, fill light, and backlight. The backlight is the least essential of these three sources. The overall character of the image is determined mainly by the relationship between the key and fill lights. The **key light** (also known as the *main*, or *source, light*) is the primary source of illumination and therefore is customarily set first. Positioned to one side of the camera, it creates hard shadows. The **fill light**, which is positioned at the opposite side of the camera from the key light, adjusts the depth of the shadows created by the brighter key light. Fill light may also come from a reflector.

The primary advantage of three-point lighting is that it permits the cinematographer to adjust the relationship and balance between illumination and shadow, the balance between the key and fill lights. That balance is known as the **lighting ratio**. When little or no fill light is used, the ratio between bright illumination and deep shadow is very high; the effect produced is known as **low-key lighting**. Low-key lighting produces the overall

High-key lighting

In *THX 1138* (1971; cinematographers Albert Kihn and David Myers), George Lucas's use of an austere setting and intense white lighting that creates a shadowless environment is as chilling as the futuristic society it records. This society has outlawed sexual relations and controls inhabitants with a regimen of mind-changing drugs. Those who rebel are thrown into a prison that is a vast, white void.

Backlighting

Backlighting can provide a dramatic sense of depth, especially when it is the sole light source, as in the projection-room scene in Orson Welles's *Citizen Kane* (1941; cinematographer Gregg Toland). The intensity of light coming from the projection booth's windows provides clear visual cues to the depth of the on-screen space by creating a deep shadow in the foreground, a bright focus in the middle ground, and murky gray in the background. The shape of the beams of light—receding to a vanishing point behind the wall—not only contributes to our sense of depth but also accentuates the two main characters in the scene: Jerry Thompson (William Alland, *left*), the reporter who prepared the "News on the March" sequence, and his boss, Mr. Rawlston (Philip Van Zandt, *right*).

gloomy atmosphere that we see in horror films, mysteries, psychological dramas, crime stories, and film noirs, where its contrasts between light and dark often imply ethical judgments.

High-key lighting, which produces an image with very little contrast between the darks and the lights, is used extensively in dramas, musicals, comedies, and adventure films; its even, flat illumination does not call particular attention to the subject being photographed. When the intensity of the fill light equals that of the key light, the result will be the highest of high-key lighting: no shadows at all.

You may have noticed that these terms—*low-key lighting* and *high-key lighting*—are counterintuitive: we increase the contrasts to produce low-key lighting and decrease them to produce high-key lighting. Cinematographers dim the fill light to achieve a higher ratio and contrast between shadow depth and illumination, and they intensify the fill light to lower the ratio and contrast.

The third source in three-point lighting is the **backlight**, usually positioned behind and above the subject and the camera and used to create highlights along the edges of the subject as a means of separating it from the background and increasing its appearance of three-dimensionality (such highlights are also known as *edge lights* or *rim lights*). In exterior shooting, the sun is often used as a backlight. Although it is less important to the three-point system than key light and fill light, backlight can be used on its own to achieve expressive effects. One effect is to create depth in a shot by separating a figure

from the background, as in the projection-room scene in Orson Welles's *Citizen Kane* (1941; cinematographer Gregg Toland), in which Mr. Rawlston (Philip Van Zandt) and Jerry Thompson (William Alland) are outlined by the strong backlight from the projector.

Lighting from underneath a character (sometimes called *Halloween lighting*) creates eerie, ominous shadows on the actor's face by reversing the normal placement of illumination and shadow. This sort of lighting is especially appropriate in the horror genre, as in James Whale's *Bride of Frankenstein* (1935; cinematographer John J. Mescall), in which the lighting thrown on Dr. Pretorius (Ernest Thesiger) from below accentuates the diabolical nature of his scientific ambitions.

Lighting thrown on a character from above can be used for many different effects, but a common result is to make a character appear vulnerable, or—in the example from Francis Ford Coppola's *The Godfather* (1972; cinematographer Gordon Willis) shown in the accompanying photo—threatening and mysterious.

Lighting from below
In this scene from *Bride of Frankenstein* (1935; cinematographer John J. Mescall), Dr. Pretorius (Ernest Thesiger), with lighting cast from below, watches his monstrous creation come to life.

Lighting from above
In the opening scene of Francis Ford Coppola's *The Godfather* (1972; cinematographer Gordon Willis)—the wedding reception of his daughter Connie—Don Vito Corleone (Marlon Brando) responds to a request from one of the guests, Signore Bonasera, an undertaker, who asks Corleone to arrange the murder of two men who beat his daughter. Don Corleone listens impassively as lighting from above puts his eyes in deep shadow, emphasizing his power and mystique. He at first gently rebukes Bonasera for not paying him respect in the preceding years, but because it is traditional to grant requests on a daughter's wedding day, he finally grants the favor. Bonasera understands the magnitude of his debt and knows he will one day be called upon to repay the favor.

Color Color is another property of light. Perhaps its most important technical aspect is color temperature, a characteristic of visible light that is important in cinematography. Any light source will emit various light rays from the color spectrum. The absolute temperature of these rays is registered on the Kelvin scale, a measure of the color quality of the light source. The movie camera does not see color the way the human eye does and thus sometimes seems to exaggerate colors. We may see an object as white, but it may turn out to look very blue or orange on the screen. Understanding the temperature of a color enables a cinematographer during shooting (or laboratory technicians in the postproduction phase) to correct the color and achieve the desired look. One way to balance color is to match the sensitivity of the film stock to the color temperature of the light source. Another way is to use a camera filter, an optical element (usually a transparent sheet of colored glass or gelatin) placed in front of the lens that alters the light by cutting out distinct portions of the color spectrum as it passes to be registered on the film stock.

The overall style of a film is determined by its **production values**, or the amount and quality of human and physical resources devoted to the image. This style includes specific decisions regarding the various properties of light we have just discussed. During the height of the classical Hollywood studio era, studios distinguished themselves from each other by adopting distinctive lighting styles and production values: for example, somber, low-key lighting in black-and-white pictures from Warner Bros.; sharp, glossy lighting in the films from 20th Century Fox; and bright, glamourous lighting for MGM's many color films, especially the musicals. The studios cultivated (and in many cases enforced) their distinct styles with an eye to establishing brand identities, and the filmmakers working for them were expected to work within the limits of the company style.

Cinematographers working within the constraints of a well-established genre often find that their decisions about lighting style are at least partly determined by the production values and lighting styles of previous films in that genre. Film noir lighting, for example, conventionally uses high-contrast white-and-black tones to symbolize the opposing forces of good and evil. The very name *film noir* (*noir* means "black" in French) implies that lighting style is an important aspect of the genre. Filmmakers working within a genre with well-established conventions of lighting must at least be aware of those conventions.

Of course, the lighting conventions that define a genre can be altered by daring and imaginative filmmakers. For example, cinematographer John Alton deviates from the film noir lighting formula in Anthony Mann's *T-Men* (1947) to develop a sense of moral ambiguity rather than a hard-edged distinction between good (light) and evil (darkness). A hard-edged crime story about U.S. Treasury Department agents' successful busting of a counterfeit ring, *T-Men* incorporates many shots made in near-total darkness—a black so deep that sometimes you can barely see the action. Bright lighting occasionally punctuates this gloom; but the overall tendency is to place everyone, cops and counterfeiters alike, in a dark and murky atmosphere. Alton lit his sets for mood rather than for making them completely visible to the viewer, and with this approach he rewrote the textbook on film noir lighting. In so doing, he also changed the expectations traditionally raised by film noir lighting in order to direct and complicate our interpretation of the film's narrative.

The various aspects of lighting—its source, quality, direction, and color—work together with other elements to determine the overall mood and meaning of a scene.

Lars von Trier's *Dogville* (2003; cinematographer Anthony Dod Mantle), a misanthropic vision of the United States in the Depression-era 1930s, is set in a town of the same name that is located high on a plateau and populated by selfish, bored losers and miscreants. Grace (Nicole Kidman) arrives out of nowhere as a "gift" to the town's residents, whose primary reactions to her presence involve humiliating and torturing her, even as she does their chores to seek their acceptance. What is this place? Who is Grace? Why is she treated as an outsider? Lighting helps us answer these questions. The town's setting is a schematic design constructed on a vast, dark studio floor and often photographed from a very high angle that permits us to see its entire layout and total isolation from the surrounding countryside (which we never see). However, in contrast to the high-key lighting that floods the overall set with an even light, the scene we are considering (which takes place in one of the "houses" outlined on the floor) uses expressively lit close-ups to record a turning point in the action.

Grace is frustrated by her lot in life and tries to provoke Jack McKay (Ben Gazzara) into taking a more open view of the world, which is ironic since he is blind. We

Aspects of lighting in *Dogville*

[1] Grace (Nicole Kidman) provokes Jack. [2] Grace faces the sunlight. [3] Grace, in profile, is transfixed by the sunlight. [4] Grace turns toward Jack, astonished at how easy it was to bring light into darkness.

are in McKay's residence, where the window is heavily draped to emphasize his condition. The scene opens with Grace sitting in a chair as she taunts Jack, telling him that she's walked outside and noticed the windows: "It must be a wonderful view." The lighting that illuminates her is a classic example of three-point lighting [1]: Grace is on the right side of the frame, in semi-profile; the light is falling on her from no identifiable source, highlighting her left cheek and the ridge of her nose; her heavily made-up eyes are in the shadows of her bangs. From this lighting, we clearly see that she is determined to get somewhere with her provocation; in addition to encouraging Jack to "see" more of the world, she may also be making sexual overtures toward him.

Next, Grace boldly takes the liberty of pulling open the drapes. Standing with her back toward us and holding the drapes apart with her widespread arms, she faces bright, almost surreal sunlight and trees (significantly, there is little other greenery in the town) as the background music builds in a soft crescendo that suggests both spiritual and sexual release [2]. The reflection of her brightly lit face in the window accentuates the passage from darkness to light. She then turns, transfixed by the light: her profile, in the far right of the frame, faces directly left and toward the sunlight, which is evenly thrown onto her face; her lips are open in an ecstatic expression; the remaining two-thirds of the screen is dark [3]. Finally, she turns toward Jack, the bright sunlight behind her (an excellent example of backlighting), her face now in shadows, but her parted lips continue to underscore her sense of astonishment at how easy it was to bring light into darkness—a microcosm of her larger hope of achieving acceptance in Dogville [4]. As the scene ends, Jack remains trapped in his blindness. It is Grace, not Jack, who is able to see the light.

Lenses

In its most basic form, a camera **lens** is a piece of curved, polished glass or other transparent material. As the "eye" of the camera, its primary function is to bring the light that emanates from the subjects in front of the camera (actors, objects, or settings) into a focused image on the film, tape, or other sensor inside the camera. This was as true of the lens in the fifteenth-century camera obscura (in which the sensor was the wall on which the image was seen) as it is of the lenses of today.

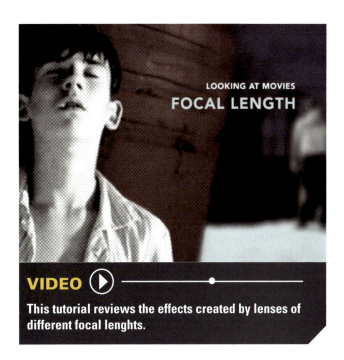

LOOKING AT MOVIES
FOCAL LENGTH

VIDEO ▶ ━━━━━━●━━━━
This tutorial reviews the effects created by lenses of different focal lenghts.

The basic properties shared by all lenses are aperture, focal length, and depth of field. The **aperture** of a lens is usually an adjustable **iris** (or diaphragm) that limits the amount of light passing through a lens. The greater the size of the aperture, the more light it admits through the lens. The **focal length** of the lens is the distance (measured in millimeters) from the optical center of the lens to the focal point on the film stock or other sensor when the image is sharp and clear (in focus). Focal length affects how we perceive perspective—the appearance of depth—in a shot, and it also influences our perception of the size, scale, and movement of the subject being shot. The four major types of lenses are designated by their respective focal lengths:

1. The **short-focal-length lens** (also known as the wide-angle lens, starting as low as 12.5mm) produces wide-angle views. It makes the subjects on the screen appear farther apart than they actually are, and because this lens elongates depth, characters or objects moving at a normal speed from background to foreground through this stretched depth might appear to be moving faster than they actually are.

2. The **long-focal-length lens** (also known as the telephoto lens; focal lengths ranging from 85mm to as high as 500mm) brings distant objects close, makes subjects look closer together than they do in

Short-focal-length lens

This shot from Stanley Kubrick's *Dr. Strangelove* (1964; cinematographer Gilbert Taylor) comically reinforces our sense of the powerlessness of Group Captain Lionel Mandrake (Peter Sellers, *facing the camera*) as he meets with his superior officer, Brigadier General Jack D. Ripper (Sterling Hayden). The resulting wide-angle composition makes Mandrake look almost like a toy doll standing on the powerful general's desk.

Middle-focal-length lens

This shot from Billy Wilder's *Sunset Boulevard* (1950; cinematographer John F. Seitz) includes the movie's three principal characters (*from left to right*): Max von Mayerling (Erich von Stroheim), with his back to us in the near left foreground; Norma Desmond (Gloria Swanson); and Joe Gillis (William Holden), in the middle ground facing us. A small orchestra is in the background. The middle-focal-length lens used to make this shot keeps the three principal subjects in normal focus, and the overall image corresponds to our day-to-day experience of depth and perspective.

real life, and flattens space and depth in the process. Thus it alters the subject's movement, so that a subject moving from the background toward the camera might appear to be barely moving at all.

3. Although the short and long extremes are used occasionally to achieve certain visual effects, most shots in feature films are made with a **middle-focal-length lens**—from 35mm to 50mm—often called the *normal lens*. Lenses in this range create images that correspond to our day-to-day experience of depth and perspective.

4. The **zoom lens**, also called the *variable-focal-length lens*, permits the cinematographer to shrink or increase the focal length in a continuous motion and thus simulates the effect of movement of the camera toward or away from the subject. However, the camera does not actually move through space but simply magnifies the image.

Short-focal-length, long-focal-length, and middle-focal-length lenses all have fixed focal lengths and are known as **prime lenses**, but zoom lenses are in their own category. Both prime and zoom lenses have their specific optical qualities, and because they are thought to produce sharper images, prime lenses are generally used more than zoom lenses. In the hands of an accomplished cinematographer, the zoom lens can produce

Long-focal-length lens

This image from Stanley Kubrick's *Barry Lyndon* (1975; cinematographer John Alcott) shows the flattening effect of a long-focal-length lens. The marching soldiers' forward progress seems more gradual as a result.

1

2

Zoom lens

In making *The Hurt Locker* (2008; cinematographer Barry Ackroyd), director Kathryn Bigelow wanted viewers to experience the Iraq war as if they were virtually involved in it. Thus, she had her camera team use lightweight Super 16mm cameras that gave them the mobility and flexibility to enter into the action and take viewers with them. One of these cameras was fitted with a zoom lens to allow its operator multiple perspectives on a scene within one shot. Overall, the movie is concerned with the highly dangerous work of a team that identifies and disables enemy roadside bombs and similar incendiary weapons. Here, the team, learning that a UN facility is apparently in danger of attack, orders the immediate evacuation of people from the building. In this shot, the camera lens begins with an extreme long shot [1] and then immediately shifts to a shorter focal length to put us among the coalition soldiers leading the frightened workers to safety [2]. The rapid, fluid movement of the lens between a neutral observation point and the people rushing toward the camera increases our involvement with the military forces and workers. In subsequent zoom-lens shots, we see the weapons team make surveillance of the immediate area, shoot a suspicious man, and disarm a vehicle loaded with bombs, thus preventing an explosion.

striking effects, but when it is used indiscriminately, as it often is by less skilled filmmakers, it not only feels artificial to an audience but can unintentionally disorient viewers. As with all other aspects of cinematography, the lens used must be appropriate for the story being told.

Depth of field is a property of the lens that permits the cinematographer to decide what **planes**, or areas of the image, will be in focus. As a result, depth of field helps create emphasis either on one or more selected planes or figures or on the whole image. The term *depth of field* refers to the distances in front of a camera and its lens in which the subjects are in apparent sharp focus. The short-focal-length lens offers a nearly complete depth of field, rendering almost all objects in the frame in focus. The depth of field of the long-focal-length lens is generally a very narrow range, and it leaves the background and foreground of the in-focus objects dramatically out

of focus. In the middle-focal-length lens, the depth of field keeps all subjects in a "normal" sense of focus.

In virtually all shooting, cinematographers keep the main subject of each shot in sharp focus to maintain clear spatial and perspectival relations within frames. One option available to cinematographers, however, is a **rack focus** (also known as *select focus*, *shift focus*, or *pull focus*)—a change of the point of focus from one subject to another. This technique guides our attention to a new, clearly focused point of interest while blurring the previous subject in the frame (see the illustration on p. 232).

The images you see on the screen are produced by a complex interaction of optical properties associated with the camera lens. Table 6.1 provides a ready reference on how the different lenses discussed here produce different images.

1 **2**

Rack focus

In this shot from Guillermo del Toro's *The Devil's Backbone* (2001; cinematographer Guillermo Navarro), the camera uses depth of field to guide our attention from one subject to another. When the shot begins, the lens is focused on the background where the villainous Jacinto (Eduardo Noriega) scans the orphanage courtyard for stray witnesses [1]. The lens then shifts focus to the foreground so that Jacinto's elusive prey, the orphan Jamie (Ìñigo Garcés), snaps into sharp relief [2].

Table 6.1 | TYPES OF IMAGES PRODUCED BY DIFFERENT LENSES	
Lens Type	**Characteristics of Images Produced by Aperture, Focal Length, and Depth of Field**
Prime lenses Short-focal-length lens (wide-angle lens)	• Produces wide-angle views. • Makes subjects appear farther apart than they actually are. • Through its nearly complete depth of field, renders almost all objects in the frame in focus.
Long-focal-length lens (telephoto lens)	• Produces deep-angle views. • Brings distant objects close. • Flattens space and depth. • Makes subjects look closer together than they actually are. • Narrow depth of field leaves most of the background and foreground of the in-focus objects dramatically out of focus.
Middle-focal-length lens (normal lens)	• Produces images that correspond to our day-to-day experience of depth and perspective. • Keeps all subjects in a normal sense of focus.
Zoom lens Zoom lens (variable-focal-length lens)	• Produces images that simulate the effect of movement of the camera toward or away from the subject. • Rather than actually moving through space, merely magnifies the image. • Can make a shot seem artificial to an audience.

Framing of the Shot

Framing is the process by which the cinematographer determines what will appear within the borders of the image during a shot. Framing turns the comparatively infinite sight of the human eye into a finite movie image—an unlimited view into a limited view. This process requires decisions about each of the following elements: the proximity to the camera of main subjects, the depth of the composition, the camera angle and height, the scale of various objects in relation to each other, and the type of camera movement, if any.

At least one decision about framing is out of the cinematographer's hands. Although a painter can choose any size or shape of canvas as the area in which to create a picture—large or small, square or rectangular, oval or round, flat or three-dimensional—cinematographers find that their choices for a "canvas" are limited to a small number of dimensional variations on a rectangle. This rectangle results from the historical development of photographic technology. Nothing absolutely dictates that our experience of moving images must occur within a rectangle; however, thanks to the standardization of equipment and technology within the motion-picture industry, we have come to know this rectangle as the shape of movies.

The relationship between the frame's two dimensions is known as its **aspect ratio** (see Figure 6.2 on p. 234), the ratio of the width of the image to its height. Each movie is made to be shown in one aspect ratio from beginning to end. The most common aspect ratios are

> 1.375:1   Academy (35mm flat)[7]

> 1.66:1   European widescreen (35mm flat)

> 1.85:1   American widescreen (35mm flat)

> 2.2:1   Super Panavision and Todd-AO (70mm flat)

> 2.35:1   Panavision and CinemaScope (35mm anamorphic)

> 2.75:1   Ultra Panavision (70mm anamorphic)

Frames within the frame

Some Japanese filmmakers experiment with the Western conventions of framing, not only by presenting more information within the frame but also by using frames within the frame. The composition of the image preceding this one from Kyoshi Kurosawa's *Charisma* (1999) deliberately directs the viewer's eye: the window to the left is dark, the tree trunk draws our eyes to the right, the fallen window screen eliminates a window we don't see. These elements subconsciously tell us to concentrate our attention on the window in the upper right corner. What happens next alerts us not to follow such suggestions lightly, because what we don't know is that the police have trapped a suspect, holding a hostage, in the room behind the window on the upper left. They storm the apartment, go through the room on the upper right, and shoot and kill both men in the adjacent room.

Feature-length widescreen movies were made as early as 1927—the most notable was Abel Gance's spectacular *Napoléon* (1927). In Hollywood, the Fox Grandeur 70mm process very effectively enhanced the epic composition and sweep of Raoul Walsh's *The Big Trail* (1930; cinematographer Arthur Edeson). Until the 1950s, when the widescreen image became popular, the standard aspect ratio for a flat film was the Academy ratio of 1.375:1, meaning that the frame is 37 percent wider than it is high—a ratio corresponding to the dimensions of a single frame of 35mm film stock. Today's more familiar widescreen variations provide wider horizontal and shorter vertical dimensions. Most commercial releases are shown in the 1.85:1 aspect ratio, which is almost twice as wide as it is high. Other widescreen variations include a 2.2:1 or 2.35:1 ratio when projected.[8]

---

7. While this ratio is still often quoted as 1.33:1, the Academy acknowledged in 1932 that the standard of the Academy ratio was widened to 1.375:1 (often referred to as 1.37:1) to provide room on the film stock for the sound track.

8. In shooting for television broadcast, cinematographers are increasingly using the 1.78:1 aspect ratio. It can be seen on a home TV set with a format of 16:9, which is universal for HDTV.

Figure 6.2 | BASIC ASPECT RATIOS

1.375:1

1.85:1

2.35:1

Architectural elements such as arches, doorways, and windows are frequently used to mask a frame. A person placed between the camera and its subject can also mask the frame, as in the opening of John Ford's *The Searchers* (see Chapter 8, p. 340). In Mike Nichols's *The Graduate* (1967; cinematographer Robert Surtees), during her initial seduction scene of Ben Braddock (Dustin Hoffman), Mrs. Robinson (Anne Bancroft) sits at the bar in her house and raises one leg onto the stool next to her, forming a triangle through which Ben is framed or, perhaps, trapped. Despite these modest attempts to

break up the rectangular movie frame into other shapes through frames within the frame, movies continue to come to us as four-sided images that are wider than they are tall.

Although filmmakers seldom use more than one aspect ratio in a movie, in shooting *The Grand Budapest Hotel* (2014), director Wes Anderson and DP Robert Yeoman shot in three different aspect ratios, one for each historical period the movie depicts. The story, which unfolds in three time periods from the 1930s to the present, is screened in the aspect ratio that would have

Architectural mask in *The Book of Eli*

In this image, the Denzel Washington character is isolated in an ar-chitectural mask formed by an opening under a destroyed highway in Albert and Allen Hughes's sci-fi thriller *The Book of Eli* (2010), a movie that contains several other excellent examples of this technique.

Masking in *The Graduate*

Mike Nichols's *The Graduate* (1967; cinematographer Robert Sur-tees) features one of the most famous (and amusing) maskings of the frame in movie history. As the scene ends, Ben Braddock (Dustin Hoffman), framed in the provocative bend of Mrs. Robin-son's (Anne Bancroft) knee, asks, "Mrs. Robinson, you're trying to seduce me . . . aren't you?"

been used in those periods. Thus the 1930s scenes—and, in fact, most of the film—are shot in the Academy ratio because they take place during that time. The period of the 1960s is shot in the 2.35:1 widescreen ratio, and the period from 1985 to the present is in the 1.85:1 wide-screen format. This unusual approach may help view-ers to remember that three difference voices are telling the story in these three different periods. Spotting this approach requires some knowledge of aspect ratios (a small reward for those reading this book—unless you know about the director's strategy, you'll probably miss it). Anderson is well known for paying meticulous atten-tion to period detail, and this movie is rich in all details, from the architecture of its buildings to their elaborate interiors, from its characters' costumes to its fairyland exteriors. Perhaps he takes similar pleasure from shoot-ing in three different aspect ratios; but it appears that only Anderson, and not the audience, gets it.

Implied Proximity to the Camera

From our earlier discussion of mise-en-scène (see Chapter 5), we know that in the vast majority of mov-ies, everything we see on the screen—including subjects within a shot and their implied proximity to each other—has been placed there to develop the narrative's outcome and meaning. Our interpretations of these on-screen spatial relationships happen as unconsciously and auto-matically as they do in everyday life.

To get a sense of the importance of proximity, imag-ine yourself on a crowded dance floor at a club or party. Among all the other distracting things in your field of

vision, you see an attractive person looking at you from the opposite end of the room. You may assign that per-son some significance from that distance, but if that same person walks up to you, virtually filling your field of vision, then the person suddenly has much greater significance to you and may provoke a much more pro-found reaction from you. Regardless of the outcome of this encounter, you have become visually involved with this person in a way that you wouldn't have if the person had remained at the other end of the room.

Similarly, the implied proximity of the camera to the subjects being shot influences our emotional involve-ment with those subjects. Think of how attentive you are during a close-up of your favorite movie actor or how shocked you feel when, as in Gore Verbinski's hor-ror movie *The Ring* (2002; cinematographer Bojan Ba-zelli), an actor moves quickly and threateningly from a position of obscurity in the background to a position of vivid and terrifying dominance of the frame. We all have favorite scenes from horror films that have shocked us in this way, violating and then virtually erasing the dis-tance between us and the screen.

Of course, nearness is not the only degree of proxim-ity that engages our emotions. Each of the possible ar-rangements of subjects in proximity to each other and to the camera has the potential to convey something meaningful about the subjects on-screen, and thank-fully, most of those meanings come to us naturally.

The following movies achieve these ends. Steve Mc-Queen's *Shame* (2011) tells a powerful story of a sex ad-dict (Michael Fassbender) who cannot have any kind of relationship with another person, and DP Sean Bobbit appropriately uses many intimate shots to record the character's solitary and sometimes secretive exploits. Paul Thomas Anderson's *The Master* (2012; cinematographer Mihai Mălaimare Jr.) records in intimate cinematography the close, needy, and perverse relationship between the father figure (Philip Seymour Hoffman) and his protégé (Joaquin Phoenix). Again, this is appropriate to the close quarters of a ship, and the shots are all the more visually powerful for being set in the 1.85:1 widescreen format. For John Korkidas's *Kill Your Darlings* (2013), a dark melodramatic account of Allen Ginsberg's (Daniel Radcliffe) evolution as a poet, DP Reed Morano captures the nearness, secrecy, and fears that fill the gay world of Ginsberg's lovers and friends in the 1950s. Similarly, in director Kaspar Munk's *You and Me and Forever* (2012), a coming-of-age drama set in Denmark, DP Søren Bay captures the familiar intensity of teenage friendships.

Shot Types The names of the most commonly used shots employed in a movie—*extreme long shot, long shot, medium long shot, medium shot, medium close-up, close-up,* and *extreme close-up*—refer to the implied distance between the camera lens and the subject being photographed. Since the best way to remember and recognize the different types of shots is to think about the scale of the human body within the frame, we'll describe them in terms of that scale. The illustrations are from Tom Hooper's *The King's Speech* (2010; cinematographer Danny Cohen). Historically, the story is familiar: King George V dies in 1936, and his son David accedes to the throne as Edward VIII. But his romantic relationship with and desire to marry Wallis Simpson, a twice-divorced American, leads to his abdication and the accession of his brother Albert ("Bertie"), the Duke

of York, to the throne as George VI. The psychological and emotional effects of Bertie's royal upbringing add depth to the story. As a boy, he developed a serious stammer due to the apparent bullying of his father and was therefore unprepared to handle the speaking engagements required of the king, both in person and over the radio. With his wife's encouragement, he meets a relatively unknown speech therapist, Lionel Logue, who uses a series of experimental vocal, physical, emotional, and psychological techniques that eventually make it possible for the future king to speak fluently and confidently in public.

> In the **extreme long shot** (**XLS** or **ELS**), typically photographed at a great distance, the subject is often a wide view of a location, which usually includes general background information. When used to provide such an informative context, the XLS is also an **establishing shot**. Even when human beings are included in such a shot, the emphasis is not on them as individuals but on their relationship to the surroundings. Image [1] shows Sandringham House, an immense country house used by the British royal family. Although several people are on the terrace, the function of the shot is to identify the house and its grandeur.

> The **long shot** (**LS**) generally contains the full body of one or more characters (almost filling the frame, but also showing some of the surrounding area above, below, and to the sides of the frame). In image [2], the archbishop and other officials of Westminster Abbey, standing amid the abbey's splendid surroundings, discuss preparations for the inauguration of King George VI.

> A **medium long shot** (**MLS**) is neither a medium shot nor a long shot, but one in between. It is used to photograph one or more characters, usually from

Shot types

[1] **Extreme long shot:** An extreme long shot of the exterior of Sandringham House, from which King George V delivers his annual Christmas address, humiliating his son in the process. [2] **Long shot:** A long shot of the interior of Westminster Abbey, where the archbishop of Canterbury and other church officials discuss the forthcoming inauguration of King George VI. [3] **Medium long shot:** A medium long shot of the interior of Lionel Logue's studio. The physical distance between the Duke of York and his mentor reflects both royal protocol and the duke's reluctance to undertake therapy. [4] **Medium shot:** A medium shot showing Mrs. Wallis Simpson greeting guests at Balmoral House, acting, quite characteristically, as if she owned the place. [5] **Close-up shot:** In this close-up shot, we see (and of course hear) King George VI, having overcome his stammer through diligent therapy, deliver the most important radio address of his reign, one that galvanized people's support of him. [6] **Medium close-up shot:** In this medium close-up shot, at the outset of the future king's lessons, we see Lionel Logue, his mentor, a figure whose poise and confidence are evident throughout the movie. [7] **Extreme close-up shot:** In this extreme close-up shot, we see one aspect of speech therapy: The Duke of York is repeatedly saying the word *father* as if to make the king's intimidation of him vanish from his consciousness.

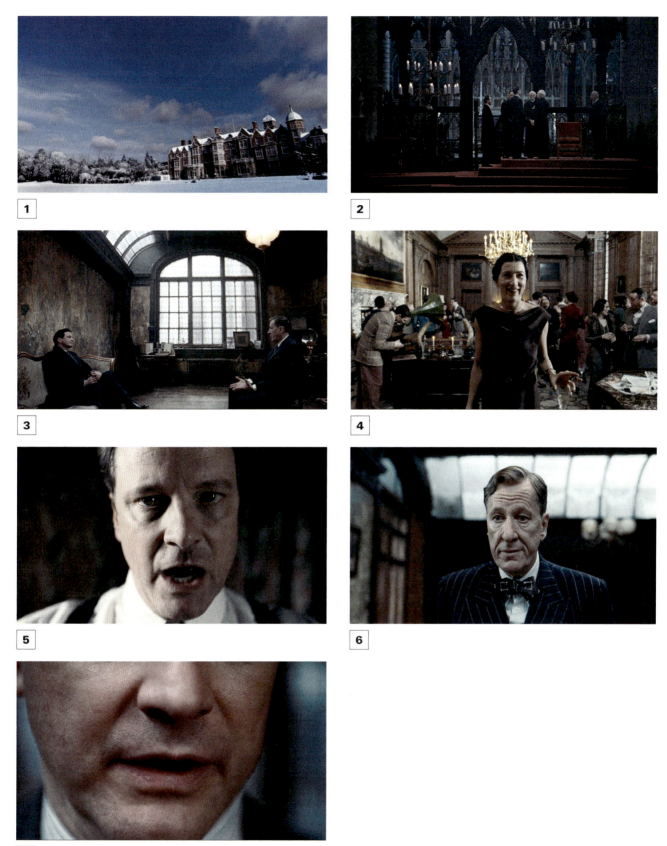

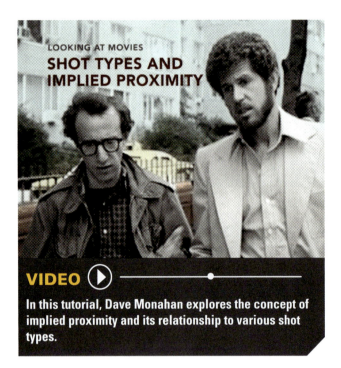

LOOKING AT MOVIES

SHOT TYPES AND IMPLIED PROXIMITY

VIDEO ▶

In this tutorial, Dave Monahan explores the concept of implied proximity and its relationship to various shot types.

the knees up, as well as some of the background. This indispensable shot permits the director to place two characters in conversation and to shoot them from a variety of angles, as in image [3], where we see a meeting between the future king (Colin Firth, *left*) and his speech therapist, Lionel Logue (Geoffrey Rush, *right*), in Logue's studio. Because the MLS is widely used in Hollywood movies, the French call this shot the *plan Américain* ("American shot").

❯ The **medium shot** (**MS**), somewhere between the long shot and the close-up, usually shows a character from the waist up. The MS is the most frequently used type of shot because it replicates our human experience of proximity without intimacy; it provides more detail of the body than the LS does. Unlike the close-up, the MS can include several characters, but it reveals more nuance in the characters' faces than can be captured in the MLS. Image [4] is a typical medium shot of Mrs. Wallis Simpson (Eve Best) greeting the duke and duchess of York at a cocktail party at a royal country house. Because she is not a member of the royal family, she is not officially entitled to take the role of host; nonetheless, her face registers her self-confidence.

❯ In a **close-up** (**CU**), the camera pays very close attention to the subject, whether it is an object or a person, but is most often used in close-ups of actors' faces. Although it traditionally shows the

full head (sometimes including the shoulders), it can also be used to show another part of the body, such as a hand, eye, or mouth. When focused on a face, the CU can provide an exclusive view of the character's emotions or state of mind, yet it can also show a face lacking emotion or thought. Director Darren Aronofsky (*Noah*, 2014; *Black Swan*, 2010) believes that the close-up was "the best invention of the twentieth century.... That you could put a camera right in front of Paul Newman's eyes and look into his soul changed storytelling."[9] In image [5] we see George VI successfully deliver a radio speech in September 1939 informing the nation that Great Britain has declared war on Germany. It is, for him, a moment of personal and professional triumph, won through his evident determination and the efforts of his mentor.

❯ The **medium close-up** (**MCU**) shows a character from approximately the middle of the chest to the top of the head. It provides a view of the face that catches minor changes in expression and gives some detail about the character's posture. Image [6] portrays speech therapist Lionel Logue as he begins his sessions with the future king of England.

❯ An **extreme close-up** (**XCU** or **ECU**), a powerful variation on the CU, is produced when the camera records a very small detail of the subject. By comparing images [5] and [7], you can see that focusing on the future king's mouth and his aggressive repetition of the word *father* show how eager he is to break the psychological hold his father maintains on him.

❯ *Note*: you can more accurately label various shots according to the number of people in them. As is obvious, a **two-shot** contains two characters, a **three-shot**, three characters, and a group shot, more than three people.

Depth

Because the image of the movie screen is two-dimensional and thus appears flat (except for movies shot with 3-D cinematography), one of the most compelling challenges faced by cinematographers has been how to give that image an illusion of depth. From the earliest years of film history, filmmakers have experimented with achieving different illusions of depth. D. W. Griffith was a master at using huge three-dimensional sets in such movies as *Intolerance* (1916; cinematographer G. W. Bitzer). A more sustained effort to make the most

9. Qtd. in Tad Friend, "Heavy Weather," *The New Yorker* (March 17, 2014), p. 48.

Depth

From the earliest years of film history, filmmakers have experimented with achieving different illusions of depth. [1] Rouben Mamoulian created an effective illusion of spatial depth in *Applause* (1929; cinematographer George Folsey) by organizing a line of burlesque dancers to move from the stage in the back of the image, across the runway that bisects the audience in the middle of the image, to the viewer—sitting, presumably, in the right-hand corner of the foreground of the screen. Even though it was not yet possible to maintain clear focus from the foreground to background, the illusion of depth is there. [2] Three years later, in his dazzling comedy *Trouble in Paradise* (1932; cinematographer Victor Milner), Ernst Lubitsch adhered to the traditional method of the time: suggesting depth by using an LS, placing the two main characters in the foreground plane and leaving the rest of the image in a soft-focus background. In both of these examples, the cinematic space is arranged to draw the viewer's eyes either away from or toward the background.

of deep-space composition began in the late 1920s. Many directors and cinematographers during this decade, especially those who were directing musicals with large casts and big production budgets, experimented with the technique of creating lines of movement from background to foreground to foster the illusion of depth.

For example, in *Applause* (1929; cinematographer George Folsey), Rouben Mamoulian created spatial depth by organizing a line of burlesque dancers to move from the stage in the back of the image, across the catwalk that ran through the audience in the middle of the image, to the viewer, sitting, presumably, in the right-hand corner of the foreground of the screen. Director Mervyn LeRoy achieved a more elaborate effect with Busby Berkeley's choreography in *Gold Diggers of 1933* (1933).

Although these elaborately choreographed scenes reveal progress toward the goal of creating a cinematic image with greater depth, during the 1930s the traditional method of suggesting cinematic depth was to use an LS and place significant characters or objects in the foreground or middle-ground planes and then leave the rest of the image in a soft-focus background. The filmmaker could also reverse this composition and place the

significant figures in the background of the image with a landscape, say, occupying the foreground and middle ground. Thus, in both of these examples, the cinematic space is arranged to draw the viewer's eyes toward or away from the background. With such basic illusions, our eyes automatically give depth to the successive areas of the image as they seem to recede in space.

Also during the 1930s, however, various cinematographers experimented with creating a deeper illusion of space through cinematographic rather than choreographic means. Of these cinematographers, none was more important than Gregg Toland, who was responsible for bringing the previous developments together, improving them, and using them most impressively in John Ford's *The Long Voyage Home* (1940) and soon after in Orson Welles's *Citizen Kane* (1941). By the time he shot these two films, Toland had already rejected the soft-focus, one-plane depth of the established Hollywood style; experimented with achieving greater depth; created sharper black-and-white images; used the high-powered Technicolor arc lights for black-and-white cinematography; used Super XX film stock, which produced a clearer image and was four times faster than previously available black-and-white stock; coated his

Deep-focus cinematography and deep-space composition in *Citizen Kane*

Gregg Toland built on the work of previous directors, such as Al-lan Dwan, one of the most formally innovative of early film direc-tors, who used deep-space composition in *The Iron Mask* (1929; cinematographers Warren Lynch and Henry Sharp), a silent swash-buckler featuring Douglas Fairbanks. Dwan could open up any shot into a complex, three-dimensional space with strategically placed foreground, middle ground, and background figures or objects. Sim-ilarly, in this beautiful deep-space composition from Orson Welles's *Citizen Kane* (1941), Toland exploits all three planes of depth along a line that draws our eye from screen right to screen left. In the foreground, we see the reporter Mr. Thompson (William Alland) in a closed telephone booth; in the middle ground, outside the booth, we see the headwaiter of the El Rancho nightclub; and in the back-ground, we see Susan Alexander Kane (Dorothy Comingore), the subject of Thompson's visit. Each character is photographed in clear focus in a unified setting, yet each is in a separate physical, psycho-logical, and emotional space.

Deep-space composition

An excellent example of the expressive potential of deep-space composition can be found in Alfred Hitchcock's *Notorious* (1946; cinematographer Ted Tetzlaff). Alicia Huberman (Ingrid Bergman), an American counterspy working in Brazil to discover enemy secrets, marries Alexander Sebastian (Claude Rains), a German spy, at the re-quest of her government. Sebastian and his mother, Madame Kon-stantin (Leopoldine Konstantin), eventually discover Alicia's duplicity, and in this scene they have already begun to kill her by poisoning her coffee. As Alicia complains of feeling ill, Madame Konstantin places a small cup on the table near her, putting it in the immediate foreground of the frame. The tiny cup is no more than a few inches tall, but it appears about as large as Alicia's head in the middle ground, thus heightening the menace facing her and raising the level of suspense.

lenses (to cut down glare from the lights); and used a camera equipped with a **blimp** so that he could work in confined spaces.

In *Citizen Kane*, these methods came together in two related techniques: a deliberate use of (1) **deep-space composition**, a total visual composition that places sig-nificant information or subjects on all three planes of the frame and thus creates an illusion of depth, coupled with (2) **deep-focus cinematography**, which, using the short-focal-length lens, keeps all three planes in sharp focus. Deep-space composition permits the filmmaker to exploit the relative size of people and objects in the frame to convey meaning and conflict.

Toland's pioneering work on *Citizen Kane* profoundly influenced the look of subsequent movies and helped to distance Hollywood even further from the editing-centered theories of the Russian formalist directors (e.g., Sergei Eisenstein); Toland also brought American moviemaking closer to the realism of such European directors as Jean Renoir. French film critic André Bazin emphasizes that deep-focus cinematography "brings the spectator into a relation with the image closer to that which he enjoys with reality" and "implies, conse-quently, both a more active mental attitude on the part of the spectator and a more positive contribution on his part to the action in progress."[10] In preserving the

10. André Bazin, "The Evolution of the Language of Cinema," in *What Is Cinema?* trans. Hugh Gray, 2 vols. (Berkeley: University of California Press, 1967–71), I, pp. 35–36.

Use of deep-space composition in *The Little Foxes*
At the climax of William Wyler's *The Little Foxes* (1941; cinematographer Gregg Toland), Horace (Herbert Marshall) responds to his wife's tirade [1], begins having a heart attack, and rises [2] while Regina (Bette Davis) remains rigidly in place [3], offering Horace no help as he staggers to his death in the background, helpless and out of focus [4].

continuity of space and time, deep-focus cinematography seems more like human perception.

Toland also understood that a scene involving deep-space composition did not necessarily have to be shot with deep-focus cinematography, as he demonstrated in William Wyler's *The Little Foxes* (1941). Perhaps the best example is found in a scene in which Regina Giddens (Bette Davis) confronts her severely ill husband, Horace Giddens (Herbert Marshall), a man she detests for his overall opposition to her scheming brothers and their plan to expand her family's wealth by exploiting cheap labor. The sequence takes place in their parlor after Horace has returned home from a long hospital stay for treatment of his serious heart condi-

tion. When Regina asks him to put more funds into strengthening the family enterprise, he tells her that he has changed his will, leaving her nothing but bonds. He does not realize that members of the family have already stolen the bonds for the same purpose. Realizing that a man she despises has unknowingly trapped her in a difficult and illegal situation, Regina retaliates by telling him that she has always hated him. During her tirade, Horace has the first seizures of a heart attack. While attempting to take his medicine, he drops the bottle; when he asks Regina to get the spare bottle upstairs, she makes the decision to let him die and sits perfectly still as he staggers toward the stairs and collapses. As Horace struggles toward the stairs behind

The rule of thirds

The rule of thirds applies to interior as well as exterior cinematography, particularly in genres such as the Western, where wide-open spaces figure significantly in a movie's meaning. Kit (Martin Sheen), the protagonist of Terence Malick's *Badlands* (1973; cinematographers Tak Fujimoto, Steven Lamer, and Brian Probyn), takes to the road on a violent killing spree, accompanied by his girlfriend Holly (Sissy Spacek). Although not a Western per se, the movie is an American classic both for its focus on the serial killers that are now, unfortunately, part of our culture and its widescreen depiction of the flat, deep badlands between the Dakotas and the Canadian border. In this image, Kit (with his arms looped over his rifle) takes stock of himself on the eve of his final spree. The rising moon occupies the deep background plane of the image; the dust-filled air of the landscape dominates the middle ground. Kit is walking toward us in the foreground, looking something like a scarecrow (an object that is frightening, but not dangerous). This character, isolated in the natural grandeur, gives no hint of what evil he will do tomorrow.

Regina, who is in the foreground, he grows more and more out of focus, but he and his actions certainly are significant subject material. He goes out of focus for a specific reason—he is dying—and the shot is still very much deep-space composition but not deep focus. Even though he is out of focus in the deep background of the frame, Horace remains significant to the outcome of the story.

The coupling of deep-space composition and deep-focus cinematography is useful only for scenes in which images of extreme depth within the frame are required, because the planning and choreography required to make these images are complex and time-consuming. Most filmmakers employ less complicated methods to maximize the potential of the image, put its elements into balance, and create an illusion of depth. Perhaps most important among these methods is the composi-

tional principle known as the **rule of thirds**. This rule, like so many other "rules" in cinema, is a convention that can be adapted as needed. It takes the form of a grid pattern that, when superimposed on the image, divides it into horizontal thirds representing the foreground, middle ground, and background planes and into vertical thirds that break up those planes into further elements. This grid assists the designer and cinematographer in visualizing the overall potential of the height, width, and depth of any cinematic space.

Camera Angle and Height

The camera's **shooting angle** is the level and height of the camera in relation to the subject being photographed. For the filmmaker, it is another framing element that offers many expressive possibilities. The

VIDEO ▶

This tutorial examines the various types of camera angles and their effects in viewers.

Eye-level shot

In John Huston's *The Maltese Falcon* (1941; cinematographer Arthur Edeson), this eye-level shot, used throughout the initial meeting of Miss Wonderly (Mary Astor) and Sam Spade (Humphrey Bogart), leads us to the false belief that the facts of their meeting are "on the level."

normal height of the camera is eye level, which we take for granted because that's the way we see the world. Because our first impulse as viewers is to identify with the camera's point of view, and because we are likely to interpret any deviation from an eye-level shot as somehow different, filmmakers must take special care to use other basic camera angles—high angle, low angle, Dutch angle, and aerial view—in ways that are appropriate to and consistent with a movie's storytelling.

The phrases *to look up to* and *to look down on* reveal a physical viewpoint and connote admiration or condescension. In our everyday experience, a high angle is a position of power over what we're looking at, and we intuitively understand that the subject of a high-angle view is inferior, weak, or vulnerable in light of our actual and cultural experiences. A filmmaker shooting from a high angle must be aware of this traditional interpretation of that view, whether the shot will be used to confirm or undermine that interpretation. Even a slight upward or downward angle of a camera may be enough to express an air of inferiority or superiority.

Eye Level An **eye-level shot** is made from the observer's eye level and usually implies that the camera's attitude toward the subject being photographed is neutral. An eye-level shot used early in a movie—as part of establishing its characters, time, and place—occurs before we have learned the full context of the story, so we naturally tend to read its attitude toward the subject as neutral. Thus when Miss Wonderly (Mary Astor) introduces herself to Sam Spade (Humphrey Bogart) at the beginning of John Huston's *The Maltese Falcon* (1941; cinematographer Arthur Edeson), the director uses an omniscient eye-level camera to establish a neutral client–detective relationship that seems to be what both characters want. This effect deliberately deceives us, as we learn only later in the film when we discover that Miss Wonderly is not the innocent person she claims to be (as the eye-level angle suggested).

By contrast, an eye-level shot that occurs in *The Grifters* (1990; cinematographer Oliver Stapleton), comes later in the movie, after director Stephen Frears has established a narrative context for interpreting his characters and their situation. From the beginning of the film, we know that Lilly Dillon (Anjelica Huston) and her son, Roy (John Cusack), are grifters, or con artists. After an eight-year estrangement they meet again, but each still regards suspiciously everything the other says or does. The eye-level shot reveals the hollow dialogue and tension of their reunion and is thus ironic, since they know, as we do, that their relationship is off balance (not "on the level").

High Angle A **high-angle shot** (also called a *high shot* or *down shot*) is made with the camera above the action and typically implies the observer's sense of superiority to the subject being photographed. In Rouben Mamoulian's *Love Me Tonight* (1932; cinematographer Victor Milner), Maurice Courtelin (Maurice Chevalier) finally

1

1

2

2

High-angle shot

[1] In this scene from Rouben Mamoulian's *Love Me Tonight* (1932; cinematographer Victor Milner), the high-angle shot has the traditional meaning of making the subject seem inferior. After Maurice Courtelin (Maurice Chevalier) admits that he is not an aristocrat but rather an ordinary tailor, the camera looks down on him as he is left to assess his future with a symbolic measuring tape in his hands. [2] This shot from Alfred Hitchcock's *North by Northwest* (1959; cinematographer Robert Burks), although taken from a high angle, makes Phillip Vandamm (James Mason) and Leonard (Martin Landau), who are planning to murder Vandamm's mistress by pushing her out of his private airplane, appear even more menacing than they have up to this point.

Low-angle shot

Two faces, both shot at low angle, convey two different meanings. [1] A low-angle shot of Radio Raheem (Bill Nunn) from Spike Lee's *Do the Right Thing* (1989; cinematographer Ernest Dickerson) puts us in the position of Sal (Danny Aiello, *not pictured*), a pizzeria owner who is intimidated and angered by his boom-box-carrying customer. [2] In Stanley Kubrick's *The Shining* (1980; cinematographer John Alcott), a low-angle shot from an omniscient point of view reveals the depth of Wendy's (Shelley Duvall) panic and despair.

admits to Princess Jeanette (Jeanette MacDonald) that he is not an aristocrat, but rather an ordinary tailor. Although the princess loves him, she runs from the room in confusion, and the camera looks down on Maurice, who is now left to assess his reduced status with the symbolic measuring tape in his hands.

Sometimes, however, a high-angle shot can be used to play against its traditional implications. In Alfred

Hitchcock's *North by Northwest* (1959; cinematographer Robert Burks), one of the villains, Phillip Vandamm (James Mason), tells his collaborator, Leonard (Martin Landau), that he is taking his mistress, Eve Kendall (Eva Marie Saint), for a trip on his private plane. Vandamm knows that Kendall is part of an American spy ring that has discovered his selling of government secrets to the enemy, and he plans to kill her by pushing her out of the

Camera angles in _M_

This scene from Fritz Lang's _M_ (1931; cinematographer Fritz Arno Wagner), in which an innocent man becomes the object of a crowd's suspicions, uses eye-level, low-angle, and high-angle shots to provide a context for us to distinguish real threats from perceived ones. [1] A neutral (and accidental) meeting between a short man and a little girl occurs in a context of suspicion (the city of Berlin has suffered a number of child murders in a short span of time). [2] From the short man's perspective, an exaggerated low-angle shot, the question "Why were you bothering that kid?" is even more ominous than the tall man's tone of voice makes it. [3] A high-angle shot from the perspective of a tall man who has brusquely asked, "Is that your kid?" reinforces the short man's modest stature and relative powerlessness. [4] Here we return to an LS as the short man protests his innocence and a crowd—soon to be a mob—gathers round.

aircraft. As he speaks, the crane-mounted camera rises to a very high angle looking down at the two men, and Vandamm concludes, "This matter is best disposed of from a great height. Over water." The overall effect of this shot depends completely on this unconventional use of the high angle: it does not imply superiority, but rather emphasizes Vandamm's deadly plan. Its ironic,

humorous effect depends as well on James Mason's wry delivery of these lines.

Low Angle A **low-angle shot** (or _low shot_) is made with the camera below the action and typically places the observer in the position of feeling helpless in the presence of an obviously superior force, as when we look up at King Kong on the Empire State Building or up at the shark from the underwater camera's point of view in *Jaws*. In Spike Lee's *Do the Right Thing* (1989; cinematographer Ernest Dickerson), Radio Raheem (Bill Nunn), who both entertains and intimidates the neighborhood by playing loud music on his boom box, appears menacing when photographed from a low, oblique angle during a confrontation with Sal (Danny Aiello), the owner of the neighborhood pizzeria.

However, filmmakers often play against the expectation that a subject shot from a low angle is menacing or powerful. In Stanley Kubrick's *The Shining* (1980; cinematographer John Alcott), Wendy (Shelley Duvall) discovers a manuscript that suggests her husband, Jack (Jack Nicholson), is insane, and a low-angle shot emphasizes her anxiety, fear, and vulnerability. The shot also reminds us that the visual and narrative context of an angle affects our interpretation of it. The shot places Jack's typewriter in the foreground, thus making it appear very large, which implies its power over her and the threatening nature of what she is seeing (even before it is revealed to us). The low angle also denies us the ability to see what is going on behind her at a moment in which we fear (and expect) the newly mad Jack to creep up behind her—thus elevating the suspense and making a character seen in extreme low angle ap-

pear more vulnerable than any high-angle shot could have.

In most scenes, obviously, different angles are used together to convey more complex meanings. Neil Jordan's *The Crying Game* (1992; cinematographer Ian Wilson), for example, uses alternating camera angles to convey and then resolve tensions between two characters. The scene begins with a confrontation between Fergus (Stephen Rea), an IRA gunman, and Jody (Forest Whitaker), a British-born black soldier whom Fergus and his terrorist cohorts have taken hostage. Power, race, and politics separate them, as confirmed by an alternating use of high- and low-angle shots from the perspectives of both characters during their dialogue. They start to relax when Jody shows Fergus a picture of his "wife," and by the time Jody talks about his experiences as a cricket player, they are speaking as men who have much in common—a transition that is signaled by a series of shots taken at eye level. These final shots help demonstrate that the men have more in common than their differences had at first suggested.

Dutch Angle In a **Dutch-angle shot** (also called a *Dutch-tilt shot* or *oblique-angle shot*), the camera is tilted from its normal horizontal and vertical position so that it is no longer straight, giving the viewer the impres-

1

2

Dutch-angle shot

In *Bride of Frankenstein* (1935; cinematographer John J. Mescall), director James Whale uses Dutch-angle shots to enhance the campy weirdness of the lab work in this film [1]. This scene culminates in one of the most famous Dutch-angle shots of all time—that of the Bride (Elsa Lanchester) first seeing the Monster [2].

sion that the world in the frame is out of balance.[11] Two classic films that use a vertiginously tilted camera are John Ford's *The Informer* (1935; cinematographer Joseph H. August) and Carol Reed's *The Third Man* (1949; cinematographer Robert Krasker). For the sequence in *Bride of Frankenstein* (1935; cinematographer John J. Mescall) in which Dr. Frankenstein (Colin Clive) and Dr. Pretorius (Ernest Thesiger) create a bride (Elsa Lanchester) for the Monster (Boris Karloff), director James Whale creates a highly stylized mise-en-scène—a tower laboratory filled with grotesque, futuristic machinery—that he shoots with a number of Dutch angles. The Dutch angles accentuate the doctors' unnatural actions, which are both funny and frightening.

Aerial View An **aerial-view shot** (or *bird's-eye-view shot*), an extreme type of point-of-view shot, is taken from an aircraft or very high crane and implies the observer's omniscience. A classic example of the aerial view comes, naturally enough, from Alfred Hitchcock's *The Birds* (1963; cinematographer Robert Burks). After showing us standard high-angle shots of a massive explosion at a gas station, the director cuts to a high aerial shot (literally a bird's-eye view) in which the circling birds seem almost gentle in contrast to the tragedy they have just caused below. Hitchcock said he used this aerial shot to show, all at once, the gulls massing for another attack on the town, the topography of the region, and the gas station on fire. Furthermore, he did not want to "waste a lot of footage on showing the elaborate operation of the firemen extinguishing the fire. You can do a lot of things very quickly by getting away from something."[12]

Scale

Scale is the size and placement of a particular object or a part of a scene in relation to the rest—a relationship determined by the type of shot used and the position of the camera. Scale may change from shot to shot. From what you learned in the preceding sections, it should be clear that the type of shot affects the scale of the shot *and* thus the effect and meaning of a scene. In *Jurassic*

Scale

In Steven Spielberg's *Jurassic Park* (1993; cinematographer Dean Cundey), [1] the reaction of Dr. Sattler (Laura Dern, *left*) and Dr. Grant (Sam Neill, *right*) to their first dinosaur sighting prepares us for an impressive image on-screen, and we are not disappointed. In placing the reaction before the action itself, Spielberg heightens the suspense of the scene. [2] The scale of the apatosaurus is exaggerated by the framing of this shot, too, which implies that the beast is so gargantuan that it can't fit into the frame.

Park (1993; cinematographer Dean Cundey), as in most of his movies, Steven Spielberg exploits scale to create awe and delight. The director knows that we really want to see dinosaurs—the stars of the film, after all—and slowly builds our anticipation by delaying this sight. When he introduces the first dinosaur, he uses the manipulation of scale and special-effects cinematography to maximize the astonishment that characters and viewers alike feel.

11. The adjective *Dutch* (as in the phrases *Dutch uncle*, *Dutch treat*, and *Dutch auction*) indicates something out of the ordinary or, in this case, out of line. This meaning of *Dutch* seems to originate with the English antipathy for all things Dutch at the height of Anglo-Dutch competition during the seventeenth century. I am grateful to Russell Merritt for clarifying this for me.

12. Alfred Hitchcock, qtd. in François Truffaut, *Hitchcock*, rev. ed. (New York: Simon & Schuster, 1985), pp. 292–294.

At Jurassic Park, jeeps carrying the group arrive on a grassy plain, clearly establishing the human scale of the scene. But Drs. Grant (Sam Neill) and Sattler (Laura Dern), preoccupied with scientific talk, take a moment to realize that Hammond (Richard Attenborough) has just introduced them to a live dinosaur, as benign as it is huge, which looks down upon them. ELSs make the dinosaur seem even taller. When the dazed Grant asks, "How did you do this?" Hammond replies, "I'll show you." It's impossible to forget what Spielberg then shows us: not just the first dinosaur but also a spectacular vista in which numerous such creatures move slowly across the screen. Creating a sense of wonder is one of Spielberg's stylistic trademarks, and his use of scale here does just that as it also helps create meaning. Because this is a science-fiction film, we are prepared for surprises when we are introduced to a world that is partly recognizable and partly fantastic. Once the dinosaurs make their actual appearance, we know that humans, however powerful in their financial and scientific pursuits, are now small in comparison and therefore highly vulnerable.

Of course, the scale of small objects can be exaggerated for meaningful effect too, as in the example from Alfred Hitchcock's *Notorious* (1946) mentioned earlier (see p. 240). When a tiny cup (or any other small object) looms larger than anything else in the frame, we can be sure that it is important to the film's meaning.

Camera Movement

Any movement of the camera within a shot automatically changes the image we see because the elements of framing that we have discussed thus far—camera angle, level, height, types of shots, and scale—are all modified when the camera moves within that shot. The moving camera, which can photograph both static and moving subjects, opens up cinematic space, and thus filmmakers use it to achieve many effects. It can search and increase the space, introduce us to more details than would be possible with a static image, choose which of these details we should look at or ignore, follow movement through a room or across a landscape, and establish complex relationships between figures in the frame—especially in shots that are longer than average. It allows the viewer to accompany or follow the movements of a character, object, or vehicle as well as to see the action from a character's point of view. The moving camera leads the viewer's eye or focuses the viewer's attention and, by moving

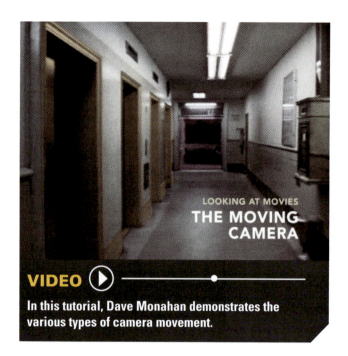

LOOKING AT MOVIES
THE MOVING CAMERA

VIDEO ▶

In this tutorial, Dave Monahan demonstrates the various types of camera movement.

into the scene, helps create the illusion of depth in the flat screen image. Furthermore, it helps convey relationships: spatial, causal, and psychological. When used in this way, the moving camera adds immeasurably to the director's development of the narrative and our understanding of it.

Within the first decade of movie history, D. W. Griffith began to exploit the power of simple camera movement to create associations within the frame and, in some cases, to establish a cause-and-effect relationship. In *The Birth of a Nation* (1915; cinematographer G. W. Bitzer), within one shot he establishes a view of a Civil War battle, turns the camera toward a woman and small children on a wagon, and then turns back to the battle. From that instinctive, fluid camera movement we understand the relationship between the horror of the battle and the misery that it has created for innocent civilians. Of course, Griffith could have cut between shots of the battle and the bystanders, but breaking up the space and time with editing would not achieve the same subtle effect as a single shot does.

In the 1920s, German filmmakers took this very simple type of camera movement to the next level, perfecting fluid camera movement within and between shots. In fact, F. W. Murnau, who is associated with some of the greatest early work with the moving camera in such films as *The Last Laugh* (1924; cinematographer Karl

Freund) and *Sunrise: A Song of Two Humans* (1927; cinematographers Charles Rosher and Karl Struss), referred to it as the *unchained camera*, thereby suggesting that it has a life of its own, with no limits to its freedom of movement. Since the 1920s, the moving camera has become one of the dominant stylistic trademarks of a diverse group of directors, including Orson Welles, Max Ophüls, Jean Renoir, Martin Scorsese, Otto Preminger, Lars von Trier, Terrence Malick, and Pedro Almodóvar.

The smoothly moving camera helped change the way movies were made as well as how we see and interpret them. But before the camera was capable of smooth movement, directors and their camera operators had to find ways to create steady moving shots that would imitate the way the human eye/brain sees. When we look around a room or landscape or see movement through space, our eyes dart from subject to subject, from plane to plane, and so we "see" more like a series of rapidly edited movie shots than a smooth flow of information. Yet our eyes and brain work together to smooth out the bumps. Camera motion, however, must itself be smooth in order for its audience to make sense of (or even tolerate) the shots resulting from that motion. The moving camera can also create suspense and even fear, as in Roman Polanski's *Rosemary's Baby* (1968; cinematographer William Fraker), where the camera moves through a luxurious Manhattan apartment, peering around corners or into rooms just enough to keep you on the edge of your seat without letting you see what you know (or think you know) is there.

There are exceptions, of course: During the 1960s, nonfiction filmmakers began what was soon to become widespread use of the handheld camera. This technique both ushered in entirely new ways of filmmaking, such as *cinéma vérité* and direct cinema, and greatly influenced narrative film style. For the most part, however, cinematographers strive to ensure that the camera does not shake or jump while moving through a shot. To make steady moving shots, the camera is usually mounted on a tripod, where it can move on a horizontal or vertical axis, or on a dolly, crane, car, helicopter, or other moving vehicle that permits it to capture its images smoothly.

The basic types of shots involving camera movement are the pan, tilt, tracking, dolly, and crane shots as well as those made with the Steadicam, the handheld camera, or the zoom lens. Each shot involves a particular kind of movement, depends on a particular kind of equipment, and has its own expressive potential.

Pan Shot A **pan shot** is the horizontal movement of a camera mounted on the gyroscopic head of a stationary tripod. This head ensures smooth panning and tilting and keeps the frame level. The pan shot offers us a larger, more panoramic view than a shot taken from a fixed camera; guides our attention to characters or actions that are important; makes us aware of relationships between subjects that are too far apart to be shown together in the frame; allows us to follow people or objects; and attempts to replicate what we see when we turn our heads to survey a scene or follow a character. Pan shots are particularly effective in settings of great scope, such as the many circus scenes in Max Ophüls's *Lola Montès* (1955; cinematographer Christian Matras) or the ballroom sequence in Orson Welles's *The Magnificent Ambersons* (1942; cinematographer Stanley Cortez), where he used several pan shots that moved almost 360 degrees.

Tilt Shot A **tilt shot** is the vertical movement of a camera mounted on the gyroscopic head of a stationary tripod. Like the pan shot, it is a simple movement with dynamic possibilities for creating meaning. Orson Welles makes excellent use of this shot in *Citizen Kane* (1941; cinematographer Gregg Toland). When Susan Kane (Dorothy Comingore) finally summons the psychological and emotional strength to leave her tyrannical husband, he reacts by destroying her bedroom. At the peak of his violent rage, he seizes the glass globe with an interior snow scene; the camera tilts upward from the ball to Kane's (Welles) face; he whispers "Rosebud" and leaves the room. The tilt links the roundness and mystery of the glass ball with Kane's round, bald head; furthermore, it reminds us that the first place we saw the glass ball was on Susan's dressing table in her rooming-house bedroom, thus further linking the meaning of *Rosebud* with her.

Dolly Shot A **dolly shot** (also known as a tracking shot or traveling shot) is one taken by a camera fixed to a wheeled support, generally known as a **dolly**. The dolly permits the cinematographer to make noiseless moving shots. When a dolly runs on tracks, the resulting shot is called a tracking shot. The dolly shot is one of the most effective (and consequently most common) uses of the moving camera. When the camera is used to **dolly in** on (move toward) a subject, the subject grows in the frame, gaining significance not only from being bigger in the

[1]

A dolly in action
Camera operators race alongside a speeding chariot on a dolly during the filming of Ridley Scott's *Gladiator* (2000; cinematographer John Mathieson).

[2]

Tilt shot
In Orson Welles's *Citizen Kane* (1941; cinematographer Gregg Toland), the camera presents the first half of this shot [1], then tilts upward to present the second half [2]. Of course, Welles could have shown us both halves, even Kane's entire body, within one static frame. The camera movement directs our eyes, however, and makes the symbolism unmistakable.

frame but also from those moments when we actually see it growing bigger.

This gradual intensification effect is commonly used at moments of a character's realization and/or decision, or as a point-of-view shot of what the character is having a realization about. The scene in Hitchcock's *Notorious* (1946), in which Alicia Huberman (Ingrid Bergman) realizes that she is being poisoned via the coffee (see p. 240), uses both kinds of dolly-in movements as well as other camera moves that explicitly illustrate cause

and effect (the camera moves from the coffee to Bergman at the moment she complains about not feeling well, for example).

The **dolly-out** movement (moving away from the subject) is often used for slow disclosure, which occurs when an edited succession of images leads from A to B to C as they gradually reveal the elements of a scene. Each image expands on the one before, thereby changing its significance with new information. A good example occurs in Stanley Kubrick's *Dr. Strangelove or: How I Learned to Stop Worrying and Love the Bomb* (1964; cinematographer Gilbert Taylor) when, in a succession of images, the serious, patriotic bomber pilot is revealed to be concentrating not on his instruments, but on an issue of *Playboy* magazine.

A **tracking shot** is a type of dolly shot that moves smoothly with the action (alongside, above, beneath, behind, or ahead of it) when the camera is mounted on a wheeled vehicle that runs on a set of tracks. Some of the most beautiful effects in the movies are created by tracking shots, especially when the camera covers a great distance. Director King Vidor used an effective lateral tracking shot in his World War I film *The Big Parade* (1925; cinematographers John Arnold and Charles Van Enger) to follow the progress of American troops entering enemy-held woods. This shot, which has a documentary quality to it because it puts us in motion beside the soldiers as they march into combat, has been repeated many times in subsequent war films.

Zoom The zoom is a lens with a variable focal length, which permits the camera operator during shooting to shift from the wide-angle lens (short focus) to the telephoto lens (long focus) or vice versa without changing the focus or aperture settings. It is not a camera movement per se, because only the optics inside the lens are moving in relation to each other and thus shifting the focal length. Still, the zoom can provide the illusion of the camera moving toward or away from the subject. One result of this shift is that the image is magnified (when shifting from short to long focal length) or demagnified by shifting in the opposite direction.

That magnification is the essential difference between **zoom-in** and dolly-in movements on a subject. When dollying, a camera actually moves through space; in the process, spatial relationships between the camera and the objects in its frame shift, causing relative changes in position between on-screen figures or objects. By contrast, because a zoom lens does not move through space, its depiction of spatial relationships between the camera and its subjects does not change. All a zoom shot does is magnify the image.

The result of zoom shots, as we've noted before, can be "movement" that appears artificial and self-conscious. Of course, there are dramatic, cinematic, and stylistic reasons for using this effect, but for the most part, the artificiality of the zoom (and the fact that viewers naturally associate the zoom effect with its overuse in amateur home videos) makes it a technique that is rarely used well in professional filmmaking. When the zoom shot *is* used expressively, however, it can be breathtaking. In *Goodfellas* (1990; cinematographer Michael Ballhaus), during the scene in which Henry Hill (Ray Liotta) meets Jimmy Conway (Robert De Niro) in a diner, director Martin Scorsese achieves a memorable effect with the moving camera and the zoom lens. He tracks *in* (while moving the zoom lens *out*) and tracks *out* (while moving the zoom lens *in*) to reflect Henry's paranoid, paralyzed state of mind. As the camera and lens move against one another, the image traps Hill inside the hermetic world of the mob and us inside a world of spatial disorientation in an ordinary diner. You have to see this brilliant zoom shot to understand and appreciate it.

Crane Shot A **crane shot** is made from a camera mounted on an elevating arm that is, in turn, mounted on a vehicle capable of moving under its own power. A

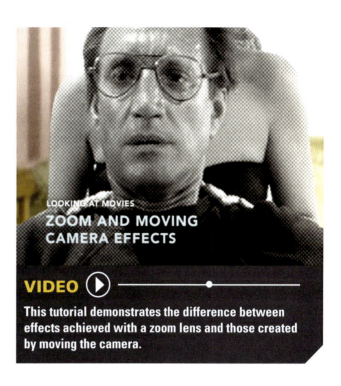

LOOKING AT MOVIES
ZOOM AND MOVING CAMERA EFFECTS

VIDEO ▶ ────────●──────────

This tutorial demonstrates the difference between effects achieved with a zoom lens and those created by moving the camera.

crane may also be mounted on a vehicle that can be pushed along tracks to smooth its movement. The arm can be raised or lowered to the degree that the particular crane permits. A crane produces shots that cannot be made with the camera mounted on a dolly or an ordinary track, because those two devices are capable of only horizontal or vertical movement. The crane moves freely both horizontally and vertically and also lifts the camera high off the ground, giving filmmakers extraordinary flexibility in choosing shots. As equipment for moving the camera has become more versatile, crane shots have become more commonplace.

Looking at Camera Movement: *Touch of Evil* Perhaps the most impressive crane shot in movie history occurs at the opening of Orson Welles's *Touch of Evil* (1958; cinematographer Russell Metty). The scene takes place at night in Los Robles, a seedy town on the U.S.–Mexico border. After the Universal International logo dissolves from the screen, we see a close-up of a man's hand swinging toward the camera and setting a timer that will make the bomb he holds explode in about three minutes. The camera pans left to reveal two figures approaching the camera from the end of a long interior corridor; the bomber, Manelo Sanchez (Victor Millan), runs left into the frame, realizes that these people are his targets, and runs out of the frame to the right as the

The crane shot in *Touch of Evil*

These stills from the opening crane shot in Orson Welles's *Touch of Evil* (1958; cinematographer Russell Metty) show the progress of the camera over a wide-ranging space through a continuous long shot that ends only when the car blows up [1–7]. A reaction shot of Mike and Susan Vargas (Charlton Heston and Janet Leigh) follows [8], and as the Vargases run toward the site of the explosion, the mystery at the heart of the movie begins to unfold.

camera pans right to follow him. He places the bomb in the trunk of a luxurious convertible, the top of which is down, and disappears screen right just as the couple enters the frame at top left; the camera tracks backward and reframes to an LS.

As the couple gets into the car, the camera (mounted on a crane that is attached to a truck) swings to an extreme high angle. The car pulls forward alongside a building and turns left at the front of the building as the camera reaches the roof level at its back. We momentarily lose sight of the car, but the camera, which has oriented us to where the car is, merely pans left and brings it back into the frame as it moves left across an alley into a main street. The camera cranes down to an angle slightly higher than the car, which has turned left and now heads toward the camera on a vertical axis moving from background to foreground. When the car pauses at the direction of a policeman, who permits other traffic to cross in the foreground on a horizontal axis, the camera begins tracking backward to keep the car in the frame. The camera continues to track backward, reframes to an XLS, and pans slightly to the left. The car stops at an intersection.

A man and a woman—"Mike" Vargas (Charlton Heston), a Mexican narcotics agent, and his newly wed wife Susan (Janet Leigh)—enter the intersection at screen right and continue across the street as the camera lowers to an eye-level LS. The car turns left onto the street where the Vargases are walking, and they scurry to get out of its way as the car moves out of the frame. They continue walking with the camera tracking slightly ahead of them; it keeps them in the frame as they pass the car, which is now delayed by a herd of goats that has stopped in another intersection. The camera continues to track backward, keeping the couple and the car in the frame; this becomes a deep-space composition with the car in the background, crossway traffic in the middle ground, and the Vargas couple in the foreground. The Vargases reach the kiosk marking the entrance to the border crossing and pass it on the right, still walking toward the camera, which now rises, reframing into a high-angle LS that reveals the car driving past the left side of the kiosk. The frame now unites the two couples (one in the car, the other walking) as they move forward at the same time to what we, knowing that the bomb is in the car, anticipate will be a climactic moment.

The camera stops and reframes to an MS with the Vargases standing on the right and the car stopped on the left. While a border agent begins to question the newlyweds, soon recognizing Vargas, a second agent checks the car's rear license plate. The agents and Vargas discuss smashing drug rings, but Vargas explains that he and his wife are crossing to the American side so that his wife can have an ice cream soda. Meanwhile, the driver of the targeted car, Mr. Linnekar (actor not credited), asks if he can get through the crossing. The Vargases walk out of the frame, continuing the discussion about drugs, then apparently walk around the front of the car and reenter the frame at the left side; the camera pans slightly left and reframes the Vargases, border agents, and Linnekar and Zita (Joi Lansing), his companion.

After a few moments of conversation, the Vargases walk away toward the back and then left of the frame; the car moves slowly forward, and Zita complains to one of the guards—in a moment of delicious black humor—that she hears a "ticking noise." As the car leaves the frame, the camera pans left to another deep-focus composition with the Vargases in the background, two military policemen walking from the background toward the camera, and pedestrians passing across the middle ground. The camera tracks forward and reframes to an MS; the Vargases embrace as the bomb explodes. Startled, they look up and see the car in flames.

The final two shots in this extraordinary sequence are, first, a rapid zoom-in on the explosion; and second, a low-angle, handheld shot of Vargas running toward the scene. These shots, more self-conscious and less polished than the preceding, fluid crane shots, cinematically and dramatically shift the tone from one of controlled suspense to out-of-control chaos that changes the normal world and sets the scene for the story's development. This is also an excellent example of how movies exploit the establishment and breaking of narrative forms.

With extraordinary virtuosity, Welles has combined nearly all types of shots, angles, framings, and camera movements. He accomplishes the changes in camera height, level, angle, and framing by mounting the camera on a crane that can be raised and lowered smoothly from ground level to an extreme high angle, reframed easily, and moved effortlessly above and around the setting (parking lot, market arcade, street, intersections, and border inspection area). Here the moving camera is both unchained and fearless, a thoroughly omniscient observer as well as a voyeur, particularly in its opening observations of the bomber. But what is the function of this cinematographic tour de force? Is it just one of Welles's razzle-dazzle attempts to grab the audience's attention, or does it create meaning?

The answer, of course, is that it serves both purposes. Its virtuosity astonishes, but has a point. In addition to witnessing the inciting device for the plot, we learn that Los Robles is a labyrinth of activity, lights, shadows, and mysteries and that the destinies of Linnekar, Zita, Vargas, and Susan are in some way tangled. The odd and extreme camera angles (at the beginning and end of the scene) reinforce the air of mystery and disorient us within the cinematic space. All the while, the bold black-and-white contrasts pull us into the deep shadows of vice, corruption, and brutal crime.

Handheld Camera The last two shots in the scene from *Touch of Evil* (1958) we described in the previous section were made with a handheld camera, a small, portable, lightweight instrument that the camera operator holds during shooting. At one time, handheld cameras were limited to 8mm or 16mm film stock, but now they can handle a variety of film stocks. In contrast to the smooth moving camera shots that we have been discussing, the inherent shakiness of the handheld camera can be exploited when a loss of control, whether in the situation or in the character's state of mind, is something the filmmaker wants to convey to the viewer. *Touch of Evil* does just that, with an elaborately choreographed and fluid moving camera sequence suddenly interrupted by an explosion that is photographed with a shaky handheld. We feel that the world has changed because the way we see the world has shifted so dramatically.

Handheld camera

The handheld camera is used to great advantage in keeping the viewer disoriented during Paul Greengrass's high-action thriller *The Bourne Supremacy* (2004; cinematographer Oliver Wood), as in this shot of Jason Bourne (Matt Damon) trying to elude the pursuing police.

However, the uses of the handheld camera go beyond this example. After nearly fifty years of viewing news coverage of unfolding events, nonfiction films in the direct cinema style, and reality television shows, audiences have been conditioned to associate the look of handheld camera shots with documentary realism—they assume that something is really happening and the photographer (and therefore the viewer) is there. Narrative feature films can also take advantage of that intuitive association to heighten or alter our experience of a particular event.

Steadicam From the beginning of the movies, movie cameras (handheld as well as those mounted on tripods, dollies, or other moving devices) have allowed filmmakers to approach their subjects, for example, when moving in for close-ups. But the handheld camera frequently produces a jumpy image, characteristic of avant-garde filmmaking and usually not acceptable in the mainstream. So mainstream filmmakers embraced the **Steadicam**, a device attached to the operator's body that steadies the camera, avoids the jumpiness associated with the handheld camera, and is now widely used for smooth, fast, and intimate camera movement. The Steadicam system is perfectly balanced and automatically compensates for any movements made by the camera operator, such as running down the stairs, climbing a hill, or maneuvering in tight places where dollies or tracks cannot fit.

The Steadicam is used so frequently that it no longer calls attention to itself. But many great, exhilarating uses of this device are worth remembering, including the work of Garrett Brown, the Steadicam operator on Stanley Kubrick's *The Shining* (1980; cinematographer John Alcott). Perhaps the most memorable and influential shot is the long sequence that follows Danny Torrance's (Danny Lloyd) determined tricycle ride through the halls of the Overlook Hotel.

Another memorable example is in *Boyhood* (2014, cinematographers Lee Daniel and Shane F. Kelly), where director Richard Linklater uses a Steadicam technique to shoot an intense head-to-head conversation between father (Ethan Hawke) and son (Ellar Coltrane) as they walk along a balcony. Linklater has great compassion for his characters and is a master of rehearsing actors, encouraging improvisation, and getting memorable shots of their intimacy. A conventional approach to filming the shot described here might have been to shoot from

different angles with the camera on a track or dolly and then cut on those angles to reshape their conversation into a whole. Linklater decided to film it as a long Steadicam two-shot with the actors talking and walking together, following the Steadicam. This technique does not call attention to itself, but rather preserves the emotional truth of the conversation.

Framing and Point of View

As the preceding discussion has illustrated, the framing of a shot—including the type of shot and its depth, camera angle and height, scale, and camera movement—has several major functions. In the most basic sense, framing controls what we see (explicitly, what is on the screen; implicitly, what we know has been left out) and how we see it (up close, far away, from above or below, and so on). Framing also calls attention to the technique of cinematography, allowing us to delight in the variety of possibilities that the director and cinematographer have at their disposal. It also implies point of view (POV), which can mean the POV of the screenwriter, director, one or more characters, or the actual POV of the camera itself. Of course, all of these POVs can be used in any one movie.

The smoothest-moving camera
The Steadicam, invented in the early 1970s, is not a camera but rather a steadying mechanism on which any motion-picture camera can be mounted. In this image of the Steadicam Ultra2 model,[13] the operator wears a harness attached to an arm that is connected to a vertical armature, here with the camera at the top and a counterbalance weight at the bottom. Unlike the handheld camera, this mechanism isolates the operator's movements from the camera, producing a very smooth shot even when the operator is walking or running quickly over an uneven surface.

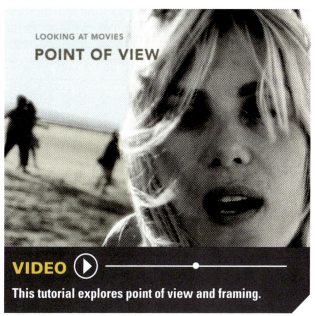

LOOKING AT MOVIES
POINT OF VIEW

VIDEO ▶
This tutorial explores point of view and framing.

13. Steadicam and Ultra2 are trademarks of the Tiffen Company.

The camera's POV, the eyes through which we view the action, depends on the physical position of the camera when shooting. In most movies, the camera is omniscient: virtually able to go anywhere and see anything, either at average human eye level or above it. Eye-level, high, and low shooting angles, however, raise questions of objectivity and subjectivity. Sometimes, as we have seen, directors use shooting angles to play against our expectations, to control or mislead us. In looking at movies, we experience frequent shifts in the camera's POV. The dominant neutral POV gives us the facts and background that are the context in which the characters live. The **omniscient POV** shows what the omniscient camera sees, typically from a high angle; a **single character's POV**, in which the shot is made with the camera close to the line of sight of a character (or animal or surveillance camera), shows what that person would be seeing of the action; and the **group POV** shows us what a group of characters would see at their level.

Julian Schnabel's *The Diving Bell and the Butterfly* (2007; cinematographer Janusz Kaminski) is a highly concentrated example of a movie shot from the mental and visual POV of a single character. Jean-Dominique Bauby (Mathieu Amalric), the editor of a French magazine, suffered a massive stroke that has left him almost totally paralyzed (he can use one of his eyes). Still, he is able to maintain his sense of humor (often black), remember and think, hear from one ear, move his face and head a little, and most important to his therapy, use his left eyelid to blink for communication (one blink for yes; two for no). He also narrates the film through his interior monologue. (That monologue actually comes from the book that Bauby "wrote" by blinking his eyes for each letter to a collaborator who put the words on paper.) What's relevant here in terms of cinematography is that much of the film is shot from the position and angle of his left eye—what he calls "the only window to my cell." (There are also extreme close-up shots of his eye from a distance of a few inches away.) The images that Bauby and the viewer see simultaneously and identically are blurred, flickering, and bleached out. Bauby is in an extreme position, and the director and cinematographer have chosen a frame that is equally extreme. This movie's visual style meets the needs of this story, which is not a record of impending death but rather the saga of Bauby's highly determined process of rebirth. The movie's consistent use of this POV might seem gimmicky with a different narrative, but here it rightly puts the emphasis on that character's eye, the "I" of his narration, and, of course, the camera's eye.

Consider a very fast and active scene in Alfred Hitchcock's *The Birds* (1963; cinematographer Robert Burks), in which a classic use of camera angle and point of view establishes and retains the viewer's orientation as the townspeople of Bodega Bay become increasingly agitated because of random attacks by birds. During one such attack, frightened people watch from the window of a diner as a bird strikes a gas-station attendant, causing a gasoline leak that results in a tragic explosion. Chief among these spectators are Melanie Daniels (Tippi Hedren) and Mitch Brenner (Rod Taylor).

The basic pattern of camera angles alternates between shots from a high angle in the restaurant, looking out and down, to those from eye level, looking from the exterior through the window of the restaurant. These alternating points of view give the sequence its power. How does Hitchcock's use of alternating points of view create meaning in the sequence? It shows us (not for the first time) that the birds really do maliciously attack unsuspecting people. It also demonstrates that, at least in this cinematic world, people close to an impending tragedy—people like Mitch, Melanie, and the man with the cigar—can do virtually nothing to stop it.

Two other interesting movies that employ a single character's POV are Robert Montgomery's *Lady in the Lake* (1947; cinematographer Paul C. Vogel), perhaps the first movie in which the camera gives the illusion of looking through a character's eyes, and Gaspar Noé's *Enter*

Types of shots in *The Birds*

In this action-packed scene from *The Birds* (1963; cinematographer Robert Burks), Alfred Hitchcock orients us by manipulating types of shots, camera angles, and points of view. It includes [1] an eye-level medium close-up of Melanie (Tippi Hedren) and two men, who [2] see a gas-station attendant hit by a bird; [3] an eye-level medium shot of Melanie and another woman, who, through high-angle shots such as this close-up [4], watch gasoline run through a nearby parking lot; [5] a slightly low-angle close-up of a group warning a man in the parking lot, seen in this high-angle long shot [6], not to light his cigar, though he doesn't hear the warning; [7] the resulting explosion and fire, seen in a long shot from high angle; and [8] Melanie watching the fire spread to the gas station [9], which the birds observe from on high [10].

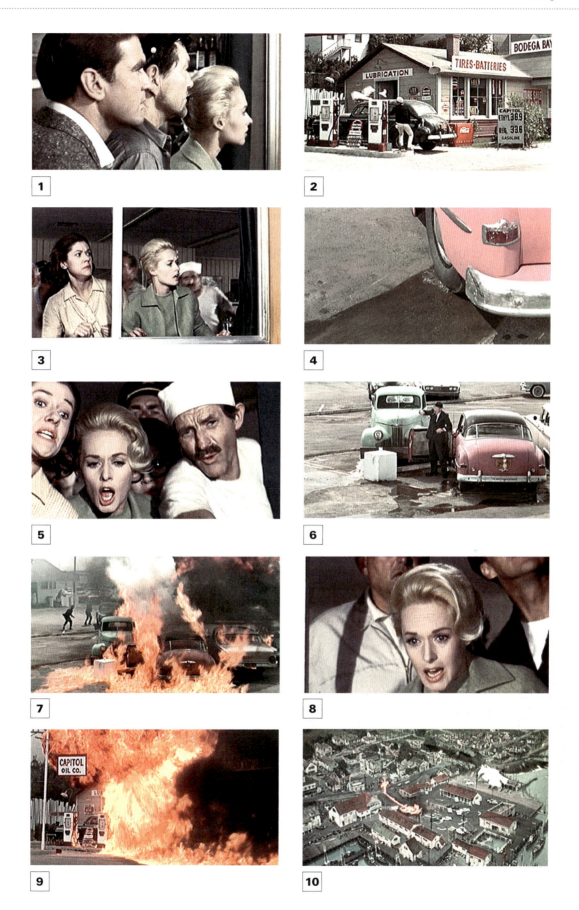

the Void (2010; cinematographer Benoît Debie), which includes dazzling camera work as the story is shot from a first-person viewpoint with psychedelic imagery reflecting the drug culture depicted.

Speed and Length of the Shot

Thus far we have emphasized the spatial aspects of how a shot is composed, lit, and photographed. But the image we see on the screen has both spatial and temporal dimensions. Its length can be as important as any other characteristic. Although a shot is one uninterrupted run of the camera, no convention governs what that length should be. Before the arrival of sound, the average shot lasted about five seconds; after sound arrived, that average doubled to approximately ten seconds. Nonetheless, a shot can (and should) be as long as necessary to do its part in telling the story.

By controlling the length of shots, filmmakers enable each shot to do its work—establish a setting, character, or cause of a following event. But they also control the relationship of each shot to the others and thus to the rhythm of the film. The length of any shot is influenced by three factors: the screenplay (the amount of action and dialogue written for each shot), the cinematography (the duration of what is actually shot), and the editing (what remains of the length of the actual shot after the film has been cut and assembled).

Here we will concentrate on the second of these factors—the relationship between cinematography and time. What kind of time does the camera record? As you know from Chapter 4, when seeing a movie, viewers are aware of basically two kinds of time: real time (time as we ordinarily perceive it in life outside the movie theater) and cinematic time (time as it is conveyed to us through the movie). With a simple adjustment of the camera's motor, cinema can manipulate time with the same freedom and flexibility that it manipulates space and light.

Slow motion decelerates action by photographing it at a rate greater than the normal 24 frames per second (fps), so it takes place in cinematic time less rapidly than the real action that took place before the camera. One effect of slow motion is to emphasize the power of memory, as in Sidney Lumet's *The Pawnbroker* (1964; cinematographer Boris Kaufman), in which Sol Nazerman (Rod Steiger), a pawnbroker living in the Bronx,

remembers pleasant memories in Germany before the Nazis and the Holocaust. Martin Scorsese frequently uses slow motion to suggest a character's heightened awareness of someone or something. In *Taxi Driver* (1976), for example, Travis Bickle (Robert De Niro) sees in slow motion what he considers to be the repulsive sidewalks of New York; and in *Raging Bull* (1980), Jake La Motta (De Niro) fondly remembers his wife, Vickie (Cathy Moriarty), in slow motion. Both films were shot by cinematographer Michael Chapman. Finally, slow motion can be used to reverse our expectations, as in Andy and Larry Wachowski's *The Matrix* (1999; cinematographer Bill Pope), where Neo (Keanu Reeves) dodges the bullets shot by Agent Smith (Hugo Weaving) while shooting back with a spray of slow-motion bullets as he does cartwheels on the walls. That scene was made possible, of course, with advanced special-effects techniques.

By contrast, **fast motion** accelerates action by photographing it at less than the normal filming rate and then projecting it at normal speed so that it takes place more rapidly on-screen. Thus fast motion often depicts the rapid passing of time, as F. W. Murnau uses it in *Nosferatu* (1922; cinematographers Fritz Arno Wagner and Günther Krampf), an early screen version of the Dracula story. The coach that Count Orlok (Max Schreck) sends to fetch his agent, Hutter (Gustav von Wangenheim), travels in fast motion, and although this effect may seem silly today, its original intent was to place us in an unpredictable landscape. In *Rumble Fish* (1983; cinematographer Stephen H. Burum), director Francis Ford Coppola employs fast-motion, high-contrast, black-and-white images of clouds moving across the sky to indicate both the passing of time and the unsettled lives of the teenagers the story portrays. In *Requiem for a Dream* (2000; cinematographer Matthew Libatique), director Darren Aronofsky uses fast motion to simulate the experience of being high on marijuana—an effect also used by Gus Van Sant in *Drugstore Cowboy* (1989; cinematographer Robert D. Yeoman).

Perhaps no modern director has used and abused slow and fast motion, as well as virtually every other manipulation of cinematic space and time, more than Godfrey Reggio in his *Qatsi* trilogy: *Koyaanisqatsi* (1982), *Powaqqatsi* (1988), and *Nagoyqatsi* (2002), all with scores by minimalist composer Philip Glass. Although Reggio's sweeping vision of the cultural and environmental decay of the modern world is lavishly depicted in poetic, even apocalyptic images, he often relies too heavily on manipulation to make his point.

1

2

Looking for meaning in what we see

Interpreting the face of Triska, a female gorilla, is what *Visitors* is all about. Or is it? We look at her [1], as do various people [2], and she looks back at us. What are we all *really* looking at? How does she regard what she is looking at? Why do we try to find meaning in what we see? Isn't *looking* enough? *Visitors* presents a provocative challenge to what we do when we are *looking at* movies.

Visitors (2013; cinematographers Trish Govoni, Graham Berry, and Tom Lowe) also uses slow-motion and time-lapse photography, but its stately pace and luscious black-and-white cinematography create a very different worldview than did its predecessors. This movie is composed mainly of single shots of faces. Here, Reggio uses only 74 shots (running time: 87 min.) to create what appears to be an intense meditation on the act of *seeing* and looking for meaning in what we see. The cast of characters consists of a gorilla and a large number of people—adults and children from all races and walks of life.

The movie opens and closes with shots of Triska, a female gorilla. She and the people appear on the screen in the same close-ups and framing: their faces are high-lighted against a black background. We see Triska only twice, and in most of the movie we see shots of people. They are a diverse group with little consistency in their facial expressions. We don't know if Triska is looking at us or at the people who stare intently at the camera; this uncertainty produces various possible meanings (see "Kuleshov effect" in Chapter 8, p. 324). The film's 74 shots are almost all shot with a stationary camera, but they are intercut in time-lapse moving shots. Viewers see an abandoned building, amusement park, and games arcade—with clouds speeding across the sky above them—as well as shots of statues of carnival clowns and puppets. Overall, there is little movement either of the camera or the characters, and the general effect is stillness. The introspective mood is enhanced by the signature repetition of Philip Glass's score. There is no other sound, although we see lips move and some people using sign language in

apparent attempts at communication, and some faces display expressive reactions.

This cross-section of humanity, and the intercut images of other subjects, make us wonder about the meaning. We learn from the ending credits that Triska is a resident of the Bronx Zoo. Are the people in the film visitors to the zoo? Is the movie commenting on evolution and the phase between primates and humans? We assume that Triska lives like most zoo animals in some kind of confinement, but we do not see it. Likewise, we don't know who the people are or where they came from. The title suggests aliens, but these people don't look like typical movie aliens. Because they are photographed several times in group shots, looking at what might be a stage or movie screen, we assume they are, unlike Triska, free to come and go. But we don't know that. When we are told at the end that she lives at the Bronx Zoo, why is that relevant? And what about the amusement park that

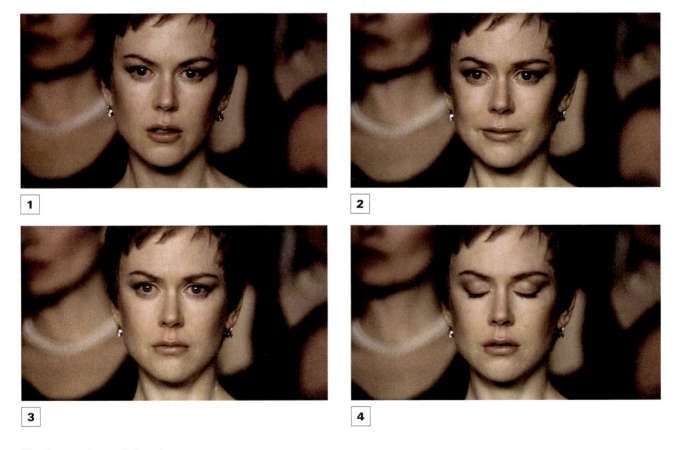

The long take and the close-up
Great cinematographers love great female beauty, as demonstrated by these four images from Jonathan Glazer's *Birth* (2004), in which cinematographer Harris Savides holds the camera steady on Nicole Kidman's face for two minutes. The slight changes in her expression and the position of her head, eyes, and lips as she listens to music that absorbs her attention reveal, however slightly, the depth of her thoughts.

has fallen into disuse? Or the huge building that might be a government office or hospital? The movie ends with a fade-out of Triska's face to white, leaving the intense black-and-white imagery as a memory and the screen blank. And still we are left with questions. What are we looking at? Are humans alone in the world in their search for meaning? *Visitors* goes right to the heart of our overall concern with *looking at movies.*

Whereas the average shot lasts ten seconds, the **long take** can run as long as there is sufficient media in the camera to record it. One of the most elegant techniques of cinematography, the long take has the double potential of preserving both real space and real time. Ordinarily, we refer to a sequence as a series of edited shots characterized by inherent unity of theme and purpose. The long take is sometimes referred to as a *sequence shot* because it enables filmmakers to present a unified pattern of events within a single period of time in one shot. However, except for such extraordinary examples as the opening of Orson Welles's *Touch of Evil* (1958; discussed earlier), the long take is rarely used for a sequence filmed in one shot. Instead, even masters of the evocative long take—directors such as F. W. Murnau, Max Ophüls, Orson Welles, William Wyler, Kenji Mizoguchi, and Stanley Kubrick—combine two or more long takes by linking them, often unobtrusively, into an apparently seamless whole.

Coupled with the moving camera, the long take also eliminates the need for separate setups for long, medium, and close-up shots. It permits the internal development of a story involving two or more lines of action without use of the editing technique called *crosscutting* that is normally employed to tell such a story. Furthermore, if a solid sense of cause and effect is essential to developing a sequence, the long take permits both the cause and the effect to be recorded in one take.

Conventional motion-picture technology limited the fluid long take that these directors were striving for, but digital technology has enabled a director to achieve it. Using a Steadicam fitted with a high-definition video camera, Russian director Aleksandr Sokurov made *Russian Ark* (2002; cinematographer Tilman Büttner), a 96-minute historical epic filmed in one continuous shot—the longest unbroken shot in film history.

Notably effective use of a long take combined with a close-up occurs in Jonathan Glazer's *Birth* (2004; cinematographer Harris Savides), a thriller that skirts the boundaries between the believable and the absurd. Anna (Nicole Kidman) plays a young widow who is torn between memories of her husband, Sean, and her obsession with a ten-year-old boy, also named Sean (Cameron Bright), who claims to be the reincarnation of her dead husband. At a concert she attends with her fiancé, Joseph (Danny Huston), Anna listens intently to a selection from an opera that is concerned partly with the incestuous relationship between two mythical characters. This theme obviously invades Anna's thoughts, as does her unnerving sexual attraction to young Sean. Cinematographer Savides devotes a full two minutes to a long take of Kidman's face, capturing the subtle shifts in her expression in a way that seems inspired by cinematographer Rudolph Maté's adoration of the face of Maria Falconetti in Carl Theodor Dreyer's *The Passion of Joan of Arc* (1928; see Chapter 7, p. 308). On one hand, Savides's haunting, long take is a declaration of love for an actor's face (one of the prime purposes of the close-up). But on the other hand, the length of the shot gives Kidman the time to convey the depth of Anna's thoughts without using dialogue or overt action. In turn, that camera is the single element that most radically differentiates the movie actor's performance.

Special Effects

Cinema itself is a special effect, an illusion that fools the human eye and brain into perceiving motion. **Special effects** (abbreviated **SPFX** or **FX**) is a term reserved for technology that creates images that would be too dangerous, too expensive, or in some cases simply impossible to achieve with the traditional cinematographic materials already discussed. As spectacular as SPFX technologies and their effects can be, however, the goal of special effects cinematography is generally to create verisimilitude—an illusion of reality or a believable alternative reality—within the imaginative world of even the most fanciful movie. Special effects expert Mat Beck says,

> The art of visual effects is the art of what you can get away with, which means you really have to study a lot about how .we perceive the world in order to find out how we can trick our perceptions to make something look real when it isn't.[14]

14. Mat Beck, qtd. in "Special Effects: *Titanic* and Beyond," *Nova,* produced for PBS by the Science Unit at WGBH Boston, November 3, 1998.

Glazer's austere sci-fi horror fantasy, *Under the Skin* (2013), is equally obsessed with the real and unreal, from its stunning pre-title sequence (in which a pinprick of light morphs into an astral disc and then an iris of an eyeball) to his direction of Scarlett Johansson as an alien predator who eventually becomes human, or seems to.

In-Camera, Mechanical, and Laboratory Effects

For audiences, a major attraction of movies has always been their ability to create illusion. Indeed, the first special effect appeared in Alfred Clark's *The Execution of Mary Stuart* in 1895 (cinematographer William Heise), the year the movies were born. To depict the queen's execution, Clark photographed the actor in position, stopped filming and replaced the actor with a dummy, then started the camera and beheaded the dummy. (Incidentally, this film involved another kind of illusion: a man, Robert Thomae, played Queen Mary.)

From that time on, special effects appeared regularly in the films of Georges Méliès, the great illusionist, who used multiple exposures and stop-motion animation. Edwin S. Porter's *The Great Train Robbery* (1903) featured matte and composite shots, and J. Searle Dawley's *Rescued from an Eagle's Nest* (1908; cinematographer Edwin S. Porter) included a mechanical eagle, created by Richard Murphy, that was the forerunner of "animatronic" creatures in contemporary films. By the mid-1920s, extraordinary effects were featured in such films as Fritz Lang's *Metropolis* (1927; cinematographers Karl Freund, Günther Rittau, and Walter Ruttmann), for which designer Otto Hunte created the city of the future in miniature on a tabletop; Cecil B. DeMille's first version of *The Ten Commandments* (1923; cinematographers Bert Glennon, J. Peverell Marley, Archie Stout, and Fred Westerberg), in which technicians could part the Red Sea because it was made of two miniature slabs of Jell-O[15]; and the first of four versions of *The Lost World* (1925; cinematographer Arthur Edeson), directed by Harry O. Hoyt. The special effects in *The Lost World* were the work of Willis H. O'Brien, who went on to create the special effects in Merian C. Cooper and Ernest B. Schoedsack's *King Kong* (1933; cinematographers Edward Linden, J. O.

Early special effects
For Fritz Lang's *Metropolis* (1927; cinematographers Karl Freund, Günther Rittau, and Walter Ruttmann), a pioneering science-fiction film, the city of the future was a model created by designer Otto Hunte. Special effects photography (coordinated by Eugen Schüfftan, who developed trick-shot techniques still in use today) turned this miniature into a massive place on-screen, filled with awe-inspiring objects and vistas.

Taylor, Vernon L. Walker, and Kenneth Peach), in which the giant ape terrorizing New York City from the top of the Empire State Building was, in fact, a puppet.

Until the advent of computer-generated imagery in the 1960s, such illusions were accomplished in essentially three ways: **in-camera effects** created in the production camera (the regular camera used for shooting the rest of the film) on the original negative, **mechanical effects** that create objects or events mechanically on the set and in front of the camera, and **laboratory effects** created on a fresh piece of film stock.

Although computer-generated graphics and animation have virtually eclipsed the way special effects are now made, as you study and analyze SPFX in movies from the past it is helpful to know how the principal types were made. Traditionally, the first category—in-camera effects—has included such simple illusory effects as fade, wipe, dissolve, and montage. (Although these are shots in themselves, together with editing they create transitional effects or manipulate time; for definitions and examples, see "Conventions of Continuity Editing" in Chapter 8.) Other in-camera effects include split screen, superimposition, models and miniatures,

---

15. DeMille's 1956 version of the parting of the Red Sea (cinematographically engineered by Loyal Griggs) cost $2 million. It was the most expensive special effect up to that time and involved matte shots, miniatures, 600 extras, and a 32-foot-high dam channeling tens of thousands of gallons of water.

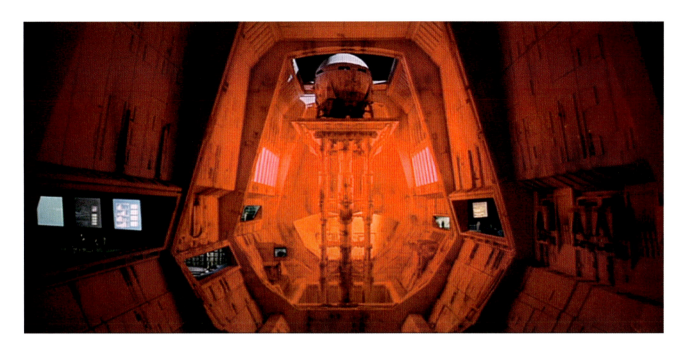

Modern special effects

The special effects in Stanley Kubrick's *2001: A Space Odyssey* (1968; special effects designer Kubrick; supervisors Wally Veevers, Douglas Trumbull, Con Pederson, and Tom Howard; cinematographer Geoffrey Unsworth) took up more than 60 percent of the movie's production budget and required nearly eighteen months to complete. These SPFX were state of the art at the time, and they add to the movie's cinematic beauty and philosophical depth. Early in the movie, Dr. Heywood R. Floyd (William Sylvester), an American scientist, is dispatched via shuttle to Clavius, a U.S. base on the moon, to investigate reports of unusual happenings there. Here we see a pod, launched from the shuttle, as it approaches its final landing via a platform moving down a red-lit shaft inside the base. Douglas Trumbull, whose technological contributions to the art of the movies were acknowledged by a special Oscar in 2012, was also responsible for the astonishing effects in Steven Spielberg's *Close Encounters of the Third Kind* (1977), Ridley Scott's *Blade Runner* (1982), and Terence Malick's *The Tree of Life* (2011).

glass shots, matte paintings, in-camera matte shots, and process shots.

The second category, mechanical effects, includes objects or events that are created by artists and craftspeople and placed on the set to be photographed. There are, of course, endless examples of such special effects, including the different Frankenstein masks used in the many movies featuring that character, such as Mel Brooks's *Young Frankenstein* (1974; cinematographer Gerald Hirschfeld; makeup artist Edwin Butterworth). Other mechanical creatures include the beast in Ishirô Honda's Japanese cult film *Godzilla* (1954; cinematographer Masao Tamai; special effects Sadamasa Arikawa) and the menacing shark in Steven Spielberg's *Jaws* (1975; cinematographer Bill Butler; special effects Robert A. Mattey and Kevin Pike).

Laboratory effects, the third category, involve more complicated procedures such as contact printing and bipack as well as blowups, cropping, pan and scan, flip shots, split-screen shots, and day-for-night shooting. These complex technical procedures are outside the scope of this book, but you can find complete information on them in the books by Raymond Fielding, Bruce Kawin, and Ira Konigsberg.[16]

Computer-Generated Imagery

In the movies, **computer-generated imagery (CGI)** is the application of computer graphics to create special effects. CGI is also widely used to create enhanced imagery in video games, art, and print media. Since its first use in film in the early 1970s, CGI has transformed the

16. Raymond Fielding, ed., *A Technological History of Motion Pictures and Television: An Anthology from the Pages of the Journal of the Society of Motion Picture and Television Engineers* (Berkeley: University of California Press, 1967); Bruce F. Kawin, *How Movies Work* (Berkeley: University of California Press, 1992); and Ira Konigsberg, *The Complete Film Dictionary*, 2nd ed. (New York: Penguin, 1997).

A wholly convincing cyber-character
The character of Davy Jones (Bill Nighy, *center*), flanked by his equally frightening shipmates, made its debut in Gore Verbinski's *Pirates of the Caribbean: Dead Man's Chest* (2006; visual effects John Knoll, Hal Hickel, Charles Gibson, and Allen Hall). A creation of the most advanced special effects—including 3-D computer-generated imagery and motion capture technology—Jones is a wholly convincing cyber-character, both human and inhuman. He is a physically and morally hideous creature who uses his many supernatural powers to inflict cruelty on virtually everyone he encounters. His head resembles an octopus whose long tentacles form a "beard." He lacks a nose, so he breathes through a tentacle on the left side of his face, and he has surprisingly blue eyes. Jones appears again in the third film of the Pirates of the Caribbean series, Verbinski's *At World's End* (2007), in which he is killed.

motion-picture industry, particularly the making of animated, fantasy, and science-fiction movies.

Over the next forty years, CGI improved rapidly. The major films that first used it now seem almost as old-fashioned as the process shot. (A **process shot** is made by filming action in front of a rear-projection screen that has on it still or moving images for the background.) Yet certain achievements are memorable for innovations that are landmarks in the development of CGI. Stanley Kubrick's *2001: A Space Odyssey* (1968; special effects designer and director, Kubrick; supervisors Wally Veevers, Douglas Trumbull, Con Pederson, and Tom Howard; cinematographer Geoffrey Unsworth) was the first film to seamlessly link footage shot by the camera with that prepared by the computer. Today, some four decades later, its look continues to amaze audiences. Indeed, it set a standard of technical sophistication, visual elegance, integration with the story, and power to create meaning that remains unsurpassed.

Today, most movies use digital imagery in one way or another. They fall into two general types. First are the live-action movies, such as James Cameron's *Avatar* or Peter Jackson's Lord of the Rings series, which

are greatly enhanced by CGI effects. Second are the fully animated features, often released in 3-D. These include Hiyao Miyazaki's *anime* features such as the Toy Story, Frozen, or Ice Age series. Animated features in 3-D appeal to surprisingly broad audience demographics and are now among the highest-grossing movies of all time. With the increasing complexity of CGI and the investment in human and technical resources required for its production, independent companies—whose artists and technicians usually work in consultation with the director, production designer, and director of photography—have become increasingly responsible for creating these effects. This artistry, now virtually a separate industry within the film industry, is expensive but has achieved astonishingly realistic effects at costs acceptable to producers. Companies include George Lucas's Industrial Light & Magic, Pixar Animation Studios (now a part of Walt Disney), Blue Sky Studios (Fox), and Pacific Data Images (DreamWorks SKG).

Motion capture (also known as motion tracking or mocap) is a specific CGI effect in which a live-action subject wears a bodysuit fitted with reflective markers that enables a computer to record each movement as digital images; they are then translated, with as much manipulation as desired, into models on which the screen figures are based. When the images include facial contours and expressions, the process is called *performance capture*. These techniques are used to create virtual reality in animated, experimental, and feature movies as well as in video games. Hironobu Sakaguchi and Moto Sakakibara's *Final Fantasy: The Spirits Within* (2001; cinematographer Sakakibara), the first major motion picture to use the technique to generate all of its "cast," broke new ground in the world of special effects by featuring characters that—while convincingly human in features and motions—were entirely computer-generated. Many other movies followed, including Peter Jackson's Lord of the Rings trilogy (2001–3; cinematographer Andrew Lesnie) and Matt Reeves's *Dawn of the Planet of the Apes* (2014). Motion capture and performance capture as well as rotoscoping, another version of motion and performance capture in which animators trace over live-action film movement for use in animated sequences, constitute a provocative sign of what might happen to the design and production of movies in years to come.

Director David Fincher's *The Curious Case of Benjamin Button* (2008; cinematographer Claudio Miranda) raises another issue related to motion and performance capture: actors' credits. The story is about a man who is born old and grows younger, and Brad Pitt, who plays the lead character, insisted on appearing as Button from old age to infancy. Since the handsome actor is relatively young, Fincher relied on electronic special effects to create the illusion of Button's reverse aging. To accomplish this, Fincher first photographed every facial expression that Pitt could make. Based on these photos, 150 visual artists created images reflecting the decrease in Button's aging (i.e., skin and hair) over the years. Second, Fincher photographed a group of "body actors"—actors whose bodies substitute for the credited actor—playing the younger and older Button. Images of Pitt's digitally altered face were then electronically inserted onto those body images to create the finished product. We know that many artists worked in the service of this single actor/character and that Pitt and six other actors actually played Benjamin Button. We also recognize that acting involves both facial expressions and physical movements, but the complex process used here raises a question: Who deserves the credit for creating the character of Benjamin Button? While all seven actors are listed in the movie's credits, only Pitt was nominated for an Academy Award for Best Actor in a Leading Role. But the "actor" in this case is an electronic compilation.

Wherever special effects take movie production in the future, the ever-present danger is that all the SPFX in action, adventure, and science-fiction films will dazzle us but do little to increase our understanding of the world we live in or the drama of human life.

Looking at Cinematography: Richard Linklater's *Boyhood*

As you read in Chapter 2, "Principles of Film Form," time and space are relative to each other on the movie screen, and we cannot separate them or perceive one without the other. But time, not space, is the central theme in *Boyhood* (2014), and it was also a significant factor in deciding how the movie would be made.

Boyhood, set in Texas, is a coming-of-age movie about Mason Evans Jr. (Ellar Coltraine) from age six to eighteen. Mason and his sister Samantha (Lorelei Linklater) live with their mother Olivia (Patricia Arquette), who is divorced from their father Mason Evans Sr. (Ethan Hawke). Soon after they move into a new house, Olivia marries Bill, a professor at the college she attends, but Bill turns out to be an abusive alcoholic and that marriage ends. Meanwhile, Mason and his sister remain in close touch with their father, who has remarried. Later, Olivia moves in with a new partner Jim, a corrections officer, but he too has an alcohol problem and they split. Under these emotionally stressful circumstances, Mason preserves his distance, common sense, and stability. He gets interested in photography, finds a girlfriend, and takes a job washing dishes in a restaurant. After graduating from high school, he leaves home for college on a scholarship and gets a taste of the life he may lead for the next four years.

Shooting *Boyhood* presented the filmmakers with some unusual challenges, and chief among them was how to visually present the passing of time. Linklater could have adopted an unorthodox approach—for example, the complex flashback structure of *Citizen*

Kane—but he instead opted for the traditional, showing moments of real life and capturing aging in real time as frankly as he could in cinematic terms. That, in essence, was his **cinematographic plan**, a visual concept for telling the story. Such plan outlines how the lighting and camera will convey emotion, relate to themes and subtexts in the script, and show character development. Most important of all, it envisions how the movie will *look*.

Boyhood's traditional plan tells the story directly and intimately, avoiding flashy camera work or special effects. The film was shot on 35mm color film stock, remarkable for capturing bright colors—clothes, lawns, buildings—under the bright Texas sun and within the evenly lighted interiors. But this brightness, which might be understood by some viewers as happiness, is often contradicted by a scene's mood and action. Indeed, this is a surprisingly bright movie for a story filled with disappointments and unhappiness. The many exterior scenes were shot largely in available light, ranging from clear Texas sunlight, to overcast skies, to the gorgeous orange sunset tones of Big Bend National Park in the film's final moments. The consistent proximity of the camera to the film's action develops the narrative's outcome and meaning, as it remains close to the characters, intimately observing them and never avoiding unpleasantness. As Linklater's camera keeps us up close to the characters, we grow to like or dislike and understand or be confused by what they do and say. As for camera angles and height, there is nothing unusual, and the cinematographer avoids moving camera shots, except in the frequent use of the Steadicam, which increases intimacy with what he is shooting.

Over a period of twelve years, Linklater and his crew shot *Boyhood* primarily from a neutral observer's point of view, using the standard shots: LS, MS, CU, as well as two- and three-shots, particularly in family scenes. It is a fiction film with a documentary look, but their continual emphasis on medium and close-up shots underscores an emphasis on the individual, not the group. Thus, with this emphasis on character, not space, the shots are predominately short, and cutting between them is frequent, further emphasizing the movie's theme: the passage of time. Finally, there are no discernible special effects. Given the director's immersion in film history and his respect for it, it's not surprising that the movie tells its fascinating story in a straightforward way. The film's production evolved as naturally as its theme.

Linklater has what he calls "this visual thing"—the ability to see the whole movie in his head (the mise-en-scène, the lighting, the angles) before shooting it—that is, a cinematographic plan. In that regard, he's like many great directors, such as Alfred Hitchcock and John Ford, both of whom confided that planning the whole film in their mind helps to avoid surprises on the set and hinders producers from making changes during editing.

Although *Boyhood* was planned and shot during the industry's conversion to digital production, Linklater shot it on 35mm film. This provided visual continuity—free from advances in digital technology—and resulted in better color consistency and flexibility in lighting exterior shots over many years of shooting. There were challenges also for the artists in production, costume, makeup, and hair design. Since the movie used the same actors throughout, who of course aged visibly in line with the roles they were playing, the designers had to make sure that the décor, clothes, makeup, and hair styles kept pace with the passing years. There were no special effects to achieve this, no prosthetics or CGI ageing effects.

Linklater's style is naturalism—a realistic cinematic depiction of young Mason growing up—and he finds the perfect moments to illuminate this passage, enabling us to see and share Mason's growth with him. According to Linklater, "If you make a film about childhood, you've got to pick a moment—you know."[17] Let's look closely

Traditional shot/reaction shots in *Boyhood*

Richard Linklater uses traditional cinematic conventions to depict the moments before Mason Jr. leaves his mother Olivia for college. [1] LS from the kitchen through the door of Mason's bedroom, where he is packing a box. He is telling his mom, seated in another room, how the college computer chooses roommates. [2] MS of mom sitting in a chair, and later, with camera following, going into the kitchen as Mason (in a voice-over) continues his comments about roommates. [3] MS of Mason holding the first photograph he ever took, saying, "Did you—did you put this in here again? I don't want it." [4] LS of the living room where mom is sitting at a table in the background looking in an eyeline shot across to kitchen counter at Mason's box of stuff, realizing that he is really going away. [5,6] MS of mom as she continues to cry as she talks. [7] MS, slightly high angle, looking down at mom sitting at the table crying with her head in her hands. [8] MLS of Mason, who is speechless.

17. Qtd. in Nathan Heller, "Moment to Moment: Why Richard Linklater Makes Movies," *The New Yorker* (June 30, 2014): 46.

at one of those moments: the scene between Mason and his mom as he prepares to leave for college. If the passage of time is the movie's major theme, resulting in character growth and change, then the sub-theme, in the view of some characters, is that this process "sucks." Mason's mother, father, and sister use that word, but significantly, he never does. His girlfriend says he's "gloomy," but in closer observation, he's thoughtful and often skeptical. This good-bye scene erupts when Olivia confronts Mason with her sad litany of disappointments: three failed marriages; a daughter who has already left the nest; and her favorite, Mason, who's about to leave for college. Moreover, Mason's biological father is happily remarried, and she's now alone. "I just thought there would be more," she confesses through her tears. He can't deal with her anguish, but earlier he said, "Mom is just as fucking confused as I am," giving us an insight into what he is thinking.

The cinematography of this scene consists of 31 shots, all made in the interior of his mom's apartment in the morning of his departure. Mason is packing in his bedroom, while his mom is in the combination living room/kitchenette, sitting at a table doing some work. The long, medium, and close-up shots are almost evenly divided between them (mom gets one more than he). Mason dominates the first part of the scene, talking about roommate selection; then there's a break when the two of them discuss whether or not he should take the first photograph he ever made with him to school; and then the final part is dominated by his mom's sorrowful outbreak. The cinematography consists of a rapid succession of shots of his mom talking and reaction shots of Mason's bewildered look.

It's a painful scene for both of them, as well as for us. Under the circumstances, both are being somewhat selfish: she's regretting her life and he just wants to get on with his. As they first speak to one another from separate rooms, the camera keeps them in separate frames, and they remain in separate frames when later, they are together in the same room, We never see them in the same frame together, the result of a cinematographic plan that

keeps it that way. They don't touch or kiss good-bye, but when he goes back to his room to get his backpack, there is a striking long shot of his mother in the empty apartment, her eyeline directed toward the box of his stuff. For the first time, we see the entire room and her loneliness within it. But while it's one of the movie's great moments, it's also ambiguous, We don't know if she's crying for herself or her son; or if he's too upset to talk, unable to deal with women (the subject of his father's last advice), or just eager to get away. Whatever he's feeling, he shows little emotion and leaves his mother sobbing.

Mason, not his family, is the focus of the narrative, and we see him off to a new adventure. He admits that college may not be "the key to my future" or "a great transforming experience," but he cautiously plunges on the first day, meeting his roommate, eating a pot-laced brownie, and finding a new girlfriend. With that, the movie ends.

But what does this add up to? What does *Boyhood*, as a fictional work beautifully crafted, mean beyond its depiction of Mason Evans's years between childhood and near-adulthood? In its depiction of a boy growing up during a succession of family breakups, no moment is more touching than when the mother realizes that she is completely alone. But there's no longing for previous years, except in some music from the 1970s. If the movie has values for our time, they rest in its universal themes of dysfunctional and functional families, parental discord, young love, disappointments, and growing up and maybe finding oneself. In an attempt to assign meaning, Linklater says, "I was trying to make a pretty anti-nostalgic piece. The view of that movie is that the times they're living in suck."[18] Like many teenagers, young Mason and his friends know that the culture in which they are growing up is not for them. They see its weaknesses, more than its strengths, and know it sucks. One of the values of casting Ellar Coltrane in the leading role was that he *was* his character: he grows up alongside Mason Evans Jr., experiencing personally the things written in the script.

---

18. Qtd. in "Moment to Moment," p. 50.

ANALYZING CINEMATOGRAPHY

This chapter has provided an overview of the major components of cinematography—the process by which a movie's mise-en-scène is recorded onto film or some other motion-picture medium. More than just a process, however, cinematography is very much a language used by directors and their collaborators (most notably, directors of photography) to convey meaning, transmit narrative information, and influence the emotional responses of viewers. Now that you know something about the basic cinematographic tools available to filmmakers, you can pay greater attention to the particulars of this language while looking at movies.

SCREENING CHECKLIST: CINEMATOGRAPHY

☐ Determine whether the cinematographic aspects of the film—the qualities of the film stock, lighting, lenses, framing, angles, camera movement, and use of long takes—add up to an overall look. If so, try to describe its qualities.

☐ Take note of moments in the film when the images are conveying information that is not reflected in characters' action and dialogue. These moments are often crucial to the development of a movie's themes, narrative, and meaning.

☐ Are special effects used in the film? To what extent? Are they appropriate to, and effective in, telling the story? Are they effective in making something look real when it isn't?

☐ Also keep track of camera angles other than eye-level shots. If there are high- or low-angle shots, determine whether they are POV shots. That is, is the high or low angle meant to represent another character's point of view? If so, what does the angle convey about that character's state of mind? If not, what does it convey about the person or thing in the frame?

☐ As you evaluate crucial scenes, pay attention to the composition of shots within the scene. Are the compositions balanced in a way that conforms to the rule of thirds, or are the elements within the frame arranged in a less "painterly" composition? In either case, try to describe how the composition contributes to the scene overall.

☐ Can you determine whether the colors of a shot or scene have been artificially manipulated through the use of color filters, different film stocks, or chemical or digital manipulation to create a mood or indicate a state of mind?

☐ Pay attention to camera movement in the film. Sometimes camera movement is used solely to produce visual excitement or to demonstrate the filmmaker's technological virtuosity. At other times it is playing an important functional role in the film's narrative. Be alert to these differences, and take note of meaningful uses of camera movement.

☐ Note when the cinematography calls attention to itself. Is this a mistake or misjudgment by the filmmaker, or is it intentional? If intentional, what purpose is served by making the cinematography so noticeable?

Questions for Review

1. What are the differences among a setup, a shot, and a take?
2. A cinematographer depends on two crews of workers. What is each crew responsible for?
3. How the lighting for any movie looks is determined, in part, by its source and direction. Explain these terms and the effect each has on the overall lighting.
4. What are the four major lenses used on movie cameras? What is the principal characteristic of the image that each lens creates?
5. Based on proximity to the camera, what are the three most commonly used shots in a movie? What principle is used to distinguish them?
6. What is the rule of thirds?
7. The movie camera can shoot from various angles. What are they? What meaning does each imply? Do these implications always hold true?
8. What are the basic types of camera movement?
9. What is a long take? What can it achieve that a short take cannot? What is the difference between a long take and a long shot?
10. Special effects create images that might not be possible with traditional cinematography. What are the basic ways to create special effects?

STUDENT RESOURCES ONLINE

digital.wwnorton.com/movies5

▶ **VIDEO**

The tutorials for this chapter provide more information about lighting, shot types, camera angles, lenses, moving camera effects, and point of view.

LOOKING AT **MOVIES**
CHAPTER 6: CINEMATOGRAPHY

LIGHTING
SHOT TYPES AND IMPLIED PROXIMITY
CAMERA ANGLES
POINT OF VIEW
ZOOM AND MOVING CAMERA EFFECTS
THE MOVING CAMERA
FOCAL LENGTH

▶ MAIN MENU

INTERACTIVE

These interactive lighting tutorials let you experience the full expressive range of four lighting techniques: quality, exposure, ratio, and direction.

BG | Back | Rim | Side | Key | Top | Bottom | Front

Wild (2014; director Jean-Marc Vallée)

CHAPTER

ACTING | **7**

LEARNING OBJECTIVES

After reading this chapter, you should be able to

✓ Explain how the coming of sound into the movie industry affected acting.

✓ Describe how movie acting today differs from that of the classical studio era.

✓ Explain why the relationship between the actor and the camera is so important.

✓ Describe the criteria used to cast actors.

✓ Explain the differences between naturalistic and nonnaturalistic movie acting.

✓ Define *improvisational acting*.

✓ Explain the potential effects on acting of framing, composition, lighting, shot types, and shot lengths.

What Is Acting?

It's actors that draw us to the movies. And today's movies are rich with talented actors, including (to name just a few) Christian Bale (*The Fighter*, 2010), Cate Blanchett (*Blue Jasmine*, 2013), Anthony Hopkins (*Hitchcock*, 2012), Viola Davis and Victoria Spencer (*The Help*, 2011), Michael Fassbender (*Shame*, 2011), Nicole Kidman (*Stoker*, 2013), Anders Danielson Lie (*Oslo, August 31st*, 2012), Paulina Garcia (*Gloria*, 2013), Daniel Day-Lewis (*Lincoln*, 2012), Emmanuelle Riva (*Amour*, 2012), Michael B. Jordan (*Fruitvale Station*, 2013), Jennifer Lawrence (*Silver Linings Playbook*, 2012), Chiwetel Ejiofor (*12 Years a Slave*, 2013), Dane De Haan (*The Place Beyond the Pines*, 2012), and Agata Trzebuchowska (*Ida*, 2013). We all have our favorite actors, and while you may not be familiar with all of these actors, you can easily check out their performances to see what great acting is all about.

It's easy to define narrative, mise-en-scène, or cinematography because those formal aspects of filmmaking depend in part on techniques and conventions that are widely accepted by filmmakers. Acting, by comparison, presents a different challenge because there is no one

way to do it; every actor is a master of his or her own technique in creating characters. Yet Joaquin Phoenix, one of today's most impressive actors, does not even try to define his work, and it's not a cliché to say that it speaks for itself. In *Her* (2013; director Spike Jonze), Phoenix plays Theodore Twombly, a lonely introvert who falls in love with Samantha, the female voice of his computer's operating system, voiced by Scarlett Johansson, whom we hear but never see. Their relationship falls apart when Samantha dumps him (she has thousands of cyberlovers just like him). It's both funny and sad when Theodore is devastated by something that is as impossible as it is peculiar. Throughout, Phoenix's portrayal of this character sustains the film's development. He is almost always on the screen, something that only a very few actors in film history have ever accomplished, and he amazes us with his control as an actor. Although he worked closely with the director, costar, and supporting actors, Joaquin Phoenix delivers the movie.[1]

Screen acting of this kind is an art in which an actor uses imagination, intelligence, psychology, memory, vocal technique, facial expressions, body language, and an overall knowledge of the filmmaking process to realize, under the director's guidance, the character created by the screenwriter. The performance and effect of that art can seem mysterious and magical when we're enjoying a movie, and acting turns out to be even more complex than we might at first assume.

Our initial interest in a movie is almost always sparked by the actors featured in it. As the critic Pauline Kael said, "I think so much of what we respond to in fictional movies is acting. That's one of the elements that's often left out when people talk theoretically about the movies. They forget it's the human material we go to see."[2] The power of some actors—Angelina Jolie or George Clooney, for example—to draw an audience is frequently more important to a movie's financial success than any other factor. For this reason, some observers regard screen actors as mere commodities, cogs in a machine of promotion and hype designed only to generate revenue. Although even the most accomplished screen actors can be used as fodder for promotional campaigns, such a

1. In *Locke* (2013; director Steven Knight), star Tom Hardy is the only actor in the film, and he carries on various telephone conversations while driving his car down a British highway. Like *Her*, this drama depends more on the voices than the visuals, but because the actor never leaves the car, it is far more claustrophobic. Alfonso Cuarón's *Gravity* (2013) is almost exclusively devoted to a space scientist (Sandra Bullock) trying to save herself, and by contrast, the visuals seem more important than the voices.

2. Leonard Quart, "I Still Love Going to Movies: An Interview with Pauline Kael," *Cineaste* 25, no. 2 (2000): 10.

The camera and the actor

English film actor Michael Caine has compared the movie camera to an impossibly attentive lover who "hangs on your every word, your every look; she can't take her eyes off you. She is listening to and recording everything you do, however minutely you do it."[3] That appears to be exactly what the camera is doing in this expressive close-up of Caine as Thomas Fowler in Phillip Noyce's *The Quiet American* (2002). The business and art of Hollywood moviemaking intersect when "bankable" stars such as Michael Caine (and in this example, his costar Brendan Fraser, *left, back to camera*) take on challenging, unglamorous roles that transcend their physical attractiveness.

view overlooks the many complex and important ways that skillful acting can influence the narrative, style, and meanings of a film. Actor Cate Blanchett believes that "when acting works, when performance works, when theater's great, when films connect—whether it's a piece of profound satire or a work of great drama—it expands what it means to be human."[4] Writer-director-producer-actor Orson Welles, who questioned nearly every other aspect of filmmaking dogma, firmly believed in the importance of acting: "I don't understand how movies exist independently of the actor—I truly don't."[5]

Despite its central importance, acting is also the aspect of filmmaking over which directors have the least precise control. Directors may describe literally what they want from their principal collaborators—for example, screenwriters or costume designers—but they can only suggest to actors what they want. That becomes quite different when a director-screenwriter like Paul Thomas Anderson writes parts specifically for the actors he casts. This approach has led to many memorable performances—for example, by Daniel Day-Lewis and

Paul Dano in *There Will Be Blood* (2007), Amy Adams and Philip Seymour Hoffman in *The Master* (2010), and Josh Brolin and Reese Witherspoon in *Inherent Vice* (2014)—in which the director, screenwriter, and actor enjoy an unusually close collaboration. However, screen actors, or at least experienced screen actors, know that the essential relationship is between them and the camera—not between them and the director or even the audience. Actors interpret the director's guidance in the area between them and the lens—an intimate and narrowly defined space that necessarily concentrates much of the actors' energy on their faces. Through composition, close-ups, camera angles and movements, and other cinematic techniques, movie actors always come closer to the audience and appear larger than actors on the stage do.

The camera makes possible an attention to detail that was impossible before the invention of cinema, mainly because stage acting forced actors to project their voices and their gestures to the back of the theater. Screen acting, as an experience, can be as tight and intimate as examining a painting at arm's length. As American screen actor Joan Crawford put it, "A movie actor paints with the tiniest brush."[6]

Movie Actors

The challenges facing movie actors in interpreting and pretending to be their characters, and the responsibilities involved in performing those characters on the screen, are very different from the challenges and responsibilities facing stage actors. Stage actors convey their interpretations of the characters they play directly to the audience through voice, gesture, and movement. By contrast, movie actors, using gesture and movement—and voice since the coming of sound—convey their characters directly to the camera. In turn, that camera is what makes the movie actor's performance so different from the stage actor's. Stage actors play to a large audience and must project their voices so they can be heard throughout the theater. They must avoid the soft speech, subtle facial expressions, or small gestures that are fundamental tools of the movie actor.

3. Michael Caine, *Acting in Film: An Actor's Take on Movie Making* (New York: Applause, 1990), p. 4.
4. Qtd. in Melena Ryzik, "Desperate Times Call for Her," *New York Times* (February 13, 2014), p. C1; www.nytimes.com/2014/02/13/movies/awardsseason/cate-blanchett-has-front-runner-oscar-status.html (accessed February 6, 2015).
5. Orson Welles and Peter Bogdanovich, *This Is Orson Welles*, ed. Jonathan Rosenbaum (New York: HarperCollins, 1992), p. 262.
6. Joan Crawford, qtd. in Lillian Ross and Helen Ross, *The Player: A Profile of an Art* (New York: Simon & Schuster, 1962), p. 66.

LOOKING AT MOVIES
PERSONA AND PERFORMANCE

VIDEO ▶

This short tutorial discusses the importance of persona to our experience of acting performances.

Stage actors, who must memorize their lines, have the advantage of speaking them in the order in which they were written. This in turn makes it much easier to maintain psychological, emotional, and physical continuity in a performance as the play proceeds. By contrast, movie actors are subject to the shooting schedule. For budgetary and logistical reasons, most shots are not made in the sequence indicated in the screenplay, so movie actors learn only those lines that they need for the moment. Therefore, movie actors bear the additional burden, particularly on their memory, of creating continuity between related shots, even though the shots may have been made days, weeks, or even months apart.

Judith Anderson had an illustrious stage career before achieving fame as a movie actor as Mrs. Danvers in Alfred Hitchcock's *Rebecca* (1940). She emphasizes how each form affects an actor's movements. On the stage she is free (to move where she wants, scratch her ear if she wants, add a bit of business if she wants), but on the screen she is constrained by the physical space before the camera, the lighting and other technical aspects, and the much greater size of the image on the screen as opposed to the natural appearance of an actor on the stage.[7]

To achieve the goal of maintaining continuity (as we will discuss in Chapter 8), editing is a major factor in putting shots together and creating the performance. During a play, the stage actor performs each scene only once; in the shooting of a movie, the actor may be asked to do many takes before the director is satisfied with the performance. Before a shot is made, the movie actor must be prepared to wait, sometimes for long periods, while camera, lighting, or sound equipment is moved or readjusted; the stage actor faces no such delays or interruptions.

Although the theater and the movies are both collaborative arts, once the curtain goes up, stage actors need not think much about the backstage crew, for the crew will perform scenery or lighting changes according to a fixed schedule. Movie actors, however, must play directly to the camera while dozens of people are standing around just outside the camera's range. These people are doing their jobs, but also watching and listening to everything the actors do. Some people are there because they have to be (e.g., the director, script supervisor, cinematographer, sound recordist, makeup artist, hairstylist); others are there waiting to make the necessary changes in scenery, properties, or lighting required for the next shot. Over the years, some temperamental actors have succeeded in closing the set to all but the most essential personnel, but that is an exceptional practice. Traditionally, however, movie sets have been closed to visitors, particularly the media.

Although there are probably as many types of actors as there are actors themselves, for the purposes of this discussion, we can identify four key types:

1. actors who take their personae from role to role (personality actors)

2. actors who deliberately play against our expectations of their personae

3. actors who seem to be different in every role (chameleon actors)

4. actors who are often nonprofessionals or people who are cast to bring verisimilitude to a part

In our everyday lives, each of us creates a persona, the image of character and personality that we want to show the outside world. For movie actors, those personae are their appearance and mannerisms of moving and delivering dialogue—unique creations that are relatively consistent from role to role and from performance to performance. Actors' personae are usually (but not always) rooted in their natural behavior, personality, and physicality. Current actors defined by their personae include Tom Cruise, Cameron Diaz, and Will Smith.

7. See interview with Anderson on Disc 2 of the Criterion Collection DVD release of *Rebecca* (2001).

Paul Giamatti is not, by Hollywood standards, a leading man, yet in Richard J. Lewis's *Barney's Version* (2010), this actor—whose persona might be described as an overweight, balding, neurotic but likable loser—channels these attributes and attitudes in a way that makes us care about his character, Barney Panofsky. Even more versatile actors, not just those who are popular action or comedy stars, rely on persona. Among them are Susan Sarandon, Sean Penn, Morgan Freeman, Jack Nicholson, William H. Macy, Chris Cooper, Ewan McGregor, and Benicio Del Toro.

For many movie actors, the persona is the key to their career as well as an important part of film marketing and why we choose particular movies over others. One reason audiences go to movies is to see a certain kind of story. That's a big part of what the concept of genre is all about. You go to a romantic comedy, an action movie, a horror film, or a comic-book adaptation because you know what to expect, and you want what you expect. Having made your choice on the basis of story, you should get familiar and appealing narrative structures, cinematic conventions, character types, dramatic situations, and payoffs.

The same thing goes for persona-identified actors like Tom Cruise. He's not only good-looking, but he projects an interesting balance of arrogance and vulnerability that appeals to many viewers. When you go to a Tom Cruise movie (the kind where the star's name is the most important factor in your choice), you have an expectation of the kind of performance he's going to give you, based on his persona. And you expect to see that performance, that persona, in the context of a certain kind of story. Part of the fun comes from seeing that persona in different kinds of movies, enjoying its interaction with a particular role or genre. So part of the reason you might go to see Cruise in Stanley Kubrick's *Eyes Wide Shut* (1999) is to see what he makes of Dr. William Harford, a Manhattan physician facing serious sexual and moral issues; or, in Michael Mann's *Collateral* (2004), how he portrays Vincent, a hit man; how he pushes the comic side of his persona and unfortunately becomes the stereotype of an end-of-the-line rock star in *Rock of Ages* (2012; director Adam Shankman); keeps his investigator/agent role going (honed perfectly in the Mission Impossible and Jack Reacher series). His foray into the science-fiction genre continues with *Edge of Tomorrow* (2014; director Doug Liman).

Sometimes an actor with a familiar, popular persona takes on a role that goes against what we expect—for example, Jack Nicholson as Warren Schmidt in Alexander Payne's *About Schmidt* (2002) or Cate Blanchett as Jude in Todd Haynes's *I'm Not There* (2007). A major factor

Cate Blanchett's complete transformation as Bob Dylan
In *I'm Not There* (2007; director Todd Haynes), Cate Blanchett transforms her glamorous self into Jude, a skinny, ragged, androgynous folksinger at the beginning of his career: Bob Dylan. In this image, Jude is responding to an obnoxious British journalist who questions his motives in switching from acoustic to electric guitar in 1965. To understand how accomplished Blanchett's portrayal is, compare her Dylan with the real Dylan as he appears in D. A. Pennebaker's *Dont Look Back* (1967) or Martin Scorsese's *No Direction Home: Bob Dylan* (2005).

affecting our enjoyment of actors in such roles is not just the role, but the strange sensation of seeing an actor whose persona we have come to know well play a totally different sort of role. In Nicholson's case, the normally crafty, strong, menacing man portrays a powerless, mundane, befuddled, and cuckolded insurance salesman. In Blanchett's career, we are astonished to see an actor known for her regal beauty in such roles as Queen Elizabeth I in Shekhar Kapur's *Elizabeth* (1998) or Lady Galadriel in Peter Jackson's The Lord of the Rings trilogy (2001–3) when she undergoes a complete physical transformation as Jude, one of six different interpretations, by six different actors, of Bob Dylan in Todd Haynes's *I'm Not There* (2007). Blanchett is famous for her ability to change her distinctly Australian accent to meet the needs of any role. She can speak the Queen's English as Elizabeth and Galadriel or, with a pitch-perfect accent redolent of New York's upper East Side, she can become Jasmine Francis, a woman on the verge of a nervous breakdown, in Woody Allen's *Blue Jasmine* (2013). In *I'm Not There*, she hits the mark squarely with her interpretation of Dylan's twangy Midwestern speech. In creating her gender-bending portrait of a diffident, slightly androgynous singer, she uses every technique in the actor's stock besides her voice: movements and gestures, wig, makeup, eyeglasses, costumes, and props.

On the other side of the acting scale is the chameleon actor, named for the lizard that can make quick, frequent changes in its appearance in response to the environment. Chameleon actors adapt their look, mannerisms, and delivery to suit the role. They surprise us as persona actors when they are cast, as Jack Nicholson or Charlize Theron often are, in a role we do not expect—one that extends their range. For example, Jeff Bridges often looks so different in roles that he's unrecognizable at first (see p. 292): Starman/Scott Hayden in John Carpenter's *Starman* (1984), Preston Tucker in Francis Ford Coppola's *Tucker: The Man and His Dream* (1988), Obadiah Stane in John Favreau's *Iron Man* (2008), or Rooster Cogburn in Ethan and Joel Coen's *True Grit* (2010). Indeed, along with such multitalented colleagues as Leonardo DiCaprio, Brad Pitt, and Christian Bale, Bridges is a marvel of flexibility.

Johnny Depp, an actor who makes quick and frequent changes in the roles he plays, has reached star status without any fixed persona. Although he's earned the reputation as the ideal *nonnaturalistic* actor for such Tim Burton movies as *Edward Scissorhands* (1990), *Sweeney*

Todd: The Demon Barber of Fleet Street (2007), *Alice in Wonderland* (2010), and *Dark Shadows* (2012), he's also played an astonishing range of very different roles, such as Raoul Duke/Hunter S. Thompson in Terry Gilliam's *Fear and Loathing in Las Vegas* (1998); the cocaine king George Jung in Ted Demme's *Blow* (2001); Sir James Matthew Barrie, the author of *Peter Pan*, in Marc Forster's *Finding Neverland* (2004); Lord Rochester, the seventeenth-century English poet, in Laurence Dunmore's *The Libertine* (2004); and gangster John Dillinger in Michael Mann's *Public Enemies* (2009). In the current phase of his career, among other roles, he's played the over-the-top character of Captain Jack Sparrow in the Pirates of the Caribbean series (various dates and directors); a scientist in Wally Pfister's *Transcendence* (2014); Guy LaPointe, a Canadian cop, in Kevin Smith's bizarre comedy *Tusk* (2014); and Charlie Mortdecai, an eccentric art dealer in search of a stolen painting, in David Koepp's crime caper *Mortdecai* (2015).

Finally, there are the nonprofessional actors, real-life people who take roles in feature films (not documentaries) to play characters whose lives are much like their own. The earliest movies were cast with only nonprofessionals, and the tradition has remained in movies that call for such casting. Memorable examples include almost all the movies in the Italian neorealist tradition, including an entire community re-creating their daily lives in Ermanno Olmi's *The Tree of Wooden Clogs* (1978). Michel Gondry recruited a group of Bronx high school students to act as Bronx high school students in *The We and the I* (2012). Similarly, Laurent Cantet recruited François Bégaudeau, as the teacher, and a group of mixed-race students, many of them immigrants, for *The Class* (2008), his film about the challenges of teaching in a French school. In *The Best Years of Our Lives* (1946), William Wyler's powerful movie about three veterans of World War II, a nonprofessional almost steals the movie away from the professionals when Harold Russell, who lost both arms in the conflict, portrays the challenges facing such a handicapped man. In *Beasts of the Southern Wild* (2012; director Benh Zeitlin), the two leading characters are played by nonprofessionals Quvenzhané Wallis and Dwight Henry. And in Lynne Ramsay's *Ratcatcher* (1999), a haunting film about a Scottish slum kid, fledgling actor Tommy Flanagan plays the lead.

Although previous generations of stage actors knew that their duty was to convey emotion through recognized conventions of speech and gesture (mannerisms), screen actors have enjoyed a certain freedom to adopt

The versatile Johnny Depp

A contemporary actor of style and substance, Johnny Depp has exhibited impressive flexibility, both in the roles he chooses and the techniques he employs, to convey his characters' often complex emotional lives. [1] As Gilbert in Lasse Hallström's moving drama *What's Eating Gilbert Grape* (1993), he plays a man who tenderly looks after Arnie (Leonard DiCaprio, *left*), his younger brother who has developmental disability. [2] In Mike Newell's *Donnie Brasco* (1997), in a complete change of pace, Depp plays an FBI agent who, under the alias Donnie Brasco, infiltrates a New York crime family. Benjamin "Lefty" Ruggiero (Al Pacino, *left*), a minor gang member who's going nowhere in the mob, makes Donnie his protégé with the hope that he'll be successful. In this image, Lefty tells Donnie (*right*) that if he successfully kills an adversary, he'll be a "made man" (a full-fledged member of the gang). Donnie knows he's betrayed Lefty and that when this assignment is over, Lefty will be arrested. Depp masterfully shows how Donnie undergoes a fascinating psychological change, slowly becoming attracted to a life of crime rather than fighting it, but ultimately remaining true to his real job. Lasse Hallström's romantic comedy *Chocolat* (2000) is a slight tale about two free spirits who find themselves in a conservative French village, some of whose inhabitants regard them as undesirable. Depp is Roux, a roguish, Irish "river rat," seen here [3] with Vianne (Juliet Binoche), a French chocolate maker. Their affair doesn't amount to much, but Depp was born to play this kind of role, and he makes the most of it, Irish accent and all. In *The Curse of the Black Pearl*, the first movie in the Pirates of the Caribbean series, a return to the Hollywood genre involving swashbuckling heroes, Depp plays Jack Sparrow. He's seen here [4] looking unlike any pirate you've ever seen on-screen, a look reportedly inspired by guitarist Keith Richards of The Rolling Stones. His performance, enhanced by extraordinary makeup and costuming, helped make the series a major box-office hit, and Depp, one of the highest-paid actors in movie history.

individual styles that communicate emotional meaning through subtle and highly personal gestures, expressions, and varieties of intonation. American screen actor Barbara Stanwyck credited director Frank Capra with teaching her that "if you can think it, you can make the audience know it. . . . On the stage, it's mannerisms. On the screen, your range is shown in your eyes."[8] In addition, many different types of inspiration fuel screen acting; many factors guide actors toward their performances in front of the camera.

Consider the work of Meryl Streep, who has been nominated eighteen times for an Oscar. That's more nominations than any actor in the history of the Academy Awards (15 for Best Actress, 2 wins; 3 for

8. Barbara Stanwyck, qtd. in *Actors on Acting for the Screen: Roles and Collaborations*, ed. Doug Tomlinson (New York: Garland, 1994), p. 524.

Best Supporting Actress, 1 win). Despite her success in over fifty feature films, Streep, like many seasoned actors, finds it difficult to describe her talent. She says it is

> an art that I find in its deepest essence to be completely mysterious. . . . I have been smug and willfully ignorant. I've cultivated a deliberate reluctance to investigate my own method of working because I'm afraid of killing the goose. I'm afraid if I parse it I won't be able to do it anymore.[9]

Streep has played an astonishing variety of fictional and actual people on the screen. Fictional characters include Anna in Karel Reisz's *The French Lieutenant's Woman* (1981), a particularly interesting movie because Anna, a film actor, is creating the character of Sarah, a romantic of the Victorian era; Sophie Zawistowksi, a woman haunted by her Nazi-era past, in Alan J. Pakula's *Sophie's Choice* (1982); or Miranda Priestly in David Frankel's *The Devil Wears Prada* (2006), where the character, though fictional, is thought to have been influenced by Anna Wintour, the longtime editor of *Vogue*. By contrast, you might also study Streep's portrayals, often controversial with audiences, of such real people as Karen Blixen, the Danish novelist writing under the name of Isak Dinesen, in *Out of Africa* (1985; director Sydney Pollack); Julia Child, America's irresistible master of French cooking, in *Julie & Julia* (2009; director Nora Ephron); Margaret Thatcher, the British prime minister, in *The Iron Lady* (2011; director Phyllida Lloyd), or feminist Emmeline Pankhurst in *Suffragette* (2015; director Sarah Gavron). Given this variety that requires her to be different in every role, Streep says: "Acting is not about being someone different. It's finding the similarity in what is apparently different, then finding myself in there."[10]

A director's individual style plays a significant role in how actors develop their characters. The many approaches include encouraging actors to identify with characters (e.g., Elia Kazan), promoting a style loosely referred to as method acting (Terence Malick); favoring spontaneity, unpredictability, and sometimes improvi- sation (Richard Linklater); and encouraging actors to see their performances from a cinematographic point of view and explicitly imagine how their gestures and expressions will look on-screen (Alfred Hitchcock). This latter approach encourages actors to think more than to feel, to perform their roles almost as if they are highly skilled technicians whose main task is to control one aspect of the mise-en-scène (performance), much as set designers control the look and feel of sets, sound mixers control sound, directors of photography control camera work, and so on.

No matter what type a movie actor is—how definite or changeable the persona is, how varied the roles are, how successful the career is—we tend to blur the distinction between the actor on-screen and the person offscreen. The heroes of today's world are performers—athletes, musicians, actors—and a vast media industry exists to keep them in the public eye and encourage us to believe that they are every bit as fascinating in real life as they are on the screen. Inevitably, some movie actors become rich and famous without having much art or craft in what they do. Essentially, they walk through their movies, seldom playing any character other than themselves. Fortunately, for every one of these actors there are many more talented actors who take their work seriously; try, whenever possible, to extend the range of roles they play; and learn to adapt to the constantly shifting trends of moviemaking and public taste.

One definition of great acting is that it should look effortless, but that takes talent, training, discipline, experience, and hard work. It also takes the skills necessary for dealing with pressures that range from getting older (and thus becoming more apt to be replaced by a younger, better-looking actor) to fulfilling a producer's expectation that you will succeed in carrying a multimillion-dollar production and making it a profitable success.

As we continue this discussion of acting, remember that it is not actors' personal lives that count, but their ability to interpret and portray certain characters. In today's world, where the media report actors' every offscreen activity, especially indiscretions, maintaining the focus required for good acting poses a challenge.

---

9. Jennifer Greenstein Altmann, "Meryl Streep Talks about the 'Mysterious' Art of Acting" (December 1, 2006), www.princeton.edu/main/news/archive /S16/49/92S82 (accessed February 5, 2014).

10. www.goodreads.com/quotes/140679-acting-is-not-about-being-someone-different (accessed February 5, 2014). See also Karina Longworth, *Meryl Streep: Anatomy of an Actor* (London: Phaidon Press, 2014).

Although the media have always done this, the behavior of some of today's actors not only is more reckless but also is seldom covered up by a studio's public-relations department like it was in Hollywood's golden age.

The Evolution of Screen Acting

Early Screen-Acting Styles

The people on the screen in the very first movies were not actors but ordinary people playing themselves. The early films caught natural, everyday actions—feeding a baby, leaving work, yawning, walking up and down stairs, swinging a baseball bat, sneezing—in a simple, realistic manner. "Acting" was simply a matter of trying to ignore the presence of the camera as it recorded the action. In the early 1900s, filmmakers started to tell stories with their films and thus needed professional actors. Most stage actors at the time scorned film acting, however, and refused to take work in the fledgling industry.

Therefore, the first screen actors were usually rejects from the stage or fresh-faced amateurs eager to break into the emerging film industry. Lack of experience (or talent) wasn't the only hurdle they faced. Because no standard language of cinematic expression or any accepted tradition of film direction existed at the time, these first actors had little choice but to adopt the acting style favored in the nineteenth-century theater and try to adapt it to their screen roles. The resulting quaint, unintentionally comical style consists of exaggerated gestures, overly emphatic facial expressions, and bombastic mouthing of words (which could not yet be recorded on film) that characterized the stage melodramas popular at the turn of the twentieth century.

In 1908, the Société Film d'Art (Art Film Society), a French film company, was founded with the purpose of creating a serious artistic cinema that would attract equally serious people who ordinarily preferred the theater. Commercially, this was a risky step not only because cinema was in its infancy but also because, since the sixteenth century, the French had seen theater as a temple of expression. Its glory was (and remains) the Comédie-Française, the French national theater. To begin its work at the highest possible level, the Société Film d'Art joined creative forces with this revered organization, which agreed to lend its actors to the society's films. In addition, the society commissioned leading theater playwrights, directors, and designers, as well as prominent composers, to create its film productions.

Sarah Bernhardt (1844–1923), adored by her public as *la divine Sarah*, was the first great theatrical actor to appear in a movie, Clément Maurice's *Le Duel d'Hamlet* (*Hamlet*, 1900, 2 min.), a short account of Hamlet's duel with Laertes. She appeared in at least seven features, the most important of which is *Les Amours d'Elisabeth, Reine d'Angleterre* (*Queen Elizabeth*, 1912, 44 min.), directed by Henri Desfontaines and Louis Mercanton and produced by the Société Film d'Art.

As interesting as it is to see one of the early twentieth century's greatest actors as Elizabeth I, it is even more interesting to observe how closely this "canned theater" resembled an actual stage production. The space we see is that of the theater, which is limited to having actors enter and exit from stage left or right. It is unlike the cinema, where characters are not confined to the physical boundaries imposed by theater architecture. For all her reputed skill, Bernhardt's acting could only echo what she did on the stage. Thus we see the exaggerated facial expressions, strained gestures, and clenched fists of late-nineteenth-century melodrama. Although such artificiality was conventional and thus accepted by the audience, it was all wrong for the comparative intimacy between the spectator and the screen that existed even in the earliest movie theaters.

Despite its heavy-handed technique, *Queen Elizabeth* succeeded in attracting an audience interested in serious drama on the screen, made the cinema socially and intellectually respectable, and therefore encouraged further respect for the industry and its development. What remained to be done was not to teach Sarah Bernhardt how to act for the camera, but to develop cinematic techniques uniquely suitable for the emerging narrative cinema as well as a style of acting that could help actors realize their potential in this new medium.

D. W. Griffith and Lillian Gish

American film pioneer D. W. Griffith needed actors who could be trained to work in front of the camera, and by 1913 he had recruited a group that included some of the most important actors of the time: Mary Pickford, Lillian and Dorothy Gish, Mae Marsh, Blanche Sweet, Lionel Barrymore, Harry Carey, Henry B. Walthall, and Donald Crisp. Some had stage experience, some did not. All of them earned much more from acting in the movies than they would have on the stage, and they all enjoyed long, fruitful careers (many lasting well into the era of sound films).

Because the cinema was silent during this period, Griffith worked out more naturalistic movements and gestures for his actors rather than training their voices. The longer stories of such feature-length films as *The Birth of a Nation* (1915), *Intolerance* (1916), *Hearts of the World* (1918), and *Broken Blossoms* (1919) gave the actors more screen time and therefore more screen space in which to develop their characters. Close-ups required them to be more aware of the effect that their facial expressions would have on the audience, and actors' faces increasingly became more important than their bodies (although, in the silent comedies of the 1920s, the full presence of the human body was virtually essential for conveying humor).

Under Griffith's guidance, Lillian Gish invented the art of screen acting. Griffith encouraged her to study the movements of ordinary people on the street or in restaurants, to develop her physical skills with regular exercise, and to tell stories through her face and body. He urged her to watch the reactions of movie audiences, saying, "If they're held by what you're doing, you've succeeded as an actress."[11] Gish's performance in *Broken Blossoms* (1919) was the first great film performance by an actor. Set in the Limehouse (or Chinatown) section of London, the movie presents a stylized fable about the love of an older Chinese merchant, Cheng Huan (Richard Barthelmess), for an English adolescent, Lucy Burrows (Gish). Lucy's racist father, the boxer Battling Burrows (Donald Crisp), beats her for the slightest transgression. Enraged by her friendship with the merchant, Burrows drags her home, and when Lucy hides in a tiny closet, he breaks down the door and beats her so savagely that she dies soon after.

The interaction of narrative, acting, extremely confined cinematic space, and exploitation of the audience's fears gives this scene its beauty, power, and repulsiveness. Seen from various angles within the closet, which fills the screen, Lucy clearly cannot escape. Hysterical with fear, she finally curls up as her father breaks through the door. At the end, she dies in her bed, forcing the smile that has characterized her throughout the film.

Lillian Gish in *Broken Blossoms*
Lillian Gish was twenty-three when she played the young girl Lucy Burrows in D. W. Griffith's *Broken Blossoms* (1919). It was, incredibly, her sixty-fourth movie, and she gave one of her long career's most emotionally wrenching performances.

Terror and pity produce the cathartic realization within the viewer that Lucy's death, under these wretched circumstances, is truly a release.

In creating this scene, Gish invoked a span of emotions that no movie audience had seen before and few have seen since. Her performance illustrates the qualities of great screen acting: appropriateness, expressive coherence, inherent thoughtfulness/emotionality, wholeness, and unity. Amazingly, the performance resulted from Gish's own instincts—her sense of what was right for the climactic moment of the story and the mise-en-scène in which it took place—rather than from Griffith's direction:

> The scene of the terrified child alone in the closet could probably not be filmed today. To watch Lucy's hysteria was excruciating enough in a silent picture; a sound track would have made it unbearable. When we filmed it I played the scene with complete lack of restraint, turning around and around like a tortured animal. When I finished, there was a hush in the studio. Mr. Griffith finally whispered: "My God, why didn't you warn me that you were going to do that?"[12]

11. Lillian Gish with Ann Pinchot, *Lillian Gish: The Movies, Mr. Griffith, and Me* (Englewood Cliffs, NJ: Prentice-Hall, 1969), pp. 97–101, quotation on p. 101. See also Jeanine Basinger, *Silent Stars* (New York: Knopf, 1999).

12. Gish, *Lillian Gish*, p. 200. For another version of how this scene was prepared and shot, see Charles Affron, *Lillian Gish: Her Legend, Her Life* (New York: Scribner, 2001), pp. 125–131.

Gish gives a similarly powerful performance—her character shoots the man who raped her—in Victor Sjöström's *The Wind* (1928), and her work in confined spaces influenced such later climactic scenes as Marion Crane's (Janet Leigh) murder in the shower in Alfred Hitchcock's *Psycho* (1960) and Jack Torrance's (Jack Nicholson) attempt to get out of a bathroom where he is trapped in Stanley Kubrick's *The Shining* (1980).

With the discovery and implementation of the principles of screen acting, Gish (and her mentor, Griffith) also influenced excellent performances by her contemporaries: Emil Jannings in F. W. Murnau's *The Last Laugh* (1924) and Janet Gaynor and George O'Brien in Murnau's *Sunrise: A Song of Two Humans* (1927), Gibson Gowland in Erich von Stroheim's *Greed* (1924), and Louise Brooks in G. W. Pabst's *Pandora's Box* (1929).

The Influence of Sound

Not long after Griffith and Gish established a viable and successful style of screen acting, movie actors faced the greatest challenge yet: the conversion from silent to sound production. Instead of instantly revolutionizing film style, the coming of sound in 1927 began a period of several years in which the industry gradually converted to this new form of production (see Chapter 9). Filmmakers made dialogue more comprehensible by developing better microphones; finding the best placements for the camera, microphones, and other sound equipment; and encouraging changes in actors' vocal performances. At first they encased the camera, whose overall size has changed relatively little since the 1920s, in either a bulky soundproof booth or the later development known as a **blimp**—a soundproofed enclosure, somewhat larger than a camera, in which the camera may be mounted so that its sounds do not reach the microphone.

Such measures prevented the sounds of the camera from being recorded, but they also restricted how freely the camera—and the actors—could move. Actors accustomed to moving around the set without worrying about speaking now had to limit their movements to the circumscribed sphere where recording took place. Furthermore, technicians needed time to adjust to the recording equipment, which also restricted their movements. Eventually, technicians were able to free the camera for all kinds of movement and find ways of recording sound that allowed the equipment and actors alike more mobility.

Early sound-film acting
Sound technicians on the earliest sound films were challenged with recording the actors' voices with stationary microphones, which restricted their movements. This problem was solved later with microphones suspended on **booms** outside the camera's range and capable of moving to follow a character's movements. In looking backward, the classic movie musical *Singin' in the Rain* (1952; Stanley Donen and Gene Kelly, directors) found nothing but humor in the process of converting movie production to sound. In the background of this image, we see a reluctant and uncooperative actor, Lina Lamont (Jean Hagen, *right*), next to Don Lockwood (Gene Kelly, *left*). A microphone concealed in the bodice of her gown is connected by wire to the loudspeaker in the glass booth in the foreground, where the exasperated director and sound recordist discover that it has recorded only Miss Lamont's heartbeat. Obviously, they'll have to find a different microphone placement if they want to hear her voice. And if you've seen the movie, you know that her voice is so bad that she had little chance of making the transition to sound movies.

As monumental as the conversion to sound was in economic, technological, stylistic, and human terms, Hollywood found humor in it. It's the subject of one of the most enjoyable of all movie musicals: Stanley Donen and Gene Kelly's *Singin' in the Rain* (1952). This movie vividly and satirically portrays the technical difficulties of using the voice of one actor to replace the voice of another who hasn't been trained to speak, trying to move a camera weighted down with soundproof housing, and forcing actors to speak into microphones concealed in flowerpots. As film scholar Donald Crafton writes:

> Many of the clichés of the early sound cinema (including those in *Singin' in the Rain*) apply to films made during this period: long static takes, badly written dialogue, voices not quite in control, poor-quality recording, and

a speaking style with slow cadence and emphasis on 'enunciated' tones, which the microphone was supposed to favor.[13]

How did the "talkies" influence actors and acting? Although sound enabled screen actors to use all their powers of human expression, it also created a need for screenplays with dialogue, dialogue coaches to help the actors "find" their voices, and other coaches to help them master foreign accents. The more actors and the more speaking a film included, the more complex the narrative could become. Directors had to make changes, too. Before sound, a director could call out instructions to the actors during filming; once the microphone could pick up every word uttered on the set, directors were forced to rehearse more extensively with their actors, thus adopting a technique from the stage to deal with screen technology. Though many actors and directors could not make the transition from silent to sound films, others emerged from silent films ready to see the addition of sound less as an obstacle than as the means to a more complete screen verisimilitude.

An innovative production from this period is Rouben Mamoulian's *Applause* (1929; sound-recording technician Ernest Zatorsky). After several years of directing theater productions in London and New York, Mamoulian made his screen-directing debut with *Applause*, which is photographed in a style that mixes naturalism with expressionism. From the opening scene, a montage of activity that plunges us into the lively world of burlesque, the film reveals Mamoulian's mastery of camera movement. But when the camera does not move, as in the many two-shots full of dialogue, we can almost feel the limited-range microphone boom hovering over the actors, one step beyond the use of flowerpots. In contrast to the vibrant shots with the moving camera, these static shots are lifeless and made even more confusing by the loud expressionist sounds that overwhelm ordinary as well as intimate conversations.

Obviously, such limitations influence how we perceive the acting, which is *Applause*'s weak point throughout. Most likely because Mamoulian knew that symphonies of city sounds and noises would be the main impression of many scenes, the actors have little to say or do. However, the movie remains interesting thanks to a new technique in sound recording that Mamoulian introduced and that soon became common practice. Earlier, all sound in a particular shot had been recorded and manipulated on a single sound track. Mamoulian persuaded the sound technicians to record overlapping dialogue in a single shot using two separate microphones and then mix them together on the sound track. When April Darling (Joan Peers), her head on a pillow, whispers a prayer while her mother, Kitty (Helen Morgan), sits next to her and sings a lullaby, the actors almost seem to be singing a duet—naturally, intimately, and convincingly.[14]

The conversion to sound, a pivotal moment in film history that simultaneously ruined many acting careers while creating others, has long fascinated movie fans. And it has been treated with pathos as well as humor in movies other than those discussed here, including Billy Wilder's *Sunset Boulevard* (1950) and Michel Hazanavicius's *The Artist* (2011).

Acting in the Classical Studio Era

From the early years of moviemaking, writes film scholar Robert Allen, "the movie star has been one of the defining characteristics of the American cinema."[15] Most simply, a movie star is two people: the actor and the character(s) he or she plays. In addition, the star embodies an image created by the studio to coincide with the kinds of roles associated with the actor. That the star also reflects the social and cultural history of the period when that image was created helps explain the often rapid rise and fall of stars' careers. But this description reveals at its heart a set of paradoxes, as Allen points out:

13. Donald Crafton, *The Talkies: American Cinema's Transition to Sound, 1926–1931* (New York: Scribner, 1997), p. 14.

14. In his next films, Mamoulian made other innovations in sound, including the sound flashback in *City Streets* (1931) and the lavish use of contrapuntal sound in the opening of *Love Me Tonight* (1932).

15. For a study of stars in Hollywood from which this section liberally draws, see Robert C. Allen and Douglas Gomery, *Film History: Theory and Practice* (New York: Knopf, 1985), pp. 172–189, quotation, p. 174 (reprinted as Robert C. Allen, "The Role of the Star in Film History [Joan Crawford]," in *Film Theory and Criticism: Introductory Readings*, 5th ed., ed. Leo Braudy and Marshall Cohen [New York: Oxford University Press, 1999], pp. 547–561).

The star is powerless, yet powerful; different from "ordinary" people, yet at one time was "just like us." Stars make huge salaries, yet the work for which they are handsomely paid does not appear to be work on the screen. Talent would seem to be a requisite for stardom, yet there has been no absolute correlation between acting ability and stardom. The star's private life has little if anything to do with his or her "job" of acting in movies, yet a large portion of a star's image is constructed on the basis of "private" matters: romance, marriage, tastes in fashion, and home life.[16]

British actor Dirk Bogarde drew a further distinction between film stars, calling them "people with extrovert personalities and the sparkling quality that puts the glamour, the glitter and the 'stardust' into a very tough work-a-day job." He viewed film actors as "people who without being great extrovert personalities or looking particularly glamorous . . . have been trained in the craft of acting and . . . [are] sound knowledgeable technicians."[17]

The golden age of Hollywood, roughly from the 1930s until the 1950s, was the age of the movie star. Acting in American movies then generally meant "star acting." During this period, the major studios gave basic lessons in acting, speaking, and movement; but because screen appearance was of paramount importance, they were more concerned with enhancing actors' screen images than with improving their acting.

During the golden age, the studio system and the star system went hand in hand, and the studios had almost complete control of their actors. Every six months, the studio reviewed an actor's standard seven-year **option contract**: if the actor had made progress in being assigned roles and demonstrating box-office appeal, the studio picked up the option to employ that actor for the next six months and gave him or her a raise; if not, the studio dropped the option, and the actor was out of work. The decision was the studio's, not the actor's. Furthermore, the contract did not allow the actor to move to another studio, stop work, or renegotiate for a higher salary. In addition to those unbreakable terms, the contract had restrictive clauses that gave the studio total control over the star's image and services; it required an actor "to act, sing, pose, speak or perform in such roles as the producer may designate"; it gave the studio the right to change the name of the actor at its own discretion and to control the performer's image and likeness in advertising and publicity; and it required the actor to comply with rules covering interviews and public appearances.[18]

These contracts turned the actors into the studios' chattel. To the public, perhaps the most fascinating thing about making actors into stars was the process of changing their names. Marion Morrison became John Wayne, Issur Danielovitch Demsky became Kirk Douglas, Julia Jean Mildred Frances Turner became Lana Turner, and Archibald Leach became Cary Grant. Name and image came first, and acting ability often was considered secondary to an actor's screen presence or aura, physical or facial beauty, athletic ability or performance skills, or character "type." Although many stars were also convincing actors capable of playing a variety of parts (e.g., Bette Davis, Henry Fonda, Barbara Stanwyck, Jimmy Stewart), surprisingly little serious attention was paid to screen acting. As Charles Affron observes:

An almost total absence of analytical approaches to screen acting reflects the belief that screen acting is nothing more than the beautiful projection of a filmic self, an arrangement of features and body, the disposition of superficial elements. Garbo is Garbo is Garbo is Garbo. We mortals are left clutching our wonder, and victims of that very wonder, overwhelmed by our enthusiasm and blinded by the light of the star's emanation.[19]

In her comprehensive study *The Star Machine*, Jeanine Basinger offers a list of observations of what a movie star is:

A star has exceptional looks. Outstanding talent. A distinctive voice that can easily be recognized and imitated. A set of mannerisms. Palpable sexual appeal. Energy that comes down off the screen. Glamour. Androgyny.

16. Allen and Gomery, *Film History*, p. 174.

17. Dirk Bogarde, qtd. in John Coldstream, *Dirk Bogarde: The Authorised Biography* (London: Weidenfeld & Nicolson, 2004), p. 223.

18. Tino Balio, *Grand Design: Hollywood as a Modern Business Enterprise*, 1930–1939 (New York: Scribner, 1999), p. 145.

19. Charles Affron, *Star Acting: Gish, Garbo, Davis* (New York: Dutton, 1977), p. 3. See also Roland Barthes, "The Face of Garbo," in *Film Theory and Criticism*, ed. Braudy and Cohen, pp. 536–538; Alexander Walker, *Stardom: The Hollywood Phenomenon* (New York: Stein and Day, 1970); and Leo Braudy, "Film Acting: Some Critical Problems and Proposals," *Quarterly Review of Film Studies* (February 1976): 1–18.

Glowing health and radiance. Panache. A single tiny flaw that mars their perfection, endearing them to ordinary people. Charm. The good luck to be in the right place at the right time (also known as just plain good luck). An emblematic quality that audiences believe is who they really are. The ability to make viewers "know" what they are thinking whenever the camera comes up close. An established type (by which is meant that they could believably play the same role over and over again). A level of comfort in front of the camera. And, of course, "she has something," the bottom line of which is "it's something you can't define."[20]

Today, film acting has become the subject of new interest among theorists and critics in semiology, psychology, and cultural studies who wish to study acting as an index of cultural history and an aspect of ideology.[21] This approach stresses that stars are a commodity created by the studio system through promotion, publicity, movies, criticism, and commentary. As Richard Dyer notes, "Stars are involved in making themselves into commodities; they are both labour and the thing that labour produces. They do not produce themselves alone."[22] Such analyses tend to emphasize the ways in which culture makes meaning rather than the art and expressive value of acting, the ways in which actors make meaning.

Materialistic as it was, the star system dominated the movie industry until the studio system collapsed. It was replaced by a similar industrial enterprise powered essentially by the same motivation of making profits for its investors. However, because every studio had its own system, creating different goals and images for different stars, there was no typical star. For example, when Lucille Fay LeSueur (also known early in her theater career as Billie Cassin) went to Hollywood in 1925, MGM decided that her name must be changed and altered her image to be that of an ideal American "girl." Through a national campaign conducted by a fan magazine, the public was invited to submit names. The first choice, "Joan Arden," was already being used by another actress, so Lucille LeSueur became Joan Crawford, a name

What makes a movie star?

Jeanine Basinger's list of observations on what makes a movie star could have been written about Cary Grant, for her criteria fit him perfectly. Regarded by the public, as well as critics and colleagues, as the finest romantic comedian actor of his time, the handsome actor was often cast as a glamorous, high-society figure in a series of 1930s screwball comedies, including George Cukor's *The Philadelphia Story* (1940). In this image, Grant's wide-open, handsome face and laid-back manner mask the charming wiles of a man who succeeds in remarrying a former wife, played by Katharine Hepburn. He played against some of Hollywood's most glamorous stars, including Mae West, Marlene Dietrich, Audrey Hepburn, Ingrid Bergman, Doris Day, and Grace Kelly. Long before the birth of the independent production system, Grant was unique among Hollywood actors by not signing a studio contract but rather controlling every aspect of his career himself, including the directors and actors he wanted to work with and the roles he wanted to play. Perhaps the high point of his career was working with Alfred Hitchcock on *Suspicion* (1941), *Notorious* (1946), *To Catch a Thief* (1955), and *North by Northwest* (1959), films in which he still plays a lighthearted rogue. His assets—sleek good looks, ease, lack of self-consciousness, physical grace, and natural comic sense—make him one of the great movie actors of all time; some say the greatest.

that she objected to for several years. However, her new name became synonymous with the public's idea of a movie star—indeed, one proclaimed by MGM to be a "star of the first magnitude."[23]

Crawford's career soon took off, reaching a high level of achievement in the mid-1930s when she became

20. Jeanine Basinger, *The Star Machine* (New York: Knopf, 2007), pp. 3–4.

21. See Richard Dyer, *Stars*, new ed. (London: British Film Institute, 1998); and his *Heavenly Bodies: Film Stars and Society* (New York: St. Martin's Press, 1986). See also Richard deCordova, "The Emergence of the Star System in America," *Wide Angle* 6, no. 4 (1985): 4–13; Carole Zucker, ed., *Making Visible the Invisible: An Anthology of Original Essays on Film Acting* (Metuchen, NJ: Scarecrow Press, 1990); and Christine Gledhill, *Stardom: Industry of Desire* (New York: Routledge, 1991).

22. Dyer, *Heavenly Bodies,* p. 5.

23. See Richard Oulahan, "A Well-Planned Crawford," *Life* 56 (February 21, 1964), pp. 11–12.

1

2

The movie star

Elizabeth Taylor epitomizes what we mean by the term *movie star*: talent, beauty, sex appeal, and a glamour that dazzled the world. As a child star, the product of the studio system, she appeared in such movies as *Lassie Come Home* (1943) and *National Velvet* (1944). As a teenager, she came to prominence as Angela Vickers in [1] George Stevens's *A Place in the Sun* (1951), a romantic but tragic melodrama. During her most fruitful period—the 1950s and 1960s—she starred in such movies as George Stevens's *Giant* (1956), Richard Brooks's *Cat on a Hot Tin Roof* (1958), Joseph L. Mankiewicz's *Suddenly, Last Summer* (1959), and Daniel Mann's *BUtterfield 8* (1960). Her career took a brief downward spin with Mankiewicz's *Cleopatra* (1963), one of the most lavish, expensive, and unsuccessful films of all time. A survivor, she recovered in two impressive roles: Martha [2] in Mike Nichols's *Who's Afraid of Virginia Woolf?* (1966) and Katharina in Franco Zeffirelli's *The Taming of the Shrew* (1967). In all, Elizabeth Taylor appeared in more than fifty films and was awarded three Oscars as Best Actress. Long after she quit her acting career, she remained a star, lending her name and reputation to raising hundreds of millions of dollars for AIDS research and other humanitarian causes.

identified with the "woman's film." Subsequently, in a long series of films, she played women who, whether by family background or social circumstances, triumphed over adversity and usually paid a price for independence. No matter what happened to them, her characters remained stylish and distinctive in their looks—chic, self-generated survivors. Like many other stars, Crawford became indelibly associated with the roles she played. Yet she received little serious acclaim for her acting until the mid-1940s, when she left MGM for Warner Bros. For Michael Curtiz's *Mildred Pierce* (1945), her first film there, Crawford won the Academy Award for Best Actress in a Leading Role—her only Oscar, although she received two more nominations. After her success at Warner Bros., Crawford worked for various major studios and independents, shedding her image as the stalwart, contemporary American woman. Sometimes her performances were excellent, as in Curtis Bernhardt's *Possessed* (1947), David Miller's *Sudden Fear* (1952), and, costarring with Bette Davis, Robert Aldrich's *What Ever Happened to Baby Jane?* (1962).

Davis was a star of another sort, leading a principled and spirited fight against the studio and star systems'

invasion into virtually every aspect of actors' personal and professional lives. In fact, Davis's career (from 1931 to 1989) comes as close to any as demonstrating these systems at their best and worst. In the mid-1930s, when she walked out of Warner Bros. demanding better roles, the studio successfully sued her for breach of contract. She returned to work rewarded by increased respect, a new contract, and better roles. But her career sagged after World War II, for she had reached her early forties, an age at which female actors are seldom offered good parts. Ironically, playing just such a character— an older stage actress in danger of losing roles because of her age—she triumphed in Joseph L. Mankiewicz's *All about Eve* (1950), generally regarded as her greatest performance. During her long career, Davis was nominated eleven times for the Oscar for Best Actress in a Leading Role, winning for Alfred E. Green's *Dangerous* (1935) and William Wyler's *Jezebel* (1938). Nominations for an Oscar as Best Actor in a Leading Role involve a peer-review process in which only actors vote. Davis's record of nominations is exceeded only by Meryl Streep's (fifteen nominations), Katharine Hepburn's (twelve), and Jack Nicholson's (eight).

Method Acting

During the studio years, movie acting and the star system were virtually synonymous. Although acting styles were varied, the emphasis was on the star's persona and its effect at the box office—on the product, not the process, of acting. And as production processes were regularized, so too was acting. Even so, screen acting in the 1930s and 1940s was not formulaic or unimaginative; quite the contrary. On Broadway, however, stage actors were becoming acquainted with a Russian theory that became known as method acting. Method acting did not make a major impact on Hollywood until the 1950s, but it marks a significant point in the evolution of screen acting from the studio system's reliance on "star acting" in the 1930s and 1940s to a new style.

What Americans call method acting was based on the theory and practice of Konstantin Stanislavsky, who cofounded the Moscow Art Theater in 1897 and spent his entire career there. In developing what became known as the **Stanislavsky system** of acting, he trained students to start by conducting an exhaustive inquiry into their characters' background and psychology. With an understanding of those aspects, they could then work from the inside out. In other words, they had to *be* the character before successfully *playing* the character. Whether that works on the stage or screen is another issue.

Stanislavsky's ideas influenced the Soviet silent film directors of the 1920s—Sergei Eisenstein, Aleksandr Dovzhenko, Lev Kuleshov, and Vsevolod I. Pudovkin—all of whom had learned much from D. W. Griffith's work. But they often disagreed about acting, especially about how it was influenced by actors' appearances, and by editing, which could work so expressively both for and against actors' interpretations.

Among this group, Pudovkin, whose *Film Acting* (1935) was one of the first serious books on the subject, has the most relevance to mainstream movie acting today. Although he advocates an explicitly Stanislavskian technique based on his observations of the Moscow Art Theater, he writes from the standpoint of film directors and actors working together. Because film consists of individual shots, he reasons, both directors and actors work at the mercy of the shot and must strive to make acting (out of sequence) seem natural, smooth, and flowing while maintaining expressive coherence across the shots. He recommends close collaboration between actors and directors as well as long periods devoted to preparation and rehearsal. He also advises film actors to ignore voice training because the microphone makes it unnecessary, notes that the close-up can communicate more to the audience than overt gestures can, and finds that the handling of "expressive objects" (e.g., Charlie Chaplin's cane) can convey emotions and ideas even more effectively than close-ups can.

Through his teaching and books, especially *An Actor Prepares* (1936), Stanislavsky had a lasting impact on Broadway and Hollywood acting. Actor Stella Adler taught principles of method acting to members of the experimental Group Theatre, including Elia Kazan. In 1947, Kazan, now a director, helped found the Actors Studio in New York City. In 1951, Kazan was replaced by Lee Strasberg, who alienated many theater people including Kazan, Adler, Arthur Miller, and Marlon Brando. Today the studio is guided by three alumni: Ellen Burstyn, Harvey Keitel, and Al Pacino. In 1949, Adler went her own way and founded the Stella Adler Studio of Acting, where Marlon Brando was her most famous and successful student.

These teachers loosely adapted Stanislavky's ideas. They used his principle that actors should draw on their own emotional experiences to create characters as well as his emphasis on the importance of creating an ensemble and expressing the subtext, the nuances lying beneath the lines of the script. The naturalistic style that they popularized (and called **method acting**, more popularly known as the *Method*) encourages actors to speak, move, and gesture not in a traditional stage manner but just as they would in their own lives. Thus it is an ideal technique for representing convincing human behavior on the stage and on the screen. The Method has led to a new level of realism and subtlety, influencing such actors, in addition to those already mentioned, as James Dean, Montgomery Clift, Marilyn Monroe, Morgan Freeman, Robert De Niro, Jack Nicholson, Jane Fonda, Sidney Poitier, Dustin Hoffman, Daniel Day-Lewis, and Shelley Winters, among many others.[24]

To understand method acting, you have to see it. Fortunately, there are some wonderful examples, including

---

24. See Carole Zucker, "An Interview with Lindsay Crouse," *Post Script: Essays in Film and the Humanities* 12, no. 2 (Winter 1993): 5–28. See also Foster Hirsch, *A Method to Their Madness: The History of the Actors Studio* (New York: Norton, 1984); and Steven Vineberg, *Method Actors: Three Generations of an American Acting Style* (New York: Schirmer, 1991).

Elia Kazan and method acting

Elia Kazan is notable, among many other things, for directing two of the iconic method-acting achievements: Marlon Brando as Terry Malloy in *On the Waterfront* (1954)—here [1] we see Kazan (*center*) and Brando (*right*) on location during the filming—and James Dean [2] as Cal Trask, a troubled teenager, in *East of Eden* (1955).

James Dean's three movie roles—Cal Trask in Elia Kazan's *East of Eden* (1955), Jim Stark in Nicholas Ray's *Rebel without a Cause* (1955), and Jett Rink in George Stevens's *Giant* (1956). Marlon Brando gave equally legendary performances as Stanley Kowalski in Elia Kazan's *A Streetcar Named Desire* (1951), reprising the stage role that made him famous, and as Terry Malloy in Kazan's *On the Waterfront* (1954). Other notable performances, out of many, include those by Paul Newman as Eddie Felson in Robert Rossen's *The Hustler* (1961), Shelley Winters as Charlotte Haze Humbert in Stanley Kubrick's *Lolita* (1962), and Faye Dunaway as Evelyn Cross Mulwray in Roman Polanski's *Chinatown* (1974). Each of these performances exhibits the major characteristics of method acting: intense concentration and internalization (sometimes mistaken for discomfort) on the actor's part; low-key, almost laid-back delivery of lines (sometimes described as mumbling); and an edginess (sometimes highly neurotic) that suggests dissatisfaction, unhappiness, and alienation. In directing *The Misfits* (1961), with a script by playwright Arthur Miller, John Huston (not a method director) must have been bewildered by the range of acting talent in front of his camera: Clark Gable, a traditional Hollywood star in any sense of the word, who always could be counted on to deliver a reliable performance; Thelma Ritter, an equally seasoned supporting player who invariably played the role of a wisecracking sidekick; and several method actors (Eli Wallach, Montgomery Clift, and Marilyn Monroe), whose performances, by contrast with the rest of the cast, seem out of touch and clumsy. Absent here is the ensemble method acting obvious in Elia Kazan's movies.

No matter what school or style of acting is involved, it is clear that memorable acting results from hard work, skill, imagination, and discipline.

Screen Acting Today

From the earliest years, the development of movie acting has relied on synthesizing various approaches, including those already discussed. Contemporary actors employ a range of physically or psychologically based approaches. Some action stars, like Arnold Schwarzenegger or Jamie Foxx, rely entirely on physical effect; others, like Bruce Willis, rely both on physical prowess and a distinct persona that has evolved from his early wise-guy days to a more world-weary one. Directors also take different approaches toward actors. Robert Altman, for example, who was particularly good at capturing the mood of an ensemble of actors within a narrative, encouraged improvisation and the exploration of individual styles. Joel Coen, in contrast, tends to regard acting as a critical component of the highly stylized mise-en-scène within the often cartoonlike movies that he creates with his brother, Ethan.

In Altman's *The Player* (1992), Tim Robbins plays Griffin Mill, a Hollywood producer, at once emotively and satirically. He uses his big, open face and charming manner to draw us into Mill's professional and existential crises, then turns edgy enough to distance us as Mill becomes a murderer and ruthless careerist. In Altman's *Kansas City* (1996), Jennifer Jason Leigh delivers

Contemporary star power

Unlike some actors who become movie stars almost overnight, Robert Downey Jr. began appearing in avant-garde movies directed by his father at the age of five. Working in the independent era, he was able to choose a range of roles that revealed his extraordinary talent. Downey's breakthrough as a major performer came with Richard Attenborough's *Chaplin* (1992), for which he received an Oscar nomination as Best Actor. He continued to demonstrate his remarkable versatility in serious roles in Robert Altman's *Short Cuts* (1993), Oliver Stone's *Natural Born Killers* (1994), Richard Loncraine's *Richard III* (1995), and Michael Hoffman's *Restoration* (1995). Between 1996 and 2001, his acting career faltered because of his drug abuse. Except for his role in Curtis Hanson's *Wonder Boys* (2000), he was cast in relatively unimportant projects. He returned to serious roles, deserving serious attention, in such movies as George Clooney's *Good Night, and Good Luck* (2005), Dito Montiel's *A Guide to Recognizing Your Saints* (2006), Steven Shainberg's *Fur: An Imaginary Portrait of Diane Arbus* (2006), and David Fincher's *Zodiac* (2007). Downey played completely different characters in two successful, ongoing franchises: Tony Stark in the Iron Man and The Avengers series, and Sherlock Holmes in the series of that name. He also worked in two comedies: *Chef* (2014; director Jon Favreau) and *The Judge* (2014; director David Dobkin). In this image, we see Downey as the brilliant, cool, arrogant, and intense Tony Stark, aka Iron Man.

an emotional hurricane of a performance as the cheap, brassy, tough Blondie O'Hara, a Jean Harlow wannabe. Her scowl, furrowed brow, rotten teeth under big red lips, and screeching-cat voice leave no room for the kind of gently ironic distance that Robbins creates in *The Player*.

In Coen's *The Hudsucker Proxy* (1994), however, both Robbins and Leigh tailor their performances to fit the madcap mood and mannered decor of an Art Deco screwball comedy. Indeed, part of the movie's appeal lies in watching an ensemble of actors working in this style. Channeling Cary Grant and Rosalind Russell in Howard Hawks's *His Girl Friday* (1940) and Spencer Tracy and Katharine Hepburn in Walter Lang's *Desk Set* (1957), Robbins plays Norville Barnes, a goofy mailroom clerk

who becomes company president, and Leigh plays Amy Archer, a hard-boiled, wisecracking newspaper reporter. Robbins and Leigh's zany comic interaction fits perfectly in Coen's jigsaw puzzle, which lovingly pays tribute to an era when movie style often transcended substance.

Today, actors struggle to get parts and to create convincing performances, and like their earlier counterparts, seldom have the chance to prove themselves across a range of roles. Once **typecast**—chosen for particular kinds of roles because of their looks or "type" rather than for their acting talent or experience—they continue to be awarded such parts as long they bring in good box-office receipts. No star system exists to sustain careers and images, but now, as in earlier periods of movie history, some individuals use films to promote themselves. Think of the music stars, sports stars, or other celebrities who sometimes appear in a movie or two but leave no mark on the history of film acting.

The transition from studio production to independent production has markedly affected the livelihood of actors and the art of acting. The shape of the average career has fundamentally changed. Fewer major movies appear each year, so actors supplement film work with appearances on television shows, in advertisements, and in theater. (Salaries and contractual benefits, such as residual payments for television reruns, provide excellent financial security.) Moreover, actors are finding fewer quality roles because today's average movies are comedies that target the under-thirty audience (and such comedies rely on physical and often scatological humor rather than verbal wit).

Some extremely versatile actors—Chris Cooper, Russell Crowe, Benicio Del Toro, Johnny Depp, Leonardo DiCaprio, Samuel L. Jackson, Nicole Kidman, John Malkovich, Julianne Moore, Kevin Spacey, and Hilary Swank, to name a few—have, after two or three successful films, become stars quickly. The greater their drawing power at the box office, the greater the urgency to promote them to top rank and cast them in more films. As independent agents, however, they can contract for one film at a time and thus hold out for good roles rather than having to make a specific number of films for a given studio. In addition, these newcomers can negotiate a new salary for each film, and they routinely make more money from a single picture than some of the greatest stars of classical Hollywood made in their entire careers. Furthermore, they usually work under their own names. But because they maintain their status by audience

1

2

Stardom: then and now

Bette Davis, an actress who became a legend for playing strong-willed and often neurotic female characters, was in top form as Leslie Crosbie in *The Letter* (1940). In the movie's electric opening scene, she pumps five bullets into her lover [1], then pleads self-defense in court. It represents another successful collaboration between Davis and director William Wyler, who she also worked with on *Jezebel* (1938) and *The Little Foxes* (1941). Nicole Kidman, like Davis, is famous for her professionalism and versatility. Unlike Davis, however, she has almost totally controlled her career. Thus she has been far more adventurous in the roles she chooses to play, and the result is a filmography of considerable depth and range. She is well known for her willingness to take risks in highly individual movies, such as Robert Benton's *The Human Stain* (2003), Noah Baumbach's *Margot at the Wedding* (2007), and Steven Shainberg's *Fur: An Imaginary Portrait of Diane Arbus* (2006; a fictional account of the famous photographer's life). At a turning point in her career—she was forty-three, an age when most actresses have trouble securing good roles—she costarred with Aaron Eckhart in John Cameron Mitchell's *Rabbit Hole* (2010), an important drama about an upper-middle-class suburban couple trying to deal with the death of their two-year-old son in a car accident. The movie avoids the tragedy itself and focuses on the couple's very different attempts to put their marriage back together. In [2], Kidman's distinctive "blank face" allows the audience to "write" whatever it wants on her conflicting day-to-day responses to her personal grief and to a marriage going somewhat recklessly to pieces. She wants to move on, while her husband wants to keep everything that reminds him of the boy. For this moving performance, she received an Oscar nomination as Best Actress.

reaction and not a studio's publicity office, such actors often face highly unpredictable futures.

Let's look more closely at the careers and earnings of two of the most important and popular movie stars in history: Bette Davis, who was at the top during the studio era, and Nicole Kidman, who is at the top today. Although they are both well regarded for their professional approach to performances in a range of film genres—melodrama, comedy, historical and period films, and romantic dramas—their careers exhibit significant differences that result from the different production systems in which each star worked (see Chapter 11, "Filmmaking Technologies and Production Systems").

Bette Davis (1908–1989), who began her movie career on Broadway, went to Hollywood at the age of twenty-two. Over a career that spanned fifty-two years, she appeared in eighty-nine movies, fifty-nine of them under contract to Warner Bros. Her breakthrough role was in John Cromwell's *Of Human Bondage* (1934); she won

her first Oscar as Best Actress in a Leading Role in 1936 and again in 1939, when she reached the peak of her career in William Wyler's *Jezebel* (1938). She sued Warner Bros. in an attempt to get better roles in better pictures (she was forced, by contract, to make a lot of mediocre films) but lost her case. (In essence, Davis had to fight for what actors of Kidman's generation take for granted: the right to pick the roles they want to play.) However, Davis did get better roles (and unwisely rejected some juicy ones, including *Mildred Pierce* [1945] and *The African Queen* [1951]). She was so well paid in the 1940s that she was known around Hollywood as the fourth Warner brother. The years between 1939 and 1945 were marked by major successes—Edmund Goulding's *Dark Victory* (1939), Michael Curtiz's *The Private Lives of Elizabeth and Essex* (1939), William Wyler's *The Letter* (1940) and *The Little Foxes* (1941), Irving Rapper's *Now, Voyager* (1942) and *The Corn Is Green* (1945)—but by 1950, her studio career was over. As one of the first freelancers in the independent system, she revived her career with her greatest performance in Joseph L. Mankiewicz's *All about Eve* (1950). However, she was then forty-one, the "barrier" year that usually relegates women actors to character parts. She had her share of them, including Robert Aldrich's *What Ever Happened to Baby Jane?* (1962). Her career went downhill, although there were still a few good movies and loyal fans; her penultimate role was a moving performance in Lindsay Anderson's *The Whales of August* (1987). A demanding perfectionist to the end, she walked off the set of her final film just before she died. Bette Davis, a name synonymous with Hollywood stardom, ranked second (after Katharine Hepburn) on the American Film Institute's poll of the greatest female actors.

Bette Davis is an icon of movies past, and Nicole Kidman is a screen legend for today. Unconstrained by a studio contract, she is free to choose her roles. She has worked with a variety of directors, including Gus Van Sant, Jane Campion, Stanley Kubrick, Baz Luhrmann, and Stephen Daldry. Where Davis had some say over her directors (all of whom were studio employees), Kidman has worked with outsiders, insiders, kings of the megaplexes, and avant-garde experimenters. Kidman (b. 1967) began her movie career in Australia at the age of fifteen and has since made 38 films (as of 2009), all independently produced. Her breakthrough movie was Tony Scott's *Days of Thunder* (1990), after which her career took off in such films as Gus Van Sant's *To Die For* and Joel Schumacher's *Batman Forever* (1995), Jane Campion's *The Portrait of a Lady* (1996), Stanley Kubrick's *Eyes Wide Shut* (1999), Baz Luhrmann's *Moulin Rouge!* (2001), and Stephen Daldry's *The Hours* (2002), for which she won the Oscar for Best Actress in a Leading Role for her portrayal of Virginia Woolf. Another turning point came in 2003, when she made three different movies with three very different directors: Lars von Trier's *Dogville*, Robert Benton's *The Human Stain*, and Anthony Minghella's *Cold Mountain*. Kidman is willing to tackle serious melodrama (Sydney Pollack's *The Interpreter*, 2005), light comedy (Nora Ephron's *Bewitched*, 2005), edgy, experimental concepts (Steven Shainberg's *Fur: An Imaginary Portrait of Diane Arbus*, 2006), and comic drama (Noah Baumbach's *Margot at the Wedding*, 2007) as well as a serious domestic drama (*Rabbit Hole*, 2007; director John Cameron Mitchell), a psychological thriller (*Stoker*, 2013; director Chan-wook Park), and a romantic biopic (*Grace of Monaco*, 2014; director Olivier Dahan). When Bette Davis turned forty-one, her career (despite her success that year with *All about Eve*) began its downward spiral. Ironically, Kidman, now forty-seven, remains at the peak of her career and continues to get roles worthy of her experience and talent.

Let's consider their earning power. In her career, we estimate that Bette Davis earned around $6 million, which in today's money is about $10 million.[25] Until 1949, her salary was set by contract; her highest studio earnings were $208,000 for the years 1941–43. Her highest poststudio earnings came with her last movie, for which she was paid $250,000. Kidman made $100,000 on her first movie and today receives $17 million per picture. During the first twenty-five years of her ongoing movie career, Kidman has earned $230 million. That's twenty-three times what Davis earned over an entire fifty-two-year career! Davis worked under a Warner Bros. contract, and the studio kept the lion's share of profits from her films. Kidman is free to negotiate the terms of her salary and her share of the profits for her movies, terms that are determined by a far more complicated equation than a studio contract. These estimates do not include fees for television acting, advertising work, DVD sales, and so on. Stars of Davis's era made far less money from advertisements than, say, Kidman, who is the face in Chanel's print and television campaigns, for which she earns millions each year. The most revealing indicator separating the "old" from the "new" Hollywood, as far as actors are concerned, is clearly the freedom to choose roles and negotiate earnings.

Earnings are keyed to an actor's popularity with audiences. There are two basic ways of measuring this popularity: box-office receipts and popularity polls. Among the popularity polls, the Harris Poll, conducted by a leading market-research company, is probably as reliable as any poll of America's favorite movie stars. The 2013 Harris Poll results[26] are as follows:

---

25. The figures cited here are based, in part, on information provided by newspaper and magazine articles and by the online database pro.imdb.com and do not include fees for television acting, advertising work, DVD sales, etc.

26. www.harrisinteractive.com/NewsRoom/HarrisPolls/tabid/447/ctl/ReadCustom%20Default/mid/1508/ArticleId/1141/Default.aspx.

1. Denzel Washington
2. Clint Eastwood
3. Tom Hanks
4. Johnny Depp
5. Brad Pitt
6. John Wayne
7. George Clooney
8. Harrison Ford
9. Meryl Streep
10. Matt Damon

1

2

Two problems are obvious here. First, even though women constitute the bulk of the movie audience, this list includes only one woman. And considering that John Wayne died in 1979, his current popularity is amazing.

Indeed, John Wayne has been on Harris's top-ten list every year since he died. An actor of many parts, he is as durable a Hollywood legend as has ever existed. Wayne is a far better actor than many people give him credit for. He was indelibly linked to the Western and, in private life, to right-wing politics. On-screen, he represented a kind of American male virtue that many people admire. Wayne is an acting icon who has a solid place in American cultural ideology.[27] The people who were polled here neglected to vote for many fine and popular actors, but the results represent the unpredictability of Hollywood fame. When an actor who made his last movie—Don Siegel's excellent *The Shootist*—in 1974 gets sixth place today, that's stardom!

In another poll, the Vulture entertainment blog released its 2013 ranking of "the most valuable" stars, those mostly likely to positively affect a movie's gross.[28] Here are the top ten stars on its 2013 list:

A durable Hollywood legend

In a career spanning forty-six years and 180 movies, John Wayne starred in war movies, romantic comedies, and historical epics, but he is best known for his roles as the hero in great Westerns, particularly those directed by John Ford and Howard Hawks. His first starring role, at age twenty-three, was as a winsome young scout in Raoul Walsh's *The Big Trail* (1930) [1], a spectacular epic of a wagon train going west. Wayne's last film, at sixty-seven, was Don Siegel's *The Shootist* (1976). In it he plays an aging gunslinger ("shootist"), dying of cancer, out to settle some old scores [2]. Wayne himself died of cancer three years after completing the film.

1. Robert Downey Jr.
2. Leonardo DiCaprio
3. Jennifer Lawrence
4. Sandra Bullock
5. Brad Pitt
6. Will Smith
7. Christian Bale
8. Denzel Washington
9. Tom Hanks
10. Johnny Depp

27. See Garry Willis, *John Wayne's America: The Politics of Celebrity* (New York: Simon & Schuster, 1997).

28. www.vulture.com/2013/10/most-valuable-movie-stars.html3/all/vulture-rankings.

An icon of the new Hollywood
Working wholly within today's independent system of movie production, an actor like Jeff Bridges does not have the security of a
studio contract or the opportunity of developing and perpetuating a
legendary character, such as John Wayne did. Nonetheless, Bridges
has earned universal respect as one of Hollywood's most talented,
resilient actors. His characters have become legendary: Ernie in John
Huston's *Fat City* (1972), Nick Kegan in William Richert's *Winter Kills*
(1979), [1] Starman/Scott Hayden in John Carpenter's *Starman* (1984),
Jeffrey "The Dude" Lebowski in Joel Coen's *The Big Lebowski* (1998),
and Obadiah Stone in Jon Favreau's *Iron Man* (2008). [2] In Joel and
Ethan Coen's *True Grit* (2010), he played a character first developed
by John Wayne in the 1969 film of the same name. To date, Bridges
has made sixty-five films, earned six Oscar nominations (three for
supporting and three for leading roles), and won Best Actor as Bad
Blake in Scott Cooper's *Crazy Heart* (2009).

An interesting list, to be sure, and you'll find these same
names on other lists, if not in the same order. You'll notice that except for Tom Hanks, it's a younger group that
includes two women. And while Denzel Washington is
America's most popular actor, he's eighth on the list of
stars likely to bring in the most money at the box office.

Technology and Acting

As discussed in Chapter 6, "Cinematography," for every advance in the world of special effects, the narrative
and the acting that propels it lose some of their importance. Movies such as Stanley Kubrick's *2001: A Space
Odyssey* (1968) and Steven Spielberg's *E.T. the Extra–
Terrestrial* (1982) made us familiar, even comfortable,
with nonhuman creatures that had human voices and
characteristics; John Lasseter, Ash Brannon, and Lee
Unkrich's *Toy Story 2* (1999), with its shiny, computer-
generated graphics, took this process another step
forward.

Although digital technology is now affecting all aspects of filmmaking, we don't have to worry about it
replacing actors entirely. Audiences say they choose
movies that include their favorite actors. But alongside
real actors, CGI can create convincing characters such
as the avatars digitally created to interact with the Na'vi,
the blue-skinned humanoids in James Cameron's *Avatar* (2009) and its sequels. Its mix of real and computer-
generated actors did not stop *Avatar* from becoming the
highest-grossing movie of all time. We moviegoers accept digital characters who do not represent recognizable human beings and enjoy them for the imaginative
creatures that they are. The same applies to computer-
generated characters in Peter Jackson's Lord of the Rings
series, although audiences have objected to such characters in other movies along the way. Whatever developments take place when creating "actors" through
technology, one thing seems clear: CGI characters are
perfectly at home in movies where fantasy is more important than reality, as in Matt Reeves's *Dawn of the
Planet of the Apes* (2014), where actors are convincingly
transformed into apes.

Let's also note the distinction between whole characters created entirely by digital technology and real actors
transformed by digital makeup (see "Makeup and hairstyling" in Chapter 5). Director David Fincher used
both procedures when faced with the challenge of casting actors to play the real-life, identical Winkelvoss
twins in *The Social Network* (2010). Since Aaron Sorkin's screenplay is a fictional account of a true incident,
it would have been acceptable to alter the story and cast
actors as fraternal rather than identical twins. Instead,
Fincher cast Armie Hammer and Josh Pence, respectively, in the roles of the identical Winklevoss twins,
Cameron and Tyler. Throughout their scenes, Hammer
acted alongside Pence, and through the postproduction

Movie technology produces identical twins

It's not a tabloid headline but a fact. With the help of an ingenious use of technology, two different actors appear on-screen as identical twins in *The Social Network*. (You can study the process used to achieve this effect by watching *The Lot* on Disc 2 of "The Supplements," included in the DVD release of the movie.)

use of motion-capture technology and digital grafting of Hammer's face onto Pence's, they appear on the screen as identical twins, as you can see in the image above (*left to right*: Hammer as Cameron, Pence as Tyler). Using two different actors in these roles allows the actors to develop characters with different personalities; using digital grafting ensures the facial similarity necessary for depicting identical twins. While the result is totally convincing in this specific situation, there aren't many movies about identical twins.

Computer-generated characters might have the same fate as some of the other innovations that Hollywood has periodically employed to keep the world on edge, such as the short-lived Sensurround, which relied on a sound track to trigger waves of high-decibel sound in the movie theater that made viewers feel "tremors" during Mark Robson's *Earthquake* (1974); or the even shorter-lived Odorama process, involving scratch-and-sniff cards, for John Waters's *Polyester* (1981). Indeed, the use of computer technology to replace actors is one side effect of our current fascination with virtual reality. Although the evolving film technology may enable filmmakers to realize their most fantastic visions, we should

remember, as film theorist André Bazin has so persuasively argued, that such developments may extend and enrich the illusions that the movies create at the expense of the film artists themselves, including directors, designers, cinematographers, editors, *and* actors.[29]

Casting Actors

Casting is the process of choosing and hiring actors for both leading and supporting roles. In the studio system of Hollywood's golden years, casting was done in several ways, but the overall process was supervised by a central casting office.[30] Often a director, producer, writer, or studio head already had his or her own idea of an actor for a particular role. That choice could be solely based on the actors' looks, screen presence, or overall charisma. Actors were under contract (typically required to appear in seven films over five years), and studio heads, mindful of this, often based casting decisions on availability rather than suitability for the role. The "bad" movies of those years are full of such mechanical casting decisions. Studios also announced the availability of a role with

29. André Bazin, "The Myth of Total Cinema," in *What Is Cinema?* trans. Hugh Gray, 2 vols. (Berkeley: University of California Press, 1967–71), I, pp. 17–22.

30. A comprehensive, insightful look into the casting process can be seen in the documentary *Casting By* (2012; director Tom Donahue).

an "open call" that could produce crowds of applicants, many of whom were dismissed after cursory consideration. Between 1930 and 1950, hundreds of movies were produced each year, so thousands of would-be actors were living in Hollywood, hoping for the big break that would make them a movie star. Unknown actors were often given **screen tests** (filmed auditions) to see how they looked under studio lighting and how they sounded in recordings. Predatory and unscrupulous studio heads, producers, and directors also used the "casting couch" to determine which actors (both male and female) were willing to trade sex for work.

Today, casting has moved into the front office and become more professional. Independent casting directors (CDs) work under contract to independent producers or directors on a film-by-film basis. For example, Juliet Taylor, who has worked with a long list of major directors, has cast more than thirty of Woody Allen's films. The CD typically scouts talent wherever actors are working, whether it's movies, theater, or commercials, and maintains regular contact with a variety of actors. They are represented by their own professional association, the Casting Society of America (CSA), and will soon be eligible for Oscar nominations and awards.

Actors learn about casting through direct contact by CDs, producers, directors, or screenwriters, as well as through trade papers such as *Variety*, *The Hollywood Reporter*, or *Back Stage*. After initial interviews, they may be asked to read for parts, either alone or with other actors, or to take screen tests. If they are chosen for the part, negotiations in most cases are handled by their agents. But if they belong to one of the actors' unions—the Screen Actors Guild (SAG) or the American Federation of Television and Radio Artists (AFTRA)—the conditions of their participation are governed by union contract.

Factors Involved in Casting

Although casting takes many factors into account, in theory the most important is how the prospective actors' strengths and weaknesses relate to the roles they are being considered for. In reality, casting—like every other aspect of movie production—depends heavily on the movie's budget and expected revenues. An actor's popularity in one film often leads to casting in other films. As we've seen, the polls that rate actors are based on very different criteria. Still, the key factor in casting is who brings in the most money, which after all other considerations is what the movie business is all about. Just as Hollywood traditionally has repeatedly made movies in popular genres (such as action films or romantic comedies), so too has the industry repeatedly cast the same popular actors in order to sell tickets. A director may think that Robert Downey Jr. is the right person for the lead in his new film, but if the producer does not have the $50 million that Downey currently makes per film, some further thinking is needed. Yet valuable actors like Downey frequently have waived all or part of their salaries because they believe in a particular film project. In such cases, an actor might agree to accept a percentage of the profits should the movie be successful. Other general factors considered in casting include the actors' reputation and popularity; prior experience on screen or stage; chemistry with other actors, particularly if ensemble acting scenes are part of the script; results of a screen test or reading, often required for newcomers or those about whom the director and others are uncertain; and, equally important, the actor's reputation for professionalism, reliability, ability to withstand the physical challenges of filming certain productions, and personal behavior on the set.

A good CD must have a strong artistic sense of which actors are right for the roles in question, a comprehensive knowledge of all the acting talent available at a particular time for a particular movie, a memory capable of remembering an actor's achievements on-screen, and the ability to avoid playing favorites and keep the process as professional as possible. He or she must be able to coordinate a liaison between directors, producers, writers, and actors in reaching casting decisions while working with everyone from nervous newcomers to the egomaniacs among acting royalty. Although the CD can make or break an actor's career, the final decision rests with the director and/or producer. Once that decision has been made, the CD must handle the deals that determine the terms of the contract. The role and the actor's suitability for it are what count, not factors such as gender, race, ethnicity, or age, which complicated casting in earlier years. Happily, Hollywood has been able to shed a great many customs of casting that contradicted social reality. Gone are practices such as casting actors who are not of a certain race or ethnicity to portray that race or ethnicity and discriminating against older actors, especially women. Today the pool of available actors is as diverse and rich as the population itself.

Just as with African American actors, it is now possible to cast Hispanic, Latino, or Asian actors to play ethnic characters. And casting directors have large pools of talent to choose from. Across the span of film history, Hispanic and Latino actors (both living and dead) appearing primarily in American movies include, among others, Jessica Alba, Antonio Banderas, Javier Bardem, Adriana Barraza, Benjamin Bratt, Aimee Garcia, Gael García Bernal, Demian Bichir, Alexis Bledel, Sônia Braga, Mark Consuelos, Penelope Cruz, Rosario Dawson, Dolores del Rio, Benicio Del Toro, Cameron Diaz, Hector Elizondo, Gloria Estafan, Eric Estrada, José Ferrer, Andy Garcia, Luis Guzmán, Selma Hayek, Rita Hayworth, Raul Julia, Katy Jurado, Susan Kohner, Fernando Lamas, John Leguizamo, Eva Longoria, George Lopez, Jennifer Lopez, Mario Lopez, Eva Mendes, Carmen Miranda, Alfred Molino, Ricardo Montalban, Maria Montez, Catalina Sandino Moreno, Rita Moreno, Ramon Novarro, Edward James Olmos, Rosie Perez, Joaquin Phoenix, Freddie Prinze Jr., Anthony Quinn, Michelle Rodriguez, Cesar Romero, Zoe Saldana, Charlie Sheen, Martin Sheen, Jimmy Smits, Oscar Torre, Lupe Velez, and Sophie Vergara.

Hispanic and Latino directors include some of the most visionary and creative film artists of our time: Alfonso Cuarón (*Harry Potter and the Prisoner of Azkaban*, 2001; *Children of Men*, 2006; and *Gravity*, 2013); Alejandro González Iñárritu (*Amores perros*, 2000; and *Babel*, 2006, which was nominated for Best Picture and Best Director Oscars); Guillermo del Toro (*Pan's Labyrinth*, 2006, for which he was nominated for the Best Original Screenplay Oscar; and three Hobbit movies, 2012-13-14); Robert Rodriguez (*Sin City*, 2005, and *Sin City: A Dame to Kill For*, 2014, both codirected with Frank Miller; and *Spy Kids: All the Time in the World*, 2011). Pedro Almodóvar has directed nearly twenty feature films, including *Talk to Her* (2002), *Volver* (2006), *The Skin I Live In* (2011), and won the Best Foreign Language Film Oscar for *All about My Mother* (1999). Cuarón, Iñárritu, and Del Toro were born in Mexico; Rodriguez in Texas; and Almodóvar in Spain. Hispanic and Latino film artists have won twenty-one Oscars in a variety of categories.

Asian and Southeast Asian actors familiar to American audiences include Jackie Chan, Michael Paul Chan, Joan Chen, John Cho, Margaret Cho, Kenneth Choi, Sessue Hayakawa, Ken Jeong, Nancy Kwan, James Hong, Shin Koyamada, Rex Lee, Gong Li, Jet Li, Lucy Liu, Daniel Dae Kim, Keye Luke, Toshirô Mifune, Haing S. Ngor, Sandra Oh, Dev Patel, Kal Penn, Lou Diamond Phillips, Frieda Pinto, Miyoshi Umeki, Ken Watanabe, Anna May

Wong, BD Wong, Joan Wong, and Yun-Fat Chow. Asian directors working in the American film industry include Gregg Araki, Cary Fukanaga, So-yong Kim, Ang Lee, Justin Lin, Mira Nair, M. Night Shyamalan, and Wayne Wang. In the Oscars competition, Asians have won thirty-eight Oscars in a variety of categories.

Aspects of Performance

Types of Roles

Actors may play major roles, minor roles, character roles, cameo roles, and walk-ons. In addition, roles may be written specifically for bit players, extras, stuntpersons, and even animal performers. Actors who play **major roles** (also called *main, featured,* or *leading roles*) become principal agents in helping to move the plot forward. Whether stars or newcomers, they appear in many scenes and ordinarily, but not always, receive screen credit above the title.

In the Hollywood studio system, major roles were traditionally played by stars such as John Wayne, whose studios counted on them to draw audiences regardless of the parts they played. Their steadfastness was often more important than their versatility as actors, although Wayne surprises us more often than we may admit. One strength of the studio system was its grooming of professionals in all its creative departments, including actors who ranged from leads such as Henry Fonda and Katharine Hepburn to character actors such as Andy Devine and Thelma Ritter. Devine is best remembered as, respectively, the wisecracking commentator on "Jeff's" (James Stewart) actions in Alfred Hitchcock's *Rear Window* (1954) and the Ringo Kid's (John Wayne) loyal friend in John Ford's *Stagecoach* (1939). Indeed, one of the joys of looking at movies from this period comes from those character actors whose faces, if not names, we always recognize: Mary Boland, Walter Brennan, Harry Carey Jr., Ray Collins, Laura Hope Crews, Gladys George, Marjorie Main, Butterfly McQueen, Una O'Connor, Franklin Pangborn, Erskine Sanford, and Ernest Thesiger, to name a distinctive few out of hundreds.

Stars may be so valuable to productions that they have **stand-ins**, actors who look reasonably like them in height, weight, coloring, and so on and who substitute for them during the tedious process of preparing setups or taking light readings. Because actors in major roles are ordinarily not hired for their physical or athletic

Character actors

Although Franklin Pangborn was never a household name, his face was instantly recognizable in the more than 200 movies he made over a career that spanned four decades. With his intimidating voice and fastidious manners, he was best known for playing suspicious hotel clerks, imperious department-store floorwalkers, and sour-puss restaurant managers. Here he's the threatening bank examiner J. Pinkerton Snoopington in the W. C. Fields classic *The Bank Dick* (1940; director Edward F. Cline).

The importance of minor roles

In John Huston's *The Maltese Falcon* (1941), Humphrey Bogart stars as the hard-boiled private eye Sam Spade. Gladys George has a small part as Iva Archer, Spade's former lover and the widow of his business partner, Miles Archer (Jerome Cowan). In this scene, George delivers a strongly emotional performance, against which Bogart displays a relative lack of feeling that fills us in on relations between the characters. Stars' performances often depend on the solid and even exceptional work of their fellow actors. The unusually fine supporting cast in this movie includes Hollywood greats Mary Astor, Peter Lorre, and Sydney Greenstreet, who received an Oscar nomination for Best Actor in a Supporting Role.

prowess, **stuntpersons** double for them in scenes requiring special skills or involving hazardous actions, such as crashing cars, jumping from high places, swimming, and riding (or falling off) horses. Through special effects, however, filmmakers may now augment actors' physical exertions so that they appear to do their own stunts, as in Andy and Larry Wachowski's *The Matrix* (1999) and McG's *Charlie's Angels* (2000). In effect, the computer becomes the stunt double. Nonetheless, ten stunt boxers were cast for Clint Eastwood's *Million Dollar Baby* (2004), indicating, at least, that some activities cannot be faked on the screen, particularly activities that could damage an actor's looks or cause other serious injuries.

Actors who play **minor roles** (or *supporting roles*) rank second in the hierarchy. They also help move the plot forward (and thus may be as important as actors in major roles), but they generally do not appear in as many scenes as the featured players. **Bit players** hold small speaking parts, and **extras** usually appear in nonspeaking or crowd roles and receive no screen credit. **Cameos** are small but significant roles often taken by famous actors, as in Robert Altman's Hollywood satire *The Player* (1992), which features appearances by sixty-five well-known actors and personalities. **Walk-ons** are even

smaller roles, reserved for highly recognizable actors or personalities. As a favor to his friend Orson Welles, with whom he'd worked several times before, Joseph Cotten played such a role in Welles's *Touch of Evil* (1958), where he had a few words of dialogue and literally walked on and off the set.

Animal actors, too, play major, minor, cameo, and walk-on roles. For many years, Hollywood made pictures built on the appeal of such animals as the dogs Lassie, Rin Tin Tin, Asta, and Benji; the cat Rhubarb; the parakeets Bill and Coo; the chimp Cheeta; the mule Francis; the lion Elsa; the dolphin Flipper; and the killer whale Willy. Most of these animals were specially trained to work in front of the camera, and many were sufficiently valuable that they, like other stars, had stand-ins for setups and stunt doubles for hazardous work. Working with animal performers often proves more complicated than working with human actors. For example, six Jack Russell terriers, including three puppies, played the title character in Jay Russell's *My Dog Skip* (2000), a tribute to that indomitable breed.

Preparing for Roles

In creating characters, screen actors begin by synthesizing basic sources, including the script, their own experiences and observations, and the influences of other actors. They also shape their understanding of a role by working closely with their director. This collaboration can be mutually agreeable and highly productive, or it can involve constant, even tempestuous arguments that may or may not produce what either artist wants. Ideally, both director and actor should understand each other's concept of the role and, where differences exist, try to agree on an approach that is acceptable to both. Director Sidney Lumet, known for his keen understanding of how actors work, recognizes that acting is a very personal thing. He writes:

> The *talent* of acting is one in which the actor's thoughts and feelings are instantly communicated to the audience. In other words, the "instrument" that the actor is using is himself. It is *his* feelings, *his* physiognomy, *his* sexuality, *his* tears, *his* laughter, *his* anger, *his* romanticism, *his* tenderness, *his* viciousness, that are up there on the screen for all to see.[31]

He emphasizes that the difference between the actor who merely duplicates a life that he or she has observed and the actor who *creates* something unique on the screen depends on how much the actor is able to reveal of himself.

Different roles have different demands, and all actors have their own approaches, whether they get inside their characters, get inside themselves, or do further research. Bette Davis, whose roles were often assigned to her by studios, said, "It depends entirely on what the assignment happens to be. . . . [But] I have never played a part which I did not feel was a person very different from myself."[32] Jack Lemmon, a method actor who generally chose his own roles, explained, "It's like laying bricks. You start at the bottom and work up; actually I guess you start in the middle and work to the outside."[33]

Building a character "brick by brick" is an approach also used by Harvey Keitel and John Malkovich, who might have varied this approach slightly when he played himself in Spike Jonze's *Being John Malkovich* (1999). Liv Ullmann and Jack Nicholson believe that the actor draws on the subconscious mind. Ullmann says, "Emotionally, I don't prepare. I think about what I would like to show, but I don't prepare, because I feel that most of the emotions I have to show I know about. By drawing on real experience, I can show them."[34] In describing his work with director Roman Polanski on *Chinatown* (1974), Nicholson says that the director "pushes us farther than we are conscious of being able to go; he forces us down into the subconscious—in order to see if there's something better there."[35] Jodie Foster works from instinct, doing what she feels is right for the character.[36] To create The Tramp, Charlie Chaplin started with the character's costume: "I had no idea of the character. But the moment I was dressed, the clothes and the make-up made me feel the person he was."[37] Alec Guinness said that he was never happy with his preparation until he knew how the character walked; Laurence Olivier believed that he would not be any good as a character unless he "loved" him[38]; and Morgan Freeman says that some of his preparation depends on the clothes he is to wear.[39]

If you are familiar with Alec Guinness only through his role as Obi-Wan Kenobi in the Star Wars films, looking at a range of his movies will provide you with a master class in the art and craft of acting. A short list would include *Kind Hearts and Coronets* (1949), *The Bridge on the River Kwai* (1957), *Our Man in Havana*

31. Sidney Lumet, *Making Movies* (New York: Knopf, 1995), pp. 59–60.

32. Bette Davis, "The Actress Plays Her Part," in *Playing to the Camera: Film Actors Discuss Their Craft*, ed. Bert Cardullo, Harry Geduld, Ronald Gottesman, and Leigh Woods (New Haven, CT: Yale University Press, 1998), pp. 177–185, quotation on p. 179.

33. Jack Lemmon, "Conversation with the Actor," ibid., pp. 267–275, quotation on p. 267.

34. Liv Ullmann, "Conversation with the Actress," ibid., pp. 157–165, quotation on p. 160.

35. See the entry on Jack Nicholson, in *Actors on Acting for the Screen*, ed. Tomlinson, pp. 404–407, quotation on p. 405.

36. See the entry on Jodie Foster, ibid., pp. 196–197.

37. Charles Chaplin, *My Autobiography* (New York: Simon & Schuster, 1964), p. 260.

38. See the entry on Alec Guinness in *Actors on Acting for the Screen*, ed. Tomlinson, pp. 232–233; and Laurence Olivier, *Confessions of an Actor: An Autobiography* (1982; repr., New York: Penguin, 1984), pp. 136–137.

39. From an interview with James Lipton, *James Lipton Takes on Three* on Disc 2 of "Special Features" in the widescreen DVD release of *Million Dollar Baby* (2004).

Actors with many faces

Alec Guinness seems to have no predictable persona, playing characters as diverse as Lawrence of Arabia and Adolf Hitler. He is also famous for playing characters who first appear to be meek and indecisive, but surprisingly turn out to have inner strength. As George Smiley in *Tinker Tailor Soldier Spy* (1979) [1], a British master spy who has all the answers, Guinness is calm and professorial with horn-rimmed glasses and a scarf to protect against a chill. He fools his smug colleagues into believing he is simply a tailor and doesn't have a clue, but in the end, he proves that appearances can indeed be misleading. Gary Oldman is another British actor noted for the wide range of different characters he plays, including two doomed celebrities (rock star Sid Vicious and playwright Joe Orton); assassin Lee Harvey Oswald; Count Dracula, a killer of another kind; Ludwig von Beethoven; and George Smiley, in the recent movie version of *Tinker Tailor Soldier Spy* (2011) [2], where he's as cool and cerebral as Guinness, but with a characterization all his own.

(1959), *Tunes of Glory* (1960), *Lawrence of Arabia* (1962; perhaps his finest performance), and *Hitler: The Last Ten Days* (1973). You might also study his performance as George Smiley in the TV series *Tinker Tailor Soldier Spy* and then compare and contrast it with Gary Oldman's in the movie version (2011). Guinness never defined acting per se; he didn't need to, for his acting says it all.

Olivier, one of the greatest stage and screen actors of the twentieth century, defined acting in various ways, including as "convincing lying."[40] Although Olivier stands out for the extraordinary range of the roles he undertook on both stage and screen, and for his meticulous preparation in creating them, this remark suggests that he had little patience with theories of acting. Indeed, when asked how he created his film performance as the king in *Henry V* (1944; directed by Olivier), he replied simply, "I don't know—I'm England, that's all."[41] Olivier had made this film to bolster British morale during the last days of World War II, and thus he wanted *Henry V* to embody traditional British values.

The great silent-era director F. W. Murnau emphasized intellect and counseled actors to restrain their feelings, to *think* rather than *act*. He believed actors to be capable of conveying the intensity of their thoughts so that audiences would understand. Director Rouben Mamoulian gave Greta Garbo much the same advice when she played the leading role in his *Queen Christina* (1933). The film ends with the powerful and passionate Swedish queen sailing to Spain with the body of her lover, a Spanish nobleman killed in a duel. In preparing for the final close-up, in which the queen stares out to sea, Garbo asked Mamoulian, "What should I be thinking of? What should I be doing?" His reply: "Have you heard of *tabula rasa*? I want your face to be a blank sheet of paper. I want the writing to be done by every member of the audience. I'd like it if you could avoid even blinking your eyes, so that you're nothing but a beautiful mask."[42] Is she remembering the past? Imagining the future? With the camera serving as an apparently neutral mediator between actress and audience, Garbo's blank face asks us to transform it into what we hope or want to see: sadness, courage, inspiration, whatever we choose. Mamoulian's influence can be seen in *The Man from London* (2007; codirectors Bela Tarr and Ágnes Hranitzky), where the

40. Olivier, *Confessions of an Actor*, p. 20.

41. Laurence Olivier, qtd. in Donald Spoto, *Laurence Olivier: A Biography* (New York: HarperCollins, 1992), pp. 111–112.

42. Rouben Mamoulian, qtd. in Tom Milne, *Rouben Mamoulian* (Bloomington: Indiana University Press, 1969), p. 74.

Laurence Olivier's *Henry V*

Laurence Olivier in the first screen adaptation of *Henry V* (1944); this very popular film, produced during a troubled time (World War II), was uniformly praised for the quality of its acting. The many previous screen adaptations of Shakespeare's plays had been mainly faithful records of stage productions, but Olivier's film, his first as a director, benefited from his understanding of cinema's potential as a narrative art, his extensive acting experience, his deep knowledge of Shakespeare's language, and his sharp instincts about the national moods in Great Britain and the United States. *Henry V* received an Oscar nomination for Best Picture, and Olivier received a nomination for Best Actor in a Leading Role as well as an Oscar for his outstanding achievement as actor, producer, and director for bringing *Henry V* to the screen.

How to read a face

In directing *The Man from London*, Béla Tarr uses many of the film noir traits: black-and-white imagery, slow-motion cinematography, long takes, and haunting close-ups. This image marks the film's ending, where Tarr holds the expression of Mrs. Brown (Agi Szirtes)—a woman who just learned of her husband's murder—for a mesmerizing length of time. What is she feeling? Despair, grief, disbelief are all possibilities. But her face holds many secrets, and we bring our own experiences watching the entire film to bear on our interpretations.

long final close-up, in high-contrast black-and-white, is of a grieving widow's expressionless face. As in the shot of Garbo, this is a face that says everything and nothing. It brings the full force of a single shot to make us think and interpret what we see.

Naturalistic and Nonnaturalistic Styles

We have all seen at least one movie in which a character, perhaps a whole cast of characters, is like no one we have ever met or ever *could* meet. Either because the world they inhabit functions according to rules that don't apply in our world or because their behaviors are extreme, such characters aren't realistic in any colloquial sense of the word. But if the actors perform skillfully, we are likely to accept the characters as believable within the context of the story. For example, consider Kathy Bates's work on such films as *Misery* (1990; director Rob Reiner), *Dolores Claiborne* (1995; director Taylor Hackford), *Midnight in Paris* (2011; director Woody Allen), *Tammy* (2014; director Stephen Herek), and *Boychoir* (2015; director François Girard). We might be tempted to call such portrayals *realistic*, but Kathy Bates is the personification of the naturalistic actor. In fact, her "acting" is so natural that it is difficult to see.

Actors who strive for appropriate, expressive, coherent, and unified characterizations can render their performances naturalistically as well as nonnaturalistically. Screen acting appears naturalistic when actors re-create recognizable or plausible human behavior for the camera. The actors not only look like the characters should (in their costume, makeup, and hairstyle) but also think, speak, and move the way people would offscreen. By contrast, nonnaturalistic performances seem excessive, exaggerated, even overacted; they may employ strange or outlandish costumes, makeup, or hairstyles; they might aim for effects beyond the normal range of human experience; and they often intend to distance or estrange audiences from characters. Frequently, they are found in horror, fantasy, and action films.

What Konstantin Stanislavsky was to naturalistic acting, German playwright Bertolt Brecht was to nonnaturalistic performance. Brecht allied his theatrical ideas with Marxist political principles to create a nonnaturalistic theater. Whereas Stanislavsky strove for realism, Brecht believed that audience members should not think they're watching something actually happening before them. Instead, he wanted every aspect of a theatrical production to limit the audience's identification with characters and events, thereby creating a psychological distance (called the **alienation effect** or **distancing effect**) between them and the stage. The intent of this approach is to remind the audience of the artificiality of the theatrical performance.

Overall, this theory has had little influence on mainstream filmmaking. After all, unlike theater, cinema can change—as often as it wants—the relationship between spectators and the screen, alternately alienating them from or plunging them into the action. However, we do see this approach when actors step out of character, face the camera, and directly address the audience (a maneuver, more common in theater than cinema, known as *breaking the fourth wall*—the imaginary, invisible wall that separates the audience from the stage). Although the distancing effect can destroy a movie if used inappropriately, breaking the fourth wall works effectively when audience members are experiencing things like the character does *and* the character has the self-confidence to exploit that empathy.

In the late 1920s in Berlin, Brecht discovered Peter Lorre, who later became one of the most distinctively stylized actors on the American screen. They worked closely together on several stage productions at the same time that Lorre was preparing the lead role of Hans Beckert, a child murderer, in Fritz Lang's *M* (1931). Lorre's magnificent performance—particularly in the final scene, which is one of the most emotional in movie history—reflects the influence of Brecht's theories and directing. Lorre creates a duality—Beckert and the actor detached from the character who comments on his actions—and while it is not pure direct address (he is addressing a "jury" in a kangaroo court), we are absolutely riveted by the power and strangeness of Lorre's conception of the role.

Tom Edison (Paul Bettany) frequently addresses his idealistic views directly to the viewer in Lars von Trier's *Dogville* (2003), which in overall style owes much to Bertolt Brecht's influence. In Max Ophüls's *Lola Montès* (1955), the Circus Master (Peter Ustinov) addresses the circus audience, of which, we understand, we are members. For comic effect, Tom Jones (Albert Finney) breaks the fourth wall in Tony Richardson's *Tom Jones* (1963), as does Alfie (Michael Caine) in Lewis Gilbert's *Alfie* (1966) and (played by Jude Law) in Charles Shyer's 2004 remake. Various characters speak directly to the viewer

1

2

Naturalistic versus nonnaturalistic performances

Naturalistic and nonnaturalistic performances sometimes overlap, but these categories help us relate actors' contributions to a filmmaker's overall vision. In *Knocked Up* (2007), Seth Rogen's naturalistic performance as a reformed slacker becomes part of director Judd Apatow's clear-eyed depiction of the consequences of unprotected sex. Here [1], Rogen tells his pregnant girlfriend, who has decided to keep their baby, that he's ready to do whatever it takes to support her. He then congratulates himself by saying "awesome" in recognition of his newfound maturity. Johnny Depp's nonnaturalistic performance as the title character in *Edward Scissorhands* (1990) [2] enables director Tim Burton to draw us into the exaggerated, downright weird world of this story. Burton's film is about fantasy, the way things might be in that world. Rogen's and Depp's performances differ widely, but they suit their respective movies. Imagine how out of place either character would be in the other's world!

in Spike Lee's *Do the Right Thing* (1989). There is a much more solid tradition of direct address in the European theatrical cinema of such directors as Jean-Luc Godard, Chantal Akerman, Eric Rohmer, Ingmar Bergman, and Michael Haneke, among others.

In Buddy Giovinazzo's *No Way Home* (1996), Tim Roth gives a naturalistic performance as Joey, a slow but principled young man who is just out of prison. He has taken the rap for an assault he did not commit and returns to Staten Island to find that the people who framed him and circumstances in the community are just as rotten as they were when he left. Determined not to associate with his low-life brother and former friends or return to a life of crime, he boards a bus and heads for undiscovered country. In Boaz Yakin's *Fresh* (1994), Sean Nelson naturalistically plays the title character—a young, black Brooklynite working as a courier for a dope dealer between going to school and looking out for his older sister. In Tim Burton's *Edward Scissorhands* (1990), Johnny Depp gives a nonnaturalistic performance as the title character, a kind of Frankenstein's monster—scary, but benevolent—created by a mad inventor who died before his work was finished. Edward lives in a deteriorating Gothic castle on a mountaintop that overlooks a nightmarishly pastel suburb, to which he eventually moves. The decor and costumes identify him immediately as a metaphor for the ultimate outsider. But the challenge to Depp as an actor is not only to acknowledge just how different he appears to others ("hands," scars, makeup, hairstyle), which he does in a very self-conscious and often comic manner (e.g., using his hands to shred cabbage for cole slaw). He also has to humanize this character so that he can be accepted as a member of the community.

Improvisational Acting

Improvisation can mean extemporizing—delivering lines based only loosely on the written script or without the preparation that comes with studying a script before rehearsing it. It can also mean playing through a moment, making up lines to keep scenes going when actors forget their written lines, stumble on lines, or have some other mishap. Of these two senses, the former is most important in movie acting, particularly in the poststudio world; the latter is an example of professional grace under pressure.

Improvisation can be seen as an extension of Stanislavsky's emphasis that the actor striving for a naturalistic performance should avoid any mannerisms that call attention to technique. Occupying a place somewhere between his call for actors to bring their own ex-

periences to roles and Brecht's call for actors to distance themselves from roles, improvisation often involves collaboration between actors and directors in creating stories, characters, and dialogue, which may then be incorporated into scripts. According to film scholar Virginia Wright Wexman, what improvisers

> seem to be striving for is the sense of discovery that comes from the unexpected and unpredictable in human behavior. If we think of art as a means of giving form to life, improvisation can be looked at as one way of adding to our sense of the liveliness of art, a means of avoiding the sterility that results from rote recitations of abstract conventional forms.[43]

For years, improvisation has played a major part in actors' training. But it was anathema in the studio system, where practically everything was preprogrammed, and it remains comparatively rare in narrative moviemaking. Actors commonly confer with directors about altering or omitting written lines, but this form of improvisation is so limited in scope that we can better understand it as the sort of fertile suggestion making that is intrinsic to collaboration. Although certain directors encourage actors not only to discover the characters within themselves but also to imagine what those characters might say (and how they might act) in any given situation, James Naremore, an authority on film acting, explains that even great actors, when they improvise, "tend to lapse into monologue, playing from relatively static, frontal positions with a second actor nearby who nods or makes short interjections."[44]

Among the director-actor collaborations that have made improvisation work effectively are Bernardo Bertolucci and Marlon Brando (*Last Tango in Paris*, 1972); Robert Altman and a large company of actors (*Nashville*, 1975; *Short Cuts*, 1993; *Gosford Park*, 2001); Mike Leigh and various actors (*Another Year*, 2010); and John Cassavetes and Gena Rowlands (*Faces*, 1968; *A Woman under the Influence*, 1974; *Gloria*, 1980).

The Cassavetes–Rowlands collaboration is particularly important and impressive, not only for what it accomplished but also for the respect it received as an

43. Virginia Wright Wexman, "The Rhetoric of Cinematic Improvisation," *Cinema Journal* 20, no. 1 (Fall 1980): 29. See also Maurice Yacowar, "An Aesthetic Defense of the Star System in Films," *Quarterly Review of Film Studies* 4, no. 1 (Winter 1979): 48–50.

44. James Naremore, *Acting in the Cinema* (Berkeley: University of California Press, 1988), p. 45.

Improvisation

"You talkin' to me? . . . You talkin' to me?" Screenwriter Paul Schrader wrote no dialogue for the scene in Martin Scorsese's *Taxi Driver* (1976) in which Travis Bickle (Robert De Niro) rehearses his dreams of vigilantism before a mirror. Before filming, De Niro improvised the lines that now accompany this well-known moment in film history, a disturbing, darkly comic portrait of an unhinged mind talking to itself.

experimental approach within the largely conventional film industry. "John's theory," Rowlands explains,

> is that if there's something wrong, it's wrong in the writing. If you take actors who can act in other things and they get to a scene they've honestly tried to do, and if they still can't get it, then there's something wrong with the writing. Then you stop, you improvise, you talk about it. Then he'll go and rewrite it—it's not just straight improvisation. I'm asked a lot about this, and it's true, when I look at the films and I *see* that they look improvised in a lot of different places where I know they weren't.[45]

Improvised acting requires directors to play even more active roles than if they were working with prepared scripts, because they must elicit actors' ideas for characters and dialogue as well as orchestrate those contributions within overall cinematic visions. Ultimately, directors help form all contributions, including those of actors. Nearly all directors who employ improvisation have the actors work it out in rehearsal and then lock it

down for filming, perhaps radically changing their plans for how such scenes will be shot. This is how, for example, Martin Scorsese and Robert De Niro worked out the originally silent "You talkin' to me?" scene in *Taxi Driver* (1976).

Unless directors and actors have talked publicly about their work, we seldom know when and to what extent improvisation has been used in a film. Because we know that Cassavetes prepared his actors with precise scripts that they refined with extensive improvisational exercises, by studying the original script we can prepare to look for the improvisation, to judge its usefulness, and to determine whether improvised performances seem convincing or, ironically, less convincing than scripted ones. Other directors who use improvisation in their films include Lynn Shelton (*Your Sister's Sister*, 2011), Wes Anderson (*Moonrise Kingdom*, 2012), Ulrich Seidl (the Paradise trilogy, 2012), and Noah Baumbach (*Frances Ha*, 2013).

Directors and Actors

Directors and actors have collaborated closely since the days when D. W. Griffith established the art of screen acting with Lillian Gish. Inevitably, such relationships depend on the individuals: what each brings to his or her work, what each can do alone, and what each needs from a collaborator. Such different approaches taken by different directors in working with actors are as necessary, common, and useful as the different approaches taken by different actors as they prepare for roles.

Some veterans of the studio system, such as William Wyler and George Cukor, are known as "actors' directors," meaning that the directors inspire such confidence they can actively shape actors' performances. Although Wyler may have enjoyed the trust of Bette Davis, Fredric March, Myrna Loy, Barbra Streisand, and other notable actors, the atmosphere on the set was considerably tenser when Laurence Olivier arrived in Hollywood for his first screen role, as Heathcliff in Wyler's *Wuthering Heights* (1939). Olivier had already earned a considerable reputation on the London stage and was frankly contemptuous of screen acting, which he thought serious actors did only for the money. Wyler, on the other

45. Gena Rowlands in *Actors on Acting for the Screen*, ed. Tomlinson, p. 482.

hand, was one of Hollywood's great stylists, a perfectionist who drove actors crazy with his keen sense of acting and love of multiple takes. Everyone on the set perceived the tension between them. Wyler encouraged Olivier to be patient in responding to the challenges involved in acting for the camera, and eventually Olivier overcame his attitude of condescension to give one of his greatest film performances.

In developing his relationships with actors, director John Ford encouraged them to create their characters to serve the narrative. He preferred to work with the same actors over and over, and his working method never changed. John Wayne, who acted in many of Ford's films and has been described as the director's alter ego, said Ford gave direction "with his entire personality—his facial expressions, bending his eye. He didn't verbalize. He wasn't articulate, he couldn't really finish a sentence. . . . He'd give you a clue, just an opening. If you didn't produce what he wanted, he would pick you apart."[46] Newcomers faced a challenge in getting it right the first time. Similarly, Otto Preminger, the director of *Laura* (1944), was so predictably cruel to his actors that he was known as Otto the Ogre.

However rigid Ford's approach may at first seem, we find it in similarly fruitful collaborations between Rouben Mamoulian and Greta Garbo, Josef von Sternberg and Marlene Dietrich, John Huston and Humphrey Bogart, William Wyler and Bette Davis, François Truffaut and Jean-Pierre Léaud, Akira Kurosawa and Toshirô Mifune, Satyajit Ray and Soumitra Chatterjee, Martin Scorsese and Robert De Niro, Spike Lee and Denzel Washington, and Tim Burton and Johnny Depp. These directors know what they want, explain it clearly, select actors with whom they work well, and then collaborate with them to create movies that are characterized in part by the seamless line between directing and acting. Alexander Mackendrick, director of the classic *Sweet Smell of Success* (1957), was once asked how to get an actor to do what he needed him to do. "You don't," he said. "What you do is try to get him to *want* what you need" [emphasis added].

By contrast, the line that *can* exist between directing and acting is evident in the work of director Alfred Hitchcock, who tends to place mise-en-scène above narrative, and both mise-en-scène and narrative above acting. Hitchcock's movies were so carefully planned and rehearsed in advance that actors were expected to follow his direction closely, so that even those with limited talent (e.g., Tippi Hedren in *The Birds*, 1963; and Kim Novak in *Vertigo*, 1958) gave performances that satisfied the director.

On the other hand, Stanley Kubrick, who controlled his films as rigidly as Hitchcock, was more flexible. When directing *Barry Lyndon* (1975), a film in which fate drove the plot, Kubrick gave his principal actors, Ryan O'Neal and Marisa Berenson, almost nothing to say and then moved them about his sumptuous mise-en-scène like pawns on a chessboard. When working with a more open story, however, he encouraged actors to improvise in rehearsal or on the set. The results included such memorable moments as Peter Sellers's final monologue as Dr. Strangelove (and the film's last line, "*Mein Führer, I can walk!*") and Jack Nicholson's manic "Heeeere's Johnny!" before the climax of *The Shining* (1980). Malcolm McDowell in *A Clockwork Orange* (1971) and Tom Cruise and Nicole Kidman in *Eyes Wide Shut* (1999) are also said to have worked out their performances in improvisations with the director. Perhaps the most extreme example is director Werner Herzog, who, in directing *Heart of Glass* (1976), hypnotized the entire cast each day on the set to create what he called "an atmosphere of hallucination, prophecy, visionary and collective madness."

How Filmmaking Affects Acting

Actors must understand how a film is made, because every aspect of the filmmaking process can affect performances and the actors' contributions to the creation of meaning. At the same time, audiences should understand what a movie actor goes through to deliver a performance that, to their eyes, seems effortless and spontaneous. Here are some of the challenges an actor faces.

With some exceptions, most production budgets and schedules do not have the funds or the time to give movie actors much in the way of rehearsal. Thus actors almost always perform a character's progression entirely out of

---

46. John Wayne, qtd. in Joseph McBride, *Searching for John Ford: A Life* (New York: St. Martin's Press, 2001), p. 299.

sequence, and this out-of-continuity shooting can also force those who are being filmed in isolation to perform their parts as though they were interacting with other people. When these shots are edited together, the illusion of togetherness is there, but the actors must make it convincing. Actors must time their movements and precisely hit predetermined marks on the floor so that a moving camera and a focus puller know where they will be at every moment; they must often direct their gaze and position their body and/or face in unnatural-feeling poses to allow for lighting, camera position, and composition. These postures usually appear natural on-screen but don't feel natural to the actors performing them on the set.

Movie actors must repeat the same action/line/emotion more than once, not just for multiple takes from a single setup but also for multiple setups. This means that they may perform the close-up of a particular scene an hour after they performed the same moment for a different camera position. Everything about their performance is fragmented, and thus they must struggle to stay in character. Finally, actors are sometimes required to work with acting and dialogue coaches, physical trainers, and stunt personnel. For all the reasons listed here, delivering a convincing screen performance is very challenging.

In the following chapters we will examine editing and sound and the ways they relate to acting and meaning. Here we'll look briefly at how acting is affected by framing, composition, lighting, and the types and lengths of shots.

Framing, Composition, Lighting, and the Long Take

Framing and composition can bring actors together in a shot or keep them apart. Such inclusion and exclusion create relationships between characters, and these in turn create meaning. The physical relation of the actors to each other and to the overall frame (height, width, and depth) can significantly affect how we see and interpret a shot.

The inciting moment of the plot of Orson Welles's *Citizen Kane* (1941) and one of the principal keys to understanding the movie—for many viewers, its most unforgettable moment—occurs when Charles Foster Kane's (Welles) mother, Mary Kane (Agnes Moorehead), signs the contract that determines her son's future. It consists of only six shots, two of which are long takes. Relying on design, lighting, cinematography, and acting, Welles creates a scene of almost perfect ambiguity.

In designing the scene, Welles puts the four principal characters involved in the incident in the same frame for the two long takes but, significantly, divides the space within this frame into exterior and interior spaces: a young Charles (Buddy Swan) is outside playing with the Rosebud sled in the snow (image [1]), oblivious to how his life is being changed forever; meanwhile, Mary, her husband Jim (Harry Shannon), and Walter Parks Thatcher (George Coulouris) are in Mrs. Kane's boardinghouse (image [2]) for shots 1 through 3 (images [1] to [5]) and outside for shot 4 (image [6]). In shot 3 (image [4]), this division of the overall space into two separate physical and emotional components is dramatically emphasized after Mary signs the contract and Jim walks to the background of the frame and shuts the window, symbolically shutting Charles out of his life and also cutting us off from the sound of his voice. Mary immediately walks to the same window and opens it, asserting her control over the boy by sharply calling "Charles!" before going out to explain the situation to him.

The two long takes carry the weight of the scene and thus require the adult actors to work closely together in shot 3 (image [4]) and with the boy in shot 4 (image [6]). They begin inside the house as a tightly framed ensemble confronting one another across a small table—their bodies composed and their faces lighted to draw attention to the gravity of the decision they are making—and continue outdoors, where these tensions break into the open as young Charles learns of his fate.

The lighting also helps create the meaning. Lamps remain unlit inside the house, where the atmosphere is as emotionally cold as the snowy landscape is physically cold. Outside, the light is flat and bright; inside, this same bright light, reflected from the snow, produces deep shadows. This effect appears most clearly after the opening of shot 3 (image [4]), when Mary Kane turns from the window and walks from the background to the foreground. As she does, lighting divides her face, the dark and light halves emphasizing how torn she feels as a mother in sending Charles away.

To prepare for the long take, Welles drilled his actors to the point of perfection in rehearsals, giving them amazing things to do (such as requiring Moorehead to pace up and down the narrow room) and then letting this preparation pay off in moments of great theatrical vitality. Look closely, for example, at the performance of Agnes Moorehead, with whom Welles had worked in

radio productions.[47] Moorehead knew exactly how to use the tempo, pitch, and rhythm of her voice to give unexpected depth to the familiar melodramatic type she plays here. In the carefully designed and controlled setting—the long room, dividing window, and snowy exterior—Mrs. Kane, whose makeup, hairstyle, and costume are those of a seemingly simple pioneer woman, reveals herself to be something quite different. She is both unforgettably humane as she opens the window and calls her son sharply to the destiny she has decreed and, given that her only business experience has been in running a boardinghouse, surprisingly shrewd in obviously having retained Thatcher to prepare the contract that seals this moment. In fact, this is one of the few scenes in the movie in which a female character totally dominates the action—not surprising, for it is a scene of maternal rejection.

As Mary Kane throws open the window, she cries out, "Charles!" in a strained, even shrill, voice that reveals her anxiety about what she is doing; yet a moment later, sounding both tender and guilty, she tells Thatcher that she has had Charles's trunk packed for a week. Should we read the cold mask of her face (image [7]) as the implacable look of a woman resigned to her decision or as a cover for maternal feelings? Does it reflect the doubt, indecision, and dread any person would feel in such a situation? Is it the face of sacrifice? Is it all of these possibilities and more? And how should we read Charles, who, in the span of a moment, goes from playful to wary to angry to antagonistic (image [8])?

Although the downtrodden Jim Kane protests his wife's actions, when Thatcher coolly informs him that he and his wife will receive $50,000 per year, he feebly gives in, saying, "Well, let's hope it's all for the best"—a remark that invariably, as it should, provokes laughter from viewers. And Thatcher, wearing a top hat and dressed in the formal clothes of a big-city banker, sends contradictory signals. He's precise in overseeing Mrs. Kane's signature, dismissive of Mr. Kane, fawning as he meets Charles, and angry when Charles knocks

him to the ground. In encouraging this kind of richly nuanced acting and its resulting ambiguity, Welles shifts the challenge of interpretation to us.

As this scene shows, the long take, used in conjunction with deep-focus cinematography, gives directors and actors the opportunity to create scenes of unusual length as well as a broader and deeper field of composition. In addition, the long take encourages ensemble acting that calls attention to acting, not editing between shots. Although we tend to think of actors and their performances as acts of individual creativity, we should keep in mind that one actor's performance often very much depends on another's. Indeed, it may rely on an ensemble, or group, of actors.[48]

Ensemble acting—which emphasizes the collaborative interaction of a group of actors, not the work of an individual actor—evolved as a further step in creating a verisimilar mise-en-scène for both the stage and the screen. Typically experienced in the theater, ensemble acting is used less in the movies because it requires the provision of rehearsal time that is usually denied to screen actors. However, when a movie director such as Richard Linklater (*Boyhood*, 2014) chooses to use long takes and has the time to rehearse the actors, the result is a group of actors working together continuously in a single shot. Depending on the story and plot situation, this technique can intensify the emotional impact of a specific plot situation by having all of the involved characters on the screen at the same time.

As with so many other innovations, Orson Welles pioneered ensemble acting in *Citizen Kane* (1941) and *The Magnificent Ambersons* (1942), and its influence was quickly seen in the work of other directors, notably William Wyler in *The Little Foxes* (1941) and *The Best Years of Our Lives* (1946). More recent examples of excellent ensemble acting can be found in *The Anniversary Party* (2001; directors Alan Cummings and Jennifer Jason Leigh), *The Paperboy* (2012; director Lee Daniels), and *The We and the I* (2012; director Michel Gondry). A particularly challenging assignment for a group of

---

47. Welles reportedly called Agnes Moorehead "the best actor I've ever known"; qtd. in Simon Callow, *Orson Welles: The Road to Xanadu* (New York: Viking, 1995), p. 512.

48. Further study of the long take should consider the work of the great Japanese director Kenji Mizoguchi and notably the Lake Biwa episode in *Ugetsu* (1953). Other notable uses of the technique can be seen in Jean-Pierre Melville's *Le Doulos* (1962), which includes a virtuoso eight-minute single shot; Werner Herzog's *Woyzeck* (1979); Lisandro Alonso's *Los Muertos* (2004), where most of the movie is divided into very long takes; and Pedro Costa's *Colossal Youth* (2006), where real time and very long takes are the norm. *Avalanche* (1937), a work by Japanese director Mikio Naruse, includes a sequence of very brief shots that are edited together so seamlessly that they provide the visual equivalent of a single long take.

Boyhood's ensemble of actors celebrates a milestone

Here, we see members of the cast celebrate the principal character's (Mason Evans Jr.) high school graduation. *Left to right*: Mason Evans Sr. (Ethan Hawke), Mason Evans Jr. (Ellar Coltrane), his mother Olivia (Patricia Arquette), Olivia's mother (Libby Villari), and his sister Samantha (Lorelei Linklater). It's a milestone for them all, young and old, near the conclusion of twelve years of intermittent filming during which they all grew up together and developed as characters.

actors was Richard Linklater's *Boyhood* (2014). The film focuses on newcomer Ellar Coltrane, who's six when the movie begins and eighteen when it ends. Filmed in four-day sections over that twelve-year span, it shows what movies usually manipulate through editing: the passage of time. Coltrane's passage from a boy to a teenager is played out on the movie screen. It requires the actors, including Ethan Hawke and Patricia Arquette, to stay in character over that period as well as to be comfortable with showing their natural aging, unaltered by makeup or digital effects. It's a unique achievement in movie-making, in a minor way comparable to Michael Apted's 7 Up series of documentaries (1964–2012), which followed the lives of a group of real British seven-year-olds and recorded their progress every seven years until they reached age fifty-six.

The Camera and the Close-Up

The camera creates a greater naturalism and intimacy between actors and audience than would ever be possible on the stage, and thus it serves as screen actors' most

important collaborator. Nowhere is the camera's effect on the actor's role more evident than in a close-up. The true close-up isolates an actor, concentrating on the face; it can be active (commenting on something just said or done, reminding us who is the focus of a scene) or passive (revealing an actor's beauty). Thus actors' most basic skill is understanding how to reveal themselves to the camera during the close-up.

All great movie actors understand, instinctively or from experience, what to do and not do with their faces when the camera moves in. They must temporarily forget their bodies' expressive possibilities, stand as close to the camera as they would to a person in real life, smoothly balance their voices because the microphone is so close, and focus on the communicative power of even the slightest facial gesture.

Close-ups can shift interpretation to the viewer, as in the two-minute-long close-up of Anna (Nicole Kidman) in Jonathan Glazer's *Birth* (2004; see Chapter 6, p. 260), or they can leave little room for independent interpretation, as in Marlene Dietrich's opening scene as Amy Jolly in Josef von Sternberg's *Morocco* (1930; cinematographer Lee Garmes). On the deck of a ship bound for Morocco, the mysterious and beautiful Amy drops her handbag. A sophisticated, older Frenchman—Monsieur La Bessiere (Adolphe Menjou)—kneels at her feet to retrieve her things and then offers to assist her in any way he can when she arrives at her destination. In a relatively quick close-up, Amy looks off into space and tells him she will not need any help. Design elements further distance us from the actress and the character: Dietrich wears a hat with a veil, and thus the shot is "veiled by the 'Rembrandt' light, by the fog, by the lens, and by the diaphanous fabric."[49] Although we do not yet know who Amy is, what she does, or why she's going to Morocco, we certainly understand La Bessiere's interest.

Close-ups can also reveal both the process of thinking and the thoughts at its end. In a close-up during the climactic moment of John Ford's *The Searchers* (1956), Ethan Edwards (John Wayne) transforms from a hateful to a loving man as he halts his premeditated attempt to murder his niece, Debbie (Natalie Wood) and instead lifts her to the safety of his arms. The shot gives us no time to analyze why he has changed his mind—we see only the results of that change.

49. Naremore, *Acting in the Cinema*, p. 141.

Acting and the close-up

Carl Theodor Dreyer's *The Passion of Joan of Arc* (1928) vividly and unforgettably illustrates the power of the close-up. Most of this silent movie's running time is taken up with contrasting close-ups of Joan (played by Maria Falconetti, a French stage actress who never again appeared on film) and of her many interrogators during the course of her trial. As Joan is questioned, mocked, tortured, and finally burned at the stake, we witness an entire, deeply moving story in her face. Thus we respond to a single character's expressions as they are shaped by the drama and the camera.

In a bar scene in Elia Kazan's *On the Waterfront* (1954), Terry Malloy (Marlon Brando), playing the tough guy, tells Edie Doyle (Eva Marie Saint) his philosophy: "Do it to him before he does it to you." Up to this point, he has remained aloof after witnessing the mob's murder of Edie's brother, an attitude he continues to display until Edie, who is trying to do something about the corruption on the waterfront, asks for his help. Stopped in his tracks, Terry sits down, and a series of close-ups reveals the shakiness of his unfeeling posture. In a soft, caring, but slightly nervous voice (in this bar setting, surrounded by other tough guys, he's a little self-conscious of being tender with a woman), he tells her, "I'd like ta help" and so reveals to her, the camera, and the audience a more sensitive man under the macho mannerisms.

Acting and Editing

Because a screen actor's performance is fragmented, the editor has considerable power in shaping it. We've already emphasized that the actor is responsible for maintaining the emotional continuity of a performance,

Artistic collaboration and the close-up

In *Morocco* (1930), Marlene Dietrich's beautiful face is made to appear even more haunting and enigmatic by director Josef von Sternberg's mise-en-scène and Lee Garmes's black-and-white cinematography. Dietrich, too, instinctively understood the kind of lighting and camera placement that was right for her role and the narrative as well as for the glamorous image she cultivated in all her movies. In this MCU, she stands on the deck of a ship at night and appears distant, almost otherworldly, as she is bathed in soft, misty "Rembrandt lighting." One half of her face is bright, part of the other half is in shadow. Her face is further framed and softened by her hat and veil and by shooting her against a background that is out of focus. In all likelihood, Garmes also placed thin gauze fabric over the lens to further soften the image. This is the first appearance of Dietrich's character in the movie, so we know little about her but can already discern that she is not only alluring but mysterious. But one thing we know for sure: the Dietrich face, as it appeared on the screen, was the conscious creation of the actress, director, and cinematographer.

but even the most consistent actor delivers slightly different performances on each take. Editors can patch up mistakes by selecting, arranging, or juxtaposing shots to cover these differences. They control the duration of an actor's appearance on the screen and how that time is used. When aspects of an actor's performance that originally were deemed acceptable appear in the editing stage to interrupt the flow of the narrative, the development of the character, or the tone of the movie, the editor, in consultation with the director, can dispense with it completely by leaving that footage on the cutting-room floor. In short, the editor has the power to mold a performance with more control than most directors and even the actors themselves can.

LOOKING AT MOVIES
EDITING AND PERFORMANCE IN SNAPSHOT

VIDEO ▶

This tutorial examines the effect that editing can have on our perception of actors' performances.

Looking at Acting

Given all the elements and aspects in our discussion of an actor's performance, how do we focus our attention on analyzing acting? Before looking at some recognized criteria, let's discuss how we can bring our own experiences to the task. An actor's performance on the screen goes beyond what we see and hear; it also includes many intangibles and subtleties. That alone makes the analysis of acting much more challenging. Breaking down and cataloging other elements of cinematic language—whether narrative, mise-en-scène, production design, or cinematography—and using that information to analyze their usefulness and effectiveness is much easier than analyzing acting. Yet acting (perhaps second only to narrative) is the component most people use to assess movies. We feel an effective, natural, moving performance in a more direct way than we respond to other cinematic aspects of most films, and we feel both qualified and compelled to judge films by their performances.

What accounts for this sense of entitlement? Why are we so fixated on actors? Why do we so frequently judge the quality of the movie by the (often intangible) quality of the actors' performances? There are several reasons. First, although cinematic language has a considerable effect on the way we look at a movie, we also identify with characters and, of course, with the actors who inhabit those characters. Second, we identify with characters who pursue a goal. We get involved with this pursuit, which is driven by and embodied by the actors who inhabit the characters, because a movie narrative is constructed to exploit what most involves us. We don't even have to like the characters as long as we believe them. Third, we identify with characters because of our own behavior as people. Although cinematic language draws from our instinctive responses to everyday visual and audio information, we don't consciously notice and process it as much as we do human behavior. We are people watchers by nature, necessity, and desire. We are constantly analyzing behavior. When you say hello to a friend or ask a professor a question or order a cup of coffee from a waiter, you are noticing and processing and reacting to human behavior. Is the friend happy? Does the professor think you're stupid? Is the waiter paying attention?

Finally, our identification with characters and the actors who play them has something to do with our own personality. We too behave in a way that is consistent with our general character or state of mind, and beyond that, we are also engaged in role-playing. You present yourself differently, depending on where you are, what's going on, and who you're with. You behave differently with a police officer than you do with your mother or your professor, differently with a new friend than with an old one.

Now that we've looked at some of the reasons for our reactions to actors and acting, how do we analyze their performances? What are the criteria of a good performance? In their everyday moviegoing, people tend to appreciate acting subjectively. They like an actor's performance when he or she looks, speaks, and moves in ways that confirm their expectations for the character (or type of character). Conversely, they dislike a performance that baffles those expectations.

This approach, though understandable, can also be limiting. How many of us have sufficient life experiences to fully comprehend the range of characters that appear on the screen? What background do we bring to an analysis of the performance of the following actors? Humphrey Bogart as a cold-blooded private eye in John Huston's *The Maltese Falcon* (1941); Carlo Battisti as a retired, impoverished bureaucrat in Vittorio De Sica's *Umberto D.* (1952); Giulietta Masina as a childlike circus performer in Federico Fellini's *La Strada* (1954); Toshirô

1

2

Assessing acting performances

[1] Toshirô Mifune in the death scene of Lord Washizu in Akira Kurosawa's *Throne of Blood* (1957) and [2] Holly Hunter in Jane Campion's *The Piano* (1993), a performance for which she won the Oscar for Best Actress in a Leading Role. To analyze an actor's performance, we need to consider its context—the particular movie in which it appears. Kurosawa's film draws on a specific genre— the *jidai-geki*, or historical drama—that is traditionally full of action; Campion's film draws on history but focuses more on psychology than on action. Thus Mifune uses ritualized, nonnaturalistic facial expressions and body language; and Hunter, who speaks only in voice-over, appears more naturalistic, inner directed, subdued.

Mifune as a Japanese warlord (based on Shakespeare's Macbeth) in Akira Kurosawa's *Throne of Blood* (1957); Marlon Brando as a Mafia don in Francis Ford Coppola's *The Godfather* (1972); Holly Hunter as a mute Victorian relocated from Scotland to New Zealand in Jane Campion's *The Piano* (1993); Sissy Spacek as the mother of a murdered son in Todd Field's *In the Bedroom* (2001);

Brad Pitt as the leader of a male aggression movement in David Fincher's *Fight Club* (1999); or Philip Seymour Hoffman as author Truman Capote in Bennett Miller's *Capote* (2005).

Movie acting may be, as legendary actor Laurence Olivier once said, the "art of persuasion."[50] Yet it is also a formal cinematic element, one as complex as design or cinematography. To get a sense of how movie acting works on its own and ultimately in relation to the other formal elements, we need to establish a set of criteria more substantial than our subjective feelings and reactions.

Because every actor, character, and performance in a movie is different, it is impossible to devise standards that would apply equally well to all of them. Furthermore, different actors, working with different directors, often take very different approaches to the same material, as you can judge for yourself by comparing the many remakes in movie history. Within the world of a particular story, your goal should be to determine the quality of the actor's achievement in creating the character and how that performance helps tell the story. Thus you should discuss an actor's specific performance in a specific film, for example, by discussing how Michael Fassbender's acting in Steve McQueen's *12 Years a Slave* (2013) serves to create the character of Edwin Epps, the alcoholic, sadist plantation owner. In your analysis, tell the story of that film without being influenced by expectations possibly raised by your having seen Fassbender in other movies, including those directed by McQueen: *Hunger* (2008) and *Shame* (2011).

In analyzing any actor's performance, you might consider the following:

> *Appropriateness.* Does the actor look and act naturally like the character he or she portrays, as expressed in physical appearance, facial expression, speech, movement, and gesture? If the performance is nonnaturalistic, does the actor look, walk, and talk the way that character might or should?
>
> Paradoxically, we expect an actor to behave as if he or she were *not* acting but were simply living the illusion of a character we can accept within the context of the movie's narrative. Such appropriateness in acting is also called *transparency*, meaning that the character is so clearly recognizable—in speech, movement, and

---

50. Olivier, *Confessions of an Actor*, p. 51.

Evil, pure evil

In *12 Years a Slave*, Michael Fassbender plays Edwin Epps, as evil a character that ever appeared on screen. He's a racist, a liar, an alcoholic, and a sadist, traits that manifest themselves in his actions than in his appearance. He may not "look" evil, but his treatment of his slaves is almost unbearable to watch. Movies like these should convince us not to confuse the actor with the part.

gesture—for what he or she is supposed to be that the actor becomes, in a sense, invisible. Most actors agree that the more successfully they create characters, the more we will see those characters and not them.

> *Inherent thoughtfulness or emotionality.* Does the actor convey the character's thought process or feelings behind the character's actions or reactions? In addition to a credible appearance, does the character have a credible inner life?

An actor can find the motivations behind a character's actions and reactions at any time before or during a movie's production. They may come to light in the script (as well as in any source on which it is based, such as a novel or play), in discussions with the director or with other cast members, and in spontaneous elements of inspiration and improvisation that the actor discovers while the camera is rolling. No matter which of these aspects or combinations of them reveal the character's motivation, we expect to see the actor reflect them within the character's consciousness or as part of the illusion-making process by which the character appears. To put it another way, the characters must seem vulnerable to forces in the narrative. They must be able to think about them and, if necessary, change their mind or feelings about them.

> *Expressive coherence.* Has the actor used these first two qualities (appropriateness and inherent thoughtfulness/emotionality) to create a characterization that holds together?

Whatever behavior an actor uses to convey character, it must be intrinsic, not extraneous to the character, "maintaining not only a coherence of manner, but also a fit between setting, costume, and behavior."[51] When an actor achieves such a fit, he or she is playing in character. Maintaining expressive coherence enables the actor to create a complex characterization and performance, to express thoughts and reveal emotions of a recognizable individual without veering off into mere quirks or distracting details.

> *Wholeness and unity.* Despite the challenges inherent in most film productions, has the actor maintained the illusion of a seamless character, even if that character is purposely riddled with contradictions?

Whereas expressive coherence relies on the logic inherent in an actor's performance, wholeness and unity are achieved through the actor's ability to achieve aesthetic consistency while working with the director, crew, and other cast members; enduring multiple takes; and projecting to the camera rather than to an audience. However, wholeness and unity need not mean uniformity. The point is this: as audience members we want to feel we're in good hands; when we're confused or asked to make sense of seemingly incoherent elements, we want to know that the apparent incoherence happened intentionally, for an aesthetic reason, as part of the filmmakers' overall vision. For example, if a given character suddenly breaks down or reveals himself to be pretending to be somebody he isn't, the actor must sufficiently prepare for this change in the preceding scenes, however he chooses, so that we can accept it.

Looking at Acting: Michelle Williams

To begin applying these criteria, we'll take a look at the work of Michelle Williams in Derek Cianfrance's *Blue Valentine* (2010) for which she earned an Oscar nomination for Best Actress in a Leading Role. She is part of a long tradition of actors who play strong female characters in a man's world. A short list would include Joan Crawford, Bette Davis, Faye Dunaway, Jane Fonda, Jodie Foster, Lillian Gish, Diane Keaton, Frances McDormand, Ellen Page, Julia Roberts, Barbara Stanwyck, and Uma Thurman. Many of them—including Crawford, Davis, and Stanwyck—worked primarily in the studio system. As discussed earlier in this chapter, these actors worked under contractual obligations that severely limited their opportunities.

Michelle Williams is one of a younger generation of actors—including Carey Mulligan, Jennifer Lawrence, Lupita Nyong'o, and Jessica Chastain—who are enriching the art of acting. They work in today's independent production system and are almost completely free to choose their movies, roles, and sometimes even their directors, costars, and other collaborators. They work as often as they want, taking time off to meet the challenges of acting on the stage, to enjoy lucrative promotional opportunities, usually for luxury goods and services, and to enjoy private life.

Williams was born in Montana and raised in California, where, after completing the ninth grade, she quit school to pursue an acting career. With her gamine-like features, she began her movie career with comedies—Andrew Fleming's *Dick* and Jamie Babbitt's *But I'm a Cheerleader*, both 1999—before moving on to serious drama with Erik Skjoldbjærg's *Prozac Nation* (2001). Between 1999 and 2014, she'd completed over thirty movies. She is best known for her portrayals of intelligent, determined women, including Emily in Thomas McCarthy's *The Station Agent* (2003); Alma in Ang Lee's *Brokeback Mountain* (2005), for which she earned an Oscar nomination for Best Supporting Actress; Wendy in Kelly Reichardt's *Wendy and Lucy* (2008); and Emily in Reichardt's *Meek's Cutoff* (2010). Her other movies include *Deception* (2008; director Marcel Langenegger), *Synecdoche, New York* (2008; director Charlie Kaufman), *Shutter Island* (2010; director Martin Scorsese). After *Brokeback Mountain*, another turning point in Williams's career was her portrayal of Marilyn Monroe in Simon Curtis's *My Week with Marilyn* (2011), for which she garnered an Oscar nomination for Best Actress. Other movies include *Oz the Great and Powerful* (2013; director Sam Raimi) and *Suite Française* (2014; director Saul Dibb). In 2014, taking time off from her movie career, she costarred as Sally Bowles in a Broadway revival of the musical *Cabaret*. Her work in *Blue Valentine* is the subject of the following discussion.

Blue Valentine is a story about a marriage that was off course from the beginning, a union of Cindy (Michelle Williams), a talented, promising young woman, and Dean (Ryan Gosling), a romantic who is contented with only being her husband, not striving for more. His love for her is genuine, hers isn't, and it's clear from almost the beginning that she is not committed. It is basically

***My Week with Marilyn* is a week to remember**
Eddie Redmayne plays Colin Clark, a young film school graduate who lands a job as an assistant to Marilyn Monroe (Michelle Williams), who is making a movie in London. Williams gives an outstanding performance as the screen goddess, in all her fragility and craziness, as well as vulnerability in falling for Eddie, a naïve, love-sick puppy. The week they spend together, much of it alone, may be something many men dream about, but it's based on a true story. When Monroe's movie work is finished, she returns to Hollywood and her new husband, Arthur Miller. Although she leaves Colin with a broken heart, Michelle Williams's versatile portrayal of Monroe provides some level of understanding.

a two-person story that requires two superb actors to handle the characters' development from needy teenagers to disillusioned parents. She's a pre-med student living at home and looking after her aging grandmother; he works for a moving company. He may be a high school dropout, but he doesn't lack intelligence, sensitivity, or a desire to be a good husband and father. But it doesn't help their situation that she's running away from her unhappy parents, that he hasn't seen his parents in some time, that their child was fathered by Cindy's high school boyfriend, or that she attempted to abort it before agreeing to start a family with Dean.

They move to rural Pennsylvania, where Cindy works as an aide in a doctor's office and Dean as a house painter, a job that he jokingly says allows him to starting drinking at eight in the morning. She soon becomes disillusioned with him and their life together. From the marriage to the ultimate breakup, their situation changes dramatically, and the movie charts those changes through frequent flashbacks that show her falling for his boyish charm and promise of a life together to the nasty fight that ends it all. Their happy memories of the time before they were married are contrasted to a climactic weekend spent in the "Future Room" of a theme motel, an arrangement that Dean hopes will rekindle their love. When it doesn't, he provokes an ugly argument at the

Cindy and Dean are married

Cindy and Dean's wedding takes place in the office of a justice of the peace. She wears a white lace dress and cries tears of joy as she looks up at Dean and repeats the vows. The couple has taken a great risk in getting married, but they are happy as they begin their life together. The director chose to shoot all scenes of the couple's past on film stock, and the bright light flooding the office fades the colors of her face and Dean's jacket (*right*), making the image look old, as was intended.

1

2

The marriage falls apart

Two incidents, among others, indicate that Cindy and Dean's marriage is falling apart. In [1], Cindy, upset when their pet dog is killed by a passing car, watches stoically as Dean buries the body in their yard. It's an omen of what's to come, just as Dean's attempt to rekindle their marriage in the "Future Room" of a motel backfires. Soon, looking haggard [2], Cindy has one last fight with Dean. She's determined not to give in to his pleas for another chance and, within minutes, he walks out of her life. The use of digital cinematography for these scenes gives them the real-life look of a documentary film.

doctor's office where she works; consequently, she is fired, and he walks off into the distance, with their young daughter begging him to come back, as the movie ends.

Such a story—so unlike *Stella Dallas* and so recognizable in our time—requires two actors who can truthfully convince us of the characters' range of intellect and emotions as they watch their marriage crumble. Williams and Gosling were so committed to bringing the story to the screen that they served as the film's executive producers. Thus they helped to formulate the process by which the movie would be shot. Indeed, this is an excellent example of how filmmaking affects acting, especially in a low-budget, independent movie such as *Blue Valentine*. The actors and director agreed that the film would be made in three stages. As we've already noted, the movie relies heavily on continual flashbacks that contrast the first part of this couple's relationship, which was happy, with the last part, which was not. So the first stage was to shoot those happy scenes, all together, with seldom more than one take for each. There were no rehearsals. And the director, Derek Cianfrance, chose to shoot on traditional film stock because it lends a romantic quality to the footage. The second stage began when the two principal actors—joined by Faith Wladyka, who plays Frankie, their daughter—spent a month "liv-

ing" their parts in the house used for the actual shooting. (They simulated this marriage here only during the day, returning to their real-life homes at night.) In this unusual mode of working, they ripped apart the happy years, determining what they would have been like in the subsequent years, and then improvised much of the dialogue for the next stage of shooting. The third stage was to shoot the marriage as it dissolves, this time on digital media, which is bright and clinical in its look, contrasting markedly from the film footage. Here, the director shot many takes. Intercutting both kinds of footage gives the movie a discernible texture that helps the viewer separate past from present. Also, to emphasize the status of the marriage, you'll notice that in the first part of the film, the cinematographer almost always uses two-shots with the couple together in the frame, and in the second part, shoots them in separate frames.

Blue Valentine is the director's second feature film—Cianfrance's previous experience was mostly with television documentaries—and while he uses a unique method of creating the film, he also intuitively understands how to let Williams and Gosling work together to create their characters. They built on mutual trust and spent eight hours a day living together in a fully functional house where Gosling and Williams, like Dean and Cindy, did nothing but bicker with each other. After a month, they were all ready to shoot "the present" and were so fully prepared in their parts that they didn't have to act. (Cianfrance also directed Gosling in *The Place Beyond the Pines* [2013], an ambitious, complex story about fathers and sons.)

In her role as Cindy in *Blue Valentine*, Williams uses her intelligence and insight to create a character who is determined to make the best of her life, but whose stoic acceptance of reality prevails until she can stand it no longer. The director takes this strong story, of which he is a co-screenwriter, and lets it run an emotional course that is clearly established by the spontaneous interaction of the two principal actors. Its measured pace builds slowly to the ultimate blowup. Of the two characters, many viewers will find Gosling to be the more sympathetic. He emphasizes Dean's loyalty, sense of humor, kind heart, and genuine but failed efforts to understand his wife's unhappiness. He makes it clear that Dean is incapable of evolving or changing. Like the cigarette that is perpetually dangling from his lower lip, he's predictable. But while Cindy is the more determined of the two to reverse her discontent, she does it at the cost of destroying Dean. It's a grim story, hard to watch in the rawness of its emotions and in its ambiguous ending. Shattered, Dean walks off; Cindy is now a single mother with no job and an uncertain future. But she has not been defeated.

Using those characteristics that we have just defined as the key to analyzing an actor's performance, we can see that Williams looks and acts naturally, as we would expect of the character that she defines. Cindy keeps a messy house and takes little notice of her appearance, but she is engaged in something more important: balancing her tender empathy for Dean with her strong resolve to change her life. At first, their sexual life together seems satisfactory, but she soon regards it mechanically and then with resentment. They're both caring parents, but Dean works harder at it than she does. She's initially and passively resentful of Dean's lack of ambition, and then, in despair, challenges him to be more than he is (or could be). Williams conveys the thought process and feelings behind Cindy's actions and reactions primarily through gesture and physical movement: you can feel her physical resentment for her husband when he tries to make love to her. And the dialogue, which was improvised, has the honest rawness to be convincing. The frequent flashbacks to happier times require the actors to break the unity of their performances to accommodate the changes that have occurred between them then and now. Because Dean doesn't change, Cindy most clearly registers these changes. We see them in her appearance, voice, and mannerisms. In high school she's a sweet, passive kid, foolishly in love with the wrong man. Williams finds great joy in Cindy's singing and dancing in the street with Dean and dressing up for their wedding. But in later life, there is little joy, and she makes Cindy into a hard, resentful, unforgiving woman. Shooting as they did, Williams (and Gosling) faced difficult challenges in maintaining expressive coherence. Ultimately, she creates a characterization that has the wholeness of its contradictory parts.

Finally, there's a truthfulness that comes with her seemingly effortless performance, a naturalness that only a born actor can create. Williams not only looks and acts like such a character in physical appearance, facial expression, speech, movement, and gesture but also understands—and can make us understand—all kinds of feelings, ranging from vulnerability to strength.

ANALYZING ACTING

Our responses to actors' performances on-screen are perhaps our most automatic and intuitive responses to any formal aspect of film. Thus it is easy to forget that acting is as much a formal component of movies—something made—as mise-en-scène, cinematography, and editing are. And yet, acting is clearly something that must be planned and shaped in some manner; the very fact that films are shot out of continuity demands that actors approach their performances with a rigor and consciousness that mirrors the director's work on the film as a whole. This chapter has presented several different things to think about as you watch film acting in other movies. Using the criteria described in the previous section, remaining sensitive to the context of the performances, and keeping the following checklist in mind as you watch, you should be able to incorporate an intelligent analysis of acting into your discussion and writing about the movies you screen for class.

SCREENING CHECKLIST: ACTING

☐ Why was this actor, and not another, cast for the role?

☐ Does the actor's performance create a coherent, unified character? If so, how?

☐ Does the actor look the part? Is it necessary for the actor to look the part?

☐ Does the actor's performance convey the actions, thoughts, and internal complexities that we associate with natural or recognizable characters? Or does it exhibit the excessive approach we associate with nonnaturalistic characters?

☐ What elements are most distinctive in how the actor conveys the character's actions, thoughts, and internal complexities: body language, gestures, facial expressions, language?

☐ What special talents of imagination or intelligence has the actor brought to the role?

☐ How important is the filmmaking process in creating the character? Is the actor's performance overshadowed by the filmmaking process?

☐ Does the actor work well with fellow actors in this film? Do any of the other actors detract from the lead actor's performance?

☐ How, if at all, is the actor's conception of the character based on logic? How does the performance demonstrate expressive coherence?

☐ Does the actor's performance have the expressive power to make us forget that he or she is acting? If it does, how do you think the actor achieved this effect?

Questions for Review

1. How does movie acting today differ from movie acting in the 1930s through the 1960s?
2. Why is the relationship between the actor and the camera so important in making and looking at movies?
3. How did the coming of sound influence movie acting and actors?
4. What's the difference between movie stars and movie actors? Why do some critics emphasize that movie stars are a commodity created by the movie industry?
5. What factors influence the casting of actors in a movie?
6. How are naturalistic and nonnaturalistic movie acting different?
7. What is improvisational acting?
8. How do framing, composition, lighting, and the long take affect the acting in a movie?
9. Given the range of techniques available to movie actors, why do we say that their most basic skill is understanding how to reveal themselves to the camera during the close-up?
10. What do you regard as the most important criteria in analyzing acting?

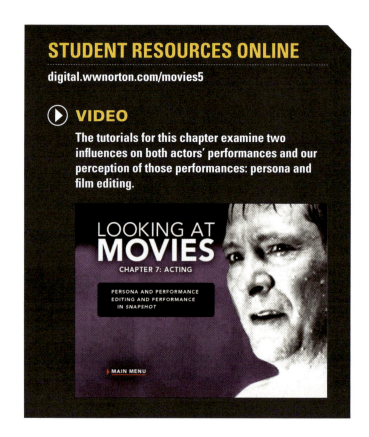

Inglorious Bastards (2009; director Quentin Tarantino, editor Sally Menke)

>>>>>

EDITING

What Is Editing?

Editing, the basic creative force of filmmaking, is the process of selecting, arranging, and assembling the essential components of a movie—visual, sound, and special effects—to tell a story in a unique way. The director and his on-set collaborators capture those elements, but it is the editor who shapes them into the movie you experience. The editor controls what you see, when you see it, its speed and pace, and what you understand and feel about all this. Indeed, editing is what distinguishes the movies from the other dramatic and visual arts, a point that cannot be overemphasized. It involves far more than an assembly process, for film editing controls the creative and expressive power of the movies. But what is good editing? There are many hallmarks, depending on the genre, narrative, cinematography, and acting. The viewers don't know what was left on the cutting room floor after the final cut, and we have become accustomed

to the excellent and almost invisible editing of today's movies, so we tend to trust it. But editing is not invisible, for everything you see on the screen is there because the director and editor agreed that it should be. As you read this chapter, you'll learn that the editing style of any movie must fit the story it is helping to tell.

There are many masters of the art, and good editing is not hard to find. You know it when you see it in such movies as *The Talented Mr. Ripley* (1999; director Anthony Minghella, editor Walter Murch), *We Need to Talk About Kevin* (2011; director Lynne Ramsay, editor Joe Bini), or *Trance* (2013; director Danny Boyle, editor Jon Harris). Like good editing, poor editing also calls attention to itself, as in these two movies: *Broken* (2012; director Rufus Norris, editor Victoria Boydell) is an interesting British middle-class family drama, but its many plots are so muddled at the end that the editing is unable to unravel them; and *Kill Your Darlings* (2013; director John Krokidas, editor Brian A. Kates) tells two stories—the coming-out of poet Allen Ginsberg (played by Daniel Radcliffe) during his college years and his relations with some truly rotten people around him, especially Lucien Carr (played brilliantly by Dane DeHaan). Carr murders a man who stands in the way of his intended affair with Ginsberg. The movie's fast-paced editing keeps the two stories apart but does not know how to reconcile the ending, which is happy and inconsistent with the beginnings of the counterculture Beat movement.

Film editor and scholar Ken Dancyger distinguishes among the technique, the craft, and the art of editing. The technique (or method) involves cutting the desired shots from the exposed roll of film or digital storage device and then joining them together so that they form a continuous whole. Before digital editing, this manual and often tedious process was called **cutting** and **splicing**, because the editor used scissors to sever the shots from the roll of film before using glue or tape to splice them together. Editors were responsible primarily for visual images. With digital editing, the work is simpler, cleaner, and easier to manage, and editors are now frequently responsible for editing all elements of the film, including the visual, sound, and special effects elements. The craft (skill) is the ability to join shots and produce a meaning that does not exist in either one of them individually. The art of editing, Dancyger declares, "occurs when the combination of two or more shots takes meaning to the next level—excitement,

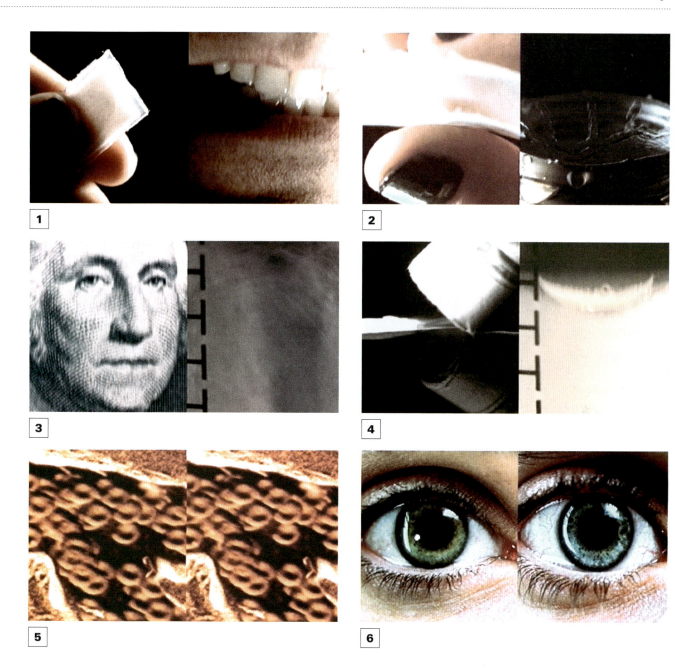

The power of editing

These images, taken from a roughly half-minute sequence from Darren Aronofsky's *Requiem for a Dream* (2000; editor Jay Rabinowitz), illustrate the potential power of film editing. As pictures are juxtaposed—in this case, literally placed side by side using an editing technique called *split screen*—the meaning of one affects the meaning of the other. Together the shots influence our creation of their meaning, and their combined meaning then affects how we see the following two halves, whose meaning undergoes a transformation similar to that of the first two, and so on. This interpretive process goes on through the sequence, into the following shot, the following sequence, and ultimately the entire movie. Our creation of meaning proceeds incrementally, though at a much faster rate of calculation than this caption can convey.

All of these images, in this context, relate to drug use. Focusing on minute details of the rituals of drug use, the sequence seeks to approximate the characters' frantic experience and to represent the perceptual changes that accompany their intake of narcotics. Through the language of editing, Aronofsky has given us a fresh look at a phenomenon that is often portrayed in clichéd and unimaginative ways.

As an experiment, try to imagine different juxtapositions of these same images, taken not in sequence but in isolation. Outside the context of drugs, what might George Washington's image on a dollar bill next to a widened, bloodshot eye mean? What might gritting teeth next to that reddish flow mean? For that matter, to what use might someone, maybe the creator of television commercials or public service messages, put each image alone?

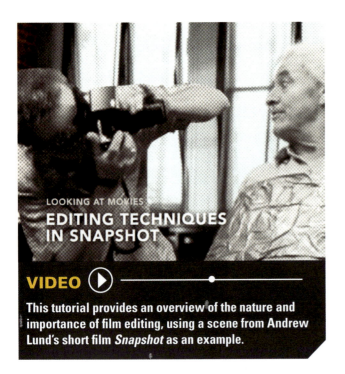

LOOKING AT MOVIES

EDITING TECHNIQUES IN SNAPSHOT

VIDEO ▶

This tutorial provides an overview of the nature and importance of film editing, using a scene from Andrew Lund's short film *Snapshot* as an example.

insight, shock, or the epiphany of discovery."[1] That is the essence of editing.

The basic building block of film editing is the **shot** (as defined in Chapter 6), and its most fundamental tool is the cut. Each shot has two explicit values: the first value is determined by what is within the shot itself; the second value is determined by how the shot is situated in relation to other shots. The first value is largely the responsibility of the director, cinematographer, production designer, and other collaborators who determine what is captured on film. The second value is the product of editing.

The early Soviet film theorists and filmmakers, particularly Dziga Vertov, Sergei Eisenstein, Lev Kuleshov, and Vsevolod I. Pudovkin (see "1924–1930: The Soviet Montage Movement" in Chapter 10), were concerned with not only individual shots, but the relationship of those shots within their context. Kuleshov reputedly demonstrated the fundamental power of editing by producing a short film (now lost, unfortunately) in which an identical shot of an expressionless actor appeared after

each of these shots: a dead woman, a child, and a dish of soup. The audience viewing this film reportedly assumed that the actor was reacting to each stimulus by changing his expression appropriately—showing sorrow (for the dead woman), tenderness (for the young child), and hunger (for the food)—when in fact his expression remained the same. (See "Kuleshov effect" on p. 324.)

Likewise, Pudovkin showed that the meaning of a shot will vary with its order (or, to use his word, *linkage*) in the context created by the surrounding shots. In one of his experiments, he took three close-ups (CUs) and arranged them differently. In the first experiment, he placed the order of shots as follows: in shot A, a man is smiling; in shot B, a pistol is being pointed; and in shot C, the man looks frightened. In the second experiment, Pudovkin arranged the shots as follows: in shot A, a man looks afraid; in shot B, a pistol is being pointed; and in shot C, the man is smiling. As you can see, to change the meaning, the editor simply changed the order of shots. This achievement was significant in asserting the film editor's power as well as drawing on the flexibility of the viewers' psychology. Thus shot order also serves a narrative purpose. This tendency of viewers to interpret shots in relation to surrounding shots is the most fundamental assumption behind all film editing. Editing takes advantage of this psychological tendency to accomplish various effects: to help tell a story, to provoke an idea or a feeling, or to call attention to itself as an element of cinematic form. No matter how straightforward a movie may seem, you can be sure that (with rare exceptions) the editor made difficult decisions about which shots to use and how to use them.

The Film Editor

The person primarily responsible for such decisions is the film editor.[2] In theory, the bulk of the film editor's work occurs after the director and collaborators have shot all of the movie's footage. In fact, in many major film productions, the editor's responsibilities as a collaborator begin much earlier in the process. During

---

1. Ken Dancyger, *The Technique of Film and Video Editing: Theory and Practice*, 2nd ed. (Boston: Focal Press, 1997), pp. xiv–xv.

2. For a documentary that explores editing through interviews with many leading editors (including Thelma Schoonmaker, Mathilde Bonnefoy, George Lucas, and Sarah Flack), see *Edge Codes.com: The Art of Motion Picture Editing* (2004; director: Alex Shuper). Edge codes (also called edge numbers or footage numbers) are the numbers printed along the edge of film stock and the magnetic sound track to assist the editors in locating images quickly and matching audio and visual images.

preproduction and production, even from the moment the movie is conceived, an editor may make suggestions to the director and cinematographer for composition, blocking, lighting, and shooting that will help the editing itself. Editors literally work behind the scenes, but their contributions can make the difference between artistic success and artistic failure, between an ordinary movie and a masterpiece.

The film editor also supervises and works closely with the editing department, whose size can vary depending on the type and scope of the production. Today's digital editing department requires a different level of technical expertise than previously needed, mainly because the computer equipment and digital process is more technically (if not creatively) complex. Nonetheless, a digital editing suite is a much tidier and better organized facility than the pre-digital ones, where loops of film hung all over to form a celluloid jungle. The basic crew consists of coeditors who draft scenes and sequences in consultation with the lead editor; assistant editors responsible for transferring, labeling, importing, organizing, and archiving terabytes of digital video files; and a postproduction supervisor who shepherds the entire process through the initial picture editing as well as the subsequent steps required before the final digital export: scoring, sound design, sound mixing, visual effects, and color grading and correction.

A good film editor must be focused, detail oriented, well organized, disciplined, able to work for long stretches of time, and willing to take as much time as necessary to fulfill the director's vision. Throughout their work, film editors must collaborate with the director and be resilient enough to withstand the producer's interference. In short, a good editor practices a rigorous craft. Even in a well-planned production, when the director has a clear vision of what to shoot and how it will look, the editor faces countless difficult decisions about what to use and what to cut.

That has always been the case, but today's movies run longer and contain more individual shots than movies did fifty years ago, so the editor's job has become more involved. For example, a typical Hollywood movie made in the 1940s and 1950s runs approximately 1 to 1½ hours long and is composed of about 1,000 shots; today's movies typically run between 2 and 3 hours, but because they consist of around 2,000 to 3,000 shots, they have a faster tempo than earlier films had. That factor alone increases the editor's work of selecting and arranging the footage. It is common for the ratio between unused and used footage in a Hollywood production to be as high as 20 to 1, meaning that for every 1 minute you see on the screen, 20 minutes of footage has been discarded. The postproduction problems that really challenge editors, however—the ones we sometimes read about in the press—tend to overinflate this ratio of unused to used footage.

Perhaps the best-known extreme example is Francis Ford Coppola's *Apocalypse Now* (1979). Working for two years, Walter Murch and his editorial team eventually shaped 235 hours of footage into a (mostly) coherent movie that runs 2 hours 33 minutes (resulting in a ratio of unused to used footage of just under 100 to 1). Sifting through the mountain of footage to find the best shots, making thousands of little decisions along the way, Murch and his team gave narrative shape to what many people at the time—sometimes even Coppola himself—considered a disaster of directorial self-indulgence. Twenty-two years later, Coppola asked Murch and his team to restore 49 minutes that they had originally cut; that version, known as the "director's cut," was released in 2001 as *Apocalypse Now Redux*.

Clearly, the creative power of the editor comes close to that of the director. But in most mainstream film productions, that creative power is put in service of the director's vision. "One gives as much as possible," says film editor Helen van Dongen, "as much as is beneficial to the final form of the film, without overshadowing or obstructing the director's intentions. . . . The editor working with a great director can do no better than discover and disclose the director's design."[3]

Consider, for example, the challenges faced by David Tedeschi, the editor of Martin Scorsese's *Shine a Light* (2008), which documents two Rolling Stones concerts in New York. Robert Richardson, the director of photography, supervised eighteen camera operators and dozens of camera assistants and lighting technicians. The editor was faced with selecting and arranging the thousands of feet of live footage that, in the finished movie, is intercut with archival footage of the group's career. (Similar challenges face the editor of any large concert

3. Helen van Dongen, qtd. in Richard Barsam, "Discover and Disclose: Helen van Dongen and *Louisiana Story*," in *Filming Robert Flaherty's "Louisiana Story": The Helen van Dongen Diary*, by Helen Durant, ed. Eva Orbanz (New York: Museum of Modern Art, 1998), p. 86.

Editing thousands of feet of footage for *Shine a Light*
A remote-controlled, crane-mounted camera (*right*) was one of eighteen cameras used to record a 2008 Rolling Stones concert for Martin Scorsese's *Shine a Light* (2008). The editor, David Tedeschi, met the overwhelming challenge of creating a record from the thousands of feet of footage recorded by those cameras. The result is one of the most vibrant, yet intimate rock movies ever made.

movie, such as Michael Wadleigh's *Woodstock* [1970], of which Scorsese was an editor.) If any one word could describe the Rolling Stones, it's probably the *energy* generated by the band's propulsive rhythms and stage movements. Mick Jagger rarely stops moving, which is a delight for audiences but a major challenge for camera operators and editors who have to contain him within the frame. Multiple cameras—stationary, moving, hand-held—produced footage from many different angles and positions on the stage, in the audience, in the balcony, and backstage. The editor then had to edit that footage to maintain on the screen, as much as possible, the continuity and energy of Jagger's movements on the stage. Tedeschi cuts with grace and ease. He manages, almost miraculously, to keep the star of the show on full screen when he is singing, thus preserving the integrity of each song as well as cutting to other musicians and the audience. *Shine a Light* was released in standard 70mm

and in the IMAX format, the size of which magnifies every shot. There's no hiding a weak cut when the image is 72 feet wide and 53 feet high (and sometimes even larger). The cinematographers capture the Rolling Stones' essential energy, and the editor repackages it and keeps it going for the two-hour length of the movie.

Although cinematic conventions can guide a film-maker, there are no rules—or at least no rules that can't be broken. Simply put, shooting a movie and editing it can be a seamless process. You can see this in Richard Linklater's *Boyhood* (2014; editor Sandra Adair), a movie about the passing of time that covers twelve years in a boy's life (running time 2 hrs. 44 min.). Sometimes, the only way to know that a year or two has passed is to see the subtle changes in a character's appearance. And it's the image, not the nearly invisible cutting, that makes you aware of that elapsed time.[4]

4. It would be instructive to compare and contrast the editing of other films dealing with the passage of time in a young person's life, for example, François Truffaut's *The 400 Blows* (1959).

However, there are as many approaches to editing as there are editors, and directors, and editor-director partnerships, and directors who are editors, and so on. Here's how two legendary directors look at editing. John Ford, like Alfred Hitchcock, said that he edited the movie in the camera; in other words, he visualized beforehand how the movie would look and then shot only the footage necessary. As a result, Ford's editors had few choices. This approach works on two levels: it was the artistic creed of a great storyteller who did not make up things as he went along; but it was also the tactic of a shrewd player in Hollywood's golden age when the studio (overriding the director and editor) reserved the right to take over the editing of a film after it was completed. Thanks to the success of his amazingly long career, Ford had earned the right to edit his own films, but he did not need to do much.

By contrast, Orson Welles arrived in Hollywood never having made a feature-length film, but he learned from Ford's example and shot *Citizen Kane* with such a clear vision of how he wanted it to look on the screen that his editor, Robert Wise, could only put his own touches on memorable sequences in the film. Welles understood the importance of a good working relationship with his editor. For example, the brilliant "breakfast table" scene was Welles's idea on every level, but Wise gave it the rhythm that seals its power. Welles, too, was a great storyteller, and he loved the editing process: "I don't know of any more fun than making a movie, and the most fun of all comes in the cutting room when the shooting is over."[5] A totally different approach comes from Thelma Schoonmaker, who has edited almost all of Martin Scorsese's movies and is used to working with far more footage than she needs: "It's hard for people to understand editing. . . . It's absolutely like sculpture. You get a big lump of clay, and you have to form it—this raw, unedited, very long footage."[6]

The length (2 hrs. 19 min.) of Terence Malick's *The Tree of Life* (2011) made some audiences impatient and led some critics to complain that its five editors should have been able to make it shorter. Malick's films have a definite philosophical aspect; this one is about *time*, which we know has no end. Yet, we're conditioned to expect a movie to have an ending, even if it's as arbitrary as Malick's. *The Tree of Life* puts our expectations to the test. Novelist Henry James wisely counseled readers to "grant the writer his *donnée* [what's given or fixed]," grant him the world he establishes, its starting and ending place. With that in mind, we must grant that Malick's movie is *his* world. If you accept that, you'll find this movie to be demanding, even taxing, but it's also an unforgettable and challenging experience to see time objectified on the screen.

As you continue reading this chapter, you'll see there are many ways to edit a movie—to shape cinematic space and time.

The Editor's Responsibilities

The film editor has both stylistic and technical responsibilities in the telling of a movie's story. He or she is an artist, a full partner in creating a movie's expressive qualities. In terms of technique, the editor is responsible for managing the following aspects of the final film:

❯ spatial relationships between shots

❯ temporal relationships between shots

❯ the overall rhythm of the film

Let's examine these responsibilities more closely.

Spatial Relationships between Shots One of the most powerful effects of film editing is to create a sense of space in the mind of the viewer. When we are watching any single shot from a film, our sense of the overall space of the scene is necessarily limited by the height, width, and depth of the film frame during that shot. But as other shots are placed in close proximity to that original shot, our sense of the overall space in which the characters are moving shifts and expands. The juxtaposition of shots within a scene can cause us to have a fairly complex sense of that overall space (something like a mental map) even if no single shot discloses more than a fraction of that space to us at a time.

For example, as the opening titles roll in Kimberly Peirce's *Boys Don't Cry* (1999; editor Lee Percy), through a short sequence of tightly framed shots we see cars dangerously passing one another on a rural highway, the exterior of a trailer park, an interior of a trailer where

---

5. Qtd. in Orson Welles and Peter Bogdanovich, *This Is Orson Welles* (New York: HarperCollins 1992), p. 149.

6. Qtd. in Eric Hynes, "Cut Here, Cut There, But It's Still 3 Hours," *New York Times* (January 19, 2014), pp. AR10, 21.

Teena Brandon (Hilary Swank) is getting a haircut to make her look like a teenage boy, the exterior of a skating rink, and finally the refashioned young woman inside introducing herself to her female blind date as "Brandon." The shots themselves and the manner in which they are edited introduce the space clearly, tightly, and unambiguously. These shots also introduce characters, mood, and conflict. The foreboding mood is established by the steady rhythm of the editing and the equally steady drumbeat on the sound track. There seems to be no turning back for Teena, and as a result, we sense that a conflict may arise over this young woman's identification of her gender.

The power of editing to establish spatial relationships between shots is so strong, in fact, that filmmakers have almost no need to ensure that a real space exists whose dimensions correspond to the one implied by editing. Countless films, especially historical dramas and science-fiction films, rely heavily on the power of editing to fool us into perceiving their worlds as vast and complete even as we are shown only tiny fractions of the implied space. Because our brains effortlessly make spatial generalizations from limited visual information, George Lucas was not required, for example, to build an entire to-scale model of the *Millennium Falcon* to convince us that the characters in *Star Wars* are flying (and moving around within) a vast spaceship. Instead, a series of cleverly composed shots filmed on carefully designed (and relatively small) sets could, when edited together, create the illusion of a massive, fully functioning spacecraft.

In addition to painting a mental picture of the space of a scene, editing manipulates our sense of spatial relationships among characters, objects, and their surroundings. For example, the placement of one shot of a person's reaction (perhaps a look of concerned shock) after a shot of an action by another person (falling down a flight of stairs) immediately creates in our minds the thought that the two people are occupying the same space, that the person in the first shot is visible to the person in the second shot, and that the emotional response of the person in the second shot is a reaction to what has happened to the person in the first shot. The central discovery of Lev Kuleshov, the Soviet film theorist mentioned at the beginning of this chapter, was that these two shots need not have any actual relationship at all to one another for this effect to take place in a viewer's mind. The effect of perceiving such spatial

LOOKING AT MOVIES
THE KULESHOV EXPERIMENT

VIDEO ▶ ━━━━●━━━━

In this tutorial, Dave Monahan attempts to re-create the Kuleshov effect.

relationships even when we are given minimal visual information or when we are presented with shots filmed at entirely different times and places is sometimes called the **Kuleshov effect**.

Temporal Relationships between Shots You have already learned that the plot of a narrative film is often shaped and ordered in a way that differs significantly from the film's underlying story. In fact, the pleasure that many contemporary movies give to viewers has its source in the bold decisions made by some filmmakers to manipulate the presentation of the plot in creative and confusing ways. Films such as Christopher Nolan's *Memento* (2000; editor Dody Dorn), Spike Jonze's *Adaptation* (2002; editor Eric Zumbrunnen), or Michel Gondry's *Eternal Sunshine of the Spotless Mind* (2004; editor Valdis Óskarsdóttir) are interesting in part because their plots are presented in a fragmented, out-of-order fashion that we as viewers must reshuffle them to make sense of the underlying story. But even in more traditional narrative films whose plots are presented more or less chronologically, editing is used to manipulate the presentation of plot time on-screen.

For example, **flashback** (the interruption of chronological plot time with a shot or series of shots showing an event that has happened earlier in the story) is a common editing technique. Used in virtually all movie genres, it is a traditional storytelling device that typically

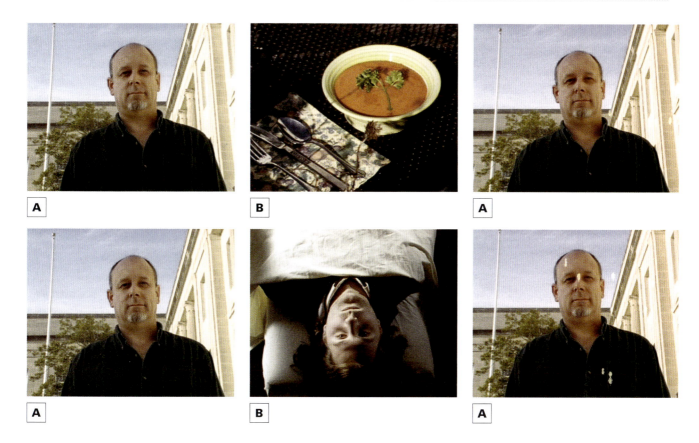

The Kuleshov effect

In the 1920s, Soviet film pioneer Lev Kuleshov conducted an experiment to investigate how editing can create new meaning. He juxtaposed a shot of an actor wearing a neutral expression and looking offscreen with a number of other shots and then screened them in sequence for a test audience. When the viewers watched a series of shots like the ABA sequence above (from the DVD tutorial re-creation of Kuleshov's experiment), they interpreted the character in shot A as looking at the soup and assumed he was hungry. When shown a sequence using the same shot of the expressionless actor but juxtaposed instead with the image of a dead man, viewers assumed a relationship between the character and the corpse and felt the actor was expressing grief or remorse. With this simple experiment, Kuleshov demonstrated a creative capacity of film editing that editors still use: the juxtaposition of images to create new meaning not present in any single shot by itself.

explains how a situation or character developed into what we see at the present time.

The flashback can be as stimulating as it is in Orson Welles's *Citizen Kane* (1941; editor Robert Wise), where our sense of Charles Foster Kane is created by the memories of those who knew him, or as straightforward as Walter Neff's (Fred MacMurray) on-screen narration of Billy Wilder's classic film noir *Double Indemnity* (1944; editor Doane Harrison); in fact, the flashback is frequently used in film noir. It can also serve as the backbone for the structure of a complicated narrative, as in Alain Resnais's *Hiroshima mon amour* (1959; editors Jasmine Chasney, Henri Colpi, and Anne Sarraute) or Quentin Tarantino's *Pulp Fiction* (1994; editor Sally Menke).

Much less common than the flashback is the **flashforward**, the interruption of present action by a shot or series of shots that show images from the plot's future.

Often, flash-forwards reflect a character's desire for someone or something, a premonition of something that might happen, or even a psychic projection. Flashforward is a problematic element in any film that strives for realism, because it implies that the film's characters are somehow seeing the future. Once employed, flash-forward sends the signal that the movie we are watching is at least partly fantastical and that we should be ready to suspend our disbelief.

The most common manipulation of time through editing is **ellipsis**, an omission between one thing and another. In a quotation, for example, an ellipsis mark (. . .) signifies the omission of one or more words. In filmmaking, an ellipsis generally signifies the omission of time—the time that separates one shot from another. Ellipsis in movies is chiefly a practical tool; it economizes the presentation of plot, skipping over portions

1

2

Flashbacks can help to develop characters

Director Terrence Malick makes poignant use of flashbacks in *The Thin Red Line* (1998; editors Billy Weber, Leslie Jones, and Saar Klein), his epic account of a crucial World War II battle in Asia. He knows that the depiction of soldiers—from Homer's *Iliad* to the movies—often includes their longing for home, wives, and family, a longing for safety and peace. Malick uses a series of such flashbacks to develop the characters of Pvt. John Bell (Ben Chaplin) and his wife, Marty (Miranda Otto). The flashbacks emphasize how war has interrupted their deep, idyllic emotional and sexual relationship. In [1], talking to Cpl. Geoffrey Fife (Adrien Brody, *left*), Bell says that he never touched another woman and wouldn't feel the desire to do so; this is followed by a flashback to a romantic, nighttime image of Marty staring out their bedroom window, as if longing for him [2]. Such an interpretation would be romantic, but Bell soon receives a letter from Marty saying that she is tired of waiting for him and wants a divorce so that she can marry a man she has fallen in love with. Here, the flashback is used ironically, to contrast John's illusions about the past—virtually his reason for living and fighting in the war—with the reality of the present wartime conditions.

1

2

Flash-forward clues us in on a murder yet to happen

The flash-forward creates an ironic context in Sydney Pollack's *They Shoot Horses, Don't They?* (1969; editor Fredric Steinkamp), a melodrama about the marathon dance contests that were a fad in the 1930s during the Great Depression. Gloria (Jane Fonda) and Robert (Michael Sarrazin), who meet and agree to dance together in the competition, want to win this grueling ordeal for the prize money and are seemingly in it until the bitter end—or almost. They are ill-matched: Gloria is a self-destructive aspiring actress; and Michael, who was deeply affected as a boy by seeing a horse shot after breaking its leg, is the more optimistic. The colorful contest is punctuated several times with highly stylized flash-forwards, shot in an entirely different mise-en-scène and color, depicting Robert in jail or at his trial for murder. They suggest that there is more to this easygoing young man than we expect. In [1], we see the couple, physically and emotionally exhausted from an ordeal that has run for more than 1,000 hours; [2] is a flash-forward to Robert being sentenced for murder. We don't know if this trial really happened—the blue-gray image seems expressionistic, even surreal—and we don't know whom he has murdered. Soon the couple, who have fallen for one another, walk out, disillusioned because the contest is dishonest. In the final scene, Gloria takes a pistol from her purse and attempts to kill herself; unable to pull the trigger, she asks Robert to do it—and he does! The flash-forwards, eerie as they are, foreshadow an action that contradicts everything we know about Robert, whose final words are those of the title.

1

2

3

Ellipsis causing disorientation

Steven Soderbergh's *Erin Brockovich* (2000; editor Anne V. Coates) demonstrates how an ellipsis can be used to cause the viewer's momentary disorientation. A sharp cut leads from [1] Erin Brockovich's car being hit broadside to [2] Ed Masry (Albert Finney) being told by his secretary (Conchata Ferrell) that Brockovich is waiting to see him. Next [3], Masry is seen greeting Brockovich (Julia Roberts), who is wearing a neck brace. Images [2] and [3] take place sequentially; although we don't know how much time has elapsed between images [1] and [2], it was at least enough to permit Brockovich to get the brace and make an appointment to see a lawyer.

of the underlying story that do not need to be presented on-screen to be understood or inferred. But its use requires the filmmaker to have carefully established the time, place, location, characters, and action so that viewers are able not only to follow what they see but also to make the intuitive inferences that fill in the material that was left out. This is what happens in Gus Van Sant's *Drugstore Cowboy* (1989; editors Mary Bauer and Curtiss Clayton) when a policeman asks Bob (Matt Dillon), a heroin addict, "Are you going to tell us where you hid the drugs, or are we going to have to tear the place apart bit by bit?" When the next shot shows Bob's house torn apart, the cut implies an ellipsis of time, and it presents us with everything we need to know about the period of story time that has elapsed.

The effect of an ellipsis on viewers is determined by how much story time is implied between shots as well as by the manner in which the editing makes the transition from the first shot to the second. In some cases, such as the example from *Drugstore Cowboy* just mentioned, an ellipsis can seem very natural and may signal a straightforward cause-and-effect relationship. In others, an ellipsis may span a much longer period of

implied story time, or the transition may be so unexpected and sudden that the effect on viewers is shock or disorientation.

For example, in Steven Soderbergh's *Erin Brockovich* (2000 editor Anne V. Coates), the title character (played by Julia Roberts), while driving away from an unsuccessful job interview, is hit broadside. We don't see what happens as the immediate result of this incident, for there is a sharp elliptical cut to a scene in which lawyer Ed Masry (Albert Finney) arrives at his office and is told by his secretary that a woman named Erin Brockovich is waiting to see him: "car accident; not her fault, she says." When he enters his office, he sees Erin wearing a neck brace. However, we don't know how much time has elapsed between the accident and this meeting.

Playing with time, and particularly with ellipses of all kinds, has become one of Soderbergh's stylistic trademarks. In *The Limey* (1999; editor Sarah Flack), the time and space of the entire movie are edited to be disori. enting. The narrative is driven by continual use of the ellipsis for shock and/or disorientation. England and California are constantly juxtaposed, as are the present, past, and future as well as memory, imagination, flashbacks,

Ellipsis for comic effect

An ellipsis shortens the time between two actions, but it can also have comic implications. In Steven Soderbergh's *Out of Sight* (1998; editor Anne V. Coates), Karen Sisco (Jennifer Lopez), a federal marshal, starts out to nab an escaped convict, Jack Foley (George Clooney), but instead is pulled into a bathtub and kisses him [1]. While she may be romantically overwhelmed, note that she still has her gun firmly in hand. A quick cut, an obvious ellipsis, shows her later in a hospital bed with a nasty bruise on her forehead [2]. Considering that she thinks little about being in a bathtub with a convicted felon, we might reach various fanciful conclusions—until we remember that she was put in that hospital earlier in the movie for another reason.

and flash-forwards. Some shots identify characters in full frames; others do not. We are never sure where or when the action is taking place. However, the cumulative progress of disorientation eventually leads us to put the pieces together, to see repeating patterns, and to become oriented.

Whether sudden and unexpected or seemingly natural, ellipses are also frequently used to provide an instant, sometimes comic, resolution to a situation. In *Out of Sight* (1998; editor Anne V. Coates), for example,

director Soderbergh tells the story of an improbable romance between two highly attractive people: Jack Foley (George Clooney), a notorious bank robber, and Karen Sisco (Jennifer Lopez), a federal marshal. Sisco has witnessed Foley and a buddy bust out of prison, and they take her hostage, but she escapes. The next day, she learns that Foley is in Miami, and, with gun in hand, she enters his hotel room and discovers him relaxing in the bathtub. As she bends over him with her gun pointed at his head, he pulls her into the water on top of him, she lays down the gun, and they kiss.

There is a quick cut, and an obvious ellipsis, for the next shot is of Sisco's father standing over her as she lies in a hospital bed with a dark bruise on her forehead. From earlier in the movie, we know that she got to the hospital because of a car crash that occurred during her escape from Foley and his buddy. However disorienting this ellipsis may be, it is also funny. In such romantic comedies, it is conventional for opposites to fall for one another, perhaps even to become partners in crime, à la Bonnie and Clyde, whose portrayals on the screen (in Arthur Penn's *Bonnie and Clyde*, 1967) Sisco and Foley have previously discussed with admiration.

Another method for controlling the presentation of time in a film is **montage**. *Montage*—from the French verb *monter*, "to assemble or put together"—is French for "editing." French film theorist André Bazin defines montage as "the creation of a sense or meaning not proper to the images themselves but derived exclusively from their juxtaposition."[7] In the former Soviet Union in the 1920s, *montage* referred to the various forms of editing that expressed ideas developed by Eisenstein, Kuleshov, Vertov, Pudovkin, and others. In Hollywood, beginning in the 1930s, *montage* designates a sequence of shots, often with superimpositions and optical effects, that shows a condensed series of events. For example, a montage of flipping calendar pages was a typical (if trite) way to show the passage of time. In Wes Anderson's *Rushmore* (1998; editor David Moritz), after the headmaster identifies Max Fischer (Jason Schwartzman) as "one of the worst students we've got," a twenty-one-shot montage unexpectedly shows Max as the key person in virtually every club at the school.

Danny Boyle's brilliant *Trainspotting* (1996; editor Masahiro Hirakubo) is a movie so full with life—more specifically, the process of choosing a life—that we are

7. André Bazin, *What Is Cinema?* ed. and trans. Hugh Gray, 2 vols. (Berkeley: University of California Press, 1967–1971), I, p. 25.

LOOKING AT MOVIES
THE EVOLUTION OF EDITING: MONTAGE

VIDEO ▶

This tutorial explores montage and discontinuity editing in Sergei Eisentein's film *The Battleship Potemkin.*

surprised to find that its characters have chosen heroin addiction as their existence. But instead of producing an antidrug tirade full of dire warnings, Boyle has produced a colorful, lively film that is great fun to watch. These characters, four young Scottish men who are always high, live in squalor (the film's colors are unique and symbolic), stealing liberally to support their habits. The style of the design, mise-en-scène, cinematography, and acting is frenzied, and the rhythm of the editing is set by an extravagant use of montage. In fact, the first of the movie's two parts consists of one montage after another, each of them full of life on the edge.

The opening montage, with its voice-over narration by the lead character Renton (Ewan McGregor), establishes the movie's look and pace—colorful and fast. In the second part of the movie, perhaps the most impressive montage depicts the boys and their girls going nightclubbing. With its relentless beat, the loud sound track of "druggy" music—especially by Iggy Pop—helps (with editing that matches) to create the illusion of fast-passing time, from the evening's wild antics to the next morning's hangovers. (You have to see this montage to enjoy it, for it is impossible to illustrate here.) The montage reaffirms that Renton and his mates live for heroin while in reality their lives are marked by bad drug experiences, rehab attempts, gruesome withdrawals,

cheating on one another, theft and sex of all kinds, arrests, illegal drug deals, and death.

Near the end, the boys sell stolen drugs for thousands of pounds and celebrate accordingly, ending up asleep in a seedy hotel room. In the final montage, Renton escapes with all of the loot. And in a voice-over narration that parallels the opening one, he vows to live a stable life that he knows will be materialistic and commonplace, totally different from the life depicted in the film's many montage sequences. The Russian filmmakers who invented the technique would have loved it.

For these various editorial manipulations of time to be understandable to viewers, editors must employ accepted conventions of editing that signal the transitions from shot to shot. Luckily, our minds are able to understand these conventions and to infer correctly the progression of plot and story from them, even when the plot is presented in nonchronological order and is riddled with ellipses. It's not entirely clear why our brains are able to do this, but for the sake of film history, it's a good thing. As Walter Murch puts it:

> When you stop to think about it, it is amazing that film editing works at all. One moment we're on top of Mauna Kea and—*cut!*—the next we're at the bottom of the Mariana Trench. The instantaneous transition of the cut is nothing like what we experience as normal life, which seems to be one continuous shot from the moment we wake until we close our eyes at night. It wouldn't have been surprising if film editing had been tried and then abandoned after it was found to induce a kind of seasickness. But it doesn't: we happily endure, in fact even enjoy, these sudden transitions for which nothing in our evolutionary history seems to have prepared us.[8]

Rhythm Among other things, editing determines the **duration** of a shot. Thus it controls the length of time you can look at each shot and absorb the information within it. Film editors can control the rhythm (or beat) of a film—the pace at which it moves forward—by varying the duration of the shots in relation to one another, and thus they can control the speed (tempo) and accents (stress or lack of it on certain shots). Sometimes the editing rhythm allows us time to think about what we see; at other times, it moves too quickly to permit thought.

8. Michael Ondaatje, *The Conversations: Walter Murch and the Art of Editing Film* (New York: Knopf, 2002), p. 49.

The musical analogy is useful, but only to a point, because a movie serves a narrative while rhythm seldom does. However, there are some landmarks in the development of movie editing—among them the "Odessa Steps" sequence in Sergei Eisenstein's *Battleship Potemkin* (1925; editors Grigori Akesandrov and Eisenstein), the diving sequence in Leni Riefenstahl's *Olympia* (1938; editor Riefenstahl), Jean-Luc Godard's *Breathless* (1960; editors Cécile Decugis and Lila Herman), Andy and Larry Wachowski's *The Matrix* (1999; editor Zach Staenberg), and Tom Tykwer's *Run Lola Run* (1998; editor Mathilde Bonnefoy)—in which the editing (its patterns, rhythms, etc.) almost seems more important than the narrative. A movie narrative has its own internal requirements that signal to the editor how long to make each shot and with what rhythm to combine those shots. Many professional editors say that they intuitively reach decisions on these matters.

What happens, however, when the rhythm is imposed autocratically before a film is made? To find out, you might look at Jørgen Leth and Lars von Trier's *The Five Obstructions* (2003; editors Daniel Dencik, Morten Højbjerg, and Camilla Skousen). In the movie, von Trier, one of the founders of the Danish Dogme movement, views Leth's 12-minute film *The Perfect Human* (1967). In an interesting reversal of roles—Leth was one of von Trier's idols—he "orders" the older director to remake the film five times, each version tightly controlled by limitations ("obstructions") that he specifies. The first version is to be composed of single shots of no more than twelve frames, each shot appearing for approximately half a second on the screen. The result, a charming look at Cuba, closely resembles a television advertisement or an MTV spot.

Of course, the images tell a kind of story simply by the rhythm that links them. But this rigid imposition of a fixed rhythm makes traditional editing, and thus traditional storytelling, impossible. Why? Because editing requires the editor to make decisions about shot length, rhythm, emphasis, and the like; von Trier's formula (as successfully applied by Leth) ties the editor's hands and puts all of the decision making in the mind of the viewer. In looking at *The Five Obstructions*, we can understand the value of experimentation, particularly for those who prefer intellectual schematics to be applied to art.

Experimentation in editing does not have to be formulaic, as demonstrated by Mathilde Bonnefoy, the editor of Tom Tykwer's *Run Lola Run* (1998). Bonnefoy handles the editor's traditional tasks—fixing the duration and frequency of shots and thus controlling the film's emphasis on a person, setting, or object—with such a sense of joy that the movie is more about the editing than about the narrative. In the opening sequence, Lola (Franka Potente) receives a phone call from her boyfriend, Manni (Moritz Bleibtreu), who implores her to help him return $100,000 to the criminal gang for which he works. If he does not do so in 20 minutes, the gang will kill him. Lola hangs up, imagines what her task will involve, and then sets off, running through the rooms of her apartment, down the stairs, and out into the city streets.

Although the principal action is composed of shots of Lola running, there are breaks in that rhythm for scenes of other action that introduce several of the characters relevant to Lola's quest. Tykwer uses a constantly moving camera, live and animated footage, time-lapse cinematography, slow motion and fast motion, different camera positions and angles, hard cuts, dissolves, jump cuts, and ellipses. Accents within the shots create their own patterns: different camera angles and heights, changes in the direction that Lola is running on the screen (e.g., left to right, right to left, toward us, away from us, or diagonally across the frame). Underscoring the resulting visual rhythm is an equally exciting sound track. Basically, it is the familiar disco beat scored for a synthesizer, piano, and percussion, with accents of glass breaking and camera shutters clicking, and Lola's voice repeating, "I wish I was a . . . ," and other voices chanting "Hey, hey, hey."

Together, editing and sound create the steady pace of Lola's run, make us empathize with her dilemma, and establish suspense (will Lola get the money? will

Patterns in *Battleship Potemkin*

Soviet filmmaker and theorist Sergei Eisenstein helped pioneer the expressive use of patterns in movies by using a dynamic form of editing called *montage*. Eisenstein's montage during the "Odessa Steps" sequence in *Battleship Potemkin* (1925; editors Grigori Aleksandrov and Eisenstein) brings violence to a climax in both what we see and how we see it. After Cossacks fire [1] on a young mother [2], she collapses [3], sending her baby's carriage rolling [4]; an older woman reacts [5] to the carriage's flight down a series of steps [6], and a student cries out [7] as the carriage hits bottom [8]. The pattern of movement from shot to shot accentuates the devastating energy contained in this scene.

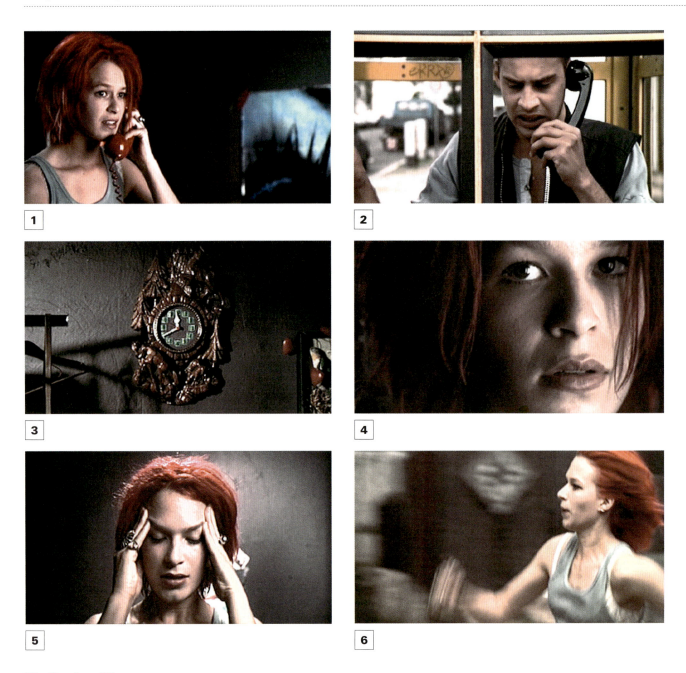

Rhythm in editing

In Tom Tykwer's *Run Lola Run* (1998; editor Mathilde Bonnefoy), the title character (played by Franka Potente) [1] receives word that her boy-friend, Manni (Moritz Bleibtreu) [2], is in a dire situation—a matter of money and time [3], which is running out. Close-ups show Lola facing facts [4] and imagining the possibilities [5]. Finally, she has no choice but to run for help [6]. From here on, the pace and rhythm of the editing will match the pace and rhythm of dramatic developments and Lola's sometimes split-second decision making.

she save Manni?) that continues until the last moment of the film. Editor Bonnefoy's handling of the complex rhythms in this scene dazzles us with its pacing while keeping the focus on what Lola is doing and why. The editing of this movie—its rhythm in particular—has been especially influential for such films as Paul Greengrass's *The Bourne Supremacy* (2004; editors Richard Pearson and Christopher Rouse).

The tempo of a movie can also be strictly measured in slow rather than fast terms, as it is in another Tykwer work, *Heaven* (2002; editor Mathilde Bonnefoy), a moral fable-cum-thriller based on a script by the great Polish director-writer Krzysztof Kieslowski. Here the action—a bomb going off in the wrong place, a woman admitting responsibility for placing it, a police officer falling in love with the woman because of her sense of moral duty, the destruction of critical evidence by a corrupt police captain, a jailbreak and flight from the police—all takes place at a very deliberate pace established by a piano and violin score that is heard in virtually every shot in the movie. The music and editing have a measured tempo that is also devoid of accents, causing the viewer to wonder when something will happen to break that tempo, signal a turning point, or provide a climax. Then, in the final moment, in a burst of gunfire, the two fugitives seize a helicopter and rise slowly toward heaven until they are out of sight. The movie ends on a note of elation that contrasts with the previously unwavering tempo established by the rhythms of both the editing and the music.

Varying the duration and rhythm of shots guides our eyes just as varying the rhythm in jazz guides the almost involuntary tapping of our fingers or feet as we listen to it. But when the visual images move with a rhythm that has little or nothing to do with the sound, we intuitively recognize and react to that rhythm. In the scene where the gulls attack a gas station attendant in *The Birds* (1963; see Chapter 6, p. 257), director Alfred Hitchcock and his editor, George Tomasini, masterfully use the rhythm of editing to build up excitement. Try to tap the rhythm with your finger at each of the thirty-nine cuts in the scene, and you'll be able to keep a discernible rhythm at first. But as the scene reaches its climax, you'll find that you can barely keep pace with the cuts.

The editor's choices regarding the rhythm of scenes can, in turn, create larger patterns of shot duration. These patterns can be built and broken for dramatic emphasis and impact, as in Sergio Leone's *Once upon a Time in the West* (1968; director's-cut DVD version released in 2003; editor Nino Baragli). During the opening title and credits, the editor has created a sequence of almost 15 minutes that is extraordinary for the patterns of what we see (an isolated railroad station on the prairie where three desperate-looking characters are waiting for a train to arrive) and what we hear (an equally extraordinary montage of sounds, whose slow, steady rhythm establishes an ominous mood).

These visual and aural images establish a slow, deliberate pattern of duration, sound, and movement. The shots of waiting for the train's arrival last a very long time, made to seem even longer by views of the vast prairie on the widescreen format, but they feature little or no action or movement by the characters. With this long sequence, Leone calls our attention to the **content curve**, which in terms of cinematic duration occurs when we have absorbed all we need to know in a particular shot and are ready to see the next shot. Because we get very little information from this sequence, ordinarily we would expect the director to use shots of a shorter duration and to cut more quickly from one to the next. However, Leone frustrates our expectations by not cutting and traps us in each shot, making us wait along with the bored desperadoes.

The montage of natural sounds in the opening sequence of Leone's film has a different rhythm from that of the visual images; its purpose is to underscore the tedium of the wait. The duration of each sound is shorter than the duration of the shots, and what we hear are repetitions of the same sounds: wind, squeaking windmill, footsteps, telegraph machine, water dripping, fly buzzing, knuckles cracking, and silence. Suddenly this pattern, pace, and mood are broken by a shot—taken from a camera positioned beneath the tracks—of a train speeding toward the station. The pattern of editing speeds up. The movie cuts between close-ups of three men loading their guns; the train approaching at a dramatic angle, its sounds now overpowering the others; and finally the train coming to a stop at a right angle to the screen, in front of the camera, wheels grinding to a halt and whistle blowing. In a moment, the train departs, leaving behind Harmonica (Charles Bronson).

The short, abrupt change in editing associated with the train's arrival takes on added significance because of Harmonica, who is to become one of the heroes of the film. In completing this scene, Leone returns to the overall pattern established in this sequence: slow, quiet, static shots of the four-way face-off between Harmonica and the desperadoes build up to a rapid-fire shooting sequence (in the action being filmed as well as the camera shots that are capturing it) in which every gunman, even Harmonica, catches a bullet.

Major Approaches to Editing: Continuity and Discontinuity

Because the editing of most contemporary narrative movies is made to be as inconspicuous as possible, the process and the results of editing may not be apparent to people unfamiliar with filmmaking. In the editing of such movies, the point is to tell the story as clearly, efficiently, and coherently as possible. This style of editing, called **continuity editing**, is certainly the most

7

8

9

10

Continuity editing in *Casablanca*, a classic Hollywood movie

Ten frames from a sequence in *Casablanca* illustrate continuity editing. [1] The sequence opens with an exterior shot of Rick's Café Americain; [2] inside, a moving camera pans across the main room, showing its customers and well-known piano player; [3] this diverse crowd includes an Arab customer, smoking a water pipe, and his waiter; [4] a man complains to a friend that all he does is wait, that he will never get out of Casablanca; [5] a woman, obviously in need of cash, sells her diamonds for less than they are worth; [6] two men, apparently spies or criminals, quietly discuss some impending event while being watchful of those around them; [7] a refugee (*left*) buys an exit visa for a large sum of cash; [8] the camera pans past a group of Asians at a table to an Englishman having a drink at the bar; [9] a female member of a large party asks the waiter to ask Rick to have a drink with them and is told that he never drinks with customers; and [10] a medium close-up of a hand approving a customer's charge; we see the bold signature "Rick" as the camera pans up to a middle shot of Rick Blaine (Humphrey Bogart). This sequence, flowing smoothly and rhythmically from shot to shot, shows that each shot has a meaning directly related to those before and after it. The sequence tells us exactly where we are, establishes the customers' unique problems, and suggests that at least one person— Rick, who runs his café with an iron hand—may be able to solve them. Indeed, Rick will hold in his grasp the fate of several major characters.

LOOKING AT MOVIES
THE EVOLUTION OF EDITING:
CONTINUITY AND CLASSICAL CUTTING

VIDEO (▶)

This tutorial explores the history of the major innovations in continuity (or classical) editing in early cinema.

prevalent in mainstream filmmaking, and it's the sort of editing that we'll spend most of this chapter discussing. Continuity editing seeks to achieve logic, smoothness, sequential flow, and the temporal and spatial orientation of viewers to what they see on the screen. It ensures the flow from shot to shot; creates a rhythm based on the relationship between cinematic space and cinematic time; creates filmic unity (beginning, middle, and end); and establishes and resolves the characters' problems.

In short, continuity editing tells a story as clearly and coherently as possible, as in the example on pages 334–335 from Michael Curtiz's *Casablanca* (1942; editor Owen Marks). The movie opens by explaining that, before the outbreak of World War II, the French Moroccan city of Casablanca was a major rendezvous for Europeans seeking exit visas that would permit them to flee the Nazi offensive. In an atmosphere of intrigue over the buying and selling of such visas there is civil unrest, including murder, as a major Nazi official arrives in town. The continuity editing, represented by this panel of images, establishes that Rick's Café Americain is an elegant, sophisticated rendezvous for everyone, a place for all nationalities and languages, and that its proprietor, Rick Blaine (Humphrey Bogart), is and will be at the center of the story.

But this is not the only approach to film editing. **Discontinuity editing** breaks the rules of continuity ed-

iting by seeking to achieve transitions between shots that are not smooth, continuous, or coherent. It permits a filmmaker to make abrupt shifts between shots, resulting in mismatches in the location of characters or objects, the direction or speed of movement, mise-en-scène, lighting, camera angles, or even colors. Instead of invisibly propelling the film forward, and unlike continuity editing, it calls attention to itself as an element of cinematic form. It was pioneered by Soviet filmmakers. (See "1924–1930: The Soviet Montage Movement" in Chapter 10, pp. 421–423.) And greatly influenced the French New Wave directors, including Jean-Luc Godard in *Breathless* (1960). Discontinuity editing has become a standard tool of today's filmmakers.

Like the tension between realism (verisimilitude) and antirealism more generally, continuity and discontinuity are not absolute values but are instead tendencies along a continuum. An average Hollywood movie may exhibit continuity in some parts and discontinuity in others, even if the movie's overall tendency is toward classical continuity. Similarly, an avant-garde film that is mostly discontinuous can include scenes that employ continuity editing. We need to look no further than Michel Gondry's *Eternal Sunshine of the Spotless Mind* (2004; editor Valdis Óskarsdóttir) or Fernando Meirelles and Kátia Lund's *City of God* (2002; editor Daniel Rezende), to cite just two cases, to find examples that use both of these major approaches to editing as well as many of the specific tools of editing described in this chapter.

Conventions of Continuity Editing

Continuity editing, now the dominant style of editing worldwide, seeks to achieve logic, smoothness, sequential flow, and the temporal and spatial orientation of viewers to what they see on the screen. As with so many conventions of film production, the conventions of continuity editing remain open to variation, but in general, continuity editing ensures that

> what happens on the screen makes as much narrative sense as possible.

> screen direction is consistent from shot to shot.

> graphic, spatial, and temporal relations are maintained from shot to shot.

The two fundamental objectives of continuity editing are to establish coverage of the scene through the master scene technique and to maintain screen direction through the 180-degree system.

Master Scene Technique This technique is based on the principle of **coverage**, meaning that a scene is photographed with a variety of individual shots, running from the general to the specific (long shot/medium shot/close-up), and taken from various distances and angles; in other words, all the shots that comprise the cinematography of that scene. Coverage is, at heart, a strategy employed specifically with the editing in mind. Usually, directors begin shooting a single scene with a long shot (sometimes known as the **master shot**) that covers the characters and action in one continuous take. The master scene technique then proceeds to covering the scene with whatever additional shots (medium shots, close-ups, etc.) the editor might need to create the finished scene. Covering the action in this comprehensive way gives the editor the tools, as well as the creative freedom, to choose the shot types and angles needed to tell the story as effectively as possible.

Typically, an editor starts a scene or sequence of shots with the master shot in order to establish location, situation, spatial relationships, and so on. Then the editor cuts in on various subjects as the drama and action dictate, regularly cutting back to the master to reacquaint viewers with location, what's happening, who's doing it, and how the characters are positioned in relation to one another.

Some of today's mainstream directors are far more experimental with continuity (we discuss several in this chapter) and do not always follow the conventions of master scene technique. But note that those conventions are common in films in which place is paramount, such as Westerns. For example, John Ford opens *The Searchers* (1956; editor Jack Murray) with a master shot of spectacular Monument Valley framed in the doorway of a darkened house. The point of view is that of Martha Edwards (Dorothy Jordan), who has an instinct that someone is outside, coming to her house. This orients and prepares us to understand the following shots. She steps out on her porch and, in an extreme long shot, soon sees a horseman riding in her direction. An exterior shot shows us the isolation of her house in the vast landscape, and we will soon learn why she has had this intuition and why this horseman is so important in her life.

Martha is joined by her husband, Aaron (Walter Coy), and their children, and by then they sense also that the lone rider is Ethan Edwards (John Wayne), her husband's brother. In a few shots of great economy, Ford establishes that Ethan has been away for a long period of time but that, somehow, his home is here. These shots establish two motifs—the vastness of the desert valley and the intimacy of the pioneer home—that Ford will develop throughout the movie.

Screen Direction In its early years, filmmaking evolved to require taking many shots from varying angles, especially in movies with action shots and chase scenes. Filmmakers needed a way to maintain consistent **screen direction**—the direction that a figure or object moves on the screen. Their search resulted in a system that was established as early as 1903 and used with occasional inconsistencies, often for deliberate comic purposes, until about 1912. At that time, filmmakers first began using the **180-degree system** (also called the *180-degree rule*, the **axis of action**, the *imaginary line*, and the *line of action*).

The axis of action, an imaginary horizontal line between the main characters being photographed, determines where the camera should be placed to preserve screen direction and thus one aspect of continuity (see Figure 8.1 on p. 341). Once this axis of action is determined, the camera must remain on the same side of the line. The resulting shots orient the viewer within

LOOKING AT MOVIES
THE 180-DEGREE RULE

VIDEO ⏵ ───────●────

This tutorial illustrates the 180-degree system by analyzing its use in a scene from Alfred Hitchcock's *Vertigo.*

9

10

11

12

Discontinuity editing in *Breathless*

Consider this panel of the movie's opening images: [1] man A leaning against a storefront background; [2] woman B, against another background, who points her chin to signify something to someone; [3] man A seems oblivious to the woman; [4] woman B gestures more emphatically; [5] man C and woman D exit a car, located against a third background; [6] another shot of man A against the storefront; [7] a shot of woman B, again beckoning, with man C and woman D moving away into the background; [8] man A, folding his newspaper and apparently getting ready to move; [9] a boat in a harbor, confusing because no spatial relationship was established between the previous shots and this one; [10] man A hot-wiring the car seen in [5], the first time we can reliably associate him with his accomplice, woman B; [11] woman B hurrying toward someone or something; [12] woman B asking the man, who is now in the stolen car, to take her with him. He has no further use for her and speeds away. Discontinuity editing has become a familiar convention, so this sequence may not seem as surprising as it did when the film was first released some 50 years ago. Yet because director Jean-Luc Godard does not orient us to the time or place of the action (see "Master Scene Technique" on p. 337) and disregards the 180-degree line, the sequence still confuses us because we don't know the place, time, identity of the four characters, their surroundings, or their relationship to them. Although [12] reveals that the woman is an accomplice to the man's car theft, we have no sense of where the narrative is going from here. *Breathless* continues to tell the story of the man, Michel (Jean-Paul Belmondo), a charming but ruthless criminal who, within a few minutes, will kill a policeman and, once in Paris, will lie and steal cars or whatever else he needs whenever necessary. Eventually, the police hunt him down and kill him as he tries to escape. The opening sequence helps us to understand the story by establishing that he seems sinister, uses people, and takes life as it comes. Equally important, the director trusts us to put the pieces together.

The master scene technique

These six shots from the opening of John Ford's *The Searchers* (1956; editor Jack Murray) economically establish both the place and some of the themes of this complex movie: the vastness of the desert valley in which Aaron and Martha Edwards's home is situated; the intimacy of family life in this isolated spot; and the return home of Ethan Edwards, who became a mercenary soldier in the Civil War after his brother married Martha, who nonetheless still yearns for Ethan, as he does for her. [1] Martha (Dorothy Jordan), framed in the doorway, looks out at Monument Valley in the background; [2] she stands on the porch; [3] she shields her eyes to try to focus on someone approaching; [4] Ethan Edwards (John Wayne) rides toward the house; [5] Martha is joined by her husband, Aaron (Walter Coy), and their children; finally, [6] the two brothers meet for the first time in years.

Figure 8.1 | THE 180-DEGREE SYSTEM

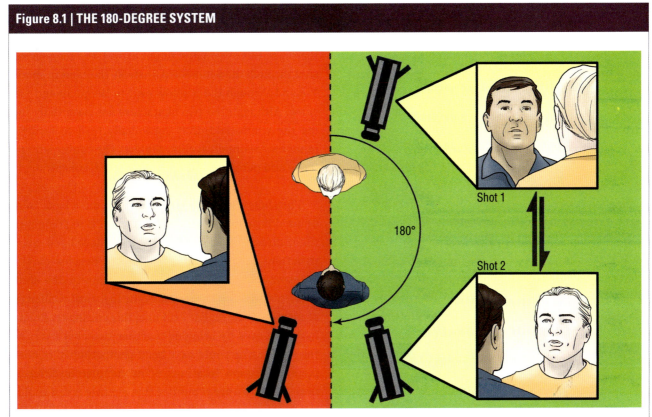

Shots 1 and 2 are taken from positions within the same 180-degree space (green background). When viewers see the resulting shots on-screen, they can make sense of the actors' relative positions to one another. If a camera is placed in the opposite 180-degree space (red background), the resulting shot reverses the actors' spatial orientation and thus cannot be used in conjunction with either shot 1 or shot 2 without confusing the viewer.

the scene, ensure consistent screen direction across and between cuts, and establish a clear sense of the space in which the action occurs (because something, an object or person, remains consistent in the frame to identify the relations between sequential spaces). The axis of action shifts, though, as the characters move within the frame and as the camera moves.

To summarize, in reaching the goals of continuity, the 180-degree system depends on three factors working together in any single shot: (1) the action in a scene must move along a hypothetical line that keeps the action on a single side of the camera; (2) the camera must shoot consistently on one side of that line; and (3) everyone on the production set—particularly the director, cinematographer, editor, and actors—must understand and follow this system.

This means that in a scene of dialogue, say, in which character A is on the left and character B is on the right, the viewer is oriented to that spatial relationship between them because the camera stays on one side of the imaginary line; however, if the camera crosses the imaginary line between the characters and moves to a position 180 degrees opposite its original position, the position of the characters in the image is reversed: character A is now on the right, character B is on the left.

Screen direction can also suggest meaning in an abstract or symbolic way. For example, the earlier discussion of *Run Lola Run* described how Lola runs against a deadline. If you study the patterns of her running, you'll see that she actually does run *against* time by continuously going in a counterclockwise pattern. Thus the screen movement and rhythm of editing reinforce the major theme: her need to beat the clock if she's going to save her boyfriend's life.

The 180-degree system remains a convention (not a rule) that can be broken if the director desires. Sometimes, for example, the director might wish to use a **reverse-angle shot** (shooting at an angle that is opposite to that in a preceding shot) or to dolly or zoom out to include more people or actions. But if the director asks the cinematographer to cross the line, the shooting and editing must be done carefully so as not to confuse the audience.

Confusing viewers can ruin their experience. Oliver Stone's *Alexander* (2004; editors Yann Hervé, Gladys Joujou, Alex Marquez, and Thomas J. Nordberg), a sword-and-sandal epic that attempts to tell the story of Alexander the Great, is plagued by bad editing decisions. Constant flashbacks disjoint the plot flow, and even though the battle scenes are marvelous, the editing has not observed the basic principles of screen direction and thus loses us in the disorder.

Editing Techniques That Maintain Continuity

In addition to the fundamental building blocks—the master shot and maintaining screen direction with the 180-degree system—various editing techniques are used to ensure that graphic, spatial, and temporal relations are maintained from shot to shot.

Shot/Reverse Shot A **shot/reverse shot**, one of the most common and familiar of all editing patterns, is a technique in which the camera (and editor) switches between shots of different characters, usually in a conversation or other interaction. When used in continuity editing, the shots are typically framed over each character's shoulder to preserve screen direction. Thus, in the first shot the camera is behind character A, who is looking right, and records what character B says to A; in the second shot, the camera is behind character B, who is looking left, and records that character's response.

Michael Mann's *The Insider* (1999; editors William Goldenberg, David Rosenbloom, and Paul Rubell) provides a good example. In one of their first discussions, Dr. Wigand (Russell Crowe) and Mr. Bergman (Al Pacino) are sitting in the close confines of Wigand's car. As their conversation begins, Wigand is on the right of the frame, in the driver's seat, and Bergman is in the front passenger's seat; the imaginary line is the backs of the seats. But as you first might expect, the scene is not shot through the windshield. Instead, the camera shoots Wigand through the window next to Bergman and vice versa. Although the two characters are essentially facing the windshield, they continually turn to face the other and maintain eyeline contact. The conversation is tense and perfectly suited to this closed, conspiratorial space.

The shot/reverse shot is among the most basic of all filmmaking conventions, and because it is so frequently used, directors over the years have developed many variations on this editing technique. Besides playing an essential role in maintaining continuity, the shot/reverse shot helps ease some of the logistical challenges of making a movie. For example, this editing technique fools our eyes by bringing together two characters on the screen who could have been photographed in completely different locations or at completely different times. Thus we are reminded that a movie is not shot in the order we see it on the screen and that the editor has the power to make us think that it was.

Match Cuts **Match cuts**—those in which shot A and shot B are matched in action, subject, graphic content, or two characters' eye contact—help create a sense of continuity between the two shots. There are several kinds of match cuts. Technically, they are identical; they differ only in what they depict.

David Lean's *Lawrence of Arabia* (1962; editor Anne V. Coates) features a match cut that is legendary in film history. Call it elliptical, poetic, or simply brilliant, it both wows us and moves the story forward. T. E. Lawrence (Peter O'Toole) is charged to make a perilous journey by Mr. Dryden (Claude Rains), a British officer in Cairo; as he listens, Lawrence lights Dryden's cigarette. He holds up the match and watches the flame burn closer and closer to his fingers (he enjoys such pain), responds to Dryden's skepticism about the assignment by saying, "No, Dryden, it's going to be fun," and blows out the match. The editor cuts to the rising of the sun above the desert horizon, thus "matching" two flares of light in two different places and time. Film critic Anthony Lane writes, "It was a moment that Steven Spielberg saw at the age of fifteen, and which, he says, ignited his determination to make films. If you don't *get* this cut, if you think it's cheesy or showy or over the top, and if something inside you doesn't flare up and burn at the spectacle that Lean has conjured, then you might as well give up the movies."[9]

Match-on-Action Cut A **match-on-action cut** shows us the continuation of a character's or object's motion through space without actually showing us the entire action. It is a fairly routine editorial technique for economizing a movie's presentation of movement. Of course, the match-on-action cut has both expressive and practical uses.

Graphic Match Cut In a **graphic match cut**, the similarity between shots A and B is in the shape and form of what we see. In this type of cut, the shape, color, or texture of objects matches across the edit, providing continuity. The prologue of Stanley Kubrick's *2001: A Space Odyssey* (1968; editor Ray Lovejoy) contains a memorable example of a graphic match cut in which the action continues seamlessly from one shot to the next: a cut that erases millions of years, from a bone weapon of the Stone Age to an orbiting craft of the Space Age. The weapon and the spacecraft have matching tubular shapes and rotations.

Alfred Hitchcock gives us another classic example of the graphic match cut in *Vertigo* (1958; editor George Tomasini) when John "Scottie" Ferguson (James Stewart) places a necklace around the neck of Judy Barton (Kim Novak). This action occurs in a sequence: a medium shot of Barton and Ferguson in front of a mirror as Ferguson fastens the necklace is followed by a dolly-in right to a close-up of him looking at her reflection; a cut to a dolly-in to a close-up of the necklace on Barton's neck is followed by the match cut to a dolly-out from a close-up of a similar necklace in a portrait.

Graphic matches often exploit basic shapes—squares, circles, triangles—and provide a strong visual sense of design and order. For example, at the end of the shower murder sequence in *Psycho* (1960; editor George Tomasini), Hitchcock matches two circular shapes: the eye of Marion Crane (Janet Leigh), tears streaming down, with the round shower drain, blood and water washing down—a metaphorical visualization of Marion's life ebbing away.

1

2

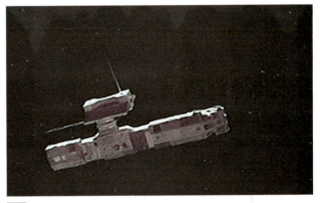

3

Graphic match cut in *2001: A Space Odyssey*

In the opening scene of Stanley Kubrick's *2001: A Space Odyssey* (1968; editor Ray Lovejoy), an ape-man [1] rejoices in his newfound weaponry, a bone, by tossing it into the air [2], at which point it becomes technology of a far more sophisticated kind [3]. This astonishing leap of space and time introduces several of the movie's principal themes: the relativity of time, the interaction of inventiveness and aggressiveness, and the desire of the human race to conquer the unknown.

9. Anthony Lane, "Master and Commander: Remembering David Lean," *The New Yorker* (March 31, 2008), p. 116.

1

2

Legendary match cut in *Lawrence of Arabia*

Director David Lean and his editor, Anne V. Coates, created a legendary match cut in *Lawrence of Arabia* (1962) by literally cutting from a shot of a match flame [1] to a shot of the sun rising on the desert [2]. Although Lean wrote, "I am not *absolutely* convinced that the match incident is worth the footage involved [less than a minute],"[10] once you've seen it, you'll no doubt disagree. To make this shot even more interesting, Lean created a sound bridge to link the two images. He said: "I thought Lawrence should blow out the match, and I wanted the sound to blow in the desert. What I did was this. He [Peter O'Toole, who plays T. E. Lawrence in the film] holds up the match and he blows. Now, I laid the first half of the blow over Peter and the last half over the sunrise in the desert, so that the blow noise carried from his close-up over to the long shot. He was still blowing on the long shot. If I'd had him blow out the match and after the sound had faded I cut to the long shot, it wouldn't have had the same effect."[11]

1

2

Match-on-action cut

Near the conclusion of John Ford's *Stagecoach* (1939; editors Otho Lovering and Dorothy Spencer), the Ringo Kid (John Wayne) intends to avenge his father's murder by the Plummer gang by shooting those responsible for it: Luke Plummer and his two brothers. To avert what might not turn out the way Ringo plans it, Doc Boone (Thomas Mitchell) enters a bar in Lordsburg with the intention of persuading Luke Plummer to give up his shotgun. There follows an excellent match-on-action shot. In [1], he points to a bottle of whiskey, says "Can I have that?" and Luke slides it across the bar toward him. In [2], he catches the bottle and pours himself a drink.

10. Lean, qtd. in Kevin Brownlow, *David Lean: A Biography* (New York: St. Martin's, 1996), pp. 471–472.
11. Lean, qtd. ibid., p. 116.

Eyeline match cut in *Now, Voyager*

As we know from looking at "old" movies, everyone smoked in them. For one thing, tobacco companies paid the studios to feature stars with cigarettes, cigars, or pipes; for another, public censorship of smoking was decades away. Today, we seldom see stars smoking on-screen, but in early years Bette Davis was Hollywood's most memorable smoker. In Irving Rapper's *Now, Voyager* (1942; editor Warren Low), the affair between Charlotte Vale (Davis) and Jerry Durrance (Paul Henreid) is repeatedly punctuated by his signature custom of lighting two cigarettes and giving one to her. In the eyeline match cut pictured here, as Charlotte asks for Jerry's help, he says, "Shall we just have a cigarette on it?" This signals the viewer that he will do all she asks, even if it means that their relationship is going up in a puff of smoke.

Eyeline Match Cut An **eyeline match cut** joins shot A, in which a person looks at someone offscreen, and shot B, the object of that gaze looking back. In Irving Rapper's *Now, Voyager* (1942; editor Warren Low), Jerry Durrance (Paul Henreid) lights two cigarettes, one for him, the other for Charlotte Vale (Bette Davis). As he hands one to her and looks into her eyes, an eyeline match cut joins a shot of her eyes looking into his, in the culmination of an intensely romantic moment that, ironically, ends their relationship.

Parallel Editing **Parallel editing** (or **crosscutting**) is the cutting together of two or more lines of action that occur simultaneously at different locations.

Joel Coen's *Raising Arizona* (1987; editor Michael R. Miller) uses crosscutting to link several simultaneous actions: Hi (Nicolas Cage) fleeing the police after robbing a convenience store; the police chasing him; his enraged wife, Ed (Holly Hunter), rescuing him from the police; the hapless clerk at the convenience store reacting to Hi's robbery; and a pack of runaway dogs also pursuing Hi. The complex choreography of this scene, accentuated by the brilliant crosscutting, creates a hilarious comic episode.

Intercutting is the editing of two or more actions that take place at different locations and/or different times but give the impression of one scene. Director Steven Soderbergh uses intercutting to foretell the outcome of a cozy scene in *Out of Sight* (1998; editor Anne V. Coates). We met Jack Foley (George Clooney) and Karen Sisco (Jennifer Lopez) earlier in this chapter; she's a federal marshal, he's an escaped convict. They meet under circumstances that viewers must see to believe. Soon these circumstances separate them, and then they meet again, this time in a hotel bar, where they recount their meeting. By intercutting their conversation (in present time) with shots of them undressing (in future time), the editor signals the predictable outcome even before it happens. There is something matter-of-fact, even comic, about this scene, which pays tribute to a similar scene in Nicolas Roeg's thriller *Don't Look Now* (1973).

Parallel editing enables us to experience at least two sides of related actions, and it has long been a familiar convention in chase or rescue sequences (as we saw earlier in D. W. Griffith's *Way Down East* [1920]; see Chapter 2, p. 42). Intercutting brings together two directly related actions, often slowing them down or speeding them up and sometimes omitting some action that might have occurred between the two actions, thus also creating a sort of ellipsis.

Point-of-view editing in *Rear Window*

Alternating subjective and omniscient shots in Alfred Hitchcock's *Rear Window* (1954; editor George Tomasini): [1, 3, 5, 7] From his wheelchair, L. B. "Jeff" Jefferies (James Stewart) observes his neighbors: [2] a dancer (Georgine Darcy), known as Miss Torso; [4] a sculptor (Jesslyn Fax), known as Miss Hearing Aid because she adjusts hers to silence the noise of Miss Torso's dancing; [6] a songwriter (Ross Bagdasarian); and [8] Lars Thorwald (Raymond Burr) and his wife, Anna (Irene Winston).

Point-of-view editing in *The Night of the Hunter*

In Charles Laughton's *The Night of the Hunter* (1955; editor Robert Golden), Harry Powell (Robert Mitchum) confronts Rachel (Lillian Gish) [1], who is providing refuge for the children he seeks. As one of the children (Pearl, played by Sally Jane Bruce) enters the scene [2], she drops a doll containing something very valuable to Harry and runs to him. Harry, clearly more interested in the doll than in Pearl, betrays his true interest by looking directly at the doll [3], as we see in the shot of the doll that follows [4].

Point-of-View Editing **Point-of-view editing** is the process of editing different shots together in such a way that the resulting sequence makes us aware of the perpective or point of view of a particular character or group of characters. Most frequently, it starts with an objective shot of a character looking toward something offscreen and then cuts to a shot of the object, person, or action that the character is supposed to be looking at.

In *Rear Window* (1954; editor George Tomasini), Hitchcock uses this editing technique, alternating between subjective and omniscient shots in an ABABAB pattern. As we watch the temporarily sidelined photographer L. B. "Jeff" Jefferies (James Stewart) sitting near the window of his apartment and watching the activities of his neighbors, one of whom he believes has committed a murder, we begin to realize that this movie is partly about what constitutes the boundaries of our perceptions and how ordinary seeing can easily become snooping, even voyeurism.

To emphasize this concept, one of the movie's principal design motifs is the frame within a frame—established when we see the opening titles framed within a three-panel window frame in which blinds are raised automatically to reveal the setting outside. Similarly, Jefferies, immobilized in his chair by a broken leg, has his vision limited by the height and position of his chair as well as by the window frame. This frame within a frame (or inner frame) is used throughout the movie, determining—along with the point-of-view editing—what we see and further defining the idea of perception that is at the movie's core.

Other Transitions between Shots

The Jump Cut   The **jump cut**, made popular by French New Wave directors of the 1960s, presents an instantaneous reverse or advance in the action. It's a sudden, perhaps illogical, often disorienting ellipsis between two shots caused by the absence of a portion of the film that would have provided continuity. Because such a jump in time can occur either on purpose or because the filmmakers have failed to follow continuity prin-

ciples, this type of cut has sometimes been regarded more as an error than as an expressive technique of shooting and editing.

In *Taxi Driver* (1976; editors Tom Rolf and Melvin Shapiro), director Martin Scorsese, who often makes unconventional use of cinematic conventions, uses a jump cut, not to advance an action—the more familiar procedure—but to reverse and repeat it.

The jump cut and the freeze-frame (which we'll discuss later) had an important influence on the New American Cinema of the 1960s, including Arthur Penn's *Bonnie and Clyde* (1967; editor Dede Allen) and Sam Peckinpah's *The Wild Bunch* (1969; editor Lou Lombardo), by introducing new cinematic techniques to supplant the conventions that had dominated filmmaking since the 1930s.

1

2

3

4

Reverse jump cut in *Taxi Driver*

In this scene, Travis Bickle (Robert De Niro) is acting out his plans to take revenge on the evils of a society that sickens him. Talking to an imaginary adversary, he repeats the same warning twice. This is captured in two shots, which are deliberately separated here into four images so that you can see the character's movements. In [1] he faces screen left and turns (within the shot) to face the camera [2]. At this point, a jump cut takes us back to where he started, and again, Bickle is photographed facing screen left [3] and turning to face the camera [4]. (Remember that the reverse jump occurs between two shots, not four.) The effect of this cut is to call attention to Bickle's cool preparation and determination.

1

2

3

Fade-in and fade-out

In *Cries and Whispers* (1972; editor Siv Lundgren), Ingmar Bergman builds the emotional intensity of his story by cutting back and forth between scenes of the past and the present and ending most of those scenes with a fade-out to a blood-red screen. Bergman has said that he thinks of red as the color of the human soul, but it also functions here as a symbolic system that has much to do with the film's focus on women. Just before this brief scene, Agnes (Rosanna Mariano, playing her as a child) has been hiding behind a curtain watching her mother (Liv Ullmann, who also plays Agnes's sister); when her mother sees Agnes, she summons the girl to her side. Agnes fears that she will be reprimanded, but instead, Bergman gives us a moment of great simplicity and tenderness that unfolds in three shots: [1] Agnes touches her mother; [2] her mother is moved by the caress; [3] the image fades to the blood-red screen. Can we find words to explain the purpose of this fade-out to red?

Fade The **fade-in** and **fade-out** are transitional devices that allow a scene to open or close slowly. In a fade-in, a shot appears out of a black screen and grows gradually brighter; in a fade-out, a shot grows rapidly darker until the screen turns black for a moment. Traditionally, such fades have suggested a break in time, place, or action.

Fades can be used within a scene, as in John Boorman's *The General* (1998; editor Ron Davis). Martin Cahill, aka "The General" (Brendan Gleeson), is one of Dublin's most notorious criminals, as famous for his audacious capers as he is for his ability to outwit the police. In one scene, he enters the house of a wealthy couple when almost everyone is asleep and steals several valuable items. The scene opens with a fade-in and closes with a fade-out; in between are eleven brief segments, each separated by a fade-out or fade-in. Cahill's stealth and self-confidence are underscored by the almost buoyant rhythm of these fades, and his evident arrogance and satisfaction are echoed on the sound track: Van Morrison's "So Quiet in Here," which contains the lyric "This must be what paradise is like, so quiet in here, so peaceful in here." The fades convey both the passage of time and the character's thoughts.

Because editing conventions are not rules, variations are welcome, especially in the hands of a master filmmaker like Ingmar Bergman. In his *Cries and Whispers* (1972; editor Siv Lundgren), he not only shoots the fades in color but also uses them between scenes of past and present. In this dreamlike movie, Agnes (Harriet Andersson) is dying, attended by her two sisters, Karin (Ingrid Thulin) and Maria (Liv Ullmann), and a servant, Anna (Kari Sylwan). Color is central to understanding the fades and the film, for the predominant reds hold a key to its meanings, suggesting the cycles of life, love, and death that the story is concerned with. Whole rooms are painted red, and the plot, which moves back and forth across the lives of these women, is punctuated with frequent fades to a completely blood-red screen (sometimes the next scene begins with a fade-in from such a red screen).

Dissolve Also called a *lap dissolve*, the **dissolve** is a transitional device in which shot B, superimposed, gradually appears over shot A and begins to replace it midway through the process. Like the fades described earlier, the dissolve is essentially a transitional cut, primarily one that shows the passing of time or implies a connection or relationship between what we see in shot A and shot B. But it is different from a fade in that the process occurs simultaneously on the screen, whereas a black screen separates the two parts of the fade. Fast dissolves can imply a rapid change of time or a dramatic contrast between the two parts of the dissolve. Slow dissolves can mean a gradual change of time or a less dramatic contrast.

In John Ford's *My Darling Clementine* (1946; editor Dorothy Spencer), a dissolve establishes a thematic connection between its parts. In the first scene, on the prairie outside of Tombstone, Wyatt Earp (Henry Fonda)

1

2

and his brothers discuss the troublemakers who have killed their younger brother. After a fast dissolve to the wide-open town of Tombstone, we instinctively understand that the troublemakers might be there. This dissolve makes an important connection for our understanding of Earp, who quells a ruckus in a saloon and, as a result, is made the town's sheriff.

Wipe Like the dissolve and the fade, the **wipe** is a transitional device—often indicating a change of time, place, or location—in which shot B wipes across shot A vertically, horizontally, or diagonally to replace it. A line between the two shots suggests something like a windshield wiper. A soft-edge wipe is indicated by a blurry line; a hard-edge wipe, by a sharp line. A jagged line suggests a more violent transition.

Although the device reminds us of early eras in filmmaking, directors continue to use it. Such diverse movies as Lewis Milestone's original version of *Ocean's Eleven* (1960; editor Philip W. Anderson), George Lucas's *Star Wars* (1977; editors Richard Chew, Paul Hirsch, and

Iris-in and iris-out

Volker Schlöndorff's *The Tin Drum* (1979; editor Suzanne Baron) contains an excellent sequence of two iris shots that single out a character and denote the passing of time in her life. The character, Anna, the narrator's mother, sells her farm produce in the municipal market. In an iris-in to a full-screen image, we see the young, prosperous Anna (Tina Engel) selling freshly killed geese [1]. This image quickly irises out; then (with a superimposition of [2]) there is an iris-in of the older Anna (Berta Drews), who, during the First World War, has only turnips to sell. Thus this succession of iris shots encompasses the passing of time, the aging of a principal character, and the narrator's vibrant memories as well as the changing economic and social circumstances of Germany before and during the war.

Iris-out shot for comic emphasis

In Gus Van Sant's *To Die For* (1995; editor Curtiss Clayton), Nicole Kidman plays Suzanne Stone Maretto, a clueless woman who wants to be a celebrity so badly that she'll do anything, eventually including murder, to get there. At a low point in her unhappy marriage to Larry (Matt Dillon), her husband uncharacteristically tries to take control of the situation by proposing that she abandon her pipe dreams and help him carry out a plan to improve the image of his father's restaurant, where he works. Her head is swimming with ideas of becoming the next hot thing on television, and she stares incredulously as he emphasizes that they are a family. Family is the last thing on Suzanne's mind, so, through an iris-out, reflecting her mental point of view, she cuts him down to size, providing a microscopic view of a man for whom she has nothing but contempt.

1

2

3

Freeze-frame

Freeze-frames are often used to underscore a significant emotional change in a character—to "freeze" time, as it were, for the character's reflection on what's happening. In the final moments of François Truffaut's *The 400 Blows* (1959; editor Marie-Josèphe Yoyotte), Antoine Doinel (Jean-Pierre Léaud), having escaped from reform school, arrives at a beach. Doinel runs along the shore, the camera following, until he abruptly turns and heads straight toward the camera. The freeze-frame [1] that ends the movie clearly doesn't tell us where Doinel goes next, but it conveys just how unsure he feels, here and now, about the possibilities that surround him. In Alfonso Cuarón's *Y Tu Mamá También* (2001; editors Cuarón and Alex Rodríguez), Julio Zapata (Gael García Bernal) feels "great pain" at learning of his best friend's betrayal in having sex with an older woman whom Julio adores, and he sinks below the surface of the leaf-filled swimming pool [2] to think about it. During this freeze-frame from Martin Scorsese's *Goodfellas* (1990; editors Thelma Schoonmaker and James Y. Kwei) [3], we actually hear young Henry Hill (Christopher Serrone) tell us what he thinks of his father's beating him for being a truant from school and working for the mob: "I didn't care. The way I saw it, everybody takes a beating sometimes." At roughly the same age as the other two boys described here, Henry has the greater self-realization at this moment of epiphany in his life.

Marcia Lucas), and Guy Ritchie's *Snatch* (2000; editor Jon Harris) continue to make imaginative use of this transitional technique.

Iris Shot An **iris shot** appears on the screen in two ways: the **iris-out** begins with a large circle that closes in around the subject, while the **iris-in** begins with a small circle and expands to a partial or full image. It is both a shot and an editing technique because it functions as a transition to the next shot and thus involves an editor's decision. (Because it is named for the iris diaphragm, which controls the amount of light passing through a camera lens, it is usually circular but can be any shape.) Filmmakers can create it in the camera, with special effects, or with a *mask*. The obvious function of the iris is to draw our attention to a particular place on the screen, thus emphasizing what we see there.

Freeze-Frame The **freeze-frame** (also called *stop-frame* or *hold-frame*) is a still image within a movie, created by repetitive printing in the laboratory of the same frame so that it can be seen without movement for whatever length of time the filmmaker desires. It stops time and functions somewhat like an exclamation point in a sentence, halting our perception of movement to call attention to an image. In Alfonso Cuarón's *Y Tu Mamá También* (2001; editors Cuarón and Alex Rodríguez), freeze-frame is used to emphasize an important moment of passage in a young man's life. Julio Zapata (Gael García Bernal) has just felt what he calls "great pain" at learning of his best friend's getting the advantage over him with a woman they both desire. He retreats to a swimming pool. In an overhead shot, we see him sink underwater through a surface covering of brown leaves, a traditional symbol of the change that comes with autumn; the screen freezes as we hear a rooster crowing, underscoring Julio's realization of change.

Cuarón uses the freeze-frame here, in all likelihood, to pay homage to one of the most famous uses of the freeze-frame: the conclusion of François Truffaut's *The 400 Blows* (1959; editor Marie-Josèphe Yoyotte).

The poignant freeze-frame close-up of young Antoine Doinel (Jean-Pierre Léaud) that concludes the movie stops his movement on a beach, but it also points toward the uncertainty of his future. In both examples, the freeze-frame ironically underscores a significant emotional change in the characters depicted.

Martin Scorsese uses the freeze-frame in *Goodfellas* (1990; editors Thelma Schoonmaker and James Y. Kwei) to show a character who actually acknowledges an emotional change as it is happening. The scene begins with young Henry Hill (Christopher Serrone) doing odd jobs for the mob, as his offscreen narration tells us that this makes him feel like a grown-up. At home, when Henry lies about his school attendance, his father (Beau Starr) savagely beats him with a belt. During an unusually long freeze-frame (15 seconds) that suspends the beating, Henry continues his narration, and then the violence resumes. The effect is ironic: while the film "stops" the violence (as Henry's mother cannot) so that we linger on its wrath, the boy continues his narration in a matter-of-fact voice suggesting his awareness that domestic violence and mob violence are now part of his life.

Split Screen The **split screen**, which has been in mainstream use since Phillips Smalley and Lois Weber's *Suspense* (1913), produces an effect that is similar to parallel editing in its ability to tell two or more stories at the same cinematic time, whether or not they are actually happening at the same time or even in the same place. Among its most familiar uses is to portray both participants in a telephone conversation simultaneously on the screen. Unlike parallel editing, however, which cuts back and forth between shots for contrast, the split screen can tell multiple stories within the same frame.

The split screen was used by other early filmmakers (e.g., D. W. Griffith and Erich von Stroheim), but never on the scale or with the technical ingenuity displayed by Buster Keaton in *The Play House* (1921), for which he invented a process (later, the industry standard) that split the screen into nine slivers of space. Buster plays all the parts, including actors, stagehands, and audience; he does drag and a dazzling imitation of a monkey. At one point, he portrays nine characters on the screen at once.

In *Napoléon* (1927; editor Gance), Abel Gance introduced Polyvision, a multiscreen technique, as in the epic pillow fight between the young Napoléon (Vladimir

The split screen as would-be matchmaker
The Rules of Attraction is about several pairs of people who want, or think they want, to be together but haven't learned the so-called rules of attraction. Sean Bateman (James Van Der Beek) receives love notes from an anonymous admirer whom he believes to be Lauren Hynde (Shannyn Sossamon), simply because he's in love with her. And Lauren is attracted to Sean, but backs off when she discovers him in bed with her roommate. In fact, the letters were written by a desperate young woman who kills herself after a series of encounters in which Sean pays no attention to her. Both Sean and Lauren plan to attend a special Saturday tutorial, and in a long, lyrical sequence of shots, edited into a split screen, we follow him (*left*) and her (*right*) as they walk from their dorms across the campus and into the classroom building. Here, in an image from the sequence, Sean walks toward us, as does Lauren, who's just learned that the professor has canceled the session. Still in split screens, the two meet at the corner where the two hallways join and these long shots become two close-ups that fill each screen. After they talk briefly, recognizing each other's names and finding a few things they have in common, a special editing effect literally pulls the two together in medium shot in a single frame. This transition suggests that editing can be a matchmaker—they might become a couple after all—but that never happens.

Roudenko) and other boys in their school dormitory. The fight begins on a single screen; continues on a screen split into four equal parts, then on one split into nine equal parts; reaches its climax on a single screen with multiple, superimposed full-size images; and ends, as it began, on a single screen.

The split screen has figured prominently in other films, including Norman Jewison's *The Thomas Crowne Affair* (1968; editors Hal Ashby, Byron Brandt, and Ralph E. Winters), in which the editors cut between many small screens that expand to fill the entire screen and then return to their smaller place within the composition; Gus Van Sant's *To Die For* (1995; editor Curtis Clayton), which uses 1, then 4, and then 64 screens near the end of the movie; Mike Figgis's *Timecode* (2000; editor uncredited), in which the screen is divided into quarters that simultaneously show four different 90-minute shots (see the image in Chapter 4, p. 145); and Hans Canosa's *Conversations with Other Women* (2005; editor Canosa), a movie shot so that the footage could be edited into a work consisting entirely of split screens. In *The Rules of Attraction* (2002; editor Sharon Rutter), a dark satire about college life, sex, and love, director Roger Avary uses various editing techniques, including the split screen, to emphasize people who want to be together, or think they do, but never make it.

Looking at Editing

When you watch a movie, you see the mise-en-scène, design, and acting, you hear the dialogue, music, and sound effects, but you *feel* the editing, which has the power to affect you directly or indirectly. Good editing—editing that produces the filmmakers' desired effects—results from the editor's intuition in choosing the right length of each shot, the right rhythm for each scene, the right moment for cutting to create the right spatial, temporal, visual, and rhythmic relationships between shots.

In answer to the question, "What is a good cut?" Walter Murch, an editor and theorist of editing, says:

> At the top of the list is Emotion . . . the hardest thing to define and deal with. *How do you want the audience to feel?* If they are feeling what you want them to feel all the way through the film, you've done about as much as you can ever do. What they finally remember is not the editing, not the camerawork, not the performances, not even the story—it's how they felt.[12]

You can most effectively analyze an editor's contributions to a film by examining individual scenes and trying to understand how their parts—the shots that make up those scenes—fit together. One useful tool for helping you to see the parts clearly and analyze their relationship to the whole is to create a shot-analysis chart similar to the one in Table 8.1 (pp. 355–357). By carefully noting details about each shot in a sequence—including its length, shot type (long, medium, close-up, etc.), and

details about the actions it includes—you can "map" a scene to get a better sense of its shape and rhythm.

The example we've provided in Table 8.1 lays out the shots in the famous scene from D. W. Griffith's *The Birth of a Nation* (1915; editors Griffith, Joseph Henabery, James Smith, Rose Smith, and Raoul Walsh) that recreates the assassination of Abraham Lincoln. We can see that the scene consists of thirty-nine shots running just under 3½ minutes. Perhaps the first thing we notice about this sequence of shots is that they are all fairly short. The average length of a shot in this scene is approximately 5 seconds, and no shot lasts longer than 14 seconds. All of these short shots convey a heightening of dramatic tension, an effect that is especially important when the audience already knows what will happen (obviously, everyone watching the film knows that Abraham Lincoln will be shot in the head by the end of the scene). By looking at the descriptions of each shot, we can also see that Griffith rarely carries the action over from shot to shot but instead presents a cumulative series of details from different viewpoints. According to British film editor and director Karel Reisz, who has written extensively on editing, this style of editing has two advantages:

> Firstly, it enables the director to create a sense of depth in his narrative: the various details add up to a fuller, more persuasively life-like picture of a situation than can a single shot, played against a constant background. Secondly, the director is in a far stronger position to guide the spectator's reactions, because he is able to choose what particular detail the spectator is to see at any particular moment. . . .
>
> Griffith's fundamental discovery, then, lies in his realisation that a film sequence must be made up of incomplete shots whose order and selection are governed by dramatic necessity.[13]

As an innovator of film form, Griffith obviously cared about what happened within shots. But he also cared about what happened between shots. Through cinematography, Griffith constructed credible visual representations of the sights surrounding the assassination of Lincoln at Ford's Theatre and re-created the actions of the assassination as faithfully as possible at the time.

12. *In the Blink of an Eye: A Perspective on Film Editing* (Los Angeles: Silman-James Press, 1995), p. 18.
13. Karel Reisz and Gavin Millar, *The Technique of Film Editing*, 2nd ed. (London: Focal Press, 1968), pp. 22, 24.

Shots from the assassination scene in *The Birth of a Nation*
[1] is from shot 21, [2] is from shot 22, [3] is from shot 32, [4] is from shot 33, [5] is from shot 38, and [6] is from shot 39.

Table 8.1 | THE ASSASSINATION SEQUENCE FROM *THE BIRTH OF A NATION*

INTERTITLE: *"And then, when the terrible days were over and a healing time of peace was at hand . . . came the fated night of 14th April, 1865."*

Two short scenes follow: Benjamin Cameron (Henry B. Walthall) fetches Elsie Stoneman (Lillian Gish) from the Stonemans' house and they leave together. Next seen in a theater, they are attending a special gala performance at which President Lincoln is to be present. The performance has already begun.

INTERTITLE: *Time: 8:30*
  The arrival of the president, Mrs. Lincoln, and party.

Shot	Description	Length (sec.)	Type of Shot*
1	Lincoln's party as, one by one, they reach the top of the stairs inside the theater and turn off toward the president's box. Lincoln's bodyguard comes up first, Lincoln last.	7	MS
2	The president's box, viewed from inside the theater. Members of Lincoln's party appear inside.	4	MS
3	Lincoln, outside his box, giving up his hat to an attendant.	5	MS
4	The president's box [as in shot 2]. Lincoln appears in the box.	4	MS
5	Elsie Stoneman and Ben Cameron sitting in the auditorium. They look up toward the president's box, then start clapping and rise from their seats.	7	MS
6	View from the back of the auditorium toward the stage. The president's box is to the right. The audience, backs to the camera, are standing in foreground, clapping and cheering the president.	3	LS
7	The president's box [as in shot 4]. Lincoln and Mrs. Lincoln bow to the audience.	3	MS
8	As in shot 6.	3	LS
9	The president's box [as in shot 7]. Lincoln enters the box and sits down.	5	MS

INTERTITLE: *Lincoln's personal bodyguard takes his post outside the presidential box.*

10	After coming into the passage outside the box and sitting down, the bodyguard starts rubbing his knees impatiently.	10	MS
11	View from the back of the auditorium toward the stage. The play is in progress, but the audience stands and greets the president.	5	LS
12	The president's box [as in shot 9]. Lincoln takes his wife's hand and acknowledges the audience's greeting.	9	MS
13	Standing, the audience waves white handkerchiefs at the president.	4	MLS
14	Closer view of the stage. The play continues.	10	MLS

INTERTITLE: *To get a view of the play, the bodyguard leaves his post.*

15	The bodyguard [as in shot 10]. He is clearly impatient.	4	MS
16	Close view of the stage [as in shot 14].	2	MLS
17	The bodyguard [as in shot 15]. He gets up and puts his chair away behind a side door.	6	MS

Table 8.1 | THE ASSASSINATION SEQUENCE FROM *THE BIRTH OF A NATION* (*continued*)

Shot	Description	Length (sec.)	Type of Shot*
18	The theater viewed from the back of the auditorium [as in shot 6]. Camera is shooting toward the box of Lincoln's party, next to the president's box, as the bodyguard enters and takes his place. (This shot is framed exactly as shot 6, but a closing-iris effect is added to isolate our gaze toward the bodyguard arriving at the box.)	3	LS
19	Within a circular mask, we see a closer view of the action of shot 18. The bodyguard takes his place in the box. The closing iris of the previous shot is repeated in this closer shot, consolidating continuity.	5	MS
INTERTITLE: *Time: 10:13* *Act III, Scene 2*			
20	General view of the theater from the back of the auditorium. A diagonal mask leaves only Lincoln's box visible.	5	LS
21	Elsie and Ben. Elsie points to something in Lincoln's direction.	6	MS
INTERTITLE: *John Wilkes Booth*			
22	The head and shoulders of John Wilkes Booth is seen in an iris shot.	3	MS
23	Elsie looks in Lincoln's direction [as in shot 21].	6	MS
24	Booth [as in shot 22].	2.5	MS
25	View showing both the president's box and the one next to it, with Booth waiting by the door.	5	MLS
26	Booth [as in shot 24].	4	MS
27	Close view of the stage [as in shot 14].	4	MLS
28	Close view of the president's box. Lincoln smiles approvingly at the play. He makes a gesture with his shoulders as if he were cold and starts to pull a shawl over his shoulders.	8	MS
29	Booth [as in shot 22] moves his head up in the act of rising from his seat.	4	MS
30	Shot 28 continued. Lincoln finishes pulling on his shawl.	6	MS
31	The theater viewed from the back of the auditorium [as in shot 20]. The mask spreads to reveal the whole theater.	4	LS
32	Within a circular mask [as in shot 19], the bodyguard, enjoying the play, with Booth leaving that box, right behind the bodyguard.	1.5	MS
33	Booth comes through the door at the end of the passage outside the president's box. He stoops to look through the keyhole into Lincoln's box, then pulls out a revolver and braces himself for the deed.	14	MS
34	Booth cocks the revolver.	3	CU
35	Shot 33 continued. Booth comes up to the door, has momentary difficulty in opening it, then steps into the president's box.	8	MS
36	Close view of the president's box [as in shot 28]. Booth appears behind Lincoln.	5	MS
37	The stage [as in shot 14]. The actors are performing.	4	MLS

Shot	Description	Length (sec.)	Type of Shot*
38	Booth shoots Lincoln in the head [as in shot 36]. Lincoln collapses. Booth climbs onto the side of the box and jumps over onto the stage.	5	MS
39	Booth on the stage. He throws up his arms and shouts.	3	LS
INTERTITLE: *"Sic Semper Tyrannis!"* ("Thus always to tyrants"—motto of the State of Virginia)			

*CU = close-up; LS = long shot; MLS = medium long shot; MS = medium shot

Note: John Wilkes Booth, who assassinated President Lincoln on Good Friday, April 14, 1865, was an actor who won wide acclaim for his Shakespearean roles. He was also an ardent Confederate sympathizer who hated the president. After he shot Lincoln and jumped onto the stage, fracturing his leg in the process, he shouted, *"Sic semper tyrannis!"*—adding, as Griffith does not, "The South is avenged."

Source: Chart prepared by Emanuel Leonard and Gustavo Mercado, revised from material in Karel Reisz and Gavin Millar, *The Technique of Film Editing*, 2nd ed. (London: Focal Press, 1968), pp. 20–22.

But the realistic tableaux and choreography that Griffith constructed within the shots come alive only through his editing of these shots, which makes us feel the fateful pace of the impending tragedy.

Now, let's look closely at a contemporary film to see how editing has evolved (or not) since Griffith's time.

Fernando Meirelles and Kátia Lund's *City of God*

City of God (2002), codirected by Fernando Meirelles and Kátia Lund and edited by Daniel Rezende, also relies on editing to tell its story. But the filmmakers take a very different approach from Griffith's. The movie opens with a section titled "Chasing the Chicken." The film's title and credits appear over this sequence, beginning with "A Film by Fernando Meirelles" and then running for 3 minutes, 7 seconds until the movie's second section begins. The movie, set in a violent, drug-ridden quarter of Rio de Janeiro, is narrated from the point of view of Rocket (Alexandre Rodrigues). In this opening sequence, we are introduced to Rocket and Li'l Zé (Leandro Firmino da Hora), a drug lord who has murdered Rocket's brother and for whom violence is an everyday thing. The tension between the two young men—exacerbated by Rocket's desire to free himself from the drugs, gangs, and violence and pursue a career as a photographer—establishes one of the existential challenges faced by all the young people in this movie.

This brief section exemplifies several of the movie's major themes: the violence and lawlessness of the city, the struggle to escape it, and the hopelessness that plagues most of the people who live there. That so much should be established in a sequence that runs underneath the credits is both a familiar cinematic convention and a reminder to watch every movie carefully from the moment it begins.

"Chasing the Chicken" is comprised of two parts. For the purposes of discussion, we'll call the first "The Preparation" (1 minute, 9 seconds), because it focuses on the various activities of preparing a chicken stew, including slaughtering several chickens. We'll call the second part "The Chase" (2 minutes, 8 seconds), because one of the chickens escapes its apparent fate and provokes a wild chase through the neighborhood. The imagery of the chickens is an allegory for the film's attitude toward human captivity and hope for escape. Rocket believes that murder is the fate of anyone who tries to escape this living hell in this city. Yet *this* chicken, which the camera and the editing quickly make into a "character" we empathize with, actually escapes! Let's look more closely at these two parts of the opening sequence to see how the editing, in particular, helps to tell the story.

Part 1, "The Preparation," is a montage composed of hundreds of repeated shots. They are primarily close-ups from handheld cameras and include a man sharpening a knife; chickens waiting to be slaughtered and put into the pot; men playing musical instruments; and people dancing, cleaning vegetables, making drinks, and lighting gas flames under the pot. If this were all that was going on here in terms of content, you might think you were watching documentary footage of these activities. But an analysis of the editing shows that much

1

2

3

***City of God*: editing in Part 1, "The Preparation"**

In [1], a man sharpens a knife (notice the dismembered chicken claw in the background); in [2], a man beheads a chicken with a knife; and in [3], we meet the chicken that is the "star" of this sequence. (Here you should remember the principle of the Kuleshov experiment: two or more juxtaposed shots need not have any actual relationship to one another for meaning to occur when they are juxtaposed.) We're watching the action, but in another sense we're also watching the chicken as she watches the same action. We assume that she sees the knife being sharpened and one of her fellow birds being killed, and thanks to the editing of these two shots, she understands her possible fate. The chicken's state of mind (her instinct for survival) is conveyed in [3], in which she stretches her neck and head and rapidly moves her eyes. She appears nervous and aware of her possible fate. In subsequent shots, she loosens the string that holds her captive and calmly walks away. We feel comfortable with identifying the chicken's state of mind in this way because it is suggested by the editing. It seems to be the conclusion the editor wants us to reach.

more than that is happening here. Instead of cataloging all the shots here (as we did with the sequence in *The Birth of a Nation*), we will look for patterns in the editing that make meanings. For example, repetitive shots of a man sharpening a knife (taken from different camera angles) form a pattern that raises our expectations about the future use of that knife—will it be used in cooking or in violence against others?

Suddenly, Li'l Zé, who we are seeing for the first time, appears on the screen saying, "Fuck, the chicken's got away! Go after that chicken, man!" We don't have time to wonder why he would care so much about one escapee, but we soon realize that it's the chase—more precisely, winning the chase—that matters, not the chicken.

In Part 2, "The Chase," a group of boys and girls (teenage and younger) begin the chase. When we see that many of them are carrying guns, we have our first clue that there may be violence. In fact, the children are members of Li'l Zé's gang. The chase begins in the yard from which the chicken escaped and ends in a confrontation with the police in another part of the neighborhood. In between, we see a great deal of the gang's frenzied running after the bird. The cinematography includes overhead shots that show the area where the

chase is taking place, moving shots from a handheld camera as the gang (and the camera operators) run through the streets, and ground-level shots from the chicken's point of view. The chicken is running through a maze of lanes and alleyways, so the director uses middle and long shots (some of them high angle) to give us a wider perspective on the chase and to verify the forward movement of its direction. The bird is running for its life, and the camera work and editing make sure we don't forget that. The continuity editing makes all this action coherent.

The editor now cuts away from the chase (an editing convention as old as the movies themselves) to introduce Rocket and begin a sequence of parallel action, cutting between Rocket and Li'l Zé. Unaware of the chase, Rocket and a friend are strolling through the area. Rocket says that he'll risk his life to get a good photograph; although we wonder what he means, we later

City of God: editing in Part 2, "The Chase"

This part of the scene begins with a shot of the chicken running through the streets [4], probably taken with a Steadicam from a ground-level point of view; the cut is to a low-angle shot of the armed gang running after the bird [5]; the editor then cuts to another shot of the chicken, ahead of its pursuers [6]. Not just in these three shots, but throughout this part of the sequence, the continuity cutting, going back and forth between shots of the chicken and its pursuers, maintains screen direction from shot to shot. Although the pace of the editing here remains rapid, to convey the urgency of the pursuit, it is not as rapid as the cutting of "The Preparation." However, this is not traditional continuity cutting because—like the chase sequences in the movies that make up the Bourne cycle (2002–7)—it's highly fragmented and contains many otherwise jarring spatial leaps that do not stress a smooth flow from one shot to the next. Yet we accept it as one continuous, coherent action.

learn that he is interested equally in the drug dealers, the armed children, and the corrupt police. He hopes that by getting photographs of any of them, he could get a good job at a newspaper. This is a comparatively calm moment in which the camera remains stationary in a long take. The editor now cuts back to Li'l Zé and the chase. His gang has only one thing on its mind—to obey the order to get the chicken—and as they rampage through the streets, they use their guns to threaten anyone in their path. Li'l Zé pulls his gun on a street vendor but does not shoot. Suddenly, the scene turns surreal as every kid seems armed. Meanwhile, the chicken has outwitted them, sometimes flying short distances that put a gap between it and the pursuers. A police van passes over the chicken, and again the chicken escapes death. All of these shots—and the way they are edited—keep us focused on the gang plunging down the streets after the chicken and the chicken's miraculous survival. The action reaches its climax as Li'l Zé and his gang meet up with Rocket. The shot of Li'l Zé's entrance into the frame is shot in slow motion, and the subsequent short shots build in an escalating rhythm. He struts like he's already won, calls Rocket a "melonhead" and a "fag," and orders him to "get that chicken."

In contrast to the shots of Rocket, which are relatively stable and of longer duration, the shots of Li'l Zé are heavily fragmented; made with a handheld camera, they emphasize his instability. The parallel action also enables us to experience each element in a new, heightened way. When we are with Rocket, our experience of his actions is colored by our fear that this calm, likeable guy must be about to encounter the seemingly bloodthirsty Li'l Zé. Likewise, our time with Li'l Zé isn't just about catching the chicken; it's also about waiting for the inevitable collision with Rocket.

Rocket, realizing that he has no choice in the matter, gently tries to capture the bird as the gang, brandishing its guns and itching for violence, looks on. Anyone who has ever tried to catch a bird understands Rocket's predicament, and the editing builds suspense around the tense moment. Meanwhile, the cops arrive on the scene, jumping from their cars with machine guns. A standoff occurs: the cops at the background of the frame, Rocket in the middle ground, and the gang in the foreground.

8

9

City of God: final confrontation

The shot that introduces Rocket (*left*) and a friend [7] is of relatively long duration and slower rhythm than the immediately preceding entrance of the gang leader. The friend says to Rocket, "If Li'l Zé catches you, he'll kill you," to which Rocket responds, "Yeah, well, he's gotta find me first." In the next shot [8], Li'l Zé (*second from right*) enters the frame in slow motion, brandishing his gun and a big smile. After several more shots (not shown here) that establish the space, he spots Rocket [9] and orders him to capture the chicken.

Everyone but Rocket has a gun; his weapon, a camera, is hanging around his neck. He recognizes the dangerous spot he's in, and his thoughts appear in a subtitle: ". . . in the City of God, if you run away, they get you, and if you stay, they get you too. It's been that way ever since I was a kid." As the camera circles Rocket, suggesting that he's trapped, the editor allows him to "escape" by using a match-on-action cut to a shot of a much younger Rocket moving in a circle. This ends the movie's first sequence.

To understand the editing of any movie, we need to answer these three questions:

1. What action occurs in the scene under analysis?
2. How has the scene been photographed?
3. What editing pattern holds the shots together?

If we know the answers to these questions, we can reach conclusions about the editing. As for the first question, we have described the basic action of this sequence and how it establishes several of the movie's major themes. Second, we have briefly summarized its cinemato-graphic plan, which includes the use of a moving hand-held camera and furtive camera angles, and reflects the bold, you-are-there graphic style of the documentary cinema. Third, the key elements of the editing pattern that hold all this footage together are fast and slow motion, freeze-frames, **swish pans**, and a montage influenced by the editing principles of the Soviet silent cinema. (Elsewhere in the movie, the editor uses the split screen, fast fade-ins/fade-outs, and superimpositions.)

Finally, what conclusions do we reach about the editing? First, we see that the editor's goal was to create a highly formal structure, one in which the cinematic conventions used are suited to the depiction of a violent youth/drug culture. These conventions add up to a coherent formal whole, and none of them are more (or less) important than the others. Second, the editor grabs and holds our attention on the violence. Third, the filmmakers, who are not out to make us squirm with disgust at the squalor and violence or feel guilty about the injustice of this Brazilian city—ironically called the "City of God"—make us not only see but *feel* the life depicted on the screen.

ANALYZING EDITING

When we watch a movie, we see the mise-en-scène, design, and acting; we hear the dialogue, music, and sound effects; but we feel the editing, which has the power to affect us directly or indirectly. Good editing—editing that produces the filmmakers' desired effects—results from the editor's intuition in choosing the right length of each shot, the right rhythm of each scene, the right moment for cutting to create the right spatial, temporal, visual, and rhythmic relationships between shots A and B.

As a viewer, you can best understand the overall effects of an editor's decisions by studying a film as a creative whole. But you can most effectively analyze an editor's contributions to a film by examining individual scenes, paying attention to the ways in which individual shots have been edited together. Indeed, the principles of editing are generally most evident within the parts that make up the whole.

SCREENING CHECKLIST: EDITING

☐ Does the editing overall seem to create continuity or discontinuity? If the editing is mostly creating continuity, are there nonetheless moments when the editing creates discontinuity? What is the significance of those moments?

☐ As each shot cuts to the next shot in the movie or clip, tap your finger on a tabletop or other surface to get a feeling for the rhythm of the editing. How would you describe that rhythm? Does it stay constant, or does it speed up or slow down? How does the rhythm affect your emotional response to the movie?

☐ Keep track of the types of transitions from shot to shot. Does the editor use one transitional effect more than others? Are the transitions seamless and nearly unnoticeable, or do they call attention to themselves?

☐ Look for the different types of match cuts in the film. What sort of visual or narrative information is each match cut conveying?

☐ Are there any moments in the movie in which the traditional conventions of Hollywood continuity editing—including use of the master shot, the 180-degree system, shot/reverse shot, match cuts, and parallel editing—are violated in some way? Describe how these moments appear on-screen. What do you think is the significance of these moments in the film?

☐ Does the editing seem to indicate what the filmmakers want the audience to feel? What is that intended feeling? Do you feel it? Is it an appropriate feeling for the narrative and themes of the movie?

Questions for Review

1. What is editing? Why is it regarded as a language?
2. What is the basic building block of film editing? What is film editing's fundamental tool?
3. What are the film editor's principal creative and technical responsibilities?
4. What is continuity editing? What does it contribute to a movie?
5. What is the purpose of the 180-degree system? How does it work?
6. What is discontinuity editing? Given the dominance of continuity editing in mainstream filmmaking, what role does discontinuity editing usually play?
7. Name and describe the various types of match cuts.
8. How does the match cut differ from and compare to parallel editing?
9. What is a jump cut? What is the typical effect of a jump cut on a viewer?
10. Given the magnitude of the editor's overall responsibility during the postproduction stage of filmmaking, why is it considered desirable, if not essential, that the editor also collaborate during the preproduction phase?

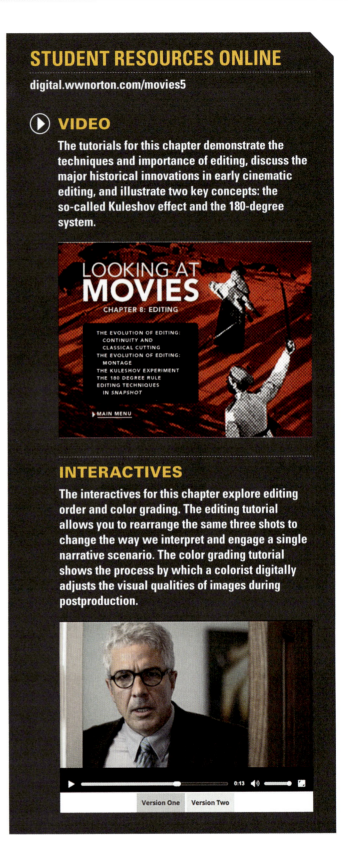

STUDENT RESOURCES ONLINE

digital.wwnorton.com/movies5

▶ VIDEO

The tutorials for this chapter demonstrate the techniques and importance of editing, discuss the major historical innovations in early cinematic editing, and illustrate two key concepts: the so-called Kuleshov effect and the 180-degree system.

LOOKING AT **MOVIES**
CHAPTER 8: EDITING

THE EVOLUTION OF EDITING: CONTINUITY AND CLASSICAL CUTTING
THE EVOLUTION OF EDITING: MONTAGE
THE KULESHOV EXPERIMENT
THE 180 DEGREE RULE
EDITING TECHNIQUES IN *SNAPSHOT*

▶ MAIN MENU

INTERACTIVES

The interactives for this chapter explore editing order and color grading. The editing tutorial allows you to rearrange the same three shots to change the way we interpret and engage a single narrative scenario. The color grading tutorial shows the process by which a colorist digitally adjusts the visual qualities of images during postproduction.

0:13

Version One   Version Two

>>>>>

SOUND

What Is Sound?

The movies engage two senses: vision and hearing. Although some viewers and even filmmakers assume that the cinematographic image is paramount, what we hear from the screen can be at least as significant as what we see on it, and sometimes what we hear is more significant. Director Steven Spielberg says, "The eye sees better when the sound is great." Sound—talking, laughing, singing, music, and the aural effects of objects and settings—can be as expressive as any of the other narrative and stylistic elements of cinematic form. What we hear in a movie is often technologically more complicated to produce than what we see. In fact, because of the constant advances in digital technology, sound may be the most intensively creative part of contemporary moviemaking. Spielberg, for one, has also said that, since the 1970s, breakthroughs in sound have been the movie industry's most important technical and creative innovations. He does not mean "using the technology to show off" by producing gimmicky sounds that distract you from the story being told, but rather sound used as an integral storytelling element.[1]

As the success of action movies and 3-D animated features grows each year, sound and music are playing a larger role in telling their stories. For one thing, these movies are often visual spectacles that require an equally spectacular sound track. For another, they usually feature nonrealistic heroes, whose characterization requires every sound element—narration, dialogue, sound effects, and music—to make them come alive. Sound has played an important role in helping to define Harry Potter, Spider-Man, and Shrek in the series of films devoted to them as well as Woody and Buzz Lightyear and their friends in the *Toy Story* movies. Likewise, where would such characters as James Bond, Benjamin Button, Superman, Indiana Jones, or Jamal Malik be without sound to establish their worlds and adventures? Without a powerful sound design that is an integral part of the movie's artistic vision, both the story and the characters would be less fascinating.

Christopher Nolan's *Inception* (2010) is a case in point. As seems appropriate for a science-fiction action movie about the creative powers of the human mind—how our thoughts and dreams create imaginary worlds—the story is complex and intellectually challenging. And the sound design, which shifts seamlessly between imagination and reality, and our perceptions of them, is equally caught up in its own intricacies. Richard King is responsible for the memorable sound editing of *Inception* and many other distinguished movies, including *War of the Worlds* (2005; discussed later in this chapter). His style produces sound that is multilayered and deeply textured, incorporating a bold and aggressive mix of sounds and music that complement the vivid visual and special effects. Virtually all of the sounds were produced in the studio, including the incredible sounds of the weapons, vehicles, explosions, and scenes of destruction.

Stanley Kubrick's *The Shining* (1980; sound by Dino Di Campo, Jack T. Knight, and Winston Ryder) opens with a series of helicopter point-of-view shots that, without the accompanying sound, might be mistaken for a TV commercial. In these shots, we see a magnificent landscape, a river, and then a yellow Volkswagen driving upward into the mountains on a winding highway. Whereas we might expect to hear a purring car engine, car wheels rolling over asphalt, or the passengers' conversation, instead we hear music: an electronic synthesis by composers Wendy Carlos and Rachel Elkind of the *Dies Irae*, one of the most famous Gregorian chants, which became

---

1. Rick Lyman, "A Director's Journey into a Darkness of the Heart," *New York Times* (June 24, 2001), sec. 2, p. 24.

Sound as meaning

Inception is about an illegal espionage project that enters the subconscious minds of its targets to gain valuable information. Dominic Cobb (Leonardo DiCaprio, *right*), the leader of the team, has hired Ariadne (Ellen Page, *left*), a gifted young architecture student, to design labyrinthine dreamscapes for this work, but she (like the viewer) is still in the learning stage. In this image, they sit in a Parisian café that is part of a larger street scene exploding all around them. Ariadne (like the viewer) is astonished to see that they sit unhurt while the perceivable world is destroyed around them, but then Ariadne awakens in the design studio to realize that she has been dreaming this episode. The action is crafted with such visual and aural detail that everything we see—flower pots, people, wine glasses, tables, chairs, automobiles—explodes in its own unique way and with its own unique sound. Every sight and sound image has been created and implanted in Ariadne's dream to show her (and the viewer) the power of the "dreams within dreams" project in which she is now a key player. Richard King, the sound designer and editor, and his sound mixers (Lora Hirschberg, Gary A. Rizzo, and Ed Novick) won Oscars for the movie's richly textured sound design.

the fundamental music of the Roman Catholic Church. The *Dies Irae* (literally, "the day of wrath") is based on Zephaniah 1:14–16, a reflection on the Last Judgment. It is one section of the Requiem Mass, or Mass for the Dead. Experiencing the shots together with the sound track, we wonder about the location, the driver, and the destination. What we hear gives life to what we see and offers some clues to its meaning. The symbolic import and emotional impact of this music transforms the footage into a movie pulsating with portentous energy and dramatic potential. Once we identify this music, we suspect it is warning us that something ominous is going to happen before the movie ends. Thus forewarned, we are neither misled nor dissatisfied.

The sound in the scenes just described (or in any movie scene) operates on both physical and psychological levels. For most narrative films, sound provides cues that help us form expectations about meaning; in some cases, sound actually shapes our analyses and interpretations. Sound calls attention not only to itself but also to silence, to the various roles that each plays in our world and in the world of a film. The option of using silence is

one crucial difference between silent and sound films; a sound film can emphasize silence, but a silent film has no option. As light and dark create the image, so sound and silence create the sound track. Each property—light, dark, sound, silence—appeals to our senses differently.

In film history, the transition to sound began in 1927. It brought major aesthetic and technological changes in the way movies were written, acted, directed, and screened to the public (see Chapters 10 and 11). After the first few sound movies, where sound was more of a novelty than a formal element in the telling of the story, a period of creative innovation helped integrate sound—vocal sounds, environmental sounds, music, and silence—into the movies. The results of this innovation can be seen and heard in some of the great movies of the 1930s, including King Vidor's *Hallelujah!* (1929; sound by Douglas Shearer), Rouben Mamoulian's *Applause* (1929; sound by Ernest Zatorsky), G. W. Pabst's *Westfront 1918* (1930; sound by W. L. Bagier Jr.), Fritz Lang's *M* (1931; sound by Adolf Jansen), and Ernst Lubitsch's *Trouble in Paradise* (1932; no sound credit). Comparing one or more of these movies to several silent classics will help you to understand how profoundly sound changed the movies.

Like every other component of film form, film sound is the product of specific decisions by the filmmakers. The group responsible for the sound in movies, the **sound crew**, generates and controls the sound physically, manipulating its properties to produce the effects that the director desires. Let's look more closely at the various aspects of sound production controlled by the sound crew.

Sound Production

Sound production consists of four phases: design, recording, editing, and mixing. Although we might suppose that most of the sounds in a movie are the result of recording during filming (such sounds are called *production sounds*), the reality is that most film sounds are constructed during the postproduction phase (and thus are called *postproduction sounds*). But before any sounds are recorded or constructed, the overall plan for a movie's sound must be made. That planning process is called *sound design*.

Design

Sound design is the art of creating the sound for a film. In the past it was the responsibility of a sound crew composed of the artists and technicians who record, edit, and mix its component parts into the **sound track**. In conventional filmmaking with film stock, the sound track is a narrow band to one side of the image on which the sound is recorded. In digital filmmaking, depending on the recording method being used, the sound track basically consists of a digital code being placed somewhere on the digital recording medium.

As motion-picture sound has become increasingly innovative and complex, the result of comprehensive sound design, the sound designer's role has become more well known. Given its name by film editor Walter Murch—the sound designer for such movies as Francis Ford Coppola's *The Conversation* (1974) and *Apocalypse Now* (1979), and Anthony Minghella's *The English*

Patient (1996) and *Cold Mountain* (2003)—sound design combines the crafts of editing and mixing and, like them, involves matters both theoretical and practical.[2]

Although many filmmakers continue to understand and manipulate sound in conventional ways, sound design has produced major advances in how movies are conceived, made, viewed, and interpreted. Until the 1970s, the vast majority of producers and directors thought about sound only after the picture was shot. They did not design films with sound in mind and frequently did not fully recognize that decisions about art direction, composition, lighting, cinematography, and acting would ultimately influence how sound tracks would be created and mixed. They considered sound satisfactory if it could distract from or cover up mistakes in shooting and create the illusion that the audience was hearing what it was seeing. They considered sound great if it was loud, either in ear-splitting sound effects or in a heavily orchestrated musical score.

By contrast, the contemporary concept of sound design rests on the following basic assumptions:

> Sound should be integral to all three phases of film production (preproduction, production, and postproduction), not an afterthought to be added in postproduction only.

> A film's sound is potentially as expressive as its images.

> Image and sound can create different worlds.

> Image and sound are co-expressible.

A sound designer treats the sound track of a film the way a painter treats a canvas. For each shot, the designer first identifies all the sounds necessary to the story and plot. The next step is laying in all the background tones (different tones equal different colors) to create the support necessary for adding the specific sounds that help the scene to function. According to Tomlinson Holman (the creator of Lucasfilm's THX technology), "Sound design is the art of getting the right sound in the right place at the right time."[3] Today, many directors—Joel Coen and David Lynch, among others—are notable for their comprehensive knowledge and expressive use of sound.

2. Randy Thom, "Designing a Movie for Sound" (1998), www.filmsound.org/articles/designing_for_soundelder.htm (accessed February 4, 2006).
3. Tomlinson Holman, *Sound for Film and Television* (Boston: Focal Press, 1997), p. 172.

Before sound design was widely accepted, the responsibilities for sound were divided among recording, rerecording, editing, mixing, and sound-effects crews; these crews sometimes overlapped but often did not. In attempting to integrate all aspects of sound in a movie, from planning to postproduction, the sound designer supervises all these responsibilities—a development initially resented by many traditional sound specialists, who felt their autonomy was being compromised. It is now conventional for sound designers (or supervising sound editors) to oversee the creation and control of the sounds (and silences) we hear in movies. They are, in a sense, advocates for sound.

During preproduction, sound designers encourage directors and other collaborators to understand that what characters hear is potentially as significant as what they see. This is especially true for point-of-view shots, which focus characters' (and audiences') attention on specific sights or sounds. Sound designers encourage screenwriters to consider all kinds of sound; working with directors, they indicate in shooting scripts what voices, sounds, or music may be appropriate at particular points. They also urge their collaborators to plan the settings, lighting, cinematography, and acting (particularly the movement of actors within the settings) with an awareness of how their decisions might affect sound. During production, sound designers supervise the implementation of the sound design. During postproduction, after the production sound track has been cut along with the images, they aid the editing team. But although their results may far exceed the audience's expectations of clarity and fidelity, sound designers keep their eyes and ears on the story being told. They want audiences not only to regard sound tracks as seriously as they do visual images but also to interpret sounds as integral to understanding those images.

Excellent example of sound design that make you sit up and listen is *Stoker* (2013; director Park Chan-wook; sound designers Chuck Michael and John Morris). The film treats the classic theme of revenge, and however implausible its story may be, the movie's values are in its savage beauty and mind-bending sound track. Sharp eyes and ears will see it also as an homage to Alfred Hitchcock's movies, especially *Shadow of a Doubt* (1943), *Psycho* (1960), and *The Birds* (1963). Lynne Ramsay's *We Need to Talk About Kevin* (2011; sound designer Paul Davies) uses expressive colors in its set design, and its sound is designed to create the strange and impenetrable world

of a hostile young man who uses his bow and arrow to murder untold numbers of people at his high school. Davies's sound design helps to portray the weird worlds of two of Ramsay's other films: *Ratcatcher* (1999) and *Morvern Callar* (2002).

Recording

The process of recording sound for the movies is very similar to the process of hearing. Just as the human ear converts sounds into nerve impulses that the brain identifies, so the microphone converts sound waves into electrical signals that are then recorded and stored. The history of recording movie sound has evolved from optical and magnetic systems to the digital systems preferred in today's professional productions. With his introduction of noise reduction and multichannel "surround sound" to film production in the 1970s, Ray Dolby revolutionized a sound technology that dated back to the late 1930s. In production, the **Dolby system** enhances fidelity by electronically reducing the hiss generated by analog sound recording and enables the technicians to match a movie's sound to the emotional intensity of its pictures. In exhibition, Dolby's theater systems produced sound superior to anything audiences had heard before. The **digital format** offers greater flexibility in recording, editing, and mixing and thus is fast becoming the standard. Of the various types of film sound (which will be described later in the chapter), dialogue is the only type typically recorded during production. Everything else is added in the editing and mixing stages of postproduction.

The recording of production sound is the responsibility of the production sound mixer and a team of assistants, which includes, on the set, a sound recordist, a sound mixer, a microphone **boom** operator, and gaffers (in charge of the power supply, electrical connections, and cables). This team must place and/or move the microphones so that the sound corresponds to the space between actors and camera and the dialogue will be as free from background noise as possible. **Double-system recording** is the standard technique of recording film sound on a medium separate from the picture. At one time, sound was recorded directly on the film, but now the various media used to record sound include digital audiotape, compact discs, or computer hard drives. This system, which synchronizes sound and image, allows both for maximum quality control and for the manifold manipulation of sound during postproduction editing, mixing, and synchronization. Once the sound has been recorded and stored, the process of editing it begins.

Editing

The editor is responsible for the overall process of editing and for the sound crew, which consists of a supervising sound editor, sound editors (who usually concentrate on their specialties: dialogue, music, or sound effects), sound mixers, rerecording mixers, sound-effects personnel, and Foley artists. The editor also works closely with the musical composer or those responsible for selecting music from other sources. In the editing room, the editor is in charge; but producers, the director, screenwriters, actors, and the sound designer may also take part in the process. In particular, the producer and director may make major decisions about editing.

The process of editing, of both pictures and sounds, usually lasts longer than the shooting itself. Sound editing takes up a great deal of that time, because a significant portion of the dialogue and all of the sound effects and music are created and/or added during postproduction. Included in this process is adding Foley sounds (discussed later in the chapter) for verisimilitude and emphasis and creating and layering ambience with traffic, crowd voices, and other background sounds.

Filmmakers first screen the **dailies** (or rushes), which are synchronized picture/sound work prints of a day's shooting. From these they select the usable individual shots from among the multiple takes, sort out the **outtakes** (any footage that will not be used), log the usable footage so it is easy to follow through the rest of the process, and decide which dialogue needs recording or rerecording and which sound effects are necessary. **Rerecording** of sound first recorded on the set (sometimes called *looping* or *dubbing*) can be done manually: the actors watch the footage, synchronize their lips with it, and reread the lines. Today, most rerecording is done by computer through **automatic dialogue replacement (ADR)**—a faster, less expensive, and more technically sophisticated process.

If ambient or other noises have marred the quality of the dialogue recorded during photography, the actors are asked to come back, view the faulty scene, and perform the dialogue again as closely as possible. When an acceptable rerecording take has been made, an ADR

ADR in action

For the American version of Hayao Miyazaki's animated movie *Spirited Away* (2001), it was necessary to rerecord the characters' voices using English-speaking actors and the ADR (automatic dialogue replacement) system. Here, Jason Marsden (the voice of Haku), standing in front of a microphone and holding his script, lip-synchs his lines to coordinate with the action on the monitor in the background.

editor inserts it into the movie. Finally, the sound-editing team synchronizes the sound and visual tracks. Because the entire editing and mixing process is now done digitally, a certain amount of overlap can occur between the sound editing and mixing stages.

Mixing

Mixing is the process of combining different sound tracks onto one composite sound track synchronous with the picture. Each type of sound occupies an individual sound track. *Mixing* is used in several different ways. Here the term refers to a single element (one track for vocals, one for sound effects, one for music, etc.) that can be combined in a multitrack sound design. However, the term is also familiarly used to describe a compilation of music included in a movie and typically released for consumers on a CD.

The number of sound tracks used in a movie depends on the kind and amount of sound needed to tell each part of the story; thus, filmmakers have an unlimited resource at their disposal. No matter how many tracks are used, they are usually combined and compressed during the final mixing. Working with their crew, sound mixers adjust the loudness and various aspects of sound quality; filter out unwanted sounds; and create, according to the needs of the screenplay, the right balance of dialogue, music, and sound effects. The result may be an "audio mise-en-scène" that allows the filmmaker and the viewer to distinguish between background and significant elements that are arranged in relation to one another.

This resembles the typical recording process for popular music, in which drums, bass, guitars, vocals, and so on are recorded separately and then mixed and adjusted to achieve the desired acoustic quality and loudness. The ideal result of sound mixing is clear and clean, so whatever the desired effect is, the audience will hear it clearly and cleanly. Even if what the filmmakers want is distorted or cluttered sound, the audience will hear that distortion or clutter perfectly.

Several movies have featured people involved in the art of sound recording and mixing, including Michael Powell's *Peeping Tom* (1960), Brian de Palma's *Blow Out* (1981), Wim Wenders's *Lisbon Story* (1994), Steven Ho's *Soundman* (1998), Ry Russo-Young's *Nobody Walks* (2012), and Peter Strickland's *Berberian Sound Studio* (2012). Each of them, in one way or another, associates sound recording with violence because films about horror use sound to scare us. Strickland's movie features Toby Jones as a memorable (and almost silent) British sound mixer who is hired to finish an Italian slasher movie. In his old-fashioned analog world, he dutifully spools tapes, fidgets endlessly with his console, consults dubbing charts, and fixes microphones, but is nevertheless insulted by the producer whenever he makes a suggestion. Eventually he is emotionally overwhelmed by the film's content, the producer's ideas, and the bizarre working conditions of this assignment. Nonetheless, this movie makes the point that sound artists and technicians have the power to confuse and deceive us. Other excellent examples of sound mixing can be found in *The Man from London* (2007; codirectors Béla Tarr and Ágnes Hranitzky) and *You, The Living* (2007; director Roy Andersson), while *Margaret* (2011; director Kenneth Lonergan) shows the confusion that follows when the sound mixing is too aggressive.

With this background on the four basic stages of sound production—what goes on during sound design, recording, editing, and mixing—we're ready now to look more closely at the actual characteristics that make up the sounds we hear in real life as well as in the movies.

Describing Film Sound

When talking or writing about a movie's sound, you should be able to describe a sound in terms of its perceptual characteristics (determined by its pitch, loudness, quality, and fidelity), its source (where it comes from), and its type (vocal or musical, for example). To that end, let's take a closer look at the perceptual characteristics of sound.

Pitch, Loudness, Quality

The **pitch** (or level) of a sound can be high (like the screech of tires on pavement), low (like the rumble of a boulder barreling downhill), or somewhere between these extremes. Pitch is defined by the **frequency** (or speed) with which it is produced (the number of sound waves produced per second). Most sounds fall somewhere in the middle of the scale. But the extremes of high and low, as well as the distinctions between high pitch and low pitch, are often exploited by filmmakers to influence our experience and interpretation of a movie.

In Victor Fleming's *The Wizard of Oz* (1939; sound by Douglas Shearer), the voice of the "wizard" has two pitches—the high pitch of the harmless man behind the curtain and the deep, booming pitch of the magnificent "wizard." Each helps us to judge the trustworthiness of the character's statements. Similarly, in the "all work and no play" scene in Stanley Kubrick's *The Shining* (1980), the pitch of the accompanying music changes from low to high to underscore Wendy's (Shelley Duvall) state of mind as she discovers Jack's (Jack Nicholson) writing (the low pitch corresponds to her anxiety and apprehension; the high pitch signals that her anxiety has turned into sheer panic).

Sound moves through the air in a wave that is acted upon by factors in the physical environment. Think of this as analogous to the wave that ripples outward when you throw a rock into a pond—a wave that is acted upon by the depth and width of the pond. The **loudness** (or volume or intensity) of a sound depends on its **amplitude**, the degree of motion of the air (or other medium) within the sound wave. The greater the amplitude of the sound wave, the harder it strikes the eardrum and thus the louder the sound. Again, although movies typically maintain a consistent level of moderate loudness throughout, filmmakers sometimes use the extremes (near silence or shocking loudness) to signal something

Exploiting the perceptual and physical characteristics of sound

Francis Ford Coppola's *Apocalypse Now* (1979; sound designer Walter Murch) opens with horrific images of war and continues with a scene of a very agitated Captain Benjamin L. Willard (Martin Sheen) in his Saigon hotel room. The first words in his voice-over narration—"Saigon. Shit!"—introduce the movie's counterintuitive logic. Between missions, Willard is distraught not because he has not returned home to the United States, but because he is "still only in Saigon." The jungle is where he really wants to be. Intercut with shots of Willard, here seen upside down, are shots of his ceiling fan, the jungle, helicopters, napalm fires, and so on—all of them represented in a ferocious and hugely ambitious sound track that combines sonic details, noise, dialogue, voice-over, and music. Together, pictures and sound prepare us for many of the movie's key themes, including the hellishness and surreality of the Vietnam War, the devastating power of military technology to destroy human beings and natural resources, and the complex roles within 1960s American society of countercultural forces such as rock music, drugs, and psychedelia.

important or to complement the overall mood and tone of a scene. In *The Shining*, during the scene in which Wendy and Jack argue and she strikes him with a baseball bat, Kubrick slowly increases the loudness of all the sounds to call attention to the growing tension.

The **quality** (also known as timbre, texture, or color) of a sound includes those characteristics that enable us to distinguish sounds that have the same pitch and loudness. In music, the same note played at the same volume on three different instruments (say, a piano, violin, and oboe) will produce tones that are identical in frequency and amplitude but very different in quality. The sound produced by each of these instruments has its own **harmonic content**, which can be measured as wavelengths. In talking about movie sounds, however, we do not need scientific apparatus to measure the harmonic content, because most often we see what we hear.

In the opening sequence of Francis Ford Coppola's *Apocalypse Now* (1979; sound designer Walter Murch), the sound comes from many sources—including helicopters, the fan in a hotel room, explosions, jungle noises, a smashed mirror, the Doors' recording of "The End," voice-over narration, and dialogue—each contributing its own qualities to an overall rich texture. Although many of these sounds are distorted or slowed down to characterize both the dreamlike, otherworldly quality of the setting and Captain Benjamin L. Willard's (Martin Sheen) state of mind, they have been recorded and played back with such accuracy that we can easily distinguish among them.

Fidelity

Fidelity is a sound's faithfulness or unfaithfulness to its source. Ang Lee's *The Ice Storm* (1997; sound-effects designer Eugene Gearty) faithfully exploits the sounds of a violent ice storm to underscore the tragic lives of two dysfunctional Connecticut families, the Hoods and the Carvers. At the climax of the movie, in the midst of the storm, Lee meticulously observes the phenomena and records the sounds of icy rain as it falls on the ground or strikes the windows of houses and cars, icy branches that crackle in the wind and crash to the ground, and the crunch of a commuter train's wheels on the icy rails. As the marriage of Ben and Elena Hood (Kevin Kline and Joan Allen), which is already on the rocks, completely falls apart, the ice storm has a powerful, even mystical effect on the lives of these characters, and its harsh

Nonfaithful sound

In *Mean Streets* (1973; sound mixer Don Johnson), Martin Scorsese uses nonfaithful sound when Charlie (Harvey Keitel), after making love to Teresa (Amy Robinson, *back to the camera*), playfully points his fingers at her as if they were a gun and pulls the "trigger." We hear a gunshot, but there is no danger, for this is just a lovers' quarrel.

breaking sounds serve as a metaphor for their frail lives while providing an audibly faithful reminder of the power of nature.

An excellent early example of a sound effect that is not faithful to its source occurs in Rouben Mamoulian's *Love Me Tonight* (1932; sound by M. M. Paggi). During the farcical scene in which "Baron" Courtelin (Maurice Chevalier) tells Princess Jeanette (Jeanette MacDonald), whom he is wooing, that he is not royalty but just an ordinary tailor, pandemonium breaks out in the royal residence. As family and guests flutter about the palace singing of this deception, one of the princess's old aunts accidentally knocks a vase off a table. As it hits the floor and shatters, we hear the offscreen sound of a bomb exploding, as if to suggest that the aristocratic social order is under attack.

Sources of Film Sound

By *source*, we mean "the location from which a sound originates." Obviously, as mentioned already, most of the sounds heard in a movie literally originate from postproduction processes. But when we talk about source, we're speaking of the implied origin of that sound, whether it's a production sound or a postproduction sound. For example, the sound of footsteps that accompany a shot of a character walking along a sidewalk may have been constructed by Foley artists in a sound studio

after filming was completed, but the source of that sound is implied to be on-screen—created by the character while walking.

The terms used to describe the source of a movie sound are *diegetic* or *nondiegetic*, *on-screen* or *offscreen*, and *internal* or *external*. Let's look at how these sounds are used in movies.

Diegetic versus Nondiegetic

As you know from the "Story and Plot" section in Chapter 4, the word *diegesis* refers to the total world of a film's story, consisting perceptually of figures, motion, color, and sound. **Diegetic sounds** come from a source within a film's world; they are the sounds heard by both the movie's audience and characters. **Nondiegetic sounds**, which come from a source outside that world, are heard only by the audience. Most diegetic sound gives us an awareness of both the spatial and the temporal dimensions of the shot from which the sound emanates; most nondiegetic sound has no relevant spatial or temporal dimensions. For example, the electronic music that plays during the opening sequence of Stanley Kubrick's *The Shining* (1980) is completely nondiegetic: we're not supposed to assume that the music is coming from the

Diegetic sound in action

In John Schlesinger's *Midnight Cowboy* (1969), right after stepping in front of an oncoming car (which screeches to a halt and honks its horn), "Ratso" Rizzo (Dustin Hoffman, *right*) interrupts his conversation with Joe Buck (Jon Voight, *left*) to shout one of the most famous movie lines of all time: "I'm walkin' here!" Even surrounded by everyday Manhattan pedestrian and traffic noise, Rizzo's nasal voice and heavy "Noo Yawk" accent help characterize him as the extremely eccentric and comic foil to Buck, a new and unseasoned arrival in the big city.

Incongruous nondiegetic sound emphasizes an incongruous scene

Inappropriate and out-of-place things are responsible for much of the comedy in Alfred Hitchcock's extremely lighthearted thriller *North by Northwest* (1959; sound by Franklin Milton). Mount Rushmore provides one of the movie's most incongruous—and therefore comic—settings as the expensively dressed and perfectly coiffed Eve Kendall (Eva Marie Saint) and Roger Thornhill (Cary Grant) attempt to escape their pursuer and defy death by climbing all over the national monument. Bernard Herrmann, who wrote scores for seven Hitchcock films and is considered the quintessential Hitchcock composer, uses lively Spanish dance music here. (The same music provides the "Overture" under Saul Bass's title sequence.) Perfectly irrational in this setting, the music seems to come from some other world entirely, signaling that the situation's improbability is part of the fun.

sky, or playing on the car radio, or coming from any location in the scene on-screen (see p. 364).

Diegetic sound can be either internal or external, on-screen or offscreen, and recorded during production or constructed during postproduction. The most familiar kind of movie sound is diegetic, on-screen sound that occurs simultaneously with the image. All of the sounds that accompany everyday actions and speech depicted on-screen—footsteps on pavement, a knock on a door,

the ring of a telephone, the report from a fired gun, ordinary dialogue—are diegetic.

Nondiegetic sound is offscreen and recorded during postproduction, and it is assumed to be inaudible to the characters on-screen. The most familiar forms of nondiegetic sound are musical scores and narration spoken by a voice that does not originate from the same place and time as the characters on the screen. When Redmond Barry (Ryan O'Neal) attracts the attention of the countess of Lyndon (Marisa Berenson) in Stanley Kubrick's *Barry Lyndon* (1975; sound by Robin Gregory and Rodney Holland) during a visually magnificent scene accompanied by the equally memorable music from the second movement of Franz Schubert's Trio no. 2 in E-flat Major (D. 929, op. 100) for violin, cello, and piano, the instrumentalists are nowhere to be seen; furthermore, we do not expect to see them. We accept, as a familiar convention, that this kind of music reflects the historical period being depicted but does not emanate from the world of the story.

Nondiegetic music is used comically in Alfred Hitchcock's *North by Northwest* (1959; sound by Franklin Milton; music by Bernard Herrmann) when we see Roger Thornhill (Cary Grant) and Eve Kendall (Eva Marie Saint) climbing across the presidential faces sculpted on Mount Rushmore and hear Bernard Herrmann's fandango score, music that is not only nondiegetic but also completely absurd given the danger facing these two characters.

The standard conventions of diegetic and nondiegetic sound may be modified for other effects. In Bobby and Peter Farrelly's *There's Something about Mary* (1998; supervising sound editor Michael J. Benavente), for example, the "chorus" troubadour, Jonathan (Jonathan Richman), exists outside the story, which makes him and his songs nondiegetic even though we can see him. The Farrellys play with this concept by having Jonathan get shot accidentally in the climactic scene and thus become part of the story.

On-Screen versus Offscreen

On-screen sound emanates from a source that we can see. **Offscreen sound**, which can be either diegetic or nondiegetic, derives from a source that we do not see. When offscreen sound is diegetic, it consists of sound effects, music, or vocals that emanate from the world of the story. When nondiegetic, it takes the form of a musical score or narration by someone who is not a character in the story. Note that on-screen and offscreen sound are also referred to, respectively, as simultaneous and nonsimultaneous sound. **Simultaneous sound** is diegetic and on-screen; **nonsimultaneous sound** occurs familiarly when a character has a mental flashback to an earlier voice that recalls a conversation or a sound that identifies a place. We recognize the sound too because its identity has previously been established in the movie.

Somewhere between on-screen and offscreen sound is **asynchronous sound**. We are aware of it when we sense a discrepancy between the things heard and the things seen on the screen. It is either a sound that is closely related to the action but not precisely synchronized with it or a sound that either anticipates or follows the action to which it belongs. Because we cannot see its source, asynchronous sound seems mysterious and raises our curiosity and expectations. Thus it offers creative opportunities for building tension and surprise in a scene.

Asynchronous sound was used expressively in some of the first sound movies by such innovators as King Vidor, Rouben Mamoulian, and René Clair. For example, in his classic *Le Million* (1931), director René Clair uses asynchronous sound for humorous effect when we see characters scrambling to find a valuable lottery ticket and hear the sounds of a football game. Another classic example (with a variation) occurs in Alfred Hitchcock's *The 39 Steps* (1935; sound by A. Birch). A landlady enters a room, discovers a dead body, turns to face the camera, and opens her mouth as if to scream. At least, that's what we expect to hear. Instead, as she opens her mouth, we hear the high-pitched sound of a train whistle, and then Hitchcock cuts to a shot of a train speeding out of a tunnel. The sound seems to come from the landlady's mouth, but this is in fact an asynchronous sound bridge linking two simultaneous actions occurring in different places (see p. 391).

Most movies provide a blend of offscreen and on-screen sounds that seems very natural and verisimilar, leading us to almost overlook the distinction between them. Some uses of sound, however, call attention to themselves; for example, when a scene favors offscreen sounds or excludes on-screen sounds altogether, we usually take notice. The total absence of diegetic, on-screen sound where we expect it most can be disturbing, as it is in the concluding, silent shots of a nuclear explosion

in Sidney Lumet's *Fail-Safe* (1964; sound by Jack Fitzstephens). It also can be comic, as in the conclusion of Stanley Kubrick's *Dr. Strangelove or: How I Learned to Stop Worrying and Love the Bomb* (1964; sound by John Cox) when the otherwise silent nuclear explosion is accompanied by nondiegetic music (Vera Lynn singing "We'll Meet Again").

In Robert Bresson's *A Man Escaped* (1956; sound by Pierre-André Bertrand), a member of the French Resistance named Lieutenant Fontaine (François Leterrier) is being held in a Nazi prison during World War II. Once he has entered the prison, he never sees outside the walls, although he remains very aware, through offscreen sound, of the world outside. In fact, sounds of daily life—church bells, trains, trolleys—represent freedom to Fontaine.

Internal versus External

An **internal sound** occurs whenever we hear what we assume are the thoughts of a character within a scene. The character might be expressing random thoughts or a sustained monologue. In the theater, when Shakespeare wants us to hear a character's thoughts, he uses a soliloquy to convey them, but this device lacks verisimilitude. Laurence Olivier's many challenges in adapting *Hamlet* for the screen included making the title character's soliloquies acceptable to a movie audience that might not be familiar with theatrical conventions. Olivier wanted to show Hamlet as both a thinker whose psychology motivated his actions and a man who could not make up his mind. Thus in his *Hamlet* (1948; sound by Harry Miller, John W. Mitchell, and L. E. Overton), Olivier (as Hamlet) delivered the greatest of all Shakespearean soliloquies—"To be, or not to be"—in a combination of both spoken lines and **interior monologue**. This innovation influenced the use of internal sound in countless other movies, including subsequent cinematic adaptations of Shakespeare's plays.

External sound comes from a place within the world of the story, and we assume that it is heard by the characters in that world. The source of an external sound can be either on-screen or offscreen. In John Ford's *My Darling Clementine* (1946; sound by Eugene Grossman and Roger Heman Sr.), Indian Charlie (Charles Stevens, uncredited) is drunk and shooting up the town of Tombstone. The townspeople are afraid of Charlie, and the sheriff (actor uncredited) resigns rather than confront

Internal sound in *Hamlet*

To be, or not to be; that is the question:
Whether 'tis nobler in the mind to suffer
The slings and arrows of outrageous fortune,
Or to take arms against a sea of troubles,
And, by opposing, end them.[4]

Few lines cut deeper into a character's psyche or look more unflinchingly into the nature of human existence, and yet it's not hard to imagine how ineffective these well-known lines might be if simply recited at a camera. In his *Hamlet* (1948), actor-director Laurence Olivier fuses character and psyche, human nature and behavior, by both speaking his lines and rendering them, in voice-over, as the Danish prince's thoughts while simultaneously combining, in the background, music and the natural sounds of the sea. Olivier's version of *Hamlet* was the first to apply the full resources of the cinema to Shakespeare's text, and his innovativeness is especially apparent in the sound.

him, so Wyatt Earp (Henry Fonda)—who is both on- and offscreen during the scene—is appointed sheriff and takes it upon himself to stop the chaos that Charlie has created.

The scene effectively combines both on- and off-screen sounds. The characters (and the viewer) hear the offscreen sounds of Charlie shooting his gun inside the saloon followed by the offscreen sounds of women screaming; then the women appear on-screen as they run from the saloon with Charlie right behind them, still shooting his gun. When Earp, on-screen, starts to enter the building through an upstairs window, we hear the offscreen screams of the prostitutes who are in the room

as he says, "Sorry, ladies." Offscreen, Earp confronts Charlie and conks him on the head, for we hear the thud of Charlie falling to the saloon floor. This is followed by an on-screen shot of Earp dragging Charlie out of the saloon to the waiting crowd. This use of sound demonstrates Earp's courage and skill while treating his serious encounter with Charlie with a comic touch.

Types of Film Sound

The types of sound that filmmakers can include in their sound tracks fall into four general categories: (1) vocal sounds (dialogue and narration), (2) environmental sounds (ambient sound, sound effects, and Foley sounds), (3) music, and (4) silence. As viewers, we are largely familiar with vocal, environmental, and musical sounds. Vocal sounds tend to dominate most films because they carry much of the narrative weight, environmental sounds usually provide information about a film's setting and action, and music often directs our emotional reactions. However, any of these types of sound may dominate or be subordinate to the visual image, depending on the relationship that the filmmaker desires between sound and visual image.

Vocal Sounds

Dialogue, recorded during production or rerecorded during postproduction, is the speech of characters who are either visible on-screen or speaking offscreen—say, from an unseen part of the room or from an adjacent room. Dialogue is a function of plot because it develops out of situations, conflict, and character development. Further, it depends on actors' voices, facial expressions, and gestures and is thus also a product of acting. By expressing the feelings and motivations of characters, dialogue is one of the principal means of telling a story. In most movies, dialogue represents what we consider ordinary speech, but dialogue can also be highly artificial.

During the 1930s, screwball comedies invented a fast, witty, and often risqué style of dialogue that was frankly theatrical in calling attention to itself. Among the most exemplary of these films are Ernst Lubitsch's *Trouble in Paradise* (1932; screenwriters Grover Jones and Samson

---

4. William Shakespeare, *The Tragedy of Hamlet, Prince of Denmark*, act 3, scene 1.

Raphaelson), Howard Hawks's *Bringing Up Baby* (1938; screenwriters Dudley Nichols and Hagar Wilde), and Preston Sturges's *The Lady Eve* (1941; screenwriters Sturges and Monckton Hoffe). Each of these movies must be seen in its lunatic entirety to be fully appreciated, but they nonetheless provide countless rich individual exchanges. Today the screwball comedy genre has been transformed in such movies as Nora Ephron's *You've Got Mail* (1998) and Joel Coen's *Intolerable Cruelty* (2003). David Mamet, who writes and directs his own movies (e.g., *The Spanish Prisoner*, 1997; and *Heist*, 2001), is noted for dialogue that calls attention to itself with its sharp, terse, and often profane characteristics.

Movie speech can take forms other than dialogue. For example, French director Alain Resnais specializes in spoken language that reveals a character's stream of consciousness, mixing reality, memory, dream, and imagination. In Resnais's *Providence* (1977; screenwriter David Mercer; sound by René Magnol and Jacques Maumont), Clive Langham (John Gielgud), an elderly novelist, drinks heavily as he drifts in and out of sleep. Through the intertwining strands of his interior monologue, we learn of his projected novel—about four characters who inhabit a doomed city—and of his relationships with members of his family, on whom his fictional characters are evidently based. Langham's monologue and dialogues link the fantasy to the reality of what we see and hear; in this way, sound objectifies what is ordinarily neither seen nor heard in a movie.

Narration, the commentary spoken by either offscreen or on-screen voices, is frequently used in narrative films, where it may emanate from a third-person narrator (thus not one of the characters) or from a character in the movie. In the opening scene of Stanley Kubrick's *The Killing* (1956; sound by Rex Lipton and Earl Snyder), when Marvin Unger (Jay C. Flippen) enters the betting room of a racetrack, a third-person narrator describes him for us. This offscreen narrator knows details of Unger's personal life and cues us to the suspense of the film's narrative.

In Terrence Malick's *Badlands* (1973; sound by Maury Harris), the character of Holly (Sissy Spacek) narrates the story in first-person voice-over, helping us understand her loneliness, her obsession with Kit (Martin Sheen), her participation in a series of brutal murders, and her inability to stop. This technique enhances our appreciation of her character because rather than simply reinforcing what we are seeing, Holly's understanding

and interpretation of events differ significantly from ours. She thinks of her life with Kit as a romance novel rather than a pathetic crime spree.

In *The Magnificent Ambersons* (1942; sound by Bailey Fesler and James G. Stewart), Orson Welles uses both offscreen and on-screen narrators. Welles himself is the offscreen, omniscient third-person narrator who sets a mood of romantic nostalgia for the American past while an on-screen "chorus"—a device that derives from Greek drama—of townspeople gossip about what is happening, directly offering their own interpretations. Thus the townspeople are both characters and narrators.

Multiple voice-over narrators are also used effectively in two movies where such narration underscores the solitude and stress of characters living in small towns: Paolo and Vittorio Taviani's *Padre Padrone* (1977; sound by Petrantonio Federico, Giovanni Sardo, and Adriano Taloni), a documentary-like account of the lives of sheepherders in the Sardinian countryside, and Atom Egoyan's *The Sweet Hereafter* (1997; sound designer Steve Munro). Egoyan's eloquent, disturbing movie concerns the fatal crash of a school bus and its aftereffects on the townspeople who have lost children. Two principal characters voice the narration—the bus driver Dolores Discolt (Gabrielle Rose) and Nicole Burnell (Sarah Polley), a teenager who survived the crash. In scenes

On-screen narration

Billy Wilder's *Double Indemnity* (1944; sound by Stanley Cooley and Walter Oberst) uses on-screen narration in a unique way. Walter Neff (Fred MacMurray), a corrupt insurance investigator, is pictured here recording his confession of murder on an office Dictaphone. His story leads to flashbacks that fill us in on events leading to that confession.

where these two are giving sworn testimony, Egoyan brilliantly employs the contrasts between the women in age, experience, and honesty. Since we have seen the crash in flashback, we know that Dolores gives an accurate account of the last moments before the crash; however, Nicole, who has promised to tell the truth but is determined to cover up her incestuous relationship with her father, deliberately lies as she accuses the bus driver of speeding and causing the crash.

Nicole's narration is made all the more haunting because she reads (both on-screen to two children and offscreen to underscore the narrative) from the Robert Browning translation of *The Pied Piper of Hamelin* (1888), the legendary German folktale about a piper, masquerading as a rat catcher, who lures a town's children to their death in a river. Although there are parallels between this story and the movie narrative, Nicole's voice-over at the movie's conclusion shows that she has mixed fiction and fact, truth and lies. Angry about what life has handed her—an abusive father and an accident that has crippled her for life—she reads the fictional account of a "strange and new . . . sweet hereafter" and lies not only to conceal the secret and save her father from the consequences but also to prevent him from gaining damages from a lawsuit. The sound of her innocent, pure voice reading the grim folktale masks a tragedy as powerful as the bus crash itself.

Environmental Sounds

Ambient sound, which emanates from the ambience (or background) of the setting or environment being filmed, is either recorded during production or added during postproduction. Although it may incorporate other types of film sound—dialogue, narration, sound effects, Foley sounds, and music—ambient sound should not include any unintentionally recorded noise made during production, such as the sounds of cameras, static from sound-recording equipment, car horns, sirens, footsteps, or voices from outside the production. Filmmakers regard these sounds as an inevitable nuisance and generally remove them electronically during postproduction. Ambient sound helps set the mood and atmosphere of scenes, and it may also contribute to the meaning of a scene.

Consider the ambient sound of the wind in John Ford's *The Grapes of Wrath* (1940; sound by Roger Heman Sr. and George Leverett). Tom Joad (Henry Fonda),

who has just been released from prison, returns to his family's Oklahoma house to find it empty, dark, and deserted. The low sound of the wind underscores Tom's loneliness and isolation and reminds us that the wind of dust-bowl storms reduced the fertile plains to unproductive waste and drove the Joads and other farmers off their land. In Satyajit Ray's "Apu" trilogy—*Pather Panchali* (1955), *The Unvanquished* (1956), and *The World of Apu* (1959)—recurrent sounds of trains establish actual places, times, and moods, but they poetically express characters' anticipations and memories as well. These wind and train sounds, respectively, are true to the physical ambience of Ford's and Ray's stories, but filmmakers also use symbolic sounds as a kind of shorthand to create illusions of reality. In countless Westerns, for example, tinkling pianos introduce us to frontier towns; in urban films, honking automobile horns suggest the busyness (and business) of cities.

Sound effects include all sounds artificially created for the sound track that have a definite function in telling the story. All sound effects, except those made on electronic equipment to deliberately create electronic sounds, come from "wild" recordings of real things, and it is the responsibility of the sound designer and the sound crew to pick and combine these sounds to create the hyperreality of the film's sound track. (*Wild recording* is any recording of sound not made during synchronous shooting of the picture.) In Ray's *Pather Panchali* (sound by Bhupen Ghosh), two children, Apu (Subir Bannerjee) and Durga (Uma Das Gupta), find their family's eighty-year-old aunt, Indir Thakrun (Chunibala Devi), squatting near a sacred pond and think she is sleeping. As Durga shakes her, the old woman falls over, her head hitting the ground with a hollow sound—a diegetic, on-screen sound effect—that evokes death.

In the 1930s Jack Foley, a sound technician at Universal Studios, invented a special category of sound effects: **Foley sounds**. There are two significant differences between Foleys and the sound effects just described. The first is that traditional sound effects are created and recorded "wild" and then edited into the film, whereas Foleys are created and recorded in sync with the picture. To do this, the technicians known as Foley artists have a studio equipped with recording equipment and a screen for viewing the movie as they create sounds in sync with it. The second difference is that traditional sound effects can be taken directly from a library of prerecorded effects (e.g., church bells, traffic noises, jungle sounds)

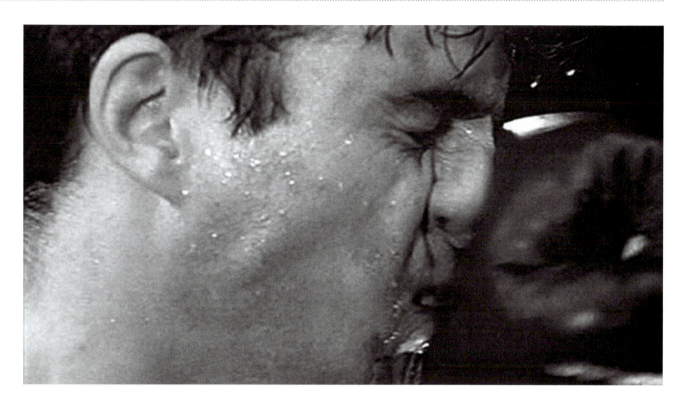

Sound effects in *Raging Bull*

The boxing film against which all others are measured is Martin Scorsese's *Raging Bull* (1980; sound by Frank Warner). Based on former middle-weight champion Jake La Motta's memoir of the same title, this movie fully employs every aspect of filmmaking technology as it re-creates the experience of being in the ring. Close-ups don't get much more vivid than this one, in which La Motta's (Robert De Niro) glove slams into and breaks fighter Tony Janiro's (Kevin Mahon) nose; blood spurts and sweat flies. The image moves from powerful to unbearable, however, when accompanied by the Foley sounds of impact, collapse, and explosion.

or created specifically for the movie. By contrast, Foley sounds are unique. As an example of the latter, the sound technicians working on Peter Jackson's *The Lord of the Rings: The Fellowship of the Ring* (2001; sound designer David Farmer) needed the sounds of arrows shooting through the air, so they set up stationary microphones in a quiet graveyard and shot arrows past the mikes to record those sounds.

Foley artists use a variety of props and other equipment to simulate everyday sounds—such as footsteps in the mud, jingling car keys, the rustling of clothing, or cutlery hitting a plate—that must exactly match the movement on the screen. Such sounds fill in the soundscape of the movie and enhance verisimilitude, but they also convey important narrative and character information. Although these sounds match the action we see on the screen, they can also exaggerate reality—both loud and soft sounds—and thus may call attention to their own artificiality. Generally, however, we do not consciously notice them, so when they are truly effective, we cannot distinguish Foley sounds from real sounds.

In Martin Scorsese's *Raging Bull* (1980; sound by Frank Warner), brutal tape-recorded sounds from boxing matches are mixed with sounds created in the Foley studio. Many different tracks—including a fist hitting a side of beef, a knife cutting into the beef, water (to simulate the sound of blood spurting), animal noises, and the whooshes of jet airplanes and arrows—all work together to provide the dramatic illusion of what, in a real boxing match, would be the comparatively simpler sound of one boxer's gloves hitting another boxer's flesh.

Today's movies are particularly rich in their uses of sound. That includes musicals: Bill Condon's *Dreamgirls* (2006); fantasy adventure films: Peter Jackson's *King Kong* (2005) or Michael Bay's *Transformers: Revenge of the Fallen* (2009); war films: Kathryn Bigelow's *The Hurt Locker* (2008); dramas: Danny Boyle and Loveleen Tandan's *Slumdog Millionaire* (2008) or Tom Hooper's *The King's Speech* (2010); and animated features: Andrew Stanton's *WALL-E* (2008).

The artistry involved in using all the various sources and types of sound has permanently established the role

Music and dancing in *Slumdog Millionaire*

This social and romantic drama, which presents a harrowing view of growing up in modern India, is a far cry from the generic Hollywood musical, but it ends happily: the hero, Jamal, wins the grand prize in a TV game show and is reunited with his childhood sweetheart, Latika, who has escaped her criminal captor. To celebrate, the movie concludes with a musical extravaganza. Led by Latika (Freida Pinto, in yellow, *left*) and Jamal Malik (Dev Patel, in blue shirt, *right*), the entire cast dances and sings "Jai Ho" on the platforms of the Mumbai train station. This scene, made memorable by its vibrant sounds, provides a very creative background for the closing credits.

of the sound designer and exponentially increased the number of sound-related job titles, and therefore new employment, in the field of movie sound. All of these jobs are reflected in the large number of sound artists and technicians receiving screen credit. Furthermore, these roles have made necessary the invention and development of new equipment for sound recording, editing, and mixing and have brought change to many theaters, which have had to install expensive new equipment to process the superb sound made possible by the digital revolution.

Music

Music is used in many distinct ways in the movies, but in this discussion we are concerned principally with the kind of music that Royal S. Brown, an expert on the subject, describes as "dramatically motivated . . . music composed more often than not by practitioners specializing in the art to interact specifically with the diverse facets of the filmic medium, particularly the narrative."[5]

Such music can be classical or popular in style, written specifically for the film or taken from music previously composed for another purpose, written by composers known for other kinds of music (e.g., Leonard Bernstein, Aaron Copland, Philip Glass, and Igor Stravinsky) or by those who specialize in movie scores (e.g., Elmer Bernstein, Carter Burwell, Georges Delerue, Bernard Herrmann, Ennio Morricone, David Raksin, Miklós Rózsa, Tôru Takemitsu, and John Williams, among many others). It also can be music played by characters in the film or by offscreen musicians, diegetic or nondiegetic. The first film score was written by French composer Camille Saint-Saëns for the 1908 movie *The Assassination of the Duke de Guise* (codirectors André Calmettes and Charles Le Bargy).

Female composers of feature films form a relatively new group, given the overall history of the male-dominated musical world in Hollywood. In 1987, Abigail Mead (Vivian Kubrick) scored her father's *Full Metal Jacket*, and Shirley Walker did John Carpenter's *Memoirs of an Invisible Man* (1992). Rock star Björk did the

5. Royal S. Brown, *Overtones and Undertones: Reading Film Music* (Berkeley: University of California Press, 1994), p. 13.

music for Lars von Trier's *Dancer in the Dark* (2000), and Wendy Carlos scored two Stanley Kubrick movies: *A Clockwork Orange* (1971), where music itself plays a major role, and *The Shining* (1980). Since she began film work in the 1960s, Rachel Portman has scored dozens of films, including director Lasse Hallström's *The Cider House Rules* (1999) and *Chocolat* (2000), Jeremiah S. Chechik's *The Right Kind of Wrong* (2013), Amma Asante's *Belle* (2014), and Charles Martin Smith's *Dolphin Tale 2* (2014). Portman, the first woman to earn an Oscar for Best Original Score, won for *Emma* (1996; director Douglas McGrath).

Some of Hollywood's most prolific contemporary composers were formerly rock musicians: Oingo Boingo's Danny Elfman has scored many Tim Burton movies, including *Corpse Bride* (2005); Devo's Mark Mothersbaugh, another prolific composer, scored Catherine Hardwicke's *Lords of Dogtown* (2005) and Wes Anderson's *The Life Aquatic with Steve Zissou* (2004). Songwriter and singer Randy Newman, equally prolific, scored Gary Ross's *Seabiscuit* (2003) and Jay Roach's *Meet the Fockers* (2004). Jonny Greenwood, the lead guitarist of the English alternative rock group Radiohead, is also the composer of the unearthly, beautiful score for Paul Thomas Anderson's *There Will Be Blood* (2007). His score for Anderson's *The Master* (2012) is a tender compilation of some of the great songs of the post–World War II era in which the movie is set. The songs of lost loves, longing, and regret echo the characters' moods and deepen the story's nostalgic feeling that, somehow, life was better then.

Like other types of sound, music can be intrinsic, helping to tell the story, whether it pertains to plot, action, character, or mood; indeed, music plays an indispensable role in many movies. Perhaps the most familiar form of movie music is the large symphonic score used to set a mood or manipulate our emotions.[6] Few old-Hollywood films were without a big score by masters of the genre such as Max Steiner (who scored Victor Fleming's *Gone with the Wind*, 1939). Although recent movies have relied mainly on less ambitious scores, they are still used when large stories call for them. These movies include Ridley Scott's *Gladiator* (2000; composers Hans Zimmer and Lisa Gerrard); Peter Jackson's *The Lord of the Rings* trilogy (2001–3; composer Howard Shore); Ang Lee's *Brokeback Mountain* (2005) and

Music and ideas

In the funeral procession that opens Orson Welles's *The Tragedy of Othello: The Moor of Venice* (1952), the composers, Alberto Barberis and Angelo Francesco Lavagnino, use heavy piano chords, insistent drums, and a chorus to underscore the director's interpretation that fate caused the deaths of Othello (Welles) and Desdemona (Suzanne Cloutier).

Alejandro González Iñárritu's *Babel* (2006), both scored by composer Gustavo Santaolalla; Joe Wright's *Atonement* (2007) and Cary Fukunaga's *Jane Eyre* (2011), both scored by composer Dario Marianelli; James Cameron's *Avatar* (2009; composer James Horner); Wes Anderson's *The Grand Budapest Hotel* (2014; composer Alexandre Desplat); and the Harry Potter movies (2001–11; various directors; composers include John Williams [films 1–3], Patrick Doyle [4], Nicholas Hooper [5–6], and Alexandre Desplat [7–8]).

Movie music can be equally effective when it creates or supports ideas in a film, as in Orson Welles's *The Tragedy of Othello: The Moor of Venice* (1952; music by Alberto Barberis and Angelo Francesco Lavagnino; 1999 sound-restoration supervisor John Fogelson; 1999 music-restoration supervisor Michael Pendowski). Welles takes a deterministic view of Othello's fate, but he depicts the two central characters, Othello (Welles) and Desdemona (Suzanne Cloutier) as being larger than life, even as they are each destined for an early death.

Accompanying their funeral processions is a musical score that leaves no question that these tragic circumstances are the result of fate. In fact, in their

---

6. See Larry M. Timm, *The Soul of Cinema: An Appreciation of Film Music* (New York: Simon & Schuster, 1998), ch. 1.

cumulative power the sights and sounds express the inexorable rhythm of all great tragedies. The complex musical score covers several periods and styles, but to most ears it resembles medieval liturgical music. Deep, hard, dirgelike piano chords combine with the chanting of monks and others in the processions, spelling out (even drawing us into) the title character's inevitable deterioration and self-destruction.

For John Curran's *We Don't Live Here Anymore* (2004), a dark melodrama about marital infidelities, composer Michael Convertino has written a score that builds with the suspense and establishes the mood of anxiety that hangs over everyone involved. By contrast, Don Davis's score for Andy and Lana Wachowski's *The Matrix* (1999) uses the sounds of brass and percussion instruments and songs by the Propellerheads and Rage against the Machine to match the world of the story's synthetic technological environment. Davis also scored the music for the two sequels (*The Matrix Reloaded* and *The Matrix Revolutions*, both 2003).

Irony often results from the juxtaposition of music and image because the associations we bring when we hear a piece of music greatly affect our interpretation of a scene. Take, for example, composer Ennio Morricone's juxtaposition of "Ave Maria" with shots of Brazilian natives and missionary priests being slaughtered by Portuguese slave traders in Roland Joffé's *The Mission* (1986); Quentin Tarantino's use of Stealers Wheel's carefree, groovy "Stuck in the Middle with You" to choreograph the violent cop-torture scene in *Reservoir Dogs* (1992); or Pier Paolo Pasolini's *Accatone* (1961), where the director contrasts urban gang violence with themes from the *St. Matthew Passion* by Johann Sebastian Bach. Another memorable juxtaposition of violent imagery with music (Bach's "Passacaglia and Fugue in C Minor" for organ) is used in *The Godfather* (see Chapter 2, p. 49). Perhaps the boldest experiment in juxtaposing music and image occurs in Sergei Eisenstein's *Alexander Nevsky* (1938), which depicts the thirteenth-century conflict between Crusader knights and the Russian people. Here, using a complex graph, the director integrated Sergei Prokofiev's original musical score, note by note, with the visual composition, shot by shot. This mathematical and theoretically rigorous experiment results, at its best, in a sublime marriage of aural and visual imagery, which has been influential, particularly in such epic movies as Stanley Kubrick's *Spartacus* (1960) and Irvin Kershner's *The Empire Strikes Back* (1980).

Neil Jordan makes a more sustained use of such juxtaposition in *The Crying Game* (1992), a political and psychological thriller that is also a frank, revealing movie about loneliness, desire, and love. Its music helps underscore the surprises in its story. Fergus (Stephen Rea) is interested in Dil (Jaye Davidson), who appears to be an attractive black woman until Dil reveals that he is a transvestite. The personal and political plot twists are too complicated to discuss in this context, but Fergus falls in love with Dil and, because of his love, takes a prison rap for him. At the end of the movie, Dil is visiting Fergus in prison, and as the camera pulls back to the final fade-out and closing credits, we hear Tammy Wynette and Billy Sherrill's country-western classic "Stand by Your Man," sung by Lyle Lovett. (This irony would be missed if the viewer did not stay for the credits, which today increasingly include music or other information vital to understanding the overall movie.) It's funny and touching at the same time, but especially ironic in light of the music under the opening credits: Percy Sledge singing the R&B classic "When a Man Loves a Woman" (by Cameron Lewis and Andrew Wright). It is the perfectly ironic introduction, although we do not know it at the time, to this story of desperate love.

Among directors, Tom Tykwer is notable for his use of music to enhance the pace, or tempo, of *Run Lola Run* (1998; music by Reinhold Heil, Johnny Klimek, and Tykwer), in which the relentless rhythm of the techno-music matches the sped-up, almost surreal pace of the action. Significantly, this music does not change with developments in the action, so it takes on a life of its own. Indeed, any action movie with many exciting chase sequences, such as Paul Greengrass's *The Bourne Supremacy* (2004; composer John Powell), could become routine if the music did not change significantly to suit the participants, location, and outcome of each chase. In *The Bourne Supremacy*'s spectacular chase through Moscow traffic, Jason Bourne (Matt Damon), whose own musical theme is played by a bassoon, successfully eludes the Russian police—but not before many vehicles are destroyed. The sound in this scene is an expressive mix of ambient sounds, Foley sounds, sound effects, and Powell's score. Indeed, it's impossible to disentangle these elements. The loud sounds of sirens, screeching tires, shattered glass, gunshots, and revving car engines accentuate the violent action. Meanwhile the music, which is softer in volume, is a full orchestral score mixed with Russian folk themes and electronic

Songs inspire a movie

Miraculous things happen, and people and events connect in unexpected ways, throughout Paul Thomas Anderson's *Magnolia* (1999; sound designer Richard King). Part of what inspired Anderson in writing his screenplay was hearing then-unreleased recordings by American pop-rocker Aimee Mann. In some cases, connections between the songs and the narrative are explicit, as when the lyrics to "Deathly" (Now that I've met you / Would you object to / Never seeing each other again) become a line of dialogue: "Now that I've met you, would you object to never seeing me again?" At the film's emotional climax, [1] Claudia Wilson Gator (Melora Walters), [2] Jim Kurring (John C. Reilly), [3] Jimmy Gator (Philip Baker Hall), [4] Quiz Kid Donnie Smith (William H. Macy), [5] "Big Earl" Partridge (Jason Robards, *left*) and his nurse, Phil Parma (Philip Seymour Hoffman, *right*), and [6] Stanley Spector (Jeremy Blackman)—all in different places and different situations—sing along with Mann's "Wise Up."

sounds, including techno-music. The chase ends with a final smashup and silence.

Many directors use music to provide overall structural unity or coherence to a story. In Wes Anderson's *Moonrise Kingdom* (2012; music by Alexandre Desplat), *Noye's Fludde* (Noah's Flood), a children's opera by British composer Benjamin Britten, is at the heart of the story. As a boy, Anderson was in a production of the opera, which made a very strong impression, and he says, "It is the colour of the movie in a way."[7] This music is used when a local church is putting on the opera with a cast of children. Audiences hear it again when a hurricane threatens the island and townspeople gather in the church, where a recording of the opera is being played. Then, amid songs by Hank Williams and Françoise Hardy, Desplat interpolates another familiar Britten work, *The Young Person's Guide to the Orchestra*, with his own take on that work, into the final credits sequence.

7. Qtd. in www.brittenpears.org/page.php?pageid=771 (accessed September 8, 2014).

Great music, bad boy

A principal theme of Stanley Kubrick's *A Clockwork Orange* (1971; sound editor Brian Blamey), the loss of moral choice through psychological conditioning, is developed by a focus on Alex (Malcolm McDowell) [1], a worthless, violent character, here staring at a poster of the German classical/Romantic composer Ludwig van Beethoven [2]. Alex's only good trait is his love for Beethoven's Ninth Symphony—especially the setting of Friedrich von Schiller's "Ode to Joy," music that represents all that is most noble in the human spirit, in its finale. Here, however, this music is used ironically to underscore Alex's desire to preserve his freedom to do what he wants (which consists mostly of violent acts), even though society tries to socialize him away from these acts (using a fascistic treatment that attempts to turn him into a "clockwork orange"). In the somewhat muddled world of this controversial film, we're supposed to be glad that Alex is still sufficiently human to embrace Beethoven *and* resist brainwashing.

This passage is so fresh and imaginative that it's almost worth the price of admission. Furthermore, if you tend to walk out during the final credits, it should cure you of that bad habit forever.

A movie such as Stephen Daldry's *The Hours* (2002), which tells a story spanning some eighty years in three different settings with three different women, presents a unique challenge to a musical composer to find some way to unify all these elements. The movie's narrative concerns the different ways these three women are affected by Virginia Woolf's 1925 novel *Mrs. Dalloway*, including the novelist herself (played by Nicole Kidman) in the 1920s; an American housewife, Laura Brown (Julianne Moore), in the 1940s; and a New York professional woman, Clarissa Vaughan (Meryl Streep), in the present. Therefore, viewers might expect a three-part musical score with one distinct sound for each historical period and location, and perhaps even a distinct theme for each principal character. However, composer Philip Glass takes a very different course.

A New Age classical composer with minimalist tendencies, Glass links the three stories with recurring musical motifs played by a chamber orchestra of a pianist and five string players. To create further unity among the lives of the three women, Glass emphasizes the bond that Woolf's novel has created among them by avoiding music from the periods in which they lived. The tensions in the score pull between the emotional and cerebral, underscoring the tensions that the characters experience in this psychological melodrama.

Finally, film music may emanate from sources within the story—a television, a radio or stereo set, a person singing or playing a guitar, an orchestra playing at a dance. For example, Ridley Scott's *Black Hawk Down* (2001) depicts a complex and failed attempt by a group of U.S. Army Rangers to depose a Somalian warlord—a conflict between Americans and African Muslims. For this film, composer Hans Zimmer decided against writing the sort of score we hear in other classic war movies, such as Coppola's *Apocalypse Now* (1979; composers Carmine and Francis Ford Coppola) or Oliver Stone's *Platoon* (1986; composer Georges Delerue).

Instead of using familiar classical themes for theatrical effect, Zimmer relies heavily on diegetic music that emanates from soldiers' radios, street musicians, or mosques. Thus the score juxtaposes Western and African music, Irish tunes, and songs by Elvis Presley and popular groups such as Alice in Chains, Stone Temple Pilots, and Faith No More on the one hand, and traditional Muslim prayer music and chants, mournful piano and strings, African pop music, and tribal drums on the other. At times, such as the beginning of the attack on

Diegetic music

Debra Granik's *Winter's Bone* (2010) is a horrific narrative film that shows how methamphetamine abuse destroys the lives of people in the rural Ozarks. Actor Jennifer Lawrence gives a brilliant performance as Ree Dolly, a teenager who takes charge and tries to keep her family together under the worst of circumstances. Her efforts are hampered by local traditions of patriarchy, secrecy, and resistance to authority, but in this image, when she listens to local bluegrass musicians, including Merideth Sisco singing "High on a Mountain," she momentarily forgets the strife. Here, a traditional folk song offers her and the others a moment of peace and reveals a creative side of their culture.

the marketplace, Zimmer fuses elements of both. His "score" goes beyond music to include many sound effects that function as rhythmic elements (the constant hum of military and civilian vehicles, the beating of helicopter rotor blades, the voices of American soldiers and African crowds). In this expanded sense of a musical score, Zimmer and Jon Title, the sound designer, worked together to create an original, seamless entity that makes few distinctions between music and other sounds. Of course, in *Black Hawk Down* sometimes music is just music and sound effects are just sound effects. But the major achievement here is the fusion of sounds.

With this score, Zimmer does not make conflict appear to be the work of godlike warriors (such as the helicopter gunships in *Apocalypse Now*) but rather conveys the hell of war, reinforces the bond among the soldiers, and helps us understand the agony they suffer on each other's behalf. Near the end, we hear his "Leave No Man Behind," a beautiful tapestry of piano and strings that includes familiar patriotic musical motifs, and his soft, martial arrangement of the heartbreaking Irish ballad "Minstrel Boy," sung by Joe Strummer and the Mescaleros. This score, derived from many sources—both diegetic and nondiegetic—is not background music but

central to portraying the movie's almost unbearable tension.

Although a movie's characters and its viewers hear diegetic music, which can be as simple as sound drifting in through an open window, only viewers hear nondiegetic music, which usually consists of an original score composed for the movie, selections chosen from music libraries, or both. John Carney's *Once* (2006; score by Glen Hansard and Markéta Irglová) is a contemporary love story about a "Guy" (Glen Hansard) and a "Girl" (Markéta Irglová). Its song lyrics virtually replace the meager dialogue. The story is simple enough: boy meets girl, boy sings to girl, girl helps boy to perfect his songs, boy gets music contract and leaves girl to make his first recording. Its goofy charm depends almost completely on this diegetic music.

Nondiegetic music is recorded at the very end of the editing process, so that it can be matched accurately to the images. In recording an original score, the conductor and musicians work on a specially equipped recording stage that enables them to screen the film and tailor every aspect of the music's tempo and quality to each scene that has music (similar to the way that Foley sounds are created). Further adjustments of the sounds of individual musicians, groups of musicians, or an entire orchestra are frequently made by sound technicians after these recording sessions and before the final release prints. Similar efforts are made to fit selections taken from music libraries with the images they will accompany.

Silence

As viewers, we are familiar with all the types of film sound that have been described in this chapter, but we may be unfamiliar with the idea that silence can be a sound. Paradoxically, silence has that function when the filmmaker deliberately suppresses the vocal, environmental, or musical sounds that we expect in a movie. When so used, silence frustrates our normal perceptions. It can make a scene seem profound or even prophetic. Furthermore, with careful interplay between sound and silence, a filmmaker can produce a new rhythm for the film—one that calls attention to the characters' perceptions. *The Silence before Bach* (2007; sound by Albert Manera), a film by the legendary Spanish surrealist director Pere Portabella, does just that. It's a feast for the ears and eyes, providing an avant-garde filmmaker's look at how the music of Bach and the contemporary world might interact.

A similar achievement distinguishes Carlos Reygadas's *Silent Light* (2007; sound by Raúl Locatelli), a film that is as visually beautiful as it is aurally spare. It records a year in the lives of Flemish Mennonite farmers living in Mexico, God-fearing people who are as silent as the extraordinary sunlight in which they work. It is not a documentary, but a celebration of the life cycle, reminiscent of Ermanno Olmi's *The Tree of Wooden Clogs* (1978) and Terrence Malick's *The Tree of Life* (2011). Another most unusual movie, Pat Collins's *Silence* (2012; sound design by Collins), follows a sound recordist who wanders the fields of Ireland in search of pure sound—natural, not man-made. This hybrid feature/documentary takes place amid magnificent scenery. And, based on the theories of American composer John Cage, the sound design results in a film that has a quiet intensity. The sound design of Malgorzata Szumowska's *In the Name Of* (2013) is uncredited, perhaps because it is mainly a silent movie composed of such powerful images that little sound is required. The story—about a priest who cannot reconcile his calling with his sexual attraction to young men—is also about a man who cannot, because of his vows, talk freely about his feelings. The perfection of the mise-en-scène, acting, and use of natural sounds help the director to tell this difficult story.

Classic directors such as Ingmar Bergman (e.g., *Wild Strawberries*, 1957) and Michelangelo Antonioni (e.g., *The Red Desert*, 1964) control their own sound designs, imaginatively using silence to evoke the psychological alienation of their characters. Akira Kurosawa's *Dreams* (1990; sound by Kenichi Benitani) consists of eight extremely formal episodes, each based on one of the director's dreams. The third episode, "The Blizzard," tells of four mountain climbers trapped in a fierce storm. We hear what they hear when they are conscious, but when they are exhausted and near death, they (and we) hear almost nothing.

As the episode begins, we hear the climbers' boots crunching the snow, their labored breathing, and the raging wind. They are exhausted, but the leader warns them that they will die if they go to sleep. Nonetheless, they all lie down in the snow. The previous loud sounds diminish until all we hear is the low sound of the wind. Then, out of this, we hear the sweet, clear, high sounds of a woman singing offscreen. The leader awakens to see a beautiful woman on-screen—the specter of Death—who says, "The snow is warm. . . . The ice is hot." As she covers the leader with shimmering fabrics, he drifts in and

Yummy.

The sound of silence

In *Uncle Boonmee Who Can Recall His Past Lives* (director Apichatpong Weerasethakul), there is silence everywhere in the Thai settings. In this tranquil image, Boonmee (Thanapa Saisaymar, *right*) and his sister-in-law Jen (Jenjira Pongpas, *left*) are sampling honey harvested at Boonmee's farm. Except for a few words, the only sound we hear is the soft hum of the bees and some distant ambient sound, perhaps a gentle wind or small river. This aesthetic pervades the entire movie, especially in the scenes where ghosts from Boonmee's family appear. Of course, we cannot call this a "silent film," but it powerfully demonstrates how to tell a story primarily with visual images.

out of sleep, trying to fight her seductive powers—all in silence.

Ultimately, Death fails to convince the leader to give up. When it's clear that he has regained his consciousness and strength, he is able to hear the loud storm again. Death disappears, accompanied by wind and thunder. Perhaps her beauty has given the leader the courage to resist death and thus save the group. The other men awaken; they, of course, have not seen or heard any of this. We then hear muted trumpets, horns, and alpine music—all nondiegetic sounds signifying the climbers' victory over the weather and death. Ironically, when they awaken in the bright sunshine, the climbers recognize that they have slept in the snow only a few yards away from the safety of their base camp. What is the meaning of this dream? Perhaps that life equals consciousness and, in this instance, awareness of sound.

While movies such as *Dreams*, Jean-Pierre Melville's *Le Cercle Rouge* (1970), or Patrice Chéreau's *Gabrielle* (2005) are important for calling our attention to the imaginative use of silence, no other contemporary movie has done this better than Joel and Ethan Coen's *No Country for Old Men* (2007; sound designer Craig Berkey). Although Carter Burwell is credited for the score, the sound track of this tense, bloody thriller has only 16 minutes of music. Likewise, there is very little dialogue. In this absence, the sound effects are particularly striking and memorable: gunshots, the prairie winds, car doors slamming and engines roaring, the scrape of a chair or footsteps in a creepy hotel, and the beeping tracking device that facilitates the movie's violent ending. When long sections of a movie are as conspicuously silent as this one, audiences automatically are obliged, perhaps ironically, to listen more carefully. However, unlike the approach in many thrillers, where sound creates suspense and even helps the audience to anticipate what might happen, we don't have that to guide us here. Indeed, many of the movie's characters also have to strain to hear and identify sounds. Together with *No Country for Old Men*, Lance Hammer's *Ballast* (2008; sound designer Kent Sparling)—another outstanding movie with little dialogue, music, or sound effects—suggests a reawakened interest in telling a story primarily with visual images.

In *Uncle Boonmee Who Can Recall His Past Lives* (2010; sound by Richard Hocks), the acclaimed Thai director Apichatpong Weerasethakul has made a film about reincarnation that may also seek to transform cinema itself by emphasizing silence rather than sound. Significantly, it won the Palme d'Or for the best feature film at the 2010 Cannes Film Festival, and it is like nothing you have ever seen or heard on the screen. The story, based on the Buddhist belief in reincarnation, is about Boonmee, who is dying of kidney disease and believes that he can see ghosts from his past. His belief is powerful enough to call forth apparitions of his late wife, with whom he discusses the afterlife. It's all treated very matter-of-factly with superimposed images of the dead appearing on the screen. Thus we (and some other characters) see the wife too, just as she was in life. One ghost returns reincarnated as a monkey, another as a catfish. The director's radical vision involves a careful observation of ordinary life in scenes shot in long takes and real time and using very austere sound design. He does not reject sound, for we hear the standard types of film sound, all of them diegetic, including vocal sounds (some dialogue, a short offscreen interior monologue, monks' prayers), music (from a TV melodrama, a stringed instrument), and environmental sounds of all kinds, including jungle noises, insects, water, and rainfall. Indeed, the combination of long takes in which there is little action and the soft, low tones of these sounds is hypnotic. Perhaps ironically, the overwhelming and calming silence of this place

defines it. The silence of the perceivable world and the afterworld is Weerasethakul's most powerful sound.

Types of Sound in Steven Spielberg's *War of the Worlds*

Let's take a close look at how important sound is to one movie in particular: Steven Spielberg's *War of the Worlds* (2005; sound designer Richard King; musical score John Williams). To do this, we'll catalog the types of sounds we hear in the movie. Because the sound design of this movie is so complex, it would be impossible to identify every sound that we hear, but the following discussion offers a sense of the many types of sound incorporated into the overall sound design.

The movie begins with shots of protoplasm as seen through a microscope, accompanied by the deep, soothing voice of the narrator (Morgan Freeman) speaking the opening lines of H. G. Wells's 1898 novel *The War of the Worlds*, on which the screenplay was loosely based:

> No one would have believed in the last years of the nineteenth century that this world was being watched keenly and closely by intelligences greater than man's and yet as mortal as his own; that as men busied themselves about their various concerns they were scrutinised and studied, perhaps almost as narrowly as a man with a microscope might scrutinise the transient creatures that swarm and multiply in a drop of water.

Sounds introduce conflict

At the beginning of Steven Spielberg's *War of the Worlds* (2005; sound designer Richard King), we hear loud, high-pitched sounds (accompanying eerie atmospheric effects) and realize that something terrible is going to happen. Here, Ray Ferrier (Tom Cruise) and his daughter, Rachel (Dakota Fanning), brave the roaring winds to watch the darkening skies.

The ominous nature of this text, along with the grave voice of the narrator, lets us know that we're in for a thrilling story. Furthermore, these few lines establish the basis of the sound design. Those "intelligences greater than man's" inhabit the colossal tripods, which make thunderous noises. By contrast, humankind is a puny thing, prone to making incredulous assumptions about what is happening and then whimpering or crying about it. Big/little, loud/soft: that's the pattern underscoring this conflict.

As the action begins with Ray Ferrier (Tom Cruise) working at a New Jersey container port, we hear the ambient sounds of this industrial operation: traffic in and around the area; the television in Ray's apartment (bringing an ominous news report of violent lightning strikes in Ukraine); and dialogue between Ray, his ex-wife Mary Ann (Miranda Otto), and their children (Rachel, played by Dakota Fanning, and Robbie, played by Justin Chatwin), who are spending the weekend with their father. From this point on, however—when the movie rapidly enters the surreal world of the story—most of the sounds we hear are the work of sound engineers and technicians: the violent lightning storm that incites the action, sudden winds that make the laundry flap wildly on the line, shattering glass as a baseball breaks a window, the earthquake that splits the streets and enables the giant tripods to emerge, electrical flashes that emanate from the tripods, and the sounds of explosions, falling debris, shattered glass, and people being vapor-

ized as the tripods wreak havoc. There are also implied sounds, such as what Robbie is listening to on his iPod, that we cannot hear.

As the crisis in this New Jersey town worsens, we are overwhelmed by the sounds of fires, explosions, bridges and highways collapsing, and the screeching tires of the car as Ray drives frantically out of town. When Ray and his children reach the temporary safety of his ex-wife's new house, there are more lightning storms, heavy winds, and the sounds of a jet aircraft crashing on the front lawn. Many of these sounds were produced in the Foley lab.

During a lull before the tripods appear again, we hear more ambient sounds: Rachel's shrill screams, a radio report on the status of the emergency broadcast system, a passing convoy of army tanks and trucks, and car horns in the heavy traffic as the Ferriers approach a ferry on the Hudson River. At the ferry landing we hear the deafening roar of a freight train as it passes in the night, the jangling of the warning bells at the train's crossing, a female ferry employee shouting instructions through a megaphone, and the ferry's deep-sounding horns. The crowd there is furious at Ray for having a car in which to escape and begins to attack it; we hear loud crowd noises, individual voices, gunshots, and the sounds of the car's windows being smashed. Amid all this pandemonium, Rachel looks up to the sky and hears geese honking as they fly by—a classic omen of the horror to come. There is very little music in this part of the film

The tripods' warning
For the first time, Ferrier sees and hears the foghorn-like warning "voice" of the tripods. He and his neighbors, who do not yet understand what's happening, seem stunned by the tripods—as much by their massive size as by their ominous sounds.

Flight from terror
Ferrier, driving a van that he has stolen, and his two children (who are hiding from danger on the floor of the car) flee their New Jersey town as it is destroyed by the tripods. Notable here are the sound effects of crumbling steel bridges, vaporizing concrete highways, and debris falling everywhere.

Panic

The tripods cause a whirlpool that capsizes a ferry overcrowded with people trying to escape. Sounds here include the hornlike "voices" of the tripods, the screams of the crowd (those still on deck and those who have fallen or dived into the river), the buckling steel of the ferryboat, underwater sounds, and John Williams's musical score.

Armageddon

As the tripods attack the fleeing crowds and devastate the landscape, military jets and missiles fail in their attempts to subdue them. We hear the sounds of the tripods and the chaos they create. Aircraft, music, and various electronic sounds add to the doomsday atmosphere.

(the rising action of the plot), but we hear from a radio somewhere the sound of Tony Bennett singing "If I Ruled the World." Since viewers know that a new demonic force now rules the world, it's a particularly ironic use of music.

The Ferriers manage to get on the ferryboat, but their escape is thwarted when the boat is caught in a whirlpool and capsizes, throwing cars and passengers overboard. The sounds of this action are faithful and vivid. We also see and hear people thrashing underwater as they seek safety. By now, the tripods are on the scene, their huge tentacles (with their own peculiar noises) grabbing people out of the Hudson and gobbling them up into their nasty "mouths." Of course, the three members of the Ferrier family escape all of this.

On the riverbank, we see an Armageddon-like scene—what might be the final conflict between the tripods and humanity—and hear the sounds of the massive tripods crashing through the landscape, army tanks firing missiles at them, and helicopters and fighter jets above also firing missiles and dropping bombs. The scene is complete chaos, and we hear ambient noises of the crowds rushing back and forth. While all this is happening, Robbie Ferrier pleads with his father for independence and escapes into the fray.

As the crowds disperse, and a semblance of quiet and order returns, Ray and Rachel are welcomed into the basement of a nearby farmhouse by Harlan Ogilvy (Tim Robbins). Soon the sounds of his sharpening a large

blade provide another omen that the battle is not yet over and that this man may also become an evil force for Ray to reckon with. We even suspect that Ogilvy is a murderer and that Ray and Rachel are in harm's way, but in fact he just wants to annihilate the tripods.

The basement is full of sounds that further establish the imminent evil: scurrying rats; the soft, whirring sound of a tripod's tentacle as it searches the labyrinth of rooms; rippling water that is pooling there; and the sounds of the stealthy grasshopperlike creatures that have emerged from inside the tripods. Meanwhile, as Rachel continues to scream, her father attempts to calm her by singing; she sings also. But Harlan has now decided to take on the tripods himself—an act that Ray knows will prove fatal for him and his daughter—so Ray kills Harlan (offscreen), apparently beating him to death with a shovel, as indicated by the accompanying heavy drumlike sound.

When Ray and his daughter emerge from the basement, they are confronted with a desolate landscape and an entire arsenal of eerie sounds associated with the tripods and other creatures. For an instant all is quiet (a rare moment in this very noisy movie), and then the tripods strike again with all the familiar sounds we have come to expect. Ray attempts to hide in a car, which is smashed by the tripods; Rachel and Ray scream as they are grabbed separately by the tentacles that are swirling everywhere like giant snakes.

It is already clear, though, that the Ferriers can withstand anything. Fulfilling that expectation, they once

Farmhouse refuge
Rachel and her father take shelter in the house of Harlan Ogilvy (Tim Robbins, *far right*). Their initial meeting is a moment of comparative quiet that's rare for this movie; all we hear is Harlan's soft voice and the offscreen sounds of distant battles being fought outside.

Rachel captured
As her father screams, "No! No!" a tentacle of one of the tripods swoops down and captures Rachel. Other sounds include Rachel's screams and the ominous, insistent musical score that suggests the inevitability of this incident.

again escape—to Boston, where the tripods self-destruct in violent explosions and fireworks. We hear the last sputtering bursts of flame, the gushing red fluid, and the last gasps of the creatures. At the conclusion, as leaves blow across a Boston street (reminding us of the winds in New Jersey at the beginning of this adventure), Rachel and Robbie reunite with their mother, who has been visiting her own mother for the weekend. We hear somber piano music and soft, muted horns as the camera surveys the dead landscape.

The musical score for *War of the Worlds* was written by John Williams, the most famous composer of film music alive today. But the movie's sound effects, more than its music, produce the fright that is the heart of the story. Contrary to viewers' expectations (if we are familiar with Williams's other work), Williams does not create a musical theme for each of the major characters—although there is a recurring, low-key motif for the tripods. Nor does he leave us with one of his memorable "wall of sound" experiences. We are frightened when we see the unfamiliar tripods, and Williams underscores that fear with atonal music, but he also understands that what we see in this movie demands a level of sound effects that necessarily assigns music a secondary role.

It's interesting to compare Steven Spielberg's movie adaptation of *War of the Worlds* with Orson Welles's classic radio adaptation. Spielberg spent some $135 million to make the movie and employed hundreds of artists and technicians in the fields of sound and special effects. Welles's budget (estimated at $2,000) paid for his eleven-person radio cast, small crew, and studio orchestra. We

cannot easily compare a blockbuster movie released in 2005 with a radio show broadcast in 1938, not only because of the differences in the two media but also because the radio audience then was less media-savvy than movie audiences of today. But for anyone who has turned off the lights and listened to Welles's production—the most famous of all radio broadcasts—it's clear how he was able to convince millions of people in the audience that aliens had actually landed and that humankind was in mortal danger. At some level Spielberg instinctively understood this because, like Welles, ultimately he created fright through sound.

Home, devastated home
At the conclusion of Spielberg's *War of the Worlds*, Ray, his daughter, Rachel, and his son, Robbie, are reunited with the children's mother. The soft, muted horns suggest a happy ending, but as Ray and his family tearfully celebrate their reunion, the camera reveals the full extent of the havoc wrought by the alien invaders. Whatever future the Ferriers may have is uncertain.

Functions of Film Sound

Primarily, sound helps the filmmaker tell a movie's story by reproducing and intensifying the world that has been partially created by the film's visual elements. A good sound track can make the audience aware of the spatial and temporal dimensions of the screen, raise expectations, create rhythm, and develop characters. Either directly or indirectly, these functions give the viewer clues to interpretation and meaning. Sounds that work directly include dialogue, narration, and sound effects (often Foley sounds) that call attention (the characters' or ours) to on- or offscreen events.

In John Ford's *My Darling Clementine* (1946; sound by Eugene Grossman and Roger Heman Sr.), "Doc" Holliday (Victor Mature) tosses his keys noisily on the hotel desk to underscore his desire to leave town if Clementine (Cathy Downs) won't keep her promise to leave before him. In Charles Laughton's *The Night of the Hunter* (1955; sound by Stanford Houghton), Harry Powell (Robert Mitchum) covets the large sum of money that he knows is hidden somewhere around the farm. His stepchildren, John (Billy Chapin) and Pearl (Sally Jane Bruce), have kept the money hidden inside Pearl's doll, but Pearl is too young to understand what's going on and has cut two of the bills into figures that she calls "Pearl" and "John." When Harry comes out of the house to tell the children that it's bedtime, they quickly restuff the crackling bills into the doll. Although we hear this sound, Harry doesn't; but a moment later, in a small but easily missed visual moment in the wide frame, we see and hear the two "Pearl" and "John" bills blowing across the path toward Harry. This ominous coincidence adds tension to the scene because we fear that Harry will surely hear it too, look down, and discover the children's secret. Happily, at least for the moment, he doesn't. The sound effects in both of these films were created by Foley artists.

Sounds that function indirectly help create mood and thus may help the audience interpret scenes subconsciously. Tomlinson Holman, a sound expert, points out that viewers differentiate visual elements in a movie far more easily and analytically than they do sound elements. The reason is that they tend to hear sound as a whole, not as individual elements. Filmmakers can take advantage of viewers' inability to separate sounds into constituent parts and use sound to manipulate emotions, often via the musical score. In *Bride of Frankenstein* (1935; composer Franz Waxman), director James

Whale uses low-pitched music to accentuate the terror of the scene in which a lynch mob pursues the Monster (Boris Karloff) through the woods. In Steven Spielberg's *Jaws* (1975), composer John Williams uses four low notes as the motif for the shark—the sound of fear being generated in an otherwise placid environment.

Whether direct or indirect, sound functions according to conventions, means of conveying information that are easy to perceive and understand. In this section, we look at some of these conventions.

Audience Awareness

Sound can define sections of the screen, guide our attention to or between them, and influence our interpretation. *Once upon a Time in the West* (1968; sound engineers Fausto Ancillai, Claudio Maielli, and Elio Pacella), Sergio Leone's masterfully ironic reworking of the Western genre, begins with a scene at the Cattle Corner railroad stop somewhere in the Arizona desert. This scene is notable for an overall mise-en-scène that emphasizes the isolation of the location and the menacing behavior of three desperadoes waiting for a man called Harmonica (Charles Bronson) to arrive on the Flagstone train. Within that setting, the director and his sound engineers have created a memorable audio mise-en-scène for the opening scene. Running approximately 14 minutes, this sequence uses various diegetic sounds that we perceive as emanating from very specific points on and off the screen.

This scene is worth studying both for its montage of sounds and for its convincing way of pinpointing their sources. This sound tapestry is composed almost entirely of sound effects: a creaking door inside the crude station, the scratch of chalk as the station agent writes on a blackboard, a squeaking windmill, the clackety-clack of a telegraph machine, water slowly dripping from the ceiling, a man cracking his knuckles, various animals and insects (a softly whimpering dog, loudly buzzing fly, and chirping bird in a cage), the distant sound of a train approaching and the closer sounds of its chugging steam engine, the music from Harmonica's harmonica, and the sounds of the shootout in which Harmonica swiftly kills the three waiting desperadoes.

We see and hear clearly the source of each of these sounds. Because we are in the desert, there is no background sound per se (except the sound of the train approaching); at two brief moments we hear voices and,

1

2

Sound that defines cinematic space

The tapestry of sounds that underscores the opening of Sergio Leone's *Once upon a Time in the West* (1968; sound engineers Fausto Ancillai, Claudio Maielli, and Elio Pacella) is based on recurring sounds (squeaking windmill) [1], sounds heard only once (whimpering dog), sounds that advance the narrative (an approaching train), sounds that emphasize the tension of the situation in which three desperadoes wait for a train (buzzing fly, dripping water), and sounds that remind us of the outside world (the clackety-clack of the telegraph—until it is disabled by one of the desperadoes) [2].

at the end, only a hint of Ennio Morricone's musical score. This sound design helps us distinguish the individual sounds and also helps us understand how they are arranged in relation to one another. Furthermore, it creates a brooding suspense and raises fundamental questions about the narrative and characters: Who are these desperadoes? Who are they waiting for? Why do they seem to betray Harmonica the moment he arrives? Why does he kill them?

In addition to directing our attention to both the spatial and temporal dimensions of a scene, as in *Once upon a Time in the West*, sound creates emphasis by how it is selected, arranged, and (if necessary) enhanced. In Robert Altman's *The Player* (1992; sound by Michael Redbourn), sound helps us eavesdrop on the gossip at one table in a restaurant and then, even more deliberately, takes us past that table to another in the distance where the protagonist is heading and where the gossip

will be confirmed. Because the scene takes place on the terrace of an exclusive restaurant in Beverly Hills—the guests all seem to be in the motion-picture business—the sound makes us feel as if we're among them, able to see the rich and famous come and go and, more relevant here, able to hear what they're saying, even if they think they aren't being overheard.

Audience Expectations

Sounds create expectations. For example, in a scene between a man and a woman in which you hear quiet music, the sounds of their movements, and a subtle sound of moving clothes, you might expect intimacy between the characters. However, in a similar scene in which the characters are not moving and you cannot hear their clothes—and instead you hear the harsh sound of traffic outside or a fan in the room—you might expect something other than intimacy. Sound also requires precise timing and coordination with the image. For example, when a simple scene of meeting in a doorway is accompanied by a musical chord, we know that the incident is significant, even if we do not know how it will evolve. But in a scene where a small boy is taken away by a bad guy at a carnival, and we hear only the carnival music and loud crowd sounds and then see the look of terror on the parents' faces when they realize their child is gone, dramatic music is probably not needed.

When a particular sound signals an action and that sound is used repeatedly, it plays on our expectations. In Ridley Scott's *Alien* (1979; sound by Jim Shields), sound (along with visual effects) plays an impressive role in helping to create and sustain the suspenseful narrative. This science-fiction/horror movie tells the story of the crew of a commercial spacecraft that takes on board an alien form of "organic life" that ultimately kills all but one of them, Lieutenant Ellen Ripley (Sigourney Weaver).

One device used to sustain this suspense is the juxtaposition of the familiar "meow" sounds made by Ripley's pet cat, Jonesy, against the unfamiliar sounds made by the alien. After the alien disappears into the labyrinthine ship, three crew members—Ripley, Parker (Yaphet Kotto), and Brett (Harry Dean Stanton)—attempt to locate it with a motion detector. This device leads them to a locked panel that, when opened, reveals the cat, which hisses and runs away from them. Because losing the cat is Brett's fault, he is charged with finding it by himself.

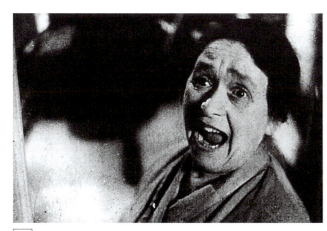

1

2

Sound that thwarts audience expectations

A classic example of sound thwarting audience expectations occurs in Alfred Hitchcock's *The 39 Steps* (1935; sound by A. Birch). A landlady (actor not credited) enters a room, discovers a dead body, turns to face the camera, and opens her mouth as if to scream [1]. At least, that's what we expect to hear. Instead, as she opens her mouth we hear a sound that resembles a scream but is slightly different—a sound that, because it is out of context, we may not instantly recognize. Immediately, though, Hitchcock cuts to a shot of a train speeding out of a tunnel [2], and the mystery is solved: instead of a scream, we have heard the train whistle blaring a fraction of a second before we see the train.

We hear his footsteps as he proceeds warily through the craft, calling "Here, kitty, kitty . . . Jonesy, Jonesy," and we are relieved when Brett finds the cat and calls it to him. Before the cat reaches Brett, however, it sees the alien behind him, stops, and hisses. Alerted, Brett

turns around, but he is swiftly killed by the creature. This sound motif is repeated near the end of the film, when Ripley prepares to escape on the craft's emergency shuttle but is distracted by the cat's meow.

Expression of Point of View

By juxtaposing visual and aural images, a director can express a point of view. In countless movies, for example, the sounds of big-city traffic—horns honking, people yelling at one another, taxis screeching to a halt to pick up passengers—express the idea that these places are frenetic and unlivable. Similarly, when a movie is set in other distinct environments—seashore, desert, mountain valley—the natural sounds associated with these places (the placid, turbulent, and stormy rhythms of the sea; the howling winds of the desert sands; the cry of a lone wolf in an otherwise peaceful valley) reflect the director's point of view of landscape and often the thoughts or emotional mood of the characters.

Alfred Hitchcock is a master of expressing his point of view through sound. In *The Birds* (1963), for example, one of the few of his movies that does not have background music, Hitchcock uses a design of electronic bird sounds (by Remi Gassmann and Oskar Sala) to express his point of view about the human chaos that breaks out in an unsuspecting town that has been attacked by birds. Bernard Herrmann, who composed the scores for many Hitchcock movies including *Psycho* (1960), was the uncredited sound designer on this one. Its highly stylized sound track consists of a juxtaposition of natural sounds and computer-generated bird noises. Elisabeth Weis, an authority on film sound, writes:

[In] *The Birds*, screeches are even more important than visual techniques for terrorizing the audience during attacks. Indeed, bird sounds sometimes replace visuals altogether. . . . Hitchcock carefully manipulates the sound track so that the birds can convey terror even when they are silent or just making an occasional caw or flutter. . . . Instead of orchestrated instruments there are orchestrated sound effects. If in *Psycho* music sounds like birds, in *The Birds* bird sounds function like music. Hitchcock even eliminates music under the opening titles in favor of bird sounds.[8]

8. Elisabeth Weis, *The Silent Scream: Alfred Hitchcock's Sound Track* (Rutherford, NJ.: Fairleigh Dickinson University Press, 1982), pp. 138–139.

Directors of visionary movies—those that show the past, present, or future world in a distinctive, stylized manner—rely extensively on sounds of all kinds, including music, to create those worlds. In *2001: A Space Odyssey* (1968), where the world created comes almost totally from his imagination, Stanley Kubrick uses sounds (and the absence of them) to help us experience what it might be like to travel through outer space. The barks and howling of the apes in the prologue reflect Kubrick's point of view that aggression and violence have always been a part of the world—indeed, that such behavior removes the distinction between such concepts as *primitive* and *civilized*. The sounds of switches, latches, and doorways on the space shuttles have a peculiar hollow sound all their own. The electronic sounds emanating from the monolith reflect its imposing dignity but also mirror the awe and fear of the astronauts who approach it.

Although Werner Herzog usually shoots his visionary movies with direct sound (meaning that it is recorded on-site), he frequently augments that sound with haunting musical scores by the German group Popol Vuh. These sounds, as well as Herzog's very deliberate use of silence, are part of what elevates such films as *Aguirre: The Wrath of God* (1972), *Nosferatu the Vampyre* (1979), and *The Enigma of Kasper Hauser* (1974) beyond being mere poetic movies to being philosophical statements about human life. *Aguirre* recounts the failed attempt of Don Lope de Aguirre (Klaus Kinski), a sixteenth-century Spanish explorer, to conquer Peru and find the fabled city of El Dorado. From the opening to the closing moments of this extraordinary movie, it is clear that Aguirre is mad. Indeed, Kinski's performance as Aguirre leaves no doubt that he is possessed by ruthless ambition and greed.

Herzog's style is frequently called hallucinatory (as well as visionary) because it produces a feeling in the viewer of being somewhere between fantasy and reality, which is exactly where Aguirre is. In the opening scene, in which Aguirre and his forces slowly descend a steep mountainside toward a river, most of the action is shot in real time, helping us to understand just how arduous and dangerous the expedition will be. The primary sounds are people's low voices, footsteps on the path, and Popol Vuh's minimalist score, which mixes electronic and acoustic sources with choral monotones. This music makes clear Herzog's view of the futility of Aguirre's quest. Thus at the end, when Aguirre is alone on a drifting raft spinning slowly out of control on the river (photographed impressively from a helicopter,

which, of course, we do not hear), we are not surprised to hear this musical score again—except that now Aguirre too seems to understand the futility of his quest. This reuse of music reinforces the prophetic nature of the director's point of view.

Rhythm

Sound can add rhythm to a scene, whether it's accompanying or juxtaposed against movement on the screen. In *Citizen Kane* (1941; sound by Bailey Fesler and James G. Stewart), in the comic scene in which Kane moves into the *Inquirer* office, Orson Welles uses the rhythms within overlapping dialogue to create a musical composition—one voice playing off another in its pitch, loudness, and quality (see "Looking at (and Listening to) Sound in Orson Welles's *Citizen Kane*" later in this chapter). In Atom Egoyan's *The Sweet Hereafter* (1997; sound by Steve Munro), two conversations overlap, joined in time but separated in on-screen space: Wendell and Risa Walker (Maury Chaykin and Alberta Watson) talk with each other while Mitchell Stevens (Ian Holm) speaks with his daughter, Zoe (Caerthan Banks), on a cell phone.

A **montage** of sounds is a mix that ideally includes multiple sources of diverse quality, levels, and placement and usually moves as rapidly as a montage of images. Such a montage can also be orchestrated to create rhythm, as in the famous opening scene of Rouben Mamoulian's *Love Me Tonight* (1932; sound by M. M. Paggi)—one of the first films to use sound creatively—in which the different qualities of sounds made by ordinary activities establish the "symphony" that accompanies the start of the day in an ordinary Parisian neighborhood.

Jean-Pierre Jeunet and Marc Caro pay homage to Mamoulian's sound montage in *Delicatessen* (1991; sound by Jérôme Thiault). One comic scene in the film functions like a piece of music, with a classic verse-chorus-verse-chorus-verse-chorus pattern. When a butcher, Monsieur Clapet (Jean-Claude Dreyfus) makes love to his mistress, Mademoiselle Plusse (Karin Viard), the mattress and frame of the bed squeak noisily and in an increasing rhythm that matches their increasing ardor. As the tempo increases, we expect the scene to end climactically. Playing on our expectations, though, Jeunet and Caro cut back and forth between the lovers and other inhabitants of the building, who hear the squeaking bed and subconsciously change the rhythm of their daily chores to keep time with the sounds' escalating pace. The sequence derives its humor from the way it

Sound and characterization

The opening montage in Francis Ford Coppola's *Apocalypse Now* (1979; sound designer Walter Murch) sets a high visual and sonic standard. But Coppola and his collaborators meet and perhaps exceed that standard during the "helicopter attack" scene, in which the lunatic Lieutenant Colonel Kilgore (Robert Duvall, *standing*, in image [6]) leads a largely aerial raid on a Vietnamese village. Accompanying horribly magnificent images of destruction and death are the sounds of wind, footsteps, gunfire, explosions, airplanes, helicopters, crowd noise, shouting, dialogue, and Richard Wagner's "Ride of the Valkyries." Although the grand operatic music gives unity, even a kind of dignity, to the fast-moving, violent, and disparate images, its main effect is to underscore Kilgore's megalomania.

satisfies our formal expectations for closure (the sexual partners reach orgasm) but frustrates the tenants, who just become exhausted in their labors.

On a far grander scale—matching the scope of the story—Francis Ford Coppola's *Apocalypse Now* (1979; sound designer Walter Murch) includes a mix of more than 140 sound tracks during the exciting, horrifying helicopter assault on the beach of a Vietcong stronghold; prominent in the mix is "Ride of the Valkyries" from Richard Wagner's opera *Die Walküre* (1856). In a later film about Vietnam, Oliver Stone's *Platoon* (1986; sound designer Gordon Daniel), the personal hatreds that divide a platoon are underscored by a montage that includes the roar of the helicopters, voices of frightened men, screams of the dying, and repeated excerpts from composer Samuel Barber's grief-stricken *Adagio for Strings* (1936).

Characterization

All types of sound—dialogue, sound effects, music—can function as part of characterization. In Mel Brooks's *Young Frankenstein* (1974; sound by Don Hall), when Frau Blücher's (Cloris Leachman) name is mentioned, horses rear on their hind legs and whinny. It becomes clear in context that she is so ugly and intimidating that even horses can't stand to hear her name, so for the rest of the movie, every time her name is mentioned, we hear the same sounds.

In *Jaws* (1975; sound by John R. Carter), Steven Spielberg uses a sound effect to introduce Quint (Robert Shaw), the old shark hunter. When Quint enters a community meeting called in response to the first killing of a swimmer by the shark, he draws his fingernails across a chalkboard to show his power and bravery: he is affected neither by a sound that makes most people cringe nor, by extension, by the townspeople or sharks. We might also observe that this sound is as abrasive as Quint is.

Musical themes are frequently associated with a character's thoughts, as in Lasse Hallström's *My Life as a Dog* (1985), where Björn Isfalt's score reflects the melancholic state of mind of a boy yearning for his dead mother, or in Joseph L. Mankiewicz's *The Ghost and Mrs. Muir* (1947), where Bernard Herrmann's score reflects a widow's loneliness in an isolated house on a cliff overlooking the sea. Musical themes can also help us to understand the setting in which characters live. Miranda July's *Me and You and Everyone We Know* (2006) is an offbeat indie feature that tells the overlapping stories of a diverse group of people living in Los Angeles and looking for love, affection, or whatever they can find. These people—young, old, married, single, black, Hispanic, and white—are poignant in their somewhat goofy yearnings, and Michael Andrews's whimsical musical score—including solo guitar, solo piano, solo organ, pop songs, and a hymn—reflects their casual lifestyles and provides the perfect comment on their activities. Animals can also be identified by a significant musical theme, as with John Williams's memorable one for Hedwig, Harry's owl in the *Harry Potter* series.

Musical themes often identify characters, occurring and recurring on the sound track as the characters make their entrances and exits on the screen. But music can also underscore characters' insights. In Sam Mendes's *American Beauty* (1999; composer Thomas Newman), for example, Lester Burnham (Kevin Spacey) is having

Music supporting characterization
Richard (John Hawkes) and Christine (Miranda July) are just two of the endearing characters looking for love in *Me and You and Everyone We Know*. When they meet initially, nothing clicks, at least not for Richard. But later they discover that they live in the wacky world of LA and view it in the same detached way. The musical score does not create a theme for them; instead, it echoes their casual way of living and loving.

a midlife crisis. Although a wide variety of diegetic popular music helps identify the musical tastes of the Burnham family, it is an original theme that helps identify and sustain Lester's longing for a different life, literally a "bed of roses"—and roses are the symbol of Lester's lust for his daughter's friend Angela (Mena Suvari). Lying on his bed, Lester has this fantasy—shots of rose petals floating on him are intercut with shots of Angela naked among the rose petals on the ceiling above him—and we hear a peaceful theme played by a Javanese gamelan orchestra. The repetitiveness and quality of this music emphasize Lester's mood of wanting to escape to another world.

Continuity

Sound can link one shot to the next, indicating that the scene has not changed in either time or space. **Overlapping sound** carries the sound from a first shot over to the next before the sound of the second shot begins. Charles Laughton's *The Night of the Hunter* (1955; sound by Stanford Houghton) contains an effective sound bridge: Harry Powell (Robert Mitchum), a con man posing as an itinerant preacher, has murdered his wife, Willa (Shelley Winters), placed her in an automobile, and driven it into the river. An old man, Birdie Steptoe (James Gleason), out fishing on the river, looks down and discovers the crime.

Through shot A, an underwater shot of great poetic quality in which we see Willa in the car, her floating hair mingling with the reeds, we hear Harry singing one of his hymns; that music bridges the cut to shot B, where Harry, continuing to sing, is standing in front of their house looking for his stepchildren. Hearing Harry's hymn singing over Willa's submerged body affects the meaning of this scene in two ways: it both adds to the shot's eerie feeling of heavenly peace (with her gently undulating hair, diffused light, etc.) associated with what should be a grisly image and connects Harry directly to the murder. In addition, his calm, satisfied, even righteous attitude reinforces the interpretation that he sees his killings as acts of God. When the picture catches up with the sound to reveal Harry calmly stalking the murdered woman's children, the dramatic tension is increased because of the association between Harry and Willa's body that the sound bridge has reinforced.

Joel Coen's *The Man Who Wasn't There* (2001; sound designer Eugene Gearty) is a dark, twisted neo-noir film. It contains a smoothly edited sequence of fifteen shots, thirteen of which are linked by overlapping, non-diegetic bits of a Beethoven piano sonata and two of which show Ed Crane (Billy Bob Thornton) listening to Rachael Abundas (Scarlett Johansson) playing the sonata (diegetic music). In a life filled with conflict and tragedy, Ed has found "peace" listening to Rachael play

this particular sonata, and this sequence is made all the more peaceful by its lyrical theme. But Carter Burwell, the movie's composer, must have chosen this sonata—no. 8 in C Minor, op. 13—for its subtitle, *Pathétique*, as a pointedly ironic reminder that Crane sees himself as a loser and so does everyone else.

Overlapping sound can also be used to link and provide unity between disparate scenes, as in Roy Andersson's *You, the Living* (2007; sound by Jan Alvemark, Günther Friedhoff, Robert Sörling), a stylish black comedy composed of 50 long takes and set in Sweden, which uses lively music and sound bridges that help the story move and make sense.

Emphasis

A sound can create emphasis in any scene: it can function as a punctuation mark when it accentuates and strengthens the visual image. Although some movies treat emphasis as if it were a sledgehammer, others handle it more subtly. In Peter Weir's *The Truman Show* (1998; sound by Lee Smith), Truman Burbank (Jim Carrey) unknowingly has lived his entire life in an ideal world that is in fact a fantastic television set contained within a huge dome. When after thirty years he realizes the truth of his existence, he overcomes his fear of water and attempts to sail away. To deter him, the television producer orders an artificial storm, which temporarily disables Truman. But the sun comes out, he wakes up, and he continues his journey, thinking he is free. Suddenly the boom of one of his sails pierces the inside of the great dome with a sound that is unfamiliar to him—indeed, one of the most memorable sounds ever heard in a movie. His first reactions are shock, anguish, and disbelief. How could there be an "end" to the horizon?

Distinct as this sound is, it has nothing of the sledgehammer effect. Rather, it underscores Truman's quiet, slow epiphany of who and where he is. His next reaction is the awareness that something is very wrong with his world. Cautiously touching the dome's metal wall, he says, "Aah," indicating a further insight into his situation. He walks along the edge of the "horizon," mounts a surreal staircase, pauses for a moment to talk with the show's producer, and finally walks through an exit door to the first free day of his life. The unique sound of the boom piercing the metal dome, underscored by the chord progressions of Burkhard Dallwitz's score, is nothing like the ordinary sound of a boat bumping

1

2

3

4

5

Overlapping music

A fifteen-shot sequence in Joel Coen's *The Man Who Wasn't There* (2001; sound designer Eugene Gearty) documents a futile attempt by Ed Crane (Billy Bob Thornton) to find a man who has swindled him out of $10,000. The sequence is one of many in the movie that show the decent but ineffectual Crane coming to grips with his life as an ordinary barber while his wife and everyone else around him set higher goals. The sequence is underscored with the nondiegetic and diegetic sounds of Beethoven's *Pathétique* piano sonata. Here are five shots from the middle of the sequence: Crane [1] tries to locate Creighton Tolliver, the swindler (played by Jon Polito), by phone; [2] checks the man's business card; and [3] listens to Rachael "Birdy" Abundas (Scarlett Johansson), a teenage neighbor, playing a Beethoven piano sonata. [4] Rachael's father, Walter (Richard Jenkins), also listens. [5] Crane is back at his job in the barber shop. When he asks, "How could I have been so stupid?" we understand the appropriateness of the filmmakers' choice of this Beethoven sonata to underscore his self-insight.

against a dock. And although it is a real sound, it is not a natural one. This is a symbolic sound that both emphasizes Truman's captivity and heralds his liberation from a world of illusion.

In Adrian Lyne's version of *Lolita* (1997; sound by Michael O'Farrell), the sexual ambiguity of a confrontation between Humbert Humbert (Jeremy Irons) and his nemesis, Clare Quilty (Frank Langella), is punctuated by the insistent sound of an electric bug zapper. In action movies, such as *Sin City* (2005; directors Frank Miller

and Robert Rodriguez; sound designer Paula Fairfield), the sounds of violent action are greatly emphasized so that fists hit with a bone-crunching "thunk" and cars crash with a deafening noise. The same exaggerated emphasis applies to many animated movies, in which the violence is loud but usually harmless.

Looking at (and Listening to) Sound in Orson Welles's *Citizen Kane*

During the 1930s, the first decade of sound in film, many directors used sound as an integral part of their movies. Their innovations were all the more significant because most of them had little or no prior background in sound. Between 1933 and 1938, Orson Welles established himself as one of the most creative innovators in American radio broadcasting. Before Welles, radio broadcasting had been a wasteland lacking in creativity, but Welles approached the medium the way he approached the theater and, later, the movies: experimenting and making things different.

As always, Welles was a one-man show: writer, director, producer, actor. As writer, he specialized in making modern adaptations of classic literary works; as producer, he cast famous stage and movie actors, generally saving the most important part for himself; and as director, he orchestrated voices, sound effects, narration, and music in a complex mix that had never been tried before, at least on the scale that he created. There was no commercial television broadcasting at the time, and Welles understood the power of pure sounds, without images, to entertain, educate, and engage listeners. He also understood the power of radio to shock people, as his notorious 1938 production of H. G. Wells's *The War of the Worlds* proved. Indeed, the awesome imagination behind that one radio broadcast made Orson Welles world famous overnight and was instrumental in his recruitment by Hollywood.

Welles's complex sound design for *Citizen Kane* (1941; sound by Bailey Fesler and James G. Stewart) is a kind of deep-focus sound that functions much like deep-focus cinematography. Indeed, we can confidently call Welles the first sound designer in American film history for his comprehensive use of sound to establish, develop, and call our attention to the meanings of what we see. In this discussion, we will look more closely at the impressive uses of sound in the party scene that celebrates Kane's acquisition of the *Chronicle* staff for the *Inquirer*. In addition to the combined staff of reporters, musicians, waiters, and dancers, the principal characters are Charles Foster Kane (Welles), Mr. Bernstein (Everett Sloane), and Jed Leland (Joseph Cotten). The setting for the party is the *Inquirer*'s offices, which have been

Sound mise-en-scène

The mise-en-scène of this party scene from Orson Welles's *Citizen Kane* (1941; sound by Bailey Fesler and James G. Stewart) clearly reflects what's going on both visually and aurally. Leland (Joseph Cotten) and Bernstein (Everett Sloane) are talking, and even though there are competing sounds around them, their voices are distinct because they have been placed close to a microphone in a medium shot. Note that Kane (Welles), both visually and aurally, dominates this scene through his presence in the middle background of each shot.

decorated for the occasion. The room is both deep and wide, designed to accommodate the deep-focus cinematography. Welles made his complicated sound design possible by covering the ceilings with muslin, which concealed the many microphones necessary to record the multiple sounds as the scene was shot.

We hear these multiple sounds simultaneously, distinctly, and at the proper sound levels in relation to the camera's placement, so that the farther we are from the sound, the softer and less distinct the sound becomes. When Bernstein and Leland are talking, for example, they appear in medium shots, and their dialogue is naturally the loudest on the sound track. However, they literally have to shout to be heard because of the pitch, loudness, and quality of the competing sounds: the music, the dancing, the crowd noise.

We can say that the sound has its own mise-en-scène here. Although these diegetic, on-screen sounds were recorded directly on the set, some additions were made during the rerecording process. Reversing the ordinary convention of composing the music after making the rough cut of a film, Bernard Herrmann wrote the music first, and Robert Wise edited the footage to fit the music's rhythm.

Sources and Types

The sound in this scene is diegetic, external on-screen. It was recorded during both production and postproduction and is diverse in quality, level, and placement. The types of sound include overlapping voices, ordinary dialogue, and singing; music from an on-screen band; sound effects; and ambient noise. Welles's handling of

sound dominates this scene: he makes us constantly aware of the sources, the types, and the mix and (unsurprisingly) doesn't use much silence. However, two signs mounted on walls read "SILENCE" and thus, as relics of an earlier period, remind us how quiet these same offices were before Kane took over from the previous editor. Through this visual pun, Welles employs a touch of silence during the loudest sequence in *Citizen Kane*.

Functions

Given what was possible in sound design and recording in 1941, the sound montage in this party scene is an extraordinary achievement. It creates the spatial, temporal, emotional, and dramatic setting of the action, and also heightens our expectations and fears about Kane's future in journalism and politics. This complexity set it far ahead of its time and deeply influenced the development of movie sound. The sound montage in this party scene functions in many ways. Here are some notable ones:

> Guides our attention to all parts of the room, making us aware of characters' relative positions (e.g., the contrast between Kane and the others)

Sound creates mood

At this party, where spirits are high, almost everyone joins in the act, including Kane, the performers, and Kane's staff of reporters, here pretending as if they were members of the band.

Complex mix of sound

In addition to the distinctive voices of the three main characters and the voices of the guests and performers, there is a brass marching band—all of this constituted a sound design and mix that was very advanced for its time.

Who is this man?

"Who is this man," a line in Kane's campaign song "There Is a Man," might function as a subtitle for the movie itself and allows Kane—singing, dancing, and mugging his way through the act—to show a lighter side of his many-faceted personality.

Sound effects

Welles rarely missed an opportunity to use sound effects expressively, as here, where the bright light of the old-fashioned flash unit illuminates the scene and punctuates his bragging about acquiring the *Chronicle* staff: "I felt like a kid in a candy store!"

> Helps define the spatial and temporal dimensions of the setting and the characters' placement within the mise-en-scène (e.g., the sound is loud when the source is closer to the camera)

> Conveys the mood and the characters' states of mind (e.g., the sound is frantic and loud and gains momentum until it almost runs out of control, underscoring the idea that these men, Kane and reporters alike, are being blinded and intoxicated by their own success)

> Helps represent time (e.g., the sound here is synchronous with the action)

> Fulfills our expectations (e.g., of how a party of this kind might sound and of the fact that Kane is continuing on his rapid rise to journalistic and political power)

> Creates rhythm beyond that provided by the music (within the changing dramatic arc that starts with a celebration involving all the men and ends with one man's colossal display of ego)

> Reveals, through the dialogue, aspects of each main character (e.g., establishes a conflict between Kane and Leland over personal and journalistic ethics, one in which Bernstein predictably takes Kane's side)

> Underscores one principal theme of the entire movie (e.g., the song "There Is a Man" not only puts "good old Charlie Kane" in the spotlight—he sings and dances throughout it—but also serves as the campaign theme song when he runs for governor and becomes a dirge after his defeat; at the same time, while the lyric attempts to answer the question "Who is this man?" it has no more success than the rest of the movie)

> Arouses our expectations about what's going to happen as the film evolves (e.g., the marching band signals both that the *Inquirer* won over the *Chronicle* and that the *Inquirer* "declares" war on Spain—a war the United States will win)

> Enhances continuity with sound bridges (the smooth transitions from shot to shot and scene to scene within the sequence)

> Provides emphasis (e.g., the sound of the flashlamp when the staff's picture is taken punctuates Kane's bragging about having gotten his candy; after Kane says, "And now, gentlemen, *your complete attention*, if you please," he puts his fingers in his mouth and whistles; the trumpets' blare)

> Enhances the overall dramatic effect of the sequence

This overwhelming sound mix almost tells the story by itself.

Sound aids characterization in *Citizen Kane*

[1] Standing at opposite ends of the banquet table, Bernstein (*background*) and Kane (*foreground*) banter back and forth as if they were a comedy duo. [2] Welles dominates the scene with sound. Putting his fingers between his lips, Kane gets the attention of his guests and loudly calls for their "complete attention." [3] Bernstein (*left*) and Leland (*right*) join in the singing of "There Is a Man," but Leland, now disillusioned with Kane, sings only to be polite.

Characterization

All the functions named in the previous section are important to this particular sequence and the overall film. In this section, we will look more closely only at how the sound helps illuminate the characters of Charles Foster Kane (Orson Welles), Mr. Bernstein (Everett Sloane), and Jed Leland (Joseph Cotten). Even though their dialogue is primarily a function of the narrative, its vocal delivery brings it to life. Long after you have seen the movie, you remember the characters, what they said, and the voices of those who portrayed them. As one legacy of his radio experience, Welles planned it that way.

Each of the actors playing these characters has a distinctive speaking voice that is a major part of their characterization. Indeed, their voices are part of the key to our understanding of their characters. The depth and resonance of Welles's voice, coupled with its many

colors (or qualities) and capabilities for both nuance and emphasis, enhance his ambiguous portrayal of the character. In several distinct areas, the sound of his voice deepens our understanding of this contradictory figure. It helps Kane flaunt his wealth and his power as the *Inquirer*'s publisher: when he brags to the new reporters about feeling like a "kid in a candy store" and having gotten his candy, his remarks are punctuated by the sound of the photographer's flashlamp. However, this sound may also be interpreted as Welles's way of mocking Kane's bragging.

Kane dominates the table of guests with the announcement that he is going to Europe for his health—"forgive my rudeness in taking leave of you"—but there is in fact nothing physically wrong with him, as we learn when he calls attention to his mania for collection (and wealth) by sarcastically saying, "They've been making statues for two thousand years and I've only been buying for five." This conversation between Kane and Bernstein is directed and acted as if it were a comedy routine on a radio show or in a vaudeville theater between the "top banana" (Kane) and the "straight man" (Bernstein). The implied nature of this exchange is something that 1940s audiences would have instinctively understood.

The sound in this scene helps Kane build on his power, not only as the boss and host of the party—"And now, gentlemen, *your complete attention*, if you please"— but also as the flamboyant and influential publisher: "Well, gentlemen, are we going to declare war on Spain, or are we not?" He's in charge because he's the boss, and the boss's voice also dominates his employees. As he asks this question, the band enters, playing "Hot Time in the Old Town Tonight," and is followed by women dancers carrying toy rifles. When Leland answers, "The *Inquirer* already has," Kane humiliates him by calling him "a long-faced, overdressed anarchist." Even though he says this humorously, he uses the tone of his voice, as well as his words, to humiliate his subordinate.

The song about "good old Charlie Kane"—here the excuse for more of Welles's vocal theatrics—later becomes his political campaign theme, so the sound in this scene connects us with later scenes in which we hear this musical theme again. By participating in the singing and dancing, Kane continues to call "complete attention" (his words) to himself. Through both visual and aural imagery, Kane remains in the center of the frame for most of the scene, either directly on-screen himself or indirectly reflected in the windows. His voice dominates all the other sounds in this scene because it always seems to be the loudest.

Leland and Bernstein are different from one another in family background, education, level of sophistication, and relationship to Kane, and their conversation about journalistic ethics establishes another major difference: these characters' voices are also quite different from Kane's voice. Leland has the soft patrician voice of a Virginia gentleman, while Bernstein's voice reflects his New York immigrant-class upbringing. Leland gently questions Kane's motives in hiring the *Chronicle*'s staff and wonders why they can change their loyalties so easily, but the pragmatic Bernstein bluntly answers, "Sure, they're just like anybody else. . . . They got work to do, they do it. Only they happen to be the best in the business." Their reading of these lines embodies one of the movie's major themes: journalistic ethics. Even their singing sets them apart. Bernstein sings as if he's having a good time, but Leland seems to sing only to show his good manners. Their differences, including the differences in their voices, ultimately determine their future relationship with Kane.

Themes

Sound serves many functions in this scene, including the development of several major themes and concerns:

> *Kane's youthful longings fulfilled.* A major strand of the narrative conveys Kane's lifelong bullying of others, mania for buying things, and egomania as a reaction to being abandoned by his parents at an early age. Here he begins the scene by addressing the new reporters and likening his acquisition of the *Chronicle* staff to a kid who has just gotten all the candy he wants. This statement is punctuated by the sound of a flashbulb.

> *Kane's ruthless ambition.* The mix of burlesque dancing, loud music, and serious conversation about ethics only underscores Kane's determination to do whatever is necessary to attain his goals.

> *Kane's disregard for ethics and principles and his relation with his two closest associates.* Kane's domination of the scene is made personal by his humiliation of Leland (throwing his coat at Leland, as if Leland were a lackey) and teasing of Bernstein ("You don't expect me to keep any of those promises, do you?"), a further reference to the "Declaration of Principles" that Kane flamboyantly writes and prints on the first page of the *Inquirer*. The dialogue in this scene (and those scenes that precede and follow it) further clarifies the relationships among Kane, Bernstein, and Leland.

The care and attention that Welles and his colleagues enthusiastically gave to the sound design of this scene was virtually unprecedented in 1941 and was seldom equaled until the 1970s. In giving this rowdy party the appearance of a real event, not something staged for the cameras, the sound—along with the visual design, mise-en-scène, acting, and direction, of course—plays a major role in depicting a crucial turning point in the narrative.

ANALYZING SOUND

By this point in our study of the movies, we know that like everything else in a movie, sound is manufactured creatively for the purposes of telling a story. As you attempt to make more informed critical judgments about the sound in any movie, remember that what you hear in a film results from choices made by directors and their collaborators during and after production, just as what you see does. This chapter has provided a foundation for understanding the basic characteristics of film sound and a vocabulary for talking and writing about it analytically. As you screen movies in and out of class, you'll now be able to thoughtfully appreciate and describe how the sound in any movie either complements or detracts from the visual elements portrayed on-screen.

SCREENING CHECKLIST: SOUND

☐ As you analyze a shot or scene, carefully note the specific sources of sound in that shot or scene.

☐ Also keep notes on the types of sound that are used in the shot or scene.

☐ Note carefully those moments when the sound creates emphasis by accentuating and strengthening the visual image.

☐ Does the sound in the shot, scene, or movie as a whole help develop characterization? If so, how does it do so?

☐ In the movie overall, how is music used? In a complementary way? Ironically? Does the use of music in this movie seem appropriate to the story?

☐ Do image and sound complement one another in this movie, or does one dominate the other?

☐ Does this film use silence expressively?

☐ In this movie, do you hear evidence of a comprehensive approach to sound—one, specifically, in which the film's sound is as expressive as its images? If so, explain why you think so.

Questions for Review

1. What is sound design? What are the responsibilities of the sound designer?
2. Distinguish among recording, rerecording, editing, and mixing.
3. What is the difference between diegetic and nondiegetic sources of sound?
4. What are the differences between sounds that are internal and external? on-screen and offscreen?
5. Is a movie limited to a certain number of sound tracks?
6. How do ambient sounds differ from sound effects? How are Foley sounds different from sound effects?
7. Can the music in a movie be both diegetic and nondiegetic? Explain.
8. How does sound call our attention to both the spatial and temporal dimensions of a scene?
9. Cite an example of sound that is faithful to its source and an example that is not.
10. What is a sound bridge? What are its functions?

STUDENT RESOURCES ONLINE

digital.wwnorton.com/movies5

▶ **VIDEO**

This chapter's tutorial discusses the sound editing in Andrew Lund's short film *Snapshot*.

INTERACTIVE

In this interactive tutorial, see how sound plays a major role in how movies convey meaning, mood, and narrative. Experience a single silent scene in several very different ways, thanks to three distinct soundscapes created by a professional sound designer.

Citizen Kane (1941; director Orson Welles); pictured: Orson Welles

FILM HISTORY

What Is Film History?

In just over a hundred years, the cinema, like the classical art forms before it—architecture, fiction, poetry, drama, dance, painting, and music—has developed its own aesthetics, conventions, influence, and, of course, history. Broadly defined, film history traces the development of moving images from early experiments with image reproduction and photography through the invention of the movies in the early 1890s and subsequent stylistic, financial, technological, and social developments in cinema that have occurred up to now.

To get some idea of the scope and depth of that record, you should start looking at as many as possible of the movies that made history. Because that could take years, a good way to start is by seeing one or both of the following compilation films. The first is *Histoire(s) du cinéma* (1998) by Jean-Luc Godard, one of the world's great film directors. Consistent with Godard's argumentative reputation, this highly original account, whose title correctly suggests that there is more than one way to look at this subject, is full of clips that will challenge your thinking. The second is Mark Cousins's *The Story of Film: An Odyssey* (2011), a 15-hour series made for British television. Cousins, an Irish filmmaker and critic, has gathered a highly personal list of movies

as radical and provocative as Godard's. Also you might browse through a comprehensive history of film, such as the ten-volume *History of American Cinema* series (University of California Press). Such comprehensive histories are written over many years, and often by many people. Because of this, most film historians don't undertake such massive projects. Most people who practice film history instead focus their energies on studying specific moments, movements, and phenomena. Jeanine Basinger's *I Do and I Don't: A History of Marriage in the Movies* (New York: Knopf, 2012) provides a masterful account of its subject. C. S. Tashiro's *Pretty Pictures: Production Design and the History of Film* (Austin: University of Texas Press, 1998) focuses on just one aspect of film production—production design—even as it ranges widely over the full chronology of film history. In both broad and specific studies, the film historian is interested equally in change—those developments that have altered the course of film history—and stability, meaning those aspects that have defied change. Film history is not, to quote film historians

A major turning point in film history

Billy Wilder's *Sunset Boulevard* (1950) is a haunting film noir about film history. Norma Desmond (Gloria Swanson), an aging silent-movie star who (in the 1950s) still represents the glamour and allure of the silent era, hopes to revive her career in the sound era with the help of Joe Gillis (William Holden), an aspiring screenwriter. Her fantasies are apparent in one of her most famous (and unintentionally funny) lines: "I am big. It's the movies that got small." Unfortunately, she isn't big anymore, and the movies just kept getting bigger and better after the conversion to sound, one of the major turning points in film history. All Desmond has left is her dreams, and *Sunset Boulevard* is all the more poignant because Gloria Swanson herself was actually one of the greatest stars of the silent era.

Robert C. Allen and Douglas Gomery, "a list of film titles or an academically respectable trivia contest. It has the much more important and complex task of explaining the historical development of a phenomenon on which billions of dollars and countless hours have been spent."[1]

Like other historians, film historians use artifacts to study the past. These artifacts include the various machines and other technology—cameras, projectors, sound recording devices, and so on—without which there would be no movies. Artifacts might include notes from story conferences, screenplays, production logs, drawings, outtakes, and other objects relevant to the production of a particular movie. Of course, they might also include first-person accounts by people involved with the movie, newspaper and magazine articles, and books about the production and the people involved in it. Obviously, the most important artifacts to the film historian are the movies themselves.

Film history includes the history of technologies, the people and industrial organizations that produce the movies, the national cinemas that distinguish one country's movies from another's, the attempts to suppress and censor the movies, and the meanings and pleasure that we derive from them. Gaining knowledge about these and other aspects of film history is pleasurable and interesting in itself. But as you graduate from merely watching movies to looking at movies in a critically aware way, your knowledge of film history will also give you the perspective and context to understand and evaluate the unique attributes of movies from the past as well as the more complex phenomena of today's movies.

Basic Approaches to Studying Film History

There are many approaches to studying film history, including studies of production, regulation, and reception.

But the beginner should know the four traditional approaches: the aesthetic, technological, economic, and social. In what follows, we describe each approach and cite one or two studies that exemplify each approach.[2]

The Aesthetic Approach

Sometimes called the *masterpiece approach* or *great man approach*, the aesthetic approach seeks to evaluate individual movies and/or directors using criteria that assess their artistic significance and influence. Ordinarily, historians who take this approach will first define their criteria of artistic excellence and then ask the following questions: What are the significant works of the cinematic art? Who are the significant directors? Why are these movies and these directors important?

Historians who take the aesthetic perspective do not necessarily ignore the economic, technological, and cultural aspects of film history—indeed, it would be impossible to discuss many great movies without considering these factors—but they are primarily interested in movies that are not only works of art but also widely acknowledged masterpieces.

The most comprehensive, one-volume international history that takes an aesthetic approach is David A. Cook's *A History of Narrative Film*, 4th ed. (New York: Norton, 2004). Other aesthetic studies are on the auteur theory, which holds that great movies are the work of a single creative mind; one outstanding study in this field is James Naremore's *On Kubrick* (London: BFI, 2007).[3]

The Technological Approach

All art forms have a technological history that records the advancements in materials and techniques that have affected the nature of the medium. Of all the arts, though, cinema seems to rely most heavily on technology. Historians who chart the history of cinema

1. Robert C. Allen and Douglas Gomery, *Film History: Theory and Practice* (New York: Knopf, 1985), p. 21.
2. These four traditional categories are covered in Allen and Gomery, chs. 4–7. Jon Lewis and Eric Smoodin, eds., *Looking Past the Screen: Case Studies in American Film History and Method* (Durham, NC: Duke University Press, 2007), pp. 4–5, identify four other categories: industrial systems, regulatory systems, reception, and representation.
3. Film critic Andrew Sarris defines the auteur theory in his *The American Cinema: Directors and Directions, 1929–1968* (New York: Dutton, 1968), pp. 19–37. See also Pauline Kael's famous rebuttal, "Circles and Squares," in *Film Theory and Criticism: Introductory Readings*, ed. Gerald Mast and Marshall Cohen, 2nd ed. (New York: Oxford University Press, 1979), pp. 666–691. Sarris's essay is also included in this anthology (pp. 650–665), but it should be read in the context of his pioneering 1968 study, cited here.

technology examine the circumstances surrounding the development of each technological advance as well as subsequent improvements. They pose questions such as: When was each invention made? Under what circumstances, including aesthetic, economic, and social, was it made? Was it a totally new idea or one linked to the existing state of technology? What were the consequences for directors, studios, distributors, exhibitors, and audiences?

By studying how the major developments (including the introduction of sound, the moving camera, deep-focus cinematography, color film stock, and digital cinematography, processing, and projection) occurred, historians show us how the production of movies has changed and can also evaluate whether that change was significant (like widescreen processes) or transitory (like Smell-O-Vision). This approach cuts across artists, studios, movements, and genres to focus on the interaction of technology with aesthetics, modes of production, and economic factors.

An excellent example of such a study is by David Bordwell, Janet Staiger, and Kristin Thompson, *The Classical Hollywood Cinema: Film Study and Mode of Production to 1960* (New York: Columbia University Press, 1985). For a study of a specific technological subject, see John Belton's *Widescreen Cinema* (Cambridge, MA: Harvard University Press, 1992).

The Economic Approach

The motion-picture industry is a major part of the global economy. Every movie released has an economic history of its own as well as a place in the economic history of its studio (policies of production, distribution, and exhibition) and the historical period and country in which it was produced.

Historians interested in this subject help us to understand how and why the studio system was founded, how it adapted to changing conditions (economic, technological, social, historical), and how and why different studios took different approaches to producing different movies, how these movies have been distributed and exhibited, and what effect this had on film history. They study how and why the independent system of production superseded the studio system and what effect this

has had on production, distribution, and exhibition. They are also concerned with such related issues as management and organization, accounting and marketing practices, and censorship and the rating system. Finally, they try to place significant movies within the nation's economy as well as within the output of the industry in general and the producing studio in particular.

Excellent studies include Douglas Gomery's *The Hollywood Studio System: A History* (London: BFI, 2005), Joel W. Finler's *The Hollywood Story*, 3rd ed. (London: Wallflower, 2003), and Tino Balio's *Grand Design: Hollywood as a Modern Business Enterprise, 1930–1939*, History of the American Cinema series, vol. 5 (Berkeley: University of California Press, 1995).

The Social History Approach

Because society and culture influence the movies, and vice versa, the movies serve as primary sources for studying society. Writing about movies as social history continues to be a major preoccupation of journalists, scholars, and students alike. Historian Ian Jarvie suggests that, in undertaking these studies, we ask the following basic questions: Who made the movies, and why? Who saw the films, how, and why? What was seen, how, and why? How were the movies evaluated, by whom, and why?[4]

In addition, those interested in social history consider such factors as religion, politics, and cultural trends and taboos. They ask to what extent, if any, a particular movie was produced to sway public opinion or effect social change. They are also interested in audience composition, marketing, and critical writing and reviewing in the media, from gossip magazines to scholarly books. Overall, they study the complex interaction between the movies—as a social institution—and other social institutions, including government, religion, and labor.

Landmark studies include Robert Sklar's *Movie-Made America: A Cultural History of American Movies*, rev. and updated ed. (New York: Vintage, 1994), and Richard Abel's *Americanizing the Movies and "Movie-Mad" Audiences, 1910–1914* (Berkeley: University of California Press, 2006).

Although some areas in the study of film history may require experience and analytic skills beyond those

---

4. This paraphrase of Ian Jarvie comes from Allen and Gomery, *Film History*, p. 154.

possessed by most introductory students, you can use your familiarity with film history in writing even the most basic analysis for a class assignment.

Which approach—aesthetic, technological, economic, or social—will we take in this chapter? Where they are relevant, we will consider them all.

A Short Overview of Film History

Precinema

Before we discuss the major milestones of film history, let's look at some of the key technological innovations that made movies possible.[5] First among these is photography.

Photography In one sense, movies are simply a natural progression in the history of photography. The word **photography** means, literally, "writing with light" and technically, "the static representation or reproduction of light." The concept has its beginnings in ancient Greece. In the fourth century BCE, the Greek philosopher Aristotle theorized about a device that later would be known as the **camera obscura** (Latin for "dark chamber"; Figure 10.1). In the late fifteenth century, Leonardo da Vinci's drawings gave tangible form to the idea. Both simple and ingenious, the camera obscura may be a box or it may be a room large enough for a viewer to stand inside. Light entering through a tiny hole (later a lens) on one side of the box or room projects an image from the outside onto the opposite side or wall. An artist might then trace the image onto a piece of paper.

Photography was developed during the first four decades of the nineteenth century by Thomas Wedgwood, William Henry Fox Talbot, and Sir John Herschel in England; Joseph-Nicéphore Niépce and Louis-Jacques-Mandé Daguerre in France; and George Eastman in the United States. In 1802, Wedgwood made the first recorded attempt to produce photographs. However, these were not camera images as we know them, but basically silhouettes of objects placed on paper or leather sensitized with chemicals and exposed to light. These images faded quickly, for Wedgwood did not know how to fix (stabilize) them. Unaware of Wedgwood's work, Talbot devised a chemical method for recording the images he observed in his camera obscura. More important was the significant progress he made toward fixing the image, and he invented the **negative**, or negative photographic image on transparent material, that makes possible the reproduction of the image.

Niépce experimented with sunlight and the camera obscura to make photographic copies of engravings as well as actual photographs from nature. The results of this heliographic ("sun-drawn") process—crude paper prints—were not particularly successful. But Niépce's discoveries influenced Daguerre, who by 1837 was able to create, on a copper plate treated with chemicals, an image remarkable for its fidelity and detail. In 1839, Herschel perfected hypo (short for hyposulfite thiosulfate, or sodium thiosulfate), a compound that fixed the image on paper and thus arrested the effect of light on it. Herschel first used the word *photography* in 1839 in a lecture at the Royal Society of London for the Promotion of Natural Knowledge. What followed were primarily technological improvements on Herschel's discovery.

In 1851, glass-plate negatives replaced the paper plates. More durable but heavy, glass was replaced by gelatin-covered paper in 1881. The new gelatin process reduced, from 15 minutes to 0.001 second, the time necessary to make a photographic exposure. This advance made it possible to record action spontaneously and simultaneously as it occurred. In 1887, George Eastman began the mass production of a paper "film" coated with gelatin emulsion; in 1889, he improved the process by substituting clear plastic (film) for the paper base. Although other technological improvements followed, this is the photographic film we know today.

This experimentation with optical principles and still photography in the nineteenth century made it possible to take and reproduce photographic images that could simulate action in the image. But simulation was not enough for the scientists, artists, and members of the general public who wanted to see images of life in motion. The missing step between still photography and cinematography was discovered with the development of series photography.

---

5. This discussion of early film technologies is necessarily brief. For more on key filmmaking technologies, see Chapter 11, "How the Movies Are Made."

Figure 10.1 | CAMERA OBSCURA

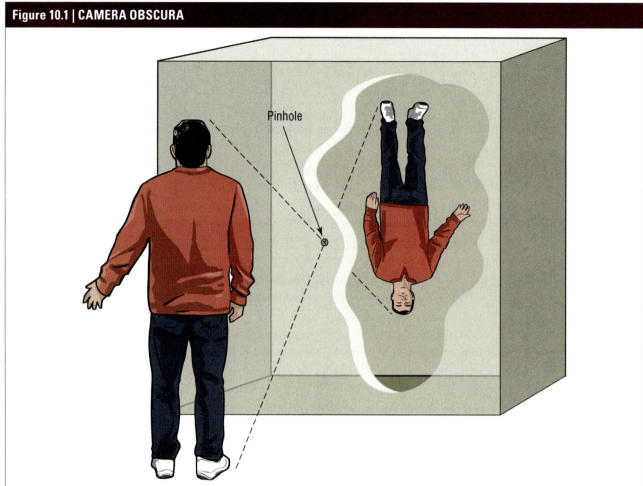

Pinhole

Before the advent of photosensitive film, the camera obscura was used to facilitate lifelike drawing. In this simple schematic, for example, the interior "wall" upon which the upside-down image is projected was usually whitened; an artist could place a piece of drawing paper on the wall and trace the image onto it.

Series Photography **Series photography** records the phases of an action. In a series of still photographs, we see, for example, a man or a horse in changing positions that suggest movement, though the images themselves are static. Within a few years, three men—Pierre-Jules-César Janssen, Eadweard Muybridge, and Étienne-Jules Marey—contributed to its development.

In 1874, Janssen, a French astronomer, developed the **revolver photographique** (or chronophotographic gun), a cylinder-shaped camera that creates exposures automatically, at short intervals, on different segments of a revolving plate. In 1877, Muybridge, an English photographer working in California, used a group of electrically operated cameras (first twelve, then twenty-four) to produce the first series of photographs of continuous motion. On May 4, 1880, using an early projector known as the **magic lantern** and his **zoopraxiscope** (a version of

the magic lantern, with a revolving disc that had his photographs arranged around the center), Muybridge gave the first public demonstration of photographic images in motion—a cumbersome process, but a breakthrough.

In 1882, Marey, a French physiologist, made the first series of photographs of continuous motion using the **fusil photographique** (another form of the chronophotographic gun), a single, portable camera capable of taking twelve continuous images. Muybridge and Marey later collaborated in Paris, but each was more interested in using the process for his own scientific studies than for making or projecting motion pictures as such. Marey's invention solved the problems created by Muybridge's use of a battery of cameras, but the series was limited to forty images—a total of 3 or 4 seconds.

The experiments that Janssen, Muybridge, and Marey conducted with various kinds of moving pictures

1   **2**

Series photography

Eadweard Muybridge's famous series of photographs documenting a horse in motion were made possible by a number of cameras placed side by side in the structure pictured here [1]. The cameras were tied to individual trip wires. As the horse broke each wire, a camera's shutter would be set off. The result of this experiment—a series of sixteen exposures [2]—proved that a trotting horse momentarily has all four feet off the ground at once (see the third frame). Series photography has been revived as a strategy for creating special effects in contemporary movies.

were limited in almost every way, but the technologies needed to make moving pictures on film were in place and awaited only a synthesis.

1891–1903: The First Movies

Who invented the movies?[6] Historic milestones such as this are seldom the result of a few persons working together on a single idea but rather the collaborative product of many dreams, experiments, and inventions. It did not occur in one moment, but rather took place in four major industrialized countries—the United States, France, England, and Germany—in the years just before 1895. Furthermore, in attempting to answer the question, we must distinguish between moving pictures that were projected onto a surface for an audience and those that were not.

In 1891, William Kennedy Laurie Dickson, working with associates in Thomas Edison's research laboratory, invented the **Kinetograph** (the first motion-picture camera) and the **Kinetoscope** (a peephole viewer). The first motion picture made with the Kinetograph, and the earliest complete film on record at the Library of

Congress, was Dickson's *Edison Kinetoscopic Record of a Sneeze* (1894), popularly known as *Fred Ott's Sneeze*, which represents, on Edison and Dickson's part, a brilliant choice of a single, self-contained action for a single, self-contained film of very limited length. Edison's staff made their movies, including *Fred Ott's Sneeze*, inside a crude, hot, and cramped shack known as the **Black Maria**. The Black Maria was really the first movie studio, for it contained the camera, technicians, and actors. The camera was limited in its motion, able only to move closer to or away from the subject on a trolley. Light was provided by the sun, which entered through an aperture in the roof, and the entire "studio" could be rotated to catch the light. Edison demonstrated the Kinetoscope to various audiences, public and private. And in April 1894, the first Kinetoscope parlor opened in New York City, thus inaugurating the history of commercial movies.

Although the visual image seen in the Kinetoscope peephole viewer was moving, it could be enjoyed by only one person at a time. In the same month, the Lathams—Woodville and his two sons, Grey and Otway, former Edison employees—used their movie projector, the Eidoloscope, to show a movie to the press. Although Edison

6. An invaluable history of the invention of the movies, and one on which this section draws, is Charles Musser's *The Emergence of Cinema: The American Screen to 1907*, History of the American Cinema, vol. 1 (New York: Scribner, 1990; repr., Berkeley: University of California Press, 1994).

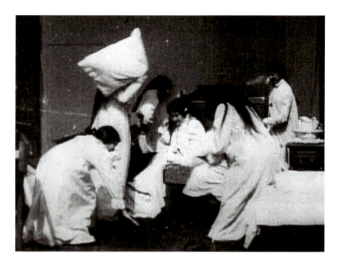

Short records of real life

Before narrative or editing, Thomas Edison's first movies (about 30 seconds in length) were simple records of ordinary people and events: a man and woman kissing, a young woman dancing, a man getting a shave and haircut in a barber shop, and a woman and child feeding doves in a barnyard. In *Seminary Girls* (1897), we see young girls having a rare moment of fun in a harmless pillow fight until the school's matron interrupts them. The scene, obviously staged for the stationary camera, was photographed in Edison's first studio, the Black Maria.

Edison's Kinetograph and the Black Maria

These images show Thomas Edison's Black Maria, the first motion-picture "studio," pictured from the outside [1] and the inside [2]. The interior view shows how awkward and static the Kinetograph was thanks to its bulk and its need to be tethered to a power source. In addition, the performers had very little room to move, and the environment was hot and airless. The makeshift quality of the studio, as well as its relatively modest size, is evident from the external view.

put down the significance of this demonstration, it was the first time an invited audience had seen projected motion pictures in the United States. Meanwhile, in November in Germany, another pair of brothers, Max and Emil Skladanowsky, projected short films in Berlin. Coincidentally, in France, two brothers (teams of brothers

figure significantly in this story) named Auguste and Louis Lumière invented the Cinématographe, a far more sophisticated device than either the Kinetoscope or the Eidoloscope. In December 1895, they used it to project a movie on a screen set up in a small room inside a public café that was converted into a theater. (They had already projected it throughout Europe for small, invited audiences). Although that movie, *Employees Leaving the Lumière Factory* (1895), which the Lumières called an *actualité* (a documentary view of the moment), was only 1 minute in length, it captivated the audience with its depiction of a spontaneous event. The Cinématographe—a hand-cranked device that served as camera, projector, and film printer—was equally amazing. In 1896, Edison unveiled his own projector, the Vitascope, in a New York City theater.

The projection of moving pictures to a paying audience ended the prehistory of cinema and freed it to become the art form of the twentieth century. Aesthetically, the work of the first filmmakers cannot compare in any way with today's movies, yet they managed, in a few years' time, to establish the basic types of movies: short narratives, documentary depictions of real life,

Real life as seen through the artists' lens

At first glance, Auguste and Louis Lumière's *Children Digging for Clams* (1896) may seem similar to Edison's *Seminary Girls* as a simple record of an ordinary activity. But the differences between them show that the Lumières were artists with a natural sense of style. Not only was it longer (44 seconds) and shot outdoors (with a stationary camera), but it also employs a deep composition. Across the foreground, in a diagonal line, we see the clam-digging children; in the middle ground, we see adults, probably their parents, keeping an eye on them; and in the background, we see other people, the shoreline, and the horizon. As far as composition goes, nothing could be simpler; but by shooting it outdoors in a natural landscape, the Lumières provide an aesthetically pleasing interpretation of an actual event rather than just a documentary record.

Méliès the magician

Georges Méliès, who was by trade a magician, took naturally to motion pictures, which are primarily an illusion. He quickly understood that he could make the camera stop and start (what we now call stop-motion photography) and, with this technique, make things vanish and reappear (sometimes in a new form). Like all magicians, he reveled in fooling the public. In *Long Distance Wireless Photography* (1908), Méliès plays the inventor of a process for transmitting photographs from one place to another and dupes his clients. When a man and woman ask for a demonstration, he photographs them and, behind them, projects unflattering images of them. Annoyed at this deception, they try to destroy the studio, but are chased away in a scene of slapstick comedy. Here, Méliès shows a prophetic but comic insight into two events that were decades away: the electronic transmission of photographs and television. The action is staged for the camera as if it were happening on a theater stage; and the movie, which is nearly 6 minutes in length, tells a complete story.

and experimental movies with special effects that foreshadow today's animation. In addition, they recognized that the movies—like the contemporary steam engine, electricity, and the railroad—would attract paying customers and make them a great deal of money. What they probably did not envision was the power of the movies to shape attitudes and values.

After a few years of experimenting with very short movies, a minute or two in length and hardly more than a novelty, Edison, the Lumière brothers, and other new filmmakers realized that the cinema needed new forms and conventions. It was clear that the movies needed to be less a curiosity that the public would soon tire of and more a durable and successful commercial entertainment. They had to compete with and draw from other popular art forms, such as literature and theater.

Paramount among the early innovators of film form was a Frenchman, Georges Méliès. In the late 1890s he began to make short narrative movies based on the theatrical model of short, sequential scenes shot from a fixed point of view. The only editing within these self-contained scenes was for cuts or in-camera dissolves. Rudimentary as these movies were, according to film historian David A. Cook, Méliès was "the cinema's first narrative artist,"[7] famous for innovating many technical and narrative devices. He is best known for his use of special effects—still captivating today—in such landmark films as *A Trip to the Moon* (1902) and *The Impossible Voyage* (1904).

---

7. David A. Cook, *A History of Narrative Film*, 4th ed. (New York: Norton, 2004), p. 14.

The beginnings of cinematic narrative
Realizing that they needed to tell stories, the early filmmakers began to develop conventions of cinematic narrative. Among these artists were Georges Méliès in France, G. A. Smith in England, and Edwin S. Porter in the United States. In *Life of an American Fireman* (1903) and *The Great Train Robbery* (1903), Porter broke away from the prevailing step-by-step, one-shot-one-scene editing of Méliès and invented an early form of continuity editing in which he built a scene made up of shots that seemed chronologically continuous from one shot to the next. We make sense of this, as well as create meaning, by mentally connecting the shots into a logical narrative. Porter also cuts back and forth in time, showing simultaneous events taking place in different locations. For example, the robbers begin their heist by shooting and tying up a telegraph operator at a train station; then they board the next train, rob the passengers, uncouple the engine, and head off. As they reach what they think is safety, Porter cuts back to the telegraph office, where (as shown here) a little girl, presumably the operator's daughter, discovers her father and revives him. Porter then cuts directly to a barn dance, where the operator and the little girl report what has happened. Porter then jumps ahead to the outlaws and the final shoot-out, continuing to use ellipsis when necessary to keep the action moving to the conclusion.

Another early pioneer, Edwin S. Porter, was a director working with Edison, who by 1903 had established a relatively sophisticated approach to narrative filmmaking in such pioneering films as *The Great Train Robbery* (1903; 12 min.), which used multiple camera positions, interior and exterior settings, and crosscutting (intercutting) that made it possible to depict parallel actions occurring simultaneously. He also established the concept that the shot was the basic structural unit of a movie

and pioneered the idea of continuity editing. *The Great Train Robbery* was the first major milestone in the development of the American narrative film as well as the first "Western."

1908–1927: Origins of the Classical Hollywood Style—The Silent Period

The "silent era" of film history is distinguished by Edwin S. Porter's and D. W. Griffith's developments in narrative form, the crystallization of the classical Hollywood style, the ascendance of Hollywood as the center of the world's motion-picture industry, the development of movie genres, and early experiments with color and animation.

The "classical Hollywood cinema"[8] refers here to the traditional studio-based style of making motion pictures in both the silent and sound periods. Although the rudiments of the classical style can be seen in the work of Edwin S. Porter, it began its ascendancy with the release of D. W. Griffith's *The Birth of a Nation* (1915) and continues, with various modifications, to identify the cinematic conventions used by most filmmakers today.

The classical Hollywood style is built on the principle of "invisibility" that we discussed in Chapter 1. This principle generally includes two parts. The first is that the movie's form (narrative, cinematography, editing, sound, acting, and so forth) should not call attention to itself. That is, the narrative should be as economical and seamless as possible, and the presentation of the narrative should occur in a cinematic language with which the audience is familiar. The second part is the studio system itself, a mode of production that standardized the way movies were produced. Management was vertically organized, meaning that a strong executive office controlled production, distribution, and exhibition; hired all employees, including directors and actors; and assigned work to them according to the terms of their contracts, thus ensuring a certain uniform style for each studio. While we know that such principles were sometimes ignored in practice, they nonetheless serve a purpose in helping us chart the course of stylistic history. Thus, for example, we can understand and appreciate just how radical Orson Welles's approach was in *Citizen*

8. A concept popularized by film scholars David Bordwell, Kristin Thompson, and Janet Staiger in *The Classical Hollywood Cinema: Film Style and Mode of Production to 1960* (New York: Columbia University Press, 1985).

Kane (1941) when he deliberately called attention to technique and, in so doing, challenged the perceived limitations of the classical Hollywood style and the studio system itself.

By 1907, a small film effort had started in and around Hollywood, its founders lured by the favorable climate and variety of natural scenery. While they were nearly all uneducated immigrants, their business practices were consistent with the ruthless tactics of other Gilded Age entrepreneurs. D. W. Griffith made his first movie there in 1910; in 1911, the first studio was built; and by 1912, some fifteen film studios were operating. By 1914, the American film industry was clearly identified with Hollywood. As a forward-looking sign of this growth, the industry invested heavily in movie theaters, some of which were dubbed "palaces" for their imposing architecture, lavish interiors, and seating for hundreds and sometimes thousands of people. It also established other "firsts," including trade journals, movie fan magazines, movie reviews in general-circulation newspapers, the star system, and a film censorship law.

During this period, filmmakers began to replace short films (generally one reel in length) with feature-length movies (four or more reels). The term *feature* came to mean major works that stood out on a program that might include shorter films as well. In these early days, the length of one reel was 10–16 minutes, depending on the speed of projection. The longer format permitted filmmakers to tackle more complicated narratives and also emphasized the quality of the production, including mise-en-scène, cinematography, acting, and editing. The growing middle-class audience liked longer narratives and more polished productions and was willing to pay more to see such movies. Accordingly, producers could book them for extended runs and, of course, make more money. The transformation of the nickelodeon into the movie palace, which exceeded in splendor any legitimate theater and thus had an attraction all its own, further established the cinema as a serious artistic endeavor. Thus, with changes in a film's length, content, quality, and exhibition came the first major restructuring of the movie industry. The second was to come with the advent of sound, and the third with the development of the independent system of production. The movies took on the modern production system and the cinematic conventions that, however much they have changed, we know today.

A great silent movie challenges the American dream
King Vidor was one of several important directors working in the early 1920s who learned his art from D. W. Griffith. In *The Crowd* (1928), Vidor dared—in the Roaring Twenties, a period of relative prosperity before the stock-market crash of 1929—to make a social critique of the American dream of opportunity and getting ahead. It tells the tragic story of a man who refuses to conform in the New York business world, suggested by the office environment pictured here, which reduces him and other employees to nonentities. The story seems to end with the promise of future happiness for the man and his wife, but it's really ambiguous, leaving us to use our own values and experiences to come to grips with the characters' fate. In the silent-movie period, exhibitors were sometimes offered the choice of alternate endings, particularly for movies with a controversial conclusion. Vidor shot seven different endings for *The Crowd* and offered two of them to the theater owners. (Here we refer to what the director called the "realistic" ending.)

The first multiple-reel movies included J. Stuart Blackton's *The Life of Moses* (1909, five reels), D. W. Griffith's *Enoch Arden* (1911; 34 min.), *The Loves of Queen Elizabeth* (1912; directors Henri Desfontaines and Louis Mercanton, 44 min.), a film from France, and such Italian epics as *Dante's Inferno* (1911, 5 reels; director unknown), Enrico Guazzoni's *Quo Vadis?* (1913; 120 min.), and Giovanni Pastrone's *Cabiria* (1914; 181 min.). In 1914, clearly the turning point, Edwin S. Porter released *Tess of the Storm Country* (1914; 80 min.) and directed an astonishing twenty features before retiring from film directing the next year. Cecil B. DeMille, another industry founder, began his feature film career with *The Squaw Man* (1914; 74 min.) and made fourteen features

The first female director

Among early filmmakers, Alice Guy Blaché stands out as the first female director in film history. Born in France, where she worked with the Gaumont Film Company, she came to the United States shortly after 1907, founded her own studio, and made dozens of narrative films, most of which are lost. *Making an American Citizen* (1912; 16 min.) is unremarkable in its theatrical staging and acting but is well photographed and edited. What's most important is its outspoken feminist message. It tells the story of Ivan and his wife, new Russian emigrants. Ivan believes in the Old World custom of wife abuse. In this shot, a well-dressed New Yorker threatens Ivan when he catches him beating his wife (note the Statue of Liberty in the background). This and other encounters with liberated American males (including a judge who sentences him to prison) convince him to love and respect his wife. With the happy ending, he is, as the title card proclaims, "Completely Americanized." Guy Blaché was not only ahead of her time as a film director but also highly optimistic in her views about American male-female relationships.

in 1915 alone. Griffith's *Judith of Bethulia* (61 min.) was released in 1914 and *The Birth of a Nation* (187 min.) in 1915.

Every ten years since 1952, the influential British publication *Sight & Sound* asks a large panel of international film critics to choose the ten greatest movies. In polls between 1952 and 2002, the list always included at least one silent film (there were five in 1952). The latest poll (2012) listed three silent films: 5: *Sunrise* (1927; director F. W. Murnau), 8: *Man with the Movie Camera* (1929; director Dziga Vertov), and 9: *The Passion of Joan of Arc* (1928; director Carl Theodor Dreyer). All were

released at the high point of the silent era, between 1926 and 1930, when sound was slowly transforming the movie industry. Many other outstanding silent films from that period also deserve mention: *The Crowd* (1926; director King Vidor), *Berlin: Symphony of a Metropolis* (1927; also called *Symphony of a Great City*; director Walter Ruttmann); *An Italian Straw Hat* (1927; director René Clair), *The Circus* (1928; director Charles Chaplin); *The Wind* (1928; director Victor Seastrom); *Un chien Andalou* (1928; directors Luis Buñuel and Salvador Dali); *Pandora's Box* (1929; director G. W. Pabst); *A Cottage on Dartmoor* (1929; director Anthony Asquith); and *Earth* (1930; director Alexander Dovzhenko).[9]

The social impact of the silent movies during this period established trends that continue today. They appealed to all socioeconomic levels and stimulated the popular imagination through their establishment and codification of narrative genres and character stereotypes, particularly those that reinforced prejudices against Native Americans, African Americans, and foreigners in general. Their depiction of certain types of behavior considered immoral provoked calls for censorship, which would become an even bigger problem in the next decade and on into today and raised issues of movie content and violence. Although most jobs in the film industry remained male-dominated for the next fifty years, at least acting jobs for women were plentiful from the beginning. Two female directors were at work—Lois Weber and Alice Guy Blaché—and the African American actor Bert Williams starred in his first movie in 1915.

The movie director was central to developing the art of the motion picture in these early years. D. W. Griffith would soon emerge as the most important of these figures, and *The Birth of a Nation* would become known as one of the most important and controversial movies ever made. While its racist content is repugnant, its form is technically brilliant. Griffith, who borrowed freely from other early filmmakers, was an intuitive and innovative artist. In this legendary movie we see him perfecting and regularizing (if not inventing) a style that included a dazzling set of technical achievements: the 180-degree system; cutting between familiar types of shots (close-up, medium shot, long shot, extreme long shot, and soft-focus shot); multiple camera setups, accelerated montage, and panning and tilting; and the exploitation of

9. Christie, Ian. "The Peak of Silent Cinema," *Sight & Sound* 23, no. 11 (November 2013), 42–50.

camera angles, in-camera dissolves and fades, the flash-back, the iris shot, the mask, and the split screen. He also highly valued using a full symphonic score and, more important, developing screen acting by training actors for the special demands of the silent cinema. At that time the longest (3 hours) and most expensive ($2.7M) American movie yet made, *The Birth of a Nation* attracted enormous audiences, garnered the critics' praise, and earned, within five years of its opening, approximately $178M (both are 2014 figures adjusted for inflation). However, the social and political stance of this film's story had another impact.

Born in Kentucky, Griffith was in sympathy with the antebellum South. He tells his story by distorting history and reaffirming the racist stereotypes of his time and background. The movie provoked controversy and riots and was banned in many Northern states. Yet this profoundly American epic, a work of vicious propaganda, is also a cinematic masterpiece that garnered international prestige for American silent movies. Unfortunately for the future history of the movies, it demonstrated how a manipulative movie could appeal to the public's worst prejudices and make a fortune as a result. Griffith made other films, including such silent masterpieces as *Intolerance* (1916), *Broken Blossoms* (1919), *Way down East* (1920), *Orphans of the Storm* (1921), and *Dream Street* (1921), a very early but unsuccessful attempt to add recorded voices to a movie. Nonetheless, his career was virtually finished by 1931.

The most successful American silent feature movies were epics (Erich von Stroheim's *Greed*, 1924), melodramas (King Vidor's *The Big Parade*, 1925), and comedies. Comedy in particular was a major factor in Hollywood's early success. These films starred gifted comic actors (Buster Keaton, Charles Chaplin, Roscoe "Fatty" Arbuckle, Harold Lloyd, Stan Laurel, and Oliver Hardy) and had innovative directors (Mack Sennett and Hal Roach). They included such enduring silent movies (shorts, series, and features) as Chaplin's *The Gold Rush* (1925) and Keaton's *The General* (1926).

According to a 2013 study by the Library of Congress, almost 70 percent of the silent feature films made in the United States are lost due to various reasons, including neglect, poor cataloguing, or the natural deterioration of film negatives. Efforts are continually being made to find

The Birth of a Nation

The turning point in D. W. Griffith's great epic (1915) comes in the middle of the movie, as the title card says: "And then, when the terrible days were over and a healing time of peace was at hand . . . came the fated night of April 14, 1865." The scene is Ford's Theatre in Washington, D.C., where a gala performance is being held to celebrate General Robert E. Lee's surrender. In this shot, President and Mrs. Abraham Lincoln enter and greet the enthusiastic audience. Moments later, he is assassinated, ending Part I, "War," and opening Part II, "Reconstruction," a saga of Southern white racism that is the most controversial part of the movie.

copies of these films in foreign countries, but it is a sad ending to one of America's great artistic achievements.[10]

Other notable films produced in this period include Robert J. Flaherty's *Nanook of the North* (1922), regarded as the first significant documentary film. The art of animation progressed in the hands of such artists as Otto Messmer (the Felix the Cat series), Walt Disney, who made his first cartoons in 1922, and Max and Dave Fleischer, who experimented with color and sound in the early 1920s and whose most endearing character was Betty Boop. Benefiting from Griffith's enormous influence, other filmmakers made improvements in design, lighting, cameras and lenses, the use of color, special effects, and editing equipment. Nothing, of course, would be more important than the experiments with sound that led to the complete transformation of the movie industry after 1927. In the meantime, however, international developments were influencing film history.

10. See http://carpetbagger.blogs.nytimes.com/2013/12/04/majority-of-silent-films-are-lost-study-finds/ (accessed December 18, 2013).

1919–1931: German Expressionism

During part of the period just discussed, Eastern and Western Europe were engulfed in chaos. The First World War (1914–18), in which many millions of people died, pitted the United Kingdom, Russia, Italy, and the United States against Germany, Austria-Hungary, the Ottoman Empire, and Bulgaria. (The United States, isolationist and opposed to the war, did not enter the conflict until 1917.) In March 1917, the Russian Revolution overthrew Czar Nicholas II. These events changed the world order.

By the end of the war, Germany had suffered a humiliating defeat. But a new democratic government emerged, known unofficially as the Weimar Republic. Seeking to revitalize the film industry and create a new image for the country, the government subsidized the film conglomerate known as UFA (Universum-Film AG). Its magnificent studios, the largest and best equipped in Europe, enabled the German film industry to compete with those of other countries as well as attract filmmakers from around the world. This organization led to Germany's golden age of cinema, which lasted from 1919 to Adolf Hitler's rise to power in 1933. Its most important artistic component was the German Expressionist film, which flourished from 1919 to 1931.

German film artists entered the postwar period determined to reject the cinematic past and enthusiastically embrace the avant-garde. Expressionism had flourished in Germany since the early twentieth century in painting, sculpture, architecture, music, literature, and theater. After the war, it reflected the general atmosphere in postwar Germany of cynicism, alienation, and disillusionment. German Expressionist film presents the physical world on the screen as a projection, or expression, of the subjective world, usually that of the film's protagonist. Its chief characteristics are distorted and exaggerated settings; compositions of unnatural spaces; the use of oblique angles and nonparallel lines; a moving and subjective camera; unnatural costumes, hairstyles, and makeup; and highly stylized acting. The classic examples are Robert Wiene's *The Cabinet of Dr. Caligari* (1920), Paul Wegener and Carl Boese's version of *The Golem* (1920), F. W. Murnau's *Nosferatu, a Symphony of Horror* (1922)—the first vampire film—and *The Last Laugh* (1924), Fritz Lang's *Metropolis* (1927) and *M* (1931), G. W. Pabst's *Pandora's Box* (1929), and Josef von Sternberg's *The Blue Angel* (1930).

The most famous expressionist film, and the one traditionally cited as the epitome of the style, is Wiene's *The Cabinet of Dr. Caligari*. What we remember most about

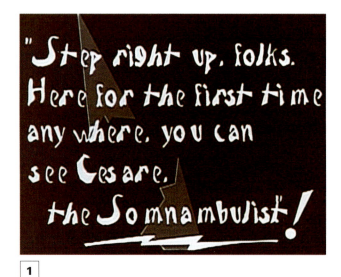

1

2

Inside *The Cabinet of Dr. Caligari*

In Robert Wiene's eerie, foreboding movie (1920), Dr. Caligari (Werner Krauss) operates a carnival attraction featuring a somnambulist (sleepwalker) named Cesare (Conrad Veidt); the "cabinet" in the title refers to the type of early freak show called a "cabinet of curiosities" as well as to the coffinlike box in which Cesare "sleeps" until Caligari awakens him and orders him to commit murders. The title card [1], written in exaggerated letters, speaks in a folksy tone while echoing the graphics of the movie's painted settings. The power of these settings is evident when we see [2] Dr. Caligari (*left*) attempting to rouse Cesare (*right*), who is presumably "asleep" while standing upright in Caligari's cabinet.

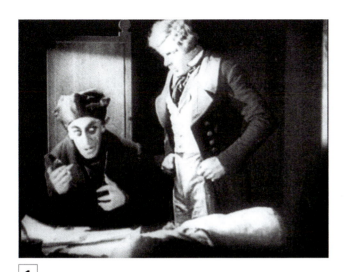

1

2

The Cabinet of Dr. Caligari's influence

Robert Wiene's *The Cabinet of Dr. Caligari* (1920) is traditionally cited as the best example of German Expressionist film. But expressionist elements also figure strongly in F. W. Murnau's *Nosferatu, a Symphony of Horror* (1922), the first of many film adaptations of the Dracula story, and *The Last Laugh* (1924), a charming fable about social justice. Their narratives could not be more different, yet these films are linked by their reliance on expressionist design. In contrast to *Dr. Caligari*, where the expressionism relies mostly on graphic effects, those in *Nosferatu* rely primarily on cinematic effects: low camera angles, makeup and costume design, lighting, and editing create an eerie mise-en-scène [1]. And even though the vampire figure is truly scary (Nosferatu is played by the memorable Max Schreck, who, pictured here with Gustav von Wangenheim as the real-estate agent, looks like a rat), the movie also manages to make him a sympathetic human being. [2] Far more sympathetic—and far more realistic—is the principal character of *The Last Laugh*, an unnamed hotel porter played equally memorably by Emil Jannings. Here, expressionism can be seen in the mise-en-scène and actor's movements as well as in the composition, play of light and shadow, and exaggerated costume, all of which are subtler than what we see in either *Dr. Caligari* or *Nosferatu*. *The Last Laugh* is also important for its impressive use of the moving camera and the camera's subjective point of view.

this disturbing, complicated story of fantasy and horror told by a madman is its design. The floors, walls, and ceilings of the interior sets are sharply angled; windows admit no natural light, though shafts of illusionistic light and shadow are painted on the walls and floors of the sets; dim staircases seem to lead nowhere; the calligraphy of the titles is bizarre, as is the color tinting—blue, sepia, rose, and green (in the 1996 restored DVD edition). All this differentiates night from day and underscores the different moods. The exterior sets are equally artificial; buildings, piled on top of one another, jut upward at strange angles.

German Expressionist film was a short-lived but unforgettable phenomenon that disappeared within ten years after it began. There are aesthetic, political, economic, and social reasons for this. Even though these films gave birth to the horror-film genre, German audiences did not crave a steady diet of them. As far as politics goes, because expressionism emphasized the inner

rather than the outer world, Hitler (now rising to power) saw it as a revolt against the traditional values that he sought to preserve. With their lavish studio settings, expressionist films were expensive to make. Furthermore, foreign films were taking an increasing share of the German market, prompting the German film industry to copy them in order to hold its market share. When the government tightened control of UFA, it became clear that Hitler would curtail freedom of expression when he came to power in 1933. Thus many great German filmmakers were lured to the United States, stimulating the aesthetics of Hollywood production for decades to come. Soon, certain tendencies of the expressionist look became evident in Hollywood's psychological dramas, horror movies, and most notably, the film noir. To quote film historians Gerald Mast and Bruce F. Kawin, "It is difficult to imagine the history of American cinema without this infusion of both visual imagery and thematic commentary from Weimar Germany."[11]

11. Gerald Mast and Bruce F. Kawin, *A Short History of the Movies*, 10th ed. (New York: Pearson/Longman, 2008), p. 193.

1918–1930: French Avant-Garde Filmmaking

In the 1920s, Paris was the world's center of avant-garde experimentation in painting, literature, drama, music, and film. It was a time when the philosophical approaches of surrealism, cubism, dadaism, and expressionism led to an explosion of artistic styles and movements. The French Avant-Garde film movement included both intellectuals and artists who took their inspiration not only from Karl Marx and Sigmund Freud but also from the experimental French filmmakers who preceded them in the earliest years of the movies: Georges Méliès, Ferdinand Zecca, Max Linder, Émile Cohl, Jean Durand, and Louis Feuillade, pioneering artists who influenced the course of avant-garde and experimental filmmaking around the world.

The French movies that we will discuss tend to fit into one of three different types: (1) short dadaist and surrealist films of an anticonventional, absurdist nature; (2) short naturalistic psychological studies; or (3) feature-length films that also emphasize pure visual form.

Dada and surrealism were two European movements in the arts that sought, provocatively and irreverently, to shock the viewer with surprises and unexpected juxtapositions. Specifically, they attempted to re-create the free play of the mind in its perceptions, dreams, or hallucinations. Dadaist and surrealist cinema attacks normal narrative conventions by eliminating causality, emphasizing chance and unexpected occurrences, and creating strange and shocking relationships among images. The result is a visual world that appears to be neurotic, unnatural, and illogical, resisting analysis and conclusion by the viewer. And because it emphasizes free association over conventional cinematic language, it attracted painters who were visual artists first and filmmakers second. (Although dada preceded surrealism, they coexisted in the 1920s to such an extent that the two words are often used interchangeably to describe works that demonstrate these characteristics.)

In France, the major filmmakers working in these movements included the American-born Man Ray (*Emak-Bakia*, 1926); Jean Epstein, whose *The Fall of the House of Usher* (1928), inspired by one of Edgar Allan Poe's most famous tales, uses dreamy, impressionistic visual effects (slow motion, out-of-focus shots, multiple exposures, and distortions); René Clair (*Entr'acte*, 1924); Fernand Léger (*Ballet mécanique*, 1924); and Germaine Dulac, one of the cinema's first female artists, whose

Surrealism on film
Inspired by Edgar Allan Poe's famous story, Jean Epstein's *The Fall of the House of Usher* (1928) remains captivating with its complex psychological themes, haunting exteriors and interiors, and overall dreamlike quality. In this image, Madeleine Usher (Marguerite Gance) returns from the tomb in which she was buried alive by her brother, Sir Roderick Usher (Jean Debucourt), who dies from fright when she falls upon him.

The Seashell and the Clergyman (1928) is one of the two acknowledged masterpieces of surrealist cinema.

The other masterpiece is *An Andalusian Dog* (1929), created by two Spanish artists working in Paris: painter Salvador Dalí and filmmaker Luis Buñuel. Here, the logic is that of a dream. Its visual effects include an opening sequence in which we see a razor slitting a woman's eyeball (for an image of this famous shot, see Chapter 3, p. 82). While Dali soon returned to painting his surrealist masterpieces (including his version of Leonardo's *Mona Lisa* with his own face replacing hers), Buñuel became one of the very few major directors to continue making surrealist feature movies, including *Viridiana* (1961), *Belle de Jour* (1967), and *The Discreet Charm of the Bourgeoisie* (1972).

The second type of French Avant-Garde filmmaking in the 1920s consists of psychological studies that emphasize naturalism, the idea that an individual's fate is determined by heredity and environment, not free will. This form becomes very powerful in a film such as *Rien que les heures* (1926), by the Brazilian-born Alberto Cavalcanti. A multilayered study of Paris over the course of a day, the film employs cinematic effects, including bold wipes, freeze-frames, double exposures, and split screens. It also reflects the influence of Soviet Montage

Turning of *The Wheel*

The movies have always been fascinated by trains, but Abel Gance's *The Wheel* (1923) is obsessed with them. Its extraordinary mise-en-scène is a world surrounded by locomotives, tracks, smoke, and railroad workers. This highly melodramatic story contains elements that remind us of classical tragedy, and its sweeping vision of life is matched by a vividly avant-garde style, creating an unforgettable milestone in French cinema.

in its juxtapositions and linkages of shots, some through contrast, others through irony, and still others unrelated. The overall impression of this film, which fits into a small, impressive category of films known as "city symphonies," is that of a mosaic: the images relate only when they are considered in connection to the whole picture. Also impressive are Dimitri Kirsanoff's *Ménilmontant* (1926) and Marcel L'Herbier's *L'Argent* (1928).

All of the films discussed so far in this section in one way or another emphasize visual form for its own sake, have a comparatively short duration, and for the most part were made independently of the French film industry. There was, however, another type of French Avant-Garde filmmaking of the 1920s—narrative, often feature-length movies far more ambitious in their scope, length, and overall visual effect. These include Abel Gance's *The Wheel* (1923), which embodies naturalistic philosophy and reflects Griffith's editing style, and *Napoléon* (1927), an almost 6-hour epic of astonishing cinematic beauty and power; Jean Cocteau's *The Blood of a Poet* (1930); Jean Vigo's *À propos de Nice* (1930); René Clair's *An Italian Straw Hat* (1928); and the strangely powerful films of Danish-born Carl Theodor Dreyer, particularly his

formalist masterpiece *The Passion of Joan of Arc* (1928). All these films, especially the short ones often screened in film history courses, offer an excellent introduction to the diverse art of the French silent movie in the 1920s.

1924–1930: The Soviet Montage Movement

The Soviet Montage movement represents, with the German Expressionist film movement, one of the twin high points of cinematic experimentation, innovation, and achievement in the years between the end of the First World War in 1918 and the coming of sound in 1927. After the Bolshevik (Communist) Revolution of October 1917, led by Vladimir Ilyich Lenin, the challenge was to reunify a shattered nation. Lenin famously proclaimed that cinema would be the most important of the arts in this effort and valued the movies' power to both attract and indoctrinate audiences. He nationalized the film industry and established a national film school to train filmmakers to make propaganda films in a documentary style. Between 1917 and 1929, the Soviet government supported the kind of artistic experimentation and expression that is most effectively seen in the work of four directors: Dziga Vertov, Lev Kuleshov, Sergei Eisenstein, and Vsevolod I. Pudovkin. What they all share in varying degrees is a belief in the power of montage (they adopted the French word for "editing") to fragment and reassemble footage so as to manipulate the viewer's perception and understanding.

Vertov was the first great theorist and practitioner of the cinema of propaganda in documentary form. In 1922, the year of Robert J. Flaherty's *Nanook of the North*, Vertov launched *kino-pravda* (literally, "film truth"). He was influenced by the spirit of Flaherty and the Lumières, which focused on everyday experiences, as well as by the avant-garde pursuit of innovation. Vertov is best known today for *The Man with the Movie Camera* (1929).

Kuleshov, a legendary teacher who was influenced by the continuity editing in Griffith's *Intolerance* (1916), built significantly on Griffith's ideas. As a result, he became less interested in how editing helps to advance the narrative than in how it can create nonliteral meaning. He was thus more interested in discontinuity rather than continuity. Among his many feature-length films is *The Extraordinary Adventures of Mr. West in the Land of the Bolsheviks* (1924).

A day in the life of the Russians

Dziga Vertov's *The Man with the Movie Camera* (1929) is about how the Russians live and how movies are made. On first viewing, it does not seem to distinguish between the two. In this image, we see the real subject: the man with the movie camera. As a record of human life, it is the prototypical movie. Vertov shows us how to frame reality and movement: through the human eye and the camera eye, or through windows and shutters. But to confound us, he also shows us—through such devices as the freeze-frame, split screen, stop-action, slow motion, and fast motion—how the cinematographer and editor can transform the movements of life into something that is unpredictable. He proves that the camera has a life of its own while also reminding us of the editor, who is putting all of this footage together. Reality may be in the control of the artist, his camera, and its tricks, but it is also defined by the editor's presentation and ultimately the viewer's perception.

Pudovkin took a third approach to montage, one based on the idea that a film was not shot, but rather built up from its footage. This style is reflected in his film *Mother* (1926), which uses extensive crosscutting of images, such as a sequence of shots showing a prison riot intercut with shots of ice breaking up on a river (a reference to Griffith's *Way down East* [1920]). Because Pudovkin's approach emphasized the continuity of the film, where the shots are connected like the links in a chain, it is called *linkage.*

In the first two decades after the birth of the movies, two pioneering geniuses tower above all other filmmakers: D. W. Griffith and Sergei Eisenstein. While they share several notable characteristics—chiefly, inventing new modes of cinematic expression and producing epic historical movies—they are very different artists.

Griffith was an American, a capitalist in his entrepreneurial production activities, and a Southern sentimentalist at heart. Unlike Eisenstein, he was self-taught (there were no film schools in the United States until the 1930s); he was not an intellectual, and he was influenced primarily by English literature and theater, in which he worked as an actor and director before turning to film. He did not write theory, but rather produced movies that exemplified his concepts.

By contrast, Eisenstein, a Russian Orthodox Christian, was also a Marxist intellectual whose propaganda movies were financed by the Soviet government. He studied to be an engineer, but after the 1917 revolution joined an avant-garde theater group, where he was shaped by many powerful influences, including the theory and practice of world-famous directors Konstantin Stanislavsky and Vsevolod Meyerhold, by Marx and Freud, and by contemporary German, Russian, and American movies, including those of Griffith. From these varied sources, he developed his own theories of how an aesthetic experience can influence a viewer's psychological and emotional reactions. Unlike Griffith, Eisenstein was a modernist with a commitment to making cinema an art independent from the other forms of creative expression. His films, few in number, are stirring achievements: *Strike* (1925), *The Battleship Potemkin* (1925), *October* (*Ten Days That Shook the World*, 1928), *Alexander Nevsky* (1938; codirected by Dmitri Vasilyev), *Ivan the Terrible, Parts I and II* (1944, 1958), and *Que Viva México* (1930–32, uncompleted and unreleased).

Eisenstein regarded film editing as a creative process that functioned according to the dialectic of Karl Marx as well as the editing concepts of Griffith and Kuleshov. In theory, Eisenstein viewed the process of historical change as a perpetual conflict of opposing forces, in which a primary force (thesis) collides with a counterforce (antithesis) to produce a third force (synthesis), a new contradiction that is more than the sum of its parts and will become the basis of a new conflict.

In filmmaking practice, one shot (thesis) collides with another shot of opposing content (antithesis) to produce a new idea (synthesis). The result emphasizes a dynamic juxtaposition of individual shots that calls attention to each of these shots while forcing the viewer to reach conclusions about the interplay between them. This "montage of attractions," as Eisenstein called it, presents arbitrarily chosen images (some of them independent of the action) to create the maximum psychological impact. Thus conditioned, viewers would have in their consciousness the elements that would lead them to the overall concept that the director wanted to communicate. Artfully handled, of course, this is manipulation of the highest order, propaganda created to serve the Soviet state. The purest, most powerful example of this approach to filmmaking is *Battleship Potemkin* (1925).

Eisenstein's *Battleship Potemkin* is one of the fundamental landmarks of cinema. Indeed, it has become so popular from screenings in film-studies courses that, over the years, its ability to surprise has diminished. Nevertheless, it is essential to know why this movie is important to film history. It depicts two events—the 1905 workers' mutiny on the *Potemkin* and the subsequent slaughter of ordinary citizens on the Odessa Steps. Through its dramatic reenactment of those events,

the movie presents a successful example of revolution against oppression. Overall, the film's classic five-part structure emphasizes the need for unity in such struggles. But most people remember the "Odessa Steps" sequence, even though its impact may lessen when seen out of context, as it so often is. The sequence, set in Odessa on the wide steps leading from the town to the harbor, depicts czarist troops brutally killing ordinary citizens who are celebrating the successful mutiny on the *Potemkin*. Indeed, although the mass is the protagonist, it is the individual faces that we remember. The movie's brutal form (jump cuts and montage editing) perfectly matches the brutality of the massacre. Many directors have been influenced by Eisenstein's theory of montage; some pay homage to the "Odessa Steps" sequence, and others spoof it.

Battleship Potemkin is a great film not only because of its individual elements—the depth of Eisenstein's humanity, the historical and social significance of its story, the formal perfection of its rhythm and editing, and its worldwide influence—but also because of the synergy by which each of these elements is enhanced by the others.

Eisenstein's battle spectacle *Alexander Nevsky*
Sergei Eisenstein's *Alexander Nevsky* (1938) stands out among Eisenstein's other movies, concerned chiefly with the class wars, for its emphasis on nationalism and patriotism. Focusing on Alexander Nevsky, a Russian prince who defended Russia's northwest territories against invading Teutonic hordes in the thirteenth century, the movie's parallels to contemporary events (i.e., the threat of invasion of Russia by Nazi Germany) were unmistakable. But the movie is far more than a political parable. The movie's set piece—the "Battle on the Ice" sequence, choreographed to Sergei Prokofiev's stirring score—has influenced many other movie battle scenes (e.g., battles in the *Star Wars* saga), particularly in its massing of forces, brutal warfare, and defining costumes. Noteworthy is Eisenstein's reversal of traditional iconography: throughout, as in this image, the bad guys (the Teutons) are in white while the Russian forces are in black.

The beginnings of a revolution
In the first part of *Battleship Potemkin* (1925), Sergei Eisenstein steadily builds a case for the crew members' discontent with their lot—a discontent that will lead to violent revolt. Among other things, the sailors are unhappy with the ship's food. In this image, they examine a slab of the rotten meat they are forced to eat: "We've had enough rotten meat. It's not fit for pigs." Although the meat is crawling with maggots, the ship's doctor tells them that it will be edible if they just wash it off.

1927–1947: Classical Hollywood Style in Hollywood's Golden Age

The golden age of Hollywood was the most powerful and prolific period of film history yet. It is notable for the transition from silent to sound production, consolidation of the studio system, exploitation of familiar genres, imposition of the Motion Picture Production Code, changes in the look of movies, and the economic success of feature-length narrative films. Yet it was less a movement than a force, for in this period, the movies became inextricably linked with the development of American culture and society. From this point forward, the movies defined America, and America defined itself through the movies. (The formidable technological and organizational challenges that enabled these achievements are covered in Chapter 11.)

None of this could have been achieved without the efficiency of the studio system, which standardized the way movies were produced. It provided a top-down organization with management controlling everything, especially the employees, who regardless of their status were treated as employees, not artists, and whose careers were subject to the strict terms of their contracts. The transition to sound began in 1926 with the production of some short as well as feature films with recorded sound, and earlier experimental "talkies" were well known back to 1900. But once audiences saw Al Jolson—who in his prime was known as "the world's greatest entertainer"—in Alan Crosland's *The Jazz Singer* (1927), with its synchronized music score and a few sequences of synchronized sound, they wanted more. Its appeal was probably due less to the few moments of sound than to Jolson's exciting screen persona and his unexpected vocal ad-libbing. The first all-talking film was a routine gangster melodrama, Brian Foy's *The Lights of New York* (1928).

Populism and popcorn

Frank Capra's *Mr. Deeds Goes to Town* (1936), *Mr. Smith Goes to Washington* (1939), and *Meet John Doe* (1941) are often described as a populist trilogy. Indeed, they are emblematic of populism in their belief that ordinary people have the right and power to struggle against the privileged elite. *Mr. Smith Goes to Washington* offers a sentimental vision of America, filled with stereotypes. Yet it was very successful with the American public, which was dissatisfied with Washington at the end of the Great Depression. In this image, Smith (James Stewart) finishes his filibuster before the U.S. Senate by pleading with his fellow senators to stand up and fight the corruption that is preventing the realization of his dream to finance a national camp for boys. Considering the national situation, this is a small issue indeed. And while it is almost impossible to imagine a similar incident paralyzing Washington today, it gives hope that the common man still has a voice in the direction of our country.

"Wait a minute. You ain't heard nothin' yet!"

While these are not the first words we hear Jack Robin (Al Jolson) speak in *The Jazz Singer* (1927; director Alan Crosland), they are the most memorable. Imagine the excitement of the 1927 audience hearing—for the first time—actors speaking in a movie. This is the melodramatic story of a young Jewish boy, Jakie Rabinowitz, who does not want to follow in his father's footsteps and become a cantor; instead, he becomes Jack Robin, a famous "jazz singer" in Broadway shows. It's a classic show-business movie, and Jolson, the country's biggest star in the 1920s, gracefully sings, whistles (image), and dances his way through it. His performance of several songs in blackface makeup may lead us today to make assumptions about Jolson's attitudes about race. Those songs are misleading, however, because Jolson was a prominent leader in the fight against show-biz segregation and was influential in promoting the careers of African American actors, singers, songwriters, and writers.

Screwball comedy

The genre of screwball comedy was popular during the Great Depression in the 1930s because it offered an escape from reality. It continues to exist today (in movies such as Joel and Ethan Coen's *Intolerable Cruelty* [2003] and George Clooney's *Leatherheads* [2008]), but without the wit or sting of the original. Its principal characteristics include stories of mistaken identity, often involving a person of the working class who accidentally (or not so accidentally) meets with someone from the upper class and, contrary to all expectations, becomes romantically involved; rapid, witty dialogue; and farcical, even fantastic, rags-to-riches plot situations. Mitchell Leisen's *Easy Living* (1937) easily fits the bill. Its script by Preston Sturges, a master of the genre, begins when tycoon John Ball (Edward Arnold), who resents his wife's buying a new sable coat, throws it from his penthouse roof. It lands on Mary Smith (Jean Arthur), an office worker who is riding on the top of a Fifth Avenue double-decker bus (behind her, the man in the turban is a classic bit of screwball incongruity). Seeing the coat, people assume she is rich, and she quickly learns to enjoy that illusion as she is enticed into a world of glamour and falls improbably in love with John Ball Jr. (Ray Milland).

Censorship threatens the release of *Baby Face*

The censors would have found plenty to dislike in Alfred E. Green's *Baby Face* (1933). It's the story of Lily Powers (Barbara Stanwyck), a Depression-era gold digger who sleeps her way to the top, both figuratively and literally, of a Manhattan skyscraper where she works. At each new floor, she finds a powerful new lover and, as a result, gets a better job. Eventually, she's in deeper than she thinks when one of her lovers murders another. Because the Motion Picture Production Code was not yet fully in power, the studio tried to get away with this version, but the New York State Censorship Board rejected it, so it trimmed some scenes and added a new ending that conformed with the code's principle that movies should endorse morality, not exploit it for entertainment purposes.

Once the conversion to sound was completed in 1930, weekly attendance at the movies and box-office receipts had increased by 50 percent, again proving the Hollywood principle that profits derive from giving the public what it wants. Between 1927 and 1941 (when film production was reduced sharply due to wartime considerations), Hollywood produced over 10,000 movies, an average of 744 each year (compared to 349 produced in 2013). The genres dominated production: screwball comedies, musicals, gangster movies, historical epics, melodramas, horror movies, Westerns, and biographies. Many of these movies were forgettable, but others are some of Hollywood's most important, influential, and memorable creations.

The moguls ran a tight, highly profitable business within their fortresslike studio walls. But outside there were calls for censorship, which, if not answered, threatened those profits. During the early 1920s, after several years of relatively frank portrayals of sex and violence on-screen (while the industry also suffered a wave of scandals), Hollywood faced a credible threat of censorship from state governments and boycotts from Catholic and other religious groups.

In 1922, in response to these pressures, Hollywood producers formed a regulatory agency called the Motion Picture Producers and Distributors of America (MPPDA, later the Motion Picture Association of America, or MPAA), headed by Will Hays. Originally conceived of as a public-relations entity to offset bad publicity and deflect negative attention away from Hollywood, the Hays Office (as the agency was commonly known) in 1930 adopted the Motion Picture Production Code, a detailed set of guidelines concerning acceptable and unacceptable subject matter. Nudity, adultery, homosexuality, gratuitous or unpunished violence, and religious

The golden age at its popular best:
Gone with the Wind

Many people think of *Gone with the Wind* (1939; director Victor Fleming) as *the* enduring symbol of the golden age of Hollywood. Its romantic story is told against the sweep of the Civil War, its cast is formidable, its mise-en-scène and music are memorable, and it was the first movie to dominate the Oscars. Furthermore, it has won every award imaginable, and while it isn't a great movie in purely cinematic terms, it is a great crowd-pleaser, as attested to by its periodic theatrical revivals and television screenings. It also reflects the highest possible production values for its time—the studio system at its best—a tribute to the extraordinary commitment of its producer, David O. Selznick, who maintained tight, demoralizing control over every aspect of production. For example, the process of casting Scarlett O'Hara, which was not typical of Hollywood at the time (or at any time), involved a two-year process in which Selznick tested nearly twenty-five major Hollywood and Broadway actors. Ironically, this quintessentially American role went to Vivien Leigh (*left*), a British actress virtually unknown in the American film industry.

blasphemy were among the many types of content that the code strongly discouraged. Perhaps even more significant, the code explicitly stated that art can influence, for the worse, the morality of those who consume it (an idea that Hollywood has been reconsidering ever since).

Adherence to the Motion Picture Code remained fundamentally voluntary until the summer of 1934, when Joseph Breen, a prominent Catholic layman, was appointed head of the Production Code Administration (PCA), the enforcement arm of the MPPDA. After July 1, 1934, all films would have to receive an MPPDA seal of approval before being released. For at least twenty years, the Breen Office rigidly controlled the general character and the particular details of Hollywood storytelling. After a period of practical irrelevance, the code was

officially replaced in 1968, when the MPAA adopted the rating system that remains in use today.

Movies produced during Hollywood's golden age were made to be entertaining and successful at the box office, and the result was a period of stylistic conformity, not innovation. If an idea worked once, it usually worked again in a string of similar movies. The idea was to get the public out of the house and into the theater, give people what they wanted (entertainment, primarily), and thus help them forget the Depression and the anxieties caused by the events leading up to the Second World War. The values stressed in these movies were heroism, fidelity, family life, citizenship, community, and of course, fun. Movies with important ideas were most often softened with comic touches and happy endings. So despite the large output, it is hard to find more than a few movies in Hollywood's golden age that stretched cinematic conventions, challenged prevailing social concepts, or provoked new ways of looking at the world. Hollywood during the golden age was not Europe, with its passion for the avant-garde, the revolutionary, or the film as art; few of those factors were part of the predominant American movie culture before the Second World War.

In the realm of cinematic style, narrative and editing conventions adapted to the challenges of sound production. Significant innovations were made in design, cinematography, lighting, acting, and editing, some related to sound, others not. Black-and-white film remained the industry standard through the early 1950s despite some interesting feature movies in Technicolor, which would become the new industry standard. Other technological advancements during the golden age included improvements in lighting, makeup, and film stock. While the predominant cinematographic style of the 1930s was soft-focus, the new lighting and film stock made it easier to achieve greater depth of focus, which created the illusion of perspective.

With the release of *Citizen Kane* in 1941, some forty-six years after the invention of motion pictures, everything changed. Orson Welles's film revolutionized the medium and has since been considered the most important movie ever made. *Citizen Kane* is noteworthy for many reasons, but its reputation is due to Welles's genius as an artist and his vision of a new kind of cinema. He was twenty-four when he began the project, his first movie. While the story of newspaper magnate Charles Foster Kane rests firmly in the biopic genre, Welles tells it with a complex plot consisting of nine sequences (each using a different tone and style), five of which are flashbacks. Including the omniscient camera, the movie has seven narrators—some of them unreliable—who, taken together, present a modern psychological portrait of a megalomaniac. Released just seven months before the United States declared war in December 1941, this was a radical film for Hollywood. And while the movie is open to various interpretations (the Freudian interpretation of young Charlie's relationship to his mother remains influential), *Citizen Kane* carries a strong antifascist message. It warns against Kane's arrogant abuse of the First Amendment right of freedom of speech and press, one of the many evils that Americans, reading their own newspapers, associated with Hitler.

Citizen Kane was also radical in its handling of the prevailing cinematic language of its time. We see this in the astonishing complexity and speed of the narrative. It may not seem so radical today, but that is only because it influenced the structure and pace of nearly every significant movie that came after it. In the other elements of cinematic form, Welles was equally innovative. The movie's stark design is heavily influenced by German Expressionism, as seen in the size, height, and depth of the rooms and other spaces at Xanadu. Through deep-space composition, lighting, deep-focus cinematography, and long takes, cinematographer Gregg Toland achieved the highest degree of cinematic realism yet seen. In contrast to the prevailing soft look of 1930s movies, *Citizen Kane* has a hard finish. The omniscient, probing, and usually moving camera, emphasizing its voyeuristic role, goes directly to the heart of each scene. The editing is mainly conventional, most often taking place within the long takes (and thus within the camera). Welles avoids such avant-garde techniques as Soviet Montage, for example, unless he wants to call attention to the editing, as he does in the "News on the March" sequence and the pans and swipes that create the passing of time during the famous breakfast-table sequence. Before going to Hollywood, Welles revolutionized American radio broadcasting, and his sound design for *Kane* creates an aural realism equivalent to the movie's visual realism. He frequently uses overlapping sound, which, like the deep-space composition, bombards us with a lightning mix of information that challenges us to choose what to listen to (just as in real life). The film is also much louder than the typical movie of the time, which is another innovation, and the

Cinematic innovation in *Citizen Kane*
Citizen Kane (1941; director Orson Welles) is marked by brilliant innovations that changed cinematic language forever. Among these is deep-focus cinematography, pioneered by Gregg Toland, which permits action on all three planes of the image. Here, the action is focused both on the foreground and background. As Signor Matiste (Fortunio Bononova, *standing second from left*) becomes increasingly frustrated in his efforts to train the voice of Susan Alexander Kane (Dorothy Comingore), her husband, Charles Foster Kane (Orson Welles), standing in the background, registers his impressions of the rehearsal. Husband, wife, and vocal coach are all participating in a long take, making cutting between them unnecessary. However, Kane will soon make it clear—however small he may look in this image—that he, not Matiste, is in charge of his wife's singing career. She, of course, has nothing to say about it. This is only one of Kane's egotistical mistakes that help to ruin the couple's careers and marriage.

bravado of its dialogue, sound effects, and music puts it in your ears as well as in your face. Bernard Herrmann's musical score was spare, modernist, and completely ahead of its time. In the film's acting, Welles called on his stage and radio experiences to break another Hollywood convention. Actors did not normally rehearse their lines except in private or for a few minutes with the director before shooting, but Welles rehearsed his cast for a month before shooting began, so his ensemble of actors could handle long passages of dialogue in the movie's distinctive long takes. And the performances, including Welles as Kane, are unforgettable.

Citizen Kane has been enormously influential on filmmakers around the world. Martin Scorsese said that Welles influenced more young people to become film directors than anyone else in film history. References to its unique style have been quoted in dozens of other films, but Welles's overall style has never been fully imitated. Even after repeated viewings, its tantalizing story, courageous political stance, provocative ambiguity, and razzle-dazzle style continue to exert their hold.

1942–1951: Italian Neorealism

With German Expressionism, Soviet Silent Realism, and the French New Wave movements, Italian Neorealism stands as one of the most vital movements in the history of world cinema. Developed during the Second World War, neorealism rose to prominence after the war and then flourished for a relatively short period before ending abruptly.

Benito Mussolini, the Fascist dictator who ruled Italy from 1922 to 1943, believed, as did Lenin, in the propaganda power of film. To revive Italy's lackluster film industry, he instituted government subsidies and control, banned American movies, established a national film school, and constructed vast new studios. Although the Italian movies produced during his regime were commercially successful (audiences had no choices), they were artistically inferior to what the French were producing before the war. After Mussolini was driven from power in 1943 and executed in 1945, an opportunity arose to revitalize Italian cinema.

In 1942, Cesare Zavattini, a prolific Marxist screenwriter, launched what came to be known as the neorealist movement, influenced its style and ideology, and led a group of young filmmakers to make film history. The group was also influenced by French poetic realism, a movement that consisted of filmmakers seeking freedom in the increasingly repressive French society of the 1930s, and by two contemporary Italian films: Luchino Visconti's *Ossessione* (1943) and Roberto Rossellini's *Rome, Open City* (1945). Rossellini's film most clearly exhibits every characteristic of neorealism and became the standard for the films that followed.

In cinema, as well as the other visual arts, realism is often an elusive concept. It is nothing more or less than the depiction of subjects as they appear to the artist in everyday life, without adornment or interpretation. In postwar period neorealism, this definition adhered, but the movement was revolutionary because it deliberately broke with the Fascist past and adopted an ideology that reflects Marxist, Christian, and humanist values. Neorealist filmmakers placed the highest value on the lives of ordinary working people; decried such postwar

conditions as widespread unemployment, poverty, child labor, government corruption, and inadequate housing (the results of Fascist rule); and focused on the struggle for a decent life in the postwar world. Politically, neorealism is antiauthoritarian, skeptical of the Catholic Church, antibureaucratic, and socialist. But overall, because it has no inherent political purpose, it is traditionally regarded more as a style than an ideology.

Stylistically, the characteristics of neorealism are specific. Despite the lavish production facilities available at the large studios that Mussolini built (or perhaps because of them), the neorealists sought simplicity in their working methods. They used actual locations rather than studio sites and hired nonprofessional actors. Their films had a documentary visual style that included shooting in the streets with natural light and lightweight cameras, using long takes to preserve real

An early influence on neorealism
Luchino Visconti's *Ossessione* (1943) represents a transition between the lackluster Italian cinema of the pre–Second World War period and the brief but significant flowering of neorealism. It reflects the older traditions in several ways: it uses professional actors, is based on an American novel, and is known mainly for its torrid love story. Soon after the two lovers—Giovanna (Clara Calamai), an unhappily married woman, and Gino (Massimo Girotti), a drifter—first meet, they become obsessively involved with one another. *Ossessione* foreshadows neorealism in its depiction of the daily routines of ordinary people, its focus on rural Italy, and its consistent use of long shots to preserve real time and emphasize how the setting constrains the characters from becoming independent. Mostly, though, its austere realism, in form and content, influenced the neorealist filmmakers. The film was remade in the United States twice, both times as *The Postman Always Rings Twice* (1946, director Tay Garnett; 1981, director Bob Rafelson).

time, and employing deep-space cinematography to maintain the look of the actual spaces where shooting occurred. All of these characteristics broke with the prevailing cinematic conventions in Italy.

Zavattini was primarily a screenwriter, but he was also responsible for pioneering a kind of documentary film, *Love in the City* (1953). In that film, he and several other young filmmakers (Michelangelo Antonioni, Federico Fellini, Carlo Lizzani, and Dino Risi, each of whom became a prominent director) worked with nonprofessional actors who played themselves in dramatizing an aspect of their lives. This approach, a sort of staged documentary, would later influence the development of *cinéma vérité* in France, free cinema in England, and direct cinema in the United States.

The most indispensable neorealist films are Vittorio De Sica's *Shoeshine* (1946), *The Bicycle Thieves* (1948; also known as *The Bicycle Thief*), and *Umberto D.* (1952), which marks the end of the movement; Cesare Zavattini wrote the screenplays for all of these.

The Bicycle Thieves, the movement's masterpiece, is set in Rome two years after the end of the war. It recounts three consecutive days in the life of Antonio Ricci (Lamberto Maggiorani), a laborer, Maria (Lianella Carell), his wife, and Bruno (Enzo Staiola), his son, who looks about eight years old but nonetheless works twelve hours a day at a gas station. The story is simple but powerful. Antonio is out of work but, at the beginning of the movie, is offered a job (hanging movie posters) on the condition that he has a bicycle. Because his bicycle is in a pawnshop, his wife takes the family linen to the pawnshop so that he can reclaim his bicycle and take the job. On his first morning at work, the bicycle is stolen. His friends help him search for it, but they have no luck. When Antonio spots the thief, the Mafia protects that man. Social forces such as the church and fortunetellers cannot help him. Faced with a practical dilemma, he too becomes a bicycle thief (hence the movie's title) and is caught and publicly humiliated. At the end of the film, Antonio is in exactly the same dilemma as when the film began. This, then, is the story of a good man caught in a seemingly hopeless world, told with insightful observation and compassion. Its ending, true to the neorealist credo, is ambiguous.

In this film the stylistic characteristics of neorealism—the long takes, the actual locations, the spare dialogue, and so on—allow De Sica to show reality without necessarily interpreting it. Nonetheless, he took com-

The Bicycle Thieves: a neorealist masterpiece
A three-day chronicle comprises the plot of *The Bicycle Thieves* (1948; director Vittorio De Sica), which tells the story of Antonio Ricci's (Lamberto Maggiorani) desperate search for his dignity. Bruno (Enzo Staiola), his son, is the one person who stands by him. Through hardship after hardship, their shared bond of love and faith is challenged but never broken. Bruno gives his father the courage to survive one heartbreaking moment after another, and although the movie ends ambiguously, there is no question that father and son will remain friends. In this image, we see Bruno waving good-bye to his father as they both begin their workday. When director De Sica cast Staiola, an unknown boy from the streets, in this part, he found a natural actor who gave the world an unforgettable performance.

plete control over the setting, cinematography, lighting, acting, and sound. Even though it is a sound film, much of its power comes from its relative silence, particularly its lack of voices. Like many films made before the coming of sound, *The Bicycle Thieves* demonstrates the intensity of silent acting.

One definition of a "classic" movie is that it can mean different things to different people at different times in their lives. *The Bicycle Thieves* is a classic and powerful film because of the director's spare style, humanist treatment of the story, and willingness to trust his viewers to make up their own mind about what it means.

Although neorealist films were innovative, they were not popular with Italians, who preferred the more upbeat American movies. Consequently, they were not successful at the box office (economic success was not one of the movement's primary goals). Critics, furthermore, said the films gave a false, even sentimental, portrayal of Italian society, one inconsistent with a country eager for prosperity and change. The government discouraged the neorealists' interest in social problems by not subsidizing them. Instead, it supported domestic films that focused on the new prosperity of the postwar society and implemented taxes and quotas on foreign movies.

By 1952 the Italian Neorealism movement was finished, yet it had an enormous impact on later Italian and world cinema. In fact, a handful of neorealist films helped rekindle greater awareness among filmmakers worldwide of the need to observe real life and to abandon, insofar as possible, the make-believe world of the movie studio. The movement also helped launch the careers of many great Italian directors, including De Sica, Rossellini, Visconti, Fellini, Antonioni, and Pietro Germi. Neorealism also influenced Italian directors who were not directly involved, including Pier Paolo Pasolini, Bernardo Bertolucci, Ermanno Olmi, and Paolo and Vittorio Taviani. Filmmakers as different as Satyajit Ray in India and Martin Scorsese in the United States regarded neorealism as the principal inspiration in beginning their careers. Today you'll see its influence in such different movies as Jean-Pierre and Luc Dardenne's *L'Enfant* (2005), John Carney's *Once* (2006), and even Matt Reeves's *Cloverfield* (2008).

1959–1964: French New Wave

After the Second World War, France, which had been occupied by the Nazis between 1940 and 1944, faced a unique set of problems, both foreign and domestic. Abroad, it was engaged in two wars with French-controlled territories: the French Indochina War (1946–54), which ended in a divided but independent Vietnam, and the Algerian War of Independence (1954–62), which led to Algeria's independence from France. At home, President Charles de Gaulle's government faced many challenges in dealing with myriad social, political, racial, ethnic, and cultural differences produced in part by the twin forces of collaboration and resistance during the Nazi occupation. Everywhere, calls for change were coming from students, artists, intellectuals, and philosophers—particularly the existentialists, who called for a new world in which individuals would be more responsible for their actions. The French New Wave was born within this broad context.

The originators of the New Wave were influenced by several movements. The first was the French cinema itself, including the 1930s cinematic style known as

poetic realism. The term applied to movies that treated everyday life with a moody sensitivity to mise-en-scène as well as to the more contemporary films of Jean-Pierre Melville. The second influence was the philosophy of Jean-Paul Sartre, the leading figure in French philosophy in the postwar period. Sartre believed that contemporary artists should rebel against the constraints of society, traditional morality, and religious faith; should accept personal responsibility for their actions; and should thus be free to create their own world. His existentialist views helped shape the new French cinema's depiction of modern human beings, while his Marxist views helped form its interpretations of society and history. Finally, the movement learned much from film critic and director Alexandre Astruc. He declared that a filmmaker should use the camera as personally as the novelist uses a pen, thus inspiring the idea of the movie director as auteur.

Other influences on the French New Wave include Italian Neorealism, the contemporaneous British Free Cinema (discussed on pp. 434–435), and contemporary developments in the French documentary film. While the Italians and the British offered models of how to make narrative films that told real stories about real people, *cinéma vérité* evolved in France in the early 1960s as a documentary style (the name, which means "film truth," pays homage to Dziga Vertov's *kino-pravda* work in the Soviet Montage movement). Among other things, this style advocated using the lightweight, portable filmmaking equipment that enhanced a filmmaker's mobility and flexibility. Stylistically, its films had a rough, intimate look that often reflected the informality of the filmmaking process. Filmmakers appeared onscreen, cameras jiggled, framing was often informal, scenes were generally unscripted, and continuity was provided primarily through lots of close-ups and sound tracks that continued under the shots. Later, such stylistic innovations would characterize many New Wave movies.

Film theorist André Bazin, known as the father of the New Wave, synthesized these concepts into the coherent model on which the New Wave was established. This interaction of intellect and creativity recalls the origins of several movements you've already encountered: the German, Soviet, and French film movements of the 1920s. Bazin cofounded *Cahiers du cinéma,* which became the leading French film journal of the time, and

French New Wave: beginnings

Among the first New Wave movies were François Truffaut's *The 400 Blows* (1959) and Jean-Luc Godard's *Breathless* (1960). Truffaut's protagonist, Antoine Doinel (Jean-Pierre Léaud), is a boy in his early teens who, as we see him here [1], has just escaped from a juvenile detention center; Godard's Michel Poiccard (Jean-Paul Belmondo) is a man in his early thirties who is preparing to steal a car and will shortly murder a policeman [2]. Antoine is just a boy prankster facing an unknown future, but Michel is a dangerous criminal whom the police will soon recognize and shoot in cold blood as he attempts to flee capture. Noteworthy is that Truffaut wrote the original treatment of *Breathless* and, after his great success with *The 400 Blows*, made a gift of it to Godard, suggesting that he submit it as the idea for his own first film.

in his capacity as editor, he became the intellectual and spiritual mentor of the New Wave. His followers included *Cahiers'* contributors, many of whom would become directors: Jean-Luc Godard, François Truffaut, Claude Chabrol, Jacques Rivette, and Eric Rohmer. Others went directly into filmmaking: Chris Marker, Alain Resnais, Agnès Varda, and Louis Malle. (There were other major directors in postwar France who were not directly involved in the New Wave movement, including Jean Cocteau, Robert Bresson, Jean Renoir, Jacques Tati, Jacques Becker, and Max Ophüls.)

Bazin's central tenets were realism, mise-en-scène, and authorship (the director's unique style). For him, the most distinctive nature of a movie was its form rather than its content. Accordingly, he encouraged his followers to see as many films as possible, looking particularly at the relationship between the director and the material. In viewing these films, great and otherwise, the young critics and would-be filmmakers developed a particular fascination with those Hollywood films that seemed to prove what Bazin, following Astruc, was saying about the director-as-author. They recognized

that most directors of Hollywood films had little say over most aspects of production, but they believed that through his style, particularly the handling of mise-en-scène, a great director could undermine studio control and transform even the most insignificant Western or detective story into a work of art.

Obviously, the New Wave was based on a theory that advocated a change in filmmaking practices. Truffaut's 1954 *Cahiers* essay "A Certain Tendency of the French Cinema" elaborated on the auteur concept and started a critical controversy that has not yet abated.[12] The issue remains: is it the director or the entire collaborative team, including the director, that makes a movie? Truffaut idolized directors who made highly personal statements in their films—directors such as Jean Renoir, Jean Cocteau, and Max Ophüls in France, and Orson Welles, Alfred Hitchcock, Howard Hawks, Fritz Lang, John Ford, Nicholas Ray, and Anthony Mann in Hollywood— so his answer was clear: the director was the primary "author" of the work. In another influential *Cahiers* essay, "The Evolution of the Language of Cinema," Bazin described mise-en-scène by stressing that everything

---

12. See François Truffaut, "A Certain Tendency of the French Cinema," in *Movies and Methods: An Anthology*, ed. Bill Nichols, 2 vols. (Berkeley: University of California Press, 1976), I, pp. 224–237.

Hitchcock's influence on the New Wave

Alfred Hitchcock's movies were greatly admired by New Wave directors. Claude Chabrol, who carefully studied the movies of the master of suspense and surprise, is noted also for movies that combine romance with gory murders. In *The Butcher* (1970), thought by many to be his masterpiece, a group of schoolchildren accompany Hélène (Stéphane Audran), their teacher, to see a magnificent cave that contains prehistoric drawings. Afterward—in the image here—as they enjoy their picnic lunch, blood drips onto one girl's bread from a fresh corpse on a cliff above. When Hélène sees the body, she suspects that it is yet another woman who has been victimized by the local butcher, a man with whom the teacher has a platonic relationship. After that, the suspense—whose effect Chabrol learned well from Hitchcock—becomes almost unbearable.

Time and mortality in the New Wave

Agnès Varda, one of the few women in the New Wave movement, was a unique force in shaping it. Her experiments in the handling of cinematic time influenced such contemporaries as Jean-Luc Godard and Alain Resnais. And her concern with the cinematic perception of women is beautifully realized in *Cleo from 5 to 7* (1962). It follows two hours in the life of Cléo (Corinne Marchand), a pop singer who wanders aimlessly around Paris while waiting for the results of a biopsy. Her story is told in near–real time, as she grapples with such issues as the meaning of friendship, her work, and mortality. Just before going to the hospital to meet her doctor—fearing that she has cancer—Cléo drops her purse; picking up the pieces, she interprets her broken mirror as an omen of death. To call attention to Cléo's ordeal of killing time, Varda titles each episode and indicates its precise running time (here, translated into English): "Chapter 11—CLÉO from 6:04 to 6:12."

we see on the screen has been put there by the director for a reason.[13]

The New Wave directors excelled at demonstrating that cinematic form is more important than content; their films were self-reflexive, focusing attention on them *as* movies and diverting our attention away from their narratives. In this, they manipulate our perceptions and keep an aesthetic and psychological distance between us and their movies. The style, substance, and achievements of the French New Wave directors had an invigorating effect on world cinema, and their movies remain very popular. Among their most important films are Jean-Luc Godard's *Breathless* (1960), François Truffaut's *The 400 Blows* (1959), Claude Chabrol's *The Butcher* (1970), Jacques Rivette's *Celine and Julie Go Boating* (1974), Eric Rohmer's *My Night at Maud's* (1969), Chris Marker's *La Jetée* (1962), Alain Resnais's *Last Year at Marienbad* (1961), Agnès Varda's *Cleo from 5 to 7* (1962), and Louis Malle's *Murmur of the Heart* (1971).

Although the movement was finished by 1964, many of these directors continued to make films.

If one movie symbolizes the fresh, innovative spirit of the New Wave, it is Godard's *Breathless* (1960). This work offers a comprehensive catalog of the movement's stylistic traits: rapid action, use of handheld cameras, unusual camera angles, elliptical editing, direct address to the camera, acting that borders on the improvisational, anarchic politics, and emphasis on the importance of sound, especially words. It is not any one of these techniques that defines the filmmaker's style, but rather the imagination and energy with which he uses them. *Breathless*, a movie that asserts Godard's personality and ideology, virtually defines what is meant by an auteur film. It tells a conventional crime story in an unconventional manner, rejecting the traditional cinematic values of

13. Among Bazin's essays, students should know "The Myth of Total Cinema," "The Evolution of the Language of Cinema," and "Theater and Cinema," in André Bazin, *What Is Cinema?* ed. and trans. Hugh Gray, 2 vols. (Berkeley: University of California Press, 1967–71), I, pp. 17–22, 23–40, 76–124.

unity and continuity in favor of discontinuity and contrast. Godard called his work a cinema of "reinvention," meaning that he generally kept all kinds of cinematic language in mind as he created his own. Consequently, by employing the iris-out, Godard not only offers homage to D. W. Griffith but also reminds modern audiences of a seldom-used visual device. Dedicating the film to Monogram Pictures (one of Hollywood's "B" or "Poverty Row" studios), Godard evokes the Hollywood film noir through allusions, direct and indirect, to tough films with tough leading men. He also pays homage to French film director Jean-Pierre Melville, a major influence on the New Wave, by casting him in the movie and patterning the role of his leading male character on the model in Melville's *Bob le flambeur* (1956). Finally, Godard includes allusions to writers, composers, and painters. Through this broad range of intertextual reference, or pastiche (making one artwork by mixing elements from others), Godard audaciously links his low-budget film noir with the works of some of the greatest artists of all time.

Most important, though, is Godard's editing, which is central to the telling of this narrative. Here, working in the radical tradition started by Eisenstein and his contemporaries—collision between and among images—Godard consciously and deliberately manipulates the images with such editing techniques as jump cuts and nondiegetic inserts. Thus he deliberately avoids such devices as crosscutting, which traditional directors would have used in cutting between the good guys and bad guys in the film's chase scenes, as well as the familiar sequence used to set up a scene—an establishing shot, long shot, medium shot, and close-up, generally in that order. The restless rhythm of the editing is perfectly suited to the restless mood of the story and the indecisiveness of the movie's two major characters.

While the term *New Wave* began with the French, its spirit soon spread internationally. These efforts were significantly bolstered in many of the countries discussed later by the establishment of state-supported filmmaking schools and film societies as well as the availability of lightweight filmmaking equipment. In the United States, the New Wave influence was noticeable early on—in Arthur Penn's *Bonnie and Clyde* (1967) and recently in Wes Anderson's *The Royal Tenenbaums* (2001) and Michel Gondry's *Eternal Sunshine of the Spotless Mind* (2004), to cite but three examples.

Many of the techniques pioneered by the French New Wave filmmakers have become commonplace, especially in today's independent cinema. Godard's films from the early 1960s still look very modern, and the unusually stylized treatment of time and subjectivity in a film like Alain Resnais's *Last Year at Marienbad* remains cutting-edge to this day, confusing and alienating many viewers used to traditional cinematic conventions.

1947–Present: New Cinemas in Great Britain, Europe, and Asia

World War II, fought mainly in Europe and Asia but involving virtually every country in the world, was the most destructive war in history. Between 40 million and 50 million people were killed, and millions of others fled from their homes or countries. The war destroyed many historic cities, shattered economies, and left the specter of the Holocaust to redefine the concept of a civilized world. It was impossible for many countries to return to normal, even though the victory over Fascism held the promise of establishing a new and more just society.

How did filmmakers react to the war? They all knew that whatever they did with their movies, the international landscape had changed utterly and that they must acknowledge the horrors, postwar challenges, and hopes for the future. For some filmmakers, it was an opportunity to express their nation's identity through what we call a *national cinema*. While this term is used generally to describe the films identified by and associated with a specific country—for example, through financing, language, or culture—it remains a subject of debate among film scholars and critics.

In the following pages, we differentiate between two kinds of countries. First are those that resumed filmmaking pretty much as usual after the war, albeit with a different perspective, audience, and set of responsibilities (e.g., Canada, Australia, New Zealand, Ireland, Italy, Sweden, Spain, Russia and the Soviet Union, Hungary, the former Czechoslovakia and former Yugoslavia, Romania, Bulgaria, and many countries in Central and Latin America, Asia, Africa, and the Middle East). The second type of country includes those that established the new wave movements we discuss in this section: Great Britain, Denmark, Germany, Japan, and China. Today, new cinemas are also emerging in Albania, Bosnia, Slovenia, Serbia, Hungary, Estonia, Turkey, and the Czech Republic. (We emphasize the new wave movements because they represent pockets of resistance to dominant filmmaking traditions and have revitalized the cinemas of their respective countries with a distinctive stylistic effect.)

In making this simple distinction and in choosing to discuss the new wave movements, we do not overlook the profound achievements of such British and European directors as Ingmar Bergman, Andrzej Wajda, Michelangelo Antonioni, Satyajit Ray, David Lean, or Federico Fellini, to name only a few. The work of those artists significantly altered the psychological and imaginative landscape of postwar filmmaking. Nor do we overlook more recent directors—such as Jane Campion, Pedro Almodóvar, Abbas Kiarostami, or Ousmane Sembene—whose films, although they don't fall within a definable movement or trend, are widely recognized as modern masterpieces.

Like the original new wave of directors in France, each of the movements described next attempted to (1) make a clean break with the cinematic past, (2) inject new vitality into filmmaking, and (3) explore cinema as a subject in itself.

England and the Free Cinema Movement

The British Free Cinema movement developed between 1956 and 1959. Like Dziga Vertov and the Italian Neorealists, these British directors rejected prevailing cinematic conventions; in so doing, they also rejected an obstinately class-bound society, turned their cameras on ordinary people and everyday life, and proclaimed their freedom to make films without worrying about the demands of producers and distributors or other commercial considerations.

Because the films of the Free Cinema movement were entirely the expression of the people who made them, they serve as another manifestation of the growing postwar movement in Europe toward a new cinema of social realism. Its primary effect was a small but impressive body of documentary films, including Lindsay Anderson's *Every Day Except Christmas* (1957), an affectionate look at the people who make the Covent Garden market such a tradition; Karel Reisz's *We Are the Lambeth Boys* (1958), an attempt to understand working-class youth;

***Victim*: the first major movie about gay rights**
The British Free Cinema dealt courageously with controversial issues of class, race, gender, and sexual orientation. Basil Dearden's *Victim* (1961) was the first commercial British film to show that homosexuality existed at every level of contemporary society. At the time, homosexual acts between consenting adults were illegal in Great Britain, and gays suffered widespread discrimination and blackmail. In *Victim*, Dirk Bogarde gave a moving performance as Melville Farr, a distinguished lawyer who is exposed by a blackmailing ring for having had an emotional, but nonsexual, gay affair before he married. In this image, he sees the photograph that triggered the blackmail. Outraged by the widespread injustices against homosexuals, he agrees to help the police by giving evidence in court, knowing that sensational newspaper publicity could ruin his career. Bogarde, then one of England's major stars, was lauded for his personal courage in helping to break a social barrier, and *Victim* was instrumental in changing the social and legal climate. In 1967, Great Britain legalized homosexual acts between consenting adults.

and Tony Richardson and Karel Reisz's *Momma Don't Allow* (1955), an admiring view of the emerging British pop culture in the mid-1950s.

After the war, the British class system began its slow disintegration, and Anderson understood the inherent challenges facing the country, as well as the role that movies might play in the transition, when he defined his approach to filmmaking: "I want to make people—ordinary people, not just Top People—feel their dignity and their importance, so that they can act from these principles. Only on such principles can confident and healthy action be based."[14]

This sentiment and Free Cinema movies helped to inspire the British New Cinema of the 1960s, an almost unique situation in which the documentary form was the catalyst for a revived spirit in narrative filmmaking.

14. Lindsay Anderson, qtd. in Richard M. Barsam, *Nonfiction Film: A Critical History,* rev. and exp. ed. (Bloomington: Indiana University Press, 1992), p. 252.

Memorable socialist-realist films were outspoken on the subjects of gender, race, and economic disparities among the classes, including Jack Clayton's *Room at the Top* (1959), Karel Reisz's *Saturday Night and Sunday Morning* (1960), Basil Dearden's *Victim* (1961), Tony Richardson's *The Loneliness of the Long Distance Runner* (1962), Lindsay Anderson's *if . . .* (1968), Joseph Losey's *The Servant* (1963), Richard Lester's *A Hard Day's Night* (1964), and Ken Loach's *Kes* (1969).

Denmark and the Dogme 95 Movement

Postwar Danish cinema is noted primarily for the Dogme 95 movement. It was founded in 1995 by three directors, including Lars von Trier, the one best known outside Denmark. The movement was based on the Dogme 95 manifesto of ten rules (known as "The Vow of Chastity"), with which participating directors were required to affirm their compliance. These are

1. Shooting must be done on location. Props and sets must not be brought in (if a particular prop is necessary for the story, a location must be chosen where this prop is to be found).

2. The sound must never be produced apart from the images or vice versa. (Music must not be used unless it occurs where the scene is being shot.)

3. The camera must be hand-held. Any movement or immobility attainable in the hand is permitted. (The film must not take place where the camera is standing; shooting must take place where the film takes place.)

4. The film must be in colour. Special lighting is not acceptable. (If there is too little light for exposure the scene must be cut or a single lamp be attached to the camera.)

5. Optical work and filters are forbidden.

6. The film must not contain superficial action. (Murders, weapons, etc. must not occur.)

7. Temporal and geographical alienation are forbidden. (That is to say that the film takes place here and now.)

Breaking the rules in *Breaking the Waves*
The Dogme rules are rigid, but Lars von Trier's *Breaking the Waves* (1996) demonstrates that a director can subvert them to facilitate production. Although the cinematographer used the requisite hand-held camera, many of the scenes were shot not in real locations, but in studio settings. The story takes place in the past, not the here and now; and contrary to Dogme rules, the movie contains nondiegetic music. Furthermore, von Trier takes full credit for his role as director. Nonetheless, a major reason for seeing it is the astonishing performance by Emily Watson as Bess, a simple, childlike woman. When her husband, seriously injured in an oil-rig accident, fears that their sex life has ended, he encourages her to have sexual relations with other men. However, she believes, from voices that she hears, that what she is doing is God's wish. These voices—if indeed she hears them—often come to her in a deserted church.

8. Genre movies are not acceptable.

9. The film format must be Academy 35mm.

10. The director must not be credited.[15]

This statement of principles brought considerable attention to the country's cinema with such movies as von Trier's *The Idiots* (1998), *Breaking the Waves* (1996), *Dancer in the Dark* (2000), *Dogville* (2003), and *The Five Obstructions* (2003). These rules were rigid, and directors often broke their vows, as seen in such Dogme films as Harmony Korine's *Julien Donkey-Boy* (1999), Lone Scherfig's *Italian for Beginners* (2000), Martin Rengel's *Joy Ride* (2001), and Susanne Bier's *Open Hearts* (2002). The Dogme movement—clearly as bold, if not as significant, as the French New Wave—influenced some avant-garde directors in Europe and the United States. Its emphasis on freedom is relevant to filmmakers with access to digital video, home computers, and advanced editing software.

15. http://www.dogme95.dk/the_vow/vow.html (accessed March 24, 2015).

Germany and Austria

Following the Second World War and until 1990 (when it was reunified as the German Democratic Republic), Germany was split into a western and eastern part. In West Germany, the Federal Republic reestablished independent film production, even though German audiences preferred Hollywood movies. In East Germany, film production remained under Soviet control, and little of significance was produced, except in the work of Kurt Maetzig, whose films helped Germans on both sides of the Wall to understand the Nazi past. In many feature films and documentaries, he dealt with Fascism, anti-Semitism, and the complicity of German corporations with the Nazi government. He founded East Germany's main film studio, which operated under the ideological dictates of the Communist Party, and he made films about life under that regime. He also made the most popular film of the postwar period—*Marriage in the Shadows* (1947)—as well as some that were banned, including *The Rabbit Is Me* (1965), a blunt criticism of the East German judicial system.

In 1962 a movement called *das neue Kino* (the New German Cinema) was born, and it flourished until the 1980s. Its founders, a group of young writers and filmmakers, recognized that any attempt to revive the German cinema must deal with two large issues: the Nazi period and the brutal break that it made in the German cultural tradition; and the reemergence of postwar Germany as a divided country whose western part was known, like Japan at the same time, as an "economic miracle." This group also knew the Italian, French, and British New Cinemas that preceded them and had a genuine affection for established genres in Hollywood, particularly melodrama. Like all serious radical groups, it issued a manifesto:

> The collapse of the conventional German film finally removes the economic basis for a mode of filmmaking whose attitude and practice we reject. With it the new film has a chance to come to life. . . .
>
> We declare our intention to create the new German feature film.
>
> This new film needs new freedoms. Freedom from the conventions of the established industry. Freedom from the outside influence of commercial partners. Freedom from the control of special interest groups.

Das neue Kino and Hollywood

German New Wave filmmakers had a genuine affection for Hollywood genres, including film noir. In Wim Wenders's *The American Friend* (1977), a crime thriller and neo-noir (shot in color), the title refers to the character of Tom Ripley, played by the American actor Dennis Hopper, shown here. Also appearing in the movie are two distinctly American movie directors: Nicholas Ray (who directed Hopper in *Rebel without a Cause* [1955]) and Samuel Fuller (*Pickup on South Street* [1953]). Although the film was shot mostly in Germany, some scenes were photographed in New York City.

> We have concrete intellectual, formal, and economic conceptions about the production of the new German film. We are as a collective prepared to take economic risks.
>
> The old film is dead. We believe in the new one.[16]

This 1962 document (known as the Oberhausen Manifesto) fused economic, aesthetic, and political goals. It sought to create a new cinema free from historical antecedents, one that could criticize bourgeois German society and expose viewers to new modes of looking at movies. A short list of the early work of the most significant directors includes Volker Schlöndorff's *Young Torless* (1966); Alexander Kluge's *Artists under the Big Top: Perplexed* (1968); and Margarethe von Trotta's *The German Sisters/Marianne and Juliane* (1981; von Trotta is perhaps the most important of a large group of female directors). Also included are Rainer Werner Fassbinder's *The Marriage of Maria Braun* (1979), *Fear of Fear* (1975), and *Berlin Alexanderplatz* (1980—a television series, released theatrically in a 15½-hour version, the longest narrative movie ever made); Wim Wenders's *The Goalie's Anxiety at the Penalty Kick* (1972), *The American Friend* (1977), and *Paris, Texas* (1984); and Werner

---

16. For the full text and list of signatories, see www.oberhausener-manifest.com/en/ (accessed June 15, 2015).

Herzog's *Even Dwarfs Started Small* (1970), *Aguirre: The Wrath of God* (1972), *Heart of Glass* (1976), and *Nosferatu the Vampire* (1979). Ultimately, the movement sparked a renaissance in German filmmaking by encouraging the production of quality films that created considerable excitement in the international cinema community. Its bold treatments of such contemporary issues as sexuality, immigration, and national identity have significantly influenced filmmakers worldwide.

The history of Austrian cinema includes a rich legacy from various film artists, such as Ernst Lubitsch and Billy Wilder, who emigrated during the 1930s and enriched the cinemas of Great Britain, France, and the United States. In the twenty-first century, a young generation of filmmakers has begun to create its own legacy with films that are uniquely Austrian in subject and style. These include Michael Haneke, arguably the best-known and most important Austrian filmmaker, with such films as *Funny Games* (1997; U.S. remake in 2008), *The Piano Teacher* (2001), *The White Ribbon* (2009), and *Amour* (2012); as well as Ulrich Seidl, *Import/Export* (2007) and his 2012 trilogy, *Paradise: Love, Paradise: Faith*, and *Paradise: Hope*; Jessica Hausner, *Lonely Rita* (2001), *Hotel* (2004), and *Lourdes* (2009); and Jan Schütte, *Love Comes Lately* (2007).

Japan

The movies were popular in Japan as early as 1896, a year after they were invented in the West. The Japanese film industry flourished, albeit with a highly stylized form of filmmaking that owed a great deal to Japanese literary and theatrical traditions as well as something to Western cinematic traditions, until World War II.

When the war ended in 1945, much of the country lay in ruins and was under occupation by the Allied powers. As the film industry began to revive, it was strongly influenced by such Hollywood masters as John Ford, Howard Hawks, and Orson Welles. However, filmmakers were limited, both by the occupying powers and by a film industry lacking money, to making films that extolled the freedoms made possible by democracy, particularly the emancipation of women. The three Japanese directors most familiar in the West are Akira Kurosawa, Kenji Mizoguchi, and Yasujiro Ozu. Mizoguchi and Ozu began their directing careers in the 1920s, but it was not until 1950 that Kurosawa launched the golden age of Japanese filmmaking with *Rashomon*.

To Western viewers, Akira Kurosawa is the most recognizable Japanese director, both for the quality of his work and because he, among his contemporaries, was most familiar with the conventions of Hollywood filmmaking, especially the work of John Ford. However, aside from familiar cinematic technique, his films are thoroughly Japanese in their fatalistic attitude toward life and death. He initiated the postwar rebirth of Japanese cinema with *Rashomon* (1950), which tells a single story—the rape of a woman—from four different points of view. Kurosawa shows us that we all remember and perceive differently and that truth is relative to those telling their stories. With this profound statement on the power of cinema, he produced a body of work that

Kurosawa's *Ran*: "a scroll of hell"
Ran, Kurosawa's adaptation of Shakespeare's *King Lear*, pushes the play to extremes. The word *ran* literally means "turmoil" or "chaos" and suggests rebellion, riot, or war. Kurosawa's *ran* is full of blood, violence, suffering, and death, qualities depicted in twelfth- and thirteenth-century Japanese scrolls known as "scrolls of hell," the term Kurosawa used to describe the movie itself. The director has transformed *King Lear*'s three daughters into the three sons of powerful warlord Hidetora Ichimonji. Lady Kaede, the wife of Taro, one of the sons, is a lethal schemer who wants her husband to become leader of the clan. She fails, however, and at the end, she is confronted by a clan loyalist, who tells her, "Vixen . . . you have destroyed the house of Ichimonji, now you should know the shallowness and stupidity of a woman's wisdom." But Kaede has the last word: "It is not shallow or stupid. I wanted to see this castle burn and the House of Ichimonji ruined by the long grudge of my family. I wanted to see all this." We do not see Kaede beheaded, but in this spectacular image, her spattered blood is running down the wall. A maid crouches to the left and the assailant stands at the right; Kaede's body is on the floor. The image resembles a Japanese scroll; overall, it is framed by pots of flowers in the middle ground; in the background, the gruesome composition is framed by sliding doors. Ironically, the dripping blood recalls various abstract modern paintings.

Painterly composition in Mizoguchi's *Sansho the Bailiff*

Nothing could be further from the color and chaos of Kurosawa's *Ran* than the calm compositions of Kenji Mizoguchi's *Sansho the Bailiff*. After her husband is banished to a distant province, an aristocratic woman named Tamaki (Kinuyo Tanaka), her lone servant, and her children are forced to wander from place to place. In this image, the wife (*center right*), who cannot find shelter elsewhere, builds a structure of branches and reeds under the spreading limbs of a tree as the servant and children help her. The black-and-white composition of this image shows why Mizoguchi is revered as a master of mise-en-scène. The tree is theatrically perfect, as is the light through the upper branches of the tree, on the mother and daughter, and on the grasses at the right and left of the image. This pictorially pleasing image gives no hint of what's to come: the children are sold into slavery, and Tamaki is exiled to an island where she is forced to become a prostitute. Despite the loss of her daughter and her other hardships, Tamaki perseveres; finally, blind and alone, she is reunited with her son. Overall, the movie demonstrates Mizoguchi's interest in issues of freedom and women's place in society.

is notable for its interest in Japanese tradition, especially the samurai culture of medieval Japan, and for its spectacle, action, and sumptuous design. As John Wayne represented John Ford's idea of the ideal hero, so did Toshiro Mifune for Kurosawa, who used him in 16 of his films. In addition to *Rashomon*, there are many other masterpieces among Kurosawa's 30 films: *Ikiru* (1952), *Seven Samurai* (1954), *Throne of Blood* (1957), his version of Shakespeare's *Macbeth*, *Yojimbo* (1961), *Kagemusha* (1980), and *Ran* (1985), his stylized version

of Shakespeare's *King Lear*. In creating these works, Kurosawa was a classic auteur, involved in every phase of filmmaking.

If Kurosawa is the master of the samurai as well as contemporary social problem films, then Kenji Mizoguchi, a sublime artist, is the master of mise-en-scène, pictorial values, the long shot, and the moving camera. His stories are about place as much as anything else, and his films, no less than Kurosawa's, have had worldwide influence. Although they are much less known in the

Unique camera placement in Ozu's *Tokyo Story*

Set in postwar Japan, this unforgettable movie tells a familiar and touching story about Shukichi (Chishu Ryu, *left*) and Tomi Hirayama (Chieko Higashiyama, *middle*), two elderly parents who visit their children in Tokyo only to find that they are in the children's way. However, Noriko (Setsuko Hara, *right*), the couple's widowed daughter-in-law, who is less busy, cheerfully takes charge of entertaining them. In this image, their first meeting, the three are traditionally seated on the floor, where the low placement of Ozu's static camera (*behind and to the left of* Noriko) gives us Noriko's perspective. The image, with its deep-space composition, permits us to see the rooms behind this group. While it's a simple story, and Ozu observes it with calm detachment, its ending reminds us of the oneness of humanity and helped to make this film an international success.

***In the Realm of the Senses*: sex and violence**

When Nagisa Oshima's most provocative movie, *In the Realm of the Senses* (1976), was released, it was banned (or cut) in many parts of the world. It explores various sexual activities, including the power dynamics between a man and a woman obsessed with one another, and ends in one of the most disturbingly violent incidents in movie history. This image, a comparatively tame moment, depicts eroticism in eating, where actor Tatsuya Fuji is playfully fed a rare mushroom by his lover. The overall movie is based on a true story involving death-obsessed eroticism and is widely thought to be pornography.

United States than they deserve to be, that may be so because they were less influenced by Western filmmaking conventions than Kurosawa's were. Unlike Kurosawa, he had a flourishing career before the war. Mizoguchi's films are highly regarded for their treatment of women. Indeed, his major concerns are women's social, psychological, and economic positions (or lack of them), the differences between women and men, male-female relations, and the idea that a man can be saved by a woman's love. These themes characterize his greatest postwar movies: *The Life of Oharu* (1952), *Ugetsu* (1953), *Sansho the Bailiff* (1954), and *Street of Shame* (1956).

Of these three directors, the films of Yasujiro Ozu are considered by the international film community as the most Japanese in their modes of expression and values. Like Mizoguchi, he began his career long before World War II. His best films are concerned not with the traditional world of the samurai but with contemporary family life; indeed, the values of the lower-middle-class families who are the staple of his movies represent a

microcosm of postwar society. And since most of them take place within the family home, their look is influenced by Japanese domestic customs and architecture. Because the Japanese often sit on the floor and thus make eye contact with others at that level, Ozu placed his camera similarly, pulling Western audiences immediately into a different world. His compositions are very formal, and his camera seldom moved; his editing consisted primarily of cuts rather than, say, fades or dissolves. Unlike Kurosawa, he did not seek to create Western-style continuity. Furthermore, his distinctive style included the use of offscreen space, meaning that his compositions force our eyes to consider the world outside the frame and as a result, heighten our sense of a movie's reality. Like Kurosawa, he was an auteur, infusing his movies with a distinct style unlike any other. While that style might at first seem austere or rigid, the subject of his films is anything but. Many Western viewers find them difficult to watch and understand due to the differences in culture. Notable among his 54 films are *Late Spring* (1949), *Early Summer* (1951), *The Flavor of Green Tea over Rice* (1952), *Tokyo Story* (1953), *Early Spring* (1956), *Floating Weeds* (1959), and *An Autumn Afternoon* (1962).

Between the 1950s and 1970s, there arose an extreme new movement (*Nubero Bagu*) that was significantly influenced by the French New Wave in its emphasis on upsetting cinematic and social conventions. Its representative directors were Hiroshi Teshigahara, Yasuzo Masumura, and Nagisa Oshima, among others, and their movies are full of brutality and nihilism. Oshima is, perhaps, the best known of the group, a provocative filmmaker whose work is often compared to that of Jean-Luc Godard. His movies include *Cruel Story of Youth* (1960), full of violent passion, *In the Realm of the Senses* (1976), a disturbing exploration of human sexuality, and *Merry Christmas, Mr. Lawrence* (1983), a film about intercultural communication in a Japanese prisoner-of-war camp that established Oshima's international reputation as a director who could also communicate across cultures.

Also well known in the United States is the work of the experimental filmmaker Nobuhiko Obayashi, who is best known for *House* (1977). This stylistically bizarre horror film demonstrates a strong familiarity with French, British, and Italian cinema of the 1960s as well as Japanese film history and silent film tradition. Although a short-lived movement, the Japanese New Wave—along with the postwar filmmakers of China—influenced the style and content of the New American Cinema (discussed on pp. 447–452).

China

After the Second World War, film production resumed in the People's Republic of China (often referred to as mainland China) as well as in two distinct political entities: Taiwan (the Republic of China), which asserts its independence from the People's Republic, and Hong Kong (a British colony until 1997, when it was transferred by treaty to the People's Republic). The People's Republic, a vast country with the world's largest population, is ostensibly Communist. Taiwan, an island off the southern coast of China, has a democratic government that desires independence even in the face of mainland China's threats of reunification. And Hong Kong, a small island near China's south coast is—by terms of the treaty that reunified it with the People's Republic—a limited democracy with considerable sovereignty compared to

the other regions of China. The tripartite Chinese film industry is thus clearly affected by these circumstances of history, ideology, and geography.

The People's Republic Postwar government-subsidized filmmaking here has reflected the shifting ideological climate that developed after the 1949 Communist Revolution. Since 1976, with the death of Party Chairman Mao Ze-dong and Premier Zhou Enlai, filmmakers have focused less on party doctrines and become more concerned with individuals, and the Chinese film industry has become more oriented to the Western market. The most important directors are Chen Kaige, Yimou Zhang, and Tian Zhuangzhuang, each of whom has managed, within a repressive society, to make films about traditionally taboo subjects. Among their best-known movies are Chen's *Farewell My Concubine* (1993), about an extramarital love triangle; Yimou's *Raise the Red Lantern* (1991), which, among other subjects, is concerned with the struggle for women's rights; and Tian's *The Horse Thief* (1986), a brilliant study of China's ethnic minorities.

But the Chinese movies that are most popular and influential outside China—the action movies inspired by

***Farewell My Concubine*: sex and politics**
The Beijing Opera, one of China's major cultural treasures, forms the backdrop for two major contemporary Chinese movies, including Hark Tsui's *Peking Opera Blues* (1986). Chen Kaige's *Farewell My Concubine* (1993) tells the lengthy, complicated story of two of the opera's male actors, whose happiness together onstage and off is threatened by a prostitute. The turbulence of this personal story is mirrored by the political upheavals of the period from the 1920s to Mao's Cultural Revolution. The movie was banned in China not because of its treatment of politics, but because of its homosexual subject matter. The Beijing Opera is known for its lavish productions, exotic costumes, and stylized makeup as well as for its ancient tradition of using males to play the female roles.

various martial arts—are produced in Hong Kong and, to a lesser extent, Taiwan. Director Jia Zhangke found a way to build on this subject, taking the style of the classic martial arts movie (*wuxia*) and applying it to a study of one of the social problems growing out of the country's transformation into a global economic power: the growth of rebellious one-on-one violence. Even in a society that strictly censors its movies, he was able speak out, perhaps because the problem was making newspaper headlines and thus was widely familiar. In *A Touch of Sin* (2013), his sixth feature, he recounts stories of four ordinary Chinese, one of them a furious mine worker, who under extreme circumstances goes on a shooting rampage against his boss. It's as bloody as it can get, and a departure from the director's previous work, but a signal that Chinese cinema may be opening up.

Hong Kong The Hong Kong martial-arts action movies stem from a venerable tradition in Chinese film history that, from the 1920s to the 1970s, shifted between two basic styles: wuxia (or wushu) and kung fu. Both of them combine, to varying degrees, these disparate elements: an intricate, sometimes incomprehensible, melodramatic plot; philosophical codes of honor based on mystical beliefs; spectacular violence; brilliantly choreographed fight sequences; the conflict between cops and gangsters; speeding vehicles; and lavish production values. Their formal characteristics include spectacular studio settings and natural locations, saturated colors, moody lighting, constant motion (slow and fast), disjointed editing techniques, and extensive computer manipulation of images and motion.

Between the late 1970s and early 1980s, a New Wave of Hong Kong cinema emerged in the work of such directors as Ann Hui, Yim Ho, Hark Tsui, Allen Fong, Patrick Tam, Clifford Choi, Dennis Yu, and others. Although many of these artists were trained in U.S. or U.K. film schools, they made movies that dealt with local experiences in a distinctly individual style. Remarkably, they worked in both mainstream cinema and television. This movement also stimulated change in the film industries of the People's Republic and Taiwan. Important early titles are Yim Ho's *The Extras* (1978), Ann Hui's *Vietnam Trilogy* (1980–1981), Hark Tsui's *The Butterfly Murders* (1979), Patrick Tam's *A Spectrum of Multiple Stars: Wang Chuanru** [*sic*] (1975), Alex Cheung's *The First Step: Facing Death* (1977), and Allen Fong's *Father and Son* (1981).

Bands of bloody brothers
A Better Tomorrow (1986), directed by John Woo, is considered a classic example of Hong Kong cinema: violent action depicted in brilliantly choreographed scenes. The image here, from the movie's spectacular conclusion, exemplifies Woo's style: bright colors, gymnastic feats, dozens of blazing guns, exploding firestorms, blood galore, overwrought male bonding, and a certain sly humor that suggests a surreal world. Woo was influenced by such action directors as Sergio Leone and Sam Peckinpah (see *The Wild Bunch*, p. 450) and in turn had wide influence on both Chinese and American directors, including Quentin Tarantino, Robert Rodriguez, and the Wachowskis.

During this time, the film culture in Hong Kong expanded to include popular film clubs and academic programs in film studies and filmmaking. However, the strong personal style of the New Wave movies clashed with the prevailing commercial nature of the island's cinema; by 1985, the New Wave spirit had become diluted, and the movement was absorbed into the mainstream cinema. Important titles from this period include Hark Tsui's *Peking Opera Blues* (1986), Allen Fong's *Just Like Weather* (1986), Ringo Lam's *City on Fire* (1987), John Woo's *A Better Tomorrow* (1986), and Kar Wai Wong's *Ashes of Time* (1994). Superstar performers like Bruce Lee, Jackie Chan (also a writer and director), Yun-Fat Chow, and Jet Li were an equally vital component of the success of these movies, one reason that they all went to Hollywood. Hong Kong directors who have worked in Hollywood include John Woo and Sammo Hung.

While the Hong Kong New Wave was short-lived, it stimulated cinematic innovations throughout China, encouraged the movement of directors between television and mainstream cinema, introduced new genres, and tackled formerly taboo subjects. The influence between Hong Kong and Hollywood has gone both ways. The Chinese have learned from such action directors as Sam Peckinpah and Sergio Leone and then influenced

Flying warriors in *Crouching Tiger, Hidden Dragon*
The films of Taiwan-born Ang Lee are known for their diversity (comedies, melodramas, traditional Chinese martial action), their ability to provoke discussion (e.g., *Brokeback Mountain* [2005]), and their almost universal acclaim. *Crouching Tiger, Hidden Dragon* (2000) has it all: a traditional intrigue-filled story about a legendary sword, magnificent exterior and interior settings, beautiful costumes, a love story, and astonishing swordplay. It is a fantastic feat of movie magic, distinguished by the exquisite choreography and special effects that give the illusion of its principal characters in flight. In this image, two female principals, Jade Fox (Cheng Pei-pei) and Jen (Zhang Ziyi) engage in a deadly battle.

such Hollywood directors as Quentin Tarantino (*Reservoir Dogs*, 1992, and the *Kill Bill* movies, 2003–4), Robert Rodriguez (*Desperado*, 1995), Sam Raimi (*A Simple Plan*, 1998), the Wachowskis (*The Matrix* trilogy, 1999–2003), Brett Ratner (the *Rush Hour* films, 1998–2007), and Rob Minkoff (*The Forbidden Kingdom,* 2008). Action choreographer Yuen Woo-ping played a major role in many of these movies.

Taiwan By following European models, particularly the Italian Neorealism movement, postwar Taiwanese cinema developed independently of Hong Kong and the People's Republic. In contrast to the action movies of earlier decades, it was concerned with realistic depictions of ordinary people. Excellent examples are Hsiao-hsien Hou's *A City of Sadness* (1989) and *Flight of the Red Balloon* (2007), Edward Yang's *Taipei Story* (1985), Tsai Ming-liang's *Vive l'amour* (1994), and Stan Lai's *The Peach Blossom Land* (1992). The first films of Ang Lee, the most familiar Taiwanese director—*The Wedding Banquet* (1993) and *Eat Drink Man Woman* (1994)—were so successful in the West that Lee went to Hollywood, where he showed an affinity for Western lit-

erature and themes and made, among other films, *Sense and Sensibility* (1995), *The Ice Storm* (1997), *Brokeback Mountain* (2005), and *Lust, Caution* (2007). In between, he returned to Taiwan to make *Crouching Tiger, Hidden Dragon* (2000), a spectacularly beautiful martial-arts action movie in the venerable Chinese tradition.

Postwar Chinese filmmaking was too diverse, aesthetically and politically, to represent a unified movement such as the French New Wave, but its movies—particularly the Hong Kong action movies—have spoken in a distinct visual language across cultural and linguistic barriers and have had a dynamic effect on filmmaking worldwide, especially in the United States.

India

Despite the worldwide success of *Slumdog Millionaire* (2008), an Anglo-Indian production, and the fact that the Indian film industry—producing more than 1,200 feature movies and an even larger number of documentaries every year—is the world's largest, Indian films are little known in the United States except in cities with a large Indian population. Indeed, India ranks first in annual film production, followed by Hollywood and China.

India, a vast country with some sixteen official languages, has a regional cinema that speaks to its many different audiences in social, political, cinematic, and linguistic terms it can understand. Thus a social protest film made in Chennai, in the South, might never be seen by those who live in Mumbai. These audiences not only speak a different dialect but seemingly prefer the lavish musicals made by Bollywood, as the Mumbai film industry is known. When Indian films are screened theatrically in the United States, the audiences are typically Indians, who understand the culture in which the movie was made and the language spoken in it. For others who want to learn more about this vast, diverse body of filmmaking, there are annual Indian (and South Asian) film festivals in such U.S. cities as New York, Boston, Chicago, and San Francisco. In these settings, the films are likely to be dubbed into English or have English subtitles.

The one exception to this description is director Satyajit Ray, the dominating figure in Indian cinema as it is known in the West. He was always unique among Indian filmmakers and, to the moviegoing public in the West, the only Indian director whose name they recognize. In that respect, he very much resembles Akira Kurosawa; both were instinctive filmmakers who made powerful and personal films with recurring themes. Ray and Kurosawa, two of the most individually unique filmmakers the world has ever produced, greatly admired each other's work. Of Ray, Kurosawa said, "Not to have seen the cinema of Ray means existing in the world without seeing the sun or the moon."

Ray was a Bengali, born in the Indian state of West Bengal, the capital of which is Kolkata (Calcutta). The principal influences on his cinematic style come from the literature and art of Bengali culture as well as from four great filmmakers: Vittorio De Sica, Akira Kurosawa, Jean Renoir, and John Ford. This helps to explain why his films are very Indian in content but the least Indian in their cinematic form.

Ray's most formative influence was Italian Neorealism, *The Bicycle Thieves* (1949) in particular. It convinced him to make a film about everyday Indian life exactly as De Sica had made his; the characteristics of this approach are discussed earlier in this chapter. The result was not one but three films, a trilogy known as the Apu trilogy for the name of its central character: *Pather Panchali* (*Song of the Little Road*, 1955), *Aparajito* (*The Unvanquished*,

The eye as symbol of consciousness in *Pather Panchali*

Director Satyajit Ray is known for his attention to detail in the lives of ordinary people and for the subtle, detached angle at which he views them in his movies. His "Apu" trilogy, of which *Pather Panchali* is the first, recounts a series of small but significant episodes in the life of Apu, who lives with his impoverished family in a Bengali village. The trilogy spans the years from his childhood through his early twenties, but here he is a boy of six or seven. Near the beginning of the movie, Apu's sister Durga tries to awaken him so that he can get ready for school. She shakes him, but he does not budge. But then, poking her fingers through a hole in his blanket, she tenderly pries open a closed eye. We would be wrong to think that Ray will henceforth see things from Apu's point of view, for we are seeing the opening of Apu's consciousness of the world around him. He is a curious boy, delighted by everything he sees and hears—traveling entertainers, a freight train, a pond—and he also learns about life and death when realizing that his father is incapable of supporting the family and by witnessing the death of his aged aunt. Careful, connected observation characterizes both Apu and his creator.

1956), and *Apar Sansar* (*The World of Apu*, 1959). As a chronicle of a family, and particular Apu's growth from a boy to a man, they are unparalleled in their humanistic insight and wonder at the natural world. (Note: Both Indian and English titles are given because they are cited in variant ways.) For these reasons, as well as for their cinematography and acting, the three films were recognized worldwide as landmarks of modern cinema. Ray, a true auteur, wrote, produced, and directed all three; he even scored the music.

In all, Ray made some 34 films, most of which were successful both in India and worldwide. Besides the Apu trilogy, his films include *Jalsaghar* (*The Music Room*, 1958), *Devi* (*The Goddess*, 1960), *Charulata* (*The Lonely*

Wife, 1964), *Shatranj-ke-Khilari* (*The Chess Players,* 1977), *Ghare-Baire* (*The Home and the World,* 1984), and *Agantuk* (*The Stranger,* 1992).

Ray's work represented the beginnings of a "new Indian cinema," or Parallel Cinema, meaning that it exists alongside the mainstream commercial industry. Leading this movement were Ritwik Ghatak and Mrinal Sen—like Ray, Bengalis; but unlike Ray, Marxists. Western audiences are familiar with the work of these directors, primarily because of their political views. Ghatak, in particular, influenced several young Marxist directors. Ghatak's most distinctive works are *Ajantrik* (*Pathetic Fallacy,* 1958) and *Jukti Takko Aar Gappo* (*Reason, Debate and Story,* 1974). Sen, the most prolific and experimental of the two, is best known for *Bhuvan Shome* (*Mr. Shome,* 1969), *Parasuram* (*Man with the Axe,* 1978), *Kharji* (*The Case Is Closed,* 1982), *Khandaar* (*The Ruins,* 1983), and *Antareen* (*The Confined,* 1993). Shyam Benegal's reputation as the most commercially successful director in the Parallel Cinema is largely due to his quartet of socially conscious films: *Ankur* (*The Seedling,* 1973), *Nishant* (*Night's End,* 1975), *Manthan* (*The Churning,* 1976), and *Bhumika* (*The Role,* 1977). He created a large body of documentaries, including two biographies: *Satyajit Ray, Filmmaker* (1985) and *Nehru* (1985).

The twenty regional cinemas of India—separate industries in virtually every major state that make movies in their own language—are marked by a vibrant diversity of aesthetic styles and political commitments. In the 1980s, for example, there was a resurgence of the Malayalam cinema of the state of Kerala, including films that appealed to an international audience, particularly Shaji N. Karun's *Piravi* (1989) and Rajiv Anchal's *Guru* (1997). Similar commercial success, both inside and outside India, has been made by some Tamil and Oriya films as well as by such commercial Hindi directors as Mira Nair, Nagsh Kukunoor, Nandita Das, and Sudhir Mishra. Bollywood has developed a new genre called Mumbai noir, urban films by such directors as Anurag Kashyap (*Black Friday,* 2004) and Deva Katta (*Prasthanam,* 2010). Finally, with such films as Homi Adajama's *Being Cyrus* (2005) and Sooni Taraporevala's *Little Zizou* (2009), the English-language cinema continues to be a part of India's multilanguage film industry. Indeed, Kashyap's two-part *Gangs of Wasseypur* (2010), a crime thriller about the Indian mafias' control of the coal industry, is, with its bold and murderous plot, the "Godfather" of the country's movies.

Contemporary Middle Eastern and North African Cinema

From its beginnings, cinema has been a part of the culture of many Middle Eastern and North African countries. But recent widespread civil unrest, revolution, and repression in these countries have had a negative impact on artistic freedom. This, as well as heavy restrictions and censorship by the governments of some of these countries—especially Iran—has not stopped the creation of serious movies, a large number of which were directed by women. Western films are often banned in these countries, leaving room for the development of a cinema rich in social, cultural, and political themes.

For the countries of Algeria, Egypt, Iraq, Iran, Israel, Lebanon, and Palestine, we have compiled a short list of contemporary films to introduce you to the work of directors who have earned a place in world cinema. Other Middle Eastern and North African countries—Bahrain, Jordan, Kuwait, Libya, Morocco, Oman, Saudi Arabia, Somalia, Sudan, Syria, Tunisia, Western Sahara, and Yemen—produce a comparatively smaller output of films that, in turn, are less well known in the West. Many excellent books are available to help you learn more about the films of all these countries.

Algeria *Days of Glory* (2006; director Rachid Bouchareb), *Masquerades* (2008; director Lyès Salem), and *Outside the Law* (2010; director Rachid Bouchareb).

Egypt *Sleepless Nights* (2003; director Hani Khalifa), *The Yacoubian Building* (2006; director Marwan Hamed), *Scheherazade, Tell Me a Story* (2009; director Yousry Nasrallah), and *Asmaa* (2011; director Amr Salama).

Iraq *Muhammad and Jane* (2003; director Usama Alshaibi), *Jani Gal* (2007; director Jamil Rostami), and *Son of Babylon* (2009; director Mohamed Al Daradji).

Iran *Offside* (2006; director Jafar Panahi), *Persepolis* (2007; directors Vincent Paronnaud and Marjane Satrapi), *Women without Men* (2009; directors Shirin Neshat and Shoja Azari), *Circumstance* (2011; director Maryam Keshavarz), *Like Someone in Love* (2012; director Abbas Kiarostami), and *This Is Not a Film* (2012; directors Jafar Panahi and Mojtaba Mirtahmasb). Mania Akbari, an Iranian filmmaker, has been self-exiled in

London since 2012, when the Iranian government severely tightened the restrictions on artists. Her distinctive, feminist view of Iranian society in movies where women's and family's issues are inextricably linked include *10 + 4* (2007), a sort of sequel to Abbas Kiarostami's *Ten* (2002), in which she starred; *One. Two. One* (2011); *In My Country Men Have Breasts* (2012); and *I Slept with My Mother, My Father, My Brother and My Sister in a Country Called Iran* (2012).

Israel *Meduzot* (2007; directors Shira Geffen and Etgar Keret), *The Band's Visit* (2001; director Eran Kolirin), and *Footnote* (2011; director Joseph Cedar).

Lebanon *Stray Bullet* (2010; director Georges Hachem), *Where Do We Go Now?* (2011; director Nadine Labaki), and *A Play Entitled Sehnsucht* (2011; director Roy Badran).

Palestine *Chronicle of a Disappearance* (1996; director Elia Suleiman), *A Ticket to Jerusalem* (2002; director Rashid Masharawi), and *Slingshot Hip Hop* (2008; director Jackie Reem Salloum).

Latin American Filmmaking

Many countries in Latin America—primarily Argentina, Brazil, Cuba, and Mexico—have produced movies since the silent era, when traveling exhibitions of work by the Lumière brothers and others captivated audiences there as elsewhere around the world. Today cinema is vibrant in those countries as well as in Chile, Costa Rica, Peru, and Venezuela. Historically, their subject matter was largely political and largely controlled by dictators and religious groups. But since the 1960s, directors have been able to turn to more personal stories concerning ordinary life and such previously taboo subjects as sex and sexual identity. While the sociopolitical foundations of these movies make them more influential within Latin America than in other countries, they are successful with audiences in theaters and at international festivals. We'll take a brief look at filmmaking in the four countries first mentioned.

Argentina A historical pattern emerges in Argentina that is applicable to filmmaking in almost every Latin American country: a pre-sound era consisting of experiments with cinematic technique and subject matter, fol-

lowed by a golden age of popular filmmaking and lapsing into the state-funded production of sociopolitical films. In Argentina that's not saying much in aesthetic terms, because the two major influences on the industry were the Catholic Church and the dictator Juan Perón and his wife Evita. The Argentine film industry made conventional crime dramas, comedies, and adaptations of literary classics, all still under the watchful eye of the church and state. The turmoil of the Perón years yielded little of cinematic quality, and the international community did not begin to pay attention until *The Hour of the Furnaces* (1968), a film by Octavio Getino and Fernando Solanas about the country's struggle for freedom from neocolonialism and violence. Along with Patricio Guzman's *The Battle of Chile* (1975–1979), Getino's movie established a template for future radical, revolutionary filmmaking across Latin America. Leopoldo Torre Nilsson's *The Revolution of the Seven Madmen* (1973) was also highly regarded by foreign audiences.

A tentative "New Cinema" was born in the 1960s and 1970s. After democracy was established in 1983, Argentine filmmakers began making serious movies about the country's turbulent past, including Jeanine Meerapfel's *The Friend* (1988), to name but one. Today, the movies in this country tackle a broader range of subjects—family dramas, love stories, and crime dramas. *The Secret in Their Eyes* (2009; director Juan José Campanella) won the Oscar for Best Foreign Language Film.

Brazil Here, the cinema developed to the point where its most unique actress, Carmen Miranda, appeared in Hollywood movies to great acclaim. Its success continued into the 1960s, when *Cinema Novo* ("New Cinema") was born in the spirit of Italian Neorealism and the French New Wave. The movement was deeply influenced by the political and aesthetic theories of director Glauber Rocha, whose most important movie is *Black God, White Devil* (1964). Its advocates included directors such as Carlos Diegues (*Bye Bye Brazil*, 1979) and Nelson Pereira dos Santos (*Memoirs of Prison*, 1984). Production of documentaries and experimental films flourished, as did the importance of female directors such as Carla Camurati, whose *Carlota Joaquina, Princess of Brazil* (1995), an offbeat look at Brazilian history, was a great success there and abroad.

Through the years, Brazilian cinema has been largely state supported, which accounts for its somewhat uneven history. When there's money, there are films, many of them good; but when the money dries up, so does creativity. Nonetheless, many Brazilian cinema has gained international recognition as well as an Oscar nomination for Best Foreign Language Film for *The Given Word* (1962; director Anselmo Duarte). In the years when state funding dried up, independent filmmakers tackled such problems as poverty and hunger—never very popular with the masses. When the support returned, it encouraged entrepreneurial filmmakers to produce movies with questionable value and importance to the country's film history. Today there is a revival of serious filmmaking, as seen in such works as *City of God* (2002; codirectors Fernando Meirelles and Kátia Lund) and Fernando Coimbra's *The Wolf at the Door* (2013).

Cuba Although the Cuban cinema was a significant industry, producing its own movies but relying heavily on Hollywood imports, it changed profoundly with the 1959 revolution led by Fidel Castro. Consistent with its Marxist principles—and adhering to Lenin's familiar remark, "cinema, for us, is the most important of the arts"—the Cuban government, in one of its first moves, established the Cuban Institute for Cinematographic Art and Industry (ICAIC) to encourage, improve, and support filmmaking at all levels.

Alfred Guevera, the father of modern Cuban cinema, headed the organization until 1980, when ideological differences between the Castro government and the ICAIC forced his ouster. (He returned later in a lesser capacity.) State funding has its price, and Cuban cinema suffered until it was revitalized by a movement known ironically as Imperfect Cinema. This experimental effort affected all aspects of Cuban filmmaking as long as it valued ideological content over aesthetic form. The party line remained dominant. But the movement's films were colorful, provocative, and very popular with the Cuban people, particularly those who supported the revolution and remained in the country. The movement died out in the mid-1970s. The end of this effort, coupled with the government's sharp reduction of production subsidies, had a negative effect on both the levels and quality of the Cuban cinema. It has been revitalized somewhat by international coproductions, especially with Mexico and Spain.

The 1959 revolution created a vast diaspora of disaffected Cubans (including many filmmakers) who emigrated to the United States and Latin American countries. There, they were free to make films critical of the Castro regime, and while these efforts did not have much impact in Cuba, some are well-known worldwide. These movies include Orlando Jiménez Leal's *The Other Cuba* (1983), *Amigos* (1986; director Iván Acosta), *Lejanía* (1985; director Jesús Diaz), and *Honey for Oshún* (2001; director Humberto Solás). Leal's *Improper Conduct* (1984; codirected by Néstor Almendros, one of the world's great cinematographers) focuses on the regime's imprisonment and mistreatment of dissidents and undesirables, particularly homosexuals. Other films on the plight of LGBT Cubans include *Strawberry and Chocolate* (1993; directors Tomás Gutiérrez Alea and Juan Carlos Tabío), which was nominated for an Oscar as Best Foreign Language Film. It's important to note that many talented Cuban exiles—writers, directors, cinematographers, and actors—have remained away from Cuba and enriched the international film world.

Other notable Cuban films—again more popular outside and than inside the country—are Tomás Gutiérrez Alea's *Memories of Underdevelopment* (1968), a brilliant film about a man who remains in Cuba rather than follow his family and friends into exile; Humberto Solás's *Lucía* (1969); and Miguel Coyula's *Memories of Overdevelopment* (2010). This movie, playing on Solás's film, concerns a man who leaves underdeveloped Cuba only to be confronted by the challenges in an overdeveloped United States.

Mexico Like other Latin American countries, Mexico had an early cinema as well as a golden age. It was dominated by film stars, such as Cantinflas and Dolores del Rio, who were also popular in the United States, and brought to the world's attention when the great Russian director Sergei Eisenstein began to make *Que Viva Mexico* there in 1931. He attempted an epic account of Mexico's history, but for various reasons it remained unfinished. Equally important, this film left a large Marxist influence on subsequent Mexican cinema. The country's films dominated the Latin American market during the 1940s, bringing attention to the early work of directors Emilio Fernández and Luis Buñuel, but this presence weakened in the 1960s and 1970s. Mexican directors had not yet found a voice for their national cinema, and audiences were distracted by popular American movies. But as we have seen, there was a fresh burst of innovative filmmaking after World War II in countries across the globe. In Mexico, the New Mexican Cinema was founded with the help of government support.

The success of this movement is seen in Arturo Ripstein's *No One Writes to the Colonel* (1999), based on a novel by Gabriel García Márquez; Alfonso Arau's *Like Water for Chocolate* (1992); Alfonso Cuarón's *Y Tu Mamá También* (2001); Guillermo del Toro's *The Devil's Backbone* (2001) and *Pan's Labyrinth* (2006); and Alejandro González Iñárritu's *Amores Perros* (2000), which not only introduced the popular actor Gael García Bernal but was also nominated for an Oscar as Best Foreign Language Film. Iñárritu was nominated as Best Director for *Babel* (2005) and is the first Mexican director to be in the running for that award. In 2015, his *Birdman,* or *The Unexpected Virtue of Ignorance* (2014), won nine Oscars, including Best Director and Best Picture. Iñárritu, Cuarón, and Del Toro have moved easily into the international filmmaking world. They have won major awards—as did Luis Buñuel, who worked primarily in Spain and France and was notable for his biting surrealist comedies such as *The Discreet Charm of the Bourgeoisie* (1972).

Gabriel Figueroa, a cinematographer, was another prominent Mexican film artist to achieve international fame. A superb artist, he shot dozens of important movies, including Emilio Fernández's *La Perla* (1947), Buñuel's *Los Olvidados* (1950) and *Simon of the Desert* (1965), and John Huston's *The Night of the Iguana* (1964) and *Under the Volcano* (1984). Many other Mexican film artists have also worked in Hollywood: they include cinematographers Rodrigo Prieto and Emmanuel Lubezki (who shot *Gravity* and several Terrence Malick movies), and actors Selma Hayek, Anthony Quinn, and Katy Jurado, among many others. Today Mexico continues to produce important movies with a social consciousness, including José Luis Valle's *Workers* (2013) and Amat Escalante's *Heli* (2013).

Finally, let's look briefly at films from other Latin American countries—Bolivia, Chile, Colombia, Haiti, Paraguay, and Peru. Widely varied in type and quality, these movies have achieved regional success and are beginning to be noticed worldwide. Many are concerned with local political issues, others with entertainment. A movie that is concerned with both is *Gloria* (2013; director Sebastián Lelio), about a middle-aged divorcée looking for some stability and love in a large Chilean city. Paulina Garcia plays the lead, who—even though she is attractive, has a good job, and is very independent—is eager to meet a man she can trust. The man who wins her heart turns out to be a rat—a lying, henpecked married man looking for some excitement. She bounces back from his deceit, though not without damage, and once more heads for the bar. We see her there, dancing to the Rolling Stones version of Van Morrison's "Gloria," sung in Italian by Umberto Tozzi. Just when you might begin to feel sorry for her, she changes the ball game. We can't make any assumptions about this mysterious, enigmatic person. And the actress is a marvel to watch.

The globalization of economies means the globalization of industries such as filmmaking. One result of this change is that great directors have influence both inside and outside their countries. They are truly international directors, and the list of those working today includes, among others, Bernardo Bertolucci (Italy), Nuri Bilge Ceylan (Turkey), Park Chan-wook (South Korea), Alfonso Cuarón (Mexico), Jean-Luc Godard (France), Michael Haneke (Germany), Roman Polanski (Poland, France), Steven Spielberg (USA), Quentin Tarantino (USA), and Béla Tarr (Hungary).

1965–1995: The New American Cinema

Twenty years after the end of the Second World War, the United States began to face political, cultural, and social challenges that were unprecedented in its history. It was now the most powerful and influential country in the world, yet it was locked with the Soviet Union in a "cold war." The next forty years would be marked by anti-Communist vehemence; the Korean War; the beginnings of the feminist, gay/lesbian/transgender, and environmental movements; the Vietnam War; and resolute antiwar and civil rights movements. There was also an unusually high level of violence, including the assassinations of President John F. Kennedy in 1963 and Senator Robert F. Kennedy and the Reverend Martin Luther King Jr. in 1968; the killing of four Kent State University students, who were protesting the Vietnam War, by the Ohio National Guard in 1970; assassination attempts on Presidents Gerald Ford and Ronald Reagan and Pope John Paul II; and terrorist attacks on the World Trade Center in 1993 and an Oklahoma City courthouse in 1995. Other major events included the U.S. landing on the moon, the beginnings of a vibrant popular music culture, the Watergate crisis, and the resignation in disgrace in 1974 of President Richard M. Nixon. The 1980s saw the emergence of the AIDS virus, and in 1991 the Soviet Union collapsed.

Against such a fast-moving, turbulent background, it is not surprising that a New American Cinema emerged. The "new" Hollywood encompasses too many transitions from the "old" Hollywood to be simply called a movement. In describing the changes that affected the American film industry—and the resulting ripples that spread throughout the international film community—the term *phenomenon* is both more accurate and appropriate. These changes were hastened by the collapse of the old studio system, which was replaced by scattered enterprises known as "independent filmmakers." This event had both negative and positive implications.

The negative factors included declining audiences, caused in part by competition from television; the escalating costs of producing films independently rather than in the studios, where the permanent physical and human support structure was very cost-effective; and the forced retirement or relocation of studio personnel. However, these were outweighed by the positive factors. The new Hollywood adapted conventions of classical genres to conform to new modes of expression and meet audience expectations, abandoned the code for a new rating system, and did more shooting on location; the result was a more authentic look for the movies.

Furthermore, though the studios retained their names and kept their production facilities open to ensure the smoothness of the established preproduction/production/postproduction matrix, they have changed ownership frequently over the years. Movies are now made in complex deals involving the studios and independent production companies headed by individual producers, many of whom invested capital in their own work. The "star machine" collapsed as well, ushering in decades of new talent whose careers, which once would have been meticulously planned and monitored, were now subject to market forces. Marketing of movies remained a precise tool, carefully adapted to meet the needs of new audiences.

A positive effect of this transition was the increase in audience members who, because of college film-study classes and an overall greater awareness of film, had a better understanding of cinematic conventions than their parents and were attracted to films by a new breed of American directors, also trained in university film schools. With the old labor-dominated system gone,

Stranger Than Paradise: a milestone in the New American Cinema

Jim Jarmusch's *Stranger Than Paradise* (1984) did more than any other movie to define the New American Cinema. It tells a distinctly American story; it was made in a fresh, easy style clearly influenced by American movies as well as the new waves in European and Asian cinema; and it was produced by a film-school graduate using funds from various sources, both American and foreign. Although unusual in production, form, and content, this art film was surprisingly successful at the box office. It is a distinctly marginal effort, but in winning the Cannes Film Festival prize for best first feature, it encouraged independent filmmakers and the reception of their work. *Stranger Than Paradise* was shot in a series of long takes, which are structured into three stages of a journey undertaken by three offbeat travelers. They are Willie (John Lurie), a hipster living in New York City; his cousin Eva (Eszter Balint), who comes from Hungary to visit him and their aunt in Ohio; and Willie's friend Eddie (Richard Edson). Eva's visit to New York is the first stage; the second, which takes place a year later, recounts a trip that Willie and Eddie make to Cleveland to visit Eva and the aunt; and the third stage follows them to the "paradise" of Florida. Their travels through the bleak landscape, shot in washed-out black and white, ultimately show that they are going nowhere, but they have a good time, and so do we. Here, we see the trio in Florida—(*left to right*) Eddie, Eva, and Willie—putting on their new sunglasses so they can look like "real tourists."

producers could hire artists from anywhere in the world, and American production was greatly enhanced by their contributions. Finally, to seal the death of the "old" Hollywood, New York and other cities in the United States and Canada emerged as thriving centers of film production.

Unlike the French New Wave, the New American Cinema was not born in theory but rather out of the more practical need to adapt to the values of its time. However, like the French New Wave, the prevailing spirit was innovation. But with so many auteurs, some from the old Hollywood and some from film schools, no single defining style emerged. Indeed, there was a range of styles, resulting in personal, highly self-reflexive films; edgy, experimental, low-budget movies; movies that played homage to great European directors; and, of course, those that still adhered to the conventions of the golden age. Thus diversity and quality are the only links among such directors as Woody Allen, Robert Altman, Tim Burton, John Cassavetes, Joel and Ethan Coen, Francis Ford Coppola, Brian De Palma, Clint Eastwood, George Roy Hill, Jim Jarmusch, Diane Keaton, Stanley Kubrick, Spike Lee, Sidney Lumet, David Lynch, Terrence Malick, Gordon Parks, Sam Peckinpah, Roman Polanski, John Sayles, Paul Schrader, Martin Scorsese, Steven Spielberg, and Gus Van Sant. Typical of Hollywood, males outnumber females. But that ratio is changing. In a reversal of the Hollywood tradition, female as well as African American, Hispanic, and Asian directors have begun to write and direct movies.

Their guiding principle was not to discard cinematic conventions, but adapt them to the new audience. In terms of content, the most noticeable changes were in the predominance of sex and violence and in the nature of the protagonists, both male and female. To quote film historians Bruce F. Mast and Gerald Kawin, "In most cases, the protagonists . . . were social misfits, deviates, or outlaws; the villains were the legal, respectable defenders of society. The old bad guys became the good guys; the old good guys, the bad guys."[17] In a further twist of traditional gender roles, the female protagonists in two of the most distinctive movies of the period, Arthur Penn's *Bonnie and Clyde* (1967) and Roman Polanski's *Chinatown* (1974)—both insightful analyses of America in the 1930s—were as evil as the men, if not more so. Although sex and violence still dominate U.S. movies, there is a large, appreciative audience for films that tackle the other serious issues that once were mainly the province of foreign movies that played only in small "art houses."

Regarding form, the strongest influences were such contemporary directors as Ingmar Bergman, Michelangelo Antonioni, Orson Welles, Jean-Luc Godard, and François Truffaut. Plots became more complex in structure and embodied new storytelling techniques. For example, Penn's *Bonnie and Clyde* (1967) tells the story of

Femmes fatales in the New American Cinema

Faye Dunaway stars in two of the most important movies of the New American Cinema: Arthur Penn's *Bonnie and Clyde* (1967) and Roman Polanski's *Chinatown* (1974). As Bonnie Parker [1], she participates fully in a bank robbery with two other members of the fearless, violent Barrow gang: (*left to right*) Buck Barrow (Gene Hackman) and Clyde Barrow (Warren Beatty). In *Chinatown*, she plays Evelyn Mulwray [2], the neurotic, scheming liar who tries to outwit J. J. Gittes (Jack Nicholson, *pictured left*). In both cases, thanks in part to the rising feminist movement, these characters are at least the equals of their male counterparts. But Dunaway is also beautiful and seductive, preserving the role of the classic film noir femme fatale.

two notorious bank robbers that could have been taken from a 1930s Hollywood model. The audience easily read it as a comic/tragic parable of violent, amoral dissent against an authoritarian social order. Its style reflects not only the director's experience as a Hollywood veteran but also the dynamic of Eisenstein's montage and the surprise of Kurosawa's slow-motion violence.

Stories became palpably more sexual and violent in such movies as Penn's *Bonnie and Clyde* (1967), Dennis

17. Mast and Kawin, *A Short History of the Movies*, p. 517.

The Wild Bunch: blood bath and beyond[18]

The New American Cinema ushered in a wave of movies as famous for good stories and superb filmmaking as they were for sex and violence. Director Sam Peckinpah, nicknamed "Bloody Sam," is noted for a string of graphically violent movies, including *The Wild Bunch* (1969), *Straw Dogs* (1971), and *Bring Me the Head of Alfredo Garcia* (1974). His brand of stylized violence reflects the influence of Arthur Penn's *Bonnie and Clyde* (1967) and in turn influenced many Hong Kong action movies as well as a host of American directors whose films include violent action—Martin Scorsese, Brian De Palma, and Francis Ford Coppola. At the conclusion of *The Wild Bunch*, the American gang of the title attempts to claim one of its men from Mapache, a Mexican rebel leader; when Mapache kills the man, he provokes one of the bloodiest battles in movie history. In an impressively choreographed gunfight between the rebel army and the gang members, most of the characters are killed, including the gang's leader, Pike (William Holden). While manning a vicious machine gun, Pike is struck by a bullet fired by a boy and dies in blood-drenched action.

Hopper's *Easy Rider* (1969), Peter Bogdanovich's *The Last Picture Show* (1969), Sam Peckinpah's *The Wild Bunch* (1969), Bob Rafelson's *Five Easy Pieces* (1970), and Terrence Malick's *Badlands* (1973). Continuity editing remained the norm, but there was an increased use of such techniques as jump cuts, split screens, slow and fast motion, simulated "grainy" documentary footage, and a mixture of color and black-and-white footage. Stanley Kubrick's *2001: A Space Odyssey* (1968) used very long takes and an absence of editing that calls attention to itself to introduce us to outer space, where time shifts in unfamiliar ways.

Cinematography also adapted as more films were shot on location rather than soundstages, and the old Hollywood ideal of visual perfection gave way to a depiction of recognizable actuality. A new generation of cinematographers—including Néstor Almendros, John Alonzo, Conrad Hall, Geoffrey Unsworth, Haskell Wexler, Gordon Willis, and Vilmos Zsigmond, to name but a few—brought a familiarity with European techniques in framing, lighting, camera movement, shot duration, and, especially, an experimental approach to color. Under the particular influence of such directors as Coppola and Lucas, there was also major experimentation with sound design, multichannel sound recording and reproduction, including the Dolby Digital system. Orchestral-type scores gave way to popular music, whose sounds and lyrics often more directly underscore a movie's action. Finally, for actors there a seismic shift from the highly groomed stars of the studio system to a large influx of new actors and a definite reliance on naturalistic acting styles.

In addition to these new directions in the narrative film, important advances took place in documentary

18. "Blood Bath and Beyond" is the title of A. O. Scott's review in the *New York Times* of Quentin Tarantino's *Kill Bill: Vol. 1* (October 10, 2003).

1

2

Documentary and experimental films as pure cinema

Both Albert and David Maysles's *Grey Gardens* (1975) [1] and Stan Brakhage's *Dog Star Man* (1962–64) [2] stand out in their respective fields—documentary and experimental films—as superb examples of cinematic form. *Grey Gardens* is a candid, intimate, and often funny look into the lives of two extraordinary women who live together: Mrs. Edith Beale ("Big Edie") and her unmarried daughter, Edith ("Little Edie"). The filmmakers (directors-as-editors) let the film's content shape its form. The women constantly bicker and disagree with one another, so the editing pattern, which juxtaposes the women with each other—the younger woman with the older—creates a line between them and their views of the past and the present. The audience is left to put the pieces together and decide the nature of this power struggle. *Dog Star Man*, like *Grey Gardens*, does not fit a categorical mold, although it is considered a classic experimental film. Stan Brakhage's techniques include superimposing four sequences at once—a kind of visual juxtaposition similar to that used by the director-editors of *Grey Gardens* in creating multiple meanings—and cutting into the frame to add new material to it. Both movies are pure cinema: work that explores the meaning and experiments with potential of the medium, challenging our perceptions. Films such as these help us understand that the work of Stanley Kubrick, another maverick director, is also pure cinema. They involve, to quote the title of one of Brakhage's films, "the act of seeing with our own eyes."

film—notably in Direct Cinema, essentially an American adaptation of *cinéma vérité* (by such filmmakers as Robert Drew, Albert and David Maysles, and Don Alan Pennebaker)—and in experimental films by such artists as Andy Warhol, Ken Jacobs, Bruce Baillie, Carolee Schneemann, Stan Brakhage, and Hollis Frampton. Of late, feature-length animated films have thrived as never before. All of these efforts have had a liberating influence on mainstream filmmaking.

In the arena of industry economics and practices, American cinema saw many new independent producers, a new financing system by which actors independently arranged their contracts and compensation, a new rating system, and the ability of consumers to rent, buy, or stream movies for home screenings. Combined, these had an impact on production, distribution, exhibition, and profits.

The New American Cinema is significant for these many changes, both large and small, that have transformed the complete structure of the American film industry. Such redefinition and reorganization constitutes a new era, comparable in many ways to the golden age. It is dependent on tradition, eager for innovation, adapts to new audiences, and always keeps its eye on the bottom line.

Film history presents an impressive record of achievement, ranging from the first modest efforts to record images on film to the sophisticated movies of today. Even as photography has remained the basis of cinema, in a little more than one hundred years film artists, technicians, and businesspeople have proved themselves flexible enough to meet, with innovative responses, each challenge facing the medium.

When audiences demanded movies with stories as complex as those in the novel and theater, the industry developed the full-length narrative film. When the public wanted to hear actors speak as they did on the stage, the industry was transformed with sound recording. And so it goes with other innovations: color film stock, images with greater width and depth, genres to please virtually any audience, and a star system that created every conceivable type of actor. At the same time, major improvements were made in the techniques of cinematography, editing, special effects, acting, and sound recording as well as in new cameras, lenses, film stocks, lighting equipment, and editing devices.

Today's artists continue to create new techniques, technologies, and cinematic conventions. They work not just in Hollywood, London, Paris, or Berlin but also in Calcutta, Tokyo, Hong Kong, and Moscow—indeed, in virtually every country and culture in the world. The result—a cinematic language that is universally understood—enables the films of Satyajit Ray, Ingmar Bergman, Steven Soderbergh, Michelangelo Antonioni, or Andrei Tarkovsky to reach an international audience.

The historical development of film is a dynamic process that has created a constantly evolving art form. As you will see in Chapter 11, the systems of production have kept pace with this aesthetic evolution. In this short history of the movies, we emphasize the films that explore every aspect of this language and in many cases are regarded as cinematic masterpieces. However, not all movies are masterpieces. Like novelists, painters, or composers, film artists can produce work that is mediocre. But despite their weaknesses, such films please vast audiences and produce the profits that make the film industry a vital part of the world's economy. The history of the movies reveals, among many other things, that art and commerce can coexist.

Looking at *Citizen Kane* and Its Place in Film History

When you finish this chapter, you will be familiar with the major trends in form and content shaping film history worldwide. In looking at some of the movies that have made this possible, you will know what made them important. And you may also come across the fact that, for many years, Orson Welles's *Citizen Kane* (1941) was considered "the best movie of all time." That conclusion represents the views of hundreds of international filmmakers, critics, and scholars and is one measure of its global influence. How can that be, when the movie is so *old*? When you may never have heard of it? There are obviously many things we want you to learn from this book, and one of them is to evaluate a movie not by its age but rather by its quality within the cinematic art as a whole (in other words, film history). There is something judgmental about *old* that has little place in a discussion of art.

Citizen Kane is important to your study of the movies because, within the borders of film history—1895 to the present—it marks a major turning point between the films produced before it and those produced after. To say that Welles revolutionized moviemaking is no understatement. Since the 1950s, when his movie became familiar worldwide, dozens of young people have said that they became filmmakers because of Welles's approach in *Citizen Kane*. The movie's influence can be measured not necessarily by the specific cinematic effects in the films that followed (although that is often quite apparent), but rather by how it transformed people's overall thinking about making movies. Thus we began to talk favorably about the Wellesian aspects of certain films, whether that influence is in the cinematography, sound recording, or editing.

But you can't know this about *Citizen Kane*, and you certainly can't understand it, unless you've seen a few of its predecessor films and become familiar with their cinematic conventions. To do this, give yourself an enjoyable crash course by looking at *You Can't Take It with You* (1938; director Frank Capra), *Stagecoach* (1939; director John Ford), *Rebecca* (1940; director Alfred Hitchcock), and *The Maltese Falcon* (1941; director John Huston). Then, in that context, watch *Citizen Kane*.

Although most critics loved it, the movie was so unpopular with contemporary audiences that it virtually disappeared until the early 1950s, when the French New Wave filmmakers discovered it and declared it a masterpiece. For those contemporary audiences, what set *Citizen Kane* apart from the movies that they knew? Let's answer by describing it in light of the elements of cinematic form we emphasize: narrative, mise-en-scène, cinematography, acting, editing, and sound.

The movie's story, while in the familiar biography genre, is not told in a conventional manner. Instead of a chronological plot that follows Charles Foster Kane from his impoverished youth to his status as one of the world's richest and most powerful men, it begins with his death and works its way backward and forward in his life through a series of interviews with people who knew him. This approach was so influential for French director Jean-Luc Godard that it could have been the source of his memorable remark: "A story should have a beginning, a middle and an end, but not necessarily in that order." Welles's handling of cinematic time broke the mold—indeed, many people were confused by this and walked out. But today it's commonplace for a movie to cut seamlessly between past, present, and future, and not necessarily in that order—a legacy from *Citizen Kane*.

Its mise-en-scène owes far more to the theater than the movies, using an art form that Welles helped revolutionize before going to Hollywood to make his first movie. A major difference between looking at movies and looking at theater is that, in the former, audiences are accustomed to the frequent use of close-ups; in the latter, they see two or more people on the stage most of the time. But Welles also wanted depth in his sets, and so he used deep-focus cinematography to capture a pictorial depth that effectively allowed actors to move around the set whenever and however they wanted. This way of shooting also opens up the power of the long take to record this movement in depth as well as enables the actors to produce an entire scene uninterrupted by editing. Previous directors had used deep-focus cinematography in a limited way to achieve limited results, but Welles's achievement overshadowed all of those efforts. No longer would audiences see actors working chiefly in the foreground; now they moved easily from fore- to background. Today, picturing depth (including the increasing use of 3-D technology) surprises no one; indeed, we expect it, because it's how the human eye sees naturally. Despite some experiments, no directors before Welles used deep-space composition and deep-focus cinematography in such sustained creative brilliance as Welles. That, too, is another reason for the importance of *Citizen Kane*.

In his editing and sound, Welles also broke away from Hollywood conventions. He shot the film in the usual Hollywood way (nonchronologically), but instead of editing it into a chronological format, he devised an elaborate flashback structure that posed great challenges for editing the footage and establishing rhythm. For the sound, he called on his vast radio experience to emphasize the immediacy and spontaneity of every scene. Except for Bernard Herrmann's musical score, most sounds come from the world of the story. Although the prevailing convention in Hollywood in 1940 was to re-record in the studio virtually all sound that had first been recorded on the set, Welles insisted on direct sound recording made on the set. He was certainly not the first to do this, but the design of the setting itself—allowing for hidden microphones to catch every sound—helped considerably to make it work smoothly. The sound includes single and overlapping voices, music, and ambient sounds. He also uses sounds to help transitions from shot to shot and scene to scene, to define the *space* and the characters' placement within the mise-en-scène, and, when it is synchronous with the action, to help to represent *time*.

Welles's innovations had their roots, but not their equivalents, in previous film history. He built on the work of others, extending, refining, and redefining techniques. He is one of cinema's greatest directors because he had the vision to do something differently and the talent to inspire collaborators to experiment and help him realize that vision. While countless directors adopted and refined those innovations, they claim him as their master, and many others say it was his example that encouraged them to become filmmakers. His innovations in *Citizen Kane* had their influence almost immediately in changing the look, sound, and overall effect of Hollywood movies. And though it lacks many of the features audiences expect today—color, widescreen, 3-D, fast-paced action, violence, and sex—many of its aspects make it a classic. These include a timeless story of egomania, greed, and cruelty; brilliant use of the flashback to tell that story; and an unforgettable look. Today, nearly seventy-five years after its release, *Citizen Kane* is the one movie you must know if you are to understand film history. Is it the best movie in the history of cinema? That's up to you to decide. But one thing is certain: it's the movie that changed the movies forever.

ANALYZING FILM HISTORY

From this short history of the movies, we can reach several conclusions. First, the movies—in their formal qualities, modes of expression, technologies, and audiences—have changed radically in the course of little more than a hundred years. Second, in many cases, the artists, technicians, and businesspeople responsible for these changes adapted or perfected the achievements of previous filmmakers to reach the next level of development. Third, working in different countries and cultures, they produced an art that spoke to a diverse audience in a cinematic language that was universally understood. While there are obviously other common threads unifying the complex course of film history, these should encourage you—when you become excited about a particular movie—to learn more about its place in film history (if it's an older film) or to be alert to a contemporary movie's explicit or implicit connection to other eras of film history and/or particular movies in that history. As you continue to look at movies, whether in class or on your own, you will see the rewards of appreciating, say, a 1927 masterpiece for what it is, where it came from, and how it influenced subsequent film history rather than thinking of it merely as an "old" movie. Likewise, you will also be able to appreciate the latest release for what it is, identifying how those who made it were influenced by past masters as well as what they contributed that seems new. With this approach, you'll understand that there are no "old" or "new" movies, just a continuum of innovation and tradition composed of those movies that we treasure and others that we'd rather forget.

SCREENING CHECKLIST: FILM HISTORY

☐ As you study a particular film or filmmaker, explore their historical context. What year was it made? Who was likely to have seen it? What elements of the historical context are reflected in the film itself?

☐ What is the film's aesthetic context? Is it part of a film movement or a reaction to prevailing tradition of the period? How does it measure up to the ideals of the movement? How does it compare or contrast with the era's mainstream aesthetic?

☐ Consider the history of the filmmakers who created the movie. Does the director have a recognizable style or pattern of subjects? How does this film fit into that pattern? How has the cinematographer approached the subject, and is it different from past work? How does the costume design reflect both the period depicted on-screen and the era when the film was made?

☐ Does the film depict a notable moment in history, like the Great Depression, Watergate, or 9/11? Learn as much as you can about the historical context. What does the film portray of these eras? What does it leave out? Does it seem "accurate"? If not, in what way?

☐ Does the film seem notable for its innovations in cinematic language or technology? Have you seen antecedents to it in other films? Have you seen its influence on films that followed? Who created the innovation (the director, the sound designer, etc.)?

☐ Does the film deal with a topic, such as gay rights, differently than the films that preceded or followed it? Can you trace how the presentation of its subject on film has changed over time?

Questions for Review

1. What is meant by the term *film history*? Why is a knowledge of it invaluable in looking at movies and analyzing them?
2. What are the four traditional approaches to film history? What are the specific concerns of each?
3. What stylistic movements made cinematic innovations that, as a result, changed the course of film history?
4. The simplest approach to film history is to divide it into the eras of silent and sound production. What was the general state of filmmaking in each of these periods, and how and why does that explain the way movies were made?
5. What (a) was the state of moviemaking in the golden age of the American studio system in the late 1930s, and (b) what film(s) besides Orson Welles's *Citizen Kane* (1941) had a profound effect on filmmakers following its release? What effect(s) did they have?
6. What are the principal differences between the following sets of stylistic movements? (a) German Expressionism and Soviet Silent Montage; (b) the classical Hollywood style and the New American Cinema; and (c) Italian Neorealism and the French New Wave.
7. The term *New Wave* is used to describe many film movements after the Second World War. What are several of these movements, and what general stylistic characteristics do they have in common?
8. Who, in your understanding, are three of the most innovative and influential directors in film history? What are their contributions?
9. Of the historic events occurring since the invention of the movies, which were most influential in providing subject matter for the movies? Discuss at least two events, and identify two movies for each event.
10. From the "prehistory" of the movies, what are the key technological innovations that made the movies possible? Who were three important inventors or innovators, what did they accomplish, and in what countries did they work?

300 (2006; director Zack Snyder)

HOW THE MOVIES ARE MADE

11

Money, Methods, and Materials: The Whole Equation

The art of the movies—the primary concern of this book—is inseparable from its business practices, film-making technologies, and production systems. In his novel *The Last Tycoon*, F. Scott Fitzgerald attempted to explain how Hollywood works:

> You can take Hollywood for granted like I did, or you can dismiss it with the contempt we reserve for what we don't understand. It can be understood too, but only dimly and in flashes. Not half a dozen men have ever been able to keep the whole equation of pictures in their heads.[1]

In fact, however, that equation is simple: moviemaking is, above all, a moneymaking enterprise.[2]

In the movie industry, costs and profits can be measured in hundreds of millions of dollars. Today's feature films cost anywhere from $1 million (e.g., *Transcendence*, 2014; director Wally Pfister) to $424 million (*Avatar*, 2009; director James Cameron). The cost of producing the "average" film is roughly $50 to $200 million, plus 50 percent of those costs for marketing and distribution. So, a $150 million movie will cost $225 million before it earns anything. Thus the individuals and financial institutions that invest in the production of films, and the producers and studios they invest in, care first about money (ensuring the safety and potential return of their investments) and second—often a distant second—about art. They focus on movies as commodities. For that reason, they often consider release dates, distribution, and marketing as more important than the products themselves. In view of this reality, it is all the more impressive, then, that the movie industry produces a small number of films each year that can be appreciated, analyzed, and interpreted as genuine works of art rather than simply as commercial products to be consumed.

Why do films cost so much? It's like everything else: labor and materials. Today's films (particularly blockbuster films) require hundreds of people at all levels of the actual production who are trained to use highly advanced digital technology. The next time you look at the rolling credits at the end of an action movie, you'll see dozens of job titles that did not exist before digital filmmaking. And the more Hollywood gives the audience, the more the audience wants, so when the industry adds such features as screening in the 3-D or IMAX formats, it is generating audience excitement but also increasing ticket prices.

Because movie production involves a much more complicated and costly process than do most other artistic endeavors, very few decisions are made lightly. Unlike some arts—painting, for example—in which the materials and the process are relatively inexpensive, every decision in filmmaking has significant financial ramifications. Painters may paint over pictures many times without incurring steep costs, so their decisions can be dictated almost entirely by artistic inspiration. Movies, in contrast, involve a constant tug-of-war between artistic vision and profitability.

A great movie generally requires two key ingredients: a good script and a director's inspiration, vision, intelligence, and supervision (but not necessarily control) of all aspects of the film's production. Because the director plays the paramount role in the production process and in most cases has final authority over the result, we ordinarily cite a film in this way: Sam Mendes's

1. F. Scott Fitzgerald, *The Last Tycoon: An Unfinished Novel* (New York: Scribner's, 1941), p. 3.

2. David Thomson takes a nonfiction approach to defining the equation in *The Whole Equation: A History of Hollywood* (New York: Knopf, 2005).

Skyfall (2012). But although movie history began with staunchly individual filmmakers, movies have been carried forward through the years by teamwork. From the moment the raw film stock is purchased through its exposure, processing, editing, and projection, filmmakers depend on a variety of artists, technologies, technicians, and craftspeople. And no matter how clear filmmakers' ideas may be at the start, their work will change considerably, thanks to technology and teamwork, between its early stages and the final version released to the public.

Many movie directors—working under such pressures as producers' schedules and budgets—have been known for taking their power all too seriously. They are difficult on the set, throw tantrums, scream at and even physically assault members of the cast and crew, and rag at the front office. Still, moviemaking is essentially a collaborative activity.[3] Even then, as film scholar Jon Lewis observes, "What ends up on the screen is not only a miracle of persistence and inspiration but also the result of certain practical concessions to the limitations of the studio system."[4]

Film production is complicated by the cost-effective, standard practice of shooting movies out of chronological order. This means that the production crew shoots the film not in the order of what we see on the screen, but in an order that allows the most efficient use of human and financial resources. During production, a script supervisor stays as close to the director as possible, for this person is an invaluable source of information about the shooting. The script supervisor records all details of continuity from shot to shot; he or she ascertains that costumes, positioning and orientation of objects, and placement and movement of actors are consistent in each successive shot and, indeed, in all parts of the film.

Overall, the pattern of production includes securing and developing a story with audience appeal; breaking the story into units that can be shot most profitably; shooting; establishing through editing the order in which events will appear on-screen; and then adding the sound, music, and special effects that help finish the movie. The use of a video assist camera permits a director to review each take immediately after shooting, when it is much easier to match details from shot to shot.

The process once took place in the vast, factory-like studios that dominated Hollywood and other major film-production centers around the world. Today it happens in the self-contained worlds of individual production units, which often operate in leased studio facilities.

The differences between these two modes of production are, in a sense, reflected in movies' production credits. In older films, all the (brief) production credits generally appear at the beginning, and the names of the leading actors are sometimes repeated in (and constitute) the closing credits. Today opening credits vary widely, but closing credits are lengthy and often include hundreds of names, accounting for virtually everyone who worked on the film or had something to do with it (e.g., caterers, animal handlers, accountants). Collective-bargaining agreements between producers and various labor unions—representing every person who works on a union production—impose clear definitions of all crewmembers' responsibilities as well as the size and placement of their screen credits. These credits properly and legally acknowledge people's contributions to films.[5]

This chapter introduces readers to the history of motion-picture technologies and production systems, showing that Hollywood is very much a product of its past. Today's Hollywood reflects how well the industry has adapted to the challenges of changing content, technologies, audiences, and exhibition opportunities. It remains one of the world's largest industries, and the impact of American movies is felt around the globe. Today Hollywood faces major challenges, most of which will be decided almost entirely on the relationship between costs and profits, the only equation (see "Production in Hollywood Today," on pp. 483–489).

To understand certain aesthetic judgments made by film producers, directors, and their collaborators, you should be familiar with the fundamentals of how a

3. Insights into the long hours and hard work that go into movie production are provided in movies about making movies. Such films show us that, in a world of large egos, collaboration can be a myth and many things go wrong on most movie sets. See also Rudy Behlmer and Tony Thomas, *Hollywood's Hollywood: The Movies about the Movies* (Secaucus, NJ: Citadel, 1975).

4. Jon Lewis, *Whom God Wishes to Destroy . . . : Francis Coppola and the New Hollywood* (Durham, NC: Duke University Press, 1995), p. 4.

5. Because nonunion crews make many independent films, these conventions of the division of labor and screen credit do not necessarily apply to independent films. Often on such films, crew members may be relatively inexperienced, not yet qualified for union membership, or unwilling to play several roles in return for the experience and screen credit. Government agencies and volunteer individuals or organizations may also be credited for their contributions.

movie is made—in particular, with the two filmmaking technologies (film and digital) and the three phases of the moviemaking process (preproduction, production, and postproduction).

Film and Digital Technologies: An Overview

Here, we cover the two major technologies used in film-making at a time when the film industry is undergoing a costly conversion from film to digital technology. This conversion has created significant opposition, but at this writing, it remains clear that digital has won. Even though *film stock* and *film projectors* may not be familiar items to some readers—and, indeed, may one day be obsolete—we believe it is useful to describe briefly what is involved in film and digital technologies, both of which are currently in use.

Looking at movies is more about what is on the screen than the technology that is unique to this art form. And since that technology is far less complicated than you might think, knowing something about it should further enhance your understanding of how movies are made. Motion-picture technology—and the production systems it serves—has developed in a simple, straight line from the early 1890s until recently.

Film Technology

When we refer to film technology, we mean that film stock is the medium on which the image is recorded. Film is an **analog** medium in which the camera (1) creates an image by recording through a camera lens the original light given off by the subject, and (2) stores this image on a roll of negative film stock. That stock, coated with an emulsion containing silver crystals, yields an image that closely resembles what the human eye sees. We call it *analog* because the image is analogous, or proportional, to the input. Put another way, once the film is processed (or "developed"), the negative image (on the negative stock) becomes a positive image (on positive stock); the first image is analogous to the second.

Unlike the newer technologies, film involves a mechanical system that moves this film stock through several machines: a camera, a processor, and a projector. These three machines bring images to the screen in three distinct stages, and light plays a vital role throughout.

In the first stage, **shooting**, the camera exposes film to light, allowing that radiant energy to burn a negative image onto each frame. These single, discrete images are shot at a standard (for theatrical movies, anyway) 24 frames per second. In the second stage, **processing**, the negative is developed into a positive print that the filmmaker can then screen in order to plan the editing, a process that produces the final print. In the third stage, **projecting**, the final print is run through a projector, which shoots through the film a beam of light intense enough to reverse the initial process and project a large image on the movie screen. (This account greatly condenses the entire process to emphasize, at this point, only the cycle of light common to all three stages.)

Projecting a strip of exposed frames at the same speed—traditionally 16 frames per second (fps) for silent film, 24 fps for sound—creates the illusion of movement. Silent cameras and projectors were often hand-cranked, and so the actual speed of the camera, which then had to be matched by the projectionist, might vary from 12 to 24 fps. Cameras and projectors used for making and exhibiting professional films are powered by electric motors that ensure perfect movement of the film (Figure 11.1). As digital technology replaces this mechanical process (Figure 11.2), it is changing the equipment and media on which the images are captured, processed, and projected. But the role of light remains the same essential component.

A movie film's **format** is the gauge, or width, of the film stock and its perforations (measured in millimeters) and the size and shape of the image frame as seen on the screen (Figure 11.3). Formats extend from Super 8mm through 70mm and beyond into such specialized formats as IMAX (ten times bigger than a conventional 35mm frame and three times bigger than a standard 70mm frame). The format chosen depends on the type of film being made, the financing available to support the project, and the overall visual look that the filmmaker wants to achieve. For example, a low-key, fairly low-budget, and intimate narrative film (such as Phil Morrison's *Junebug* [2005]) might be shot in 16mm or 35mm format, but an action-filled, broad, and expensive nonfiction film (such as Luc Jacquet's *March of the Penguins* [2005]) might require a 70mm or IMAX format. The **film-stock length** is the number of feet (or meters) or the number of reels being used in a particular film. The **film-stock speed** (or *exposure index*) indicates the degree to which the film is light-sensitive. This speed ranges from very fast, at which the film requires little

Figure 11.1 | THE MOTION-PICTURE CAMERA

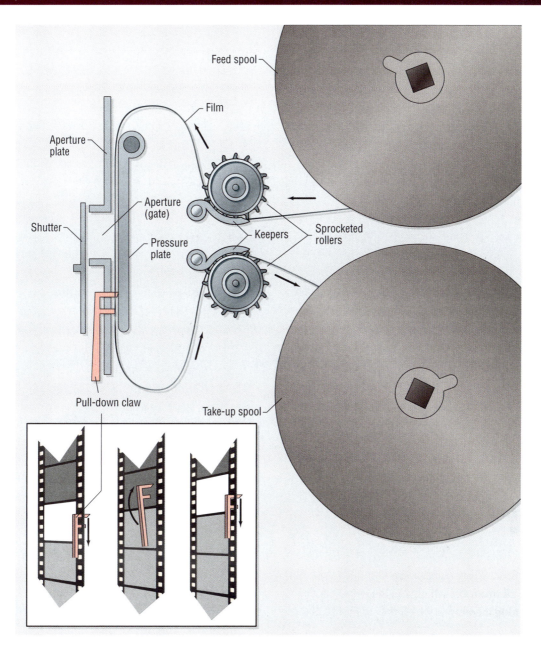

The motion-picture camera moves unexposed film from one storage area, called the **feed spool** (or, in professional cameras today, the portion of the magazine that stores unexposed film), along the **sprocketed rollers**. The rollers control the speed of the film as it moves through the camera and toward the lens, which focuses the image on the film as it is exposed. The **aperture** (or gate) is essentially the window through which each frame of film is exposed. The **shutter**—a mechanism that shields the film from light while each frame is moved into place—is synchronized with the motion of the **pull-down claw**, a mechanism used in both cameras and projectors to advance the film frame by frame. The pull-down claw holds each frame still for the fraction of a second that the shutter allows the aperture to be open so that the film can be exposed. The **take-up spool** (or, again, the portion of the magazine that stores exposed film) winds the film after it has been exposed.

Figure 11.2 | THE DIGITAL MOVIE CAMERA

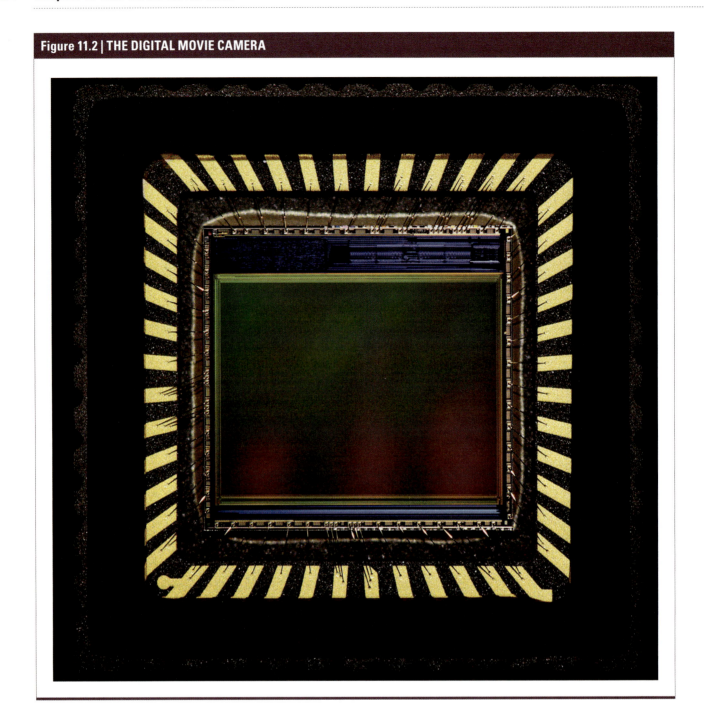

light, to very slow, at which it requires a lot of light. Film is also categorized into black-and-white and color stock.

In traditional film production, cinematographers control the photographic image in many ways: with their choice of stock; the amount and color of the lighting of each shot, the **exposure** (the length of time that the film is exposed to light), and the opening of the lens aperture (this regulates the amount of light that passes through the lens onto the surface of the film); the **resolution** (the capacity of the camera lens, film stock, and processing to provide fine detail in an image); the instructions provided to the processing laboratory, including special effects; and in the postproduction effort, through possible involvement in the editing process.

Professional motion-picture photography is a complex, time-consuming, and expensive process, but many filmmakers think it's worth it because it is the only way they can achieve the rich "look" that we traditionally

Figure 11.3 | STANDARD FILM GAUGES

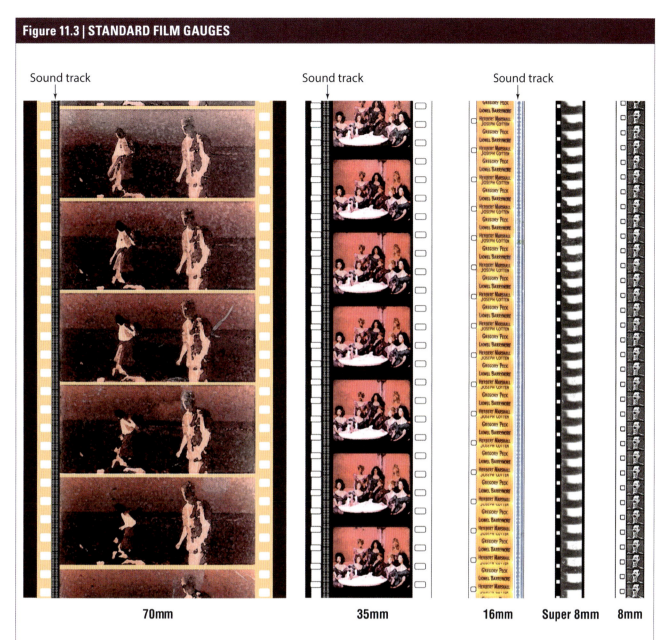

70mm   35mm   16mm   Super 8mm   8mm

The most common variations on standard motion-picture film gauges. Digital technology does not use film, so the size of the film gauge is determined by the sensor, a central component in determining visual qualities. (See the following section on "Digital Technology.")

associate with the movies. However, as we will discuss below, film and digital images are now virtually indistinguishable—just one factor spurring the momentum of making feature movies in digital technology.

Digital Technology

Digital technology involves an electronic process that creates its images through a numbered system of pixels (which we can think of as the binary numbers 0 and 1). Unlike the analog images, digital images do not have a physical relationship to the original. Indeed, they are not exactly images but rather thousands of digits stored on a **flash card** or a computer hard drive. These digits are reconstructed into visual images each time the movie is edited or shown and, unlike film stock, can be manipulated endlessly. For example, filmmakers can make many alternate versions of any scene in searching for the perfect arrangement or timing of shots. They can also adjust and manipulate the light, color, and quality of the image.

Digital technology, like film technology, is used in all three stages of filmmaking: preproduction, production, and postproduction. And there are many significant similarities between the film and digital processes. When making conventional theatrical motion pictures, both systems shoot single, discrete images at a standard 24 frames per second. Every camera uses a lens, an aperture, shutter speed, frame rate, and so on—whether it shoots film or digital.[6] The essential difference comes down to how the light is captured as an image. Digital uses a sensor, which transfers light as data onto a memory chip; film uses silver nitrate particles embedded on celluloid. In shooting a movie, digital cameras have different sizes of sensors recording the image and transferring it into electronic signals (see Figure 11.2). Instead of using different sizes of film gauges to determine the resolution and other visual performance/quality factors (such as depth of field, color retention, etc.), a digital camera uses the sensor for this work. In both film and digital processes, it all boils down to the size of the little square that the camera is focusing light onto. The bigger the gauge or sensor, the more information can be recorded with each frame.

Film versus Digital Technology

Before we proceed, let's summarize the strengths and weaknesses of both technologies. Film stock is a physical thing; digital is virtual representation. Film stock runs through a mechanical device and is subjected to a chemical reaction when light from the lens strikes silver-nitrate crystals (or whatever) on the stock, which must be kept locked away from light and must be processed by a lab and edited on a work print (which allows the editor to see only one version of any scene or sequence at any one time). Digital takes that same light from the lens and processes it through a sensor chip into pixels, which were traditionally put on various types of tape but increasingly are now recorded directly onto a flash card or a computer hard drive. It doesn't have to go through a laboratory for processing and can be manipulated with complete freedom on the computer.

What is the current state of digital production, distribution, and exhibition of films? Because the conversion to digital is under way, precise figures are changing monthly. However, it appears that as of 2014, approximately 62 percent of all U.S. live-action feature films are shot digitally; 100 percent of those films are edited and otherwise prepared for release digitally; and 92 percent of the approximately 40,000 U.S. theaters have digital projection capabilities of one kind or another.[7] Theaters without digital projection are usually in small towns, where the level of business may not warrant the costly conversion. It's clear that there is almost universal acceptance of the conversion to digital technology on both the creative and business sides of the industry. However, there is small but significant opposition on the creative side from directors and cinematographers, in particular, who say they will continue to shoot on film. And the industry cannot afford to neglect people like Tim Burton, Martin Scorsese, or Christopher Nolan, who are dedicated to film's particular aesthetic: its film grain, its depth of color and shadow, even its imperfections.

That opposition created a problem, because Fuji stopped manufacturing motion-picture film in 2013. Eastman Kodak is now the only major company producing it. Faced with rapidly falling sales, Kodak was ready to follow Fuji. In 2014, a coalition of studios found a solution and made a deal with Kodak to ensure that the company will continue manufacturing motion-picture film for the next several years. Studios will buy a guaranteed quantity of that film and make it available to directors who wish to use it. The finished film, transferred to digital media and edited digitally, will be screened in theaters using digital projection. This arrangement preserves, in what we see, the visual quality of motion picture film stock that many prefer.

Another strength of digital technology is that it uses less light than film technology and involves no processing. Overall, digital is much more versatile, easier, and (beyond the initial investment in new equipment) cheaper

---

6. For a documentary film on the transition from celluloid to digital capture, including interviews with many important Hollywood figures, see Chris Kenneally's *Side by Side* (2012).

7. In 2014, Paramount became the first major Hollywood studio to supply its films to theaters in only a digital format.

to work with than film. Film is fragile and disintegrates over time; digital copies (such as DVDs) can be scratched, but compared to a film print, they are easily duplicated and virtually indestructible under normal conditions. Archival copies of both film and digital movies are costly.

When it comes to film editing, everyone involved seems to be convinced by the efficiency and flexibility of the new technology. Virtually 100 percent of all feature films are digitally edited. That's understandable, considering that digital editing suites are reasonably priced. In distribution and exhibition (getting the movie to the theaters and up on the screens), there has been measurable progress in converting theaters. As you might expect, the key factors are economic. The major obstacle is the cost of converting a theater's projection and sound systems, estimated at anywhere from $75,000 to $150,000 or more per screen (remember that a single multiplex can have 12 or more screens, and the projector for each screen would need converting).

While theater owners are less willing to upgrade than studios might be, there is a substantial potential for distributors and exhibitors to realize great savings by converting to digital technology. These savings would occur in distribution costs, the availability of a wider range of content for the audiences, and significant control of movie piracy. In contrast to traditional methods of distributing movies to movie theaters, digital distribution seems cost-effective. In traditional film-distribution processes, new film prints, costing around $1,200, must be made for each theater (and must also be replaced regularly, because a print deteriorates as it runs through a projector). If this movie were distributed to 25,000 screens (out of the 40,000 total in the United States), that cost would be $30 million, not including the cost of shipping the bulky, heavy cans that contain these prints. By contrast, downloading a digital copy of a film to a theater's computer system (which could simply be a hard drive costing several hundred dollars) costs virtually nothing. Converting to digital projection could save the film industry $1 billion a year or more. The advent of the DVD and the home theater system was once regarded as a threat to the future of the movie theater. However, since both theater admissions and the number of movie screens have, according to the latest available information, remained stable since 2006, it seems highly likely that the development of digital technology will give us the options of looking at movies at home, in theaters, or both.

Digitally equipped theaters are able to offer more than feature films, including sports, entertainment, and cultural events. Even independent movies that might not otherwise seem profitable could be more or less subsidized for short runs in a multiplex. Such an expanded range of content can be particularly valuable in areas where there are no alternative theaters and few cultural opportunities.

With digital distribution, a blockbuster movie could be released and screened simultaneously in all areas of the United States, even around the world, thus maximizing the audience. Such instantaneous, widespread exposure might curtail the market for pirated copies made surreptitiously inside a theater by a thief using a camcorder and then duplicated in cheap copies sold on the streets. However, the industry also fears that digital exhibition will foster the theft and subsequent pirating of the digital release prints themselves.

Furthermore, digital technology is changing so rapidly that long-term preservation of digital movies will remain problematic until stable standards can be established. By contrast, the 35mm film format was rapidly standardized in the 1890s within a few years of the technology's invention and has remained stable, with various improvements, until today. Preservation of those films is now a major issue.

Finally, the motion-picture industry is traditionally very conservative about investing money that will diminish profits and is not uniformly convinced about the relative strengths and weaknesses of digital technology. Perhaps because of these factors, the industry has yet to take a united position in converting to digital technology the way it did when making the conversion to sound in the late 1920s. Distributors and exhibitors have the most to lose, because they realize the competitive power of such alternative ways of delivering movies as direct downloading to homes. As a result, they have made significant progress in converting theaters.[8]

8. Producers, distributors, and exhibitors incur additional costs when a movie is made and shown in the increasingly popular 3-D format.

How a Movie Is Made

The making of a movie, whether by a studio or an independent producer (as we'll discuss later) and whether it is shot on film or a digital medium, proceeds through three basic phases: preproduction, production, and postproduction.

Preproduction

The first stage, **preproduction**, consists of planning and preparation. It takes as long as necessary to get the job done—on average, a year or two. Initially, filmmakers develop an idea or obtain a script they wish to produce. They may secure from a publisher the rights to a successful novel or buy a writer's "pitch" for a story.

The opening segment of the late Robert Altman's *The Player* (1992) provides a comic view of the start of a studio executive's typical day. The executive, Griffin Mill (Tim Robbins), has the responsibility of listening to initial pitches from writers and recommending to his boss the ones he likes. Moving blithely through a world of business politics, intrigue, and power games, he hears from people with and without appointments, losers, hangers-on, hacks, and even experienced authors. Everyone he meets wants to be a screenwriter, and everyone wants to cast Julia Roberts. The pitches are mostly desperate attempts to make a new movie out of two previously successful ones: one scriptwriter, who cannot even agree with her partner on what they're talking about, summarizes a proposal as "*Out of Africa* meets *Pretty Woman*." The final pitch before the opening credits end, about a political thriller, serves as a transition to the thriller at the heart of Altman's film. One of Hollywood's most inventive and successful independent directors, Altman clearly knew the territory well enough to satirize it.

Once the rights to producing a story have been contracted and purchased, the producers can spend months arranging the financing for a production. How easily they accomplish this, and the funds that they secure, depends largely on the film they offer to their backers and its projected financial returns. As we'll see, a director may spend another month or more discussing the script with the screenwriter and the key people responsible for design, photography, music, and sound. Another two or three months may be spent rewriting the script.

Throughout the preproduction period, the producers continually estimate and reestimate the budget. The final budget, which should cover all foreseeable expenses, also reflects their marketing strategy. As one example, the producers of *Inception* (2010) allocated a production budget of $160 million and an advertising budget of $100 million, a shrewd calculation considering the movie was a major box-office success and was also nominated for an Academy Award for Best Picture.

During this process of previsualization, before the cameras start to roll, the director and the chief collaborators decide how they want the film to look, sound, and move. At least two to three weeks more can be devoted to organizational issues and details such as scheduling studio space and scouting locations, obtaining permissions to use those locations, and arranging for the design and construction of sets, costumes, and properties. Just before shooting begins, another two weeks will probably be devoted to rehearsals with the cast and crew.

Up to this point, likely almost a year has elapsed—assuming all has gone smoothly. Though the entire process of making a movie may seem straightforward, this description does not take into account the inevitable delays, the continuing difficulties in pulling together the financial package, and the countless details that must be attended to. For example, a film made at the peak of the Hollywood studio system would have been carefully planned, budgeted, and supervised by the producer in the front office, whether it was shot in a studio or on location. Daily reports to and from the set ensured that everyone knew, to the minute and to the dollar, the progress and the cost.

Orson Welles extensively composed and planned the shots of his first film, *Citizen Kane* (1941). It was photographed entirely in the RKO studio and miraculously (considering Welles's later reputation as a spendthrift independent director) was completed in less than a year and almost within the allotted budget. By contrast, Francis Ford Coppola, already a highly experienced director by the time he made *Apocalypse Now* (1979), began without a clear plan of what he wanted to achieve, worked as an independent producer with financing from United Artists, and shot the film in a foreign country under very difficult conditions. Ultimately, 115 hours of film were exposed for every hour actually used. During the four years it took to complete the film, Coppola spent more than twice his original budget.

In making a film, meticulous preparation is everything, and key people take the time to think out alternatives and choose the one that seems best for the film. Thorough planning does not stifle further creativity or improvisation during production but rather encourages it, because planning makes the alternatives clear. Director Sidney Lumet emphasizes the logistics:

> Someone once asked me what making a movie was like. I said it was like making a mosaic. Each setup is like a tiny tile [a *setup*, the basic component of a film's production, consists of one camera position and everything associated with it]. You color it, shape it, polish it as best you can. You'll do six or seven hundred of these, maybe a thousand. (There can easily be that many setups in a movie.) Then you literally paste them together and hope it's what you set out to do. But if you expect the final mosaic to look like anything, you'd better know what you're going for as you work on each tiny tile.[9]

Production

Production, the actual shooting, can last six weeks to several months or more. Although the producer and director continue to work closely together, the director ordinarily takes charge during the shooting. The director's principal activities during this period are conducting blocking and lighting rehearsals on the set with stand-ins, followed by rehearsals with the cast; supervising the compilation of the records that indicate what is being shot each day and informing cast and crew members of their assignments; placing and, for each subsequent shot, replacing cameras, lights, microphones, and other equipment; shooting each shot as many times as necessary until the director is satisfied and calls "print"; reviewing the results of each day's shooting (called *rushes* or *dailies*) with key creative personnel and cast; and reshooting as necessary.

Every director works differently. Ordinarily, however, the director further breaks down the shooting script into manageable sections and then sets a goal of shooting a specified number of pages a day (typically, three pages is a full day's work). This process depends on the number of setups involved. Most directors try to shoot between fifteen and twenty setups a day when they're in the studio, where everything can be controlled; for exterior shooting, the number of setups varies. In any event, everyone involved in the production works a full day—usually from about 8:00 a.m. to about 6:00 p.m. (depending on their jobs and contracts), five days a week, with overtime when necessary. When complicated makeup and costuming are required, the actors may be asked to report for work early enough to finish that preparation before the crew is due to report. After each day's shooting, or as soon as the processing laboratory can deliver them, the director and others review the rushes. (Movies shot digitally or with a video assist camera can be reviewed immediately, allowing retakes to be made with the same setup or a different one.)

At a recent movie shoot in a Manhattan store, which was closed for the day to give the crew maximum access, any observer would have seen why it takes longer than might be expected to complete even the simplest shot. By actual count, forty crew members were there to support the director and four actors, who were ready to work. After the first setup was blocked, rehearsed, and lit, the director made three takes. This process took three hours. However, the rest of the day's schedule was abandoned because the lighting that had been brought in for the shoot failed. Why? The gaffer, the chief electrician, had neglected to ensure that the store's electrical capacity could support it. By the time generators were located and trucked to the site, two hours had been lost. Of course, any one of a dozen problems—human and technical—could have kept the director and crew from meeting their schedule.

During production, the number of people required to film a particular shot depends on the needs of that shot or, more precisely, on the overall scene in which the shot occurs. Many factors determine the size of the crew for any shot or scene, including the use of studio or exterior locations, day or night shooting, shooting on an uncrowded exterior location or a crowded city street, camera and lighting setups, and the extent of movement by the camera and the actors. For example, a scene that involves two people in a simple interior setting, with a basic camera and lighting setup, may require a minimal crew, while a scene involving many people in an exterior setting, with several camera positions and carefully choreographed movement, normally requires a large crew.

---

9. Sidney Lumet, *Making Movies* (New York: Knopf, 1995), p. 58.

The creation of artificial weather (rain, wind, or snow) and the use of animals or crowds are all expensive efforts that require additional personnel. Shooting on exterior locations is usually more expensive than shooting in a studio because it involves transportation and food, sometimes requires hotel accommodations, and depends largely on the weather.

To better understand what's involved in shooting, let's look briefly at the production of Robert Zemeckis's *Cast Away* (2000). The movie features Tom Hanks as Chuck Noland, a FedEx systems engineer based in Memphis, Tennessee. While he is en route from Moscow to the Far East, his plane crashes in the ocean. Chuck, the only survivor, washes ashore on a desert island. After sustaining himself physically, emotionally, and spiritually for four years, Chuck builds a raft and attempts to return to civilization. Overwhelmed by the elements and near death, he is picked up by a freighter and returned to Memphis, where he faces yet another emotional challenge.

In making *Cast Away*, the production crew faced daunting physical and logistical problems. Their largest challenge was to make the most efficient use of human, financial, and physical resources. The film, which cost $85 million to produce, was shot on soundstages in Hollywood as well as on actual locations in Texas, Tennessee, Russia, and the Fiji island of Monuriki in the South Pacific. The task of planning the overall production schedule was relatively routine, however. Although the largest part of the film's three-part structure is set on Monuriki and features only one actor (Hanks), the cast actually includes nearly sixty other actors. The credits list another 123 members the production crew, most of them involved in creating the visual and special effects.

When shooting on Monuriki, the crew had to endure real winds, storms, and floods. When nature did not cooperate with their shooting schedule, they had to create their own bad weather. Furthermore, their work depended on the tides and available sunlight (Chuck would not have had artificial light on the island). The airplane crash was simulated in Hollywood, where considerable shooting was done underwater, and the scenes of Chuck's attempted escape by raft were shot on the ocean as well as in the perilous surf off another Fiji island. After one month's shooting on Monuriki, capturing footage that established Chuck's overall challenge, the crew took a yearlong hiatus while Hanks lost the fifty pounds he had gained to portray Chuck in the early part of the film. This change helped create the illusion that

Chuck had spent four years on the island. Meeting these challenges as successfully as the filmmakers did (while maintaining visual consistency within the footage) was central to maintaining the film's verisimilitude.

Postproduction

When the shooting on a film has been completed, **postproduction** begins. Postproduction consists of three phases: editing, preparing the final print, and bringing the film to the public (marketing and distribution).

In brief, editing consists of assembling the visual images and sound recordings, adding the musical score and sound effects, adding the special effects, assembling the sound tracks, and doing any necessary dubbing. Preparing the final print consists of timing the color print, which involves inspecting each shot of a film and assigning color corrections and printer light values to maintain consistency of brightness and color from shot to shot; completing the first combined picture and sound print, in release form, of a finished film; possibly previewing the film; then possibly making changes in response to the comments of preview audiences. Bringing the film to the public consists of determining the marketing and advertising strategies and budgets, setting the release date and number of theaters, finalizing distribution rights and ancillary rights, and finally exhibiting the film.

In your study of movies, keep in mind that the art of the movies has been influenced not only by changes in technology and cinematic conventions but also by changes in the production process. Thus the Hollywood studio-system process that created F. W. Murnau's *Sunrise: A Song of Two Humans* (1927) was very different from the independent production process that created Alexander Payne's *Nebraska* (2013). The history of Hollywood production systems can be easily understood as comprising three basic periods: the studio system, the independent system, and a system today that manages to combine them. Let's look more closely at each of them.

The Studio System

Organization before 1931

The studio system's roots go back to the first decade of the twentieth century and the pioneering attempts of men such as Thomas Edison, Carl Laemmle, Thomas H. Ince, and D. W. Griffith to make, distribute, and exhibit movies. In 1905, Laemmle began to distribute and exhibit films, but by 1909 his efforts were threatened by the Motion Picture Patents Company (MPPC—not to be confused with the Motion Picture Production Code), a protective trade association (or trust) controlled by Edison, which sought both to control the motion-picture industry completely and to eliminate competition by charging licensing fees on production and projection equipment. However, widespread resistance to the MPPC encouraged competition and laid the groundwork for both the studio and independent systems of production. The U.S. government broke the MPPC monopoly in 1915.

Between 1907 and 1913, a large number of movie production companies in New York and New Jersey migrated to various spots in warmer climates, including Florida, Texas, and New Mexico. But eventually the main companies settled in southern California, in and around Hollywood. They did so to take advantage of the year-round good weather, the beautiful and varied scenery, the abundant light for outdoor shooting, and the geographic distance from the greedy MPPC.[10] Soon these companies had a critical mass of both capital and talent on which to build an industry. By 1915, more than 60 percent of the American film industry, employing approximately 15,000 workers, was located in Hollywood.

The early studios relied on a system dominated by a central producer, a person in charge of the well-organized mass production system that was necessary for producing feature films. This system of central production began in 1912 and was the dominant practice by 1914. At his Hollywood studio, Inceville, Thomas H. Ince was the first studio head to insist that the authority and responsibilities of the producer, as executive head of a movie production, were distinctly different from those of the director.

Before 1931, typical Hollywood studios were dominated by central producers such as Irving Thalberg at Metro-Goldwyn-Mayer, Adolph Zukor at Paramount, and Harry and Jack Warner at Warner Bros. These men—known as moguls, a reference to the powerful Muslim Mongol (or Mogul) conquerors of India—controlled the overall and day-to-day operations of their studios. Executives in New York, generally called the "New York office," controlled the studios financially; various personnel at the studios handled the myriad details of producing films. Central producers, such as Thalberg, supervised a team of associate supervisors (not yet called producers), each with an area of specialization such as sophisticated comedies, Westerns, and so on. The associate supervisors handled the day-to-day operations of film production, but the central producer retained total control.

By the late 1920s, the film industry had come to see that the central-producer system encouraged quantity over quality and that less-than-stellar movies did not draw audiences into theaters. As a result, the industry sought a new system, one that would value both profits and aesthetic value.

Organization after 1931

In 1931, the film industry adopted the producer-unit system, an organizational structure that typically included a general manager, executive manager, production manager, studio manager, and individual production supervisors.[11] Each studio had its own configuration, determined by the New York office. The producer-unit system as it functioned at MGM in the 1930s illustrates the structure. (Figure 11.4 indicates the basic form and responsibilities of the producer-unit system. Note that the titles of these team members are generic; the actual titles varied with each studio.)

The general manager, Irving Thalberg, who had been supervising MGM's production since 1924, continued this work in the new unit. At the time, MGM's annual output was some fifty films. Reporting directly to Thalberg was a staff of ten individual unit production supervisors, each of them responsible for roughly six to eight films per year; the actual number varied widely based on the scope and shooting schedules of different productions. Each producer, who usually received screen

---

10. This peculiar mixture of art, geography, and economics is the subject of Allen J. Scott's *On Hollywood: The Place, the Industry* (Princeton, NJ: Princeton University Press, 2005).

11. The material in this section was drawn from David Bordwell, Janet Staiger, and Kristin Thompson, *The Classical Hollywood Cinema: Film Style and Mode of Production to 1960* (New York: Columbia University Press, 1985), pts. 2 and 5; Thomas Schatz, *The Genius of the System: Hollywood Filmmaking in the Studio Era* (1988; repr., New York: Holt, 1996), pts. 2 and 3; Joel Finler, *The Hollywood Story*, 3rd ed. (New York: Wallflower, 2003), pt. 2; and Douglas Gomery, *The Hollywood Studio System: A History* (London: British Film Institute, 2005).

Figure 11.4 | PRODUCER-UNIT SYSTEM AT MGM

General Manager
Irving Thalberg

Thalberg supervised the overall production of some fifty films each year: his responsibilities included selecting the property, developing the script (either by himself or in collaboration with writers), selecting the actors and key production people, editing the film, and supervising marketing. Thus, without ever leaving his office to visit the set, he could be intimately involved in every phase of every production at the studio. He generally received screen credit as "producer."

Executive Manager

Responsible for the studio's financial and legal affairs as well as daily operations.

Production Manager

Responsible for all pre- and postproduction work; key liaison among the general manager, studio manager, and individual production supervisors.

Studio Manager

Responsible for the support departments (research, writing, design, casting, cinematography, marketing research, etc.) representing almost 300 different professions and trades.

Individual Unit Production Supervisors

Ten men (e.g., Hunt Stromberg and Bernard Hyman) were each responsible for planning and producing six to eight films per year. Films were assigned by the general manager and production manager. These ten were often called *associate* or *assistant producers* and sometimes given screen credit as such. Each producer was sufficiently flexible to be able to handle various types of movies.

credit with that title, was able to handle various types of movies. Such flexibility also enabled the general manager to assign these producers according to need, not specialization. This producer-unit management system (and its variations) helped create an industry that favored standardization, within which workers were always striving for the ideal relationship between cost and quality.

The system produced movies that had a predictable technical quality, often at the cost of stylistic sameness, or what we call the studio "look." It resulted in an overall output that inevitably, since hundreds of films were produced each year, valued profitability above all else. Yet although it could be stifling, standardization allowed for creative innovation, usually under carefully controlled

circumstances. To help ensure such creativity, unit producers received varied assignments.

Hunt Stromberg and Bernard Hyman were two of Thalberg's individual unit production supervisors. In 1936, a busy year for MGM, the studio released six movies for which Stromberg received screen credit as producer: two musicals, two romantic comedies, and two *Thin Man* movies. Hyman also produced four equally diverse films that year.

Although Hyman regularly produced fewer films each year than Stromberg, both were members of Thalberg's inner group. Reliable if not particularly imaginative (exactly what Thalberg liked in his subordinates), these producers made movies that enhanced MGM's reputation for producing quality films, kept its major stars in the public eye, and satisfied the studio's stockholders. That's what the studio system was all about. Finally, these producers were forerunners of what today we call a *line producer*, the person responsible for supervising the daily operations of a film production.

The Hollywood studio system established the collaborative mode of production that dominated American filmmaking during its golden age while influencing the mode of film production worldwide. The studio system also established an industrial model of production through which American filmmaking became one of the most prolific and lucrative enterprises in the world. Furthermore, although its rigidity ultimately led to its demise after some forty years, the system contained within itself the seeds—in the form of the independent producers that would replace it—to sustain American film production until the present day.

Organization during the Golden Age

By the mid-1930s, Hollywood was divided into four kinds of film production companies: majors, minors, "B" studios, and independent producers (Table 11.1).[12] The five major studios—Paramount, MGM, Warner Bros., 20th Century Fox, and RKO—were all vertically integrated companies, meaning that they followed a top-down hierarchy of control, vesting ultimate managerial authority in their corporate officers and boards of directors. These managers were in turn responsible to those who financed them: wealthy individuals (e.g., Cornelius Vanderbilt Whitney or Joseph P. Kennedy), financial

institutions (e.g., Chase National Bank in New York or Bank of America in California), corporations related to or dependent on the film industry (e.g., RCA, manufacturers of sound equipment used in movie production), and stockholders (including studio executives and ordinary people who purchased shares on the stock market). Controlling film production through their studios and, equally important, film distribution (the marketing and promotion of a film) and exhibition (the actual showing of a motion picture in a commercial theater) through their ownership of film exchanges and theater chains, they produced "A" pictures, meaning those featured at the top of the double bill (ordinarily, for the price of a single admission, moviegoers enjoyed almost four hours of entertainment: two feature films, a cartoon, a short subject, and a newsreel).

The three minor studios—Universal, Columbia, and United Artists—were less similar. Universal and Columbia owned their own production facilities but no theaters, and thus depended on the majors to show their films. By contrast, United Artists (UA)—founded in 1919 by Mary Pickford, Charles Chaplin, Douglas Fairbanks, and D. W. Griffith—was considered a studio even though it was essentially a distribution company established by these artists to give them greater control over how their movies were distributed and marketed. During the 1930s, however, UA was distributing the work of many other outstanding producers, directors, and actors. Although UA declined during the 1940s, it was revived in the 1950s and today is part of MGM.

The five B studios (sometimes called the *poverty row studios* because of their relatively small budgets) were

Table 11.1	STRUCTURE OF THE STUDIO SYSTEM UNTIL 1950			
Major Studios	**Minor Studios**	**Most Significant "B" (Poverty Row) Studios**	**Most Significant Independent Producers**
1. Paramount	1. Universal Studios	1. Republic Pictures	1. Samuel Goldwyn Productions
2. Metro-Goldwyn-Mayer	2. Columbia Pictures	2. Monogram Productions	2. David O. Selznick Productions
3. Warner Bros.	3. United Artists	3. Grand National Films	3. Walt Disney Studios
4. 20th Century Fox		4. Producers Releasing Corporation	
5. RKO		5. Eagle-Lion Films	

12. See David A. Cook, *A History of Narrative Film*, 4th ed. (New York: Norton, 2004), pp. 239–255.

Republic Pictures, Monogram Productions, Grand National Films, Producers Releasing Corporation, and Eagle-Lion Films. Their B movies filled in the bottom half of double bills.

The most important independent producers in the 1930s, when independent production was still a relatively unfamiliar idea, were Hollywood titans Samuel Goldwyn, David O. Selznick, and Walt Disney. Each producer owned his own studio but released pictures through his own distribution company, one of the majors, or United Artists. Disney produced his classic animated films, such as *Pinocchio* (1940), at the Walt Disney studios and released them through his own distribution company, Buena Vista Productions. Goldwyn produced such major pictures as William Wyler's *The Best Years of Our Lives* (1946), which he released through RKO. In 1936, Selznick left MGM to establish Selznick International Pictures. In 1940, three of his films—Victor Fleming's *Gone with the Wind* (1939), Alfred Hitchcock's *Rebecca* (1940), and Gregory Ratoff's *Intermezzo* (1939)—together earned some $10 million in net profits, more than all the films of any of the majors, each of which produced roughly fifty-two films that year. Although he released his films through the major studios, including MGM, Selznick's prestige pictures and remarkable profits established the independent producer as a dominant force in Hollywood for the next sixty years and beyond.

The **producer** guides the entire process of making the movie, from its initial planning to its release. This person is chiefly responsible for the organizational and financial aspects of the production, from arranging the financing to deciding how the money is spent. The studio system was dominated by producers who, in turn, depended on directors who were under studio contract to direct a specific number of films in each contract period.

The work of the **director** is to determine and realize on the screen an artistic vision of the screenplay; cast the actors and direct their performances; work closely with the production designers in creating the look of the film, including the choice of locations; oversee the work of the cinematographer and other key production personnel; and in most cases, supervise all postproduction activity, including the editing. Although some studio system directors—Alfred Hitchcock, John Ford, and Vincente Minnelli, for example—could be involved completely from preproduction through postproduction, most were expected to receive a script one day and begin filming shortly thereafter. They were seasoned professionals capable of working quickly and were conversant enough with various genres to be able to handle almost any assignment.

The career of Edmund Goulding, who directed thirty-eight movies, clearly exemplifies the work of a contract director. After starting in silent films in 1925 and directing several films at Paramount Pictures, Goulding made an auspicious start as a director at MGM with *Grand Hotel* (1932), an all-star blockbuster. He followed that with *Blondie of the Follies* (1932), a comedy featuring Marion Davies; the melodrama *Riptide* (1934), starring Norma Shearer; and *The Flame Within* (1935), also a melodrama. From MGM, Goulding moved to Warner Bros. There, as a contract director, he made *That Certain Woman* (1937), *Dark Victory* (1939), and *The Old Maid* (1939), all starring Bette Davis; *The Dawn Patrol* (1938), a World War I action film; *'Til We Meet Again* (1940), a wartime romance; and *The Constant Nymph* (1943), a romantic drama.

After World War II, Goulding moved to 20th Century Fox, where the declining quality of the movies he was assigned truly reflects the challenges facing a contract director. Starting with *The Razor's Edge* (1946; a quasi-philosophical movie nominated for an Oscar as Best Picture of 1946) and *Nightmare Alley* (1947), a melodramatic film noir, he went on to direct *We're Not Married!* (1952), an episodic comedy featuring Marilyn Monroe; *Teenage Rebel* (1956), a drama; and for his last film, *Mardi Gras* (1958), a teenage musical starring Pat Boone. Goulding made the most of the challenges inherent in such variety. He was also popular with actors and noted for his screenwriting, which accounts for some of the gaps between pictures (most contract directors were expected to make three or four movies per year). Goulding was also noteworthy as an openly gay man who successfully pursued his career at a time when most Hollywood gays and lesbians remained in the closet.[13]

The actual, physical studios, called "dream factories" by anthropologist Hortense Powdermaker, were complex operations.[14] If you were fortunate enough to get past a studio's high walls and through its guarded

---

13. See William J. Mann, *Behind the Screen: How Gays and Lesbians Shaped Hollywood, 1910–1969* (New York: Viking, 2001).

14. See Hortense Powdermaker, *Hollywood, the Dream Factory: An Anthropologist Looks at the Movie-Makers* (Boston: Little, Brown, 1950).

gates, you would find yourself in a vast industrial complex. MGM, for example, the largest studio, covered 117 acres, over which 10 miles of paved streets linked 137 buildings. There were 29 soundstages—huge airconditioned and soundproofed production facilities, the largest of which had a floor area of nearly an acre. The studio was a self-contained community with its own police and fire services, hospital, film library, school for child actors, railway siding, industrial section capable of manufacturing anything that might be needed for making a movie, and vast backlot containing sets representing every possible period and architecture. In the average year, MGM produced fifty full-length feature pictures and one hundred shorts. Depending on the level of production, the workforce consisted of 4,000 to 5,000 people. The other major studios had smaller but similar operations.

The Decline of the Studio System

Fostered by aggressive competition and free trade, the studio system grew to maturity in the 1930s, reached a pinnacle of artistic achievement and industrial productivity in the 1940s, and then declined at the beginning of the 1950s. We can see this trajectory clearly by looking at the actual number of films produced and released by American studios during that downward swing. As Table 11.2 indicates, the average number of films annually produced and released in the United States from 1936 to 1940 was 495; from 1941 to 1945, the war years, that number fell to 426; in the immediate postwar period, 1946–1950, it fell even further, to 370. In 1951, the total number of U.S. films was 391, the highest it would be until 1990, when 440 films were released. In looking at these data, remember that the total film releases in any one year usually reflect two kinds of production: those begun in that year and those begun earlier. In any case, one thing is clear: total Hollywood production between 1936 and 1951 fell by 25 percent.

By the mid-1930s, in fact, the system had reached a turning point because of three intertwined factors. First, the studios were victims of their own success. The two most creative production heads—Darryl F. Zanuck, who dominated production at 20th Century Fox from 1933 until 1956, and Irving Thalberg, who supervised production at MGM from 1923 until his death in 1936— had built such highly efficient operations that their studios could function exceptionally well, both stylistically

Table 11.2 | FEATURE FILMS PRODUCED AND RELEASED IN THE UNITED STATES, 1936–1951	
Year	Number of Feature Films Released
1936	522
1937	538
1938	455
1939	483
1940	477
1941	492
1942	488
1943	397
1944	401
1945	350
1946	378
1947	369
1948	366
1949	356
1950	383
1951	391

Note: These figures do not include foreign films released in the United States.
Source: Joel Finler, *The Hollywood Story* (New York: Crown, 1988), p. 280.

and financially, without the sort of micromanaging that characterized David O. Selznick's style at Selznick International Pictures. In a very real sense, these central producers and others had made themselves almost superfluous.

Second, several actions taken by the federal government signaled that the studios' old ways of doing business would have to change. President Franklin D. Roosevelt's plan for the economic revitalization of key industries—the 1933 National Industrial Recovery Act— had a major impact on Hollywood. On the one hand, it sustained certain practices that enabled the studios to control the marketing and distribution of films to their own advantage; on the other, it fostered the growth of the labor unions, perennially unpopular with the studio heads, by mandating more thoroughgoing division of labor and job specialization than Hollywood had yet experienced. In 1938, however, the federal government began trying to break the vertical structure of the major studios—to separate their interlocking ownership of production, distribution, and exhibition—an effort that finally succeeded in 1948.

Third, the studios began to reorganize their management into the producer-unit system. Each studio had its own variation on this general model, each with strengths and weaknesses. Although the resulting competition among the units increased the overall quality of Hollywood movies, the rise of the unit producer served as a transition between the dying studio system and the emergence of the independent producer.

Three additional factors further undercut the studio system. The first was a shift in the relations between top management and creative personnel that loosened the studios' hold on the system. From the mid-1930s on, actors, directors, and producers sought better individual contracts with the studios—contracts that would give them and their agents higher salaries and more control over scripts, casting, production schedules, and working conditions. For example, in the early 1950s actor James Stewart had an agreement whereby he would waive his usual salary for appearing in two films (then $200,000 per picture) in exchange for 50 percent of the net profits. Equally significant, these profits would extend through the economic life of the film, whether it was shown on a theater screen, broadcast on television, or distributed via other formats.

The second factor was World War II, which severely restricted the studios' regular, for-profit operations (they were also making movies that supported government initiatives, such as films instructing people how to cope with food rationing or encouraging them to buy war bonds). As noted already, the production of feature films fell precipitously during the war. Because many studio employees (management and labor alike) were in the armed services and film stock was being rationed to ensure the supply needed by armed-services photographers, there were fewer people and materials to make films. Thus, even though audiences went to the movies in record numbers, fewer films were available for them to see.

The third blow to the studio system was the rise of television, to which Hollywood reacted slowly. When the federal government made the studios divest themselves of their theater holdings, it also blocked their plans to replicate this dual ownership of production and distribution facilities by purchasing television stations. At first, the major studios were not interested in television production, leaving it to the minors and to such pioneering independents as Desilu Productions (Desi Arnaz and Lucille Ball, producers). By 1955, though, the majors were reorganizing and retooling what remained of their studios to begin producing films for television. Some efforts were more successful than others, but even more profitable was the sale both of their real estate—on which the studios were built—for development and of the valuable films in their vaults for television broadcasting. Universal Studios had the best of both worlds, continuing to use part of its vast property at the head of the San Fernando Valley for film and television production and devoting the rest to a lucrative theme park dedicated to showing how movies are made.

The Independent System

Through the 1930s and 1940s, the independent system of production—sometimes called the *package-unit system*—coexisted with the studio system, as it continues to do with a much different set of studios. The package-unit system, controlled by a producer unaffiliated with a studio (independents such as Samuel Goldwyn, David O. Selznick, Walt Disney, and others), is a personalized concept of film production that differs significantly from the industrial model of the studio system. Based outside the studios but heavily dependent on them for human and technical resources, the package-unit system governs the creation, distribution, and exhibition of a movie (known as the *package*). The independent producer does what a movie producer has always done: chooses the right stories, directors, and actors to produce quality films.

Depending on many factors, the producer may also choose to be involved in creative responsibilities, ranging from developing the property, revising the screenplay, assembling the key members of the production team, supervising the actual production (including the editing), and marketing and distributing the finished product. Consider the career of Sam Spiegel, one of the most successful independent producers; his movies included John Huston's *The African Queen* (1951), Elia Kazan's *On the Waterfront* (1954), David Lean's *The Bridge on the River Kwai* (1957) and *Lawrence of Arabia* (1962), Joseph L. Mankiewicz's *Suddenly, Last Summer* (1959), and Elia Kazan's *The Last Tycoon* (1976), inspired by the life of his fellow producer Irving Thalberg. Spiegel controlled the money and thus the production. Although that attitude may seem arrogant, it makes excellent business sense to a producer responsible for films like Spiegel's, which were characterized by high costs, high artistic caliber, and high profits.

The producer's team may include an **executive producer**, **line producer**, and **associate** or **assistant producers**. These variations on the overall title of producer reflect the changes that have occurred since the studio system collapsed and, in different ways, reinvented itself. By the nature of film production, titles must be flexible enough to indicate greater or fewer responsibilities than those listed here. Unlike the members of the craft unions—cinematographers or editors, for example—whose obligations are clearly defined by collective bargaining agreements, producers tend to create responsibilities for themselves that match their individual strengths and experiences.

At the same time, the comparative freedom of independent filmmaking brings new benefits. Creative innovation is both encouraged and rewarded; actors, writers, and directors determine for themselves not only the amounts of compensation but also the ways in which they receive it; and though the overall number of movies produced each year has decreased, the quality of independently produced films has increased considerably from year to year. Whereas the producer helps transform an idea into a finished motion picture, the director visualizes the script and guides all members of the production team, as well as the actors, in bringing that vision to the screen.

The director sets and maintains the defining visual quality of the film, including the settings, costumes, action, and lighting. Those elements produce the total visual impact of the movie's image, its look and feel. When a film earns a profit or wins the Oscar for Best Picture, the producer takes a large share of the credit and accepts the award (true under the studio system also), but the director usually bears artistic responsibility for the success or failure of a movie. When a film loses money, the director often gets most of the blame.

Because creativity at this high level resists rigid categorization, we cannot always neatly separate the responsibilities of the producer and the director. Sometimes one person bears both titles; at other times the director or the screenwriter may have initiated the project and later joined forces with the producer to bring it to the screen. But whatever the arrangement, both the producer and the director are involved completely in all three stages of production.

A quick snapshot of a few differences between the studio and independent systems will give you an idea of how moviemaking has changed. At first, each studio's facilities and personnel were permanent and capable of producing any kind of picture, and the studio owned its own theaters, guaranteeing a market for its product. Now, by contrast, an independent producer makes one film at a time, relying on rented facilities and equipment and a creative staff assembled for that one film. Even figuring for those cost-saving elements, the expenses can be staggering.

Moviemaking entails various kinds of "costs." In both the old and the new American film industry, the total cost of a film is what it takes to complete the postproduction work and produce the release negative as well as one or two positive prints for advance screening purposes. But this "total cost" does not include the cost of marketing or of additional prints for distribution, so it is useful only for the special purposes of industry accounting practices. You will generally see this figure referred to as the negative cost of a movie, where *negative* refers to the costs of producing the release negative.

Contemporary filmmakers have found creative ways to reduce costs and increase profits. For example, in making *Minority Report* (2002), producer Steven Spielberg and his star Tom Cruise agreed to receive only minimal fees up front rather than their usual large salaries—a practice that Spielberg began with Tom Hanks in *Saving Private Ryan* (1998) and is now standard in the film industry. According to a clause in their contracts, Spielberg and Cruise were each guaranteed 17.5 percent of the studio's first-dollar gross profit, meaning that 35 cents of each dollar earned on the film went to them. The movie reportedly cost more than $100 million to make, and earned approximately $358 million in worldwide box office return and sales of 4 million DVDs, promotional products, and movie rights. Thus, it is conservatively estimated that each man earned $55 million. As in any other industry, costs and revenues are controlled by supply and demand. As costs increase for making the kind of blockbuster films that return sizable revenues, producers make fewer films, forcing people who work in the industry to become financially creative in negotiating the contracts that preserve their jobs.

Labor and Unions

Before the industry was centralized in Hollywood, movie production was marked by conflicts between management and labor. Strikes led to the formation of guilds and unions, which led to the division of labor; that development, as much as anything, led a hodgepodge of relatively small studios to prosper and grow into one of the world's largest industries. In 1926, the major studios and unions stabilized their relations through the landmark Studio Basic Agreement, which provided the foundation for future collective bargaining in the industry.[15]

Workers in the industry formed labor unions for the standard reasons: they sought worker representation, equity in pay and working conditions, safety standards, and job security. For example, the Screen Actors Guild, established in 1933, is the nation's premier labor union representing actors. In the 1940s, it fought the attempt of the studio system to break long-term engagement contracts; today, it faces new challenges in protecting artists' rights amid the movie industry's conversion to digital production. In addition, because of the uniquely collaborative nature of their jobs, industry workers needed a system that guaranteed public recognition of their efforts. Contracts between the labor unions and the studios covered the workers' inclusion in screen credits. Executive managers often had similar contracts.

In any manufacturing enterprise, division of labor refers to breaking down each step in that process so that each worker or group of workers can be assigned to and responsible for a specialized task. Although this system was designed to increase efficiency in producing steel, cars, and the like, it was applied very successfully in the film industry. Indeed, Hollywood has often been compared to Detroit. Both of these major industrial centers are engaged in the mass production of commodities. Detroit's output is more standardized, though manufacturer and model differentiate the automobiles that roll off the assembly line.

Like automobile manufacturers, each studio during the studio era specialized in certain kinds of films in its own distinctive style (e.g., MGM excelled in musicals; Warner Bros., in films of social realism); but unlike the Detroit product, each film was a unique creative accomplishment, even if it fit predictably within a particular genre such as film noir. For the most part, each studio had its own creative personnel under contract, though studios frequently borrowed talent from each other on a picture-by-picture basis. Once a studio's executive management—board of directors, chairman, president, and production moguls—determined what kinds of films would most appeal to its known share of the audience, the studio's general manager (here titles varied among studios) developed projects and selected scripts and creative personnel consistent with that choice.

In Hollywood, the activities in the three phases of making a movie—preproduction, production, and postproduction—are carried out by two major forces: management and labor. Management selects the property, develops the script, chooses the actors, and assigns the key production people; but the actual work of making the film is the responsibility of labor (artists, craftspeople, and technicians belonging to labor unions). Members of management receive the highest salaries; the salaries of labor depend on the kind and level of skills necessary for each job. Such a division of labor across the broad, collaborative nature of creating a film shapes the unavoidable interaction between the work rules set by union contracts and the standards set by professional organizations.

Professional Organizations and Standardization

Beyond the labor unions, other organizations are devoted to workers in the motion-picture industry, including the American Society of Cinematographers (founded in 1918; chartered in 1919), the Society of Motion Picture and Television Engineers (1916), and the American Cinema Editors (1950), which set and maintain standards in their respective professions.

These organizations engage in the activities of a traditional professional organization: conducting research related to equipment and production procedures; standardizing that equipment and those procedures; meeting, publishing, and consulting with manufacturers in the development of new technologies; promulgating professional codes of conduct; and recognizing outstanding

15. An excellent account of the power of labor unions in Hollywood, including the pervasive presence of organized crime, is Connie Bruck's *When Hollywood Had a King: The Reign of Lew Wasserman, Who Leveraged Talent into Power and Influence* (New York: Random House, 2003).

achievement with awards. Although they do not represent their membership in collective bargaining, as do labor unions, they voice opinions on matters relevant to the workplace.

Membership in these societies has its distinctions. For example, members of the American Cinema Editor are nominated and elected on the basis of their professional achievements and commitment to the craft of editing. Membership entitles them to place "ACE" after their name in a movie's credits.

In 1927, the industry established the Academy of Motion Picture Arts and Sciences, which seeks, among its stated objectives, to improve the artistic quality of films, provide a common forum for the various branches and crafts of the industry, and encourage cooperation in technical research. Since ancient times, an *academy* has been defined as a society of learned persons organized to advance science, art, literature, music, or some other cultural or intellectual area of endeavor. Although profits, not artistic merit, are the basic measure of success in the movie industry, using the word *academy* to describe the activities of this new organization suited early moviemakers' strong need for social acceptance and respectability.

A masterful stroke of public relations, the Academy is privately funded from within the industry and is perhaps best known to the public for its annual presentation of the Academy Awards of Merit, or Oscars, as they are commonly known. Membership in the Academy is by invitation only. Now numbering around 5,800, members fall into sixteen categories: actors, art directors, cinematographers, directors, documentary, executives, film editors, makeup artists and hairstylists, music, producers, public relations, short films and feature animation, sound, visual effects, members-at-large, and writers. Members in each category make the Oscar nominations and vote to determine the winners. All voting members are also eligible to vote for the Best Picture nominees.

Currently, Academy members award Oscars for the "best" in these 24 categories: Actor in a Leading Role, Actor in a Supporting Role, Actress in a Leading Role, Actress in a Supporting Role, Animated Feature, Animated Short Film, Art Direction, Cinematography, Costume Design, Director, Documentary Feature, Documentary Short Subject, Film Editing, Foreign Language Film, Live Action Short Film, Makeup and Hairstyling, Original Score, Original Song, Picture, Sound Editing, Sound Mixing, Visual Effects, Writing—Adapted Screen-

play, and Writing—Original Screenplay. In addition, the Academy has the option to present honorary awards, scientific and technical awards, special-achievement awards, and the Jean Hersholt Humanitarian Award and Irving G. Thalberg Memorial Award. Various attempts to add the following new categories have not been approved: Casting, Stunt Coordination, and Title Design.

Financing in the Industry

The pattern for financing the production of motion pictures, much like the establishment of labor practices, developed in the industry's early years. Within the two decades after the invention of the movies, there were two major shifts: first from individual owners of small production companies (e.g., Edison and Griffith) to medium-sized firms and then to the large corporations that not only sold stock but also relied heavily on the infusion of major capital from the investment community. Because prudent investors have traditionally considered producing films to be a risky business, the motion-picture industry recognized that it would need efficient management, timely production practices, and profitable results to attract the capital necessary to sustain it. As Hollywood grew, its production practices became more and more standardized. Today, producers aggressively seek the support of a newer breed of investors.

From the beginning, however, the vertical organizational structure of the studios was challenged by independent producers. Although the studios dominated the distribution and exhibition of films (at least until 1948, when the federal government broke that monopoly), the independents did have access to many movie theaters and could compete successfully for the outside financing they required. The early success of independent producers—such as David O. Selznick in gaining the financing for such major undertakings as *Gone with the Wind* (1939)—demonstrates their individual strengths as well as the viability and possible profitability of their alternative approach to the studio system.

No rule governs the arranging of financing. Money may come from the studio, the producer, the investment community, or (most probably) a combination of these. Nor does one timetable exist for securing money. By studying the production credits of films (known as the billing block), you can see just how many organizations may back a project.

Figure 11.5 | PRODUCERS' CREDITS ON *GODS AND MONSTERS*

UNIVERSAL

[Title superimposed over company logo]

LIONSGATE FILMS
SHOWTIME and FLASHPOINT
in association with
BBC FILMS
Present

A
REGENT ENTERTAINMENT
PRODUCTION

in association with
GREGG FIENBERG

A
BILL CONDON
FILM

Next, separate titles list the principal members of the cast, film title, and major members of the production crew.

LINE PRODUCERS
JOHN SCHOUWEILER
&
LISA LEVY

CO-EXECUTIVE PRODUCERS
VALORIE MASSALAS
SAM IRVIN
SPENCER PROFFER

EXECUTIVE PRODUCERS
CLIVE BARKER
&
STEPHEN P. JARCHOW

EXECUTIVE PRODUCERS
DAVID FORREST
&
BEAU ROGERS

PRODUCED BY
PAUL COLICHMAN
GREGG FIENBERG
MARK R. HARRIS

For example, Figure 11.5 lists the opening credits of Bill Condon's *Gods and Monsters* (1998) in the order of their appearance on the screen. Universal Studios released the film, which involved the financial as well as creative input of six entities: Lionsgate Films, Showtime, Flashpoint, BBC Films, Regent Entertainment, and Gregg Fienberg. Separate title screens identify two line producers, three co-executive producers, two executive producers, and two more executive producers. Finally, a "Produced By" screen credit lists three more names. Each person receiving credit as a producer was affiliated with one of the six entities listed at the beginning of the film and may also have had some creative responsibility beyond her or his financial and organizational concerns.

With thirteen people listed as producers at one title or another on *Gods and Monsters,* you might wonder about the hierarchy among these names, who the *actual* producers are, and what they do. You would not be alone in feeling confused. Apparently, the Producers Guild of America (e.g., the producers' union) saw that confusion and, in 2012, adopted the "producers' mark," a designation (p.g.a.) that appears on the screen following the names of those producers receiving the "produced by" credit in motion pictures. This mark signifies that those persons have met the guild's standard of undertaking "a majority of producing duties on a motion picture" so that, should their movie win the Academy Award for Best Picture, each would receive an Oscar statuette.[16]

Some producers will have enough start-up financing to ensure that the preproduction phase can proceed with key people on the payroll; others will not be able to secure the necessary funds until they present investors with a detailed account of anticipated audiences and projected profits. Whether a movie is produced independently (in which case it is usually established as an independent corporation) or by one of the studios (in which case it is a distinct project among many), financial and logistical control is essential to making progress and ultimately completing the actual work of production as well as to holding down costs. Initial budgets are subject to constant modification, so budgeting, accounting, and auditing are as important as they would be in any costly industrial undertaking.

In the old studio system, the general manager, in consultation with the director and key members of the production team, determined the budget for a film, which consisted of two basic categories: direct costs and indirect costs. Direct costs included everything from art direction and cinematography to insurance. Indirect costs, usually 20 percent of the direct costs, covered the studio's overall contribution to "overhead" (such items as making release prints from the negative, marketing, advertising, and distribution). Table 11.3 shows the summary budget for Michael Curtiz's *Casablanca* (1942), including a line-item accounting for each major expense. Direct costs were 73 percent of the total budget.

Today, in the independent system, budgeting is done differently. Usually the producer or a member of the producer's team prepares the budget with the assistant director. The total cost of producing the completed movie generally breaks down into a ratio of 30 percent to 70 percent between above-the-line costs (the costs of the preproduction stage, producer, director, cast, screenwriter, and literary property from which the script was developed) and below-the-line costs (the costs of the production and postproduction stages and the crew).[17] Categorizing costs according to where they are incurred in the three stages of production is a change from the studio-system method.

Costs also vary depending on whether union or nonunion labor is being used. In some cases, producers have little flexibility in this regard, but usually their hiring of personnel is open to negotiation within industry standards. Finally, we must always remember that no matter what approach is taken to making movies, movie-industry accounting practices traditionally have been as creative as, if not more creative than, the movies themselves.

Marketing and Distribution

After screening a movie's answer print (the first combined print of the film, incorporating picture, sound, and special effects) for executives of the production

---

16. See Ben Schott, "Assembling the Billing Block," *New York Times* (February 24, 2013), Sunday Review section. www.nytimes.com/interactive /2013/02/24/opinion/sunday/ben-schott-movies-billingblocks.html (accessed September 22, 2014).

17. An excellent source of information on current budgeting practices is Deke Simon with Michael Wiese, *Film and Video Budgets*, 4th ed. (Studio City, CA: Michael Wiese Productions, 2006).

Table 11.3 | SUMMARY BUDGET FOR *CASABLANCA*			
	Subtotals	**Totals**	**Grand Totals**
DIRECT COSTS			**$638,222**
Story		$67,281	
Story	$20,000		
Continuity and treatment (writers, secretaries, and script changes)	$47,281		
Direction		$83,237	
Director: Michael Curtiz	$73,400		
Assistant Director: Lee Katz	$9,837		
Producer: Hal Wallis		$52,000	
Cinematography		$11,273	
Camera operators and assistants	$10,873		
Camera rental and expenses	$400		
Cast		$217,603	
Cast salaries: talent under contract to studio, including Humphrey Bogart, Sydney Greenstreet, Paul Henreid, and others	$69,867		
Cast salaries: outside talent, including Ingrid Bergman, Claude Rains, Dooley Wilson, Peter Lorre, and others	$91,717		
Talent (extras, bits, etc.)	$56,019		
Musicians (musical score, arrangers, etc.)		$28,000	
Sound expenses		$2,200	
Sound operating salaries		$8,000	
Art department		$8,846	
Wardrobe expenses		$22,320	
Makeup, hairdressers, etc.		$9,100	
Electricians		$20,755	
Editors' salaries		$4,630	
Special effects		$7,475	
Negative film stock		$8,000	

	Subtotals	Totals	Grand Totals
Developing and printing		$10,500	
Property labor		$10,150	
Construction of sets		$18,000	
Standby labor		$15,350	
Striking (dismantling sets and storing props)		$7,000	
Property rental and expenses		$6,300	
Electrical rental and expenses		$750	
Location expenses		$1,252	
Catering		$1,200	
Auto rental expenses and travel		$5,000	
Insurance		$2,800	
Miscellaneous expenses		$3,350	
Trailer (preview)		$2,000	
Stills		$850	
Publicity		$3,000	
INDIRECT COSTS			**$239,778**
General studio overhead (35%)		$223,822	
Depreciation (2.5%)		$15,956	
GRAND TOTAL COST (release negative)			**$878,000**

Source: Adapted from Joel Finler, *The Hollywood Story* (New York: Crown, 1988), p. 39.

company as well as for family, friends, and advisers, the producer may show it to audiences at previews. Members of preview audiences are invited because they represent the demographics of the audience for which the film is intended (e.g., female teenagers).

After the preview screening, preview viewers are asked to complete detailed questionnaires to gauge their reactions. At the same time, the producer may also have chosen a smaller focus group from this audience and will meet with them personally after the screening to get their reactions firsthand. After analyzing both the questionnaires and the responses of the focus group, the person in charge of the final cut—either the producer or the director—may make changes in the film.

Although this procedure is presumably more "scientific" than that employed in previous years by the studios, it reflects the same belief in designing a film by the numbers. Since most major movies are intended as entertainment for the largest, broadest audience possible, the strategy makes business sense. Films intended to appeal to smaller, more homogeneous audiences must attract them through publicity generated by media coverage, festival screenings and awards, and audience word of mouth.

Today's movie audiences are composed primarily of young people, whose preferences are reflected in the various lists that you can find by searching for them on the Internet (i.e., highest grossing films for a particular year or for all time). These lists are often contradictory for several reasons: (1) there is no standard for announcing gross or net figures in Hollywood; (2) the variables are too many; and (3) the studios are notoriously protective of their financial information. When you consult these lists, keep in mind that they are rarely adjusted for such factors as ticket-price inflation, population size, or ticket purchasing trends.

The mode of production determines how the activities in this final phase of postproduction are accomplished. Under the studio system, in the days of vertical integration, each studio or its parent company controlled production, distribution, and exhibition. Independent producers, however, have never followed any single path in distributing films. A small producer without a distribution network has various options, which include renting the film to a studio (such as Paramount) or to a producing organization (such as United Artists or Miramax) that will distribute it. These larger firms can also arrange for the film to be advertised and exhibited.

Deciding how and where to advertise, distribute, and show a film is, like the filmmaking process itself, the work of professionals. During the final weeks of postproduction, the people responsible for promotion and marketing make a number of weighty decisions. They determine the release date (essential for planning and carrying out the advertising and other publicity necessary to build an audience) and the number of screens on which the film will make its debut (necessary so that a corresponding number of release prints can be made and shipped to movie theaters). At the same time, they finalize domestic and foreign distribution rights and ancillary rights, contract with firms who make DVDs, schedule screenings on airlines and cruise ships, and for certain kinds of films, arrange marketing tie-ins with fast-food chains, toy manufacturers, and so on.

The model for distributing and exhibiting a movie depends on the product itself. For example, there are exclusive and limited releases (a first-run showing in major cities, often used to gauge public response before a wider release), key-city releases (a second-tier release that further measures public response), and wide and saturated releases on hundreds or thousands of screens in the major markets as good reviews and word of mouth build public awareness and demand. In addition, based on the mode of release, there are complex formulas for establishing the rental cost of a print (or digital download), ticket prices, length of run, up-front guarantees, and box-office grosses. The latter do not reflect what a theater or studio earns, but rather what the public spends to see a film. What part of a movie's gross goes to the producers, investors, and those (directors, writers, actors, etc.) who have a share of the gross included in their contracts remains one of Hollywood's most mysterious dealings.

In a further attempt to create new revenue streams for studios and new viewing options for consumers, Hollywood is planning to bring movies to homes at the same time (or close to it) that they are released in theaters. Such distribution practices are not yet proven to be economically or technically feasible, and in any event, are likely to throw the current method of theatrical distribution into turmoil. But as Netflix, for example, has significantly raised its prices for mail-order DVDs and encouraged its subscribers to stream videos at home, we have already begun to make major changes in the way, time, cost, and place that we look at movies.

Some or all of this activity is responsive to the voluntary movie-rating system administered by the Motion Picture Association of America (MPAA), the trade association of the industry. Because the rating helps determine the marketing of a film and thus the potential size of its audience, it is very important.[18] But ratings should also tell parents all they need to know to make wise choices about what their children see, and that's where they fall short, especially with the PG-13 ratings. Such films have increasing amounts of violence, profanity, and nudity, factors that are often played down by the rating system. Since movies rated PG-13 appeal to a teenage audience—especially boys, whose attendance is vital to their success at the box office—the rating language has become less useful (see Table 11.4).

---

18. Kirby Dick's documentary *This Film Is Not Yet Rated* (2006) provides valuable insight into the workings of the rating system.

Table 11.4 | MPAA MOVIE-RATING SYSTEM

Rating Category	Explanation
G: General Audience	Nothing that would offend parents for viewing by children.
PG: Parental Guidance Suggested	Parents urged to give "parental guidance." May contain some material parents might not like for their young children.
PG-13: Parents Strongly Cautioned	Parents are urged to be cautious. Some material may be inappropriate for preteenagers.
R: Restricted	Contains some adult material. Parents are urged to learn more about the film before taking their young children with them.
NC-17: No One 17 and under Admitted	Clearly adult. Children are not admitted.

Source: From www.mpaa.org/film-ratings/ (accessed August 2014). See also Dave Banks, "Today's MPAA Ratings Hold Little Value for Parents," www.wired.com/geekdad/2012/04/mpaa-ratings/ (accessed August 2014).

Once initial marketing and distribution decisions have been made, all that remains is to show the film to the public, analyze the reviews in the media and the box-office receipts of the first weekend, and make whatever changes are necessary in the distribution, advertising, and exhibition strategies to ensure that the movie will reach its targeted audience.

Production in Hollywood Today

The production system in Hollywood today is an amalgam of (1) a studio system that differs radically from that of the golden age described earlier and (2) independent production companies, many of which are "small picture" or "prestige" (nongenre) divisions of the larger studios. The term *studio system* no longer means what it once did: a group of vertically integrated, meticulously organized factories that employ large numbers of contract employees in the creative arts and crafts. Today there is no "system," and the studios exist to make and release movies, one at a time. In addition, now that almost every studio has its own prestige "indie" division, very few producers are truly independent.

In 2014, as Table 11.5 shows, there are seven major studios and several independent producers (known in Hollywood as mini-majors). The best known of these mini-majors are Lionsgate, The Weinstein Company, and Relativity. More important in numbers and earning power, there are lots of other independent producers too numerous to list. Altogether in 2013 (latest information available), these three groups released 659 theatrical movies that grossed $10.9 billion. Of that total number of films, 114 were produced by the major studios (17 percent) and 545 (83 percent) by the independents, some of whom are subsidiaries of the majors. These figures alone show how dramatically production has changed in Hollywood.[19]

Dominating the market worldwide, the major studios continue to define movie production in the United States. When one of these smaller studios has a larger corporate owner, the parent firm is usually the distributor. In addition, countless independent producers must distribute their movies through the "big six" studios if they want the largest possible audience and the maximum profits on their investments.[20]

To get a better sense of how this arrangement works today, consider Table 11.6, which shows how the nine Oscar nominees for Best Picture of 2013 were produced and released. All nine were independent productions involving multiple coproduction deals. Six were released by major studios, and three by divisions of major studios: *Nebraska*, *Dallas Buyers Club*, and *Philomena*. In one way or another, the major studios kept control of the box office.

19. *Sources*: Motion Picture Association of America, "Theatrical Market Statistics 2013" (www.mpaa.org/wp-content/uploads/2014/03/MPAA-Theatrical-Market-Statistics-2013_032514-v2.pdf); and Film L.A., "2013 Feature Film Production Report" (www.filmla.com; accessed August 2014).
20. Compaine and Gomery, *Who Owns the Media?* p. 373.

Table 11.5 | HOLLYWOOD STUDIOS AND INDEPENDENT PRODUCTION COMPANIES TODAY

Major Studios	Owner	Independent Production Company Owned by Studio
21st Century Fox	News Corporation	Fox Searchlight Pictures
Warner Bros. Pictures	Time Warner Inc.	New Line Cinema; Picturehouse
Columbia Pictures	Sony Corporation of America	Sony Pictures Classics
Universal Studios	Comcast	Focus Features; Working Title Films
Walt Disney Pictures	Walt Disney Company	
Paramount Pictures	CBS Corporation/Viacom	Paramount Classics
DreamWorks	Reliance ADA Group	
Mini-Major Production Companies		
Lionsgate	Lions Gate Entertainment Corporation	
The Weinstein Company	Bob Weinstein and Harvey Weinstein	
Relativity	Ryan Kavanaugh, Ron Burkle, Colbeck Capital	

Table 11.6 | PRODUCTION AND DISTRIBUTION DATA FOR THE 2013* OSCAR NOMINEES FOR BEST PICTURE

Title	Producers*	Number of Coproduction Companies	U.S. Distributors
American Hustle	Charles Roven, Richard Suckle, Megan Ellison, Jonathan Gordon	3	Columbia Pictures
Captain Phillips	Scott Rudin, Dana Brunetti, Michael De Luca	3	Columbia Pictures
Dallas Buyers Club	Robbie Brenner, Rachel Winter	5	Focus Features
Gravity	Alfonso Cuarón, David Heyman	3	Warner Bros.
Her	Megan Ellison, Spike Jonze, Vincent Landay	1	Warner Bros.
Nebraska	Albert Berger, Ron Yerxa	5	Paramount Vantage
Philomena	Gabrielle Tana, Steve Coogan, Tracey Seaward	9	Anchor Bay Entertainment
12 Years a Slave	Brad Pitt, Dede Gardner, Jeremy Kleiner, Steve McQueen, Anthony Katagas	5	21st Century Fox
The Wolf of Wall Street	Martin Scorsese, Leonard DiCaprio, Joey McFarland, Emma Tillinger Koskoff	5	Paramount Pictures

*Names recognized by the Academy of Motion Picture Arts and Sciences for legal and award purposes.

Today, with its reorganization into a production system dominated by independent producers and its ongoing conversion to digital technology, Hollywood is in a strong position to face the future. But television is attracting new audiences with programs of content that rival Hollywood in sophistication, violence, and previously untouched subjects. The traditional networks and cable companies have been joined in such production by Netflix and Amazon, whose efforts are in the early stages. In addition, new delivery systems have been developed for both movie and television content, including streaming video and renting movies on demand as well as experiments with renting movies on demand while they are also still in the theaters. These systems are sure to negatively affect DVD and Blu-ray sales. While formats remain the same, it's still an open question whether 3-D movies are here to stay. Producers face problems with production and distribution technology, particularly the retrofitting of movie theater screens. And, so far, 3-D has been used almost exclusively in movies for youngsters or for those that depend on action and violence.

As the following discussion shows, Hollywood is also facing other challenges: new sources of production and distribution, the importance of movie franchises to the whole equation, new movie content, shifting demographics in audiences, and new delivery systems.

Audience Demographics

While Hollywood is aggressively planning its future in various ways, it must also be able to attract a broad audience globally as well as in the United States. The 2013 U.S. box office of $20.9 billion was up 1 percent over 2012 but down 3 percent from 2008. This increase was due to higher ticket prices. More women (51 percent) than men went to the movies, and the overall demographic composition was 64 percent white, 18 percent Hispanic, 12 percent African American, and 6 percent Asian and others. Interestingly, the largest share of the audience was in two groups: 2- to 11-year-olds and 50- to 59-year-olds, with shrinking figures in the 25–39 age group. However, the top five grossing films (all action and adventure) attracted a overwhelmingly male audience, while family films attracted a majority female audience. Despite an increase in 3-D production, the 3-D box office was down 1 percent from 2012. Figures such as these play an incalculable role in planning and making movies.

Franchises

Action/adventure movies, often in established series or franchises, continue to dominate the box office. Literally, a movie franchise involves the licensing of an original work to others, such as the licensing of the Harry Potter novels to the extensive Warner Bros. series of films. A franchise offers a fertile if not always fresh source of content. The movie franchise is almost as old as the movies themselves, and, as we noted earlier, a significant number of the twenty-five top-grossing films of 2013 were in this category.

But there is another sort of franchise with an open-ended movie potential, one that is original and not tied to existing sources, proven brands, or well-known characters. James Cameron's "Avatar" project is just such a franchise. The original 3-D spectacle (2009) is the best-selling movie in history. He plans three successive Avatar movies to be released between 2016 and 2018. The original movie brought in $2.8 billion at the box office as well as $345 million in sales of DVD and Blu-ray discs and additional revenue from television screenings. Its producers can only predict box-office numbers at this point, but much is riding on this project's success.

In the 1930s and 1940s, franchises in such movie genres as Westerns and horror were very popular. When a movie featuring a certain type of character or story is successful, Hollywood tries to repeat that success with a sequel, as many as the market will bear. The list of such characters is endless. Among the most long-lasting and successful of these franchises, both live action and animation, are the Harry Potter, Star Trek, and James Bond movies, as well as those featuring (in various guises, settings, and plots) characters such as Iron Man, Sherlock Holmes, Batman, Shrek, the Monsters, the Wolverine, the Pirates of the Caribbean, vampires and zombies from every quarter imaginable, animals such as Lassie, and cartoon characters such as Bugs Bunny. Movie franchises also feed off the success of such TV franchises as *The Sopranos*, *Mad Men*, *Arrested Development*, and *Breaking Bad*. It is apparent that audiences enjoy following the development of a particular story over a long course of time.

A brief discussion of several representative series that rank among the top fifty franchise films of all time will provide the model followed by many other series, including those that are less successful. The X-Men series is based on the Marvel Comics character Logan/Wolverine, played by Hugh Jackman. At this writing, the series includes *X-Men* (2000) and *X2* (2003; both directed by Bryan Singer), *X-Men: The Last Stand* (2006; director Brett Ratner), *X-Men: Origins: Wolverine* (2009; director Gavin Hood), *X-Men: First Class* (2011; director Matthew Vaughn), *The Wolverine* (2013; director James Mangold); and *X-Men: Days of Future Past* (2014; director Bryan Singer).

The popular Die Hard series includes five movies: *Die Hard* (1988; director John McTiernan), *Die Hard 2* (1990; director Renny Harlin), *Die Hard with a Vengeance* (1995; director McTiernan), *Live Free or Die Hard* (2007; director Len Wiseman), and *A Good Day to Die Hard* (2013; director John Moore). Featuring Bruce Willis as New York City Police Lieutenant John McClane, the action in this series never stops.

The Iron Man series, also based on a Marvel Comics character, is perhaps the most polished in its form, the most sophisticated in its story, and among the highest-grossing series of all time. For these reasons, the three movies made so far—*Iron Man* (2008; director Jon Favreau), *Iron Man 2* (2010; director Jon Favreau), and *Iron Man 3* (2013; director Shane Black)—have also been well received by audiences and critics. The excellent cast, including Robert Downey Jr., Gwyneth Paltrow, and Don Cheadle, has not yet worn themselves out with the series, and Downey has made cameo appearances in two related films: *The Incredible Hulk* (2008; director Louis Leterrier) and *The Avengers* (2012; director Joss Whedon).

Older audiences are responding positively at the box office to updates and remakes of older movie icons, often comic book heroes being remade for the 21st century. *Man of Steel* (2013; director Zack Snyder) is the latest in the Superman series based on a DC Comics character and starring Henry Cavil as Clark Kent/Superman. In three of the five Superman movies that preceded it, Christopher Reeve played the title role; these include *Superman* (1978; director Richard Donner), *Superman II* (director Richard Lester; a 2006 release restored the original Richard Donner production), *Superman III* (1984; director Richard Lester), and *Superman IV: The Quest for Peace* (1987; director Sidney J. Furie). Brandon Routh played the lead in *Superman Returns* (2006; director Bryan Singer) and, in a variation on the role, Helen Slater played the title role in *Supergirl* (1984; director Jeannot Szwarc). Two other Superman series were produced:

Superman (1948; a fifteen-part serial released in theaters) and *The Adventures of Superman* (1952–58; a television series).

A remake of *The Lone Ranger* (2013; director Gore Verbinski) failed at the box office, even though the characters were long-time favorites.

The rivalry for comic book superheroes is intense. The character Tarzan, from comic books based on the popular Edgar Rice Burroughs novels, influenced one of the most enduring movie series ever made. Between 1918 and 2013, Tarzan, "the ape man," was featured in some ninety feature and animated movies. Popular as these movies were, the Tarzan characters seem absurd in today's world. Other comic book characters that have been the subject of movie (and television) series include Flash Gordon, Popeye, Zorro, and Dick Tracy. The comic book characters in the Archie series have been the subject of numerous TV shows, and a feature film production is now in the planning stages.

LGBT Movies

The year 2013 marked a breakthrough for LGBT (lesbian, gay, bisexual, transgender) cinema, both in its variety and quality. At one end of the spectrum are Steven Soderbergh's *Behind the Candelabra*, a made-for-TV movie featuring Michael Douglas and Matt Damon, dealing with a period in the life of Liberace, an entertainer who was a great favorite with U.S. television audiences; *Blue Is the Warmest Colour* (director Abdellatif Kechiche), a movie about lesbians; two films about transgendered people: *Laurence Anyways* (director Xavier Dolan) and *Dallas Buyers Club* (director Jean-Marc Vallée); *Museum Hours* (director Jem Cohen); and two films on gay marriage: Linda Bloodworth-Thomason's *Bridegroom* (2013) and Glenn Gaylord's *I Do* (2012).

Somewhere in the middle of the spectrum is *Out in the Dark* (director Michael Mayer), an Israeli production about two star-crossed gay lovers—one Palestinian, the other Israeli—trying to find love and happiness against a tragic political background; and at the other end of the spectrum are two psychologically dark dramas: *Stranger by the Lake* (director Alain Guiraudie) and *Truth* (director Rob Moretti).

Finally, there is *Lilting* (2014; director Hong Khaou), a touching drama made in England, not Hollywood, about a non-English-speaking Chinese woman living in London with her gay son, Kai. She senses his involvement with another man, Richard (Ben Whishaw), but Kai is reluctant to come out to her in either English or Mandarin, leaving her hurt and lost in a world of language and cultural differences. When Kai is killed in an accident, Richard attempts to befriend her—in effect, to be her new son—but not understanding his intentions, she rebuffs him. It's a tragedy of such delicacy and familiarity that it sets a new standard for movies about coming out.

African American Movies

In the first decade of the new century, an increasing number of African American movies were released. Their stories, cast, and crew reflect a continuously growing diversity of race, gender, and background.

The blockbuster franchises were Richard Donner's Lethal Weapon series (1987, 1989, 1992, 1998), Michael Bay's Bad Boys films (1995, 2003), Barry Sonnenfeld's Men in Black series (1997, 2002), Brett Ratner's Rush Hour franchise (1998, 2001, 2007), and the eight films in Tyler Perry's Madea franchise (2005–2013).

Other notable films in this period were Jim Sheridan's *Get Rich or Die Tryin'* (2008), Peter Berg's *Hancock* (2008), Lee Daniels's *Precious* (2009) as well as *The Butler* and *The Paperboy* (both 2012), Tate Taylor's *The Help* (2011), *Let's Stay Together* (2011; director Joshua Bee Alafia), Quentin Tarantino's *Django Unchained* (2012), *Think Like a Man* (2012; director Tim Story), Benh Zeitlin's *Beasts of the Southern Wild* (2012), *Fruitvale Station* (2013; director Ryan Coogler), and Justin Chadwick's *Mandela: Long Walk to Freedom* (2013).

In the short period of two years, we had the two greatest movies ever made about African Americans: Steve McQueen's *12 Years a Slave* (2013) and Steven Spielberg's masterpiece *Lincoln* (2012). The first movie dramatically shows slavery as we've never seen it depicted before; the second documents the behind-the-scenes drama of the president's efforts, in the last four months of his life, to get the Thirteenth Amendment to the U.S. Constitution passed—in other words, to abolish slavery in the United States.

Foreign Influences on Hollywood Films

Of the $35.9 billion global box office in 2013, 70 percent came from foreign audiences, among which China was the largest. Hollywood faces a great challenge to make movies that will continue to sell to these audiences. Studios try to enhance the appeal of their movies in various ways by collaborating with local producers, hiring more foreign actors in blockbusters, rewriting scripts to enhance a story's global appeal, and concentrating on producing action movies that are the most successful.

Also significant is the growth of multinational productions in which, say, the United States shares financing with Germany, Britain, or France. These movies, which are truly international in story as well as casting, include *Slumdog Millionaire* (2008), *The Artist* (2011), and *The King's Speech* (2010), all of which won the Oscar for Best Picture, and *A Most Wanted Man* (2014). All of these and others include directors from various countries and international casts, chosen to appeal to global audiences.

Looking at the Future of the Film Industry

Among the major U.S. industries—including manufacturing, banking, chemicals, mining utilities, and health care—one of the most resilient is the entertainment industry (particularly the movies). Since the founding of this industry in the early years of the twentieth century, film studios have opened and closed, and creative talent has come and gone. But the production of movies has never stopped, although it slowed considerably during World War II. Unlike the car manufacturing or banking industries, the movies have avoided large-scale government surveillance, takeovers, and bailouts. Hollywood realized early in the 1930s that self-regulation through various but relatively ineffective ratings systems was better than government censorship, no matter what it was called. Because the movie industry is continually adapting to new technological and market forces, because it enjoys a high rate of consumer satisfaction, and because its profits (despite its voodoo accounting methods) please its investors, it remains a significant part of the U.S. industrial economy.

We know that today's movie industry is more concerned with explosions. Moviegoers are seeing more digital demolition per movie than ever before. But director Steven Spielberg recently warned that the failure of six or so $250 million movies would cause an implosion—a violent inward collapse—that could alter the industry forever. Director George Lucas agreed that the film industry is going through a period of extraordinary turmoil, and he predicted a virtual trifecta of doom: fewer films would be released and they would stay in theaters longer (about a year), and ticket prices would be much higher. Books appeared with titles like *Do the Movies Have a Future?* (2012) and *Film after Film: Or, What Became of 21st Century Cinema?* (2012).

People have been predicting the death of the film industry for as long as it has existed. Of all the major industries, it is probably the one most vulnerable to the ups and downs created by technological changes, particularly the rapid development of alternative digital means of getting the movie to the viewer; available financing for production; and unpredictable customer tastes. When sound came in, industry analysts predicted that theater owners would go broke in refitting their theaters with new projectors and sound systems; they were wrong. The advent of color caused die-hard traditionalists to argue that movies were supposed to be made in black-and-white. Depending on your preferences, they may have been right; depending on the creative opportunities afforded by shooting on color film stock (as a contrast to black-and-white), they were completely correct. When television came in, analysts predicted that people would stay home to watch movies on television and shun the theaters; they were partly right and partly wrong. The tales of gloom and doom go on.

So what happened to all these predictions? While a significant number of blockbusters failed, the studios continued to make them and to be unfazed by such colossal 2013 wrecks as Gore Verbinski's *The Lone Ranger*, starring Johnny Depp, or Marc Forster's *World War Z*, starring Brad Pitt. There always have been, and always will be, big-budget stumbles. The studios know that the blockbuster strategy works. And, as for digital technology, the fast-paced conversion continues without any studio or theater chains going bankrupt or out of business. The cinema, in this country and around the world, is neither dying nor dead. Hollywood is sticking with the two strategies that work most effectively—producing blockbusters and movies that are part of a successful franchise. But it is also producing the kind of carefully budgeted, star-driven movie that many say isn't being made anymore, such as Steven Soderbergh's *Side Effects* (2013), as well as a healthy list of **art house** movies, such as Alexander Payne's *Nebraska* (2013). A film critic for the *Wall Street Journal* says, "The future for films of

quality is breaking good."[21] Large capital investments are ensuring a steady digital conversion. Enrollments in film production schools have never been higher, and we are seeing a growing list of new directors including Derek Cianfrance, Ryan Coogler, Ava DuVernay, Andrew Haigh, Barry Jenkins, Terence Nance, Sarah Polley, and Dee Rees.

Statistics support this careful, optimistic outlook.[22] In 2013 (the last year for which authoritative figures are available), U.S. box office income was up, thanks to increased ticket prices, while admissions fell by 1 percent. Although more than two-thirds of the population went to the movies at least once in that year, the share of tickets sold to 2- t o 11-year-olds was at its highest point ever, as was the share sold to people in the 50–59 age bracket. In the 25–39 age group, ticket sales have been declining.

Because the movie industry is driven by the box office numbers, the following analysis of the twenty-five top-grossing movies of 2012 will provide a good idea of what audiences were seeing.

> Overall, 21 (84 percent) of these 25 movies were live-action features; 4 were animated features
>   - Six movies (24 percent) were in the action/adventure genre.
>   - Five (20 percent) were in the action/adventure genre with some secondary overlap in one or more of the following genres: comedy, drama, fantasy, sci-fi, mystery, and crime.
>   - Five (20 percent) were comedies.
>   - Four (16 percent) were animated features.
>   - Three (12 percent) were dramas.
>   - One (4 percent) was a history film.
>   - One (4 percent) was a horror movie.

> Percentages of total by rating:
>   - One (4 percent) rated G
>   - Four (16 percent) rated PG
>   - Fourteen (56 percent) rated PG-13
>   - Six (24 percent) rated R

> Eleven (44 percent) of the total 25 movies were part of a franchise series.

> Three (12 percent) of the total 25 movies were based on a comic book.

21. Joe Morgenstern, "In Defense of the Movies" (September 20, 2013), sec. D1, p. 1.
22. MPAA "Theatrical Market Statistics 2013."

The movies in this list offer plenty of good entertainment for all ages. But there are other movies in all genres, from all parts of the world, that help us to track other trends in contemporary film production. For example, the annual poll conducted by *Sight & Sound*, the international film magazine, produced the following list of the top films of 2012 (with director and countries of production):

> *The Act of Killing* (Joshua Oppenheimer; Denmark et al.)

> *Gravity* (Alfonso Cuarón; US and Mexico)

> *Blue Is the Warmest Colour* (Abdellatif Kechiche; Belgium, Spain, and France)

> *The Great Beauty* (Paolo Sorrentino; France and Italy)

> *Frances Ha* (Noah Baumbach; US and Brazil)

> *A Touch of Sin* (Jia Zhangke; China) tied with *Upstream Color* (Shane Carruth; US)

> *The Selfish Giant* (Clio Barnard; UK)

> *Norte, the End of History* (Lav Diaz; Philippines)

> *Stranger by the Lake* (Alain Guaraudie; France)

By comparing this short list, based on an international poll, with the longer list (based on the twenty-five top-grossing movies in the United States), you will see that there is no overlap; indeed, only *Gravity* made the U.S. list of the 100 top-grossing films of 2013. Further complicating the issue of what audiences see and what they and critics like are the countless wonderful movies that reach limited audiences, usually those interested in movies of serious content and challenging form.

THINKING ABOUT HOW THE MOVIES ARE MADE

Understanding and appreciating what can, and has been, achieved in a particular movie is closely linked to understanding the technology and production systems that existed at the time it was made. Major—sometimes revolutionary—advances in technology and production systems (the how and where movies are made) have generally been made when a director or producer asks for a stylistic effect for which neither technique nor technology currently exist. Sometimes, the response is "That's impossible" or "That's not the way we do things here." Fortunately, though, such requests throw down challenges to the artists and technicians working on the movie. For example, even though Orson Welles had never made a movie before *Citizen Kane*, he knew what he wanted and was sufficiently enthusiastic and persuasive to convince his crew to improve existing technologies (e.g., in deep-focus cinematography) or invent new ones (e.g., in sound recording). The result, of course, radically changed the prevailing conventions of moviemaking. But even *Citizen Kane*, revolutionary as it was, has its weaknesses. Take, for example, the special effects used throughout the movie. Although the effects represent the state of the art in 1940, they are not seamlessly integrated into the images and so, in contrast to what we see today, are clumsy. Understanding what could (and could not) be achieved at a particular time in film history helps us to understand the current state of film art and the opportunities (and limitations) available to filmmakers. Keeping this perspective is vital today as we watch the film industry making its first steps toward what most experts agree will be an almost total conversion to digital technologies. Yesterday's movies are being digitally remastered to restore the visual depth and sparkle of the original 35mm prints, and while those movies today that are being shot digitally do not necessarily improve the image, they are challenging our visual perception and thus the way we look at movies.

SCREENING CHECKLIST: HOW THE MOVIES ARE MADE

☐ In studying a particular movie, learn as much as you can about the prevailing cinematic conventions and state of the filmmaking art at the time it was made. In particular, do some research on the major creative personnel to determine if any of them are known for particular innovations. For example, if you are studying the influence of F. W. Murnau's *Sunrise: A Song of Two Humans* (1927) on Hollywood conventions, it's important to know his key role in the development of the German Expressionist film as well as his pioneering use of the moving camera.

☐ Movies made during the height of the studio system in Hollywood and those made in the independent system that followed are often quite similar in their look. However, the studio system had some space for mavericks, the independent system relies heavily on traditional methods of moviemaking, and the production system in place today is very much a hybrid of the two. In studying a movie, try to determine how much the production system affected its production. You might, for example, examine such related aspects as design, lighting, and cinematography.

☐ Today we have seven major studios (six of them carryovers from the golden age) as well as one relative newcomer (DreamWorks). Take a close look at a movie by one studio that was produced near the beginning of that studio's history, and then compare it to another made more recently. From this comparative viewing, what can you say about how and to what extent that studio has changed from its beginnings?

☐ An interesting way to gain insight into the production of an independent movie is to examine its financing, particularly the nature and investment of each producer and/or production company. This and other related information can be found in such publications as the *Wall Street Journal*, *Variety*, and the *Hollywood Reporter* as well as online at IMDbPro (www.pro.imdb.com). From this information, you can see the hierarchy of financial influences behind the film and pose questions about how they might have affected the movie's content and form.

☐ The conversion to digital technology is a key factor in the overall future of the production, distribution, and exhibition systems of the international film industry. As such, a study of the challenges, costs, and implications of just one of these areas is an excellent subject for your further study, perhaps even a term paper. One way to look at this phenomenon is in the context of the conversion to sound in the late 1920s and early 1930s.

Questions for Review

1. What are the key technological milestones that laid the foundation for the invention of the movies?
2. How do the two filmmaking technologies—film and digital—differ from each other?
3. What are the strengths and weaknesses of film and digital technology?
4. Why are some filmmakers less than enthusiastic about digital technology?
5. What are the challenges and benefits involved in converting the film industry to digital technology in the areas of production, distribution, and exhibition?
6. How was the studio system organized in the golden age, and what factors contributed to its decline?
7. In what major ways does the independent system differ from the studio system?
8. What are the principal activities in each of the three basic phases of making a movie: preproduction, production, and postproduction?
9. How is a movie financed, and why are today's movies so expensive to make?
10. How are movies marketed and distributed? Have these aspects changed between the studio and independent systems?
11. Who were three major Hollywood producers—in both the studio and independent systems—and what are the similarities among them?

GLOSSARY

AC See **assistant cameraperson**.

ADR See **automatic dialogue replacement**.

additive color systems In early filmmaking, techniques used to add color to black-and-white images, including hand-coloring, stenciling, tinting, and toning. Compare **subtractive color systems**.

aerial-view shot Also known as *bird's-eye-view shot*. An omniscient point-of-view shot that is taken from an aircraft or extremely high crane and implies that the observer can see all.

alienation effect Also known as *distancing effect*. A psychological distance between audience and stage for which, according to German playwright Bertolt Brecht, every aspect of a theatrical production should strive, by limiting the audience's identification with characters and events.

ambient sound Sound that emanates from the ambience (background) of the setting or environment being filmed, either recorded during production or added during post-production. Although it may incorporate other types of film sound—dialogue, narration, sound effects, Foley sounds, and music—ambient sound does not include any unintentionally recorded noise made during production.

American shot See **medium long shot**.

amplitude The degree of motion of air (or other medium) within a sound wave. The greater the amplitude of the sound wave, the harder it strikes the eardrum, and thus the louder the sound. Compare **loudness**.

analog Film is an analog medium in which the camera creates an image by recording through a camera lens the original light given off by the subject and stores this image on a roll of negative film stock. Opposite of **digital**.

animated film Also known as *cartoon*. Drawings or other graphical images placed in a series photography–like sequence to portray movement. Before computer graphics technology, the basic type of animated film was created through drawing.

animatronics Basically a mechanized puppet programmed or remotely controlled by computers or humans. Existing before digital special effects, it is used to create human figures or animals that do not exist, and action that is too risky for real actors or animals or too fantastic to be possible in real life.

antagonist The character, creature, or force that obstructs or resists the protagonist's pursuit of her or his goal. Compare **protagonist**.

antihero An outwardly unsympathetic protagonist pursuing a morally objectionable or otherwise undesirable goal.

antirealism A treatment that is against or the opposite of realism. However, realism and antirealism (like realism and fantasy) are not strict polarities. Compare **realism**.

aperture Also known as *gate*. The camera opening that defines the area of each frame of film exposed.

apparent motion The movie projector's tricking us into perceiving separate images as one continuous image rather than a series of jerky movements. Apparent motion is the result of such factors as the phi phenomenon and critical flicker fusion.

art director The person responsible for transforming the production designer's vision into a reality on the screen, assessing the staging requirements for a production, and arranging for and supervising the work of members of the art department.

art house A movie theater featuring independent or foreign movies that appeal to small, discerning audiences. While the term is somewhat outdated, it frequently appears in industry business publications.

aspect ratio The relationship between the frame's two dimensions: the width of the image related to its height.

assistant cameraperson (AC) Member of the camera crew who assists the camera operator. The *first AC* oversees everything having to do with the camera, lenses, supporting equipment, and the material on which the movie is being shot. The *second AC* prepares the slate that is used to identify each scene as it is being filmed, files camera reports, and feeds film stock into magazines to be loaded into the camera.

associate (or assistant) producer Person charged with carrying out specific responsibilities assigned by the producer, executive producer, or line producer.

asynchronous sound Sound that comes from a source apparent in the image but is not precisely matched temporally with the actions occurring in that image.

auteurism A film theory based on the idea that the director is the sole "author" of a movie. The application of auteurism frequently takes two forms: a judgment of the whole body of a film director's work (not individual films) based on style, and a classification of great directors based on a hierarchy of directorial styles.

automatic dialogue replacement (ADR) Rerecording done via computer—a faster, less expensive, and more technically sophisticated process than rerecording done with actors.

avant-garde film See **experimental film**.

axis of action An imaginary line connecting two figures in a scene that defines the 180-degree space within which the camera can record shots of those figures. See **180-degree system**.

backlight Lighting, usually positioned behind and in line with the subject and the camera, used to create highlights on the subject as a means of separating it from the background and increasing its appearance of three-dimensionality.

backstory A fictional history behind the cinematic narrative that is presented on-screen. Elements of the backstory can be hinted at in a movie, presented through narration, or not revealed at all.

best boy First assistant electrician to the gaffer on a movie production set.

bird's-eye-view shot See **aerial-view shot**.

bit player An actor who holds a small speaking part.

Black Maria The first movie studio—a crude, hot, cramped shack in which Thomas Edison and his staff began making movies.

blimp A soundproofed enclosure somewhat larger than a camera, in which the camera may be mounted to prevent its sounds from reaching the microphone.

blockbuster A movie that, whatever its cost, has exceptionally large box office receipts.

blocking The actual physical relationships among figures and settings. Also, the process during rehearsal of establishing those relationships.

boom A polelike mechanical device for holding the microphone in the air, out of camera range. A boom can be moved in almost any direction.

cameo A small but significant role often played by a famous actor.

camera crew Technicians that make up two separate groups: one concerned with the camera, and the other concerned with electricity and lighting.

camera obscura Literally, "dark chamber." A box (or a room where a viewer stands), in which light entering (originally through a tiny hole, later through a lens) on one side of it projects an image from the outside onto the opposite side or wall.

camera operator The member of the camera crew who does the actual shooting.

cartoon See **animated film**.

casting The process of choosing and hiring actors for a movie.

catalyst Also known as the *inciting incident*. The event or situation during the exposition stage of the narrative that sets the rest of the narrative in motion.

causality The relationship between cause and effect. Compare **narrative**.

celluloid roll film Also known as *motion-picture film* or *raw film stock*. A material for filming that consists of long strips of perforated cellulose acetate on which a rapid succession of frames can be recorded. One side of the strip is layered with an emulsion consisting of light-sensitive crystals and dyes, and the other side is covered with a

backing that reduces reflections. Each side of the strip is perforated with sprocket holes that facilitate the movement of the stock through the sprocket wheels of the camera, the processor, and the projector.

character An essential element of film narrative; any of the beings who play functional roles within the plot, either acting or being acted on. Characters can be flat or round; major, minor, or marginal; protagonists or antagonists.

characterization The process of developing a character in a movie. Characterization is the collaborative result of the creative efforts of the actor, the screenwriter, and the director.

character role An actor's part that represents a distinctive character type (sometimes a stereotype): society leader, judge, doctor, diplomat, and so on.

chiaroscuro The use of deep gradations and subtle variations of lights and darks within an image.

chronophotographic gun See **revolver photographique**.

cinéma vérité See **direct cinema**.

cinematic conventions Accepted systems, methods, or customs by which movies communicate. Cinematic conventions are flexible; they are not "rules."

cinematic language The accepted systems, methods, or conventions by which the movies communicate with the viewer.

cinematic time The passage of time within a movie, as conveyed and manipulated by editing. Compare **real time**.

cinematographic plan A visual concept for telling the story.

cinematography The process of capturing moving images on film or some other medium.

climax The highest point of conflict in a conventional narrative; the protagonist's ultimate attempt to attain the goal.

closed frame An approach to framing a shot that implies that neither characters nor objects may enter or leave the frame, rendering them hemmed in and constrained. Compare to **open frame**.

close-up (CU) A shot that often shows a part of the body filling the frame—traditionally a face, but possibly, a hand, eye, or mouth.

color As related to sound, see **quality**.

color grading In postproduction, the process of altering and enhancing the color of a motion picture (or video or still image) with electronic, photochemical, or digital techniques.

colorization The use of digital technology to "paint" colors on movies meant to be seen in black and white; a process similar to hand-tinting.

composition The organization, distribution, balance, and general relationship of stationary objects and figures—as well as of light, shade, line, and color—within the frame.

computer-generated imagery (CGI) The application of computer graphics to create special effects. Compare **in-camera effect** and **laboratory effect**.

content The subject of an artwork. Compare **form**.

content curve In terms of cinematic duration, the point where we have absorbed all we need to know in a particular shot and are ready to see the next shot.

continuity editing A style of editing (now dominant throughout the world) that seeks to achieve logic, smoothness, sequential flow, and temporal and spatial orientation of viewers to what they see on the screen. Continuity editing ensures the flow from shot to shot, creates a rhythm based on the relationship between cinematic space and cinematic time, creates filmic unity (beginning, middle, and end), and establishes and resolves a problem. In short, continuity editing tells a story as clearly and coherently as possible. Compare **discontinuity editing**.

costumes The clothing worn by an actor in a movie; sometimes called *wardrobe,* a term that also designates the department in a studio in which clothing is made and stored.

cover shot See **master shot**.

coverage The use of a variety of shots of a scene—taken from multiple angles, distances, and perspectives—to provide the director and editor a greater choice of editing options during postproduction.

crane shot A shot that is created by movement of a camera mounted on an elevating arm (crane) that in turn is mounted on a vehicle that, if shooting requires it, can move on its own power or be pushed along tracks.

crisis A critical turning point in a story when the protagonist must engage a seemingly insurmountable obstacle.

critical flicker fusion A phenomenon that occurs when a single light flickers on and off with such speed that the individual pulses of light fuse together to give the illusion of continuous light. See also **apparent motion**.

crosscutting Also called *parallel editing.* Editing that cuts between two or more lines of action, often implied to be occurring at the same time but in different locations.

CU See **close-up**.

cut A direct change from one shot to another as a result of cutting; that is, the precise point at which shot A ends and shot B begins.

cutting In a process that predated digital editing, editors used scissors to cut shots out of a roll of film before splicing them together with glue to form a continuous whole.

cutting on action Also known as *match-on-action cut.* A continuity editing technique that smoothes the transition between shots portraying a single action from different camera angles. The editor ends the first shot in the middle of a continuing action and begins the subsequent shot at approximately the same point in the matching action.

dailies Also known as *rushes.* Usually, synchronized picture/sound work prints of a day's shooting that can be studied by the director, editor, and other crew members before the next day's shooting begins.

decor The color and textures of the interior decoration, furniture, draperies, and curtains of a set.

deep-focus cinematography The process of rendering the figures on all planes (background, middle ground, and foreground) of a deep-space composition in focus.

deep-space composition An approach to composition within the frame that places figures in all three planes (background, middle ground, and foreground) of the frame, thus creating an illusion of depth. Deep-space composition is often, though not always, shot with deep-focus cinematography.

depth of field The distance in front of a camera and its lens, in which objects are in apparent sharp focus.

design The process by which the look of the settings, props, lighting, and actors is determined. Set design, decor, prop selection, lighting setup, costuming, makeup, and hairstyle design all play a role in shaping the overall design.

dialogue The lip-synchronous speech of characters who are either visible on-screen or speaking offscreen, say from another part of the room that is not visible or from an adjacent room.

diegesis (adj. diegetic) The total compilation of a story—events, characters, objects, settings, and sounds—that form the world in which the story occurs. Compare **story**.

diegetic element An element—event, character, object, setting, and sound—that helps form the world in which the story occurs. Compare **nondiegetic element**.

diegetic sound Sound that originates from a source within a film's world. Compare **nondiegetic sound**.

digital An electronic process that creates its images through a numbered system of pixels (which can be thought of as the binary numbers 0 and 1) that are stored on a flash card or a computer hard drive. Opposite of **analog**.

digital animation Animation that employs computer software to create the images used in the animation process, as opposed to analog techniques that rely on stop-motion photography, hand-drawn cels, and so on.

digital format A means of storing recorded sound made possible by computer technology in which each sound wave is represented by combinations of the numbers 0 and 1.

digital imaging technician (DIT) Working in collaboration with the cinematographer, during production the DIT is responsible for managing media capture that will result in the highest image quality; if necessary, further manipulation may occur during the postproduction period.

direct address narration A form of narration in which an on-screen character looks and speaks directly to the audience.

direct cinema An approach to documentary filmmaking that employs an unobtrusive style in an attempt to give viewers as truthful and "direct" an experience of events as possible. Used interchangeably with *cinéma vérité.*

director The person who determines and realizes on the screen an artistic vision of the screenplay; casts the actors and directs their performances; works closely with the production design in creating the look of the film, including the choice of locations; oversees the work of the cinematographer and other key production personnel; and in most cases, supervises all postproduction activity, especially editing.

discontinuity editing A style of editing (less widely used than continuity editing, and often but not exclusively used in experimental films) that joins shots A and B in ways that upset the viewer's expectations and cause momentary disorientation or confusion. The juxtaposition of shots in films edited for discontinuity can often seem abrupt and unmotivated, but the meanings that arise from such discordant editing often transcend the meanings of the individual shots that have been joined together. Compare **continuity editing**.

dissolve Also known as *lap dissolve*. A transitional device in which shot B, superimposed, gradually appears over shot A and begins to replace it at midpoint in the transition. Dissolves usually indicate the passing of time. Compare **fade-in/fade out**.

distancing effect See **alienation effect**.

documentary film A film that purports to be nonfictional. Documentary films take many forms, including instructional, persuasive, and propaganda. Compare **narrative film**.

Dolby system Invention of Ray Dolby that marked the change from analog to digital movie sound. It reduced noise, enabled a movie's sound to have the same emotional intensity as its pictures, and gave audiences sounds superior to anything they had heard before.

dolly A wheeled support for a camera that permits the cinematographer to make noiseless moving shots.

dolly in Slow movement of the camera toward a subject, making the subject appear larger and more significant. Such gradual intensification is commonly used at moments of a character's realization and/or decision, or as a point-of-view shot to indicate the reason for the character's realization. See also **zoom in**.

dolly out Movement of the camera away from the subject, often used for slow disclosure that occurs when an edited succession of images leads from shot A to B to C as they gradually reveal the elements of a scene. Each image expands on the one before, thereby changing its significance with new information.

dolly shot Also known as *traveling shot*. A shot taken by a camera fixed to a wheeled support called a dolly. When the dolly runs on tracks (or when the camera is mounted to a crane or an aerial device such as an airplane, a helicopter, or a balloon), the shot is called a *tracking shot*.

double-system recording The standard technique of recording film sound on a medium separate from the picture. This technique allows for both maximum quality control of the medium and the many aspects of manipulating sound during postproduction editing, mixing, and synchronization.

down shot See **high-angle shot**.

dubbing See **rerecording**.

duration A quantity of time. In any movie, we can identify three specific kinds of duration: story duration (the time that the entire narrative arc—whether or not explicitly presented on-screen—is implied to have taken), plot duration (the time that the events explicitly shown on-screen are implied to have taken), and screen duration (the actual time elapsed while presenting the movie's plot—that is, the movie's running time).

Dutch-angle shot Also known as *Dutch shot* or *oblique-angle shot*. A shot in which the camera is tilted from its normal horizontal and vertical positions so that it is no longer straight, giving the viewer the impression that the world in the frame is out of balance.

ECU See **extreme close-up**.

editing The process by which the editor combines and coordinates individual shots into a cinematic whole; the basic creative force of cinema.

ellipsis In filmmaking, generally an omission of time—the time that separates one shot from another—to create dramatic or comedic impact.

ELS See **extreme long shot**.

ensemble acting An approach to acting that emphasizes the interaction of actors, not the individual actor. In ensemble acting, a group of actors work together continuously in a single shot. Typically experienced in the theater, ensemble acting is used less in the movies because it requires rehearsal time that is usually denied to screen actors.

establishing shot A shot whose purpose is to briefly establish the viewer's sense of the setting of a scene—the relationship of figures in that scene to the environment around them. This shot is often, but not always, an extreme long shot. See **master shot**.

executive producer Person responsible for supervising one or more producers, who in turn are responsible for individual movies.

experimental film Also known as *avant-garde film*, a term implying a position in the vanguard, out in front of traditional films. Experimental films are usually about unfamiliar, unorthodox, or obscure subject matter, and ordinarily made by independent (even underground) filmmakers, not studios, often with innovative techniques that call attention to, question, and even challenge their own artifice.

explicit meaning Everything that a movie presents on its surface. Compare **implicit meaning**.

exposition The images, action, and dialogue necessary to give the audience the background of the characters and the nature of their situation, laying the foundation for the rest of the narrative.

exposure Exposing the recording media (film or digital) in a camera to light in order to produce a latent image on it, the quality of which is determined primarily by the source and amount of light. The cinematographer can further control that image by the choice of lens and film stock, use of filters, and the aperture that regulates the amount of light passing through the lens. Normally, it is desirable to have images that are clear and well defined, but sometimes the story requires images that are overexposed (very light) or underexposed (dark or dense).

exposure index See **film-stock speed**.

external sound A form of diegetic sound that comes from a place within the world of the story, which we and the characters in the scene hear but do not see. Compare **internal sound**.

extra An actor who usually appears in a nonspeaking or a crowd role and receives no screen credit.

extreme close-up (ECU, XCU) A very close shot of a particular detail, such as a person's eye, a ring on a finger, or a face of a watch.

extreme long shot (ELS, XLS) A shot that is typically photographed far enough away from the subject that the subject is too small to be recognized, except through the context we see, which usually includes a wide view of the location as well as a general background information. When it is used to provide such informative context, the extreme long shot is also referred to as an *establishing shot*.

eye-level shot A shot that is made from the observer's eye level and usually implies that the observer's attitude is neutral toward the subject being photographed.

eyeline match cut An editing transition that shows us what a particular character is looking at. The cut joins two shots: the character's face, with his or her eyes clearly visible, then whatever the character is looking at. When the second shot is of another character looking back at the character in the first shot, the resulting reciprocal eyeline match cut and the cuts that follow establish the two characters' proximity and interaction, even if only one character is visible on-screen at any one time.

factual film A documentary film that usually presents people, places, or processes in a straightforward way meant to entertain and instruct without unduly influencing audiences. Compare **instructional film**, **persuasive film**, and **propaganda film**.

fade-in/fade-out Transitional devices in which a shot fades in from a black field on a black-and-white film or from a color field on a color film, or fades out to a black field (or a color field). Compare **dissolve**.

familiar image Any image that a director periodically repeats in a movie (with or without variations) to help stabilize the narrative.

fast motion Cinematographic technique that accelerates action on-screen. It is achieved by filming the action at a rate *less* than the normal 24 frames per second (fps). When the shot is then played back at the standard 24 fps, cinematic time proceeds at a more rapid rate than the real action that took place in front of the camera. Compare **slow motion**.

featured role See **major role**.

feed spool The storage area for unexposed film in the movie camera.

fiction film See **narrative film**.

fidelity The faithfulness or unfaithfulness of a sound to its source.

figure Any significant thing—person, animal, or object—that moves on the screen.

fill light Lighting, positioned at the opposite side of the camera from the key light, that can fill in the shadows created by the brighter key light. Fill light may also come from a reflector board.

film criticism Evaluating a film's artistic merit and appeal to the public. Film criticism takes two basic forms: reviews written for the general audience and appearing in popular media, and essays published in academic journals for a scholarly audience. Compare **film theory**.

film speed See **film-stock speed**.

film stock Celluloid used to record movies. There are two types: one for black-and-white films and the other for color. Each type is manufactured in several standard formats.

film-stock length The number of feet (or meters) of film stock, or the number of reels used in a particular film.

film-stock speed Also known as *film speed* or *exposure index*. The rate at which film must move through the camera to correctly capture an image. Very fast film requires little light to capture and fix the image, whereas very slow film requires a lot of light.

film theory Evaluating movies from a particular intellectual or ideological perspective. Compare **film criticism**.

first AC See **assistant cameraperson**.

first-person narration Narration by an actual character in the movie. Compare **third-person narration** and **voice-over narration**.

flashback A device for presenting or reawakening the memory of the camera, a character, the audience, or all three. In a flashback, the action cuts from the narrative present to a past event, which may already have appeared in the movie either directly or through inference. Compare **flash-forward**.

flash card A fast, portable, shock-resistant memory card, housed in a small plastic or metal case, that is used as a storage medium in such battery-powered devices as digital cameras, mobile phones, and portable digital assistants.

flash-forward A device for presenting the anticipation of the camera, a character, the audience, or all three. In a flash forward, the action cuts from the narrative present to a future time, when, for example, the omniscient camera either reveals directly or a character imagines from his or her point of view, what is going to happen. Compare **flashback**.

flat character A relatively uncomplicated character exhibiting few distinct traits. Flat characters do not change significantly as the story progresses.

floodlight A lamp that produces soft (diffuse) light. Compare **focusable spotlight**.

focal length The distance from the optical center of a lens to the focal point—the film plane that the cameraperson wants to keep in focus—when the lens is focused at infinity.

focusable spotlight A lamp that produces hard, mirrorlike light that can be directed to precise locations. Compare **floodlight**.

Foley sound A sound belonging to a special category of sound effects, invented in the 1930s by Jack Foley, a sound technician at Universal Studios. Technicians known as Foley artists create these sounds in specially equipped studios, where they use a variety of props and other equipment to simulate sounds such as footsteps in the mud, jingling car keys, or cutlery hitting a plate.

form The means by which a subject is expressed. The form for poetry is words; for drama, it is speech and action; for movies, it is pictures and sound; and so on. Compare **content**.

formal analysis Film analysis that examines how a scene or sequence uses formal elements—narrative, mise-en-scène, cinematography, editing, sound, and so on—to convey the story, mood, and meaning.

format Also called *gauge*. The dimensions of a film stock and its perforations, and the size and shape of the image frame as seen on the screen. Formats extend from Super 8mm through 70mm and beyond, into such specialized formats as IMAX, but they are generally limited to three standard gauges: Super 8mm, 16mm, and 35mm.

frame A still photograph that when recorded in rapid succession with other still photographs, creates a motion picture.

framing The process by which the cinematographer determines what will appear within the borders of the moving image (the frame) during a shot.

freeze-frame Also known as *stop-frame* or *hold-frame*. A still image within a movie created by repetitive printing in the laboratory of the same frame, so that it can be seen without movement for whatever length of time the filmmaker desires.

frequency The speed with which a sound is produced (the number of sound waves produced per second). The speed of sound remains fairly constant when it passes through air, but it varies in different media and in the same medium at different temperatures. Compare **pitch**.

full-body shot See **long shot**.

fusil photographique A form of the chronophotographic gun—a single, portable camera capable of taking twelve continuous images. See **revolver photographique**.

FX See **special effects**.

gaffer The chief electrician on a movie production set.

gate See **aperture**.

gauge See **format**.

generic transformation The process by which a particular genre is adapted to meet the expectations of a changing society.

genre The categorization of narrative films by form, content, or both. Examples of genres are musical, comedy, biography, Western, and so on.

goal A narratively significant objective pursued by the protagonist.

graphic match cut A match cut in which the similarity between shots A and B is in the shape and form of the figures pictured in each shot; the shape, color, or texture of the two figures matches across the edit, providing continuity.

grip All-around handyperson on a movie production set, most often working with the camera and electrical crews.

group POV A point of view captured by a shot that shows what a group of characters would see at their level. Compare **omniscient POV** and **single character's POV**.

harmonic content The wavelengths that make up a sound. Compare **quality**.

high-angle shot Also known as *high shot* or *down shot*. A shot that is made with the camera above the action, and typically implies the observer's sense of superiority to the subject being photographed. Compare **low-angle shot**.

high-key lighting Lighting that produces an image with very little contrast between darks and lights. Its even, flat illumination expresses virtually no opinion about the subject being photographed. Compare **low-key lighting**.

high shot See **high-angle shot**.

hold-frame See **freeze-frame**.

hub A major event in a plot; a branching point in the plot structure that forces a character to choose between or among alternate paths. Compare **satellite**.

ideological meaning Meaning expressed by a film that reflects beliefs on the part of filmmakers, characters, or the time and place of the movie's setting. Ideological meaning is the product of social, political, economic, religious, philosophical, psychological, and sexual forces that shape the filmmakers' perspectives.

imaginary line See **180-degree system**.

implicit meaning An association, connection, or inference that a viewer makes based on the given (explicit) meaning conveyed by the story and form of a film. Lying below the surface of explicit meaning, implicit meaning is closest to our everyday sense of the word *meaning*. Compare **explicit meaning**.

improvisation Actors' extemporization—that is, delivering lines based loosely on the written script or without the preparation that comes with studying a script before rehearsing it. Or "playing through" a moment—that is, making up lines to keep scenes going when actors forget their written lines, stumble on lines, or have some other mishap.

in-camera effect A special effect that is created in the production camera (the regular camera used for shooting the rest of the film) on the original negative; examples include montage and split screen. Compare **computer-generated imagery (CGI)** and **laboratory effect**.

inciting incident Also known as the **catalyst**. The narrative event that presents the protagonist with a goal that sets the rest of the narrative in motion.

insert/insert shot A shot containing visual detail (an object or figure not from the scene) that is inserted between one shot and another to establish a story point or to provide additional information or dramatic emphasis. For example, shot A might be an establishing shot of a room (giving us the place); shot B, the insert, might be a close-up of a clock photographed on a wall (giving us the time); and shot C would logically return us to the room.

insert titles/intertitles Words (printed or handwritten) inserted into the body of a film, such as "The day after" or "Saturday morning"; in common usage today, but used extensively in silent movies.

instructional film A documentary film that seeks to educate viewers about common interests, rather than persuading them with particular ideas. Compare **factual film**, **persuasive film**, and **propaganda film**.

intercutting Editing technique that juxtaposes two or more distinct actions to create the effect of a single scene.

interior monologue A variation on the mental, subjective point of view of an individual character that allows us to see the character and hear his or her thoughts in their own voice, even though the character's lips don't move.

internal sound A form of diegetic sound in which we hear the thoughts of a character we see on-screen but other characters cannot hear them. Compare **external sound**.

iris A circular cutout made with a mask that creates a frame within a frame. Also, an adjustable diaphragm that limits the amount of light passing through the lens of a camera.

iris-in Iris shot that begins with a small circle and expands to a partial or full image.

iris-out Iris shot that begins with a large circle and contracts to a smaller circle or total blackness.

iris shot Optical wipe effect in which the wipe line is a circle; named after the iris of a camera.

jump cut The removal of a portion of a film, resulting in an instantaneous advance in the action—a sudden, perhaps illogical, and often disorienting ellipsis between two shots.

key light Also known as *main light* or *source light*. The brightest light falling on a subject.

kinesis The aspect of composition that takes into account everything that moves on the screen.

Kinetograph The first motion-picture camera.

Kinetoscope A peephole viewer, an early motion-picture device.

Kuleshov effect The discovery of Lev Kuleshov, a Soviet film theorist, that two shots need not have any actual relationship to one another for viewers to perceive a spatial relationship. For example, the placement of one shot of a person's reaction (a look of shock) after a shot of an action by another person (falling down a flight of stairs) immediately creates the perception that the two are occupying the same space.

laboratory effect A special effect that is created in the laboratory through processing and printing. Compare **computer-generated imagery (CGI)** and **in-camera effect**.

lap dissolve See **dissolve**.

leading role See **major role**.

lens The piece of transparent material in a camera that focuses the image on the film being exposed. The four major types of lenses are short-focal-length lens, middle-focal-length lens, long-focal-length lens, and zoom lens.

lighting ratio The relationship and balance between illumination and shadow—the balance between key light and fill light. If the ratio is high, shadows are deep, and the result is called *low-key lighting*. If the ratio is low, shadows are faint or nonexistent and illumination is even, and the result is called *high-key lighting*.

line of action See **180-degree system**.

line producer The person, usually involved from preproduction through postproduction, who is responsible for the day-to-day management of the production operation.

long-focal-length lens Also known as *telephoto lens*. A lens that flattens the space and depth of an image and thus distorts perspectival relations. Compare **middle-focal-length lens**, **short-focal-length lens**, and **zoom lens**.

long shot (LS) Also known as *full-body shot*. A shot that shows the full human body, usually filling the frame and some of its surroundings.

long take Also known as *sequence shot*. A shot that can last anywhere from 1 to 10 minutes. Between 1930 and 1960, the average length of a shot was 8 to 11 seconds; today, it's 6 to 7 seconds, signifying that directors are telling their stories with a tighter pace.

looping See **rerecording**.

loudness The volume or intensity of a sound, which is defined by its amplitude. Loudness is described as either loud or soft.

low-angle shot Also known as *low shot*. A shot that is made with the camera below the action, and typically places the observer in a position of inferiority. Compare **high-angle shot**.

low-key lighting Lighting that creates strong contrasts; sharp dark shadows, and an overall gloomy atmosphere. Its contrasts between light and dark often imply ethical judgments. Compare **high-key lighting**.

low shot See **low-angle shot**.

magic lantern An early movie projector.

main light See **key light**.

main role See **major role**.

major character One of the main characters in a movie. Major characters make most things happen or have most things happen to them. Compare **marginal character** and **minor character**.

major role Also known as *main role, featured role*, or *leading role*. A role that is a principal agent in helping move the plot forward. Whether movie stars or newcomers, actors playing major roles appear in many scenes and—ordinarily, but not always—receive screen credit preceding the title. Compare **minor role**.

makeup artist A person responsible for using makeup to enhance or alter (positively or negatively) an actor's appearance.

marginal character A minor character that lacks both definition and screen time.

mask An opaque sheet of metal, paper, or plastic (with, for example, a circular cutout, known as an iris) that is placed in front of the camera and admits light through that circle to a specific area of the frame to create a frame within a frame.

master shot Also known as a *cover shot*. A shot that covers the action of a scene in one continuous take. Master shots are usually composed as long shots so that all the characters are on-screen during the action of the scene. Editors rely on the master shot to provide coverage, so that, if other shots of the scene's action (medium shots, close-ups, etc.) fail to provide usable footage of certain portions of the scripted scene, there is no need to reshoot the scene.

match cut A cut that preserves continuity between two shots. Several kinds of match cuts exist, including eyeline match cut, graphic match cut, and match-on-action cut.

match-on-action cut Also called *cutting on action*. A match cut that shows us the continuation of a character's or object's motion through space without actually showing the entire action. This is a fairly routine editorial technique for economizing a movie's presentation of movement.

mechanical effect A special effect created mechanically by an object or event on the set and in front of the camera.

mediation An agent, structure, or other formal element, whether human or technological, that transfers something, such as information in the case of movies, from one place to another.

medium close-up (MCU) A shot that shows a character from the middle of the chest to the top of the head. A medium close-up provides a view of the face that catches minor changes in expression, as well as some detail about the character's posture.

medium long shot (MLS) Also known as *plan américain* or *American shot*. A shot that shows a character from the knees up and includes most of a person's body.

medium shot (MS) A shot showing the human body, usually from the waist up.

method acting Also known simply as the *Method*. A naturalistic acting style, loosely adapted from the ideas of Russian director Konstantin Stanislavsky by American directors Elia Kazan and Lee Strasberg, that encourages actors to speak, move, and gesture not in a traditional stage manner, but in the same way they would in their own lives. An ideal technique for representing convincing human behavior, method acting is used more frequently on the stage than on the screen.

middle-focal-length lens Also known as *normal lens*. A lens that does not distort perspectival relations. Compare **long-focal-length lens, short-focal-length lens**, and **zoom lens**.

minor character A supporting character in a movie. Minor characters have fewer traits than major characters, so we know less about them. They also may be so lacking in definition and screen time that they can be considered marginal characters.

minor role Also known as *supporting role*. A role that helps move the plot forward—and thus may be as important as a major role—but played by an actor who does not appear in as many scenes as the featured actors do. Compare **major role**.

mise-en-scène Also known as *staging*. The overall look and feel of a movie—the sum of everything the audience sees, hears, and experiences while viewing it.

mixing The process of combining different sound tracks onto one composite sound track that is synchronous with the picture.

montage In France, from the verb *monter*, means editing, "to assemble or put together." In the former Soviet Union in the 1920s, it refers to the various forms of editing that expressed ideas developed by theorists and filmmakers, such as Sergei Eisenstein. In Hollywood, beginning in the 1930s, it refers to a sequence of shots, often with superimpositions and optical effects, showing a condensed series of events.

motion capture Also known as *mocap, motion tracking,* or *performance capture*. An elaborate process in which the movements of objects, or actors dressed in special suits, are recorded as data that computers subsequently use to render the motion of CGI characters on-screen.

motion picture film See **celluloid roll film**.

motif A recurring visual, sound, or narrative element that imparts meaning or significance.

movie star A phenomenon, generally associated with Hollywood, comprising the actor, the characters played by that actor, an image created by the studio to coincide with the kind of roles associated with the actor, and a reflection of the social and cultural history of the period in which that image was created.

moving frame The result of the dynamic functions of the frame around a motion-picture image, which can contain moving action but also can move and thus change its viewpoint.

narration The act of telling the story of the film. The primary source of a movie's narration is the camera, which narrates the story by showing us the events of the narrative on-screen. When the word narration is used to refer more narrowly to *spoken* narration, the reference is to the commentary spoken by either an offscreen or on-screen voice. When that commentary is not spoken by one of the characters in the movie, it is omniscient narration; when spoken by a character within the movie, it is first-person narration.

narrative A cinematic structure in which content is selected and arranged in a cause-and-effect sequence of events occurring over time. Compare **plot** and **story**.

narrative film Also known as *fiction film*. A movie that tells a story—with characters, places, and events—that is conceived in the mind of the film's creator. Stories in narrative films may be wholly imaginary or based on true occurrences, and may be realistic, unrealistic, or both. Compare **documentary film**.

narrator Who or what that tells the story of a film. The primary narrator in cinema is the camera, which narrates the film by showing us events in the movie's narrative. When referring to the more specific action of voice narration, the narrator may be either a character in the movie (first-person narrator) or a person who is not a character (omniscient narrator).

negative A negative photographic image on transparent material that makes possible the reproduction of the image.

nondiegetic element Something that we see and hear on the screen that comes from outside the world of the story, such as background music, titles and credits, and voice-over narration. Compare **diegetic element**.

nondiegetic sound Sound that originates from a source outside a film's world. Compare **diegetic sound**.

nonsimultaneous sound Sound that has previously been established in the movie and replays for some narrative or expressive purpose. Nonsimultaneous sounds often occur when a character has a mental flashback to an earlier voice that recalls a conversation, or to a sound that identifies a place, event, or other significant element of the narrative. Compare **simultaneous sound**.

normal lens See **middle-focal-length lens**.

normal world In a narrative screenplay, the state of the character and setting before the inciting incident.

oblique-angle shot See **Dutch-angle shot**.

obstacles Events, circumstances, and actions that impede a protagonist's pursuit of the goal. Obstacles often originate from an antagonist and are central to a narrative conflict.

offscreen sound A form of sound, either diegetic or nondiegetic, that derives from a source we do not see. When diegetic, it consists of sound effects, music, or vocals that emanate from the world of the story. When nondiegetic, it takes the form of a musical score or narration by someone who is not a character in the story. Compare **on-screen sound**.

offscreen space Cinematic space that exists outside the frame. Compare **on-screen space**.

omniscient Providing a third-person view of all aspects of a movie's action or characters. Compare **restricted**.

omniscient POV The most common point of view portrayed in movies. An omniscient POV allows the camera to travel freely within the world of the film, showing us the narrative's events from a godlike, unlimited perspective that no single character in the film could possibly have. Compare **group POV** and **single character's POV**.

on location Shooting in an actual interior or exterior location away from the studio. Compare **set**.

180-degree system Also known as the *180-degree rule*. The fundamental means by which filmmakers maintain consistent screen direction, orienting the viewer and ensuring a sense of the cinematic space in which the action occurs. The system depends on three factors working together in any scene: the action in a scene must move along a hypothetical line that keeps the action on a single side of the camera, the camera must shoot consistently on one side of that line, and everyone on the production set—particularly the director, cinematographer, editor, and actors—must understand and adhere to this system.

on-screen sound A form of diegetic sound that emanates from a source that we both see and hear. On-screen sound may be internal or external. Compare **offscreen sound**.

on-screen space Cinematic space that exists inside the frame. Compare **offscreen space**.

open frame A frame around a motion-picture image that, theoretically, characters and objects can enter and leave. Compare **closed frame**.

option contract During the classical Hollywood era, an actor's standard seven-year contract was reviewed every six months. If the actor had made progress in being assigned roles and demonstrating box office appeal, the studio picked up the option to employ that actor for the next six months with a raise; if not, the studio dropped the option and the actor was out of a job.

order The arrangement of plot events into a logical sequence or hierarchy. Across an entire narrative, or in a brief section of it, filmmaker can use one or more methods to arrange its plot: chronological order, cause-and-effect order, logical order, and so on.

outtake Material that is not used in either the rough cut or the final cut, but is nevertheless cataloged and saved.

overlapping sound Also known as a *sound bridge*. Sound that carries over from one shot to the next before the sound of the second shot begins.

pan shot The horizontal movement of a camera mounted on the gyroscopic head of a stationary tripod; like the tilt shot, the pan shot is a simple movement with dynamic possibilities for creating meaning.

parallel editing Also called *crosscutting* and *intercutting*, although the three terms have slightly different meanings. The intercutting of two or more lines of action that occur simultaneously; a very familiar convention in chase or rescue sequences. Compare **split screen**.

performance capture See **motion capture**.

persistence of vision The process by which the human brain retains an image for a fraction of a second longer than the eye records it.

persuasive film A documentary film concerned with presenting a particular perspective on social issues, or with corporate and governmental injustice. Compare **factual film**, **instructional film**, and **propaganda film**.

phi phenomenon The illusion of movement created by events that succeed each other rapidly, as when two adjacent lights flash on and off alternately and we seem to see a single light shifting back and forth. This cognitive phenomenon is part of the reason we see movies as continuously moving images rather than as a successive series of still images. See also **apparent motion**.

photography Literally, "writing with light." Technically, the recording of static images through a chemical interaction caused by light rays striking a sensitized surface.

pitch The level of a sound, which is defined by its frequency. Pitch is described as either high or low.

pixels Short for "picture elements." These are the small dots that make up the image on a video screen. The dots (denoted by the binary numbers 0 and 1) are meaningless in themselves, but when they are arranged in order, like the pieces in a jigsaw puzzle, they form a picture.

plan américain See **medium long shot**.

plane Any of three theoretical areas—foreground, middle ground, and background—within the frame. See also **rule of thirds**.

plot The specific actions and events that filmmakers select, and the order in which they arrange those events and actions to effectively convey on-screen the movie's narrative to a viewer. Compare **narrative** and **story**.

plot duration The elapsed time of the events within a story that a film chooses to tell. Compare **screen duration** and **story duration**.

plot point Significant events that turn the narrative in a new direction.

point of view (POV) The position from which a film presents the actions of the story; not only the relation of the narrator(s) to the story, but also the camera's act of seeing and hearing. The two fundamental types of cinematic point of view are omniscient and restricted.

point-of-view editing The process of editing different shots together-so that the resulting sequence makes us aware of the perspective or POV of a particular character or group of characters. Most frequently, it starts with an objective shot of a character looking toward something outside the frame and then cuts to a shot of the object, person, or action that the character is supposed to be looking at.

postproduction The third stage of the production process, consisting of editing, preparing the final print, and bringing the film to the public (marketing and distribution). Postproduction is preceded by preproduction and production.

POV See **point of view**.

preproduction The initial planning and preparation stage of the production process. Preproduction is followed by production and postproduction.

prime lens A lens that has a fixed focal length. The short-focal-length, middle-focal-length, and long-focal-length lenses are all prime lenses; the zoom lens is in its own category.

processing The second stage of creating motion pictures, in which a laboratory technician washes exposed film that contains a negative image with processing chemicals. Processing is preceded by shooting and followed by projecting.

process shot Live shooting against a background that is front- or rear-projected on a translucent screen.

producer The person who guides the entire process of making the movie from its initial planning to its release, and is chiefly responsible for the organizational and financial aspects of the production, from arranging the financing to deciding how the money is spent.

production The second stage of the production process—the actual shooting. Production is preceded by preproduction and followed by postproduction.

production designer A person who works closely with the director, art director, and director of photography in visualizing the movie that will appear on the screen. The production designer is both an artist and an executive responsible for the overall design concept (the *look* of the movie) as well as individual sets, locations, furnishings, props, and costumes; and for supervising the heads of the many departments—art, costume design and construction, hairstyling, makeup, wardrobe, location, and so on—that create that look.

production value The amount of human and physical resources devoted to the image, including the style of lighting. Production value helps determine the overall style of a film.

projecting The third stage of creating motion pictures, in which edited film is run through a projector that shoots through the film a beam of light intense enough to project a large image on the movie-theater screen. Projecting is preceded by shooting and processing.

propaganda film A documentary film that systematically disseminates deceptive or distorted information. Compare **factual film**, **instructional film**, and **persuasive film**.

properties Also known as *props*. Objects used to enhance a movie's mise-en-scène by providing physical tokens of narrative information.

protagonist The primary character whose pursuit of the goal provides the structural foundation of a movie's story. Compare **antagonist**.

pull-down claw Within the movie camera and projector, the mechanism that controls the intermittent cycle of shooting and projecting individual frames and advances the film frame by frame.

pull focus See **rack focus**.

quality Also known as *timbre, texture*, or *color*. The complexity of a sound, which is defined by its harmonic content. Described as simple or complex, quality is the characteristic that distinguishes a sound from others of the same pitch and loudness.

rack focus Also known as *select focus, shift focus,* or *pull focus*. A change of the point of focus from one subject to another within the same shot. Rack focus guides our attention to a new, clearly focused point of interest while blurring the previous subject in the shot.

raw film stock See **celluloid roll film**.

realism An interest in or concern for the actual or real; a tendency to view or represent things as they really are. Compare **antirealism**.

real time The actual time during which something takes place. In real time, screen duration and plot duration are exactly the same. Many directors use real time within films to create uninterrupted "reality" on the screen, but they rarely use it for entire films. Compare **cinematic time**, **stretch relationship**, and **summary relationship**.

reflector board A piece of lighting equipment, but not really a lighting instrument because it does not rely on bulbs to produce illumination. Essentially, a reflector board is a double-sided board that pivots in a *U*-shaped holder. One side is a hard, smooth surface that reflects hard light, and the other side is a soft, textured surface that reflects softer fill light.

reframing A movement of the camera that adjusts or alters the composition or point of view of a shot.

repetition The number of times that a story element recurs in a plot. Repetition signals that a particular event has noteworthy meaning or significance.

rerecording Also known as *looping* or *dubbing*. The replacing of dialogue, which can be done manually with the actors rereading the lines while watching the footage, synchronizing their lips with it; or, more likely today, through computerized automatic dialogue replacement (ADR). (Dubbing can also refer to the process of replacing foreign language dialogue with English, or the reverse, throughout a film.)

reshoot To make additional takes of a shot to meet the director's standards, or as supplemental material for production photography.

resolution The concluding narrative events that follow the climax and celebrate, or otherwise reflect upon, story outcomes. Also, the capacity of the camera lens, film stock, and processing to provide fine detail in an image.

restricted Providing a view from the perspective of a single character. Compare **omniscient**.

restricted narration Reveals information to the audience only as a specific character learns of it.

reverse-angle shot A shot in which the angle of shooting is opposite that of the preceding shot.

revolver photographique Also known as *chronophotographic gun*. A cylinder-shaped camera that creates exposures automatically, at short intervals, on different segments of a revolving plate.

rising action The development of the action of the narrative toward a climax.

rough-draft screenplay Also known as *scenario*. The step after a treatment, the rough-draft screenplay results from discussions, development, and transformation of an outline in sessions known as *story conferences*.

round character A complex character possessing numerous, subtle, repressed, or contradictory traits. Round characters often develop over the course of a story.

rule of thirds A principle of composition that enables filmmakers to maximize the potential of the image, balance its elements, and create the illusion of depth. A grid pattern, when superimposed on the image, divides the image into horizontal thirds representing the foreground, middle ground, and background planes, and into vertical thirds that break up those planes into additional elements.

rushes See **dailies**.

satellite A minor plot event in the diegesis (or world of the narrative) but detachable from it; removing a satellite may affect the overall texture of the narrative. Compare **hub**.

scale The size and placement of a particular object or a part of a scene in relation to the rest—a relationship determined by the type of shot used and the placement of the camera.

scenario See **rough-draft screenplay**.

scene A complete unit of plot action incorporating one or more shots; the setting of that action.

scope The overall range of a story.

score music Nondiegetic music that is typically composed and recorded specifically for use in a particular film, and is used to convey or enhance meaning and emotion.

screen direction The direction of a figure's or object's movement on the screen.

screen duration The amount of time that it has taken to present the movie's plot on-screen—that is, the movie's running time. Compare **plot duration** and **story duration**.

screen test A filming undertaken by an actor to audition for a particular role.

script supervisor The member of the crew responsible for ensuring continuity throughout the filming. Although script supervisors once had to maintain detailed logs to accomplish this task, today they generally rely on the video assist camera for this purpose.

second AC See **assistant cameraperson**.

select focus See **rack focus**.

sequence A series of edited shots characterized by inherent unity of theme and purpose.

sequence shot See **long take**.

series photography The use of a series of still photographs to record the phases of an action.

set A constructed space used as the setting for a particular shot in a movie. Sets must be constructed both to look authentic and to photograph well. Compare **on location**.

set decorator A person in charge of the countless details that go into furnishing and decorating a set.

setting The time and space in which a story takes place.

setup One camera position and everything associated with it. Whereas the shot is the basic building block of the film, the setup is the basic component of the film's production.

shift focus See **rack focus**.

shooting The first stage of creating motion pictures in which images are recorded on previously unexposed film as it moves through the camera. Shooting is followed by processing and projecting.

shooting angle The level and height of the camera in relation to the subject being photographed. The five basic camera angles produce aerial-view shots, Dutch-angle shots, eye-level shots, high-angle shots, and low-angle shots.

shooting script A guide and reference point for all members of the production unit in which the details of each shot are listed and can thus be followed during filming.

short-focal-length lens Also known as *wide-angle lens*. A lens that creates the illusion of depth within a frame, although with some distortion at the edges of the frame. Compare **long-focal-length lens**, **middle-focal-length lens**, and **zoom lens**.

shot One uninterrupted run of the camera. A shot can be as short or as long as the director wants, but it cannot exceed the length of the film stock in the camera. Compare **setup**.

shot/reverse shot One of the most prevalent and familiar of all editing patterns, consisting of parallel editing (or cross-cutting) between shots of different characters, usually in a conversation or confrontation. When used in continuity editing, the shots are typically framed over each character's shoulder to preserve screen direction.

shutter A camera device that shields the film from light at the aperture during the film-movement portion of the intermittent cycle of shooting.

simultaneous sound Sound that is diegetic and occurs on-screen. Compare **nonsimultaneous sound**.

single character's POV A point of view that is captured by a shot made with the camera close to the line of sight of one character (or surveillance camera), showing what that character would be seeing of the action. Compare **group POV** and **omniscient POV**.

slate The board or other device that is used to identify each scene during shooting.

slow motion Cinematographic technique that decelerates action on-screen. It is achieved by filming the action at a rate *greater* than the normal 24 frames per second (fps). When the shot is then played back at the standard 24 fps, cinematic time proceeds at a slower rate than the real action that took place in front of the camera. Compare **fast motion**.

sound Transmitted vibrations received by the ear and thus heard by the recipient. In cinematic terms, the expressive use of auditory elements, such as dialogue, music, ambience, and effects.

sound bridge See **overlapping sound**.

sound crew The group that physically generates and controls a movie's sound, manipulating its properties to produce the effects that the director desires.

sound design A state-of-the-art concept, pioneered by director Francis Ford Coppola and film editor Walter Murch, combining the crafts of editing and mixing and, like them, involving both theoretical and practical issues. In essence, sound design represents advocacy for movie sound, to counter some people's tendency to favor the movie image.

sound effect A sound artificially created for the sound track that has a definite function in telling the story.

soundstage A windowless, soundproofed, professional shooting environment that is usually several stories high and can cover an acre or more of floor space.

sound track A separate recording tape occupied by one specific type of sound recorded for a movie—one track for vocals, one for sound effects, one for music, and so on.

source light See **key light**.

special effects (FX, SPFX) Technology for creating images that would be too dangerous, too expensive, or in some cases, simply impossible to achieve with traditional cinematographic materials. The goal of special effects cinematography is generally to create verisimilitude within the imaginative world of even the most fanciful movie.

speed See **film-stock speed**.

SPFX See **special effects**.

splicing In pre-digital editing, the act of gluing or taping shots together to form a continuous whole. See **cutting**.

split screen A method—created either in the camera or during the editing process—of telling two stories at the same time by dividing the screen into different parts. Unlike parallel editing, which cuts back and forth between shots for contrast, the split screen can tell multiple stories within the same frame.

sprocketed rollers Devices that control the speed of unexposed film as it moves through the camera, printer, or projector,

staging See **mise-en-scène**.

stakes In a conventional narrative, that which is at risk due to the protagonist's pursuit of the goal.

stand-in An actor who looks reasonably like a particular movie star or an actor playing a major role—in height, weight, coloring, and so on—and substitutes for that actor during the tedious process of preparing setups or taking light readings.

Stanislavsky system A system of acting, developed by Russian theater director Konstantin Stanislavsky in the late nineteenth century, that encourages students to strive for realism, both social and psychological, and to bring their past experiences and emotions to their roles. This system influenced the development of method acting in the United States.

Steadicam A camera suspended from an articulated arm that is attached to a vest strapped to the cameraperson's body, permitting the operator to remain steady during "handheld" shots. The Steadicam removes jumpiness and is now used for smooth, fast, and intimate camera movement.

stock See **film stock**.

stop-frame See **freeze-frame**.

stop-motion cinematography A technique that allows the camera operator to stop and start the camera to facilitate changing the subject while the camera is not shooting.

Frequently used for claymation and other forms of physical animation.

story In a movie, all the events we see or hear on the screen, as well as all the events that are implicit or infer to have happened but are not explicitly presented. Compare **diegesis**, **narrative**, and **plot**.

storyboard A scene-by-scene (or sometimes shot-by-shot) breakdown that combines sketches or photographs of how each shot is to look and written descriptions of the other elements that are to go with each shot, including dialogue, sound, and music.

story conference One of any number of sessions during which the treatment is discussed, developed, and transformed from an outline into a rough-draft screenplay.

story duration The implied amount of time taken by the entire narrative arc of a movie's story—whether or not explicitly presented on-screen. Compare **plot duration** and **screen duration**.

stream of consciousness A literary style that gained prominence in the 1920s in the hands of such writers as Marcel Proust, Virginia Woolf, James Joyce, and Dorothy Richardson, that attempted to capture the unedited flow of experience through the mind.

stretch relationship A time relationship in which screen duration is longer than plot duration. Compare **real time** and **summary relationship**.

stuntperson A performer who doubles for another actor in scenes requiring special skills or involving hazardous actions, such as crashing cars, jumping from high places, swimming, or riding (or falling off) horses.

subplot A subordinate sequence of action in a narrative, usually relevant to and enriching the plot.

subtractive color systems Adopted in the 1930s, this technique involved shooting three separate black-and-white negatives through three light filters, each representing a primary color (red, green, blue). Certain color components were subtracted or removed from each of the three emulsion layers, creating a positive image in natural color. Compare **additive color systems**.

summary relationship A time relationship in which screen duration is shorter than plot duration. Compare **real time** and **stretch relationship**.

supporting role See **minor role**.

surprise A taking unawares that is potentially shocking. Compare **suspense**.

suspense The anxiety brought on by partial uncertainty—the end is certain, but the means are not. Compare **surprise**.

swish pan A type of transition between two or more scenes made by moving the camera so rapidly that it blurs the moment of transition, thus suggesting (1) that the two actions are happening simultaneously, for example, in Billy Wilder's *Some Like It Hot* (1959; editor Arthur P. Schmidt), a swish pan separates an amorous scene involving Tony Curtis and Marilyn Monroe from a scene of Jack Lemmon, dressed as a woman, dancing with Joe E. Brown; or (2) that

several years have elapsed between the scenes, for example, those that comprise the breakfast-table sequence of Orson Welles's *Citizen Kane* (1941; editor Robert Wise).

synopsis See **treatment**.

take An indication of the number of times a particular shot is taken (e.g., shot 14, take 7).

take-up spool A device that winds the film inside the movie camera after it has been exposed.

telephoto lens See **long-focal-length lens**.

texture As related to sound, see **quality**.

theme A shared, public idea, such as a metaphor, an adage, a myth, a familiar conflict, or personality type.

third-person narration Narration delivered from outside the diegesis by a narrator who is not a character in the movie. Compare **first-person narration** and **voice-over narration**.

three-point system Perhaps the best-known lighting convention in feature filmmaking, a system that employs three sources of light—key light, fill light, and backlight—each aimed from a different direction and position in relation to the subject.

three-shot A shot in which three characters appear; ordinarily, a medium shot or medium long shot.

tilt shot The vertical movement of a camera mounted on the gyroscopic head of a stationary tripod. Like the pan shot, the tilt shot is a simple movement with dynamic possibilities for creating meaning.

timbre As related to sound, see **quality**.

tracking shot See **dolly shot**.

traveling shot See **dolly shot**.

treatment Also known as *synopsis*. An outline of the action that briefly describes the essential ideas and structure for a film.

two-shot A shot in which two characters appear; ordinarily a medium shot or medium long shot.

typecasting The casting of actors because of their looks or "type" rather than for their acting talent or experience.

variable-focal-length lens See **zoom lens**.

verisimilitude A convincing appearance of truth. Movies are verisimilar when they convince you that the things on the screen—people, places, and so on; no matter how fantastic or antirealistic—are "really there."

video assist camera A tiny device, mounted in the viewing system of the film camera, that enables a script supervisor to view a scene on a video monitor—and thus compare its details with those of surrounding scenes to ensure visual continuity—before the film is sent to the laboratory for processing.

viewfinder On a camera, the little window that the cameraperson looks through when taking a picture; the viewfinder's frame indicates the boundaries of the camera's point of view.

voice-over narration Narration heard concurrently and over a scene but not synchronized to any character who may be talking on-screen. It can come from many sources, including a third person, who is not a character, to bring us up-to-date; a first-person narrator commenting on the action; or in a nonfiction film, a commentator. Compare **first-person narration** and **third-person narration**.

walk-on A role even smaller than a cameo, reserved for a highly recognizable actor or personality.

wardrobe See **costumes**.

wide-angle lens See **short-focal-length lens**.

widescreen aspect ratio Any aspect ratio wider than 1.33:1, the standard ratio until the early 1950s.

wipe A transitional device between shots in which shot B wipes across shot A, either vertically or horizontally, to replace it. Although (or because) the device reminds us of early eras in filmmaking, directors continue to use it.

XCU See **extreme close-up**.

XLS See **extreme long shot**.

zoom in A shot in which the image is magnified by movement of the camera's lens only, without the camera itself moving. This magnification is the essential difference from the dolly in.

zoom lens Also known as *variable-focal-length lens*. A lens that is moved toward and away from the subject being photographed, has a continuously variable focal length, and helps reframe a shot within the take. A zoom lens permits the camera operator during shooting to shift between wide-angle and telephoto lenses without changing the focus or aperture settings. Compare **long-focal-length lens**, **middle-focal-length lens**, and **short-focal-length lens**. See also **prime lens**.

zoopraxiscope An early device for exhibiting moving pictures—a revolving disk with photographs arranged around the center.

PERMISSIONS ACKNOWLEDGMENTS

Chapter 1

p. 1: Everett Collection; **p. 2:** *Brokeback Mountain,* © 2005 Alberta Film Entertainment; **p. 4:** *The Imposter,* © 2012 Film4 Productions; **p. 5:** *Chennai Express,* © 2013 Red Chillies Entertainment; **p. 7 (top left):** *Sweeney Todd: The Demon Barber of Fleet Street,* © 1979; **(all):** *Sweeney Todd,* 2007 Dreamworks Pictures; **p. 8 (all):** *Juno,* © 2007 Dancing Elk Productions/FOX; **p. 9 (all):** *Juno,* © 2007 Dancing Elk Productions/FOX; **p. 10 (all):** *Juno,* © 2007 Dancing Elk Productions/FOX; **p. 11 (both):** *Juno,* © 2007 Dancing Elk Productions/FOX; **p. 12:** *Juno,* © 2007 Dancing Elk Productions/FOX; **p. 13 (top):** *Juno,* © 2007 Dancing Elk Productions/FOX; **(bottom):** *Back to the Future,* © 1985 Universal Pictures; **p. 14:** *Juno,* © 2007 Dancing Elk Productions/FOX; **p. 15 (both):** *Juno,* © 2007 Dancing Elk Productions/FOX; **p. 16 (all):** *Juno,* © 2007 Dancing Elk Productions/FOX; **p. 17 (all):** *Juno,* © 2007 Dancing Elk Productions/FOX; **p. 18 (all):** *Juno,* © 2007 Dancing Elk Productions/FOX; **p. 19 (both):** *Juno,* © 2007 Dancing Elk Productions/FOX; **p. 20 (top left):** *Way Down East,* 1920 D.W. Griffith Productions; **(top right):** *The Miracle of Morgan's Creek,* 1944 Paramount Pictures; **(middle left):** *Rosemary's Baby,* 1968 William Castle Productions; **(middle right):** *Knocked Up,* © 2012 Apatow Productions; **(bottom left):** *Waitress,* © 2007 Fox Searchlight Pictures; **(bottom right):** *Obvious Child,* © 2014 Rooks Nest Entertainment; **p. 22:** *The Hunger Games* © 2012 Lions Gate/Color Force; **p. 23 (both):** *The Hunger Games* © 2012 Lions Gate/Color Force; **p. 24:** *The Hunger Games* © 2012 Lions Gate/Color Force; **p. 25 (first row):** Wikimedia Commons; **(second row):** *The Hunger Games: Catching Fire* © 2013 Lions Gate/Color Force; **(third row):** Wikimedia Commons; **(fourth row):** *The Hunger Games: Catching Fire* © 2013 Lions Gate/Color Force; **p. 26 (all):** *The Hunger Games: Catching Fire* © 2013 Lions Gate/Color Force; **p. 27 (all):** *The Hunger Games: Catching Fire* © 2013 Lions Gate/Color Force; **p. 28 (all):** *The Hunger Games: Catching Fire* © 2013 Lions Gate/Color Force; **p. 29 (all):** *The Hunger Games: Catching Fire* © 2013 Lions Gate/Color Force; **p. 30 (all):** *The Hunger Games: Catching Fire* © 2013 Lions Gate/Color Force; **p. 31 (all):** *The Hunger Games: Catching Fire* © 2013 Lions Gate/Color Force; **p. 32:** *Harry Potter and the Half-Blood Prince,* © 2009 Warner Bros. Pictures; **p. 34:** *Juno,* © 2007 Dancing Elk Productions/FOX.

Chapter 2

p. 35: Everett Collection; **p. 36:** Steven K. Tsuchida, © 2005 Spam-Ku; **p. 37 (all):** *Juno,* © 2007 Dancing Elk Productions/FOX; **p. 38 (top left):** Erich Lessing/Art Resource, NY; **(right and bottom left):** ANNEBICQUE BERNARD/CORBIS SYGMA; **p. 39:** *Zero Dark Thirty,* © 2012 Colombia Pictures; **p. 40:** *The Searchers,* © 1956 C.V. Whitney Pictures/Warner Bros.; **p. 41 (both):** *Bonnie and Clyde,* © 1967 Tatira-Hiller Productions/Warner Bros.; **p. 42 (all):** *Way Down East,* © 1920 D.W. Griffith Productions; **p. 43 (all):** *The Silence of the Lambs,* © 1991 Orion Pictures Corporation; **p. 44 (all):** *The New World,* © 2005 New Line Cinema; **p. 46 (all):** *The Grapes of Wrath,* © 1940 Twentieth Century-Fox Film Corporation; **p. 47 (all):** *Atonement,* © 2007 Work-

ing Title Films/Universal Pictures; **p. 50 (all):** *The Gold Rush,* © 1925 Charles Chaplin Pictures; **p. 51 (top left and right):** *Boyhood,* © 2014 IFC Films; **(middle left):** *Locke,* © 2013 Shoebox Films; **(middle right):** *Edge of Tomorrow,* © 2014 Warner Bros. Pictures; **(bottom left):** *Spring Breakers,* © 2012 A24; **(bottom right):** *X Men: Days of Future Past,* © 2014 20th Century Fox; **p. 52:** *City of God,* © 2002 O2 Films; **p. 53 (all):** *The Killer,* © 1989 Film Workshop; **p. 54 (all):** *The Matrix,* © 1999 Warner Bros. Pictures; **p. 55 (both):** Wikimedia Commons; **p. 56 (left):** *Beasts of the Southern Wild,* © 2012 Fox Searchlight Pictures; **(top and bottom right):** *L'Enfant,* © 1987 Rondo Caprioso; **p. 57 (left):** Geoffrey Clements/CORBIS; **(right):** The Louise and Walter Arensberg Collection; **p. 58 (left):** *Let the Right One In,* © 2008 EFTI; **(right):** *Kick-Ass,* © 2010 Lionsgate; **p. 60:** *Jane Eyre,* © 2011 Focus Features; **p. 61:** *Donnie Darko,* © 2001 Pandora Cinema; **p. 62 (all):** *Donnie Darko,* © 2001 Pandora Cinema; **p. 63 (all):** *Donnie Darko,* © 2001 Pandora Cinema; **p. 66:** Steven K. Tsuchida, © 2005 Spam-Ku.

Chapter 3

p. 67: Jasin Boland/©Warner Bros. Pictures/Courtesy Everett Collection; **p. 69 (all):** *Star Wars,* © 1977 Lucas Arts; **p. 70 (all):** *Slacker,* © 1991 Orion Classics; **p. 72 (top):** *Mulholland Dr.,* © 2001 Les Films Alain Sarde; **(middle):** *Syriana,* © 2005 Warner Bros. Pictures; **(bottom):** *Rango,* © 2011 Blind Wink Productions; **p. 73:** *Nanook of the North,* © 1922 Pathe Exchange; **p. 74 (both):** *Triumph of the Will,* © 1935 Reichsparteitag-Film; **p. 75 (top left):** *American Movie,* © 1999 Bluemark Productions; **(top right):** *Hands on a Hard Body,* © 1997 Idea Entertainment; **(bottom left):** *The King of Kong: A Fist Full of Quarters,* © 2007 LargeLab; **p. 76 (both):** *Grey Gardens,* © 1975 Portrait Films; **p. 77 (left):** *Exit Through the Gift Shop,* © 2012 Paranoid Pictures; **(right):** *The Act of Killing,* © 2012 Final Cut for Real DK; **p. 80 (all):** *Tribulation 99: Alien Anomalies under America,* © 1992 Other Cinema; **p. 81 (all):** *Ballet Mecanique,* © 1923; **p. 82 (all):** *An Andalusian Dog,* © 1929 Luis Bunuel; **p. 83:** *Removed,* © 1995 Naomi Uman; **p. 84 (top left):** *Borat,* © 2006 Four by Two; **(top right):** *Under the Skin,* © 2013 Studio Canal; **(bottom row):** *Symbiopsychotaxiplasm,* © 1968 Take One Productions; **p. 85:** *The Tree of Life,* © 2011 Cottonwood Pictures; **p. 86 (top left):** *Mean Streets,* © 1973 Taplin-Perry-Scorsese Productions; **(top right):** *Goodfellas,* © 1990 Warner Bros. Pictures; **(bottom left):** *The Wolf of Wall Street,* © 2013 Paramount Pictures; **p. 87:** *2001: A Space Odyssey,* © 1968 Metro-Goldwyn-Mayer; **p. 90 (top):** *Iron Man 2,* © 2010 Paramount Pictures; **(middle):** *Her,* © 2013 Warner Bros. Pictures; **(bottom):** *Hitchcock,* © 2012 Fox Searchlight Pictures; **p. 92:** *The Godfather,* © 1972 Alfran Productions/Paramount Pictures; **p. 93:** *White Heat,* © 1949 Warner Bros. Pictures; **p. 94 (left):** *Double Indemnity,* © 1944 Paramount Pictures; **(right):** *Sunset Boulevard,* © 1950 Paramount Pictures; **p. 95 (top left):** *Brick,* © 2005 Bergman Lustig Productions; **(top right):** *Fargo,* © 1996 PolyGram Filmed Entertainment; **(bottom left):** *Insomnia,* © 2002 Alcon Entertainment; **p. 97 (left):** *Close Encounters of the Third Kind,* © 1977 Colombia Pictures Corporation;

Chapter 4

Chapter 5

Chapter 6

© 1934 Paramount Pictures; **p. 226 (left):** *THX 1138*, © 1971 American Zoetrope; **(right):** *Citizen Kane*, © 1941 Mercury Productions; **p. 227 (top):** *Bride of Frankenstein*, © 1935 Universal Pictures; **(bottom):** *The Godfather*, © 1972 Alfran Productions; **p. 228 (all):** *Dogville*, © 2003 Zentropa Entertainments; **p. 229:** *Devil's Backbone*, © 2001 El Deseo S.A.; **p. 230 (top):** *Dr. Strangelove*, © 1964 Hawk Films; **(bottom left):** *Sunset Boulevard*, © 1950 Paramount Pictures; **(bottom right):** *Barry Lyndon*, © 1975 Peregrine; **p. 231 (both):** *Hurt Locker*, © 2008 Voltage Pictures; **p. 232 (both):** *Devil's Backbone*, © 2001 El Deseo S.A.; **p. 233:** *Charisma*, © 1999 King Record Co.; **p. 235 (left):** *The Book of Eli*, © 2010 Alcon Entertainment/Silver Pictures; **(right):** *The Graduate*, © 1967 Embassy Pictures Corporation; **p. 237 (all):** *King's Speech*, © 2010 The Weinstein Company; **p. 238:** *Annie Hall*, © 1977 United Artists; **p. 239 (left):** *Applause*, © 1929 Paramount Pictures; **(right):** *Trouble in Paradise*, © 1932 Paramount Pictures; **p. 240 (left):** *Citizen Kane*, © 1941 Mercury Productions; **(right):** *Notorious*, © 1946 Vanguard Films; **p. 241 (all):** *The Little Foxes*, © 1941 The Samuel Goldwyn Company; **p. 242:** *Badlands*, © 1973 Warner Bros. Pictures; **p. 243 (left):** *The Shining*, © 1980 Hawk Films; **(right):** *The Maltese Falcon*, © 1941 Warner Bros. Pictures; **p. 244 (top left):** *Love Me Tonight*, © 1932 Paramount Pictures; **(top right):** *Do the Right Thing*, © 1989 40 Acres & A Mule Filmworks; **(bottom left):** *North by Northwest*, © 1959 Metro-Goldwyn-Mayer; **(bottom right):** *The Shining*, © 1980 Hawk Films; **p. 245 (all):** *M*, © 1931 Nero-Film AG; **p. 246 (both):** *Bride of Frankenstein*, © 1935 Universal Pictures; **p. 247 (both):** *Jurassic Park*, © 1993 Universal Pictures; **p. 248:** *Taxi Driver*, © 1976 Colombia Pictures; **p. 250 (top and bottom left):** *Citizen Kane*, © 1941 Mercury Productions; **(right):** *Gladiator*, © 2000 Dream Works SKG; **p. 251:** *Jaws*, © 1975 Universal Pictures; **p. 252 (all):** *Touch of Evil*, © 1958 Universal International Pictures; **p. 254:** *The Bourne Supremacy*, © 2004 Universal Pictures; **p. 255 (left):** Courtesy of Photofest; **(right):** *The Diving Bell and the Butterfly*, © 2007 Pathe; **p. 257 (all):** *The Birds* © 1963 Universal Pictures; **p. 259 (both):** *Visitors*, © 2013 Cinedigm; **p. 260 (all):** *Birth* © 2004 New Line Cinema; **p. 262:** *Metropolis* © 1927 Universum Film (UFA); **p. 263:** *2001: A Space Odyssey* © 1968 Metro-Goldwyn-Mayer; **p. 264:** *Pirates of the Carribean: Dead Man's Chest* © 2006 Walt Disney Pictures; **p. 267 (all):** *Boyhood*, © 2014 IFC Films; **p. 270 (top):** *Do the Right Thing*, © 1989 40 Acres & A Mule Filmworks; **(bottom):** Provided by Dave Monahan.

Chapter 7

p. 271: Anne Marie Fox/TM and Copyright © Fox Searchlight. All rights reserved/Courtesy Everett Collection; **p. 273:** *The Quiet American*, © 2002 Figaro; **p. 274 (left):** *One Flew Over the Cuckoo's Nest*, © 1975 United Artists; **(center):** *The Shining*, © 1980 Hawk Films; **(right):** *Batman*, © 1989 Warner Bros.; **p. 275:** *I'm Not There*, © 2007 Killer Films; **p. 277 (top left):** *What's Eating Gilbert Grape?* © 1993 Paramount Pictures; **(top right):** *Donnie Brasco* © 1997 Mandalay Entertainment; **(bottom left):** *Chocolat* © 2000 Miramax Films; **(bottom right):** *Pirates of the Carribean: Dead Man's Chest* © 2006 Walt Disney Pictures; **p. 280:** *Broken Blossoms* © 1919 D.W. Griffith Productions; **p. 281:** *Singin' in the Rain* © 1952 Metro-Goldwyn-Mayer; **p. 284:** *The Philadelphia Story* © 1940 Metro-Goldwyn-Mayer; **p. 285 (left):** *A Place in the Sun* © 1951 Paramount Pictures; **(right):** *Who's Afraid of Virginia Woolf?* © 1966; **p. 287 (top):** *On the Waterfront*, © 1954 Colombia Pictures; **(bottom):** *East of Eden*, © 1955 Warner Bros.; **p. 288:** *Iron Man*, © 2004 Paramount Pictures; **p. 289 (left):** *The Letter*, © 1940 Warner Bros.; **(right):** *The Rabbit Hole*, © 2010 Lionsgate; **p. 291 (top):** *The Big Trail*, © 1930 Fox Film Corp.; **(bottom):**

The Shootist, © 1976 Paramount Pictures; **p. 292 (top):** *Starman*, © 1984 Colombia Pictures; **(bottom):** *True Grit*, © 2010 Paramount Pictures; **p. 293:** *The Social Network*, © 2010 Colombia Pictures; **p. 296 (left):** *The Bank Dick*, © 1940 Universal Pictures; **(right):** *The Maltese Falcon*, © 1941 Warner Bros. Pictures; **p.298 (top):** *Tinker Tailor Soldier Spy*, © 1979 BBC Worldwide; **(bottom):** *Tinker Tailor Soldier Spy*, © 2011 StudioCanal UK; **p. 299 (top):** *Henry V*, © 2012 Neal Street Productions; **(bottom):** *Man From London*, © 2007 Fortissimo Films; **p. 300 (top):** *Knocked Up*, © 2012 Apatow Productions; **(bottom):** *Edward Scissorhands*, © 1990 20th Century Fox; **p. 302:** *Taxi Driver*, © 1976 Colombia Pictures; **p. 305 (all):** *Citizen Kane*, © 1941 Mercury Productions; **p. 307:** *Boyhood*, © 2014 IFC Films; **p. 308 (left):** *The Passion of Joan of Arc*, © 1928 Society General Films; **(right):** *Morocco*, © 1930 Paramount Pictures; **p. 309:** *Snapshot*, © 1979 Filmways; **p. 310 (top):** *Throne of Blood*, © 1957 Toho; **(bottom):** *The Piano*, © 1993 Bac Films; **p. 311:** *12 Years a Slave*, © Fox Searchlight Pictures. **p. 312:** *My Week with Marilyn*, © 2011 Entertainment Films Distributors; **p. 313 (all):** *Blue Valentine*, © 2010 Weinstein Company; **p. 316:** *American Beauty*, © 1999 DreamWorks Pictures.

Chapter 8

p. 317: The Kobal Collection/Universal Picture/Art Resource, NY; **p. 319 (all):** *Requiem for a Dream*, © 2000 Artisan Entertainment; **p. 320:** *Snapshot*, © 1979 Filmways; **p. 322:** *Shine a Light*, © 2008 Paramount Classics; **p. 324:** Provided by Richard Barsam; **p. 325 (all):** Wikimedia Commons; **p. 326 (top row):** *The Thin Red Line*, © 1998 20th Century Fox; **(bottom row):** *They Shoot Horses, Don't They?* © 1969 ABC Pictures; **p. 327 (all):** *Erin Brockovich*, © 2000 Universal Pictures; **p. 328 (both):** *Out of Sight*, © 1998 Universal Pictures; **p. 329:** *Battleship Potemkin*, © 1925 Soviet Union; **p. 330 (all):** *Battleship Potemkin*, © 1925 Soviet Union; **p. 332 (all):** *Run, Lola, Run*, © 1981 Sony Pictures Classics; **p. 334 (all):** *Casablanca*, © 1942 Warner Bros.; **p. 335 (all):** *Casablanca*, © 1942 Warner Bros.; **p. 336:** *Trip to the Moon*, © 1902 Georges Méliès; **p. 337:** *Vertigo*, © 1958 Paramount Pictures; **p. 338 (all):** *Breathless*, © 1960 UGC; **p. 339 (all):** *Breathless*, © 1960 UGC; **p. 340 (all):** *The Searchers*, © 1956 Warner Bros.; **p. 343 (all):** *2001: A Space Odyssey*, © 1968 Metro-Goldwyn-Mayer; **p. 344 (top row):** *Lawrence of Arabia*, © 1962 Colombia Pictures; **(bottom row):** *Stagecoach*, © 1939 Walter Wanger Productions; **p. 345 (both):** *Now, Voyager*, © 1942 Warner Bros.; **p. 346 (all):** *Rear Window*, © 1954 Paramount Pictures; **p. 347 (all):** *Night of the Hunter*, © 1955 United Artists; **p. 348 (all):** *Taxi Driver*, © 1976 Colombia Pictures; **p. 349 (all):** *Cries and Whispers*, © 1972; **p. 350 (top and bottom left):** *The Tin Drum*, © 1979 United Artists; **(right):** *To Die For*, © 1995 Academy Entertainment; **p. 351 (top):** *The 400 Blows*, © 1959 Cocinor; **(middle):** *Y Tu Mama Tambien*, © 2001 20th Century Fox; **(bottom):** *Goodfellas*, © 1990 Warner Bros. Pictures; **p. 352:** *The Rules of Attraction*, © 2002 Lions Gate Films; **p. 354 (all):** *The Birth of a Nation*, © 1915 Epoch Producing Co.; **p. 358 (all):** *City of God*, © 2002 O2 Filmes; **p. 359 (all):** *City of God*, © 2002 O2 Filmes; **p. 360 (all):** *City of God*, © 2002 O2 Filmes; **p. 362 (top):** *Battleship Potemkin*, © 1925 Soviet Union; **(bottom):** Provided by Dave Monahan.

Chapter 9

p. 363: GHOULARDI FILM COMPANY/THE KOBAL COLLECTION; **p. 365:** *Inception*, © 2010 Warner Bros.; **p. 368:** *Spirited Away*, © 2001 Studio Ghibli; **p. 370 (all):** *Apocalypse Now*, © 1979 United

Artists; **p. 371 (left):** *Mean Streets*, © 1973 Taplin-Perry-Scorsese Productions; **(right):** *Midnight Cowboy*, © 1969 United Artists; **p. 372 (both):** *North by Northwest*, © 1959 Metro-Goldwyn-Mayer; **p. 374:** *Hamlet*, 1948; **p. 375:** *Double Indemnity*, © 1944 Paramount Pictures; **p. 377:** *Raging Bull*, © 1980 United Artists; **p. 378:** *Slumdog Millionaire*, © 2009 Fox Searchlight Pictures; **p. 379:** *Tragedy of Othello*, © 1952; **p. 381 (all):** *Magnolia*, © 1999 New Line Cinema; **p. 382 (both):** *A Clockwork Orange*, © 1971 Warner Bros.; **p. 383:** *Winter's Bone*, © 2010 Roadside Attractions; **p. 384:** *Uncle Boonmee Who Can Recall His Past Lives*, © 2010 Kick the Machine; **p. 385:** *War of the Worlds*, © 2005 Paramount Pictures; **p. 386 (both):** *War of the Worlds*, © 2005 Paramount Pictures; **p. 387 (both):** *War of the Worlds*, © 2005 Paramount Pictures; **p. 388 (all):** *War of the Worlds*, © 2005 Paramount Pictures; **p. 390 (both):** *Once Upon a Time in the West*, © 1968 Paramount Pictures; **p. 391 (both):** *39 Steps*, © 1939; **p. 393 (all):** *Apocalypse Now*, © 1979 United Artists; **p. 394:** *Me and You and Everyone We Know*, © 2005 IFC Films; **p. 395:** *Snapshot*, © 1979 Filmways; **p. 396 (all):** *The Man Who Wasn't There*, © 2001 USA Films; **p. 397 (both):** *Citizen Kane*, © 1941 Mercury Productions; **p. 398 (both):** *Citizen Kane*, © 1941 Mercury Productions; **p. 399 (both):** *Citizen Kane*, © 1941 Mercury Productions; **p. 400 (all):** *Citizen Kane*, © 1941 Mercury Productions; **p. 403 (top):** *Snapshot*, © 1979 Filmways; **(bottom):** Provided by Dave Monahan.

Chapter 10

p. 405: Mercury Productions; **p. 406:** *Sunset Boulevard*, © 1950 Paramount Pictures; **p. 411 (both):** University of PA; **p. 412 (all):** Courtesy of Museum of Modern Art/Film Stills Archive, New York; **p. 413 (left):** *Children Digging for Clams*, © 1896 Lumière; **(right):** Image Entertainment; **p. 414:** *The Great Train Robbery*, © 1903 Edison Manufacturing Company; **p. 415:** *The Crowd*, © 1928 MGM; **p. 416:** Solax Film Company; **p. 417:** *The Birth of a Nation*, © 1915

Epoch Producing Co.; **p. 418 (both):** *The Cabinet of Dr. Caligari*, © 1920 Decla-Bioscop AG; **p. 419 (left):** *Nosferatu*, © 1922 Film Arts Guild; **(right):** *The Last Laugh*, © 1924 UFA; **p. 420:** *The Fall of the House of Usher*, © 1928; **p. 421:** *Turning the Wheel*, © 1923; **p. 422:** *The Man with the Movie Camera*, © 1929; **p. 423 (left):** *Alexander Nevsky*, © 1938; **(right):** *Battleship Potemkin*, © 1925 Soviet Union; **p. 424 (left):** *Mr. Deeds Goes to Town*, © 1939 Colombia Pictures; **(right):** *The Jazz Singer*, © 1927; **p. 425 (left):** *Easy Living*, © 1937 Paramount Pictures; **(right):** *Baby Face*, © 1933 Warner Bros.; **p. 426:** *Gone with the Wind*, © 1939 Selznick International Pictures; **p. 427:** *Citizen Kane*, © 1941 Mercury Productions; **p. 428:** *Ossessione*, © 1943 Industrie Cinematografiche Italiane; **p. 429:** *The Bicycle Thief*, © 1948 Produzioni De Sica; **p. 431 (left):** *The 400 Blows*, © 1959 Cocinor; **(right):** *Breathless*, © 1960 UGC; **p. 432 (left):** *The Butcher*, © 1970 Cinerama Releaseing Corporation; **(right):** *Cleo from 5 to 7*, © 1962; **p. 434:** *The Victim*, © 1961 Rank Film Distributors; **p. 435:** *Breaking the Waves*, © 1996; **p. 436:** *The American Friend*, © 1977 Axiom Films; **p. 437:** *Ran*, © 1985 Toho; **p. 438:** *Sansho the Bailiff*, © 1954 Daiei Film; **p. 439 (left):** *Tokyo Story*, © 1953 Shochiku; **(right):** *In the Realm of the Senses*, © 1976 Argos Films; **p. 440:** *Farewell My Concubine*, © 1993 Beijing Film Studio; **p. 441:** *A Better Tomorrow*, © 1986 Cinema City & Films Co.; **p. 442:** *Crouching Tiger Hidden Dragon*, © 2000 Asia Union Film & Entertainment Ltd.; **p. 443:** *Pather Panchali*, © 1955 Aurora Film Corporation; **p. 448:** *Stranger Than Paradise*, © 1984 The Samuel Goldwyn Company; **p. 449 (top):** *Bonnie and Clyde*, © 1967 Tatira-Hiller Productions/Warner Bros.; **(bottom):** *Chinatown*, © 1974 Paramount Pictures; **p. 450:** *The Wild Bunch*, © 1969 Warner Bros.; **p. 451 (left):** *Grey Gardens*, © 1975 Portrait Films; **(right):** *Dog Star Man*, © 1961.

Chapter 11

p. 457: The Kobal Collection/Warner Bros./Legendary Pictures/Art Resource, NY; **p. 462:** Science Source.

INDEX

Page numbers in *italics* refer to illustrations and captions; those in **boldface** refer to main discussions of topics.

Writing About

MOVIES

FOURTH EDITION

Writing About
MOVIES
FOURTH EDITION

KAREN M. GOCSIK
University of California, San Diego

RICHARD BARSAM
Emeritus, Hunter College

DAVE MONAHAN
University of North Carolina, Wilmington

W. W. NORTON & COMPANY
New York • London

W. W. Norton & Company has been independent since its founding in 1923, when William Warder Norton and Mary D. Herter Norton first published lectures delivered at the People's Institute, the adult education division of New York City's Cooper Union. The firm soon expanded its program beyond the Institute, publishing books by celebrated academics from America and abroad. By midcentury, the two major pillars of Norton's publishing program—trade books and college texts—were firmly established. In the 1950s, the Norton family transferred control of the company to its employees, and today—with a staff of four hundred and a comparable number of trade, college, and professional titles published each year—W. W. Norton & Company stands as the largest and oldest publishing house owned wholly by its employees.

Editors: Peter Simon and Spencer Richardson-Jones
Managing editor, College: Marian Johnson
Production manager: Andy Ensor
Design director: Rubina Yeh
Series design: Chris Welch
Composition and project management: Westchester Publishing Services
Manufacturing: Maple Press

ISBN: 978-0-393-26523-1

W. W. Norton & Company, Inc., 500 Fifth Avenue, New York, N.Y. 10110-0017
www.wwnorton.com
W. W. Norton & Company Ltd., Castle House, 75/76 Wells Street, London W1T 3QT

1 2 3 4 5 6 7 8 9 0

Brief Contents

Part I: Preparing to Write

Part II: The Writing Process

Part III: Resources

Contents

Part I: Preparing to Write

Contents

Contents

Part II: The Writing Process

Contents

Contents

Contents

Part III: Resources

Writing About

MOVIES

FOURTH EDITION

Part I

PREPARING
TO WRITE

1

The Challenges of Writing About Movies

What's so hard about writing about movies? After all, we all "know" movies. Most of us could recite the plot of *The Hunger Games* more easily than we could recite the Gettysburg Address. We know more about the fictional characters who inhabit "Middle Earth" in *The Lord of the Rings* trilogy than we know about many of the people who inhabit our own lives.

It's precisely our familiarity with film, however, that presents our greatest writing challenge. Film is so familiar and so prevalent in our lives that we are often lulled into viewing movies passively. As a result, certain aspects of films are often invisible to us. Caught up in the entertainment, we sometimes don't "see" the camera work, composition, editing, or lighting. Nor do we "hear" the sound design. Nor do we observe the production struggles that accompany every film—including the script's many rewrites, the drama of getting the project financed, the casting challenges, and the hundreds of other decisions that were strung together to make the film reach the screen.

However, when your film professor asks you to write about film, it's precisely those "invisible" aspects that you're expected to see and hear. You need to pay attention to the way the camera moves. Observe the composition (the light, shadow, and arrangement) within the frame. Think about how the film was edited. Note the sound design. In short, consider the elements that make up the film and examine how they function, separately and together. In breaking down the film into its constituent parts, you'll be able to *analyze* what you see.

You might also think about the film in the context of when it was made, how, and by whom. Considering the context of the film's production, its reception by viewing audiences, and its relationship with the culture in which it was made and released, you'll be able to *synthesize* your analysis of the film and its context. In short, you'll be able to write a paper that transforms your thoughts and responses into writing that is appropriately academic.

Before we get into the thick of this subject, let's tackle the most general question of all.

What Is Academic Writing?

Simply put, academic writing (sometimes called "scholarship") is writing done by scholars for other scholars—and that includes you. As a college student, you are engaged in activities that scholars have been engaged in for centuries: you read about, think about, argue about, and write about great ideas. Of course being a scholar requires that you read, think, argue, and write in certain ways. You will need to make and support your claims according to the customary expectations of the academic community.

How do you determine what these expectations are? The literary theorist Kenneth Burke has famously described scholarship as an ongoing conversation, and this metaphor may be helpful. Imagine you have just arrived at a dinner party. The discussion (which in this case is about cinema) has already been going on for quite a while when you arrive. What do you do? Do you sit down and immediately voice your opinions? Or do you listen, try to gauge the lay of the land, determine what contribution you might make, and only then venture to make it?

The etiquette that you would employ at the dinner party is precisely the strategy that you should use when you write academic papers. In short, listen to what other scholars are saying. Familiarize yourself with the scholarly conversation before jumping in. Pay attention to both *what* is said and *how* it is said. A book like the one you're reading now can be a helpful "dinner companion" that helps get you up to speed and fills you in on the conversation that preceded you. But you should make use of other resources, too. Your professor, for instance, is a living, breathing expert on what film scholars care about. Books, journals, and reputable Internet sites also offer an opportunity to eavesdrop on the ongoing scholarly conversation about movies. Once you understand the substance of that conversation, you can begin to construct informed arguments of your own.

Getting Started

CONSIDER WHAT YOU KNOW

A short paper written in response to a viewing of Alfred Hitchcock's *Rear Window* (1954), for example, may not require you to be familiar with Hitchcock's other films or to have a broad familiarity with film's formal elements.

However, if you're asked to write an academic paper on the film, you'll want to know more. You'll want to have a firm grasp of the technical and formal elements of film so that you can explain how Hitchcock and his collaborators created the movie. You'll want to be familiar with Hitchcock's other films so that you can understand what themes are important to Hitchcock and his work. Finally, if you're watching this film in an upper-level film class, you'll want to be aware of different critical perspectives on Hitchcock's films and on films in general, so that you can "place" your argument within the ongoing critical conversation.

CONSIDER WHAT YOU THINK

The aim in thinking about your topic is to come up with fresh observations. After all, it's not enough to summarize in a paper what's obvious, what's already known and discussed. You must also add something of your own to the conversation.

Understand, however, that "adding something of your own" is not an invitation to allow your personal associations, reactions, or experiences to dominate your paper. To create an informed argument, you must first recognize that your writing should be analytical rather than personal. In other words, your writing must show that your associations, reactions, and experiences of a film have been framed in a critical, rather than a personal, way.

This is not to say that your personal responses to a movie are irrelevant. Indeed, your personal responses are often a good starting point for the academic work to come. For instance, being terrified by *The Babadook* (2014; director: Jennifer Kent) can be the first step on the way to a strong analysis. Interrogate your terror. Why are you scared? Which elements of the film contribute most to your fear? How does the film play with the horror genre in order to evoke a fear that is fresh and convincing?

Interrogating your personal responses is the first step in making sure that your argument will be appropriately academic. To help ensure that your responses are critical rather than personal, subject them to the following critical thinking processes: summary, evaluation, analysis, and synthesis.

SUMMARIZE

The first step in thinking critically about any film is to summarize what the film presents onscreen. You can construct several different summaries, depending on your goals, but beware: even the most basic of summaries—the plot summary—isn't as simple as it seems. It's difficult to write both economically and descriptively, to discern what's essential to your discussion and what's not.

Consider this: Orson Welles's *Citizen Kane* (1941) has a very complex plot using seven narrators and consisting of nine parts (five of which include flashback sequences). Further complicating matters is that the story duration is about seventy years, while the plot duration is one week of a reporter's research. *Citizen Kane* is a notoriously difficult film to sum up—though the following plot summary by Jesse Garon, taken from the Internet Movie Database (IMDb), does an excellent job:

> Multimillionaire newspaper tycoon Charles Foster Kane dies alone in his extravagant mansion, Xanadu, speaking a single word: "Rosebud." In an attempt to figure out the meaning of this word, a reporter tracks down the people who worked and lived with Kane; they tell their stories in a series of flashbacks that reveal much about Kane's life but not enough to unlock the riddle of his dying breath.

What makes this summary effective? It follows the basic structure of any film: a conflict/riddle/problem is proposed;

someone tries to solve the problem, meeting obstacles along the way; finally, the problem is resolved. The writer of this summary traces the conflict without being sidetracked by the many plot complications. He sticks to the theme and to the basic conflict/resolution structure. He also makes sure that his sentences are simple and clear. In the end, he produces a summary that is faithful to the film but that doesn't overwhelm the reader with details.

The exercise of summarizing a film in this manner is a useful one. In most student film essays, plot summary is an important touchstone for the rest of the paper's argument: it helps to ground your argument in concrete details. Summarizing a film's plot helps you to see its structure, conflicts, and themes. But if you choose to provide a plot summary in your own writing, use it judiciously—as a tool that aids your analysis, not as an excuse to avoid analysis. A common beginner's error is to hand in a paper that claims to offer an argument about a film but instead merely retells the movie's story. You can avoid this by resisting the urge to structure your paper around the movie's narrative chronology. Use the narrative events to support your argument, but don't allow those events to overwhelm it.

When thinking critically about a film, you needn't limit yourself to plot summary. Equally useful, depending on your purpose, are summaries of a film's production values (lighting, editing, sound), its production history (financing, casting, distribution), or its critical reception (reviews, scholarship, and so on). The point is that summarizing is useful in helping you clarify what you know about a film, laying the foundation for the more complex processes to come.

EVALUATE

Evaluation is an ongoing process. You can evaluate a film the moment you encounter it, and you can continue to evaluate and to reevaluate as you go along. It's important to understand that evaluating a movie is different from reacting to it. When you evaluate for an academic purpose, you must find and articulate the reasons for your personal response. What in the film is leading you to respond a certain way? Which influences that are not in the movie might be contributing to your response? Watching *Citizen Kane*, for instance, you might find yourself caught up in the film's suspense. What in the film is making you feel this way? The editing? The acting? The script? Something else? Can you point to a moment in the film that is particularly successful in creating suspense? In asking these questions, you are straddling two intellectual processes: experiencing your own personal response, and analyzing the film.

Evaluation also encourages you to compare a film with other films that you've seen. How does the acting in *Citizen Kane* compare with the acting in other films from the same era? What about the editing? The composition and design of the images in the frame? The sound? The story? How do they compare? Evaluating what's special about a film allows you to isolate those aspects that are most interesting—and most fruitful—to investigate further.

ANALYZE

In the analysis stage of constructing an informed argument, your first task is to consider the parts of your topic that most interest you, then examine how these parts relate to one another or to the whole. To analyze *Citizen Kane*, you will want to break the film down by examining particular scenes, point of view, camera movements, sound, and so on. In short, you'll want to ask, What are the components of Welles's film, and how do these components contribute to the film's theme? How do they contribute to Welles's work as a whole?

Films are filled with so much information that it is difficult to see even a small part of their formal and narrative arrangement in one viewing. You can learn a good deal by carefully analyzing individual shots and scenes, viewing them several times, taking notes each time. Multiple viewings enable you to recognize how the parts of a film interrelate, how some elements recall previous events and foreshadow others, how motifs and subplots function, and how actors create characters through voice, gesture, and expression. When analyzing complex scenes, you might focus on one particular formal or narrative element in each viewing: lighting, editing, camera movement, setting, costume, dialogue, music, sound effects, and so forth.

When you analyze, you break the whole into parts so that you might see the whole differently. When you analyze, you find things to say.

SYNTHESIZE

When you synthesize, you look for *connections* between ideas. Consider once again *Citizen Kane*. In analyzing this film, you might come up with elements that seem initially disparate. You might have some observations that at first don't seem to jell. Or you might have read various critical perspectives on the film, all of them in disagreement with one another. Now would be the time to consider whether these disparate elements or observations might be reconciled, or synthesized. This intellectual exercise requires that you create an *umbrella argument*—a larger argument under which several observations and perspectives might stand.

In an analysis of *Citizen Kane*, for example, an author might observe a series of elements that initially seem at odds with one another. For instance, he might note the range of conflicting emotions that the actors experience (each shifts among various feelings that include tenderness, joy, annoyance, guilt, and rage), and how the interior and exterior actions contradict our typical expectations (whereas outside in the snow the boy Charles plays gleefully, inside the house, which one would expect to be warmer, the lamps remain unlit and the action is cold and strained). The point that the author might make by calling our attention to these conflicting aspects of the film is that Welles is constructing a scene in which appearances are deceiving. Through this scene, an author is warned that her own interpretations of the film's surface details might be mistaken. This warning leads the author to think more broadly about what Welles might be saying—about appearances, and about the secrets that we hold within. The author might then be inspired to look for other examples in which Welles seems to be commenting on appearances, and synthesize them into a broader observation of the film. In this way, the author might transform a list of observations into a powerful and intriguing argument.

Adopting a Rhetorical Stance

When writing an academic paper, you must consider not only what you want to say but also the audience to whom you're saying it. In other words, it's important to determine not only what you think about a topic but also what your audience is likely to think. What biases does your audience have? What values, expectations, and knowledge do they possess? For whom are you writing, and for what purpose?

When you begin to answer these questions, you have started to reckon with what has been called the "rhetorical stance," which refers to the position you take as a writer in terms of both the subject and the reader of your paper.

CONSIDER YOUR POSITION

Let's first consider your relationship to the topic you're writing about. When you write a paper, you take a stand on a topic. You determine whether you're for or against it, passionate or cool-headed. Because few issues can be reduced to pro and con or black and white, you'll also want to consider the nuances of your position. Finally, you may wish to consider whether or not your position takes a particular critical perspective (e.g., feminist). All of these considerations will enable you to refine your stance on a topic.

To ensure that your stance is appropriately analytical, you should ask yourself some questions. Begin by asking why you've taken this particular position. For instance, why did you find some elements of the film more important than others? Does this prioritizing reflect a bias or preconception on your part? If you dismissed part of the film as boring or unimportant, why did you do so? Do you have personal issues or experiences that might lead you to be impatient with certain elements? Might any part of your response to the movie cause readers to discount your paper as biased or uncritical? If so, you might want to reconsider your position, or, if you feel strongly about the argument you're trying to make, you will want to carefully plan how you will support that argument with evidence from the film.

CONSIDER YOUR AUDIENCE

Your position on a topic does not, by itself, determine your rhetorical stance. You must also consider your readers. In the college classroom, the audience is usually the professor or your classmates—although occasionally your professor will instruct you to write for a more particular or more general audience. No matter who your readers are, you'll want to consider them carefully before you start to write.

What do you know about your readers and their stance toward your topic? What are they likely to know about the topic? What biases are they likely to have? Moreover, what effect do you hope to have on the readers? Is your aim to be controversial? Informative? Entertaining? Will the readers appreciate or resent your intention?

Once you've determined who your readers are, you will want to consider how you might best reach them. If, for example, you're an authority on a particular subject and you're writing to readers who know little or nothing about that subject, you'll want to take an informative stance. If you aren't yet confident about a topic and you have more questions than answers, you might want to take an inquisitive stance.

In any case, when you're deciding on a rhetorical stance, choose one that allows you to be sincere. You don't want to take an authoritative stance on a subject if you cannot be confident about what you're saying. On the other hand, you don't want to avoid taking a position on a subject; readers are very often frustrated by writers who refuse to take a clear stance. What if you are of two minds on a subject? Declare that to the reader. Make ambivalence your clear rhetorical stance.

Finally, don't write simply to please your professor. Though some professors find it flattering to discover that all of their students share their positions on a subject, most of us are hoping that your argument will engage us by telling us something new about your topic—even if that "something new" is simply a fresh emphasis on a minor detail. Moreover, it's impossible for you to replicate the ideal paper that exists in your professor's head. When you try, you risk having your analysis compared to your professor's own. Is that really what you want?

Considering Tone and Style

So now you understand what's required of you in an academic paper. You need to be analytical. You need to create an informed argument. You need to consider your relationship to the topic and to the reader. But what about finding an appropriate academic tone and style?

The tone and style of academic writing might at first seem intimidating. But that needn't be the case. Professors want students to write clearly and intelligently on matters that they, the students, care about. What professors don't want is imitation scholarship—that is, exalted gibberish that no one cares to read. If the student didn't care to write the paper, the professor probably won't care to read it. The tone of an academic paper, then, must be inviting to the reader, even while it maintains an appropriate academic style.

Remember that professors are human beings, capable of boredom, laughter, irritation, and awe. They have lives outside of their duties as teachers, and they don't appreciate having their time wasted any more than you do. Understand that you're writing to a person who will be delighted when you make your point clearly, concisely, and persuasively. Understand, too, that she will be less delighted if you have inflated your prose, pumped up your page count, or tried to impress her by using terms that you didn't take the time to understand. (For more on how to craft an appropriate but engaging academic tone and style, see "Attending to Style," later in this guide.)

2

Looking at Movies

Before you start writing anything about a movie, you must first look at it—closely, with an analytical eye, and armed with the specialized vocabulary that is an integral part of serious film study. Looking closely at movies, and taking notes as you do so, is the first step to having something interesting to say about them. This chapter should help you get the process started.

Public and Private Screenings

Most film courses require attendance at public screenings, and often the movies being viewed are the ones that your professor wants you to write about. Even if public screenings aren't required by your instructor, viewing a movie with an audience in a theater is something that every student of film should experience. The reaction of your fellow audience members may, after all, be different from yours. Being alert to their reactions could help you to notice things about the film that you might have overlooked if your only screening happened in the privacy of your own room. Use the time in a public screening to enjoy the experience along with the audience, but also to note those moments when the audience reacts strongly to what's happening onscreen. If you can manage it, take shorthand notes (as discreetly as possible) about what was happening onscreen immediately before, during, and after those moments. These notes will be valuable when you later view the movie in private.

There was a time not so long ago when scholars, critics, and students of film were forced to write about movies without the benefit of private viewings after public screenings. Relying on notes and memory, they often got the details wrong, sometimes in ways that undercut the arguments they were attempting to make. Thankfully, those days are past. Most of the movies that instructors assign in film courses are also available in digital formats for private viewing. These formats have been tremendously popular with consumers, obviously, but they are also a godsend for film scholars and film students, who can rewind, fast-forward, pause, and select specific scenes as often as they need to.

The benefits of private viewings and these simple playback options for film analysis can't be overstated. The pause button, for example, allows you to look carefully at the composition of a shot, to note details of the setting, design, lighting, and individual characters' appearance. The ability to watch a scene first with the sound on, then with the sound off, and then to close your eyes and listen only to the sound in that scene, can help you isolate the effects of the visual and auditory elements individually, and thus understand how that scene "works" with more precision. Even fast-forwarding through a film that you've already viewed can reveal things about the movie: for instance, the repetition of certain patterns, motifs, or visual themes that might not have been obvious when viewed at regular speed.

Not only do digital formats allow you to view movies in a more accurate and productive way, but they also frequently give you access to contextual information about the film that might be difficult to find otherwise. Many DVDs, for example, provide special features that document the film's production background, the intentions and plans of its creators, and the technological innovations and techniques that made certain things happen onscreen. They also often include scenes and shots that were cut from the film. Viewing unused footage provides further insight into the decision-making process of the filmmakers. Sometimes, a scene is cut because of a poor acting performance, or an entire subplot is removed because it doesn't seem to work. Other times, very good scenes and strong performances are left on the cutting room floor. The decision to remove such scenes sometimes reflects the desires of a director to tell the story more concisely or simply, and other times is a signal that a producer or other executive has pushed for a shorter running time. Since many deleted scenes were dropped before they underwent sound editing, effects work, and color corrections (that is, they are *rough cuts*), this unused footage also provides dramatic evidence of the degree to which film studios polish the final product—a useful reminder that the supposed "realism" of the final release is always a carefully crafted construction.

Coupled with the wealth of information on the Internet, special DVD features provide film students with an abundance of material once reserved only for industry insiders or researchers lucky enough to be granted access to studios, film libraries, and special collections. You should take advantage of this material as much as is relevant to your writing assignment.

The Importance of Taking Notes

Taking notes is an essential part of preparing to write about movies. Whether you are recording your observations during a public or personal screening, copying key points of a classroom lecture or group discussion, or jotting down stray ideas over the course of your day, note taking can capture observations, attitudes, and insights that you may otherwise not recall when it comes time to actually compose your paper. Memory is less perfect than we often assume, and realizing that "memory," especially in academic settings, exists no less in documents than between our ears should encourage you to adopt good note-taking practices. There are no rules for note taking, but here are a few useful hints to start:

Make your notes as succinct as possible.

Resist the temptation to record all of your observations at once. Focus instead on significant turning points and details. You can always return to the film for more detail later.

Make rough sketches of shots that you want to discuss. These will prove very useful when you begin to write. If you're viewing on a computer, you can also use an inexpensive software program to grab images from the movie and insert them into your paper as illustrations.

Use shorthand for describing what you see onscreen (a list of suggested shorthand notations is provided at the end of the book). This shorthand will not only speed up the process but will get you in the habit of using film terms.

If you're viewing the movie on a player of some sort, make note of the timing of each shot that you want to discuss—for instance, 09:43—so that you can easily find it again if you need to. If you're watching in a theater, note the approximate timing (e.g., "approx. 10:00").

Review and organize your notes according to any patterns or categories that may appear. Do this while the viewing is still fresh in your mind. Many students come up with ideas for their papers when they reorganize the observations in their notes.

Taking notes is a highly personal activity. Some people meticulously record information in a systematic way, while others haphazardly scrawl ideas and doodles. You should adopt whatever method works for you. That said, there are a few strategies for note taking that have proven useful to film scholars and students that you might consider using or adapting to your own purposes:

ASKING WHY

When viewing a film for the first time all the way through, the most important thing to do is to be alert to things about the film that strike you as different, memorable, or puzzling at the moment. Taking note of these things, and framing your notes about them in the form of questions, will prompt you during your viewing(s) to return to those moments to see if you can answer that question, and thus perhaps discover something about the movie that is interesting enough to write about. Here are some concrete examples of questions about specific films that a student might ask:

Why are the first ten minutes or so [of Lars von Trier's
The Antichrist] in black-and-white and in slow motion?
Why do the credits run at the beginning [of Stanley
Kubrick's *Spartacus*] rather than at the end?
Why is the last shot [in François Truffaut's *The 400 Blows*]
a freeze-frame?
Why is the first running sequence [in Tom Tykwer's *Run
Lola Run*] partly done in animated cartoon form?

Why does the camera "look away" at the moment that Vic Vega cuts off Marvin Nash's ear [in Quentin Tarantino's *Reservoir Dogs*]?

Why is the dialogue so hard to hear [in Terrence Malick's *The Tree of Life*]?

Why are there two actresses playing the same role in the same scene [in Luis Buñuel's *That Obscure Object of Desire*]?

Questions such as these will plant the seeds for productive re-viewing, analysis, and writing.

PLOT SEGMENTATION

If you suspect, after your first question-generating note-taking session, that you will need to understand the structure of the movie's narrative system in order to write your paper, then you may want to create a *plot segmentation*—a scene-by-scene outline of the entire film—during your first re-viewing. In a plot segmentation, each scene should be described briefly in a separate line, with whatever details strike you as worth noting (for example, the nature of the transition from one scene to another, the setting in time and place, any significant difference in this scene's mood, etc.). How will you know when you've gone from one scene to another? When a film significantly shifts in time, space, or action, a new scene has begun.

Once you've mapped out the individual scenes, you should have a document that is no longer than a few pages. If you find yourself on a pace to produce a ten-page document, stop—you have probably confused individual *shots* for *scenes*. Here's an excerpt from a plot segmentation of John Ford's *Stagecoach* (1939):

{Title, cast names, and principal production credits}

I. MORNING OF THE FIRST DAY IN TONTO IN THE 1870s

A. The U.S. cavalry office receives telegraph warning that Apache warriors, under the command of Geronimo, are cutting telegraph wires, a sign that they're preparing to attack the white settlers.

B. Six passengers, the driver, and the sheriff board the stagecoach, which is accompanied by a cavalry escort.

FIRST STAGE OF THE JOURNEY TO LORDSBURG

Conversations establish the passengers' basic antipathy toward one another.

A rifle shot announces the appearance of the Ringo Kid; he surrenders his rifle, and the sheriff arrests him as an escaped convict.

Ringo enters the coach.

The journey resumes without interruption.

One of the first things a plot segmentation shows you is the boundaries of each scene. Seeing these boundaries laid out in one document helps reveal the movie's overall structure (e.g., the number of "acts," the presence of a thematic pattern) and its smallest details (e.g., a consistent use of a certain type of transition between scenes). A plot segmentation is best done during a re-viewing of the film, and with the assistance of the fast-forward button.

SHOT-ANALYSIS CHARTS

Sometimes, your instructor will tell you to pay special attention to a particular scene in the movie you're writing about. Or, if the topic of your paper is yours to determine, you may realize after a few viewings that a particular scene in a movie may be critically important to your paper. Either way, a useful note-taking strategy when you want to analyze a specific scene is the *shot-analysis chart*. A shot-analysis chart, like the plot segmentation, is a "map" of sorts that allows you to see the shot-by-shot structure of a scene, and thus to understand better how the scene works.

The simplest version of a shot-analysis chart would offer four columns and as many rows as there are discrete shots. The columns would be as you see in the sample chart that follows of the beginning of the "assassination" scene in D. W. Griffith's *The Birth of a Nation* (1915): one column for numbering each shot, one that describes each shot in enough detail that you'll be able to recall its details when you later write about it, one that specifies the duration of the shot, and finally, one that

Shot number	Description	Length (sec.)	Type of shot
1	Lincoln's party enter their viewing box.	7	MS *
2	Members of Lincoln's party appear inside the box.	4	MS
3	Lincoln tips his hat to an attendant.	5	MS
4	Lincoln's party in the box; Lincoln appears in it.	4	MS
5	Elsie Stoneman and Ben Cameron sitting in auditorium; they see Lincoln, clap, and rise from their seats.	7	MS
6	View from the back of the auditorium toward the stage. The audience is standing, clapping, and cheering Lincoln.	3	LS **
7	The president's box (as in shot 4); Lincoln and Mrs. Lincoln bow to the audience.	3	MS
8	As in shot 6.	3	LS
9	The president's box (as in shot 7); Lincoln enters the box and sits down.	5	MS

* Medium shot
** Long shot

specifies the type of shot (using a shorthand notation). While the shot-analysis chart might initially seem too technical and detailed for your work as a novice film analyst, you'll find that taking the time to create this chart will actually save you time when you start putting together your analysis—you won't have to keep returning to the film to note the shot sequence, duration, and so on.

You might choose to get into more detail by adding other columns. To chart a particularly kinetic scene, for example, you might want to describe the movement of the camera and the movement of figures within the frame. If you suspect that the setting of each shot in a scene is somehow crucial to the argument that you'll want to make, then you probably should add a column specifically dedicated to a description of the setting. If the sound in the film seems to be playing a crucial role in the scenes you're analyzing, then you will want to add a column that allows you to specify the types and sources of sound in each shot. Whether spare or detailed, the main purpose of a shot-analysis chart is to accurately map the progress from one shot to another in the scene. This sort of note taking will help you be precise in your descriptive analysis when you finally write your paper.

USING SHORTHAND NOTATION

No matter what sort of note-taking system or strategy you adopt, it's helpful to have a list of shorthand notations you can use to quickly describe what you are seeing and hearing onscreen. The list included at the back of this book, "Shorthand Notation for Screenings," can get you started, but of course any set of shorthand notations, as long as you apply them consistently, can do the trick.

What Are You Looking For?

You may wonder at this point just what all these tools and tips amount to. What, exactly, are you *looking for*? What's the *point*?

To answer these questions, first we need to recognize that every movie is a complex synthesis—a combination of many separate, interrelated elements that form a coherent whole. Anyone attempting to comprehend a complex synthesis must rely on analysis—the act of taking something complicated apart to figure out what it is made of and how it all fits together.

A chemist, for example, breaks down a compound substance into its constituent parts to learn more than just a list of ingredients. The goal usually extends to determining how the identified individual components work together toward some sort of outcome: What is it about this particular mixture that makes it taste like strawberries, or grow hair, or kill cockroaches? Likewise, film analysis involves more than breaking down a sequence, a scene, or an entire movie to identify the tools and techniques that are used to create it. The investigation is also concerned with the function and potential effect of that combination: Why does it make you laugh, or prompt you to tell your friend to see it, or incite you to join the Peace Corps? The search for answers to these sorts of questions boils down to one essential inquiry: What does it mean?

Intriguingly, movies have a way of hiding their methods and meanings. When movies are consumed the way they were designed to be consumed (i.e., as entertainment, in one uninterrupted sitting), then their methods, and even their underlying meanings, fade into the background—they become "invisible" to the viewer.

The moving aspect of moving pictures is one reason for this invisibility. Movies simply move too fast for even the most diligent viewers to consider everything they've seen. When we read a book, we can pause to ponder the meaning of any word, sentence, or passage. Our eyes often flit back to review something we've already read. Similarly, we can stand and study a painting or sculpture for as long as we require in order to absorb whatever meaning we need or want from it. But up until very recently, our relationship with movies has been transitory. We experience movie shots—each of which is capable of delivering multiple layers of visual and auditory information—for the briefest of moments before they are taken away and replaced with another, and another, and another. If you're watching a movie the way it's designed to be experienced, you're absorbed in what you're seeing. There's no time (and perhaps no desire) to contemplate the layers of meanings that a single movie moment might present.

Recognizing a spectator's tendency to identify with the camera's viewpoint (which may be omniscient or that of an individual or group), early filmmakers created a film grammar (or cinematic language) that draws upon the way we interpret visual or audio information in our real lives, thus allowing audiences to absorb movie meaning intuitively and instantly.

Cinematic language is a verbal and nonverbal method of communication that uses formal elements to express a movie's thoughts and feelings. These elements are narrative, mise-en-scène (the sum of everything the audience sees, hears, and experiences while viewing), cinematography, acting, editing, and sound.

In the hands of film artists, the flexibility of this language is what makes movies some of the most visceral experiences that art has to offer. For example, the more you learn about the properties of the movie camera, the more you will understand how rich its potential is, not only to record, but also to manipulate the world we see on the screen. And this is why we say that everything you see (or hear) has been put there for a reason, whether it's the way an actor performs, an editor creates rhythm in a sequence, or the sound technicians enhance emotion with tone or volume. The film artist commands cinematic language with a power equal to that of an author writing a novel. Indeed, it is a greater power, for the director works with many artistic and technical collaborators, while the author ordinarily works alone.

So, what are you looking for? In short, you are looking for specific examples of cinematic language that will support the principal idea of your paper. Let's say that you have chosen to write about how Spike Lee develops the theme of power in *Do the Right Thing* (1989), a classic film about racial and ethnic tensions in a New York City neighborhood. Lee made a film rather than a novel because sight and sound seemed to him to be the most realistic ways to capture the vigorous movement and energy of a large city and colorful cast of characters. He tells his story using cinematic language (or film grammar), meaning that instead of telling us, as a novelist does, he shows us with such expressive elements as cinematography, acting, editing, and sound that create not only shots, but also meaning.

Let's say that from your classroom discussions and background preparation, you have reached two hypotheses: that each of Lee's characters have their own ideas about power, and that their individual ideas play out in larger conflicts between a range of opposing forces of race, ethnicity, family, gender, culture, and philosophy. So, in your first analytical screening, you will be looking for examples of how ideas of power are expressed in cinematography, editing, or sound. As you watch the film, you find that the camera is almost always moving as it records the characters' continuous activity; the editing maintains that pace; and the sound, which is realistic and diegetic, often from a boom box, is loud and vibrant. There is *power* in this movement and volume.

This is just a start. Although these examples demonstrate the interdependent relationship of cinematic form and content, *Do the Right Thing* is not a film that should be evaluated strictly on just formal standards. Its meanings are also a product of social contexts bigger than what's on the screen. Remember that your examples must not only support your position but also consider your readers—what sort of context would they bring to a reading of *Do the Right Thing*?

Armed with some tips and techniques to analyze the formal elements that make up a movie's cinematic language, you will be better able to appreciate the complex way in which they blend to convey meaning. There's no way of knowing what your instructor will require in a writing assignment, but chances are that it will involve analyzing the interaction of form and content—for example, how editing helps to create meaning in Alfred Hitchcock's *The Birds* (1963).

3

Formal Analysis

In the previous chapter, we focused on the elements of movies that are there on the screen for us to see. Analyzing those elements—a process sometimes referred to as *formal analysis*—is an important part (in many cases even the *dominant* part) of the process of writing about movies. But it isn't the only approach you'll want to consider. In this chapter, we will briefly describe the various analytical approaches—starting with formal analysis—that serious students of film are asked to employ in their writing.

What Is Formal Analysis?

Careful analysis of a film's form is an essential skill for any student of cinema. Nearly every essay about movies will employ formal analysis, even ones that are written primarily from another perspective.

So what is formal analysis? Formal analysis dissects the complex synthesis of cinematography, sound, composition, design, movement, performance, and editing as they are orchestrated by screenwriters, directors, cinematographers, actors, editors, sound designers, and art directors, as well as the many craftspeople who implement their vision. This synthesis seems complex because it is: the meaning of a movie is expressed through the complicated interplay of its many formal elements. These elements range from matters as straightforward as where and when a particular scene takes place, to the subtler issues of mood, tone, and what a character is thinking or feeling.

While it is certainly possible for the overeager analyst to read more meaning into a particular visual or audio component than the filmmaker intended, you should consider that cinematic storytellers exploit every tool at their disposal. Every element in every frame exists for a reason. Your task, as a formal analyst, is to carefully consider the narrative intent of each of these elements. You'll want to consider how the parts of a film interrelate; how some elements recall previous events and foreshadow others; how motifs and subplots function; how actors create characters through voice, gesture, and expression; and how directors, cinematographers, sound technicians, and editors create mood and convey meaning.

When analyzing complex scenes, you might focus on one particular element: lighting or editing, camera movement or costume, music or sound effects, and so forth. While not all scenes will reward such close attention, most films contain segments that are layered with meaning and significance. If you take the time to examine the way that form and content work together to create meaning, you'll certainly find interesting ideas that can serve as the foundation for your paper.

DESCRIBING FILM FORM

Whatever formal element or elements you choose to write about, you need to offer your reader dynamic, detailed, descriptive writing. In other words, you need to *show*, not merely *tell*, your readers what happens. While your essays cannot provide your reader images twenty feet tall or offer up enhanced surround sound, they can evoke—through language—something of the film's form and your experience of it. Also important to note is that a good description can be analytical: the way you *describe* a scene or shot can convey your *analysis* of that scene or shot. For these reasons it's important to craft your descriptions with great care.

Let's look at a few descriptions of the opening sequence of Alfred Hitchcock's *Vertigo* (1958). In the first example, notice that although the writer has something to say, the writing offers very little detailed imagery:

> The theme of vertigo can be seen even in the opening credits. The close-up of a woman's face and the music make one think of psychological problems. The circles that begin to appear seem like a vertigo of some kind. The opening makes it clear that the movie *Vertigo* will be about more than just the fear of heights.

This writing doesn't offer a vivid description of the opening of the film. We don't get a sense of what the woman's face looks like. Nor do we know what sort of music might be playing that would make us understand that we are looking at a woman who is unstable. Moreover, this description doesn't connect the descriptive details to the analysis: the writer *tells* us what we should be thinking, but doesn't *show* us why we should be thinking that way. In sum, the writer has squandered an opportunity to write a description that also shapes her analysis.

The next example, by the film critic and scholar Robin Wood, is more descriptive. Note that Wood not only practices the principle of *Show, don't tell*; he also shapes his description in order to make his analytical points:

> One aspect of the theme of *Vertigo* is given to us by Saul Bass's credit designs. We see a woman's face; the camera moves in first to lips, then to eyes. The face is blank, mask-like, representing the inscrutability of appearances: the impossibility of knowing what goes on behind the mask. But the eyes dart nervously from side to side: beneath the mask are imprisoned unknown emotions, fears, desperation. Then a vertiginous, spiraling movement begins in the depths of the eye, moving outward as if to involve the spectator. Before the film has begun, we are made aware that the vertigo of the title is to be more than a literal fear of heights.[1]

[1] Robin Wood, *Hitchcock's Films Revisited* (New York: Columbia University Press, 1989), 110.

Wood's analysis of the opening credit sequence works both because he helps us to *see* the opening sequence, and because he illustrates the theme of vertigo—an abstraction—via his concrete description of what is projected onscreen.

Whatever formal element or elements you focus on when you analyze a film, make sure that you use language that is as vivid and descriptive as possible. Tie the concrete details and the carefully constructed observations to larger themes and ideas as you see fit, but always make sure that the particulars within the film back you up. Getting the details right is the heart and soul of formal analysis.

DOING FORMAL ANALYSIS: A SCREENING CHECKLIST

As you examine a movie's formal elements, keep in mind the following questions and considerations. For your convenience, we've crafted this list according to the primary categories of film form: narrative, mise-en-scène, cinematography, acting, editing, and sound. If you are uncertain about the meaning of any of the terms used in the following pages, you should consult the "Illustrated Glossary of Film Terms" at the end of this book. If you're eager for more complete discussions of these terms, you should consult a more comprehensive text, such as *Looking at Movies: An Introduction to Film*.

In general

Whenever you prepare a formal analysis of a scene's use of film grammar, start by considering the filmmakers' intent. Remember that filmmakers use every cinematic tool at their disposal. Very little in any movie moment is left to chance. So before analyzing any scene, first ask yourself some basic questions:

What is this scene about?

After watching this scene, what do I understand about the character's thoughts and emotions?

How did the scene make me feel?

What tools and techniques did the filmmakers use in order to communicate these feelings?

Are there elements of the film that I might not have picked up on in the first viewing?

Did I have any expectations of the movie before I watched it? What were these expectations? Where did they come from? How did they shape my reaction to the movie?

What can I learn from the movie's title? What did the title suggest to me before I saw the movie? What does it suggest now that I've seen it? Has my understanding of the title (or the movie) changed?

Narrative

Narrative is not only the story being told on the screen but also the cinematic and other devices that help tell that story.

Analyzing narrative means examining the effect of a narrator, the relationships of characters, heroes pursuing goals and villains thwarting their progress; it means taking stock of individual scenes and how they fit into the overall plot, and the sequence in which plot points are arranged in cause-and-effect relationships. Questions that can help you examine narrative elements closely include:

- Do I see any narrative or visual patterns recurring? If so, what are these patterns, and why is the director repeating them?
- Who is the movie's protagonist? What motivates or complicates that character's actions?
- What might I learn from categorizing the movie's characters according to their depth (round characters versus flat characters) and motivation?
- Is the camera the only narrator of the film (in other words, is the camera the vehicle by which viewers are "told" the story of the movie)? Or is there another narrator, provided to the viewer by voice-over or direct address?
- Does the movie use restricted narration to limit the viewer's perspective? If so, what is the effect on the viewer's understanding?
- What is the movie's narrative structure? What is the inciting incident? What goal does the protagonist pursue? What obstacles does the protagonist encounter,

and how does she handle them? How is the problem resolved?

Are the plot events presented in chronological order? If not, how are events ordered? Why were they ordered this way?

What can I learn from the movie's subplot? What does this subplot add to the movie? Why is it there?

What nondiegetic elements (voice-overs, for example) are essential to the movie's plot? Do they seem natural and appropriate to the film, or do they appear to be "tacked on" to make up for a shortcoming in the narrative?

Are there scenes that create a noticeable summary relationship between story duration and screen duration? How do these scenes complement or detract from the overall narrative?

Is any major plot event presented onscreen more than once? If so, why do you think the filmmaker has chosen to repeat the event?

Mise-en-scène

Mise-en-scène ("staging or putting on an action or scene" in French) refers to the complete look and feel of a movie—the sum of everything the audience sees, hears, and experiences while viewing it. Aspects of mise-en-scène include the design of sets, costumes, makeup, and props, as well as the composition of shots (i.e., how characters and objects are framed and their organization, balance, distribution, and movement within that frame). The interplay of design and composition, and the relative emphasis of some elements of both, help create meaning in each shot and scene. The following questions can help you deduce which elements of the mise-en-scène help create this overall feel and thus your response to a movie:

How am I responding emotionally to the movie's design and mise-en-scène? Am I comforted or made anxious by what I see onscreen?

What elements contribute to my emotional response?

Does the movie's design feel coherent to me? Do the various elements of the design (the sets, props, costumes, makeup, hairstyles, etc.) work together, or do some elements work against others? What is the effect either way?

Do the design and mise-en-scène evoke the correct times, spaces, and moods? Or is there something not quite "right" that distracts me?

Does it seem as though the filmmakers were attempting to achieve a "realistic" look with the design and mise-en-scène of this film? If so, have the filmmakers succeeded in that goal?

If making the mise-en-scène seem "realistic" doesn't seem to be important in this movie, what were the filmmakers attempting to accomplish with their design?

How are the individual shots framed? What is the composition within the frame? Where are the figures placed? What is the relationship among the figures in the foreground, middle ground, and background?

Does the film employ an open frame or a closed frame? What visual clues suggest that the framing is open or closed? What is the effect of this framing on the viewer's understanding?

Does the use of light call attention to itself? What effect does the lighting have on the overall meaning of the scene? On the overall meaning of the movie?

Does the shot or scene employ lots of movement? Very little movement? How does this movement complement or detract from the narrative?

Cinematography

Broadly speaking, cinematography is the process of capturing moving images on film. Movies have their own language, and cinematography could be called film's grammar—how that language works to make meaning. Cinematography consists of a filmmaker's choices about the types of shots, quality of lighting, camera angles, and special effects to create the language of cinema, in much the same way a writer picks her nouns, verbs, and adjectives to create meaning on a page. And just as specific words have different connotations, different choices in the cinematography of a film create different meanings and associations on the screen. When analyzing a film's cinematography, consider some of the following questions:

Is the film shot so that I identify with the camera lens? If so, what does the director compel me to see? What is left to my imagination? In sum, how does the director's use of the camera help to create the movie's meaning?

Do the cinematographic aspects of the film—the qualities of the film stock, lighting, lenses, framing, camera angles, camera movement, and use of long takes—add up to an overall look? How can I describe that look?

Which moments in the film convey information that is not reflected in characters' action and dialogue? How do these scenes convey that information?

Are special effects used in the film? To what extent? Are they appropriate to, and effective in, telling the story? Are they effective in making something look real when it isn't?

What kinds of shots am I noticing? Is the cinematographer employing shots other than the medium shot—for instance, extreme close-ups or extreme long shots? What role are these shots playing in the film?

Is the cinematographer deviating from eye-level shots? If there are high-angle shots or low-angle shots, are these shots meant to represent a particular point of view (i.e., are they *POV shots*)? If so, what does the angle convey about that character's state of mind? If not, what does it convey about the person or thing in the frame?

What can I note about the composition of shots within a scene? Are the compositions balanced in a way that conforms to the so-called "rule of thirds," or are the elements within the frame arranged in a less "paint-erly" composition? How does the composition contribute to the scene overall?

Have the colors of a shot or scene been artificially manipulated through the use of color filters, different film stocks, or chemical or digital manipulation in order to create a mood or indicate a state of mind? What effect is achieved?

Does the cinematography ever call attention to itself? Is this a mistake or misjudgment on the filmmaker's part, or is it intentional? If intentional, what purpose is served by making the cinematography so noticeable?

Acting

Acting can encompass everything from an actor's performance in a movie to the aura of a movie star's persona in a film. The look, voice, gestures, and interpretation of a character by an actor can contribute enormously to a film's effect on the viewer. And as styles of acting have evolved over more than a century since the movies began, the analysis of acting is dependent on when a film was made, too. The following questions can help guide your response to the acting in a movie:

Why was this actor, and not another, cast for the role?
Does the actor's performance create a coherent, unified character? If so, how?

Does the actor look the part? Is it necessary for the actor
to look the part? Why or why not?

What elements are most distinctive in how the actor
conveys the character's thoughts and internal complexities: body language, gestures, facial expressions,
language? Did the actor use these elements successfully?

Does the actor seem to work well with fellow actors in
this film? Put another way, is there chemistry? How do
the actors make us feel that chemistry? Conversely, do
any of the actors detract from the lead actor's
performance?

Does the actor's performance have the expressive power
to make me forget that he or she is acting? If so, how
did the actor achieve this effect? If the actor is a movie
star like Tom Cruise, do I forget that I am watching
Tom Cruise, or am I acutely aware that this is a Tom
Cruise movie? What are the implications either way?

Editing

Editing is the process of selecting, arranging, and assembling the essential components of a movie—visual, sound, and
special effects—to tell a film's story. It creates relationships
between different shots and between the components of a shot,
and from these relationships emerges a film's meaning. The
different types and pacing of edits a filmmaker can make, from
flashbacks, montages, rapid cuts or long tracking shots, jump
cuts, cross-cutting, and more, contribute enormously to how

we perceive a movie and its story. By asking some of the following questions, you can assess the effectiveness of editing in a film:

Does the movie's editing manipulate my experience of time? Is this condensing, slowing, speeding, repeating, or reordering of time simply practical (as in removing insignificant events), or is it expressive (in that it creates another layer of meaning)? If the play with time is expressive, just what is being expressed?

Does the editing overall seem to create continuity or discontinuity? If the editing is mostly creating continuity, are there nonetheless moments when the editing creates discontinuity? What is the significance of those moments?

What kind of transitions am I seeing from shot to shot (e.g., types of cuts, dissolves, wipes, etc.)? Does the editor use one transitional effect more than others? Are the transitions seamless and nearly unnoticeable, or do they call attention to themselves? Why does the editor use these techniques? What is their effect?

As each shot cuts to the next shot, I'll tap my finger on a tabletop or other surface to get a feeling for the rhythm of the editing. How might I describe that rhythm? Does it stay constant, or does it speed up or slow down? How does the rhythm affect my emotional response to the movie?

Considering the different types of match cuts in the film, what visual or narrative information is each match cut conveying?

Do I see any moments in the movie in which the traditional conventions of Hollywood continuity editing—including use of the master shot, the 180-degree system, shot/reverse shot, match cuts, and parallel editing—are violated in some way? Where and how do these moments appear onscreen? What is the significance of these moments?

Sound

The sound we hear in a film—its music, dialogue, and sound effects—creates meaning just as much as what we see. Sound helps the filmmaker tell a movie's story by reproducing and intensifying the world that has been partially created by the film's visual elements. The choices made for dialogue, music, ambient sounds, and even silence can alter our impression of a scene completely, even if the visuals we see remain the same. Elements to consider when analyzing a film's sound include:

Which sounds are diegetic sounds? Which are nondiegetic? Which are onscreen sounds and which are offscreen sounds?

What types of sound (vocal sounds, ambient sounds, sound effects, music, silence) are used in this shot or scene? To what effect?

Are there moments when the sound creates emphasis by
accentuating and strengthening the visual image?
What is the purpose of this use of sound?
How does the sound develop characterization?
How is music used? In a complementary way? Ironically?
Is the music nondiegetic, or are the characters within
the shot or scene able to hear it?
Do image and sound complement one another in this
movie, or does one dominate the other?
Does this film use silence expressively? How so?
In this movie, do I hear evidence of a comprehensive
approach to sound—one, specifically, in which the
film's sound is as expressive as its images? If so, what's
going on?

Exploring Meaning

FORM AND CONTENT

Even though we've been spending a great deal of time asking
you to consider a movie's formal elements, it's important for
us to acknowledge that there is another aspect of any movie
that goes hand in hand with its form, a component that shapes
and is shaped by form: namely, the movie's *content*.

The terms *form* and *content* crop up in almost any scholarly
discussion of the arts. But what do they mean, and why are
they so often paired? At the most basic level, we can define

content as the subject of an artwork (what the work is about), and form as the means by which that subject is expressed and experienced. The two terms are often paired because works of art need them both. Content provides something to express; form supplies the methods and techniques necessary to present content to the audience.

However, form doesn't just allow us to *see* the subject/content; it lets us see that content *in a particular way*. Form enables the artist to shape both our experience and our interpretation of that content. As we try to understand how the movie we're analyzing *works*, we thus become more aware of how form and content interplay to make *meaning*. In other words, we come to see *form as content*, in that formal elements convey something important about content. We come to see *content as form*, in that content is shaped by the form it takes.

Complicating the matter futher is that, in addition to the story that any movie tells, there are cultural values, shared ideals, and other ideas that lie just below the surface of that movie. These cultural contents—the story, the assumptions, the values, the ideas—as well as the particular form they take, create various layers of meaning within the movie. These layers of meaning overlap, intersect, and inform one another. The notion that any movie contains layers upon layers of meaning may make the process of looking at movies seem intimidating. But you'll find that the process of observing, identifying, and interpreting a movie's meanings will become considerably less mysterious once you grow accustomed to actively looking at movies rather than just watching them. It might also help to keep in mind that, no matter how many different layers of meaning there may be in a movie, each layer is either *explicit* or *implicit*.

EXPLICIT AND IMPLICIT MEANING

By explicit meaning, we mean a message that the movie presents right on its surface. The central facts of a story, for instance, are explicit. An implicit meaning, by contrast, lies below the surface of a movie's story and presentation, and is closest to our everyday sense of the word *meaning*. In this sense, implicit meaning is an association, connection, or inference that a viewer makes on the basis of the explicit meanings available on the surface of the film.

To tease out the difference between these two levels of meaning, let's look at two statements about *Juno* (2007). First, let's imagine that a friend who hasn't seen the movie asks us what the film is about. Our friend doesn't want a detailed plot summary; she simply wants to know what she'll see if she decides to watch the film. In other words, she is asking us for a statement about *Juno*'s explicit meaning. We might respond to her question by explaining: "The movie's about a rebellious but smart sixteen-year-old girl who gets pregnant and resolves to tackle the problem head-on. At first, she decides to get an abortion. But after she backs off that choice, she gets the idea to find a couple to adopt the kid after it's born. She spends the rest of the movie dealing with the implications of that choice."

Now what if our friend hears this statement of explicit meaning and asks, "Okay, sure, but what do you think the movie is trying to say? What does it *mean*?" In a case like this, when someone is asking about the meaning of an entire film, he or she is seeking something like the film's overall message or "point." In essence, our friend is asking us to *interpret* the movie—to say something arguable about it—not simply to make a statement of obvious surface meaning that everyone can agree on. In other words, she is asking us for our sense of the movie's implicit meaning. One possible response might be: "A teenager faced with a difficult decision makes a bold leap toward adulthood but, in doing so, discovers that the world of adults is no less uncertain or overwhelming than adolescence."

At first glance, this statement might seem to have a lot in common with our summary of the movie's explicit meaning—as, of course, it does. After all, even though a meaning is under the surface, it nonetheless has to relate to the surface. Our interpretation of the film's implicit meaning therefore needs to be grounded in the surface's explicitly presented details. Nevertheless, if you compare the two statements closely, you can see that the second one is more interpretive than the first, more concerned with what the movie "means."

Explicit and implicit meanings need not pertain to the movie as a whole, and not all implicit meaning is tied to broad messages or themes. Smaller doses of both kinds of meaning are present in virtually every scene. For example, Juno's application of lipstick before she visits the adoptive father, Mark, is explicit information. The meaning of this action—that her admiration for Mark is beginning to develop into something approaching a crush—is implicit. Later, Mark's announcement that he is leaving his wife and does not want to be a father sends Juno into a panicked retreat. On her drive home, a crying jag forces the disillusioned Juno to pull off the highway. She skids to a stop beside a rotting boat abandoned in a ditch. The discarded boat's decayed condition and the incongruity of a watercraft adrift in an expanse of grass are explicit details that convey implicit meaning about Juno's isolation and alienation. In the end, our ability to understand and appreciate the film depends on our ability to make the associations between its explicit and implicit messages.

4

Cultural Analysis

As we've already said, filmmakers use the conventions of cinematic language to make the inner workings of a movie "invisible" to us as viewers. They want us to be immersed in the imaginative world they've created, not distracted by the technical mechanisms that they've employed to create that world.

The same commercial instinct that inspires filmmakers to hide their methods and mechanisms from our view also compels them to favor stories and themes that reinforce viewers' shared belief systems. For the most part, the mainstream film industry seeks to entertain, not to provoke, its customers. A key to entertaining one's customers is to "give them what they want"—to tap into and reinforce their most fundamental desires and beliefs. Even movies deemed "controversial" or "provocative" can be popular if they trigger emotional responses from their viewers that reinforce yearnings or beliefs that lie deep within. Because so much of this response occurs on an unconscious, emotional level, the casual viewer may be blind to the implied political, cultural, and ideological messages that help make the movie so appealing.

Of course, this cultural invisibility is not always a calculated decision on the part of the filmmakers. Directors, screenwriters, and producers are, after all, products of the same society inhabited by their intended audience. Oftentimes, the people making the movies may be just as oblivious of the cultural attitudes shaping their cinematic stories as the people who watch them.

Thus, the layers of implicit meaning in any film include not only those that the filmmakers have consciously crafted, but also those that they have not intended. This fact can be liberating for you as you write about film: you are not limited to deciphering the filmmaker's intent but can explore the unintended messages of the film, as well as the effect the film has on its audiences. Having taken this time to explain what we mean when we talk about "meaning," we can now turn to the next general approach to film analysis: *cultural analysis*.

What Is Cultural Analysis?

Scholars of cinema look not only at the surface of a film to understand how it "works"; they also examine the layers of implicit meaning that reflect any cultural assumptions that the filmmakers and audience might take for granted.

The tools that scholars use to analyze films in this manner are borrowed from critical theories first developed by social theorists, cultural critics, and philosophers. While these theoretical perspectives are the "tools of the trade" for professional scholars of film, they can prove challenging to students who are just beginning their studies. You needn't feel pressured to master film theory before writing your paper. Even a basic understanding of the theoretical perspectives commonly used by film scholars can be useful to novice writers. First, these theories can show you how to cast a more analytical eye on the unspoken assumptions and ideals that seem to be taken for granted in the movies you write about. Second, these theories can be used to jump-start a paper by giving you different frames through which you can view a film.

The most important theoretical frames in film studies include *Marxism*, *feminism*, *race and ethnicity studies*, and *queer theory*. When applied to film, these perspectives offer a critical lens through which you can examine a movie's portrayal of socioeconomic status (Marxism), gender (feminism), racial, ethnic, or national identities (race and ethnicity studies), and sexual orientation (queer theory). Let's look at each of these categories to see how they might serve your film analyses.

SOCIOECONOMIC STATUS

The stories that human beings tell each other cannot avoid issues of socioeconomic status. Characters are rich, or poor, or somewhere in between, and the concrete realities of their existence determine both the way they are developed as characters and the challenges the narrative throws their way.

Depending on the filmmaker's perspective and the culture in which the film is made and screened, a movie can portray a particular social class negatively, approvingly, or anywhere in between. The film may offer explicit or implied messages about the rightness (or wrongness) of the social hierarchies portrayed onscreen. Or, it may seem as though the filmmakers and the characters are willfully blind to the tensions that exist across and among various socioeconomic classes.

The theoretical perspective that concerns itself with issues of socioeconomic class in cinema is *Marxist film analysis*. This framework focuses on the ways that movies either reinforce or undermine the dominant power structures in a society. Based on the extensive philosophical/economic writings of Karl Marx (1818–1883), this form of theoretical analysis sees movies not as innocent entertainment, but rather as an important means by which the social status quo is either maintained (most of the time) or disrupted (occasionally).

Marx himself saw the arts (along with law, religion, and other institutions) as part of the *superstructure* of society—an overlay of ideas and ideologies that reflects the perspective of those at the highest levels of power. According to Marx, popular art forms (including movies) typically lure the working classes and the poor to rally around the ideas that perpetuate the power of those at the very top of the social ladder. When there is broad consensus among the working classes and the poor that the status quo, while unfair to them, is inevitable and proper, then they are exhibiting, to use Marx's phrase, "false consciousness." The values they subscribe to are working directly against their socioeconomic interests. In Marx's view, popular art is one of the means by which the powerful lure the poor and working classes to embrace false consciousness, and to internalize the dominant culture's values and ideas.

Of course, any work of art may work against some aspects of the dominant power structure even as it buttresses others. There is always the potential for works of art to break free of the dominant narrative and to introduce perspectives that inspire us to see "the way things are" with fresh eyes. Nevertheless, according to this theory, the very powerful pull of one's social milieu prevents even the most radical artist from breaking entirely free from accepted ideas and expressions.

Following this line of thinking, many contemporary film scholars examine movies to uncover their unspoken ideas about power and class. Marxist analysis examines the ways that social classes are represented in a film, as well as what messages the film seems to be sending about each class and its place in the hierarchy. When looking at films that set out specifically to undercut the dominant ideology, Marxist analysis examines both the ways that the film succeeds in doing so, and the ways that it inadvertently reinforces existing social structures.

If you are interested in considering issues of socioeconomic status as a springboard for your analysis, you might consider asking the following questions:

Does the socioeconomic status of each character play a significant role in the narrative? How so?

> Are people from a particular class portrayed negatively (or positively) in this movie? If so, what seems to be the point of that portrayal?
>
> Does this film seem to set out to critique the socioeconomic status quo? In what ways does it do so? What aspects of the status quo does it leave unquestioned?
>
> Is nearly everything of value in this movie something that can be bought and sold (i.e., a *commodity*)? Or does the film portray values that fall outside the realm of economics? Overall, what values are being argued for in this film? How is this argument being presented?

Since the movies began, money has been a favorite subject in countless gangster movies, as well as such films as *Greed* (1924; director: Erich von Stroheim), *Citizen Kane* (1941; Orson Welles), *There Will Be Blood* (2007; Paul Thomas Anderson), and *The Social Network* (2010; David Fincher). Money motivates both men and women from all races, creeds, and backgrounds. That's no surprise in the United States, a country that prizes entrepreneurship and success.

Interestingly, movies about sports often concern the role that money and socioeconomic status play in winning. Take, for example, *The Color of Money* (1986; director: Martin Scorsese), *Raging Bull* (1980; Martin Scorsese), or *Jerry Maguire* (1996; Cameron Crowe). *Foxcatcher* (2014; Bennett Miller) is another. It's about the particular (some would say peculiar) desire of a real-life character, John du Pont (Steve Carell), to spend whatever amount it takes to create a U.S. wrestling team for the Olympics. For du Pont, an heir to one of the world's largest fortunes, this seems easy, even a foregone conclusion. So, with stubborn determination and substantial financial incentives, he recruits a group that includes brothers Mark and Dave Schultz (Channing Tatum and Mark Ruffalo, respectively), star wrestlers from the opposite end of the socioeconomic scale. Here, old money = power, while young wrestlers = talent. It is a story that begins with promises of glory and ends in tragedy when du Pont murders Dave, seemingly out of jealousy, because Dave has the admiration of his brother, as well as a loving wife and children.

In a movie where money is so important, socioeconomic forces might have been responsible, at least in part, for this ending. Is du Pont's money more important than the sport he loves? Does money buy happiness? Is money the "root of all evil"? Does money corrupt sports? Is du Pont portrayed as evil? Are the needy boys portrayed as vulnerable commodities being used for du Pont's dreams of glory? To what extent does money define a family's values? What is the difference, if any, between du Pont's legendary "dynasty" and the Schultzes' developing sports dynasty?

GENDER

Like socioeconomic status, gender is a part of every story ever told. In fact, most of the world's most popular stories hinge on some aspect of gender—whether the story is about what it means to be a man or a woman, or the often-fraught relations between the sexes, or the social roles that are traditionally assigned to one gender or another.

The theoretical lens through which these issues are analyzed by film scholars is *feminism* (or *gender studies*). Feminist film theory brings to the study of movies the same overall concerns that mark the feminist movement as a whole: namely, a desire for equality with men, in society and in the arts; a critical examination of the roles that women have traditionally been expected to fill in society; and a sensitivity to (and critical perspective on) the representations of women and men that reinforce stereotypes and that make the status quo seem "natural" and inevitable.

Feminist film critics have focused their attention particularly on representations of women as passive objects of male desire. Such portrayals back female characters into a corner where their very identities are defined primarily by men, who either validate them or reject them based on their sexual attractiveness. But even more interestingly, we, members of the audience—whether we're male or female—do so as well. In her landmark essay, "Visual Pleasure and Narrative Cinema" (1975), the film scholar Laura Mulvey takes the position that movies lure audiences to identify with the male protagonist's (and the camera's) "gaze," and to thereby judge the worth of the female character as we would any beautiful object to be looked at—i.e., based on desirability.

There are other traditional "types" of female characters in art, of course—the virginal naïf, the helpless "damsel in distress," the femme fatale, etc.—but these, too, according to feminist critics, have their origins in prejudicial stereotypes constructed by and for men. A core task of feminist critique, therefore, is to identify and to deconstruct these stereotyped portrayals wherever and whenever they appear in the movies.

Because of the work of feminist critics at least since the 1960s, women are now producing more films, and otherwise influencing the portrayals of women onscreen, than they ever have before. Some feminist critics are therefore devoting at least part of their efforts to writing about filmmakers whose work breaks with past stereotypes, portraying women in less passive, more diverse and fully realized ways. These critics advocate on behalf of films that are more nuanced in their portrayal of gender.

If you are interested in investigating how gender plays out in movies, here are a few questions you can ask yourself to jump-start your thinking:

Are the main female characters in this movie as fully realized as the male characters? What characteristics do the female characters possess? Which do they lack? What does this tell us about how the filmmakers are positioning women?

Is the identity of the main female character (or characters) defined primarily by her (or their) sex appeal? What are the implications of this portrayal?

Does this movie's narrative seem to suggest that the relations between the sexes are "natural" and proper, or

does it seem to critique the status quo? If the latter,
what is the nature of the critique?
Does this film reflect or work against the assumptions
about gender roles that prevailed in the time when this
movie was made and screened? How so?
Do the formal aspects of this movie (the cinematography,
the editing, etc.) cause you to see the female characters
from the perspective of a male protagonist? In what
way does this perspective limit your understanding of
the characters?
Do you find yourself sympathizing with the main female
character(s) in this film? Why or why not?

Although worldwide feminist movements hold at least one
objective in common—equality for women and men—there
are countries where women have responsibilities unique to
their society, ones that do not always involve equality. We see
this in *Fill the Void* (2012), director Rama Burshtein's intimately
observed drama about a predicament faced by an Orthodox
Hasidic family in Israel. The title refers to the challenge faced
by Yochay (Yiftach Klein), whose wife, Esther, dies in childbirth and leaves him with the dilemma of what to do about
raising their baby. An observant Jew (as are all the characters),
he understands the rigid rules and traditions by which this
ancient community lives, including arranged marriages. In
almost every way, the men and women lead very different lives
from one another. The director, an affirmed feminist, shows

that, however disturbing the practice of arranged marriage may be to some audiences, the woman has the final choice of whom she will marry, even though she is presented with many obstacles in reaching her decision. *Fill the Void* was released to audiences both inside and outside the Orthodox community.

In "filling the void," which suggests a mechanical rather than a meaningful way to find a new wife, Yochay has two choices: marry his 18-year-old sister-in-law, Shira Mendelman (Hadas Yaron)—who has already been looking after the child but is hoping for an arranged marriage with a young man she likes—or an older woman in Belgium whom he has known since childhood but who does not appear in the film. It is not an easy choice for him, and there is no shortage of advice from family, rabbinical elders, and busybodies about what he (and Shira) should do. To some, it would appear that there is only room in this community for tradition, obligation, and interference, but not for love.

Indeed, Yochay and Shira have many serious discussions about their reasons for marrying, but neither mentions love. In this confusion, each is hurt in one way or another by selfishness, misread intentions, and masked emotions. Finally, after much thought, ritual, and prayer, love seems to transfigure both of them, but still neither says the word. The director deliberately leaves the interpretation to us. It is a feeling, not a fact. Nonetheless, the decision to marry is Shira's, and hers alone. They marry, and the film ends as they enter their new apartment.

The movies gives us sufficient information about this community to enable us to study the dilemma as we see it and reach some opinions of our own about the role that gender plays in it. The challenge is to understand, not to judge. In this process, you might consider the following:

Has the process of thought, discussion, and decision changed Shira? If so, how?

Outside of the relatively closed community in which Shira lives, is she a recognizable female character?

Is her character development believable? Or is she a sterotype?

The director is female. From what perspective does she portray the characters, both male and female? In particular, does she photograph the women differently from the men?

Regardless of your gender, do you sympathize with the women and men in the film, Shira and Yochay in particular?

At the end of the movie, Yochay shuts the door of their new apartment while Shira stands timidly. Does this door have symbolic value in relation to their new life together?

Shira is a young woman in a closed community with a fixed way of life, but we also see that the larger society outside is changing culturally. Does her age give her an advantage in dealing with her decision?

RACE, ETHNICITY, AND NATIONAL ORIGIN

Many films in the long history of American cinema present only (or primarily) white characters onscreen. Others have a diverse cast of characters but present racial or ethnic minorities in a mildly unflattering, or even blatantly prejudicial, manner. In contemporary cinema, the perspectives of people of various racial, ethnic, and national origins are very much present, more than they have ever been before. And yet, mainstream Hollywood movies, even now, often stumble into caricature and stereotypical representations of people whose race, ethnicity, or place of origin differs from what the producers of those movies assume are their primary audience.

When societies are composed of a majority population that shares certain characteristics, real or imagined, there is a tendency to privilege that majority's perspective. The perspectives of minority populations are either ignored or "othered," thereby asserting the superiority of the majority group and its values. Such beliefs make it difficult for members of any other group to be seen, heard, or treated with respect.

Film scholars and critics who are sensitive to these issues bring a wide range of analytical and theoretical tools to their work, so it's more difficult than it was above to give a name to some specific theoretical perspective that these critics adopt when they write about film. Professional criticism about cultural portrayals of race, ethnicity, and origin generally depends on a wide familiarity with core concepts in psychology, sociology, and philosophy, and on a broad understanding of cultural and political history.

For beginning students of film, a sensitivity to the relevant issues (or a direct experience with having been viewed as an "other") can enrich any analysis of a movie that portrays tensions or imbalances across the boundaries of race, ethnicity, or national origin. Merely asking pointed questions about these movies can lead you to observations that add significant interest and weight to your analysis. Here are a few questions you might ask to get yourself started.

Given what you know about the place or time portrayed in the movie, are there groups of people not shown or barely acknowledged in the movie who were nonetheless significant and visible there and then? Why do you think they aren't portrayed in this movie?

Does the movie use visual cues—in lighting, camera angles, editing decisions, costume, makeup, or actors' gestures—to establish that a character or a group of characters is clearly an "other"—a strange, foreign, or menacing type of person who falls outside of the "normal" majority? If so, what are the cues and how do they work?

Is the movie seemingly content to reinforce traditional stereotypes of minority characters? Or does it seem to be working against them? How so?

Does the movie portray racial, ethnic, or cross-cultural relations as complex and contradictory social interactions? Or does the film offer, literally and figuratively, a "black-and-white" worldview? What is the effect of the complex or simplistic portrayal of these relations?

With today's national concerns about race, law enforcement, and immigration laws, we see American movies attempting to deal seriously and honestly with the subjects of race, ethnicity, and national origin, including (to name a few) *An Oversimplification of Her Beauty* (2012; director: Terence Nance), *Django Unchained* (2012; Quentin Tarantino), *Fruitvale Station* (2013; Ryan Coogler), *12 Years a Slave* (2013; Steve McQueen), *Lee Daniels' The Butler* (2013; Lee Daniels), *Mandela: Long Walk to Freedom* (2013; Justin Chadwick), and *Selma* (2014; Ava DuVernay). These films depict slavery, the civil rights movement, and domestic situations that were largely ignored throughout American film history. And their directors, both white and black, depict racial, ethnic, or cross-cultural interactions with multiple perspectives. To be sure, a film like *12 Years a Slave* represents a black-and-white worldview of evil white plantation owners versus victimized black slaves, but it also provides other perspectives, including those of whites opposed to slavery, and blacks who betray each other.

Tate Taylor's *The Help* (2011) presents a dense tangle of stories, at the heart of which is a clear-eyed, level-headed examination of how white women treated their black female servants ("the help") in 1960s Jackson, Mississippi, one of the most troubled spots in the South. These middle-class white women have little to do besides host card parties and boss around their black servants, who not only do all their domestic chores but also care for their children. The movie depicts the racism of this little town so thoroughly that we understand that these women have never known any way of life apart from white supremacy. But there are exceptions. Eugenia "Skeeter" Phelan (Emma Stone), a young white woman, returns from college and encourages the maids to tell their stories for a book she is compiling. When it's published, it exposes their employers and blows the town wide open. Two other white women, long ingrained in the town's culture, are strong enough to change their attitudes: Skeeter's mother (Allison Janney) changes almost too late, but the mother (Sissy Spacek) of the film's most obnoxious hostess has long opposed her daughter's behavior. The leading black characters (Viola Davis, Octavia Spencer, and Cicely Tyson) must behave as their employers demand, but they do not reinforce stereotypes of black servants. We see the impact of the town's low wages, hard discipline, segregated buses and housing, and reduced educational opportunities on these women and their families. And in both the black and white communities, the director shoots with an almost documentary precision to show us how each side lives, never exaggerating or simplifying to make a point. It's as if we are there, seeing it for our own eyes, and it has to be that way, for most of us have never experienced firsthand a town like Jackson. Taylor's approach makes it very difficult not to trust his vision.

The Help depicts a place and time that we know is still deeply flawed in its racial attitudes, and its characters, both black and white, are shown honestly. It is primarily a film about women, and the decor of their homes, as well as their appearance, speech patterns, and manners, clearly distinguish between the leisure and working classes. Although the movie ends on a hopeful note, we know that however accurate its depictions may be (and not all would agree on this point), it has presented a world that heretofore Hollywood has peopled with stereotypes, often comic nannies and maids.

SEXUAL ORIENTATION

When it comes to human sexuality, what is "normal"? What is "deviant"? There's no question that these categories are of great interest to many people, and that public attitudes about the boundaries between the various categories of sexual practice are always in flux.

Scholars who critique movie portrayals of "deviant" sexualities or who look critically at the tendency in mainstream cinema to reinforce the idea that heterosexuality is the sole "normal" variety of human sexual identity use a broad array of theoretical tools to conduct their analyses. The umbrella that encompasses all of this work is often called "queer theory."

Film scholars who use queer theory as their lens of analysis focus their attention on cinematic portrayals of alternative sexualities and on the various ways that movies convey "heteronormative" messages (i.e., the subtle or not-so-subtle messages that support the view that only heterosexuality deserves to be considered "normal"). These scholars are often interested in presentations of transgressive phenomena such as drag, cross-dressing, camp, and transsexuality, chiefly because these phenomena cast in high relief the conventions of gender that are clearly "performative" and therefore easily (and often quite entertainingly) parodied. Another obvious task of queer theory is to critique omissions, distortions, and stereotypes of alternative sexual identities wherever they appear.

It's interesting to note that many film artists throughout history who were gay, lesbian, transgender, or otherwise outside the societally defined "norm" of sexual identity have kept this aspect of their identity under wraps. Queer theorists often uncover or make more apparent the fact of these film-makers' sexual identities, analyzing the ways that their films reflect (or conceal) their identities.

If you're interested in analyzing a film through the lens of sexual orientation or identity, you might begin by asking the following questions:

Does the movie present a straightforward and uncomplicated portrait of heterosexual relationships? Or does it
introduce narrative elements that portray alternative
sexual identities? In either case, what comments about
sexuality is the film making?

If the movie does portray alternative sexualities, does it
present people as social deviants, as comic foils, or as

otherwise "abnormal" characters? Or are these characters portrayed as fully realized human beings?

If a movie seems primarily occupied with portraying heterosexuality as the norm to be emulated and celebrated, does it nonetheless contain subtle narrative or visual elements that undermine that portrait of normalcy? What are these elements, and how are they in play?

What function, if any, do performative aspects of gender and sexuality have in the film? Are there camp elements? Drag? Cross-dressing? Are they meant to be merely laughed at or dismissed as deviant, or do they move the movie's narrative in an interesting direction?

If you watch a film made by or starring a film artist who was eventually revealed to be gay, lesbian, bisexual, transgender, or of some other alternative sexual identity, what aspects of the film seem to flow from this identity, and which aspects seem to contradict it?

In writing about a film on money, you would first need to recognize your perspective as, say, a person raised in middle-class circumstances—neither poor nor rich—as a vantage point from which to evaluate it. So it is when writing about a film concerned with sexual orientation. You should acknowledge in your writing at least two things: your gender and your sexuality. Sexual orientation is a sensitive subject, and your reader should know your perspective.

We have long passed the time when homosexuality was a taboo subject in popular culture. Indeed, the word *homosexuality* has given way to the acronym LGBT (lesbian, gay, bisexual, and transgender), although it is not completely inclusive of the varieties of sexual orientation and expression that currently exist. No matter. The subject is out of the closet and widely represented in books, theater, music, television shows, and movies. In the past decade, there have been more feature movies dealing with LGBT issues than we can easily list here, and that does not include documentaries, avant-garde, or animated films. Among other issues, these films deal with parental and societal discrimination, the coming-out process, and the actions and attitudes of all concerned. They represent a cross-section of LGBT characters and societies in countries both East and West—including England, France, Germany, Israel, Arab states, the United States, Japan, Hong Kong, Taiwan, South Korea, Thailand, the Philippines, and India— although the primary focus to date has been on gay men. They are both ordinary men (real and fictional) and politicians (Harvey Milk), writers (Truman Capote), artists (Francis Bacon), athletes (Glenn Burke), and celebrities (Liberace). Among the feature films about lesbians are *Go Fish* (1994; director: Rose Troche), *Heavenly Creatures* (1994; Peter Jackson), *Kissing Jessica Stein* (2002; Charles Herman-Wurmfeld), *Monster* (2003; Patty Jenkins), *The Kids Are All Right* (2010; Lisa Cholodenko), and *Blue Is the Warmest Color* (2013, Abdellatif Kechiche). The characters in these films represent the entire spectrum of race, gender, ethnicity, religion, and sexual orientation. And their stories have been told in all genres, whether drama, melo-drama, or comedy, true or fictional.

Some of these movies have reached a wide audience, while others have appealed to most specialized groups. But the one movie about sexual orientation that almost everyone knows is Jean-Marc Vallée's *Dallas Buyers Club* (2013), which tells a true story about gay and transgender Texans in the 1980s and the AIDS epidemic. (The first major film about AIDS was Jonathan Demme's *Philadelphia* [1993].) The movie vividly depicts the Dallas gay scene—not only the drinking, drug abuse, casual sex, and rowdy clubs, but more importantly the devastating effects of the HIV virus before anti-viral drugs were developed to treat it. It had wide exposure and won Academy Awards for Matthew McConaughey as Best Actor (Ron Woodruff) and Jared Leto as Best Supporting Actor (Rayon).

Woodruff, once a loud, violent homophobe, learns that he has AIDS and channels all his energy into importing the drug AZT and selling it to the afflicted. He is initially hostile toward Rayon, a drug-addicted, HIV-positive transgender woman, who eventually joins him in running the buyers club. Rayon, who is a delightful and thoughtful contrast to Woodruff, dies during the course of the movie; an onscreen note informs us that Woodruff died in 1992, but not before playing a signifi-cant role in convincing the Food and Drug Administration to test and approve the first anti-viral drugs.

The challenge in writing about this movie is not the story, but rather the director's vision and the performances of the two leading actors. Various directors (and actors) were considered before the final choices were made. Jean-Marc Vallée was chosen as director, perhaps because his film *C.R.A.Z.Y.* (2005), based on his own experiences, depicts a young man dealing with homophobia. An interesting array of actors was considered before final casting of McConaughey and Leto. Both play characters who are extreme in their respective appearances and attitudes, and each is larger than live in his own way: Woodruff is very theatrical in his attempts to help his fellow men, and Rayon brings color, humor, and reason to a character who has nothing to lose. Both actors lost about 50 pounds in order to look convincing as people dying from AIDS.

The LGBT world encompasses many types of people and behavior, some of which have become stereotyped through the mass media. But the film is set exclusively in Dallas in the late 1980s, a long time before the more recent successes achieved by the gay rights movement. The more you are familiar with the LGBT world and its citizens, the easier it will be for you to write about this movie. But for those who are not familiar with this world and are challenged by trying to interpret and understand it, it may be reassuring to know that, although the movie was rated R by the Hollywood rating system, it is less about sexuality than about moral outrage and action politics.

Whatever your perspectives on the LGBT world, you will need to determine for yourself the director's perspective in telling the story and directing the actors. How does the director visually depict the city, citizens, the health-care system of Dallas? Does he present the operators or patrons of the buyers club as deviants or stereotypes? The buyers club depicted in the movie is a humanitarian effort that operates outside the law; does this status affect your thinking about it? And you would need to determine the effectiveness with which the two leading actors play their roles. Leto's appearance as Rayon involves an elaborate transformative look (the film won a third Academy Award for makeup and hairstyle); how does this affect your interpretation of the character? Does McConaughey make a convincing change from a stereotyped villain to a studious and effective activist? Is he believable in the role?

Genre Study

Film scholars may analyze a movie based on a wide range of criteria, including its specific aesthetic style, the artists who created it, its country or region of origin, its apparent ideologies, or the cinematic movement from which it emerged. But one of the most enduring criteria that has determined how movies are studied and analyzed is *genre*—the categorization of narrative films by the stories they tell and the ways they tell them.

Commonly recognized movie genres include westerns, horror films, science fiction, musicals, and gangster films. But this list is far from complete. The film industry also produces action movies, biographies (biopics), melodramas, thrillers, romances, romantic comedies, fantasy films, and many others that fall within some genre or subgenre.

Whether or not your paper focuses on a film's genre, nearly any kind of film analysis will benefit from an awareness of it. Understanding some basic principles about film genres, and about their importance in the film industry and in film scholarship, will help you develop interesting critiques even if your analysis is primarily about some other aspect of the movie(s) you are analyzing.

THE EMERGENCE OF FILM GENRES

Unlike film movements (such as French New Wave or Dogme 95), in which a group of like-minded filmmakers conspire to create a particular approach to film style and story, film genres tend to spring up organically—not through any conscious plan, but rather because of a cultural need to explore and express certain ideas. Cultural conditions inspire artists to tell certain kinds of stories, the nature of which motivates certain technical and aesthetic approaches. Eventually the accumulation of like-minded movies is detected, labeled, studied, and explicated by cinema scholars.

Of course, academic scholars are not the only movie lovers who find it useful to categorize films by genre. Genre has a significant effect on how audiences choose the movies they attend, rent, or purchase. Genre films have been prevalent since the earliest days of cinema because, contrary to popular perceptions, most movie viewers value predictability over novelty. Elements of certain genres appeal to us, so we seek to repeat an entertaining or engaging cinema experience by viewing a film that promises the same surefire ingredients. We get a certain pleasure from seeing how different filmmakers and performers have rearranged and interpreted familiar elements. We also enjoy seeing how a filmmaker or performer might deviate from the usual path. To put this relationship into gastronomic terms: the most common pizza features a flour-based crust topped with tomato sauce and mozzarella cheese, but it's the potential variety within that familiar foundation that has made pizza one of America's favorite foods.

A less obvious explanation for the persistent prevalence of genre lies in the deep roots genre has in our society. Any given genre naturally emerges not because Hollywood thinks it'll sell, but because it gives narrative voice to something essential to our culture. The film industry may ultimately exploit our love of certain genres, but it's our interests in certain kinds of movies that create genres in the first place. No studio executive decided (for instance) to invent horror movies out of thin air. Rather, these films exist because of our collective fear of death and the human psyche's need for catharsis. Westerns endorse ideas about America that Americans need to believe. We go to these movies not only to celebrate the familiar, but to enforce fundamental beliefs. As our world evolves and audience perspectives change, genre movies adapt to reflect these cultural shifts. A western made during the can-do patriotism of World War II is likely to express its themes differently than one produced at the height of the Vietnam War.

PREDICTABILITY AND INNOVATION

Once a particular genre has crystallized, then of course Hollywood executives use the newly emergent category to help them decide which projects to bankroll. Genres, once recognized and defined, offer familiar story formulas, conventions, themes, and conflicts, as well as immediately recognizable visual icons, all of which together provide a blueprint for creating and marketing a type of film that has proven successful in the past. Studios and distributors can develop genre-identified stars; select directors on the basis of proven proficiency in a particular genre; piggyback on the success of a previous genre hit; and even recycle props, sets, costumes, and digital backgrounds. Just as important, the industry counts on genre to predict ticket sales, to pre-sell markets, and to cash in on recent trends by making films that allow consumers to predict they'll like a particular movie. In other words: give people what they want, and they will buy it. This simple economic principle helps us understand the phenomenal growth of the movie industry from the 1930s on, as well as the mind-numbing mediocrity of so many of the movies the industry produces. The kind of strict adherence to genre convention driven solely by economics often yields derivative and formulaic results.

If genre films are prone to mediocrity, why are so many great filmmakers drawn to making them? The beginning of the answer can be found, of all places, in a statement by the Nobel Prize–winning poet T. S. Eliot, who wrote: "When forced to work within a strict framework, the imagination is taxed to its utmost—and will produce its richest ideas." Eliot was talking about poetry, but the same concept can be applied to cinema. Creatively ambitious writers and directors often challenge themselves to create art within the strict confines of genre convention. A genre's so-called rules can provide a foundation upon which the filmmaker can both honor traditions and innovate change. The resulting stories often fulfill some expectations while surprising and subverting others. Indeed, genre has intrigued so many of our greatest American and European filmmakers that many entries in the canon of important and transformative movies are genre films.

It should be clear by now that genre films provide lots of opportunities for interesting analyses. If you're convinced that grappling with a specific genre film or with a genre overall is something you'd like to do in your own writing, here are some basic principles of genre to keep in mind:

GENRE CONVENTIONS

Movie genres are defined by sets of conventions. These conventions include aspects of storytelling such as themes, situations, settings, character types, and story formula, as well as aspects of presentation such as decor, lighting, and sound. Even the movie stars associated with a particular genre can be considered one of these defining conventions. Keep in mind that these conventions are not enforced; filmmakers don't follow mandated genre checklists. While every movie within any particular genre will incorporate some of these elements, few genre movies attempt to include every possible genre convention.

Story Formulas. The way a movie's story is structured—its plot—also helps viewers determine what genre it belongs to. For example, gangster films—from Howard Hawks's *Scarface* (1932) to Ridley Scott's *American Gangster* (2007)—tend to share a plot structure in which an underprivileged and disrespected immigrant joins (or forms) an organized-crime syndicate; works his way to the top with a combination of savvy, innovation, and ruthlessness; becomes corrupted by his newfound power and the fruits of his labors; and as a result is betrayed, killed, or captured. Romantic-comedy plots are structured around characters in love as they couple, break up, and reconnect. When they first meet, the two characters (usually a man and a woman) are at odds. They fall in love in spite of—or sometimes because of—this seeming incompatibility, then must overcome obstacles to their relationship in the form of misunderstandings, competing partners, social pressures, or the aforementioned incompatibility. Eventually the romance will appear doomed, but one half of the couple will realize they are meant for each other and make a grand gesture that reunites the romantic duo.

Themes. A movie's *theme* is a unifying idea that the film expresses through its narrative or imagery. Not every genre is united by a single, clear-cut thematic idea, but the western comes close. Nearly all westerns share a central conflict between civilization and wilderness: settlers, towns, schoolteachers, cavalry outposts, and lawmen stand for civilization; free-range cattlemen, Indians, prostitutes, outlaws, and the wide-open spaces themselves fill the wilderness role. Many classic western characters exist on both sides of this conflict. For example, the Wyatt Earp character played by Henry Fonda in John Ford's *My Darling Clementine* (1946) is a former gunfighter turned lawman turned cowboy turned lawman. He befriends an outlaw but falls in love with a schoolteacher from the East. Early westerns tend to sympathize with the forces of civilization and order, but many of the westerns from the 1960s and 1970s valorize the freedom-loving outlaw, cowboy, or Native American hero.

Gangster films are shaped by three well-worn but obviously resonant themes that can each be summarized in a phrase: "rags to riches"; "crime does not pay"; and "absolute power corrupts absolutely." The thematic complexity made possible by the tension between these aspirational and moralistic ideas can provide the viewer a more meaningful experience than one might expect from a genre dedicated to career criminals.

Character Types. While most screenwriters strive to create individuated characters, genre films are often populated by specific character "types." Western protagonists personify the tension between order and chaos in the form of the free-spirited but civilized cowboy or the gunslinger turned lawman. Female characters also personify this tension, but only on one side or the other—as schoolmarm or prostitute, and only rarely as a combination of both. Other western character types include the cunning gambler, the greenhorn, the sidekick, and the settler. John Ford packed nearly every western character type into a single wagon in his classic western *Stagecoach* (1939). The horror and science fiction film antagonist is almost always some form of "other"—a being utterly different from the movie's protagonist (and audience) in form, attitude, and action. Many of these movie monsters look like large, malevolent bugs—the more foreign the villain's appearance and outlook, the better. When the "other" is actually a human, he often wears a mask designed to accentuate his otherness.

Setting. Where a movie's action is located and how that environment is portrayed—otherwise known as *setting*—is also a common genre convention. Obviously, westerns are typically set in the American West, but setting goes beyond geography. Most classic westerns take place in the 1880s and 1890s, an era of western settlement when a booming population of Civil War veterans and other eastern refugees went west in pursuit of land, gold, and cattle trade. The physical location of Monument Valley became the landscape most associated with the genre, not because of any actual history that occurred there, but because the scenic area was the favorite location of the prolific western director John Ford. Since science fiction films are speculative and, therefore, look forward rather than backward, they are usually set in the future: sometimes in space, sometimes in futuristic Earth cities, sometimes in a post-apocalyptic desolation, but almost always in an era and place greatly affected by technology. While gangster films are almost always urban in setting, horror films seek the sort of isolated locations—farms, abandoned summer camps, small rural villages—that place the genre's besieged protagonists far from potential aid.

Presentation / iconic imagery. Many genres feature elements of cinematic language that communicate tone and atmosphere and that viewers come to associate with those genres more than others.

Horror films take advantage of lighting schemes that accentuate and deepen shadows. While the resulting gloom helps to create an eerie mood, horror films are more than just dark; filmmakers use the hard-edged shadows as a dominant compositional element to convey a sense of oppression, to distort our sense of space, and to conceal narrative information. Film noir, a genre that also seeks to disorient the viewer and convey a sense of unease (although for very different thematic and narrative reasons), employs many of the same lighting techniques.

Westerns, a genre clearly associated with setting, feature a great many exterior shots that juxtapose the characters with the environment they inhabit. The human subject tends to dominate the frame in most movie compositions, but many of these western exterior shots are framed so that the "civilized" characters are dwarfed by the overwhelming expanse of wilderness around them.

Movies in the action genre often shoot combat (and other high-energy action) from many different angles to allow for a fast-paced editing style that presents the action from a constantly shifting perspective. These highly fragmented sequences subject the viewer to a rapid-fire cinematic simulation of the amplified experiences of the characters fighting onscreen.

Such iconic imagery often becomes so intimately entwined with a genre that when filmmakers later use these images, they signal that either they are making a joke, or that they are making an explicit homage to the original genre or to the particular filmmaker who pioneered the iconic imagery.

Stars. Even the actors who star in genre movies factor into how the genre is classified, analyzed, and received by audiences. In the 1930s and 1940s, actors worked under restrictive long-term studio contracts. With the studios choosing their roles, actors were more likely to be "typecast" and identified with a particular genre that suited their studio-imposed persona. Thus, John Wayne is forever identified with the western, Edward G. Robinson with gangster films, and Boris Karloff with horror. These days, most actors avoid limiting themselves to a single genre, but several contemporary actors have become stars by associating themselves almost exclusively with action films. Arnold Schwarzenegger, Chuck Norris, Steven Seagal, and others have benefited from the genre's preference for physical presence and macho persona over acting ability. That's not to say that genre stars can't act. In fact, an actor who has become identified with one genre will often receive extra attention and accolades for performing outside of it. For example, Bill Murray became a star while acting in screwball comedies, but his subtle performances in the dramas *Lost in Translation* (2003; director: Sofia Coppola) and *Broken Flowers* (2005; Jim Jarmusch) made him an actor worthy of movie critics' praise.

EVOLUTION OF GENRES

As the major film genres have evolved, filmmakers working within them have begun to display greater self-consciousness of the history and conventions of genre. This development is visible in such simple touches as a brief reference or homage to a previous film. Consider, for instance, Wes Craven's *Scream* (1996), which self-consciously echoes, recasts, and parodies such classic horror films as Alfred Hitchcock's *Psycho* (1960), John Carpenter's *Halloween* (1978), and the horror genre itself.

The process of genre transformation is as organic as the process that sprouts new genres. Existing genres change with the times and adapt to audience expectations, which are in turn influenced by many factors—technological, cultural, social, political, economic, and so on. Arguably, genres that don't evolve lose the audience's interest quickly and fade away.

And of course new genres continue to emerge. For example, blockbuster franchises like Jon Favreau's *Iron Man* movies and Christopher Nolan's *Dark Knight* series, as well as lower-budget entries like *Kick-Ass* (2010) and *Scott Pilgrim vs. the World* (2010) are all comic-book movies, a rapidly emerging genre that has grown darker and more effects-laden since the modern genre's birth in Richard Donner's *Superman* (1978). In a related vein, some movies take a free hand with the conventions of specific genres, combining them to create hybrids (such as the horror-comedy that *Scream* represents) or films that somehow transcend genre categorization (such as the *Kill Bill* series by Quentin Tarantino, which freely and ingeniously combines elements from a handful of disparate genres).

When studying any genre film, be sensitive to its ratio of inventiveness to conventionality, its expression of genre elements, the ways that it reflects its historical and cultural moment, and the degree to which it self-consciously asserts its status *as* genre. These questions can help you get started in your analysis:

Does the film you're analyzing seem to fit into a particular genre? In what way(s)?

Does the film fulfill your expectations about that genre, or does it seem to work against some of the traditional conventions of the genre? Again, in what way(s)?

Which conventions of the genre does the movie place greatest emphasis on? Themes? Character types? Setting? Iconographic imagery? Casting of actors well-known in the genre?

Which conventions of the genre does the movie underplay or ignore?

In viewing two films from the same genre made at different times, what differences do you see? What do those differences suggest to you about the evolution of the genre during the years between the two films?

If the film doesn't seem to fit into an identifiable genre, does it nonetheless borrow or blend elements from other genres? If so, how does it use those elements? What is the purpose of this borrowing and blending?

Historical Analysis

In just over a hundred years, the cinema, like the classical art forms that preceded it—architecture, fiction, poetry, drama, dance, painting, and music—has developed its own aesthetics, conventions, influence, and, of course, history. Broadly defined, film history traces the development of moving images from early experiments with photography, through the invention of the movies in the early 1890s, to the subsequent stylistic, financial, technological, and social developments in cinema that have occurred up to now.

To get some idea of the scope and depth of that record, you might browse through a comprehensive history of film, such as the ten-volume History of American Cinema series (University of California Press). Such comprehensive histories take many years, and often the efforts of many people, to get written. Because of this, most film historians don't undertake such massive projects. Most people who practice film history instead focus their energies on studying specific moments, movements, and phenomena. Jeanine Basinger's *The Star Machine* (New York: Knopf, 2007), for example, provides a masterly account of the Hollywood studio system during a very specific era (the so-called "golden age") and how it created its stars. C. S. Tashiro's *Pretty Pictures: Production Design and the History of Film* (Austin: University of Texas Press, 1998) limits its scope to focus on one aspect of film production—production design—even as it ranges widely over the full chronology of film history. In these studies and others like them, the film historian is interested equally in change—those developments that have altered the course of film history—and stability—those aspects that have defied change.

Like other historians, film historians use artifacts to study the past. These artifacts include the various machines and other technology—the cameras, projectors, sound recording devices, etc.—without which there would be no movies. They might also include notes from story conferences, screenplays, production logs, drawings, outtakes, and other objects relevant to the production of a particular movie. Obviously, the most important artifacts to the film historian are the movies themselves.

Film history includes the history of technologies, the people and industrial organizations that produce the movies, the national cinemas that distinguish one country's movies from another's, the attempts to suppress and censor the movies, and the meanings and pleasure that we derive from watching a good film. Gaining knowledge about these and other aspects of film history is pleasurable and interesting in and of itself. But as you graduate from merely watching movies to looking at movies in a critically aware way, your knowledge of film history will also provide you with the perspective and context to understand and evaluate the unique attributes of movies, both past and present.

BASIC APPROACHES TO FILM HISTORY

Although there are many approaches to studying film history (including studies of production, regulation, and reception), the beginner should know the four traditional approaches: the aesthetic, technological, economic, and social. In what follows, we describe each approach and cite one or two studies as exemplary models of each.

The aesthetic approach

Sometimes called the *masterpiece approach* or *great man approach*, this approach seeks to evaluate individual movies and/or directors using criteria that assess their artistic significance and influence. Ordinarily, historians who take this approach will first define their criteria of artistic excellence and then ask the following questions: What are the significant works of the cinematic art? Who are the significant directors? Why are these movies and these directors important? Historians who take the aesthetic perspective do not necessarily ignore the economic, technological, and cultural aspects of film history—indeed, it would be impossible to discuss many great movies without considering these factors—but they are primarily interested in movies that are not only works of art, but are also widely acknowledged masterpieces. The most comprehensive, one-volume international history that takes an aesthetic approach is David A. Cook's *A History of Narrative Film* (New York: Norton, 2015).

Auteurism. Within the category of the aesthetic approach is an approach called *auteurism*. The auteur theory postulates the film director as the *auteur* (author) of a film. Its application usually takes one of two forms: a judgment of the whole body of a film director's work based on style, or a classification of directors based on directorial styles. Auteurist criticism can be a useful exercise when one is trying to understand, for example, what makes a film a "Hitchcock" (or for that matter, a "Tarantino") film. A director must have made a significant body of films to be considered an auteur. Auteurists believe, to varying degrees, that a film director's style can (and should, according to Alexandre Astruc, one of the approach's leading advocates) be as distinctive as a novelist's. If the director is the visionary, the one person who makes a film what it is, then cinematic style is the DNA by which that "author" can be identified.

The idea of the author's presence in a cinematic work has been long debated. Whereas some critics argue that a work's coherence depends on the vision and decisions of a single person, critics in the opposing camp believe that it's the structure of a work—and not the personality that created it—that we can justly address.

Complicating the matter further is the fact that film is a collaborative medium. It's important to understand that no one person can control the product. The director of photography, the screenwriters (often many), the wardrobe and makeup people, the head of the studio—all these and others have a hand in determining the final product of a film.

Still, auteur criticism is widely practiced and is useful in helping us understand the common themes and aesthetic decisions in films by the same director (or producer, or star). Keep in mind, however, that the best of the auteur criticism draws on other sources, like film history or formal analysis, to ensure that the critique is not simply an examination of the private life or the psychology of the auteur. A fine example of the auteurist approach is James Naremore's *On Kubrick* (London: BFI, 2007).

The technological approach

All art forms have a technological history that records the advancements in materials and techniques that have affected the nature of the medium. Of all the arts, though, cinema seems to rely most heavily on technology. Historians who chart the history of cinema technology examine the circumstances surrounding the development of each technological advance, as well as subsequent improvements. They pose questions such as: When was each invention made? Under what circumstances—including aesthetic, economic, and social—was it made? Was it a totally new idea or one linked to the existing state of technology? What were the consequences for directors, studios, distributors, exhibitors, and audiences? By studying major developments (including the introduction of sound, the moving camera, color film stock, and digital cinematography), historians show us how the production of movies has changed. They can also evaluate whether or not that change was significant (like widescreen processes) or transitory (like Smell-O-Vision).

An excellent example of a study that explores technological history in conjunction with other aspects of film history is David Bordwell, Janet Staiger, and Kristin Thompson, *The Classical Hollywood Cinema: Film Study and Mode of Production to 1960* (New York: Columbia University Press, 1985). A wonderful example of a study of a specific technological subject is John Belton's *Widescreen Cinema* (Cambridge, Mass.: Harvard University Press, 1992).

The economic approach

The motion-picture industry is a major part of the global economy. Every movie released has an economic history of its own, as well as a place in the economic history of its studio and the historical period and country in which it was produced. Historians interested in this subject help us to understand how and why the studio system was founded, how it adapted to changing conditions (economic, technological, social, historical), why different studios took different approaches to producing different movies, how these movies have been distributed and exhibited, and what effect this particular economic history had on film history. Scholars who take an economic approach study how the independent system of production superseded the studio system, and what effect this has had on production, distribution, and exhibition. They are also concerned with such related issues as management and organization, accounting and marketing practices, and censorship and the rating system. Excellent examples of such studies include Douglas Gomery's *The Hollywood Studio System: A History* (London: BFI, 2005), Joel W. Finler's *The Hollywood Story*, 3rd ed. (London: Wallflower, 2003), and Tino Balio's *Grand Design: Hollywood as a Modern Business Enterprise, 1930–1939*, History of the American Cinema series, vol. 5 (Berkeley: University of California Press, 1995).

Film as social history

Because society and culture influence the movies and vice versa, the movies are good sources for studying society. Writing about movies as social history continues to be a major preoccupation of journalists, scholars, and students alike. Historian Ian Jarvie suggests that, in undertaking these studies, we ask the following basic questions: Who made the movies, and why? Who saw the films, how, and why? What was seen, how, and why? How were the movies evaluated, by whom, and why? In addition, those interested in social history consider such factors as religion, politics, cultural trends, and taboos, asking to what extent a particular movie was produced to sway public opinion or effect social change.

These social historians are also interested in audience composition, marketing, and criticism as it appeared in all media, from gossip magazines to scholarly books. Overall, they study the complex interaction between film as a social institution and other social institutions, including government, religion, and labor. Landmark studies include Robert Sklar's *Movie-Made America: A Cultural History of American Movies*, rev. and updated ed. (New York: Vintage, 1994), and Richard Abel's *Americanizing the Movies and "Movie-Mad" Audiences, 1910–1914* (Berkeley: University of California Press, 2006).

Here are some ways that you can make your film analyses— regardless of their primary topic or approach—more historically aware:

As you study a particular film (or film artist, style, or movement), learn as much as you can about its historical context: the year in which it was made/released; the country of origin; why, if relevant, that year was important to that country's history; how, if relevant, the movie deals with the events of that period; the means of production (e.g., studio, independent, government-sponsored); the audience for which it was intended; its reception by the public and critics alike. Isolate and identify the movie as closely as you can within this overall context.

Also learn about the film's aesthetic context: Was it made as part of a particular film movement (e.g., Italian neorealism), or does it break from the prevailing tradition of the period? If it is representative of a movement, how does it measure up against the movement's ideals and achievements? Is it part of a "national cinema" with its own aesthetic, political, and cultural values?

Learn something about its director's overall body of work. Is he regarded as an auteur? If so, how is this movie similar to, or different from, his other films? Since you may not have time to see many of the director's movies, you might compare the director's most famous movie with the one you are analyzing.

Similarly, you may want to study the history of a creative artist in the historical context of a particular genre. A few suggestions are Hayao Miyazaki's anime style within the history of animation, Preston Sturges's screenplays for 1930s screwball comedies, Freddie Young's cinematography for the historical epics directed by David Lean, Ann Roth's approach to designing costumes for period movies, Walter Murch's sound designs for the movies of Francis Ford Coppola, or the production design of films about the Civil War, from D. W. Griffith's *The Birth of a Nation* (1915) to Anthony Minghella's *Cold Mountain* (2003).

When movies have been inspired by a historical period or event (e.g., the Great Depression, the Vietnam War, the rise and fall of Rome), you have a rich opportunity to analyze and understand those cinematic interpretations. First, you should understand the complexity of this historical event by taking notes on how different historians have treated it—in other words, you should work to understand that all historical accounts are themselves interpretations of events. Your notes will help you establish a context for determining the scope, thoroughness, and effectiveness of the movies inspired by the event.

Have you found that a particular movie has made important innovations in cinematic language or in the use of technology? If so, what are they? Who was principally responsible for these innovations (e.g., the director, sound designer, cinematographer)? Was this a momentary blip on film history's screen, or did it become a permanent part of cinematic technique or language?

If the movie you are analyzing was the product of a particular Hollywood studio, find out if that studio had a unified style for most of its movies or if it encouraged its directors to use different styles. If the former, how well does the movie evoke that style? If the latter, how is it different? And did this film influence subsequent studio productions?

The "reception" of a film can be as interesting as its form. Some movies, such as *Gone With the Wind* (1939), were instant successes, as popular with audiences at the time as they have proven to be over the years since first release. Others, such as *Night of the Hunter* (1955), languished in theaters during their initial release but became more highly regarded and more popular as time passed. Whatever movie you analyze, take some time to familiarize yourself with its reception-history. Consider the early reviews and audience responses, the box-office receipts, the "buzz" that accompanied the release (or didn't), and the longer-term critical and popular opinion about the film.

Nearly any film essay can make use of historical facts and references. Keeping a historical perspective in the back of your mind can inform your writing even if the assignment calls primarily for a formal analysis. The typical film paper is a vehicle for exploring and explicating film form, perhaps with some use of theory, or perhaps with an eye to exploring cultural issues through films. But film history—if your instructor encourages you to pursue it—is a rich source of information that can transform a film paper into a work of considerable interest and achievement.

Now that we've looked at the wide-ranging field of film study and have discussed the various tools and concerns film scholars bring to their own writing, let's look at the *process* of writing academic papers in film courses. The following chapters will offer you good advice that you can use not only in your film courses, but in many of your other courses as well. As you read about and practice the following strategies, pay attention to which work best for you, and which might become strategies that you can use more broadly in all of your writing.

Part II

THE WRITING
PROCESS

5

Generating Ideas

I n some ways writing about film is similar to writing on any subject: you must choose a topic, generate ideas, research your topic, craft a thesis, structure your argument, and find the proper tone. But each of these more general tasks requires you to perform some tasks that are specific to the study of film. For instance, you must look at movies with a more critical and analytical eye (which the preceding three chapters are intended to help you do), you must be able to use specialized language appropriately, and you must know how to use research resources effectively. The following section combines general advice with suggestions specific to film studies, with the aim of helping you produce better papers for your film class.

Generating Ideas

While viewing the movie you've chosen or that was assigned to you, you will usually come up with some ideas worth writing about. But what if you've watched the film a few times and you still haven't found anything that you feel is worth exploring? Or what if you've found an idea for writing, but you haven't yet discovered how you might develop that idea? In any of these situations you might want to take the time to try one of the following strategies for generating ideas.

CONVERSATION

After seeing a movie, we typically talk about it with others as soon as we leave the venue. Those conversations often leave us thinking about the movie in new and interesting ways. Note, however, that the kinds of conversations that we have with our friends—which are often freewheeling, opinionated, and more emotional than intellectual—mark just the beginning of scholarly inquiry. Still, talking with friends can be useful in exploring differences of opinion and in encouraging you to articulate and back up your point of view.

BRAINSTORMING

Another way to formulate ideas is to brainstorm. Brainstorming is useful because it is a quick and efficient way of laying out what you know about a subject. By brainstorming, you might also see what you don't know about a topic, which might move you to read and think further.

Suppose you decided to brainstorm for a paper on the film *Brokeback Mountain* (2005; director: Ang Lee). You might make a list like the one we offer here:

Brokeback Mountain
- Is controversial in its subject matter
- Is beautifully shot
- Has a lonely feeling
- Is in some ways pretty conventional
- Has the sweeping panoramas of the western
- Has minimal dialogue, typical of the western
- Has the plot structure of a doomed love story
- Portrays the women as helpless
- Won the Academy Award for directing but not for best picture

As this list illustrates, *brainstorming* is an informal strategy for invention in which you jot down, as quickly as you can, ideas concerning your topic. The ideas don't have to be connected—though sometimes looking for connections will yield a paper topic. For instance, you might want to write a paper arguing that *Brokeback* is a more conventional film than most people think. Or you might want to write about how the spaces and silences of the film contribute to conveying the characters' essential loneliness.

Remember that you can also stop at any point in the writing process to brainstorm, especially when you feel that you're stuck or that you have to fill in some gaps in your argument. In short, when you brainstorm you freely explore your topic without the pressure of structure, grammar, or style. In the process, ideas for an essay (or a paragraph, or even a footnote) evolve unhindered.

FREEWRITING

Freewriting is similar to brainstorming in that it is a quick and informal way to develop an idea. But whereas brainstorming most often involves making a list of ideas, freewriting requires that you try to elaborate on these ideas by writing about them, without paying close attention to syntax or grammar. In this way, freewriting can get you "unstuck" when coming up with ideas is difficult.

Here's an example (and note that this freewriting, since it is meant for the writer's eyes only, is very informal—with spelling, grammar, and punctuation errors intact):

OK, so i just saw apocalypse now and, wow, i'm supposed to write a paper on it but i have no idea what i'm going to say. the film hit me in a place where language doesn't live but still i gotta come up with something. where to start? maybe i should begin at the beginning, because from the first scene coppola grabs you and pulls you in, not just into vietnam but also into the mind of the protagonist, willard. I mean from the start you know that it's all insane— willard's insane and so is vietnam and somehow the two insanities are the same, one is causing the other in a crazy vicious cycle. how does coppola do this? hmmmm. i guess that a lot of it has to do with the sound mix. first of all there's the great song by the doors—"the end"—which is apocalyptic and reminds us how crazy the sixties were. And willard is in this hotel room and this song is going on and we see willard sweating in this hot hotel room in Hanoi, losing his mind, and then we hear the ceiling fan that swoops menacingly overhead. And the fan blurs with the sounds of helicopters and the other sounds of the war. And you feel like the sounds outside and the sounds inside are all blending into each other. And then at the height of the insanity willard tears up the hotel room, breaks a mirror, bleeds on the sheets, and lets out a howl, which you don't hear. that's cool. you watch willard fall apart but you don't hear him screaming. you hear all the other stuff but you don't hear the scream. i wonder why coppola decided to do it this way? maybe i could think more about the sound editing in that first scene, maybe do a paper on that and how coppola manages to use sound to show the inner and outer insanities? hmmmm. i guess this was a pretty successful freewrite. all i had to do was push buttons and some ideas popped out. pushing buttons is a lot more fun than just sitting and staring at a blank screen.

DISCOVERY DRAFT

A discovery draft is another strategy for coming up with or developing your ideas. A discovery draft is similar to freewriting in that you can write freely, with little thought to the structure and the development of your ideas for the time being. You can also forget about matters of syntax and style. However, writing a discovery draft is different from freewriting in that a discovery draft makes a conscious attempt to focus on and develop an idea or a cluster of ideas. In other words, a discovery draft is like freewriting with an agenda. And because you have an agenda, a discovery draft tends to be more structured than freewriting, and to be written more or less coherently, in complete sentences.

Think of writing a discovery draft as writing a letter to an imaginary friend about your paper. Suppose that you've just seen *Memento* (2001). You might first summarize, for your friend's benefit, the film and the issues it presents. You might then raise questions about the film. You might challenge the filmmaker on certain points. You might note continuity problems or contradictions. You might point out a certain part of the film that you found compelling. You might address and then work out any confusion that you have about the topic. In writing the discovery draft you might have an aha! moment, in which you see something you hadn't seen before, and break off mid-sentence to explore it.

In a sense, the aha! moment is the point of the discovery draft. When writing the discovery draft, your thoughts are focused on your topic. You're giving language to your questions and observations. In this process, the mind almost always stumbles across something new—makes a *discovery*. And with this discovery, a paper is often launched.

Creating a discovery draft is more formal than a freewriting exercise. It always uses complete sentences and correct grammar, and it follows a logical train of thought. However, it's still not nearly as formal as a paper that you would hand in to your professor. It uses casual, colloquial language, and it doesn't state ideas as strongly as it might (because as you write a discovery draft, you're often still trying to figure out what, exactly, those ideas are). It also typically uses some of the thoughts that showed up in the freewrite. Freewriting helps you find ideas that might be useful in your paper; the discovery draft helps you figure out how they're useful and what you might say about them. A student who takes the time to do a freewriting exercise and to compose a discovery draft will be well on the way to a solid, working thesis.

FIVE *W*S AND AN *H*

Journalism has provided us with perhaps the simplest and most familiar way of coming up with a topic: simply ask questions such as *who, what, when, where, why,* and *how.* Answering these questions initially doesn't seem very hard—at least until one gets to the *why* and *how.* Then it gets tricky.

Let's use this method to try to generate ideas, once again, for a paper on Francis Ford Coppola's *Apocalypse Now* (1979).

Maybe when you were watching *Apocalypse Now* you got interested in Coppola's use of voice-over, so you have a topic you want to explore. Now begin your interrogation:

Where in the film does Coppola use voice-over? (Mark the scenes.)

Who is speaking during the voice-over?

What was happening in those moments? (Summarize the action.)

How is the voice-over used? (Analyze. Is Coppola using the voice-over to restore order when the narrative slips into chaos?)

When does the voice-over work best? (Evaluate its effectiveness. Is order really restored?)

Why does the film end without a final voice-over comment? Why does it end in silence?

These are tough questions. But it's precisely when you have difficulty answering a *why* question that a real paper is beginning. When the answer comes too easily, you're on familiar ground, so you're probably not saying anything interesting. Cultivate a taste for confusion. Then cultivate a strategy for clearing up confusion. Only when you ask a question that initially confuses you can real thinking and real writing begin.

TAGMEMICS

Tagmemics is a system that allows you to look at a single object from three different perspectives. One of these perspectives (or even all three) can help you determine a subject for writing. By extending an analogy regarding the different ways physicists think about light, tagmemics involves seeing your topic

as a particle (as a thing in itself);
as a wave (as a thing changing over time);
as part of a field (as a thing in its context).

Suppose you want to write a paper on Cooper and Schoedsack's *King Kong* (1933). If you use tagmemics as a system of invention, you will begin by looking at *King Kong* as a thing in itself. In other words, what elements of this 1933 film are worth noting?

Next you might consider how the film has changed over time. How was the film received in its day? How does this reception compare to current assessments of the film? Consider the Peter Jackson remake (2005). What elements of the film have changed in the remake? How has the approach to the King Kong story changed over time?

Finally, consider *King Kong* (1933) as a thing in context. Relate it to its culture, to its moment in time. What was happening in the world in 1933? Even unlikely events and figures may provide an interesting context. For instance, in 1933 the United States was in the middle of the Great Depression, and Hitler was named chancellor of Germany. Might these events be reflected in the film in some way? How? And why?

ARISTOTLE'S TOPOI

As one of the fathers of rhetoric, Aristotle worked to formalize a system for conceiving, organizing, and expressing ideas. We're concerned here with what Aristotle called the "topoi"— a system of specific strategies for invention. Think of the topoi as a series of questions that you might ask of a work of literature—questions that might lead you to interesting paper topics. The topoi are especially helpful when you're asked to explore a topic that seems very broad. Consider, for instance, how using the topoi can help you write a paper on the importance of *Star Wars* to the sci-fi genre.

Use Definition

You can use definition in two ways to come up with or develop a topic. First, you might look at *genus*, which Aristotle explains as defining a general idea within specific limits. For example, you could define the sci-fi genre with the intent of showing how *Star Wars* (1977) epitomizes the elements of that genre.

The second way to use definition is to think in terms of *division*. In other words, try to think of your subject in terms of its parts. For example, consider the elements of *Star Wars* that are most significant in earning it the reputation of the most important science fiction film in movie history.

Use Comparison

You can generate ideas by making comparisons in two ways. The first is to look for *similarities* and/or *differences*. For example, you might determine how *Star Wars* stands apart from other important sci-fi films.

The second method is to compare *degree*. In other words, you might consider how something is better or worse than something else. For example, is *Star Wars* more important to the genre than *The Matrix* (1999)? Is it less important to the genre than *2001: A Space Odyssey* (1968)?

Explore Relationships

Aristotle determined four ways of exploring relationships as a way of coming up with ideas for writing. The first is to consider either the *cause* of your subject or its *effects*. For example, you might research the effects that *Star Wars* had on subsequent sci-fi films.

Second, you might consider a subject's *antecedent* and *consequences*. In other words, you might ask this question of your subject: If this, then what? For example, if *Star Wars* hadn't been made, would science fiction movies still be stuck in the B movie genre?

Third, you might examine *contraries*, or make an argument by proving its opposite. An example is to say that war is bad in order to convey the idea that peace is good. Along these lines, you might argue that *Star Wars* was the most significant sci-fi film of all time by showing how others miss the mark.

Finally, you might look for *contradictions, incompatible statements,* or *controversy.* For example, some critics feel that *Star Wars* is the greatest sci-fi film of all time; others feel that it's overrated. You can explore the controversy and stake a claim of your own.

Examine Circumstances

In seeking an idea for a paper, you can examine circumstances in two ways. The first is to consider the possible and the impossible. Sometimes you can construct an interesting argument by considering what's possible and what's not. For example, it's impossible to find a sci-fi series that is more influential to the genre than the *Star Wars* series.

The second strategy is to consider the past or to look to the future. For example, in what ways does *Star Wars* influence the sci-fi films being produced today? What trends do we see that might allow us to predict the direction of future sci-fi films?

Rely on Testimony

The opinions of others can be a source for your paper. Look to authorities, testimonials, statistics, maxims, laws, and precedents. For example, read what Joseph Campbell says on the mythic/heroic structure of *Star Wars*. Find other authorities and listen to what they have to say. For instance, what does the box-office history of *Star Wars* tell us about its success?

Developing Your Ideas

You've done some preliminary brainstorming. Perhaps you've even completed a discovery draft. The problem sitting before you now is that you have too many ideas and you don't know what to do with them, or the ideas you've come up with don't seem to be adequately academic. What do you try next?

NUTSHELLING

Nutshelling is the simple process of trying to explain the main point of your observations in a few sentences—in a nutshell. When you put your thoughts in a nutshell, you come to see just how those thoughts fit together. You see how each thought is relevant to the others, and what the overall point is. In short, nutshelling helps you transform your observations or information into something meaningful, focused, and coherent.

Imagine, for example, that you're asked in an assignment to consider whether or not, from your point of view, Philip Seymour Hoffman deserved to win the Best Actor Oscar for his portrayal of Truman Capote in the film *Capote* (2005). You actually have a lot to say about this. First, though Hoffman's performance was superb (in fact, you loved it), you think that Heath

Ledger's portrayal of a gay cowboy in *Brokeback Mountain* was more Oscar-worthy. Why? Well, when you were watching *Brokeback*, you forgot you were watching Heath Ledger play a gay cowboy; when you were watching *Capote*, you were always aware that you were watching Hoffman taking on Capote's skin. In your opinion, making the audience forget that they're watching a celebrity is harder than imitating (however brilliantly) another celebrity. But you're pretty sure the academy doesn't agree with you. After all, they recently gave the Oscar to Nicole Kidman for playing Virginia Woolf, and to Jamie Foxx for playing Ray Charles.

In a nutshell, what is your take on the matter? After considering all of your feelings on the subject, you decide that, although Philip Seymour Hoffman's performance was Oscar-worthy, his win over Heath Ledger reveals how celebrity-obsessed the voting members of the academy are. Stated more fully,

> When actors in biopics meet the challenges of re-creating a character, they dazzle us: it seems as if they've managed to resurrect their subjects before our very eyes. And yet this resurrection shouldn't be the determining criterion for awarding the Oscar, as it has been in the last few years. Philip Seymour Hoffman's win over Heath Ledger in the 2006 Oscar race illustrates the tendency of Oscar voters to reward celebrities playing other celebrities, indicating the Academy's own obsession with celebrity culture.

In the process of nutshelling you've done more than come up with a promising idea for a paper; you've also come up with a promising plan for your entire introduction. Nutshelling has proven to be a successful prewriting strategy in this case.

BROADENING YOUR TOPIC

What happens when you've put your thoughts in a nutshell and they seem too "small"? You may have come up with a topic that's too narrow, too particular to support a sustained conversation.

Say, for example, that you've been asked to watch a film and to observe the makeup and costuming. You've noticed that the filmmaker seems to focus on women and lipstick. The film has a key scene of women discussing their sex lives as they try on lipstick at a cosmetics counter. Throughout the film, the director makes sure that we notice lipstick by offering lingering close-ups of women putting on lipstick, of lipstick stains on glasses, and so on.

You've made notes about these lipstick scenes, and you think that you can write an essay that chronicles the use of lipstick as a metaphor in this film. But it's not enough simply to chronicle the appearance of lipstick in the film. Instead, you have to talk about *how* the director uses these images and then make a declaration about what this recurring image *means*.

After writing your discovery draft, you come up with the idea that the filmmaker uses lipstick to call attention to the fact that the characters are trying to mask their feelings. Though this observation is a promising one, it still isn't "big" enough. Why not? Because it remains an observation, not an argument; it lists *how* A, B, and C mask their feelings without addressing the matter of *why* this masking is important to consider. How do you broaden your topic so that you feel you have something important to say?

First, try to make connections. Do the characters rely on other ways of masking themselves? Is masking one of the film's central themes? In what other ways does the director explore the idea of masking?

Second, turn your idea inside out. Consider the other side of the matter. For example, lipstick might be part of a character's mask, but it also calls attention to that character. Lipstick doesn't give her a mask to hide behind; instead it screams, "Hey! Look at me!" This is interesting. Perhaps the character exaggerates certain qualities in order to hide others. Is this sleight of hand (reveal/conceal) at work elsewhere in the film?

Third, consider the context. There are, of course, at least two contexts to consider: the context *within* the film, and the context *without*. Within the film, you might seek a context for lipstick. What's happening, exactly, when the characters put lipstick on? Is this act presented by the filmmaker as being positive or negative? What values does the film assert, and how does the use of lipstick reflect or challenge these values? What is the film's theme, and how does lipstick reflect or challenge that?

Without the film are other contexts. Consider, for instance, the filmmaker's other works. Is masking an important issue there? Consider some of the cultural forces at work. What larger social issue might the filmmaker be highlighting? Finally, masking is an ancient practice. What can you find out about the history of masking that is relevant to the matter at hand?

All of these questions might help you broaden your topic so that your discussion is substantial and interesting.

NARROWING/FOCUSING YOUR TOPIC

What if your topic seems too big to handle? What do you do then?

Let's consider the hypothetical film that we were just discussing.

Perhaps after doing the various prewriting exercises, you've concluded that all the characters in this film seem to wear masks. Although this observation is potentially fruitful, you should resist the temptation to be satisfied with it. After all, a paper showing that Mary wears a mask and Johnny wears a mask and Caroline wears a mask will probably bore the reader. It will seem like a string of obvious and general observations. How do you focus your topic?

First, test your claim. A statement as broad as this one is probably not always true. Do all the characters wear masks, or just some of them? You might discover that only the female characters wear masks. Or you might discover that, while these women wear makeup (a kind of physical mask), it's the men in the film whose feelings are most concealed. These more focused observations lead to a more interesting, more manageable topic.

Then look for examples. Remember that broad is also *vague*. Focusing on specific examples can make a topic clearer. For example, you might want to consider when, specifically, the characters try to mask themselves. Do they mask themselves in every moment of the film, or only at those moments that are crucial to their destinies? Are they cowards, or is the filmmaker trying to say that it's right for people to try to protect themselves from the cruelty of fate?

Look for more examples. How do people mask themselves? Reconsider the lipstick idea. Perhaps the use of lipstick in the film signifies the impulse to mask.

Finally, consider the context. Just as a consideration of context can help you broaden an idea, it can also help you focus it. "Everybody masks" can therefore become, "Historically, people have used masks in these particular ways. Filmmaker X uses masks in similar ways to argue Y." Then show (1) how the characters use masks in traditional ways, and (2) what the filmmaker is trying to illustrate through these allusions to the historical uses of the mask.

Essentially, you are looking for details that support your specific claim while simultaneously weeding out other parts of the film because they're not important to your argument.

If you fail to go through that process, you may end up including extraneous information in your essay, and your instructor will likely tell you that the paper seems disorganized. If you do a good job of narrowing your focus, that won't be a problem.

Thinking Beyond the Frame

So far, we've been advising you to consider the formal aspects of a film's composition. As we pointed out earlier, however, you can write about film in several ways. Sometimes you will want to "think beyond the frame" and consider questions about how the film was made, its historical context, and so on. For example, ask yourself the following questions:

Who made the film? Find out who directed the film and what other films this director has made. If you've seen some of these other films, you'll have a better understanding of the themes and genres that interest the director.

What is the production history of the film? See if you can find out anything about the conditions under which the film was made. *Apocalypse Now*, for example, has an interesting production history, in terms of its financing, casting, writing, and so on. Knowing something about the film's production can help you understand some of the aesthetic and cinematic choices that the director has made.

What do the critics and scholars say? Reading what others have said about the film before you see it may help you focus your observations. If a film is particularly well known for the editing of a certain scene (the shower scene in Hitchcock's *Psycho* (1960), for example), you'll want to pay close attention to the editing when you view the film.

What can you learn from the film's genre? Before you see the film, think a bit about the norms and limitations of its genre. When you view the film, you can then consider how these limitations are obeyed or stretched. For example, Clint Eastwood's *Unforgiven* (1992) is a western that challenges its genre's typical notions of good guy versus bad guy. Knowing how this dynamic plays itself out in other westerns helps you understand and appreciate Eastwood's accomplishment.

Does the work reflect an interesting cultural phenomenon? Sometimes a professor will ask you to watch certain films because he wants you to examine a cultural phenomenon— for example, the phenomenon of stardom. Accordingly, you might watch Roland Joffé's *The Scarlet Letter* (1995) with the idea of viewing it as a "star vehicle," contributing to Demi Moore's star persona. Note that this sort of paper may also be a discussion of formal analysis; for example, you might discuss how Demi Moore was lit in certain scenes to emphasize her position as Hollywood star.

If asking these questions leads you to a promising topic, but you find that you don't know enough to write about the topic without reading other sources, then you will need to conduct research in order to write your paper. The next chapter provides some guidance on the research process.

6

Researching Movies

Doing research in a film class is in many ways similar to doing research for other classes: you'll visit the library, find books and journals, get a clear sense of the scholarly conversation, and then offer a perspective of your own. One important difference, though, is that when you write about movies, the film itself is typically the primary source, with film criticism (books, journal articles, and so on) serving as secondary sources.

Understanding Primary and Secondary Sources

Primary sources are defined as any text, object, photograph, film, or other medium that is the object of scholarly investigation. A *secondary source*, on the other hand, is a work that analyzes, comments on, or otherwise sheds light on the primary text, historical event, object, or phenomenon in question.

A source can be primary or secondary, depending on the purpose of your research. For instance, you might write a film paper in which the primary text is something other than a movie (e.g., a filmmaker's journal, shooting script, or shot list). Or you might write a paper in which a secondary source consists of film footage (e.g., an "extra" feature on a DVD).

As we continue this discussion about research, we'll be talking in most cases about secondary sources that comment on film—e.g., film history, film criticism, and theoretical articles.

Using Sources

Having a strategy for collecting and employing sources is a good idea. No one wants to wander from source to source trying to remember what, precisely, that source argued, or why it mattered in the first place. We therefore offer the following research tips, which we think will help you become a more effective and efficient researcher.

It may seem at first that these steps take time. "Why should I stop to summarize a source when I can simply go back to the original?" you might wonder. However, the strategies outlined here will save you time in the long run. The work you do to digest and classify your sources as you do your research will make the writing process much more focused, much more efficient, and much less painful in the end.

SUMMARIZE YOUR SOURCES

Before attempting to use any source in your paper, make sure you understand it. The best way to do this is to summarize the source. In summarizing, you accomplish a few things. First, summarizing a source requires you to put the argument in your own language. Some of your secondary sources might use language that puzzles you. When you summarize, you are, in a sense, translating an argument into language that you understand and can work with. Summarizing also helps you see whether there's any aspect of the argument that you aren't getting. If you find yourself stumbling as you attempt to summarize, go back to the original source for clarity.

Summarizing also allows you to restate an argument in terms that are relevant to your paper. Most film criticism that you will encounter is very complex and offers several ideas for consideration. Some of these ideas will be relevant to your topic, while others will not. When you summarize, you can restate the part of the argument that seems most relevant to the paper you want to write.

Summarizing can also help you organize your source material. If you've used ten sources in a research project, you've probably taken a lot of notes and gathered several quotations for your paper. This work can amount to pages and pages of text. Summaries can help you organize these notes by telling you almost at a glance which idea comes from which source. You can also include in your summaries a few of the best quotations from each source.

Finally, summarizing is helpful to the entire research process. It's not something that you should do once at the beginning of the research process and then forget about. Every time your understanding of the topic shifts or evolves, take the time to write a brief summary. You'll find that putting your thoughts into writing helps you solidify one stage of understanding before progressing to the next.

CATEGORIZE YOUR SOURCES

Once you've summarized your sources, try to place them into various categories. Remember, writing an academic essay is like taking part in a large, ongoing conversation. Although everyone has a particular point of view, it's safe to say that no one is entering the conversation as a lone wolf. Everyone is speaking from a certain critical perspective. These perspectives might be classified into different groups.

Categorizing your sources might be as simple as looking for similarities among them. Which sources seem to share a point of view? Which seem to arrive at similar conclusions? You will also discover differences among your sources. Try to define these differences and see if they seem to fall into different categories. For example, side A seems to believe X, while side B seems to believe Y. Or, side A attempts to understand the literary work from a feminist perspective, while side B is interested in interpreting the work from a socioeconomic perspective.

Once you've categorized your sources, try to understand what these differences and similarities mean to your argument. Are these categories relevant to the issues you intend to discuss? Where does your own argument fit in? Does the reader need to know about these categories for your argument to make sense? Try to articulate these matters clearly. Write a summary of what you think at this point.

INTERROGATE YOUR SOURCES

In most of the papers that you'll write in college, you'll have to do more than review what other people have said about a topic. You will be asked to present your own point of view. To do this, you'll need to interrogate your sources.

Interrogating your sources does not mean that you have to be contentious. You don't have to search like a bloodhound for the weak spot in an argument. You're not required to "take on" your source. Instead, you'll want to ask questions of your sources. Initiate a conversation: challenge, interrogate, rebut, and confirm. Some good questions to ask are the following:

Is the writer offering evidence for her claims? Is this evidence sufficient? Why or why not?

Is there something that the writer is overlooking? Omitting? If so, is the omission a matter of carelessness, or does it seem purposeful? Why?

Does the writer's argument seem reasonable? If not, can you locate places where the reasoning seems to break down? Can you locate and identify any logical fallacies?

Is the writer's language appropriate? Does she sometimes rely on a pretty phrase or a passionate claim to cover up a lack of evidence?

What can you determine about the writer's perspective? Does she seem to have any important biases? Does she seem to belong to a particular critical school of thought? Does the writer's perspective help or hinder the argument she's trying to make? Why?

Where do you stand in relation to the writer? Do you give her a round of applause? Do you feel like booing her off the stage? Are you sitting with your arms crossed, feeling skeptical? Keep notes of your personal responses to the writer, and try to translate those responses into comments or questions.

ANNOTATE YOUR SOURCES

Most scholars find it useful whenever possible to mark their texts as they read them. Marking your text enables you to enter into conversations with the author. No longer are you reading passively. Instead, you are reading actively, filling the margins with comments and questions that could blossom into a paper topic down the road. Annotating your texts also ensures that your questions and inspirations won't get lost. Entire books and dissertations have evolved from notes made in the margins. The ideas for these books and dissertations might have been lost had the writer not taken the time to write them down.

MAKE YOUR SOURCES WORK FOR YOU

Students often make a grave mistake when they write their first academic papers: overwhelmed by what their sources have to say, they permit their papers to crumble under the weight of scholarly opinion. They end up not writing an informed argument of their own but rehashing what has already been said on a topic. Such a paper might be informative. It might also be competently written. But it does not fulfill the requirements of a good academic paper.

Remember, a good academic paper must be analytical, it must be critical, and it must present a well-crafted, persuasive, informed argument.

Consider the phrase "informed argument." The word with the power in this phrase is the noun "argument." The word "informed" is merely a descriptor. It serves the noun, qualifying it, shading it. The information that you gather should serve your argument in much the same way. Make your sources work for *you*.

You can take some steps to ensure that your sources do indeed work for you without overwhelming your argument. First, don't go to the library or go online before you've thought about your topic on your own. Certainly your research will have an impact on what you think. Sometimes you might even find that you reverse your opinion. But if you go to the library before you've given your topic some thought, you risk jumping on the bandwagon of the first persuasive argument you encounter.

Second, limit your sources to those that are relevant to your topic. It's easy to be swept up in the broader scholarly conversation about your subject and to go off on tangents that don't, in the end, serve your argument.

Finally, keep track of your evolving understanding of the topic by periodically stopping to summarize. As we said earlier, summarizing your sources makes them more manageable. If you manage your sources as you go along, you will reduce the risk that they'll overwhelm you later.

Keeping Track of Your Sources

During the research process it's very important to keep track of your sources. Nothing is more frustrating than having a great quotation and not knowing where it came from. Develop a good, consistent system for keeping notes.

Every academic discipline requires that you submit with your paper a bibliography or list of works cited. A bibliography should include every work you looked at in your research, even if you didn't quote that source directly. A list of works cited, on the other hand, is just that: a list of works that you quoted, paraphrased, or alluded to in the text of your paper. Both bibliographies and lists of works cited require you to provide information that will make it easier for your reader to find these sources for herself. Consult the Modern Language Association's *MLA Handbook* for information about how to construct a proper bibliography and/or list of works cited.

Citing Sources

When you write an academic paper, you must cite all the sources that you've used, even if you don't quote them directly. If you fail to cite these sources, you will be charged with plagiarism. Plagiarism (passing off as your own the words and ideas of others, whether an entire article or just one phrase) is an academic offense for which there are serious consequences.

We can offer several good reasons not to plagiarize. First, it's very easy to get caught. Your instructors—who have spent years teaching students to write and so have read countless student essays—are keenly aware of the difference between professional and student writing. They notice when sophisticated, highly polished academic writing appears out of the blue, with seemingly no development or context. In addition, although the Internet makes plagiarism easy, it also empowers teachers, who can use sophisticated search programs to scan literally millions of documents for suspect phrases and sentences.

Second, plagiarism cheats both the reader and the writer. At a fundamental level, citing a source is an academic courtesy. Because scholarship is an ongoing conversation, you should always presume that other students or scholars could want to use your work to develop their own. If you've taken an idea from another scholar but haven't cited it (or have cited it improperly), your reader will have no easy way of finding the source of the ideas that have found their way into your work.

Perhaps the most serious problem raised when you plagiarize or fail to cite your sources is that you're cheating yourself. When you rely on the ideas of others to meet a course requirement, you're denying yourself the opportunity to have the best experience that college can offer: the opportunity to think for yourself. Writing papers can be difficult, and when deadlines loom it can be tempting to look for a shortcut and to lift ideas from scholars who clearly know more about your topic than you do. But it's *your* opinion that your instructor wants to hear. Take each writing assignment as an opportunity to explore and express your ideas. You're paying a lot for this education; you might as well get your money's worth.

7

Developing Your Thesis

Writing a Thesis Sentence

No sentence in your paper will vex you as much as the thesis sentence, and with good reason: the thesis sentence is very often the one sentence in the paper that asserts, controls, and structures the entire argument. Without a strong, persuasive, thoughtful thesis—explicit or implied—a paper might seem unfocused, weak, and not worth the reader's time.

What makes a good thesis sentence? A good thesis sentence generally has the following characteristics:

A good thesis sentence makes a claim. This doesn't mean that you have to reduce an idea to an either-or proposition and then take a stand. Rather, you need to develop an interesting perspective that you can support and defend. This perspective must be more than an observation. "The United

States of America has a violent-crime rate more than twice that of Canada" is merely an observation (verifiable by statistical records). "Americans are more violent than Canadians because they are fearful of each other" (the position that the documentary filmmaker Michael Moore makes in *Bowling for Columbine* [2002]) is an argument. Why? Because it posits a perspective. It makes a claim that engages competing claims. Put another way, a good thesis sentence inspires (rather than silences) other points of view. Someone else might argue that America is violent because of the disintegration of the traditional nuclear family. Another person might point to a third factor. In short, if your thesis is positing something that no one can (or would bother to) argue with, then it's not a very good thesis.

A good thesis sentence determines the scope of the argument. The thesis sentence determines what you're required to say in a paper. It also determines what you cannot say. Every paragraph in your paper exists to support or elaborate on your thesis. Accordingly, if one paragraph you've written seems irrelevant to your thesis, you have three choices: get rid of that paragraph, rewrite the thesis sentence, or work to make the paragraph more clearly relevant. Understand that you don't have a fourth option: you can't simply include the idea without making clear its connection to your thesis. The thesis is like a contract between you and your reader. If you introduce ideas that the reader isn't prepared for or doesn't find relevant, you've violated that contract.

A good thesis sentence provides a structure for the argument. The thesis sentence signals to the reader not only what your argument is but how it will be presented. In other words, your thesis sentence should either directly or indirectly suggest the structure of your argument to the reader. Say, for example, that you're going to argue the following idea: "Michael Moore plays on American fearfulness by using three techniques: A, B, and C." In this case the reader understands that you're going to cover three important points, and that these points will appear in a certain order. If you suggest a particular ordering principle and then abandon it, the reader could feel irritated and confused.

Alternatives to the Thesis Sentence

Sometimes the purpose of a piece of writing is not to make a claim but to raise questions. Other times a writer wants to leave a matter unresolved, inspiring readers to create their own positions. In these cases the thesis sentence might take other forms: the thesis question or the implied thesis.

As we've said, not every piece of writing sets out to make a claim. If your purpose as a writer is to explore, for instance, the reasons for the financial success of James Cameron's *Avatar* (2009) (a topic for which you're not prepared to make a claim), your thesis question might read, "What cultural forces conspired to make *Avatar* a popular success?"

Note that this question, while provocative, does not offer a sense of the argument's structure. It permits the writer to pursue all ideas, without committing to any. Although this freedom might seem appealing, in fact you will find that the lack of a declarative thesis statement requires more work: you need to tighten your internal structure and your transitions from paragraph to paragraph so that the essay is clear and the reader can easily follow your line of inquiry.

But let's suppose, for the sake of illustration, you want to use the thesis question "What forces conspired to make *Avatar* the highest-grossing film of all time?" You might start by discussing the history of the blockbuster since Steven Spielberg's *Jaws* (1975). You might also talk about how the themes of the movie—most prominently, the concerns among young people about environmental devastation—tapped into the zeitgeist at the time of the movie's release. You might expand your discussion to look at the appeal of technological innovations in movies, especially pathbreaking special effects techniques and the visual spectacles that they make possible.

You can see that there's a lot of material to cover here—perhaps too much. If you don't know where the paper will lead or what your conclusions will be, you might find it difficult to avoid digressing into irrelevant tangents. Therefore, if you're going to use a thesis question, make sure that it's a clearly articulated question and that you can structure a well-ordered investigation in response. If the paper starts to feel unwieldy, you might decide instead to use the question as the beginning of a discovery draft. Your findings in the discovery draft can then lead to a declarative thesis for the essay.

THE IMPLIED THESIS

One of the most fascinating things about a thesis sentence is that it is the most important sentence in a paper—even when it's not there.

Some of the best writers never explicitly declare a thesis. In some essays you'll find it difficult to point to a single sentence that declares the argument. Still, the essay is coherent and makes a point. In these cases the writers have used an implied thesis.

Writers use an implied thesis when they want readers to come to their own conclusions about the matter at hand. However, just because the writer doesn't declare the thesis doesn't mean that she is working without one. Good writers will clearly state a thesis—either in their own minds or in their notes for the paper. They may elect not to put the thesis in the paper, but each paragraph, each sentence that they write, is controlled by the thesis all the same.

If you decide to write a paper with an implied thesis, be sure that you have a strong grasp of your argument and its structure. Also be sure that you supply adequate transitions so that the reader can follow your argument with ease.

When you begin writing, you should have a solid, well-articulated thesis. The thesis will tell your readers the purpose of your essay, and as you write, it will help guide you. However, it's also important to keep in mind that the thesis you have when you begin is not set in stone; you can still modify it. Often you'll find that as you write, your thoughts about the issue will evolve, and you'll refine your conclusions. Sometimes it will be necessary to change your thesis to reflect those changes in your thinking. Therefore, when you begin writing, what you really have is a *working thesis*. It can change and adapt and develop as you write the paper. A working thesis doesn't necessarily become a final thesis until the paper is finished.

Turning Your Ideas into a Thesis

Now that we've looked at what you want in a thesis, let's take a moment to look at creating one based on work you've already done. Let's say you've done some brainstorming, a little freewriting, and maybe written a discovery draft, and you've come up with some interesting thoughts. After that, you spent a little time nutshelling, trying to focus your ideas. Now you just need to convert one of those focused ideas into a working thesis.

Composing a working thesis is challenging. After all, the thesis is arguably your paper's most important sentence. It cannot be crafted formulaically but must reflect the complexities of the argument that you are hoping to write. But even while no formula exists for writing a successful thesis, we can offer some advice to get you off on the right foot.

First you'll want to determine what you want to write about. Since you've already created some ideas through brainstorming, freewriting, and other exercises, you should have some options.

From the list of observations you generated during these idea-generating exercises, you'll want to find an observation that interests you. You might choose a single observation from your list and focus on it, or you might look for an idea that ties together two or three of these observations, and focus on that. Whatever you decide, don't try to squeeze everything you've observed into a single essay. To do so would require a book—and you simply don't have time to write a book before the paper is due. Determining which idea or set of ideas you want to work with will enable you to stay focused and to do justice to your ideas in the limited time that you have.

Sometimes writers are torn between two or three very good observations. If the ideas can't be synthesized into a single idea or claim, the best strategy is to pick whichever observation looks most interesting. In other words, choose the observation you can have the most fun with. Doing so will help you stay focused: you will now know not only what you'll want to discuss but what you can leave alone.

You'll also notice something interesting at this point: even though you don't yet have a thesis, the observation you've chosen to write about will help dictate which type of paper you're writing. If your observation has to do with the use of sound in a film (as in the *Apocalypse Now* example above), then you'll be writing a formal analysis paper. Realizing this helps you understand not only what you're going to do but what you're not going to do: a paper about film history, or a cultural analysis, for example.

So now you have your plan: you're going to write a specific type of paper (formal analysis) about Coppola's use of sound in *Apocalypse Now*. As we noted earlier in this guide, your goal in writing a formal analysis paper is to choose an element of the film's form and examine in detail how that element contributes to the major themes, underlying message, or overall effect of the film. At this point you need to compose a question, using this goal to guide you. After some doodling you come up with this question: How does Coppola's use of sound contribute to the overall effect of *Apocalypse Now*? Give yourself the opportunity to explore that question. Brainstorm or freewrite a response. Then try to shape your response so that you can answer the question in a couple of sentences, then a single sentence. When you can answer that question in one sentence, you'll have your working thesis.

Of course if you were writing a cultural analysis paper, you'd ask yourself a different question, based on the goals of that type of paper. The same is true for a paper that explores the place of *Apocalypse Now* in film history and cultural history. The strategy is clear: instead of trying to create a thesis out of thin air, pick an element of the movie that interests you, then ask yourself a relevant question based on the goals of the type of paper you're going to write. When you answer your own question, you'll have a working thesis.

The Thesis Sentence Checklist

In the end you may have spent a good deal of time writing your working thesis and still not know if it's a good one. As we indicated earlier, a good thesis typically evolves as the writer writes. As you write, you'll want to interrogate your thesis in order to determine how well it's holding up. Some questions to ask yourself follow:

Does the thesis sentence attempt to answer or to explore a challenging intellectual question? If your thesis doesn't challenge you, it likely won't challenge your reader either. If you find yourself bored as you write, or if you are haunted by the sense that you aren't talking about anything important, stop writing. Return to your list of observations. See if you can find some connection between the observations that might raise the intellectual stakes.

Will the point I'm making generate discussion and argument, or will it leave people asking "So what?" If your thesis doesn't generate discussion, perhaps the point you made is too obvious. Return to your list of observations. Ask of each one, "Why is this important?" The answer to that question should help you refine your thesis.

Is the thesis too vague? Too general? Should you focus on a more specific aspect of the topic? If a thesis is too broad, it's unlikely to hold the reader's interest. Take your more general idea and link it to specific observations about the text. Perhaps in that linkage you'll find the focus for your paper.

Does the thesis deal directly with the topic at hand, or is it a declaration of my personal feelings? Be careful about personal opinions: to make a claim is different from declaring an opinion. An academic paper does the former but eschews the latter.

Does the thesis indicate the direction of my argument? Does it suggest a structure for my paper? If a thesis is well constructed, it will suggest to you and to your reader where the paper is going. Look at your thesis, then look at your outline. Does your thesis reflect or suggest that outline? Can you rewrite the thesis so that the outline/structure is suggested?

Does the introductory paragraph define terms important to my thesis? Don't make your thesis do all the work. Rely on your introduction to help your thesis, especially when it comes to necessary but cumbersome tasks, such as defining terms.

If I'm writing a research paper, does my introduction place my thesis within the larger, ongoing scholarly discussion about the topic? Consider again the dinner party metaphor. What do the scholars at the table have to say about the topic? What do you have to say in response to their ideas? Is the relationship between your perspective and theirs clear to the reader? If not, how might it be made clear?

8

Considering Structure and Organization

Once you've figured out what you want to say, you're left with the problem of how to say it. How should you begin the paper? Should you address the opinions of other thinkers? And what should you do with that stubborn contradiction you've uncovered in your own thinking?

Writing papers in college requires you to come up with sophisticated, complex, and even creative ways of structuring your ideas. Accordingly, we can't offer simple formulas that will work for every paper, every time. We can, however, give you some things to think about that will help you as you consider how to structure your paper.

Let Your Thesis Direct You

Begin by listening to your thesis. If it's well written, it will tell you which way to go with your paper. Suppose, for example, that, in responding to the films of the early Soviet filmmakers, you have written a thesis that says this:

> The purpose of the early Soviet films was not only to support the ideology of the revolution, but to create *Homo sovieticus*, a new kind of human being.

This thesis provides the writer with several clues about how best to structure the paper, and it prepares readers for what they will encounter therein. First, the thesis promises readers that the paper will argue that Soviet filmmakers were interested in more than ideology. The paper will therefore begin by acknowledging that although the promotion of revolutionary values was important to them, it was not their only goal. The rest of the paper will concern the (more important) creation of *Homo sovieticus*—a new sort of human being.

We say that this idea of *Homo sovieticus* is more important than ideology not necessarily because the Soviet filmmakers said so but because the writer seems to say so in her thesis. Reread the thesis sentence. Note that the emphasis falls on the last clause: "a new kind of human being." This emphasis tells us that we will be given not simply a description of how Soviet filmmakers propagated Soviet ideology but, rather, a description of how the methods of propagating this ideology were used to create a new type of human being—a Soviet person. We understand all of this because the writer took the time to make sure that the thesis was written emphatically.

Sketching Your Argument

Although your thesis will identify your paper's general direction, it will not necessarily provide you with a plan for how to organize all of your points, large and small. Here it might be helpful to diagram or sketch your argument.

In sketching your argument, the goal is to fill the page with your ideas. Begin by writing your thesis. Put it where your instincts tell you to: at the top of the page, in the center, at the bottom. Around the thesis, cluster the points you want to make. Under each of these points, note the observations you've made and the evidence you'll use. Don't get nervous when your sketch starts to look messy. Use arrows. Draw circles. Take up colored pens. Any of these methods can help you find connections between your ideas that otherwise might go unnoticed. Working from your sketch, try to see the line of reasoning that is evolving.

Sketching is an important step in the writing process because it allows you to explore visually the connections between your ideas. If you outline a paper too early in the process, you risk missing these connections. You might line up your points—A, B, C—without fully understanding why. Sketching your argument helps you see, for example, that points A and C really overlap and need to be thought through more carefully.

Outlining Your Argument

When you've finished the sketch, you're ready to make an outline. The task of the outline is to identify the paper's best structure. By "best structure" we mean the structure that best supports the argument you intend to make.

When you're outlining a paper, you'll have many options for organization. Understand, however, that each choice you make eliminates dozens of other options. Your goal is to come up with an outline in which all your choices support your thesis.

Treat the outline as if it were a puzzle that you are putting together. In a puzzle, each piece has only one appropriate place. The same should be true of your paper. If it's easy to shift around your ideas—if several of your paragraphs could be switched around and no one would be the wiser—then you haven't yet found the best structure for your paper. Each paragraph should present a single, well-supported idea that is the logical successor to the ideas that preceded it, all of them building inexorably toward your paper's overall point—the thesis. Keep working until your outline fits your ideas like a glove.

When you think you have an outline that works, challenge it. The first outline rarely holds up to a good interrogation. When you start asking questions of your outline, you will begin to see where the plan holds and where it falls apart. Here are some questions you might ask:

Does my thesis control the direction of the outline?

Are all of my main points relevant to the thesis?

Can any of these points be moved around without changing something important about the thesis?

Does the outline seem logical?

Does the argument progress, or does it stall?

If the argument seems to take a turn midstream, does the thesis anticipate that turn?

Do I have sufficient support for each of my points?

Have I made room in the outline for other points of view about the topic?

Does this outline reflect a thorough, thoughtful argument? Have I covered the ground?

Constructing Paragraphs

Imagine that you've written the thesis. You've interrogated the outline. You know which modes of arrangement you intend to use. You've settled on a plan that you think will work. Now you have to go about the serious business of constructing paragraphs.

You were probably told in high school that paragraphs are the workhorses of a paper. Indeed they are. If a single paragraph is incoherent or weak, the entire argument might fail. It's important that you consider carefully the "job" of each paragraph. Know what you want that paragraph to do. Make sure it pulls its weight.

WHAT IS A PARAGRAPH?

A paragraph is generally understood as a single "unit" of a paper. What your readers expect when they encounter a new paragraph is that you're going to declare a point and then offer support for that point. If you violate this expectation—if your paragraphs wander aimlessly among a half dozen points, or if they declare points without offering any evidence to support them—readers will become confused or irritated by your argument. They won't want to read any further.

WHAT SHOULD A PARAGRAPH DO?

At the risk of sounding silly, we suggest that you consider this: what you look for in a boyfriend or girlfriend, a reader looks for in a paragraph. You want a partner who is supportive, strong, and considerate to others. Similarly, a good paragraph is:

- **Supportive.** Even in the most trying of times a good paragraph finds a way to support the thesis. It declares its relationship to the thesis clearly, so that the whole world knows what the paragraph intends to do. In other words, a supportive paragraph's main idea clearly develops the argument of the thesis.
- **Strong.** A good paragraph isn't bloated with irrelevant evidence or redundant sentences. Nor is it a scrawny thing, begging to be fed. It's strong and buff. You know that it's been worked on. In other words, a strong paragraph develops its main idea, using sufficient evidence.
- **Considerate.** Good paragraphs consider their relationship to other paragraphs. A good paragraph never interrupts its fellow paragraphs to babble on about its own irrelevant problems. A good paragraph waits its turn. It shows up when and where it's supposed to. It doesn't make a mess for other paragraphs to clean up. In other words, a considerate paragraph is a coherent paragraph. It makes sense within the text as a whole.

WRITING THE TOPIC SENTENCE OR GUIDING CLAIM

Just as every paper requires a thesis sentence to assert and control its argument, so also every paragraph requires a topic sentence to assert and control its main idea. Without a topic sentence, your paragraphs will seem jumbled, aimless. Your reader will become confused. Because the topic sentence plays an important role in your paragraph, it must be crafted with care. When you've written a topic sentence, ask yourself the following questions:

Does the topic sentence declare a single point of the argument? Because the reader expects that a paragraph will explore only one idea in your paper, it's important that your topic sentence not be too ambitious. If it points to two or three ideas, perhaps you need to consider developing more paragraphs.

Does the topic sentence further the argument? Give your topic sentences the same "so what?" test that you gave your thesis sentence. If your topic sentence isn't interesting, your paragraph probably won't further the argument. Your paper could stall.

Is the topic sentence relevant to the thesis? It might seem so to you, but the relevance may not be so clear to your reader. If you find that your topic sentence is taking you into brand-new territory, stop writing and consider your options. If the new territory isn't relevant to the existing thesis, either you'll have to rewrite your thesis to accommodate this new direction, or you'll have to consider excluding this paragraph from your final paper.

Is there a clear relationship between this topic sentence and the paragraph that came before? Make sure that you haven't left out any steps in the process of composing your argument. If you take a sudden turn in your reasoning, signify that turn to the reader by using the proper transitional phrase—"on the other hand," "however," or the like.

Does the topic sentence control the paragraph? If your paragraph seems to unravel, take a second look. Perhaps the topic sentence isn't adequately controlling the paragraph and needs to be rewritten. Or maybe the paragraph is moving on to a new idea that needs to be developed in a paragraph of its own.

Where have I placed my topic sentence? Readers often look for topic sentences at or near the beginning of a paragraph. Consider this: If you are skimming something quickly, which sentence do you look to in each paragraph? Likely it's the first sentence. But that doesn't mean all of your topic sentences need to be situated at the beginning of your paragraphs. Nevertheless, if you're going to place your topic sentence elsewhere, you'll need to craft your paragraph with care. You might justify putting the topic sentence in the middle of the paragraph, for example, if you have information that needs to precede it. You might also justify putting the topic sentence at the end of the paragraph if you want the reader to consider your line of reasoning before you declare your main point. Let the argument and what it needs dictate where you place your topic sentence. Wherever you place it, be strategic. Make sure that your decision facilitates your argument.

Developing Your Paragraphs

EVIDENCE

Students often ask how long a paragraph should be. To this we respond, "As long as it takes."

It's possible to make a point quickly. Sometimes it's desirable to keep it short. Notice the preceding paragraph, for example. We might have hemmed and hawed, talked about short paragraphs and long paragraphs. We might have said that the average paragraph is one-half to two-thirds of a page in length. We might have spent time explaining why the too-short paragraph is too short, and the too-long paragraph too long. Instead, we cut to the chase. After huffing and puffing through this paragraph (which is getting longer and longer all the time), we'll give you the same advice: a good paragraph is as long as it needs to be in order to illustrate, explore, and/or prove its main idea.

However, length isn't all that matters in paragraph development. What's important is that a paragraph develops its idea fully, and in a manner that readers can follow with ease.

Let's consider these two issues carefully. First, how do we know when an idea is fully developed? If your topic sentence is well written, it should tell you what the paragraph needs to do. If the topic sentence declares, for example, that there are two conflicting impulses at work in a particular fictional character, then the reader will expect the two impulses to be defined and illustrated. It might take two paragraphs to do this; it might take one. The decision will depend on how important this matter is to the discussion. If the point is important, you'll take your time, and (more likely than not) you'll use at least two paragraphs. In this case a topic sentence might be understood as controlling not only a paragraph but an entire section of text.

When you've written a paragraph, ask yourself the following questions:

Do I have enough evidence to support this paragraph's idea?

Do I have too much evidence?

Does this evidence clearly support the assertion that I'm making in this paragraph, or am I stretching it?

If I'm stretching it, what can I do to convince the reader that this stretch is worth making?

Am I repeating myself in this paragraph?

Have I defined all of the paragraph's important terms?

Can I say, in a nutshell, what the purpose of this paragraph is?

Has the paragraph fulfilled that purpose?

ARRANGEMENT

Equally important to the idea of a paragraph's development is the matter of the paragraph's arrangement. Paragraphs are arranged differently for different purposes. For example, if you're writing a paper about a film's history and wish to summarize a sequence of events, you'll likely want to arrange the information chronologically. If you're writing a paper in which you want to describe the composition or setting of a particular shot or scene, perhaps you'll choose to arrange the information spatially. If you're writing a paper about the elements of a film that make it stand out from other movies of a similar type, you might want to arrange your ideas by working from the specific to the general—and so on.

COHERENCE

So you have your thesis, your topic sentences, and truckloads of evidence to support the whole lot. You've spent three days writing your paragraphs, making sure that each paragraph argues one point and that this point is well supported with evidence. But when you read the essay back to yourself, you feel a profound sense of disappointment. Though you've followed your outline, the essay just doesn't seem to hold together. It could be that you have a problem with coherence.

A lack of coherence is easy to diagnose but not so easy to cure. An incoherent essay doesn't seem to flow. Its arguments are hard to understand. The reader has to double back again and again in order to follow the gist of the argument. Something has gone wrong. What?

Look for the following issues in your paper:

Make sure the grammatical subjects of your sentences reflect the real subject of your paragraph. Underline the subjects of all the sentences in the paragraph. Do these subjects match the paragraph's subject in most cases? Or, have you put the paragraph's subject into another, less important part of the sentence? Remember that the reader understands an idea's importance according to where you place it. If your main idea is hidden as an object of a preposition in a subordinate clause, do you really think your reader is going to follow what you're trying to say? For instance, consider the following paragraph about the way sound is used in *Apocalypse Now*. The grammatical subject of each sentence is underlined.

> Many **situations** occur in *Apocalypse Now* in which sound is the main means by which we understand characters' psychology. An excellent **example** is the scene when Sgt. Willard is in a hotel room in Hanoi. The Doors' **song** "The End" provides a sound track for Willard's psychological breakdown and Vietnam's insanity, while the sound of a fan over his head blends menacingly with the sound of helicopters and the sounds of war. One **shot** in this sequence shows Willard screaming, but we

don't hear the scream in the sound mix, and this silence makes Willard's desperation even more palpable.

Look at the four subjects: "situations," "example," "song," and "shot." Of these, only "song" is clearly related to the topic of the paragraph. Now consider this revised paragraph:

> Many times in *Apocalypse Now*, **sound** is the main means by which we understand characters' psychology. In one scene, the rhythmic **pulsing** of a ceiling fan over Sgt. Willard's head blends menacingly with the sounds of helicopters and of war, while The Doors' song "The End" provides a sound track for Willard's psychological breakdown and Vietnam's insanity. The **silence** that accompanies Sgt. Willard's scream near the end of the scene makes his desperation even more palpable.

Look at the subjects here: "sound," "pulsing," and "silence." The paragraph's string of related subjects keeps the reader focused on the topic and creates a paragraph that flows more naturally and seems much more coherent than the first one.

Make sure the grammatical subjects are consistent. Again, look at the grammatical subjects of all your sentences. How many different subjects do you find? If you have too many different sentence subjects, your paragraph will be hard to follow.

Make sure your sentences look backward as well as forward. For a paragraph to be coherent, each sentence should begin by linking itself firmly to the sentence that preceded it. If the link between sentences does not seem firm, use an introductory clause or phrase to connect one idea to the other.

Follow the principle of moving from old to new. If you put the old information at the beginning of the sentence and the new information at the end, you accomplish two things: first, you ensure that your readers are on solid ground, moving from the familiar to the unknown, and, second, because we tend to give emphasis to what comes at the end of a sentence, readers rightfully perceive that the new information is more important than the old.

Use repetition to create a sense of unity. Repeating key words and phrases at appropriate moments will give your readers a sense of coherence in your work. But don't overdo it; you'll risk sounding redundant.

Use transition markers wisely. Sometimes you'll need to announce to your readers a turn in your argument, or you'll want to emphasize one point, or you'll want to make clear a particular relationship in time. In all these cases you'll want to use transition markers. Some examples follow:

- **To give an example:** *for example, for instance*
- **To present a list:** *first, second, third, next, then*

- **To show that you have more to say:** *in addition, furthermore, moreover*
- **To indicate similarity:** *also, likewise, similarly*
- **To show an exception:** *but, however, nevertheless, on the other hand*
- **To show cause and effect:** *accordingly, consequently, therefore, because*
- **To emphasize:** *indeed, in fact, of course*
- **To conclude:** *finally, in conclusion, in the end*

Introductions and Conclusions

Introductions and conclusions are among the most challenging of all paragraphs. Why? Because they must do more than state a topic sentence and offer support. Introductions and conclusions must synthesize and provide context for your entire argument, and they must also make the proper impression on your readers.

The introduction is your chance to get readers interested in your subject. Accordingly, the tone of the paragraph has to be just right. You want to inform, but not to the point of being dull; you want to intrigue, but not to the point of being vague; you want to take a strong stance, but not to the point of alienating readers. Pay attention to the nuances of your tone. Seek out a second reader if you're not sure that you've managed to get the tone the way you want it.

Equally important to the tone of the introduction is that it needs to "place" your argument into a larger context. Some strategies follow:

Announce your topic broadly; then declare your particular take. For example, if you're interested in talking about the symbolism of Fellini's films, you might (1) begin by saying that Fellini's symbolism has posed a problem for many of his critics, (2) provide a quick definition of the problem as others have defined it, and (3) declare your thesis (which states your own position on the matter).

Provide any background material important to your argument. If you're interested in exploring how events in the 1960s influenced the work of Oliver Stone, in your introduction you'll want to provide the reader, in broad strokes, a description of the sixties. Don't include irrelevant details in your description; instead, emphasize those aspects of the culture (the assassination of John F. Kennedy, the war in Vietnam) that might have most influenced Stone.

Define key terms as you intend to make use of them in your argument. If, for example, you're writing a paper on cinema verité, it is absolutely essential that you define the term for your reader. For example, how do you understand the term *verité*? How do you understand *reality*? Begin with a definition of terms, and from there work toward the declaration of your argument.

Use an anecdote or a quotation. Sometimes you'll find a terrific story or quotation that seems to reflect the main point of your paper. Don't be afraid to begin with it. Be sure, however, that you tie that story or quotation clearly and immediately to your main argument.

Acknowledge your opponents. When you're writing a paper about a controversial matter, you might wish to begin by summarizing the point of view of your adversaries. Then state your own position in opposition to theirs. In this way you place yourself clearly in the ongoing conversation.

Remember, the introduction is the first impression that your argument will make on the reader. Take special care with your sentences so that they'll be interesting. Also take the time to consider who your readers are and what background they will bring with them to their reading. If your readers are very knowledgeable about the subject, you will not need to provide a lot of background information. If your readers are less knowledgeable, you will need to be more careful about defining terms.

Finally, you might want to consider writing the introduction after you've written the rest of the paper. Many writers find that they have a better grip on their subject once they've done a first draft. This "better grip" helps them craft an introduction that is sure-footed, persuasive, interesting, and clear. But be careful. Any changes that you make to an introduction and/or a thesis statement will affect the paper that follows. Simply adding the new introductory paragraph will not produce a "completed" paper.

Conclusions are also difficult to write. How do you manage to make the reader feel persuaded by what you've said? Even if the points of your paper are strong, the overall effect of your argument might fall to pieces if the paper as a whole is badly concluded.

Many students end their papers by simply summarizing what has come before. A summary of what the reader has just read is important to the conclusion—particularly if your argument has been complicated or has covered a lot of ground. But a good conclusion will do more. Just as the introduction sought to place the paper in the larger, ongoing conversation about the topic, so should the conclusion insist on returning readers to that ongoing conversation, but with the feeling that they've learned something more. You don't want readers to finish your paper and say, "So what?" Admittedly, writing a conclusion isn't easy.

Many of the strategies we've listed for improving introductions can help you improve your conclusions as well. In the conclusion you might do the following:

Return to the ongoing conversation, emphasizing the importance of your own contribution to it.

Consider again the background information with which you began, and illustrate how your argument has shed new light on that information.

Return to the key terms and point out how your essay has added new dimension to their meanings.

Use an anecdote or a quotation that summarizes or reflects your main idea.

Acknowledge your opponents—if only to emphasize that you've countered their positions successfully.

Remember, language is especially important to a conclusion. Your goal in the final sentences is to leave your ideas resounding in the reader's mind. Give the reader something to think about. Make your language ring.

9

Attending to Style

Most of us know good style when we see it—and *hear* it in the mind's ear. We also know when a sentence seems cumbersome to read. However, though we can easily spot beastly sentences, it is not as easy to say why a sentence—especially one that is grammatically correct—isn't working. We look at the sentence; we see that the commas are in the right places; and we find no error to speak of. So why is the sentence so awful? What's gone wrong?

When thinking about what makes a good sentence, be sure to put yourself in the reader's place. What is a reader hoping to find in your sentences? Information, yes. Eloquence, surely. But, most important, a reader is looking for clarity. Your reader does not want to wrestle with sentences. She wants to read with ease. She wants to see one idea build on another. She wants to experience, without struggling, the emphasis of your language and the importance of your idea. Above all, she wants to feel that you, the writer, are doing the bulk of the work. In short, she wants to read sentences that are persuasive, straightforward, and clear.[2]

Basic Principles of the Sentence

FOCUS ON ACTORS AND ACTIONS

To understand what makes a good sentence, it's important to understand one principle: a sentence, at its very basic level, is about actors and actions. As such, the subject of a sentence should point clearly to the actor, and the verb of the sentence should describe the important action.

This principle might seem so obvious to you that you don't think it warrants further discussion. But think again. Look at the following sentence, and then try to determine, in a nutshell, what's wrong with it:

> There is a question in the mind of some screenwriters over whether the employment of flashbacks is a sign of weakness in a script.

This sentence has no grammatical errors. But certainly it lumbers along, without any force. What are the actors? What are the actions?

---

[2] The way of teaching style that is represented here has been greatly influenced by Joseph Williams and his work. For a thorough examination of the fundamental principles of style, see Williams's *Style: Lessons in Clarity and Grace*, 10th ed. (New York: Pearson Longman, 2010).

Now consider the following sentence:

Some screenwriters question whether flashbacks signify a weak script.

What changes does this sentence make? We can point to the more obvious changes: omitting the empty *there is* phrase; replacing the abstract noun *sign* with the stronger verb *signify*; replacing a second abstract noun *weakness* with the adjective *weak*; omitting all of the prepositions that the abstract nouns require. What principle governs these many changes? Precisely the one mentioned earlier: that the *actors* in a sentence should serve as the sentence's grammatical subjects, and the *actions* should be illustrated forcefully in the sentence's verbs.

Whenever you feel that your prose is confusing or hard to follow, find the actors and the actions of your sentences. Is the actor the subject of your sentence? Is the action related, vividly, in a verb? If not, rewrite your sentences accordingly.

BE CONCRETE

Student writers tend to rely too heavily on abstract nouns: they use *expectation* when the verb *expect* is stronger; they write *evaluation* when *evaluate* is more vivid. So why use an abstract noun when a verb will do better? Many students believe that abstract nouns permit them to sound more "academic." When you write with a lot of abstract nouns, however, you risk confusing your reader. You also end up cornering yourself syntactically. Consider the following:

Nouns often require prepositions. Too many prepositional phrases in a sentence are hard to follow. Verbs, on the other hand, can stand on their own. They're cleaner; they don't box you in. If you need some proof of this claim, consider the following sentence:

> An evaluation of the footage by the director is necessary prior to our editing process.

Notice all of the prepositional phrases that these nouns require. Now look at the following sentence, which uses verbs:

> The director must evaluate the footage before we edit it.

This sentence has fewer nouns and prepositions and is therefore much easier to read—yet it still conveys all the information found in the prior sentence.

Abstract nouns often invite the *there is* construction. Consider the following sentence:

> There is a method of acting that Konstantin Stanislavsky invented in which acting students are taught about the use of past experiences to bring emotion to their roles.

We might rewrite this sentence as follows:

> Konstantin Stanislavsky invented a method that teaches actors to use past experiences to bring emotion to their roles.

The result, again, is a sentence that is more direct and easier to read.

Abstract nouns are, well, abstract. Using too many abstract nouns will leave your prose seeming ungrounded. Words such as *falsification*, *beauteousness*, and *insubstantiality* sound pompous and vague—which may be exactly what you want, if you're striving for a slightly comic, self-mocking effect. But, by and large, people simply don't talk this way. Instead, use concrete nouns, as well as strong verbs, to convey your ideas. *Lying*, *beauty*, and *flimsiness* reflect the way people really speak; these words point directly to their meanings without drawing undue attention to themselves.

Abstract nouns can obscure your logic. Note how hard it is to follow the line of reasoning in the following sentence (the nouns that might be rewritten as verbs or as adjectives are in boldface):

> **Decisions** with regard to **the dismissal** of actors on the basis of **their unwillingness** to put on weight for a role rest with the director.

Now consider this sentence:

> When actors refuse to gain weight for a role, the director
> must decide whether or not to dismiss them.

The Exception: When to Use Abstract Nouns

In some instances an abstract noun will be essential to the sentence. Sometimes abstract nouns refer to a previous sentence (*these arguments*, *this decision*, etc.). Other times they allow you to be more concise (e.g., *her argument* versus *what she argued*). And, in other cases, the abstract noun is a concept important to your argument: freedom, love, revolution, and so on. Still, if you examine your prose, you'll probably find that you overuse abstract nouns. Omitting from your writing those abstract nouns that aren't really necessary makes for leaner, "fitter" prose.

BE CONCISE

One of the most exasperating aspects of reading student texts is that most students don't know how to write concisely. Students use phrases when a single word will do, offer pairs of adjectives and verbs where one is enough, or overwrite, saying the same thing two or three times with the hope that the reader will be impressed by a point worth rephrasing and then rephrasing again.

Stop the madness! It's easy to delete words and phrases from your prose once you've learned to be ruthless about it.

Do you really need words such as *actually, basically, generally*, and so on? If you don't need them, why are they there? Are you using two words where one will do? Isn't the phrase *first and foremost* redundant? What's the point of *future* in *future plans*? And why do you keep saying, *"In my opinion"*? Doesn't the reader understand that this is your paper, based on your point of view? Does drawing attention to yourself in this way make your points any stronger—or does it have the opposite effect, coming across as insecurity or as hedging?

Sometimes you won't be able to fix a wordy sentence by simply deleting a few words or phrases. You'll have to rewrite the whole sentence. Take the following sentence, for example:

> Plagiarism is a serious academic offense resulting in punishments that might include suspension or dismissal, profoundly affecting your academic career.

The idea here is simple: *Plagiarism is a serious offense with serious consequences.* Why not simply say so? Don't be afraid to let your reader connect your ideas to the context—at its most pleasurable, good writing gives the reader a sense of collaboration, of being trusted to connect the dots.

BE COHERENT

At this point in discussing style, we move from the sentence as a discrete unit to the way that sentences fit together. Coherence (or the lack of it) is a common problem in student papers.

Sometimes a professor encounters a paper in which all the ideas seem to be there, but they're hard to follow. The prose seems jumbled. The line of reasoning is anything but linear. Couldn't the student have made this paper a bit more readable?

Although coherence is a complicated and difficult matter to address, we can offer a couple of tricks that will help your sentences "flow." Silly as it sounds, you should "dress" your sentences the way a bride might—wear, as the saying goes, something old and something new. In other words, most of the sentences you write should begin with the old—with something that looks back to the previous sentence. Then your sentence should move on to telling the reader something new. If you do this, your line of reasoning will be easier for readers to follow.

Though this advice sounds simple enough, it is not always easy to follow. Let's dissect the practice so that we can better understand how our sentences might be "well dressed."

Consider, first, the beginnings of sentences. The coherence of your paper depends largely on how well you begin sentences. "Well begun is half done," says Mary Poppins, and in this case (as in all cases, really) she's right.

Beginning a sentence is hard work. When you begin a sentence, you have three important matters to consider:

1. **Is your topic also the subject of the sentence?** When a sentence lacks coherence, usually it's because the writer

has not been careful to ensure that the topic of the sentence is also the grammatical subject of the sentence. If, for instance, you're writing a sentence whose topic is the importance of the close-up in silent films, then the grammatical subject of the sentence should reflect that idea:

A silent-film actor's **facial expressions** were more important to his success than his body language was.

If, on the other hand, you bury your topic in a subordinate clause, look what happens:

The rise of the silent-film stars, which came about **because of their facial expressions**, was not due to their control of body language.

The emphasis and focus of the sentence are obscured.

2. **Are the topics/subjects of your sentences consistent?** For a paragraph to be coherent, most of the sentence subjects should be the same. To check for consistency, pick out a paragraph and make a list of its sentence subjects. See if any of the subjects seem out of place. For example, if you're writing a paragraph about the importance of the close-up in a paper on silent films, do most of your sentence subjects reflect that paragraph topic? Or, do some of your sentences have other, tangential topics (such as "gestures"

or "body language") as the grammatical subject? Although the full-body comedy of silent film stars such as Charlie Chaplin and Buster Keaton may indeed have a place in your paper on silent films, you will confuse readers if your paragraph's sentence subjects point to too many competing ideas. Revise the sentences (perhaps the entire paragraph) for coherence.

3. **Have you marked, when appropriate, the transitions between ideas?** Coherence depends on how well you connect a sentence to the one that came before it. You'll want to make solid transitions between your sentences, using words such as *however* or *therefore*. You'll also want to signal to readers whenever, for example, something important or disappointing comes up. In these cases you'll want to use expressions such as *note that* or *unfortunately*. You might also want to indicate time or place in your argument. If so, you'll use transitions such as *then, later, earlier,* or *in the previous paragraph*. Be careful not to overuse transition phrases. Some writers think transition phrases can, all by themselves, direct a reader through an argument. Indeed, sometimes all a paragraph needs is a *however* in order for its argument suddenly to make sense. More often, though, the problem with coherence does not stem from a lack of transition phrases but from the fact that the writer has not articulated, for himself, the connections between his ideas. Don't rely on transition phrases alone to bring sense to muddled prose.

BE EMPHATIC

We've been talking about how sentences begin, but what about how they end?

If the beginnings of sentences must look over their shoulders at what came before, the ends of sentences must forge ahead into new ground. It's the end of a sentence, then, that must be courageous and emphatic. You must construct sentences so that the ends pack the punch.

To write emphatically, follow these principles:

Declare important ideas at the end of a sentence. Shift less important ideas to the front.

Tighten the ends of sentences. Don't trail off into nonsense, don't repeat yourself, and don't qualify what you've just said if you don't have to. Simply make your point and move on.

Use subordinate clauses to house subordinate ideas. Put all the important ideas in main clauses and the less important ideas in subordinate clauses. If you have two ideas of equal importance that you want to express in the same sentence, use parallel constructions or semicolons. These two tricks of the trade are perhaps more useful than any others in balancing equally significant ideas.

BE IN CONTROL

When sentences run on and on, readers know that a writer has lost control. Take command of your sentences. When you read over your paper, look for sentences that never seem to end. Your first impulse might be to take these long sentences and divide them into two (or three or four). This simple solution often works. But sometimes this strategy isn't the most desirable one; it might lead to short, choppy sentences. Moreover, if you always cut your sentences in two, you'll never learn how a sentence can be long and complex without violating the boundaries of good prose.

What do you do when you encounter an overly long sentence? First consider the point of your sentence. Usually it will have more than one point, and sorting out the points helps sort out the grammar. Consider carefully the points that you're trying to make and the connections between those points. Then try to determine which grammatical structure best serves your purpose.

Are the points of equal importance? Use a coordinating conjunction (*and, but, or*) or a semicolon to join the ideas. Try to use parallel constructions when appropriate.

Are the points of unequal importance? Use subordinate clauses (*although, while, because*, and so on) or relative clauses *(that, which)* to join the ideas, putting the less important idea in the subordinate clause.

Does one point make for an interesting aside? Insert that point between commas, dashes, or even parentheses at the appropriate juncture in the sentence.

Do these ideas belong in the same sentence? If not, create two sentences.

WRITE BEAUTIFULLY

In your career as a writer you will sometimes produce a paper that is well written but could be written better. On this happy occasion, you might wish to turn your attention to such matters as balance, parallel structure, emphasis, rhythm, and word choice. If you're interested in exploring these rhetorical tools, consult one of several excellent style books, such as Joe Williams's *Style: The Basics of Clarity and Grace*, William Strunk Jr. and E. B. White's *The Elements of Style*, or John Trimble's *Writing with Style*. You will find plenty of valuable advice in any one of these sources.

10

Revising Your Work

Why and How to Revise

Most of us who compose on a computer understand revision as an ongoing—even constant—process. Every time you hit the delete key, every time you cut and paste, and every time you take out a comma or exchange one word for another, you're revising.

Real revision, however, is more than making a few changes here and there. Real revision, just as the word implies, calls for *seeing again*; it requires that you open yourself up to the possibility that parts of your paper—even your entire paper—might need to be rethought, and rewritten.

Achieving this state of mind is difficult. First, you might be very attached to what you've written. You might be unwilling to change a word, let alone three or four paragraphs. Second, there's the matter of time: you might sense that the paper needs major work, but it's due tomorrow, or you have an exam in physics, or you're coming down with a cold and know that you need to sleep. Third, you might have difficulty understanding what, exactly, is wrong with your paper. Finally, you might simply be sick and tired of the paper. How can you make another pass through it when exhaustion has you in its grip? Why should you be bothered with (or let yourself be overwhelmed by) the process of revising?

Of course we might convince you that revision is worth the extra effort simply by saying that revising a paper will help you achieve a better grade. A good reader can sense when a piece of writing has been thoroughly considered and reconsidered. This consideration (and here we mean the word in both of its meanings) is not lost on your professor and will be rewarded.

More important than grades, however, is the fact that revising your papers teaches you to be a better writer. Professional writers know that to write is to rewrite. In the revision process you improve your reading skills and your analytical skills. You learn to challenge your own ideas, thus deepening and strengthening your argument. You learn to find the weaknesses in your writing. You may even discover patterns of error or habits of organization that are undermining your papers.

Though revising takes time and energy, it also will help you become a more efficient writer down the road. If, for example, you have discovered through the revision process that you tend to bury your topic sentences in the middle of your paragraphs, you can take this discovery with you as you draft your next paper. You may then be less likely to make that particular mistake again.

Perhaps we've answered the question "Why should I revise?" The next question, of course, is "How?" There are many different kinds of revising, including the following:

Large-scale revision. Large-scale revision means looking at the entire paper for places where your thinking seems to go awry. You might need to provide evidence, define terms, or add an entirely new step to your reasoning. You might even decide to restructure or rewrite your paper completely if you discover a new idea that intrigues you, or a structure that seems to be more effective than the one you've been using.

Small-scale revision. Small-scale revision needs to happen when you know that a certain part of your paper isn't working. Maybe the introduction needs work. Maybe one part of the argument seems weak. Once you've located the problem, you'll focus on revising that one section of your paper. When you're finished you'll want to reconsider your paper as a whole to make sure that your revisions work in the context of the entire paper.

Editing. Too often students confuse editing with revision. They are not the same processes. Editing is the process of finding minor problems with a text—problems that might easily be fixed by deleting a word or sentence, cutting and pasting a paragraph, and so on. When you edit, you're considering your reader. You might be happy with how you've written your paper, but will your reader find your paper clear, readable, and interesting? How can you rewrite the paper so that it's clearer, more concise, and, most important of all, a pleasure to read?

The very best writers revise their writing in all the ways listed here. To manage these various levels of revision, it's very important that you get an early start on your papers so that you have time to make any substantive, large-scale revisions that might be needed. Good writers also understand that revision is an ongoing process, not necessarily something that you do only after your first draft is complete. You might find, for example, that you're stuck halfway through the first draft of your paper. You decide to take a look at what you have so far. As you read, you find that you've neglected to make a point that is essential to the success of your argument. You revise what you've written, making that point clear. In the end you find that your block, your "stuckness," is gone. Why? Maybe it's gone because what was blocking you in the first place was a hole in your argument. Or maybe it's gone because you gave your brain a break. In any case, stopping to revise in the middle of the drafting process often proves wise.

Developing a Critical Eye

We have yet to address the matter of how a writer knows what she should revise. Developing a critical eye is perhaps the most difficult part of the revision process. But having a critical eye makes you a better writer, reader, and thinker. So it's worth considering carefully how you might learn to see your own work with the objectivity that is essential to successful self-criticism.

The first step in developing a critical eye is to get some distance from your work. If you've planned your writing process well, you'll have left yourself a day or two to take a break. If you don't have this luxury, even an hour of video games or a walk over to the printing center to pick up a hard copy of your draft might be enough to clear your head. Many writers find that their mind keeps working on their papers even while their attention is turned elsewhere. When they return to their work, they bring with them a fresh perspective. They also bring a more open mind.

When you return to your paper, the first thing you'll want to do is consider whether or not the paper as a whole meets your (and your professor's) expectations. Read the paper through without stopping (don't get hung up on one troublesome paragraph). Then ask yourself the following questions:

Did I fulfill the assignment? If the professor gave you instructions for this assignment, reread them and then ask yourself whether you've addressed all of the matters you're expected to address. Does your paper stray from the assignment? If it does, have you worked to make your argument relevant, or are you coming out of left field? If the professor hasn't given you explicit instructions for this paper, you'll still want to take a moment to consider what she or he expects. What books has the professor asked you to read? What position does he or she take toward your topic? Has the professor emphasized a certain method of scholarship (feminism, Marxism, etc.)? Has she or he said anything to you about research methods in his or her discipline? Does your paper seem to fit into the conversation that the professor has been carrying on in class? Have you written something that other students would find relevant and interesting?

Did I say what I intended to say? This question is perhaps the most difficult question you will ask yourself in the revision process. Many of us think that we have indeed said what we intended to say. When we read our papers, we're able to fill in any holes that might exist in our arguments with the information that we have in our minds. The problem is that our readers sometimes don't have this same information in mind. Your challenge in revising your own writing, therefore, is to forget about what you *meant* and see only what you actually *wrote*—the meaning has to be right there in the words on the page. It's very important to think carefully about what you've said—and to think just as carefully about what you haven't said. Ask yourself the following questions: Was I clear? Do I need to define my terms? Has every stage of the argument been articulated clearly? Have I made adequate transitions between my ideas? Is my logic solid—is it there for all to see? If the answer to any of these questions is no, you will want to revise your draft.

What are the strengths of my paper? In order to develop a critical eye it's just as important to know when you've written well as it is to know when you've written poorly. It helps, therefore, to make a list of what you think you've done well in your draft. It's also helpful to pick out your favorite or strongest paragraph. When you find a good paragraph, sentence, or idea, think about why it's good. You'll not only be gaining an understanding of what it means to write well, but you'll also be giving yourself a pat on the back—something that's very important to do in the revision process.

What are the weaknesses of my paper? Looking for weaknesses isn't as fun as looking for strengths, but it's necessary to the revision process. Again, try to make a list of what you haven't done well in this paper. Your list should be as specific as you can make it. Instead of writing "problems with paragraphs," you might say, "problems with unity in my paragraphs," or, even more specific, "problems with the transitions between paragraphs 3 and 4, and 12 and 13." Also force yourself to determine which paragraph (or sentence) you like least in the paper. Figure out why you don't like it, and work to make it better. Then go back through your paper and look for others like it.

Analyzing Your Work

If you've been considering the strengths and weaknesses of your paper, you've already begun to analyze your work. The process of analysis involves breaking down an idea or an argument into its parts and evaluating those parts on their merits. When you analyze your own paper, then, you're breaking down that paper into its parts and asking yourself whether or not these parts support the paper as you envision it.

The following checklist reiterates our earlier advice. Use it to analyze your whole paper, or use it to help you figure out what has gone wrong with a particular part of your work.

Consider your introduction:

If you're writing a research paper, does the introduction place your argument in an ongoing conversation?

If you're not writing a research paper, does the introduction establish context?

Does the introduction define all of your key terms?

Does the introduction draw the reader in?

Does the introduction lead the reader clearly to your thesis?

Consider your thesis:

Does the thesis say what you want it to say?

Does the thesis make a point worth considering? Does it answer the question "So what?"

Does the thesis provide the reader with some sense of the paper's structure?

Does the paper deliver what your thesis promises to deliver?

Consider your structure:

Make an outline of the paper you've just written. Does this outline reflect your intentions?

Does this outline make sense, or are there gaps in the logic—places where you've asked your readers to make leaps for which they haven't been prepared?

Is each point in the outline adequately developed?

Is each point equally developed? (That is, does your paper seem balanced overall?)

Is each point relevant? Interesting?

Underline the thesis sentence and all of the topic sentences. Then cut and paste them together to form a paragraph. Does this paragraph make sense?

Consider your paragraphs:

Does each paragraph have a topic sentence that clearly controls it?

Are the paragraphs internally coherent?

Are the paragraphs externally coherent? (That is, have you made adequate transitions between paragraphs? Is each paragraph clearly related to the thesis?)

Consider your argument and its logic:

Have you really presented an argument, an assertion worth making, or is your paper merely a series of observations, a summary?

Do you see any holes in your argument, or do you find it convincing?

Have you dealt fairly with the opposition, or have you neglected to mention other possible arguments concerning your topic for fear that they might undermine your own argument?

Have you supplied ample evidence for your arguments?

Consider your conclusion:

Does the conclusion sum up the main point of the paper?

Is the conclusion appropriate, or does it introduce a completely new idea?

Does the language resonate, or does it fall flat?

Have you inflated the language in order to pad a conclusion that is empty and ineffective?

Does the conclusion leave the reader with something to think about?

The final step that you'll want to take before submitting your paper is to make sure that the grammar, spelling, and punctuation throughout the paper are correct and that you've formatted it appropriately. These details may seem frustratingly minor, but errors often cause readers to grow impatient with otherwise well-written essays. So be sure to take the time to carefully proofread your essay.

When you proofread, you need to slow down your reading, allowing your eye to focus on every word, every phrase of your paper. Reading aloud is the most effective way to make yourself see and hear what you actually *wrote*, not just what you *meant*. Remember, a computer spell-checker is not an editor; for example, the spell-checker will see the word "form" as spelled correctly, even if you meant "from." As you read, look for common errors—spelling errors, faulty subject-verb agreement, unclear pronoun antecedents, *its/it's* confusion, *their/there* confusion, and so on. If you have time, get the opinion of a second reader. Treat the proofreading stage as you would a word search or Sudoku puzzle—that is, as a puzzle to be solved. No doubt, some errors are lurking in your prose (even professional writers find errors when they proofread their own work). Make it your mission to find them and root them out.

You'll also want to format the paper correctly. Some instructors provide explicit directions about constructing a title page, choosing a font, setting margins, paginating, footnoting, and so on. Be sure to follow these instructions carefully. If the instructor does not provide directions, consult the *MLA Handbook*—the standard reference for writers in the humanities—for specific advice. Instructors appreciate papers that are not only well written but also beautifully presented. In academic writing, "beauty" equals simplicity: no needless ornamentation, no fancy fonts, and nothing to distract the reader from the sound of your writer's voice and the clarity of your thoughts.

Part III

RESOURCES

Illustrated Glossary
of Film Terms

aerial-view shot. Also known as bird's-eye-view shot. An omniscient-point-of-view shot that is taken from an aircraft or extremely high crane.

An aerial-view shot from Alfred Hitchcock's *The Birds* (1963).

ambient sound. Sound that seems to the viewer to emanate from the ambience (background) of the setting or environment being filmed, either recorded during production or added during postproduction.

angle. The perspective from which the camera shoots a figure. If the camera shoots from below the subject's eye level upward, the resulting shot is a *low-angle shot*. If it is positioned above the subject and shooting downward, the resulting shot is a *high-angle shot*.

animation. The process of creating an illusion of motion from a series of rapidly displayed still images. Common methods of animation include stop-motion photography, drawn animation (otherwise known as cartoons), and digital animation.

antagonist. The character, creature, or force that obstructs or resists the protagonist's pursuit of a goal.

antihero. An outwardly unsympathetic protagonist pursuing a morally objectionable or otherwise undesirable goal.

aperture. Also known as gate. The camera opening that defines the area of each frame of film exposed.

art director. The person responsible for transforming the production designer's vision into a reality on the screen, assessing the staging requirements for a production, and arranging for and supervising the work of the members of the art department.

aspect ratio. The relationship between the film frame's two dimensions: the width of the image related to its height.

Three common aspect ratios: 1.33:1 (the "Academy" ratio); 1.85:1 (U.S. widescreen); and 2.35:1 (Cinemascope widescreen).

asynchronous sound. Sound that comes from a source apparent in the image but that is not precisely matched temporally with the actions occurring in that image.

auteurism. A film theory based on the idea that the director is the sole "author" of a movie. The application of auteurism frequently takes two forms: a judgment of the whole body of a film director's work (not individual films) based on style, and a classification of great directors based on a hierarchy of directorial styles.

axis of action. An imaginary line connecting two figures in a scene that defines the 180-degree space within which the camera can record shots of those figures. See *180-degree system*.

B

backlight. Lighting usually positioned behind and in line with the subject and the camera, used to create highlights on the subject as a means of separating it from the background and increasing its appearance of three-dimensionality.

Backlight

An example of extreme backlighting, from an instructional video about lighting methods.

backstory. A fictional history behind the cinematic narrative that is presented onscreen. Elements of the backstory can be hinted at in a movie, presented through narration, or not revealed at all.

bird's-eye-view shot. See *aerial-view shot*.

blocking. The actual physical relationships among figures and settings. Also, the process during rehearsal of establishing those relationships.

boom. A polelike mechanical device for holding the microphone in the air, out of camera range, that can be moved in almost any direction.

C

cameo. A small but significant role often played by a famous actor.

camera crew. Technicians that make up two separate groups—one concerned with the camera, the other concerned with electricity and lighting.

camera operator. The member of the camera crew who does the actual shooting.

casting. The process of choosing and hiring actors for a movie.

cel. A transparent sheet of celluloid or similar plastic on which drawings or lettering may be made for use in animation or titles.

celluloid roll film. Also known as motion picture film or raw film stock. A material for filming that consists of long strips of perforated cellulose acetate on which a rapid succession of frames can be recorded. One side of the strip is layered with an emulsion consisting of light-sensitive crystals and dyes; the other side is covered with a backing that reduces reflections. Each side of the strip is perforated with sprocket holes that facilitate the movement of the stock through the sprocket wheels of the camera, the processor, and the projector.

CGI. Computer-generated imagery.

character. An essential element of film narrative; any of the beings who play functional roles within the plot, either acting or being acted on. Characters can be flat or round; major, minor, or marginal; protagonists or antagonists.

characterization. The process of developing a character in a movie. Characterization is the collaborative result of the creative efforts of the actor, the screenwriter, and the director.

character POV. A point of view (POV) that is captured by a shot made with the camera close to the line of sight of one character (or other figure capable of sight), showing what that person (or figure) would be seeing of the action. Compare *omniscient POV* and *group POV.*

character role. An actor's part that represents a distinctive character type (sometimes a stereotype): society leader, ingenue, mobster, femme fatale, and so on.

chiaroscuro. The use of deep gradations and subtle variations of lights and darks within an image.

A shot from Stanley Kubrick's *The Killing* (1956) in the chiar-oscuro style.

cinematic language. The accepted systems, methods, or conventions by which the movies communicate with the viewer.

cinematic time. The passage of time within a movie, as conveyed and manipulated by editing.

cinematography. The process of capturing moving images on film or some other medium.

climax. The highest point of conflict in a conventional narrative; the moment of the protagonist's ultimate attempt to attain the goal.

closed frame. An approach to framing a shot that implies that neither characters nor objects may enter or leave the frame—rendering them hemmed in and constrained. Compare to *open frame*.

A closed-frame shot from Akira Kurosawa's *Ikiru* (1952) shows a government bureaucrat literally framed and trapped by the books and papers in his office.

close-up (CU). A shot that often shows a part of the body filling the frame—traditionally a face, but possibly a hand, eye, or mouth.

A close-up of Thierry Guetta (aka "Mr. Brainwash") from Banksy's *Exit Through the Gift Shop* (2010).

composition. The organization, distribution, balance, and general relationship of stationary objects and figures, as well as of light, shade, line, and color, within the frame.

content. The subject of an artwork. Compare *form*.

continuity editing. A style of editing that seeks to achieve smoothness, sequential flow, and the temporal and spatial orientation of viewers—i.e., the telling of a story as clearly and coherently as possible. Compare *discontinuity editing*.

coverage. The use of a variety of shots of a scene—taken from multiple angles, distances, and perspectives—to provide the director and editor a greater choice of editing options during postproduction.

crane shot. A shot that is created by movement of a camera mounted on an elevating arm (crane) that in turn is mounted on a vehicle that, if shooting requires it, can move on its own power or be pushed along tracks.

A student film crew uses a small crane-like device, called a "jib arm," to shoot a crane shot.

crosscutting. Also called parallel editing. Editing that cuts between two or more lines of action, often implied to be occurring at the same time but in different locations.

cut. The point at which one shot ends and another shot begins.

cutting on action. Also called a match-on-action cut. An editing technique that smoothes the transition between shots portraying a single action from different camera angles. The action portrayed begins in one shot and continues into the next shot, thus implying a continuous action.

D

decor. The color and textures of the interior decoration, furniture, draperies, and curtains of a set.

deep-focus cinematography. In a deep-space composition, the process of rendering the figures on all planes (background, middle ground, and foreground) in focus.

deep-space composition. An approach to composition within the frame that places figures in all three planes (background, middle ground, and foreground) of the frame, thus creating an illusion of depth. Deep-space composition is often, though not always, shot with deep-focus cinematography.

A classic scene using both deep-space composition and deep-focus cinematography from Orson Welles's *Citizen Kane* (1941).

depth of field. The distance in front of a camera and its lens in which objects are in apparent sharp focus.

design. The process by which the look of the settings, props, lighting, and actors is determined. Set design, decor, prop selection, lighting setup, costuming, makeup, and hairstyle design all play a role in shaping the overall design.

diegesis. (adj. *diegetic*) The total world of a story—the events, characters, objects, settings, and sounds that form the world in which the story occurs.

diegetic element. An element—an event, character, object, setting, or sound—that is implied to be part of the cinematic world in which a movie's narrative occurs. Compare *nondiegetic element*.

digital animation. Animation that employs computer software to create the images used in the animation process (as opposed to analog techniques that rely on stop-motion photography, hand-drawn cels, etc.).

direct cinema. An approach to documentary filmmaking that employs an unobtrusive style in an attempt to give viewers as truthful and "direct" an experience of events as possible.

direct narration. A form of narration in which an onscreen character looks and speaks directly to the audience.

director. The person who (a) determines and realizes on the screen an artistic vision of the screenplay; (b) casts the actors and directs their performances; (c) works closely with the production designer in creating the look of the film, including the choice of locations; (d) oversees the work of the cinematographer and other key production personnel; and, (e) in most cases, supervises all postproduction activity, especially the editing.

discontinuity editing. A style of editing—less widely used than continuity editing, often but not exclusively in experimental films—that joins shots A and B in ways that upset the viewer's expectations and cause momentary disorientation or confusion. The juxtaposition of shots in films edited for discontinuity can often seem abrupt and unmotivated, but the meanings that arise from such discordant editing often transcend the meanings of the individual shots that have been joined together.

dissolve. Also known as lap dissolve. A transitional device in which shot B, superimposed, gradually appears over shot A and begins to replace it at midpoint in the transition. Dissolves usually indicate the passing of time. Compare *fade-in/fade-out*.

documentary film. A film that purports to be nonfictional. Documentary films take many forms, including instructional, persuasive, and propaganda. Compare *narrative film*.

dolly. A wheeled support for a camera that permits the cinematographer to make noiseless moving shots.

A student film crew uses a dolly on set.

dolly in. Slow movement of the camera toward a subject, making the subject appear larger in the frame. Often used to express a character's realization or epiphany.

dolly out. Movement of the camera away from a subject that is often used for slow disclosure—a process of gradually revealing the elements of a scene as the scene unfolds.

dolly shot. Also known as traveling shot. A shot taken by a camera fixed to a wheeled support called a dolly. When the dolly runs on tracks, the shot is called a tracking shot.

down shot. See *high-angle shot.*

duration. A quantity of time. In any movie, we can identify three specific kinds of duration: *story duration* (the time that the entire narrative arc—whether explicitly presented onscreen or not—is implied to have taken), *plot duration* (the time that the events explicitly shown onscreen are implied to have taken), and *screen duration* (the actual time that has elapsed to present the movie's plot, i.e., the movie's running time).

Dutch-angle shot. Also known as Dutch shot or oblique-angle shot. A shot in which the camera is tilted from its normal horizontal and vertical positions so that it is no longer straight, giving the viewer the impression that the world in the frame is out of balance.

A Dutch-angle shot from James Whale's *Bride of Frankenstein* (1935).

E

editing. The process by which the editor combines and coordinates individual shots into a cinematic whole; the basic creative force of cinema.

ellipsis. An omission of time—the time that separates one shot from another—to create dramatic or comic impact.

establishing shot. A shot whose purpose is to briefly establish the viewer's sense of the setting of a scene—the relationship of figures in that scene to the environment around them. This shot is often, but not always, an *extreme long shot.*

An establishing shot from *The King's Speech* (2010) shows us the exterior of a building, which is the implied setting for the interior scene that follows.

executive producer. Person responsible for supervising one or more producers, who in turn are responsible for individual movies.

experimental film. A film about unfamiliar, unorthodox, or obscure subject matter, typically made by independent (even underground) filmmakers, not studios, often with innovative techniques that call attention to, question, and even challenge their own artifice.

explicit meaning. Meaning that a movie presents on its surface. Compare *implicit meaning.*

external sound. A form of diegetic sound, audible to characters in the scene and to viewers, that comes from a place within the world of the story, but the source of which we do not see. Compare *internal sound.*

extra. An actor who appears in a nonspeaking or crowd role and receives no screen credit.

extreme close-up (XCU). A very close shot of a particular detail, such as a person's eye, a ring on a finger, or a watch face.

An extreme close-up from Spike Lee's *Do the Right Thing* (1989).

extreme long shot (XLS). A shot that is typically photographed far enough away from the subject that the subject is too small to be recognized, except through the context we see, which usually includes a wide view of the location, as well as general background information. When it is used to provide such informative context, the extreme long shot is also referred to as an *establishing shot*.

eye-level shot. A shot that is made from the observer's eye level and usually implies that the observer's attitude is neutral toward the subject being photographed.

An eye-level shot from John Huston's *The Maltese Falcon* (1941).

eye-line match cut. An editing transition that shows us what a particular character is looking at. The cut joins two shots: (1) the character's face, with his/her eyes clearly visible, then (2) whatever the character was looking at. When the second shot is of another character looking back at the character in the first shot, the resulting reciprocal eye-line match cut, and the cuts that follow, establish the two characters' proximity and interaction, even if only one character is visible onscreen at any one time.

Successive eye-line match cuts in *Now, Voyager* (1942) link the gazes of Bette Davis and Paul Henreid, thus accentuating the intimacy of an emotional turning point in the film.

F

fade-in/fade-out. Transitional devices in which a shot fades in from a black field on black-and-white film or from a color field on color film, or fades out to a black field (or a color field). Compare *dissolve*.

fast motion. Cinematographic technique that accelerates action onscreen. It is achieved by filming the action at a rate less than the normal 24 frames per second (fps). When the shot is then played back at the standard 24 fps, cinematic time proceeds at a more rapid rate than the real action that took place in front of the camera. Compare *slow motion*.

fill light. Lighting positioned at the opposite side of the camera from the key light and used to fill in the shadows created by the brighter key light. Fill light may also come from a reflector board.

film stock. Celluloid used to record movies. There are two types: one for black-and-white films, the other for color. Each type is manufactured in several standard formats.

film-stock speed. Also known as film speed or exposure index. The rate at which film must move through the camera to correctly capture an image; very fast film requires little light to capture and fix the image; very slow film requires a lot of light.

film theory. Evaluating movies from a particular intellectual or ideological perspective.

first-person narration. Narration by an actual character in the movie. Compare *voice-over narration*.

flashback. A manipulation of cinematic time in which the action cuts from the present within the narrative to a past event, which may or may not have already appeared in the movie either directly or through inference. Compare *flash-forward*.

flash-forward. A manipulation of cinematic time in which the action cuts from the present within the narrative to a future time in which, for example, an omniscient POV might reveal directly, or a character might imagine, from his or her point of view, what is going to happen. Compare *flashback*.

flat character. A relatively uncomplicated character that exhibits few distinct traits and that does not change significantly as the story progresses. Compare *round character*.

floodlight. A lamp that produces soft (diffuse) light. Compare *focusable spotlight*.

focal length. The distance from the optical center of a lens to the focal point (the film plane that the cameraperson wants to keep in focus) when the lens is focused at infinity.

focusable spotlight. A lamp that produces hard, mirrorlike light that can be directed to precise locations. Compare *floodlight*.

A focusable spotlight is used in this scene from Billy Wilder's *Some Like It Hot* (1959) to highlight Marilyn Monroe's face and to act as a provocative virtual neckline.

Foley sound. A sound belonging to a special category of sound effects, invented in the 1930s by Jack Foley, a sound technician at Universal Studios. Technicians known as Foley artists create these sounds in specially equipped studios, where they use a variety of props and other equipment to simulate sounds such as footsteps in the mud, jingling car keys, or cutlery hitting a plate.

form. The means by which a subject is expressed. The form for poetry is words; for drama, it is speech and action; for movies, it is pictures and sound; and so on. Compare *content*.

formal analysis. Film analysis that examines how a scene or sequence uses formal elements—narrative, mise-en-scène, cinematography, editing, sound, and so on—to convey story, mood, and meaning.

format. Also called gauge. The dimensions of a film stock and its perforations, and the size and shape of the image frame as seen on the screen. Formats extend from Super 8mm through 70mm (and beyond into such specialized formats as IMAX), but they are generally limited to three standard gauges: Super 8mm, 16mm, and 35mm.

frame. A still photograph that, recorded in rapid succession with other still photographs, creates a motion picture.

framing. The process by which the cinematographer determines what will appear within the borders of the moving image (the frame) during a shot.

freeze-frame. Also known as stop-frame or hold-frame. A still image within a movie, created by repetitive printing in the laboratory of the same frame so that it can be seen without movement for whatever length of time the filmmaker desires.

full-body shot. See *long shot*.

FX. See *special effects*.

G

gate. See *aperture.*

gauge. See *format.*

genre. The categorization of narrative films by form, content, or both. Examples of genres are musical, comedy, biography, western, and so on.

goal. A narratively significant objective pursued by the protagonist.

graphic match cut. A match cut in which the similarity between shots A and B is in the shape and form of the figures pictured in each shot. The shape, color, or texture of the two figures matches across the edit, providing continuity.

A classic graphic match cut from Stanley Kubrick's *2001: A Space Odyssey* (1968) that first shows a bone [1] that has just been thrown into the air by an ape man, followed by a space ship [2] floating in outer space.

group POV. A point of view (POV) captured by a shot that shows what a group of characters would see, but at the group's level, not from the much higher omniscient point of view. Compare *character POV*.

H

handheld shot. A shot taken from a camera held by a camera operator either on the shoulder or in the hands. The resulting shot generally shows movement that suggests the perspective of someone running or walking—i.e., a *character POV*.

high-angle shot. Also known as high shot or down shot. A shot that is made with the camera above the action and that typically implies the observer's sense of superiority to the subject being photographed. Compare *low-angle shot*.

A high-angle shot from Fritz Lang's *M* (1931).

high-key lighting. Lighting that produces an image with very little contrast between darks and lights, producing an even, flat illumination of the subject. Compare *low-key lighting*.

This shot of Grace Kelly in Alfred Hitchcock's *Rear Window* (1954) is the result of high-key lighting.

high shot. See *high-angle shot.*

hold-frame. See *freeze-frame.*

I

implicit meaning. An association, connection, or inference that a viewer makes on the basis of the *explicit meaning* conveyed by the form and content of the film. Lying below the surface of explicit meaning, implicit meaning is closest to our everyday sense of the word *meaning.*

improvisation. 1. Actors' extemporization—that is, delivering lines based only loosely on the written script or without the preparation that comes with studying a script before rehearsing it. 2. "Playing through" a moment—that is, making up lines to keep scenes going when actors forget their written lines, stumble on lines, or have some other mishap.

in-camera effect. A special effect that is created in the production camera (the regular camera used for shooting the rest of the film) on the original negative. Examples include *slow motion* and *fast motion*. Compare *laboratory effect* and *CGI*.

inciting moment. The narrative event or situation that presents the protagonist with a goal that sets the rest of the narrative in motion.

intercutting. Editing technique that juxtaposes two or more distinct actions to create the effect of a single scene.

internal sound. A form of diegetic sound that we are to assume is heard (or imagined) by one character but is not audible to other characters. Compare *external sound*.

intertitles. Words—printed or handwritten—inserted into the body of a film in between shots to provide additional exposition or dialogue. Not in common usage today, but used extensively in silent movies.

iris. 1. A circular cutout made with a mask that creates a frame within a frame. 2. An adjustable diaphragm that limits the amount of light passing through the lens of a camera.

iris shot. Optical wipe effect in which the wipe line is a circle; named after the iris of a camera. The iris-in begins with a small circle, which expands to a partial or full image; the iris-out begins with a large circle, which contracts to a smaller circle or total blackness.

An iris shot from Charles Laughton's *Night of the Hunter* (1955).

J

jump cut. The removal of a portion of a film, resulting in an instantaneous advance in the action—a sudden, perhaps illogical, often disorienting ellipsis between two shots.

K

key light. Also known as main light or source light. The brightest light falling on a subject.

kinesis. The aspect of composition that takes into account everything that moves on the screen.

L

laboratory effect. A special effect that is created in the laboratory through processing and printing. Compare *in-camera effect* and *CGI*.

lens. The piece of transparent material in a camera that focuses the image on the film being exposed. The four major types of lenses are the *short-focal-length lens*, the *middle-focal-length lens*, the *long-focal-length lens*, and the *zoom lens*.

lighting ratio. The relationship and balance between illumination and shadow—the balance between key light and fill light. If the ratio is high, shadows are deep; the result is called *low-key lighting*; if the ratio is low, shadows are faint or nonexistent and illumination is even; the result is called *high-key lighting*.

long-focal-length lens. Also known as telephoto lens. A lens that flattens the space and depth of an image and thus distorts perspectival relations. Compare *middle-focal-length lens, short-focal-length lens,* and *zoom lens*.

This shot from Stanley Kubrick's *Barry Lyndon* (1975) was shot with a telephoto lens. The many rows of soldiers are compressed by the long-focal-length lens, flattening the depth of the scene.

long shot (LS). Also known as full-body shot. A shot that shows the full human body, usually filling the frame, and some of its surroundings.

A long shot from Orson Welles's *Citizen Kane* (1941).

long take. Also known as sequence shot. A shot that can last anywhere from one minute to ten minutes.

low-angle shot. Also known as low shot. A shot that is made with the camera below the action and that typically places the observer in a position of inferiority. Compare *high-angle shot*.

A low-angle shot from Spike Lee's *Do the Right Thing* (1989).

low-key lighting. Lighting that creates strong contrasts, sharp, dark shadows, and an overall gloomy atmosphere. Its contrasts between light and dark often imply ethical judgments. Compare *high-key lighting*.

A shot from Alexander Mackendrick's *Sweet Smell of Success* (1957) makes use of low-key lighting.

M

major role. Also known as main role, featured role, or leading role. A role that is a principal agent in helping move the plot forward. Whether movie stars or newcomers, actors playing major roles appear in many scenes and—ordinarily, but not always—receive screen credit preceding the title. Compare *minor role*.

mask. An opaque sheet of metal, paper, or plastic with a cutout (for example, a circular cutout, known as an iris), which is placed in front of the camera and admits light through that cutout to a specific area of the frame, to create a frame within a frame.

master shot. Also known as a cover shot. A shot that covers the action of a scene in one continuous take. Master shots are usually composed as *long shots* so that all of the characters in the scene are onscreen during the action of the scene. Editors rely on the master shot to provide *coverage* so that, if other shots of the scene's action (medium shots, close-ups, etc.) fail to provide usable footage of certain portions of the scripted scene, the director won't need to reshoot the scene.

match cut. A cut that preserves continuity between two shots. Several kinds of match cuts exist, including the *eye-line match cut*, the *graphic match cut*, and the *match-on-action cut*.

match-on-action cut. Also called cutting on action. A *match cut* that shows us the continuation of a character's or object's motion through space without actually showing us the entire action. This is a fairly routine editorial technique for economizing a movie's presentation of movement.

A classic example of a match-on-action cut from John Ford's *Stagecoach* (1939). Doc Boone enters a bar, points to a bottle of whiskey, and asks, "Can I have that?" [1] Another character slides the bottle down the bar toward him. A cut to a second shot [2] shows Doc Boone catching the bottle and pouring himself a drink.

mechanical effect. A special effect created by an object or event mechanically on the set and in front of the camera.

medium close-up (MCU). A shot that shows a character from the middle of the chest to the top of the head. A medium close-up provides a view of the face that catches minor changes in expression, as well as some detail about the character's posture.

A medium close-up of Gloria Swanson from Billy Wilder's *Sunset Boulevard* (1950).

medium long shot (MLS). Also known as *plan américain* or American shot. A shot that shows a character from the knees up and includes most of a person's body.

A medium long shot from Fred Zinnemann's *High Noon* (1952).

medium shot (MS). A shot showing the human body, usually from the waist up.

A medium shot from Tom Hooper's *The King's Speech* (2010).

middle-focal-length lens. Also known as normal lens. A lens that does not distort perspectival relations. Compare *long-focal-length lens*, *short-focal-length lens*, and *zoom lens*.

minor role. Also known as supporting role. A role that helps move the plot forward (and thus may be as important as a major role) but that is played by an actor who does not appear in as many scenes as the featured players do.

mise-en-scène. Also known as staging. The overall look and feel of a movie—the sum of everything the audience sees, hears, and experiences while viewing it.

mixing. The process of combining different sound tracks onto one composite sound track that is synchronous with the picture.

montage. 1. In France, the word for editing, from the verb *monter*, "to assemble or put together." 2. In the former Soviet Union in the 1920s, the various forms of editing that expressed ideas developed by theorists and filmmakers such as Sergei Eisenstein. 3. In Hollywood, beginning in the 1930s, a sequence of shots, often with superimpositions and optical effects, showing a condensed series of events.

motif. A recurring visual, sound, or narrative element that imparts meaning or significance.

motion picture film. See *celluloid roll film*.

movie star. A phenomenon, generally associated with Hollywood, comprising the actor and the characters played by that actor, an image created by the studio to coincide with the kind of roles associated with the actor, and a reflection of the social and cultural history of the period in which that image was created.

moving frame. The result of the dynamic functions of the frame around a motion-picture image, which can contain moving action but can also move and thus change its viewpoint.

N

narration. The act of telling the story of the film. The primary source of a movie's narration is the camera, which narrates the story by showing us the events of the narrative onscreen. When the word "narration" is used to refer more narrowly to spoken narration, the reference is to commentary spoken by either an offscreen or onscreen voice. When that commentary is not spoken by one of the characters in the movie, it is *omniscient*. When spoken by a character within the movie, the commentary is *first-person narration*.

narrative. A cinematic structure in which content is selected and arranged in a cause-and-effect sequence of events occurring over time.

narrative film. Also known as fiction film. A movie that tells a story—with characters, places, and events—that is conceived in the mind of the film's creator. Stories in narrative films may be wholly imaginary or based on true occurrences, and they may be realistic, unrealistic, or both.

narrator. Who or what tells the story of a film. The primary narrator in cinema is the camera, which narrates the film by showing us events in the movie's narrative. When referring to the more specific action of voice narration, the narrator may be either a character in the movie (a first-person narrator) or a person who is not a character (an *omniscient* narrator).

nondiegetic element. Something that we see and hear on the screen that comes from outside the world of the movie's story (including background music, titles and credits, and voice-over narration). Compare *diegetic element*.

nonsimultaneous sound. Sound that has previously been established in the movie and replays for some narrative or expressive purpose. Nonsimultaneous sounds often occur when a character has a mental flashback to an earlier voice that recalls a conversation or to a sound that identifies a place, event, or other significant element of the narrative. Compare *simultaneous sound*.

normal lens. See *middle-focal-length lens*.

O

oblique-angle shot. See *Dutch-angle shot*.

obstacles. Events, circumstances, and actions that impede a protagonist's pursuit of a goal. Obstacles often originate from an antagonist and are central to a narrative conflict.

offscreen sound. A form of sound, either diegetic or nondiegetic, that derives from a source we do not see on the screen. When diegetic, it consists of sound effects, music, or vocals that emanate from the world of the story. When nondiegetic, it takes the form of a musical score or a voice-over narration by someone not present onscreen. Compare *onscreen sound*.

offscreen space. Cinematic space that exists outside the frame. Compare *onscreen space*.

omniscient. Providing a third-person point of view or perspective on the movie's action or characters. Compare *restricted*.

omniscient POV. The most common point of view portrayed in movies. An omniscient POV allows the camera to travel freely within the world of the film, showing us the narrative's events from a godlike, unlimited perspective that no single character in the film could possibly have. Compare *character POV* and *group POV*.

180-degree system. Also known as the 180-degree rule. The fundamental means by which filmmakers maintain consistent *screen direction*, orienting the viewer and ensuring a sense of the cinematic space in which the action occurs. The system depends on three factors working together in any scene: (1) the action in a scene must move along a hypothetical line that keeps the action on a single side of the camera; (2) the camera must shoot consistently on one side of that line; and

(3) everyone on the production set—particularly the director, cinematographer, editor, and actors—must understand and adhere to this system.

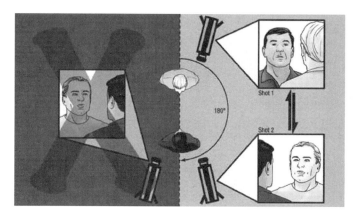

This diagram illustrates how the 180-degree system would apply to a hypothetical shoot featuring two actors facing each other. Shots 1 and 2 are taken from positions within the same 180-degree space. When viewers see the resulting shots onscreen, they can make sense of the actors' relative positions to one another. If a camera is placed in the opposite 180-degree space, the resulting shot reverses the actors' spatial orientation and thus cannot be used in conjunction with either shot 1 or shot 2 without confusing the viewer.

on location. Shooting in an actual interior or exterior location away from the studio. Compare *set*.

onscreen sound. A form of diegetic sound that emanates from a source that we both see and hear. Onscreen sound may be internal sound or external sound. Compare *offscreen sound*.

onscreen space. Cinematic space that exists inside the frame. Compare *offscreen space*.

open frame. A frame around a motion-picture image that, theoretically, characters and objects can enter and leave. Compare *closed frame*.

This shot from Robert Zemeckis's *Cast Away* (2000), set in a vast open space, is framed in a way that suggests that Tom Hanks's character has the freedom to move about as he chooses, and to leave the film frame accordingly.

outtake. Material that is not used in either the rough cut or the final cut, but is cataloged and saved.

overlap editing. An editing technique that expands viewing time and adds emphasis to an action or moment by repeating it a number of times.

overlapping sound. Sound that carries over from one shot to the next before the sound of the second shot begins.

P

pan shot. The horizontal movement of a camera mounted on the gyroscopic head of a stationary tripod.

parallel editing. Also called crosscutting. The intercutting of two or more lines of action that occur at different places. These lines of action are often (though not always) made to look as though they are occurring simultaneously. A very familiar convention in chase or rescue sequences, parallel editing often results in the convergence of the various lines of action.

persistence of vision. The process by which the human brain retains an image for a fraction of a second longer than the eye records it.

phi phenomenon. The illusion of movement created by events that succeed each other rapidly, as when two adjacent lights flash on and off alternately and we seem to see a single light shifting back and forth. This cognitive phenomenon is part of the reason we see movies as continuous moving images, rather than a successive series of still images.

plan américain. See *medium long shot*.

plane. Any of three theoretical areas—foreground, middle ground, and background—within the frame. See also *rule of thirds*.

plot. The specific actions and events that the filmmakers select and the order in which they arrange those events and actions to effectively convey onscreen the movie's narrative to a viewer. Compare *narrative* and *story*.

plot duration. The time that the narrative events explicitly shown onscreen are implied to have taken. Compare *screen duration* and *story duration*.

plot point. A significant event that turns the narrative in a new direction.

point of view (POV). The position from which a film presents the actions of the story; not only the relation of the narrator(s) to the story but also the camera's act of seeing and hearing. The two fundamental types of cinematic point of view are *omniscient* and *restricted*.

point-of-view editing. The process of editing different shots together in such a way that the resulting sequence makes us aware of the perspective or POV of a particular character or group of characters. Most frequently, it starts with an objective shot of a character looking toward something outside of the frame and then cuts to a shot of the object, person, or action that the character is supposed to be looking at.

In this sequence of shots from *Night of the Hunter* (1955), a young girl enters the scene and reaches out to Robert Mitchum [1], who seems to be looking down at her [2], but then we see that his gaze is fixed on the doll that the girl has dropped [3]. This POV editing sends a clear signal about Robert Mitchum's priorities and intentions.

postproduction. The third stage of the production process, consisting of editing, preparing the final print, and bringing the film to the public (marketing and distribution). Postproduction is preceded by *preproduction* and *production*.

POV. See *point of view*.

preproduction. The initial, planning-and-preparation stage of the production process. Preproduction is followed by *production* and *postproduction*.

prime lens. A lens that has a fixed focal length. The short-focal-length, middle-focal-length, and long-focal-length lenses are all prime lenses; the zoom lens, which has a variable focal length, is in its own category.

process shot. Live shooting against a background that is front- or rear-projected on a translucent screen.

producer. The person who guides the entire process of making the movie from its initial planning to its release and is chiefly responsible for the organizational and financial aspects of the production, from arranging the financing to deciding how the money is spent.

production. The second stage of the production process, the actual shooting. Production is preceded by *preproduction* and followed by *postproduction*.

production designer. A person who works closely with the director, art director, and director of photography in visualizing the movie that will appear on the screen. The production designer is both an artist and an executive, responsible for the overall design concept, the *look* of the movie—as well as individual sets, locations, furnishings, props, and costumes—and for supervising the heads of the many departments (art, costume design and construction, hairstyling, makeup, wardrobe, location, etc.) that create that look.

production value. The amount of human and physical resources devoted to the image, including the style of its lighting. Production value helps determine the overall style of a film.

properties. Also known as props. Objects used to enhance a movie's mise-en-scène by providing physical tokens of narrative information.

protagonist. The primary character whose pursuit of a goal provides the structural foundation of a movie's narrative. Compare *antagonist*.

pull focus. See *rack focus*.

R

rack focus. Also known as select focus, shift focus, or pull focus. A change of the point of focus from one subject to another within the same shot. Rack focus guides our attention to a new, clearly focused point of interest while blurring the previous subject in the shot.

real time. The actual time during which something takes place. In real time, *screen duration* and *plot duration* are exactly the same. Many directors use real time within films to create uninterrupted "reality" on the screen, but they rarely use it for entire films. Compare *cinematic time, stretch relationship,* and *summary relationship.*

reflector board. A piece of lighting equipment, but not really a lighting instrument, because it does not rely on bulbs to produce illumination. Essentially, a reflector board is a double-sided board that pivots in a U-shaped holder. One side is a hard, smooth surface that reflects hard light; the other is a soft, textured surface that reflects softer fill light.

reframing. A movement of the camera that adjusts or alters the composition or point of view of a shot.

reshoot. To make additional takes of a shot in order to meet the director's standards or as supplemental material for production photography.

resolution. The concluding narrative events that follow the climax and that celebrate or otherwise reflect upon the story's outcomes.

restricted. Providing a view from the perspective of a single character. For example, restricted narration reveals information to the audience only as a specific character learns of it. Compare *omniscient*.

reverse-angle shot. A shot in which the angle of shooting is opposite to that of the preceding shot.

rising action. The development of the action of the narrative toward a climax.

round character. A complex character possessing numerous subtle, repressed, or contradictory traits. Round characters often develop and change over the course of a story. Compare *flat character*.

rule of thirds. A principle of *composition* that enables filmmakers to maximize the potential of the image, balance its elements, and create the illusion of depth. A grid pattern, when superimposed on the image, divides the image into horizontal thirds representing the foreground, middle ground, and background planes and into vertical thirds that break up those planes into additional elements.

A shot from Terrence Malick's *Badlands* (1973) that exemplifies the principles of the rule of thirds. Its foreground, middle ground, and background occupy roughly equal thirds of the horizontal, while the moon, the man, and the empty space between them occupy spaces that are well balanced into three vertical bands.

S

scale. The size and placement of a particular object or a part of a scene in relation to the rest—a relationship determined by the type of shot used and the placement of the camera.

scene. A complete unit of plot action incorporating one or more shots; the setting of that action.

scope. The overall range of a story.

score. Nondiegetic music that is typically composed and recorded specifically for use in a particular film, and is used to convey or enhance meaning and emotion.

screen direction. The direction of a figure's or object's movement on the screen.

screen duration. The amount of time that it has taken to present the movie's plot onscreen, i.e., the movie's running time. Compare *plot duration* and *story duration*.

screen test. A filming undertaken by an actor to audition for a particular role.

select focus. See *rack focus*.

sequence. A series of edited shots characterized by inherent unity of theme and purpose.

sequence shot. See *long take*.

set. A constructed space used as the setting for a particular shot in a movie. Sets must be constructed both to look authentic and to photograph well. Compare *on location*.

setting. The time and space in which a story takes place.

setup. One camera position and everything associated with it. Whereas the shot is the basic building block of the film, the setup is the basic component of the film's production.

shift focus. See *rack focus*.

shooting angle. The level and height of the camera in relation to the subject being photographed. The five basic camera angles produce *eye-level shots*, *high-angle shots*, *low-angle shots*, *Dutch-angle shots*, and *aerial-view shots*.

shooting script. A guide and reference point for all members of the production unit, in which the details of each shot are listed and can thus be followed during filming.

short-focal-length lens. Also known as wide-angle lens. A lens that creates the illusion of depth within a frame, albeit with some distortion at the edges of the frame. Compare *long-focal-length lens*, *middle-focal-length lens*, and *zoom lens*.

A shot from Stanley Kubrick's *Dr. Strangelove* (1964) that employs the short-focal-length lens.

shot. One uninterrupted run of the camera. A shot can be as short or as long as the director wants, but it cannot exceed the length of the film stock in the camera. Compare *setup.*

shot / reverse shot. One of the most prevalent and familiar of all editing patterns, consisting of cuts between shots of different characters, usually in a conversation or confrontation. Sometimes the shots are framed over each character's shoulder, but other times only one character is onscreen at a time.

Two shots from Elia Kazan's *On the Waterfront* (1954), showing a classic shot / reverse shot cut between Eva Marie Saint and Marlon Brando.

simultaneous sound. Sound that is diegetic and occurs onscreen. Compare *nonsimultaneous sound.*

slate. The board or other device that is used to identify each scene during shooting.

slow motion. Cinematographic technique that decelerates action onscreen. It is achieved by filming the action at a rate greater than the normal 24 frames per second (fps). When the shot is then played back at the standard 24 fps, cinematic time proceeds at a slower rate than the real action that took place in front of the camera. Compare *fast motion.*

sound effect. A sound artificially created for the sound track that has a definite function in telling the story.

soundstage. A windowless, soundproofed, professional shooting environment that is usually several stories high and can cover an acre or more of floor space.

sound track. A separate recording tape occupied by one specific type of sound recorded for a movie (one track for vocals, one for sound effects, one for music, etc.).

source light. See *key light*.

special effects (SFX, FX). Technology for creating images that would be too dangerous, too expensive, or, in some cases, simply impossible to achieve with traditional cinematographic materials. The goal of special-effects cinematography is generally to create verisimilitude within the imaginative world of even the most fanciful movie.

speed. See *film-stock speed*.

splicing. In the pre-digital era, the act of gluing or taping together shots to form a continuous whole. See *cut*.

split screen. A method, created either in the camera or during the editing process, of telling two stories at the same time by dividing the screen into different parts. Unlike parallel editing, which cuts back and forth between shots for contrast, the split screen can tell multiple stories within the same frame.

staging. See *mise-en-scène*.

stand-in. An actor who looks reasonably like a particular movie star (or at least an actor playing a major role) in height, weight, coloring, and so on, and who substitutes for that actor during the tedious process of preparing setups or taking light readings.

Steadicam. A camera suspended from an articulated arm that is attached to a vest strapped to the cameraperson's body, permitting the operator to remain steady during "handheld" shots. The Steadicam removes jumpiness and is now often used for smooth, fast, and intimate camera movement.

stock. See *film stock*.

stop-frame. See *freeze-frame*.

stop-motion cinematography. A technique that allows the camera operator to stop and start the camera in order to facilitate changing the subject while the camera is not shooting. Frequently used for claymation and other forms of physical animation.

story. In a movie, all the events we see or hear on the screen, and all the events that are implicit or that we infer to have happened but that are not explicitly presented. Compare *narrative* and *plot.*

storyboard. A scene-by-scene (sometimes shot-by-shot) breakdown that combines sketches or photographs of how each shot is to look and written descriptions of the other elements that are to go with each shot, including dialogue, sound, and music.

story duration. The amount of time that the entire narrative arc of a movie's story—whether explicitly presented onscreen or not—is implied to have taken to occur. Compare *plot duration* and *screen duration.*

stretch relationship. A time relationship in which screen duration is longer than plot duration. Compare *real time* and *summary relationship.*

stuntperson. A performer who doubles for another actor in scenes requiring special skills or involving hazardous actions, such as crashing cars, jumping from high places, swimming, or riding (or falling off) horses.

subplot. A subordinate sequence of action in a narrative, usually relevant to and enriching the plot.

summary relationship. A time relationship in which screen duration is shorter than plot duration. Compare *real time* and *stretch relationship.*

supporting role. See *minor role.*

swish pan. A type of transition between two or more scenes made by moving the camera so rapidly that it blurs the moment of transition.

synopsis. See *treatment.*

T

take. An indication of the number of times a particular shot is taken (e.g., shot 14, take 7).

take-up spool. A device that winds the film inside the movie camera after it has been exposed.

telephoto lens. See *long-focal-length lens.*

three-point system. Perhaps the best-known lighting convention in feature filmmaking, a system that employs three sources of light—*key light, fill light,* and *backlight*—each aimed from a different direction and position in relation to the subject.

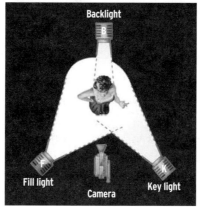

This diagram shows the setup of the classic three-point system, and this shot from Josef von Sternberg's *The Scarlet Empress* (1934) shows how the system can be used to accentuate the glamour of stars such as Marlene Dietrich.

tilt shot. The vertical movement of a camera mounted on the gyroscopic head of a stationary tripod.

tracking shot. See *dolly shot*.

traveling shot. See *dolly shot*.

treatment. Also known as synopsis. An outline of the action that briefly describes the essential ideas and structure for a film.

two-shot. A shot in which two characters appear; ordinarily a medium shot or medium long shot.

A two-shot of the Winklevoss twins from David Fincher's *The Social Network* (2010).

typecasting. The casting of actors because of their looks or "type" rather than for their acting talent or experience.

V

variable-focal-length lens. See *zoom lens.*

verisimilitude. A convincing appearance of truth; movies are verisimilar when they convince you that the things on the screen—people, places, and so on, no matter how fantastic or antirealistic—are "really there."

voice-over narration. Narration heard concurrently and over a scene but not synchronized to any character on the screen at the time. It can come from a third-person narrator (someone who is not a character) or a first-person narrator commenting on the action from somewhere outside of the shot's diegesis.

W

wide-angle lens. See *short-focal-length lens.*

widescreen. Any aspect ratio wider than 1.33:1.

wipe. A transitional device between shots in which shot B wipes across shot A, either vertically or horizontally, to replace it.

Z

zoom in. A shot in which the image is magnified by movement of the camera's lens only, without the camera itself moving. Compare to the *dolly in*.

zoom lens. Also known as variable-focal-length lens. A lens that is moved toward and away from the subject being photographed, has a continuously variable focal length, and helps reframe a shot within the take. A zoom lens permits the camera operator during shooting to shift between wide-angle and telephoto lenses without changing the focus or aperture settings. Compare *long-focal-length lens*, *middle-focal-length lens*, and *short-focal-length lens*.

Shorthand Notation
for Screenings*

Shot Proxemics/Framing

XLS	extreme long shot
LS	long shot
MLS	medium long shot
MS	medium shot
MCU	medium close-up
CU	close-up
XCU	extreme close-up
OFF	offscreen (space)
ON	onscreen
RF	rack focus

* With the exception of some abbreviations listed for shot proxemics, these suggested shorthand notations are *not* universal or standard forms—they are suggestions only, intended merely to help you economize your note-taking.

Lighting

LK	low-key lighting
HK	high-key lighting
BCK	backlighting

Point of View

Opov	omniscient POV
Cpov	specific character's POV (with name of character)
Gpov	group POV

Camera Angles

ELS	eye-level shot
HAS	high-angle shot
LAS	low-angle shot
DAS	Dutch-angle shot
AVS	aerial-view shot

Camera Movement

PAN	pan shot
TILT	tilt shot
DOLI	dolly in
DOLO	dolly out
ZM	zoom
CRA	crane shot

Speed and Length of Shot

SLO	slow motion
FST	fast motion
LT	long take

Editing Conventions

EST	establishing shot
FB	flashback
ELL	ellipsis
SRS	shot/reverse shot
MOA	match-on-action cut
GM	graphic match cut
ELM	eye-line match cut
PAR	parallel editing
POVE	point-of-view editing
JC	jump cut
FI	fade in
FO	fade out
LD	lap dissolve
FF	freeze-frame

Sound

ONS	onscreen sound
OFS	offscreen sound
DS	diegetic sound

NDS	nondiegetic sound
3VO	third-person voice-over narration
1VO	first-person voice-over narration
INSO	internal sound